# AutoCAD 2007

## One Step at a Time

**Timothy Sean Sykes**

Forager Publications
Spring, Texas
ForagerPub.com

ISBN 0-9765888-7-0 (ebook)

ISBN 0-9765888-6-2 (print)

Forager Publications

2043 Cherry Laurel

Spring, TX 77386

www.foragerpub.com

## Author's Notes

Where to Find the Required Files (and Review Questions) for Using This Text:

All of the files required to complete the lessons in this text can be downloaded free of charge from this site:

http://www.uneedcad.com/2007/Files/

Select on the file called *2007Files.zip* and save it to your computer. (Windows XP will open a zipped file. If you need a zip utility, however, I suggest the free WinZip download at: http://www.winzip.com/. The evaluation version will do to get your files. You'll have to follow WinZip procedures to unzip the files.)

Once you've downloaded the zip file, follow these instructions to unzip it with Windows XP.

1. Double-click on the file. Windows XP will display a window with the Step folder listed.
2. Right click on the Step folder and select **Copy** from the menu that appears.
3. Using Windows Explorer, navigate to the C-drive.
4. Select **Paste** from the Edit pull down menu.

To get the review questions, go to the website indicated at the end of each lesson. A PDF file will open in your Internet browser. These files are fully printable, or you can save them to your disk if you wish. The last page of each file contains the answers to the questions in that file. Note: We included review questions along with additional exercises in *AutoCAD 2007: One Step at a Time – The Workbook*. You can save some money by buying the ebook version of *The Workbook* and printing a copy.

Contacting the Author/Publisher:

Although we tried awfully hard to avoid errors, typos, and the occasional boo boos, I admit to complete fallibility. Should you find it necessary to let me know of my blunders, or to ask just about anything about the text – or even to make suggestions as to how to better the next edition, please feel free to contact me at: comments@foragerpub.com. I can't promise a fast response (although I'm usually pretty good about answering my email), but I can promise to read (almost) everything that comes my way.

An afterthought for that email address: this particular address suffers heavy spam traffic. As a result, it is severely filtered. For best results: don't try to contact me from a hotmail or yahoo address, don't use html, don't attach anything, and don't include RE or FW in the header. I promise that I won't sell, give away, or in any other way distribute your address to anyone else.

Frequently Asked Questions (and responses to less-frequently-asked but more annoying questions):

*I went to the web site but got a* Page cannot be found *error. What gives?*

This is the most common complaint I get. The fix is simple: make sure you capitalize the "Files" in the address. The web is case-sensitive.

*Where's Part II?*

Beginning with the 2007 release, we're trying a new approach. We've redone the pedagogy to reduce the size of the text to a single book. We'll include a workbook for some additional end-of-lesson exercises and review questions, but the entire text is here.

*How do I get* The Workbook*?*

We'll make *AutoCAD 2007: One Step at a Time – The Workbook* available in both printed and the less-expensive (printable) eboook formats. Check with your local retailer, our website (www.foragerpub.com) or amazon.com. I intend to keep the price for the ebook format of *The Workbook* as low as possible. Further, it'll have the same (lack of) printing restrictions as this book, so you'll be able to print a color copy of The Workbook in color if you wish, punch holes in it, and put it into a notebook for reference.

# Contents

## Chapter 15: Customizing Dimensions



## Chapter 16: Advanced Modification Techniques



## Chapter 17: Tables and Fields



## Chapter 18: Hatching and Filling



## Chapter 19: Many as One - Groups and Blocks



## Chapter 20: Advanced Blocks



## Chapter 21: Sharing Your Work with Others

# Lesson 1

Following this lesson, you will:

- ✓ *Know how to create a new drawing*
- ✓ *Know how to open an existing AutoCAD drawing*
- ✓ *Know how to partially open an existing AutoCAD drawing*
- ✓ *Know how to save and close an AutoCAD drawing*
- ✓ *Recognize the various parts of the AutoCAD User Interface*

# The Setup

*How do you begin a new drafting project?*

*The number of answers I've heard to this question over the years might surprise you. Some say you begin with the layout. Others say you begin by positioning the drawing on the page. The most experienced drafters generally come up with a quip about coffee and radio settings.*

*This doesn't mean that I was questioning bad drafters, but simply that experience has engrained the basics so deeply that good drafters don't think about these simple questions anymore.*

*So, you might say, how do you begin a drafting project?*

*Well, first you decide on the scale and units (engineering, architectural, etc.) that you'll use. Then you decide the size of the page on which you'll draw (even if your final drawing will be electronic, you'll need to set up for a page size).*

*This first lesson will introduce you to the AutoCAD User Interface – the AUI, or the screen on which you'll draw – and show you how to set up things like units and sheet size.*

## 1.1 The Groundwork: How AutoCAD Handles Scale, Units, and Paper Size

It may surprise you to learn that we won't use a scale when drawing in AutoCAD. In fact, all drawing in AutoCAD is done **full scale**! This simply means that a 3-inch line will actually be drawn 3-inches long. A line 3 miles long will be drawn 3 miles long!

Okay, so if we draw full scale, how can we put a house plan or refinery unit onto a sheet of paper unless the paper is very, very large? Well, we actually *tell* AutoCAD that we have a sheet of paper that's very, very large – a bit larger, in fact, than the house or unit we'll draw. Then later, when we plot (or print) the drawing to an actual sheet of paper, we *plot to scale*.

How do we determine the size of the paper we'll tell AutoCAD to use? I'm glad you asked!

> I've added a discussion of printing/plotting as an independent lesson (Lesson 21). The idea of making it independent is to allow students/instructors to include it at any point (after the first lesson) in their schedule.

We know the standard sizes of paper used in the design world. And we know the standard scales used. To determine what we tell AutoCAD about paper size, we need to determine how many feet or inches (or millimeters) will fit onto each size sheet at each scale. The easiest way to do this is to look at the Drawing Scales Chart in Appendix A. (You'll find a similar chart in the possession of all CAD operators.)

To use the chart, we select the scale at which we'll want the final drawing plotted, and then select the paper size for the plot. Where row and column meet, we find the width x height *limits* of your drawing. (We'll talk more about limits shortly.) There's a place for these numbers in the drawing setup.

It's probably best to jump right in. So as the heading says …

## 1.2 Let's Get Started

### Do This: 1.2.1 — Starting a Drawing Session

I. Follow these steps.

## 1.2.1: Starting a Drawing Session

1. When you loaded AutoCAD, a shortcut that looks like this  appeared on your desktop. Double-click this with your left mouse button to launch AutoCAD. AutoCAD will open (it may take a moment or two), and you'll see the AutoCAD User Interface (the AUI) shown in Figure 1.001 (without the annotations). (You may see a "Workspaces" menu next to the Layers toolbar. If so, you can right click on it and remove the check next to **Workspaces** in the menu that appears. Or you can leave it alone if it doesn't bother you.)

[If your screen doesn't look like Figure 1.001, refer to Appendix H.]

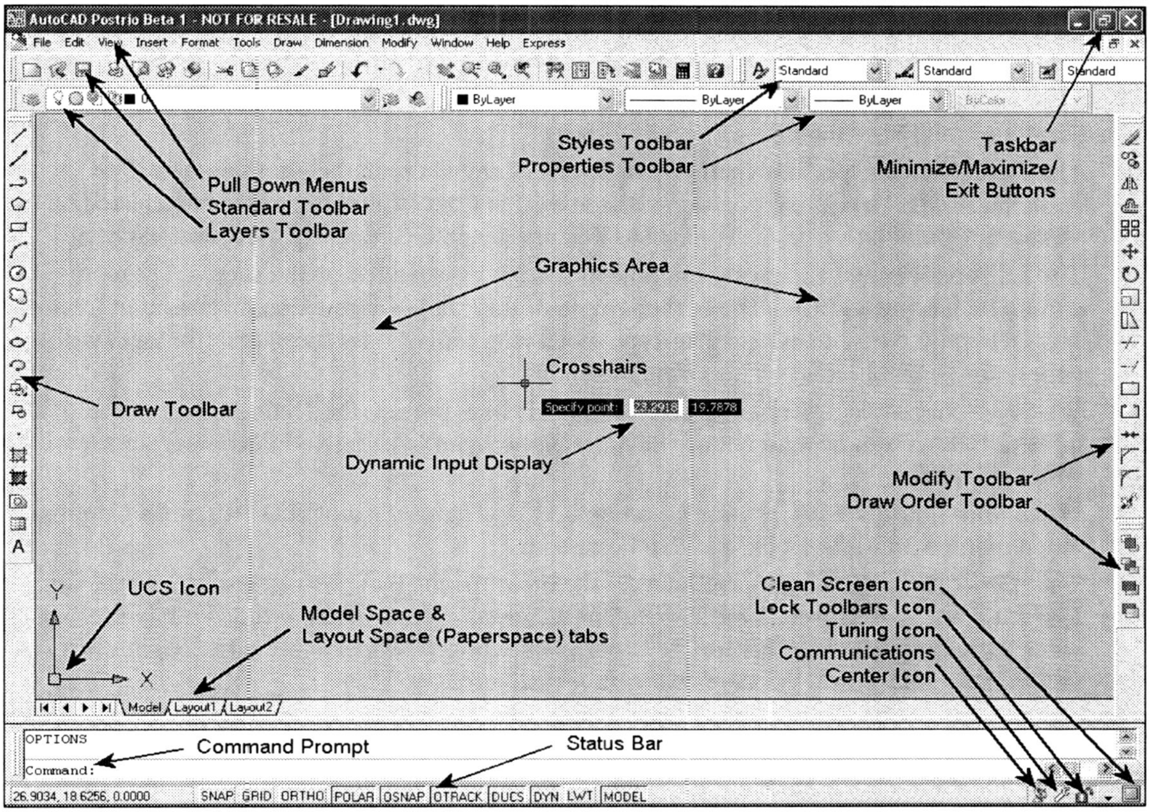


Figure 1.001

Let's take a few minutes to familiarize ourselves with what we're seeing.

### 1.2.1 Menus and Toolbars

If you're at all familiar with Microsoft Windows, or even with the Macintosh operating system, the interface will be familiar. Except for some software-specific menu items, you could almost mistake the top of the AutoCAD screen for Word, Excel, Paintbrush, or any other MS product. We find the standard title bar at the top, with three buttons on the right. These buttons will, from left to right, reduce the software to a pick on the taskbar (the gray bar across the bottom of the Windows screen), make the size of the AutoCAD window adjustable, and exit the software.

Below the title bar, we find the pull-down menu bar. This begins with the conventional Windows menus: **File**, **Edit**, and **View**. Take a minute to explore these and the other pull-down menus. You'll notice that the AutoCAD crosshairs become a cursor (an arrow) when moved out of the graphics area.

Place the cursor on one of the pull-down menus and click with the left mouse button. A menu will drop from that location showing you various options related to the selection. Picking any of these options will activate an AutoCAD macro.

A *macro* is a series of commands or events responding to a single input. Generally, you can't tell this from a single command.

One of a less apparent set of menus will appear anytime you right-click in your drawing (pick with the right mouse button). These *cursor menus* (or pop-up screen menus) help you watch the screen more and spend less time searching for the right thing to press on the keyboard!

We have to give the programmers credit for accomplishing a minor miracle with the right mouse button. They've provided one of AutoCAD's most dynamic tools. Which cursor menu appears when the right button is picked depends upon: whether or not there's a command in progress, if there are items selected on the screen, and where the cursor / crosshairs are located when the button is picked!

AutoCAD provides five basic modes (or types) of cursor menus: Default, Edit-mode, Dialog-mode, Command-mode, and Other menus.

- The Default menu appears when you right-clicks anywhere in the graphics area if no command is active and no selection set is available (that is, nothing has been selected on the screen with which to work). Tools provided are general, frequently used commands.
- The Edit-mode menu appears when objects have been selected on the screen, but no command has been given. The best example of this is the Grips menu discussed in Lesson 16. Generally, you can expect grip-type modifying tools. But object-specific tools will appear for some objects (such as dimensions).
- When you right-click in a dialog box, AutoCAD may present the Dialog-mode menu. The tools presented will depend upon which dialog box you're using and the cursor's location when you click.
- When you right-click while there's a command in progress, AutoCAD presents a Command-mode menu with tools specific to that command.
- The "Other menus" category includes all the other menus that don't fit easily into the first four categories. Right-clicking in different locations and at different times might present some surprising results. Feel free to experiment while you're in a drawing. Right-click over the different buttons on the status bar or over the toolbars.

A toolbar is a group of buttons. To remove a toolbar from the screen, undock it (see below), and then pick the "**X**" found in the upper right corner of the undocked bar. To add a toolbar, right-click on an existing toolbar and select the desired toolbar from the menu that appears.

A *docked* toolbar appears "attached" to a side, top, or bottom of the graphics window. An *undocked* toolbar appears to float over the screen. Drawing objects may exist behind an undocked toolbar, but a docked toolbar forces the drawing to move over.

To undock a toolbar, place your cursor on the two lines found on the left end (or top) of the toolbar and drag it free from its dock. (To drag an object, select it with the left mouse button, but don't release the button until you have relocated the object.)

To dock a toolbar, place your cursor in the blue title bar area and drag it to a docking site (one of the borders of the graphics area).

Once you've docked or undocked your toolbars, avoid accidentally moving them by picking the **Lock Toolbars** icon at the right end of the Status Bar. This will produce a popup menu (Figure 1.002) where you can lock one type of toolbar or all the toolbars on the screen. (Override the lock by holding down the CTRL key while dragging the toolbar.)

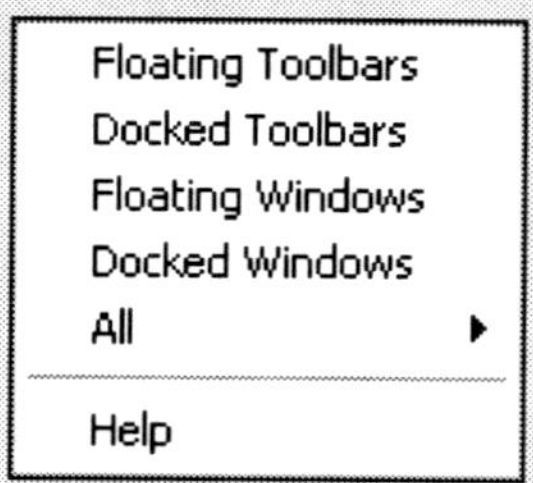

1.002

We'll spend more time exploring the cursor menus as they apply to specific areas throughout this book. But for now, let's take a look at toolbars.

Below the left end of the upper menu bar, we see the first of AutoCAD's toolbars. This *Standard* toolbar carries many of the same buttons, or tools, found in other Windows software. Reading from the left, you see the following buttons: **QNew** (or New), **Open**, **Save**, **Plot**, **Plot Preview**, **Publish**, **3DDWF**, **Cut**, **Copy**, **Paste**, and so forth. To determine the function of these or other buttons on a toolbar, place you cursor over the button and wait a second. You'll see a written description appear in a tooltip box.

Next to the Standard toolbar (to the right), lies the Styles toolbar. Here you can control text and dimension styles, and access the Text Style Manager, Table Style Manager, and the Dimension Style Manager. We'll cover basic text in Lesson 4 and basic dimensioning in Lesson 14.

Moving just below the Standard toolbar, we find the Layers toolbar. Here you can quickly manipulate layers in your drawing, as well as access the Layer Manager where you'll find more detailed controls. We'll discuss layers in more detail in Lesson 6.

To the right of the Layers toolbar rests the Properties toolbar. Here you can control color, linetype, and line weight.

Two other toolbars will bear considerably more attention than those at the top of the screen. The Draw toolbar, docked to the left of the drawing area, provides instant access to the most common drawing tools. The Modify toolbar, docked to the right, provides access to the most common editing tools.

Take a moment to look at each of the buttons on these last two toolbars; you'll become quite familiar with them before your AutoCAD course is finished! Once you've finished that, let's take a look at Tool Palettes.

## 1.2.2 Tool Palettes

If your screen doesn't display Tool Palettes (Figure 1.003) pick the **Tool Palettes** button on the Standard toolbar or enter ***toolpalettes*** at the command prompt.

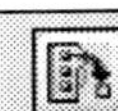
Tool Palettes Button

Tool Palettes (Figure 1.003 – next page) provide access to palettes that contain some of the same tools you found on the Draw and Modify toolbars, as well as some of the more advanced (and useful) tools you'll discover in your basic studies – hatch patterns and blocks. We'll go into more detail about these in Lessons 18 - 20; but let's take a quick look at tool palettes now.

Looking at the left side of the palette, you'll find several tabs – something like the tabs on file folders (in fact, the designers modeled the look after file folders). Selecting one (placing your cursor on one and picking with your left mouse button) will bring a different set of tools to the front of the palette.

The center and largest part of the palette contains the tools made available by the palette. As I indicated earlier, we'll discuss these in some detail in later chapters.

The right side of the palette contains a scrollbar to help access the tools, and a toolbar with some useful buttons. From the top, these include:

- The **Exit** button ("**X**") which will close the tool palette, thus removing it from the screen and allowing you better access to the drawing (graphics) area.
- An **Auto-hide** button (it looks like a pair of arrows and a line - <>|). Picking on this will hide the palettes, but leave the toolbar visible for easy access. To see the palettes, move your cursor over the toolbar. Pick on the button again to turn auto-hide off.

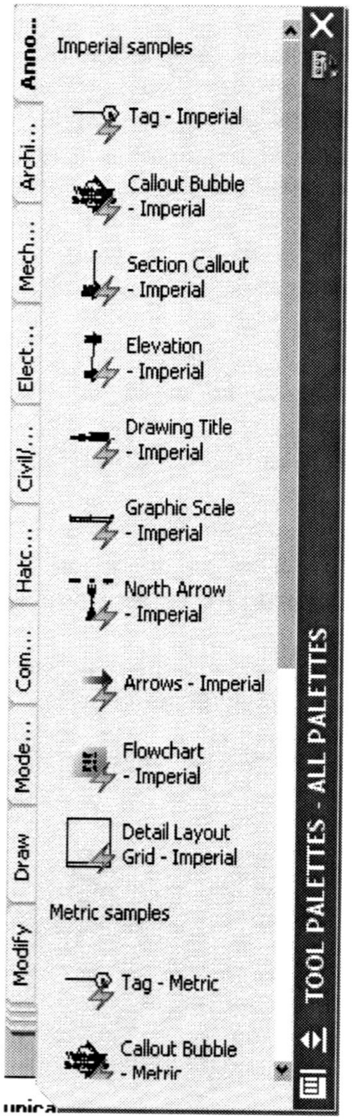


Figure 1.003

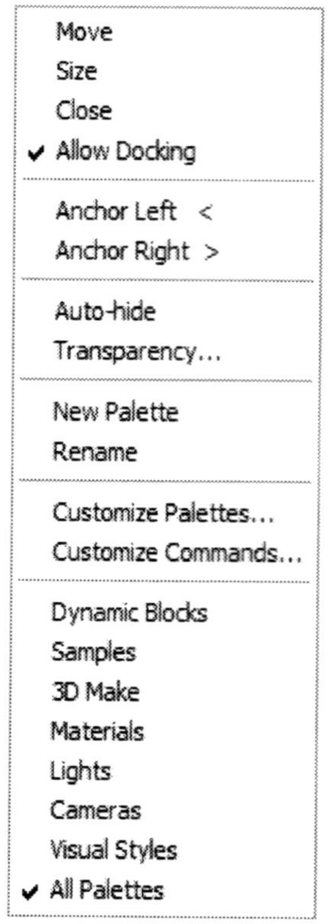


Figure 1.004

Figure 1.005

Depending on how your hardware works, you may receive a warning box instead of the Transparency dialog box presented in Figure 1.005. The warning tells you that "Palette Transparency is unavailable while using hardware acceleration." As transparent dialog boxes aren't crucial to your work, don't try to change your hardware acceleration settings.

- A **Properties** button at the bottom of the toolbar, which calls the menu shown in Figure 1.004. Let's look at the selections available here.
  - When you select **Move**, AutoCAD changes the cursor to a four-sided arrow, which you can use to drag the tool palettes to a new location without docking them.
  - The **Size** selection also changes the cursor to a four-sided arrow. This one you can use to resize the palettes (from the right or bottom only).

- Of course, **Close** does just that; it closes the tool palettes.Selecting **Allow Docking** will either check or uncheck the option. When checked, Tool Palettes can be docked (just like any toolbar) to a side of the drawing area. When unchecked, it can't be docked.
- **Anchor Left <** and **Anchor Right >** will dock the tool palettes to the side of the window as if they were toolbars.
- **Auto-hide** is a menu approach to do the same thing the **Auto-hide** button does.
- A really cool tool is the **Transparency** setting for dialog boxes and tool palettes. The three dots at the end of the **Transparency ...** selection tell you that it will provide a dialog box (Figure 1.005) to make your setup easier. Sliding the bar from left to right will increase the transparency level of the Tool Palettes Window, making it much easier to keep the palettes open while still being able to see the drawing below it.
- **New Palette** enables you to create your own tool palette with job-specific items.

- Be careful with the **Rename** selection. It enables you to rename the Tool Palettes Window, not a specific tab. When you select this option, AutoCAD will provide a text box (floating over the tool palette) wherein you can rename the window. (To rename a specific folder tab, right-click over the tab and select **Rename Palette** from the options on the cursor menu.)
- **Customize Palettes** or **Customize Commands ...** call a customize dialog box. From the Customize Palettes dialog box, you can import or export tool palettes to other AutoCAD systems, add new tool palettes, or remove existing ones. Ignore the Customize Commands dialog box (Customize User Interface) until you're more comfortable with the system.
- **Dynamic Blocks**, **Samples**, and **All Palettes** toggle between these sets of palettes (take a look at these now if you like – **All Palettes** is the default). The other options involve 3D work; you can ignore them for now.

AutoCAD's tool palettes will prove useful when we discuss blocks and hatching. For now, however, it may prove a distraction to your basic lessons. You might be better off closing it or even docking it to the side of your screen until we're ready for it. Alternately, you can dock it to one side of your screen, hide it until you need it, and close the Draw and Modify toolbars. Both palettes and toolbars provide access to the same tools.

## 1.2.3 The Graphics Area

AutoCAD dedicates the largest part of the screen – called the *graphics area* – to workspace. You'll do your drawing and editing here.

Until the recent appearance of the tool palettes, which we'll remove from the screen (or dock and hide) during most of our work time, the only item allowed to occupy the coveted space on the graphics area was the User Coordinate System (UCS) Icon. The icon serves a very useful purpose in 3-dimensional drafting. For AutoCAD beginners in the 2-dimensional world, however, it serves as a reminder of the X- and Y-planes. (We'll discuss X- and Y-planes in more detail in Lesson 2, and the UCS Icon in more detail in our 3D AutoCAD text.) You can disable the icon (turn it off) by entering ***ucsicon*** at the command prompt and responding ***off*** to the prompt as shown in the following sequence.

**Command:** ***ucsicon***

**Enter an option**

**[ON/OFF/All/Noorigin/ORigin/Properties] <ON>:** *off*

> The command sequence may also appear in the *dynamic input display* (Figure 1.001), but the sequence is the same. We'll discuss dynamic input in Lesson 2.

Repeat the command and enter ***on*** to restore the UCS Icon. You'll learn more about AutoCAD's prompts throughout this text.

> AutoCAD actually uses two coordinate systems, the UCS and the World Coordinate System (WCS), but that discussion belongs in the 3-dimensional world. The UCS and the WCS are the same for the lessons in this text.

Just below the left side of the graphics area, you'll find the **Model Space/Layout** (Paper Space) tabs. Paper Space is a more advanced tool covered in Lessons 22 & 23. For now, we'll remain on the **Model Space** tab.

> An advanced drawing environment called Paper Space enables you to work in multiple scales on the same drawing. It's also a useful plotting tool. You'll see more on this in Lessons 22/23.

## 1.2.4 The Command Window and Status Bar

Just above the bottom of the screen, you can see a window with two **Command** prompts. Like the toolbars, this window can undock, but I don't recommend it. You can also resize it by placing your cursor on the heavy line above it, picking with the left mouse button, and "dragging" the window up or down. (The cursor will become a double arrow when properly located, and you must hold the button down for this procedure.) I usually set my command window to be large enough for two lines. This allows more room for drawing.

I can't overemphasize the importance of becoming familiar with the **Command** prompt. Look closely. AutoCAD speaks to you on the left side of the colon. You respond on the right. Right now, AutoCAD is "prompting" you, or asking you what you want to do. When you respond, either by keyboard entry or mouse selection, your response will appear to the right of the colon.

Once you enter a command, AutoCAD's prompt may change, asking you for more information or input. Just follow the prompts to complete your task.

AutoCAD also provides an enhancement to the command line that's quite useful. It's called *AutoComplete* functionality. If you're unsure of a command spelling, enter the first few letters and press the TAB key until you find the command you want! You can also use the up and down arrow keys to repeat previously used commands or data entry!

> Command line messages also appear on the dynamic input display, which appears to follow your crosshairs. You can remove the command prompt from your display (and provide more working area) by entering ***CommandLineHide*** at the prompt. (Redisplay it by entering ***CommandLine*** … but be sure the **DYN** button on the status bar is depressed first! Alternately, you can hold down the CTRL button and press the '9' key on the keyboard.) I don't advise this setup. Some procedures still require the command line.
>
> You can also turn the dynamic input display on and off using the **DYN** toggle on the status bar. We'll discuss dynamic input in more detail in Lesson 2.

---

At the bottom of the screen is the *status bar*. On the left end of the status bar, you'll see a small box with three numbers in it. This Coordinate Display box shows the X, Y, and Z coordinates of the cursor in your drawing. We'll look again at AutoCAD's coordinate system in Lesson 2.

To the right of the Coordinate Display box is a series of toggles (**Snap**, **Grid**, **Ortho**, etc.). We'll look at these in some detail in Lesson 3.

On the right end of the status bar, you'll find an icon  representing AutoCAD's Communication Center. This tool will help you keep your software current by informing you of any available updates. It also gives you access to articles and tips that might make your AutoCAD experience more productive, as well as general product information about new and current Autodesk products.

You'll have to set up the Communication Center if it hasn't already been done. Here's how to do that.

| Do This: 1.2.4.1 | **Using the Communication Center** |
|---|---|

I. If you're not already in AutoCAD, double-click the AutoCAD icon on the desktop.

II. Follow these steps.

## 1.2.4.1: Using the Communication Center

1. With your left mouse button, pick once on the Communication Center icon on the right-end of your status bar. AutoCAD will present the Communication Center dialog box shown here. (If the dialog box looks different from this one, it may have already been set up and you can skip this exercise.)

2. Pick anywhere on the line that reads: **Specify your country/region and preferred update frequency**. AutoCAD presents the configuration dialog box below.

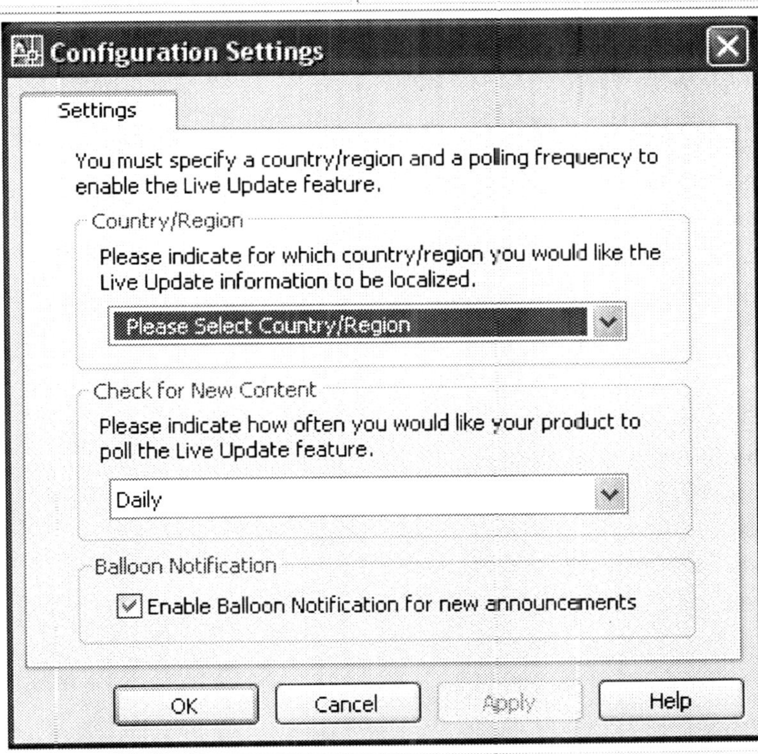

## 1.2.4.1: Using the Communication Center

3. Pick the down arrow next to the text box that reads **Please Select Country/Region**, and select a country from the drop down list. The name of the country now appears in the text box.

You can use the same procedure to change the frequency that AutoCAD will check the internet for updates in the **Check for New Content** frame below this one. If you have a slow connection, you might change it to check less frequently. We'll leave it set to **Daily** for now.

Leave the check in the **Balloon Notification** frame as well. This way, AutoCAD can let you know when something needs your attention.

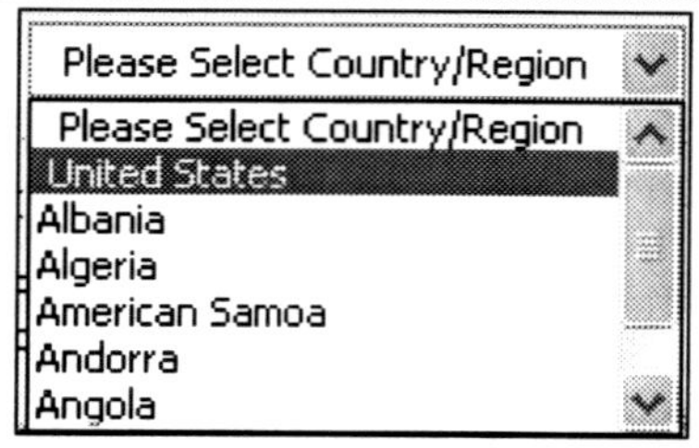


4. Pick the **Okay** button 

to complete the setup. AutoCAD returns to the Communication Center dialog box, which now looks like the figure shown here.

5. Pick on the line that reads **Connect to the Internet and download available information.**

AutoCAD pauses for moment – it may display a message box asking you to wait while it does the task. Then it places a check next to this line to show that it's been accomplished.

6. Pick on the line that reads **Specify which information channels you wish to view.**

AutoCAD takes you to the configuration settings dialog box (following figure).

Most of your options are fairly clear; but if you need a hint, rest your cursor over any of the check boxes.

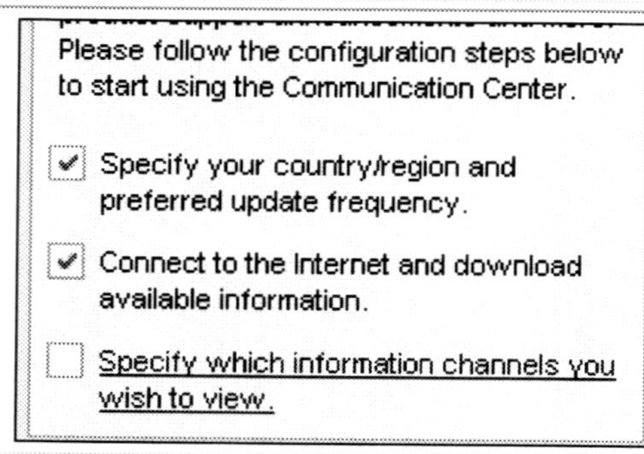

## 1.2.4.1: USING THE COMMUNICATION CENTER

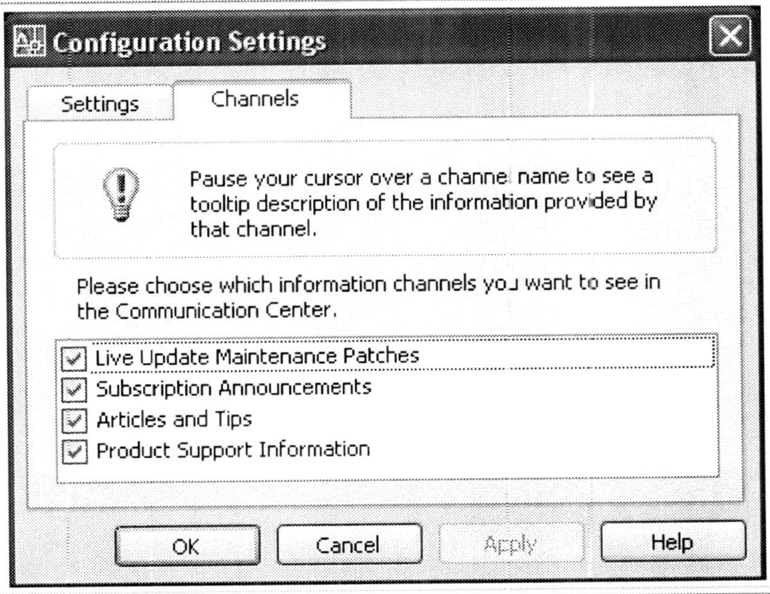


7. All of the boxes are selected by default; deselect any boxes that contain information you're not interested in, and then pick the **Okay** button OK to complete the step. AutoCAD returns to the Communication Center dialog box (shown) and will list any information that is currently available.

8. Review any tips or information you would like to see, and then pick the [X] at the right end of the title bar to exit the dialog box.

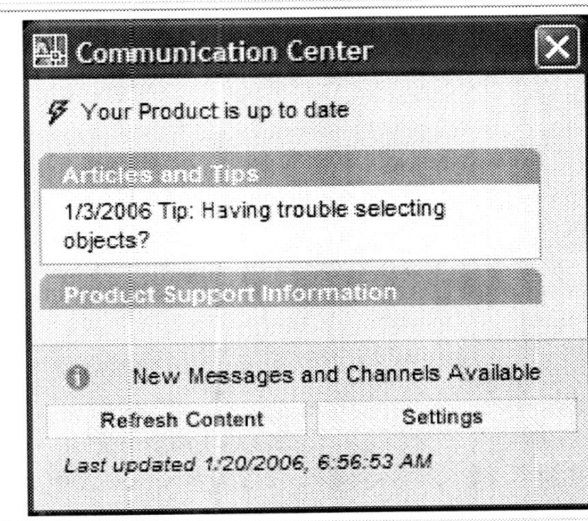


The Communication Center will automatically update its information base as often as you told it to in Step 3, or you can manually update it by picking on **Refresh Content** at any time. You can also adjust all the settings you made in the previous exercise by selecting **Settings** at the bottom of the Communication Center.

Just to the right of the Toolbar Window Position icon, you'll find a down arrow that calls the Status Bar Menu (Figure 1.006 – next page). You'll use this menu to tell AutoCAD whether or not to display the Coordinate Display box, as well as which of the various toggles you'd like to see. We'll become more familiar with these toggles in Lesson 3.

You also use the Status Bar menu to call the Tray Settings dialog box (Figure 1.007 – next page).

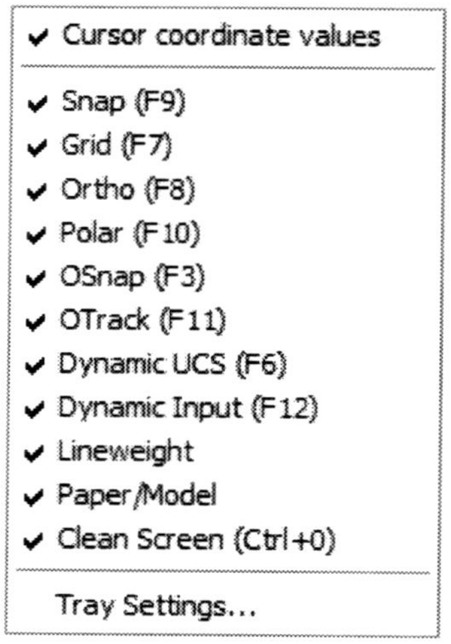


Figure 1.006

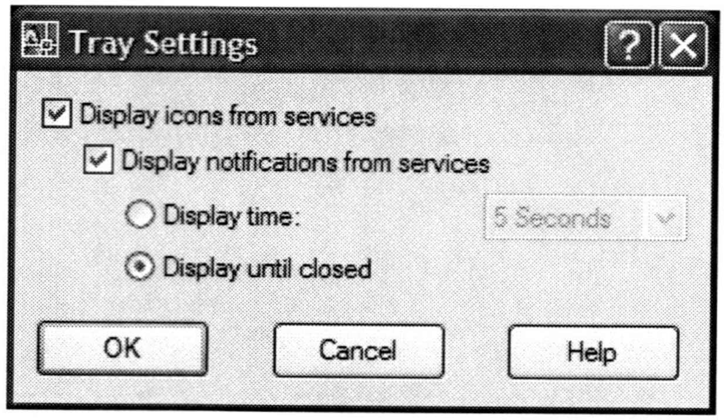


Figure 1.007

To remove the Communication Center Icon from the status bar, simply remove the check next to **Display icons from services**. If you leave the check here, as recommended, you can use the next check box to control whether or not AutoCAD will let you know about anything new that comes in by way of the Communication Center. When a check appears next to **Display notifications from services**, the Communication Center will display a bubble next to its icon whenever something needs your attention. Use the two radio buttons below this line to control how long the bubble will be displayed.

> A **Radio Button** is a round hole. Selecting a radio button places a black dot (or bullet) inside the round hole. Radio buttons usually come in small groups, but only one button in a group can hold the bullet.

Just to the right of the Communication Center icon in the status bar, you'll find the Tuner icon. This calls a dialog box that you can use to "tune" AutoCAD's performance. I suggest you leave this alone for now and allow AutoCAD's default settings to work for you.

To the extreme right of the status bar resides the Clean Screen Toggle icon. Clean Screen removes everything from the user interface except: the command window, the pull down menus, the model and layout tabs, and the status bar. This gives you more work room but limits your use of toolbars or palettes.

### 1.2.5 Workspaces

Once you're pleased with your user-interface (your *workspace*) – you have all your toolbars and palettes where you want them – you can save the layout just in case someone else comes along and changes things. (Alternately, you can have a variety of interface setups to use for your different projects.)

Use the ***WSSave*** command to save your workspace. It looks like this:

**Command:** ***wssave***

[AutoCAD presents a dialog box asking for the name of the workspace. Enter an appropriate name and pick the **Save** button.]

That's all there is to saving your workspace so you can return to it at any time. Use the ***WSCurrent*** command to restore your workspace. It looks like this:

**Command:** ***wscurrent***

**Enter new value for WSCURRENT <" ">:** ***MyWorkspace***

> Not much of a typist? Don't sweat it! Right-click on any toolbar and select **Workspaces** from the popup menu. AutoCAD will provide a toolbar with the same options presented by the ***WSSave*** and ***WSCurrent*** commands.

Well, you've read a lot of pages and have become familiar with the interface, but you haven't actually done any AutoCAD yet. Let's set up a new drawing.

## 1.3 Setting Up a New Drawing

Actually, you've already started a new drawing – back at the beginning of Section 1.2. It was just that simple to create a new drawing "from scratch" (using AutoCAD's default settings). You can begin any number of new drawings at any time in the same manner; but to make your drawing time more productive, there are a few things you should set up first – like paper size and units. Of course you could accept AutoCAD's defaults for these and just get started, but let's take a look at the procedures anyway – just in case your boss wants to use company standard settings.

> By default, AutoCAD uses the following settings:
>
> - Limits (paper size) = 12" x 9" (imperial) or 429mm x 297mm (metric)
> - Units = decimal to 4 places
> - Angles are decimal and measured counterclockwise with 0 degrees East

AutoCAD – never the shirker when it comes to redundancy – provides three methods for setting up a new drawing: templates, wizards, and of course, "from scratch." The new user will find the first two methods easier than the third, but once you've become a bit more seasoned, you may find that you prefer the third's more simplistic approach. We'll look at each and you can decide which is most comfortable for you.

Unfortunately, AutoCAD doesn't make wizards immediately available in the current release as it has in the past. You'll have to make a small adjustment to access them. You'll have to adjust a system variable – one of AutoCAD's default settings. But don't worry; it isn't difficult. The procedure will also let you see how to close a drawing session. Let's do it now.

| Do This: 1.3.1 | Change the Startup System Variable to Tell AutoCAD to Show the Startup Dialog Box |
|---|---|

I. If you're not already in AutoCAD, double-click the AutoCAD icon on the desktop.

II. Follow these steps.

| 1.3.1: CHANGE THE STARTUP SYSTEM VARIABLE |
|---|
| 1. At the command line, type ***startup***.<br>Note: Remember to hit the ***enter*** key after entering the text. Otherwise, AutoCAD won't know you've said anything.<br>**Command: *startup*** |
| 2. When AutoCAD asks you for a new value for the **Startup** system variable, enter ***1***.<br>**Enter new value for STARTUP <0>: *1*** |
| 3. AutoCAD returns to the command prompt to await your next order.<br>**Command:** |

Wasn't that easy?

Although it doesn't appear that anything has changed, you're now able to utilize some tools that weren't available to you previously. Of course, you can always follow the same procedure to reset the variable back to ***0*** after you've seen the wizards approach to setting up a new drawing.

We'll begin by entering the ***New*** command. Now that we've adjusted the **Startup** system variable, the Create New Drawing dialog box (Figure 1.008) will appear on the screen. I'll give you a brief overview of this before we take a stab at using it.

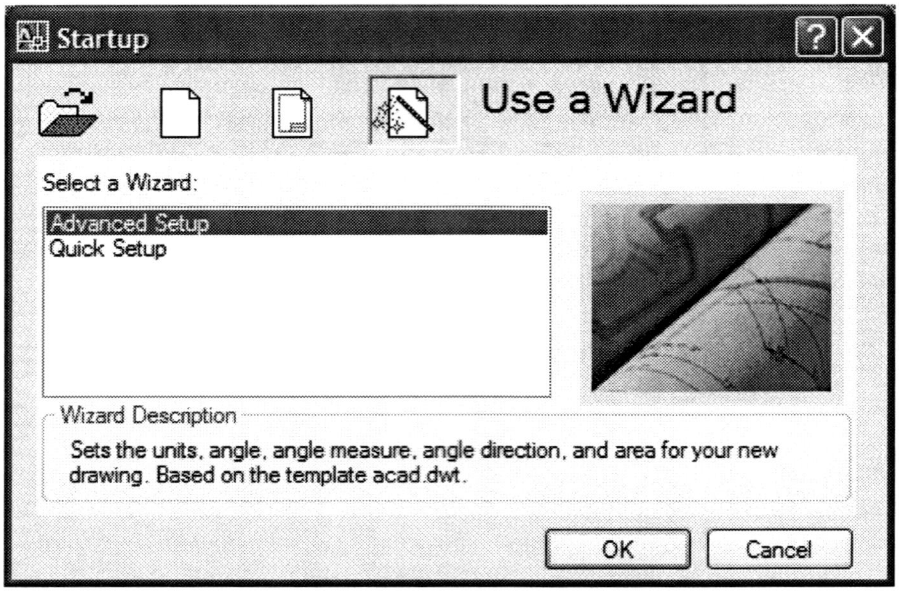


Figure 1.008

You'll find four really useful buttons across the top. These are (from the left):

- **Open** – for opening an existing drawing. (Open isn't available when you access this dialog box with the ***New*** command.)
- **Start from Scratch** – for starting a new drawing without using a template or wizard. This uses the same AutoCAD defaults that would be used if you were to start a drawing without using the dialog box. If you intend to use this button consistently, you can turn the **Startup** system variable ***Off*** and AutoCAD won't present the dialog box.
- **Use a Template** – allows you to start a new drawing using preset system variables.
- **Use a Wizard** – provides a choice of two wizards to walk you through the setup process.

Okay, that's the brief overview, now let's get busy! We'll start by setting up a drawing using a drawing wizard. We'll set up a drawing for a ¼"=1'-0" scale on a B-size (11 x 17) sheet of paper.

| Do This: 1.3.2 | Setup Procedure #1: Using the Setup Wizard to Create a New Drawing |
|---|---|

I. If you haven't already, double click the AutoCAD icon on the desktop. Notice the presence of a Startup dialog box when AutoCAD begins. (This is the same dialog box as the Create New Drawing dialog box you saw in Figure 1.010, but the **Open** button is available.) If you're still in AutoCAD, enter the ***New*** command at the command prompt.

II. Follow these steps.

**1.3.2: USING THE SETUP WIZARD**

1. Pick the **Use a Wizard** button . Notice that the dialog box changes to offer you a choice

between the **Quick Setup** wizard and the **Advanced Setup** wizard (Figure 1.008).

2. We'll use the **Advanced Setup** wizard. You can select it in one of two ways: either highlight it in the list box (by picking on it one time) and then picking the **Okay** button, or simply double click on it in the list box. Do this now.

AutoCAD presents the first of a series of dialog boxes (**Units** – figure shown below) of the **Advanced Setup** wizard.

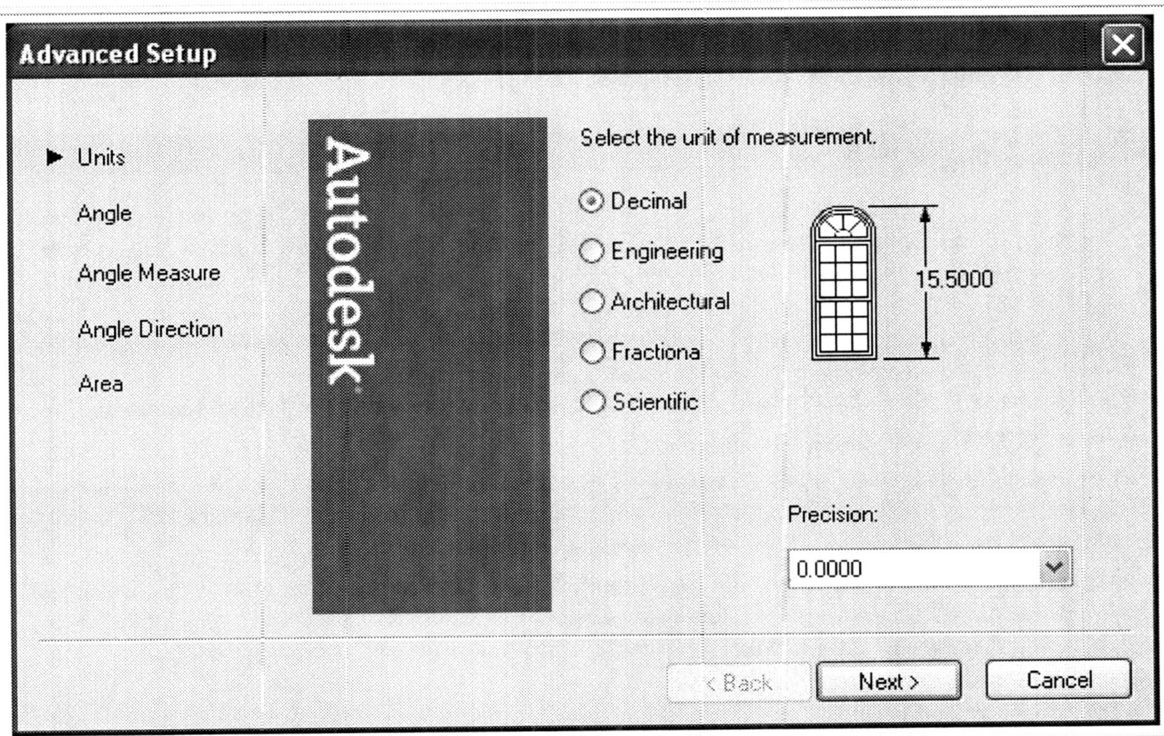


3. Notice the list down the left side of the dialog box. This list includes the settings available in the **Advanced Setup** wizard. The initial screen presents the **Units** options as indicated by the arrow.

Select **Architectural** in the center of the dialog box (as shown at left). A "bullet" appears in the radio button to the left.

You'll notice the demo to the right will change showing a sample of what architectural units look like. You may select the other buttons to see samples of them, but then reselect the **Architectural** option.

The precision of the units is already set to **1/16"**, but you can change it on this screen as well by picking the down arrow on the **Precision** control box.

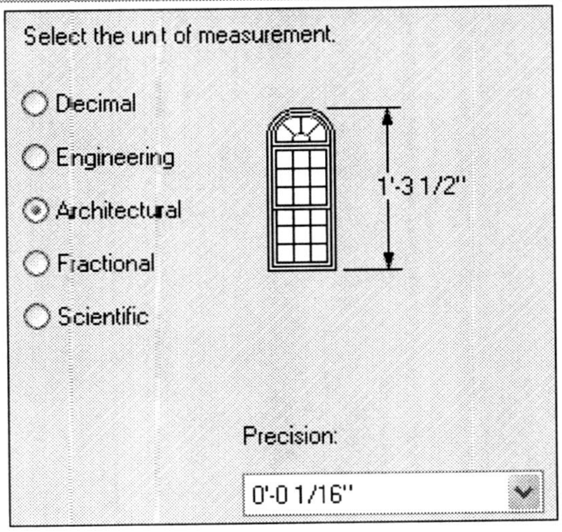

4. Pick the **Next** button 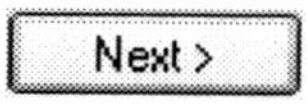

at the bottom of the dialog box. The arrow on the settings list drops to **Angle**, and the options on the right side of the dialog box change accordingly.

5. Select the different radio buttons to see how each appears in the sample image to the right. Then set the **Decimal Degrees** option (as shown). Leave the **Precision** at which you want AutoCAD to measure angles at ***0*** (for *no decimal places*).

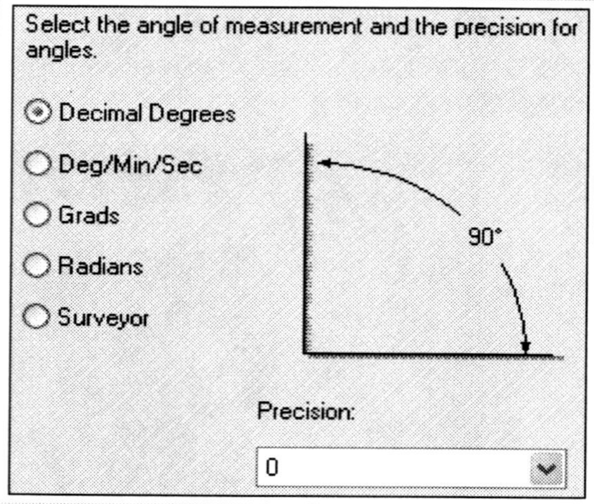


6. Pick the **Next** button 

. Your dialog box now looks like the following figure. Here we control the direction of the angles.

Most of us are familiar with the nautical way of determining degrees (a product of a good scout training). Unfortunately, many engineers apparently missed that training. The standard 0°North in the real world has changed to 0°East in the world of computer engineering.

You can change it here if you wish; but be warned, 0°East has become an engineering *convention* (unwritten standard). If another CAD operator discovers that you have changed the angles, you may be in for some grief. Many third-party programs and AutoLISP routines (as well as engineering standards) are based on 0°East.

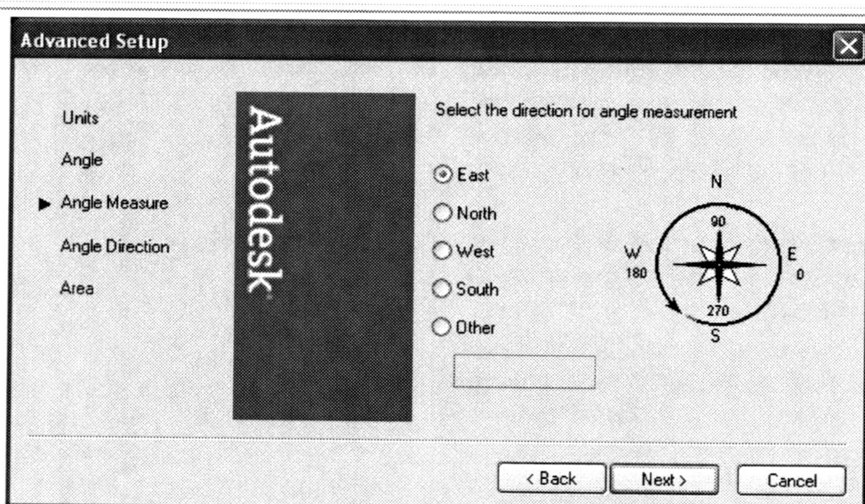


7. Pick the **Next** button 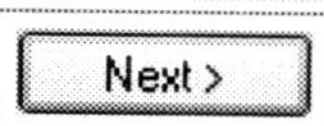

to go to the **Angle Direction** options. This one also suffers the wrath of the engineers. We must now measure our angles *counterclockwise*! Thus, 90°North, 180°West, and 270°South follow 0°East.

## 1.3.2: Using the Setup Wizard

8. Pick the **Next** button 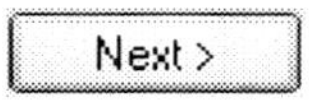

again to go to the last dialog box.

9. In the **Area** options dialog box (shown), you'll determine the size of the sheet on which you'll plot your final drawing. The default is 1' wide by 9" long, shown in the architectural units we set up in Step 4.
Look at the Drawing Scales chart (Appendix A). Determine what the drawing limits should be for the ¼" scale 11"x17" sheet we want to use. Did you come up with 44' x 68'? Excellent!
Put the 68' in the width text box and the 44' in the height text box. Why 68' and 44' instead of 44' and 68'? This is because we want the drawing to be landscaped (wider than high). [Note: Be sure to use the foot mark (') when entering the limits.]

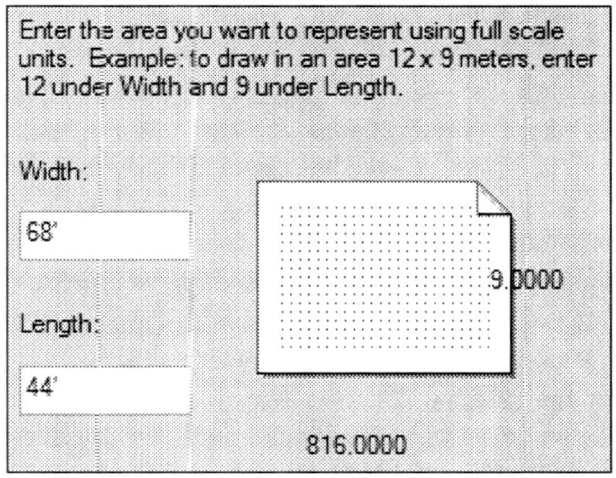


10. Pick the **Finish** button 

at the bottom of the Advanced Setup dialog box. The dialog box disappears, replaced by AutoCAD's graphic screen.

Don't close your drawing yet; we'll continue with it in our next section.

Congratulations! You've set up your first AutoCAD drawing using the **Advanced Setup** option of the Startup wizard.

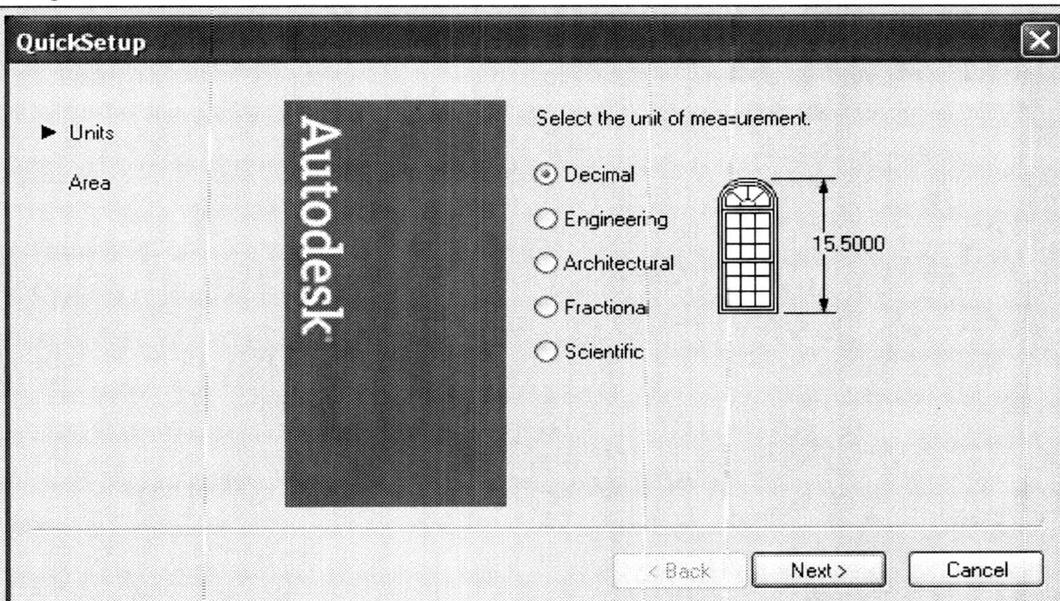


Figure 1.009

The **Quick Setup** option of the Startup wizard has only two options, as shown in Figure 1.009. These are similar to the same dialog boxes of the **Advanced Setup**. In the **Quick Setup** wizard, however, AutoCAD uses default settings for all the other options provided by the **Advanced Setup** wizard.

## 1.4 Saving and Leaving a Drawing Session

### 1.4.1 Saving a Drawing to a Local or Network Drive and Leaving the Drawing Session

Now that we've created our drawing, we need to save it. We accomplish this by using one of three commands: ***Save***, ***Saveas***, or ***Qsave***. Each behaves in a similar manner depending on the status of the drawing. That is, each will present the Save Drawing As dialog box if the drawing has not been previously saved. The ***Qsave*** command, however, will automatically save the drawing without prompting for additional information, provided it has been previously saved and given a name.

***Save*** and ***Saveas*** are available at the command prompt or under the File pull-down menu. ***Qsave*** will occur when you pick the **Save** button on the Standard toolbar.

How you end the drawing depends on whether you wish to end only the current drawing or the entire drawing session. In other words, do you want to close AutoCAD or just close this drawing? To leave the drawing without leaving AutoCAD, use the ***Close*** command. To close all drawings that are currently open, without leaving AutoCAD, use the ***Closeall*** command. Otherwise, use the ***Quit*** command or pick the **X** button on the right end of the title bar.

These commands are also available both at the command prompt and under the File pull-down menu.

Let's save and exit our drawing.

| Do This: 1.4.1.1 | Saving Your Drawing Changes |
|---|---|

I. Continue the previous drawing session.

**1.4.1.1: SAVING YOUR DRAWING**

1. Open the Save Drawing As dialog box. To do this, you must choose one of two approaches: Type ***saveas*** at the command prompt, or go to the File pull-down menu and select **Save As**. AutoCAD presents the Save Drawing As dialog box shown atop the next page.

**Command:** ***saveas***

## 1.4.1.1: SAVING YOUR DRAWING

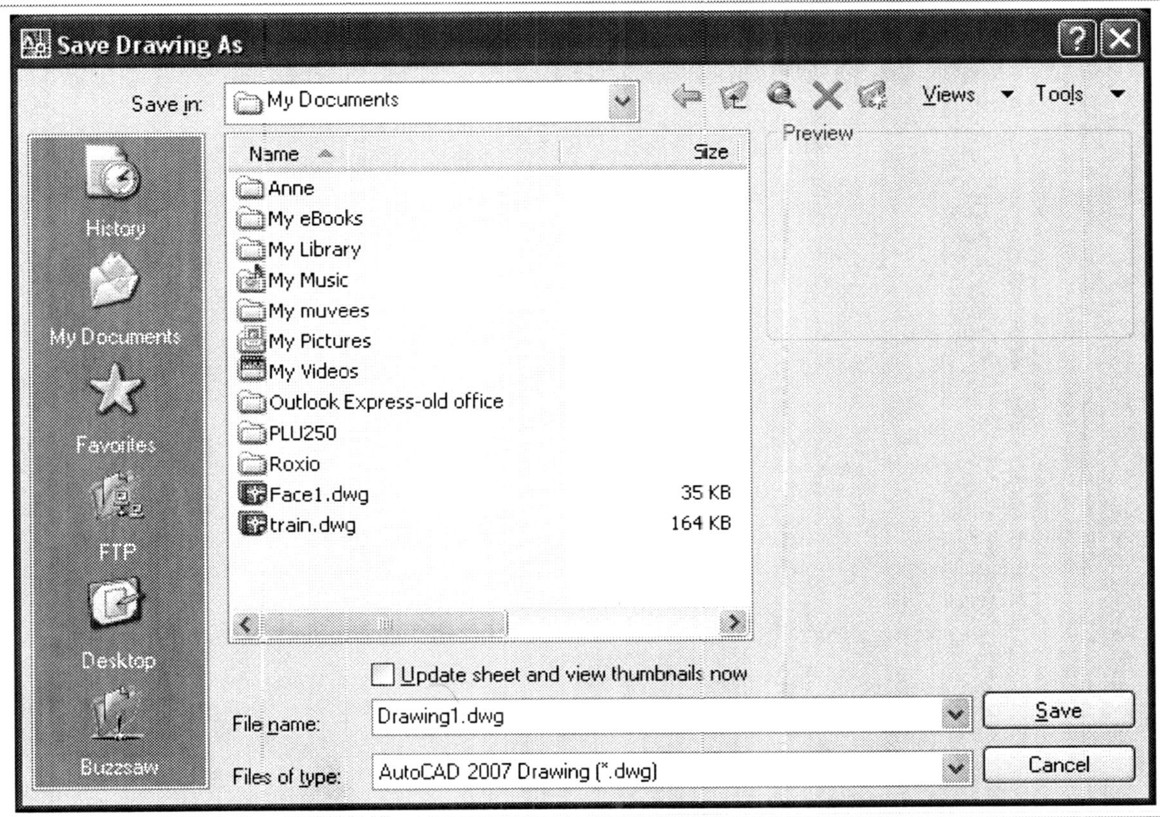


2. Next to the **Save in** control box (where you see *My Documents*), you'll find a downward-pointing arrow. Pick on that arrow to see a path showing where you are on your hard drive (as indicated). We're going to save the file to the C:\Steps\Lesson01 folder.

Pick on the computer icon next to **(C:)**. The list box below changes to show all the folders on the C-drive. (Use this procedure to save your drawing to a network drive as well. Simply pick the letter that designates the drive to which you wish to save your work.)

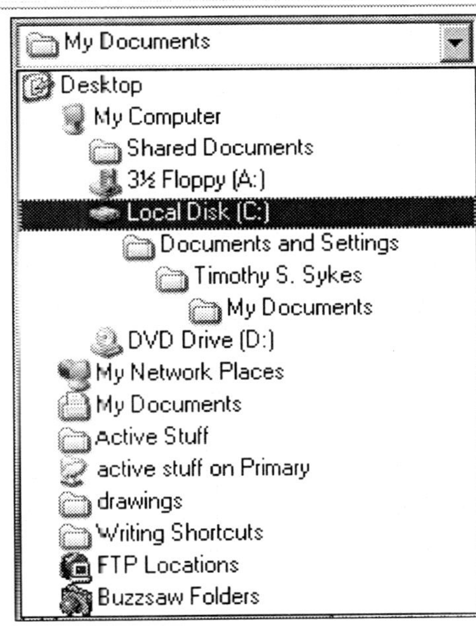


3. In the list box, double-click on the folder identified as **Steps** 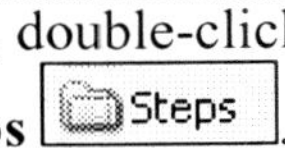

. This folder opens and the list box now shows the contents of the Steps folder.

4. Double-click on the folder identified as **Lesson01** 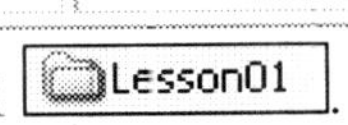

. This folder now opens. Your dialog box should now look like the figure below.

## 1.4.1.1: Saving Your Drawing

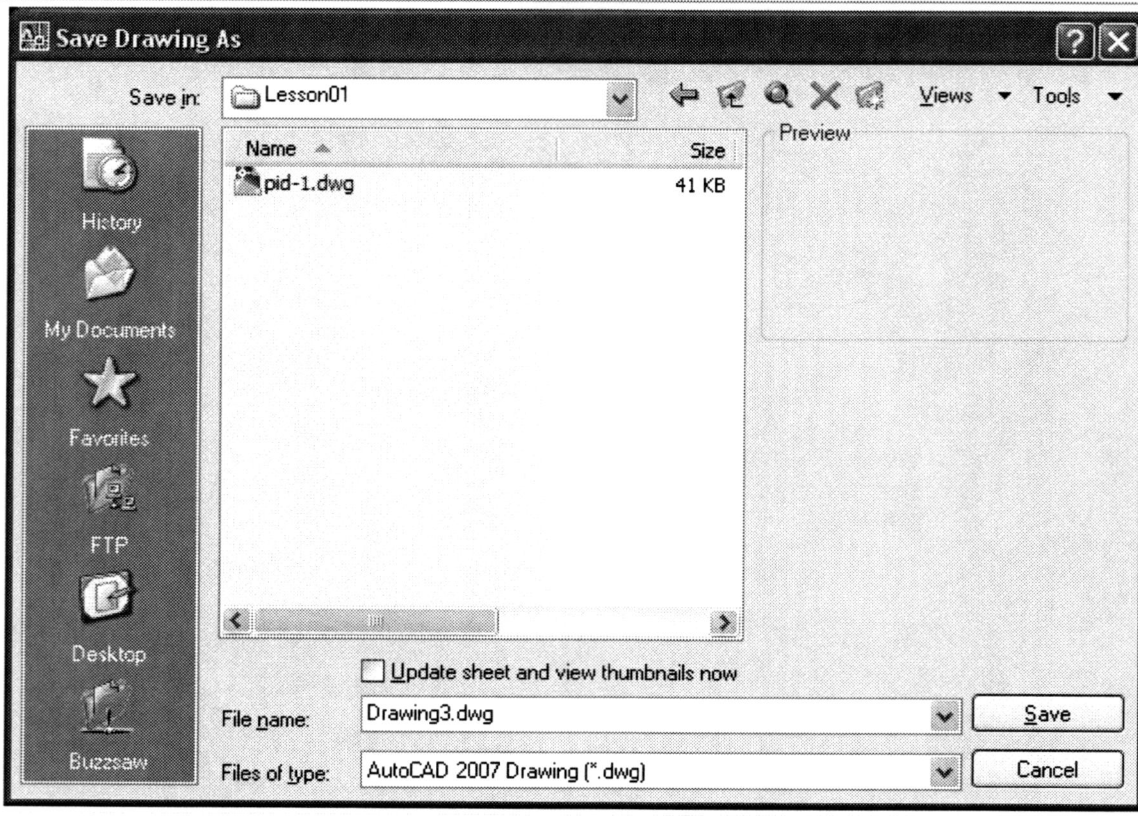


5. Type in the name *MyFirstStep* in the box next to the words **File name**.

Don't put the extension on the name; AutoCAD will do that for you.

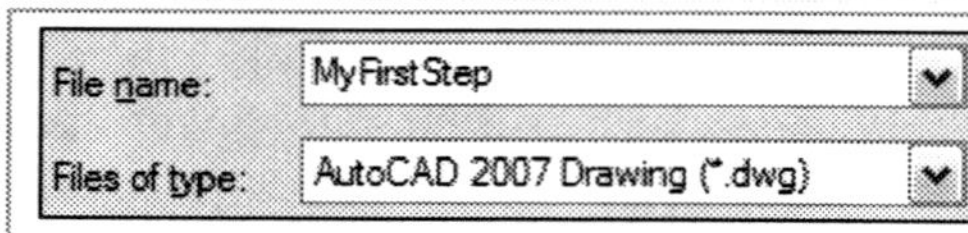


6. Notice that the type of file you'll save has been identified in the **Files of type** control box. Pick the down arrow to view the different formats available.

- The *DWG* file types make it possible to save an AutoCAD drawing so that it may be edited by earlier releases of AutoCAD.
- The *DWT* file is an AutoCAD template (we'll look more at this in a few minutes).
- *DXF* files are binary files (computer programming stuff) used to exchange AutoCAD drawings with other programs.
- Finally, the *DWS* files are used as standard files.

Leave the default **AutoCAD 2007 Drawing** selected.

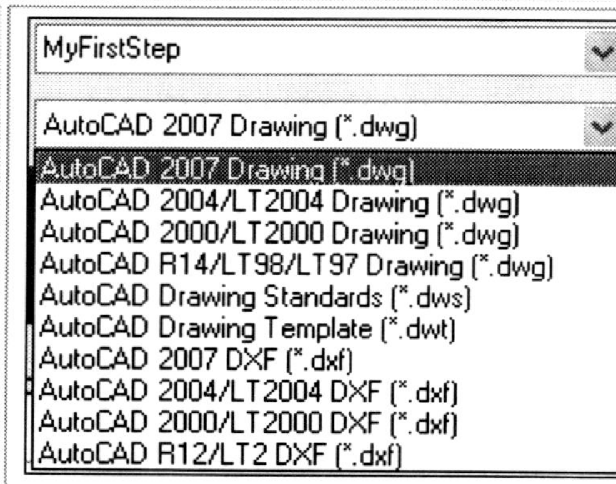

## 1.4.1.1: SAVING YOUR DRAWING

7. Pick the **Save** button [Save] in the lower right corner of the dialog box. AutoCAD saves the drawing and the dialog box closes. Notice that the title and path of the drawing now appear on the title bar.

8. Now that your drawing has been saved, you can exit the program. The easiest way to do this is to pick the **X** button on the right end of the title bar, but you can also enter ***quit*** on the command line or select **Exit** from the File pull-down menu.

**Command:** ***quit***

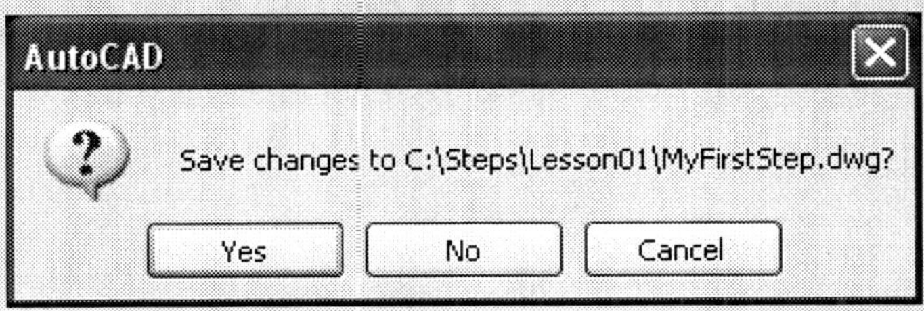


Note that leaving a drawing that has been changed, without first saving it, will cause AutoCAD to present a warning box (shown here). AutoCAD will let you know that you have not saved the drawing and ask if you'd like to save it now. If you haven't saved it before, AutoCAD will take you to the Save Drawing As dialog box that you used in Step 1 of the previous exercise.

## 1.4.2 Saving a Drawing to an Internet Location

Saving a drawing to an Internet location is simple enough; it requires that you enter a web address in the **File name** text box of the Save Drawing As dialog box. But because of Internet protocols, you can't transfer information from your computer to an *http* address. You can, however, send your file to an *ftp* address. For such a slight difference, the significance of this change should not be underestimated. Forgetting to change protocols has driven many an operator into frantic searches for more profound problems, only to wind up feeling foolish when the oversight was discovered.

Once you've entered the correct address and picked the **Save** button, AutoCAD must stop and ask you for a user ID and password. The nature of the Internet requires these to ensure the integrity of the web site. (Imagine opening a file on your web site only to discover that some unknown villain had overwritten your drawing files with Daffy Duck cartoons.)

Let's save a drawing to an Internet address.

In order to avoid thousands of stray documents finding their way to our website, you can't actually save your document to the Internet in this exercise. Instead, I'll take you to the point where the user ID and password are required, and then we'll cancel the procedure.

Before we continue, turn off the Startup dialog box. We won't need it again.

Here's how:

1. Open AutoCAD and select **Start From Scratch** on the dialog box. Pick **OK** to continue.
2. Enter the ***Startup*** command.
3. AutoCAD asks you to enter a value; enter ***0***.
4. Close AutoCAD.

## Do This: 1.4.2.1 — Saving Your Drawing to an Internet Site

I. Begin an AutoCAD session (double-click on the AutoCAD icon on the desktop).
II. Follow these steps.

### 1.4.2.1: Saving to an Internet Site

1. Begin by entering the ***Saveas*** command.

   **Command: *saveas***

2. Enter the ftp address to our Internet site (*ftp://ftp.uneedcad.com/2007/MyDrawing.dwg**).
   Notice (right) that you'll need to include the extension when saving to an Internet site.

**I used this site as an example. If you have problems with this one, any ftp site will work.*

3. Pick the **Save** button .


4. AutoCAD asks you for the network password. If you had the proper **User name** and **Password**, you would enter them here and AutoCAD would save the drawing to the appropriate Internet address. Since we can't save without the password, pick the **Cancel** button to exit the command.

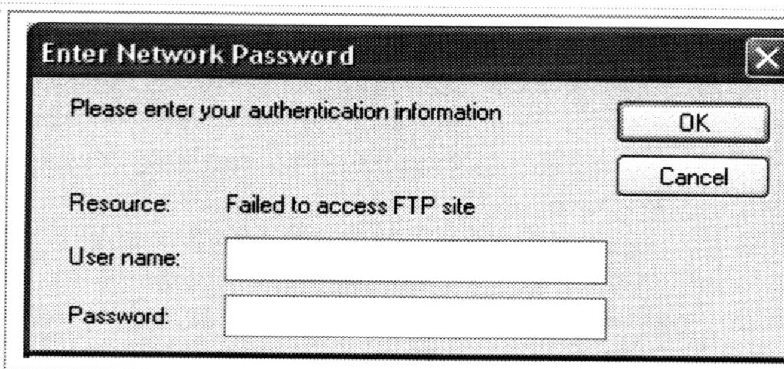


5. Close your Internet connection. (Note: If you have accessed the Internet through a company network, this may not be possible or practical. Move on to Step 6.)

6. Exit AutoCAD without saving the drawing .

   **Command: *quit***

## 1.5 Opening an Existing Drawing

How you open a drawing depends in part on where the drawing is located. Let's look at the various procedures one at a time.

### 1.5.1 Opening a Drawing from a Local or Network Drive

You won't find opening an AutoCAD file (a drawing) any different from opening a file in most Microsoft applications.

## Do This: 1.5.1.1 — Opening an Existing Local/Network Drawing

I. Begin a new AutoCAD session (double-click on the desktop icon).

II. Follow these steps.

| 1.5.1.1: OPENING A DRAWING |
| --- |
| 1. Begin by picking the **Open** button  on the Standard toolbar. (Alternately, you can enter ***open*** at the command prompt, or use the Windows method of holding down the CTRL key and typing ***o***.)<br>**Command:** ***open*** |
| 2. Navigate to the C:\Steps\Lesson01 folder just as you did in Exercise 1.4.1.1. |
| 3. Select the *pid-1* drawing file (shown below). Notice that AutoCAD previews the drawing in the area to the right. |
| 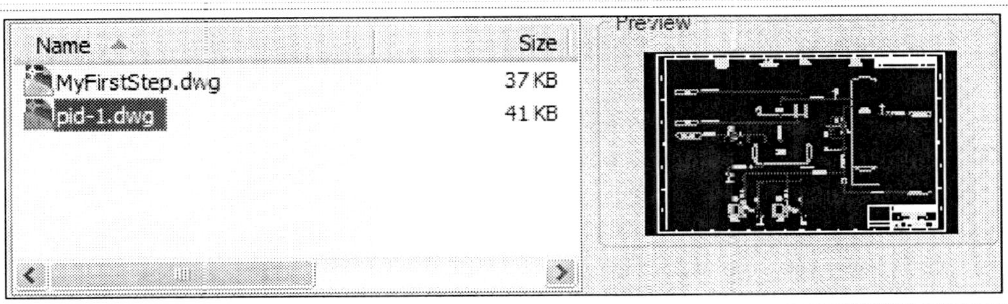  |
| 4. Now double-click on *pid-1*. AutoCAD will open the drawing for editing. |

## 1.5.2 Opening a Drawing from an Internet Site

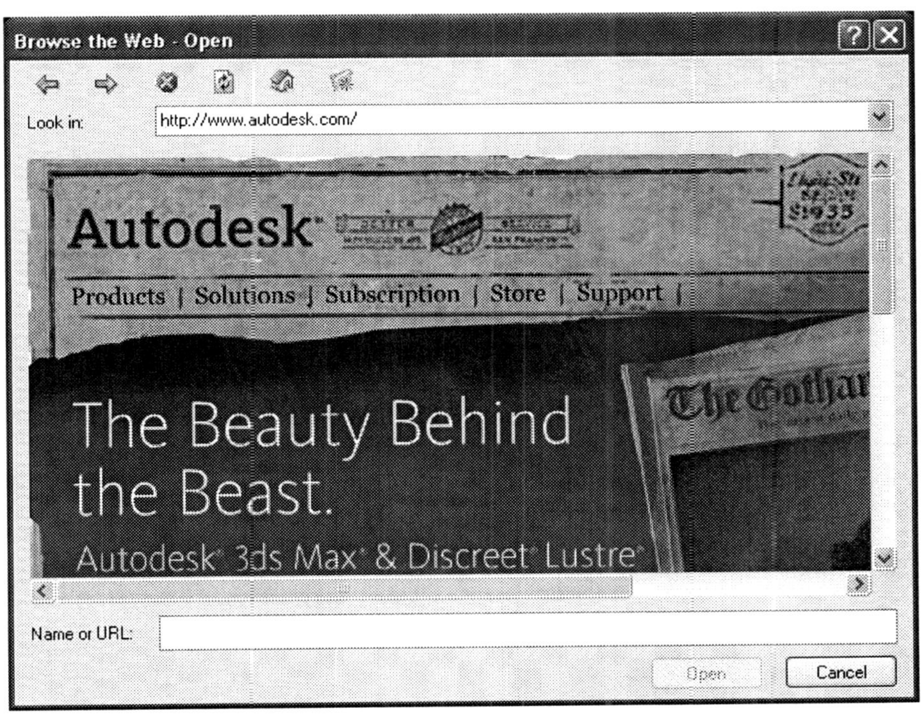


Figure 1.010

Search the Web Button

Thanks to some remarkable work by AutoCAD programmers, we may now access Internet files as easily as we access files on our own computers. But as always, we have a couple of approaches available to us. Luckily, both involve the now familiar Windows Select File dialog box.

- To access a drawing (or Xref, block, or OLE Object – all things that you'll learn about later) via the Internet, simply begin the ***Open*** command (enter ***open*** at the command prompt), and then type the file's address in the **File name** text box. Be sure to type the complete address and include the file's extension (.dwg).
- Another approach to accessing a file over the Internet involves AutoCAD's browser (Figure 1.010 – the image may vary). To open it, pick the **Search the Web** button on the Select File dialog box's toolbar (along the top of the Select File dialog box).

AutoCAD's web browser works like any other web browser – except that it makes opening a drawing a bit easier.

- Internet Explorer users will find some familiar buttons across the top of the browser. From left to right, these are:
    - **Back** – for returning to the last address.
    - **Forward** – for moving from an address reached via the **Back** button to the next address in sequence.
    - **Stop** – for stopping the browser when a search is taking too long.
    - **Refresh** – for cleaning up the screen or reloading the current address.
    - **Home** – for returning to the home page. By default, AutoCAD uses its own home page here. But you can change the home page with the ***InetLocation*** command. The command sequence is

        **Command: *inetlocation***

        **Enter new value for INETLOCATION <"http://www.autodesk.com">: *http://www.uneedcad.com***
    - **Favorites** – for opening the Windows Favorites folder.
- To go to another web site, type the address into the **Look in** text box (top of the browser). Be sure to hit enter so AutoCAD will know when you've finished entering the address.
- Once you've reached the web site, you can pick on the file name you wish to open. If the site doesn't show the file, enter the file name in the **Name or URL** text box.

In our next exercise, we'll open a drawing that's located at our UNeedCAD site.

But how can so many people open the same drawing? Simple – AutoCAD actually copies the original drawing into a temporary folder on your hard drive. You'll work on it there until you're ready to save it. This way, you don't have to maintain an open connection to the Internet indefinitely.

Let's begin.

> Although AutoCAD will automatically dial your ISP connection if Windows has been configured to do so, you may need to open the connection before trying to access a web site via AutoCAD's browser. You can do this by executing your dialup connection, or simply by opening your browser as you normally would. Many corporate offices or schools connect to the Internet via their own networks. In this situation, you probably won't need to do anything since network/Internet access is automatic.

| **Do This: 1.5.2.1** | **Opening Files on the Internet** |
|---|---|

I. Begin a new AutoCAD session. (Close any other sessions you may have open.)

II. Follow these steps.

## 1.5.2.1: Opening Files on the Internet

1. Enter the ***Open*** command at the command prompt, or pick the **Open** button on the Standard toolbar.

**Command:** ***open***

2. Type the address of the file to open into the **File name** text box. (The address is *http://www.uneedcad.com/2007/web.dwg*. Be sure to include the extension.)

3. Pick the **Open** button to continue. AutoCAD transfers the file to a local folder and opens it for you. (AutoCAD may present a File Download status box depending on the speed of your connection.) The drawing looks like the following figure.

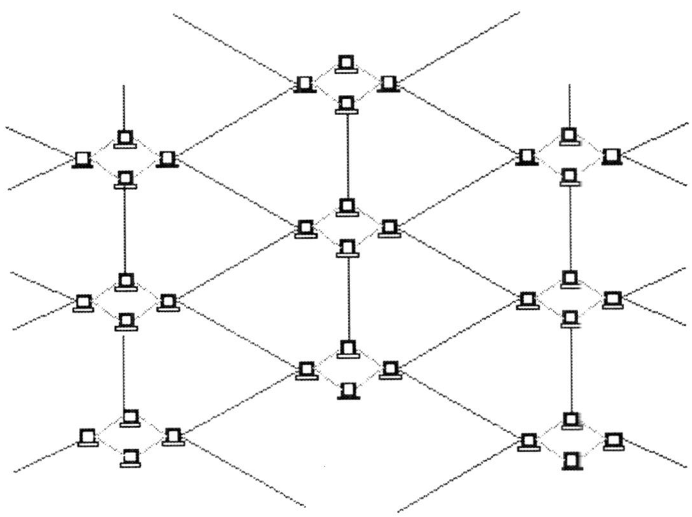

4. Now let's take a look at AutoCAD's browser. Repeat Step 1.

**Command:** ***open***

5. In the Select File dialog box, pick the **Search the Web** button (just above the **Preview** frame). (Alternately, you can hold down the ALT key while pressing the 3 key.) AutoCAD presents the browser (Figure 1.010).

6. First, we'll go to the web site. Enter the address in the **Look in** control box as indicated in the figure below. The address is: *http://www.uneedcad.com/2007*. (Be sure to hit ***enter***.)

## 1.5.2.1: OPENING FILES ON THE INTERNET

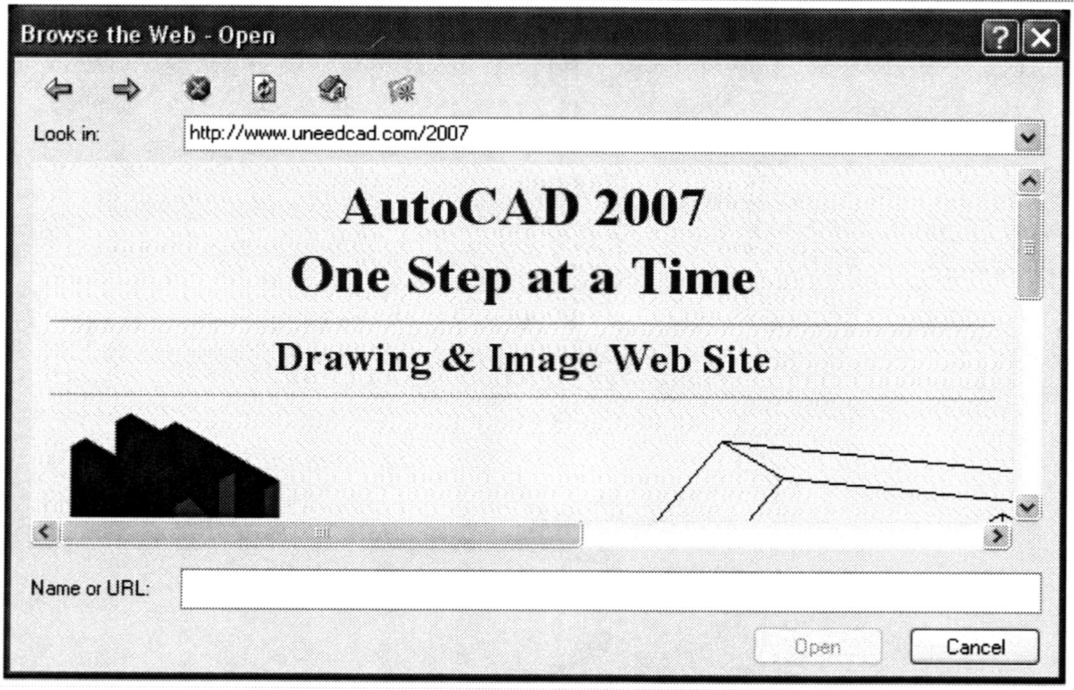


7. Scroll (use the scroll bars) until you see the *Gable.dwg* image on the right (following figure).

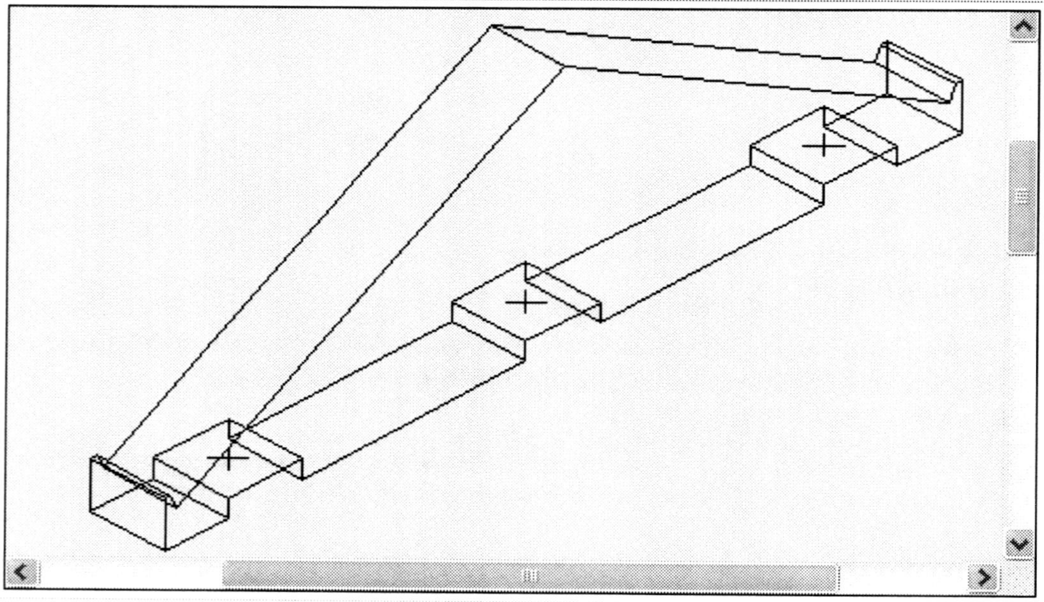

8. Pick on the *Gable.dwg* image. AutoCAD places the name and location of the drawing in the **Name or URL** text box (see figure below).

## 1.5.2.1: Opening Files on the Internet

9. Pick the **Open** button 

to open the drawing. AutoCAD will download the drawing just as it did in Step 3.

Was that easy? One way to make it even easier is to list the web site in the Favorites folder of your browser. Then you can pick the **Favorites** button on the AutoCAD browser and simply select the site from there. This saves quite a bit of typing.

# 1.6 Partial Open and Partial Load

A real timesaver has been included with AutoCAD file managing capabilities. The ***Partialopen*** command allows you to open only that part of a drawing necessary for completion of a simple task. You can specify what part of the drawing to open based on saved views or layers (more on these in Lessons 4 and 6). This ability minimizes the time spent loading or regenerating a full drawing and increases system performance by reducing the amount of memory required for the editing task.

The command sequence for ***Partialopen*** looks like this:

> **Command:** ***partialopen***
>
> **Enter name of drawing to open:** ***[enter the name of the drawing to open]***
>
> **Enter view to load or [?]<*Extents*>:** ***[enter the name of the desired view]***
>
> **Enter layers to load or [?]<none>:** ***[tell AutoCAD which layers to load, or enter a * for all layers]***
>
> **Unload all Xrefs on open? [Yes/No] <N>:** ***[unloading xrefs will save time; if they aren't pertinent to your task, type "Y" before hitting enter]***

But the easiest way to partially open a drawing is simply to select the **Partial Open** button on the Select File dialog box presented by the ***Open*** command. AutoCAD will present the Partial Open dialog box. Let's take a look at how this is done.

> What the bee-jeepers are layers and Xrefs and views you ask? It's okay to wonder at this point because these things haven't been explained yet. Don't let it bother you that it feels a bit confusing; it won't confuse you when you've finished the course. For now, you don't need any of these things, and additional explanation at this point might be more bewildering than helpful. In fact, you won't need ***Partialopen*** until you start using very large drawings. So you can relax.

| **Do This: 1.6.1** | **Partially Opening a File** |
|---|---|

I. Be sure you're in a drawing session. Close any open drawings.

II. Follow these steps.

## 1.6.1: Partially Opening a File

1. Enter the ***Open*** command 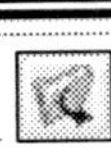. AutoCAD presents the Select File dialog box.

   **Command:** ***open***

2. Navigate to the C:\Steps\Lesson01 folder and select the *pid-1.dwg* file.

## 1.6.1: PARTIALLY OPENING A FILE

3. Pick the down arrow next to the **Open** button and select **Partial Open** from the menu. AutoCAD presents the Partial Open dialog box seen in the following figure.

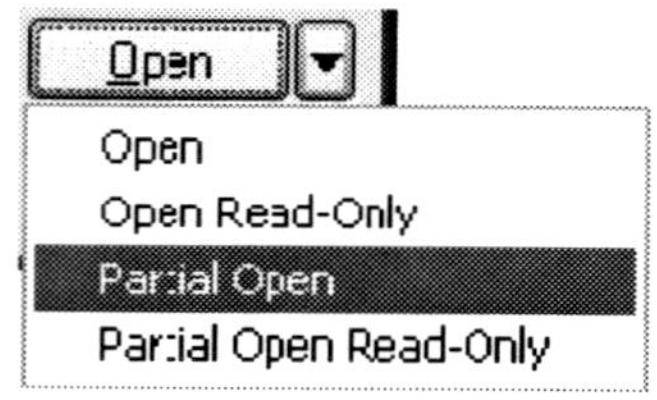


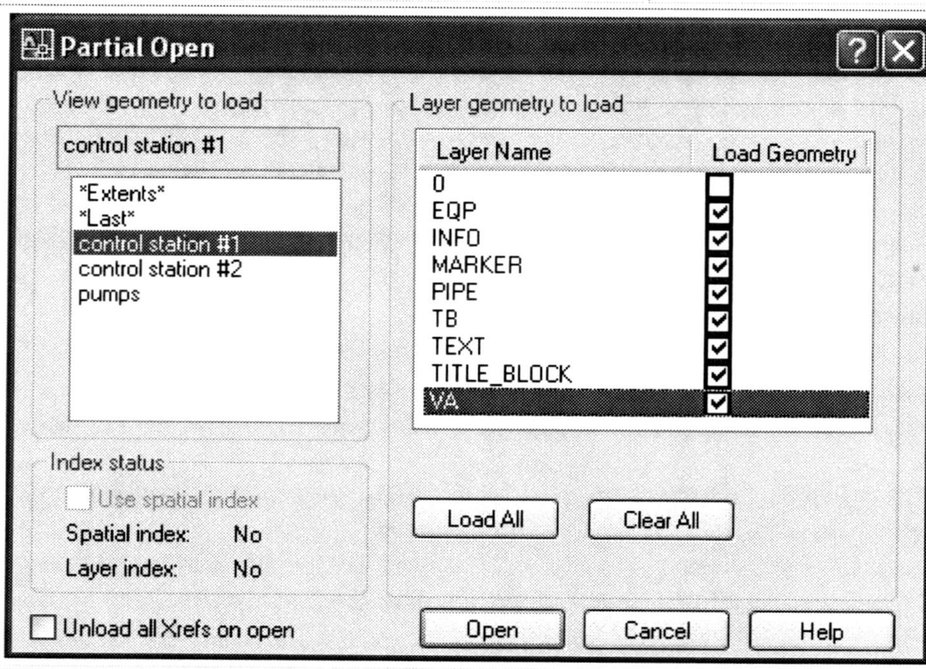


4. Select the *control station #1* view and check the layers indicated in the right frame.

5. Pick the **Open** button 

. AutoCAD opens just the part of the drawing shown below.

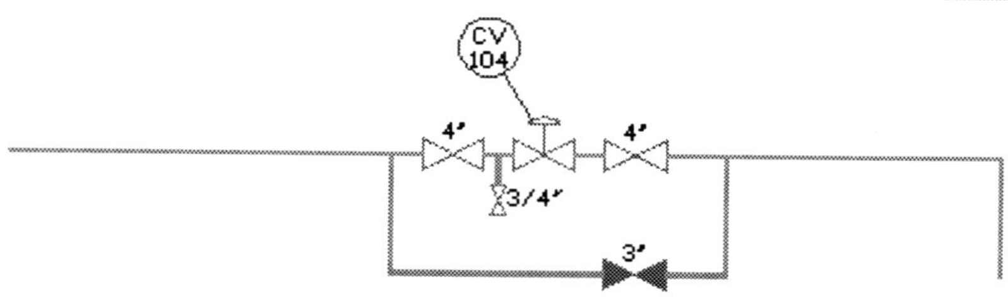


> Note that when opening a drawing that was saved in the partially opened state, AutoCAD will present a warning box giving you the opportunity to partially open it using the same settings previously used or to fully open it.

Once the drawing is partially opened, you can work on the opened section only. But there will be times when you'll discover that you need more of the drawing than originally anticipated. For this reason, AutoCAD also provides the ***Partiaload*** command. Using this command, you have the flexibility to open (or load) additional parts of the partially opened drawing. The ***Partiaload*** command works with the Partial Load dialog box, which is very similar to the Partial Open dialog box.

Let's give it a try.

| Do This: 1.6.2 | Partially Loading a File |
|---|---|

I. Be sure you're still in the *pid-1.dwg* file you partially opened in Exercise 1.6.1. If not, repeat that exercise now.

II. Follow these steps.

**1.6.2: PARTIALLY LOADING A FILE**

1. Enter the ***Partiaload*** command. AutoCAD presents the Partial Load dialog box shown in the figure following Step 2.

**Command: *partiaload***

2. Select the *pumps* view and the layers indicated in the following figure.

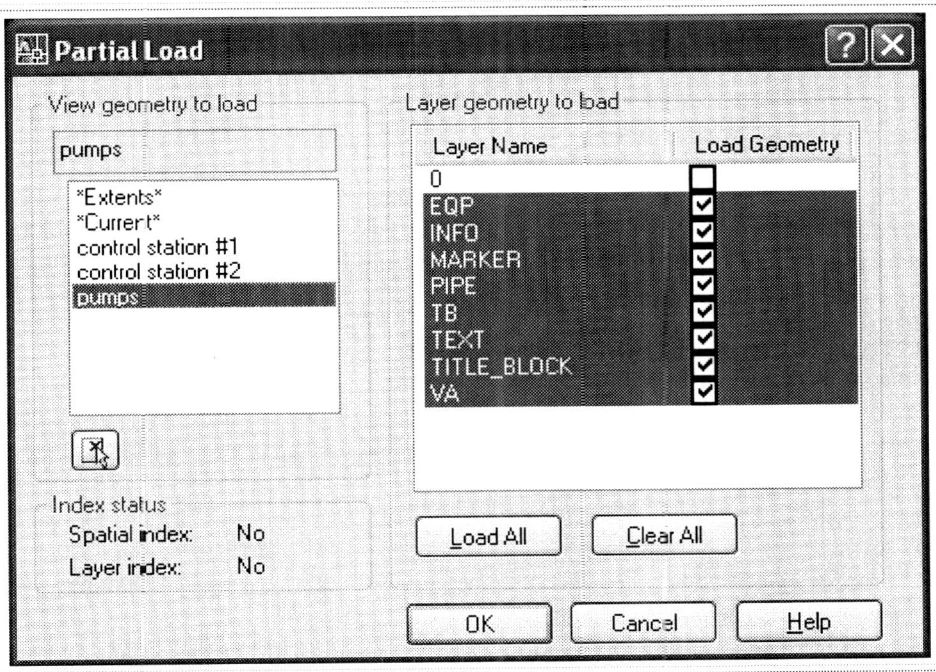


3. Pick the **OK** button 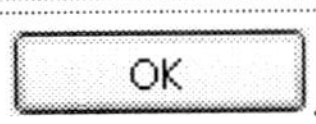
.

4. Type in the commands shown. (We'll look more closely at the ***Zoom*** command in Lesson 4.)

**Command: *zoom***

**Specify corner of window, enter a scale factor (nX or nXP), or [All/Center/Dynamic/Extents/Previous/Scale/Window/ Object] <real time>: *e***

AutoCAD displays the *pid-1* drawing as seen in the following figure.

### 1.6.2: Partially Loading a File

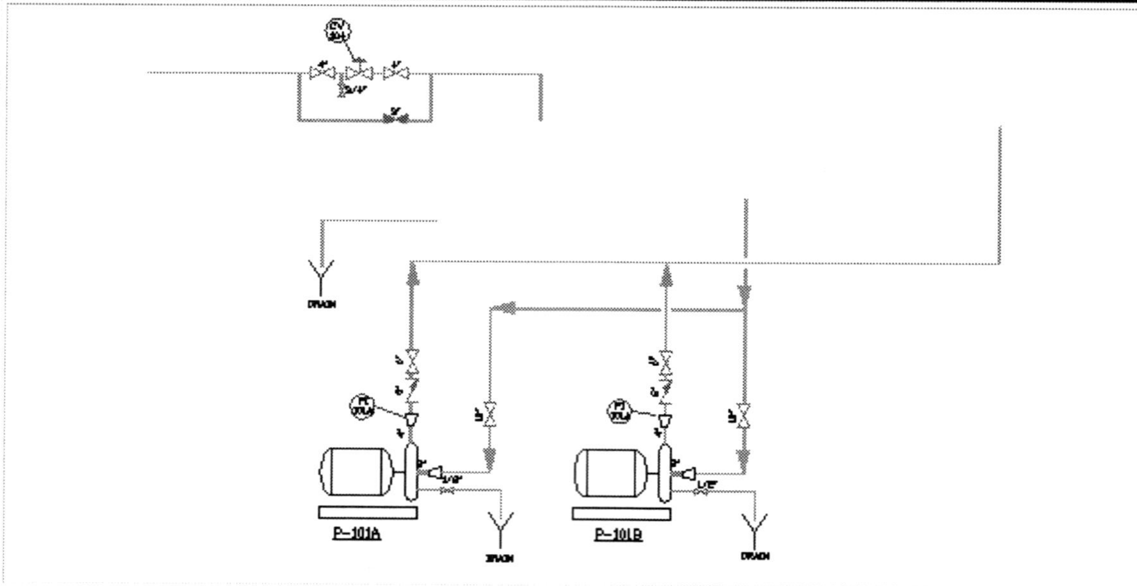


5. Quit the drawing without saving it.

   **Command: *quit***

The ***Partiaload*** command complements and serves as a fix for oversights in the ***PartialOpen*** command. Remember these timesaving tools when you're working on very large drawings.

Now let's take a look at another timesaver.

## 1.7 Creating and Using Templates

We've learned how to set up a new drawing using wizards from the Startup dialog box. But let's face it; this is a tedious procedure at best. About midway through the exercise, many students ask if "we have to do this every time." The answer is, "NO!"

You should have to set up a drawing once for each scale and sheet size you'll use. So you may have a ¼"=1'-0" drawing setup for an 11 x 17 sheet of paper, a 3/8"=1'-0" drawing for an 11 x 17 sheet, a ¼"=1'-0" for a 24 x 36, and so forth. But once set up, you should not have to set it up again regardless of how many times you may need it.

Here's how this works. Set up your drawing, but save it as a template. Then, when you need to create a drawing at that scale and with those limits (on that size sheet of paper), use the template to create the drawing. Any drawing created with that template will carry the same setup as the template. But the template will never change unless you overwrite it, so you can use it repeatedly.

Now let's see if we can create a template from the *MyFirstStep* file we created earlier. We'll see how to use the template to start a new drawing, too.

> We'll set up our template using some basic stuff – sheet size and scale. But templates can and should also include such things as dimension and text styles, plot styles, layers, and more. You'll learn about these things over the course of this text.
>
> AutoCAD also provides a host of predefined templates that can also be of use with some adjustments for project-specific details.

| Do This: 1.7.1 | Creating a Template |
|---|---|

I. Open the *MyFirstStep* file in the C:\Steps\Lesson01 folder.
II. Follow these steps.

| 1.7.1: CREATING A TEMPLATE |
|---|
| 1. Enter the ***Saveas*** command. AutoCAD presents the Save Drawing As dialog box we examined in Exercise 1.4.1.1. **Command: *saveas*** |
| 2. Pick the down arrow in the **Files of type** control box and select the **AutoCAD Drawing Template** option (as shown in the following figure). |

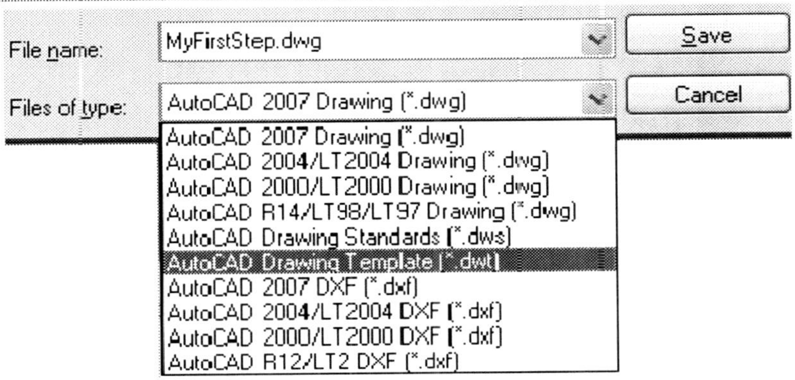


3. AutoCAD automatically changes the path to place the template in its own template folder. Change it back to save our template in the C:\Steps\Lesson01 folder.

4. Call it *MyFirstTemplate* as shown.

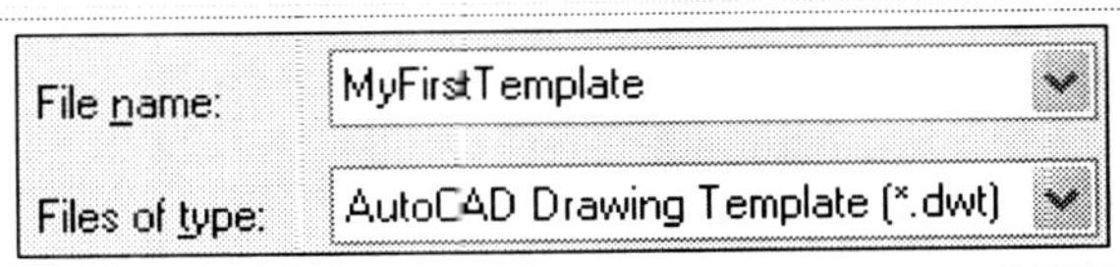


5. Pick the **Save** button 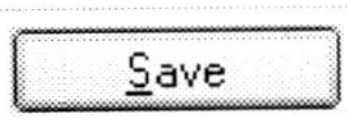

.

6. AutoCAD presents a Template Description dialog box. You can enter a description if you wish, but it isn't required. Pick the **OK** button 

to complete the procedure.

7. Close the drawing template .

**Command: *close***

That was easy! Now let's create a new drawing using the template you just created.

| Do This: 1.7.2 | Using a Drawing Template |
|---|---|

I. Begin an AutoCAD session.
II. Follow these steps.

## 1.7.2: Using a Drawing Template

1. Select **New** from the File pull down menu. Alternately, you can enter ***New*** at the command prompt.

**Command: *new***

2. A Select Template dialog box appears (similar to an Open File dialog box). Navigate to the C:\Steps\Lesson01 folder and select the *MyFirstTemplate* you created in the last exercise (see following figure).

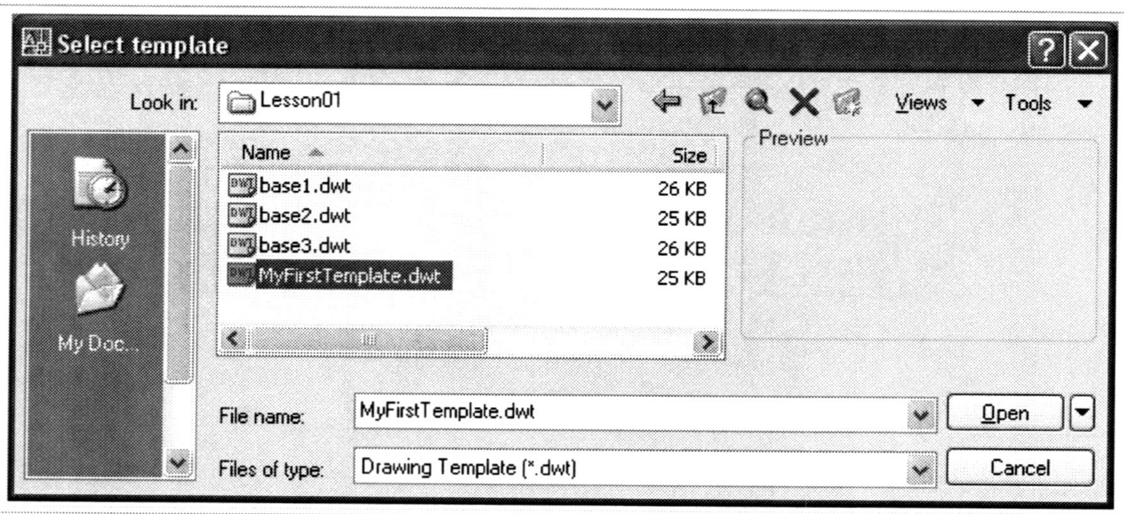


3. Pick the **Open** button  to complete the procedure.

Remember, you can use the setup in a template file as many times as you wish with this procedure. The drawing you create will contain all the information (setup, drawing, etc.) found in the template, but using the template will in no way affect the template itself.

## 1.8 Changing the Setup or Starting a New Drawing from Scratch

The possibility always exists that you may need to change your basic setup after you've already begun a drawing session. Maybe you entered the wrong sheet size or used engineering units instead of architectural. You can still adjust, even if you've already begun to draw. (Or you may, like many experienced AutoCAD drafters, simply prefer to start all of your drawings from scratch – that is, using AutoCAD's default setup – and then change the settings manually.)

To change units, enter ***Units*** at the command prompt. AutoCAD will provide the Drawing Units dialog box (Figure 1.011 – next page) where you can identify the new units and unit precision, as well as the angle type, precision, and direction.

To change the sheet size, enter ***Limits*** at the command prompt. AutoCAD will prompt you for the lower left coordinates of your drawing, using 0,0 as the default (see the following insert). Accept the default by hitting ***enter*** on you keyboard.

> Note that most companies will use 0,0 as the lower left corner of their drawings. Occasionally, however, a company may choose to use *true coordinates*. This is best explained by example.
>
> In the petrochem world, plants are divided into units. Each unit may have one or more drawings specific to that unit. Vessels and other items in the unit are located in the plant by overall *east/west* and *north/south* (*X* and *Y*) coordinates. It's often useful to identify the east/west and north/south coordinates with the X and Y coordinates in AutoCAD. This way, every item in the

plant can be quickly located in the drawings simply by doing an ***ID*** command. (We'll look at the ***ID*** command in Lesson 8.)
When using true coordinates, the absolute location of the drawing will dictate the lower left as well as the upper right corners of the drawing limits.

AutoCAD will then prompt you for the upper right coordinates. Get these from the Drawing Scales chart and enter them as ***width,height*** (no spaces). The sequence looks like this:

**Command: *limits***
**Reset Model space limits:**
**Specify lower left corner or [ON/OFF] <0.0000,0.0000>: *[enter]***
**Specify upper right corner <12.0000,9.0000>: *[enter the new width and height]***

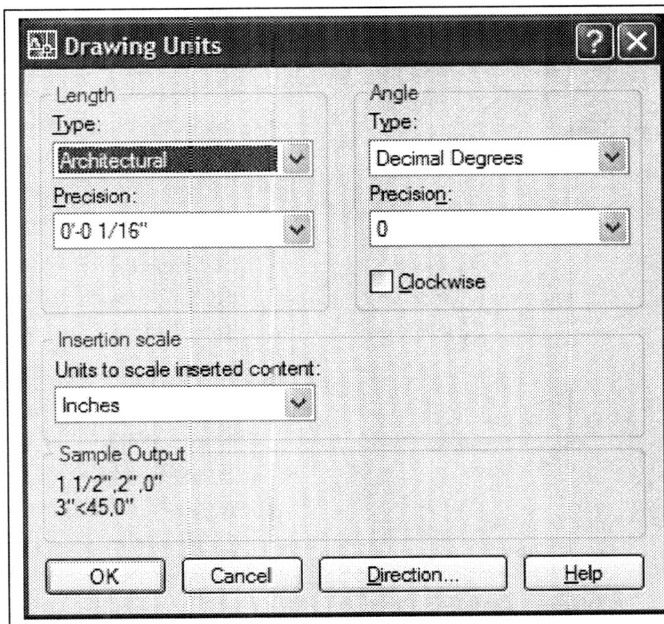


Figure 1.011

While you can make these adjustments at any time during your drawing session, I don't recommend waiting too long. It's always best to groom good habits from the very beginning.

We'll set up several drawings from scratch over the course of our text, so you'll become familiar with the ***Units*** and ***Limits*** commands.

If you're already in AutoCAD and you want to start a new drawing from scratch, pick the **New** button on the Standard toolbar. AutoCAD will open a new drawing from scratch. Alternately, you can select New from the File pull down menu or enter Newt at the command prompt. AutoCAD will open a Select Template dialog box. You can bypass the selection of a template by picking the down arrow next to the **Open** button and selecting **Open with No Template – [Imperial** or **Metric]** (shown here).

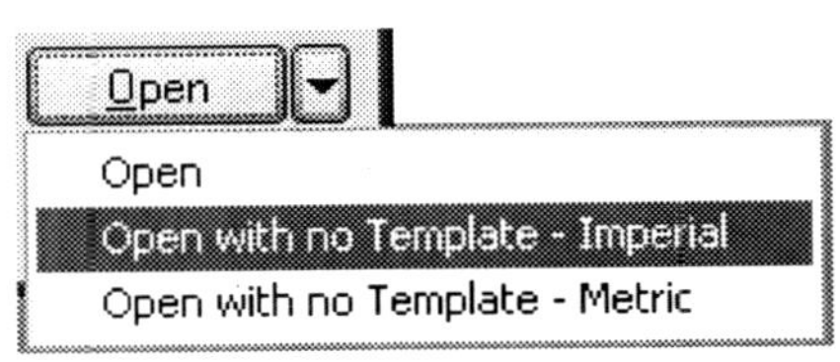


## 1.9 Extra Steps – The Info Palette

Similar in purpose (if not appearance) to Microsoft's Office Assistants, the Info Palette provides instructions, hints, and help whenever you need it. The initial screen, shown in Figure 1.012, even explains how to use the Info Palette itself!

This powerful tool works like a good reference book and a good teacher packed into one window. If you ever find yourself lost or unsure of how to proceed, simply look to the Info Palette for detailed instructions.

To display the Info Palette, select **Info Palette** from the Help pull-down menu (or type **5** while holding down the CTRL key on your keyboard). Alternately, you can use the keyboard and enter ***Assist***. Any of these approaches will activate it. Like other palettes, the Info Palette remains active until you turn it off (although you can use the Auto-hide feature to minimize its distracting presence on your screen. Of course, picking on the **X** at the top of the title bar will remove it from the screen.

While AutoCAD displays the Info Palette, you don't even have to ask for help. Just proceed through the drawing process as you normally would. The Info Palette will provide information about each and every command you enter!

Let's take a look at how to control this useful monster!

Figure 1.012

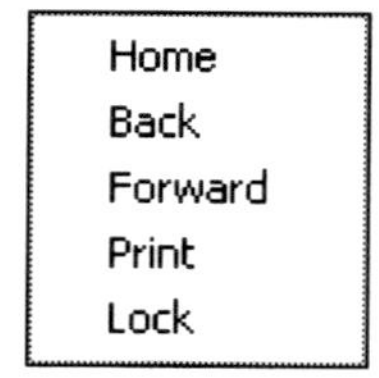

Figure 1.013

Begin by right-clicking in the palette. AutoCAD presents the cursor menu shown in Figure 1.013. You'll recognize the first four options presented as options normally found on a web browser or the Windows Explorer. They serve the same navigational purpose here. (Notice that icons for the same options appear at the top of the Info Palette.)

- **Home** returns the palette to the initial screen where you find convenient information on how to use the Info Palette.
- **Back** returns you to the previously viewed palette.
- **Forward** works only after you've used **Back** to return to previously viewed palette. It takes you forward to the next screen you've viewed.
- **Print** allows you to print the information currently displayed in the Info Palette.
- **Lock**, when checked, tells AutoCAD to stop displaying information for the commands you're giving. The constantly changing display can become a bit of an irritant unless you need the information. This helps prevent that while keeping the palette immediately available to assist you.

## 1.10 What Have We Learned?

*Items covered in this lesson include:*

- *The Info Palette*
- *The Quick and Advanced Setup Wizards*
- *Templates*
- *The AutoCAD User Interface*
- *Dynamic Input Display*
- *Commands:*
    - ***QSave***
    - ***Save***
    - ***SaveAs***
    - ***Close***
    - ***Closeall***
    - ***Quit***
    - ***Open***
    - ***PartialOpen***
    - ***Partiaload***
    - ***Units***
    - ***Limits***
    - ***InetLocation***
    - ***UCSIcon***
    - ***CommandLine***
    - ***CommandLineHide***
    - ***ToolPalettes***
    - ***WSSave***

Well, now you've gotten your feet wet. How was it?

Any road begins with a first step, and any design begins with some basic decisions; what scale should I use … what size sheet of paper do I need … should I listen to country or rock-n-roll while I draw?

We have looked at how to accomplish most of these tasks on a computer, using AutoCAD as our tool. In the next few lessons, you'll see a whole new world of possibilities opening before you as we explore this wonderful drafting tool.

But first, let's get some practice with what we have learned so far.

## 1.11 Exercises

*Using the **Quick Setup**, create a few templates to use later in this course.*

1. Create a template with these parameters:
   - 1.1.1. Use architectural units;
   - 1.1.2. Use a 1=1 scale (this requires no setup; it is the default);
   - 1.1.3. Set up for a sheet size of 8½ x11;
   - 1.1.4. Save this project as *MyBase1.dwt* in the C:\Steps\Lesson01 folder.
2. Create a new template with the following parameters:
   - 2.1.1. Use architectural units;
   - 2.1.2. Use a 1=1 scale;
   - 2.1.3. Set up for a sheet size of 11x17;
   - 2.1.4. Save the project as *MyBase2.dwt* in the C:\Steps\Lesson01 folder.
3. Create a third template with the following parameters:
   - 3.1.1. Use architectural units;
   - 3.1.2. Use a 1=1 scale;
   - 3.1.3. Set up for a sheet size of 17 x 22;
   - 3.1.4. Save the project as *MyBase3.dwt* in the C:\Steps\Lesson01 folder.

*For more exercises related to Lesson 1, please see Lesson 1 in AutoCAD 2007: One Step at a Time – Workbook.*

## 1.12 For Web-Based Review Questions, visit: http://www.uneedcad.com/2007/Files/07R1.pdf

# Lesson

# 2

Following this lesson, you will:

- ✓ *Know how to use the basic draw commands: **Line** and **Rectangle***
- ✓ *Know how to use the basic modify commands: **Erase**, **Undo**, **Redo** and **MRedo***
- ✓ *Know how to select objects using object selection, window, and crossing window methods*
- ✓ *Know how to use the display controls: **Redraw** and **Regen***
- ✓ *Know how to use AutoCAD's Cartesian Coordinate System*
- ✓ *Know how to use Dynamic Input*

# Drawing Basics – Lines & Coordinates

*We can define drafting as the placing of geometric shapes on paper to represent existing or proposed objects. Of course we're using a computer rather than the traditional paper or vellum medium, but the results are the same.*

*All geometric shapes can be formed by the constructive use of two simple objects – lines and circles. Did you know that, in a 2-dimensional CAD environment, a drafter spends only about 30% of his time placing lines and circles? He spends the vast majority of his time modifying what he has drawn and placing text on the drawing. Still, without a basic knowledge of placing lines and circles, the drafter will never leave the starting gate.*

*We'll begin this lesson learning to use the most basic geometric shape with which we can work – the line. (We'll save circles for Lesson 4.) Then we'll explore the coordinate system AutoCAD uses to identify locations within the drawing.*

## 2.1 Lines and Rectangles

AutoCAD has created commands that are really quite simple to remember. For example, to draw a line, you type ***line*** at the command prompt. To draw a circle, you type ***circle***. To erase an object, what do you think you would type? Did you say ***erase***? That's right!

But wait; it gets simpler yet! Can't type? Most commands have simple abbreviations, or *hotkeys* (also called *aliases* or *shortcuts*). To draw a line, you can type ***l***. To erase, type ***e***. I'll identify the hotkeys for each command as we progress through the book.

Of course, if you have an aversion to the keyboard, there's almost always a toolbar or palette approach to each command. We'll look at those as well.

The ***Line*** command provides a nice uncluttered approach to seeing the command prompt in action. The sequence involved in drawing a two-point line is as follows:

**Command: *line* (or *l*)**

**Specify first point: *1,1 [enter the coordinate for a point or pick a point on the screen]***

**Specify next point or [Undo]: *2,2 [again, enter the coordinate for a point or pick a point on the screen]***

**Specify next point or [Undo]: *[hit enter to complete the command, or you can click the right mouse button and select* Enter *from the cursor menu]***

> If you've toggled dynamic input on (the **DYN** toggle on the status bar is depressed), you'll see a lot happening on the screen as you type. Don't let it worry you. You can toggle it off (raise the **DYN** toggle by picking on it) if you prefer. We'll look at dynamic input in more detail in a few minutes.

Not too difficult, is it? Try it. Start a new drawing using the *Sample Template 02* template in the Lesson02 folder. (Notice that I've provided a background grid to help guide you through the drawing.) Enter the preceding sequence. Remember to hit the ***enter*** key on the keyboard after each line of information. Otherwise, AutoCAD won't know you've finished your command. The final ***enter*** tells AutoCAD that you've finished the command. The numbers represent coordinates on the drawing. We'll discuss them in Section 2.4.

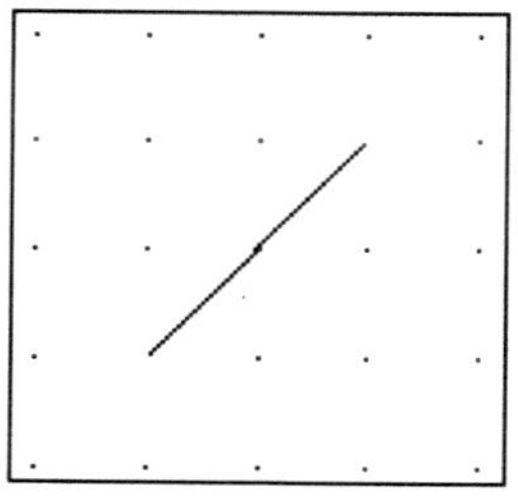

Figure 2.001

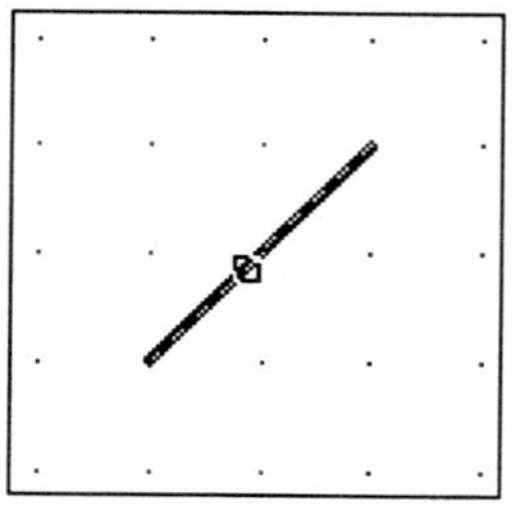

Figure 2.002

Does the lower left quadrant of your screen look like Figure 2.001? Excellent!

Okay, now erase the line. Use this sequence.

**Command: *erase* (or *e*)**

**Select objects:** ***[The crosshairs become a tiny box and the line highlights when you cross over it (Figure 2.002). Place the box over the line and pick once with the left mouse button. The line becomes dashed, or highlighted.]***

**Select objects:** ***[enter or click the right mouse button – the line disappears]***

Now try an exercise.

Try to draw the figure shown in Figure 2.003. Don't worry if you can't get the lines perfect just yet. This is your first time. Besides, we'll soon find much easier and more accurate ways of drawing.

> Your first "Hail Mary" option: You'll frequently find yourself entering a command too fast or out of order. Don't worry. If you make a mistake, use the escape key (ESC) in the upper left corner of most keyboards. You'll return to the command prompt where you can start over.

| Do This: 2.1.1 | Drawing Lines |
|---|---|

I. Start a new drawing using the *Sample Template 02* template file in the C:\Steps\Lesson02 folder.

II. We'll take this opportunity to see two different approaches to locate points in AutoCAD. Begin by turning the Polar and OTrack displays off (the **POLAR** and **OTRACK** toggles on the status bar should be raised). Then be sure the **DYN** toggle on the status bar is depressed.

III. Follow these steps.

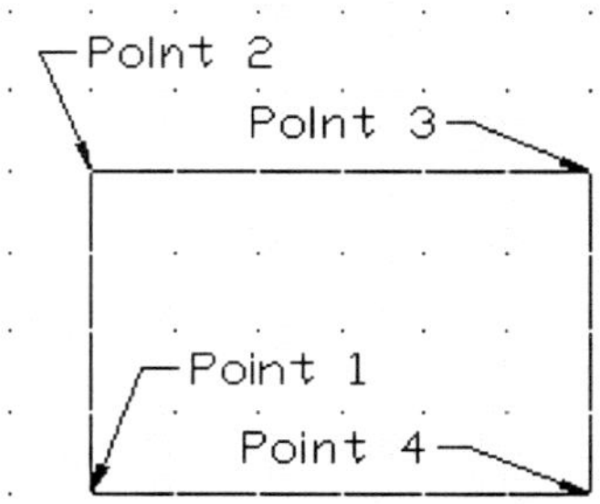


Figure 2.003

## 2.1.1: DRAWING LINES

1. Enter the ***Line*** command at the command prompt by typing ***line*** or ***l***. Alternately, you can pick the **Line** button  on the Draw toolbar or Draw palette, or select **Line** from the Draw pull-down menu.

    **Command:** ***l***

2. Using the dynamic entry display next to the crosshairs, select a point around grid reference 2,1.

    **Specify first point:** ***[pick a point near 2,1]***

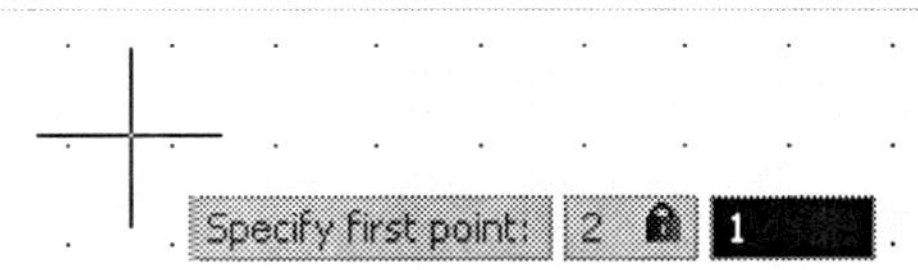


3. Now move your cursor to a point around 2,3. (Use the coordinate display at the lower left corner of your screen to help locate the proper coordinate.) Ghost dimensions have appeared (right) indicating that you've moved your crosshairs 2" at a 90° angle (the angle dimension is above the tooltip in our example). The **DYN** button on the status bar toggles this display on or off.

    Pick with the left mouse button when you're display looks like ours.

    **Specify next point or [Undo]:** ***[pick a point near 2,3]***

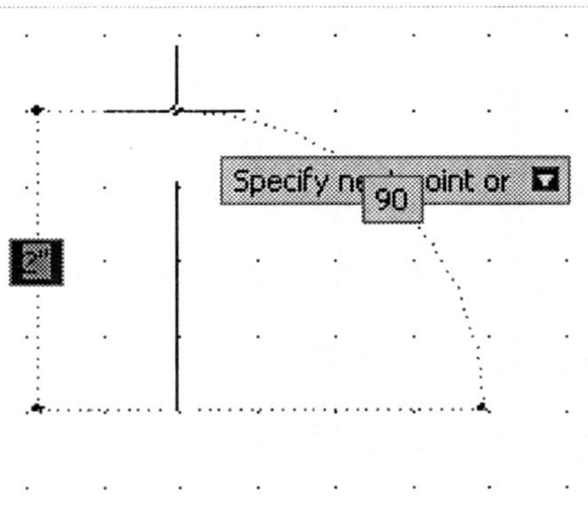

## 2.1.1: Drawing Lines

4. Pick the **DYN** toggle DYN on the status bar to turn off the dynamic display.

5. Pick the **POLAR** toggle POLAR on the status bar to turn on the polar display.

6. Now select a point around 5,3.

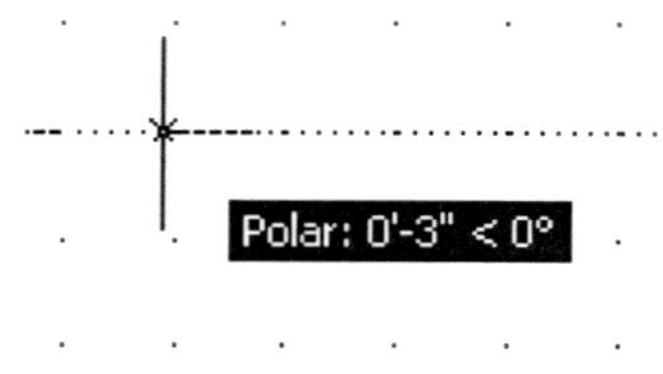


A tooltip has appeared that reads **Polar: 0'-3"<0°**. This *polar display* tells you that you've moved your cursor 3" over on the X-axis. We'll learn more about coordinate entry methods – including Polar – in Section 2.4. The **POLAR** toggle on the status bar toggles this display on or off.

Additionally, a ghost line has appeared indicating that you're moving in a true 0° direction. (These ghost lines appear for N-S-E-W directions.) The **POLAR** toggle on the status bar also controls this ghost line.

**Specify next point or [Undo]:** ***[pick a point near 5,3]***

7. And then select a point around 5,1 (about 2" straight down – or at a 270° angle).

**Specify next point or [Close/Undo]:** ***[pick a point near 5,1]***

6. Finally, type ***c*** to close the line.

**Specify next point or [Close/Undo]:** ***c***

Did you notice that last command? When used in response to a ***Line*** or ***Polyline*** command prompt, ***c*** will close the line (that is, it'll draw a line from the last point selected to the first point selected).

Using either the polar display or the dynamic display, you may find it difficult (although not impossible) to draw your lines without some accuracy. But I wouldn't use them at the same time; too much help can be a nuisance! Throughout this text, experiment with both. Then when you go to work, you can use the one you prefer.

Some things to remember when drawing lines:

- Hitting ***enter*** at the **Command** prompt will always repeat the last command regardless of what that command was. (You may also right-click in the graphics area and pick the repeat line at the top of the cursor menu.)
- Hitting ***enter*** at the **Specify first point** prompt will cause the last point selected to be the first point of the line. In other words, if you leave the line prompt before you actually finish drawing the lines you want, you can hit ***enter*** to repeat the ***Line*** command, and then hit ***enter*** again to continue from where you stopped.
- ***C*** will always draw a line from the last point selected to the first point selected during this command sequence … but only during *this* sequence. In other words, if you return to the **Command** prompt, enter the ***Line*** command again, and then continue the same line, ***C*** will draw a line from the last point selected back to the first point of the current sequence. (When entered at the **Command** prompt, ***C*** wil begin the ***Circle*** command.)

All of this will become clearer as we go.

Try some random lines and experiment with these last few statements. When you're comfortable with them, erase all the lines as explained previously. Then continue.

Let me show you an easier way to draw the same rectangle by using only two picks. We'll use the ***Rectangle*** command this time.

The ***Rectangle*** command sequence is:

> **Command:** ***rectangle*** **(or *rec*)**
>
> **Specify first corner point or [Chamfer/Elevation/Fillet/Thickness/Width]:** ***2,1 [identify the first corner of the rectangle]***
>
> **Specify other corner point or [Area/Dimensions/Rotation]:** ***5,3 [identify the opposite corner of the rectangle]***

Go ahead and try the preceding sequence. Does it look better than the one you drew using the ***Line*** command? Was it easier to draw?

Now erase it. Did you notice something different here? You only had to select one line and the entire rectangle highlighted. The rectangle is a *polyline*.

> A *polyline* is a multi-segmented line, or a line consisting of one or more than one line segment. We'll cover this more advanced line tool in Lesson 8.

Did you notice that AutoCAD gave you several options when you drew the rectangle? In the first prompt of the ***Rectangle*** command, you may select to draw a **Chamfered** (mitered) or **Filleted** (round-cornered) rectangle. Or you can use the **Width** option for a rectangle with heavier lines. The other options, **Elevation** and **Thickness**, involve 3-dimensional space. We'll cover those in the 3D text. The default choice will always precede the bracketed options. Our response in the preceding sequence accepted the default choice. AutoCAD read ***2,1*** as the **first corner point** of the rectangle.

The second prompt gave you a **Dimensions** option. After selecting the first corner of the rectangle, you can use this prompt to tell AutoCAD how large a rectangle to draw. AutoCAD will then prompt you for the orientation of the new rectangle.

Let's examine our options.

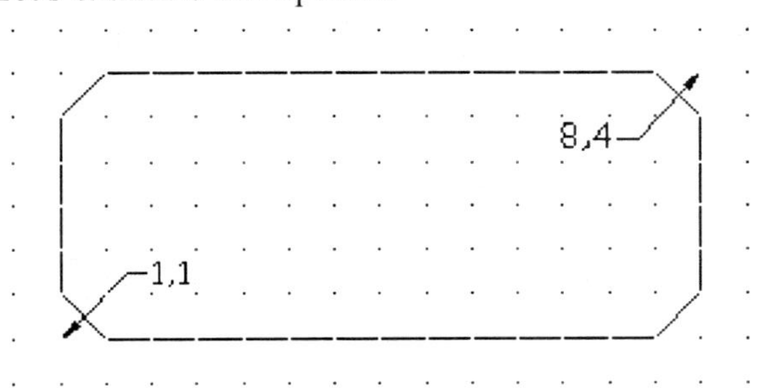


Figure 2.004

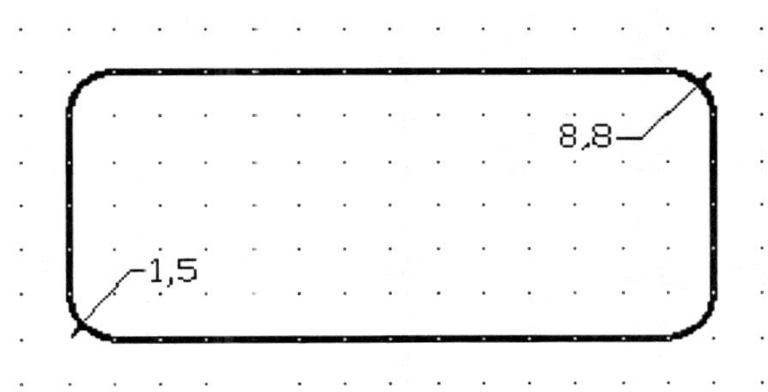


Figure 2.005

To draw a rectangle with ½" chamfered corners (Figure 2.004), use this sequence:

> **Command:** ***rectangle*** **(or *rec*)**
>
> **Specify first corner point or [Chamfer/Elevation/Fillet/Thickness/Width]:** ***c [use the Chamfer option]***
>
> **Specify first chamfer distance for rectangles <0'-0">:** ***.5***
>
> **Specify second chamfer distance for rectangles <0'-0 1/2">:** ***[hit enter to accept the default]***
>
> **Specify first corner point or [Chamfer/Elevation/Fillet/Thickness/Width]:** ***[select point 1]***
>
> **Specify other corner point or [Area/Dimensions/Rotation]:** ***[select point 2]***

The sequence for drawing a filleted rectangle is essentially the same as that of the chamfered. Here's the sequence for drawing a filleted rectangle with 1/16" wide lines (Figure 2.005).

> **Command:** ***rectangle*** **(or *rec*)**
>
> **Specify first corner point or [Chamfer/Elevation/Fillet/Thickness/Width]:** ***w [use the Width option]***

**Specify line width for rectangles <0'-0">:** ***1/16***

**Specify first corner point or [Chamfer/Elevation/Fillet/Thickness/Width]:** ***f [use the Fillet option]***

**Specify fillet radius for rectangles <0'-0">:** ***1/2***

**Specify first corner point or [Chamfer/Elevation/Fillet/Thickness/Width]:** ***[select point 1]***

**Specify other corner point or [Area/Dimensions/Rotation]:** ***[select point 2]***

The sequence for drawing a rectangle by area looks like this:

**Command:** ***rectangle*** **(or *rec*)**

**Specify first corner point or [Chamfer/Elevation/Fillet/Thickness/Width]:** ***[pick or select one of the rectangle's corners]***

**Specify other corner point or [Area/Dimensions/Rotation]:** ***a [tell AutoCAD you wish to use the Area option]***

**Enter area of rectangle in current units <100.000>:** ***[how much area should your rectangle contain?]***

**Calculate rectangle dimensions based on [Length/Width] <Length>:** ***[you can identify either the width or the length of your rectangle; AutoCAD will calculate the rest based on the area you've entered]***

**Enter rectangle length <100.000>:** ***[tell AutoCAD what length or width you'd like for your rectangle; AutoCAD will do the rest]***

The beginning of the sequence for drawing a rectangle by dimensions is identical to that for drawing a rectangle by area. The rest of the sequence looks like this:

**Specify other corner point or [Area/Dimensions/Rotation]:** ***d [tell AutoCAD to use the Dimensions option]***

**Specify length for rectangles <100.000">:** ***[how long should your rectangle be?]***

**Specify width for rectangles <100.000>:** ***[how wide should your rectangle be?]***

**Specify other corner point or [Area/Dimensions/Rotation]:** ***[this option is deceptive – you'll actually need to enter the rotation of the rectangle now; you can pick a point on the screen if you wish]***

The beginning of the sequence for drawing a rectangle by rotation is identical to that for drawing a rectangle by area or dimensions. The rest of the sequence looks like this:

**Specify other corner point or [Area/Dimensions/Rotation]:** ***r [ tell AutoCAD to use the Rotation option]***

**Specify rotation angle or [Pick points] <0>:** ***[tell AutoCAD what rotation angle to use]***

**Specify other corner point or [Area/Dimensions/Rotation]:** ***[now you can continue by picking points or using the Area or Dimensions options; AutoCAD will draw the rectangle at the angle you specified]***

Now try some rectangles.

| Do This: 2.1.2 | Drawing Rectangles |
|---|---|

I. Start a new drawing using the *Sample Template 02* template file in the C:\Steps\Lesson02 folder.

II. Follow these steps to draw a simple rectangle.

## 2.1.2: Drawing Rectangles

1. Enter the ***Rectangle*** command by typing ***rectangle*** or ***rec*** at the command prompt.

Alternately, you can pick the **Rectangle** button on the Draw toolbar or palette or select it from the Draw pull-down menu.

**Command:** ***rec***

2. Type in the lower left coordinate as shown. (We'll learn more about coordinate entry later in this lesson.)

**Specify first corner point or [Chamfer/Elevation/Fillet/Thickness/Width]:** ***1,1***

3. Type in the upper right coordinate as shown. (For clarity, we'll show command line entry throughout this book; but feel free to use dynamic entry if you prefer.) Your rectangle will look like the figure that follows.

**Specify other corner point or [Area/Dimensions/Rotation]:** ***8,4***

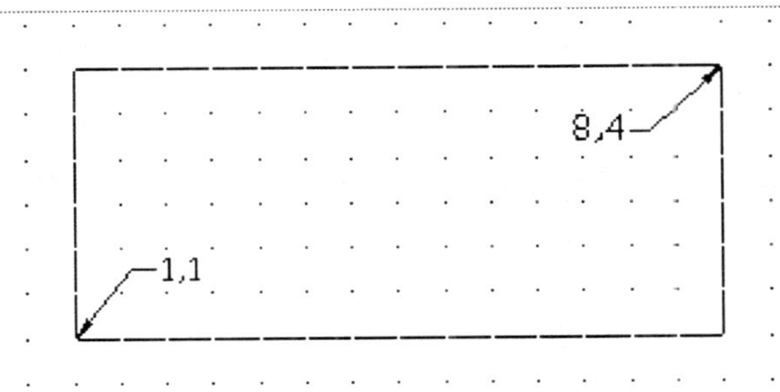


III. Now draw a ½" chamfered rectangle as follows. (This time, we'll use the **Dimensions** option.)

4. Repeat the ***Rectangle*** command.

**Command:** ***[enter]***

5. You can type ***c*** for the **Chamfer** option, but this might be a good time to see how useful a cursor menu can be. Right-click (click with your right mouse button) in the graphics area, and select **Chamfer** from the cursor menu.

**Specify first corner point or [Chamfer/ Elevation/Fillet/ Thickness/Width]:** ***c***

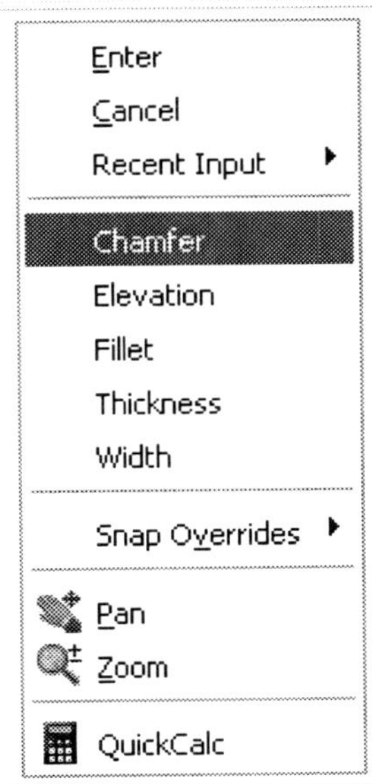


6. Tell AutoCAD what the chamfer distances should be (that is, how far back on each line of the corner to begin the angle).

**Specify first chamfer distance for rectangles <0'-0">:** ***1/2***

7. AutoCAD automatically sets the second chamfer distance the same distance as the first. You can accept by hitting ***enter***, or give a different number. Let's accept.

**Specify second chamfer distance for rectangles <0'-0 1/2">:** ***[enter]***

8. Now tell AutoCAD where to draw. Type in the lower left coordinates.

**Specify first corner point or [Chamfer/Elevation/Fillet/Thickness/Width]:** ***1,5***

## 2.1.2: Drawing Rectangles

9. When prompted for the other corner, tell AutoCAD you want to use the **Dimensions** option either by typing ***d*** at the prompt or by selecting **Dimensions** from the right-click cursor menu.

**Specify other corner point or [Area/Dimensions/Rotation]: *d***

10. AutoCAD asks you to identify the **length** and **width** of the rectangle. Enter the numbers indicated.

**Specify length for rectangles <0'-10">: 7**

**Specify width for rectangles <0'-10">: 3**

11. When AutoCAD prompts you again for the other corner, move your cursor around and see how it reorients the rectangle according to the cursor's position in the drawing. Pick a point directly above the first corner point. AutoCAD creates the rectangle shown in the following figure (without the dimensions).

**Specify other corner point or [Area/Dimensions/Rotation]:**

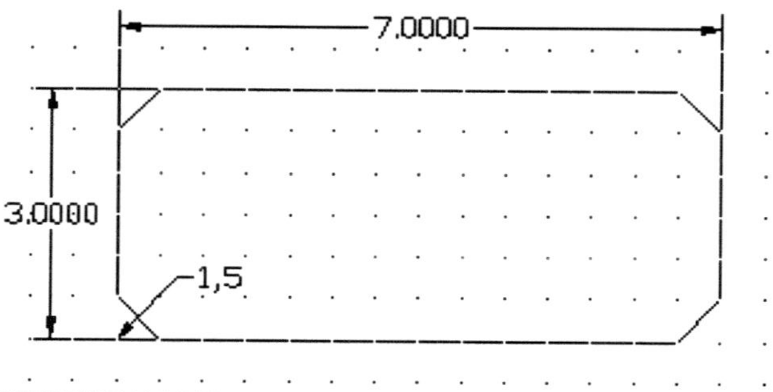


IV. Now draw a ¾" filleted rectangle with 1/16" wide lines and an area of 22 sq. in.

12. Repeat the ***Rectangle*** command 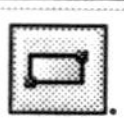.

**Command: *[enter]***

13. AutoCAD tells you that you're currently set up to draw a chamfered rectangle. It also tells you the chamfer distances. We'll change that now.

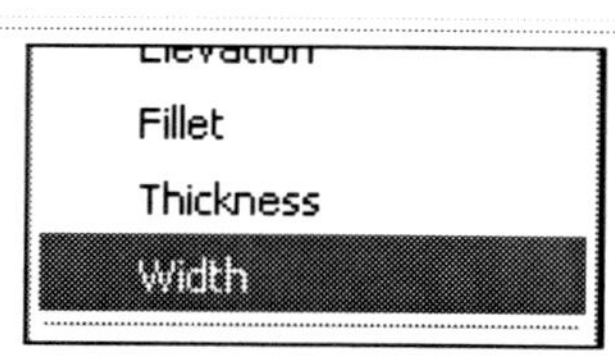


Type ***w*** for the **Width** option (or select **Width** from the cursor menu).

**Current rectangle modes: Chamfer= 0'-0 1/2" x 0'-0 1/2"**

**Specify first corner point or [Chamfer/Elevation/Fillet/Thickness/Width]: *W***

14. Tell AutoCAD how wide to make the lines.

**Specify line width for rectangles <0'-0">: *1/16***

15. Type ***f*** for the **Fillet** option (or select **Fillet** from the cursor menu).

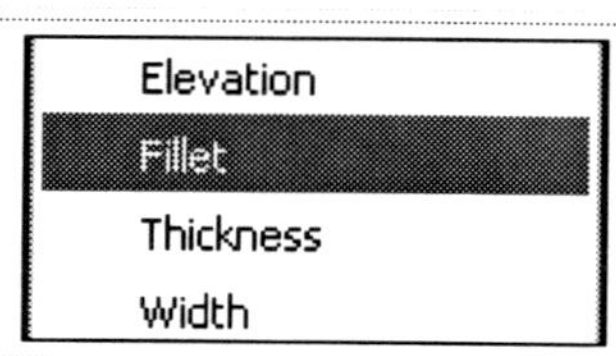


**Specify first corner point or [Chamfer/Elevation/Fillet/Thickness/Width]: *F***

### 2.1.2: Drawing Rectangles

16. Tell AutoCAD the radius you want for your fillets.

    **Specify fillet radius for rectangles <0'-0 1/2">:** *3/4*

17. Tell AutoCAD where to draw. Type in the lower left coordinates.

    **Specify first corner point or [Chamfer/Elevation/Fillet/Thickness/Width]:** *4,2.5*

18. Now tell AutoCAD to base the rectangle on an area that you'll give it.

    **Specify other corner point or [Area/Dimensions/Rotation]:** *A*

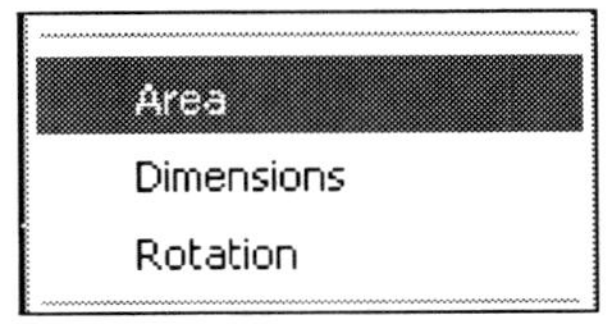


19. And tell it to make the area 22 sq. in.

    **Enter area of rectangle in square inches <100.0000>:** *22*

20. Use the **Length** option …

    **Calculate rectangle dimensions based on [Length/Width] <Length>:** *[enter]*

21. … and make the length *6*". Your rectangle will look like the following figure.

    **Enter rectangle length <0'-0">:** *6*

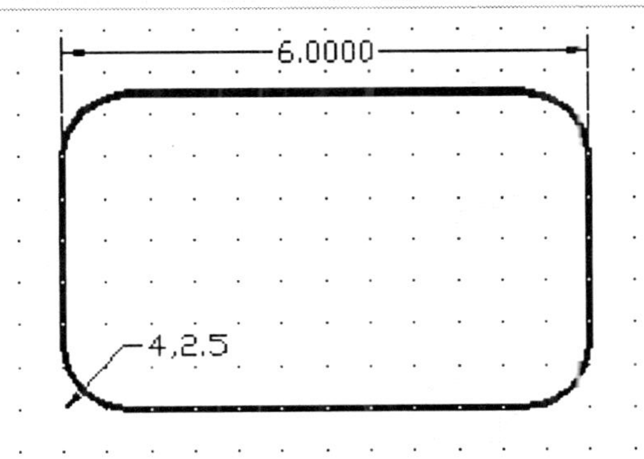


19. Leave the drawing without saving the changes .

    **Command:** *quit*

Have you noticed that you don't need to put inch marks on your numbers? We've set up our drawing using architectural units. The inch is the basic architectural unit. AutoCAD knows this, so we don't have to indicate it. We would have to indicate feet, however, with a prime (').

AutoCAD uses a rather different approach to entering feet and inches in response to a prompt. To enter one-foot-seven-and-one-half-inches, for example, type ***1'7-1/2***. Notice the lack of a dash between the feet and inch numbers. Separate these only with the foot mark (the prime, '). Use a dash to separate inches from fractions.

The reason for this is simple: AutoCAD reads a space the same way it reads ***enter***. So you can't use a space as a separator. (But you can use it instead of the **Enter** key!)

## 2.2 Fixing the Uh-Ohs: *Erase*, *Undo*, and *Redo/MRedo*

When I first studied drafting – using charcoal from the fire and drawing on the cave walls – I thought the electric eraser was the height of laziness. I mean, how spoiled could a professional be?

Then I got my first drafting job. I was assigned to removing revision clouds from old cloth drawings. I had an electric eraser (and a sore hand) by the second day.

Today, the CAD system makes erasure even easier than that old Bruning did.

You're already familiar with the command sequence for erasing a single object, or a group of objects one at a time:

> **Command:** ***erase*** **(or** ***e*****)**
>
> **Select objects:** ***[select an object]***
>
> **Select objects** ***[AutoCAD allows you to select more objects if you'd like; otherwise, hit*** **enter** ***to complete the command]***

We'll take a look at some ways to speed this up a bit in a few minutes. But first, we should look at how we fix mistakes. If, for example, your erasure was a mistake, you can use the ***Undo*** command to return your drawing to a point before the mistake occurred.

Although the ***Undo*** command hasn't changed much in the last few releases of AutoCAD, it has become significantly easier to access. Further, its counterpart – the ***Redo*** command – has been usurped by the newer and more powerful ***MRedo*** command.

We'll look at ***Undo*** first. I'll explain the command sequence; but I'll warn you up front that you'll probably never use it. Here's the sequence:

> **Command:** ***undo***
>
> **Current settings: Auto = On, Control = All, Combine = Yes**
>
> **Enter the number of operations to undo or [Auto/Control/BEgin/End/Mark/Back] <1>:** ***[enter]***

Let's look at the options.

- **Enter the number of operations to undo** (the default) – undoes the specified number of preceding commands. The default number is one, so an ***enter*** will undo a single command.
- **Auto** – undoes a menu selection as a single command. Remember that menu commands and toolbar commands cause a macro to run. If **Auto** is set to ***Off***, undo will only undo one step of the macro at a time. If it's ***On*** (the default setting), ***Undo*** will undo the entire macro at once. (The **Current settings** list before the command line prompt will tell you if **Auto** is on or off.
- **Control** – controls how **Undo** performs. It has four options: **All/None/One/Combine**.
    - **All** – allows ***Undo*** to function fully, providing virtually unlimited undos.
    - **None** – turns ***Undo*** **Off**.
    - **One** – limits ***Undo*** to the last command only.
    - **Combine** – controls whether consecutive ***Pan*** and ***Zoom*** commands are treated as a single undo or redo operation.
- **Begin** and **End** – **Begin** begins a group. All commands entered after the **Begin** option will be treated as a single command and are undone by a single ***Undo***. **End** ends the **Begin** option.
- **Mark** and **Back** – **Mark** places a mark in the command sequence. **Back** undoes back to the mark.

Now, about the ***Undo*** command … Most of these options sound good; but as I warned you, you'll never use them. I've rarely, in the years I've worked with CAD, known in advance that I would be undoing a command. How would I know to **Mark** or **Begin** a sequence for later undoing?

I advise people to learn the ***U*** command discussed next. It'll cover your needs and not require you to memorize the ***Undo*** options. Additionally, the upgraded **Undo** button on the Standard toolbar allows a much easier method to undo many commands at once.

The ***U*** command acts as a macro for the default ***Undo*** option, and assumes a number of one. If you need to use the keyboard to undo something, you'd be much better off using ***U*** rather than its more confusing cousin – ***Undo***.

Even more promising than the *U* command is the **Undo** button on the Standard toolbar (Figure 2.006). Picking the **Undo** arrow will undo the last command – just as it will in most Windows-based software. In this regard, it simply runs the *U* command one time.

But if you look to the right of the **Undo** button, you'll find a down arrow that'll list the last several commands you've run. You can select to undo from one to all of these in a single stroke!

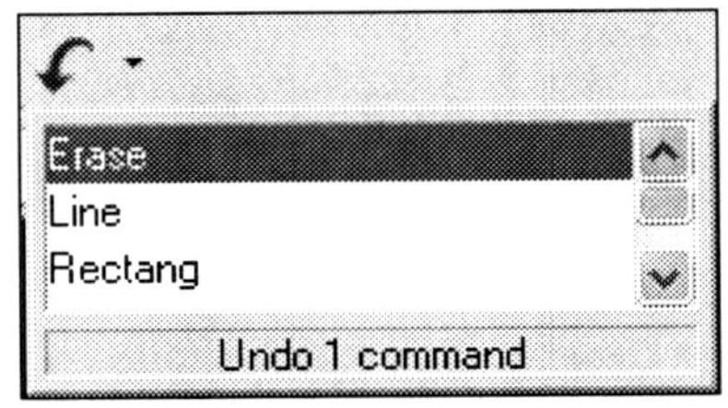

Figure 2.006

Perhaps the most important thing to remember about the ***Undo*** command family is the one thing that you can't undo; you can t undo the undo that you just did! You can, however, *redo* what you undid. (Don't worry … we'll have an exercise in a minute that'll make this a bit clearer.)

AutoCAD provides two 'redo' tools – ***Redo*** and ***MRedo***. The first – ***Redo*** – simply redoes whatever the last ***Undo*** undid. ***Redo***, however, is only good once, and only after one of the ***Undo*** commands. ***MRedo*** is a bit more flexible and allows you to redo several undos at once. Here's the sequence:

**Command:** ***mredo***

**Enter number of actions or [All/Last]:** ***[tell AutoCAD if you wish to redo only the last undo, or all the previous undos]***

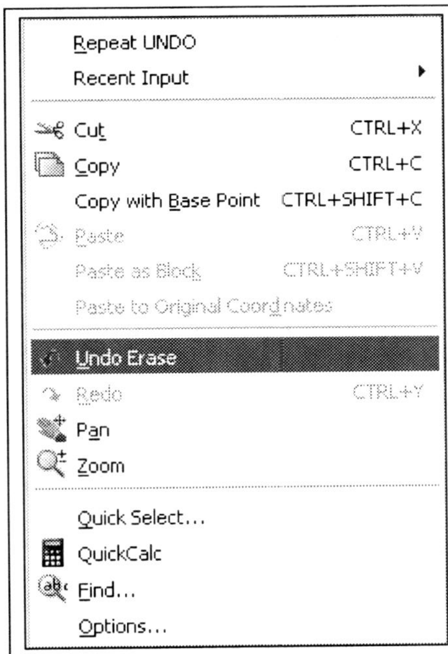

Figure 2.007

You'll also find the ***Undo*** (***U***) and ***Redo*** commands on the default cursor menu (Figure 2.007). Just right-click anywhere in the graphics area of the drawing with nothing selected and the command prompt empty.

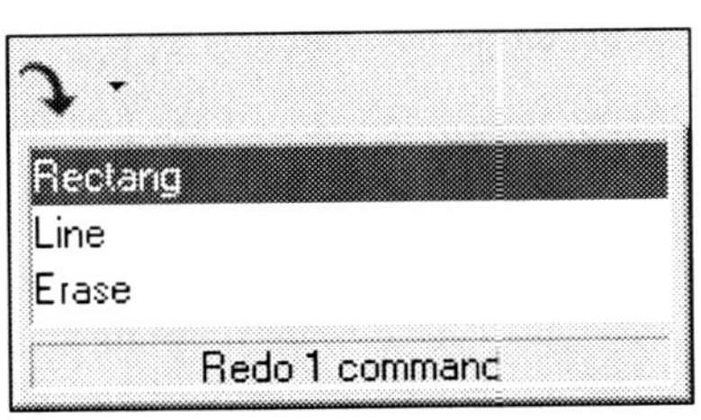

Figure 2.008

The **Redo** button to the right of the **Undo** button on the Standard toolbar (Figure 2.008) actually calls the ***MRedo*** command and sports a down arrow next to it that functions much like the down arrow next to the **Undo** button.

Now you have five of AutoCAD's "Hail Mary" procedures – Escape, ***Erase***, ***Undo***, ***Redo***, and ***MRedo***. You're probably nicely confused. Let's see if an exercise can help clear things up for you.

| Do This: 2.2.1 | Erase, Undo, and Redo |
|---|---|

I. Open drawing *erase-samp*, in the C:\Steps\Lesson02 folder.
II. Follow these steps.

**2.2.1: ERASE, UNDO, AND REDO**

1. Enter the ***Erase*** command by typing ***erase*** or ***e***. Alternately, you can pick the **Erase** button  on the Modify palette or toolbar (docked to the right of your screen), or select **Erase** from the Modify pull-down menu.

**Command: *e***

2. Pick one of the lines by placing the selection box on it and clicking the left mouse button as indicated.

3. Confirm that you've finished selecting (hit ***enter*** or use the right mouse button).

**Select objects: *[enter]***

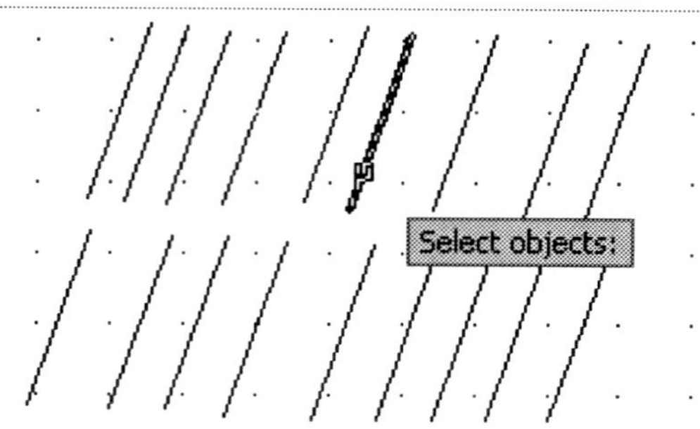


4. Undo the erasure either by typing ***U*** at the command prompt or by picking the **Undo** button  on the Standard toolbar.

Notice that the erased line returns.

**Command: *u***

5. Redo the erasure by typing ***redo*** at the command prompt or by picking the **Redo** button  on the Standard toolbar.

**Command: *redo***

6. Repeat Steps 1, 2, and 3 until you have erased another four lines. (Be sure to repeat all three steps four times.)

**Command: *e***

7. Now pick the down arrow next to the **Undo** button and select the last three ***Erase*** commands.

Notice that the last three lines you erased return to the screen.

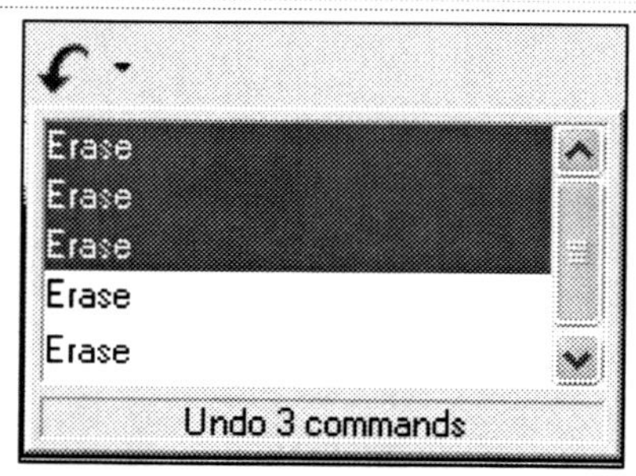


8. Pick the down arrow next to the **Redo** button and select two ***Erase*** commands.

Notice that two of the lines you erased have once again been removed from the drawing. Notice also that they were erased in the order in which they were originally selected.

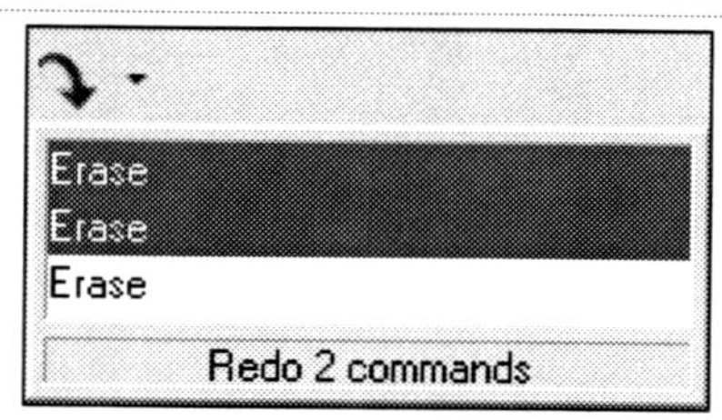

You can also take advantage of the DELETE key in much the same way you can in other Windows programs. Simply select the object to be erased (without entering a command) and then hit the DELETE key.

## 2.3 Multiple-Object Selection Made Easy

We've seen how easily we can erase a single object. But what if we want to erase 20 or 200 objects? Must we select 20 or 200 times?

The answer, of course, is no! Let's look at a couple of options that'll make multiple object selection easier.

The first option places a window around the objects to be selected (refer to Figure 2.009). What do you suppose it's called? What do you think the shortcut will be? If you said, "window" and ***w***, you were quite right. A window selection includes all the objects that are completely within a window.

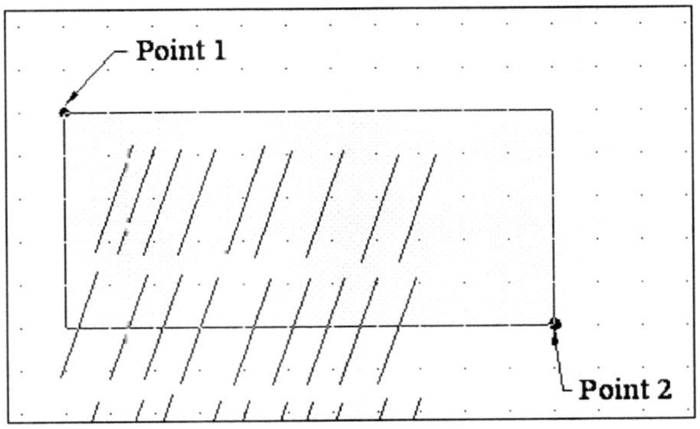

Figure 2.009

Let's give it a try.

### Do This: 2.3.1 Using a Window to Select Multiple Objects

I. Close and reopen the *erase-samp* drawing you used in the last exercise. Don't save the changes. (It's in the C:\Steps\Lesson02 folder.)

II. Follow these steps.

| 2.3.1: Window Selections |
|---|
| 1. Enter the ***Erase*** command.<br>**Command: *e*** |
| 2. Tell AutoCAD you want to use a window to make your selections by entering a ***w*** at the **Select objects** prompt.<br>**Select objects: *w*** |
| 3. Place your first corner near **Point 1** in the drawing (refer to Figure 2.009).<br>**Specify first corner:** |
| 4. Place the opposite corner near **Point 2**. (Notice that the window has a blue shade to it.)<br>**Specify opposite corner:** |
| 5. Complete the command by hitting ***enter*** at the **Select objects** prompt.<br>Notice that only the lines that were completely encircled by the window were erased.<br>**Select objects: *[enter]*** |
| 6. Undo the erasure.<br>**Command: *u*** |

The second option places a window around *and across* the objects to be selected. This one is called *crossing* and uses ***c*** as a shortcut. The difference between this and a standard window is simple. A crossing window will select everything within or *touched by* the window.

Watch this one in action.

| Do This: 2.3.2 | Using a Crossing to Select Multiple Objects |
|---|---|

I. Be sure you're still in the *erase-samp* drawing you used in the last exercise. If not, open it now. (It is in the C:\Steps\Lesson02 folder.)

II. Follow these steps.

### 2.3.2: Crossing-Window Selections

1. Enter the ***Erase*** command.

   **Command: *e***

2. Tell AutoCAD you want to use a crossing to make your selections by entering a ***c*** at the **Select objects** prompt.

   **Select objects: *c***

3. Place your first corner near **Point 1** in the drawing.

   **Specify first corner:**

4. Place the opposite corner near **Point 2.** Notice the difference in the way AutoCAD shows the window (this one uses a dashed line and is shaded green).

   **Specify opposite corner:**

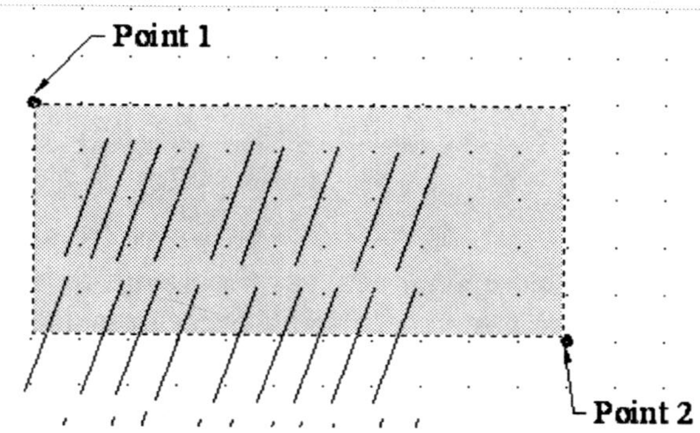


5. Complete the command by hitting ***enter*** at the **Select objects** prompt.

   Notice that the lines that were completely encircled and the lines that were touched by the crossing window were erased.

   **Select objects: *[enter]***

6. Undo the erasure.

   **Command: *u***

> To make windowing even easier, AutoCAD includes *Implied Windowing*. This means that you don't actually have to type ***w*** or ***c*** to create a window or a crossing.
>
> When you pick an empty place on your drawing at the **Select objects** prompt, AutoCAD assumes that you want to use Implied Windowing.
>
> To use a window at any **Select objects** prompt, simply pick an empty point to the left of what you want to select, then pick a second point to the right. You'll get a window.
>
> If you pick the first point to the right and the second point to the left, you'll get a crossing window.
>
> Undo the last erasure, and then try this by selecting a place near **Point 1** then near **Point 2** in the current drawing. Then try it by selecting a place near **Point 2** and then near **Point 1**.

## 2.4 The Cartesian Coordinate System

Remember suffering through plane geometry back in high school math class? That was the one with the crossing number lines, four quadrants, and probably the one that you insisted to you parents, teachers, and any else who would listen that you would never use. Look at Figure 2.010 – it's your math teacher's revenge!

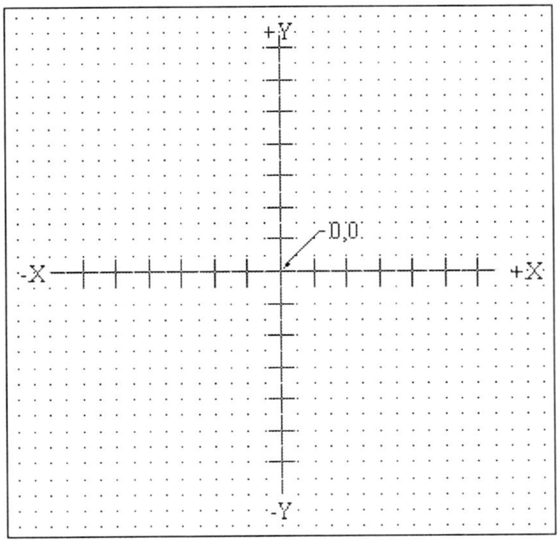


Figure 2.010

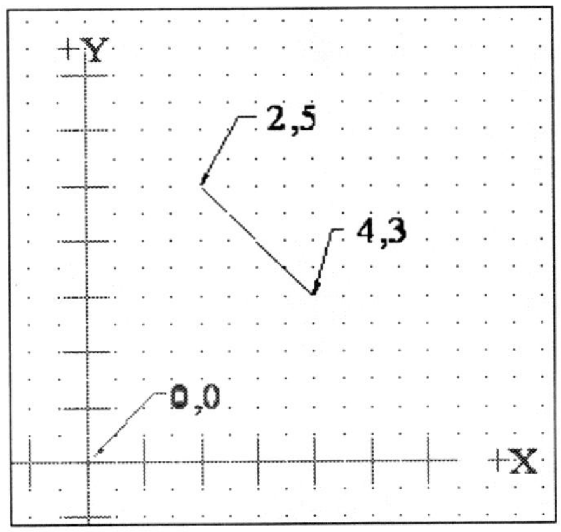


Figure 2.011

On the bright side, it's not nearly as difficult as a math teacher might wish. There are three axes – X, Y, and Z. But we're only concerned with two of them in beginning AutoCAD; so the difficulty is already cut by 1/3!

The *X-axis* runs horizontally (left to right). Everything to the right of a point we call 0 is positive (plus). Everything to the left of the 0 is negative (minus). Thus, we now have +X and –X directions identified. Each number of the X-axis (the axis is the line that runs through the 0) represents an X-*plane*. An X-plane runs infinitely up and down, crossing the X-axis.

The *Y-axis* runs vertically (up and down). Everything above the point we call 0 is positive. Everything below 0 is negative. Each number on the Y-axis represents a Y-*plane*. A Y-plane runs infinitely right and left, crossing the Y-axis.

> The X- and Y-planes also run parallel to the 3-dimensional Z-axis and might be called the XZ- and YZ-planes. But let's stick to two dimensions for now.

Are you still with me?

Okay. Where an X-plane meets a Y-plane in two-dimensional space, we have a *point*. We identify the point by its *coordinate* – or by the number of the X-plane, followed by a comma, and then the number of the Y-plane. Remember this as ***X,Y*** (no spaces). For example, point 4,3 is found 4 spaces to the right of zero and 3 spaces above, as shown in Figure 2.011.

AutoCAD provides three methods for using these coordinates: *absolute*, *relative*, and *polar*. The use of coordinates is your first step toward a drawing precision that was never possible using conventional drafting tools.

### 2.4.1 Absolute Coordinates

The Absolute System is easiest. You simply enter absolute coordinates as ***X,Y*** (remember, no spaces) whenever AutoCAD asks for a point.

Give it a try.

| Do This: 2.4.1.1 | **Using Absolute Coordinates** |
|---|---|

I. Open *ccs.dwg* in the C:\Steps\Lesson02 folder. Refer to Figure 2.010.

II. Be sure the dynamic entry is off (raise the **DYN** toggle on the status bar). By default, you cannot use absolute coordinates with dynamic entry.

III. Raise the **POLAR** toggle as well.

IV. Follow these steps.

**2.4.1.1: USING ABSOLUTE COORDINATES**

1. Enter the ***Line*** command .

   **Command: *l***

2. Enter the first absolute coordinate.

   **Specify first point: *4,3***

3. Enter the next absolute coordinate.

   **Specify next point or [Undo]: *2,5***

4. Hit ***enter*** to complete the command. Your drawing looks like Figure 2.011.

   **Specify next point or [Undo]: *[enter]***

The Absolute Coordinate System is quite easy to use, but using it means that you must know the exact X and Y value of each point you wish to use. This isn't always possible. (That's why most people don't use it). Let's look, then, at the *Relative System.*

## 2.4.2 Relative Coordinates

Use a relative coordinate anytime after identifying the first point. (Either select the first point with the mouse, or use an absolute coordinate.) The syntax for relative coordinates is ***@X,Y*** (read, "at X,Y").

Let's give the Relative System a try.

| Do This: 2.4.2.1 | **Using Relative Coordinates** |
|---|---|

I. Be sure you're still in *ccs.dwg* in the C:\Steps\Lesson02 folder. If not, open it now.

II. Erase the line you drew in the last exercise.

III. Follow these steps. (Refer to Figure 2.012.)

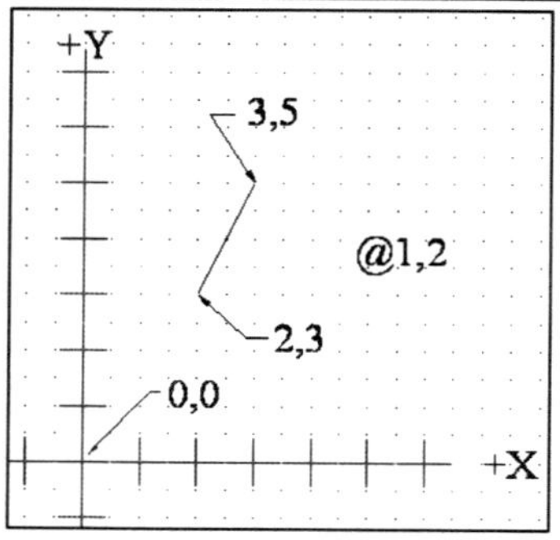


Figure 2.012

**2.4.2.1: USING RELATIVE COORDINATES**

1. Enter the ***Line*** command .

### 2.4.2.1: Using Relative Coordinates

**Command:** ***l***

2. Use absolute coordinates to enter the first point.

   **Specify first point:** ***2,3***

3. Now use relative coordinates to draw a line one space in the +X direction and 2 spaces in the +Y direction.

   **Specify next point or [Undo]:** ***@1,2***

4. Hit ***enter*** to complete the command.

   **Specify next point or [Undo]:** ***[enter]***

5. Undo the line.

   **Command:** ***u***

6. Let's look at this procedure using dynamic entry. Turn dynamic entry back on (depress the **DYN** toggle on the status bar).

7. Repeat Steps 1 and 2.

   **Command:** ***l***

8. Rather than using relative coordinates, enter the X and Y coordinate on the keyboard. Notice that the numbers appear in the dynamic display (right). (If prompted for a third coordinate – the Z-coordinate – just hit enter.) Notice that when you hit enter, AutoCAD places the @ symbol before the numbers for you.

   **Specify next point or [Undo]:** ***@1,2***

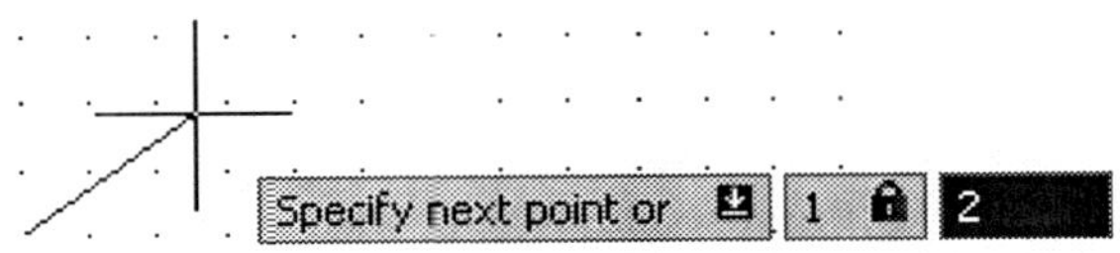


9. Hit ***enter*** to complete the command.

   **Specify next point or [Undo]:** ***[enter]***

Notice that the second point is located 1 unit to the right (a positive 1 on the X-axis) and 2 units up (a positive 2 on the Y-axis), or *at 1X and 2Y* from the last point identified. The point is *relative to* the last identified point.

Using the Relative System means you must know how far (in plus/minus terms) along each axis you want to go from where you are. You'll find this much easier than having to locate each point in absolute terms, especially on larger drawings.

> In this exercise, we used AutoCAD's default dynamic entry settings, which use relative coordinates. We'll see how to change these settings in Lesson 3.

## 2.4.3 Polar Coordinates

I find polar coordinates the most useful. But I must admit that I'll use the Relative System when needed.

Like relative coordinates, you'll use polar coordinate entry after identifying the first point required. The syntax for polar coordinates is ***@dist<angle*** (at – *distance* – at an angle of – *angle*). You must

know the distance and direction you wish to go from the last selected point. Remember, measure angles counterclockwise beginning at 0°East.

Let's take a look.

| Do This: 2.4.3.1 | Using Polar Coordinates |
|---|---|

I. Be sure you're still in *ccs.dwg* in the C:\Steps\Lesson02 folder. If not, open it now.

II. Erase the line you drew in the last exercise.

III. Turn off the dynamic display.

IV. Follow these steps. (Refer to Figure 2.013.)

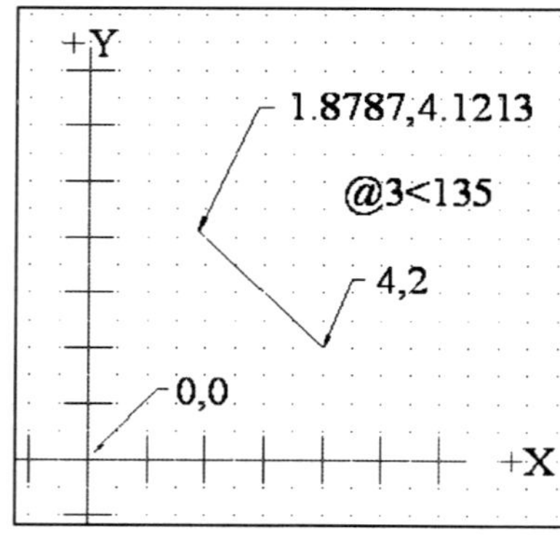


Figure 2.013

### 2.4.3.1: Using Polar Coordinates

1. Enter the ***Line*** command 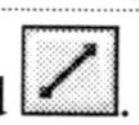.

   **Command: *l***

2. Use absolute coordinates to enter the first point.

   **Specify first point: *4,2***

3. Now use polar coordinates to draw a 3" line at an angle of 135°. (If DYN is toggled on, you'll notice that AutoCAD changes something called the **ORTHOMODE** during this procedure. You can ignore this for now; we'll look at Orthomode in Lesson 3.)

   **Specify next point or [Undo]: *@3<135***

4. Hit ***enter*** to complete the command.

   **Specify next point or [Undo]: *[enter]***

   Nothing to it, right? Let's try it with dynamic input.

5. Erase  the line you just drew.

   **Command: *e***

6. Toggle dynamic input on (depress the **DYN** toggle DYN).

7. Repeat Steps 1 and 2.

8. Enter the distance. Notice that AutoCAD places the distance between ghost dimension lines and shows the current angle in another display box.

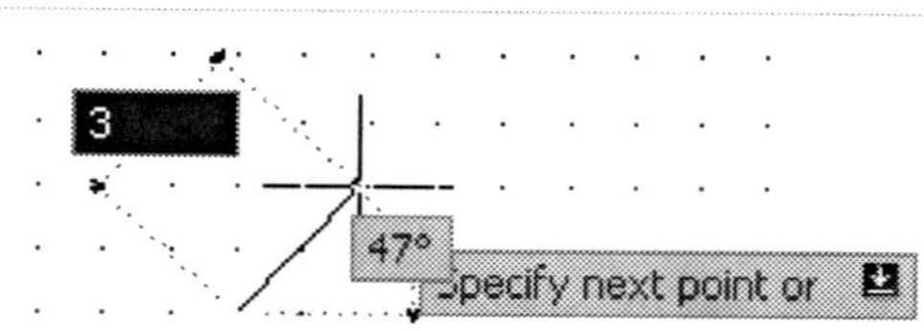


9. Hit the TAB key on your keyboard to work in the other display box.

## 2.4.3.1: Using Polar Coordinates

10. Enter the angle for your line. Hit *enter* when you've finished.

11. Complete the command.

**Specify next point or [Undo]:** ***[enter]***

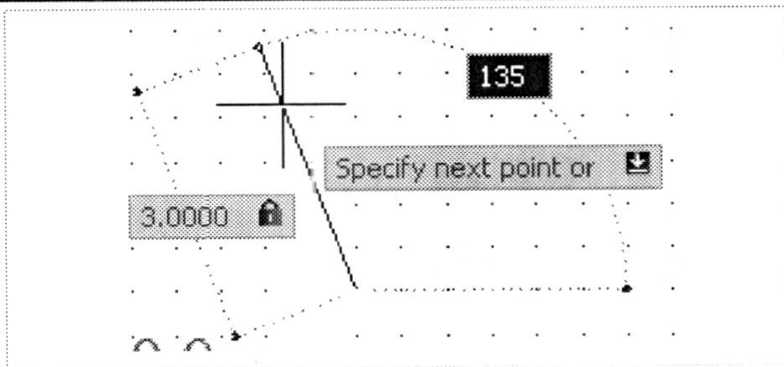


Notice that the coordinate of the second point isn't an integer. This often happens with polar entries. Remember that you're drawing the *hypotenuse* of an angle. This is why I mix my use of polar coordinates with the use of relative coordinates. Sometimes I may know how long a line I need (polar coordinates); other times I know the X and Y distances (relative coordinates).

We've seen several approaches to drawing a simple line with a great deal of precision. It's time now to practice.

| 2.4.4 | Practicing with Cartesian Coordinates |
|---|---|
| **Do This: 2.4.4.1** | **Practice** |

I. Begin a new drawing using *Sample Template 03* found in the C:\Steps\Lesson02 folder.

II. Toggle the dynamic input display off.

III. Using the chart, draw Figure 2.014. (Note: Grid marks are 1 unit apart.) Draw the figure first using absolute coordinates. Erase it. Draw it using relative coordinates. Erase it. Draw it again using polar coordinates. Erase it.

IV. Now toggle the dynamic input display back on.

V. Draw Figure 2.022 using relative coordinates. Erase it. Draw it again using polar coordinates.

| Point | Absolute (X,Y) | Relative (@X,Y) | Polar (@dist<angle) |
|---|---|---|---|
| 1 | 2,15 | 2,15 | 2,15 |
| 2 | 5,15 | @3,0 | @3<0 |
| 3 | 5,9 | @0,-6 | @6<270 |
| 4 | 6,9 | @1,0 | @1<0 |
| 5 | 8,11 | @2,2 | @2.8284<45 |
| 6 | 10,11 | @2,0 | @2<0 |
| 7 | 12,9 | @2,-2 | @2.8284 <315 |
| 8 | 13,9 | @1,0 | @1<0 |
| 9 | 13,15 | @0,6 | @6<90 |
| 10 | 16,15 | @3,0 | @3<0 |
| 11 | 16,4 | @0,-11 | @11<270 |
| 12 | 13,4 | @-3,0 | @3<180 |
| 13 | 10,7 | @-3,3 | @4.2426<135 |
| 14 | 8,7 | @-2,0 | @2<180 |
| 15 | 5,4 | @-3,-3 | @4.2426<225 |
| 16 | 2,4 | @-3,0 | @3<180 |
| Back to 1 | C | C | C |

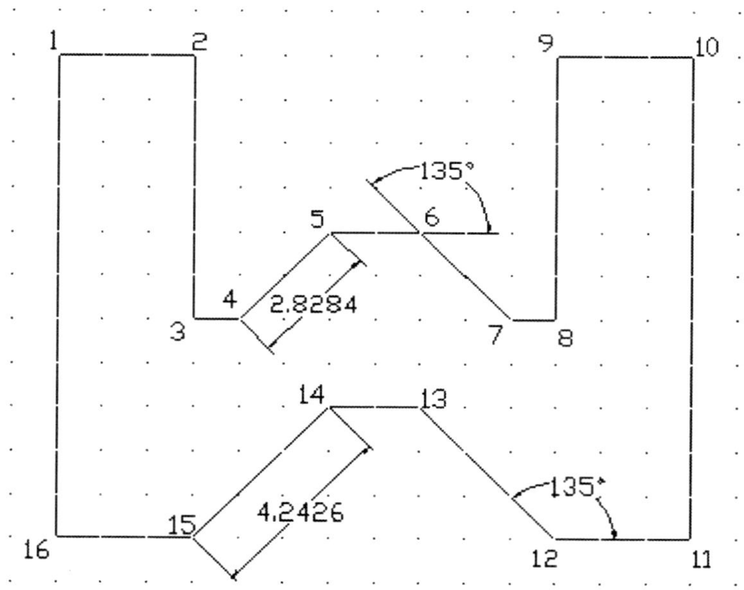


Figure 2.014

## 2.5 Extra Steps

With all the drawing and erasing you've done in this chapter, you may have noticed that you'll occasionally "lose" a line (or other object) that you thought was there. Likewise, you may notice that an object may remain highlighted even after you've canceled the command. This problem lies mostly with the video card or monitor you're using. But most programs allow you to *refresh* your screen after doing a great deal of work, to make sure all the screen pixels that should be lit, are lit.

AutoCAD calls its refresh command ***Redraw***, but that requires too much typing. When your screen needs refreshing (redrawing), type ***R*** at the command prompt and hit enter. This'll redraw the screen.

> By the way, I indicate commands and hotkeys using capital letters as a matter of convention. AutoCAD isn't case sensitive.

In the event that what you expect to see doesn't materialize after a redraw, you have one other option. Every object within an AutoCAD drawing carries with it quite a bit of information. This information includes details about the type of object, its size, location, layer, and so forth. With AutoCAD's ***Regen*** command (***Re***), AutoCAD reads and redraws every object in the drawing. You might think this would take a lot of time in a larger drawing, and in fact, it once did. Now, however, with the advent of faster computers and better programming, regens often go unnoticed.

If the object doesn't show after a regen, it doesn't exist as part of the drawing and you'll have to redraw it.

So add these two commands to your "Hail Mary" list, but don't cut it off yet. More will follow!

## 2.6 What Have We Learned?

*Items covered in this lesson include:*

- *Object selection*
- *Cartesian Coordinate System*
- *Dynamic input display*
- *Commands*
  - ***Line***
  - ***Rectangle***
  - ***Erase***
  - ***Undo / U***
  - ***Redo / MRedo***
  - ***Redraw***
  - ***Regen***

We began this lesson by describing drafting as "the placing of geometric shapes on paper to represent existing or proposed structures." We've seen how to use the "backbone" of more than half of all geometric structures – the straight line. We've seen how to draw the line with precision and accuracy using the "backbone" of AutoCAD precision – the Cartesian Coordinate System.

But if the Cartesian Coordinate System was solely responsible for precision in AutoCAD, the software might never have survived through so many releases. Let's face it, at its best, it can be time-consuming and a bit cumbersome. In Lesson 3, we'll look at some faster ways to draw that, although not replacements for Cartesian coordinates, accent them nicely. Then, in Lesson 4, we'll look at the curved line – arcs and circles – to complete the basic structures of drafting.

## 2.7 Exercises

1. Using what you've learned, fill in the blanks with the command entries needed to draw the structure in the following figure. Use each of the Cartesian coordinate methods – absolute, relative, and polar. Then draw the object using each of the methods and the dynamic methods we discussed. (Grid marks are ½" apart.) Save the drawing as *MyM.dwg* in the C:\Steps\Lesson02 folder. (Download a blank, printable table from: http://www.uneedcad.com/Files/table.pdf.)

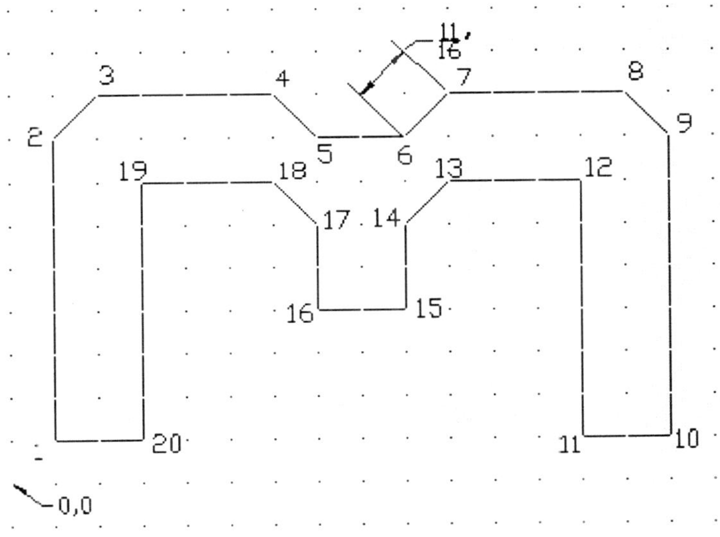


*For more exercises related to Lesson 2, please see Lesson 2 in AutoCAD 2007: One Step at a Time – Workbook.*

## 2.7 For Web-Based Review Questions, visit: http://www.uneedcad.com/2007/Files/07R2.pdf

# Lesson 3

Following this lesson, you will:

- ✓ *Know how to use the Ortho, Grid, Snap, and Tracking tools to your advantage*
- ✓ *Know how to use OSNAPs*
- ✓ *Know how to use the Direct Distance Option when you draw*
- ✓ *Be familiar with the different toggles – keyboard, function keys, and status bar – available to help you*

# Drawing Aides

*Lesson 2 showed us how to draw with accuracy. But without some additional help, we'll need to know exact coordinates or exact distances every time we draw a line or a circle. What if we want to go to a specific point – say, the end of an existing line? Must we break out the calculator every time?*

*No! AutoCAD provides many tools and drawing aids that help you minimize, though not eliminate, the need for calculation. Lesson 2 taught you to draw with accuracy. This lesson will show you how to draw with speed without sacrificing accuracy.*

## 3.1 The Simple Stuff: Ortho, Grid, Tracking, and Snap

### 3.1.1 Ortho

The first drawing aid with which you'll want to familiarize yourself is **Orthomode** (aka. **Ortho**). You may recognize the word as an aberration of the word *Orthographic*. We learned about orthographic projections in the first days of drafting class. These present views necessary to describe an item from all sides. Orthographic views include the following (Figure 3.001): front, back, right side, left side, top, and bottom. The views are placed above or below, left or right of a primary view (usually the front) depending on which view it is.

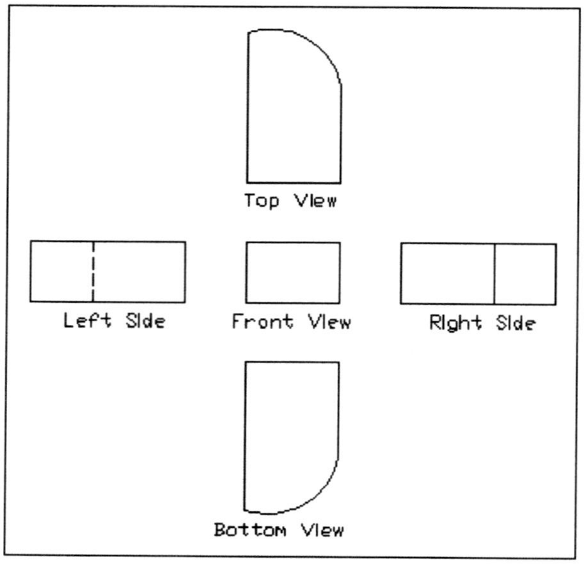


Figure 3.001

**Orthomode** restricts drawing or editing movement in a drawing to the left/right or up/down directions. When ***Ortho*** is toggled on, your lines will be drawn along the X- or Y-plane. (When drawing in the isometric mode, the X- or Y-planes will be located at 30° and 150°.) This will become clearer during our exercises.

The command sequence for **Orthomode** is

**Command: *ortho***

**Enter mode [ON/OFF] <OFF>: *on***

Toggle Ortho on or off using the **F8** function key or by clicking the **ORTHO** toggle on the status bar.

> You can temporarily toggle **Orthomode** on or off using the SHIFT key. To use this method, begin your command (say, ***Line***), pick your start point, hold down the SHIFT key, and pick your second point. If **Orthomode** is on, the SHIFT key will disable it temporarily. Conversely, if **Orthomode** is off, the SHIFT key will temporarily enable it.
> Cool, huh?

### 3.1.2 Grid

One of the drafting tricks we learned back in the pencil days was to lay a background grid sheet on our drawing board before taping down our drawing sheet. This grid served as a lettering guide and helped in aligning different items.

AutoCAD's grid can be quite useful in aligning things. But as we'll see later, it isn't necessary for sizing text.

The grid toggles on or off quite easily. And controlling the size and shape of the grid, together with some creative use of the ***Snap*** tool, will often dramatically increase your drawing speed. (We'll discuss ***Snap*** in Section 3.1.4.)

Controlling the grid size is easy. Following is the command sequence:

> **Command: grid**
> **Specify grid spacing(X) or [ON/OFF/Snap/Major/aDaptive/Limits/Follow/Aspect] <0.5000>:** ***1***

AutoCAD provides some options for the ***Grid*** command. The default option sets the grid spacing. In this example, the spacing defaulted to **0.5000** drawing units. We set the spacing to ***1*** drawing unit. Other options include:

- **ON/OFF**: Turns the grid on or off.
- **Snap**: Sets the grid spacing equal to the snap increments.
- **Major**: This new tool controls the frequency of major (when compared with minor) grid lines. By default in the setup you're using, AutoCAD uses grid points. But when the visual style has been set to anything other than **2D wireframe**, it uses grid lines. We'll learn more about visual styles in the 3D text.
- **aDaptive**: Using this, you can control the density of grid lines. Again, you must be in something other than the **2D Wireframe** visual style. We'll also discuss this in more detail in our 3D text.
- **Limits**: Tells AutoCAD to show the grid beyond the limits of the drawing.
- **Follow**: Follow tells AutoCAD to force the grid lines to follow the dynamic UCS. "What!?" You ask. Don't worry, it's another 3D thing. (All this 3D stuff gives you something to look forward to in your advanced studies!)
- **Aspect**: Enables you to set a separate spacing for the X- and Y-planes.

Toggle the grid on or off using the **F7** function key or by clicking the **GRID** toggle on the status bar.

### 3.1.3 Polar Tracking

A remarkable and intuitive tool, polar tracking was designed to assist you by placing a temporary construction line from the last point selected. Additionally, polar tracking provides a tooltip detailing distance and angle from the last point selected (Figure 3.002). This makes it much easier to locate the next point accurately and quickly with a minimal need for absolute, relative, or polar coordinate entry

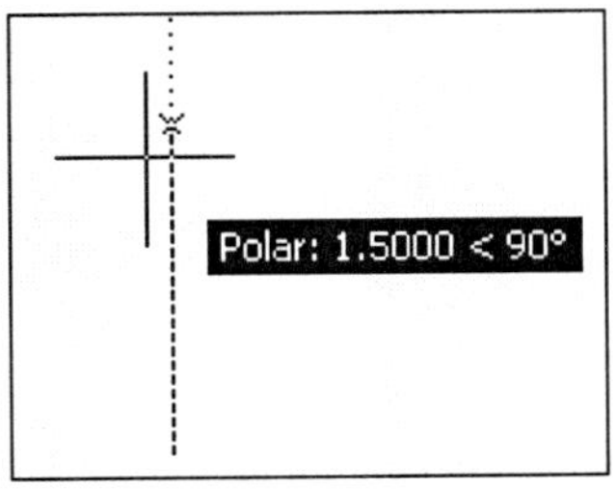


Figure 3.002

Polar tracking works on the four quadrants (0°, 90°, 180°, and 270°) by default, but you can set it to track at any angle or to override the settings on the fly. When used with **Polar Snap** (See Section 3.1.4), you can snap to any point at any angle with little or no need for the keyboard at all!

> To set your own angles, refer to Section 3.2.

Toggle polar tracking on or off using the **F10** function key or by clicking the **POLAR** toggle on the status bar.

## 3.1.4 Snap (Polar and Grid)

The grid and polar tracking by themselves are only of minimal use. So AutoCAD provides a tool that was not available back in the pencil days. The ***Snap*** tool actually pulls (or *snaps*) the crosshairs to a grid or polar reference. Controlling the snap while referencing the grid or polar tracking construction lines can provide speed to an otherwise tedious job.

Look at the ***Snap*** command.

> **Command: *snap* (or *sn*)**
>
> **Specify snap spacing or [ON/OFF/Aspect/Style/Type] <0.5000>: *[enter the desired spacing or select an option]***

What's the default spacing? Did you say **0.5000**? Correct. As in other commands, we can see the default inside the <>.

> Conventional wisdom suggests that setting the grid snap to half the grid works best for most drawings. This way, you can snap to each grid, and halfway between each. More than a single snap between grids is difficult to follow.

Snap options include:

- **ON/OFF**: For turning the snap on or off.
- **Aspect**: For setting a different snap spacing horizontally and vertically.
- **Style**: For changing from a standard grid/snap style to an isometric style (we'll look at this in more detail in Section 3.6).
- **Type**: For setting either **Polar** (to snap to points determined with the polar tracking feature) or **Grid** (to snap to grid referenced points).

Let's try an exercise using ***Grid***, ***Snap***, ***Polar Tracking***, and ***Ortho***.

> ***Grid***, ***Snap***, ***Polar Tracking***, and ***Ortho*** would not be of much use if we had to stop a drawing or editing command every time we needed to turn one **On** or **Off**. Mercifully, AutoCAD gives us toggles that will work even while we're in the sequence of another command. In other words, we can toggle the ***Grid***, ***Snap***, ***Polar Tracking***, or ***Ortho*** **On** or **Off** while drawing a line (or doing some other command).
>
> There are a few ways to toggle each of these items. They are

| | KEYBOARD | FUNCTION KEY | SCREEN | TEMP. OVERRIDE |
|---|---|---|---|---|
| Grid | Ctrl + G | F7 | Status bar | None |
| Snap | Ctrl + B | F9 | Status bar | SHIFT + d |
| Ortho | None | F8 | Status bar | SHIFT |
| Polar Tracking | None | F10 | Status bar | SHIFT + . |
| Object Snap Tracking | None | F11 | Status bar | SHIFT + q |
| Dynamic Input | None | F12 | Status bar | None |

> Find the function keys across the top of your keyboard. Identify them by the **F** followed by a number, such as **F8**. Refer to Appendix B for a complete list of AutoCAD's function keys.
>
> Status bar toggles are shown here.

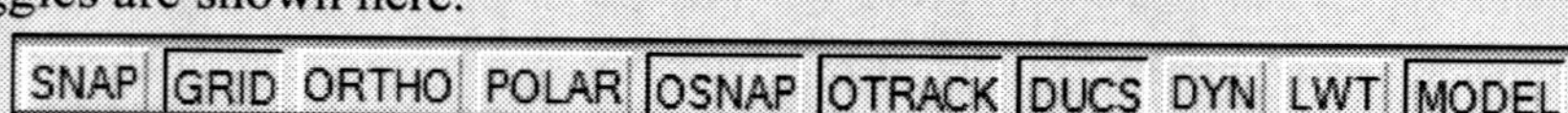


> To toggle something **On** or **Off** at the status bar, place your cursor on the item and click with the left mouse button. A "raised" item is currently off; an "indented" item is on. To define or redefine the settings of one of these toggles, right-click on it and pick **Settings** (see Section 3.2).

| Do This: 3.1.4.1 | Grid, Snap, Polar Tracking, and Ortho Practice |
|---|---|

Try drawing the "W" in Exercise #2.4.4.1 in Lesson 2 using only the four tools you've just seen.

I. Start a new drawing using the *MyBase2* template you created in Lesson 1. Alternately, you can use *Base2.dwt* in the C:\Steps\Lesson01 folder.

II. Set the ***Grid*** to 1.

III. Set the ***Snap*** to ½ and the snap **Type** to **Grid**. Be sure **Grid** and **Snap** are both toggled on.

IV. Draw the "M" toggling **Orthomode** on or off as needed during the drawing.

How much faster did you draw? Usually, at this point, my students begin planning my demise for not having shown them this approach first. I'm really not that cruel. But once these tools are known, it's exceedingly difficult to convince students to learn the Cartesian Coordinate approaches to drawing. As you'll see, both the coordinate system and these drawing tools are quite necessary for speed and accuracy. (Wait until you master OSNAPs!)

Now try drawing the rest of the Lesson 2 exercises using your own settings.

## 3.2 And Now the Easy Way - *DSettings*

We've seen the command prompt method of setting **Grid** and **Snap**. Any setting that requires several lines of entry, as these do, is a prime candidate for a dialog box, and AutoCAD hasn't disappointed.

There are several ways to display the Drafting Settings dialog box. You can enter the command ***DSettings*** (or ***DS***) at the command prompt or right-click on any of the toggles on the status bar and select **Settings** from the cursor menu that appears. AutoCAD will present the Drafting Settings dialog box seen in Figure 3.004.

This box has four tabs available to help you (Refer to the figures that follow).

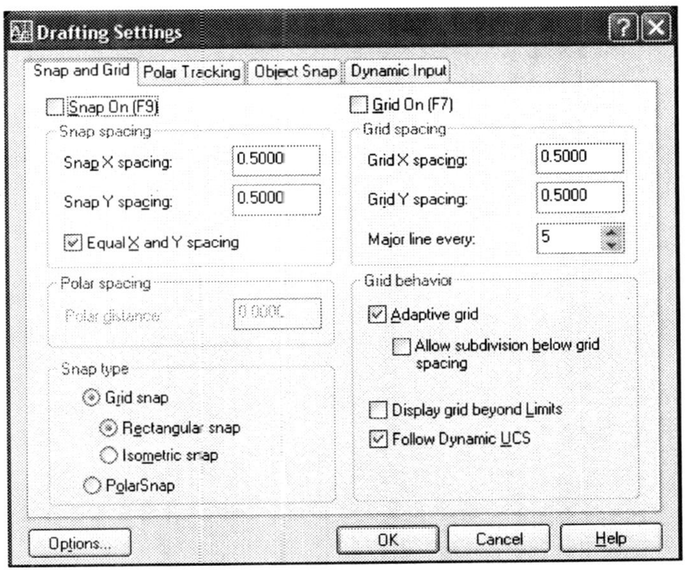


Figure 3.004

- Figure 3.004 shows the **Snap and Grid** tab on top. You'll see this when you select **Settings** from the cursor menu presented when you right-click on the **SNAP** or **GRID** toggle on the status bar. This tab presents frames where you can set increments for the **Snap** spacing (for the grid snap), the **Polar spacing** (for the polar snap), or the **Grid** spacing. This tab also provides check boxes for toggling on/off the **Snap** and **Grid**, and radio buttons for setting the type of snap (**Polar** or **Grid**, **Rectangular** or **Isometric** – more on isometric snap in Section 3.6). The Grid Behavior frame provides some new and useful tools for 3-dimensional work. You can ignore it for now.
- If you access the Drafting Settings dialog box by right-clicking on the **POLAR** toggle and selecting **Settings**, AutoCAD will place the **Polar Tracking** tab on top, as seen in Figure 3.005.

Here you can toggle **Polar Tracking** on/off using the check box. But more importantly, you can adjust the **Increment Angle** settings (the angles at which polar tracking appears) using a drop-down box, or add additional angles (not shown in the drop-down box) by picking the **New** button. **Additional angles** will appear in the list box and be used when you place a check in the check box.

You can also determine whether to use polar tracking only orthogonally (at the four quadrants – 0°, 90°, 180°, and 270°) or using **all** the **angle settings**. The **Object Snap Tracking Settings** frame provides radio buttons for each.

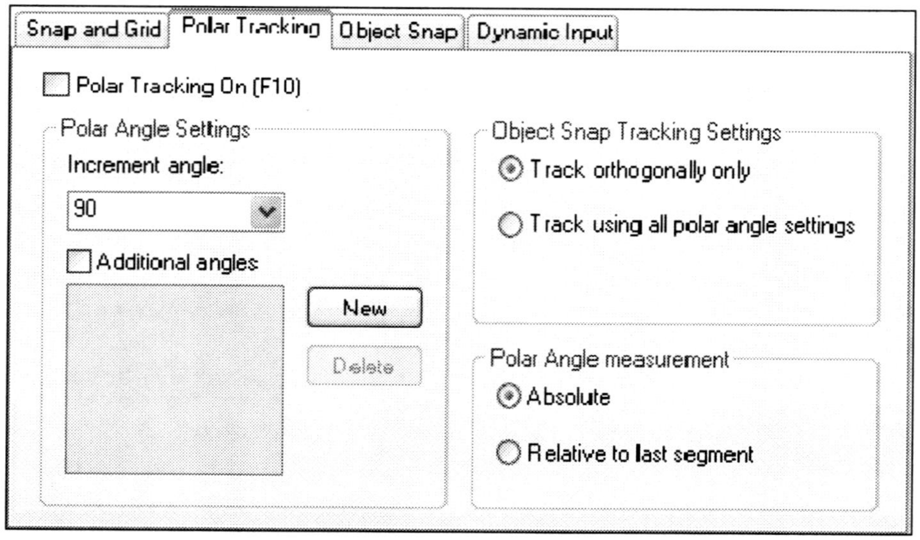

Figure 3.005

The **Polar Angle measurement** frame allows you to show polar tracking angles in absolute terms (always showing angles as they relate to AutoCAD's compass points) or relative to the last segment (showing angles as they relate to the last line segment drawn). I recommend using the default **Absolute** setting to avoid confusion.

- The **Object Snap** tab (Figure 3.006) will appear on top when the Drafting Settings dialog box is accessed by right-clicking on the **OSNAP** or **OTRACK** toggles. Here you can set Running Object Snaps (OSNAPs). We'll look at OSNAPs and Running OSNAPs in Sections 3.3 and 3.4.

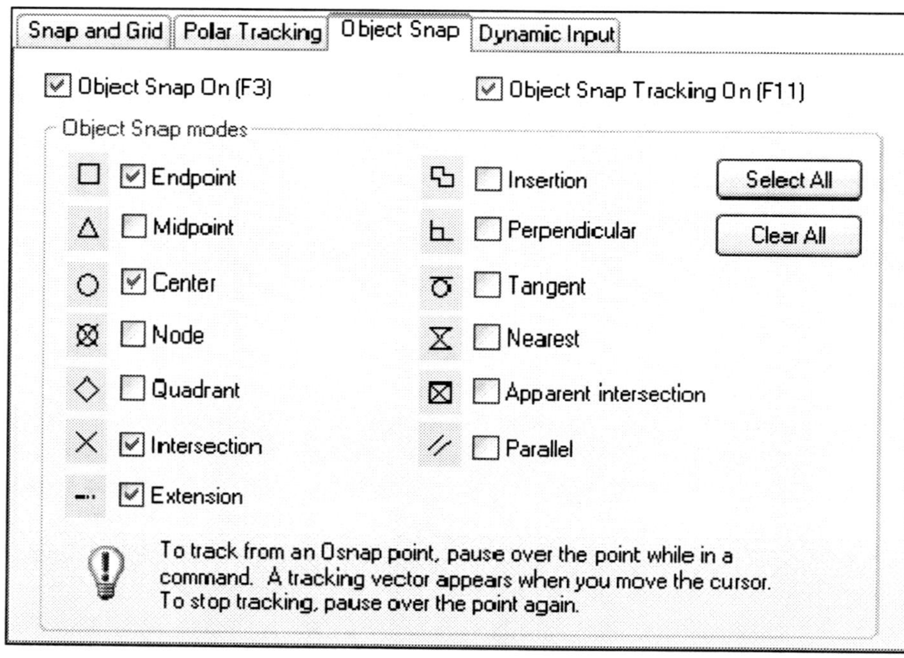

Figure 3.006

- The final tab – **Dynamic Input** (Figure 3.007) controls the appearance and function of AutoCAD's dynamic input (the information you see next to your crosshairs when the **DYN** button on the status bar is depressed).
    - The two check boxes at the top – **Enable Pointer Input** and **Enable Dimension Input where possible** – control exactly what dynamic input displays. **Enable Pointer Input** controls whether or not coordinates will display as you move your cursor about the screen. **Enable Dimension Input where possible** controls whether or not you'll see a prompt next to the crosshairs when AutoCAD needs a dimension (as when requesting a circle radius or diameter).

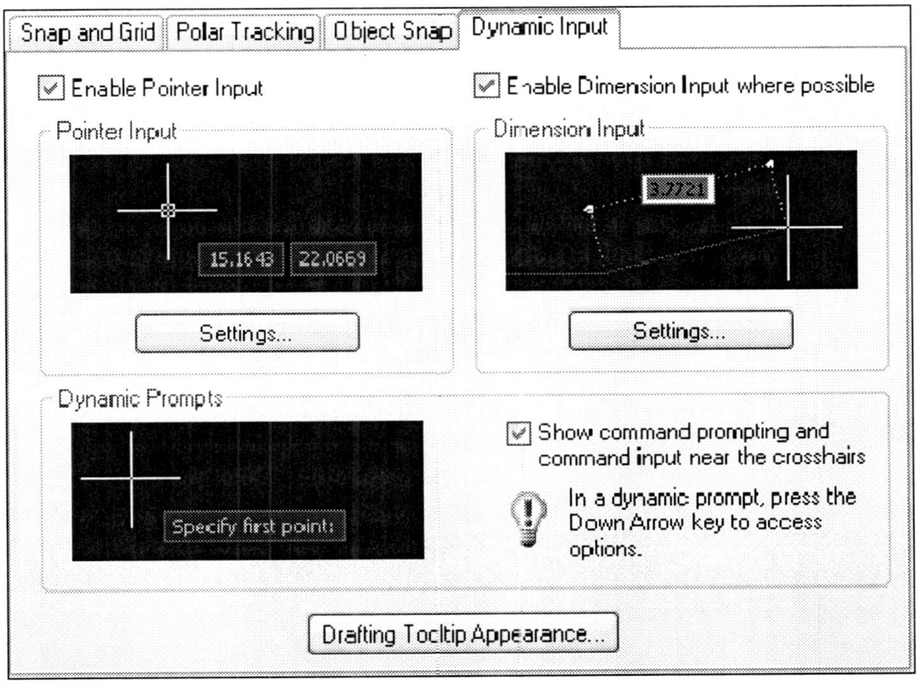


Figure 3.007

    - When **Enable Pointer Input** is on, you can control exactly what it displays with the Pointer Input Settings dialog box (Figure 3.008) reached via the **Settings** button below the check box. Here you can change the format from **Relative coordinates** to **Absolute coordinates**, or from a **Polar format** (the second point prompt in a polar-type format, or *X<angle*) to the **Cartesian format** (the second point prompt appears as a Cartesian coordinate).

      Options in the **Visibility** frame control when the tooltips will be visible.

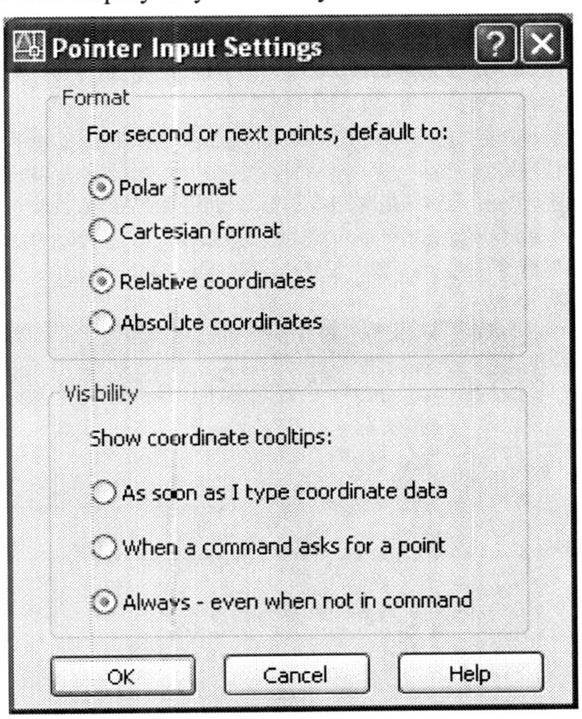


Figure 3.008

- The **Settings** button under **Enable Dimension Input where possible** provides control for stretching with grips. We'll discuss grips in some detail in Lesson 16.
- The **Dynamic Prompts** frame holds a single, handy check box – **Show command prompting and command input near the crosshairs**. I prefer to turn this off. Without it, AutoCAD prompts on the command line only (not at the crosshairs). Your screen will still display coordinates but without the additional nuisance of the prompt.
- The next thing on the **Dynamic Input** tab is the **Drafting Tooltip Appearance** button. This calls a simple dialog box that allows you to adjust the color and transparency of the tooltips.
- Finally, you'll see an **Options** button at the bottom of the tab. Please ignore this one for now. It calls the Options dialog box where a more experienced operator can adjust some of the default settings for AutoCAD. *The Options dialog box is not a place for beginners! It contains settings that can render AutoCAD inoperable if set incorrectly, so please, avoid this until you have some experience.*

## 3.3 Never Miss the Point with OSNAPs

We've now seen several ways to draw with precision. What more could we possibly need?

Well, not all of these tools lend themselves easily to large drawing environments like those found in disciplines such as architecture or petrochemical. This leads us back to a need for some tools that free us as much as possible from the Cartesian Coordinate System. Enter ObjectSnaps – OSNAPs.

These remarkable tools must and will become second nature to the successful CAD operator. After learning OSNAPs, you must engrain this $11^{th}$ Commandment into your hearts and minds: *Thou shalt not eyeball!* Because after learning OSNAPs, there will never again be a need to guess about the location of a point.

What are OSNAPs? OSNAPs are a means of responding with precision to any prompt directing you to pick a point in your drawing. They provide the means for precisely locating and selecting a point (endpoint, midpoint, center point, etc.) on (or referenced by) any existing object in the drawing – lines, circles, arcs, and so forth.

Study the following chart. The first column shows the buttons found on the OSNAP toolbar. The middle column shows the cheater symbols AutoCAD shows when trying to use an OSNAP in a drawing. The third column shows the equivalent command found when you call up the cursor menu by clicking the right mouse button (with your cursor in the drawing area), while holding down the **SHIFT** key on the keyboard. The last column shows the temporary override keys when they're available.

| OSNAP Toolbar | Symbol | Cursor Menu | Temporary Override |
|---|---|---|---|
|  | | Temporary Track Point | |
|  | | From | |
| 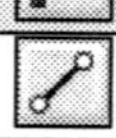 | □ | Endpoint | Shift + e |
|  | △ | Midpoint | Shift + v |
| 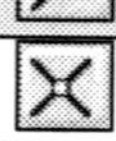 | × | Intersection | |
| 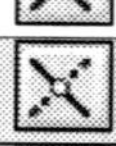 | ⊠ | Apparent Intersection | |
| 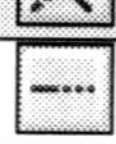 | 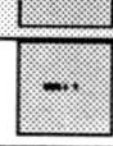 | Extension | |

| OSNAP TOOLBAR | SYMBOL | CURSOR MENU | TEMPORARY OVERRIDE |
|---|---|---|---|
| | | Center | Shift + c |
| | | Quadrant | |
| | | Tangent | |
| | | Perpendicular | |
| | | Parallel | |
| | | Insert | |
| | | Node | |
| | | Nearest | |
| | | None | |
| | | Osnap Settings | |

Most of these will become obvious once you've used them. Some will require a bit more explanation. The best way to learn how to use object snaps, though, is through a practice exercise. Follow me!

| Do This: 3.3.1 | OSNAP Practice |
|---|---|

I. Open the *train.dwg* file found in the C:\Steps\Lesson03 folder. It'll look like Figure 3.009.

II. Show the OSNAP toolbar and dock it to the right side of your screen. [Right-click on any visible toolbar and select **Object Snap** from the cursor menu. When the toolbar appears, pick and hold with the left mouse button in the blue title bar, dragging the toolbar until it docks against the right side of the graphics area.]

III. Follow these steps. For this exercise, I'll use three methods of selecting OSNAPs, but the methods are completely interchangeable.

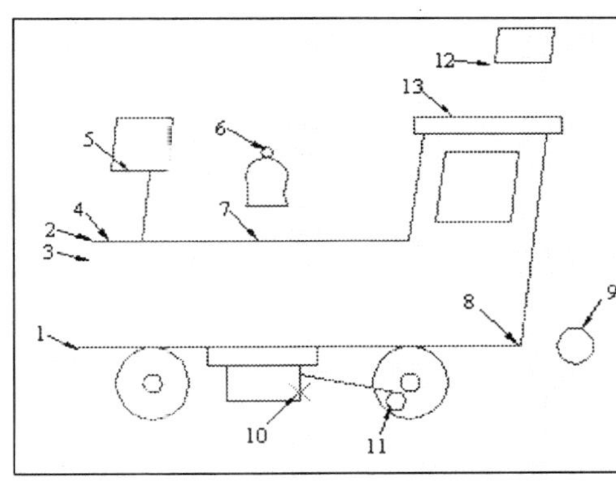

Figure 3.009

**3.3.1: OSNAP PRACTICE**

1. Check the status bar (figure below) and be sure that all the toggles shown here are raised. If any of the toggles appear depressed, pick on it once to raise it

| SNAP | GRID | ORTHO | POLAR | OSNAP | OTRACK | DUCS | DYN |
|---|---|---|---|---|---|---|---|

2. We'll begin at the front of the train. Enter the ***Line*** command .

**Command: *l***

## 3.3.1: OSNAP PRACTICE

3. Pick the **Endpoint** OSNAP button  on the OSNAP toolbar.

**Specify first point: _endp of**

4. Place the cursor at point 1. Notice how a small square (the symbol for endpoint) appears at the endpoint of the line. Pick here.

Notice that the line begins at the endpoint of the existing line.

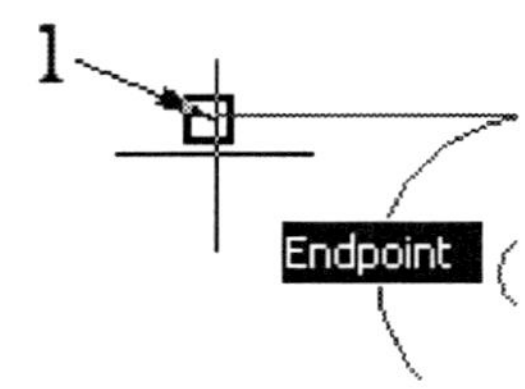


5. Select the **Endpoint** button  again.

**Specify next point or [Undo]: _endp of**

6. Place the cursor at Point 2. Notice the symbol for endpoint appears again. Pick here. Your line is drawn to the endpoint. Hit ***enter*** to complete the command.

**Specify next point or [Undo]: *[enter]***

7. Next we'll draw a cowcatcher using the ***Line*** command, the **Extension** OSNAP, and Polar Tracking. First, let's set up polar tracking. Right-click on the **Snap** toggle on the status bar, and select **Settings** from the menu.

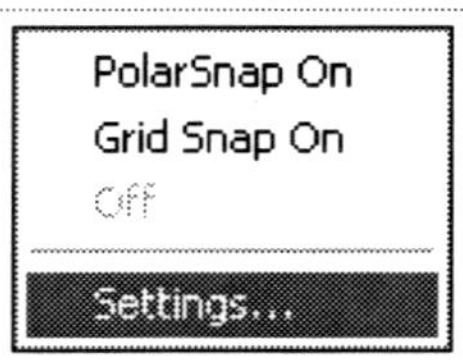


8. AutoCAD presents the Drafting Settings dialog box with the **Snap and Grid** tab on top, as seen in Figure 3.004. Place a bullet next to **Polar Snap**, and then set the **Polar distance** at ***.25*** as shown. Check the **Snap On** check box; then pick on the **Polar Tracking** tab.

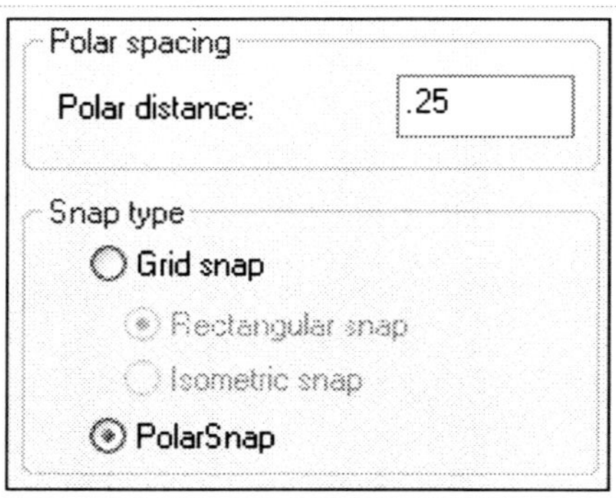


9. We'll want to use Polar Tracking on all angles, so put a bullet in the **Track using all polar angle settings** option of the **Object Snap Tracking Settings** frame as shown.

Check the **Polar Tracking On** check box; then pick the **OK** button 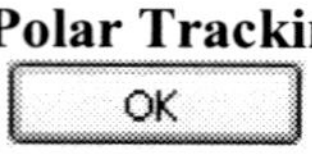 to complete the setup.

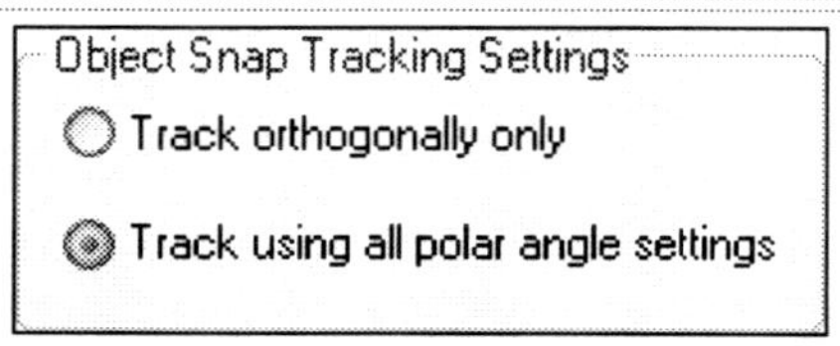


10. Begin the ***Line*** command .

**Command: *l***

11. Pick the **Extension** OSNAP button 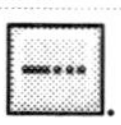.

## 3.3.1: OSNAP PRACTICE

12. Place your crosshairs over Point 1, but *don't pick.* AutoCAD will display a small plus symbol indicating that the object has been located. Move your cursor down and slightly to the left. Notice the tooltip as polar tracking helps you locate a point off of the extension of the line that you created in Steps 2 through 6.

Pick at the point located ¾" at 262° as shown.

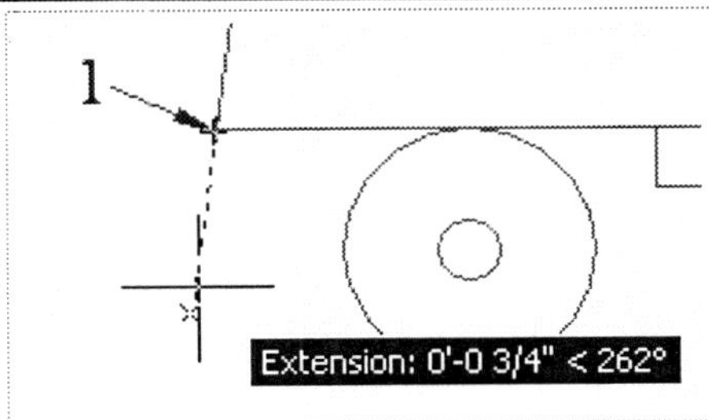


13. Now use polar tracking to create a rectangle ¼" up and 2" to the left.

14. Using the **Endpoint** OSNAP, draw a line connecting the upper right corner of the cowcatcher to Point 1, as shown in the following figure.

**Command: *l***

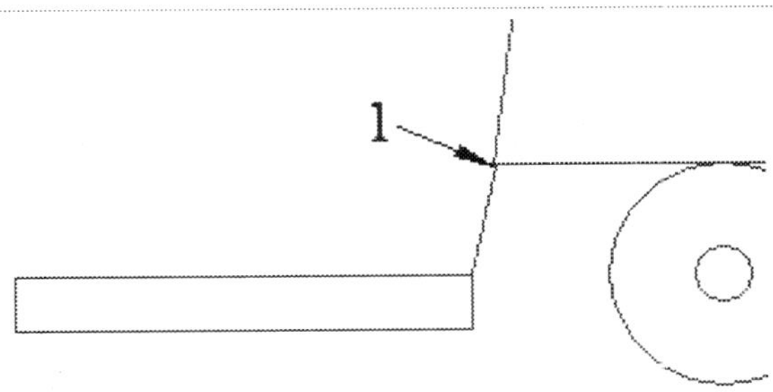


15. Use the **Endpoint** OSNAP to begin a line at the upper left corner of the cowcatcher.

**Command: *l***

**Specify first point: _endp of**

16. At the **Specify next point** prompt, type ***nea*** to tell AutoCAD you want the point nearest to where you select. (Typing "nea" is the keyboard entry method for using the **Nearest** OSNAP.) Select a point near Point 3. Notice the symbol.

**Specify next point or [Undo]: *nea***

17. Complete the command.

**Specify next point or [Undo]: *[enter]***

18. Repeat the ***Line*** command. This time we'll select a point where two lines would intersect if they were a bit longer. And we'll use the cursor menu to enter the OSNAPs.

**Command: *[enter]***

## 3.3.1: OSNAP Practice

19. Hold down the SHIFT key on the keyboard and right-click in the graphics area of the screen. You'll see a cursor menu like the one shown here. Select **Apparent Intersection**.

AutoCAD asks which nonintersecting lines you wish to use. Select the line you drew between the cowcatcher and Point 3; and then select the line at Point 4. Notice the symbols.

AutoCAD begins the line.

**Specify first point: _appint of and**

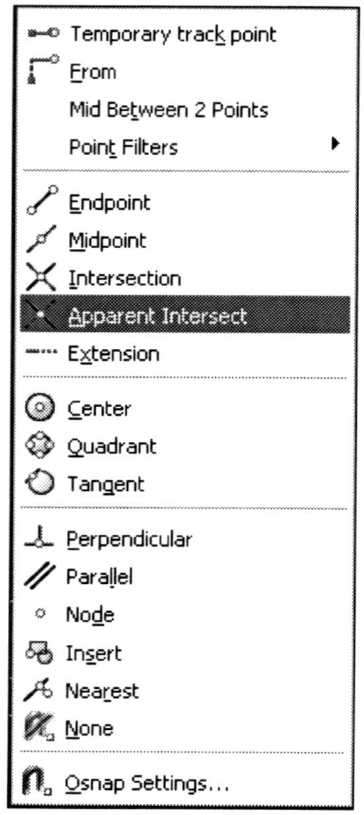


20. Now we must identify where to go with the line. Bring up the cursor menu again (as you did in Step 19), and select **Parallel**. Place your cursor over the line between Points 1 and 2 (don't pick). AutoCAD will display a symbol to let you know it has found the line.

**Specify next point or [Undo]: _par to**

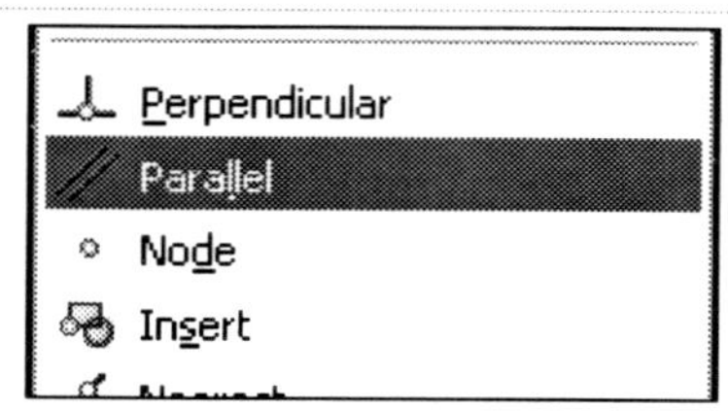


21. Move the cursor to the bottom of the smokestack. Pick when AutoCAD displays the tooltip shown. (Notice that the parallel symbol appears on the line you selected when your line is parallel to it.)

22. Complete the command. Your drawing looks like the following figure.

**Specify next point or [Undo]:** ***[enter]***

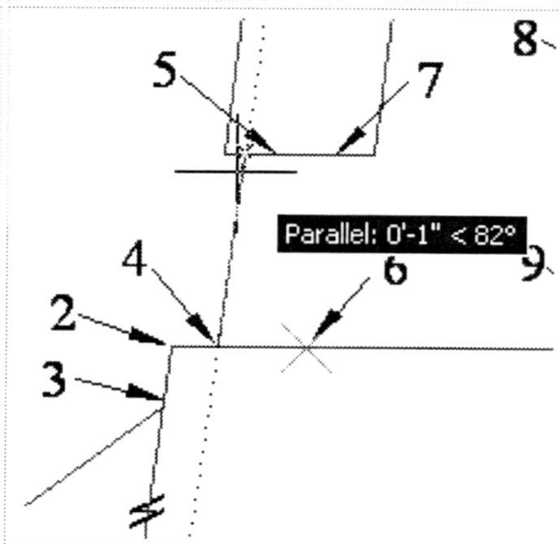

## 3.3.1: OSNAP PRACTICE

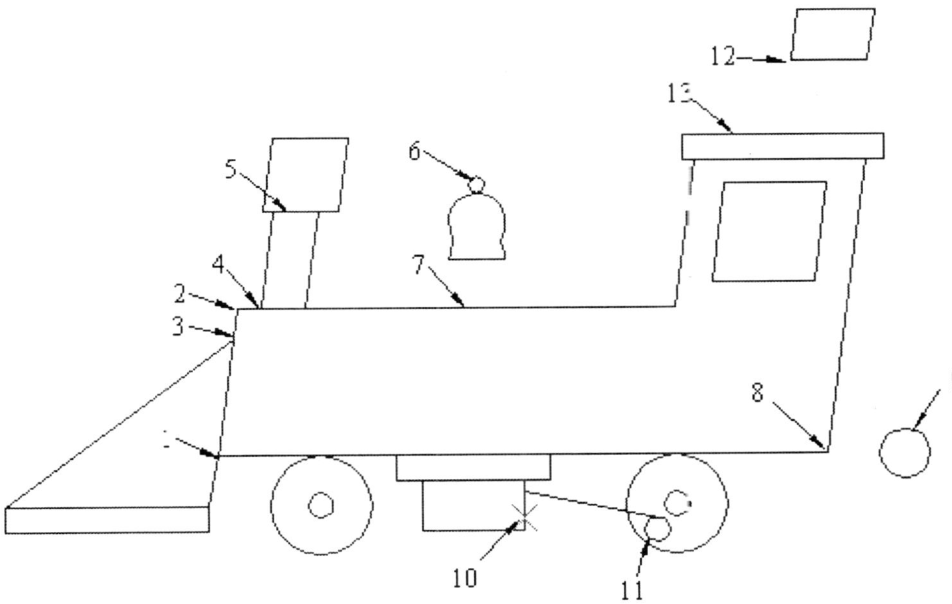


23. Repeat the ***Line*** command .

**Command:** ***[enter]***

24. We want the bell assembly to start a bit above the top of the bell. There is not a point there to snap, so we'll use the **From** OSNAP .

**Specify first point:** ***from***

25. We'll start a line ¼" above (**From**) the center  of the circle at point 6. We'll need to use polar coordinates.

**Base point:** ***cen***

**of <Offset>:** ***@.25<90***

**26.** Perpendicular  to the line at point 7.

**Specify next point or [Undo]:** ***per***

27. Complete the command. Your drawing now looks like the following figure.

**Specify next point or [Undo]:** ***[enter]***

## 3.3.1: OSNAP PRACTICE

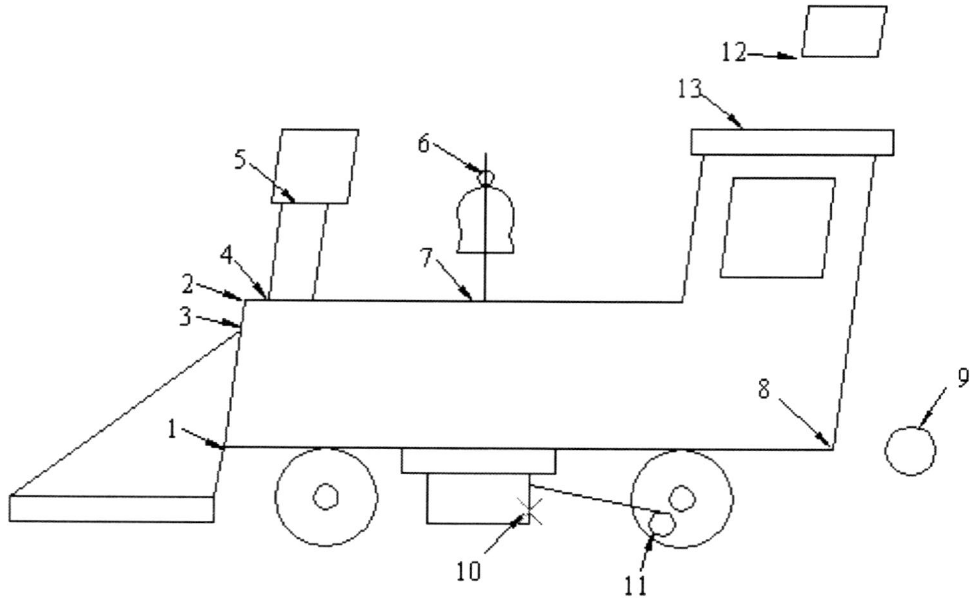


28. Repeat the ***Line*** command.

**Command: *[enter]***

29. From the **endpoint** at point 8…

**Specify first point: *end***

30. …to the **center** of the circle at point 9.

**Specify next point or [Undo]: *cen***

31. Complete the command.

**Specify next point or [Undo]: *[enter]***

32. Repeat the ***Line*** command.

**Command: *[enter]***

33. From the **node** at point 10…

**Specify first point: *nod***

34. …**tangent** to the circle at point 11.

**Specify next point or [Undo]: *tan***

35. Complete the command.

**Specify next point or [Undo]: *[enter]***

36. Now the flagpole. Repeat the ***Line*** command.

**Command: *[enter]***

## 3.3.1: OSNAP Practice

37. From the **intersection** at point 12…

**From point:** ***int***

38. …to the **midpoint** of the line at point 13.

**To point:** ***mid***

39. Complete the command. Your drawing now looks like the following figure.

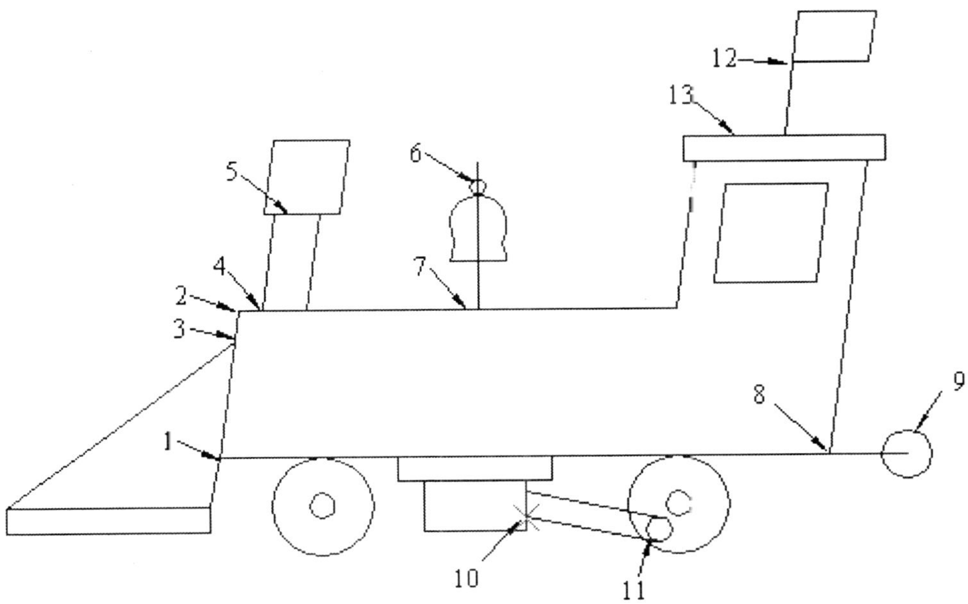


40. This next OSNAP is a secret – so secret, in fact, that it doesn't even have a button! But **m2p** (or midway between two points) has long been needed.
We'll get a sneak preview of the ***Circle*** command for this procedure. (Don't worry; I'll walk you through it). Start by entering the ***Circle*** command.

**Command:** ***circle***

41. At the prompt, use the (right-click) cursor menu to select **Mid Between 2 Points**. Alternately, you can enter ***m2p*** on the keyboard.

**Specify center point for circle or [3P/2P/Ttr (tan tan radius)]:** ***m2p***

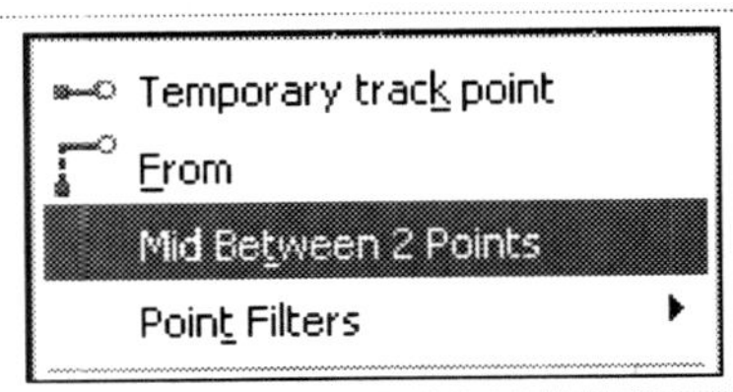


42. Using the **endpoint** OSNAP, select the upper right corner of the cabin window …

**First point of mid: _endp of**

43. … and then the lower left corner.

**Second point of mid: _endp of**

### 3.3.1: OSNAP PRACTICE

44. Give the circle a ¼" radius. Your drawing looks like the following figure. (This is by far the easiest method of locating this point, as you will soon see.)

**Specify radius of circle or [Diameter]:** ***.25***

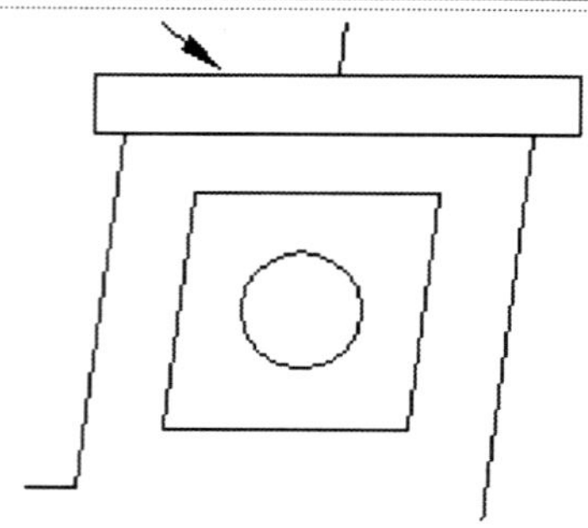

45. Save the drawing to the C:\Steps\Lesson03\ folder as *MyTrain.dwg*.

**Command:** ***saveas***

You should now be fairly familiar with three ways to call on OSNAPs – the toolbar, the keyboard, and the cursor menu.

## 3.4 Running OSNAPs

Let me show you another way to use OSNAPs. We call this one *Running OSNAPs*.

Before long, you'll discover that having to select an OSNAP every time you want to place a point is a tedious procedure at best (even if it's easier than typing coordinates). Is there not, you might ask, a way to turn OSNAPs on and leave them on? By now, of course, you know that if there weren't, I wouldn't ask.

Look at the last button on the OSNAP toolbar (or the last option on the cursor menu). The button (**OSNAP Settings** ) looks like one of those horseshoe magnets with which we played as children. This is the key to setting our running OSNAPs. Picking this button tells AutoCAD to display the Drafting Settings dialog box with the **Object Snap** tab on top (Figure 3.010).

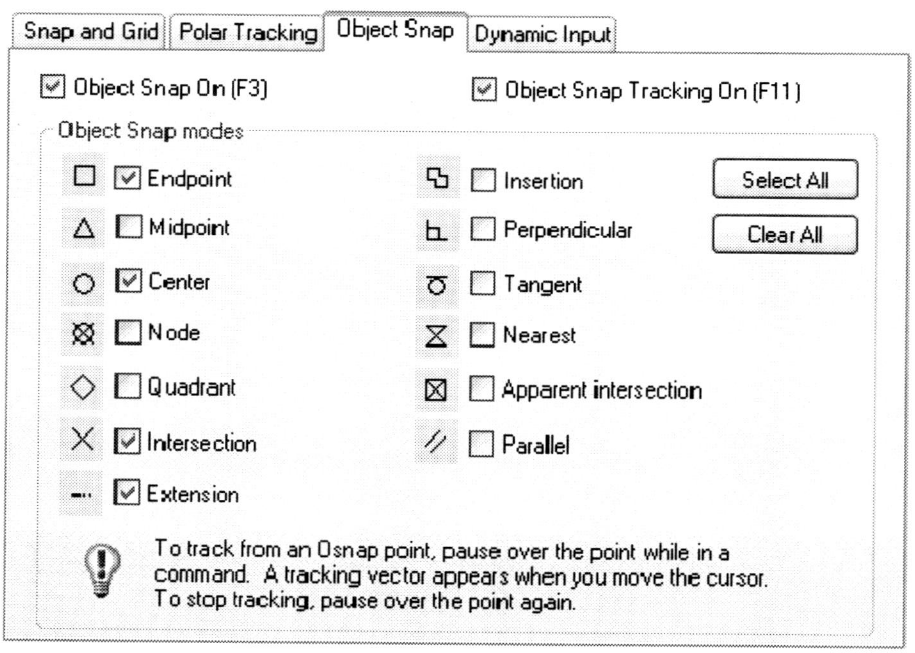


Figure 3.010

Each available OSNAP has a check box beside it. Click in the box to place a check and activate that particular running OSNAP. Look to the left of each box to see a symbol (or marker). We've seen that AutoCAD uses this symbol to indicate that you're selecting a point using this particular OSNAP.

> Other ways to access the **Object Snap** tab of the Drafting Settings dialog box include: typing ***OSNAP*** or ***OS*** at the command prompt, or right-clicking on the **OSNAP** toggle on the status bar and selecting **Settings.**

An **Options** button resides at the bottom of the dialog box. This button opens the Options dialog box with the **Drafting** tab on top (Figure 3.011). Here the user has several frames to help control the behavior of object snaps. You can control OSNAP settings from this tab, including:

- the size and color of the symbol (**Marker**);
- whether or not you want a **tooltip** when you hesitate over an OSNAP area;
- whether or not you want the crosshairs to snap to (**Magnet**) the selected OSNAP;
- whether or not you want to see tooltips.

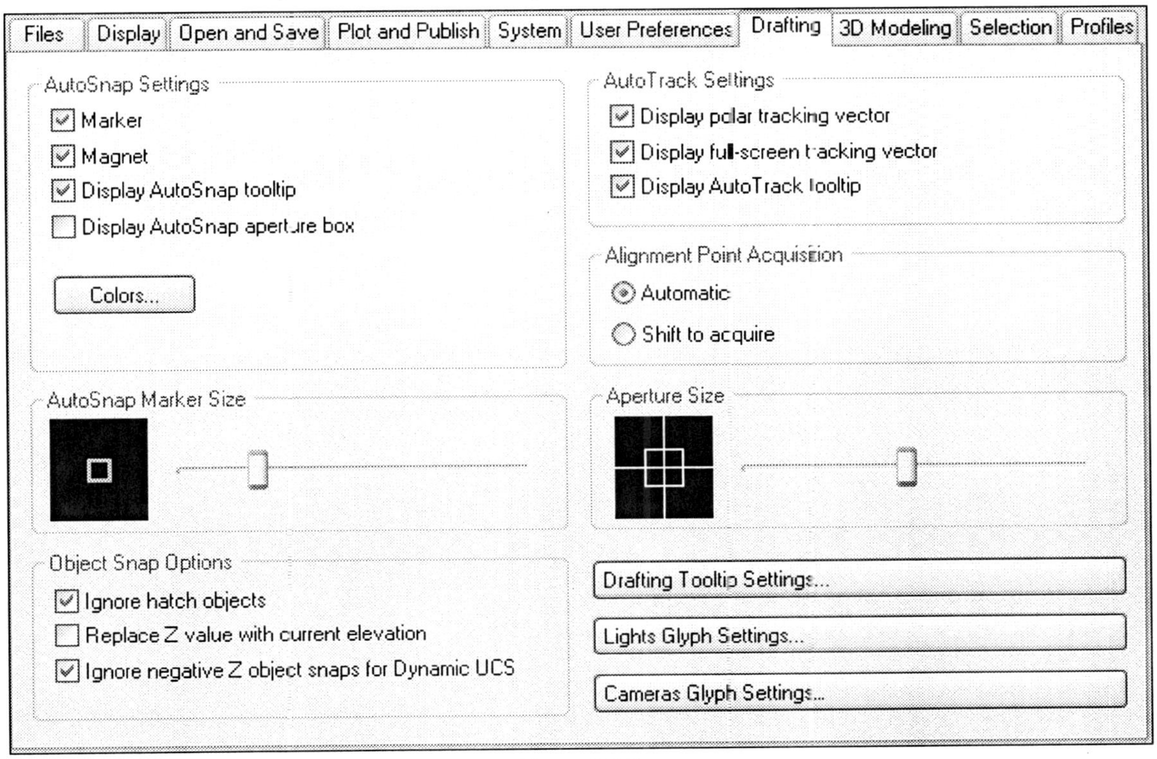


Figure 3.011

But for optimal performance, I suggest leaving all these options at their default settings. (Reminder: DON'T experiment in the Options dialog box!)

Let's try using running OSNAPs to redraw the train.

> You may notice that it's difficult to select the **center** or the **quadrant** of a circle, as AutoCAD doesn't know which you want. If you move your crosshairs over the circle and the center symbol appears instead of the quadrant symbol (or vice versa), hold the mouse steady and pick the TAB key on the keyboard. AutoCAD will toggle through the various possibilities until it finds the one you like. This procedure is quite useful for busy drawings in which AutoCAD must choose between several OSNAP possibilities.

| **Do This: 3.4.1** | **More OSNAP Practice** |
|---|---|

I. Open the *train2.dwg* file found in the C:\Steps\Lesson03 folder. This is a pristine copy of the drawing you used in the last exercise.

II. Follow these steps.

## 3.4.1: More OSNAP Practice

1. Click on the **OSNAP Settings** button on the OSNAP toolbar. Alternately, you can enter ***OSNAP*** or ***os*** at the command prompt.

**Command:** ***os***

2. Set the running OSNAPs indicated.

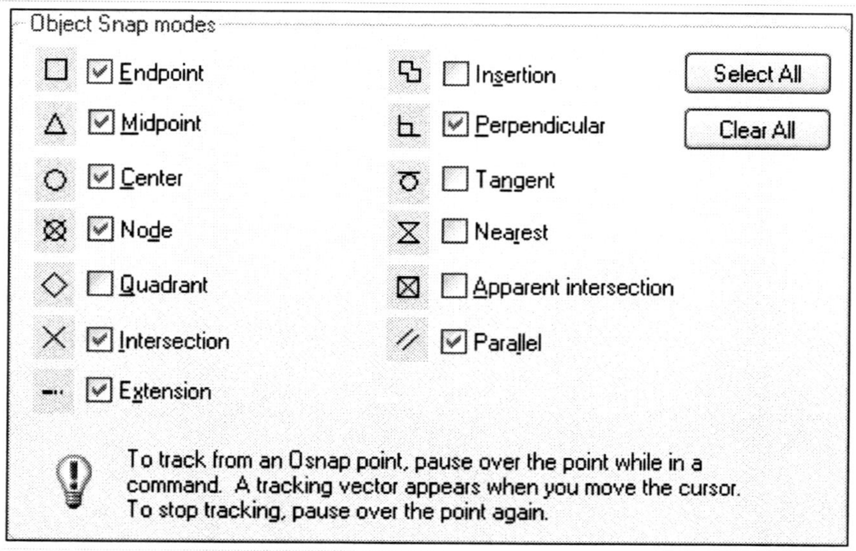


3. Now follow the instructions in Exercise 3.3.1 to draw the train. But this time, don't pick on or type in the OSNAPs (except, of course, for the ones you didn't set in Step 2). You'll notice AutoCAD automatically uses OSNAP endpoints, midpoints, and so forth. It won't, however, automatically use the **Apparent Intersection** or the **Nearest** OSNAP (you didn't set those). You'll have to select those manually as you did previously.

4. Exit the drawing without saving.

**Command:** ***quit***

> Other ways to activate/deactivate Running OSNAPs include clicking on the **OSNAP** toggle on the status bar, using the **F3** function key on the keyboard, or holding down the CTRL key on the keyboard while typing ***F***.

Was that faster? Easier?

The biggest problem my students have with running OSNAPs is that they forget to deactivate them. They can't understand why their lines or circles keep jumping to an endpoint or intersection. If this happens to you, click the **OSNAP** toggle on the status bar to deactivate Running OSNAPs.

## 3.5 Point Filters and Object Snap Tracking

Often in drafting, we find it necessary to align objects according to the location of other objects. Parallel bars, triangles, and 4H-lead guidelines made this easy on the board. But what does AutoCAD use to substitute for these proven tools?

Actually, there are two things we can use: *point filters* and *object snap tracking*.

## 3.5.1 Point Filters

Use point filters to tell AutoCAD to locate an object using the X, Y, and/or Z coordinate of an existing object. Let's see how they work. We'll redraw the stick figure in our train's cabin.

### Do This: 3.5.1.1 Introducing Point Filters

I. Open the *MyTrain.dwg* file found in the C:\Steps\Lesson03 folder.
II. Erase the figure in the cabin window.
III. Follow these steps.

**3.5.1.1: POINT FILTERS**

1. Begin with the ***Circle*** command.

**Command: *circle***

2. At the circle prompt, type ***.X*** to tell AutoCAD to use the X coordinate …

… of the midpoint of the lower horizontal line of the cab.

**Specify center point for circle or [3P/2P/Ttr (tan tan radius)]: *.x***
**of**

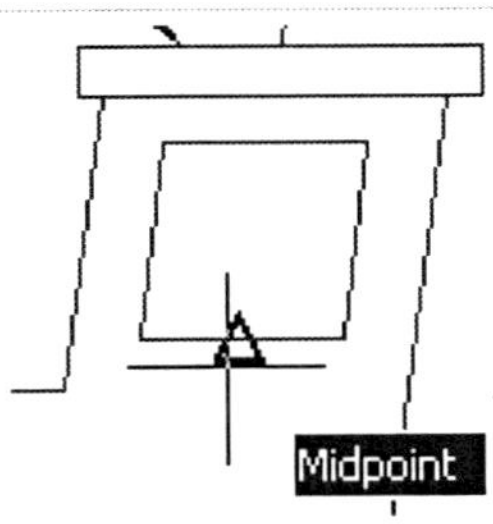


3. AutoCAD tells you that it needs the Y and Z coordinates.

Tell it to use the YZ coordinate of the midpoint of the vertical line.

**(need YZ):**

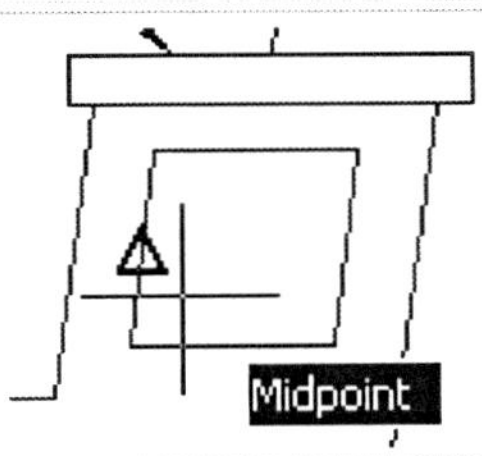


4. AutoCAD locates the center of the circle and asks you for a radius. Tell it to use a radius of ¼".

**Specify radius of circle or [Diameter]: *.25***

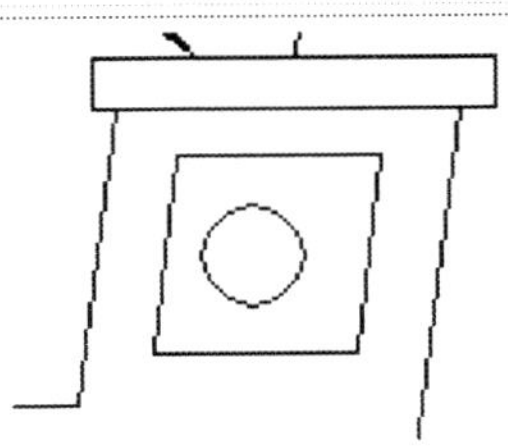

It's not as easy as **m2p**, but this is one way of acquiring coordinates from existing geometry in a drawing. But let's look at yet another, easier method.

## 3.5.2 Object Tracking

AutoCAD produced the tracking feature in response to complaints that most OSNAPs require a direct contact with an existing object, and Point Filters were too tedious. However, like Point Filters, Tracking allows you to draw in *relation to* an existing object without actually touching it. Let's see how it works. We'll redraw the stick figure in our train's cabin.

| Do This: 3.5.2.1 | Object Tracking |
|---|---|

I. Be sure you're still in the *MyTrain.dwg* in the C:\Steps\Lesson03 folder. If not, open it now.

II. Erase the circle you drew in the last exercise.

III. Follow these steps.

## 3.5.2.1: Object Tracking

1. Turn Object Tracking **On** by depressing (picking) the toggle on the status bar . Alternately, you can use the **F11** function key on your keyboard.

2. Clear all Running OSNAPs except **Midpoint** (see the figure below). Be sure to place the check in the **Object Snap On** check box to turn on running OSNAPs.

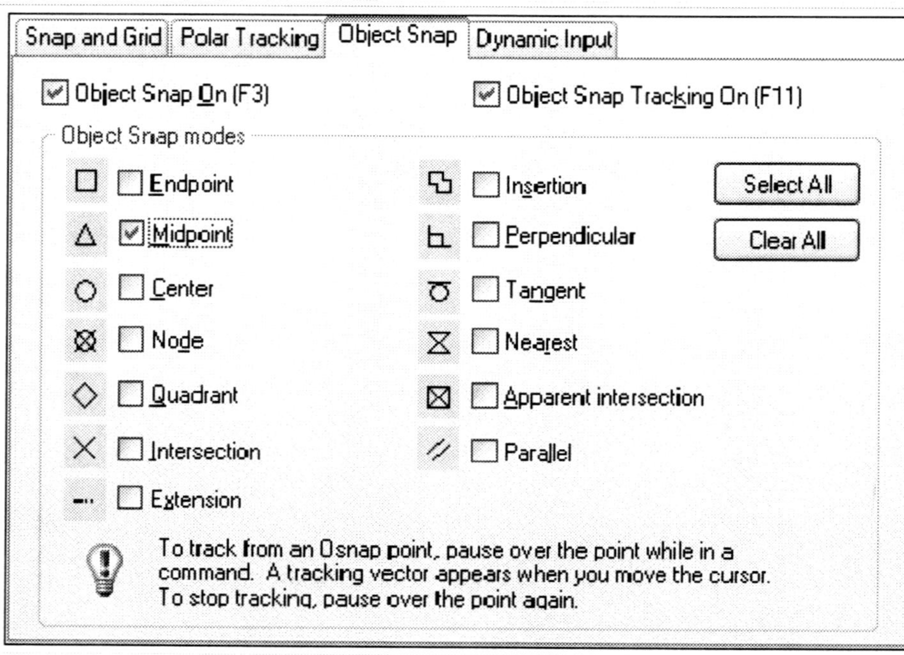


3. Enter the ***Circle*** command .

**Command: *circle***

4. At the **Specify center point** prompt, place your cursor over the midpoint of the lower horizontal line in the cab window. Hesitate for a moment (don't pick anything), and then move your crosshairs upward. Notice the tracking line.

**Specify center point for circle or [3P/2P/Ttr (tan tan radius)]:**

5. Repeat Step 4, this time placing your crosshairs over the left vertical line of the cab window and moving inward.

**Specify center point for circle or [3P/2P/Ttr (tan tan radius)]:**

## 3.5.2.1: Object Tracking

6. Move the crosshairs toward the center of the window. Pick with the left mouse button when Tracking tells you that you're located at 0° from the last point and 90° from the first point (as shown).

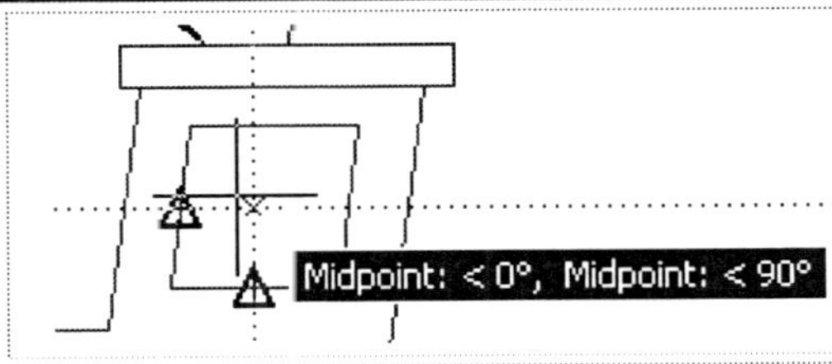


7. You'll notice that the center of the circle has been placed at a point near the center of the window.
Use polar tracking to draw a circle with a ¼" radius (as shown).

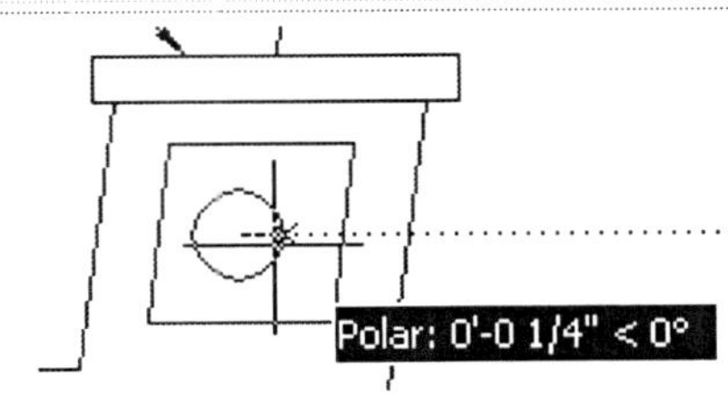


8. Draw a line 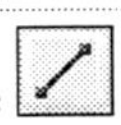 …

**Command: *l***

9. … from the lower **quadrant** 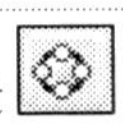 of the circle you just drew …

**Specify first point: _qua of**

10. … **perpendicular** 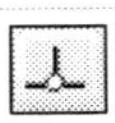 to the bottom of the window.

**Specify next point or [Undo]: _per to**

11. Complete the command.

**Specify next point or [Undo]: *[enter]***

12. Erase  the numbers and arrows. Your drawing now looks like the following figure.

**Command: *e***

## 3.6 Isometric Drafting

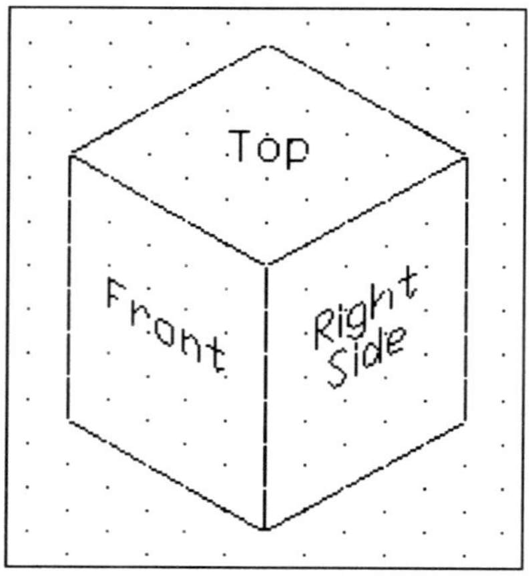


Figure 3.012

After having thoroughly confused us with orthographic projections, my old drafting instructor threw *isometric* drawings at us. (At this point, I started thinking about other ways to make a living.) I'll try to make it a bit easier than he did.

Orthographic drawings (projections) show an object from one aspect – left / right / top / bottom / front / back. An isometric drawing shows three aspects at once – left or right side / top or bottom / front or back. Standard isometrics are drawn so that the faces are seen on a plane running 30° above or below the X-axis, as shown in Figure 3.012. Of course, there are variations, but the 30° format is standard.

To draw isometrics in AutoCAD requires adjusting the grid and snap to an isometric format. This is easier than it sounds. Remember the options AutoCAD provided for the snap tool? This is where we make the switch from orthographic layout to isometric. Here's how:

**Command: *snap* (or *sn*)**

**Specify snap spacing or [ON/OFF/Aspect/Style/Type] <0.5000>: *s***

**Enter snap grid style [Standard/Isometric] <S>: *i***

**Specify vertical spacing <0.5000>: *[enter]***

That's all there is to it! AutoCAD changes the grid and snap simultaneously. Ortho will now work along the 30°/90° planes. You'll notice that even your crosshairs have changed, and you'll need a new toggle– the *isometric plane toggle*. This will adjust your crosshairs and help you draw along the 30°/90° plane, the 150°/90° plane, or the 30°/150° plane. The keyboard toggle is ***Ctrl + E***, and the function key is **F5**. As with the other toggles we've learned, these will work regardless of the command sequence we're running.

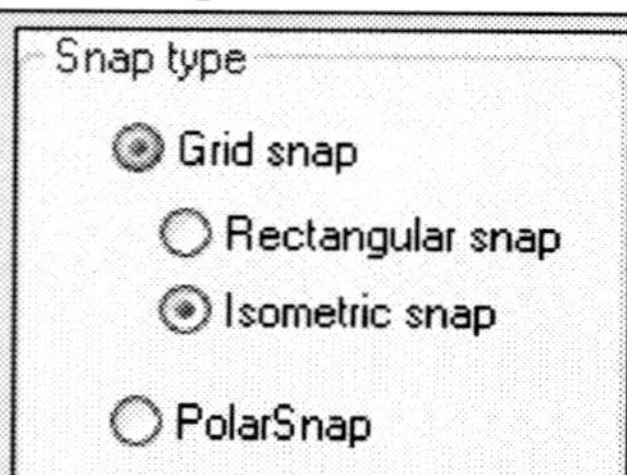


You can also set the isometric snap style on the **Snap and Grid** tab of the Drafting Settings dialog box (left). Simply right-click on the **Snap** or **Grid** toggle on the status bar, and select **Settings**.

Let's try a simple isometric drawing.

Try to draw the standard isometric shown in Figure 3.012. Don't try the text yet. We'll look at text in Lesson 4.

| **Do This: 3.6.1** | **Isometric Drafting** |
|---|---|

I. Begin a new drawing using the *MyBase1* (or *base2*) template found in the C:\Steps\Lesson01 folder.

II. Turn on dynamic input.

III. Follow these steps.

## 3.6.1: Isometric Drafting

1. Enter the ***Snap*** command by typing ***snap*** or ***sn*** at the command prompt.

   **Command: *sn***

2. We'll tell AutoCAD to change the snap **Style**, but we'll use a dynamic input trick to do it. Hit the down arrow on the keyboard and select the **Style** option from the dynamic input menu.

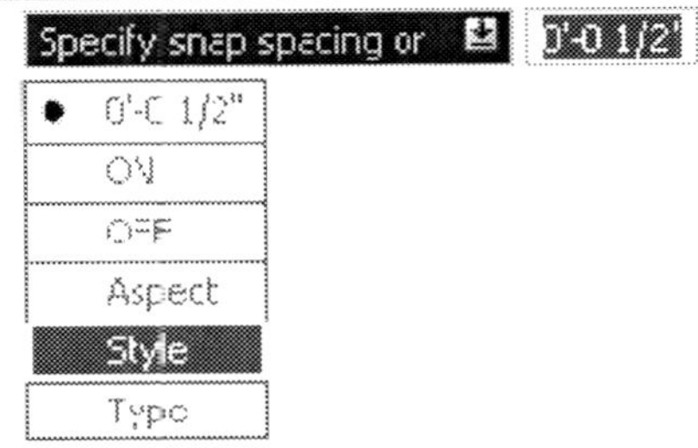


3. Set the **Style** to **Isometric** Isometric...

   **Enter snap grid style [Standard/Isometric] <S>: *i***

4. ... with a spacing of ¼".

   **Specify vertical spacing <0'-0 1/2">: *1/4***

5. Using the **F5** function key F5, set your crosshairs to a 90°/30° configuration. The crosshairs will look like the image at right.

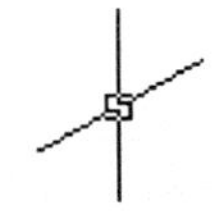

6. Depress the **Grid** and **Ortho** toggles SNAP GRID on the status bar to turn them on.

7. Right-click on the **Snap** toggle and select **Grid Snap On**. (Toggle dynamic input off if you wish.)

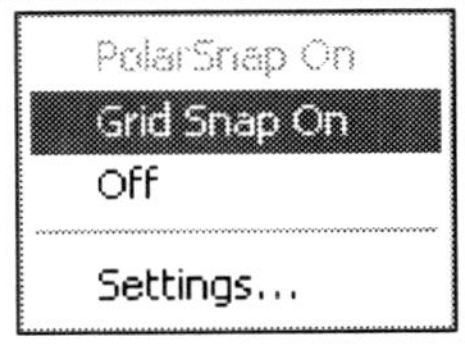


8. Draw the right side of the cube.

   **Command: *l***

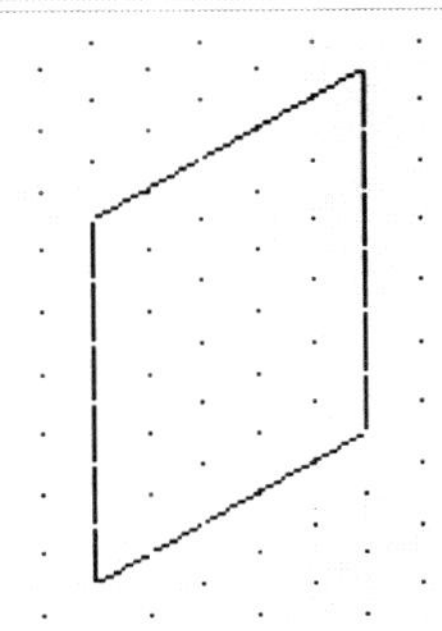

9. Toggle the crosshairs F5 to 90°/150°.

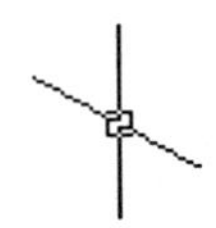

### 3.6.1: ISOMETRIC DRAFTING

10. Draw the left side of the cube.

**Command: *l***

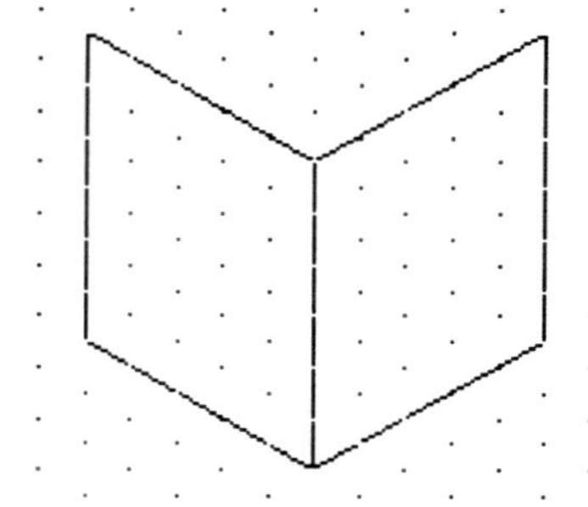

11. Toggle the crosshairs [F5] to 30°/150°.

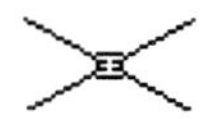

12. Draw the top of the cube.

**Command: *l***

13. Save  your drawing in the C:\Steps\Lesson03 folder as *MyCube.dwg*.

**Command: *save***

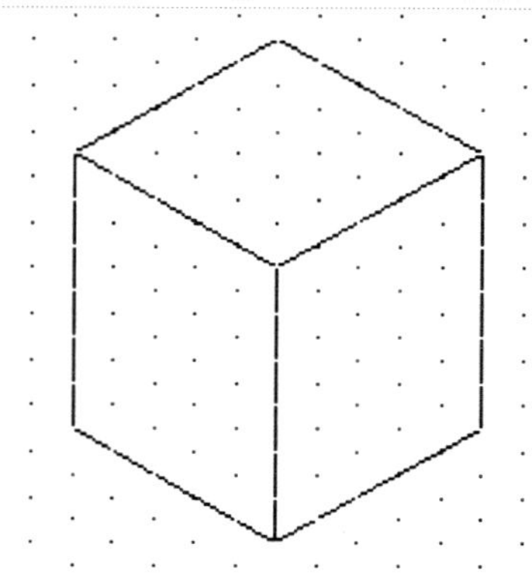

## 3.7 Extra Steps

One of the lesser-known drawing tools works similarly to the polar coordinate system, but requires less input. This is called the *Direct Distance Option*. Learn this one to amaze and confound older CAD operators.

Simply put, this is how it works. At the **Specify next point or [Undo]** prompt, you enter a distance at the keyboard, move the crosshairs in the direction you want the line to go, and then hit ***enter*** (or pick the right mouse button then select **Enter**). Let me demonstrate.

| Do This: 3.7.1 | Direct Distance Entry |
|---|---|

I. Start a new drawing from scratch. Turn off dynamic input and toggle Ortho on (**F8**).

II. Begin to draw a line from point 2,2.

III. At the **Specify next point or [Undo]:** prompt, type ***3***. Don't hit ***enter*** yet.

IV. Move your crosshairs to the right.

V. Hit ***enter***. Notice that AutoCAD has drawn a line 3 units in the direction you moved the crosshairs!

The marvels never cease!

## 3.8 What Have We Learned?

*Items covered in this lesson include:*

- *Drafting Settings: Ortho, Snap, Tracking, Grid, and dynamic input tools*
- *OSNAPs and Running OSNAPs*
- *Point Filters*
- *Object Snap Tracking*
- *Direct Distance Entry*
- *Dynamic Input*
- *Commands*
  - ***Grid***
  - ***Snap***
  - ***Ortho***
  - ***DSettings***
  - ***OSNAP***

In this lesson, we've covered the tools that'll make the difference between a computer *doodler* and a CAD *operator*. Anyone can draw lines and circles, but for CAD to be an effective tool in industry, you must have the ability to draw with speed and precision. But don't expect yourself to fly through a drawing yet. First, you must practice the material in this lesson until it becomes second nature – like a draftsman knowing how to begin a drafting project without thinking about it. So take some time to do these exercises. Do them again and again until you're quite comfortable with AutoCAD's drawing aids.

## 3.9 Exercises

1. Start a new drawing. Set it up as follows:
   1.1. Units: architectural
   1.2. Lower left limits: 0,0
   1.3. Upper right limits: 17,11
   1.4. Grid: ½
   1.5. Snap: ¼
   1.6. Snap style: isometric
   1.7. Save this as a template file called *MyIsoGrid.dwt* to the C:\Steps\Lesson03 folder.
2. For each of the drawings below, start a new drawing using the *MyIsoGrid* template file created in Exercise 3. (If this file is not available, use the *IsoGrid2* template in the same folder.) Draw the figures and save them as their figure name/number in the C:\Steps\Lesson03 folder.

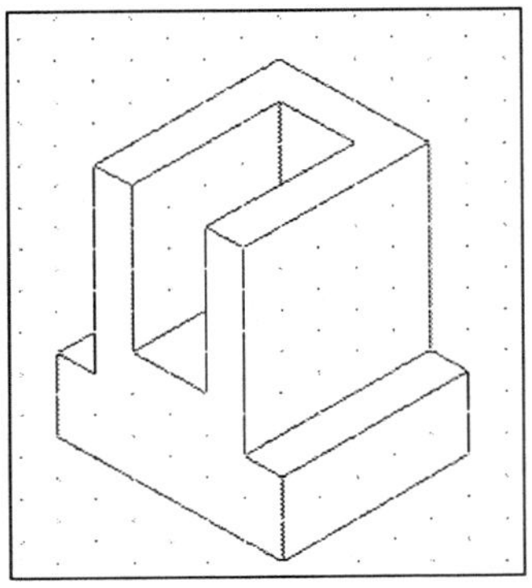

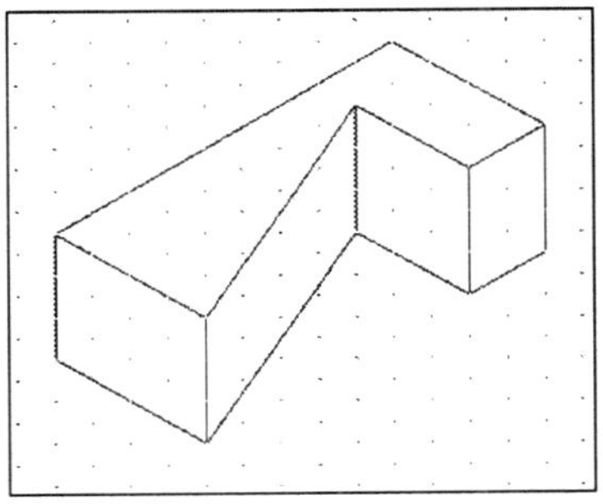

*For more exercises related to Lesson 3, please see Lesson 3 in AutoCAD 2007: One Step at a Time – Workbook.*

## 3.10 For Web-Based Review Questions, visit: http://www.uneedcad.com/2007/Files/07R3.pdf

# Lesson 4

Following this lesson, you will:

- ✓ *Know how to manipulate the screen display of your drawing through:*
  - *The **Zoom** command*
  - *The **Pan** command*
  - *The **View** command*
- ✓ *Know how to use a transparent command*
- ✓ *Know how to use Basic Text and Text Editing commands, including:*
  - ***Text/DText***
  - ***DDEdit***
  - ***Style***
  - ***Qtext***
  - ***Find***
- ✓ *Know how to load a LISP routine*

# Display Controls and Basic Text

*Our last lesson probably made you feel fairly comfortable with your new ability to create some wildly accurate drawings. But have you tried to use some of these tools in larger drawings? If you have, you might have noticed that grid and snap become difficult (if not impossible) to use as the drawing encompasses more space. You might also have noticed that those wonderful OSNAPs don't help if you can't tell which endpoint you've selected.*

*We'll begin this lesson by addressing these problems. Then we'll examine the tools available to help place text in a drawing.*

## 4.1 Getting Closer: The *Zoom* Command

One of the allowances I've had to make as I amassed all this "experience" has been the acquisition of a pair of reading glasses. At first I wore them down on my nose – a look more professorial. Now, however, I wear them closer to my eyes to get a wider field of vision. Ah, age!

For this reason, I really appreciate AutoCAD's ***Zoom*** command. With this, I can enlarge all or part of my drawing as much as I like, without having to search for my "eyes."

To appreciate the demonstrations of the ***Zoom*** command, we'll need to open the *pid* drawing in the C:\Steps\Lesson04 folder. The drawing is shown in Figure 4.001. Note that the *pid* drawing was created for a D-size sheet of paper, so viewing it on the screen (or on our book-size sheet of paper) makes it difficult to read.

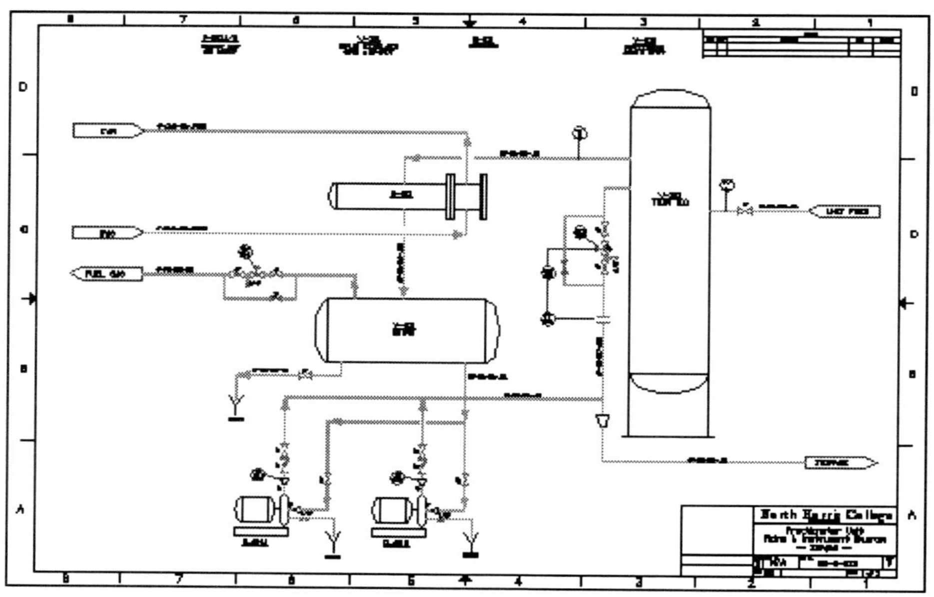

Figure 4.001

The command sequence for the ***Zoom*** command follows:

> **Command: *zoom* (or *z*)**
>
> **Specify corner of window, enter a scale factor (nX or nXP), or**
>
> **[All/Center/Dynamic/Extents/Previous/Scale/Window/Object] <real time>: *[select a corner of the window]***
>
> **Specify opposite corner: *[select the opposite corner of the window]***

***Z*** (the hotkey) will work as well as ***zoom***, or you can pick the **Zoom Window** button 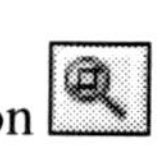 from the Standard or Zoom toolbar.

Let's look at the various ***Zoom*** options. Notice that most of the options have an equivalent button on the Zoom Window flyout toolbar.

A *flyout* toolbar button is indicated by a small triangle in the lower right corner of the button. The triangle indicates that there are more buttons below the one shown. To see the other available buttons, pick on the flyout button and hold down the mouse key. A flyout toolbar will appear. To identify what a button will do, rest your cursor on it for a moment. A tooltip will appear telling you the use of the button. To select the button, simply move your cursor to it and release the mouse key.

| **Zoom Option** | **Alternate Button** |
|---|---|
| **Realtime** appears to be the default, but it's accepted only by hitting the **ENTER** key. We'll look at realtime zooming shortly. If instead, you select an empty point on the screen, AutoCAD will assume you're placing a window around the objects you wish to view more closely. It'll then prompt you for the other corner. (Remember Implied Windowing – Section 2.3.) |  Zoom Realtime Button |
| **All** displays the limits of the drawing, unless something has been drawn outside the limits. In that case, **All** will display the extents, or *all* the objects on the drawing. |  Zoom All Button |
| **Center** prompts you for the desired center point of the display, and then adjusts the display so that the selected point is in the center of the screen. | 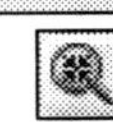 Zoom Center Button |
| One of the most forgotten zoom features, **Dynamic** provides you with the ability to place an adjustable box over that part of the drawing you want to display. When selected, AutoCAD temporarily replaces the screen with a view of the entire drawing. A view box shows what and where your current view area is. A selection box appears that you can manipulate with the mouse as you would the crosshairs. Move this box over the area you wish to view and hit the right mouse button to confirm your selection. AutoCAD redisplays the drawing with the selected area shown (this'll be clearer when we do it in Exercise 4.1.1. |  Zoom Dynamic Button |
| **Extents** brings you as close as possible to the drawing while showing *all* the objects in the drawing. |  Zoom Extents Button |
| **Previous** displays the last screen viewed. |  Zoom Previous Button |
| **Scale** can be a bit confusing. You don't have to type ***s***, but you can. If you do, AutoCAD prompts you for the scale you want. Note that this isn't the drawing scale, but the size of the drawing in relation to the graphics area. Hence, a scale of ***.5*** will cause the drawing to occupy half the graphics area of your screen.<br>If you simply type ***.5X*** at the ***Zoom*** prompt (rather than typing ***s***), the drawing will appear half its current size.<br>Notice that the ***Zoom*** prompt suggests the **X** or an **XP** procedure. (Ignore the **XP** for now. We'll cover that in detail in our discussion of Paper Space in Lesson 22.) |  Zoom Scale Button |

| Zoom Option | Alternate Button |
|---|---|
| To simplify the **Scale** option, AutoCAD provides two additional buttons – **Zoom Out** and **Zoom**. **Zoom In** zooms to a 2X scale and **Zoom Out** zooms to a .5X scale. |  Zoom Out Button  Zoom In Button |
| When you select the **Object** option of the ***Zoom*** command, AutoCAD will ask you to select an object(s). It'll then zoom in as close to that object(s) as possible while showing it in its entirety. |  Zoom Object Button |

In addition to the command line and toolbar, all the ***Zoom*** options can be found in the **Zoom** selection of the View pull-down menu and on the (right-click) cursor menu once the ***Zoom*** command has been entered.

Let's try some of these now.

Note: Beginning with this exercise, I'll show dynamic input menus in the **TOOLS** column (rather than the older cursor menu). But feel free to toggle dynamic input off and use cursor menu options if you prefer. (The options are the same.)

| Do This: 4.1.1 | Practice Zooming |
|---|---|

I. If *pid.dwg* isn't already open, please open it now. It's in the C:\Steps\Lesson04 folder.

II. Follow these steps.

**4.1.1: PRACTICE ZOOMING**

1. We'll begin with the **Window** option of the ***Zoom*** command.

Enter the ***Zoom*** command or pick the **Zoom Window** button  on the Standard toolbar.

**Command: *z***

2. Select the corners of the window as shown at right.

**Specify corner of window, enter a scale factor (nX or nXP), or [All/Center/ Dynamic/ Extents/Previous/ Scale/Window/Object] <real time>: *[select first window corner]***

**Specify opposite corner: *[select other corner]***

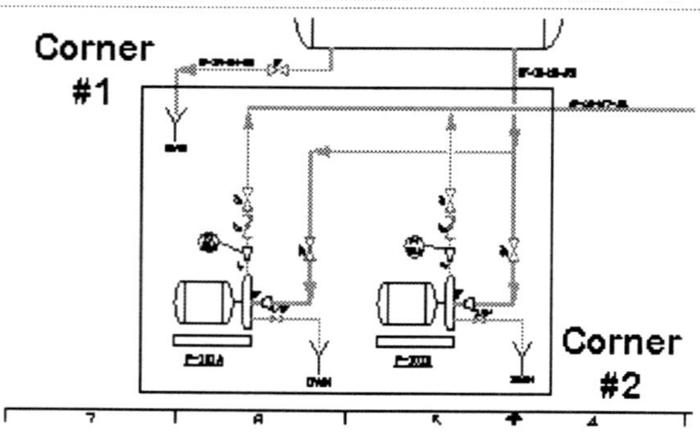


3. Now let's zoom back to where we started by using the **Previous** option or the **Zoom Previous** button  on the Standard toolbar.

**Command: *z***

**Specify corner of window, enter a scale factor (nX or nXP), or**

**[All/Center/Dynamic/Extents/ Previous/Scale/Window/Object] <real time>:** *p*

4. Zoom to a .5X scale using the **Zoom In** button on the Zoom flyout toolbar.

5. Now zoom **All** using either keyboard commands or the **Zoom All** button on the Zoom flyout toolbar. Notice the location of and the spacing around the drawing on the screen. Let's compare that to the **Extents** option.

**Command:** *z*
**Specify corner of window, enter a scale factor (nX or nXP), or**
**[All/Center/Dynamic/Extents/ Previous/Scale/Window/Object] <real time>:** *a*

6. Zoom **Extents** using keyboard or button. Notice the locat on of and spacing around the drawing on the screen now. How does it compare with the results of the zoom **All** option?

**Command:** *z*
**Specify corner of window, enter a scale factor (nX or nXP), or**
**[All/Center/Dynamic/Extents/ Previous/Scale/Window/Object] <real time>:** *e*

7. Now let's play with the **Dynamic** option. We'll select this one from the dynamic menu – enter the ***Zoom*** command and select **Dynamic** from the dynamic input menu Dynamic (Remember to use the down arrow to get to the menu. Be sure the **DYN** toggle on the status bar is depressed.)

Notice the change in the display. There is now a box over the display with an "X" in the middle. This is the *location box* (right).

**Command:** *z*

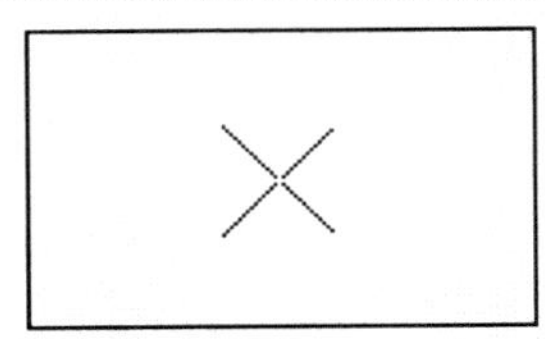

8. Pick with the left mouse button and notice how the box changes. Instead of an "X" in the middle, there is now an arrow pointing toward the right side of the box. This is the *sizing box* (right).

As you move the mouse back and forth, notice how the size of the selection box changes. When it's just large enough to enclose the exchanger (right), pick again with the left mouse button.

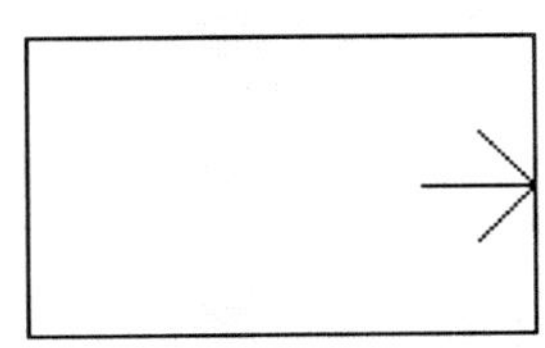

9. Now place the selection box over the exchanger and right-click. Your display now looks like the figure at right.

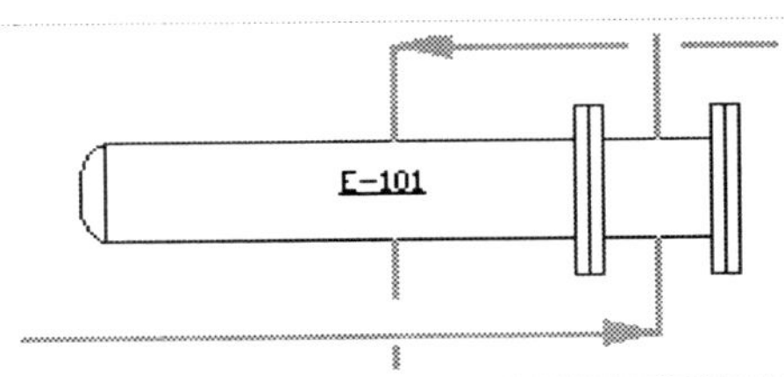


10. Now let's center our exchanger. Repeat the ***Zoom*** command and enter the **Center** option. Alternately, you can pick the **Zoom Center** button on the Zoom flyout toolbar.

**Command:** *z*
**Specify corner of window, enter a scale factor (nX or nXP), or**

## 4.1.1: Practice Zooming

**[All/Center/Dynamic/Extents/ Previous/Scale/Window/Object] <real time>:** ***c***

11. Select a point roughly in the center of the exchanger.

**Specify center point:**

12. And hit ***enter*** to complete the command.

**Enter magnification or height <X.XXXX>:** ***[enter]***

13. Let's take a look at the **Object** option. Repeat the ***Zoom*** command and select the **Object** option. Alternately, you can pick the **Zoom Object** button on the Zoom flyout toolbar.

**Command:** ***z***
**Specify corner of window, enter a scale factor (nX or nXP), or**
**[All/Center/Dynamic/Extents/ Previous/Scale/Window/Object] <real time>:** ***o***

14. AutoCAD prompts you to **Select objects**. Select the head of the exchanger (select all of the vertical lines – I used a window).

**Select objects:**

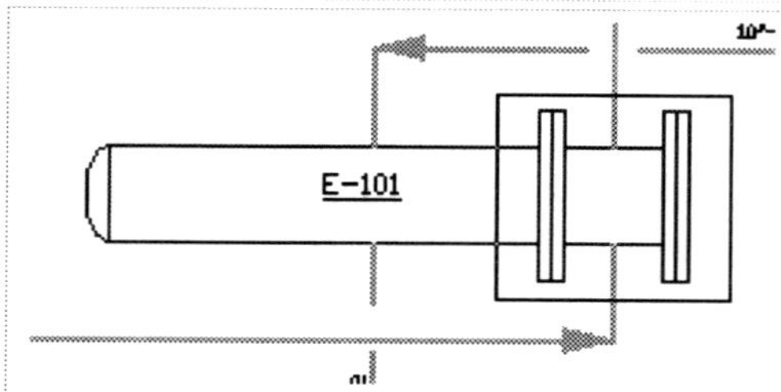


15. Hit ***enter*** to complete the command. Your drawing looks like the figure at right.

**Select objects:** ***[enter]***

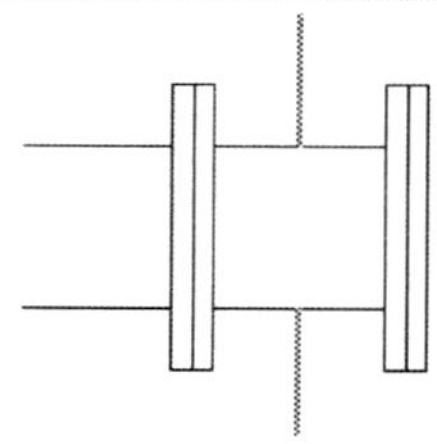

Before we proceed, there are two other aspects of display manipulation we should discuss – ***Realtime Zoom*** and ***Pan*** (aka. ***Realtime Pan***).

Realtime is just a fancy way to say, "Do it while I watch." In other words, you can judge how far you want to zoom by watching the display change as you move your mouse.

Here's the **Zoom Realtime** button? You can find it on the Standard toolbar, next to the **Zoom** flyout buttons we've been using. When you pick this button, you'll notice the crosshairs change to a cursor that resembles the button image. To use realtime zoom, pick anywhere in the graphics area of the screen with the left mouse button. While holding the button down (dragging), move the cursor up and down. Notice how the display changes. When you're happy with the display, release the left mouse button, click the right button, and pick **Exit** on the cursor menu that appears. (Alternately, you can use the **ENTER** or **ESC** keys on your keyboard.)

> AutoCAD will also make use of the wheel located between the two buttons on a wheeled mouse. Rotating the wheel forward or backward works like a ***Realtime Zoom***. If you don't have a wheeled mouse, the convenience will more than justify the expense!

You can also access realtime zoom by entering the ***Zoom*** command and then hitting ***enter*** at the first prompt.

A trick to remember when using realtime zoom is to do a zoom **Center** first. You may have noticed that realtime zoom doesn't allow you to change position during a zoom. In fact, it maintains the same center point on the display, zooming in or out about that point.

Another of AutoCAD's *realtime* features, ***Pan*** behaves as though you are panning a camera across your display. Located next to the **Zoom Realtime** button on the Standard toolbar, the **Pan Realtime** button will also change the crosshairs to a cursor that resembles the button image. Realtime pan works in much the same way as realtime zoom. Pick and drag with the left mouse button. It's like putting your hand down on your paper and sliding the paper across the drawing table.

Here again AutoCAD makes use of the wheeled mouse. Depressing the wheel between the mouse buttons and dragging the cursor across the screen appears as though you are in realtime pan. But no command line or toolbar entries are needed!

The hotkey for accessing the ***Pan*** command is ***P***. Exit realtime pan just as you did realtime zoom.

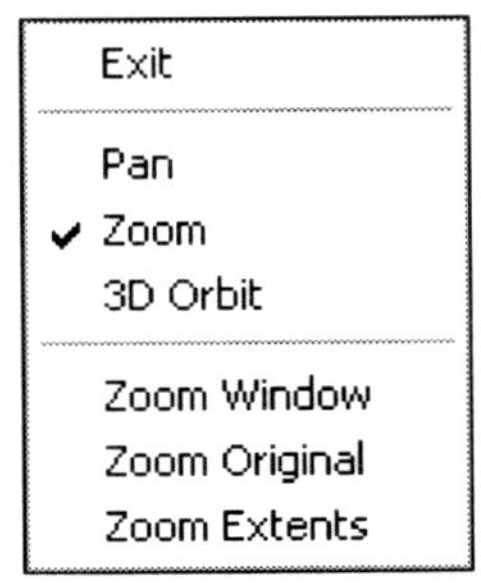


One of the really neat aspects of the realtime features is the cursor menu (shown at right) that displays with a right-click. I strongly suggest getting comfortable with this menu (especially if you don't have a wheeled mouse). Expertise with it will enable you to position yourself exactly where you want to be in a drawing, while saving the time you might otherwise spend keyboarding or toolbar-clicking.

Before continuing, take a few minutes to play with these last few features in the *pid* drawing. Note the increased speed using the realtime features as opposed to the time spent in display manipulation using the methods we learned previously.

AutoCAD's display commands – including the ***Zoom*** and ***Pan*** commands are *transparent*. That is, they may be used while at another command's prompt (or while running another command). The buttons will work as they always do; however, to enter a transparent command at a prompt other than the command prompt, precede it with an apostrophe. Thus, entering the ***Zoom*** command while at the ***Line*** command's prompt will look like this:

> **Specify next point or [Undo]:** *'z*
> **>>Specify corner of window, enter a scale factor (nX or nXP), or**
> **[All/Center/Dynamic/Extents/Previous/Scale/Window/Object] <real time>:**

The double bracket preceding the zoom prompt indicates that it's operating transparently. When the transparent command is completed, AutoCAD returns to the previous command prompt (in this case, the ***Line*** command's prompt).

## 4.2 Why Find It Twice? – The *View* Command

One of the things you'll discover after drafting on a computer for a while is that you must return frequently to certain areas of your drawing. A beginning CAD operator will use display tools like ***Zoom*** and ***Pan*** because these are simple, easily mastered, and they work. With so much to learn, who can blame them?

But AutoCAD has provided the ***View*** command to speed past these display controls. With the ***View*** command, you can create and store certain displays (views) and then restore these views at any time from any position in the drawing. Thus, using our *PID* drawing as an example, we can go directly from a display of the pumps to a display of the exchanger without the need for panning or zooming in and out.

Using ***View*** requires a bit of setup time at first; however, you can see that it will save quite a bit of time later when you might be panning and zooming all over the place.
View utilizes a dialog box (Figure 4.002) that's easier to use than it looks! Let's take a look.

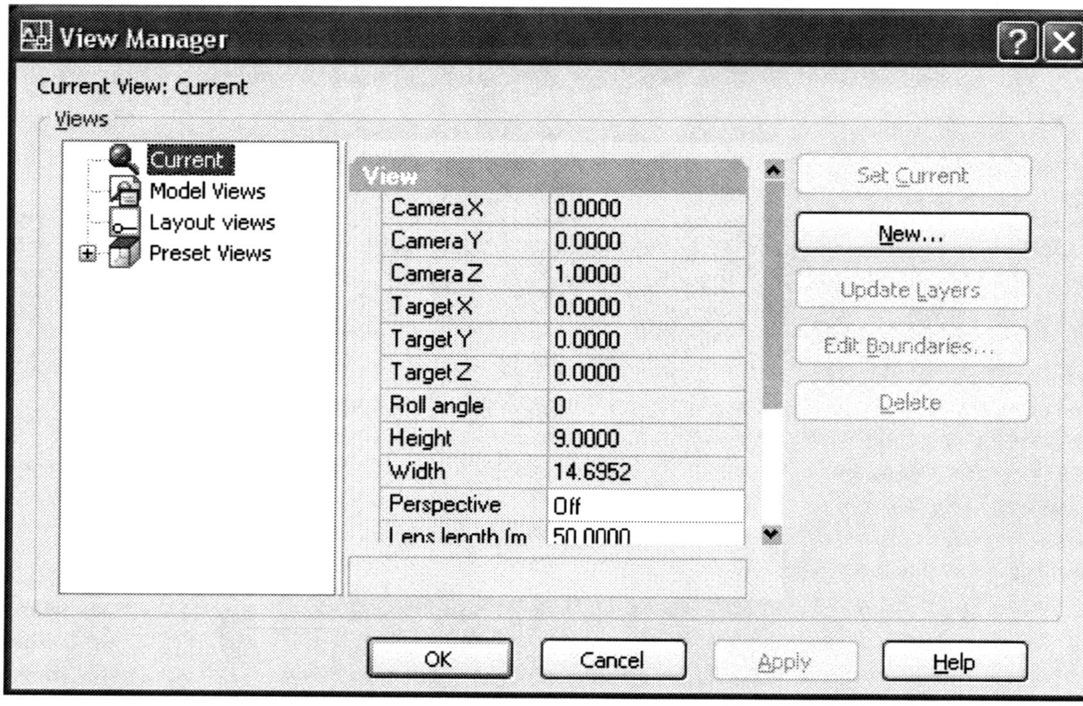


Figure 4.002

- The **Views** frame to the left lists four categories of views:
  - **Current** contains only the current view,
  - **Model Views** contains a list of named views and camera views (more on cameras when we get into 3D space). Figure 4.002 doesn't show any Model views available. The selection will have a plus next to it when you define some views. You'll be able to double-click, or select and pick the **Set Current** or **Apply** button, to make a view current on your screen. More on that in a few minutes.
  - We'll look at **Layout Views** in depth when we get into Paper Space in Lessons 22 and 23.
  - **Preset Views** contains a list that will prove valuable in 3-dimensional space.
- The center section provides a list of properties of the selected view. These serve as useful references in 3-dimensional space. (You may get tired of me referencing the 3-dimensional tools in AutoCAD, but such is the nature of the beast. Eventually, you'll appreciate those tools as well; but I won't drop you into a three-dimensional ocean until you can swim.)
- The right side of the View Manager contains several buttons – here's where the work begins.
  - **Set Current** does just that – it sets the currently selected view as the one you'll see on your screen.
  - The **New** button presents the workhorse of view procedures – the New View dialog box (Figure 4.003 – next page).
    - Here you will name your view (**View name**) and assign it a category (either selected or entered in the **View category** list box).

- In the **Boundary** frame, you can tell AutoCAD to use the **Current display**, or you can put a bullet next to the **Define window** option. (Alternately, you can pick the **Define View Window** button next to the Define window option.) When you select the Define window option (or the Define View Window button), AutoCAD returns you to the graphics screen and prompts:

  **Specify first corner:**
  **Specify opposite corner:** ***[place a window around the area to include in your view]***
  **Specify first corner:** ***[accept your selection or redefine it]***

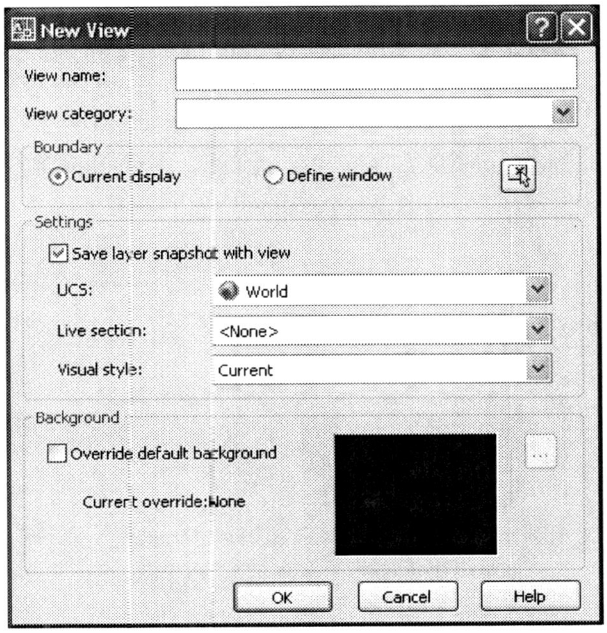


Figure 4.003

- The **Settings** frame also contains several options.
  - ◊ A check next to **Save layer snapshot with view** tells AutoCAD to save your current layer settings with the view. This can save a lot of work later, but you'll see that when we talk about layers in Lesson 6.
  - ◊ The next three selection boxes all refer to 3-dimensional tools. Ignore them for now. (I know, it puts some things off, but it makes life easier for now.)
- The final frame in the New Views dialog box – **Background** – allows you to change the background color for the newly defined view. We'll see this in our next exercise.

- o Use the next button on the View Manager – **Update Layers** – to update the layer settings associated with the view to the current settings.
- o The **Edit Boundary** button tells AutoCAD to present the drawing with the selected view highlighted. You can select opposite corners to redefine the view's boundaries until you confirm your new boundaries with the **Enter** key.
- o Finally, use the **Delete** button to delete a selected view from the drawing's database.

Let's try creating and restoring a view using the View dialog box.

> AutoCAD has several commands that at one time worked on the command line but have been replaced with dialog boxes. In order to continue allowing users to utilize the command line approach, the programmers have provided the dash-command method – simply put a dash in front of the command that normally calls a dialog box and you'll receive command line prompts instead.
>
> Throughout this book, I'll let you know which commands have undergone this metamorphosis and, where appropriate, I'll show you both command line and dialog box approaches.

| **Do This: 4.2.1** | **Creating a View** |
|---|---|

I. If you're not currently in the *pid.dwg* file, please open it now. It's in the C:\Steps\Lesson04 folder.

II. **Zoom** All and then follow these steps.

### 4.2.1: Creating a View

1. Enter the ***View*** command by typing ***view*** or ***v***. Alternately, you can pick the **Named Views** button  on the View toolbar, or **Named Views** from the View pull-down menu.

   **Command: *v***

2. Pick the **New** button 

on the View dialog box. The New View dialog box will appear (Figure 4.003).

3. Follow these instructions:

   a. Type **exchanger** in the **View name** text box.

   b. Type ***Model Views*** in the **View Category** box.

   c. Leave a check next to **Save layer snapshot with view**.

   d. Place a bullet in the radio button beside the words **Define Window**.

   The dialog boxes will disappear and AutoCAD will prompt you to locate the window.

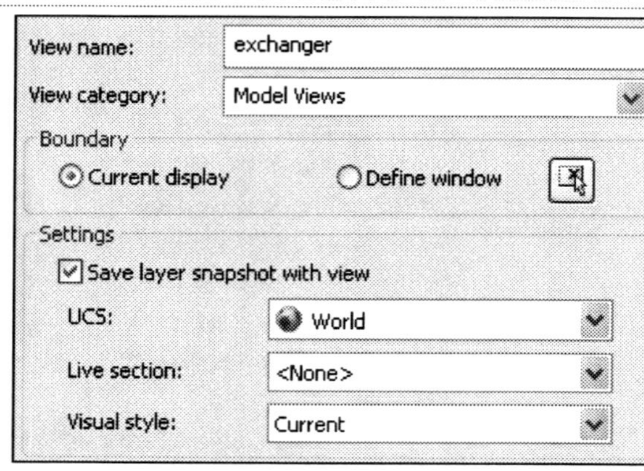


4. Place the window as shown below. The dialog box will return.

   **Specify first corner:**
   **Specify opposite corner:**
   **Specify first corner: *[enter]***

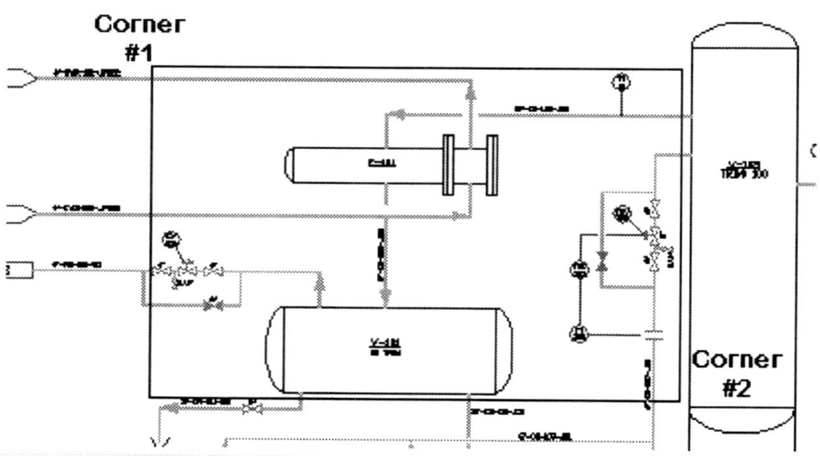

## 4.2.1: CREATING A VIEW

5. Place a check next to **Override default background** [☑ Override default background] in the **Background** frame. AutoCAD presents a Background dialog box (right). Experiment with the settings, then choose a color you like. (Pick in the **Color** box to select a new color from AutoCAD's Select Color dialog box.)

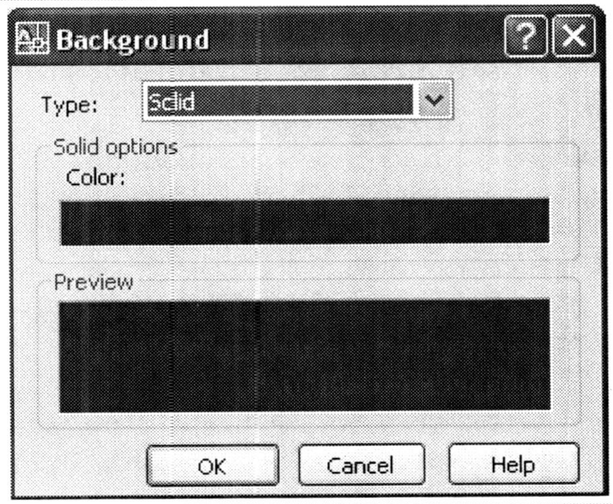


6. Pick the **OK** button [OK] to close the Background dialog box and again to close the New View dialog box.

The View dialog box returns. You see the exchanger view listed in the list box.

7. Now we'll set the exchanger view as current. Pick **exchanger** in the list box (under the **Model Views** category); then pick the **Set Current** button [Set Current]. Alternately, you can double-click on **exchanger**.

8. Pick the **OK** button [OK]. We return to the graphics screen where the exchanger view is now displayed (below).

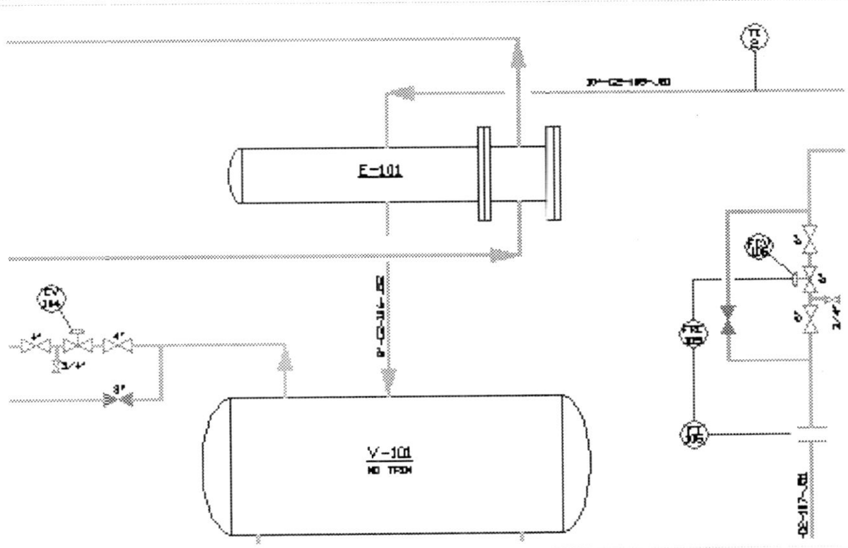


9. Save the drawing [save icon] and exit.

**Command:** ***qsave***

I really like the View dialog box (despite my first acquaintance with the command line approach) because it lists the views that are stored in the drawing, and I don't have to be concerned with remembering their names (or their *spellings!*).

(Note: For a nifty trick, see the **Extra Steps** section of this lesson.)

## 4.3 Simple Text

Placing text into an AutoCAD drawing appears quite complicated. But once you've mastered the procedures, you'll see that it isn't as difficult as it seems.

The ***Text*** command allows multiple lines of text to be entered; and it shows the text on the screen as you type.

The command sequence looks deceptively simple.

> **Command: *text* (or *dt*)**
>
> **Current text style: "Standard" Text height: 0.2000**
>
> **Specify start point of text or [Justify/Style]: *[pick the starting point of the text]***
>
> **Specify height <0.2000>: *[enter the desired text height]***
>
> **Specify rotation angle of text <0>: *[enter the desired rotation angle]***
>
> **[Here AutoCAD stops prompting and places a text entry box on the screen. Enter your text and hit the ENTER key twice to complete the command.]**

Let's look at each line.

- The first line shows that ***DT*** (for *Dynamic* Text) is the hotkey for ***Text***. Note that ***T*** is also a hotkey, but not for the ***Text*** command.
- The second line tells you what style you're using (more on style in Section 4.6) and what the current **Text height** is.
- The third line provides access to more ***Text*** options than initially meet the eye.
  - The default option – **Specify start point** – simply directs you to identify the insertion point of the text. Do this by coordinate input or picking a point on the screen with the mouse.
  - You don't actually have to select the **Justify** option (that is, you don't have to type ***J***) to justify your text. Typing J, however, will tell AutoCAD to present the various justification options as shown here.

    **Enter an option [Align/Fit/Center/Middle/Right/TL/TC/TR/ML/MC/MR/BL/BC/BR]:**

> You can use the ***JustifyText*** command to reset the justification once the text has been entered. This command won't, however, relocate the text around the insertion point.

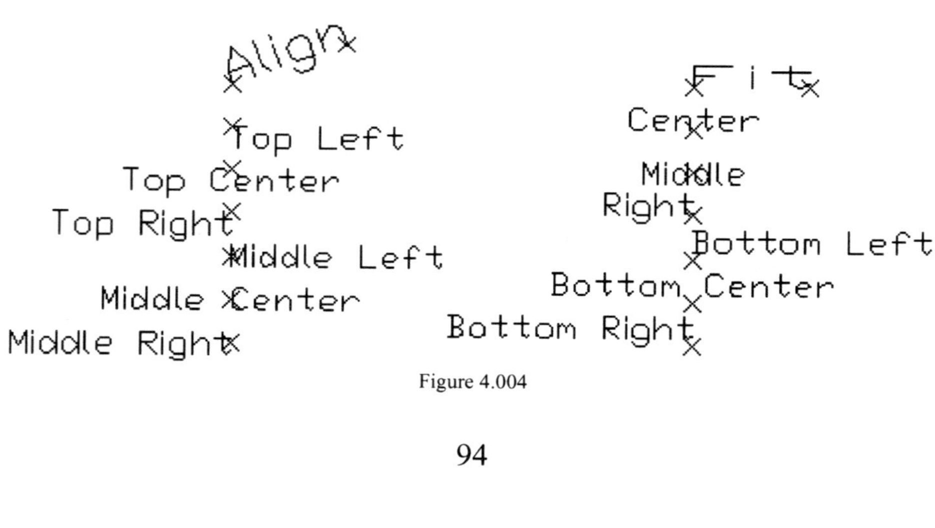


Figure 4.004

By default, AutoCAD uses the **Bottom Left** option. Refer to Figure 4.004 to see where each of the options will place the text in relation to the insertion point (the "X").

The **Align** and **Fit** justifications behave in much the same manner; however, **Align** will adjust the text height proportionally as it fits the text between the selected points, and **Fit** will maintain the user-defined height.

- o The **Style** option enables you to choose among text styles defined within the drawing. More on style in Section 4.6.

- Set the **height** of the text on the next line. This is one of the places where it's easy to make a mistake. As drafters, we're accustomed to scaling our drawing but not our text. We draw 1/8" text 1/8" high. In CAD, we do just the opposite – that is, we scale our text but not our drawing!

> Transparent commands – like ***Zoom*** or ***Pan*** – don't work while the ***Text*** prompt is showing. This way, all the keys are available while entering text.

You'll remember from Lesson 1 that we draw full-size, and then adjust for scale when we plot (print). When we adjust to plot, we downsize our drawing to fit onto a certain size sheet of paper. Well, when we downsize the drawing, the text goes with it. So we must increase the size of the text when we create it to allow for the downsizing.

Confused? It's really fairly easy to do.

Look at the Drawing Scales chart in Appendix A. The second column contains a **Scale Factor**. This is the key to creating the proper text size. Simply multiply the size you want the text to be when it's plotted by the scale factor for the final plotted scale. Use that number as your text height.

Here's an example. I'm creating a drawing that I'll plot later at 3/8"=1'-0". The factor for this scale is 32. I want my text size to be 1/8" when I plot. I multiply the 1/8 by 32 to get 4. I use 4 as my text height.

I know that may be a bit difficult to understand at this point; but believe me, it works!

> If you make a mistake in scaling your text, don't worry. You can fix the scale easily using AutoCAD's ***ScaleText*** command. The command sequence looks like this:
>
> **Command: *scaletext***
>
> **Select objects: *[select the text to rescale]***
>
> **Select objects: *[hit enter to confirm your selection]***
>
> **Enter a base point option for scaling [Existing/Left/Center/Middle/Right/TL/TC/TR/ML/MC/MR/ BL/BC/BR] <Existing>: *[accept the* Existing *insertion point unless you wish to scale from a different point]***
>
> **Specify new height or [Match object/Scale factor] <0.1250>: *[tell AutoCAD how large to make the text, or enter* M *to match the height of some existing text or* S *to enter a scale factor]***
>
> We'll see this command in our next exercise.

- The next line asks for a **rotation angle**. AutoCAD wants to know if your text will be standard read-from-the-bottom-of-the-page (left-to-right) text or something else. Remember how AutoCAD measures angles! Read-from-the-right-side-of-the-page would be entered at 90°.
- Now AutoCAD starts a text box on your screen. Here you type the desired text, hitting ***enter*** for a return (like the old-fashioned typewriters). When finished, hit ***enter*** again and the command prompt returns.

Let's try some text.

In addition to the command line, you can access the ***Text*** command by selecting **Text**, and then **Single Line Text** from the Draw pull-down menu. The **Text** button on the Draw toolbar calls the MText dialog box; so we'll avoid it for now. (***MText*** is a more advanced text tool that uses a word processor approach to enter text. We'll discuss it in Lesson 13.)

| Do This: 4.3.1 | Inserting Text |
|---|---|

I. Open the *pidtext* drawing in the C:\Steps\Lesson04 folder.

II. For this exercise, we'll want to display the Text toolbar. Right-click on any existing toolbar and select **Text** from the menu that appears. Move the Text toolbar to a convenient location on your screen.

III. Refer to the drawing in Figure 4.001 as you follow these steps.

### 4.3.1: Inserting Text

1. First let's get a bit closer. Restore the **EXCHANGER** view (Figure 4.005 – it's in the **Model Views** category). (Your drawing won't show the numbers and leaders.)

**Command: *v***

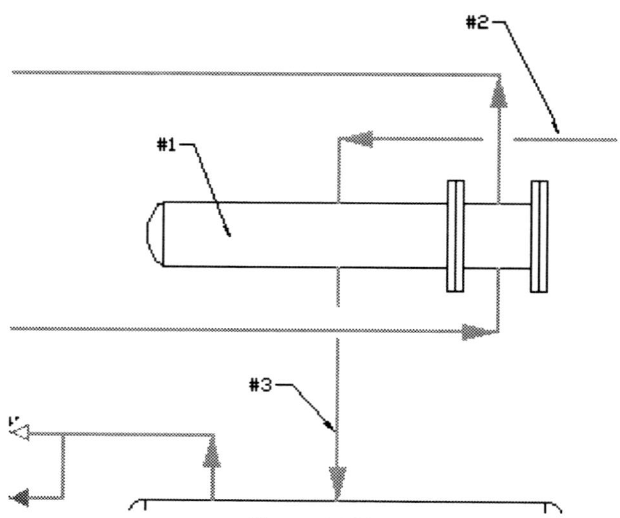


Figure 4.005

2. We'll begin by identifying the exchanger. Enter the ***Text*** command by typing ***Text*** or ***dt*** at the command prompt. Alternately, you can pick the **Single Line Text** button on the Text toolbar.

**Command: *dt***

3. Pick a point near the tip of arrow #1 (Figure 4.005). (Toggle OSNAPs **Off** if necessary.)

**Current text style: "STANDARD" Text height: 0.1250**

**Specify start point of text or [Justify/ Style]:**

4. This drawing was created with no scale on a D-size sheet of paper, so we won't have to scale the text. Assign a text height of ¼".

**Specify height <0.1250>: *.25***

## 4.3.1: Inserting Text

5. Accept the default rotation angle.

**Specify rotation angle of text <0>:** ***[enter]***

6. Enter the text shown.

7. Hit ***enter*** twice to complete the command.

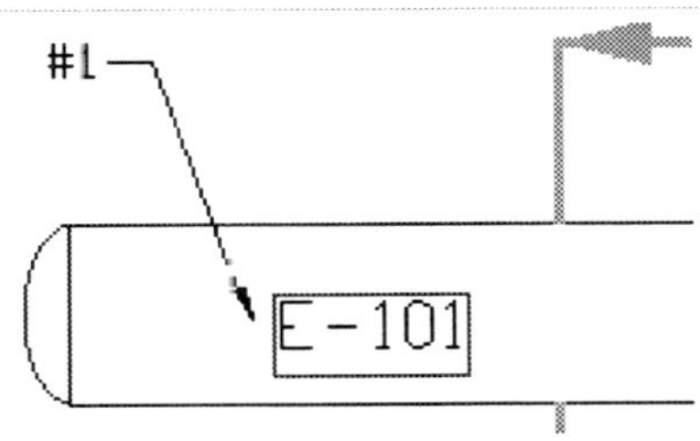


8. Now enter a line number by arrow #2 (Figure 4.005). Begin by repeating the command AI.

**Command:** ***[enter]***

9. Pick a point just above the line.

**Current text style: "STANDARD" Text height: 0.2500**
**Specify start point of text or [Justify/ Style]:**

10. Accept the default text height and rotation angle.

**Specify height <0.2500>:** ***[enter]***
**Specify rotation angle of text <0>:** ***[enter]***

11. Enter the line number.

12. Complete the command.

13. Now let's try some angled text. Repeat the command AI.

**Command:** ***[enter]***

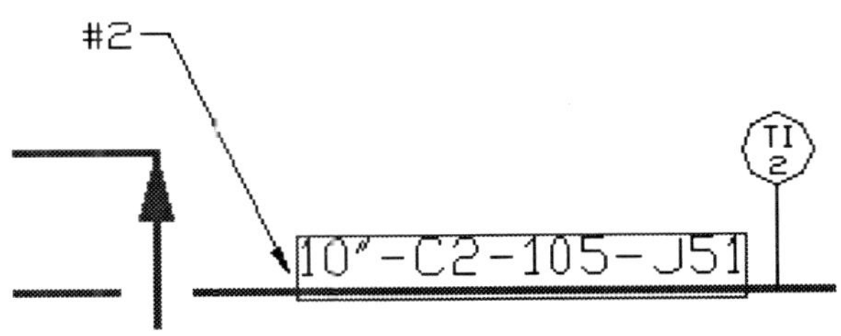


14. Pick a point just to the left of the line at arrow #3 (Figure 4.005).

**Current text style: "STANDARD" Text height: 0.25**
**Specify start point of text or [Justify/ Style]:**

15. Change the text height to 1/8" and the rotation angle to 90°.

**Specify height <0.2500>:** ***.125***
**Specify rotation angle of text <0>:** ***90***

16. Enter the text and complete the command. (Notice that the angle doesn't appear until you finish the command. This should make it easier to enter your text.) Your drawing looks like the following figure.

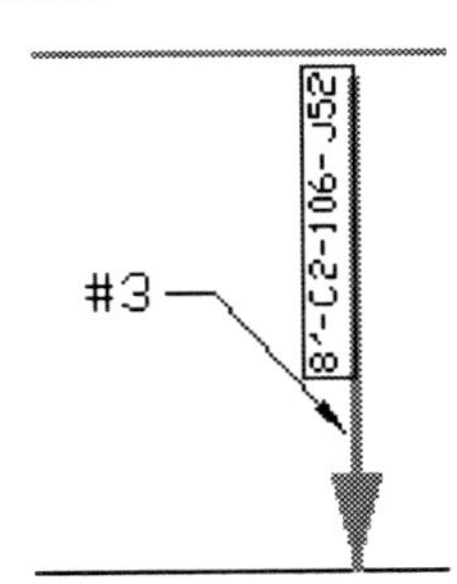

## 4.3.1: INSERTING TEXT

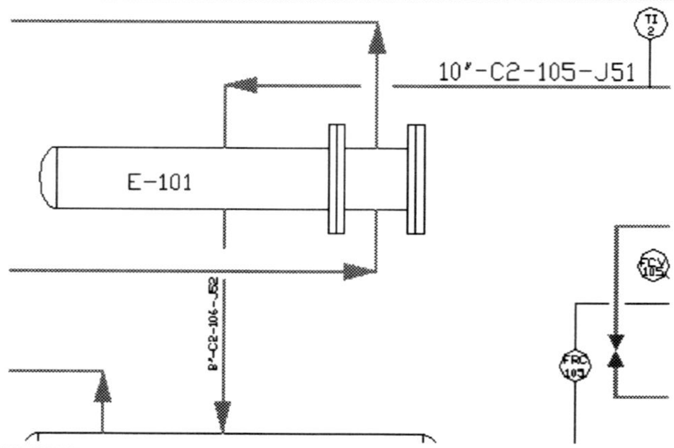


17. Notice that the text heights are inconsistent. Let's fix those now. Enter the ***ScaleText*** command. Alternately, you can pick the **Scale** button on the Text toolbar.

**Command: *scaletext***

18. Select the **E-101** text you placed in the exchanger; then confirm the selection.

**Select objects: *[select the text]***
**Select objects: *[enter]***

19. Accept the default base point for scaling.

**Enter a base point option for scaling [Existing/Left/Center/Middle/Right/ TL/TC/TR/ML/MC/MR/BL/BC/BR] <Existing>: *[enter]***

20. Tell AutoCAD to make the text 3/16" high.

**Specify new height or [Match object/Scale factor] <0.2500>: *3/16***

21. Now let's use the **Match object** option to fix the line numbers. Repeat the command .

**Command: *[enter]***

22. Select the 10" line number (at arrow #2). We'll make it 1/8" high like the 8" line number (at arrow #3). Confirm the selection.

**Select objects: *[select the text]***
**Select objects: *[enter]***

23. Accept the default base point for scaling.

**Enter a base point option for scaling [Existing/Left/Center/Middle/Right/ TL/TC/TR/ML/MC/ MR/ BL/BC/BR] <Existing>: *[enter]***

24. Tell AutoCAD you'd like to match the height of some existing text.

**Specify new height or [Match object/ Scale factor] <0.1875>: *m***

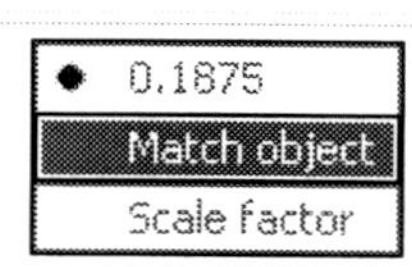


25. Select the 8" line number, which you created at a height of 1/8". Notice that AutoCAD tells you how high the text is and makes the change for you.

**Select a text object with the desired height: *[select the 8" line number]***
**Height=0.1250**

## 4.3.1: Inserting Text

26. Let's try justifying some text. Change to the **PUMPS** view (Figure 4.006).

**Command: *v***

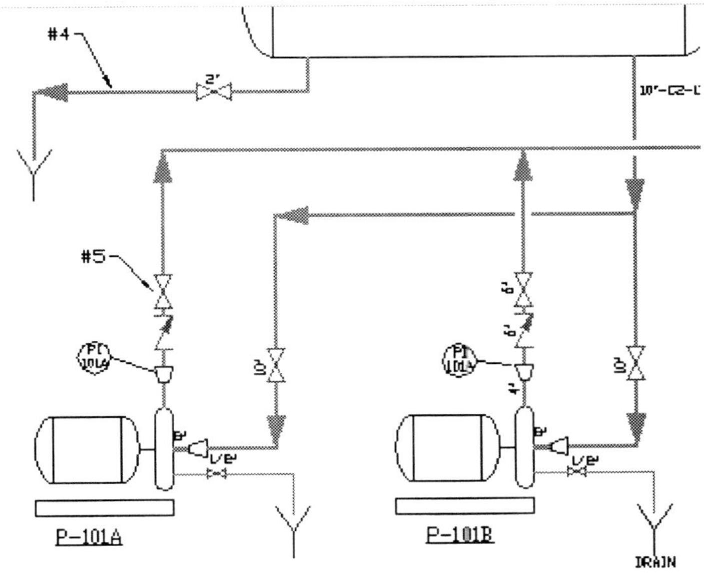


Figure 4.006

27. Begin the ***Text*** command.

**Command: *dt***

28. We don't have to go to the **Justify** prompt if we know what we want to do. So let's just type ***C*** for centered text.

**Current text style: "STANDARD" Text height: 0.1250**

**Specify start point of text or [Justify/ Style]: *c***

29. AutoCAD asks for the center point of our text. Pick a point two snaps out from the center of the valve – near the tip of arrow #5 in Figure 4.006. (Toggle the grid snap **On** or **Off** as needed.)

**Specify center point of text:**

30. Accept the defaults for **Height** and **Rotation angle**.

**Specify height <0.1250>: *[enter]***

**Specify rotation angle of text <90>: *[enter]***

31. Type ***6"*** for the size of the valve.

## 4.3.1: Inserting Text

32. Center some text next to the valve just below the last one. This is also a 6" valve (figure at right).

33. Using a 1/8" text height, place the text (***2"-DR-104-D2***) above the drain line (indicated by arrow #4 in the figure at right).

34. Now center the word ***DRAIN*** below the funnel. This area of your drawing now looks like our figure.

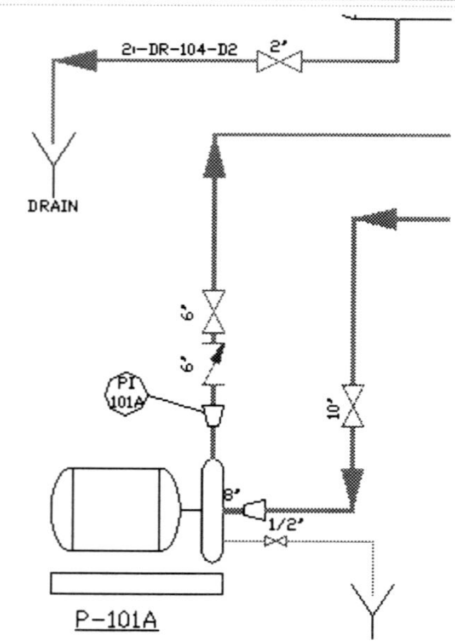


35. Save the drawing.

**Command: *qsave***

You may notice the underscoring on some of the text in our last drawing. You can accomplish this by using the word processing standard CTRL + U before and after the text to be underlined. You can also add some useful symbols using ASCII coding - %%c provides a diameter symbol, %%p provides a plus/minus symbol, and %%d places a degrees symbol in your text. If you wish to use much beyond this in the way of symbols or text formatting, I suggest you opt for the ***MText*** command rather than dynamic text. It has nearly full word processor capabilities. (We'll discuss MText in Lesson 13.)

One of the ways CAD operators used to save regeneration time was to tell AutoCAD not to regenerate the text in a drawing. As a great portion of the drawing is text, this saved time with larger drawing files. The command they used was ***QText*** and it looked like this:

**Command: *qtext***
**Enter mode [ON/OFF] <OFF>: *on***

The text in the drawing was replaced with a rectangular locator (to help the operator avoid placing geometry on top of the text).

With the advent of faster computers, the ***QText*** command really isn't necessary anymore. But there'll always be an older operator who likes to ***QText*** his drawing before passing it on to a freshman operator as a joke. So if you get a drawing with ***QText*** activated, simply enter the command and turn it off. (Remember to ***regen*** the drawing afterward.)

## 4.4 Editing Text – The *DDEdit* Command

So now you see that creating text isn't that difficult. But suppose you make a mistake or just want to change something. Let's look at AutoCAD's text editor – the ***DDEdit*** command. The command sequence is quite simple:

**Command: *ddedit* (or *ed*)**

**Select an annotation object or [Undo]:** ***[select the text to edit]***

AutoCAD highlights the text and allows you to edit it.

> In addition to the command line, you can access the ***DDEdit*** command by using the **Edit** button on the Text toolbar, or selecting **Object – Text** – and then the desired editing tool from the Modify pull-down menu.
>
> Alternately, you can select the text and then select **Edit** from the cursor menu.
>
> Want an easier method? Try just double-clicking on the text to edit!

| Do This: 4.4.1 | Editing Text |
|---|---|

I. Be sure you're still in the *pidtext* drawing in the C:\Steps\Lesson04 folder. If not, open it now.

II. Restore the **TITLEB** view shown in Figure 4.007.

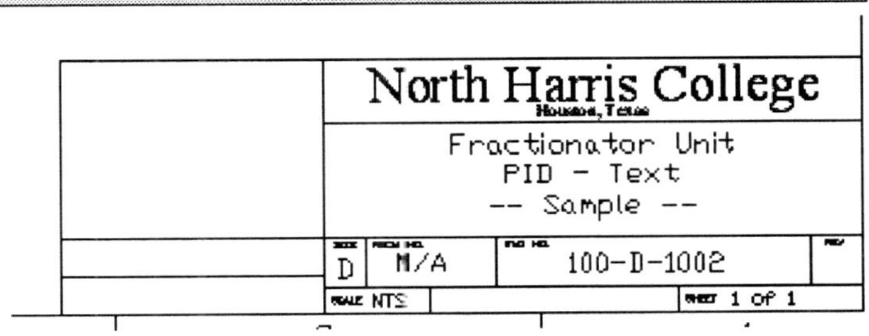


Figure 4.007

III. Notice that the middle line of the title area reads *PID-Text*. Let's edit this line.

**4.4.1: EDITING TEXT**

1. Double-click on the line to be edited (*PID-Text*). AutoCAD highlights the text so you can edit it (Figure 4.023).

   **Command:** ***[double-click on the text without entering a command]***

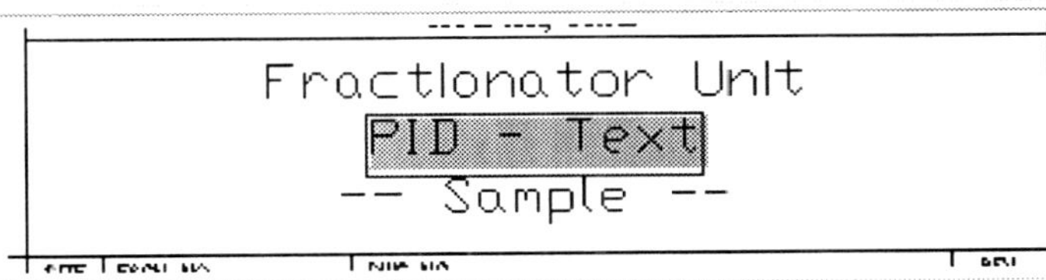


2. Type ***Piping and Instrument Diagram***, and then hit ***enter*** twice.

3. Save the drawing.

   **Command:** ***qsave***

That's all there is to editing text.

## 4.5 Finding and Replacing Text

The ***Find*** command offers the ability to search for (and replace) text in a document. To make it even easier, AutoCAD provides a simple dialog box (Figure 4.008 – next page).

In our example (Figure 4.008), we're searching for text *V-101*. We've entered the text in the **Find text string** text box and picked the **Find** button to begin our search. (The **Find Next** button replaced the **Find** button after the initial search.)

AutoCAD found one instance of the text and displayed it in the **Search Results** list box.

Had we desired to replace the text, we would've placed the replacement text in the **Replace with** text box, done our search (picked the **Find** button), and then picked either the **Replace** button (for a single replacement) or the **Replace All** button (for a universal replacement).

Note that we can also search part or all of a drawing using the **Search in** drop-down box.

We can also go to the text's location using the **Zoom in** button once the text has been located.

We'll become more familiar with these options in Lesson 13.

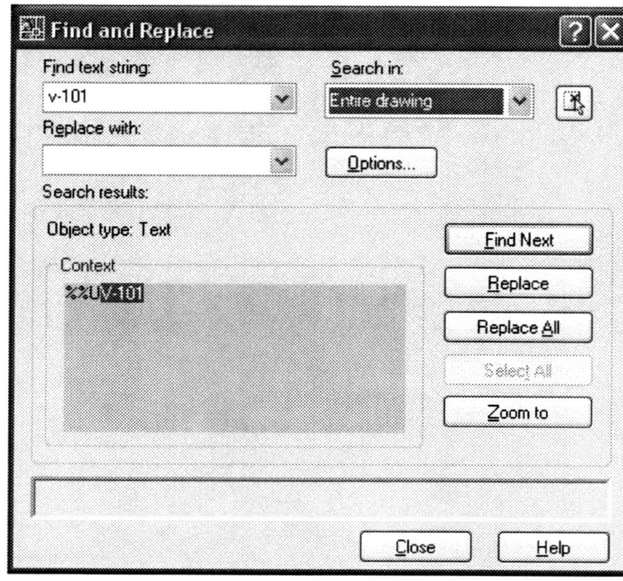


Figure 4.008

## 4.6 Adding Flavor to Text with *Style*

Although AutoCAD's default style is called *Standard*, in our next exercise, we'll create text using a style called *Times*. We'll create this style and make it current. We'll use Windows' *Times New Roman* True Type Font instead of AutoCAD's *TXT* font because it shows up better in print.

*What exactly is the difference between* style *and* font*?*

Simply put, *font* refers to the physical shape of a letter or number. *Style* refers to all of the characteristics of a letter or number (including font, size, slant, boldness, etc.).

AutoCAD has provided access to the True Type Fonts used by all the other programs on your Windows computer. So when creating a style, your drawing can be consistent with the other documents in your project.

To access the Text Style dialog box (Figure 4.009), simply type ***Style*** or ***st*** at the command prompt.

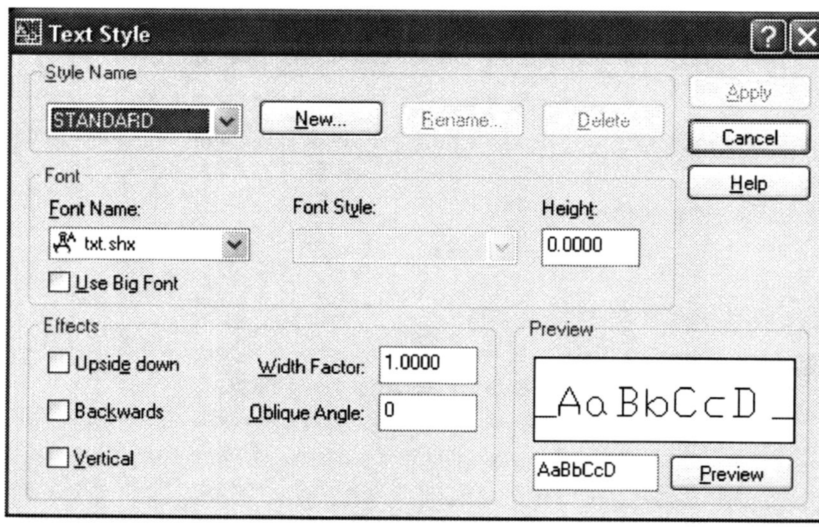


Figure 4.009

The dialog box looks intimidating, but don't let that throw you. Most of the buttons are self-explanatory – **New** to create a new style, **Rename** to rename a style, and so forth.

Let's create a few styles to see how it's done.

In addition to the command line, you can access the ***Style*** command by using the **Text Style** button on the Text toolbar, or by selecting **Text Style** from the Format pull-down menu.

| **Do This: 4.6.1** | **More Text Editing** |
|---|---|

I. Start a new drawing from scratch.

II. Follow these steps.

### 4.6.1: MORE TEXT EDITING

1. Set both the grid and the grid snap to ½". (Be sure to toggle them both **On**.) Zoom all.

**Command:** ***ds***

**Command:** ***z***

2. Accepting the default text size and rotation angle, place the text ***Standard*** in the upper left corner, as indicated in the figure here. (Don't place the rest of the text yet.)

**Command:** ***dt***

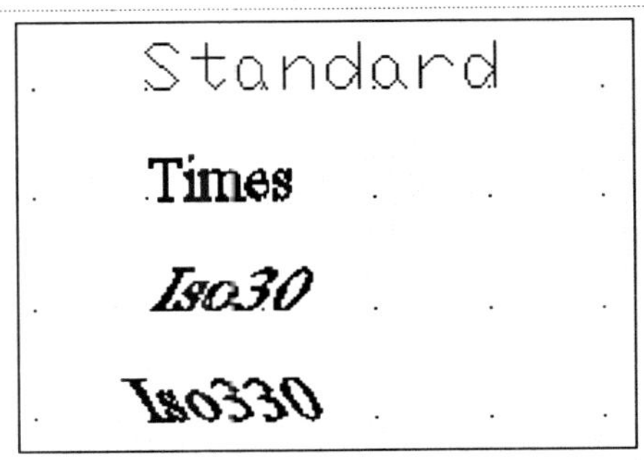


3. Open the Text Style dialog box by typing ***style*** or ***st*** at the command prompt. Alternately, you can pick the **Text Style** button on the Text toolbar.

**Command:** ***st***

4. Pick the **New** button. The New Text Style dialog box (right) will appear atop the Text Style dialog box.

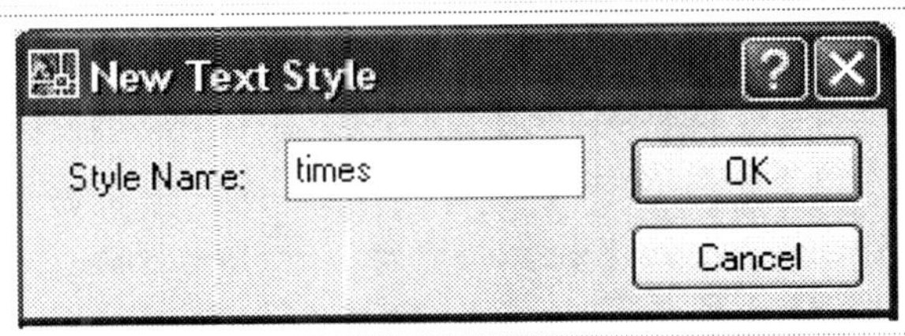


5. Type in the name ***times*** (as indicated above), then pick the **OK** button. The New Text Style dialog box will disappear and the name **times** will appear in the **Style Name** frame of the Text Style dialog box (below).

# 4.6.1: More Text Editing

6. Now let's define the style. Pick the down arrow in the **Font Name** text box (in the **Font** frame). Scroll as necessary to find **Times New Roman**. Select it as shown.

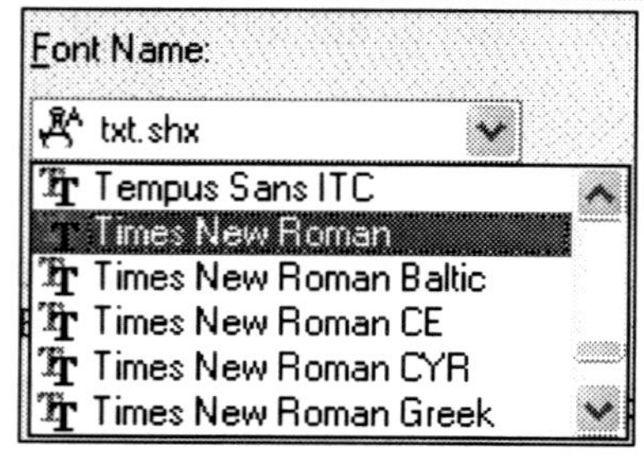


7. Notice that the word **Regular** appears in the **Font Style** text box. Pick the down arrow here to see what your other choices are (as shown), but leave it set to **Regular** for now.

8. You can set a height for your text in the **Height** text box. If you do, the text height will be what you have set whenever you use this style, *and AutoCAD won't prompt you for the height when you enter text.* I usually leave the **Height** set to ***0*** for the flexibility it allows me when I enter the text.

9. You can set additional physical characteristics for the style in the **Effects** frame of the Text Style dialog box (below). You see the options **Upside down**, **Backwards**, and **Vertical** listed on the left. I've never found a reason for entering text upside down or backward, but the options are available if you find a reason.

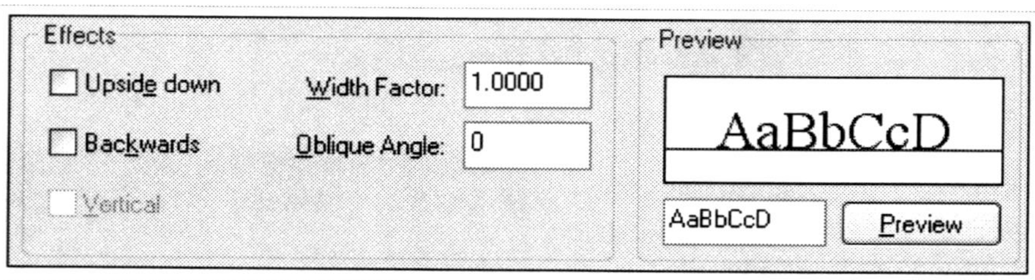


10. The **Width Factor** determines the width of each character in relation to its height (greater than one creates a wider character; less than one creates a narrower character). Most people leave this at ***1***, but let's set it to ***7/8*** 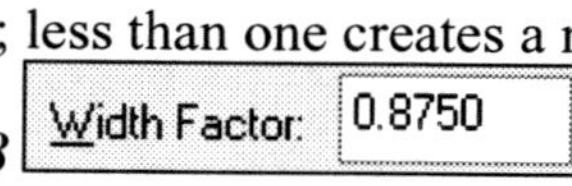

. I prefer the narrower characters because it enables me to place more text in a smaller area. The difference is imperceptible when plotted.

11. You can set the slant of the characters in the **Oblique Angle** text box. ***0*** is straight text. You'll use the obliquing angle when you set up isometric text on the next page. We'll leave the **times** style at ***0***.

12. The **Preview** panel shows you what your settings will look like (see the figure following Step 9). You can even change the sample characters in the text box next to the **Preview** button.

13. Next pick the **Apply** button 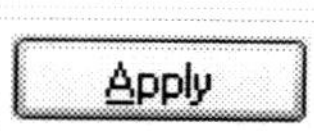

…

14. … and then the **Close** button 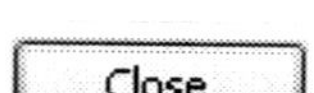

.

III. Place the word ***Times*** just below the word **Standard**. (Zoom in as necessary for a better view.) Can you see the difference (refer to Figure 4.026 – at the beginning of this exercise)?

IV. Now create two more styles with the following settings.

| Style Name | Font | Width | Oblique Angle |
|---|---|---|---|
| Iso30 | Times New Roman | 1 | 30 |
| Iso330 | Times New Roman | 1 | 330 |

V. Type the names of these styles below the names of the others. (Hint: Type ***S*** at the first text prompt to set the style.) Your drawing will look like Figure 4.026.

VI. Now let's use the *isotext* in an isometric setting. Follow these steps.

### 4.6.1: More Text Editing

15. Set your snap to **isometric**.

**Command:** ***sn***
**Specify snap spacing or [ON/OFF/Aspect/Rotate/Style/ Type] <0.5000>:** ***s***
**Enter snap grid style [Standard/Isometric] <S>:** ***i***
**Specify vertical spacing <0.5000>:** ***[enter]***

16. Set the current text style to ***Iso30***.

**Command:** ***dt***
**Current text style: "Standard" Text height: 0.2000**
**Specify start point of text or [Justify/Style]:** ***s***
**Enter style name or [?] <Standard>:** ***iso30***

17. Pick a point near the other text and enter ***30°*** as the rotation angle.

**Current text style: "Iso30" Text height: 0.2000**
**Specify start point of text or [Justify/Style]:** ***[pick a start point]***
**Specify height <0.2000>:** ***[enter]***
**Specify rotation angle of text <0>:** ***30***

18. Enter in the name of the style (***Iso30***).

19. Now repeat the preceding sequence using the **Iso330** style you created and a rotation angle of ***330°***. Your text looks like the figure at right.

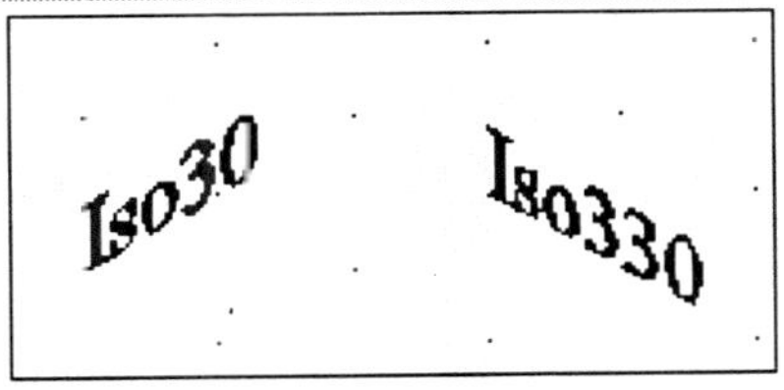


20. Quit the drawing without saving it.

## 4.7 Extra Steps

Perhaps the greatest selling point in AutoCAD's favor is its inclusion of AutoLISP as a customizing agent. Certainly, it's too early in our study of AutoCAD to be concerned with customizing it – or at least too early to learn the AutoLISP programming language (although I highly recommend it later). But one thing not included in most textbooks is how to use AutoLISP.

You can use it to your advantage quite easily, and as there are zillions of lisp routines available in most CAD environments and the Internet (just ask the guy next to you), you should at least be comfortable with loading the programs.

The command sequence is very simple:

**Command:** ***(load "C:/Steps/lesson04/views")***

That's it! Note that the parentheses are required, as are the quotation marks around the path and file name. Note also that the slashes (normally backslashes) are *front*slashes. (AutoLISP reads backslashes as pauses in its routines.)

But in these days of dialog boxes, there's another way. Go to the Tools pull-down menu and select **Load Application**. (Alternately, you can enter ***Appload*** at the command prompt.) The Load/Unload Applications dialog box will appear (Figure 4.010). Here's how to use it.

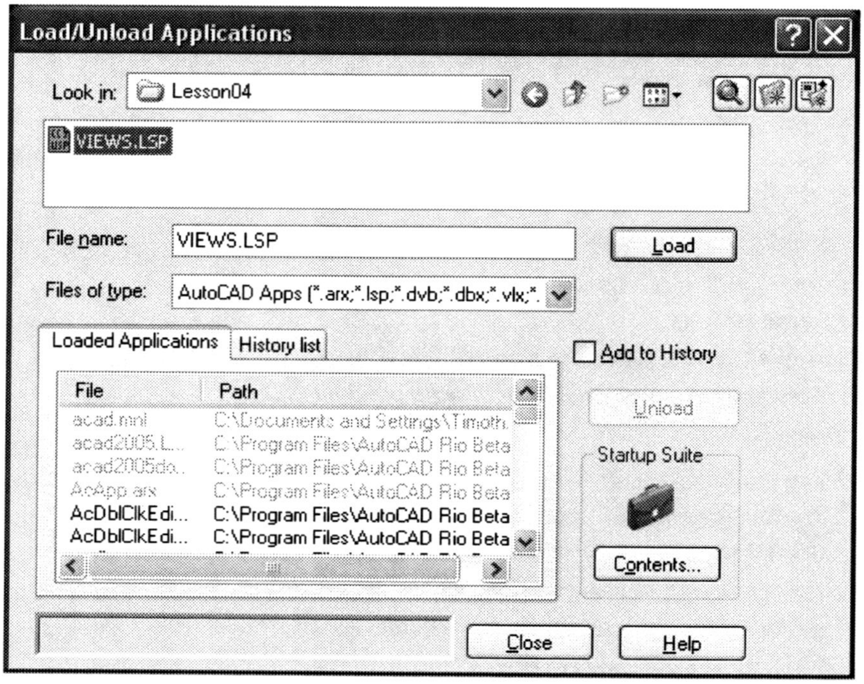


Figure 4.010

1. Use the upper half of the dialog box as you would a typical Windows Open File dialog box. Locate the file you wish to open. In Figure 4.010, I've located the *Views.lsp* file in the C:\Steps\Lesson04 folder. The name of the selected file will appear in the **File name** text box.
2. Pick the **Load** button. The file appears in the **Loaded Applications** list box in the lower half of the dialog box.
3. Pick the **Close** button to finish the procedure.

You must load each file into the drawing session every time you restart AutoCAD – unless you use the **Startup Suite** to automatically load selected files when AutoCAD begins a new session.

Each file contains one or more *programs* or *routines* intended to shorten or ease your drawing time. Accessing a routine is as easy as typing a command (the command is identified – or programmed – into the routine). Thus, typing ***VS*** after loading the *Views* routine will enable you to store a view without the dialog box. Typing ***VR*** will restore a view. Try it! You'll like it!

AutoCAD also provides access to another extremely valuable programming tool – Visual Basic. But an understanding of AutoLISP is necessary to effectively use a VB program. Once you are comfortable with the use of AutoCAD, I highly recommend a study of AutoCAD Customization (including Lisp and VB).

## 4.8 What Have We Learned?

*Items covered in this lesson include:*

- *Display commands*
  - ***Zoom***
  - ***Pan***
  - ***View***
- *Text Commands*
  - ***Text***
  - ***DDEdit***
  - ***QText***
  - ***Style***
  - ***ScaleText***
  - ***JustifyText***
  - ***Find***
- *Loading Lisp Applications*

Well, this was quite a lesson! We covered AutoCAD's display commands ***Zoom***, ***Pan***, and ***View***. Then we looked at the basic text command ***Text***. After that, we covered the ***Style*** command. We'll see that one again when we cover ***MText*** in Lesson 13. Lastly, we took a quick peek at AutoLISP and how to load and use a Lisp routine. Of all the things covered thus far, mastering these few short paragraphs will go further than any other in convincing an employer that you've mastered AutoCAD.

We covered quite a bit of material; but believe it or not, you'll soon be using these tools as second nature (just as you may now use a triangle or Ames Lettering Guide).

## 4.9 Exercises

1. Start a new drawing with the following parameters:
   1.1. Grid: 1
   1.2. Snap: ½
   1.3. Lower left limits: 0,0
   1.4. Upper right limits: 36,24
   1.5. Text Heights: 3/8", 3/16", 1/4" & 1/8"
   1.6. Create the organizational chart in the figure on the next page. Feel free to substitute names for those used.

(HINT: Most of my students spend an hour or so drawing a number of rectangles only to discover that the text won't fit; then they must redraw them after entering the text. Enter the text *first.*)

   1.7. Save the drawing as: *MyOrg* in the C:\Steps\Lesson04 folder.

*For more exercises related to Lesson 4, please see Lesson 4 in AutoCAD 2007: One Step at a Time – Workbook.*

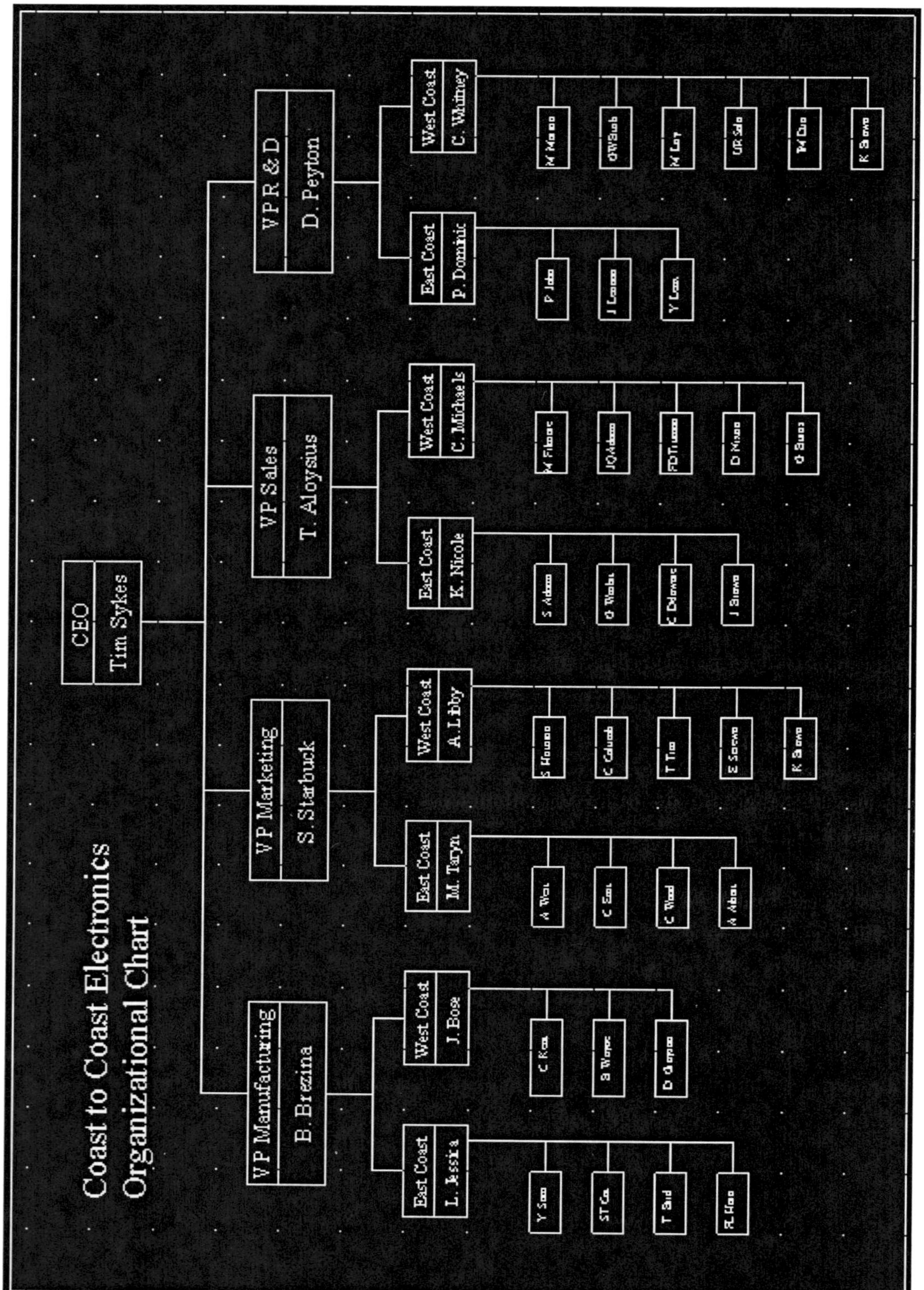


| 4.9 | For Web-Based Review Questions, visit: http://www.uneedcad.com/2007/Files/07R4.pdf |
|---|---|

# Lesson 5

Following this lesson, you will:

✓ *Know how to draw:*

- *Circles*
- *Ellipses*
- *Arcs*
- *Polygons*

✓ *Have mastered most of AutoCAD's basic 2-dimensional drawing commands!*

# Geometric Shapes (Other Than Lines and Rectangles!)

*By now, you must have tired of drawing lines and rectangles. After all, back at the beginning of the second lesson, we discussed lines and circles as the foundation for drawing geometric shapes. How about those circles?*

*In this lesson, we'll look at drawing not only circles, but arcs and ellipses as well. We'll also expand our multisided geometry from simple rectangles to include those -gons, collectively known as polygons.*

*Let's proceed.*

## 5.1 Getting Around to Circles

Next to lines, circles (and parts of circles) are the most frequent factor in geometric drawings. You might think creating such important objects should be complicated, but AutoCAD has made ***Circle*** one of the easiest of its commands. We draw lines, as you know, using the ***Line*** command. In keeping with the simple approach, draw circles by using the ***Circle*** command. Not simple enough? Okay, just type ***C*** at the command prompt!

Here's the command sequence.

> **Command: *circle* (or *c*)**
>
> **Specify center point for circle or [3P/2P/Ttr (tan tan radius)]: *[pick or identify a point on the screen]***
>
> **Specify radius of circle or [Diameter]: *[drag or type the radius]***

That seems fairly easy. Open the *cir-ell.dwg* file in the C:\Steps\Lesson05 folder and give it a try. Draw a circle in one of the open areas of the screen.

What do you think?

Okay. Let's look at some of the ***Circle*** command's options.

- The default is the **Specify center point** option. Any point selected on the screen or identified by coordinates will be the center point of the circle.
- The **3P** option allows you to draw a circle by selecting three points on the circle.
- The **2P** option allows you to draw a circle by selecting both ends of an imaginary diameter line.
- **Ttr** stands for **Tangent-Tangent-Radius** and allows you to draw the circle by selecting two objects to which the circle will be tangent and then entering the required radius.

Let's try each option.

> All of the options are also available in the **Circle** selection under the Draw pull-down menu, as well as via cursor or dynamic input menu once the ***Circle*** command has been entered.

| Do This: 5.1.1 | Circle Practice |
|---|---|

I. If you haven't yet opened *cir-ell.dwg*, open it now. it's in the C:\Steps\Lesson05 folder and looks like Figure 5.001.

II. Restore the **CIRCLES** view.

III. Follow these steps.

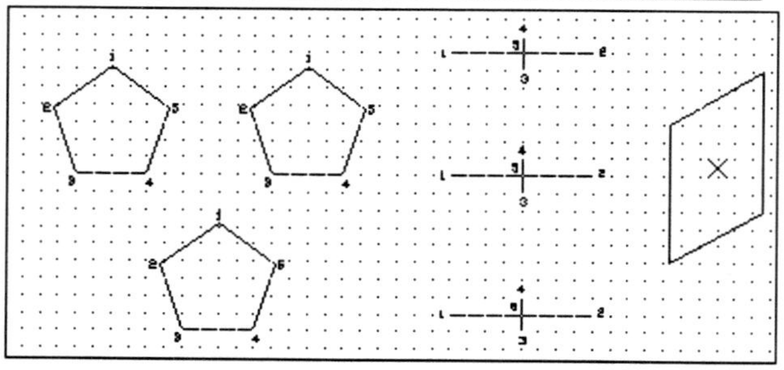

Figure 5.001

## 5.1.1: CIRCLE PRACTICE

1. Set your running OSNAPs to **Endpoint**. Clear all other settings. Turn on the Running OSNAPs, and turn off the **Snap**.

**Command:** *os*

2. Type the ***Circle*** command or the ***C*** hotkey at the command prompt. Alternately, you can pick the **Circle** button  on the Draw toolbar or tool palette.

**Command:** *c*

3. Type ***3P*** (or select it on the dynamic input or cursor menu) for the three-point option.

**Specify center point for circle or [3P/2P/Ttr (tan tan radius)]:** *3p*

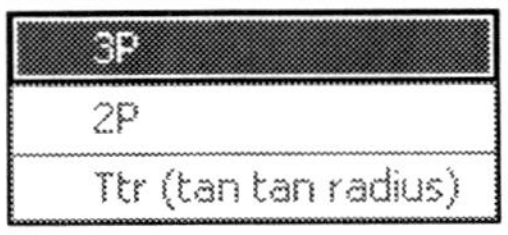


4. Select any three endpoints on the upper left polygon. The results should look like the figure shown.

**Specify first point on circle:**

**Specify second point on circle:**

**Specify third point on circle:**

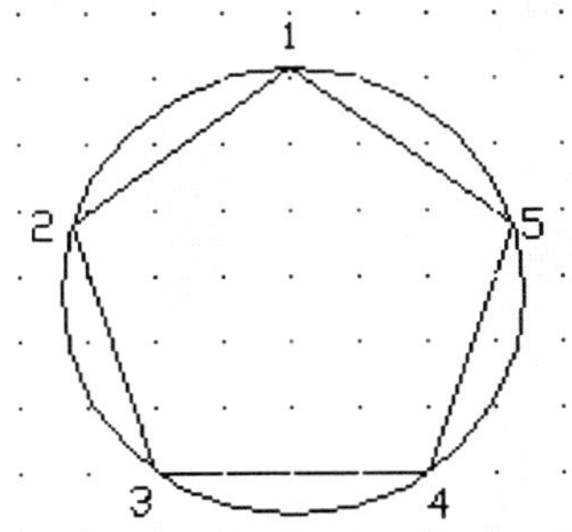


5. Repeat the ***Circle*** command.

6. Use the two-point option.

**Specify center point for circle or [3P/2P/Ttr (tan tan radius)]:** *2p*

7. Select points 2 and 5 on the upper right polygon. The results will look like the figure shown.

**Specify first end point of circle's diameter:** *[select point 2]*

**Specify second end point of circle's diameter:** *[select point 5]*

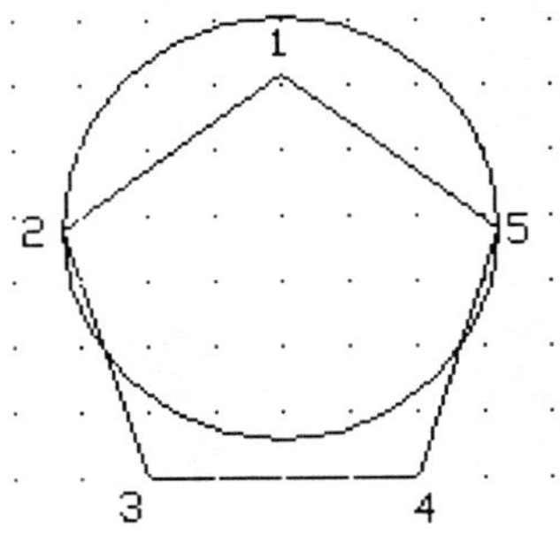


8. Repeat the ***Circle*** command.

9. Select the **Ttr** option for tangent-tangent-radius.

**Specify center point for circle or [3P/2P/Ttr (tan tan radius)]:** *t*

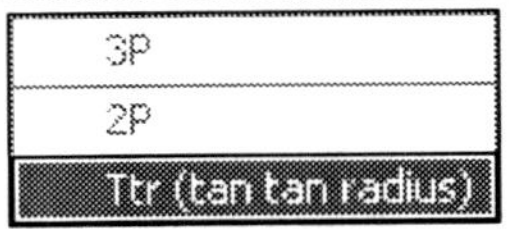


10. Select any point on line **1-2** of the remaining polygon. Notice how the OSNAP symbol for **tangent** appears when you cross the line.

**Specify point on object for first tangent of circle:**

11. Now select any point on line **2-3**.

**Specify point on object for second tangent of circle:**

### 5.1.1: Circle Practice

| | |
|---|---|
| 12. Enter a radius of ***1***. Your drawing will look like the figure shown. Notice that AutoCAD draws a 1"R circle tangent to both the selected lines.<br>**Specify radius of circle <1.6180>: *1*** | 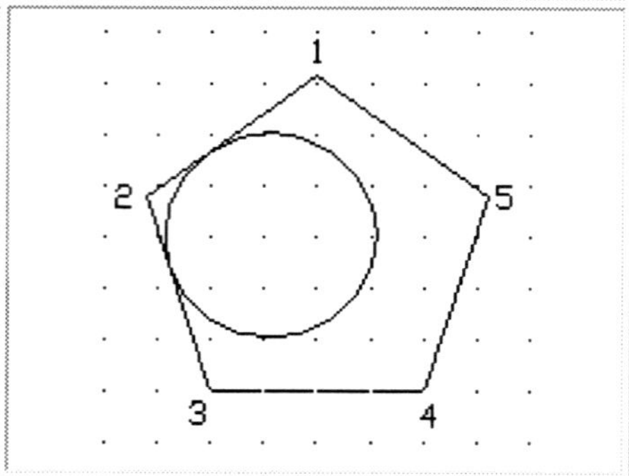 |
| 13. Save [icon] your drawing.<br>**Command: *qsave*** | |



I know. Had you known it was this easy, you'd have learned AutoCAD long ago!

## 5.2 Ellipses and Isometric Circles

I've often been amazed – and frequently aggravated – by the number of incomplete or oddball circles required in drafting. Back in my board days (bored days?), arcs were seldom a problem. I just used my circle template and drew as much as I needed. Ellipses, however, required the purchase of specific templates – often several! There were, of course, templates that tried to provide almost every dimensional ellipse the draftsman might need – from 25° to 80°, and from ¼" to 6". But the ellipse I needed would inevitably fall into an oddball degree or size.

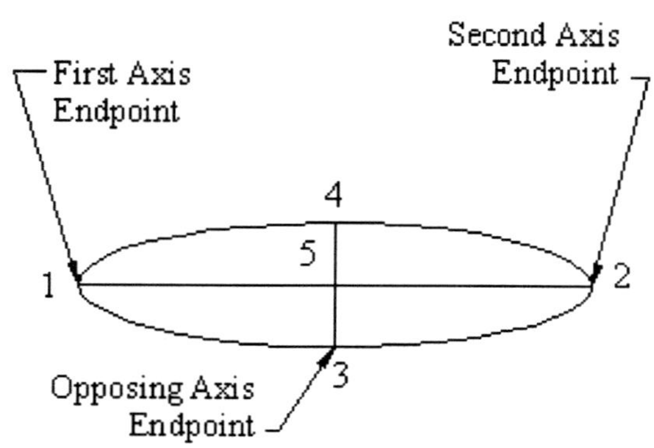


Figure 5.002

Ellipses are one of those things that AutoCAD makes quite a bit easier than plastic templates or clumsy compass attempts to create oddball shapes. Let's look at the command sequence (refer to Figure 5.002).

**Command: *ellipse* (or *el*)**

**Specify axis endpoint of ellipse or [Arc/Center]: *[select the first axis endpoint]***

**Specify other endpoint of axis: *[select the opposite axis endpoint]***

**Specify distance to other axis or [Rotation]: *[select the opposing axis endpoint]***

The basic ellipse is really very easy to draw regardless of rotation or dimension. But as you can see, we have some options to consider.

- **Specify axis endpoint** is the default. It allows you to draw the ellipse by selecting three axis endpoints, or two axis endpoints and a rotation angle.
- The **Arc** option allows you to draw partial ellipses.
- The **Center** option allows you to create an ellipse using a center point and two axis endpoints (rather than three axis endpoints).

Let's look at each of these options.

> All of the options are also available in the **Ellipse** selection under the Draw pull-down menu or on the dynamic input or cursor menu once the ***Ellipse*** command has been entered.

| Do This: 5.2.1 | Drawing Ellipses |
|---|---|

I. Be sure you're still in the *cir-ell* drawing. If not, open it now. it's in the C:\Steps\Lesson05 folder.

II. Restore the **ELLIPSE** view.

III. Be sure the Running OSNAP is still set to **Endpoint**.

IV. Follow these steps.

## 5.2.1: Drawing Ellipses

1. Enter the ***Ellipse*** command or ***el*** hotkey. Alternately, you can pick the **Ellipse** button  on the Draw toolbar or tool palette.

   **Command: *el***

2. Select the endpoint at point 1 of the top set of lines. (The lines aren't necessary; we use them here as guides only.)

   **Specify axis endpoint of ellipse or [Arc/Center]:**

3. Select the endpoint at point 2.

   **Specify other endpoint of axis:**

4. Select the endpoint at either point 3 or point 4. Your ellipse looks like the one shown here.

   **Specify distance to other axis or [Rotation]:**

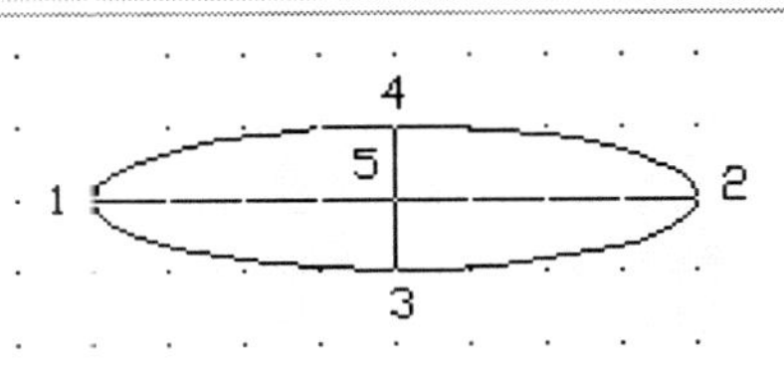


5. Repeat the ***Ellipse*** command.

6. Type ***c*** (or select **Center** on the menu) to access the **Center** option.

   **Specify axis endpoint of ellipse or [Arc/Center]: *c***

7. When AutoCAD prompts you for the center of the ellipse, select the OSNAP button for intersection , and then select point 5 of the second set of lines.

   **Specify center of ellipse: _int of**

8. Select the endpoint at either point 1 or point 2.

   **Specify endpoint of axis:**

9. Let's try the **Rotation** option. Type ***R*** or select **Rotation** on the menu .

   (**Rotation** refers to the angle at which you see the circle.)

   **Specify distance to other axis or [Rotation]: *r***

10. Type in a rotation angle of 75°. Your ellipse will look like the one in Step 4.

   **Specify rotation around major axis: *75***

11. Repeat the ***Ellipse*** command or pick the **Ellipse Arc** button  on the Draw toolbar or palette. (If you use the **Ellipse Arc** button, skip Step 12.)

   **Command: *[enter]***

### 5.2.1: Drawing Ellipses

12. Type ***a*** (or select **Arc** on the menu) to access the **Arc** option.

**Specify axis endpoint of ellipse or [Arc/Center]: *a***

13. Notice that you again have the option to select either an axis endpoint or the center of the ellipse. Let's use the default – **axis endpoint** – and select the endpoint at point 1 on the bottom set of lines.

**Specify axis endpoint of elliptical arc or [Center]:**

14. Select the endpoint at point 2.

**Specify other endpoint of axis:**

15. Here again your options are repeated. Select point 3.

**Specify distance to other axis or [Rotation]:**

16. Now you have some new options. The **Parameter** option uses a complicated formula to determine where the arc will begin and end. We'll use the default – **start angle** to give us more control of our work. Enter ***0***.

**Specify start angle or [Parameter]: *0***

17. We started our arc at angle 0. An included angle is an angle measured counterclockwise from that point. We can type ***I*** followed by the angle we wish to use to create our arc. Alternately, we can use the **end angle** approach and simply type the angle we want for the other end of the ellipse. Let's use the **end angle** default and type in ***180***°.

Your ellipse looks like the figure at right.

**Specify end angle or [Parameter/ Included angle]: *180***

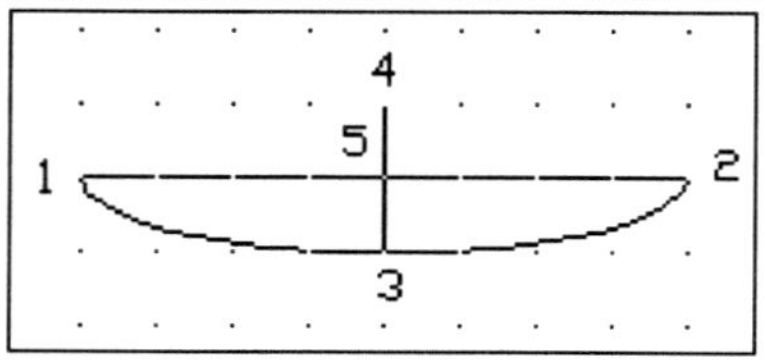


18. Save the drawing , but don't exit.

**Command: *qsave***

By default, AutoCAD draws true ellipses. This enables you to find the center with an OSNAP. The system variable **PELLIPSE** allows you to change the way AutoCAD draws ellipses. When set to the default ***0***, ellipses work the way we've seen. But set it to 1 and ellipses are drawn as polylines (just as rectangles are drawn). Both ellipses look the same, but the latter can be given width using the ***PEdit*** command. You can't, however, easily find the center of the ellipse. We'll learn about polylines and the ***PEdit*** command in Lesson 8.

You can now see that drawing ellipses isn't difficult – although mastering the various approaches may take some time.

The ellipses we've drawn thus far have all existed in a true 2-dimensional plane. But you can also use ellipses to draw *isometric circles*. The procedure is simple but requires that you be in *isometric mode*. Otherwise, the ***Ellipse*** command won't provide the **Isocircle** option.

Let's look at this.

| Do This: 5.2.2 | Drawing Isometric Circles |
|---|---|

I. Be sure you're still in the *cir-ell* drawing. If not, open it now. it's in the C:\Steps\Lesson05 folder.

II. Restore the **ISO-ELLIPSE** view.

III. Follow these steps.

### 5.2.2: Drawing Isometric Circles

1. First, set your drawing to the isometric *style*. (Accept the defaults.) Your crosshairs and the grid will change.

   **Command: *sn***

2. Begin the ***Ellipse*** command.

   **Command: *el***

3. Type ***i*** (or select **Isocircle** on the menu) to select the **Isocircle** option.

   **Specify axis endpoint of ellipse or [Arc/Center/ Isocircle]: *i***

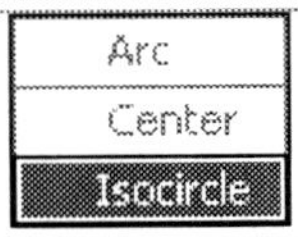


4. Pick the **Node** button from the OSNAP toolbar, and then select the node in the center of the isometric rectangle.

   **Specify center of isocircle: _nod of**

5. See how the ellipse drags with the cursor in the current isometric plane? Toggle the plane using the **F5** key [F5] to see how the ellipse changes. Stop toggling when the crosshairs return to the 90°/30° position.

6. Notice that you can specify a radius or diameter. Let's use the default (**radius**) and enter *1*. Your drawing looks like the figure shown.

   **Specify radius of isocircle or [Diameter]: *1***

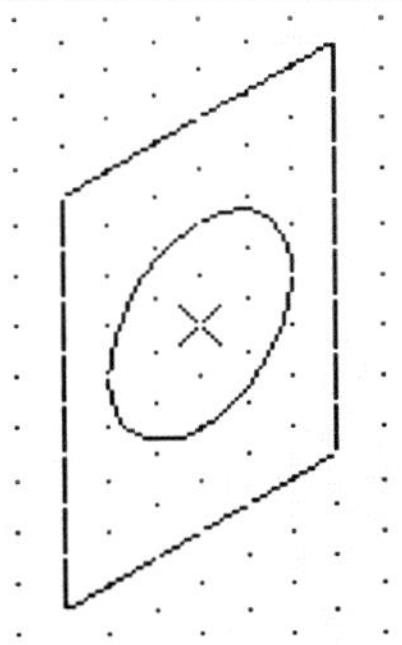

7. Save and close the drawing.

   **Command: *qsave***

We've looked at circles and "squished" circles (ellipses), ellipse arcs, and isometric circles. Let's move on then to partial circles – arcs.

## 5.3 Arcs: The Hard Way!

How's that for a section title to make you want to skip past this part of the lesson?! But wait! "There's gold in them thar pages!"

Although it'll frequently be quicker and easier to create a circle and trim away the part you don't want, there are times when there is simply no substitute for the ***Arc*** command. (Besides, we haven't learned the ***Trim*** command yet.)

Drawing an arc isn't difficult – providing you know which of the eleven available procedures to use. The command sequence is

**Command:** ***arc*** **(or *a*)**

**Specify start point of arc or [Center]:** ***[select or identify the starting point]***

**Specify second point of arc or [Center/End]:** ***select or identify a point on the arc]***

**Specify end point of arc:** ***[select or identify the endpoint]***

The best way to see each of the options is through an exercise. So fire up the computer and full speed ahead! (The next exercise uses a slightly different format, but it replaces one with over 60 steps!)

> You can find the various options of the ***Arc*** command under the Draw pull-down menu.
>
> However, you may have noticed by now that I don't always provide details about procedures using the pull-down menus. There's a reason for this.
>
> Most commands available on a pull-down menu are also available on a toolbar (Draw pull-down – Draw toolbar, etc.). However, one of the easiest (and certainly the first) parts of AutoCAD to be customized is the pull-down menu system. In the years I've worked AutoCAD in various capacities, I've never seen two companies use the same pull-down menu system. Additionally, I've never seen a company use AutoCAD's default pull-down menus.
>
> For this reason, I shy away from the pull-down menus and discourage my students from becoming too reliant on them (or any one method of doing things).
>
> You can also find the various options in the cursor menu once the ***Arc*** command has been entered.

| **Do This: 5.3.1** | **Arcs, Arcs, Arcs** |
|---|---|

I. Open the *arcs* drawing in the C:\Steps\Lesson05 folder.

II. Set the Running OSNAP to **Node** and clear any other settings.

III. You'll notice twelve squares in the drawing. Use these as a guide. First, restore the **TOP** view and regenerate the drawing. When you've finished with the first six squares, restore the **BOTTOM** view and continue.

IV. Begin in each square with the ***Arc*** command. (Enter ***Arc*** or ***a*** at the command prompt. Alternately, you can pick the **Arc** button 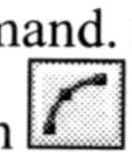 on the Draw toolbar.)

V. Follow the command/response sequences given in the chart below. You can use keyboard entry, cursor menu, or dynamic entry when making your responses.

| Square/ Procedure | Prompt/Response | Results |
|---|---|---|
| 1<br>Start – Second Point – End | **Command:** ***a***<br>**Specify start point of arc or [Center]:** ***[pick point a]***<br>**Specify second point of arc or [Center/End]:** ***[pick point b]***<br>**Specify end point of arc:** ***[pick point c]*** | 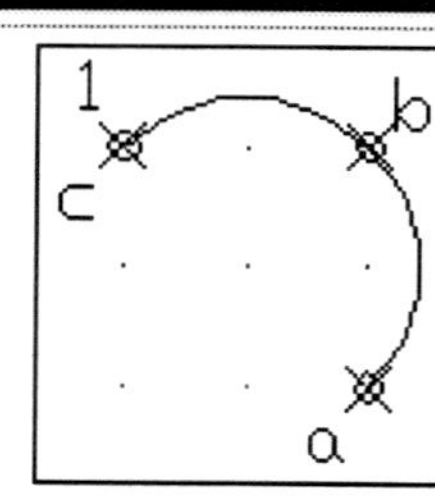 |

| Square/ Procedure | Prompt/Response | Results |
|---|---|---|
| 2<br>Start – Center – End<br>(This is the most common approach.) | **Command:** ***a***<br>**Specify start point of arc or [Center]:** ***[pick point a]***<br>**Specify second point of arc or [Center/End]:** ***c [select the*** **Center** ***option]***<br>**Specify center point of arc:** ***[pick point b]***<br>**Specify end point of arc or [Angle/chord Length]:** ***[pick point c]*** | 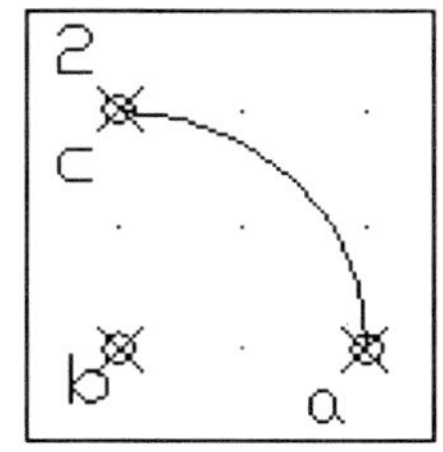 |
| 3<br>Start – Center – Angle<br>(This procedure enables you to control the included angle of the arc.) | **Command:** ***a***<br>**Specify start point of arc or [Center]:** ***[pick point a]***<br>**Specify second point of arc or [Center/End]:** ***c [select the*** **Center** ***option]***<br>**Specify center point of arc:** ***[pick point b]***<br>**Specify end point of arc or [Angle/chord Length]:** ***a [select the*** **Angle** ***option]***<br>**Specify included angle:** ***45 [enter an angle]*** | 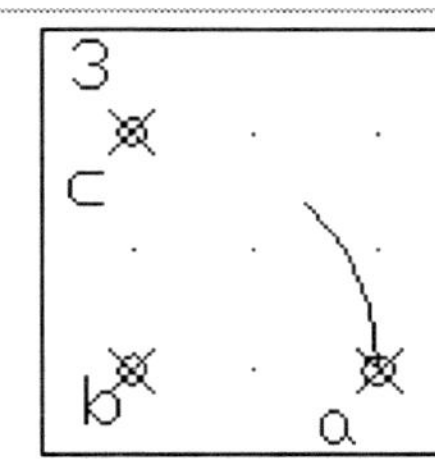 |
| 4<br>Start – Center – chord Length<br>(This procedure enables you to control the true length of the arc.) | **Command:** ***a***<br>**Specify start point of arc or [Center]:** ***[pick point a]***<br>**Specify second point of arc or [Center/End]:** ***c [select the*** **Center** ***option]***<br>**Specify center point of arc:** ***[pick point b]***<br>**Specify end point of arc or [Angle/chord Length]:** ***l [select the*** **chord Length** ***option]***<br>**Specify length of chord:** ***1.25 [enter the length of the arc]*** | 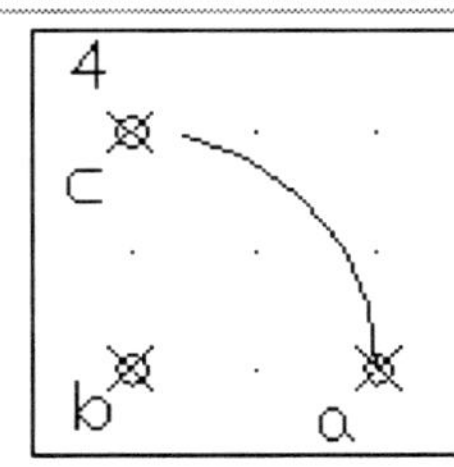 |
| 5<br>Start – End – Angle | **Command:** ***a***<br>**Specify start point of arc or [Center]:** ***[pick point a]***<br>**Specify second point of arc or [Center/End]:** ***e [ select the*** **End** ***option]***<br>**Specify end point of arc:** ***[pick point b]***<br>**Specify center point of arc or [Angle/Direction/Radius]:** ***a [select the*** **Angle** ***option]***<br>**Specify included angle:** ***45 [enter an angle for your arc]*** | 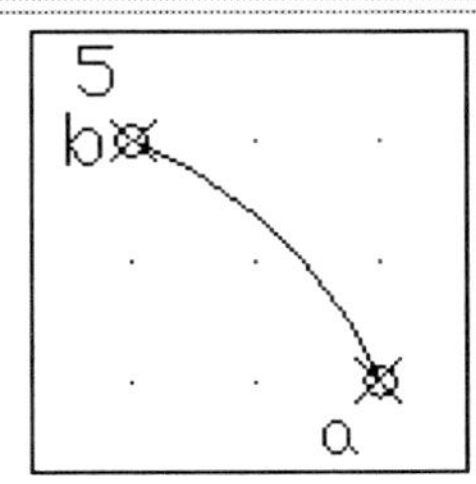 |

| SQUARE/ PROCEDURE | PROMPT/RESPONSE | RESULTS |
|---|---|---|
| 6<br>Start – End – Direction<br>(This procedure enables you to control the direction of your arc.) | **Command:** ***a***<br>**Specify start point of arc or [Center]:** ***[pick point a]***<br>**Specify second point of arc or [Center/End]:** ***e [select the* End *option]***<br>**Specify end point of arc:** ***[pick point c]***<br>**Specify center point of arc or [Angle/Direction/Radius]:** ***d [select the* Direction *option]***<br>**Specify tangent direction for the start point of arc:** ***[pick point b]*** | 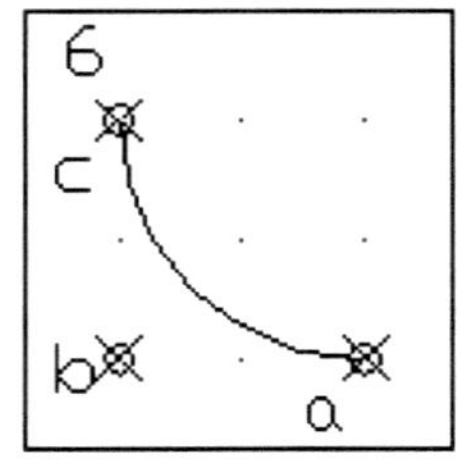 |
| **VI.** Set the **BOTTOM** view current. | | |
| 7<br>Start – End – Radius | **Command:** ***a***<br>**Specify start point of arc or [Center]:** ***[pick point a]***<br>**Specify second point of arc or [Center/End]:** ***e [select the* End *option]***<br>**Specify end point of arc:** ***[pick point b]***<br>**Specify center point of arc or [Angle/Direction/Radius]:** ***r [select the* Radius *option]***<br>**Specify radius of arc:** ***1 [tell AutoCAD what radius to use]*** | 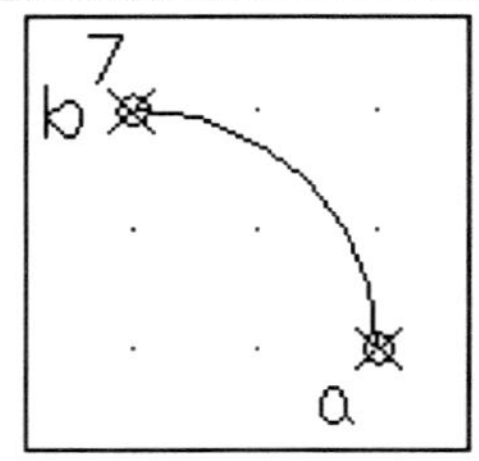 |
| 8<br>Center – Start – End | **Command:** ***a***<br>**Specify start point of arc or [Center]:** ***c [select the* Center *option]***<br>**Specify center point of arc:** ***[pick point a]***<br>**Specify start point of arc:** ***[pick point b]***<br>**Specify end point of arc or [Angle/chord Length]:** ***[pick point c]*** | 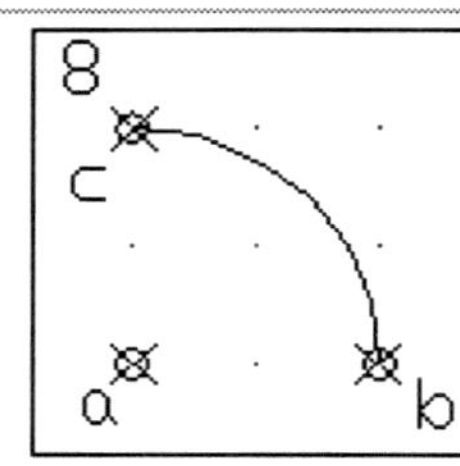 |
| 9<br>Center – Start – Angle | **Command:** ***a***<br>**Specify start point of arc or [Center]:** ***c [select the Center option]***<br>**Specify center point of arc:** ***[pick point a]***<br>**Specify start point of arc:** ***[pick point b]***<br>**Specify end point of arc or [Angle/chord Length]:** ***a [select the* Angle *option]***<br>**Specify included angle:** ***45 [enter an angle for your arc]*** | 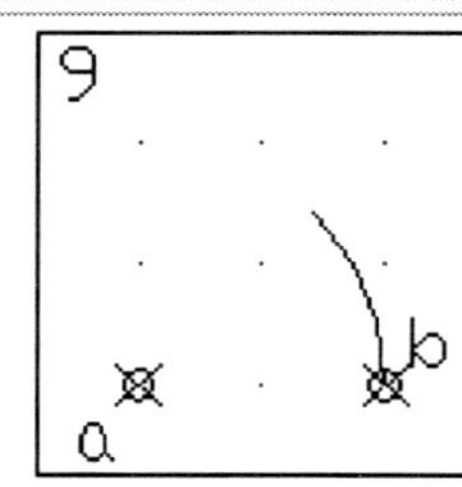 |

| SQUARE/ PROCEDURE | PROMPT/RESPONSE | RESULTS |
|---|---|---|
| 10<br>Center – Start – chord Length | **Command:** *a*<br>**Specify start point of arc or [Center]:** *c [select the Center option]*<br>**Specify center point of arc:** *[pick point a]*<br>**Specify start point of arc:** *[pick point b]*<br>**Specify end point of arc or [Angle/chord Length]:** *l [select the* **chord Length** *option]*<br>**Specify length of chord:** *1.25 [enter the length of the arc]* | 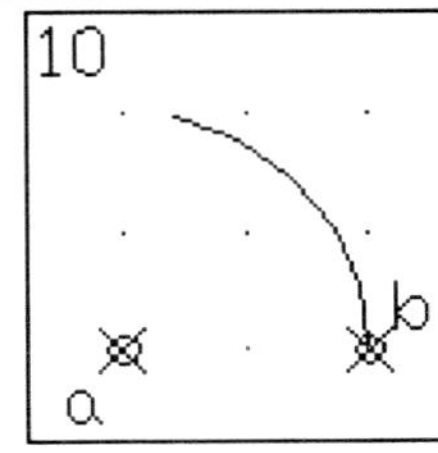 |
| 11<br>Continue Arc | *[Create an arc using the Start – Center – End method at points a – b – c.]*<br>*[Repeat the command, and then at the first arc prompt, hit enter to continue the arc. Pick point d.]* | 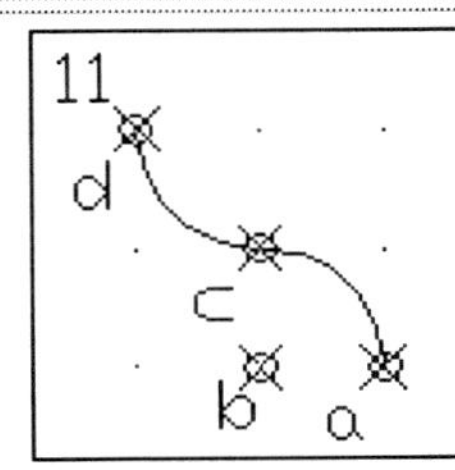 |

Wow! That was a chore! But as you can see, drawing arcs isn't difficult if you just know which method to use.

## 5.4 Drawing Multisided Figures: The *Polygon* Command

The polygon has long been one of the foundations on which our world is designed. Everything from the simple triangles of the pyramids to the hex head bolts that hold our automobiles together relies on the mathematics associated with multisided objects. Fortunately, I can leave the mathematics to those better qualified to confuse. All I must do is explain the three simple methods for drawing polygons.

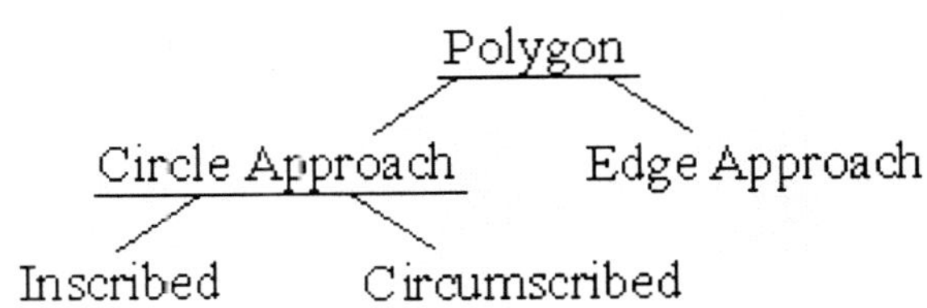

Figure 5.003

Consider the chart in Figure 5.003. It's really as simple to draw polygons as this chart suggests. Let's look at the command sequence:

> **Command:** *polygon* (**or** *pol*)
>
> **Enter number of sides <4>:** *[enter the desired number of equal sides – from 3 to 1024]*
>
> **Specify center of polygon or [Edge]:** *[either identify the location of the center of the polygon (the Circle Approach), or type* **E** *to use the Edge Approach]*
>
> **Enter an option [Inscribed in circle/Circumscribed about circle] <I>:** *[let AutoCAD know if you'll draw your polygon* **inside** *(inscribed) or* **outside** *(circumscribed) an imaginary circle]*
>
> **Specify radius of circle:** *[tell AutoCAD the radius of the imaginary circle in which (or around which) you want to draw the polygon]*

You see the first branch of the chart at the second command prompt. Find the second branch at the third prompt.

You can also access the ***Polygon*** command under the Draw pull-down menu. ***Polygon*** command options are also available on dynamic input or cursor menus once the command has been entered.

| Do This: 5.4.1 | Drawing Polygons |
|---|---|

I. Open the *polygons* drawing in the C:\Steps\Lesson05 folder. It looks like Figure 5.004.

II. Set the **Endpoint** and **Center** running OSNAPs. Clear all others.

III. Be sure the **DYN** and **OSNAP** buttons on the status bar are depressed, and that the **Snap**, **Grid**, **Ortho**, **Polar**, and **OTRACK** buttons are raised.

IV. Follow these steps.

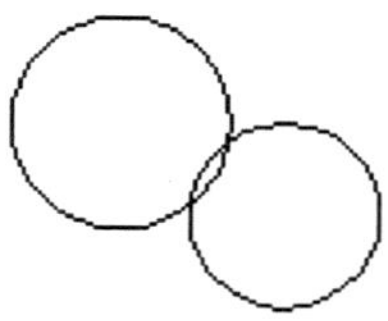

Figure 5.004

## 5.4.1: Drawing Polygons

1. Enter the ***Polygon*** command by typing ***polygon*** or ***pol*** at the command prompt.

Alternately, you can pick the **Polygon** button 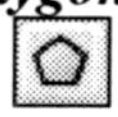 on the Draw toolbar or palette.

**Command: *pol***

2. AutoCAD asks for the number of sides needed to create the polygon. Enter ***6***.

**Enter number of sides <4>: *6***

3. Now AutoCAD needs to know how to draw the polygon. We'll accept the **center of polygon** default option. Select the center of the larger upper circle. (Let your Running OSNAPs located it.)

(Note: The circle isn't necessary for drawing the polygon. We just use it for demonstration purposes.)

**Specify center of polygon or [Edge]:**

4. We'll draw our polygon *inside* the circle **(Inscribed)**. Accept the default.

**Enter an option [Inscribed in circle/ Circumscribed about circle] <I>: *[enter]***

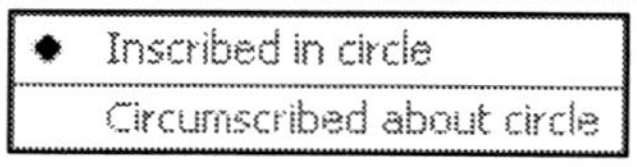


5. Enter ***1.5*** as the radius of the circle. Your drawing should look like the figure shown here.

**Specify radius of circle: *1.5***

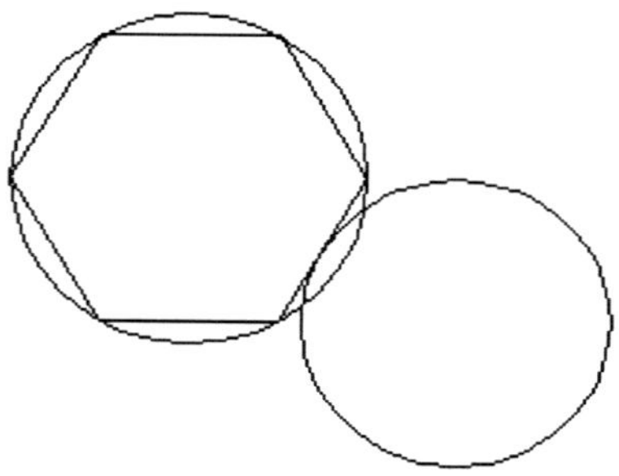

6. Repeat the ***Polygon*** command.

**Command: *[enter]***

7. This time AutoCAD defaults to six sides, as that was the last number used. Hit ***enter***.

**Enter number of sides <6>: *[enter]***

8. Select the center of the smaller circle.

**Specify center of polygon or [Edge]:**

## 5.4.1: Drawing Polygons

9. We'll circumscribe this polygon about the outside of the circle. You can type ***c*** or select **Circumscribed about circle** from the dynamic input menu.

**Enter an option [Inscribed in circle/ Circumscribed about circle] <I>: *c***

10. When prompted, use the OSNAP to select the bottom quadrant of the circle. Your drawing looks like the figure shown.

**Specify radius of circle: _qua of**

11. Now let's look at the **Edge** option. Repeat the ***Polygon*** command.

**Command: *pol***

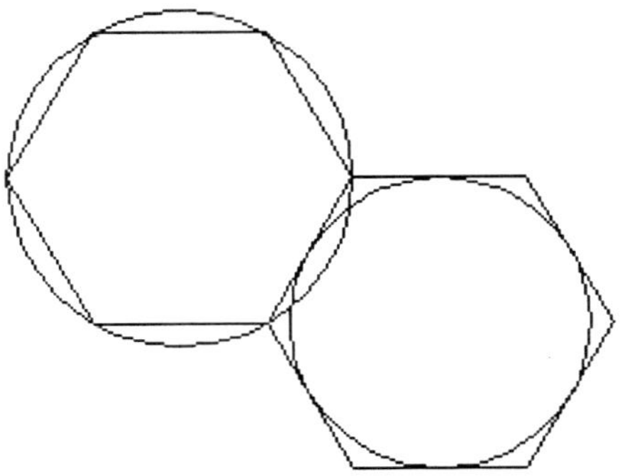

12. Accept six as the number of sides.

**Enter number of sides <6>: *[enter]***

13. Type ***e*** (or select **Edge** on the menu) to select the **Edge** option.
If the dynamic input menu doesn't show the options, use the down arrow on your keyboard to display them (see the figure below).

**Specify center of polygon or [Edge]: *e***

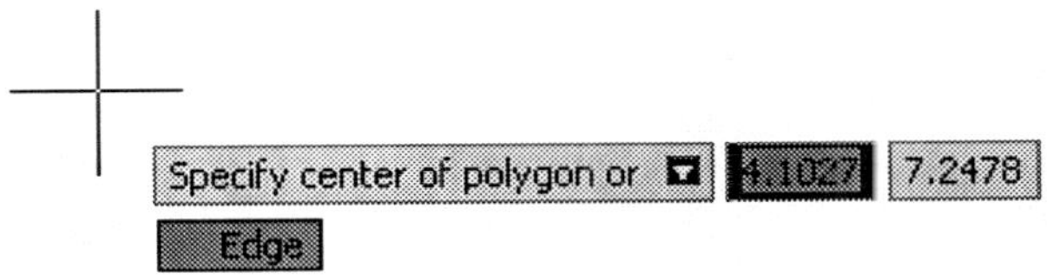


14. Select **Point 1** as indicated.

**Specify first endpoint of edge:**

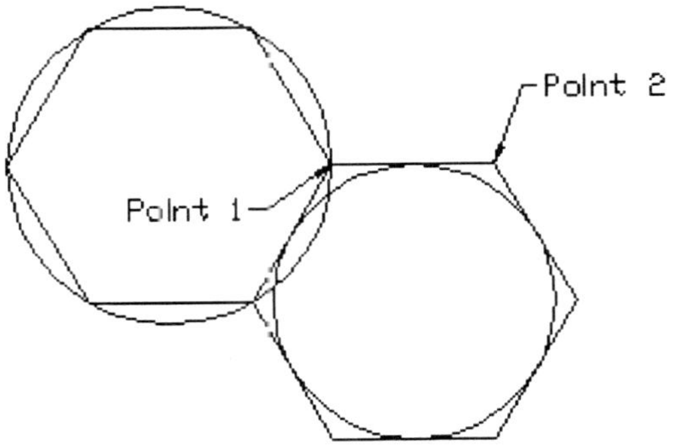

### 5.4.1: Drawing Polygons

15. Select **Point 2**. Your drawing looks like the figure shown.

**Specify second endpoint of edge:**

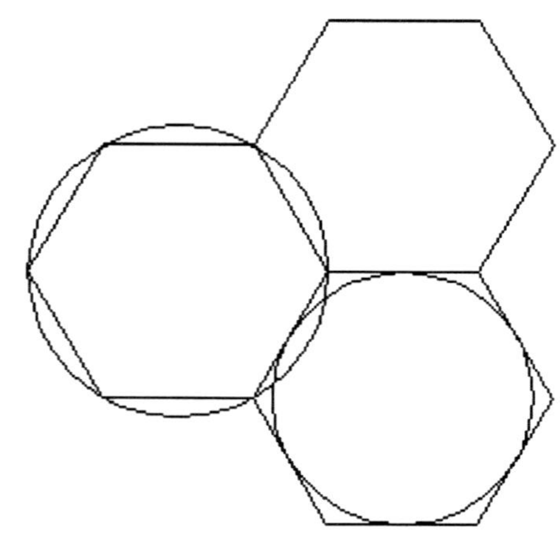

16. Save and close the drawing.

**Command:** ***qsave***

That's it for polygons! Remember, you can draw polygons with anything from 3 to 1024 sides … and you don't need an actual circle to guide you!

## 5.5 Putting It All Together

Let's try a project using what we've learned. We'll draw the Ring Stand Base shown in Figure 5.005.

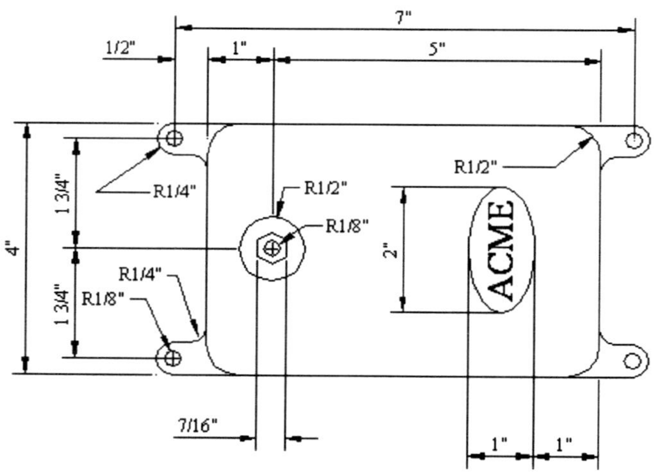


Figure 5.005

### Do This: 5.5.1 Polygons, Arcs, and Circles – The Project

I. Create a new drawing with the following setup:

- Lower left limits: 0,0
- Upper right limits: 17,11
- Units: Architectural
- Grid: ½
- Snap: ¼
- Textsize: 3/8
- Font: Times New Roman

II. Follow these steps.

## 5.5.1: The Project

1. ***Zoom* All** to see the entire drawing.

   **Command:** *z*

2. Save the drawing as *MyStand* to the C:\Steps\Lesson05 folder.

   **Command:** ***save***

3. Enter the ***Line*** command.

   **Command:** ***l***

4. Start at point ***4,2½*** and draw a 3" line upward. (Feel free to use any method of point entry you prefer – direct distance, dynamic input, coordinate entry, etc.)

   **Specify first point:** ***4,2-1/2***

   **Specify next point or [Undo]:** ***@3<90***

   **Specify next point or [Undo]:** ***[enter]***

5. Repeat the ***Line*** command. Then draw the second line as indicated.

   **Command:** ***[enter]***

   **Specify first point:** ***4-1/2,2***

   **Specify next point or [Undo]:** ***@5<0***

   **Specify next point or [Undo]:** ***[enter]***

6. Draw a third line…

   **Command:** ***[enter]***

   **Specify first point:** ***4-1/2,6***

   **Specify next point or [Undo]:** ***@5<0***

   **Specify next point or [Undo]:** ***[enter]***

7. … and a fourth line. Your drawing now looks like the figure.

   **Command:** ***[enter]***

   **Specify first point:** ***10,2-1/2***

   **Specify next point or [Undo]:** ***@3<90***

   **Specify next point or [Undo]:** ***[enter]***

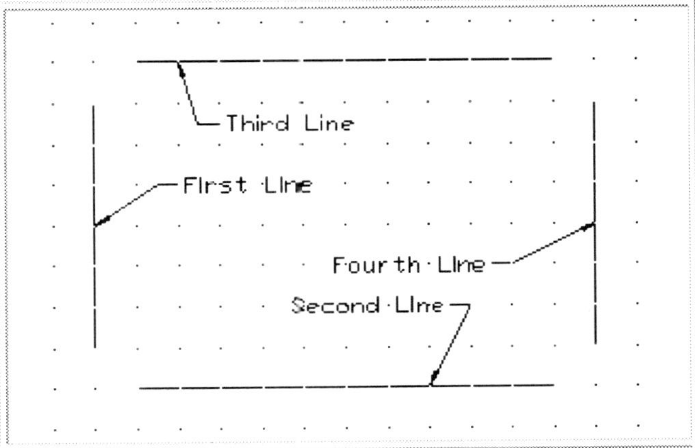


8. Set the Running OSNAP to **Endpoint**. Clear all other settings. (Remember to toggle the Running OSNAP on or off using the **F3** function key or the status bar toggle as needed!)

   **Command:** ***os***

9. Enter the ***Arc*** command.

   **Command:** ***a***

## 5.5.1: The Project

10. Select the endpoint of the second line nearest the fourth line.

    **Specify start point of arc or [Center]:**

11. Use the **Center** option.

    **Specify second point of arc or [Center/End]:** ***c***

12. Snap to the grid mark directly above the point you selected in Step 10.

    **Specify center point of arc:**

13. Select the lower endpoint of the fourth line.

    **Specify end point of arc or [Angle/chord Length]:**

14. Repeat Steps 9 through 13 to draw the other three arcs. Your drawing now looks like the figure.

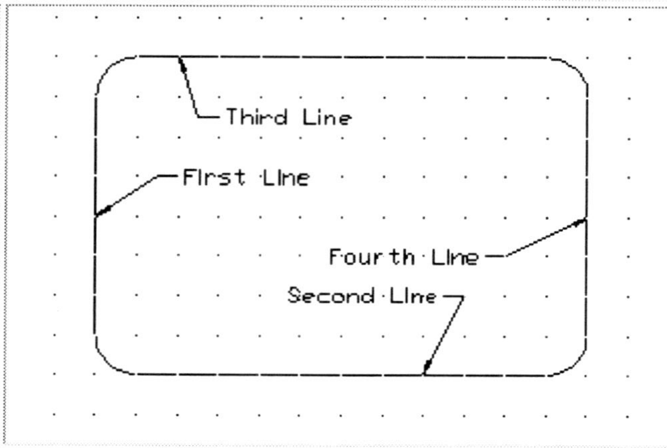


15. Repeat the ***Line*** command.

    **Command:** ***l***

16. (Refer to the figure above.) Draw a 1" line from the left endpoint of the second line in the 180° direction.

    **Specify first point:**

    **Specify next point or [Undo]:** ***@1<180***

    **Specify next point or [Undo]:** ***[enter]***

17. Repeat Step 16 at all four corners. Your drawing will look like this figure.

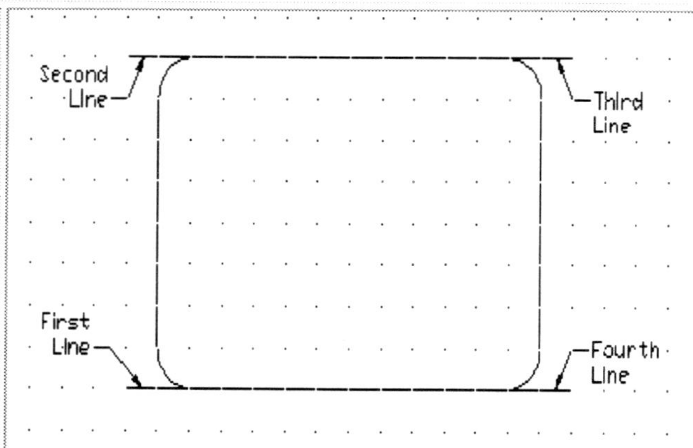


18. Now we'll draw an arc at the end of the first line. Start the command at the point indicated.

    **Command:** ***a***

    **Specify start point of arc or [Center]:** ***3-1/2,2-1/2***

19. Use the **Center** option.

    **Specify second point of arc or [Center/End]:** ***c***

20. Select a point one snap down from the point selected in Step 18.

    **Specify center point of arc:**

## 5.5.1: The Project

21. Select the endpoint of the first line.

**Specify end point of arc or [Angle/chord Length]:**

22. Repeat Steps 18 through 21 at the other four lines. Your drawing will look like the figure below.

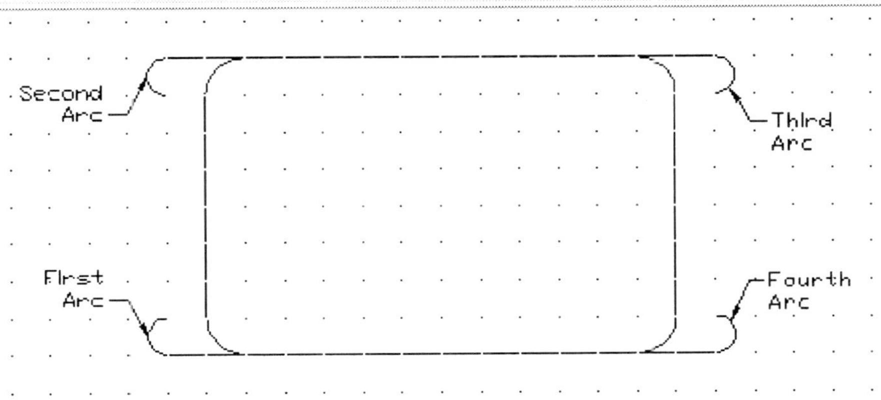


23. Now add a ¼" line at the end of the first arc.
Repeat for each arc. Your drawing will look like the figure below.

**Command:** ***l***
**Specify first point:**
**Specify next point or [Undo]:** ***@1/4<0***
**Specify next point or [Undo]:** ***[enter]***

24. Now draw arcs at the end of the new lines (refer to the figure following Step 29). We'll start at the lower left corner.

**Command:** ***a***
**Specify start point of arc or [Center]:** ***[select the endpoint of the line at the first arc]***

25. Use the **End** option.

**Specify second point of arc or [Center/ End]:** ***e***

26. The endpoint is one snap up and one snap to the right.

**Specify end point of arc:**

## 5.5.1: The Project

27. Select the **Direction** option.

**Specify center point of arc or [Angle/ Direction/Radius]:** ***d***

28. Select a point to the right of the point selected in Step 24.

**Specify tangent direction for the start point of arc:**

29. Repeat Steps 24 through 28 for the other arcs. Your drawing looks like the figure below.

30. It's a good idea to save your drawing occasionally!

**Command:** ***qsave***

31. Draw a circle in the center of the first anchor leg.

**Command:** ***c***

32. Use the **center** OSNAP to locate the center of the first arc.

**Specify center point for circle or [3P/2P/Ttr (tan tan radius)]: _cen of**

33. Use a 1/8" radius for the circle.

**Specify radius of circle or [Diameter]:** ***1/8***

34. Repeat Steps 31 through 33 for each of the anchor legs. Your drawing will look like the figure below.

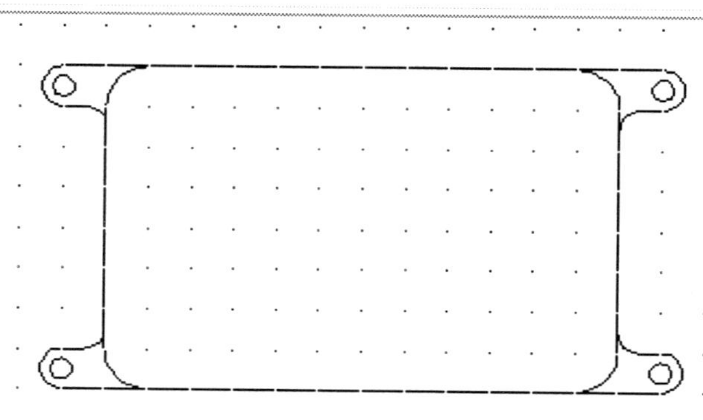

35. Now draw the 1" washer using the ***Circle*** command.

**Command:** ***c***

**Specify center point for circle or [3P/2P/Ttr (tan tan radius)]:** ***5,4***
**Specify radius of circle or [Diameter] <0'-0 1/8">:** ***1/2***

36. Draw the ¼" bolt center using the ***Circle*** command.
**Command:** ***c***
**Specify center point for circle or [3P/2P/Ttr (tan tan radius)]:** ***5,4***
**Specify radius of circle or [Diameter] <0'-0 1/2">:** ***1/8***

37. Draw the bolt using the ***Polygon*** command.
**Command:** ***pol***

38. Give it six sides.
**Enter number of sides <4>: 6**

39. Place it in the center of the last circle you drew.
**Specify center of polygon or [Edge]: _cen of**

40. Since we've a dimension on the bolt from flat side to flat side, we'll draw the polygon around a circle with that diameter. Enter ***c*** for **Circumscribed**.
**Enter an option [Inscribed in circle/Circumscribed about circle] <I>:** ***c***

41. Enter in ***7/32*** (half the given diameter). The washer and bolt look like the figure at right.
**Specify radius of circle:** ***7/32***

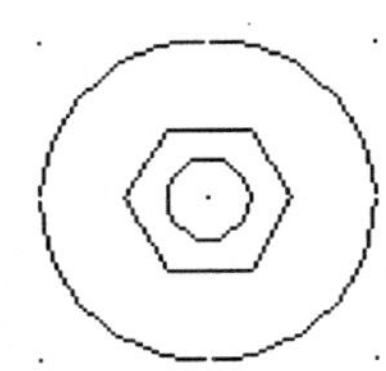

42. Now let's draw the logo plate using the ***Ellipse*** command.
**Command:** ***el***

43. Start at point ***8½,3***.
**Specify axis endpoint of ellipse or [Arc/Center]:** ***8-1/2,3***

44. The ellipse is 2" along the long axis.
**Specify other endpoint of axis:** ***@2<90***

45. It's 1" along the short axis.
**Specify distance to other axis or [Rotation]:** ***@1/2<0***

46. Add the ***ACME*** text to finish the project.
**Command:** ***dt***

47. We'll middle-justify the text in the center of the ellipse.
**Current text style: "times" Text height: 0'-0 3/8"**
**Specify start point of text or [Justify/Style]:** ***m***
**Specify middle point of text:** ***8-1/2,4***

48. If you set the **textsize** to 3/8 during the setup, it will default to that now. Otherwise, set it to ***3/8***.
**Specify height <0'-0 3/8">:** ***[enter]***

### 5.5.1: The Project

49. Set the **rotation angle** so the text may be read from the bottom of the stand.

    **Specify rotation angle of text <0>: *90***

50. Enter the text (***ACME***).

51. Save  your drawing. It should now look like the sample in Figure 5.005.

    **Command: *qsave***

## 5.6 Extra Steps

These may be the most important paragraphs in the text!

AutoCAD provides several system variables (generally called SYSVARS) including one called **Savetime**.

> SYSVARS (system variables) are one of the ways AutoCAD provides for you to configure the software for optimal performance.

The ***Savetime*** command sequence is

**Command: *savetime***

**Enter new value for SAVETIME <10>:**

The default time shown here is 10 minutes. I prefer this setting, but you can set it to whatever makes you feel comfortable. Remember that whatever number you assign to ***Savetime*** is the amount of drawing time you may lose in case of a system crash.

You don't have to worry about it overwriting a file if you don't want your changes saved. AutoCAD saves the drawing in the \Local Settings\Temp folder.

## 5.7 What Have We Learned?

*Items covered in this lesson include:*

- *Commands*
    - ***Arc***
    - ***Circle***
    - ***Ellipse***
    - ***Polygon***
    - ***Savetime***

Lines and circles (and their various complements) shape our world. With this lesson, we wrap up the basic drawing tools. You're now able to draw quite a few things in the 2-dimensional world. But remember that only about 30% of CAD is drawing. The rest is modifying what you've drawn and entering text. We'll consider many of AutoCAD's modifying tools in Lesson 7, but first, we'll look at adding a bit of flavor to our work in Lesson 6.

Work on the exercises until you're more comfortable with what you've learned so far. Then go on to the next "colorful" lesson.

## 5.8 Exercises

1. Use the *MyIsoGrid2* template you created in Lesson 3 (or the *IsoGrid2* template in the Lesson03 folder) to create the drawing in Figure 5.006. Save the drawing as *MyIsoBlockwithEllipses* in the C:\Steps\Lesson05 folder.

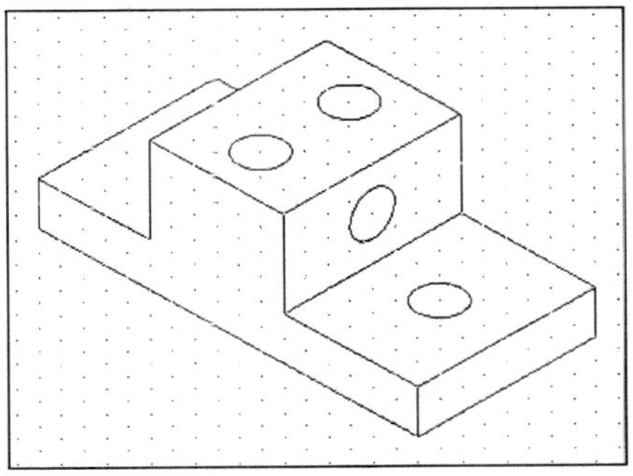

Figure 5.006: Isometric Block with Isometric Circles

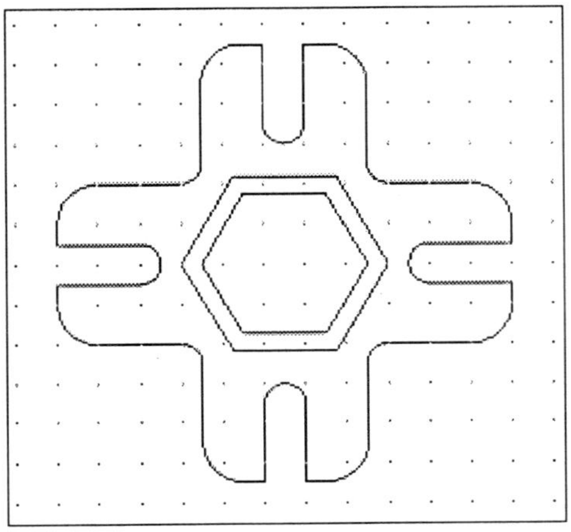

Figure 5.007: Slotted Holder

1. Using the *MyBase3* template you created in Lesson 1 (or the *Base3* template in the Lesson01 folder), create the drawing in Figure 5.007. Save the drawing as *MyHolder* in the C:\Steps\Lesson05 folder.

*For more exercises related to Lesson 5, please see Lesson 5 in AutoCAD 2007: One Step at a Time – Workbook.*

## 5.9 For Web-Based Review Questions, visit: http://www.uneedcad.com/2007/Files/07R5.pdf

# Lesson 6

Following this lesson, you will:

✓ *Know how to add color to a drawing using the* ***Color*** *command*

✓ *Know how to use linetypes in a drawing using the* ***Linetype*** *command*

✓ *Know how to use lineweights in a drawing using the* ***Lweight*** *command*

✓ *Know how to use layers in a drawing*

✓ *Know how to modify layers, linetypes, lineweights, and colors in a drawing using:*

- ***Properties*** *(and the Properties Palette)*
- ***Matchprop***

✓ *Know how to use the Autodesk Design Center*

✓ *Know how to use the Layer Translator*

# Adding Flavor to Your Drawings with Layers

*This is one of my favorite lessons to teach. It may be that I appreciate the respite from new drawing routines. It may be that I like dialog boxes. But more likely, it's just that by this point in the course, I'm really tired of looking at black-and-white drawings!*

*In the drafting world, we learn to differentiate between objects by well-established uses of linetypes and lineweights (widths). The number and spacing of dashes in a line, the width of a line, or combinations of dashes and width say a lot about what is being represented on the drawing. (For more information about specific representations, look in any basic drafting text.) We'll learn to use these tools in a CAD environment as well. But in the CAD environment, you'll have an additional tool at your disposal – color.*

*This lesson will lead you through two different methods of using linetype, lineweight, and color to differentiate between objects in your drawing; these are the direct approach (using specific commands such as* ***LType****,* ***LWeight****, and* ***Color****), and using layers. Each method should be considered exclusive; that is, you shouldn't combine them, as the results will no doubt aggravate someone.*

## 6.1 The Simple Command Approach

### 6.1.1 Adding Color with the Color Command

*"Oh, wow! The colors ... the colors!"*

*1960s Deep Thinker*

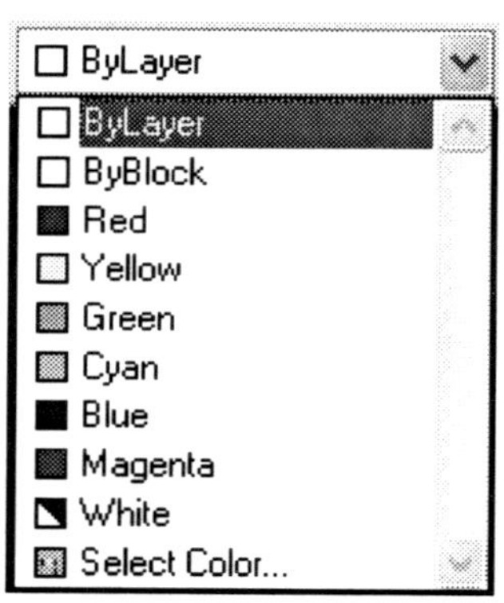


Figure 6.001

Changing the color in which you draw can be as simple as selecting the down arrow in the **Color** control box (Figure 6.001) on the Properties toolbar, and then selecting your color. Here you'll find the nine basic options including the seven basic colors AutoCAD provides. The other two are **ByLayer**, which assigns colors according to the layer setting (more on this in Section 6.2), and **ByBlock**. **ByBlock** means that objects will be drawn in basic black or white (depending on your background color). They'll keep this color until joined together as a block (more on blocks in Lessons 19 and 20). When inserted as part of the block, they'll adopt the current color setting in the drawing.

You may notice that **White** has a white/black color assignment in the **Color Control** box. The results of using this setting will depend on the background color you've set for the graphics area of your screen.

If you need more colors from which to choose, use the **Select color** option. (Alternately, you can type ***Color***, or ***Col***, at the command prompt and bypass the Properties toolbar and command line prompts altogether.) AutoCAD will prompt you with the Select Color dialog box (Figure 6.002 – next page). This has three tabs that we need to examine more closely.

- The first tab – **Index Color** – provides the traditional AutoCAD Color Index (ACI). This index provides 255 colors, shades of black and white, and the **ByLayer/ByBlock** settings we've already discussed.

  To select a color from the **Index Color** tab, simply double-click on the desired color from the palette. AutoCAD puts a number in the **Color** text box that corresponds to that color (thank goodness you don't have to remember the names of 255 colors!). You can, of course, type in the number yourself if you know it.

- The second tab – **True Color** – allows color settings using 24-bit true color (see Figure 6.003). Okay, that's computer-eze; what's it mean? Put simply, it means that you have up to 16 million colors from which to choose.

  You have two color models which you can use on the **True Color** tab – Hue, Saturation, Luminance (**HSL**) or Red, Green, Blue (**RGB**). (Select your preferences from the **Color model** list box in the upper right corner of the dialog box.) Let's take a look at these.

  - Color can be manipulated by virtue of small changes in three qualities – Hue, Saturation, or Luminance – HSL settings (Figure 6.003). Although these qualities will no doubt be familiar to those with art backgrounds, they won't be of much use to the average CAD operator. Still, a brief discussion is in order.
    - *Hue* is a measure of the dominant wavelength of light. To change the hue of your color setting, move the hue box (your cursor) from side to side over the color spectrum area of the tab. Alternately, you can change the number in the **Hue** control box from 0 to 360.
    - *Saturation* refers to the purity of a color – that's, the lack of white pollution in the color or how vivid the color appears. To change the saturation of your color setting, move the hue box up and down over the color spectrum area of the tab. Alternately, you can change the number in the **Saturation** control box from 0 to 100.

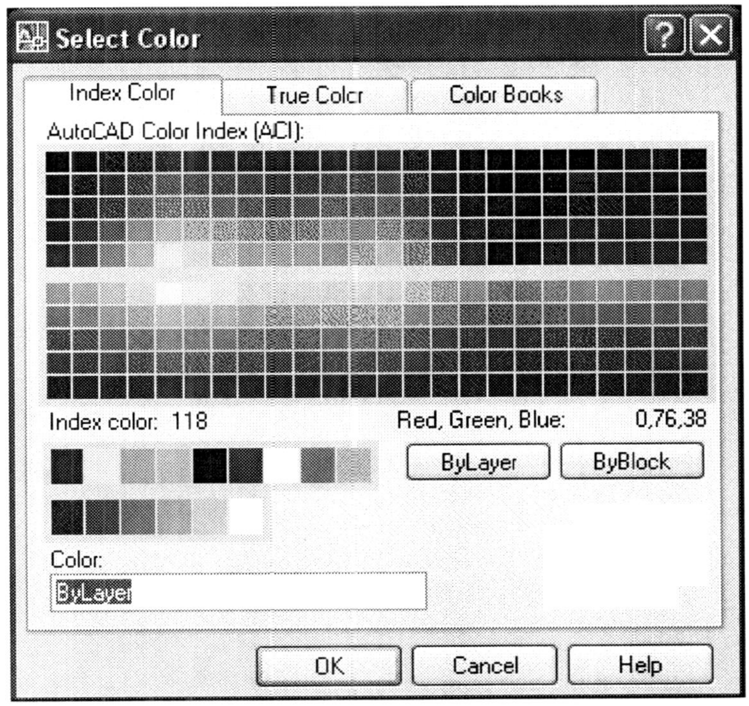


Figure 6.002

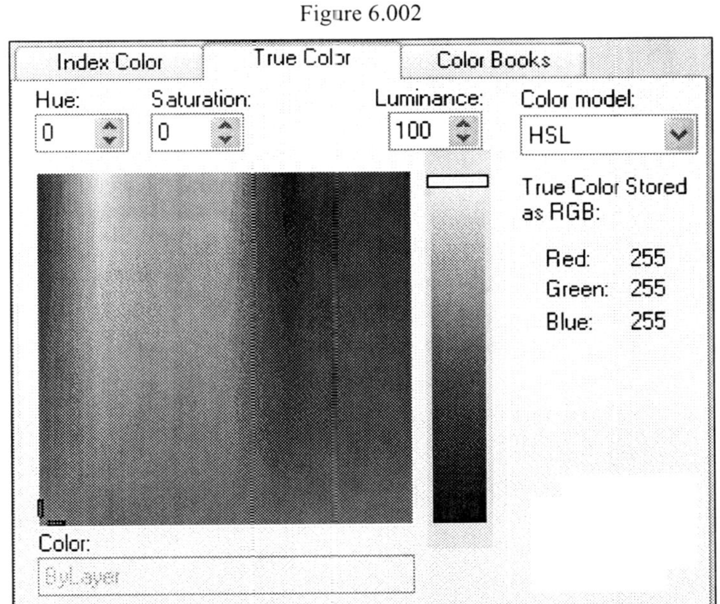


Figure 6.003

- *Luminance* refers to how the color reflects light. A value of 0 means that it doesn't reflect light (becomes black); a value of 100 means that it reflects all light (becomes white). The optimal value is 50. To change the luminance, adjust the color slider bar located at the right of the hue box. Alternately, you can enter a value from 0 to 100 in the **Luminance** control box.

  - Another method of adjusting true color would be the RGB method (Figure 6.004). You can create any color by mixing different amounts of red, green, and blue (just ask the guy who mixes your paint down at Home Depot). That's what you'll do on the **True Color** tab when you select RGB in the **Color model** list box. You can use the slider bars or fill in values (from 0 to 255) in the list boxes. Alternately, you can enter a color by entering a series of three numbers (each from 0 to 255) in the **Color** text boxes.

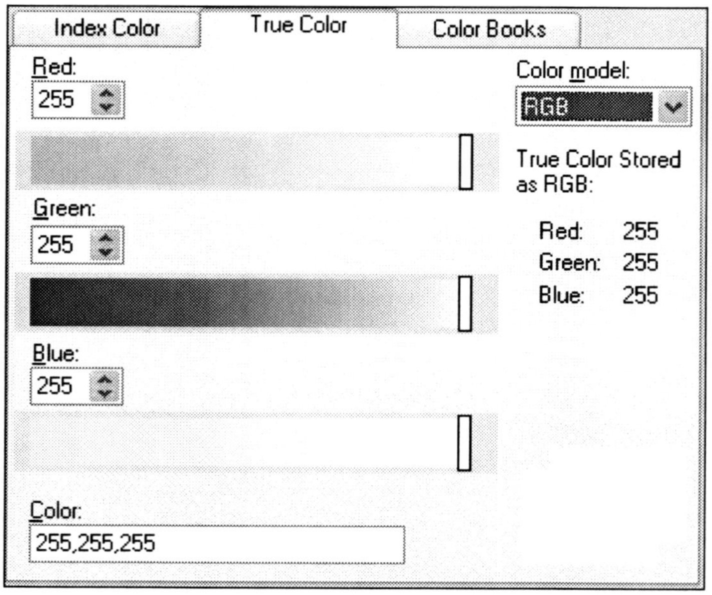


Figure 6.004

- **Color Books** (the final tab – Figure 6.005) provide an interesting addition to AutoCAD's capability. This one may come in handy for the architect or interior designer. Certain companies – by default DIC (Dai Nippon Ink color), Pantone® (a New Jersey company), and RAL (a German company) – provide color books. These tools are similar to those color cards you use at the paint store to decide what color to paint your kitchen. You select which book to use from the **Color book** list box, and then adjust the color bar (to the right of the selection box) to locate a general color. When a general color has been selected, you then select a specific color (or shade of color) from the selection box. Once you've selected the color, it appears in the **Color Control** box on the Properties toolbar. This way, you can increase the number of colors and shades of color immediately available for drawing.

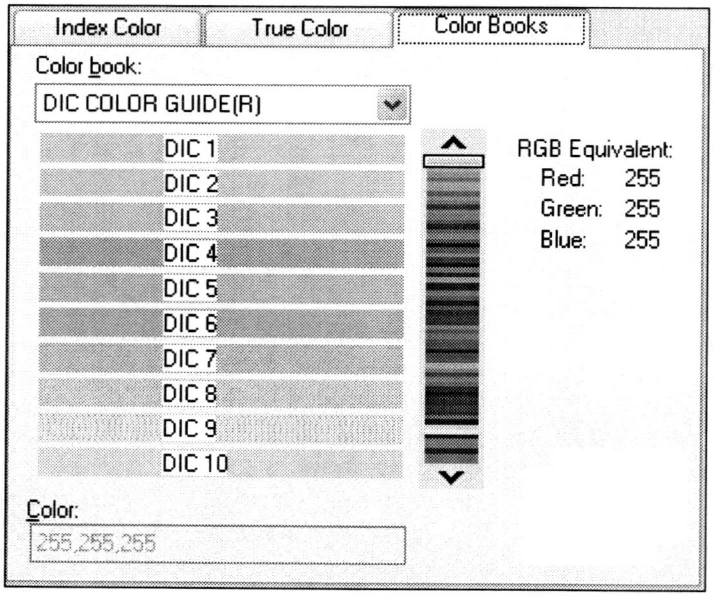


Figure 6.005

Okay, let's try to draw some lines and circles in color!

> In addition to the command line and toolbar, you can access the ***Color*** command by selection **Color** from the Format pull-down menu.

| Do This: 6.1.1.1 | Drawing in Color |
|---|---|

I. Open the *Star* drawing from the C:\Steps\Lesson06 folder. The drawing has a single circle in it.

II. Follow these steps.

**6.1.1.1: DRAWING IN COLOR**

1. Set **Cyan** as the current color using the **Color Control** box (shown) on the Properties toolbar. To do this, pick the down arrow next to the box, and select **Cyan**.

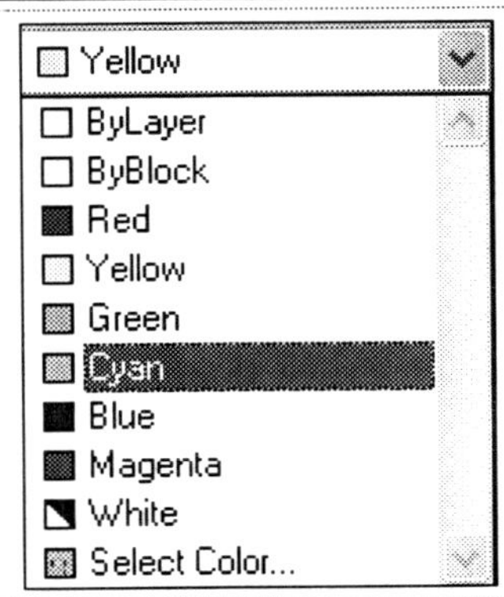


2. Draw a five-sided polygon 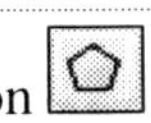 inscribed in the 3"ø circle you see on your screen. Be sure to use OSNAPs.

Your drawing looks like the figure at right.

**Command:** ***pol***
**Enter number of sides <4>:** ***5***
**Specify center of polygon or [Edge]: _cen of**
**Enter an option [Inscribed in circle/Circumscribed about circle] <I>:** ***[enter]***
**Specify radius of circle:** ***1.5***

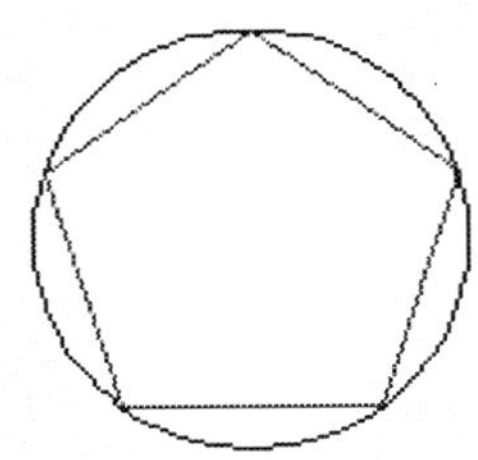

3. Call the Select Color dialog box by typing ***Color*** or ***col*** at the command prompt.

**Command:** ***col***

4. Set the color to number ***30*** by entering the number into the **Color** text box at the bottom of the dialog box, as shown.

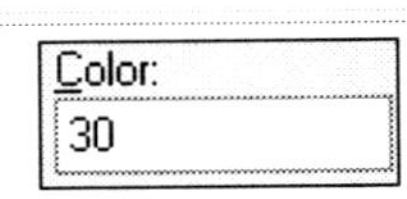


5. Pick the **OK** button 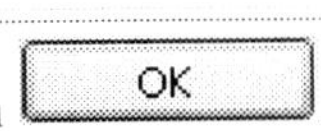.


6. Set the running OSNAP 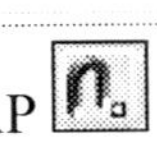 to **Endpoint**, and then draw lines  connecting the corners of the polygon to form a star. Your drawing looks like the figure shown here.

**Command:** ***os***
**Command:** ***l***

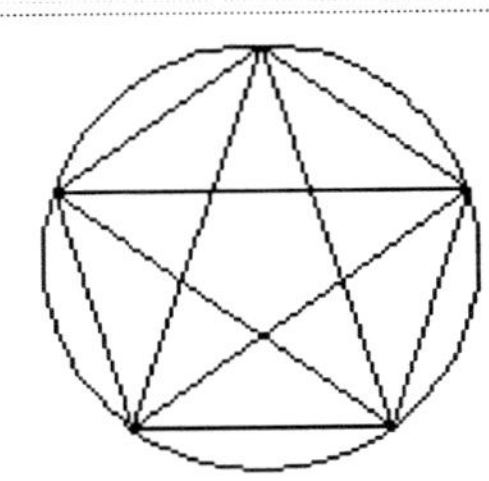

### 6.1.1.1: Drawing in Color

7. Now let's use the **RGB** method to set a new color. Call the Select Color dialog box.

   **Command:** ***col***

8. Pick on the **True Color** tab, and select **RGB** from the **Color model** list box.

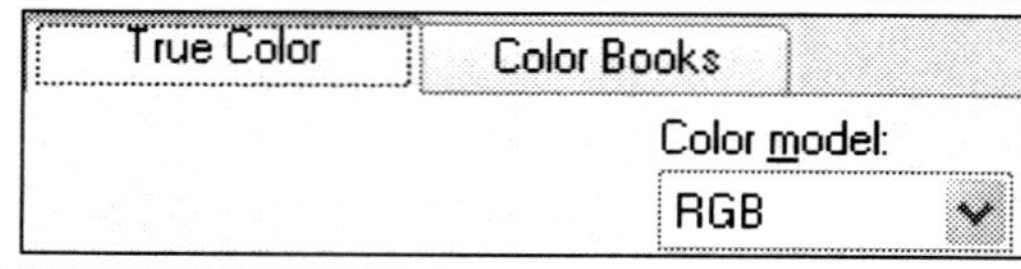


9. Enter the number ***226*** into the **Red**, ***99*** into the **Green**, and ***220*** into the **Blue** control boxes. Notice that the slider bars reposition themselves in accordance with what you've entered, and that the color indicator in the lower right corner changes to show the color you've set.

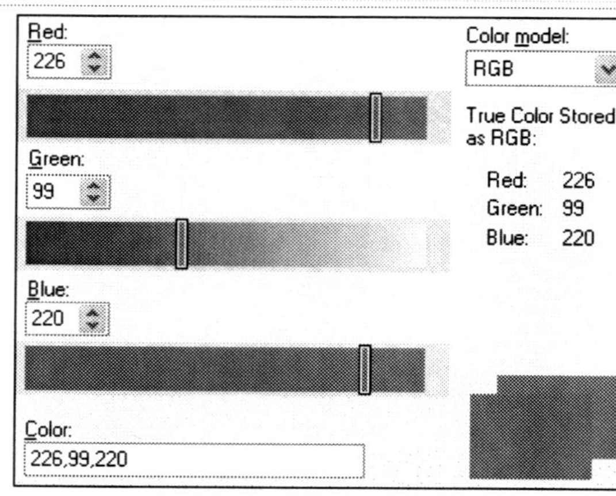


10. Pick the **OK** button 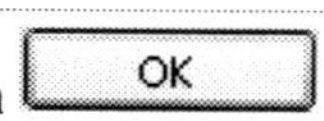 to conclude the procedure.


11. Create the text shown here. The text should be middle-justified … in the center of the circle … and make it 3/16" high.

    **Command:** ***dt***

    **Current text style: "Standard" Text height: 0.2000**

    **Specify start point of text or [Justify/ Style]:** ***m***

    **Specify middle point of text: _cen of**

    **Specify height <0.2000>:** ***3/16***

    **Specify rotation angle of text <0>:** ***[enter]***

12. Save your drawing  as *MyStar* in the C:\Steps\Lesson06 folder.

## 6.1.2 Drawing with Linetypes

What would drafting be without linetypes? *Boring!* And builders wouldn't be able to tell hidden lines from centerlines. I suppose we'd have some pretty interesting buildings out there (not to mention some OSHA nightmares).

Luckily, AutoCAD has continued all the traditional drafting tools – and even added a few. But let's look at linetypes.

The command to bring up the Linetype Manager dialog box (Figure 6.006 – next page) is, you guess it, ***Linetype***, although ***Ltype*** or ***lt*** will work as well.

As you can see in the list box, there are only three options available by default. **ByLayer** and **ByBlock** work in the same way they did with the ***Color*** command. The only other option is **Continuous**, which provides a solid line. To select one of the options, simply pick on the desired linetype, the **Current** button, and then the **OK** button. You'll notice that the **Linetype Control** box on the Properties toolbar shows your choice as current.

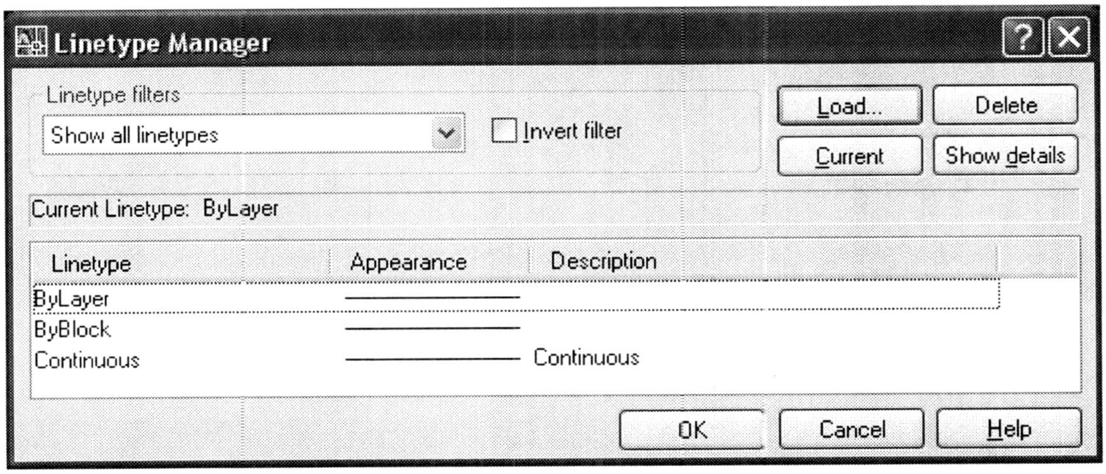


Figure 6.006

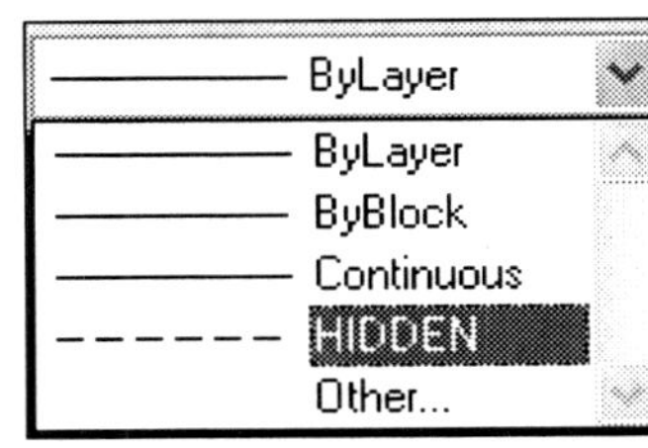


Figure 6.007

An easier way of making a *loaded* linetype current is simply to pick the down arrow next to the **Linetype Control** box (Figure 6.007) on the Properties toolbar, and select the linetype of your choice (much as you did with the **Color Control** box).

*So what if the linetype you need isn't shown?*

To avoid using a great deal of memory to hold information that may not be used, AutoCAD doesn't automatically load all the more than 45 available linetypes. But you can load them all or just the ones you want. We'll see how in our next exercise.

> You can still access the command line options of the ***Linetype*** command by typing a dash in front of it, as in ***-linetype***. The command sequence to set a linetype looks like this:
>
> **Command: *-linetype***
> **Current line type: "ByLayer"**
> **Enter an option [?/Create/Load/Set]: *s***
> **Specify linetype name or [?] <ByLayer>: *hidden***
> **Enter an option [?/Create/Load/Set]: *[enter]***
>
> The command line method is only occasionally useful; although *by using this approach, you can set a linetype current without first loading it.* (AutoCAD will load it automatically.)

> In addition to the command line and toolbar, you can access the ***Linetype*** command by selecting **Linetype** from the Format pull down menu.

| **Do This: 6.1.2.1** | **Drawing with Linetypes** |
|---|---|

I. Open *va.dwg* from the C:\Steps\Lesson06 folder. This is a valve attached to a vessel wall (Figure 6.008). We'll load some linetypes, add a centerline to the valve, and add some hidden lines to indicate pipe inside the vessel.

II. Follow these steps.

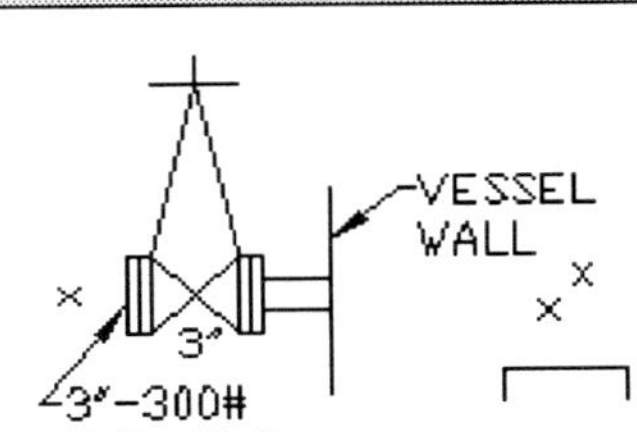


Figure 6.008

## 6.1.2.1: Drawing with Linetypes

1. Open the Linetype Manager dialog box (Figure 6.006) by typing ***Linetype***, ***Ltype***, or ***lt***. Alternately, you can select **Other** in the **Linetype Control** box.

**Command: *lt***

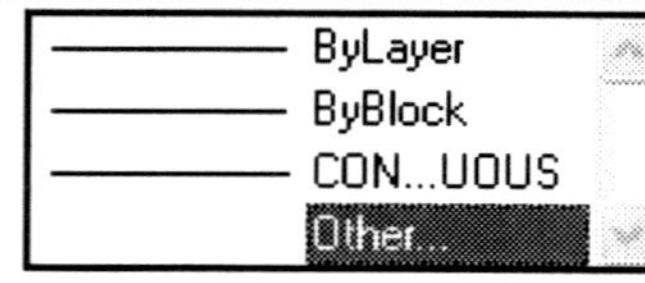


2. Pick the **Load** button 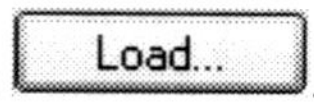

. The Load or Reload Linetypes dialog box appears (below).

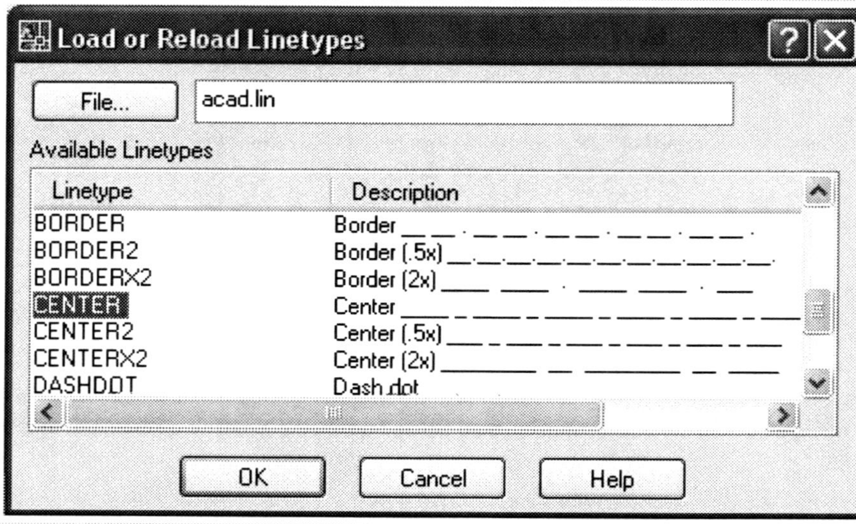


Notice the **File** button at top. AutoCAD stores its linetype definitions in a file called *acad.lin* (although there is another file – the *acadiso.lin* file used for metrics – with additional definitions).

Notice also the list of linetype names under the **Linetype** heading in the list box. A description and sample appears to the right of each. Scroll down the list as necessary to find the linetype(s) you want to load.

3. For now, scroll down until you see **CENTER**. Select it by picking on the word **CENTER**. Scroll down a bit more until you see **HIDDEN**. Holding down the CTRL key on the keyboard (to enable you to select more than one linetype at a time) select **HIDDEN**.

4. Pick the **OK** button 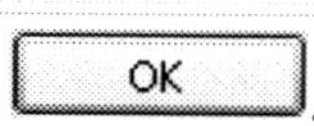

. AutoCAD closes the dialog box and lists **CENTER** and **HIDDEN** in the Linetype Manager (below).

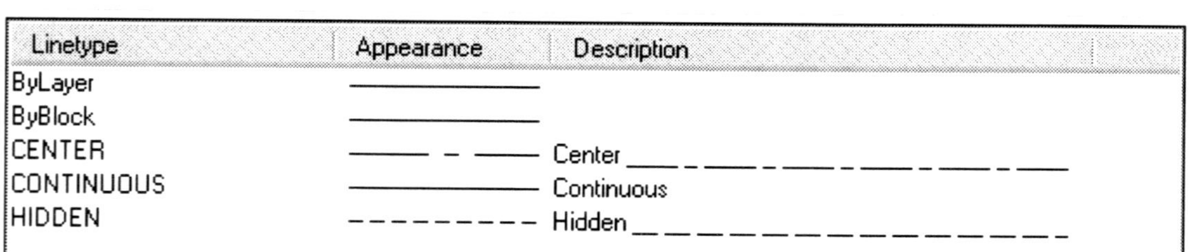


5. Complete the command 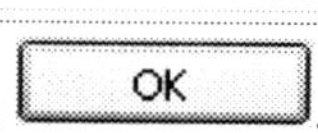

.

## 6.1.2.1: Drawing with Linetypes

6. Now let's draw some lines. First, set **CENTER** as the current linetype. Pick the down arrow in the **Linetype Control** box on the Properties toolbar, and select the **CENTER** linetype as shown.

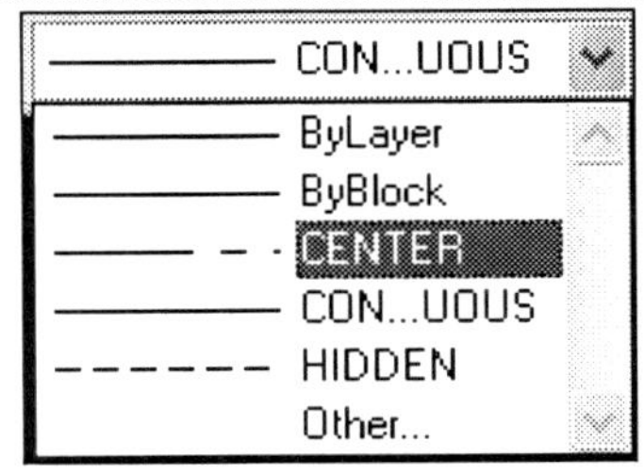


7. Draw a line from the node at **Point 1** to **Point 2** (refer to the figure following Step 8). Notice that you've drawn a centerline.

**Command: *l***

8. Now draw a line from the handwheel – **Point 3** – through the center of the valve to **Point 4** (be sure to use the appropriate OSNAP and Ortho settings). Your drawing looks like the figure below.

**Command: *[enter]***

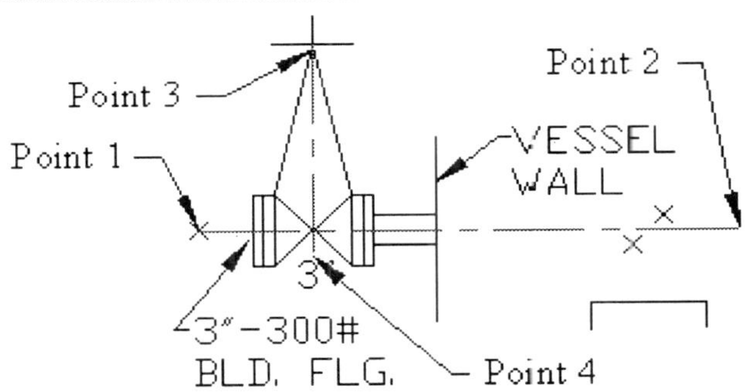


9. Set the current color to **Blue**.

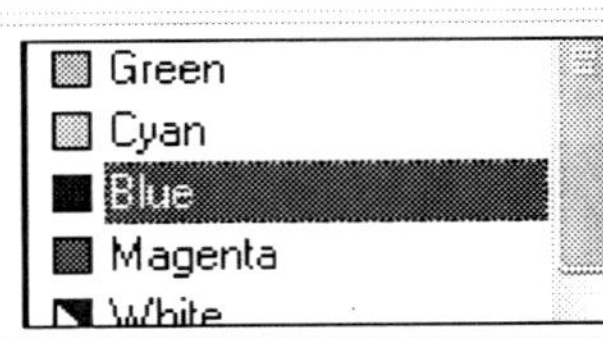


10. Set the linetype to **HIDDEN**.

11. Now draw the hidden lines to show the pipe inside the vessel (refer to the figure at right). Start at the intersection (use OSNAPs) at **Point 1** and draw to the node at **Point 2**. Continue the line perpendicular to the basin below.

Repeat the ***Line*** command and draw a line from **Point 3** to **Point 4** and down to the basin.

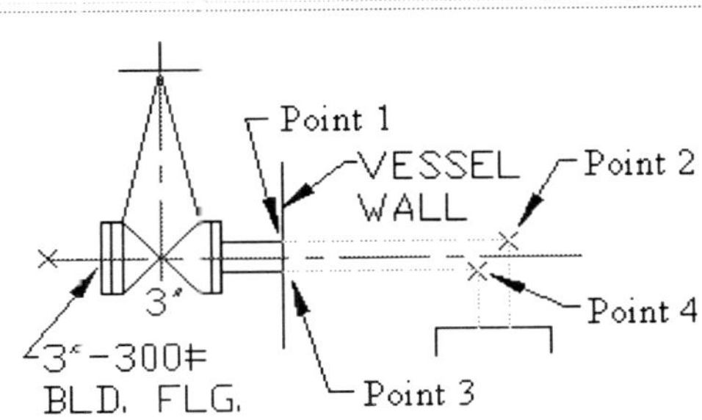


12. Save the drawing, but don't exit.

You've seen that drawing with linetypes is fairly simple. But there are some other considerations of which you must be aware. The first of these is a system variable called **LTScale**.

AutoCAD defines dashed and dotted lines by a code that details how long to make each dash and each space. You can define your own line by learning that code – but that's a topic for a customization guide. At this level, you must know how to adjust the line definitions (much as you learned to adjust the text size) to appear as dashes or dots on a larger drawing. Otherwise, a dashed line defined as having ¼" dashes separated with 1/8" spaces may appear as a solid line on a scaled drawing.

Try the ***LTScale*** command now. You'll see that it has already been set to **8** (the default is **1**). I set it here so you could see the hidden and centerlines as you drew them. Set it back to ***1*** and note the change to your drawing. Here's the command sequence.

> **Command:** ***ltscale*** **(or** ***lts*****)**
>
> **Enter new linetype scale factor <8.0000>:** ***1***

Your drawing will look like Figure 6.009 – with dashes and spaces too tiny to see.

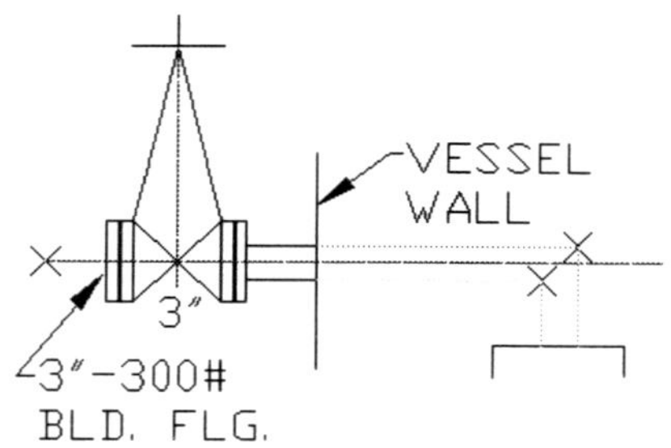

Figure 6.009

The best setting for the **LTScale** is the scale factor for the drawing (use the Drawing Scales chart in Appendix A).

The ***LTScale*** command sets the universal linetype scale factor for the drawing. All lines defined with dashes and spaces are affected. You can, however, adjust the **LTScale** specifically to a single line or linetype if you find it necessary.

We can adjust the **LTScale** from the **Details** section of the Linetype Manager dialog box. Let's look at this.

| Do This: 6.1.2.2 | More Drawing with Linetypes |
|---|---|

I. If you're not still in the *va.dwg* file, open it now. It's in the C:\Steps\Lesson06 folder.

II. Open the Linetype Manager.

III. Follow these steps.

**6.1.2.2: MORE DRAWING WITH LINETYPES**

1. Pick on the **Show details** button  to open the **Details** section (below). It appears at the bottom of the dialog box.

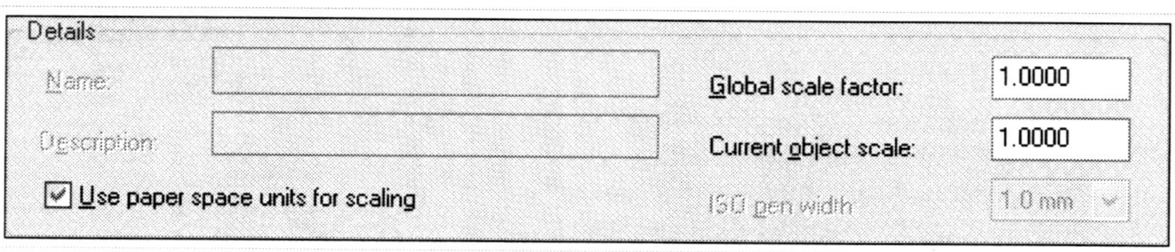


2. Notice that the **Global scale factor** is currently set to ***1.000***. Set it back to ***8*** (double-click in the text box next to the words: **Global scale factor** and then type ***8***).

3. Pick the ***OK*** button  to return to the graphics screen. Notice that dashes reappear on the drawing.

## 6.1.2.2: More Drawing with Linetypes

4. Reopen the Linetype Manager dialog box.

**Command:** ***lt***

5. Repeat Steps 2 and 3 to reset the **Global scale factor** to ***1***. Notice that dashes again disappear from the drawing.

6. Erase lines 1 and 2, as indicated.

**Command:** ***e***

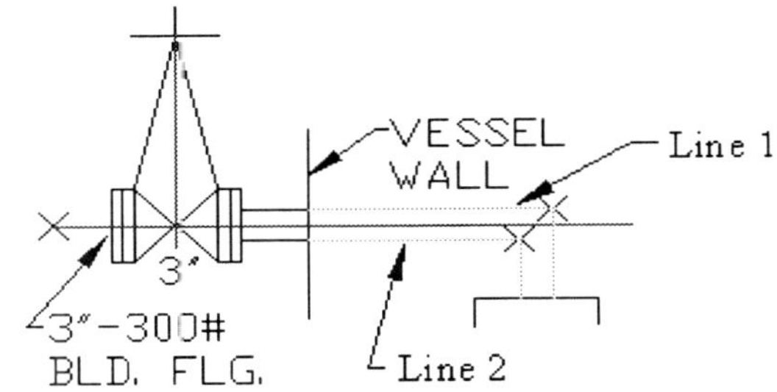


7. Reopen the Linetype Manager.

**Command:** ***lt***

8. Select the **HIDDEN** linetype from the list box. The word **HIDDEN** appears in the **Name** text box in the **Details** area. Now set the **Current object scale** to ***8*** (below).

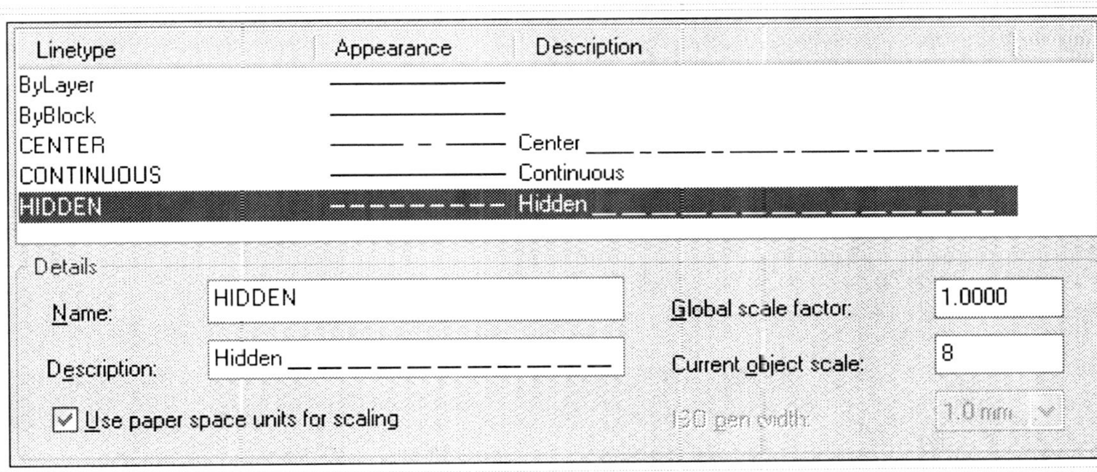


9. Pick the **OK** button [OK] to return to the screen.

10. Be sure **HIDDEN** is the current linetype [------ HIDDEN] (check the **Linetype Control** box on the Properties toolbar to be sure). Redraw lines 1 and 2 (see the figure in Step 6).

Notice that the new lines appear dashed whereas other hidden lines don't (right). *All lines drawn will have an* ***LTScale*** *equal to the product of the* ***Global scale factor*** *and the* ***Current object scale***.

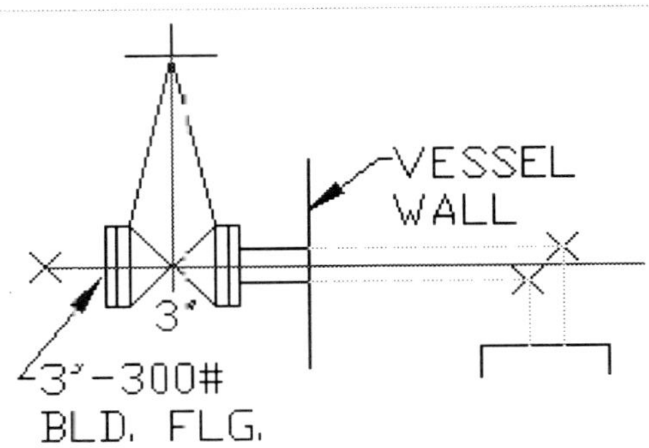


11. Save the drawing.

At the top of the Linetype Manager, you'll find a control box with the words **Linetype filters** above it (below). Use these filters to help you determine the linetype status of the current drawing by controlling what AutoCAD shows in the Linetype Manager.

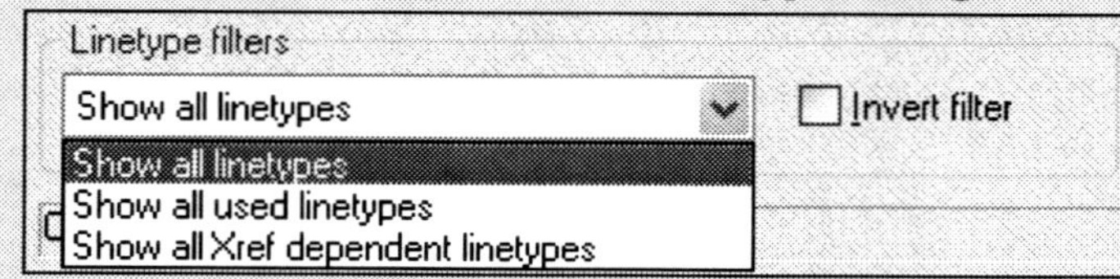


- **Show all linetypes** refers to all the linetypes loaded into the drawing;
- **Show all used linetypes** refers to only those linetypes currently in use;
- **Show all Xref dependent linetypes** refers to linetypes dependent on their Xref status (more on Xrefs in Lesson 25).

You can, at the end of a project, choose to see all the unused linetypes so you can delete them (a good way to free some memory and reduce the drawing's size). Do this by selecting the **Show all used linetypes** option, and then placing a check in the **Invert filter** check box next to the control box.

## 6.1.3 Using Lineweights

Exercise caution when using lineweights; they aren't true *WYSIWYG* objects – that is, What You See Is (not necessarily) What You Get. In Model Space, AutoCAD displays lineweight by using a relationship between pixels and lineweight. This enables you to tell that an object has weight – even if you can't tell how much weight until you plot the drawing.

Pixels are those little lights that make your monitor work. Think of them as tiny flashlights shining through colored lenses in the back of your monitor screen. The number of tiny flashlights depends on the *resolution* of your monitor (see your Windows manual). A standard resolution for AutoCAD would be 1024 x 768 – or 1024 columns of tiny flashlights and 768 rows of tiny flashlights in every square inch of your screen! (They're really tiny flashlights!)

Use the ***Lineweight*** command (or its hotkey, ***Lw***). Let's take a look at the dialog box for Lineweight Settings (Figure 6.010).

- The **Lineweights** frame on the left provides a choice of predetermined lineweights from which to select – from **0.00 mm** to **2.11 mm** (or **0.000"** to **0.083"** – depending on the units selected).

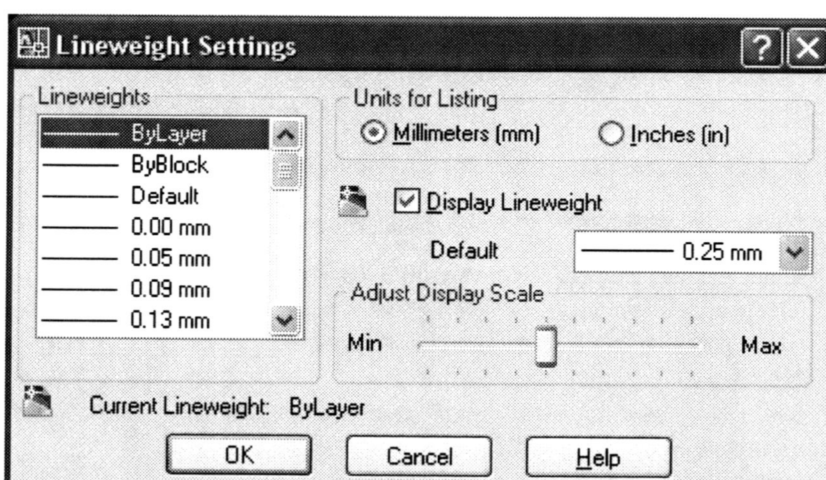


Figure 6.010

- The **Units for Listing** frame allows you to list the lineweight options in **Inches** or **Millimeters**. You can also set the units system variable at the command line by using the ***LWUnits*** command (**0** for inches or **1** for millimeters).
- The check in the box next to the line: **Display Lineweight** means that lineweights will be shown in Model Space. The weight will be determined in pixels. You can remove the check (or enter ***Off*** at the prompt after the ***LWDisplay*** command) to prevent seeing lineweights.
- The slider bar in the **Adjust Display Scale** frame allows you to control the pixels-to-lineweight ratio. In other words, slide the bar to the left to minimize (or to the right to maximize) the number of pixels used to show lineweight.

Of course, the easiest way you can set the lineweight is just as you set the color or linetype – using the **Lineweight Control** box on the Properties toolbar.

An interesting thing to note about the control boxes on the Properties toolbar – you can also use them to *change* (as well as set) lineweight, color, and linetype! Let's take a look at this.

| Do This: 6.1.3.1 | Changing the Lineweight |
|---|---|

I. If you're not still in the *va.dwg* file, open it now. It's in the C:\Steps\Lesson06 folder.

II. Follow these steps.

**6.1.3.1: CHANGING THE LINEWEIGHT**

1. Without entering a command, select the vessel wall. Notice that three tiny squares appear and the line highlights. The squares are grips (more on grips in Lesson 16).

2. Pick the down arrow on the **Lineweight Control** box; then scroll down and select **0.30mm** as shown.

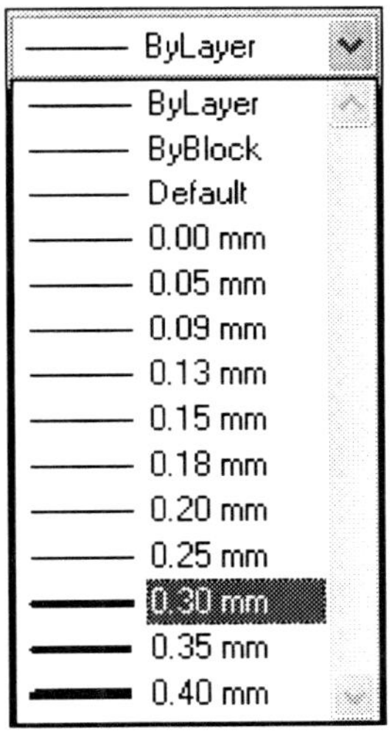


3. Right-click in the graphics area and pick **Deselect All** from the cursor menu. This will clear the selection set on the screen. (Alternately, you can simply hit the ESC key on the keyboard.)
Notice the change in the line you selected. (Remember: you can use this technique to change linetypes, colors, and layers, as well!)
(Note: If you don't see the lineweight, toggle **LWT** on the status bar on – or down.)

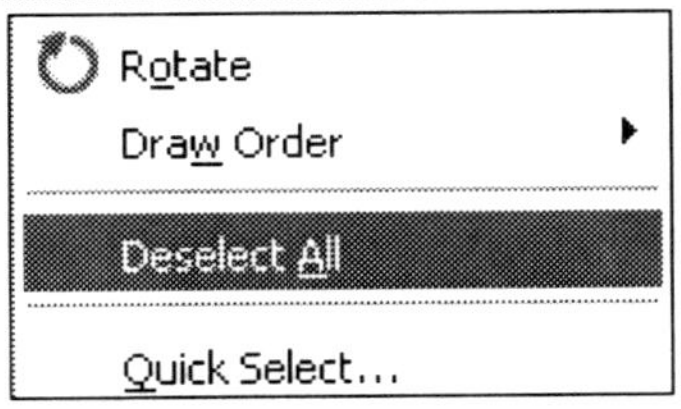


4. Leave the drawing without saving it.

**Command: *quit***

## 6.2 Color, Linetype, and So Much More - Layers

When I was a child (back when we created intricate drafting plans on the cave walls), one of the most coveted possessions of our household was a set of *Encyclopedia Britannica*. I spent hours exploring the world through those books, but my favorite site was the picture of the human body. I wasn't all that interested in anatomy – but I was fascinated by the way the body was shown. There was one page with an outline of the body. Then there were successive pages made of clear plastic overlays with the skeletal, reproductive, digestive, and circulatory systems. As these folded down atop each other, the body took shape. If one system was in the way, all I had to do was fold that sheet back.

This is the idea behind layers in AutoCAD.

You'll assign each layer a specific color, lineweight, linetype, and plot style. You should also assign a specific name to the layer – like *dim* for dimensions, *txt* for text, or *obj* for objects. All objects referenced by that name are drawn on that layer much as everything related to the skeletal system was found on a single plastic sheet. If something gets in the viewer's way during subsequent drawing sessions or discussions, the appropriate layer can be toggled **Off** or **Frozen** much as I could fold the unwanted sheet back when viewing the body.

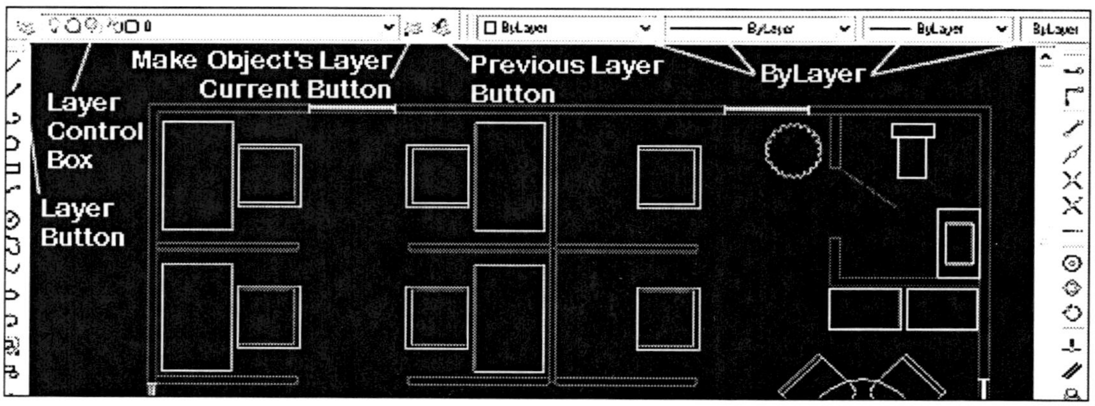


Figure 6.011

Additionally, you can organize the layers into *filtered* groups to make manipulation easier and faster. Using groups, you can change the visibility (**On/Off**, **Frozen/Thawed**), or even **lock/unlock** several layers simultaneously.

Let's take a look at layers and how they work. First, open the *flrpln.dwg* file (Figure 6.011) from the C:\Steps\Lesson06 folder.

Notice that the **Color**, **Linetype**, and **Lineweight Control** boxes each indicate the **ByLayer** setting. This will be important if layers are to work properly, as *the color, linetype, and lineweight settings will override the layer settings*. Note also where the **Layer** control box (Figure 6.012) and **Layer Properties Manager** button (indicated as **Layer Button** in Figure 6.011) are located.

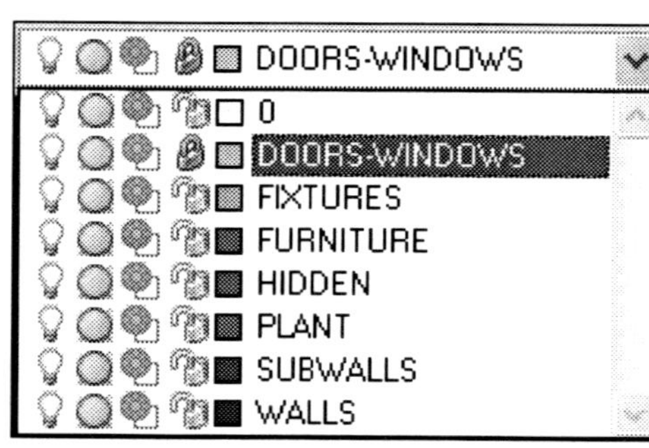


Figure 6.012

You'll do most of your layer manipulating from the **Layer** control box (Figure 6.012). It's quicker than having to open the Layer Properties Manager dialog box every time. For example, to set a layer current, simply pick the down arrow and select the layer you want. The drop down box will disappear and the name of the current layer will appear in the box. By picking on a specific icon, you can also (refer to the icons from left to right): turn a layer **On** or **Off**, **Freeze** or **Thaw** a layer, **Freeze** or **Thaw** a layer in the current viewport ((more on viewports in Lesson 22), or **Lock** or **Unlock** a layer.

Use the **Layer Properties Manager** button (or the ***Layer*** command – the hotkey is ***la***) to call the Layer Properties dialog box (Section 6.2.1). Here you'll create new layers … and much more!

But before we get too deeply involved in the Layer Properties dialog box, let's get our feet wet.

| Do This: 6.2.1 | Using Layers |
|---|---|

I. Be sure you're in the *flrpln.dwg* file in the C:\Steps\Lesson06 folder. If not, please open it now.

II. Follow these steps.

**6.2.1: USING LAYERS**

1. Pick the down arrow next to the **Layer** control box and select the **FURNITURE** layer.

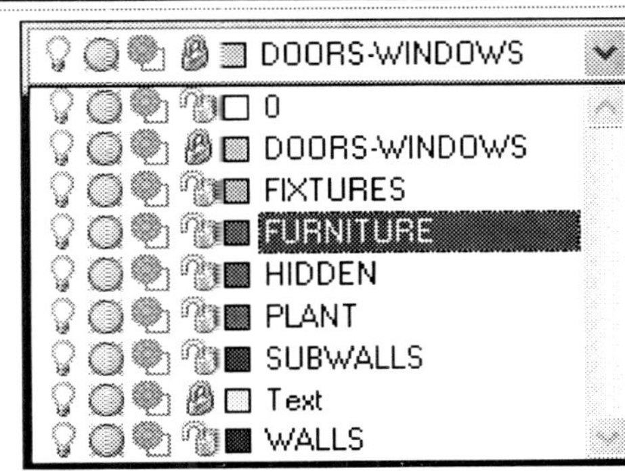


2. Now draw the two 2'-6" x 4' desks missing from the center cubicles. Use the grid and snap as needed. Notice that the desks assume the color and linetype associated with the **FURNITURE** layer. Your drawing looks like the figure below.

**Command: *rec***

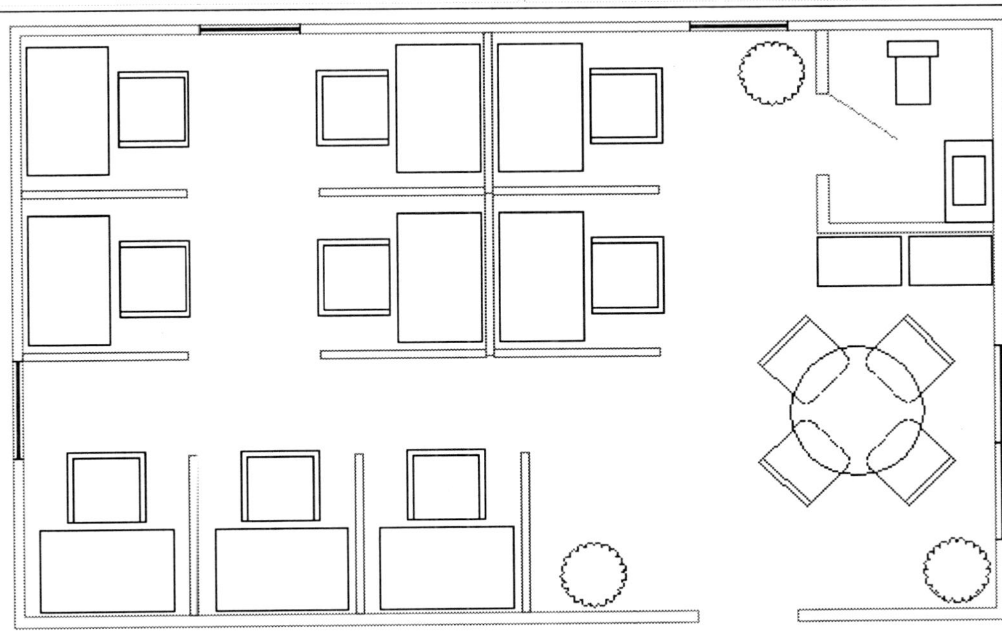

## 6.2.1: Using Layers

3. Set the **Text** layer current.

Using the default text size, add the text shown in the following figure.

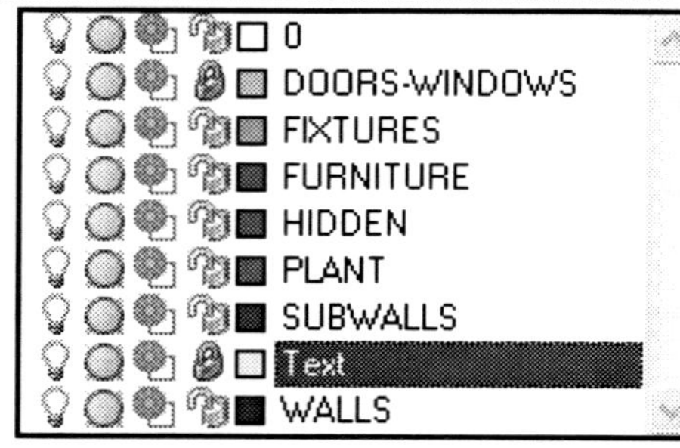


4. Save your drawing .

**Command:** ***qsave***

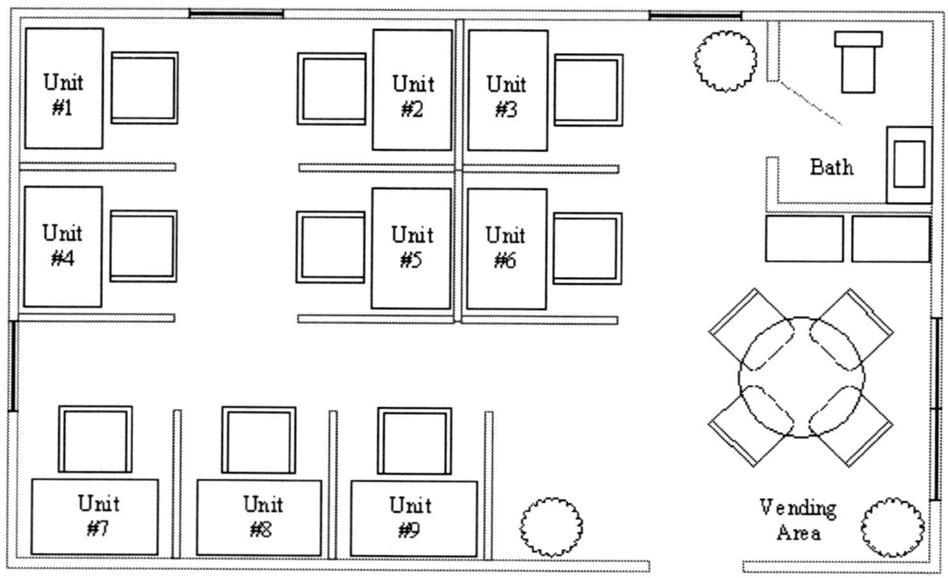


In the preceding exercise, you saw how to set a layer current. But that procedure required that you know which layer you wanted to be current. In some drawings, there may be dozens of layers from which to choose, and remembering the name of the one you want may be impossible. AutoCAD comes to the rescue again with a couple simple buttons.

When you pick the **Make Object's Layer Current** button , AutoCAD prompts:

**Command: _Laymcur**
**Select object whose layer will become current:** ***[select an object – a chair]***
**FURNITURE is now the current layer.**

Using this method, you can set a layer current by selecting something already on the desired layer – you don't even have to know which layer it is!

If you make a mistake, use the ***LayerP*** command to reset the previous layer current again.

Don't confuse the ***LayMCur*** command (**Lay**er **M**ake **Cur**rent) with the ***LayCur*** command (**Lay**er **Cur**rent). ***LayCur*** prompts:

**Command:** ***laycur***
**Select objects to be changed to the current layer:** ***[select an object]***
**Select objects to be changed to the current layer:** ***[enter to complete the selection set]***
**One object changed to layer FURNITURE (the current layer).**

Using ***LayCur***, you can change the layer of an object in the drawing to the current layer.

## 6.2.1 The Layer Properties Manager

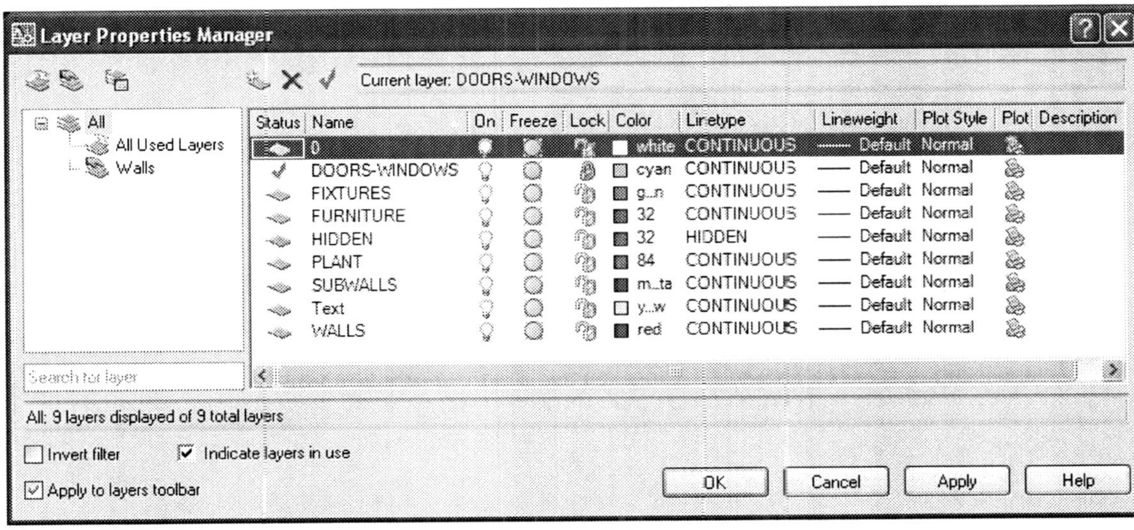


Figure 6.013

Now let's look at the Layer Properties Manager (Figure 6.013) in more detail. Open it by picking on the **Layer Properties Manager** button.

There's a lot of information here – so much, in fact, that AutoCAD had to separate it into tree view and list view areas.

- The list view area presents the layer names present in the selected group (selected in the tree view) and sorts the various properties of the layer into columns of information.

  Let's take a look at each column and its command line equivalent as well as buttons available on the Layer II toolbar.

| COL. | SYMBOL | COM. LINE | BUTTON | DESCRIPTION |
|---|---|---|---|---|
| **Status** |   | (None) | (None) | The **Status** column identifies the currently active layer with a check. |
| **Name** | (No Symbol) | (None) | (None) | The **Name** column is just what it implies – the name of the layer. |
| **On** |   | ***LayOn*** ***LayOff*** |  Layer Off Button | The **On** column shows a light bulb that's either lit (yellow) or not lit (gray). If lit, the layer is **On**; if not lit, the layer is **Off** and all objects on the layer will disappear from the screen but remain part of the drawing and be regenerated. The ***LayOn*** command turns on all layers; ***LayOff*** allows you to select an object on a layer to turn off. |

| Col. | Symbol | Com. Line | Button | Description |
|---|---|---|---|---|
| **Freeze** | Freeze | ***LayFrz*** ***LayThw*** | Layer Freeze Button | The **Freeze** column shows an image of the sun when **Thawed** or a snowflake when **Frozen**. When frozen, all objects on the layer will disappear from the screen but remain part of the drawing and *not* be regenerated. Most people prefer **Freeze** to **Off** as it speeds regeneration time. The ***LayThw*** command thaws all layers; ***LayFrz*** allows you to select an object on a layer to freeze. |
| **Lock** | Lock | ***LayLck*** ***LayUlk*** | Layer Lock Button<br>Layer Unlock Button | When a layer is **Locked**, you can't edit or erase any objects on that layer. This is a useful tool when working on a crowded drawing and selecting objects may be difficult, or when you just want to be sure that you don't accidentally move or delete something. The ***LayUlk*** command unlocks all layers; ***LayLck*** allows you to select an object on a layer to lock. |
| **Color** | Color<br>white | (None) | (None) | The **Color** column uses a box and a name or number to indicate the current color setting for that layer. |
| **Linetype** | Linetype<br>CONTINUOUS | (None) | (None) | The **Linetype** column lists the specific linetype assigned to that layer. |
| **Lineweight** | Lineweight<br>Default | (None) | (None) | The **Lineweight** column shows the specific lineweight assigned to the layer. |
| **Plot Style** | Plot Style<br>Normal | (None) | (None) | The **Plot Style** column shows how this layer will be plotted in the current plot style. (We'll discuss plotting in Lesson 21.) |
| **Plot** | Plot | (None) | (None) | The **Plot** column allows you to plot the layer or to remove all objects on the layer from the plot. (Note: This doesn't affect the layer's visibility.) |
| **Description** | No Symbol | (None) | (None) | The **Description** column provides a place for you to enter something a bit more descriptive than the name. This can come in handy for very busy drawings. |

You can select multiple layers for formatting at one time by holding down the CTRL or SHIFT key while making your selections.

At the top of the Layer Properties Manager list box, you'll find three buttons also associated with the list box. Look at the following chart for an explanation of their function.

| **BUTTON** | **DESCRIPTION** |
|---|---|
|  | The **New Layer** button enables you to create a new layer. When picked, this button creates a new layer in the list box where you can assign definitions to its properties. By default, a new layer will be white, unlocked, thawed, on, have the default lineweight and plot style, and have a continuous linetype.<br>You can, however, begin by selecting an existing layer before picking the **New Layer** button. This way, the property settings will default to the existing layer's settings (this can be a real timesaver). |
|  | Use the **Delete Layer** button to remove a layer. There can be no objects drawn on a layer to be removed. Additionally, you cannot remove layers **0**, **Defpoints**, or the current layer. Alternately, you can use the ***LayDel*** command to delete a layer along with all the objects that currently reside on it. (As with all deletion commands, use this one with caution!) |
|  | Use the **Set Current** button to set the currently selected layer current. The text box to the right of the **Set Current** button displays the current layer.<br>Of course, using the **Layer** control box on the Layers toolbar makes setting a layer current a lot faster and easier. This box works just as the **Color Control** and **Linetype Control** boxes did. |

You can use another button – **Apply** (just below and to the right of the list box) – to apply your changes without closing the Layer Properties Manager.

- The tree view area (Figure 6.014) lists all the groups of layers existing in the drawing. It also allows you to manipulate the groups by selecting options on a cursor menu. The default view will list **All** the layers in the drawing and divide that list into subgroups. When **All** is selected, all the layers in the drawing will appear in the list box. The only default subgroup is **All Used Layers**. When you select this, the list box will display only those layers, which have been used in the drawing. You can create additional subgroups of all or any existing subgroup by selecting the group and then picking the **New Group Filter** button above the tree view.

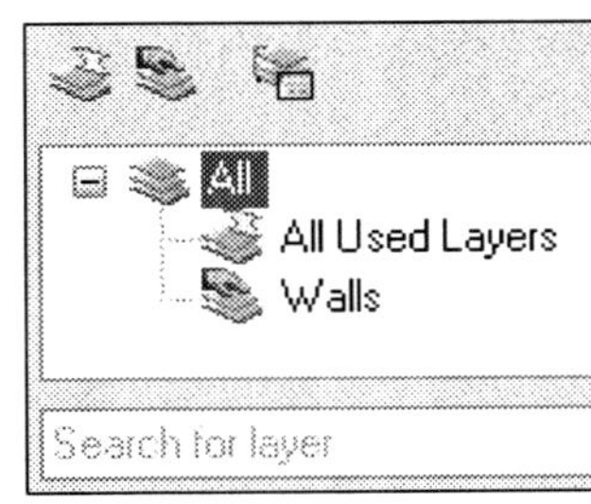

Figure 6.014

Let's take a look at the rest of the buttons above the tree view.

| **BUTTON** | **DESCRIPTION** |
|---|---|
|  | The **New Property Filter** button displays the Layer Filter Properties dialog box (Figure 6.015) that enables you to create a new layer filter based on the properties of the layers. Name the new filter in the **Filter name** text box at top. The **Filter definition** box provides a series of lookup columns (columns that list available data in a drop down box). All you have to do is select or name the filtered value for each property. The list of layers that meet the filter will appear in the **Filter preview** list below. |

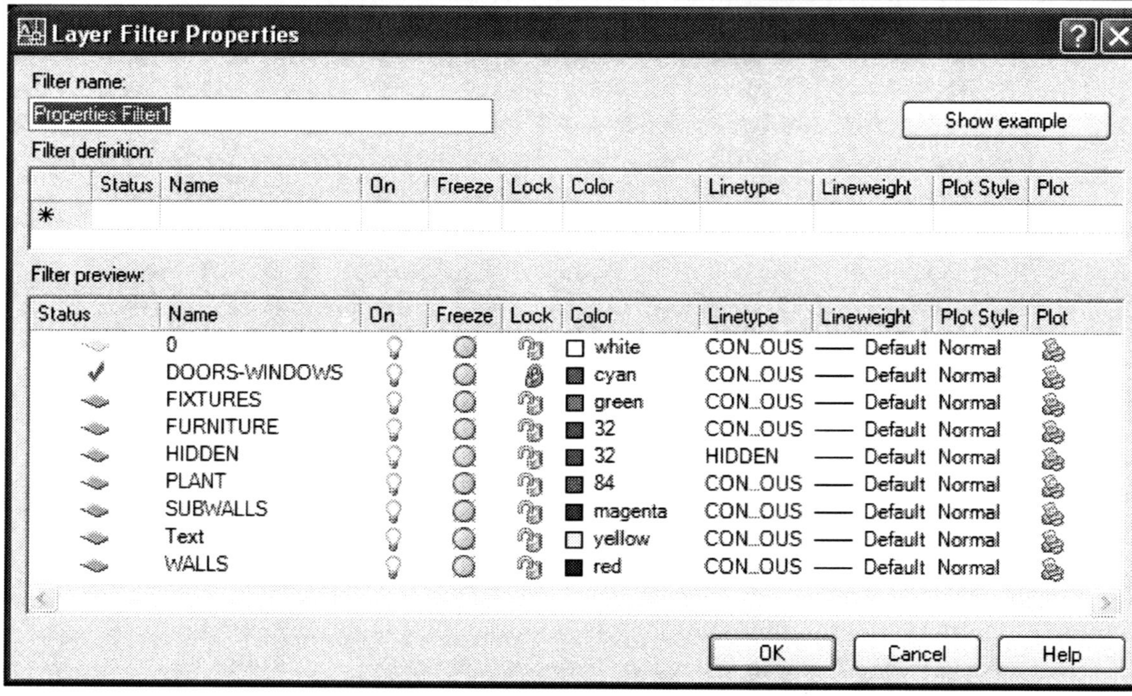


Figure 6.015

| BUTTON | DESCRIPTION |
|---|---|
|  | The **New Group** button creates a new group or subgroup in the tree view. You can manually put layers into this group using the cursor menu. |
|  | The **Layer States Manager** button calls the Layer States Manager (Figure 6.016). This handy tool lets you save the current states of layers so that you can recall them later. Creating a new layer state saves the current layer settings in a file (with a .dws extension) for later retrieval. You can even share Layer states (import/export) between drawings. When you decide to restore the settings, you can use the check boxes in the **Layer settings to restore** frame to tell AutoCAD which properties to restore (or not restore). This tool can save a tremendous amount of time in viewing certain aspects of your drawing. |

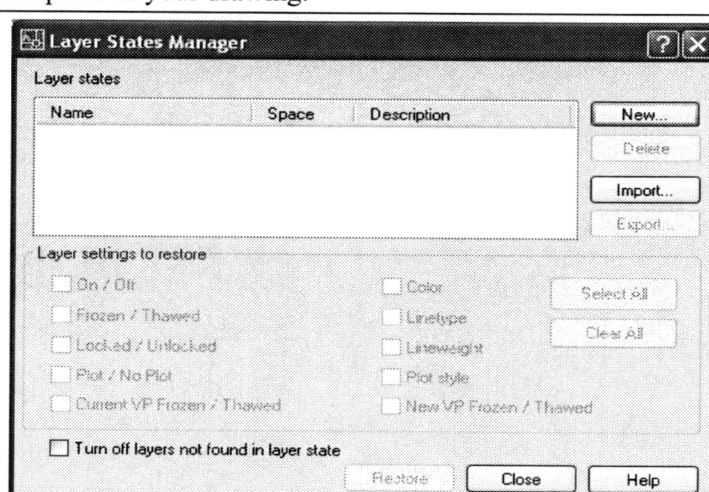


Figure 6.016

Within the tree view, AutoCAD provides a cursor menu (Figure 6.017) to manipulate all the layers within a group simultaneously. Your options include:

- **Visibility** allows you to turn a filtered group of layers on or off, or freeze/thaw the group.
- **Lock**, of course, allows you to lock all the layers in a selected group.
- It's best to leaver our discussion of viewports to Lesson 22. This will cover both the **Viewport** and **Isolate Group** options.
- The **New Properties Filter ...** and **New Group Filter** options do the same thing as picking the associated button above the tree view.

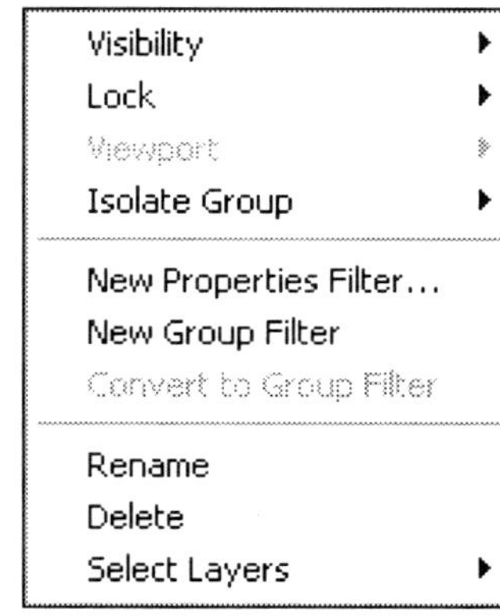

Figure 6.017

- **Convert to Group Filter** changes a selected property filter to a group filter.
- **Rename** and **Delete** do just what their names imply.
- You'll use the **Select Layers** option to manually **Add** layers to (or **Replace** all the layers in) a selected group.

At the bottom of the tree view (Figure 6.028), you'll see a small text box containing the words *Search for layer*. You can pick in this box and enter the name of a layer, which you'd like AutoCAD to display in the Layer Properties Manager. This can make working with a specific layer in a busy drawing much easier.

Let's explore some of these tools.

| Do This: 6.2.1.1 | Using the Layer Properties Manager |
|---|---|

I. Be sure you're in the *flrpln.dwg* file in the C:\Steps\Lesson06 folder. If not, please open it now.

II. Follow these steps.

**6.2.1.1: Using the Layer Properties Manager**

1. First, we'll add a new layer.

Open the Layer Properties Manager by typing ***la*** or picking the ***Layer Properties Manager*** button. The dialog box looks like Figure 6.013.

**Command:** ***la***

2. Select the **0** layer to use default settings.

3. Pick the **New Layer** button. Notice that AutoCAD creates a new layer. (If only they were all that easy!) You can give your new layer a name and set the parameters for linetype, color, etc. at this time.

4. That was too easy, let's add a layer to a group.

Notice that a subgroup for the wall layers already exists in the tree view. Pick on it now. You'll see AutoCAD list (in the list view) only those layers already associated with that group.

Right-click on **Walls** in the tree view.

5. AutoCAD presents a cursor menu (shown). Pick the **Select Layers** option, and then select **Add**.

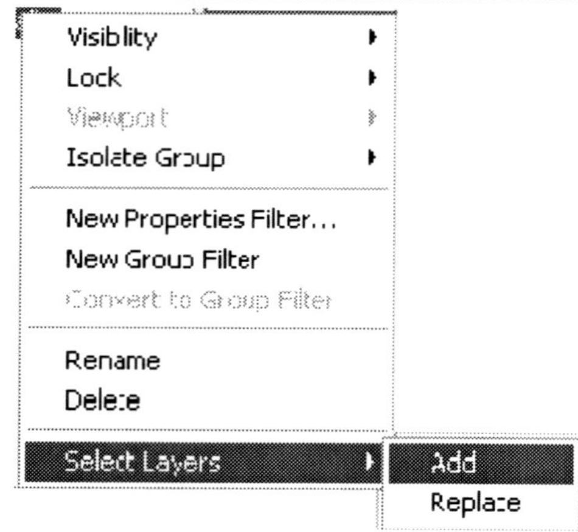


6. AutoCAD returns to the graphics screen and asks you to select an object on the layer you wish to add. Select one of the windows and hit ***enter*** to return to the Layer Properties Manager.

**Select objects:**

Notice below that AutoCAD now includes the **Doors-Windows** layer in the Walls group.

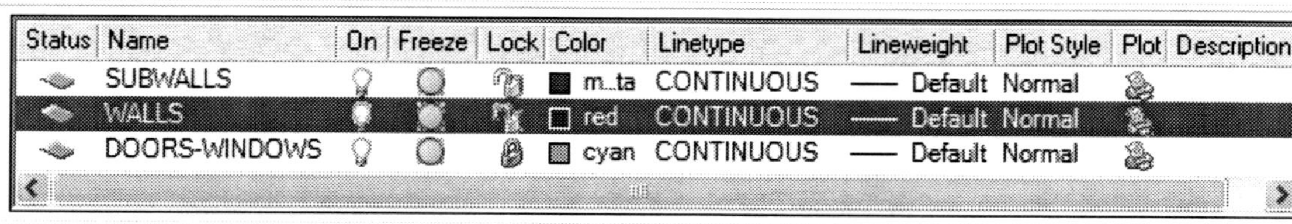


7. Pick the **Apply** button 

to complete the procedure without leaving the Layer Properties Manager.

8. Now let's freeze all the layers associated with the walls in our drawing. Right-click again on the **Walls** group. This time, select **Visibility** and then **Frozen** from the flyout menu.

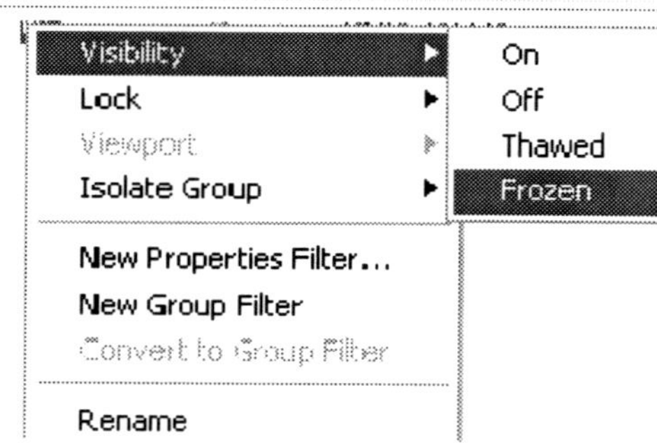


9. This time, pick the **OK** button 

to complete the procedure and close the dialog box. Notice in the following image that all of the walls, subwalls, doors and windows disappear.

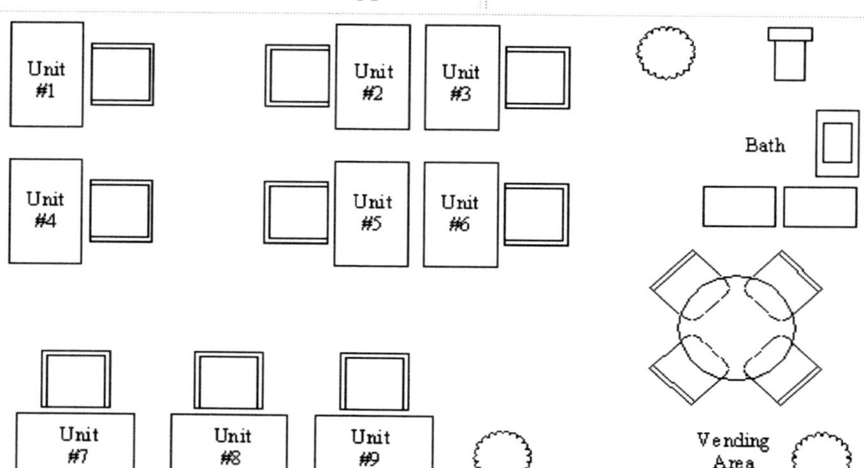

## 6.2.1.1: Using the Layer Properties Manager

10. Reopen the Layer Properties Manager and repeat Step 8, this time selecting **Thawed** from the flyout menu.

11. Pick the **Apply** button to complete the procedure without leaving the Layer Properties Manager.

12. Now let's create a group of our own. Select **All** in the list box to make all the layers available for our group.

13. Pick the **New Group Filter** button above the tree view box.

14. AutoCAD creates a new group (it's just that simple!) and gives you the opportunity to rename it. We'll call this one *Furnishings*.

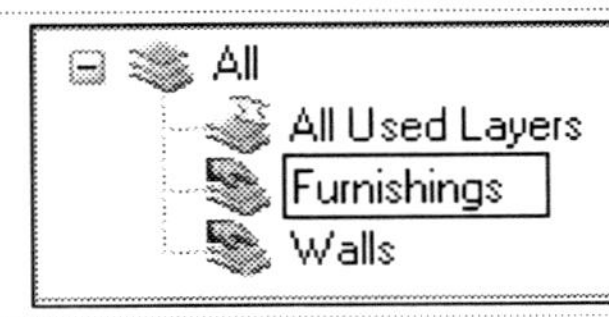


15. We'll use an easier method to add layers to our new group. Pick **All** to show all the layers.

16. Now drag-n-drop these layers atop your new group: **Fixtures**, **Furniture**, **Plant**, and **Text**.

17. Pick the **Furnishings** group to be sure your procedure worked (see below).

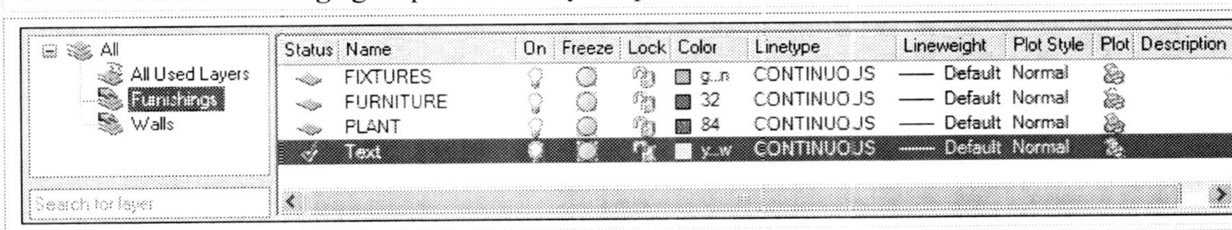


18. Reselect **All** (to be sure that AutoCAD lists all the layers in the **Layer** control box), and then pick the **OK** button to close the Layer Properties Dialog box.

19. Save the drawing but don't exit.

**Command: *qsave***

You'll notice three check boxes resting unobtrusively at the bottom left corner of the Layer Properties Manager. These quiet options can be quite powerful.

- Placing a check next to **Invert filter** causes AutoCAD to fill the list box with all the layers that do *not* meet the filter criteria for the selected group. This effectively doubles the number of groups by providing both inclusive and exclusive lists. (Pretty cool, huh?)
- A check next to **Apply to layers toolbar** (the default) means that AutoCAD will use the filters used by the currently selected group to populate the **Layer** control box. (Okay, put more simply, only the layers in the currently select group will show up in the **Layer** control box.)
- Finally, a check next to **Indicate layers in use** tells AutoCAD to change the symbol in the **Status** column for unused layers. This makes it pretty easy to purge your drawing of unwanted layers when you've finished it.

## 6.2.2 Some Other Layer Commands

With the 2007 release of AutoCAD, some additional layer tools have graduated from the list of "Express Tools" to full-fledged members of the command community. I think you'll be glad they did!

- With ***LayIso***, AutoCAD prompts:

  **Select objects on the layer(s) to be isolated or [Settings]:** ***[select an object on the layer on which you wish to work]***

  **Select objects on the layer(s) to be isolated or [Settings]:** ***[enter to confirm the selection]***

  **Layer FURNITURE has been isolated.**

  This handy tool clears a drawing of all the nuisance material by turning off all but the selected layer(s). Turn them back on with the ***LayerP*** command.

- ***LayMch*** allows you to change the layer of a selected object to a target layer of your choice. You don't need to know the name of either layer. You'll find this handy for quick fixes when you draw something on the wrong layer, too! (Of course, that'll never happen to you!)

  The prompt is

  **Select objects to be changed:** ***[select the object whose layer you wish to change]***

  **Select objects:** ***[enter to confirm the selection]***

  **Select object on destination layer or [Name]:** ***[select an object on the target layer – alternately, you can hit enter and provide the name of the target layer; but that's work]***

  **One object changed to layer "SUBWALLS"**

- Be careful when you use ***LayMrg***; it takes all the objects on a selected layer, moves them to another layer, and deletes the layer they were originally on. (Or more simply, it merges the objects on two layers and deletes one of them.)

  It works like this:

  **Select object on layer to merge or [Name]:** ***[select an object on (or provide the name of) the layer you wish to merge with another layer; you layer you select here will be deleted]***

  **Selected layers: FURNITURE.**

  **Select object on layer to merge or [Name/Undo]:** ***[enter to confirm the selection]***

  **Select object on target layer or [Name]:** ***[now select an object on (or provide the name of) the layer you wish on which you wish to place all the objects currently residing on the first layer]***

  ********** WARNING **********

  **You are about to merge layer "FURNITURE" into layer "SUBWALLS".**

  **Do you wish to continue? [Yes/No] <No>:** ***[one last chance to change your mind]***

  If you use the **Name** option at either of the prompts, AutoCAD will present a dialog box from which you can select the name of the layers you wish to merge.

- Finally, a really cool tool – ***LayWalk*** – presents a dialog box that allows you to select the layer you want to see. AutoCAD will turn off all but the selected layers allowing you to "walk" through the drawing, one layer at a time. We'll see this one in our next exercise.

I suppose we'd better try an exercise with these new tools.

| Do This: 6.2.2.1 | Newly Graduated Commands |
|---|---|

I. Open the *flrpln622.dwg* file in the C:\Steps\Lesson06 folder. The drawing is a pristine copy of the *flrpln* drawing with which you've been working.

II. Open the Layers II toolbar. (Right-click on any existing toolbar and select **Layers II** from the menu.) Position it someplace convenient on your screen.

III. Follow these steps.

## 6.2.2.1: Newly Graduated Commands

1. We'll start with the easy one, enter ***LayWalk*** at the command prompt. Alternately, you can select the **Layer Walk** button on the Layer II toolbar.

AutoCAD presents the Layer Walk dialog box (Figure 6.035).

**Command:** ***laywalk***

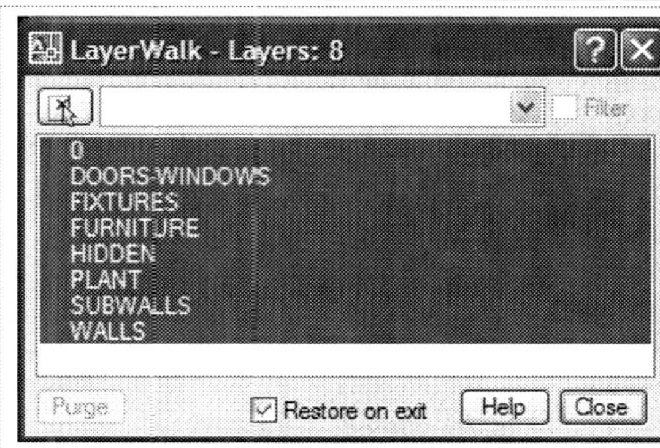


2. Select each of the layers listed in the dialog box and watch the drawing area. AutoCAD turns off all layers except the one selected.

3. Reselect the entire list (select the top of the list, then hold down the SHIFT key while selecting the bottom). Now pick the **Select Objects** button in the upper left corner of the dialog box.

AutoCAD returns to the screen and prompts you to select objects.

4. Select an object on the screen.

AutoCAD returns to the dialog box, highlights the layer on which the object resides, and turns the rest of the layers off.

**Select objects:**

**Select objects:** ***[enter]***

5. Close the dialog box Close.

6. Enter the ***LayIso*** command. Alternately, you can pick the **Layer Isolate** button on the Layer II toolbar.

**Command:** ***layiso***

7. Select an object on the layer you'd like to isolate. Notice that AutoCAD turns off all other layers to make viewing of the selected layer easier.

**Select objects on the layer(s) to be isolated or [Settings]:**

**Select objects on the layer(s) to be isolated or [Settings]:** ***[enter]***

8. Use the ***LayerP*** command to restore the layers.

**Command:** ***layerp***

### 6.2.2.1: Newly Graduated Commands

9. Now let's match a layer. Enter the ***LayMch*** command. Alternately, you can pick the **Layer Match** button on the Layers II toolbar.

**Command:** ***laymch***

10. Select the object you'd like to change – I'll select one of the desks.

**Select objects to be changed:**

**Select objects:** ***[select an object]***

**Select objects:** ***[enter to confirm]***

11. Now select an object on the layer you'd like the previously select object (the desk) to reside on. AutoCAD changes the layer of the first selected object to the layer of the second selected object.

**Select object on destination layer or [Name]:** ***[select an object on the target layer]***

**One object changed to layer "SUBWALLS"**

12. Finally, we'll see what happens when we merge a couple layers. Enter the ***LayMrg*** command. There's no button for this command.

**Command:** ***laymrg***

13. AutoCAD asks you to select an object on the layer you wish to merge to another layer. (This layer will be deleted.) Select a desk.

**Select object on layer to merge or [Name]:**

**Selected layers: FURNITURE**

**Select object on layer to merge or [Name/Undo]:** ***[enter]***

14. Now AutoCAD wants to know onto which layer you'd like to merge the objects on the selected layer. This time, let's use the dialog box. Select the **Name** option by entering *N* or selecting it from the menu.

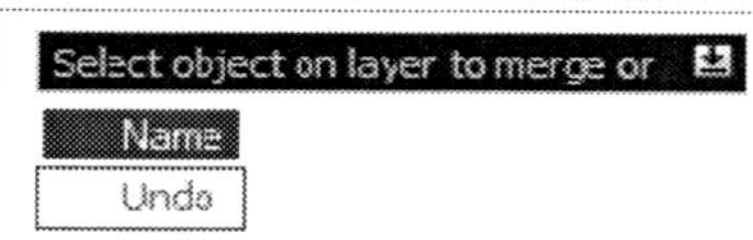


**Select object on target layer or [Name]:** ***N***

15. AutoCAD presents the Merge to Layer dialog box. Select the **SUBWALLS** layer.

Pick the **OK** button to close the dialog box.

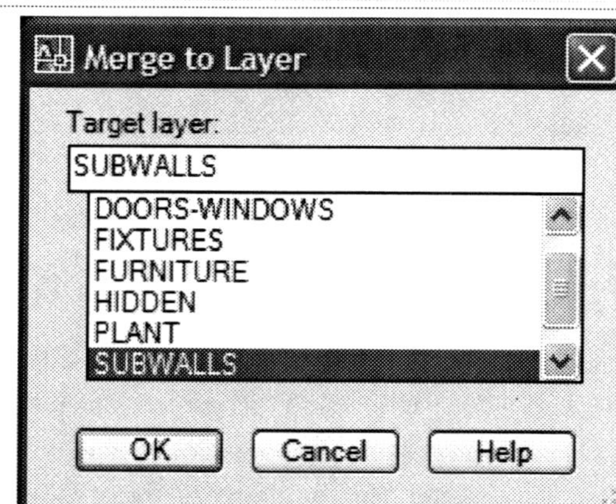

| 6.2.2.1: Newly Graduated Commands | |
|---|---|
| 16. One last chance to change your mind – pick **Yes**. AutoCAD takes all the objects on the **FURNITURE** layer and puts them on the **SUBWALLS** layer. | 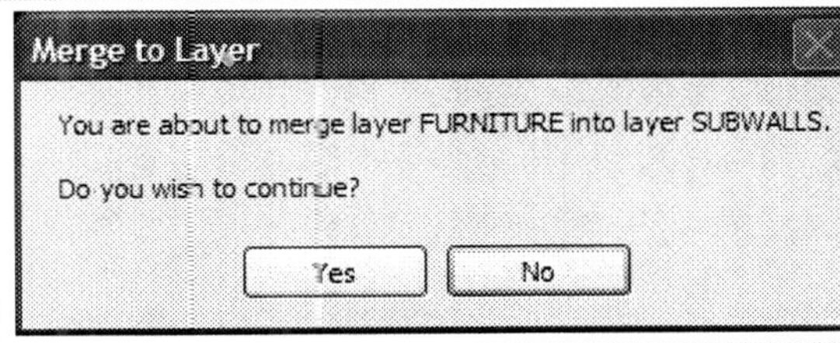  |
| 17. Check the **Layers** control box; notice that the **FURNITURE** layer has been removed. | 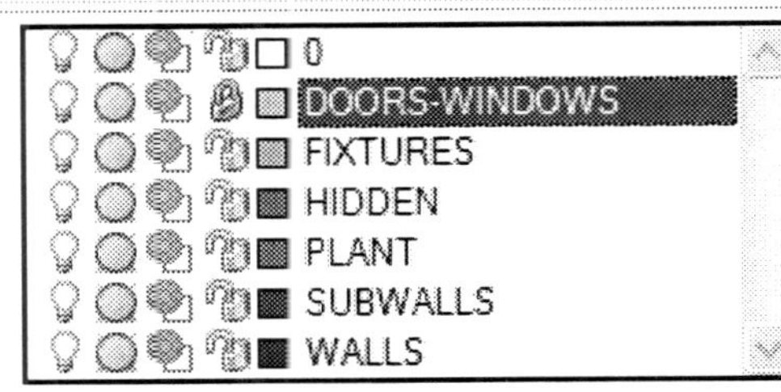  |
| 18. Close the drawing without saving. **Command:** ***close*** | |

You'll be surprised how useful these tools will be!

## 6.3 Sharing Setups: The AutoCAD Design Center and the Layer Translator

You've already seen one way to share drawing information between drawings – templates. These work well; however, AutoCAD provides two considerably more powerful tools – the AutoCAD Design Center (Figure 6.018) and (for layers only) the Layer Translator (more on the Layer Translator in a few minutes). The first – the AutoCAD Design Center (ADC) – allows you to *mine* another drawing for useful stuff – layers, blocks, text styles, dimension styles, etc. That is, you can dig into another drawing and find and retrieve the pieces you want. But unlike gold mines, the mined drawing remains unaffected by the task.

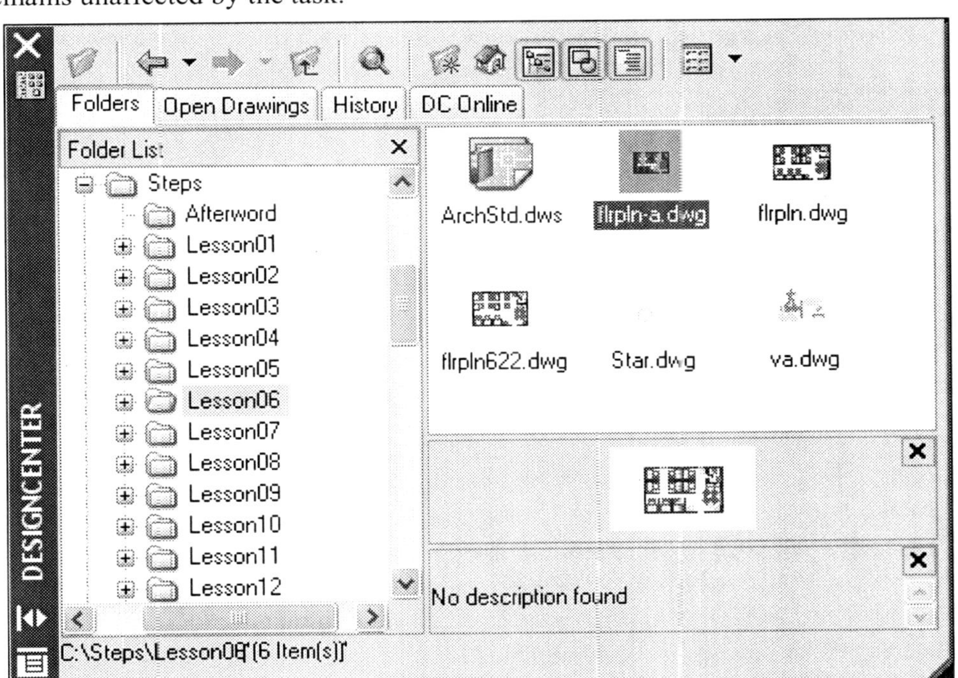


Figure 6.018

Access the ADC from the command line by entering ***ADCenter*** (or ***ADC***). AutoCAD presents the ADC floating over the screen. You can dock or undock it as you would the Tool Palettes window (Lesson 1).

Let's take a look at the ADC.

- The title bar on the left should be familiar to you after your study of the Tool Palettes window. Its function is exactly the same.
- A toolbar resides along the top of the ADC. The function of each tool follows:

| TOOL | DESCRIPTION |
|---|---|
|  | **Load** provides a standard File … Open window. With that, you can navigate to the desired folder and open the palette for the desired drawing. The palette, in this case, is simply a list of things available to you – layers, blocks, text styles, etc.) |
|  | The **Back** button returns you to the previous folder. The down arrow next to the **Back** button allows you to select from all the folders you have previously visited. |
|  | The **Next** button works conversely to the **Back** button. That is, once you have returned to a previous folder, the **Next** button allows you to navigate back to the folder you occupied prior to using the **Back** button. |
|  | **Up** is another navigation button. It changes the display to a step back (up) along the path. |
|  | **Search** presents a dialog box similar to the Windows **Find** program. Using this, you can search for drawings by date modified or included text. |
|  | **Favorites** opens the **Favorites** folder. |
|  | **Home**, of course, returns you to a pre-designated folder. By default, this is the C:\Program Files\AutoCAD\Sample\DesignCenter folder. (To reset the home location, navigate to the desired folder, right-click on it, and select **Set as Home** from the menu.) |
|  | This is a toggle button for the **Tree** view (the view seen in Figure 6.018). When depressed, your Design Center shows the folders list in a frame to the left of the window. When raised, the folders list disappears. |
|  | The **Preview** button toggles on or off the drawing preview display just below the content area to the right of the folders list. |
|  | The **Description** button toggles on or off the drawing description display just below the preview display. |
| 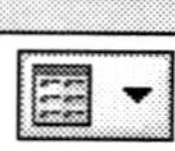 | The **Views** button works just like the **Views** button in Windows – it allows you to determine how you will see items in a folder (large icons, small icons, listed, or with details). |

- Four tabs appear below the toolbar: **Folders**, **Open Drawings**, **History**, and **DC Online**.
    - On the **Folders** tab (Figure 6.018), you see the **Tree** view. That is, like Windows Explorer, you see the path to a folder on the left (here you see C:\Steps\Lesson06). The right shows the contents of the folder, a preview frame, and a description frame. You can navigate the tree view much as you do Windows Explorer.

      Below the left frame, you see the path that's being shown and the number of items in the current folder.
    - The **Open Drawings** folder shows only those drawings that are currently open.

- The **History** folder shows the last few drawings that have been opened.
- **DC Online** takes you to the Design Center Online web site where you have access to blocks, block libraries, catalogs, and even some manufacturer's content (you'll need Internet access for this one to work).

> A useful trick to know is that, once you've navigated to a folder, you can add that folder to your **Favorites** list by selecting **Add to Favorites** on the right-click cursor menu.

Let's see just how useful the ADC can be. We'll use it to copy the layers from our *flrpln* drawing file to a new file.

| Do This: 6.3.1 | Using the AutoCAD Design Center |
|---|---|

I. Start a new drawing from scratch.

II. Follow these steps.

**6.3.1: USING THE AUTOCAD DESIGN CENTER**

1. Open the AutoCAD Design Center by entering ***ADCenter*** or ***ADC***. Alternately, you can pick the **DesignCenter** button  on the Standard toolbar.

   **Command: *adc***

2. Navigate to the C:\Steps\Lesson06 folder just as you would using Windows Explorer, and pick on the plus sign next to the *flrpln* drawing.
Pick on **Layers** as indicated in the following figure.
Notice the palette shown in the right window. Since **Layers** has been selected in the left window, the palette shows the layers in the *flrpln* drawing.

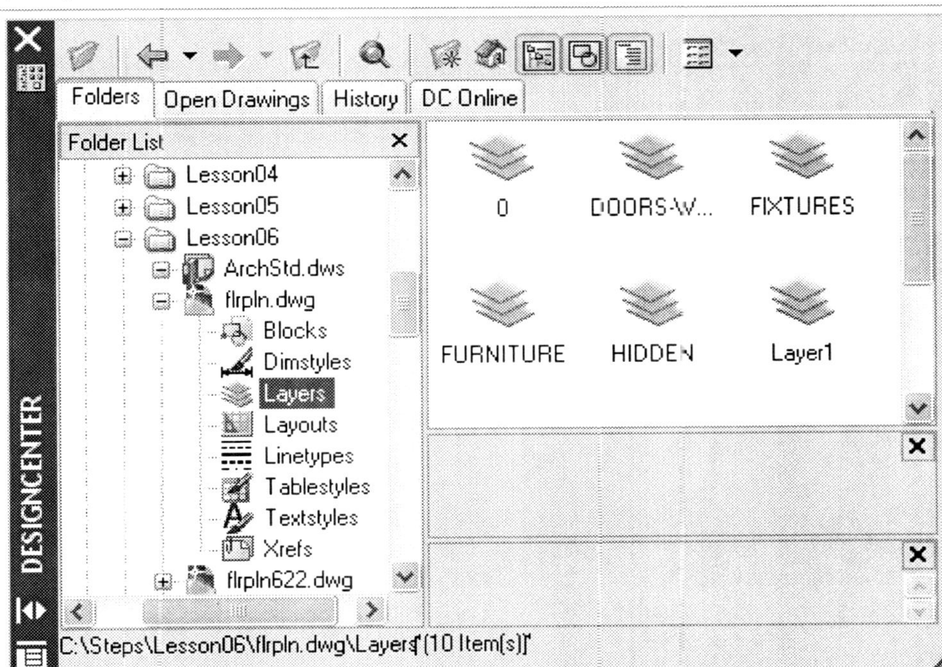

## 6.3.1: Using the AutoCAD Design Center

3. We want all the layers except **Hidden** and **0**. Holding down the CTRL key (to allow multiple selections), select the desired layers as indicated.

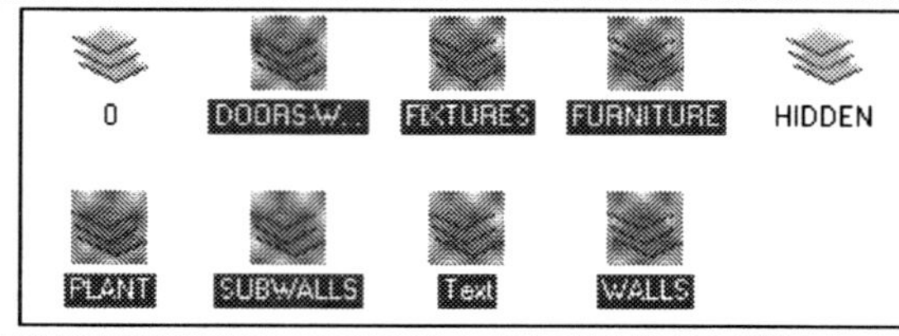


4. We'll use the drag-n-drop method. Click and hold down the left mouse button anywhere in the highlighted area. Drag the selection set into the drawing area, and then release the mouse button.

5. Check the **Layer** control box to be sure the layers have been copied to the current drawing.

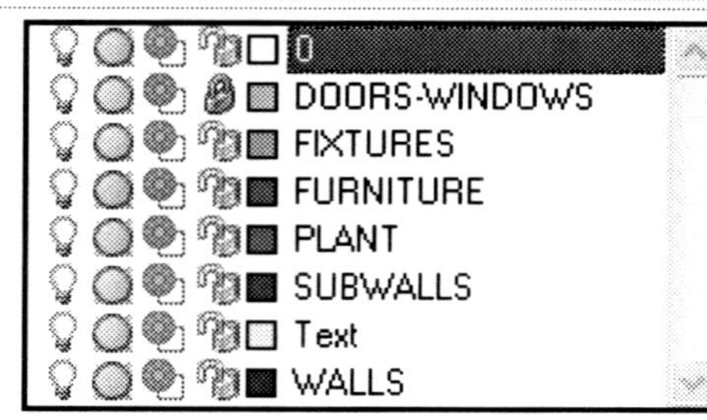


6. Close the ADC by picking on the **X** in the upper corner of the titlebar.

The ADC can be used as easily to copy blocks, dimstyles, text styles, or line types.

---

The second tool AutoCAD provides for sharing layer setups allows you to translate an existing layer or group of layers to meet a set standard. AutoCAD calls this tool the Layer Translator. The standard can be taken from an existing drawing or from a standard drawing (a drawing with a .dws extension) created to help maintain consistency throughout a project.

Let's see how the Layer Translator works.

| **Do This: 6.3.2** | **The Layer Translator** |
|---|---|

I. Begin in the *flrpln* drawing in the C:\Steps\Lesson06 folder. (Close any other drawings.)

II. Follow these steps.

## 6.3.2: The Layer Translator

1. Enter the ***LayTrans*** command.

**Command:** ***laytrans***

AutoCAD presents the Layer Translator dialog box (see the following figure). Notice that AutoCAD lists the layers in the current drawing in the **Translate From** frame.

## 6.3.2: THE LAYER TRANSLATOR

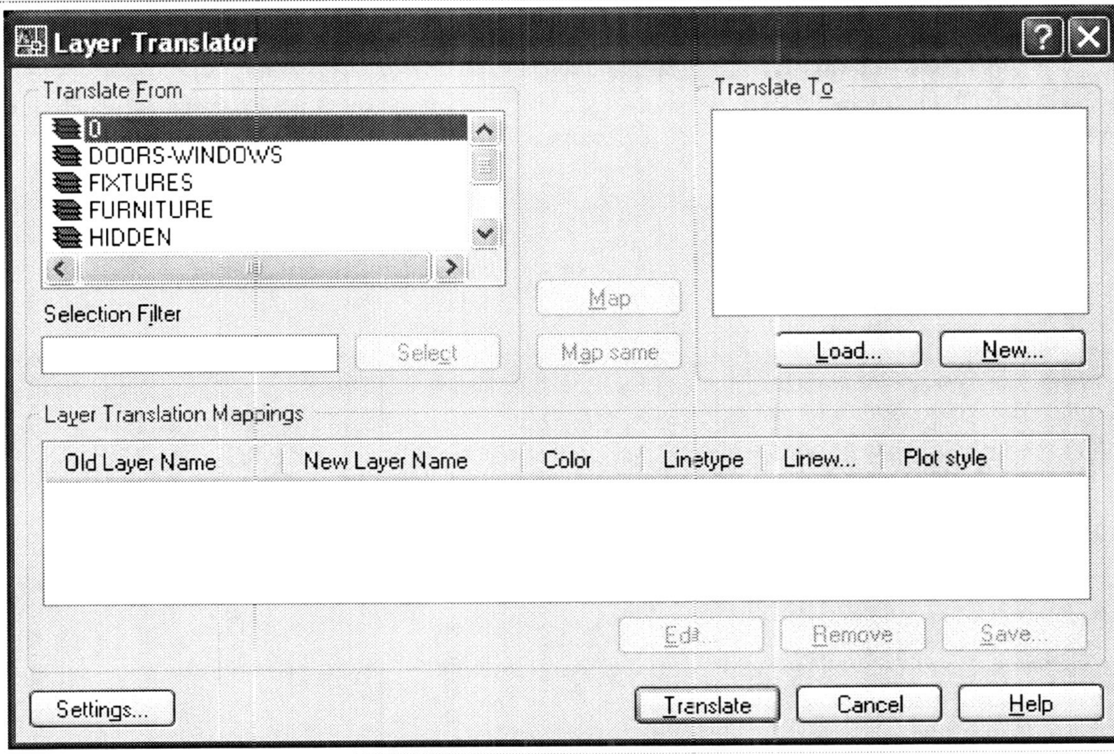


2. First, we must load a *Standards* drawing. Pick the **Load** button 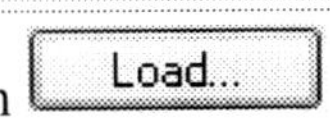 (below the **Translate To** frame).

3. AutoCAD presents a typical Select … Files dialog box. First, tell the box to look for *.dws* files as indicated.

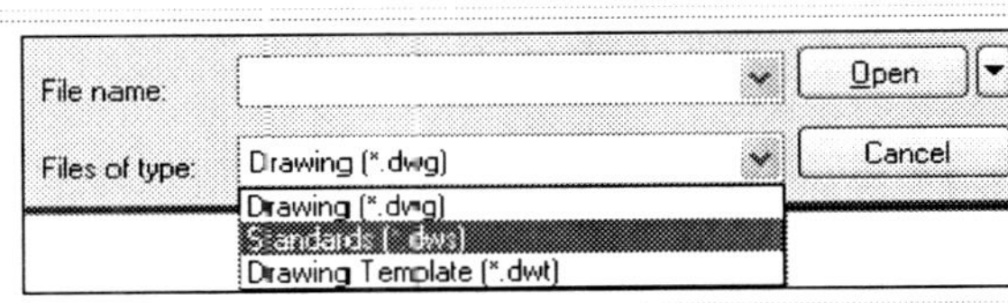


4. Now select the *ArchStd.dws* file in the C:\Steps\Lesson06 folder and pick the **Open** button 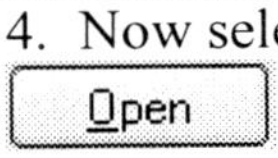. Notice now that AutoCAD provides another list of layers – this one in the **Translate To** frame (below). These are our standard layers – the ones we wish to use in our current drawing.

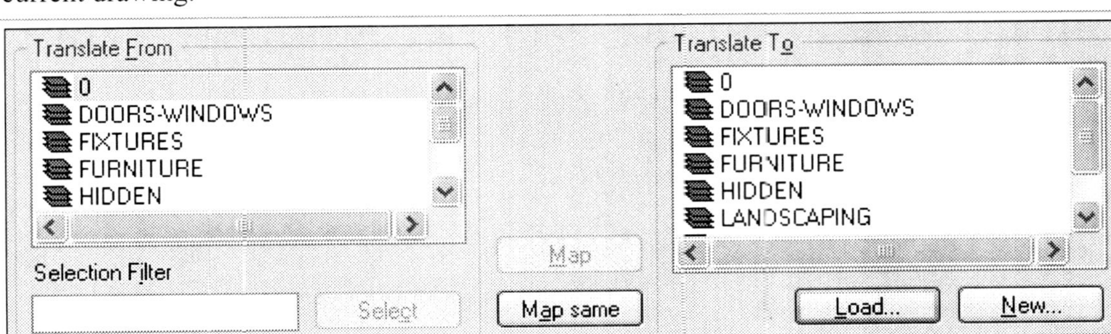


5. When we opened a standards file, AutoCAD activated the **Map same** button (between the frames). This provides a fast and easy way to tell AutoCAD to accept layers in our current

drawing that are already standardized (already match the layers in the standards file).

Pick the **Map same** button now. Notice that AutoCAD details the mapped layers in the **Layer Translation Mappings** frame (below). Notice also that the **PLANT** layer did not translate (it remains in the **Translate From** frame). The **PLANT** layer isn't a part of the standard setup.

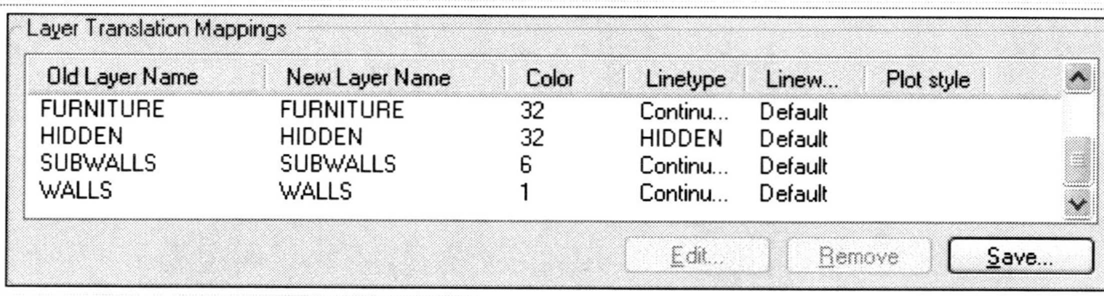


6. Let's translate the **Plant** layer to the standard **Landscaping** layer. Select **PLANT** in the **Translate From** frame. Select **LANDSCAPING** in the **Translate To** frame as shown below.

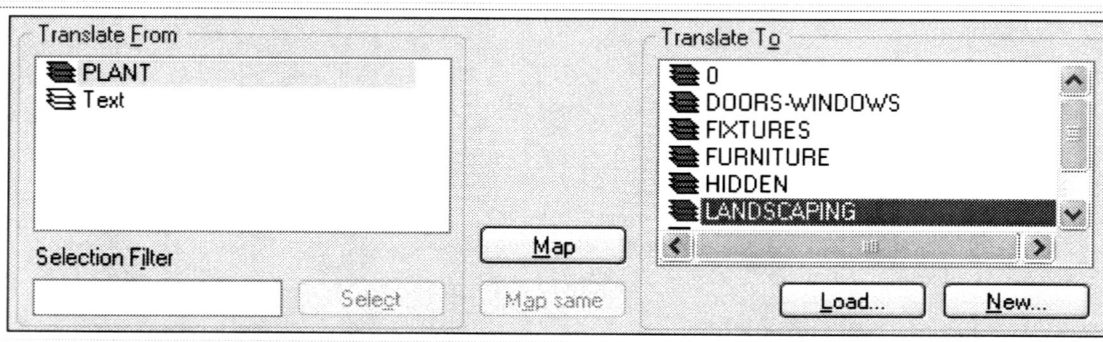


7. Pick the **Map** button to translate objects on the **PLANT** layer to objects on the **LANDSCAPING** layer.

8. Ignore the **Text** layer in the **Translate From** frame – it doesn't need to be translated. Pick the **Translate** button to complete the procedure. AutoCAD will prompt you with a message that you haven't saved your settings and allow you to do so if you wish. Pick **No** for now.

AutoCAD has translated the layer settings in the *flrpln* drawing file to match those in the project drawing standards file. How simple!

Some additional things to know about the layer translator include:

- You can create a new layer as a target (**Translate To**) layer by picking the **New** button at the bottom of the **Translate To** frame. AutoCAD provides a simple dialog box (Figure 6.019) to help you set up the new layer.
- Use the **Edit** button below the **Layer Translation Mappings** frame to change the settings (color, linetype, plotstyle) on a specific translation layer. Changes here won't affect the settings in the Standards file.
- The **Remove** button (next to the **Edit** button) will remove a mapped layer translation. The layer that had been mapped will return to the **Translate From** frame for remapping.
- The **Save** button allows you to save the current mappings for later use.

- The **Settings** button in the lower left corner of the Layer Translator calls the Settings dialog box (Figure 6.020). Here you can control exactly what happens during a layer translation.

We've learned a lot about layers; now let's see how we deal with a mistake when we use them!

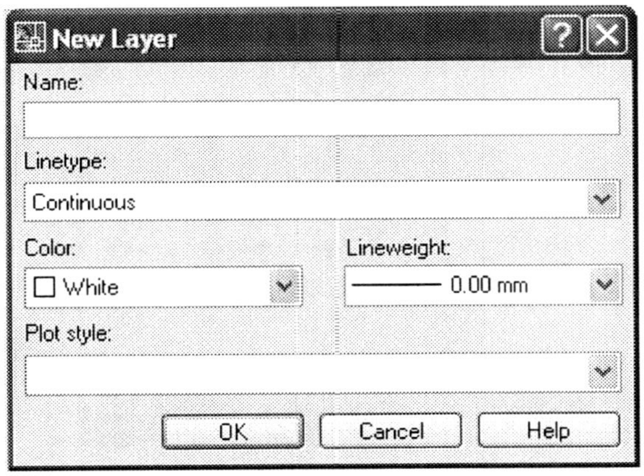

Figure 6.019

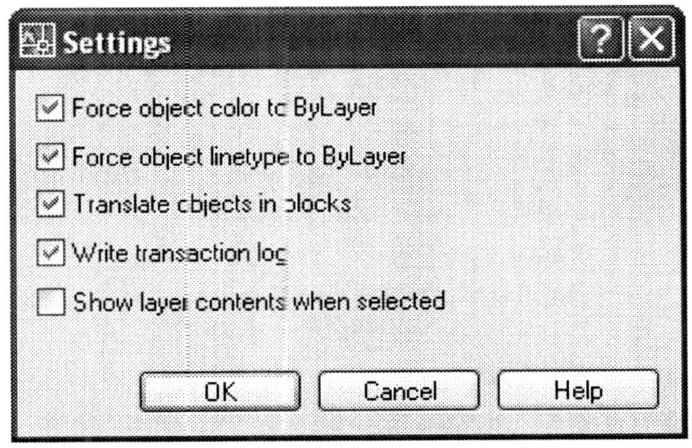

Figure 6.020

## 6.4 Un-Ohs, Boo Boos, Ah $%&#s: The Properties Palette

You'll soon discover that perhaps the easiest mistake to make in AutoCAD is drawing an object on the wrong layer. You get into a flow with your drawing and simply forget or overlook the necessity of changing layers. The same will hold true if you're using the ***Color/Linetype*** method in your drawing. A good drawing flow simply doesn't allow time for changing these things on the fly.

Fortunately, AutoCAD has a simple and wonderful tool to fix oversights. Behold the Properties Palette!

The Properties Palette takes advantage of a programming interface to provide an on-screen, editable listing of properties associated with drawing objects. For those of you who are newly computer literate, this simply means that it's really easy to change things like layers, color, linetypes, and lineweights.

The Properties Palette appears to hover above the screen, just as the ADC did. It begins looking like Figure 6.021, but the properties listed change according to the selected object.

Let's take a look.

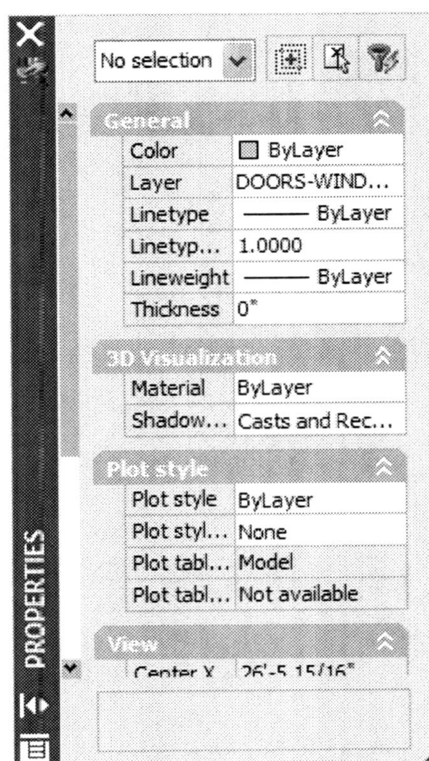

Figure 6.021

- Notice the control box at the top of the window. Use this box to select the type of objects in the drawing to edit. Alternately, you can select an object in the drawing and that object will show in the control box.
- The **PickAdd** button next to the control box toggles the **PickAdd** system variable. This determines whether or not AutoCAD will add a selection to an existing selection set (a setting of **1**) or replace the existing selection set with the new selection (**0**).
- The **Select Objects** button (to the immediate right of the **PickAdd** button) presents a **Select objects** prompt on the command line. You can use this to select specific objects whose properties will appear

on the Properties Palette. (You can also select the objects without using the **Select Objects** button. The results will be the same.) Note that, if you select two different types of objects, only those properties common to both will appear in the Properties Palette.

- The **Quick Select** button next to the **Select Objects** button allows you to filter the drawing for objects to edit.

Don't you want to see the Properties Palette in action?

| Do This: 6.4.1 | Using the Properties Palette |
| --- | --- |

I. Open the *flrpln-a.dwg* file in the C:\Steps\Lesson06 folder. The dashed lines under the table have been drawn on the **FURNITURE** layer with a hidden linetype. Let's change them to the **HIDDEN** layer.

II. Follow these steps.

### 6.4.1: Using the Properties Palette

1. Open the Properties Palette by entering ***Properties*** or ***props***. Alternately, you can pick the **Properties** button on the Standard toolbar.

   **Command: *props***

2. Pick the **Quick Select** button. AutoCAD presents the Quick Select dialog box (right).

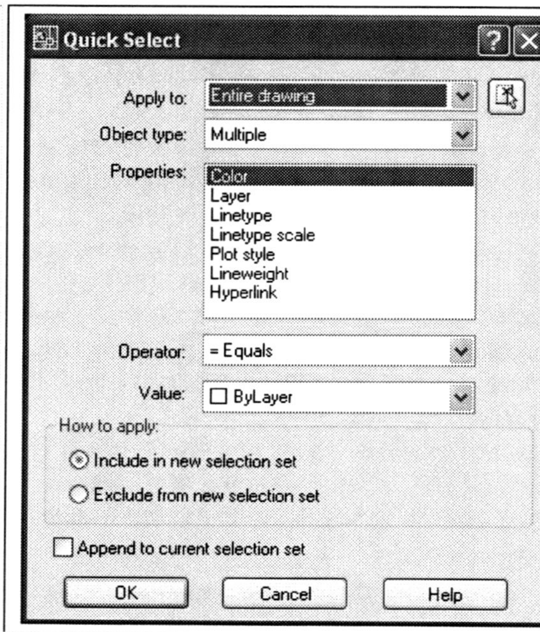

## 6.4.1: Using the Properties Palette

3. Pick the **Select objects** button. AutoCAD returns to the graphics screen and prompts you to select some objects. Select the area around the table as here.

Hit ***enter*** to complete the select set.

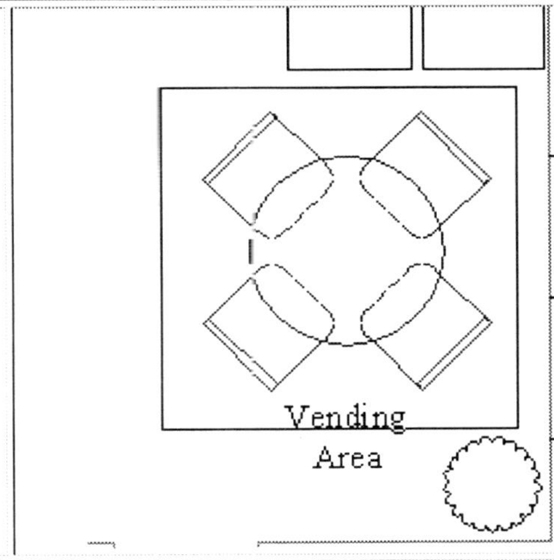


4. (Note: we'll filter multiple objects for those objects drawn with the **Hidden** linetype.)

Pick **Linetype** in the **Properties** list box, and then pick the down arrow in the **Value** control box and select **HIDDEN**, as shown.

5. Pick the **OK** button to exit the Quick Select dialog box.

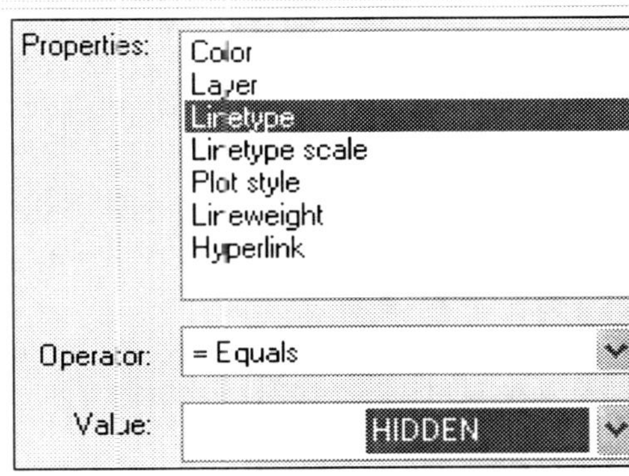


6. Change the layer of the objects using the Properties palette as follows:

- pick in the right column of the **Layer** row
- pick the down arrow and select the **HIDDEN** layer

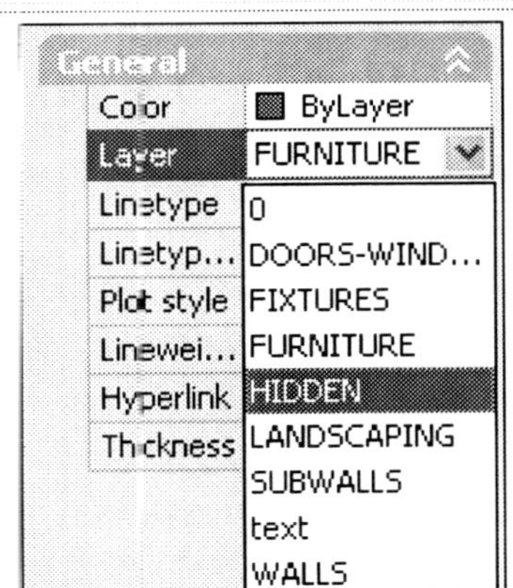

### 6.4.1: Using the Properties Palette

7. Follow the procedure in Step 6 to change the **Linetype** to **ByLayer**, as shown.

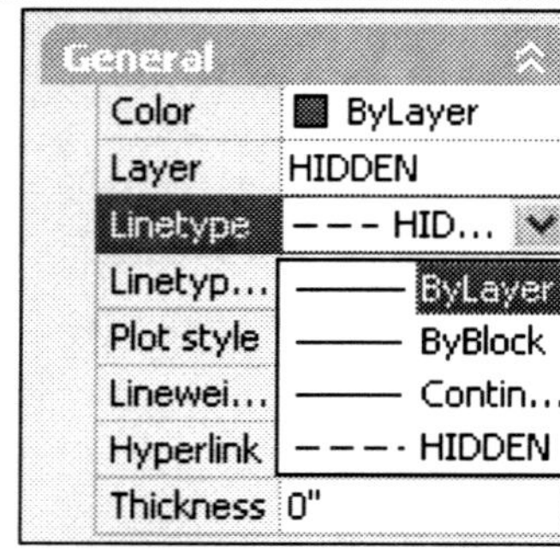


8. Close the Properties Palette.

9. Hit the ESC key to deselect the objects.

10. Save and close the drawing.

You can leave the Properties Palette open all the time if you wish – you can even dock it and minimize it much as you could the Design Center and the Tool Palettes; but unless you have a fairly large monitor, it may take up too much of your drawing area.

> In our last exercise, we used the **Quick select** button to select the objects we were going to modify. Frankly, I think the quick select approach takes longer than simply selecting the objects on the screen using a window or a pick (selection) box. Quick select works well when you must filter a large number of objects to get what you want. But otherwise, just do this:
>
> - Select what you want to modify (with an empty command prompt).
> - Right-click in the graphics area and select **Properties** from the cursor menu.
> - Make your changes in the Properties Palette.
>
> Still too difficult? Try this: double-click on the object you wish to modify. AutoCAD will automatically open the Properties Palette!

## 6.5 And Again, the Easy Way to Modify: *Matchprop*

Let's say you've drawn a chair but used the wrong layer by mistake. The chair consists of a rectangle and three lines. You need to know on what layer the chair should have been drawn. But you can't remember. You can do a ***Properties*** command on one of the other chairs just to read the layer setting, and then the ***Properties*** command on the chair you just drew … man, that's a lot of work!

> Okay, the easy way is to select the chair and read the layer in the **Layer** control box, but then I couldn't show you the ***MatchProp*** command. So just play along for now.

Try the ***Matchprop*** command.

Pick the **Match Properties** button on the Standard toolbar, type ***Matchprop*** at the command prompt, or select **Match Properties** in the Modify pull-down menu. AutoCAD prompts:

**Command: *matchprop* (or *ma*)**
**Select source object: *[select an object that was drawn on the correct layer]***
**Current active settings: Color Layer Ltype Ltscale Lineweight Thickness PlotStyle Dim Text Hatch Polyline Viewport Table Material Shadow display**
**Select destination object(s) or [Settings]: *[select the object you want to change]***
**Select destination object(s) or [Settings]: *[enter to complete the command]***

Who could ask for anything more?

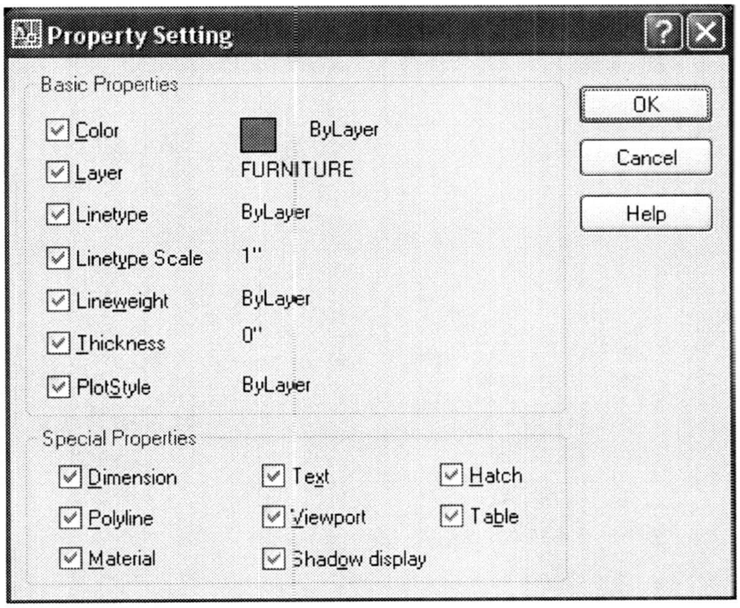


Figure 6.022

But wait! There is more! (Will the wonders never cease?!)

Notice that ***Matchprop*** gives you a **Settings** option. The line above the **Settings** option tells you what the current settings are. AutoCAD will match these properties. Selecting the **Settings** option will produce the Property Settings dialog box (Figure 6.022) in which you can tell AutoCAD the properties you do or don't want to match: **Color**, **Layer**, **Linetype**, **Linetype Scale**, and more!

Personally, I like to leave all the boxes checked. I rarely run into a situation where I might need some properties matched but not others. Still, it's nice to know that I have this option.

## 6.6 Extra Steps

Have you noticed that you repeat the same commands with some frequency? AutoCAD has provided a way to make those commands available to you in one central location without requiring you to look for on this toolbar or that drop down menu or someplace else. You'll find the tool palettes to be quite easily customized.

Try this.

Let's say you've discovered that you use the ***Line***, ***Circle***, ***Erase***, and ***DText*** commands quite often. Their buttons are on a variety of toolbars and you can't always quickly remember where to look.

Follow this procedure:

1. If it isn't already open, open the tool palettes. (There is a **Tool Palettes** button on the Standard toolbar, or you can enter ***toolpalettes*** or ***tp*** at the command prompt.)
2. Pick the **Properties** button at the bottom of the title bar and select **New Palette** from the menu.
3. AutoCAD will ask you to name the new palette; I'll call mine *My Tools.*
4. Drag a line from the drawing onto the palette. Notice that AutoCAD places a **Line** tool on the palette. (Repeat this step with other objects.)

   Try to draw something from the new palette. Notice that AutoCAD creates the object with the properties (layer, color, linetype, etc.) of the object you used to create the tool.
5. Right click on the tool and select **Properties** from the menu. Use the Tool Properties dialog box to redefine the properties of objects created with this tool.
6. Do the same for DText.

Now, anytime you need one of your more common commands, it'll be right there on your own tool palette!

## 6.7 What Have We Learned?

*Items covered in this lesson include:*

- *Using the Layer Properties dialog box*
- *Creating your own tool palette*
- *Using the AutoCAD Design Center*
- *Using the Layer translator*
- *Using the Properties Palette*
- *Commands*
  - ***Color***
  - ***Linetype***
  - ***LTScale***
  - ***LWeight***
  - ***LWUnits***
  - ***LWDisplay***
  - ***Layer***
  - ***Properties***
  - ***Laytrans***
  - ***Matchprop***
  - ***ADCenter***
  - ***LayCur***
  - ***LayDel***
  - ***LayFrz***
  - ***LayIso***
  - ***LayLck***
  - ***LayMch***
  - ***LayMCur***
  - ***LayMrg***
  - ***LayOff***
  - ***LayOn***
  - ***LayThw***
  - ***LayUlk***
  - ***CopytoLayer***

This (very long) lesson has challenged you more than any other thus far. We've taken AutoCAD from a simple drawing toy to a real drafting tool. We've seen how to use colors in our drawing (yea! – no more b&w), use linetypes and lineweights, and layers to put more into a drawing than was ever possible in the world of graphite and paper. (Did you feel like Dorothy walking into Oz?)

Next we'll begin to look at that 70% of CAD work that's *not* drawing – modifying what we've drawn. But try some exercises first and get a bit more comfortable with the material in this chapter.

## 6.8 Exercises

1. Using the layers listed in the chart and the parameters below it, create the drawing in shown atop the next page using the following setup. Save the drawing as *MyRemote* in the C:\Steps\Lesson06 folder.

| Layer Names | Color | Linetype |
|---|---|---|
| Button | 62 | continuous |
| Dim | cyan | continuous |
| Obj | 211 | continuous |
| Text | yellow | continuous |
| Toggle | blue | continuous |
| Up-Down | 211 | continuous |

1.1. Lower left limits: 0,0

1.2. Upper right limits: 6,10

1.3. Architectural units

1.4. Grid: ¼"

1.5. Snap: as needed

1.6. Font: Times New Roman

1.7. Text Height: 1/8

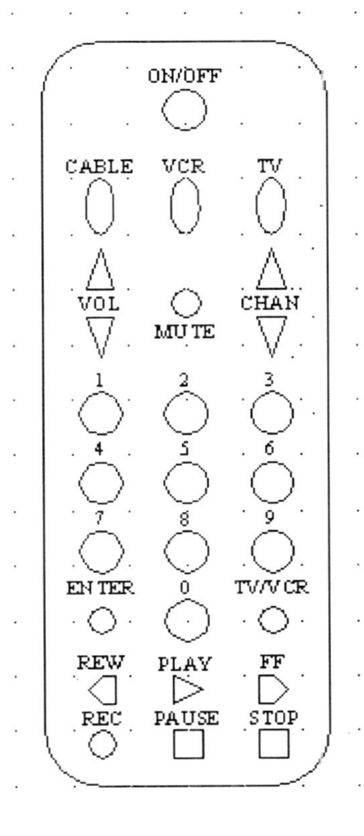


*For more exercises related to Lesson 6, please see Lesson 6 in AutoCAD 2007: One Step at a Time – Workbook.*

| 6.9 | **For Web-Based Review Questions, visit: http://www.uneedcad.com/2007/Files/07R6.pdf** |
|---|---|

# Lesson 7

Following this lesson, you will:

- ✓ *Be familiar with several modification procedures, including:*
  - o ***Trim, Extend,** & **Change***
  - o ***Break***
  - o ***Fillet** & **Chamfer***
  - o ***Move, Align,** & **Copy***
- ✓ *Be familiar with the Multiple Document Environment*
- ✓ *Be familiar with Windows' procedures for moving and copying objects between drawings*

# Editing Your Drawing – Modification Procedures

*Although we'll cover some more advanced drawing commands and techniques in later chapters, the first six lessons have made you comfortable with AutoCAD's basic approach to 2-dimensional drawing. But you probably still feel a bit clumsy with some of your work. This comes partly from the newness of AutoCAD to you, partly from the need to erase and redo an effort because of small mistakes, and partly from the need to draw the same thing over and over (in great Sisyphean efforts) as you did the remote's buttons in our last lesson's exercises. Additionally, you can't create some more complex drawings that might be simple on the drawing board – given templates and an electric eraser.*

*In this lesson, we'll tackle several commands meant to save drawing time and effort. There are many commands to cover, but they're not difficult.*

*We'll divide the basic modification routines into two groups: the* Change Group, *which will include commands designed to change an object's appearance or basic properties, and the* Location & Number Group, *which will include commands designed to move or duplicate existing objects.*

## 7.1 The Change Group

### 7.1.1 Cutting It Out with the *Trim* Command

You'll often find it easier to draw one long line across an area and then cut away the extra pieces than to draw several shorter lines. AutoCAD designed the ***Trim*** command to remove the "extra" bits of lines and circles. Here's the command sequence:

**Command: *trim* (or *tr*)**

**Current settings: Projection=UCS, Edge=None**

**Select cutting edges ...**

**Select objects or <select all>: *[select the cutting edge or hit enter to make cutting edges out of all the objects in the drawing]***

**Select objects: *[enter to confirm completion of this selection set]***

**Select object to trim or shift-select to extend or**

**[Fence/Crossing/Project/Edge/eRase/Undo]: *[select the part you wish to remove]***

**Select object to trim or shift-select to extend or**

**[Fence/Crossing/Project/Edge/eRase/Undo]: *[enter to confirm completion of this selection set]***

- The **cutting edges** are usually lines or circles to which you want to trim. In other words, as you select a **cutting edge**, say to yourself, "*I want to cut back to here.*"
- The **object to trim** is the piece of a line or circle you want to remove from the drawing. When selecting the **object to trim**, say to yourself, "*I want to get rid of this.*"
- Notice the subtle **or shift-select to extend** part of the **Select object to trim** prompt. This tells you that you can hold down the SHIFT key on your keyboard and, rather than trimming an object to the cutting edge, you can extend an object to it! This option really cuts down the time required to jump between the ***Trim*** and ***Extend*** commands.
- **Fence** allows you to select all objects touched by a *fence*. A fence behaves much like a single line crossing window.

- The **Crossing** option forces AutoCAD to use a crossing window regardless of where you pick the **first corner** and **opposite corner**.
- **Project** refers to a UCS projection – something we'll cover in our discussion of 3-dimensional drafting in our 3D text. Ignore it for now.
- **Edge** refers to one of the more useful innovations AutoCAD has provided – the ability to trim an object even if the object doesn't touch your cutting edge.
- **eRase** allows you to erase an object without leaving the ***Trim*** command. I recommend ignoring this option in favor of its command counterpart. (Just because you can do something doesn't mean that you should!)
- The **Undo** *option*, of course, will undo the last modification within the command. Remember, the ***Undo*** *command* will undo the entire ***Trim*** command modification (all the changes made by the command).

Let's experiment.

> In addition to the command line and toolbar, you'll find all of the commands in this lesson in the Modify pull-down menu.

| Do This: 7.1.1.1 | Using the *Trim* Command |
|---|---|

I. Open *trim-extend.dwg* in the C:\Steps\Lesson07 folder. The drawing looks like Figure 7.001.

II. Follow these steps.

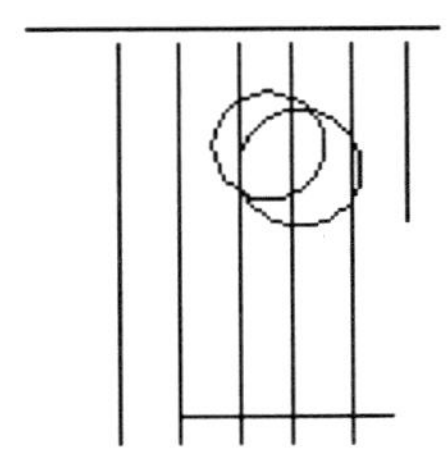

Figure 7.001

### 7.1.1.1: Using the Trim Command

1. Enter the ***Trim*** command by typing ***trim*** or ***tr***. Alternately, you can select the **Trim** button 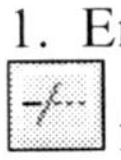 from the Modify toolbar or palette.

    **Command: *tr***

2. Select the circles at points 1 and 2, and the line at point 3 as shown.

    **Current settings: Projection=UCS, Edge=None**
    **Select cutting edges ...**
    **Select objects or <select all>:**

3. Confirm that you've completed selecting the **cutting edges**.

    **Select objects: *[enter]***

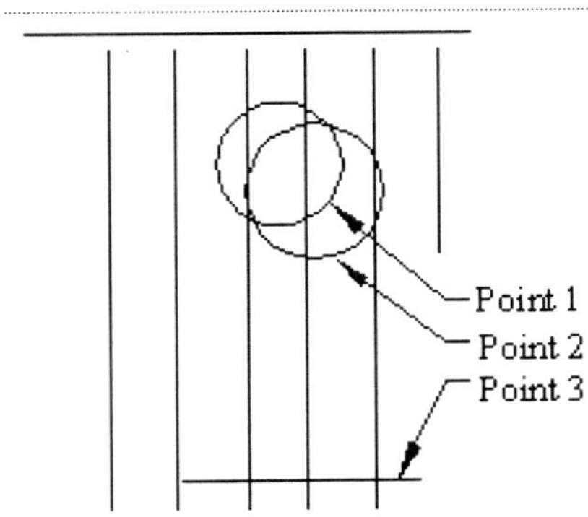

## 7.1.1.1: Using the Trim Command

4. Select what you want to trim – the circles at points 1 and 2, as shown.

**Select object to trim or shift-select to extend or [Fence/Crossing/Project/ Edge/eRase/Undo]:**

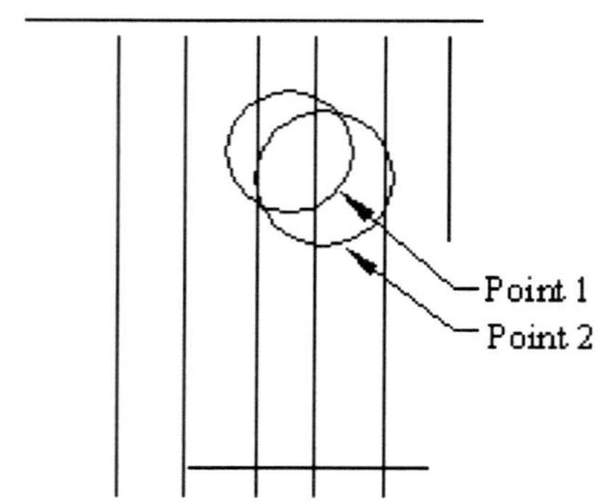


5. Now select the **Fence** option …

**Select object to trim or shift-select to extend or [Fence/Crossing/Project/ Edge/eRase/Undo]:** ***f***

6. And place a fence across the lines extending below the bottom horizontal line.

Notice that AutoCAD refuses to trim the left-two lines. Let's fix that now.

**Specify first fence point:**

**Specify next fence point or [Undo]:**

**Specify next fence point or [Undo]:** ***[enter]***

**Object does not intersect an edge.**

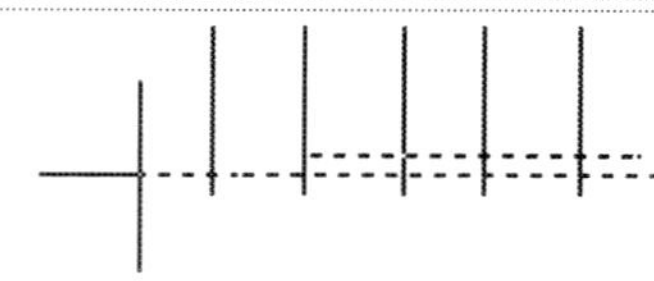

7. Without leaving the ***Trim*** command, type ***e*** to select the **Edge** option. Alternately, you can select **Edge** from the cursor or dynamic input menu.

**Select object to trim or shift-select to extend or [Fence/Crossing/Project/Edge/eRase/Undo]:** ***e***

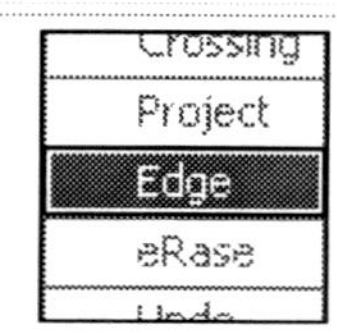


8. Type ***e*** again to select the **Extend** option. Alternately, you can select **Extend** from the cursor or dynamic input menu.

**Enter an implied edge extension mode [Extend/No extend] <No extend>:** ***e***

9. Now select again the pieces that didn't trim in Step 6. Notice the difference? In Steps 7 and 8, you told AutoCAD to extend the cutting edge as an invisible plane in both directions. AutoCAD then used that invisible edge to trim the objects.

**Select object to trim or shift-select to extend or [Fence/Crossing/Project/ Edge/eRase/Undo]:**

10. Now let's use that **shift-select** trick to extend a line. Hold down the SHIFT key and select the right-most vertical line (select it toward the bottom of the line).

**Select object to trim or shift-select to extend or [Fence/Crossing/Project/ Edge/eRase/Undo]:**

Your drawing looks like this.

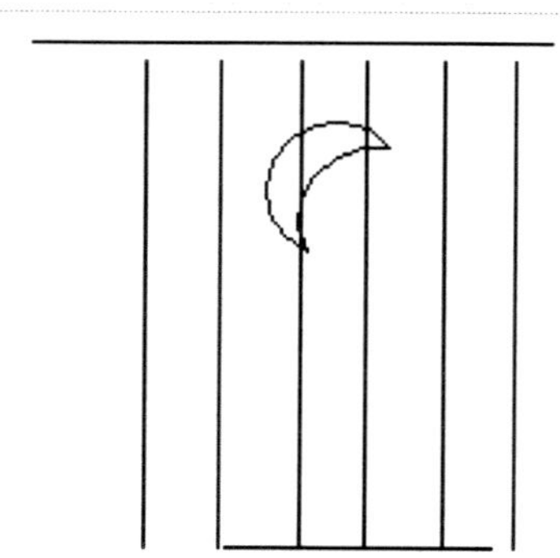

11. Complete the command.

**Select object to trim or shift-select to extend or [Fence/Crossing/ Project/ Edge/eRase/Undo]:** ***[enter]***

### 7.1.1.1: Using the Trim Command

12. Now follow the preceding procedures to trim the lines inside the moon. Your drawing will look like this.

**Command: *tr***

13. Save your drawing but don't exit.

**Command: *qsave***

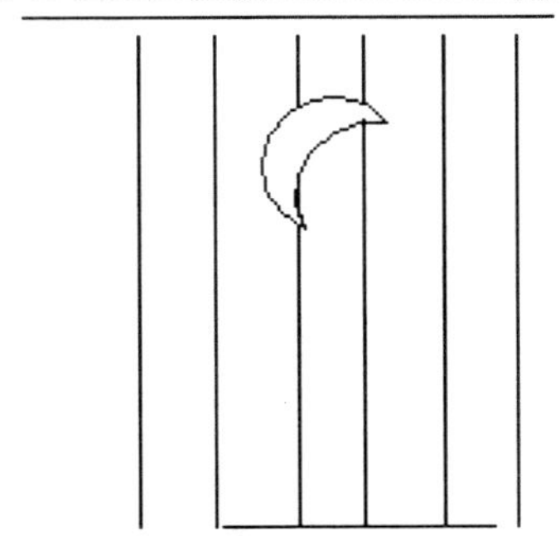

The ***Trim*** command, as useful as it is, is only one side of a coin. The opposite side is the ***Extend*** command, which is just as useful even if performing the opposite task.

## 7.1.2 Adding to It with the *Extend* Command

You don't have to enter the ***Trim*** command to extend an object as you did in our last exercise. It's certainly more logical to use the ***Extend*** command to extend a line. But considering the two procedures and how frequently they work together, placing them together should prove quite a time saver.

To be fair, AutoCAD also placed a **Trim** option in the ***Extend*** command, which it designed to extend lines that come up short of the mark.

Here is the ***Extend*** command sequence:

**Command: *extend* (or *ex*)**

**Current settings: Projection=UCS, Edge=Extend**

**Select boundary edges ...**

**Select objects or <select all>: *[select the boundary edge or hit enter to make boundaries out of all the objects in the drawing]***

**Select objects: *[enter to confirm completion of this selection set]***

**Select object to extend or shift-select to trim or**

**[Fence/Crossing/Project/Edge/Undo]: *select the object to extend]***

**Select object to extend or shift-select to trim or**

**[Fence/Crossing/Project/Edge/Undo]: *[enter to confirm completion of this selection set]***

Each step corresponds to the same step in the ***Trim*** command sequence. The only difference is that with the ***Extend*** command, you'll select a **boundary edge** – the place to which you want to extend a line or arc. (Say to yourself, "I want to extend *to here*.")

Notice that the **Edge**, while defaulting to **None** in the ***Trim*** command, now defaults to **Extend**. This is because ***Trim*** and ***Extend*** share the **Edgemode** system variable. When you set the **Edge extension mode** to **Extend** in the last exercise, you set it to **Extend** for the ***Extend*** command as well. This will become clearer as we do the next exercise.

| Do This: 7.1.2.1 | Using the *Extend* Command |
|---|---|

I. Be sure you're still in the *trim-extend.dwg* file in the C:\Steps\Lesson07 folder. If not, please open it now.

II. Follow these steps.

### 7.1.2.1: Using the Extend Command

1. Enter the ***Extend*** command. Alternately, you can select the **Extend** button 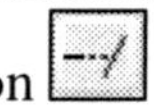 on the Modify toolbar or palette.

 **Command:** ***ex***

2. Select the top line and left vertical line as your **boundary edge**(s).

 **Current settings: Projection=UCS, Edge=Extend**
 **Select boundary edges ...**
 **Select objects or <select all>:**
 **Select objects:** ***[enter]***

3. Select the bottom horizontal line to extend. (Select it toward the left end.)

 **Select object to extend or shift-select to trim or [Fence/Crossing/Project/ Edge/Undo]:**

4. Now tell AutoCAD to use the **Crossing** option.

 **Select object to extend or shift-select to trim or [Fence/Crossing/Project/ Edge/Undo]:** ***c***

5. … and place a crossing window around the top of the six vertical lines (right).

 **Specify first corner:**
 **Specify opposite corner:**

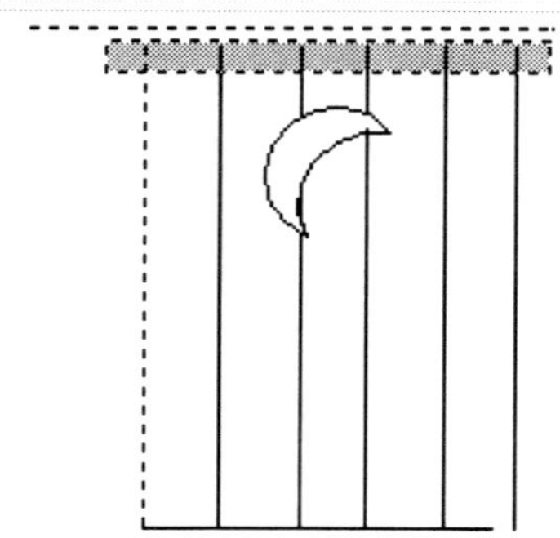

6. Confirm that you've finished.

 **Select object to extend or shift-select to trim or [Fence/ Crossing/Project/ Edge/Undo]:** ***[enter]***

Your drawing looks like this.

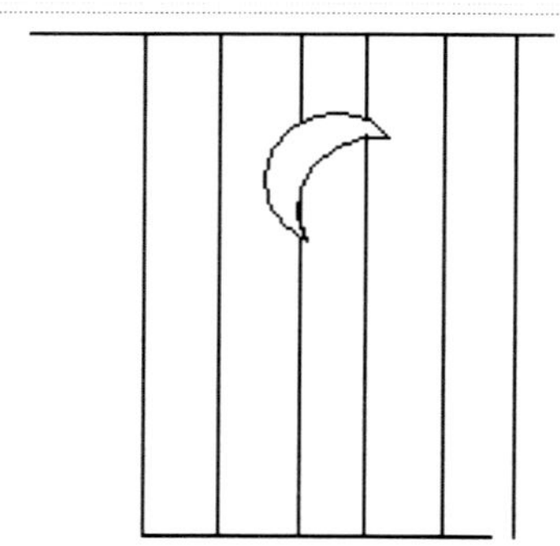

7. Save your drawing 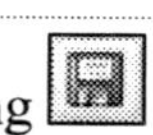 but don't exit.

 **Command:** ***qsave***

You've probably already recognized the value of these two simple commands. The ability to trim unneeded material or extend a line or arc will save a lot of redraw time.

## 7.1.3 Redundancy – Thy Name is AutoCAD: The *Break* Command

AutoCAD provides yet another way to remove parts of lines or circles. But this one is a bit more tedious than the ***Trim*** command. The ***Break*** command sequence is

 **Command:** ***break*** **(or** ***br*****)**
 **Select object:** ***[select the object to be broken]***
 **Specify second break point or [First point]:** ***f***

**Specify first break point:** ***[select the first end of the break]***

**Specify second break point:** ***[select the other end of the break]***

The section between the first and second selected points is removed.

There's only one option in this sequence – that of entering ***F*** for the **First point**. If you enter ***F***, AutoCAD prompts for the first end of the break. You can then use OSNAPs for precise selection of both first and second points. If you don't enter ***F***, AutoCAD assumes the point at which you selected the line or circle is the first point. As no OSNAP is used to select the line, there is no precision in selecting the first point. So we discover one of those unwritten rules: *always use* ***First point*** *when using the* **Break** *command.* (Of course, you know what they say about rules.)

> One of AutoCAD's lesser-known tricks concerns the ***Break*** command. You can enter an @ symbol at the **Enter second point** prompt to break the object into two pieces without removing anything. The object is broken at the point selected at the **Specify first break point** prompt.
>
> (But the easy way is to pick the **Break at Point** button on the Modify toolbar.)

Let's use the ***Break*** command to add a handle to our moon-faced door.

| Do This: 7.1.3.1 | Using the *Break* Command |
|---|---|

I. Be sure you're still in the *trim-extend.dwg* file in the C:\Steps\Lesson07 folder. If not, please open it now.

II. Follow these steps.

### 7.1.3.1: Using the Break Command

1. Zoom in to the area indicated.

   **Command:** ***z***

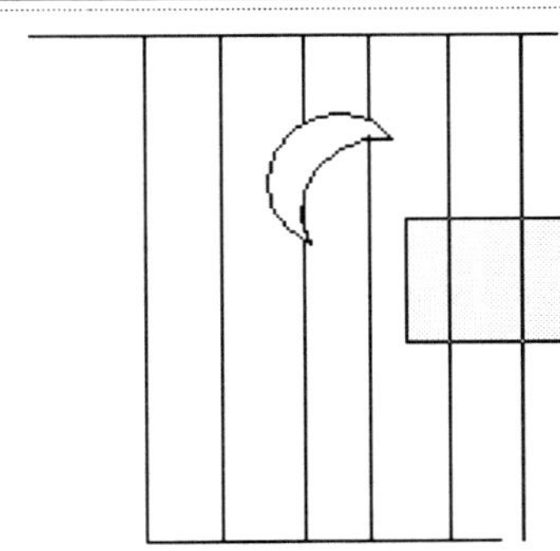

2. On the **OBJ** layer, draw two lines as indicated.

   **Command:** ***l***

   **Specify first point:** ***7.75,5***

   **Specify next point or [Undo]:** ***@2<0***

   **Specify next point or [Undo]:** ***[enter]***

   **Command:** ***[enter]***

   **Specify first point:** ***7.75,4.75***

   **Specify next point or [Undo]:** ***@2<0***

   **Specify next point or [Undo]:** ***[enter]***

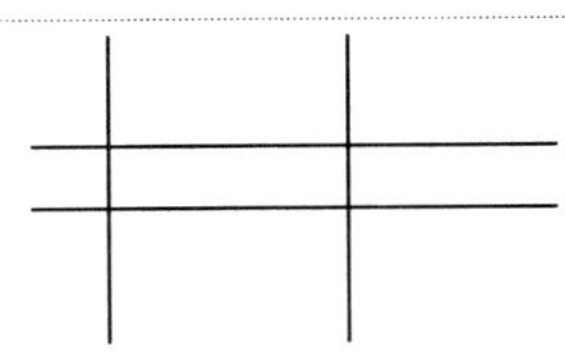

3. Enter the ***Break*** command. Alternately, you can pick the ***Break*** button from the Modify toolbar or palette.

   **Command:** ***br***

### 7.1.3.1: Using the Break Command

4. Select the left vertical line.

   **Select object:**

5. Type *f* or pick **First point** on the menu [First point].

   **Specify second break point or [First point]: *f***

6. Place the first end of the break on the vertical line at the Point 1 intersection; select the other end of the break at the Point 2 intersection. (Be sure to use OSNAPs.)

   **Specify first break point: _int of**

   **Specify second break point: _int of**

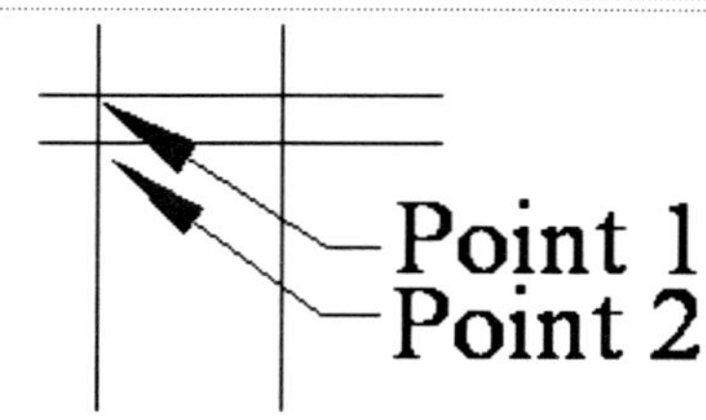


7. Repeat Steps 3 to 6 for the other line. Your drawing looks like this.

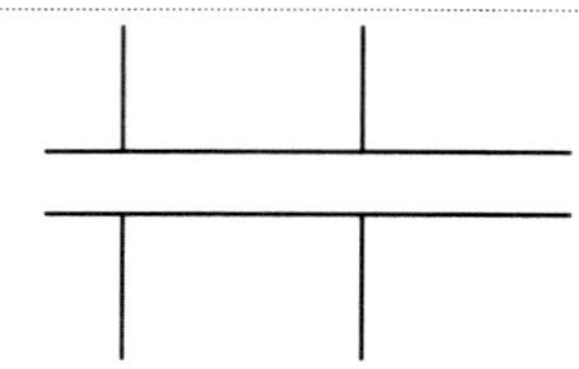

8. Save this view of your drawing as ***latch***.

   **Command: *v***

9. Save your drawing but don't exit.

   **Command: *qsave***

## 7.1.4 Now We Can Round That Corner: The *Fillet* Command

The ***Fillet*** command provides an easy way to round corners without the need for any of the ***Arc*** command's routines; or you can use it to *square* corners!

The command sequence is

> **Command: *fillet* (or *f*)**
>
> **Current settings: Mode = TRIM, Radius = 0.5000**
>
> **Select first object or [Undo/Polyline/Radius/Trim/Multiple]: *[select the first object]***
>
> **Select second object or shift-select to apply corner: *[select the second object or use shift-select to make a square corner]***

- The default radius for the ***Fillet*** command is **0.5**, but you can change that by typing ***R*** for the **Radius** option (at the **Select first object** prompt). AutoCAD will prompt:

  **Specify fillet radius <0.5000>:**

  You can type a different radius, or you can enter ***0*** for a square corner.
- The **Polyline** option allows you to fillet all the corners of a polyline at once. (We'll discuss polylines in Lesson 8.)
- The **Trim** option allows you to decide whether or not to automatically trim away the excess line, circle, arc, etc., when the ***Fillet*** operation is done.
- Normally, AutoCAD allows one fillet to be completed per command sequence. If you wish to fillet more than one corner, first select the **Multiple** option.

- The second option line provides a useful shortcut. Rather than use the default **Select second object** option (and select a second object), you can hold down the SHIFT key while selecting a second object to create a square corner.
- A final option (one that AutoCAD doesn't show in its options list) allows you to fillet parallel lines. This procedure draws an arc connecting the endpoints of both lines. We'll see how it works in the next exercise.

Let's give it a try.

| Do This: 7.1.4.1 | Using the *Fillet* Command |
|---|---|

I. Be sure you're still in the *trim-extend.dwg* file in the C:\Steps\Lesson07 folder. If not, please open it now.

II. ***Zoom* all.**

III. Follow these steps.

**7.1.4.1: USING THE FILLET COMMAND**

1. Enter the ***Fillet*** command. Alternately, you can pick the **Fillet** button 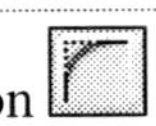 from the Modify toolbar or palette.

   **Command: *f***

2. Accept the default radius for now and select the upper and right lines at Points 1 and 2, as shown.

   **Current settings: Mode = TRIM, Radius = 0.5000**

   **Select first object or [Undo/Polyline/Radius/Trim/Multiple]:**

   **Select second object or shift-select to apply corner:**

   Notice that the edge is rounded (with a 0.5" radius arc) and the excess lines are automatically trimmed away.

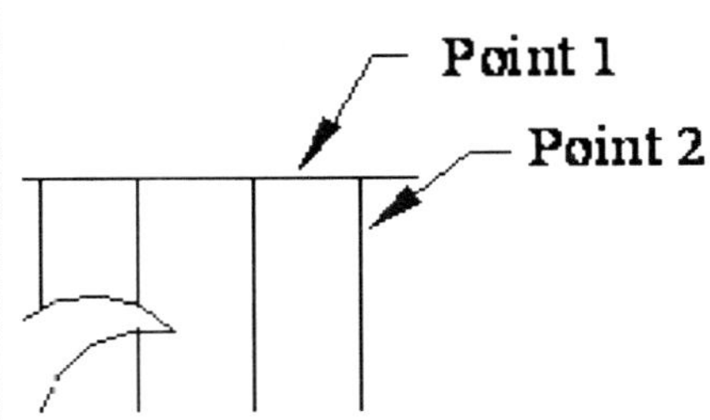


3. Repeat Steps 1 and 2 at the lower right corner of the door. Your drawing looks like this.

   **Command: *[enter]***

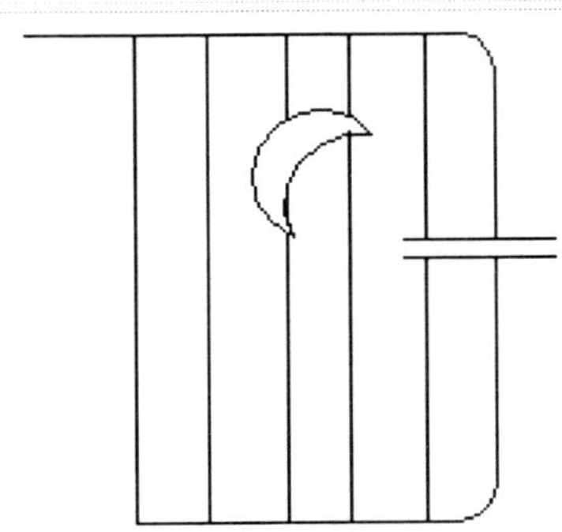

4. Now let's square the other corners. Repeat the ***Fillet*** command .

   **Command: *[enter]***

5. Enter ***M*** or select **Multiple** from the menu to use the **Multiple** option.

   **Current settings: Mode = TRIM, Radius = 0.5000**

   **Select first object or [Undo/Polyline/Radius/Trim/Multiple]: *m***

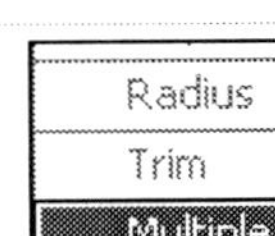

## 7.1.4.1: Using the Fillet Command

6. Select the top line at Point 1.

   **Select first object or [Undo/ Polyline/Radius/Trim/Multiple]:**

7. Now hold down the SHIFT key and select the left line at Point 2.

   **Select second object or shift-select to apply corner:**

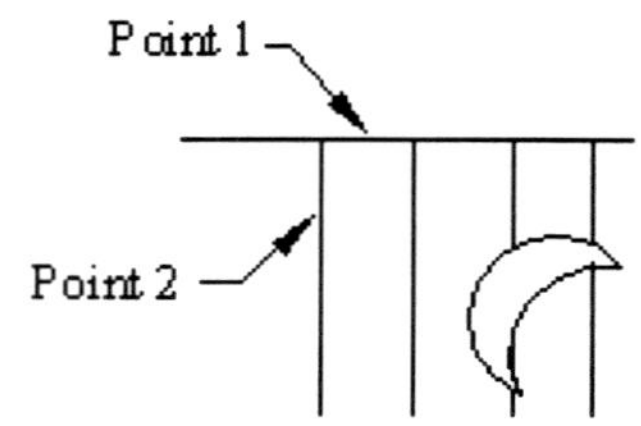


8. Fillet the lower left corner as well, and then complete the command.

   **Select first object or [Undo/Polyline/ Radius/Trim/Multiple]:**

   **Select second object or shift-select to apply corner:**

   **Select first object or [Undo/Polyline/ Radius/Trim/Multiple]:** ***[enter]***

Your drawing looks like this.

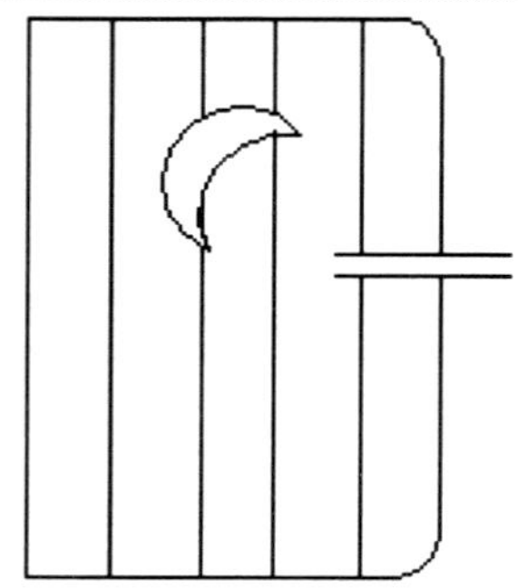

9. Restore the **latch** view you created at the end of the last exercise.

   **Command:** ***v***

10. Fillet the two lines on both ends. (Refer to the Step 11 figure.) Don't worry about the radius; AutoCAD will calculate it from the distance between the parallel lines.
(Add a couple of 0.05"R circles for an anchor and a lever if you wish.)

   **Command:** ***f***

   **Current settings: Mode = TRIM, Radius = 0.0000**

   **Select first object or [Undo/Polyline/ Radius/Trim/Multiple]:** ***m***

   **Select first object or [Undo/Polyline/ Radius/Trim/Multiple]:**

   **Select second object or shift-select to apply corner:**

   **Select first object or [Undo/ Polyline/Radius/Trim/Multiple]:** ***[enter]***

11. Zoom back out again . Your drawing will look like this.

   **Command:** ***z***

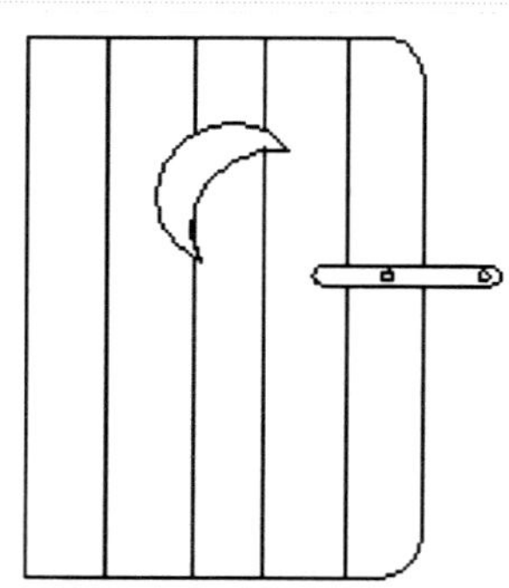

12. Save the drawing but don't exit.

   **Command:** ***qsave***

The **Trim** option, available for both the ***Fillet*** and ***Chamfer*** commands, was added to AutoCAD after users complained that they didn't always want to trim away the excess part of the lines during ***Fillet*** or ***Chamfer*** procedures. When selecting the **Trim** option, AutoCAD prompts:

**Enter Trim mode option [Trim/No trim] <Trim>:**

Notice that **Trim** is the default. AutoCAD will automatically trim away the excess. If you want to keep the excess, enter ***N***. AutoCAD sets the **Trimmode** (the system variable that controls the **Trim/No trim** option) accordingly. The objects are filleted, but the excess remains.

## 7.1.5 Fillet's Cousin: The *Chamfer* Command

***Fillet*** and ***Chamfer*** are so similar that you might get confused as to which one you want. Look at the pictures on the buttons if you're perplexed.

Where ***Fillet*** rounds corners, ***Chamfer*** provides a mitre – a flat edge at a corner – much like a carpenter achieves with a hand plane. You control the size and angle of the edge through responses to the prompts, which look like this:

**Command: *chamfer* (or *cha*)**

**(TRIM mode) Current chamfer Dist1 = 0.5000, Dist2 = 0.5000**

**Select first line or [Undo/Polyline/Distance/Angle/Trim/mEthod/Multiple]: *[select the first chamfered line]***

**Select second line or shift-select to apply corner: *[select the second chamfered line]***

- The default **Method** is **Distance** (shown in the sample sequence). Using the **Distance** option tells AutoCAD to measure a user-defined distance from the corner (real or apparent) on both lines, put a line between these two points, and **Trim** (or not – depending on the **Trimmode** setting).
- Another method is **Angle**. Here, you define one distance (as in the **Distance** method) and an angle of cut.
- You can switch between methods (**Distance** or **Angle**) using the **mEthod** option.
- The **Polyline** option can be used to chamfer entire polylines, but the results can be surprising. I tend to shy away from chamfering polylines.
- The **Multiple** option works just is it did in the ***Fillet*** command.
- Notice that last prompt? That's right; you can square a corner using the ***Chamfer*** command as easily as you did with the ***Fillet*** command!

These options will become clearer with an exercise.

### Do This: 7.1.5.1 Using the *Chamfer* Command

I. Be sure you're still in the *trim-extend.dwg* file in the C:\Steps\Lesson07 folder. If not, please open it now.

II. ***Zoom* all**.

III. Erase the arcs we created using the ***Fillet*** command.

IV. Follow these steps.

**7.1.5.1: USING THE CHAMFER COMMAND**

1. Enter the ***Chamfer*** command. Alternately, you can pick the **Chamfer** button on the Modify toolbar or palette.

**Command: *cha***

## 7.1.5.1: USING THE CHAMFER COMMAND

2. Let's change the **Dist1** and **Dist2** settings so that we can better tell what's happening. Type ***D*** or pick **Distance** on the menu.

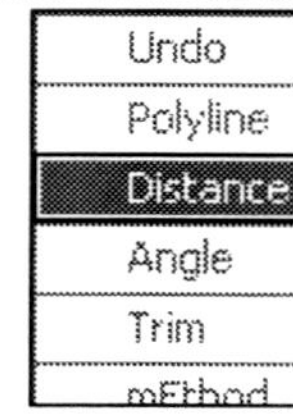


**(TRIM mode) Current chamfer Dist1 = 0.5000, Dist2 = 0.5000**

**Select first line or [Undo/Polyline/Distance/Angle/Trim/ mEthod/ Multiple]: *d***

3. AutoCAD prompts for each distance. Enter ***.25*** for the **first chamfer distance** and ***.75*** for the **second chamfer distance**.

**Specify first chamfer distance <0.5000>: *.25***

**Specify second chamfer distance <0.2500>: *.75***

4. Select the top line of our door, and then the right vertical line where indicated.

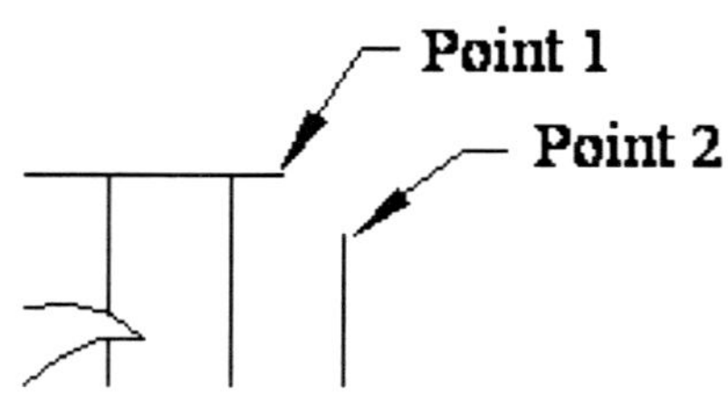


**Select first line or [Undo/Polyline/Distance/Angle/Trim/ mEthod/Multiple]:**

**Select second line or shift-select to apply corner:**

5. Now we'll chamfer the bottom corner using the **Angle** option. Repeat the command .

**Command: *[enter]***

6. Type ***a*** or pick **Angle** on the menu to select the **Angle** option.

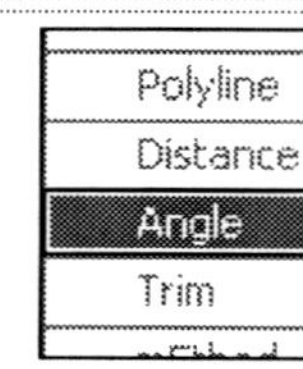


**(TRIM mode) Current chamfer Dist1 = 0.2500, Dist2 = 0.7500**

**Select first line or [Undo/Polyline/ Distance/Angle/Trim/ mEthod/Multiple]: *a***

7. Enter ***.5*** as the **chamfer length on the first line**; then enter ***60*** as the **chamfer angle from the first line**.

**Specify chamfer length on the first line <1.0000>: *.5***

**Specify chamfer angle from the first line <0>: *60***

8. AutoCAD now prompts you for the lines to chamfer. Select the right end of the bottom line and then the bottom of the right line.

**Select first line or [Undo/Polyline/ Distance/Angle/Trim/mEthod/ Multiple]:**

**Select second line or shift-select to apply corner:**

Your door looks like this.

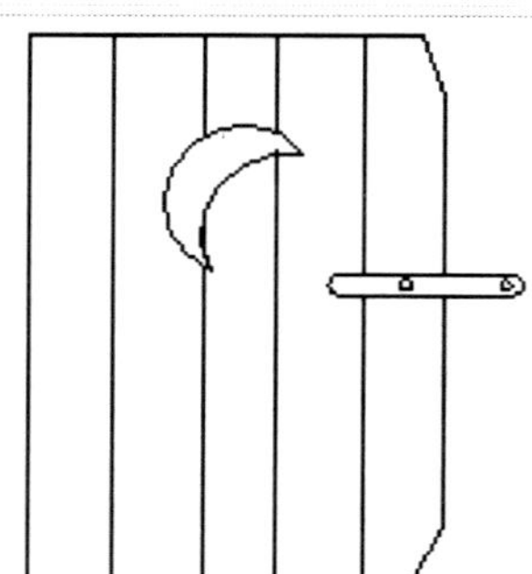

9. Save 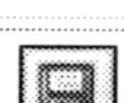 and close the drawing.

**Command: *qsave***

We've completed the six commands of the first part of this lesson. This is a lot of material to absorb with more to come. If you feel you need to practice what you've learned so far, do Exercise 1 at the end of this lesson (the *Checkers* exercise). Then return to Section 7.2.

## 7.2 The Location and Number Group

### 7.2.1 Here to There: The *Move* Command

The ***Move*** command allows you to move one or more objects from one place to another. It has one of the easiest sequences to remember:

> **Command:** ***move*** **(or** ***m*****)**
>
> **Select objects:** ***[select one or more objects]***
>
> **Select objects:** ***[enter to confirm completion of this selection set]***
>
> **Specify base point or [Displacement] <Displacement>:** ***[select the point at which you'll "pick up" the object]***
>
> **Specify second point or <use first point as displacement>:** ***[pick the target point – the place where you'll put the object "down"]***

The only options here involve the **base point** and the **displacement**.

- The easiest way to explain **base point** is this: imagine the object(s) you're moving as a solid object sitting on a table. To move the object, you must first pick it up. The **base point** is the place you grab (a corner, an edge, the middle, etc.). The **second point** is where you put it down – or the point at which you'll place the corner or edge (or whatever) you grabbed.
- Notice the **base point or [Displacement]** prompt. You have two ways to use a displacement method. (Both produce the same results.)
  - First, you can enter an X,Y (or X,Y,Z) distance at the **Specify base point** prompt. Then you'll hit **enter** at the **Specify second point** prompt. AutoCAD will move the selected objects the designated distance along the X- and Y-axes.
  - Alternately, you can hit enter at the **Specify base point or [Displacement] <Displacement>** prompt. AutoCAD will then move the object as though you'd used the relative coordinate system.

Let's try the ***Move*** command.

| Do This: 7.2.1.1 | Using the *Move* Command |
|---|---|

I. Open *Star.dwg* in the C:\Steps\Lesson07 folder. The drawing looks like Figure 7.002.

II. Follow these steps.

Figure 7.002

**7.2.1.1: USING THE MOVE COMMAND**

1. Enter the ***Move*** command. Alternately, you can pick the **Move** button on the Modify toolbar or palette.

> **Command:** ***m***

2. Put a selection window around the entire circle and all its contents. Then complete the selection set.

### 7.2.1.1: Using the Move Command

**Select objects: Specify opposite corner: 13 found**

**Select objects:** ***[enter]***

3. Select the lower quadrant  of the circle. (You can select any point, but this one is convenient.)

**Specify base point or [Displacement] <Displacement>: _qua of**

Move the circle 4 units to the right. Notice how the circle changes position.

**Specify second point or <use first point as displacement>:** ***@4<0***

4. Now we'll use the **Displacement** option to move it back. Repeat the command .

**Command:** ***[enter]***

5. Select the circle and all of its contents again.

**Select objects: Specify opposite corner: 13 found**

**Select objects:** ***[enter]***

6. Tell AutoCAD to use the **Displacement** option.

**Specify base point or [Displacement] <Displacement>:** ***[enter]***

7. Return the objects to their original location. Notice that you don't have to enter a Z-distance.

**Specify displacement <0.0000, 0.0000, 0.0000>:** ***-4,0***

As you can see, there really isn't much to the ***Move*** command. But you do need to remember things like OSNAPs and Cartesian coordinates to ensure precision in your modifications.

## 7.2.2 Okay, Move It – But Then Line It Up: the *Align* Command

A variation of the ***Move*** command, ***Align*** will move objects and then align them with something else. The command sequence is

**Command:** ***align*** **(or** ***al*****)**

**Select objects:** ***[select the object to be moved/aligned]***

**Select objects:** ***[confirm the selection]***

**Specify first source point:** ***[this is the first point where you "grab" the objects]***

**Specify first destination point:** ***[this is where you put the first grabbed point]***

**Specify second source point:** ***[this is a second point where you grab the objects – you need at least two points so that you can align the objects]***

**Specify second destination point:** ***[this is where you put the second grabbed point]***

**Specify third source point or <continue>:** ***[you can grab the object with three points, but this really isn't necessary in 2D space]***

**Scale objects based on alignment points? [Yes/No] <N>:** ***[tell AutoCAD whether or not you want to scale the source object to fit exactly between the points you've selected]***

Don't worry; it's not as complicated as it looks.

| Do This: 7.2.2.1 | Using the *Align* Command |
|---|---|

I. Open *align.dwg* in the C:\Steps\Lesson07 folder.

II. Follow these steps.

## 7.2.2.1: Using the Align Command

1. Turn on the **Endpoint** Running OSNAP. Clear all other OSNAPs.

   **Command:** ***os***

2. Enter the ***Align*** command.

   **Command:** ***al***

3. Select box 1 and the text inside.

   **Select objects:**

   **Select objects:** ***[enter]***

4. Using the endpoint OSNAP, select the points as indicated.

   **Specify first source point:** ***[pick point 1a]***

   **Specify first destination point:** ***[pick point 2a]***

   **Specify second source point:** ***[ pick point 1b]***

   **Specify second destination point:** ***[pick point 2b]***

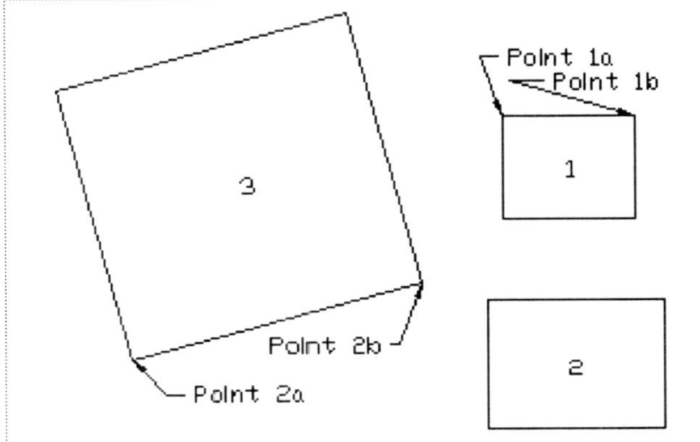


5. Completion the point selection procedure.

   **Specify third source point or <continue>:** ***[enter]***

6. Don't scale the objects.

   **Scale objects based on alignment points? [Yes/No] <N>:** ***[enter]***

   Your drawing looks like this.

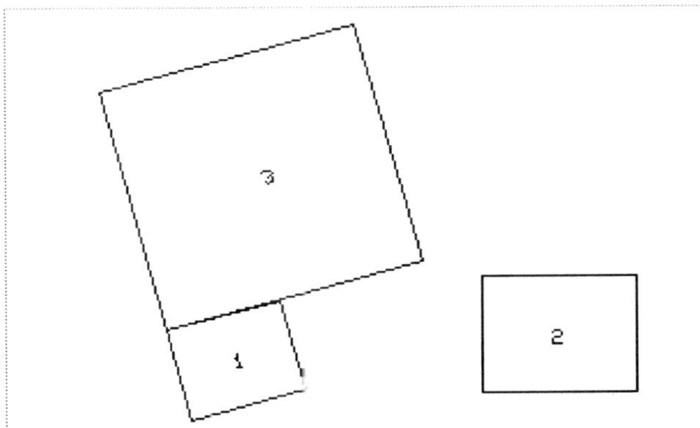


7. Repeat the ***Align*** command. Let's try it again using box 2; this time, we'll scale the objects.

   **Command:** ***[enter]***

   **Select objects:**

   **Select objects:** ***[enter]***

#### 7.2.2.1: Using the Align Command

8. Using the endpoint OSNAP, select the points as indicated.

> **Specify first source point:** ***[pick point 1a]***
> **Specify first destination point:** ***[pick point 2a]***
> **Specify second source point:** ***[ pick point 1b]***
> **Specify second destination point:** ***[pick point 2b]***

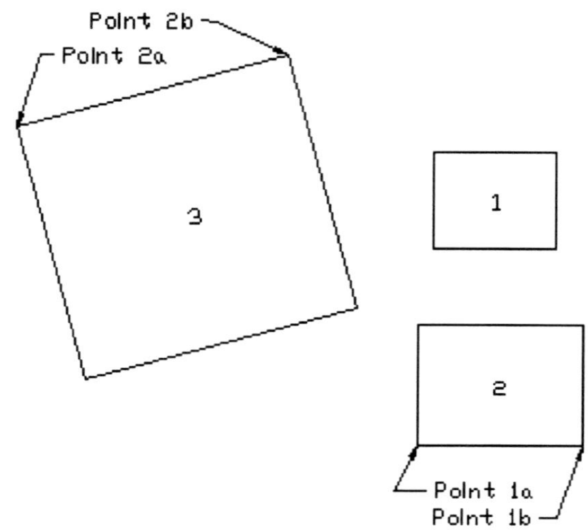


9. Scale the objects.

> **Scale objects based on alignment points? [Yes/No] <N>:** ***y***

Your drawing looks like this.

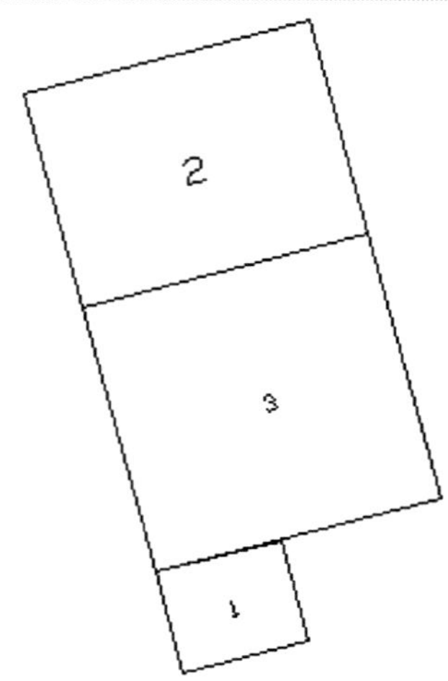


10. Save and exit your drawing.

> **Command:** ***qsave***

You can see, then, that the ***Align*** command is related to the ***Move*** command, although it's a bit more complex. You might say it's also related to the ***Rotate*** and ***Scale*** commands (we haven't studied those yet!). Wow! We'll look at the ***Rotate*** command in Lesson 9.

## 7.2.3 The *Copy* Command: From One to Many

Another command that's related to ***Move***, ***Copy*** has a command sequence that closely resembles the ***Move*** command sequence. Compare the following sequence to the ***Move*** sequence in Section 7.2.1.

> **Command:** ***copy*** **(or** ***cp*** **or** ***co*****)**
> **Select objects:** ***[select one or more objects]*** **1 found**
> **Select objects:** ***[enter to confirm completion of this selection set]***
> **Specify base point or [Displacement] <Displacement>:** ***[pick a starting (grabbing) point]***
> **Specify second point or <use first point as displacement>:** ***[pick a target point]***
> **Specify second point or [Exit/Undo] <Exit>:** ***[continue to pick target points, or enter to complete the command]***

All the options are the same as the ***Move*** command's – including **Displacement**. But ***Copy*** provides one big difference. Whereas the ***Move*** command simply moved an object, the ***Copy*** command will leave the original and place a copy at the **second point**. Want more? It'll continue to place copies until you tell it you have enough (by hitting ***enter***).

Let's give it a try!

| **Do This: 7.2.3.1** | **Using the *Copy* Command** |
|---|---|

I. Be sure you're in *Star.dwg* in the C:\Steps\Lesson07 folder.

II. Follow these steps.

**7.2.3.1: USING THE COPY COMMAND**

1. Enter the ***Copy*** command. Alternately, you can pick the **Copy** button on the Modify toolbar or palette.

   **Command: *co***

2. Put a selection window around the circle and all its contents.

   **Select objects:**

   **Select objects: *[enter]***

3. Select the lower quadrant of the circle as the **base point**.

   **Specify base point or [Displacement] <Displacement>: _qua of**

   Make a copy of the circle **4** units to the right.

   **Specify second point or <use first point as displacement>: *@4<0***

4. Complete the command.

   **Specify second point or [Exit/Undo] <Exit>: *[enter]***

   Your drawing looks like this.

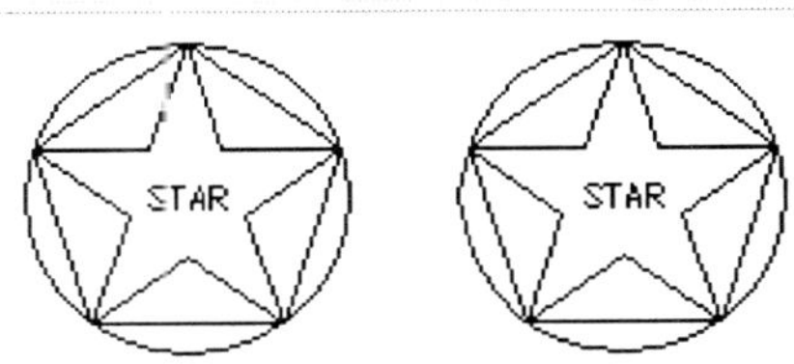


5. Erase the new circle and its contents.

   **Command: *e***

6. Now let's make **Multiple** copies. Repeat the ***Copy*** command.

   **Command: *co***

7. Select the objects as you did in Step 2.

   **Select objects:**

   **Select objects: *[enter]***

8. Select the center of the circle (just to be different) as the **base point**.

   **Specify base point or [Displacement] <Displacement>: _cen of**

9. Make three copies of the objects, as indicated.

   **Specify second point or <use first point as displacement>: *@4<0***

   **Specify second point or [Exit/Undo] <Exit>: *@8<0***

   **Specify second point or [Exit/Undo] <Exit>: *@3<90***

   **Specify second point or [Exit/Undo] <Exit>: *[enter]***

   Your drawing looks like the figure below.

### 7.2.3.1: Using the Copy Command

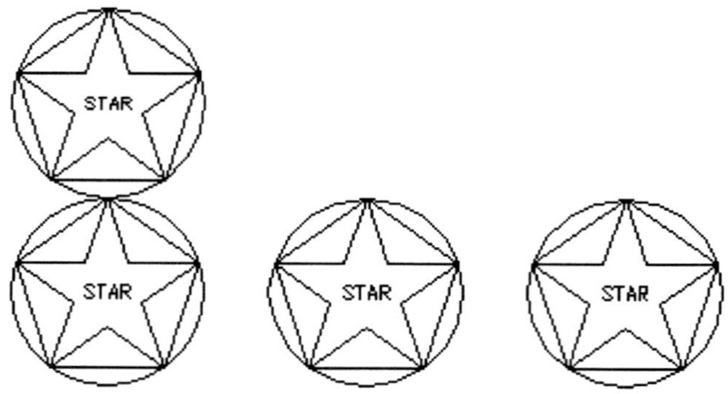


10. Save the drawing  but don't exit.

As you can see, ***Copy***, like ***Move***, requires little effort to master. But the benefits can be wondrous in terms of time and effort saved.

## 7.3 Moving and Copying Objects *between* Drawings

AutoCAD has given us the ability to move or copy objects from one drawing to another as well as within a single drawing. This feature makes use of the Windows ***Cut*** & ***Paste*** or ***Copy*** & ***Paste*** commands. It also takes advantage of AutoCAD's Multiple Document Environment (MDE), which enables you to open more than one drawing at a time. (Oh, the wonders that can happen with a little cooperation!)

You've probably seen that the ***Copy*** and ***Move*** commands can be found in the Modify pull-down menu. These, of course, are AutoCAD commands. But did you notice that the ***Copy*** command is also located in the Edit pull-down menu? This command (and the other commands in this menu) belongs to Windows. It takes advantage of the Windows clipboard (Windows' method of copying and moving objects and files within and between Windows' documents). It also makes it possible to copy and move objects between AutoCAD drawing files.

The Windows method of copying requires two steps: ***Copy*** and ***Paste***. ***Copy*** places the item(s) on the clipboard (an *imaginary* clipboard – a location in your computer's memory); ***Paste*** takes it from the clipboard and puts it into your document.

The Windows method of moving also requires two steps: ***Cut*** and ***Paste***. ***Cut*** (like ***Copy***) places the item(s) on the clipboard. But ***Cut*** also removes the item(s) from the source location. ***Paste*** puts the item(s) into your document.

AutoCAD's command line equivalents for Windows commands are:

| Windows | AutoCAD |
|---|---|
| Copy | ***copyclip*** or ***copybase*** |
| Cut | ***cutclip*** |
| Paste | ***pasteclip***, ***pasteblock***, or ***pasteorig*** |

Of course, the best way to understand all of this is to see it in action. Let's do an exercise.

| Do This: 7.3.1 | Using the MDE to Move and Copy Objects *between* Drawings |
|---|---|

I. Be sure you're in *Star.dwg* in the C:\Steps\Lesson07 folder. If not, please open it now.

II. Follow these steps.

**7.3.1: COPYING BETWEEN DRAWINGS**

1. Without closing the *star* drawing, start a new drawing from scratch 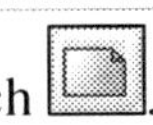.

   **Command: *new***

2. The new drawing opens atop the already open star drawing. We must position them so that we can see both at one time. Pick the Window pull-down menu and select **Tile Vertically**, as indicated.

   Notice that the two open drawings are listed at the bottom of the menu. Had you not wished to tile your drawings, you would've used these to toggle between the drawings.

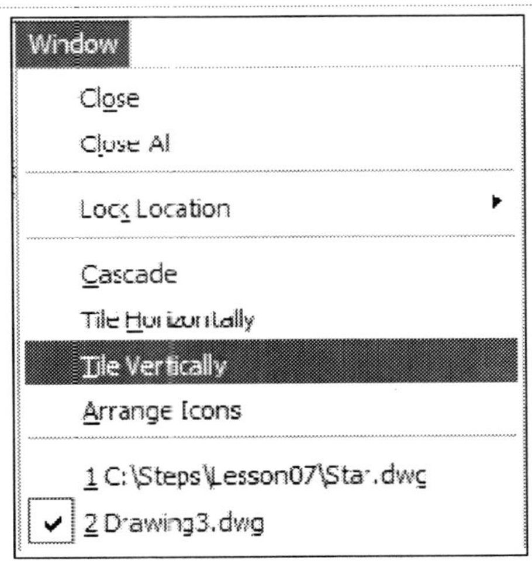


3. The drawings now appear side by side as shown below.

   Pick anywhere in the right drawing to make it active. Notice that the title bar of the active (current) drawing is solid and the other one is faded.

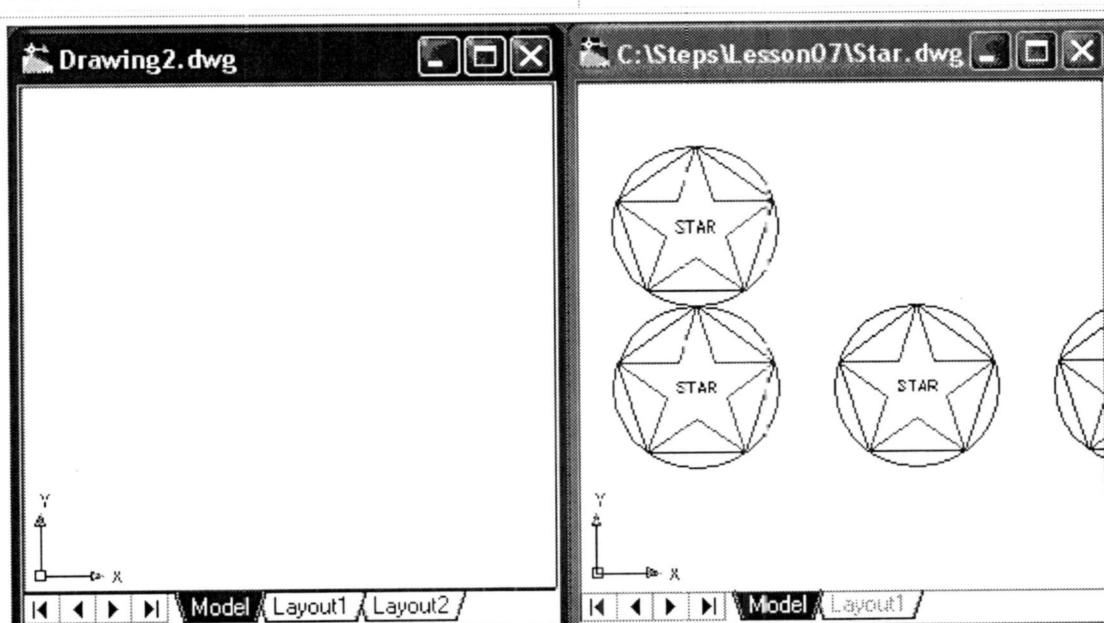

## 7.3.1: Copying Between Drawings

4. Without entering a command, place a selection window around the two circles on the left. They now appear highlighted as shown.

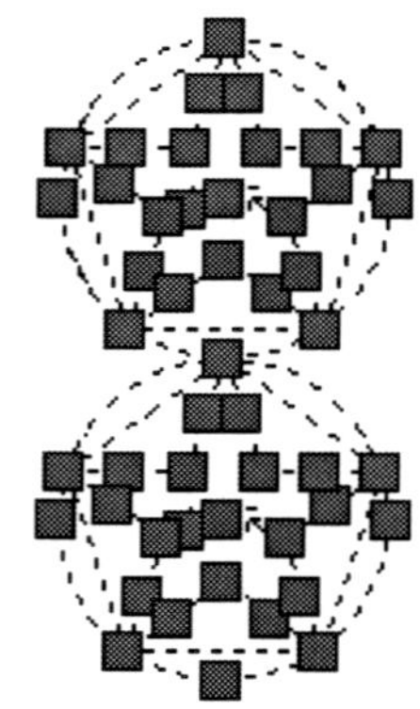

5. We could use the ***Copy*** command in the Edit pull-down menu, but the cursor menu will be more convenient. Right-click anywhere in the active document and select **Copy with Base Point** on the menu (the command line equivalent is ***Copybase***).

(Had we used the Edit menu's **Copy** command, AutoCAD would have assumed a base point in the lower-left corner of the objects selected.)

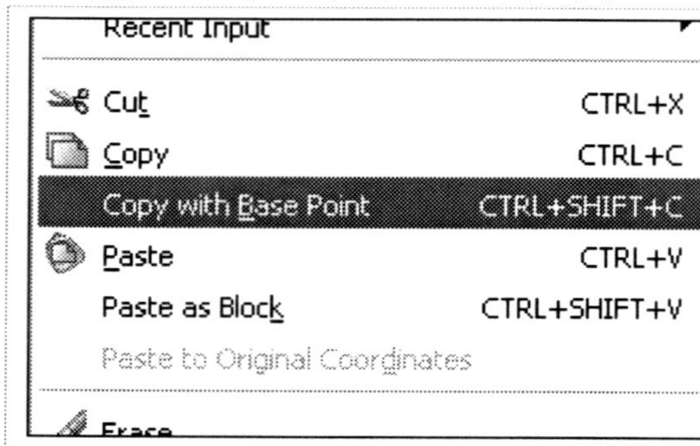


6. AutoCAD prompts you for the **base point**; use the center of the lower circle.

**Specify base point: _cen of**

7. AutoCAD returns to the command line. It doesn't appear that anything has been done, but the objects are now recorded on the Windows clipboard.

Click anywhere in the drawing on the left to activate it. Notice that its title bar becomes solid.

8. Right-click to access the cursor menu. Notice that you have three **Paste** options. The simple **Paste** (***pasteclip***) will add the objects to the new drawing as though you had copied them as you did in the last section.

**Paste as Block** (***pasteblock***) will add the objects as a block (more on blocks in Lesson 19).

**Paste to Original Coordinates** (***pasteorig***) will add the objects to the new drawing at the same coordinates at which they existed in the source drawing.

Select **Paste**.

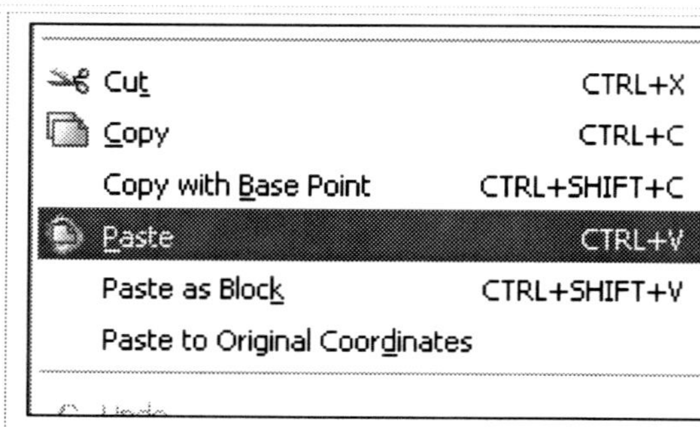


9. Paste the objects anywhere in the new drawing.

**Specify insertion point:**

10. Exit both drawings without saving.

**Command: *quit***

Some things to remember about using the Windows clipboard:

- To move objects, use the **Cut** (***Cutclip*** command) option rather than the **Copy** or **Copy with Base Point** option we used in Step 5.
- To clear the highlighting, either hit the ESC key or pick the **Deselect all** option from the cursor menu.
- Using the clipboard requires a small amount of computer memory. Keep this in mind if you use a particularly slow system (not much RAM) or have problems with your computer's memory.
- You can also use the ***Matchprop*** command from one drawing to another.
- Hitting ***enter*** to repeat a command will repeat the last command given in the active drawing (i.e., commands are active document-specific).
- *Remember to close a drawing when you've finished with it.* (Type ***Close*** or select it from the File pull-down menu.)

## 7.4 Extra Steps

After completing this lesson, spend some time experimenting with the new Lisp routines mentioned in this and other lessons. All the lisp routines included with this text are freeware. Play with them, pass them around, alter them as you see fit. Some are quite primitive; others are more advanced. But the value of each has been proved countless times since I wrote them.

Other Lisp routines will be available to you – some with this text, others where you go to work. One thing about the AutoCAD world – there is no shortage of these programs from which to pick and choose. When you get to your job site, ask around. CAD operators love to share!

## 7.5 What Have We Learned?

*Items covered in this lesson include:*

- *AutoCAD Modifying Commands*
  - ***Trim***
  - ***Extend***
  - ***Change***
  - ***Break***
  - ***Fillet***
  - ***Chamfer***
  - ***Move***
  - ***Align***
  - ***Copy***
- *AutoCAD's Multiple Document Environment (MDE)*
- *Windows' Commands*
  - ***Cut***
  - ***Copy***
  - ***Paste***

This has been a very good lesson. You've learned the basics of manipulating drawing objects to your advantage. Your drawing time will be noticeably lessened as you become more adept with these tools.

Relax for a moment and think about what you've learned. Sure, it's all still quite new to you. But when you began, did you think you would be able to draw the log cabin (Exercise 3) this soon? Draw it, then pat yourself on the back and go on to Lesson 8.

## 7.6 Exercises

1. Open the *Checkers* drawing in the C:\Steps\Lesson07 folder.
   1.1. Using the commands you've learned in this lesson, create the drawing in the figure at right from the objects provided. (Be sure to use different layers and colors to mark the different sides.)

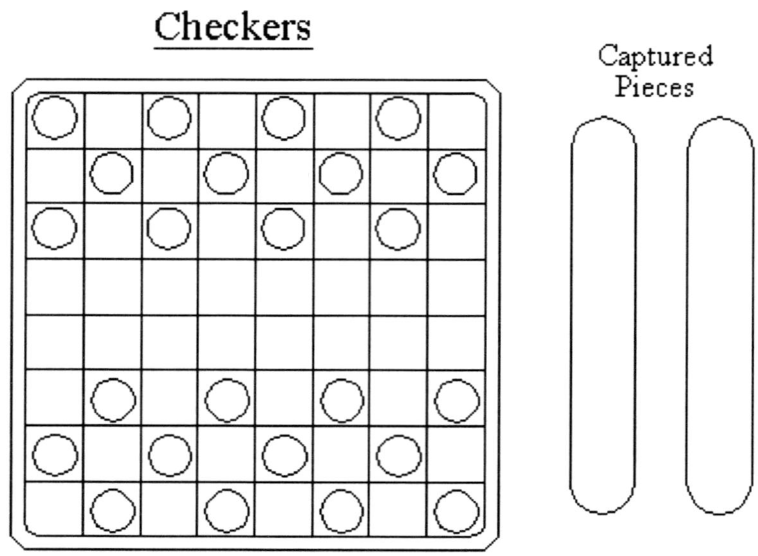


2. Using the *MyGrid3* template you created in Lesson 1 (or the *Grid3* template in the Lesson01 folder), create the drawing in the figure at right. Reset the grid to ¼" and the snap accordingly. Use the same layers you used in Exercise #3 of Lesson 6. Don't draw the dimensions.

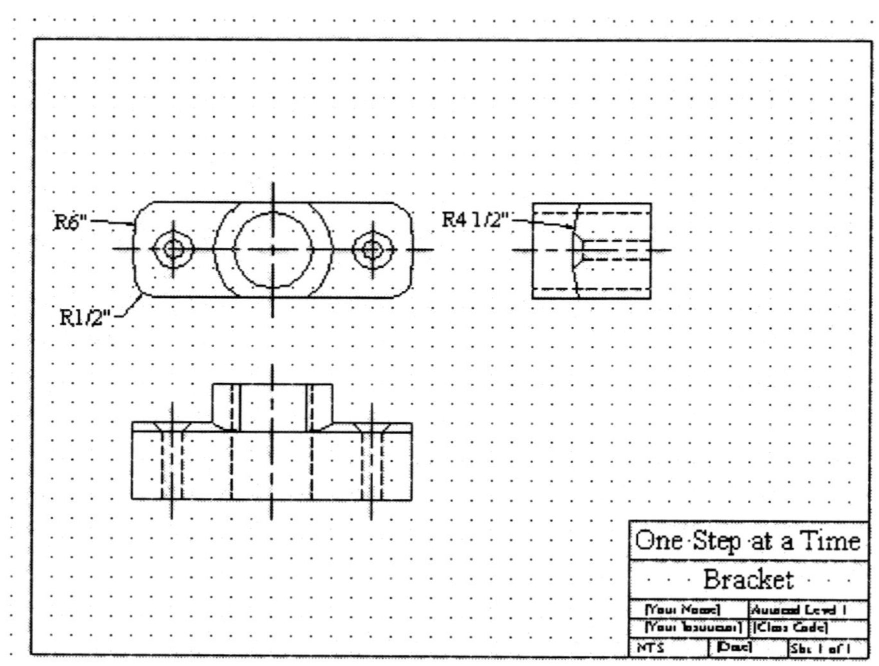


*For more exercises related to Lesson 7, please see Lesson 7 in AutoCAD 2007: One Step at a Time – Workbook.*

## 7.7 For Web-Based Review Questions, visit: http://www.uneedcad.com/2007/Files/07R7.pdf

# Lesson 8

Following this lesson, you will:

- ✓ *Know how to draw Polylines: The **PLine** command*
- ✓ *Know how to edit Polylines: The **PEdit** command*
- ✓ *Know how to convert Lines to Polylines*
- ✓ *Know how to convert Polylines to Lines: The **Explode** command*
- ✓ *Be familiar with the **Join** command*
- ✓ *Be familiar with AutoCAD's Inquiry Commands*
  - ***List***
  - ***Dist***
  - ***Area***
  - ***ID***

# Polylines and Overlooked Commands

*Back in Lesson 6, we discussed ways of differentiating among the various parts of a drawing using colors, linetypes, and layers. We also used lineweights to add width, but we had problems with them because lineweight isn't a true WYSIWYG property. In that lesson, I promised to show you how to create lines with true WYSIWYG width. Once you've conquered width – through polylines – you can combine wide lines with linetypes and layers for more complex drawings.*

*You can draw lines with width using the **PLine** command (pronounced "P-Line"). We call these lines polylines, not for their ability to show width, but for their ability to be drawn as multi-segmented lines. That is, polylines can contain many lines and still be treated as a single unit (much as you've already seen with polyline rectangles and polygons).*

> Additionally, polylines can carry information. These are known as smart polylines but are beyond the scope of this text. For more information on smart polylines, see an AutoCAD customization text.

*Polylines used to confuse the AutoCAD user because of the massive amounts of information they contained. They also dramatically increased the size of a drawing with stored information that was often never needed. For this reason, AutoCAD created the light weight polyline (lwpolyline). Capable of containing most of the information available to the polyline, the lwpolyline is much more condensed, presents its information via the **List** command (Section 8.2.1) in a much more logical and understandable manner, and takes up much less drawing memory. The **PLine** command will actually draw an lwpolyline ("L-W-Polyline") and convert automatically to a polyline if the need arises to function as the older polylines did.*

## 8.1 Using the *PLine* Command for Wide Lines and Multi-Segmented Lines

You've already made use of polylines in two commands – ***Rectangle*** and ***Polygon***; so you have some idea of how polylines behave. Each group of lines acts as a single object when modified or manipulated. With ***Rectangle***, you even saw that you could control the line width. Now we'll see how to create objects with a little more freedom than these commands allowed – by using the ***PLine*** command.

One of AutoCAD's more difficult commands, ***PLine*** contains several options. We'll look at each, but the basic sequence is

> **Command: *pline* (or *pl*)**
>
> **Specify start point: *[select a starting point]***
>
> **Current line-width is 0.0000**
>
> **Specify next point or [Arc/Halfwidth/Length/Undo/Width]: *[select the next point]***
>
> **Specify next point or [Arc/Close/Halfwidth/Length/Undo/Width]: *[you can continue to create line segments or hit enter to complete the command]***

The options appear more intimidating than they actually are.

- **Close** works just like it does with the ***Line*** command. That is, it closes the polyline. But remember, unlike lines, the entire polyline will be treated as a single unit.
- **Halfwidth** and **Width** do the same thing. These are your options for telling AutoCAD how wide to make the polyline. **Width** is how wide you want the polyline, whereas **Halfwidth** is half of the width. Why two options to achieve the same end? AutoCAD redundancy again! Each of these options provides its own prompts. The **Halfwidth** prompts are

  > **Specify starting half-width <0.0000>:**
  >
  > **Specify ending half-width <0.0000>:**

  The **Width** prompts are the same, but ask for width rather than halfwidth. Notice that the starting and ending widths can be set separately. This'll come in handy when creating arrowheads, as we'll see in our exercises.

- **Length** allows you to enter the length of a line segment. AutoCAD defines the line direction by the location of the crosshairs. You'll be happier if you ignore this option in favor of one of AutoCAD's many other methods of defining line length (direct distance, Cartesian coordinates, polar tracking, etc.). The **Length** option provides this prompt:

  **Specify length of line:**
- **Undo** will do just that. Here at the ***PLine*** prompt, it undoes the last segment drawn.
- Notice that AutoCAD repeats the list of options, always with the **Specify next point** option as the default. This makes it simple to continue drawing – selecting points – until finished while making all the other options available for *each* line segment. In other words, you can change the width, close the polyline, or switch to an arc at any time during the creation process!
- **Arc** allows you to create polyline arcs – that is, sequential arcs or arcs with width. The **Arc** option provides a second tier of prompts that behave remarkably like the options of the ***Arc*** command:

  **Specify endpoint of arc or [Angle/CEnter/CLose/Direction/Halfwidth/ Line/Radius/Second pt/Undo/Width]:**
  - The **Angle** option allows you to specify an included angle to define the arc. To more easily understand this, think of *pieces* of a circle. A circle is 360°; 45° would be 1/8 of the circle, so specifying an angle of 45° will tell AutoCAD to draw 1/8 of a circle. AutoCAD will prompt as it did in the ***Arc*** command.
  - The **CEnter** option allows you to specify the center point of the arc followed by an **Angle**, the **Length** of the arc, or the **Endpoint** of the arc. Again, pline arc prompts resemble the ***Arc*** command.
  - The **CLose** option in this tier will close the polyline using an arc. You can use this method to create circles with line-width.
  - AutoCAD normally draws an arc in a counterclockwise direction. Once you draw an arc using the ***PLine*** command, AutoCAD reverses direction but stays in the **Arc** mode until told to switch back to **Line** or to **CLose** (or exit) the ***PLine*** command. If you wish to draw a series of arcs in the same direction – like tiles on a roof – the **Direction** option allows you to specify the direction of the next arc.
  - **Halfwidth** and **Width** provide a way to change the width of the polyline from within the **Arc** option. AutoCAD prompts the same way it did for these options in the first tier of ***PLine*** options.
  - The **Line** option returns you to the first tier of ***PLine*** options. From there, you can continue the polyline or exit the command.
  - One of the easier options is the **Radius** option. With this, AutoCAD allows you to specify the radius of the arc followed by the **Angle** or **endpoint**.
  - You can draw a three-point arc, just as you did with the ***Arc*** command, by using the **Second pt** option. AutoCAD prompts for the **second point** on the arc, then the **endpoint**.
  - **Undo** performs just as it did in the upper tier.
  - The default option is simply to **Specify endpoint of arc**. When that's done, AutoCAD repeats the options until you either select the **Line** option or exit the command by hitting ***enter***.

It took a few pages to explain the various parameters of the ***PLine*** command. It's a powerful tool, but don't let the scope of the ***PLine*** command deter you from its use. Most students get the hang of it fairly quickly. Let's look at some of the options in an exercise.

In addition to the command line, toolbar, and palette, you can access the ***PLine*** command by selecting **Polyline** from the Draw pull down menu.

The various options of the ***PLine*** command are also available in the cursor and dynamic input menus once the ***PLine*** command has been entered.

| **Do This: 8.1.1** | **Drawing with Polylines** |
|---|---|

I. Start a new drawing from scratch.

II. Set the grid to ***0.5*** and the grid snap to ***0.25***. Zoom in and turn on polar tracking.

III. Follow these steps.

### 8.1.1: Drawing with Polylines

1. Enter the ***PLine*** command. Alternately, you can pick the **Polyline** button 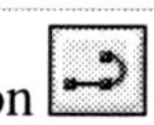 on the Draw toolbar or palette.

    **Command: *pl***

2. Select a starting point at ***6,5***.

    **Specify start point: *6,5***

3. AutoCAD tells you what the **Current line-width** setting is, and then prompts you for the next step. Type ***w*** or pick **Width** on the menu to change the line width.

    **Current line-width is 0.0000**

    **Specify next point or [Arc/Halfwidth/Length/Undo/Width]: *w***

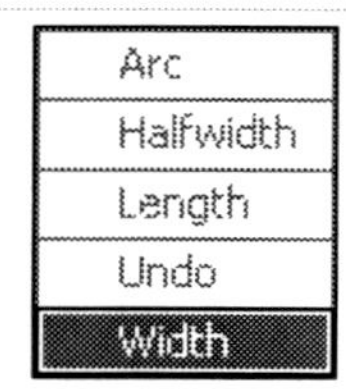


4. Set the **starting width** to 1/16.

    **Specify starting width <0.0000>: *1/16***

5. AutoCAD has set the **ending width** to match the starting width, but asks you if you want to change it. Accept the setting.

    **Specify ending width <0.0625>: *[enter]***

6. Draw the first line segment ***1.5*** units upward. Use coordinate entry or polar tracking.

    **Specify next point or [Arc/Halfwidth/Length/Undo/Width]: *@1.5<90***

7. Tell AutoCAD to draw an **Arc** next .

    **Specify next point or [Arc/Close/Halfwidth/Length/Undo/Width]: *a***

8. Accept the **endpoint of arc** option and place the endpoint ***1*** unit to the left.

    **Specify endpoint of arc or [Angle/CEnter/CLose/Direction/Halfwidth/Line/Radius/Second pt/Undo/Width]: *@1<180***

9. Select the **Line** option  to return to the first tier of options. (Note: Remember, AutoCAD isn't case-sensitive – that is, it doesn't matter if you type a capital or small letter.)

    **Specify endpoint of arc or [Angle/CEnter/CLose/Direction/Halfwidth/Line/Radius/Second pt/Undo/Width]: *l***

## 8.1.1: Drawing with Polylines

10. Continue the polyline ***1.5*** units downward as indicated.

11. Continue ***1.5*** units to the west.

**Specify next point or [Arc/Close/Halfwidth/Length/Undo/ Width]:** ***@1.5<180***

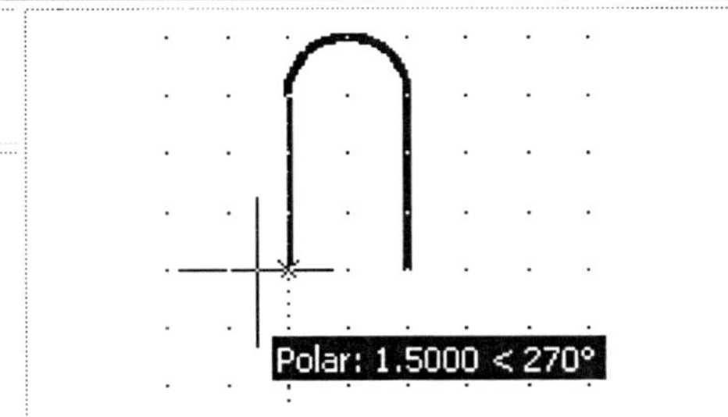


12. Use the **Arc** option again 

.

**Specify next point or [Arc/Close/Halfwidth/Length/Undo/Width]:** ***a***

13. Draw the arc with a ¼ unit **Radius** 

downward.

**Specify endpoint of arc or [Angle/CEnter/CLose/ Direction/Halfwidth/Line/ Radius/ Second pt/Undo/Width]:** ***r***

**Specify radius of arc:** ***.25***

**Specify endpoint of arc or [Angle]:** ***[select a point one grid mark due south of the current point]***

14. Let's use the **Direction** option to repeat the arc.

**Specify endpoint of arc or [Angle/CEnter/CLose/Direction/ Halfwidth/Line/Radius/ Second pt/Undo/Width]:** ***d***

15. Pick a point due west of the current point, as indicated.

**Specify the tangent direction for the start point of arc:**

16. Pick a point ½" to the south.

**Specify endpoint of the arc:** ***@.5<270***

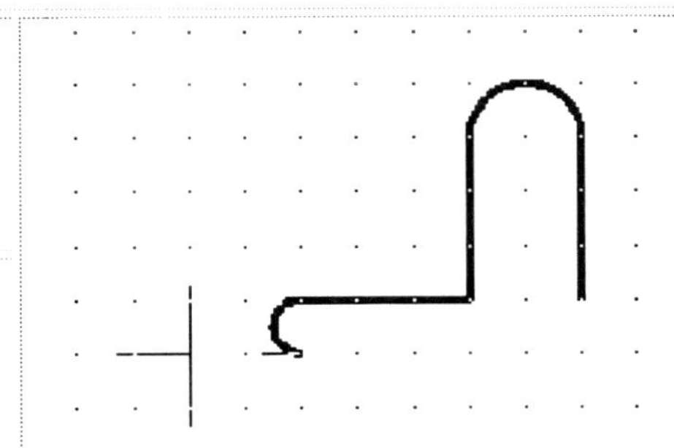

17. Return to the **Line** option.

**Specify endpoint of arc or [Angle/CEnter/CLose/Direction/ Halfwidth/Line/Radius/ Second pt/Undo/Width]:** ***l***

18. Draw the line ***1.5*** units to the right using polar tracking. Your drawing now looks like this.

**Specify next point or [Arc/Close/ Halfwidth/Length/Undo/Width]:**

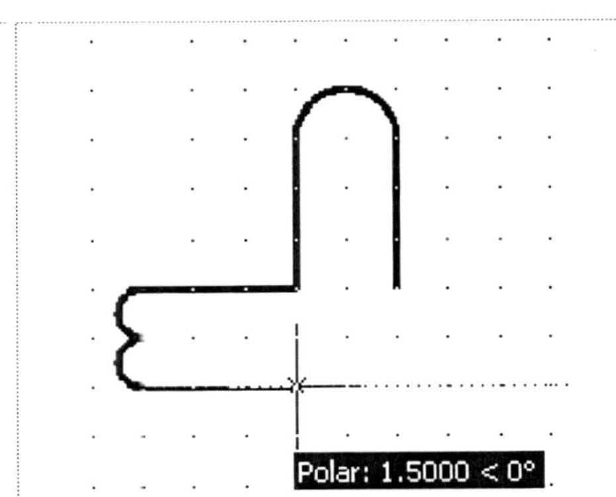

19. Using the preceding details, see if you can complete the drawing. (Remember to type ***c*** to complete the polyline.) When you've finished, it'll look like this.

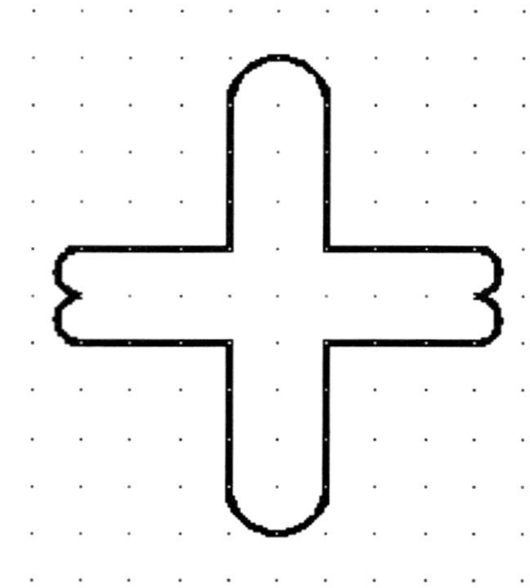

20. And now let's try something completely different. Zoom in around the center of the object you just drew. You'll be working in this area.

**Command:** *z*

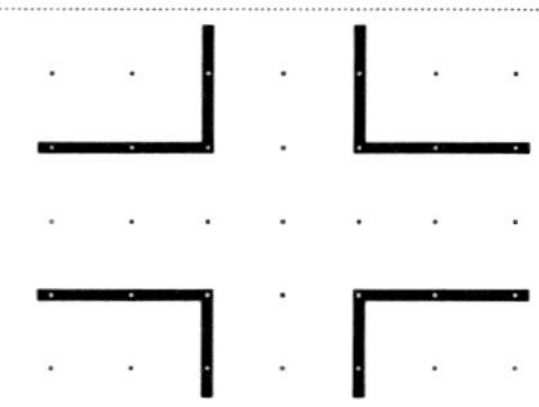

21. Repeat the ***PLine*** command.

**Command: *pl***

22. Pick the starting point indicated.

**Specify start point:** *4.75,4.5*

23. Tell AutoCAD you want to change the **Width**.

**Current line-width is 0.0625**

**Specify next point or [Arc/ Halfwidth/Length/Undo/Width]:** *w*

24. Set different **starting** and **ending widths** as indicated.

**Specify starting width <0.0625>: *0***

**Specify ending width <0.0000>: *.25***

25. Draw the line segment. Notice the arrowhead effect of your width settings.

**Specify next point or [Arc/Halfwidth/Length/Undo/Width]: *@.5<0***

26. Continue the polyline. Now AutoCAD uses just the width setting of the endpoint of the last line segment drawn.

**Specify next point or [Arc/Halfwidth/Length/Undo/Width]: *@.5<0***

27. Change the **Width** again. Accept the **0.25** default of the starting width, but change the ending width back to ***0***.

**Specify next point or [Arc/Close/Halfwidth/Length/Undo/Width]:** *w*

**Specify starting width <0.2500>: *[enter]***

**Specify ending width <0.2500>: *0***

## 8.1.1: Drawing with Polylines

28. Complete the polyline.

**Specify next point or [Arc/Close/ Halfwidth/Length/Undo/Width]:** *@.5<0*

**Specify next point or [Arc/Close/ Halfwidth/Length/Undo/Width]:** *[enter]*

Your drawing looks like this.

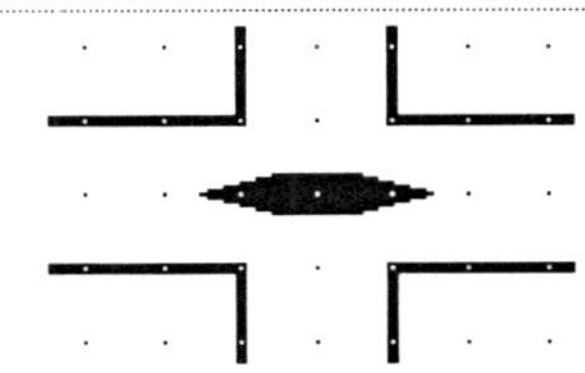

29. Complete the drawing by placing a final polyline as shown.

**Command:** ***pl***

30. Save the drawing as *MyPline* to the C:\Steps\Lesson08 folder and exit.

**Command:** ***qsave***

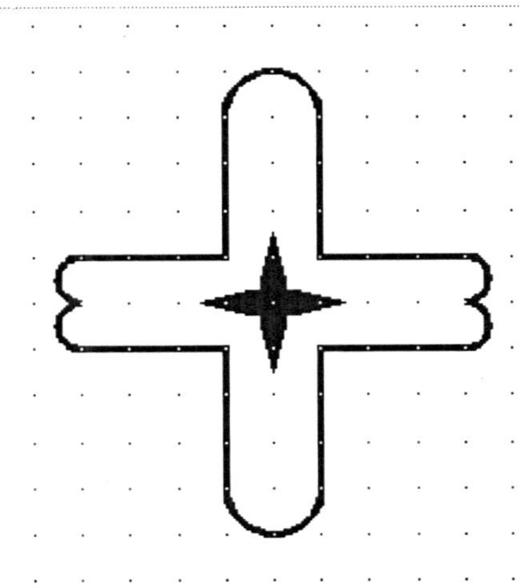

Polylines can be a bit frightening at first because of the depth of the command. But don't let too many options prevent you from using one of AutoCAD's best tools.

We'll need to spend some time with the polyline editing tools. Let's get right to it!

## 8.2 Editing Polylines – The *PEdit* Command

If you thought drawing polylines was fun, you're in for a real treat now! Remember that second tier of options? The ***PEdit*** command has one, as well, *and several smaller third tiers!* Sort of makes you want to go back to the board, doesn't it? But to encourage you, let me just say that you'll probably never need the second (or third) tier – or at least only rarely in the 2-dimensional world.

> In the 3-dimensional world, it'll often be easier to edit a polyline. When you get there, it'll be useful if you already know how to add or move a vertex (the "corners" within a polyline). We'll see how to do that here, but you probably won't need it for a while.

Two-dimensional polylines are such that it's often easier to erase and redraw than it is to edit. Still, you should be familiar with the ***PEdit*** command for those benefits that it does provide. These include the ability to change the width of the polyline and to join several polylines into a single object.

The ***PEdit*** command sequence looks like this:

**Command:** ***pedit*** **(or** ***pe*****)**

**Select polyline or [Multiple]:** ***[select the polyline(s) to edit]***

**Enter an option [Open/Join/Width/Edit vertex/Fit/Spline/Decurve/Ltype gen/Undo]:** ***tell AutoCAD how you want to edit the polyline]***

This sequence includes the first tier of options. Let's stop here to examine them.

- Use the **Multiple** option to edit more than one polyline at a time. (Note: The **Edit vertex** option isn't available during multiple polyline editing sessions.)

- The **Open** option appears if a closed polyline is selected at the **Select polyline** prompt. Conversely, a **Close** option appears if an open polyline is selected. The **Open** option removes the last line segment – the one that closed the polyline. The **Close** option adds a polyline segment between two open endpoints.
- The **Join** option enables you to join one polyline to another to form one large polyline. The ***Join*** *command* will do the same thing … and more!
- The **Width** option allows you to modify the polyline's width.
- **Fit** and **Spline** will soften corners into curves. This was once the tool of choice for drawing contour lines for topographical maps. However, AutoCAD now provides a ***Spline*** command that was specifically designed for drawing contour lines (more on this in Lesson 11). The difference between **Fit** and **Spline** is that, although **Fit** will create curves that go through each point on the polyline, **Spline**'s curves go through only the first and last point. The rest of the points "pull" the curve but don't insist that the curve touch each point.

> The system variable **Splinetype** controls the amount of curve caused by the **Spline** option. A setting of **5** will cause a more pronounced curve (called a Quadratic B-spline) that's actually tangent to the original polyline. The default setting of **6** causes a softer, less pronounced curve (a Cubic B-spline). There are only the two settings available.

- **Decurve** removes all curves on the polyline whether put there as **Arcs**, **Fits**, or **Splines**.
- **Ltype gen** regulates the placement of dashes and spaces in linetypes.

  Let me make this as simple as possible. Through some fairly complicated mathematics, AutoCAD normally balances dashes and spaces in a line so that the amount of solid line at both ends is the same. If the length of the line doesn't allow enough room for the dashes and spaces defined by the linetype, no spaces are shown. When turned **on**, **Ltype gen** calculates the placement of dashes and spaces for the overall polyline. When turned **off** (the default), the placement is calculated for each individual line segment within the polyline. This will become clearer in our exercise.
- By now you're familiar with the **Undo** option. It undoes the last modification made within the ***PEdit*** command.

We'll look in some detail at the **Edit vertex** option later in this lesson. But let's try an exercise on what we've learned so far.

> In addition to the command line, toolbar, and palette, you can find the ***PEdit*** command by selecting **Object**, and then **Polyline**, in the Modify pull-down menu. The easy way, however, is to simply double-click on the polyline you want to edit. AutoCAD will automatically start the ***PEdit*** command.
>
> The various options of the ***PEdit*** command are also available on the cursor and dynamic input menus once the ***PEdit*** command has been entered.

| **Do This: 8.2.1** | **Working with Simple Polyline Editing Tools** |
|---|---|

I. Open the *MyPline* drawing you created earlier in this lesson. If this drawing isn't available, open the *pline* drawing in the C:\Steps\Lesson08 folder.

II. Follow these steps. (Although I don't always show the option, you can use cursor or dynamic input menus at any ***PEdit*** prompt if you prefer.)

## 8.2.1: Simple Polyline Editing Tools

1. Enter the ***PEdit*** command . Alternately, you can pick the **Edit Polyline** button on the

## 8.2.1: Simple Polyline Editing Tools

Modify II toolbar or the Modify palette.

**Command:** ***pe***

2. Select the outer polyline.

**Select polyline or [Multiple]:**

3. Let's start with the **Open** option Open. Type *o* or pick **Open** on the menu. Your drawing will look like this.

**Enter an option [Open/Join/ Width/Edit vertex/Fit/Spline/ Decurve/Ltype gen/Undo]:** ***o***

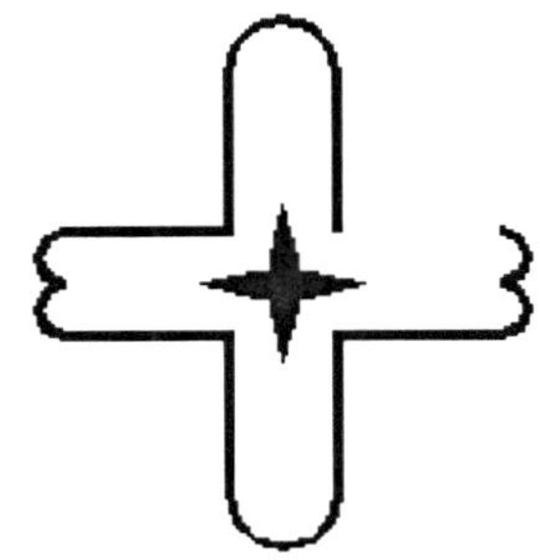

4. Notice how the prompt has changed from **Open** to **Close**. Use the **Close** option. Notice that the figure is closed and looks like it did when you started.

**Enter an option [Close/Join/Width/Edit vertex/Fit/Spline/Decurve/Ltype gen/Undo]:** ***c***

5. Select the **Width** option Width.

**Enter an option [Open/Join/Width/Edit vertex/Fit/ Spline/Decurve/Ltype en/Undo]:** ***w***

6. AutoCAD asks for a new width. Enter 1/32. Notice (right) the difference in the figure.

**Specify new width for all segments:** ***1/32***

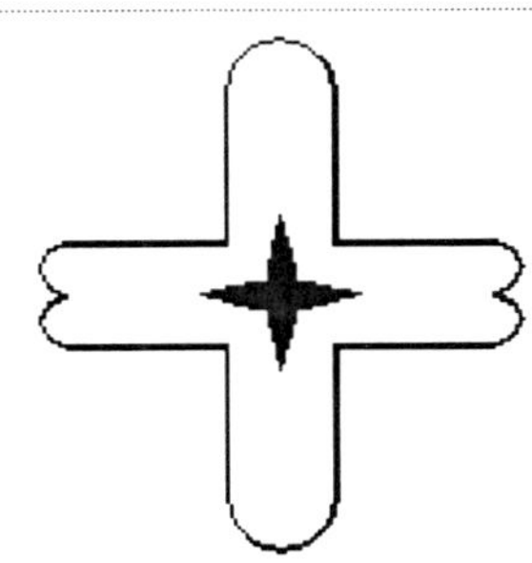

7. Note where the vertices (corners) are on the figure (use the grid if it helps), then select the **Fit** option Fit.

**Enter an option [Open/Join/Width/Edit vertex/ Fit/Spline/Decurve/Ltype gen/Undo]:** ***f***

Notice (right) that the polyline still goes through the vertices.

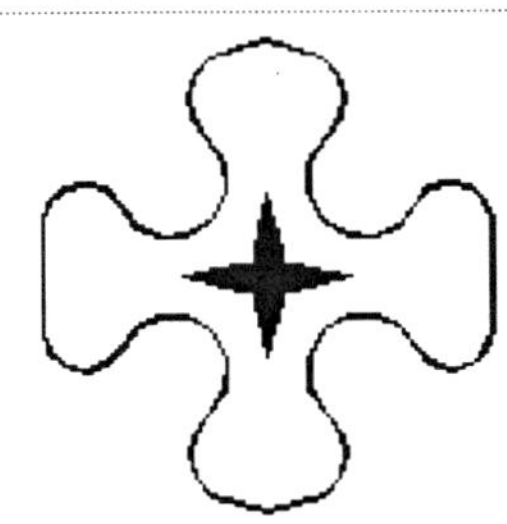

8. **Undo** Undo the last modification.

**Enter an option [Open/Join/Width/Edit vertex/Fit/Spline/Decurve/Ltype gen/Undo]:** ***u***

9. Now try the **Spline** option Spline.

**Enter an option [Open/Join/Width/Edit vertex/ Fit/Spline/Decurve/Ltype gen/Undo]:** ***s***

Notice (right) the differences between **Fit** and **Spline**.

10. Decurve the polyline Decurve.

**Enter an option [Open/Join/Width/Edit vertex/ Fit/Spline/Decurve/Ltype gen/Undo]:** ***d***

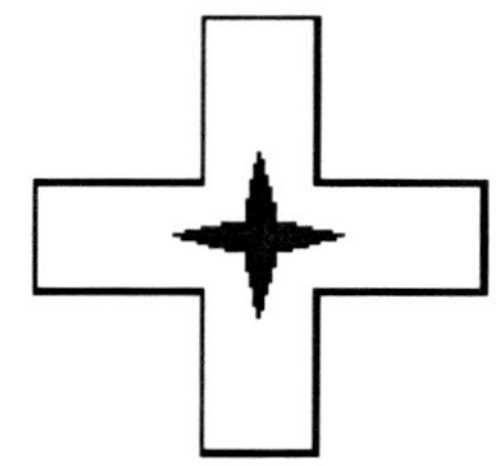

11. Undo the last two modifications. The drawing will look as it did in Step 6.

**Enter an option [Open/Join/Width/Edit vertex/Fit/Spline/Decurve/Ltype gen/ Undo]:** ***u***

**Enter an option [Open/Join/Width/Edit vertex/Fit/Spline/Decurve/Ltype gen/ Undo]:** ***u***

12. Exit the command.

**Enter an option [Open/Join/Width/Edit vertex/Fit/Spline/Decurve/Ltype gen/ Undo]:** ***[enter]***

13. Change the linetype of the polyline to **Center2.**

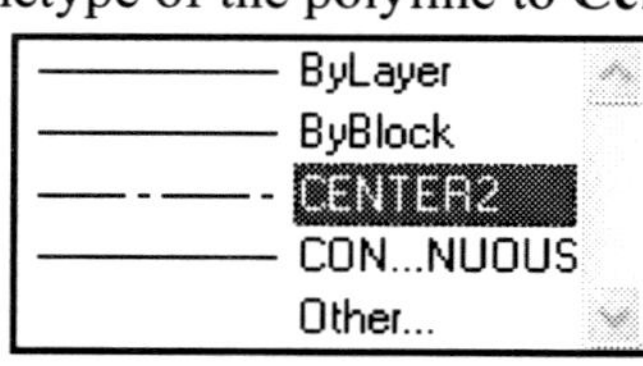


Notice (right) that there are no dashes and spaces showing in the smaller arcs.

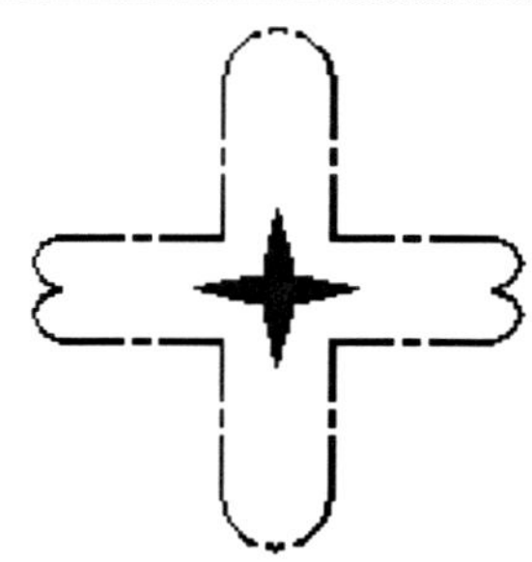

14. Repeat the ***PEdit*** command.

**Command:** ***pe***

15. Select the same polyline.

**Select polyline or [Multiple]:**

16. Now turn the **Ltype gen** option Ltype gen …

**Enter an option [Open/Join/Width/Edit vertex/Fit/Spline/Decurve/Ltype gen/ Undo]:** ***l***

## 8.2.1: Simple Polyline Editing Tools

17. … **On** 

. Notice (right) the change in the drawing dashes and spaces now show in the smaller arcs.

**Enter polyline linetype generation option [ON/OFF] <Off>:** ***on***

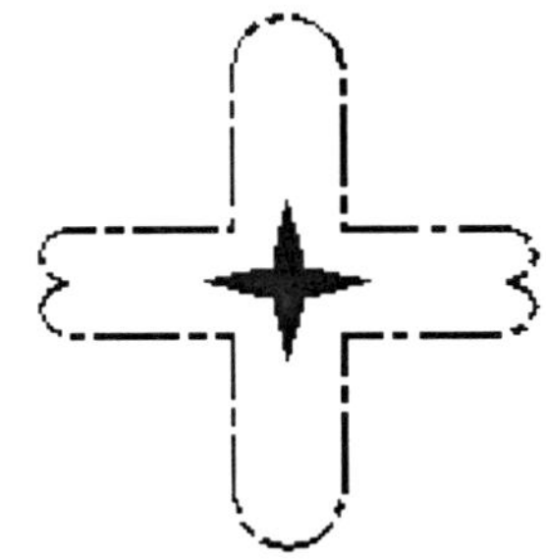

18. Exit the command.

**Enter an option [Open/Join/Width/Edit vertex/ Fit/Spline/Decurve/Ltype gen/Undo]:** ***[enter]***

19. Return the linetype to **ByLayer** 

.

As I mentioned earlier, the **Join** option allows you to join two (or more) polylines together to make a single polyline. You control how this is done. It works like this:

**Command:** ***pedit*** **(or** ***pe*****)**
**Select polyline or [Multiple]:** ***m [use the Multiple option to select more than one polyline]***
**Select objects:** ***[select the polylines you wish to join together]***
**Select objects:** ***[hit enter to complete the selection]***
**Enter an option [Close/Open/Join/Width/Fit/Spline/Decurve/Ltype gen/Undo]:** ***j [select the Join option]***
**Join Type = Extend** ***[AutoCAD tells you what type of join it'll perform]***
**Enter fuzz distance or [Jointype] <0.0000>:** ***[tell AutoCAD how far apart the polylines may be]***
**1 segments added to polyline** ***[AutoCAD tells you how many segments it has added to the polyline]***
**Enter an option [Close/Open/Join/Width/Fit/Spline/Decurve/Ltype gen/Undo]:** ***[hit enter to complete the command]***

You must make two decisions when joining polylines – the **Join Type** and the **fuzz distance**.

- **Fuzz distance** refers to how much distance separates the polylines. AutoCAD will only join polylines whose endpoints fall within the distance you specify – that is, the distance you specify is the outer limit of the polylines' proximity to each other. You can actually use this option to your advantage – joining only those polylines whose endpoints fall within a certain distance or even touch each other (a **0.0000** fuzz distance).
- The **Jointype** option will present the following prompt:

  **Enter join type [Extend/Add/Both] <Extend>:**

  Select the type of joining you would like between your polylines.
  - **Extend**, the default, will extend or trim the polylines as necessary to form the joint.
  - **Add** will add polyline segments between the endpoints of the selected polylines.
  - When using the **Both** option, AutoCAD will extend or trim the polylines whenever possible to form the joint; where this isn't possible, as in the case of parallel polylines, it'll add a polyline segment.

Let's try an exercise to see the **Join** option in action.

| Do This: 8.3.2 | Joining Polylines |
|---|---|

I. Open the *Join* drawing in the C:\Steps\Lesson08 folder. It looks like Figure 8.001.

II. Follow these steps.

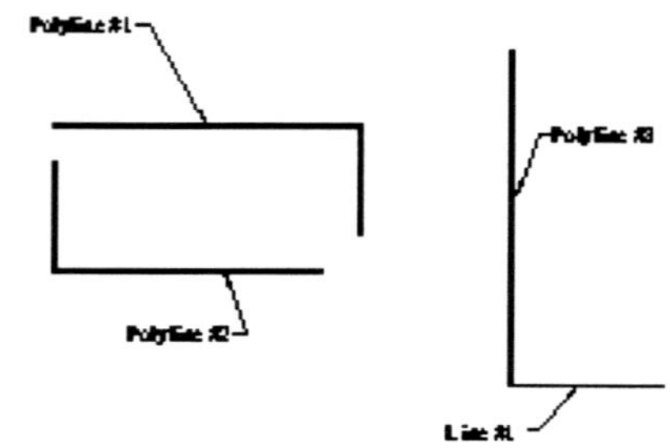

Figure 8.001

## 8.3.2: Joining Polylines

1. Enter the ***PEdit*** command 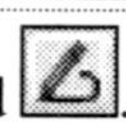.

   **Command: *pe***

2. Use the **Multiple** option 

, and select **Polyline #1** and **Polyline #2**.

   **Select polyline or [Multiple]: *m***
   **Select objects:**
   **Select objects: *[enter]***

3. Use the **Join** option 

.

   **Enter an option [Close/Open/Join/Width/Fit/Spline/Decurve/Ltype gen/ Undo]: *j***

4. The grid in this drawing is 0.5. The proximity of one set of endpoints is less than 0.6; the proximity of the other set is greater that 0.6. Set the **fuzz distance** to ***0.6***.

   **Join Type = Extend**
   **Enter fuzz distance or [Jointype] <0.0000>: *.6***

5. AutoCAD tells you how many segments it added to the polyline. Hit ***enter*** to complete the command. You now have a single polyline consisting of four segments (right).

   **2 segments added to polyline**
   **Enter an option [Close/Open/Join/Width/Fit/ Spline/Decurve/Ltype gen/Undo]: *[enter]***

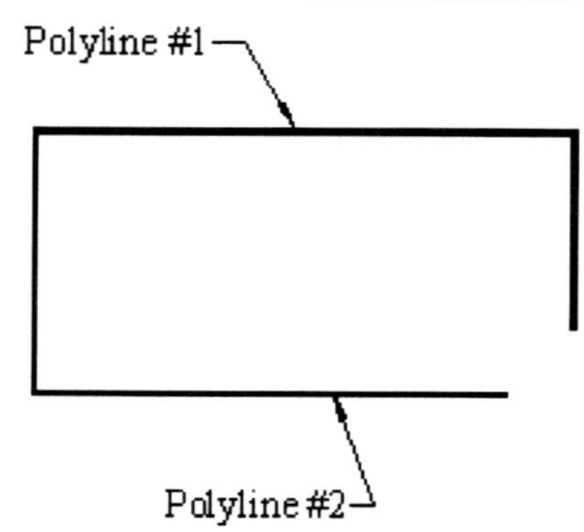


6. Let's repeat this procedure using **Polyline #3** and the **Line**. Repeat Steps 1 and 2, this time selecting these objects.

   **Command: *pe***
   **Select polyline or [Multiple]: *m***
   **Select objects:**

## 8.3.2: JOINING POLYLINES

7. Because one of the objects you selected was not a polyline, AutoCAD asks if you'd like to convert it to one. Accept the offer. (This is how you convert from a line to a polyline.)

**Convert Lines and Arcs to polylines [Yes/No]? <Y>** ***[enter]***

8. Again, use the **Join** option 

.

**Enter an option [Close/Open/Join/Width/Fit/Spline/Decurve/Ltype gen/ Undo]:** *j*

9. Reset the **fuzz distance** to ***0*** and complete the command.

The objects don't look any different; but if you try to erase one, you'll notice that both area selected. Both segments are now part of a single polyline!

**Join Type = Extend**

**Enter fuzz distance or [Jointype] <0.6000>:** ***0***

**1 segments added to polyline**

**Enter an option [Close/Open/Join/Width/Fit/Spline/Decurve/Ltype gen/ Undo]:** ***[enter]***

10. Close the drawing without saving.

**Command:** ***close***

In addition to the **Join** option of the ***PEdit*** command, AutoCAD has added a ***Join*** command to its repertoire. Use this to join objects such as:

- Line segments – Line segments must be collinear (that is, they should lie along the same infinite line whether real or imaginary), but they can have gaps.
- Polylines – Polylines must be touching at endpoints and be on the same XY-plane. Polyline line segments or arcs can be joined.
- Arcs or Elliptical Arcs – Arcs which are part of the same (real or imaginary) circle can be joined or closed into a circle. Arc segments can have gaps.
- Splines – Splines must be in the same plane and have touching endpoints. (More on Splines in Lesson 11.

We've just about covered the first tier of options in the ***PEdit*** command. The only remaining option is the key to the next tier – **Edit vertex**. As a beginning CAD operator in a 2-dimensional world, you'll rarely find the need to edit a vertex. But the option comes in quite handy for very complex polylines and 3-dimensional polylines. Choosing **Edit vertex** will result in the following list of second-tier options:

**Enter a vertex editing option [Next/Previous/Break/Insert/Move/Regen/Straighten/ Tangent/Width/eXit] <N>:**

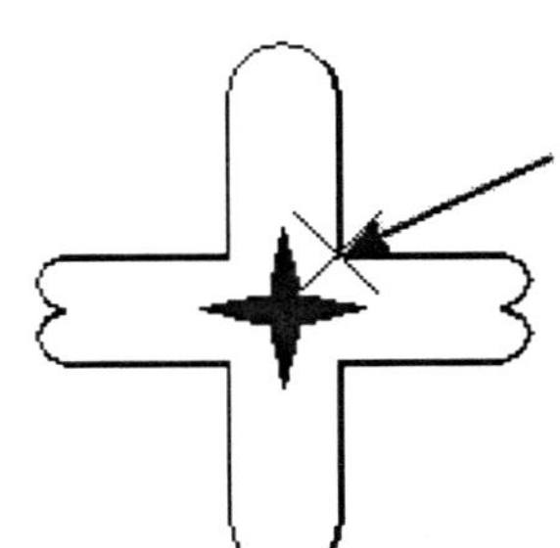

Figure 8.002

You'll notice that, when you enter this level of the ***PEdit*** command, a small "X" appears on the polyline you're editing (Figure 8.002). The X is a locator to let you know which vertex is being edited.

- The **Next** (default) and **Previous** options move the locator forward and backward to each vertex around the polyline.
- Use the **Break** option just as you used the ***Break*** command – to remove part of a polyline.

- **Insert** enables you to define a new vertex on the polyline and **Straighten** allows you to remove an existing vertex.
- **Move**, of course, enables you to move a vertex, thus reshaping the polyline.
- In the event that too much editing causes the polyline to display oddly on your screen, you can **Regen** just the polyline while still within the editing session. This saves you from having to leave the command, regen the drawing, and then return to the ***PEdit*** command.
- The **Tangent** option allows you to assign a tangent direction for AutoCAD to use when it fits the polyline (with the **Fit** option on the upper tier).
- The **Width** option on the first tier of choices allowed you to change the width for the entire polyline. The **Width** option on the second tier allows you to change the width for a specific segment of the polyline.

Let's look at some of these options.

| **Do This: 8.3.3** | **More Complex Polyline Editing Tools** |
|---|---|

I. If you're not already in the *MyPline* or *pline* drawing, please open one of them now. Refer to Figure 8.003 for this exercise. (I've shown the numbers of the vertices on all of the graphics in this exercise to make it easier for you to follow. If you wish to display them in your drawing, open the *pline* drawing and thaw the **TEXT** layer.)

II. Follow these steps. (Again, feel free to use cursor or dynamic input menus to display the ***PEdit*** options.)

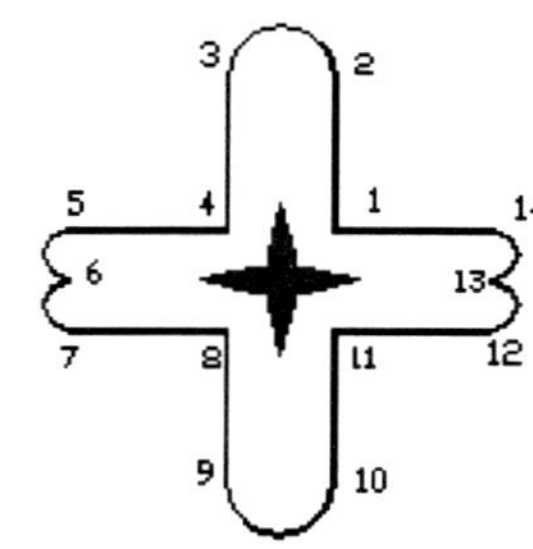


Figure 8.003

**8.3.3: MORE COMPLEX POLYLINE EDITING TOOLS**

1. Enter the ***PEdit*** command .

    **Command: *pe***

2. Select the outer polyline.

    **Select polyline or [Multiple]:**

3. Use the **Edit vertex** option  to access the next tier of options.

    

    **Enter an option [Open/Join/Width/Edit vertex/Fit/Spline/Decurve/Ltype gen/ Undo]: *e***

4. Reposition the locator to point 2. Notice the default option is **N**. This is the **Next** option, so just hit ***enter*** to reposition the locator.

    **Enter a vertex editing option [Next/Previous/Break/Insert/ Move/Regen/ Straighten/Tangent/Width/eXit] <N>: *[enter]***

5. Select the **Break** option 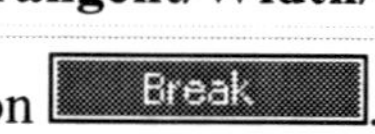.

    

    **Enter a vertex editing option [Next/Previous/Break/Insert/Move/Regen/ Straighten/Tangent/Width/ eXit] <N>: *b***

6. Notice that AutoCAD drops to a third tier of options.

- **Next** and **Previous** work as they do in the second tier.
- **Go** executes the option that dropped you to this level (in this case, the **Break** option).

- **Exit** to leave this level without executing the level two option.

Hit ***enter*** to accept the **Next** default. The locator will move to point 3.

**Enter an option [Next/Previous/Go/eXit] <N>: *[enter]***

7. Use the **Go** option to execute the **Break** option. The segment between points 2 (where you began the **Break** option) and 3 (where you are now) is removed as shown.

**Enter an option [Next/ Previous/Go/eXit] <N>: *g***

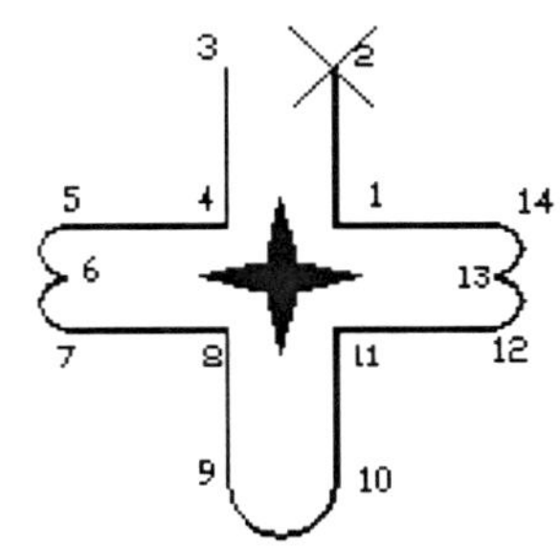


8. Use the **eXit** option to return to the primary tier, and then hit ***enter*** to leave the command.

**Enter a vertex editing option [Next/Previous/Break/Insert/Move/Regen/ Straighten/Tangent/Width/ eXit] <N>: *x***

**Enter an option [Close/Join/Width/ Edit vertex/ Fit/Spline/Decurve/Ltype gen/Undo]: *[enter]***

9. Repeat Steps 1, 2, and 3.

**Command: *[enter]***

10. Now let's **Insert** a vertex.

Notice that AutoCAD provides a rubber band (a line from the currently selected vertex) to help guide you.

**Enter a vertex editing option [Next/Previous/Break/Insert/ Move/Regen/ Straighten/Tangent/Width/eXit] <N>: *i***

11. Place the new vertex midway between points 3 and 4 (right). Use your OSNAPs! Notice the locator appears at this new point.

**Specify location for new vertex: _mid of**

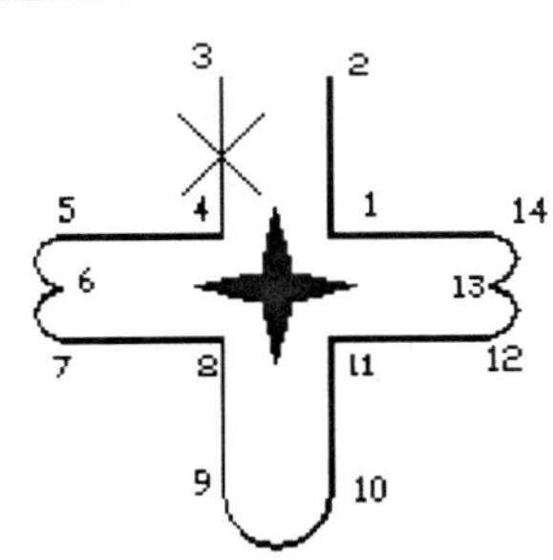

## 8.3.3: MORE COMPLEX POLYLINE EDITING TOOLS

12. Now move 

the new vertex a single unit to the west (see figure right).

**Enter a vertex editing option [Next/Previous/Break/Insert/Move/Regen/ Straighten/Tangent/Width/ eXit] <N>:** ***m***

**Specify new location for marked vertex:** ***@1<180***

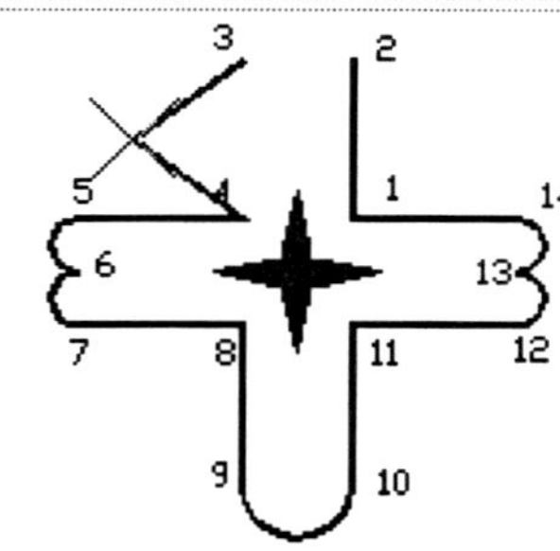


13. Now we'll remove the new vertex. Return the locator to point 3 (use the **Previous** option).

**Enter a vertex editing option [Next/Previous/Break/Insert/Move/Regen/ Straighten/Tangent/Width/ eXit] <N>:** ***p***

14. Use the **Straighten** option 

.

**Enter a vertex editing option [Next/Previous/Break/Insert/Move/Regen/ Straighten/Tangent/Width/ eXit] <P>:** ***s***

15. Hit ***enter*** until the locator moves to point 4. Then use **Go** to execute the **Straighten** option. The new vertex disappears and the drawing appears as it did in Step 7.

**Enter an option [Next/Previous/ Go/eXit] <N>:** ***[enter]***

**Enter an option [Next/Previous/ Go/eXit] <N>:** ***g***

16. Now use the **Width** option 

to change the width of a single line segment.

**Enter a vertex editing option [Next/Previous/Break/Insert/Move/Regen/ Straighten/Tangent/Width/ eXit] <P>:** ***w***

17. Set the starting width to ***0*** and the ending width to ***1/8***. Your drawing will look like this.

**Specify starting width for next segment <0.0313>:** ***0***

**Specify ending width for next segment <0.0000>:** ***.125***

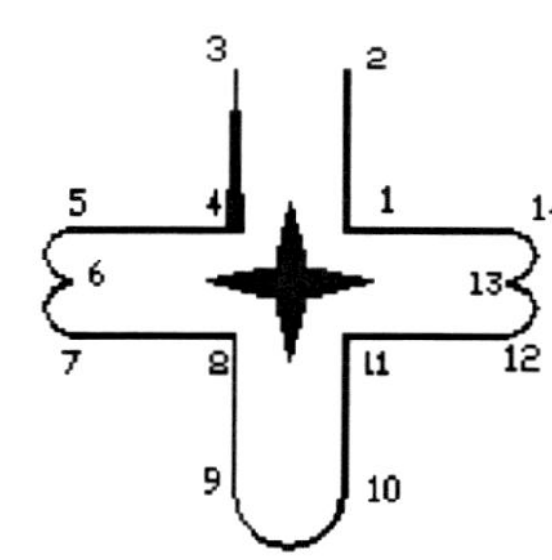


18. Exit the ***PEdit*** command, and then exit the drawing  without saving your changes.

**Command:** ***quit***

One other consideration of the ***PEdit*** command is its effect on non-polyline lines and arcs. You've seen what happens when you select a line or arc at the **Select polyline** prompt. AutoCAD will ask if you want to turn it into a polyline. This is the conversion method for lines or arcs to polylines.

To convert polylines to lines or arcs, simply use the ***Explode*** command. (Alternately, you can use the "X" hotkey or the **Explode** button 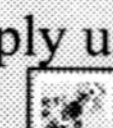 on the Modify toolbar). AutoCAD prompts:

**Select objects:**

The prompt will repeat until you confirm the selection set. Be aware, however, that only a polyline can show WYSIWYG width. An exploded polyline becomes a line or arc and loses its width.

## 8.3 AutoCAD's Inquiry Commands

AutoCAD provides four commands – ***List***, ***Dist***, ***Area***, and ***ID*** – whose simplicity has led to their being almost completely forgotten. We'll cover them quickly because they're so simple; but I do recommend them as possible residents of monitor stick'ems (those tiny bits of paper taped to the side of your monitor with cheater notes).

### 8.3.1 Tell Me About It – The *List* Command

One of the problems you may run into on occasion is a modifying command not working exactly as you might expect. The object you're modifying not being what you think it is frequently causes this. For example, you may try to edit a polyline arc only to receive a message from AutoCAD that the object isn't a polyline; or you may freeze a layer only to discover that something you thought was on that layer doesn't freeze. When something unexpected like this happens, do a ***List*** on the object to see if you can spot the problem. Look at some examples.

In addition to the command line and toolbar, you can find *all* the Inquiry commands listed in the Inquiry section of the Tools pull-down menu.

**Do This: 8.3.1.1 Listing an Object's Properties**

I. Open the *samples.dwg* file from the C:\Steps\Lesson08 folder. The drawing looks like Figure 8.004.

II. Follow these steps.

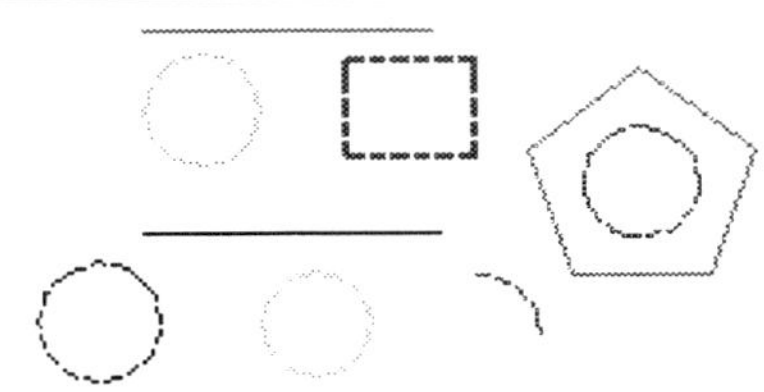

Figure 8.004

**8.3.1.1: LISTING AN OBJECT'S PROPERTIES**

1. Enter the ***List*** command by typing ***list*** or ***ls***. Alternately, you can use the **List** button on the Inquiry toolbar.

**Command: *ls***

2. Select the upper red line, and then confirm that you've finished selecting.

**Select objects:**

**Select objects: *[enter]***

AutoCAD switches to the *text screen* and displays the following information.

```
          LINE      Layer: "FRED"
                    Space: Model space
           Handle = 26
      from point, X=   2.5424  Y=    7.7686  Z=    0.0000
        to point, X=   7.4140  Y=    7.7686  Z=    0.0000
  Length =    4.8717,  Angle in XY Plane =      0
          Delta X =    4.8717, Delta Y =    0.0000, Delta Z =    0.0000
```

Here we see: the type of object (**Line**), its layer (**Fred**), that it was drawn in Model Space, its Handle (for programmers), and its beginning and ending point, length, and angle.

#### 8.3.1.1: Listing an Object's Properties

3. Return to the graphics screen either by hitting the **F2** key [F2] or by picking on the **X** in the upper right corner of the text screen.

4. Let's repeat the procedure with another object.

   **Command:** ***[enter]***

5. Select the dashed rectangle.

   **Select objects:**

   **Select objects:** ***[enter]***

AutoCAD again switches to the text screen and displays the following information.

```
                LWPOLYLINE  Layer: "0"
                         Space: Model space
                 Color: 6 (magenta)     Linetype: "HIDDEN"
                 Handle = 28
          Closed
  Constant width     0.0625
            area    3.5494
       perimeter    7.6074

        at point  X=    5.9830  Y=    7.2213  Z=    0.0000
        at point  X=    8.1448  Y=    7.2213  Z=    0.0000
        at point  X=    8.1448  Y=    5.5794  Z=    0.0000
        at point  X=    5.9830  Y=    5.5794  Z=    0.0000
```

Again, we see the type of object and layer. But since this object is a multi-segmented lwpolyline, we also see that: the lwpolyline is **Closed,** its width, the beginning and ending points of each segment, and the area and perimeter of the lwpolyline.

Note that the linetype and color characteristics of this object weren't assigned by layer. We assigned these characteristics using the ***Color*** and ***Linetype*** methods. As a result, the ***List*** command also shows **Color** and **Linetype**. It'll show these only when the layer doesn't define them.

6. Repeat the ***List*** command for the rest of the objects in this drawing. (It's best to list objects one at a time.) Notice that ***List*** provides slightly different information for each.

## 8.3.2 How Long or How Far – The *Dist* Command

Another useful tool helps determine just what its name implies – *distance*. How long is a line or how far is it from here to there?

### Do This: 8.3.2.1 Determining Distance

I. If you're not still in *samples.dwg*, please open it now. It's in the C:\Steps\Lesson08 folder.

II. Follow these steps.

#### 8.3.2.1: Determining Distance

1. Enter the ***Dist*** command by typing ***dist*** or ***di***. Alternately, you can pick the **Distance** button

## 8.3.2.1: Determining Distance

 on the Inquiry toolbar.

**Command:** ***di***

2. Using OSNAPs, pick the western endpoint of the cyan line. Then pick the center of the lower blue circle (right).

**Specify first point: _endp of**

**Specify second point: _cen of**

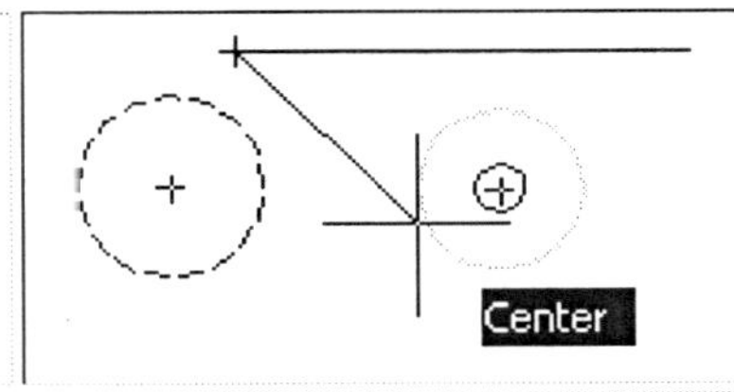


3. AutoCAD returns the following information on the command line. If you can't see all of the information, toggle to the text screen with the **F2** key [F2]. (Close the text screen when you've finished.)

```
Distance = 2.0267,  Angle in XY Plane = 319,  Angle from XY Plane = 0
Delta X = 1.5216,  Delta Y = -1.3388,   Delta Z = 0.0000
```

Here, AutoCAD shows the true distance, the 2-dimensional angle *in* the XY plane, the 3-dimensional angle *from* the XY plane, the distance along the X-plane (shown as **Delta X**), the distance along the Y-plane (shown as **Delta Y**), and the distance along the 3-dimensional Z-plane (shown as **Delta Z**).

Aren't these cool commands?! But wait – the best is yet to come!

## 8.3.3 Calculating the Area

The ***List*** command provides the area of closed rectangles, polygons, and circles as you saw in Section 8.3.1. But the boundaries in which we need to determine area aren't always closed objects. Sometimes, we need an area bounded by simple lines or even multiple objects. For this reason, AutoCAD provides the ***Area*** command.

The ***Area*** command sequence is

**Command:** ***area*** **(or** ***aa*****)**

**Specify first corner point or [Object/Add/ Subtract]:** ***[select the first corner of the area's boundary]***

**Specify next corner point or press ENTER for total:** ***[continue selecting corners – this prompt repeats until you hit enter]***

**Area = 3.5494, Perimeter = 7.6074**

The options are fairly clear.

- The **Specify first corner point** option is the default and simply instructs you to select the first boundary point of the area to be calculated. AutoCAD follows with **Specify next corner point** prompts until the boundary is defined and you complete the command. AutoCAD then shows values for the **Area** within and **Perimeter** around the boundary. (Note: You must identify at least three points to define an area. If you don't "close" the area, AutoCAD will assume a line between the last point selected and the first point selected and calculate the area accordingly.)
- The **Object** option allows you to select an object – a circle, polygon, and so forth – and defines the boundary from the edges of the object.

- **Add** and **Subtract** are ways to keep a running total of several areas or to get the area of a bounded site minus a smaller site – such as the area of a plot of land minus the house sitting on it.

| Do This: 8.3.3.1 | Calculating Area |
|---|---|

I. If you're not still in *samples.dwg*, please open it now. It's in the C:\Steps\Lesson08 folder.

II. Follow these steps.

### 8.3.3.1: Calculating Area

1. Enter the ***Area*** command. Alternately, you can pick the **Area** button  on the Inquiry toolbar.

   **Command: *aa***

2. Tell AutoCAD you want to use the **Object** option 

.

   **Specify first corner point or [Object/Add/Subtract]: *o***

3. Select the circle in the center of the polygon (right).

   **Select objects:**

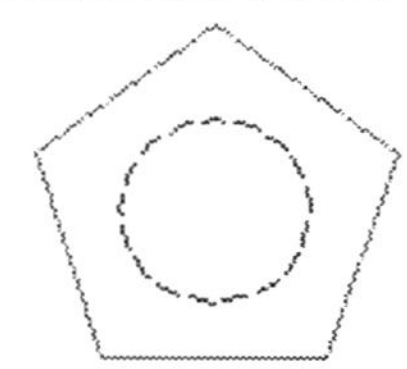

AutoCAD returns this information on the command line.

   **Area = 3.1416, Circumference = 6.2832**

4. Repeat the command .

   **Command: *[enter]***

5. Select the five points on the polygon (use OSNAPs).

   **Specify first corner point or [Object/Add/Subtract]:**

   **Specify next corner point or press ENTER for total:**

AutoCAD returns this information on the command line.

   **Area = 9.5106, Perimeter = 11.7557**

6. Repeat the command .

   **Command: *[enter]***

7. Tell AutoCAD you want to use the **Add** option 

.

   **Specify first corner point or [Object/Add/Subtract]: *a***

8. AutoCAD prompts again for points or objects. Pick the five points of the polygon as you did in Step 5.

   **Specify first corner point or [Object/Subtract]:**

   **Specify next corner point or press ENTER for total (ADD mode):**

9. After selecting the fifth point, hit ***enter*** to complete the polygon.

   **Specify next corner point or press ENTER for total (ADD mode): *[enter]***

AutoCAD tells you what the **Area** and **Perimeter** are so far, and the **Total area** defined during this command. It then prompts again as it did previously.

   **Area = 9.5106, Perimeter = 11.7557 Total area = 9.5106**

| 8.3.3.1: Calculating Area |
|---|
| 10. Select the **Object** option .<br>**Specify first corner point or [Object/Subtract]:** ***o*** |
| 11. Select the upper blue circle.<br>**(ADD mode) Select objects:**<br>AutoCAD tells you the **Area** and **Circumference** of the circle, and then adds the area of the circle to the **Total Area**.<br>**Area = 2.9741, Circumference = 6.1134 Total area = 12.4846**<br>Then it prompts again. |
| 12. Hit ***enter*** to leave the **Add mode**.<br>**(ADD mode) Select objects:** ***[enter]*** |
| 13. Now tell AutoCAD you want to **Subtract** <br>**Specify first corner point or [Object/Subtract]:** ***s*** |
| 14. We want to subtract an **Object** .<br>**Specify first corner point or [Object/Add]:** ***o*** |
| 15. Select the circle inside the polygon.<br>**(SUBTRACT mode) Select objects:**<br>AutoCAD tells you the **Area** and **Circumference** of the circle, and then subtracts the area from the **Total Area** (the polygon and blue circle, less the area of the dashed circle).<br>**Area = 3.1416, Circumference = 6.2832 Total area = 9.3430** |
| 16. Hit ***enter*** twice to leave the command.<br>**(SUBTRACT mode) Select objects:** ***[enter]***<br>**Specify first corner point or [Object/Add]:** ***[enter]*** |

## 8.3.4 Identifying Any Point with *ID*

The last of these simple tools enables you to identify any point in a drawing. This can prove particularly beneficial to the drafter who works in true coordinates (see the insert in Section 1.8 for an explanation of true coordinates) or someone working with the Ordinate system. We'll discuss the Ordinate system in Lesson 14.

The command sequence for ***ID*** is

**Command: id**

**Specify point:** ***[select a point in the drawing]***

**X = 0.0000 Y = 0.0000 Z = 0.0000**

As you can see, AutoCAD responds with the X,Y,Z coordinate location of the selected point.

| Do This: 8.3.4.1 | Identifying Coordinates in a Drawing |
|---|---|

I. If you're not still in *samples.dwg*, please open it now. It's in the C:\Steps\Lesson08 folder.

II. Follow these steps.

### 8.3.4.1: Identifying Coordinates

1. Enter the ***ID*** command. Alternately, you can pick the **Locate Point** button on the Inquiry toolbar.

    **Command: *id***

2. Select the center point of the upper blue circle.

    **Specify point: _cen of**

AutoCAD returns the coordinates locating the center of the circle.

**X = 3.5472 Y = 6.3395 Z = 0.0000**

3. Exit the drawing. Don't save your changes.

    **Command: *quit***

## 8.4 Extra Steps

I've included another Lisp routine – *pe-w.lsp* – in the C:\Steps\Lesson08 folder. This routine includes two commands – ***W*** and ***PLW*** – both designed to help you change a polyline's width without having to enter the frightening world of the ***PEdit*** command. ***W*** will prompt you for the desired width of a polyline, and then prompt you to select lines, arcs, or polylines to change. It saves a bit of time over the ***PEdit*** method. ***PLW*** allows you to select a polyline that has the desired width, and then select a polyline to change.

## 8.5 What Have We Learned?

*Items covered in this lesson include:*

- *AutoCAD Inquiry Commands:*
    - ***List***
    - ***Dist***
    - ***Area***
    - ***ID***
- ***Join*** *command*
- *Creating and Editing Polyline Commands:*
    - ***PLine***
    - ***PEdit***
    - ***Explode***

This has been a difficult lesson. But polylines are exceptionally powerful tools, and I suppose the nature of the beast requires the multi-leveled structure of both the ***PLine*** and ***PEdit*** commands. Take some time to review the lesson. Repeat the exercises as needed to make yourself comfortable. I can guarantee that polylines will be an important part of your CAD future, so get comfortable with them now.

We also discussed some other important commands. Do you remember what they were? Remember, we discussed that they were so simple they are often overlooked and forgotten. Do you forget them already? I'm talking, of course, about ***List***, ***Dist***, ***Area***, and ***ID***. Remember to put that cheater sheet on your monitor!

## 8.6 Exercises

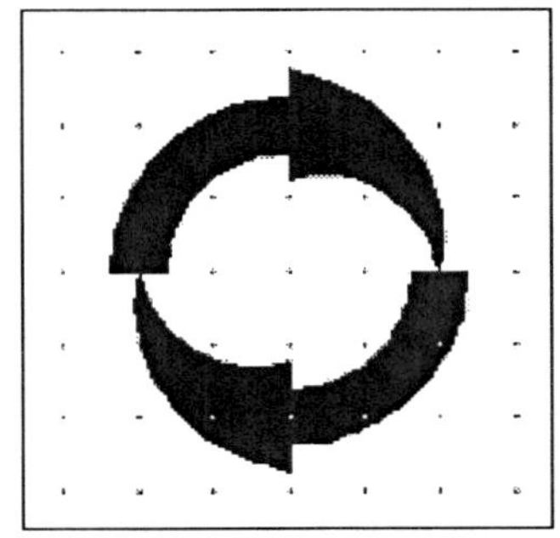

1. Start a new drawing from scratch. Set the grid to ¼" and create the image at right. Save the drawing as *MyArrows* in the C:\Steps\Lesson08 folder.

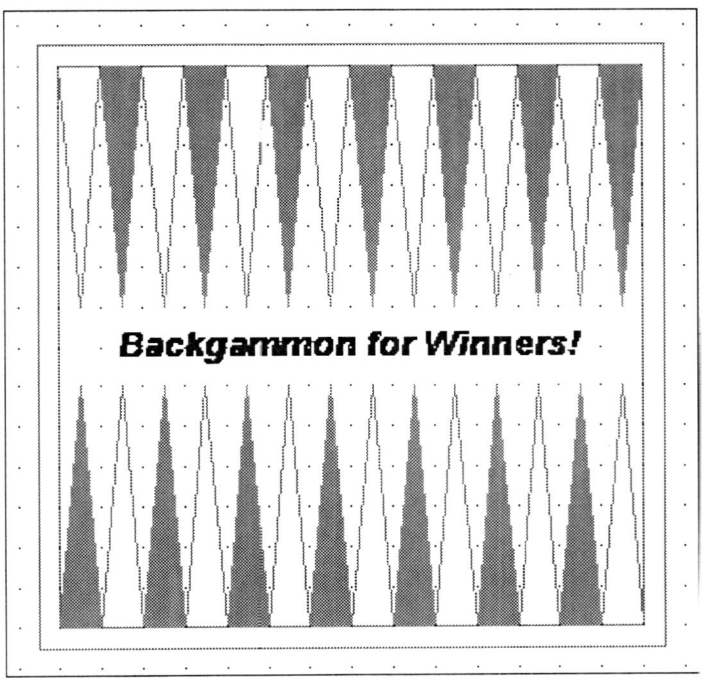


2. Set up a new drawing with the following parameters:
   2.1. Lower left limits: 0,0
   2.2. Upper right limits: 16,16
   2.3. Grid: 1
   2.4. Snap: as needed
   2.5. Textsize: 5/8
   2.6. Text style: Arial font, Bold and Italicized
   2.7. Layers: as needed
   2.8. Create the backgammon board shown. Save the drawing as *MyBoard* in the C:\Steps\Lesson08 folder.

*For more exercises related to Lesson 8, please see Lesson 8 in AutoCAD 2007: One Step at a Time – Workbook.*

## 8.7 For Web-Based Review Questions, visit: http://www.uneedcad.com/2007/Files/07R8.pdf

# Lesson 9

Following this lesson, you will:

- ✓ *Know how to use the advanced copy commands:*
  - o ***Offset***
  - o ***Array***
  - o ***Mirror***
- ✓ *Know how to use the **Lengthen** command*
- ✓ *Know how to use the **Stretch** command*
- ✓ *Know how to use the **Rotate** command*
- ✓ *Know how to use the **Scale** command*
- ✓ *Know how to use the **Cloud** command*

# More Editing Tools

*In Lesson 7, we discussed several modification tools that make computer drafting easier. In this lesson, we'll see some more modifying tools also designed to speed and simplify the drafting process. To keep it simple, we'll use the same two groupings we began in Lesson 7 –* Location and Number *and* Change. *Let's begin where we left off – with the Location and Number group.*

## 9.1 Location and Number

### 9.1.1 Parallels and Concentrics – The *Offset* Command

We ended Lesson 7 with a study of AutoCAD's various approaches to copying objects. ***Offset*** gives us another way to create one or many copies of a single object (line, polyline, circle, arc, etc.). The copies will be either parallel (lines and polylines) or concentric (circles & arcs) to the existing object. The command sequence is

**Command: *offset* (or *o*)**

**Current settings: Erase source=No Layer=Source OFFSETGAPTYPE=0**

**Specify offset distance or [Through/Erase/Layer] <Through>: *[either specify an offset distance or hit enter to accept the default (Through)]***

**Select object to offset or [Exit/Undo] <Exit>: *[select the object to offset]***

**Specify through point or [Exit/Multiple/Undo] <Exit>: *[select a point through which the copy should pass]***

**Select object to offset or [Exit/Undo] <Exit>: *[hit enter to complete the command]***

AutoCAD begins by showing you the current ***Offset*** command settings. Consider the options.

- The first ***Offset*** prompt asks you for an **Offset distance**. This option allows you to specify *a perpendicular distance away from* the original object to place the copy.
- The **Through** option allows you to select a point in the drawing *through which* the copy will pass. AutoCAD then prompts for the direction in which to place the copy.
- By default, AutoCAD leaves the source object of an offset in the drawing. The **Erase** option allows you to remove the source object once it's been offset. It prompts:

  **Erase source object after offsetting? [Yes/No] <No>:**
- The **Layer** option lets you choose where you place the new object – either on the current layer or the layer of the source object (the default). It prompts

  **Enter layer option for offset objects [Current/Source] <Source>:**
- The **Exit** and **Undo** options perform their usual function.
- When offsetting an object, the **Multiple** option (of the **Specify through point** prompt) allows you to make more than a single copy of the source object.

Let's try it.

> In addition to the command line, toolbar, and palette, you'll find all of the commands in this lesson in the Modify pull-down menu (unless noted otherwise).

| Do This: 9.1.1.1 | Using the *Offset* Command |
|---|---|

I. Open the *star+* drawing in the C:\Steps\Lesson09 folder. The drawing looks like Figure 9.001.

II. Follow these steps.

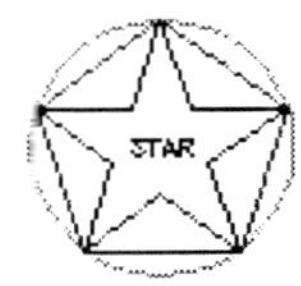


Figure 9.001

### 9.1.1.1: Using the Offset Command

1. Enter the ***Offset*** command. Alternately, you can pick the **Offset** button on the Modify toolbar or palette.

   **Command: *o***

   **Current settings: Erase source=No Layer=Source OFFSETGAPTYPE=0**

2. Accept the default option.

   **Specify offset distance or [Through/Erase/Layer] <Through>: *[enter]***

3. Select the circle around the star.

   **Select object to offset or [Exit/Undo] <Exit>:**

4. Select the endpoint of the upper line.

   **Specify through point or [Exit/Multiple/Undo] <Exit>: _endp of**

5. Complete the command.

   **Select object to offset or [Exit/Undo] <Exit>: *[enter]***

   Notice (right) that the new circle resides on the same layer as the source object.

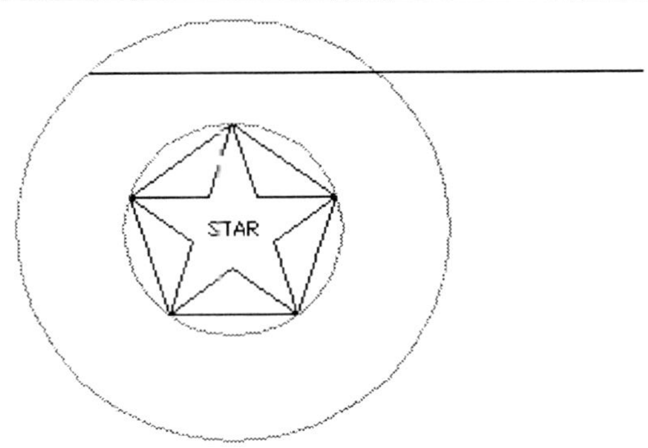


6. Repeat the command.

   **Command: *o***

7. Use the **Layer** option Layer…

   **Specify offset distance or [Through/Erase/Layer] <Through>: *l***

8. … and tell AutoCAD to place offset copies on the **Current** layer Current.

   **Enter layer option for offset objects [Current/Source] <Source>: *c***

9. AutoCAD returns to the **Specify offset** prompt. Accept the default **Through** option.

   **Specify offset distance or [Through/Erase/Layer] <Through>: *[enter]***

10. Select the horizontal line above the circle.

    **Select object to offset or [Exit/Undo] <Exit>:**

## 9.1.1.1: Using the Offset Command

11. Select the center of the circle.

**Specify through point or [Exit/Multiple/Undo] <Exit>: _cen of**

12. Complete the command.

**Select object to offset or [Exit/Undo] <Exit>: *[enter]***

AutoCAD has offset a copy of the source object onto the current layer.

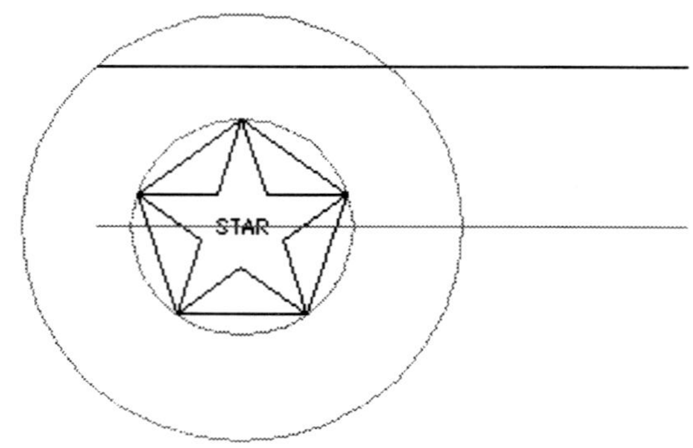


13. Erase the new line and circle.

**Command: *e***

14. Now let's try a specific distance for our offsets. Repeat the ***Offset*** command.

**Command: *o***

15. Tell AutoCAD to offset each object ¼ unit.

**Specify offset distance or [Through/Erase/Layer] <Through>: *.25***

16. Select the upper line.

**Select object to offset or [Exit/Undo] <Exit>:**

17. Tell AutoCAD to make multiple copies Multiple.

**Specify point on side to offset or [Exit/Multiple/Undo] <Exit>: *m***

18. Pick a point above the line. Continue to pick until you have four lines.

**Specify point on side to offset or [Exit/Undo] <next object>:**

19. Tell AutoCAD to move on to the **next object**.

**Specify point on side to offset or [Exit/Undo] <next object>: *[enter]***

20. Now select the circle and repeat Step 18 until you have four circles.

**Select object to offset or [Exit/Undo] <Exit>:**

**Specify point on side to offset or [Exit/Undo] <next object>: *[enter]***

21. Complete the command.

**Specify object to offset or [Exit/Undo] <next object>: *[enter]***

22. Erase the new objects. Don't exit.

**Command: *e***

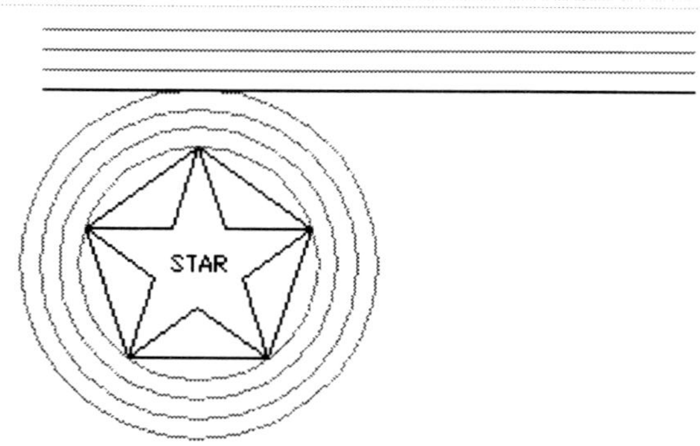


Nothing to it, right? ***Offset*** became a bit more complicated with changes to the 2006 release, but the changes only make it handier!

Let's look at something that can make multiple objects at one time.

## 9.1.2 Rows, Columns, and Circles – the *Array* Command

Many times we find that not only do we need several copies but also that the copies must be arranged in rows, columns, or even circles. Using a normal ***Copy*** command, this can evoke groans of tedium from CAD operators. Fortunately, the ***Array*** command was designed to prevent these groans.

AutoCAD provides a handy dialog box approach to the ***Array*** command. Let's take a look.

> There's also an older command line approach for the ***Array*** command – reached by adding the now familiar dash in front of the command. But it has fewer options and the smart user will opt for the simplicity of the dialog box.

By way of radio buttons across its top, the Array dialog box (Figure 9.002) provides two distinct types of arrays– the **Rectangular Array** and the **Polar Array**.

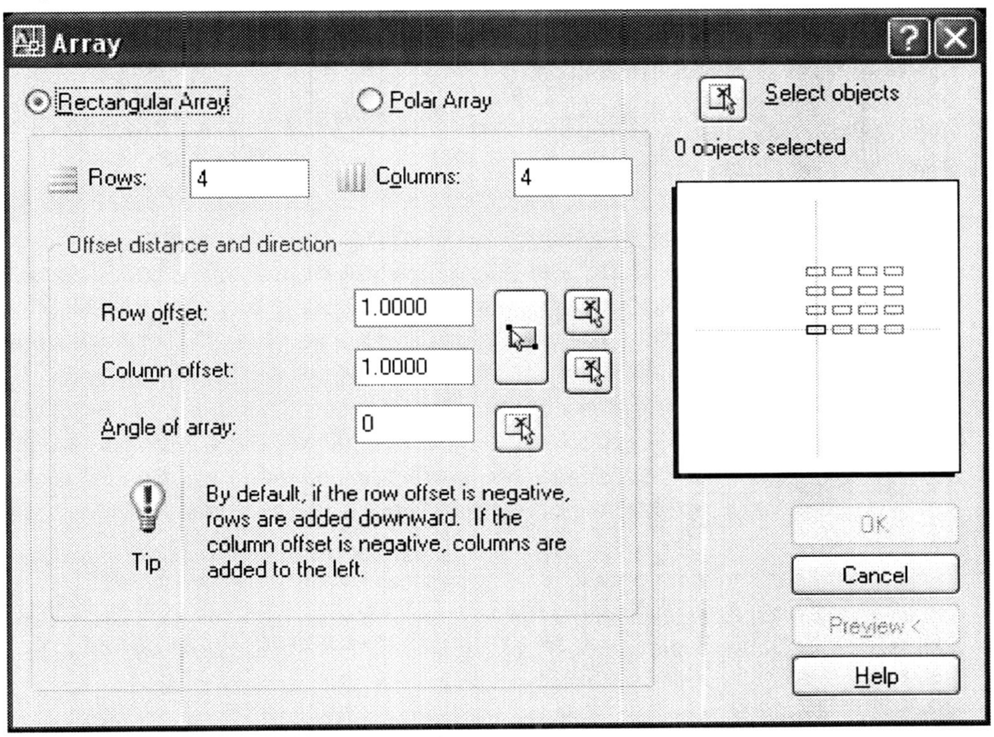


Figure 9.002

- When creating a **Rectangular Array** (rows and columns), you'll need to tell AutoCAD how many **Rows** and **Columns** to create in the corresponding text boxes.

  You can enter the distance between rows or columns in the **Row offset** and **Column offset** boxes. Alternately, you can use the pick buttons to indicate a distance by selecting points on the screen. (Notice that AutoCAD provides three buttons – one each to **Pick Row Offset** and **Pick Column Offset**, and a third, larger button that will allow you to **Pick Both Offsets** at one time.)

  The dialog box also allows you to define the **Angle of array** by entering the angle in a text box of picking points on the screen to define it. (This option isn't available on the command line.)

  Watch the preview box in the right side of the dialog box to see a graphics representation of how the array settings will work.

- The **Polar Array** option presents the choices seen in Figure 9.003.

  Here you can enter the coordinates for the **Center point** of the array in the appropriate text boxes, or you can use the **Pick Center Point** button (to the right of the **X** and **Y** text boxes) to pick the **Center Point** on the screen.

  The Array dialog box allows you to define a polar array in one of three ways using the **Method** control box (**Methods and values** frame):

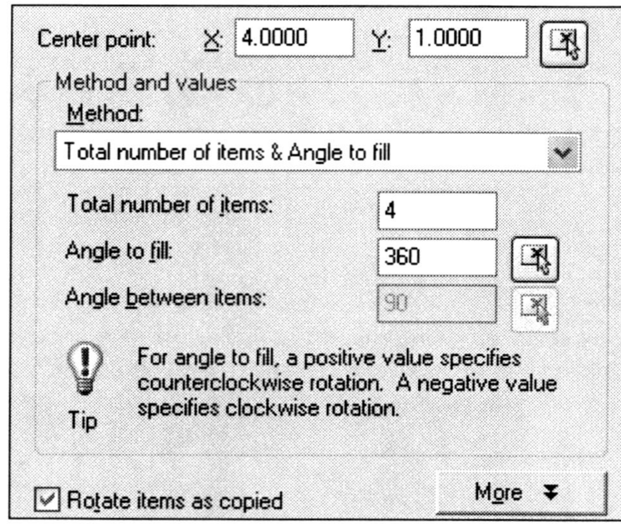


Figure 9.003

  - Using the default **Total number of items & Angle to fill** method, you'll define your array by telling AutoCAD how many items you want in the array and what portion of a circle you want to use. Use the **Total number of items** and **Angle to fill** text boxes (or the **Pick Angle to Fill** button).
  - Use the **Total number of items and Angle between items** method to define the array by telling AutoCAD how many items you want in the array and how to space them using angles. Here you'll use the **Total number of items** and the **Angle between items** text boxes (or the **Pick Angle between Items** button).

    This method offers you some flexibility.
  - Use the **Angle to fill & Angle between items** method when you know the area you want to fill with copies of selected objects but aren't sure how many objects it'll take. Here you'll use the **Angle to fill** and the **Angle between items** text boxes (or their associated buttons).

  The **Polar Array** option has a couple other items that require some attention.

  - Just below the **Method and values** frame, you'll find a check box that enables you to **Rotate** [the arrayed] **items as** [they're] **copied**. This valuable tool will come in quite handy!
  - Notice the **More** button to the right of the **Rotate** check box. This presents the options seen in Figure 9.004. Here you can reset the **base point** of the selected objects for the array. The base point can be critical to the final appearance of your array. This is the point at which you'll 'grab' the objects being arrayed and the point that will define the location of the arrayed objects in relation to the settings on the dialog box.

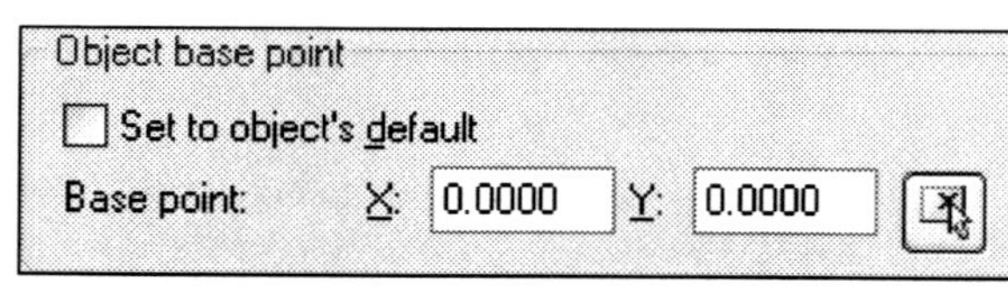


Figure 9.004

  Use the **Object base point** frame (revealed by the **More** button) to reset the base point of the selected objects for the array.

- The other options available in the Array dialog box include:
  - The **Select objects** button to the right of the **Rectangular Array / Polar Array** radio buttons. Use this to return to the screen to select the objects you wish to array.
  - A **Preview** button (in the button group below the preview display box) that enables you to see the results of the array before committing to any changes.

Let's see the Array dialog box in action.

| Do This: 9.1.2.1 | Using the *Array* Command |
|---|---|

I. Be sure you're still in the *star+* drawing in the C:\Steps\Lesson09 folder.

II. Freeze the **Line** layer.

III. Follow these steps.

**9.1.2.1: USING THE ARRAY COMMAND**

1. Enter the ***Array*** command by typing ***array*** or ***ar***. Alternately, you can pick the **Array** button 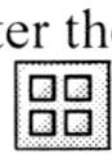 on the Modify toolbar or palette.

    **Command: *ar***

AutoCAD presents the Array dialog box (Figure 9.002).

2. Set up the array as shown:
    - Be sure the **Rectangular Array** option has been selected.
    - Create two rows and four columns.
    - Offset the rows by **3"**.
    - Offset the columns by **3.5"**.

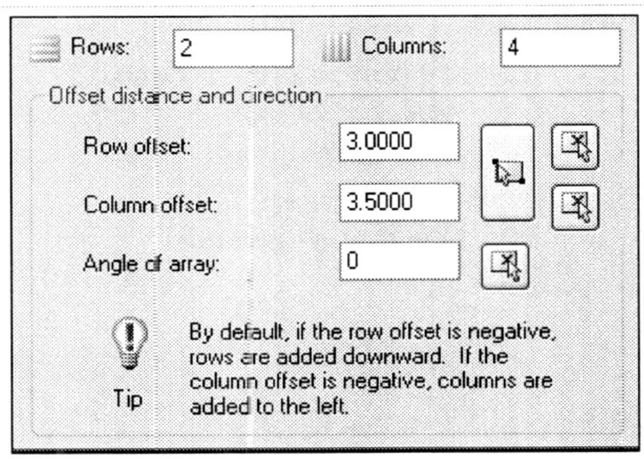


3. Pick the **Select objects** button  to return to the graphics area.

4. Select the circle and all of its components. Confirm the selection set.

    **Select objects:**

    **Select objects: *[enter]***

AutoCAD returns to the Array dialog box.

5. Preview [Preview <] the array. (See the following figure for the preview.)

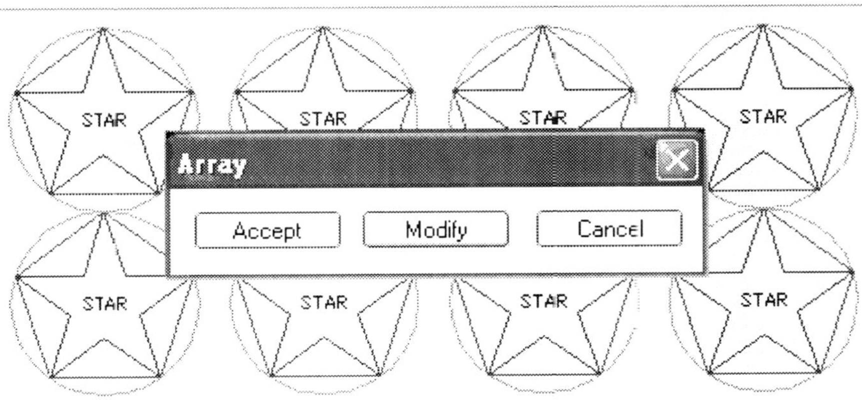

6. Pick the **Accept** button. AutoCAD creates the array and returns to the command line.

7. Undo the changes.

**Command: *u***

8. Let's try a **Polar array**. Repeat the ***Array*** command.

**Command: *ar***

9. Set up the array as shown:
   - Be sure the **Polar Array** option has been selected.
   - Set the **Center point** to ***5,5***.
   - Use the **Total number of items and Angle to fill** method.
   - Create five items and fill a 360° angle.
   - Don't **Rotate the items as** [they're] **copied**.

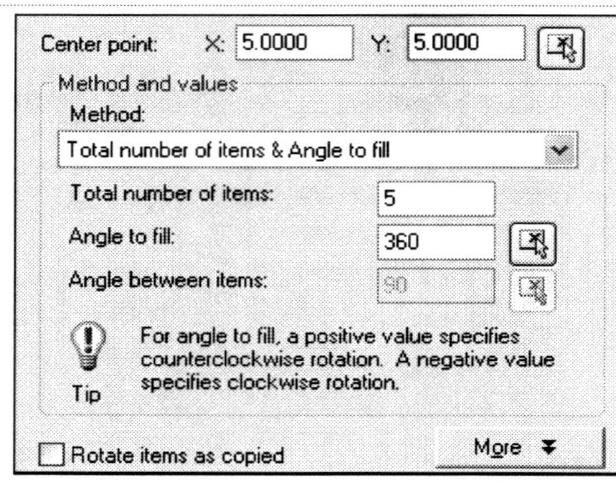


10. Pick the **More** button. AutoCAD presents the **Object base point** frame (Figure 9.004).

11. Be sure the **Set to object's default** check box is clear, and then pick the **Pick Base Point** button.

12. AutoCAD returns to the graphics screen and prompts you for the base point. Select the center of the circle.

**Specify the base point of objects: _cen of**

AutoCAD returns to the Array dialog box and shows the coordinates of the base point in the **Object base point** frame (right).

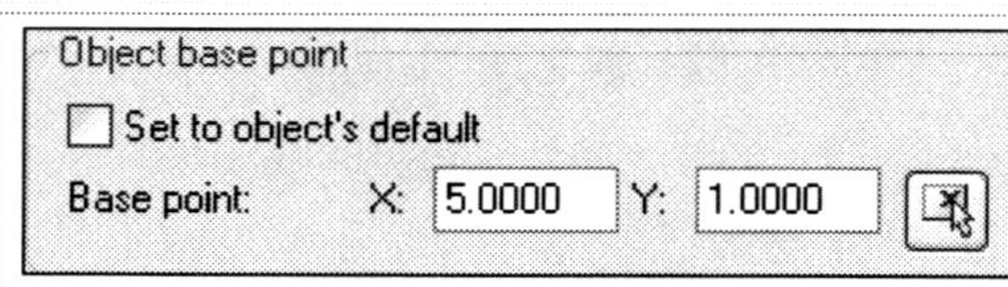


13. Pick the **Select objects** button to return to the graphics area.

14. Select the circle and all of its components.

**Select objects:**
**Select objects: *[enter]***

15. Pick the **OK** button to complete the procedure. The array appears in the following figure.

## 9.1.2.1: Using the Array Command

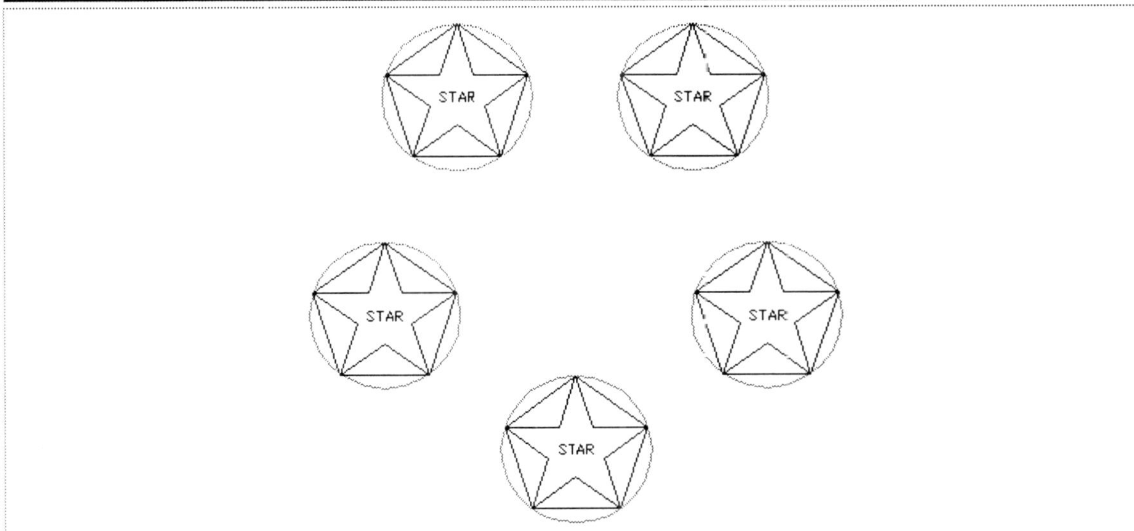


16. Undo the changes 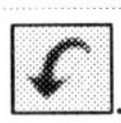.

    **Command:** ***u***

17. Repeat Steps 8 through 16, but this time rotate the copies (Step 9). Notice the difference?

## 9.1.3 Opposite Copies – the *Mirror* Command

Occasionally, you'll run into a situation where you not only need to copy an object, but you need to completely reverse its orientation. This isn't a true rotating of the object(s), which would just stand it on its head. What you see is an opposite or a *mirror* image of the original.

The ***Mirror*** command is one of AutoCAD's simplest:

**Command:** ***mirror*** **(or** ***mi*****)**

**Select objects:** ***[select the object(s) to be mirrored]***

**Select objects:** ***[confirm completion of the selection set]***

**Specify first point of mirror line:** ***[pick the first point of the mirror line]***

**Specify second point of mirror line:** ***[pick the second point of the mirror line]***

**Erase source objects? [Yes/No] <N>:** ***[do you want to keep the original object(s)?]***

You may have difficulty understanding the "mirror line" in this sequence. Refer to Figure 9.005. Consider this: To see a mirror image of an object as it lies on a table, you'll lay a mirror alongside the object (at a bit of an angle so as to reflect the object). The mirror *line* is the edge of the mirror where it meets the surface of the table. In AutoCAD, your screen is the table. You must define the *line* (the edge of the mirror) by identifying *two* points on it.

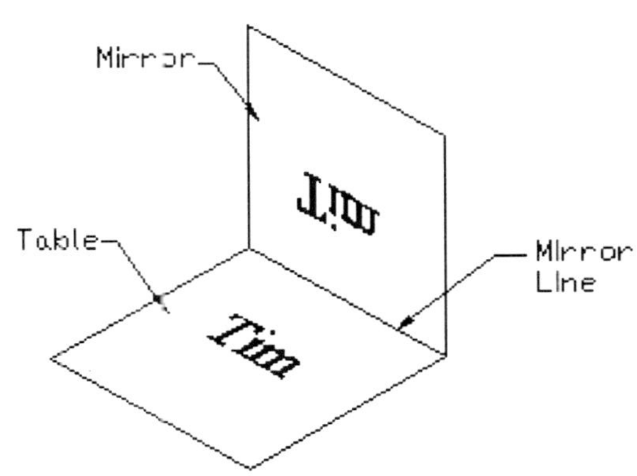


Figure 9.005

Let's give it a try.

| Do This: 9.1.3.1 | Mirroring an Object |
|---|---|

I. Be sure you're still in the *star+* drawing in the C:\Steps\Lesson09 folder.
II. Follow these steps.

| 9.1.3.1: Mirroring an Object | |
|---|---|
| 1. Enter the ***Mirror*** command. Alternately, you can pick the **Mirror** button  on the Modify toolbar or palette.<br>**Command: *mi*** | |
| 2. Select the circle and all of its contents.<br>**Select objects:**<br>**Select objects: *[enter]*** | |
| 3. Pick the **first point of mirror line** around coordinate ***7,3***, and then (with the **Ortho** on) pick a **second point** to the left (or west) of the first point, as shown.<br>**Specify first point of mirror line: *7,3***<br>**Specify second point of mirror line:** | 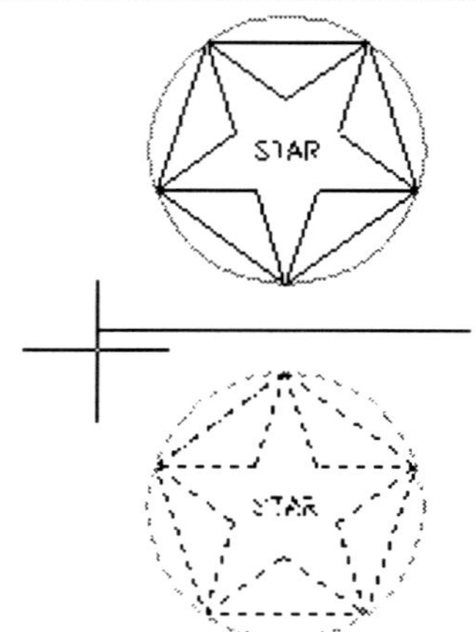 |
| 4. AutoCAD asks if you wish to delete the original. Accept the default – **No**.<br>**Erase source objects? [Yes/No] <N>: *[enter]***<br>Notice (right) that everything mirrored *except* the text. See the following insert for more details on this behavior. |  |
| 5. Undo the changes 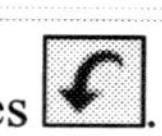.<br>**Command: *u*** | 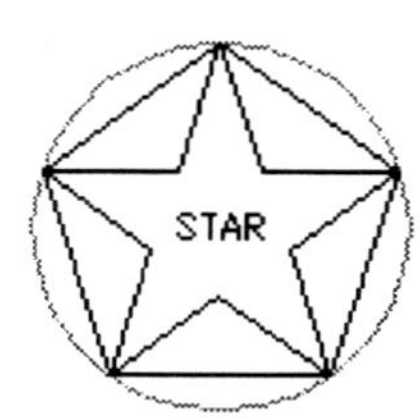 |

By default, AutoCAD will mirror all objects *except text*. This default will help you avoid the frustration of having to redo all the text in an object just because you needed a mirror image.

If, however, you want the text mirrored as well, you can change the system variable that controls mirrored text – **Mirrtext**. Here's how:

**Command: *mirrtext***

**Enter new value for MIRRTEXT <0>: *1***

Turn on the **Mirrtext** system variable (set it to ***1*** as indicated), and then redo the previous exercise. Notice the difference? (Be sure to reset it to ***0*** when you've finished.)

## 9.2 More Commands in the Change Group

### 9.2.1 Two Ways to Change the Length of Lines and Arcs – The *Lengthen* and *Stretch* Commands

Prior to the inclusion of the ***Lengthen*** command, AutoCAD relied on the ***Stretch*** command to lengthen or shorten one or several lines. The ***Stretch*** command is still reliable and is really quite simple once you understand the need to use a crossing window to select objects. The command sequence is

**Command: *stretch* (or *s*)**

**Select objects to stretch by crossing-window or crossing-polygon...**

**Select objects: Specify opposite corner: *[note the instruction on the previous line – select the object(s) to be stretched using a* crossing *window]***

**Select objects: *[enter to confirm completion of the selection set]***

**Specify base point or [Displacement] <Displacement>: *[pick a base point]***

**Specify second point or <use first point as displacement>: *[pick a target point]***

The line instructing you to **Select objects to stretch by crossing-window or crossing-polygon...** is easily overlooked as it appears above the actual prompt. But don't overlook its importance. You must select objects using a crossing window (or crossing-*polygon*, which we'll discuss in Lesson 10). Unfortunately, AutoCAD doesn't default to a crossing window, so you must enter ***c*** (or use implied windowing) to create a crossing window for object selection.

Notice that you have the same option provided by the ***Copy*** and ***Move*** commands – that is, you can select a **Base point or [Displacement]**. To review how these work (as well as the **Second point of displacement**), see the discussion in Section 7.2.1.

Let's experiment with the ***Stretch*** command.

| Do This: 9.2.1.1 | Stretching Objects |
|---|---|

I. Be sure you're still in the *star+* drawing in the C:\Steps\Lesson09 folder.

II. Be sure the **Line** layer is still frozen.

III. Follow these steps.

| 9.2.1.1: STRETCHING OBJECTS | |
|---|---|
| 1. Enter the ***Stretch*** command. Alternately, you can pick the **Stretch** button  on the Modify toolbar or palette.<br>**Command: *s*** | |
| 2. Place a crossing window around the upper part of the star as shown.<br>**Select objects to stretch by crossing-window or crossing-polygon...**<br>**Select objects:** | 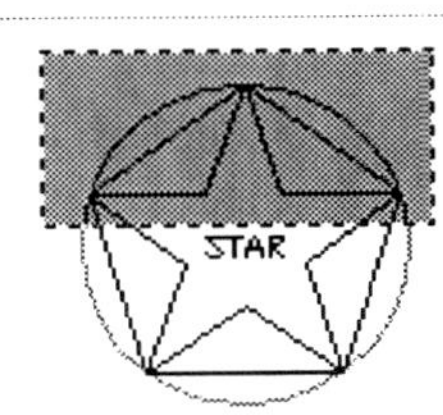  |
| 3. Complete the selection set.<br>**Select objects: *[enter]*** | |

## 9.2.1.1: Stretching Objects

4. Use the **displacement** option and enter a displacement of ***0,2***.

   **Specify base point or [Displacement]**
   **<Displacement>:** ***[enter]***

   **Specify displacement <0.0000, 0.0000, 0.0000>:** ***0,2***

Your drawing looks like this.

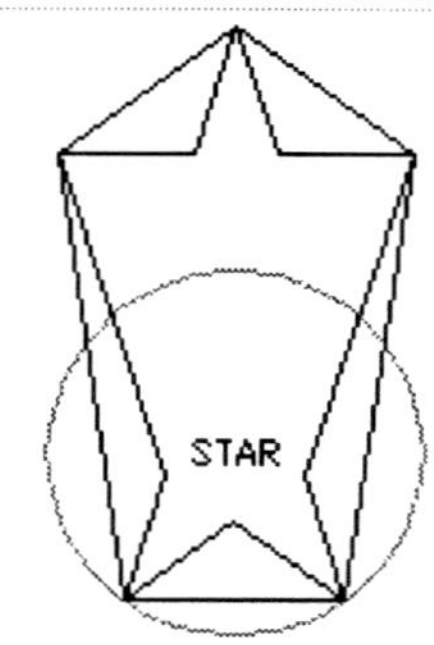


6. Undo your changes .

   **Command:** ***u***

Of course, AutoCAD doesn't limit you to one direction or even one object with the ***Stretch*** command. So in some ways, it still exceeds the newer ***Lengthen*** command. But the ***Lengthen*** command has its good points, too. Let's look at the command sequence:

**Command:** ***lengthen*** **(or** ***len*****)**

**Select an object or [DElta/Percent/Total/ DYnamic]:** ***[tell AutoCAD what you what to do with the object or select a line or arc; subsequent prompts will depend on which option you select]***

**Current length: X.XXXX** ***[if you select an object, AutoCAD tells you the current length; if you select an arc, it'll tell you the included angle as well]***

**Select an object or [DElta/Percent/Total/ DYnamic]:** ***[enter to complete the command]***

The command includes four fairly simple options.

- **DElta** (the old Greek word for "change") means change. When selected, it prompts:

  **Enter delta length or [Angle] <1.0000>:** ***[enter the amount of change you wish]***

  **Select an object to change or [Undo]:** ***[select the object closest to the end at which you wish to add the length (use a negative number to shorten the line or arc]***

  If you select the **Angle** choice of the **DElta** option, you can add to an arc by specifying the angle of the arc to add.

- **Percent** allows you to change the length of the selected object by percent. AutoCAD prompts:

  **Enter percentage length <100.0000>:**

  Note that 100% means no change. More than 100% increases the length of the object and less than 100% decreases the length. Length is added or removed from the end closest to where you select the object.

- **Total** simply means, "How long do you want the object to be?" AutoCAD will add or remove as necessary (again, from the selected end) to make the object as long as you have specified.

- **DYnamic** allows you to manually (or *dynamically*) stretch the object to the desired length. AutoCAD prompts:

  **Select an object to change or [Undo]:**

  **Specify new end point:**

  Select the **object to change** and specify a new **end point**.

Let's see what we can do with the ***Lengthen*** command.

| Do This: 9.2.1.2 | Using the *Lengthen* Command |
|---|---|

I. Be sure you're still in the *star+* drawing in the C:\Steps\Lesson09 folder.
II. Thaw the **Line** and **Arc** layers.
III. Zoom all. Notice the line and arc.
IV. Follow these steps.

### 9.2.1.2: Using the Lengthen Command

1. Enter the ***Lengthen*** command.

   **Command: *len***

2. Select the arc.

   **Select an object or [DElta/Percent/Total/DYnamic]:**

3. AutoCAD reports the true length of the arc and the included angle.

   **Current length: 1.5708, included angle: 90**

4. Use the **DElta** option 

 to change the length.

   **Select an object or [DElta/Percent/Total/DYnamic]: *de***

5. AutoCAD asks if you want to make a change by **Angle** or **length**. Enter a length of **1**.

   **Enter delta length or [Angle] <0.0000>: *1***

6. Select the upper end of the arc.

   **Select an object to change or [Undo]:**

   AutoCAD adds one unit to the upper end. It now looks like this.

7. Now select the left end of the horizontal line. Notice that AutoCAD adds a piece one unit long to the end.

   **Select an object to change or [Undo]:**

8. Complete the command.

   **Select an object to change or [Undo]: *[enter]***

9. Repeat the command.

   **Command: *[enter]***

10. Let's make an adjustment by the **Percent** method. Select the **Percent** option 

.

    **Select an object or [DElta/Percent/Total/DYnamic]: *p***

11. Let's cut the objects in half. Enter ***50*** for the **percentage length**.

    **Enter percentage length <100.0000>: *50***

12. Select the lower end of the arc; then select the right end of the line.

    **Select an object to change or [Undo]:**

    Complete the command.

    **Select an object to change or [Undo]: *[enter]***

    The objects now look like this.

13. Repeat the command.

### 9.2.1.2: Using the Lengthen Command

14. This time we'll set the **Total** length of arc and line. Select the **Total** option 

.

**Select an object or [DElta/Percent/ Total/DYnamic]:** ***t***

15. Enter ***4*** to set a total length of four units.

**Specify total length or [Angle] <1.0000)>:** ***4***

16. Select the left end of the arc; then select the right end of the line.

**Select an object to change or [Undo]:**

Finally, complete the command.

**Select an object to change or [Undo]:** ***[enter]***

Notice (right) that **Total** added to the arc but subtracted from the line.

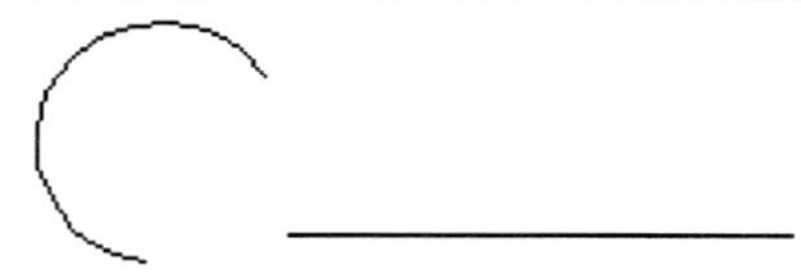

17. Repeat the command.

**Command:** ***[enter]***

18. Using the **Dynamic** option 

, select the line and watch how it changes as you move the cursor back and forth. Then try it with the arc.

**Select an object or [DElta/Percent/ Total/DYnamic]:** ***dy***

**Select an object to change or [Undo]:**

**Specify new end point:**

19. Close the drawing without saving the changes.

**Command:** ***quit***

The greatest differences between the ***Lengthen*** and ***Stretch*** commands are twofold. First, there's an easy precision allotted by the ***Lengthen*** command; and second, the ***Stretch*** command allows you to modify more than one object at a time.

I'm more prone to use the ***Stretch*** command partly because, more often than not, I must modify multiple objects. But I use it also out of habit. For such a simple command, it's remarkably versatile and quite useful.

## 9.2.2 "Oh, NO! I Drew It Upside Down!" – The *Rotate* Command

Okay. So this'll probably never happen to you (then again, you might just be surprised). Still, it's not unusual to find a need to rotate text for a better fit or to rotate a piece of equipment or furniture for a more efficient layout. Either way, the ***Rotate*** command offers a simple solution to problems that, on a drawing board, might cause a redraw.

The ***Rotate*** command sequence is

**Command:** ***rotate*** **(or** ***ro*****)**

**Current positive angle in UCS: ANGDIR=counterclockwise ANGBASE=0**

**Select objects:** ***[select the object(s) to rotate]***

**Select objects:** ***[hit enter to confirm the selection set]***

**Specify base point:** ***[select a point around which to rotate]***

**Specify rotation angle or [Copy/Reference] <0>:** ***[how much do you want to rotate the objects?]***

- AutoCAD begins by telling you something about the setup:

- The **Current positive angle in UCS:** line refers to 3-dimensional space. You can ignore it for now.
- **ANGDIR** simply reminds you that angles are measured counterclockwise (unless you changed it during the setup procedure for the drawing).
- **ANGBASE** refers to a system variable that allows you to change the angle from which AutoCAD begins to measure. For example, if you tell AutoCAD to use a reference angle of 45°, it'll add 45 to the value of the **Angbase** system variable.

- The default option – **Rotation angle** – simply means, "How much do you want to rotate?" Type in an angle or drag the object on the screen (use Ortho to rotate at 90° increments).
- The next option – **Reference** – prompts again:

  **Specify the reference angle <0>: *[tell AutoCAD what the current rotation is]***

  **Specify the new angle or [Points] <0>: *[tell AutoCAD what you want the rotation to be either by entering an angle or specifying two points]***

  Use this option when you know what the current rotation angle is and what you want it to be. If you don't know what it is but do know what you want it to be, use the **Points** option and select two points on a line that represent the current rotation. AutoCAD will determine the angle from the line you select and rotate to the **new angle**.
- Use the **Copy** option to create a rotated copy of the selected objects.

This may be confusing. Let's try an example.

| Do This: 9.2.2.1 | Rotating Objects |
|---|---|

I. Reopen the *star+* drawing in the C:\Steps\Lesson09 folder.

II. Freeze the **Arc** and **Line** layers.

III. Follow these steps.

**9.2.2.1: ROTATING OBJECTS**

1. Enter the ***Rotate*** command. Alternately, you can pick the **Rotate** button  on the Modify toolbar or palette.

   **Command: *ro***

2. Select the circle and all the objects within it.

   **Current positive angle in UCS: ANGDIR=counterclockwise ANGBASE=0**

   **Select objects:**

   **Select objects: *[enter]***

3. Select the center point  of the circle.

   **Specify base point: _cen of**

4. Tell AutoCAD to rotate the objects ***90°***.

   **Specify rotation angle or [Copy/Reference] <0>: *90***

   The star looks like this.

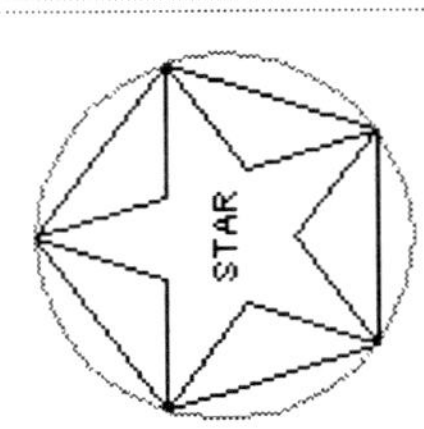


5. Let's make a rotated copy. Repeat the ***Rotate*** command 

**9.2.2.1: ROTATING OBJECTS**

6. Select the circle and all the objects within it.

    **Current positive angle in UCS: ANGDIR=counterclockwise ANGBASE=0**
    **Select objects:**
    **Select objects: *[enter]***

7. Specify a point one unit to the left of the object as the base point.

    **Specify base point: *3,1***

8. Tell AutoCAD to make a **Copy** [Copy] of the object to rotate.

    **Specify rotation angle or [Copy/Reference] <90>: *c***

9. AutoCAD lets you know it'll be rotating a copy of the selected objects.

Now tell it to use the **Reference** option [Reference].

    **Rotating a copy of the selected objects.**
    **Specify rotation angle or [Copy/Reference] <90>: *r***

10. We rotated the objects by 90° in Step 4, so tell AutoCAD that the current angle (or reference angle) is ***90***.

    **Specify the reference angle <0>: *90***

11. Tell AutoCAD to rotate all objects to an angle of ***270°***.

    **Specify the new angle or [Points] <0>: *270***

The stars now look like this.

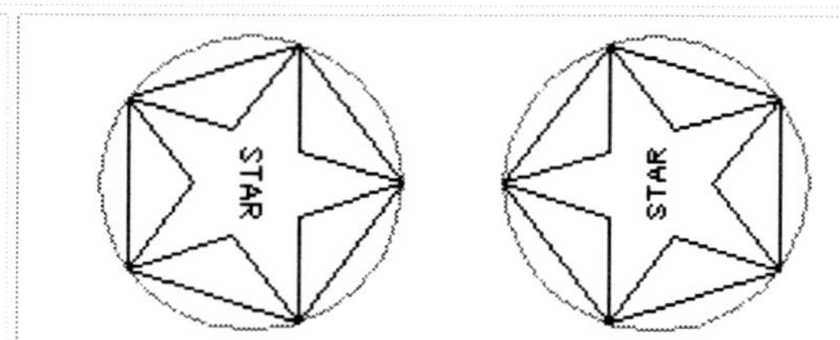


12. Undo all the changes in this exercise.

    **Command: *u***

If only they were all that easy!

## 9.2.3 "Okay. Give Me Three Just Like It, But Different Sizes." The *Scale* Command

No, that doesn't mean you have to draw it two more times. You simply need to make two copies and then scale (or resize) the copies to meet the customer's requirements. The command sequence is one of the easy ones:

**Command: *scale* (or *sc*)**
**Select objects: *[select the object(s) to scale]***
**Select objects: *[confirm completion of the selection set]***
**Specify base point: *[pick the base point]***
**Specify scale factor or [Copy/Reference] <1.0000>: *[enter the scale factor]***

**Copy** and **Reference** work just like they did in the ***Rotate*** command. Let's see ***Scale*** in action.

### Do This: 9.2.3.1 Scaling Objects

I. Be sure you're still in the *star+* drawing in the C:\Steps\Lesson09 folder.

II. Be sure the **Line** and **Arc** layers are still frozen.

III. Follow these steps.

### 9.2.3.1: Scaling Objects

1. Use the ***Pan*** command to center the circle in the lower area of the screen.

   **Command: *p***

2. Enter the ***Scale*** command. Alternately, you can pick the **Scale** button on the Modify toolbar or palette.

   **Command: *sc***

3. Select the circle and all the objects within it.

   **Select objects:**
   **Select objects: *[enter]***

4. Select the bottom quadrant of the circle as the **base point**. Notice how the objects change as you move the cursor.

   **Specify base point: _qua of**

5. Tell AutoCAD you want to scale the objects by a factor of two. The objects look the same but are twice as large.

   **Specify scale factor or [Copy/Reference] <1.0000>: *2***

6. Repeat Steps 2 through 4, but select only the outer circle.

   **Command: *[enter]***

7. Tell AutoCAD you want to scale a copy Copy.

   **Specify scale factor or [Copy/Reference] <2.0000>: *c***
   **Scaling a copy of the selected objects.**

8. Scale the copy to 1.5x the original.

   **Specify scale factor or [Copy/Reference] <2.0000>: *1.5***

   Your drawing looks like this.

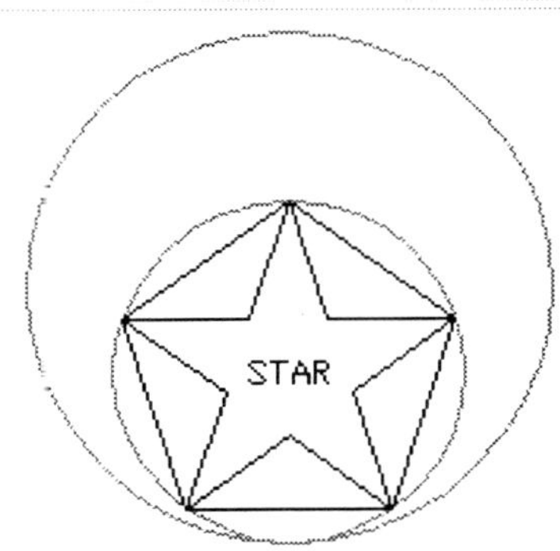


10. Quit the drawing. Don't save your changes.

    **Command: *quit***

## 9.3 Identifying the Changes – The *Revcloud* Command

Creating a revision cloud on a paper drawing has always been one of the easiest chores in drafting – simply turn the paper over and scribble a cloudy line around your changes (then add a revision triangle to identify the change). It'll no doubt please you to know that AutoCAD's revision cloud is just as easy as the cloud you put on paper!

Here's the command sequence:

**Command: *revcloud***
**Minimum arc length: 0.5000 Maximum arc length: 0.5000 Style: Normal**

**Specify start point or [Arc length/Object/Style] <Object>:** ***[Pick the start point for your cloud]***

**Guide crosshairs along cloud path...** ***[Move your crosshairs along the path you want your cloud to take – no need to pick, AutoCAD will automatically draw the cloud]***

**Revision cloud finished.** ***[When you move the crosshairs back to the beginning of the cloud, AutoCAD will automatically close it for you!]***

This remarkably easy tool has a couple options you might want to review.

- You have the ability to change the **Arc length** if you wish. The default **0.5000** works quite well, and AutoCAD automatically multiplies it by the **Dimscale** (more on dimension variables in Lesson 15).
- The **Object** option allows you to convert any existing closed object (polyline, circle, polygon, or spline) into a cloud.
- The style option gives you two choices:

  **Select arc style [Normal/Calligraphy] <Normal>:**

  Normal simply draws a polyline cloud.

  Calligraphy makes the cloud a bit fancier. Other than that, it works just the same as a normal cloud.

You really have to see this tool in action!

| Do This: 9.3.1 | Adding Revision Clouds |
|---|---|

I. Reopen the *star+* drawing in the C:\Steps\Lesson09 folder.

II. Make the **OBJ1** layer current and turn ORTHO off.

III. Follow these steps.

### 9.3.1: Adding Revision Clouds

1. Enter the ***Revcloud*** command. Alternately, you can pick the **Revcloud** button on the Draw toolbar or palette. (Note: The Standard toolbar has a similar button, but it serves a different purpose.)

   **Command:** ***revcloud***

2. AutoCAD tells you what the arc lengths will be and asks you where you'd like to start the cloud. Pick a point above the circle.

   **Minimum arc length: 0.5000 Maximum arc length: 0.5000 Style: Normal**

   **Specify start point or [Arc length/Object/Style] <Object>:**

3. Trace the path of the cloud around it.

   **Guide crosshairs along cloud path...**

   **Revision cloud finished.**

   Your drawing will look something like this.

4. Erase the cloud. Notice that it's a polyline and a single pick will select the entire cloud.

   **Command:** ***e***

5. Let's try the **Object** and **Calligraphy** options. Repeat the ***Revcloud*** command.

   **Command:** ***revcloud***

6. Select the **Style** option, and then select **Calligraphy**.

**Specify start point or [Arc length/Object/Style] <Object>:** ***s***

**Select arc style [Normal/ Calligraphy] <Normal>:** ***c***

7. Now accept the **Object** option.

**Minimum arc length: 0.5000   Maximum arc length: 0.5000**

**Arc style: Calligraphy**

**Specify start point or [Arc length/Object/ Style] <Object>:** ***[enter]***

8. Select the circle.

**Select object:**

9. Don't reverse the direction of the cloud this time (we'll do that in a minute).

**Reverse direction [Yes/No] <No>:** ***[enter]***

**Revision cloud finished.**

Your drawing looks like this.

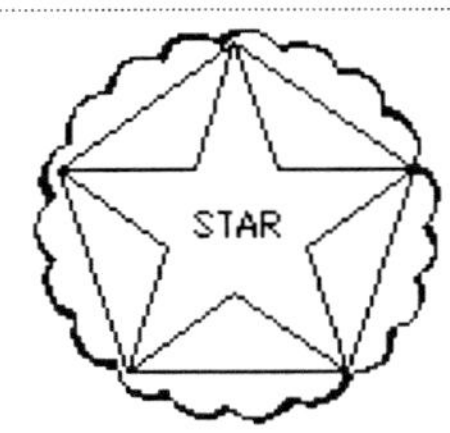


10. Undo the last command.

**Command:** ***u***

11. Let's try the **Object** option on a polyline. Repeat the ***Revcloud*** command.

**Command:** ***revcloud***

12. Select the **Object** option.

**Minimum arc length: 0.5000   Maximum arc length: 0.5000**

**Arc style: Calligraphy**

**Specify start point or [Arc length/Object] <Object>:** ***[enter]***

13. Select the polygon just inside the circle.

**Select object:**

14. This time, let's reverse the direction of the cloud.

**Reverse direction [Yes/No] <No>:** ***y***

**Revision cloud finished.**

Your drawing looks like this.

15. Experiment with the ***Revcloud*** command on the other objects in the drawing. On which will the command work? On which will it not work? Why/Why not?

As you've seen, ***Revcloud's*** **Object** option will replace the selected object with a revision cloud. You can prevent the removal of the selected object by changing the **Delobj** system variable from its default of **1** to **0**.

Did you notice what the ***Revcloud*** command doesn't do? I know, it was so simple that you just hate to hear that it lacks anything … but it's missing one key ingredient for revisions. It doesn't provide a revision *triangle* to allow you to identify the changes you made! You'll have to provide this yourself (use the ***Polygon*** command)!

Okay, I couldn't let you go like that. I created a lisp routine (called *Revtriangle.lsp* – the command is ***RevT***) and put it in the C:\Steps\Lesson09 folder. You can use it to insert your revision triangles.

## 9.4 Putting It All Together

We've covered several new modification tools in this lesson using our star for demonstrations. Although the star is perfect for these demonstrations, let's try a more practical exercise and use several of these tools to create something.

### Do This: 9.4.1 A Practical Exercise

I. Open the *grad_cyl* drawing from the C:\Steps\Lesson09 folder.

II. Follow these steps.

**9.4.1: PRACTICE EXERCISE**

1. Adjust your view to the one shown.

   **Command: *z***

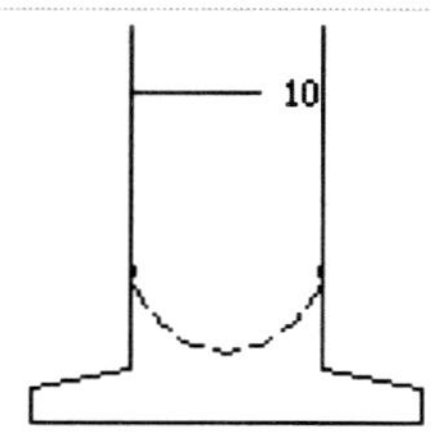


2. Use the ***Array*** command to make four copies (five lines in all) of the cyan line below the one shown. The spacing should be -0.1.

   **Command: *ar***

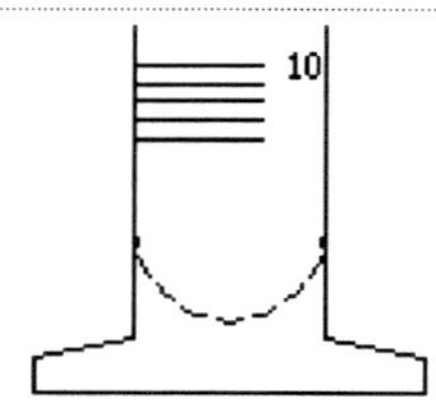


3. Use the ***Lengthen*** command to adjust the length of the top line to .75".

   **Command: *len***
   **Select an object or [DElta/Percent/Total/DYnamic]: *t***
   **Specify total length or [Angle] <1.0000)>: *.75***
   **Select an object to change or [Undo]:**
   **Select an object to change or [Undo]: *[enter]***

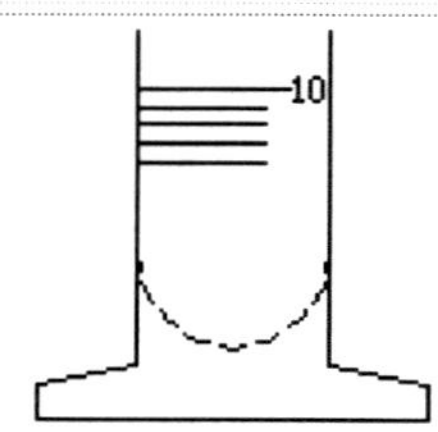


4. Copy the lines upward ½" for a total of 10 lines.

   **Command: *cp***
   **Select objects:**
   **Select objects: *[enter]***
   **Specify base point or [Displacement] <Displacement>: *0,.5***
   **Specify second point or <use first point as displacement>: *[enter]***

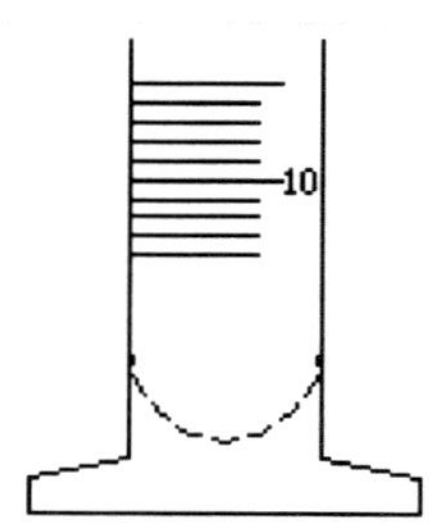

## 9.4.1: Practice Exercise

5. Use the ***Lengthen*** command to adjust the length of the top line to 11/16".

**Command:** ***len***

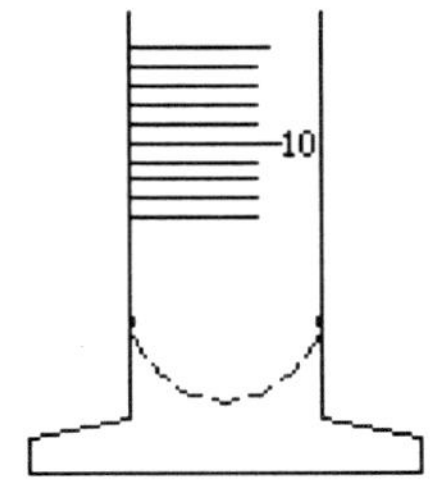


6. Restore the previous  view.

**Command:** ***z***

7. Use the ***Array*** command 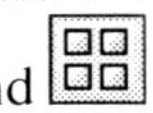 to place the graduations on the cylinder (see the left figure below). (The distance between sections is 1".)

**Command:** ***ar***

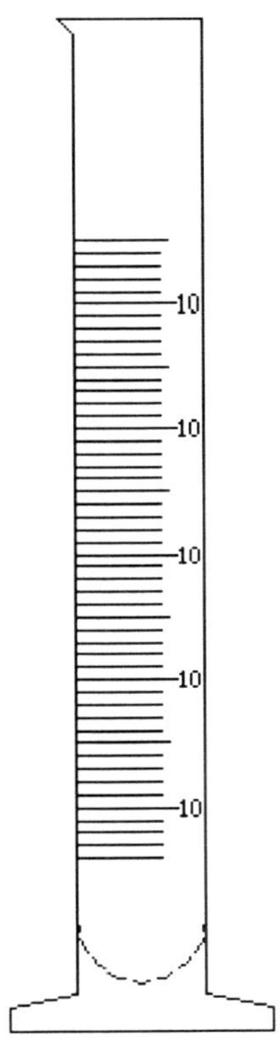


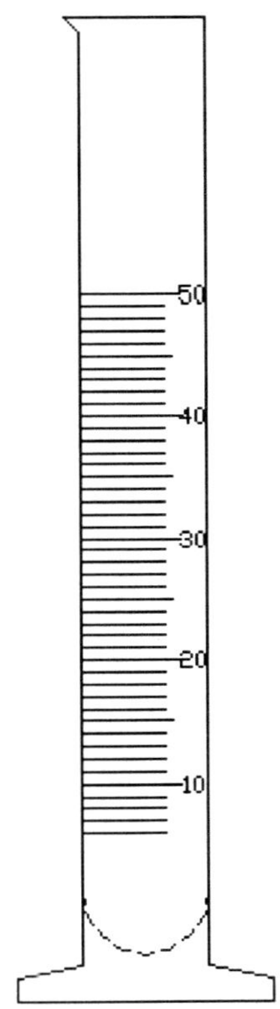


8. Use the text editor  to change the numbers to read 10, 20, 30, 40, and 50. Erase the lines above 50.

**Command:** ***ed***

**Command:** ***e***

Your drawing looks like the right figure above.

Your graduated cylinder is finished. Good job! Now let's draw a speedometer.

## 9.4.1: Practice Exercise

9. Now adjust your view to get closer to the circle on the right.

**Command:** ***z***

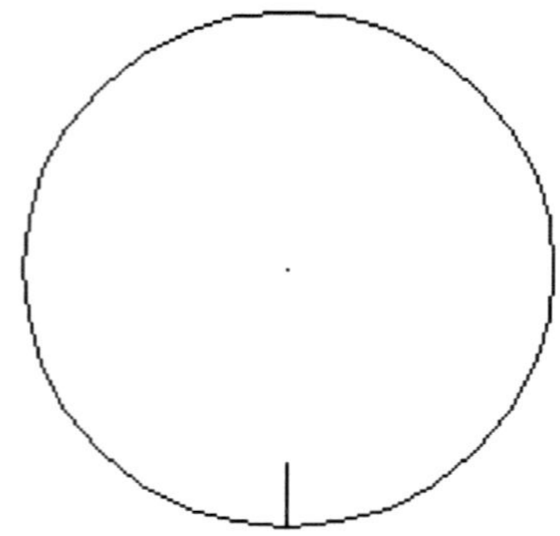

10. Use the ***Offset*** command to copy the circle inward twice at .17" increments.

**Command:** ***o***

**Current settings: Erase source=No Layer=Source OFFSETGAPTYPE=0**

**Specify offset distance or [Through/Erase/Layer] <Through>:** ***.17***

**Select object to offset or [Exit/Undo] <Exit>:** ***[select the circle]***

**Specify point on side to offset or [Exit/Multiple/Undo] <Exit>:** ***m***

**Specify point on side to offset or [Exit/Undo] <next object>:**

**Select object to offset or [Exit/Undo] <Exit>:** ***[enter]***

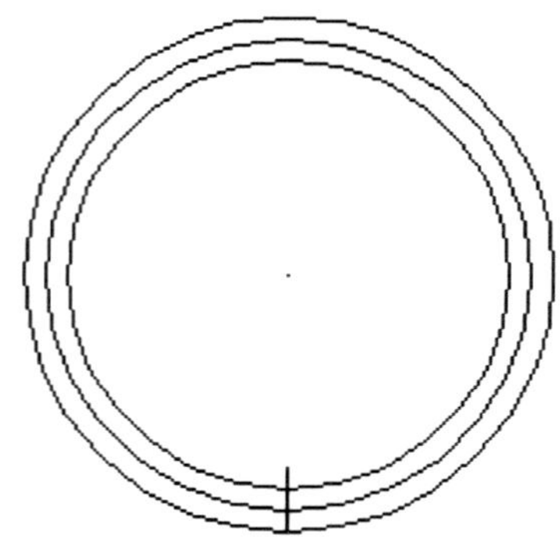

11. Use the ***Array*** command to make 10 copies (11 lines altogether) of the line along a 36° arc.

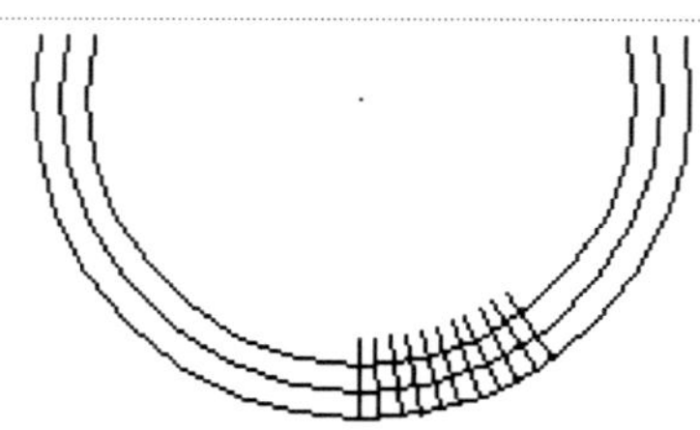

12. Using the inner circles as cutting edges, ***trim*** the lines, as shown. (Erase the right-most line.)

**Command:** ***tr***

13. ***Erase*** the two inner circles.

**Command:** ***e***

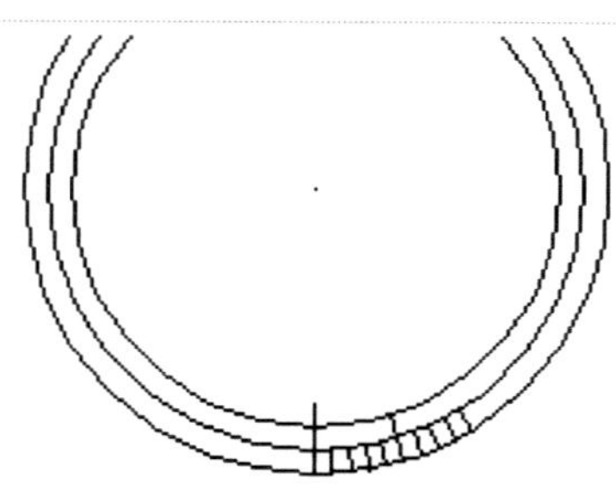

## 9.4.1: Practice Exercise

14. Array the lines as shown. (Make 9 copies – 10 sets – and fill a 360° angle.)

**Command:** ***ar***

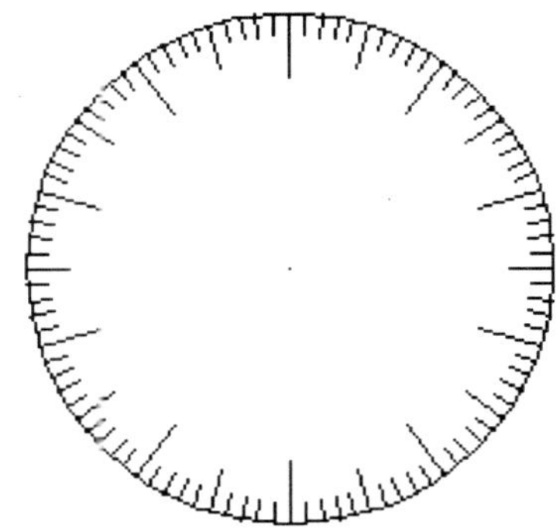

15. Erase the bottom set of lines as shown.

**Command:** ***e***

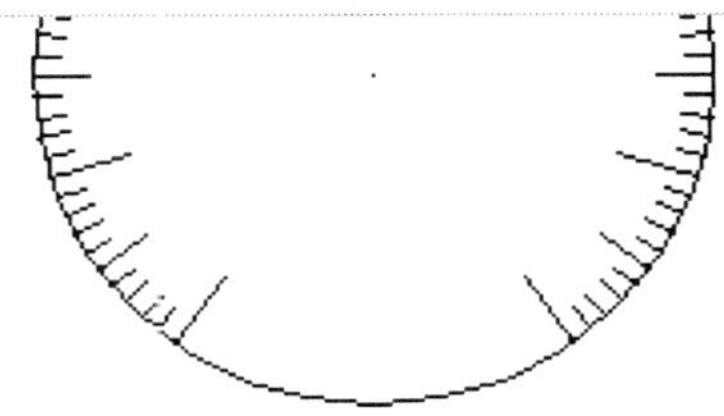

16. Add text and polylines (use the appropriate layers and a text height of **0.2**) to complete the speedometer. (Hint: Draw the pointer pointing downward using Ortho, and then rotate it.)

17. Save the drawing.

**Command:** ***qsave***

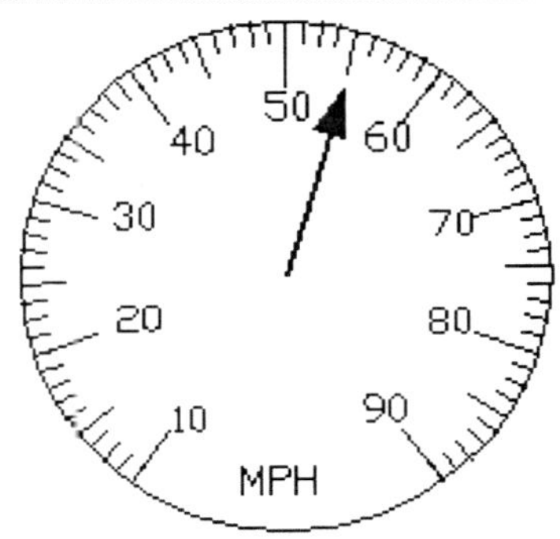


## 9.5 Extra Steps

*When All Else Fails – Ask for Help!*

- My Wife (When I couldn't find the right exit)

*I'm convinced that we learn more through exploration, experimentation, and error than by any other means.*

- Anonymous

We're really making progress through our course! Have you noticed the Help pull-down menu yet? Have you tried to use it?

One of the smartest things you (or any student) can do is to know what resources are available to help you when you get into a bind.

Make a list of the resources available to you – begin with this text. Add your instructor (if you're in a classroom environment), the smart guy sitting next to you, the Info Palette, and any other classroom references (handouts, books, tests, etc.). Most importantly – add *your willingness to explore and experiment with the software* (never underestimate the power of trial and error as a learning tool).

Now take a look at the Help pull-down menu. The first thing you may notice is the number of selections available to you. Let's look at some of these:

- **Help** provides access to a standard Windows Help dialog box. Tabs provide access to information using a table of contents format, a subject index format, and a word search format. Tabs also include **Ask Me**, which enables you to simply ask a question based upon the (hopefully) familiar *Ask Jeeves* tool (www.ask.com).

  I suggest starting with the subject index – simply enter the subject for which you're searching and pick the **Display** button. If that doesn't provide a solution, try the word search **(Search)** tab.
- **Info Palette** calls the Info Palette.
- The **New Feature Workshop** helps if you're already familiar with AutoCAD but new to this release.
- As so many software companies are doing now, AutoCAD also provides access to Online Resources. These are useful mostly for upgrades and expansion of your software … online support, while often cheaper than telephone support, is generally quite slow.

## 9.6 What Have We Learned?

*Items covered in this lesson include:*

- *AutoCAD Modify Commands:*
  - ***Offset***
  - ***Array***
  - ***Mirror***
  - ***Lengthen***
  - ***Stretch***
  - ***Rotate***
  - ***Scale***
  - ***Revcloud***
- *AutoCAD System Variables:*
  - ***Mirrtext***
  - ***Angdir***
  - ***Angbase***
  - ***Delobj***

Have you noticed that the easiest of AutoCAD's tools are invariably modification commands?

With the conclusion of this lesson, you'll have learned all of the more common drawing and editing techniques AutoCAD has to offer the 2-dimensional drafter. We'll go next to a discussion of some fairly useful drawing tricks and toys. Then we'll start our study of some more advanced techniques that you'll need to master before venturing into the third dimension (or applying for that CAD position).

## 9.7 Exercises

1. Create a drawing template with the following parameters:
   - 1.1. Lower left limits: 0,0
   - 1.2. Upper right limits: 17,11
   - 1.3. Grid: ½
   - 1.4. Snap: ¼
   - 1.5. Layers: At right
   - 1.6. Save the template as *BwLay.dwt* in the C:\Steps\Lesson09 folder.

| LAYER | COLOR | LINETYPE |
|---|---|---|
| Obj | red | continuous |
| Cl | cyan | center2 |
| Hidden | magenta | hidden2 |
| Text | yellow | continuous |
| Dim | blue | continuous |

2. Start a new drawing using the *BwLay.dwt* template. (You created this in Exercise #1.)
   2.1. Create the drawing below. You're allowed to draw one box and the outline of the wall. You may use the following commands to help: ***Copy***, ***Rotate***, ***Scale*** and ***Stretch***. The size of each window is 1.75x the size of the smaller window next to it. Feel free to add layers if you think it necessary.

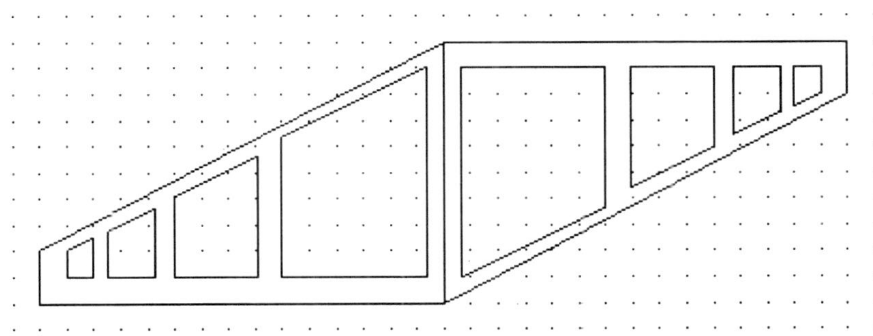

*For more exercises related to Lesson 9, please see Lesson 9 in AutoCAD 2007: One Step at a Time – Workbook.*

| 9.8 | **For Web-Based Review Questions, visit: http://www.uneedcad.com/2007/Files/07R9.pdf** |
|---|---|

# Lesson 10

Following this lesson, you will:

- ✓ *Know how to use **Divide** and **Measure***
- ✓ *Know how to draw with these commands:*
  - ***Point***
  - ***Solid***
  - ***Donut***
- ✓ *Be familiar with these Advanced Selection Methods:*
  - *WindowPoly*
  - *CrossingPoly*
  - *Last*
  - *All*
  - *Previous*
  - *Add and Remove*
- ✓ *Know how to use Quick Select Filters*
- ✓ *Know how to use AutoCAD's Calculator*

# Some Useful Drawing Tricks

*You've come a very long way since learning the Cartesian Coordinate System so many lessons ago. You've learned the basic 2-dimensional tools for drawing and modifying most objects. You've learned to draw with a precision you probably never dreamt possible on a drawing board. Did you know that this drawing precision enables manufacturers to create products directly from your drawing? It's a system called CAM (Computer Aided Manufacturing). CAD-CAM is one possible direction your career might take if you pursue AutoCAD into the 3-dimensional world.*

*This lesson allows you to relax a bit and take a look at some of AutoCAD's tricks and toys meant to enhance the productivity of its users. Some of the toys you may never use; some you might rarely use. But all are full of possibilities.*

*Let's begin.*

## 10.1 Equal or Measured Distances – The *Divide* and *Measure* Commands

Both these commands serve to place markers (nodes) at certain locations on an object. ***Divide*** places equally spaced nodes along the object. ***Measure*** places a node at user-set distances along the object. (Note: Neither command actually breaks the object. Rather, both place nodes along the object.)

> We defined a *point*, you will recall, as the place where an X-plane intersects a Y-plane. A *node* is an object that occupies a single point. It serves primarily as an identifier or locator in the drawing. CAD operators frequently use the terms *point* and *node* interchangeably when referring to a single point. It isn't that important to remember the difference, but this might help:
>
> I snap to a **n**ode (**o**bject) that occupies a poi**nt** (**i**dea).

The command sequences are very simple. Here's the ***Divide*** command:

**Command: *divide* (or *div*)**

**Select object to divide: *[select the object to divide]***

**Enter the number of segments or [Block]: *[tell AutoCAD how many segments you want]***

The **Block** option allows you to place a predefined block rather than a node at the end of each segment. We'll study blocks in Lessons 19 and 20.

The ***Measure*** command sequence is

**Command: *measure* (or *me*)**

**Select object to measure: *[select the object to divide]***

**Specify length of segment or [Block]: *[tell AutoCAD how far apart to place the nodes]***

Let's see these commands in action.

> These commands are also available in the Draw pull-down menu. Follow this path:
>
> *Draw – Point – Divide (or Measure)*

### Do This: 10.1.1 Dividing and Measuring

I. Open the *mea-div* drawing in the C:\Steps\Lesson10 folder. The drawing looks like Figure 10.001.

II. Follow these steps.

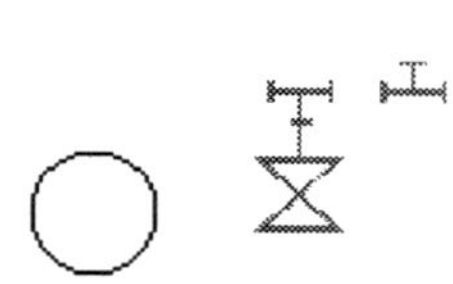

Figure 10.001

## 10.1.1: Dividing and Measuring

1. Zoom in around the circle.

   **Command: *z***

2. Set **MARKERS** as the current layer.

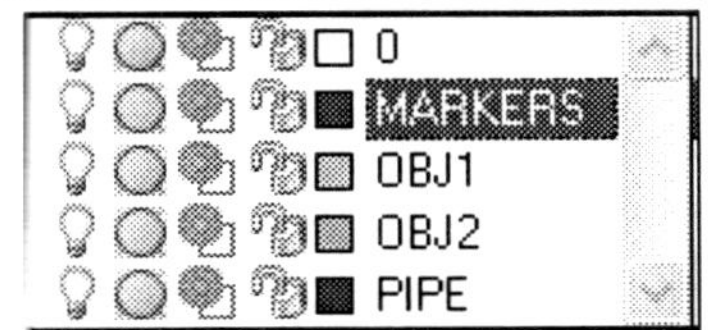


3. Enter the ***Divide*** command.

   **Command: *div***

4. Select the circle.

   **Select object to divide:**

5. Tell AutoCAD you want five equal divisions marked off on the circle.

   **Enter the number of segments or [Block]: *5***

Your drawing looks like this.

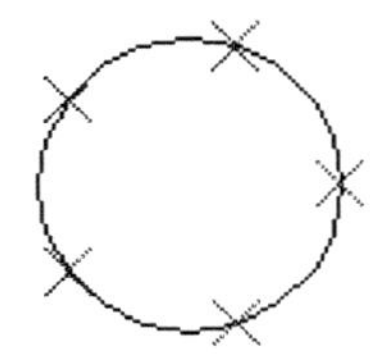

6. Set the Running OSNAP to **Node**. Clear all other settings.

   **Command: *os***

7. Set the current layer to **OBJ2**.

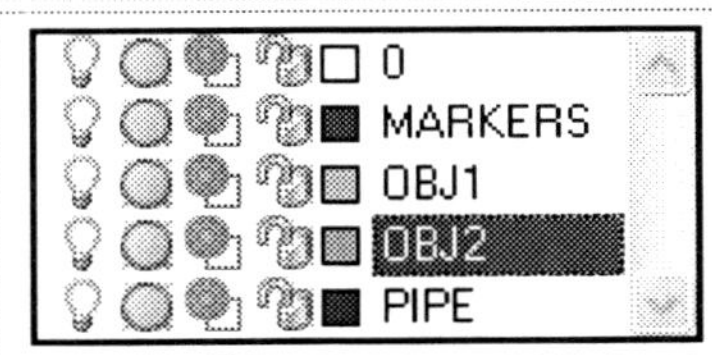


8. Draw lines connecting the nodes so that your drawing looks like this.

   **Command: *l***

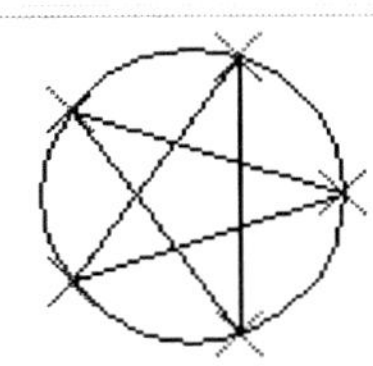

9. Save your drawing, but don't exit.

   **Command: *qsave***

Remember the last star we drew? We used a polygon inside a circle to locate the points. This trick is a bit faster and simpler than the polygon procedure. But the ***Divide*** command in this exercise requires a circle whereas the ***Polygon*** command did not.

III. Let's take a look at the ***Measure*** command.

10. Zoom out to your previous screen.

    **Command: *z***

11. Set the **MARKERS** layer current.

12. Enter the ***Measure*** command.

    **Command: *me***

## 10.1.1: Dividing and Measuring

13. Select the horizontal line. (Select the left end of the line.)

    **Select object to measure:**

14. Tell AutoCAD you want the nodes placed 6" apart as shown below.

    **Specify length of segment or [Block]: *6***

AutoCAD placed the first mark 6" from the left, then placed marks every 6" thereafter. Notice there's a bit of leftover space at the other end. This space will always be shorter than the specified distance.

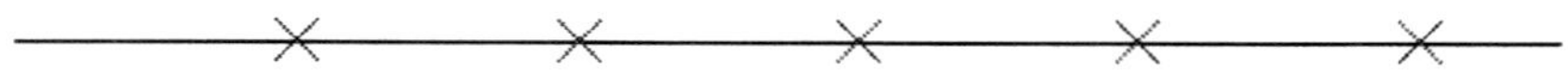

15. Move the *Tee* to the middle node as shown below.

    **Command: *m***

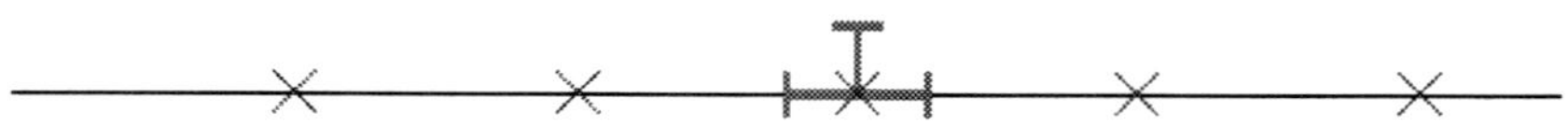

16. Now copy the *Tee and Valve* to each of the remaining nodes.

    **Command: *co***

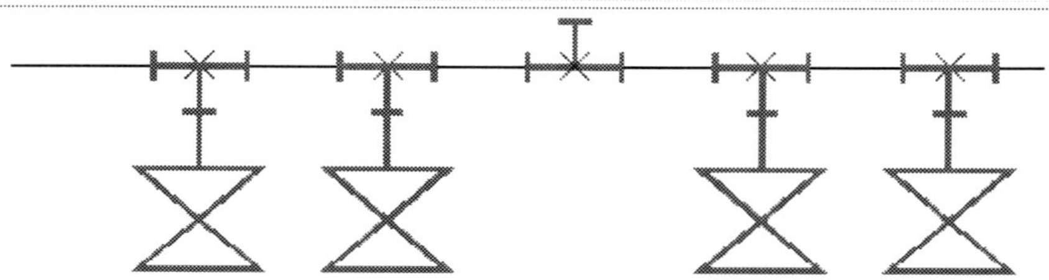

17. Using the modify tools you know, complete the header drawing, as shown below. (Note: The *pipe* is 1/8" wide and goes on the **PIPE** layer.)

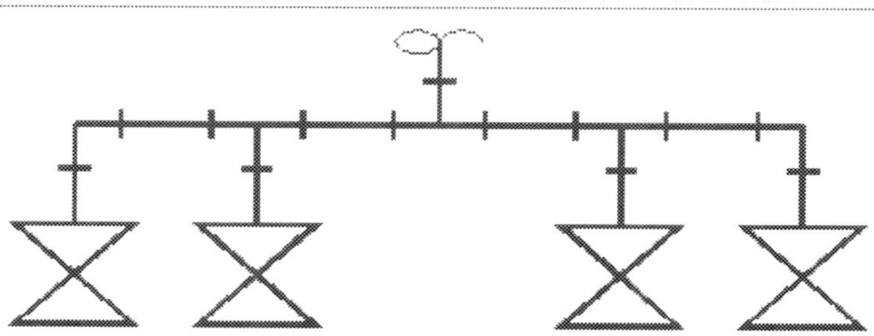

18. Save your drawing, but don't exit.

    **Command: *qsave***

## 10.2 So Where's the *Point*?

But are these the only tools that make use of those nifty nodes? Of course not. Nodes are a favorite tool of third-party software. I've even included a couple of Lisp routines that make use of nodes. But you can place nodes anywhere you think they might be useful with the ***Point*** command.

> Third-party software refers to any of a myriad of products designed to work within the AutoCAD environment to make life easier for you. Products are available for most industries.

The ***Point*** command sequence is

**Command:** ***point*** **(or** ***po*****)**

**Current point modes: PDMODE=3 PDSIZE=0'-0"** ***[AutoCAD tells you how the nodes are currently set to appear – more on this after the exercise]***

**Specify a point:** ***[pick the location]***

You really can't get any easier than this one. But remember to always use OSNAPs for precise placing of your nodes.

> This command is also available in the Draw pull-down menu (as well as the toolbar and palette). Follow this path:
>
> *Draw – Point – Single Point (or Multiple Point)*

| Do This: 10.2.1 | Making a Point |
|---|---|

I. Be sure you're still in the *mea-div* drawing in the C:\Steps\Lesson10 folder.

II. Set the **MARKERS** layer current.

III. Follow these steps.

### 10.2.1: Making a Point

1. Zoom in around the circle.

   **Command:** ***z***

2. Place a node …

   **Command:** ***po***

3. … in the center of the circle.

   **Current point modes: PDMODE=3 PDSIZE=0'-0"**

   **Specify a point: _cen of**

4. Erase the circle. Now you can still find the center of the star by using the node.

   **Command:** ***e***

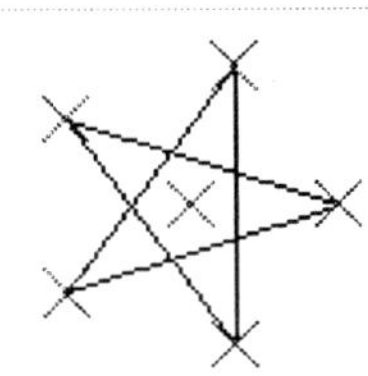

5. Save your drawing, but don't exit.

   **Command:** ***qsave***

We've been using an "X" to mark our nodes. I set this symbol in the drawing when I created it. But it isn't the only (or even the default) symbol available to show a node. To see the various symbols available, or to change the symbol you use, enter ***DDPType*** at the command prompt or select **Point Style** from the Format pull-down menu. AutoCAD provides a dialog box (Figure 10.002 – next page) to help your selection.

To change the node symbol you're using, simply pick the symbol you want to use.

Note that the second symbol on the top row is blank. This is an important "symbol" as it clears all the nodes in the drawing without removing them. *You should set the node symbol to blank before plotting a drawing!*

You can set the point (or node) size **Relative to Screen** or in **Absolute Units**. I recommend the former. AutoCAD will resize the nodes to keep them **Relative** when you alter views (zoom in or out). If they don't automatically resize, regenerate the drawing. **Absolute** nodes can be easily lost if you zoom out too far. I also recommend leaving the **Point Size** at its default. This is large enough to be seen but won't cause your nodes to dominate the screen.

Experiment with the different symbols to see which you prefer. Remember that you must ***regen*** to see each new setting.

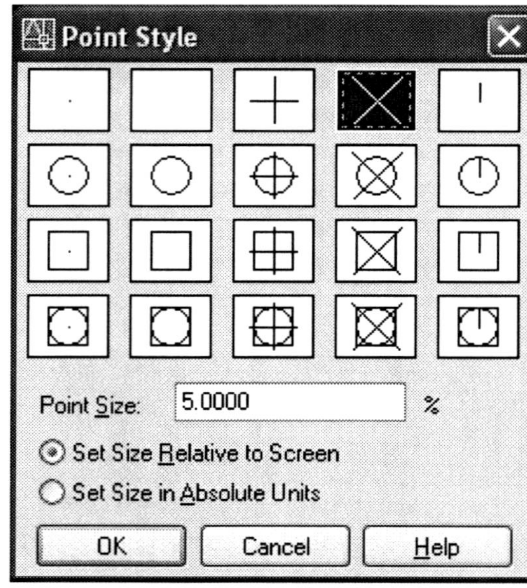


Figure 10.002

> AutoCAD stores the point type you select in a system variable called **PDMode**. If you know the number code of the symbol you want to use, you can set it like this:
>
> **Command:** ***pdmode***
>
> **Enter new value for PDMODE <0>:** ***3***

## 10.3 From Outlines to Solids – The *Solid* and *Donut* Commands

Tired of drawing stick figures (outlines)?

The only tool we've seen thus far for drawing objects with width is the polyline. This tool can create most of the objects on which we need to show width. But wait ... there are others! There are even tools that are easier to use than the polyline! Find that hard to believe? Read on!

Two easy tools for showing a solid surface in the 2-dimensional world are the ***Solid*** command and the ***Donut*** command. With the ***Solid*** command, you can fill triangular areas. With the ***Donut*** command, you can fill round areas.

Let's start with the ***Solid*** command. The sequence follows:

**Command:** ***solid*** **(or** ***so*****)**

**Specify first point:** ***[pick the first corner of the area to fill]***

**Specify second point:** ***[pick the second corner of the area to fill]***

**Specify third point:** ***[pick the third corner of the area to fill – if there are four corners or more, select the corner nearest the first corner]***

**Specify fourth point or <exit>:** ***[AutoCAD repeats the third and fourth corner until you end the command by hitting enter]***

**Specify third point:** ***[enter]***

Let's try it.

> This command is also available in the Draw pull-down menu. Follow this path:
>
> *Draw – Surfaces – 2D Solid*

| Do This: 10.3.1 | Creating Solids |
|---|---|

I. Be sure you're still in the *mea-div* drawing in the C:\Steps\Lesson10 folder.
II. Set the **OBJ1** layer current.
III. Set the running OSNAP to **Node** and **Intersection**. Clear all other settings.
IV. Follow these steps.

### 10.3.1: CREATING SOLIDS

1. Enter the ***Solid*** command.

**Command:** ***so***

2. Select points 1, 2, and 3 as shown.

**Specify first point:** ***[select point 1]***
**Specify second point:** ***[select point 2]***
**Specify third point:** ***[select point 3]***

Then hit ***enter*** twice to exit the command.

**Specify fourth point or <exit>:** ***[enter]***
**Specify third point:** ***[enter]***

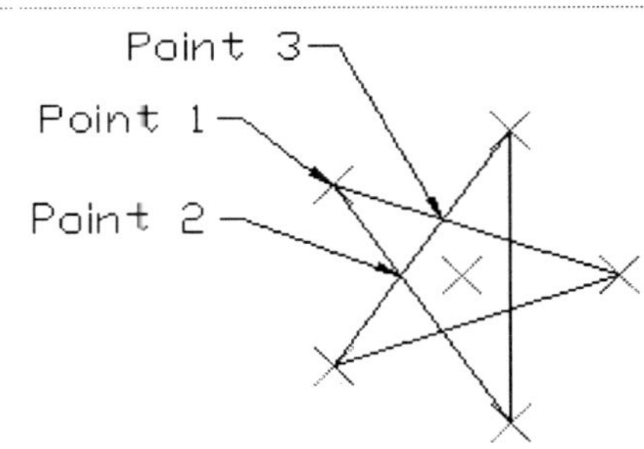


3. Add solids at each of the points of the star.

**Command:** ***so***

Your drawing now looks like this.

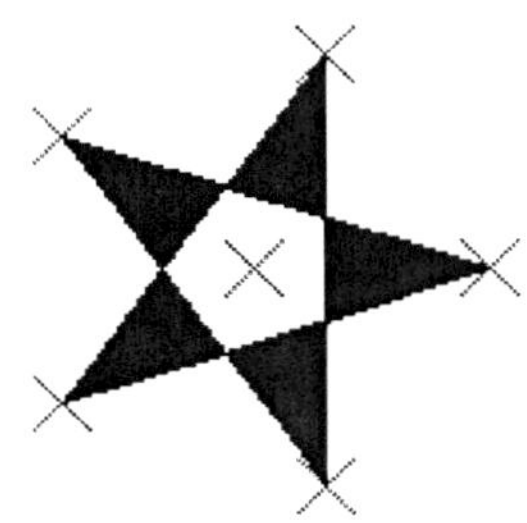

4. Save your drawing 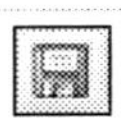 but don't exit.

**Command:** ***qsave***

You see that drawing solids isn't difficult. Try drawing a rectangle next to the star, and then placing a solid inside. Pick your corners first in clockwise direction. Notice the hourglass shape of the solid (Figure 10.003).

Figure 10.003

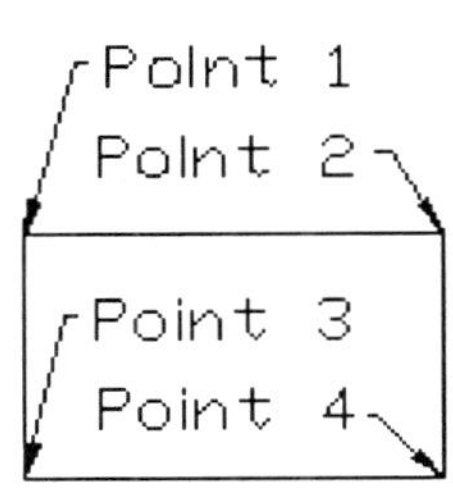


Figure 10.004

Figure 10.005

Now undo that and create your solid, picking the points in the order shown in Figure 10.004. Notice the difference? You should always reverse Points 3 and 4 from the direction taken from Point 1 to Point 2 (that is, work in triangles) in order to create a full solid, as shown in Figure 10.005.

---

You can draw donuts as easily as solids. But the ***Donut*** command does ask a couple questions.

**Command:** ***donut*** **(or** ***do*****)**

**Specify inside diameter of donut <0'-0 1/2">:** ***[set the diameter of the donut hold]***
**Specify outside diameter of donut <0'-1">:** ***[set the outer diameter of the donut]***
**Specify center of donut or <exit>:** ***[place the donut]***
**Specify center of donut or <exit>:** ***[enter to complete the command]***

The prompts are self-explanatory, so let's look at donuts in action.

> This command is also available in the Draw pull-down menu. Follow this path:
> *Draw - Donut*

| **Do This: 10.3.2** | **Using Donuts** |
|---|---|

I. Be sure you're still in the *mea-div* drawing in the C:\Steps\Lesson10 folder.
II. Follow these steps.

**10.3.2: USING DONUTS**

1. Enter the ***Donut*** command.
   **Command:** ***do***
2. Set the **inside diameter** to ***0*** …
   **Specify inside diameter of donut <0'-0 1/2">:** ***0***
3. … and the **outside diameter** to ***2.25***.
   **Specify outside diameter of donut <0'-1">:** ***2.25***
4. Place the **center of donut** at the **node** in the center of the star.
   **Specify center of donut or <exit>:**
5. Complete the command.
   **Specify center of donut or <exit>:** ***[enter]***

   Your drawing looks like this.

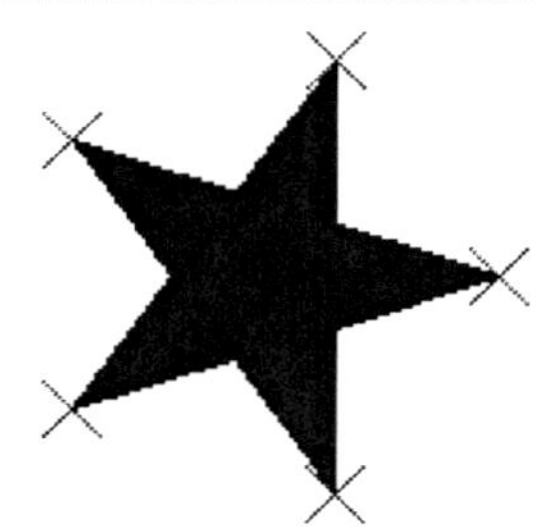

6. Let's place some other donuts. Repeat the command.
   **Command:** ***[enter]***
7. Make the inside diameter ***.25*** and the outside diameter ***.5***.
   **Specify inside diameter of donut <0'-0">:** ***.25***
   **Specify outside diameter of donut <0'-2 1/4">:** ***.5***
8. Place donuts at each of the points of the star. Your drawing looks like this.
   **Specify center of donut or <exit>:**
   **Specify center of donut or <exit>:** ***[enter]***

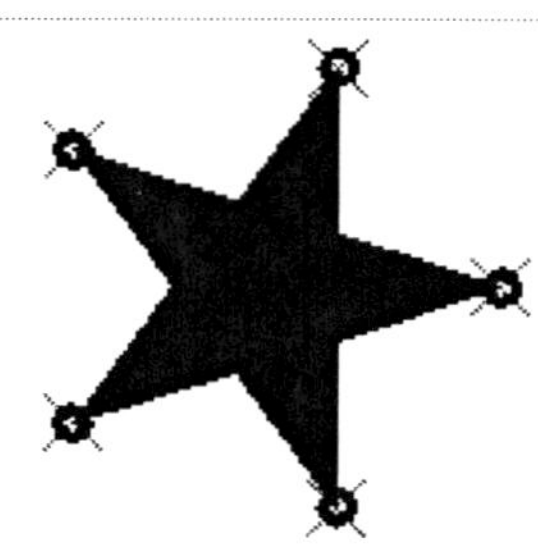

9. Save your drawing.
   **Command:** ***qsave***

I must admit that my piping profession offered little opportunity to use solids or donuts. Still, had I been using a computer at the time, these commands would have been quite handy when I was designing those little houses that Santa sits in down at the mall!

Solids and donuts can cause a bit of a slowdown in regeneration time. They can also suck the ink right out of your plotter!

But the programmers were smart; they provided a way to save time and ink. Until you're ready for that final plot, set your **Fillmode** system variable to ***0***, then regenerate the drawing to see the results (Figure 10.006).

AutoCAD hides the filled area of solids and replaces the filled area of donuts with *wireframing* (more on wireframing in the 3D text). Set the **Fillmode** back to ***1*** for the final plot. (Note: The **Fillmode** system variable controls the fill on polylines as well.)

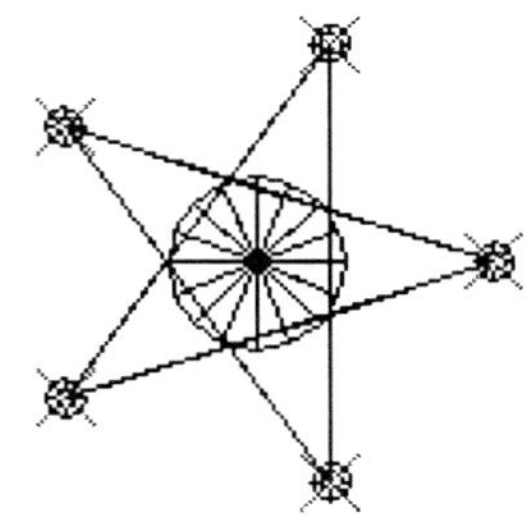

Figure 10.006

## 10.4 More Object Selection Methods

As our drawings get busier, selecting multiple objects for erasure or modification becomes more difficult. Fortunately, AutoCAD has provided several additional methods to create a selection set. These are **WindowPoly (wp)**, **CrossingPoly (cp)**, **Last**, **All**, **Previous**, **Add**, and **Remove**. You'll find it easy to master each.

- **WindowPoly** and **CrossingPoly** behave like **Window** and **Crossing Window**, except that you line out each side of the window. Neither is restricted to the four-sided windows of their non-poly counterparts.
- **Last** refers to the last object drawn.
- **Previous** refers to the last active selection set.
- Be careful with the **All** tool. **All** places *all* the thawed objects in the drawing in the selection set. Erasing **All**, then, may empty your drawing if you're not careful.
- **Remove** allows you to remove objects from the selection set. It's often easier to remove one or two objects from a selected group than it is to individually select multiple objects around the one or two you want to keep.
- **Add** enables you to put objects into a selection set. Use this when you've made your selection, removed an object, and then decided to add something else.

Let's see these in action.

| Do This: 10.4.1 | Selection Practice |
|---|---|

I. Open the *sel-prac* drawing in the C:\Steps\Lesson10 folder. It looks like Figure 10.007.

Notice that the lines exist on different layers with different colors and linetypes. The objects between the lines are nodes.

II. Turn OSNAPs off.

III. Follow these steps.

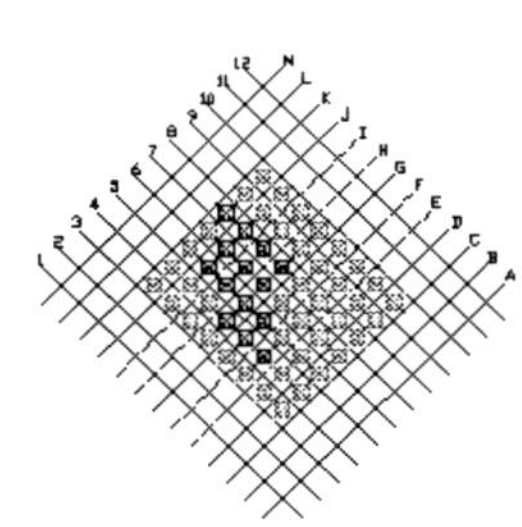

Figure 10.007

**10.4.1: SELECTION PRACTICE**

1. Enter the ***Erase*** command .

**Command: *e***

## 10.4.1: Selection Practice

2. Tell AutoCAD you wish to select objects using a **WindowPoly** by entering ***wp*** at the prompt.

**Select objects: *wp***

3. AutoCAD tells you to draw a polygon around the objects you wish to select. Draw the polygon around the light yellow nodes. (Be sure your OSNAPs are off.) AutoCAD will continue to prompt until you hit ***enter*** to tell it that you've completed the set.

**First polygon point:**

**Specify endpoint of line or [Undo]:**

4. AutoCAD tells you how many objects it has found and repeats the **Select objects** prompt. Complete the command.

**14 found**

**Select objects: *[enter]***

Your drawing looks like this.

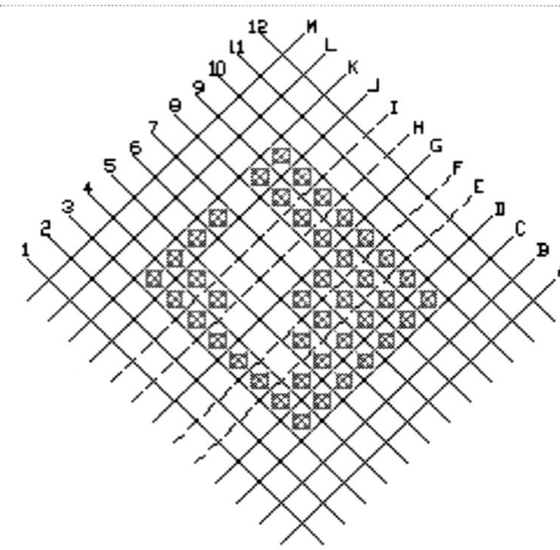


5. Undo the changes.

**Command: *u***

6. Draw a rectangle in the drawing, as shown.

**Command: *rec***

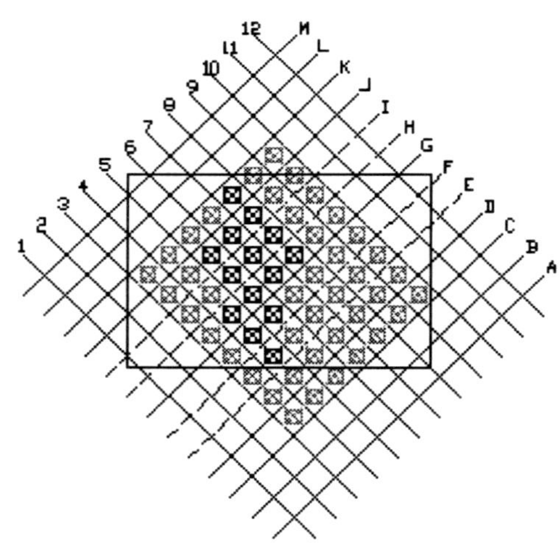


7. Now enter the ***Trim*** command.

**Command: *tr***

8. Select the rectangle as your cutting edge, but do it by typing ***l*** for ***Last***.

**Current settings:**
**Projection=UCS, Edge= Extend**
**Select cutting edges ...**
**Select objects or <select all>: *l***

AutoCAD selects the last object you drew. Complete the selection.

**Select objects: *[enter]***

## 10.4.1: Selection Practice

9. Tell AutoCAD you want to use a **Fence** to select the objects to trim. Then draw the fence line around the outside edge of the rectangle. Be sure to cross all the lines.

> **Select object to trim or shift-select to extend or [Fence/Crossing/ Project/Edge/eRase/Undo]:** ***f***
>
> **Specify first fence point:**
>
> **Specify next fence point or [Undo]:**

Hit ***enter*** when you've finished.

> **Specify next fence point or [Undo]:** ***[enter]***

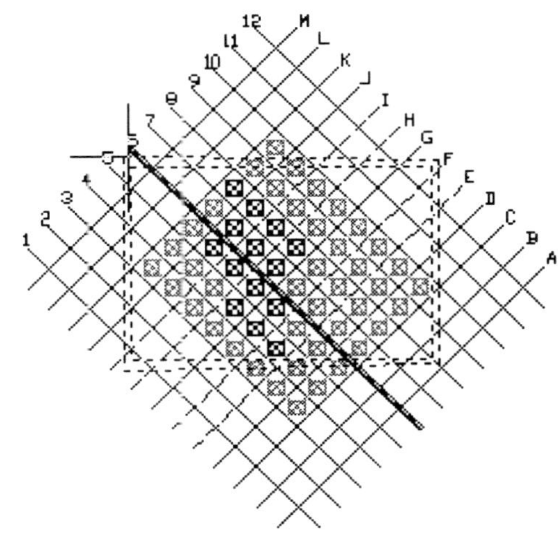

10. AutoCAD trims the lines, then prompts for more selection. Hit ***enter*** to confirm completion of the command.

> **Select object to trim or shift-select to extend or [Fence/ Crossing/Project/Edge/eRase/ Undo]:** ***[enter]***

Does your drawing look something like this? Notice that not all the lines were trimmed. Remember that the **Fence** method isn't always reliable.

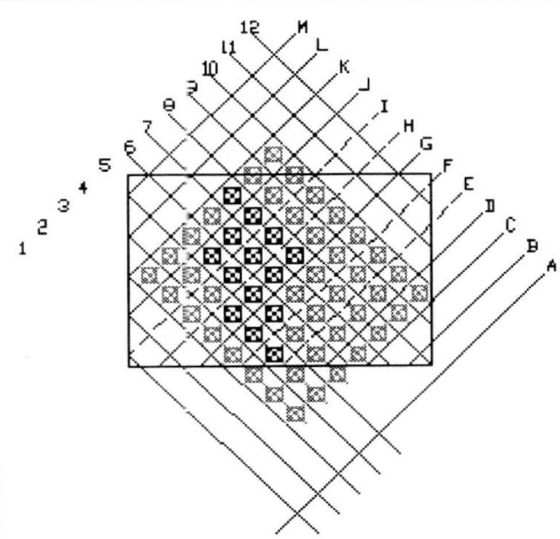

11. Erase the rectangle now, but tell AutoCAD you want to erase the **Previous** selection set.

> **Command:** ***e***
>
> **Select objects:** ***p***
>
> **Select objects:** ***[enter]***

AutoCAD remembers that you selected the rectangle in your last modification and removes it.

12. Undo all the changes.

> **Command:** ***u***

13. This time, let's use the **CrossingPoly** method. Enter the ***Erase*** command and tell AutoCAD to use a **CrossingPoly** as indicated.

> **Command:** ***e***
>
> **Select objects:** ***cp***

## 10.4.1: Selection Practice

14. Draw a polygon that crosses all the lines but doesn't touch the numbers.

**First polygon point:**

**Specify endpoint of line or [Undo]:** ***[this line repeats]***

**Specify endpoint of line or [Undo]:** ***[enter]***

**81 found**

15. Now tell AutoCAD to remove some objects from the selection set.

**Select objects:** ***r***

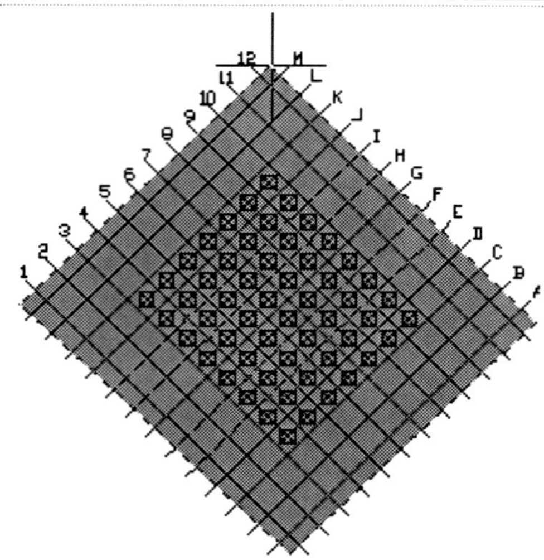

16. Use a **Fence** to select the objects to remove, and place it across lines **E** through **I** as shown.

**Remove objects:** ***f***

**Specify first fence point:**

**Specify next fence point or [Undo]:**

**Specify next fence point or [Undo]:** ***[enter]***

17. Now tell AutoCAD you want to **Add** one of the lines back into the selection set, then select line **G**.

**Remove objects:** ***a***

**Select objects:**

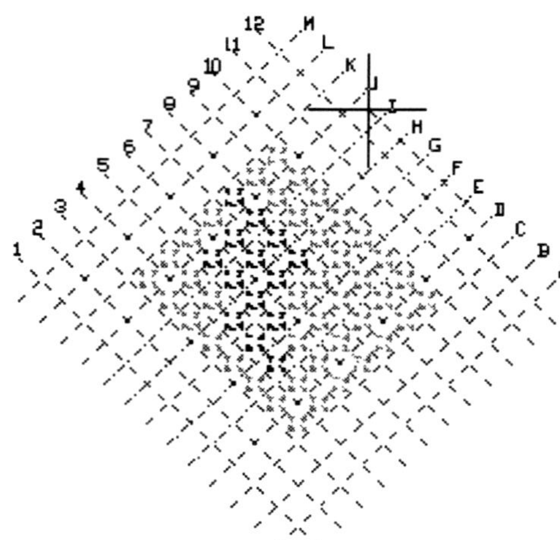

18. Complete the ***Erase*** command.

**Select objects:** ***[enter]***

Your drawing looks like this.

19. Undo all the changes 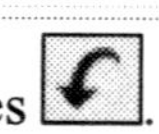.

**Command:** ***u***

20. This last method is the easiest, but I must again caution you. It erases *everything*! Enter the ***Erase*** command 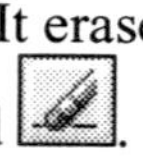.

**Command:** ***e***

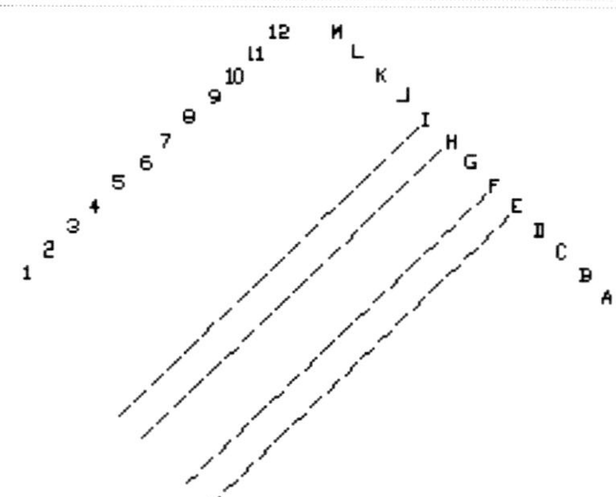


21. At the prompt, type ***all*** and hit ***enter*** at the next prompt. See that AutoCAD has removed all the objects in the drawing.

**Select objects:** ***all***

**Select objects:** ***[enter]***

## 10.4.1: Selection Practice

22. Quit the drawing without saving your changes.

**Command:** ***quit***

Well, now you've used all of AutoCAD's selection techniques. What do you think? They sure beat the simple windows we've used up to now, don't they? Certainly, you'll almost always use those simple windows and single-object selection boxes in your work. But occasionally, you'll be ever so glad to have learned these advanced selection tricks.

## 10.5 Object Selection Filters – Quick Filters

Selection filters have been available to CAD operators for quite some time; but the introduction of the Quick Select dialog box makes them friendly, convenient, and easy to use!

Use the ***QSelect*** command to access the dialog box (Figure 10.008). The dialog box may appear a bit frightening at first; but once mastered, you'll find it irreplaceable.

Let's take a look.

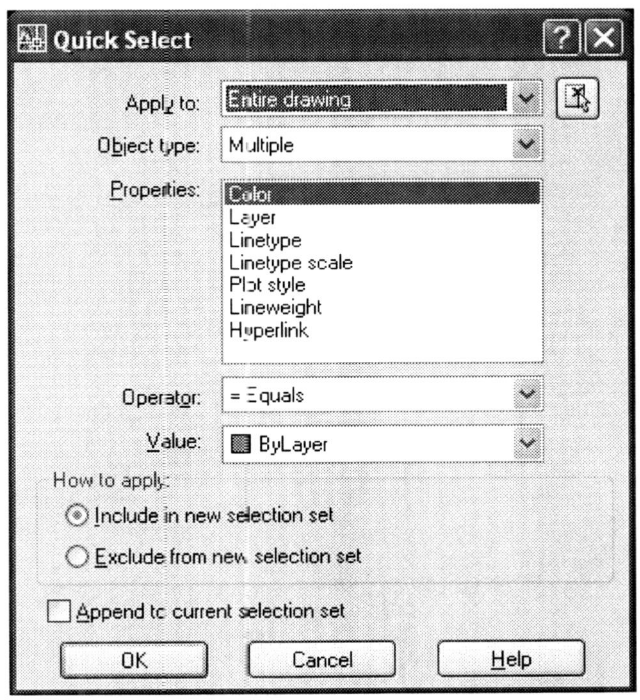


Figure 10.008

- At the top of the box, you find the **Apply to** control box. Here, AutoCAD allows you to apply the data listed in the rest of the dialog box to the **Entire drawing** or to the **Current selection** (once a selection has been made).
- Create a selection set to which you can apply the data listed in the dialog box by picking on the **Select objects** button to the right of the **Apply to** control box. AutoCAD will return you to the graphics area where you can select the objects with which you want to work.
- The **Object type** control box acts as your first filter. Picking the down arrow will produce a list of the objects currently in use in the drawing (or the selection set). You can select the type of object with which to work, or **Multiple** if you wish to apply the filters to more than one type of object.
- The **Properties** box allows you to filter the selection by specific properties.
- The **Operator** and **Value** control boxes work together. The **Operator** box allows you to set the filter: *equal to*, *not equal to*, *less than* or *greater than* the value set in the **Value** box. The properties shown in the **Value** box depend on the property selected in the Properties box.
- The **How to apply** frame allows you to use the filters above to include or exclude objects from the selection set.

It really isn't as difficult as it sounds. Let's use filters to repeat what we did in the first part of our last exercise.

| Do This: 10.5.1 | Selection Practice with Filters |
|---|---|

I. Reopen the *sel-prac* drawing in the C:\Steps\Lesson10 folder.

II. Follow these steps.

## 10.5.1: Selection Practice – Filters

1. Open the Quick Select dialog box. Alternately, you can pick **Quick Select** from the Tools pull-down menu or the cursor menu.

   **Command: *qselect***

2. Tell AutoCAD you want to select some nodes – pick the down arrow in the **Object type** control box and pick **Point**.

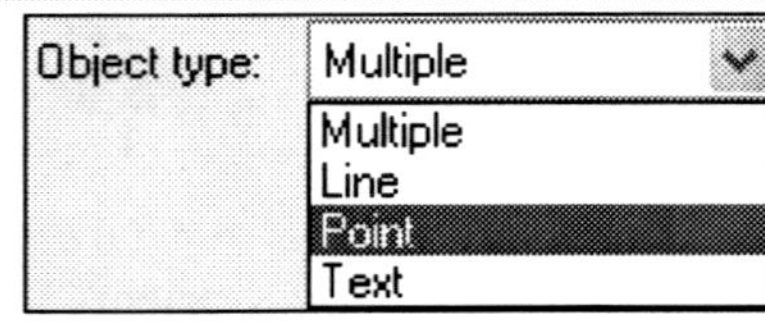


3. We'll filter the nodes by layer. Select **Layer** in the **Properties** box.

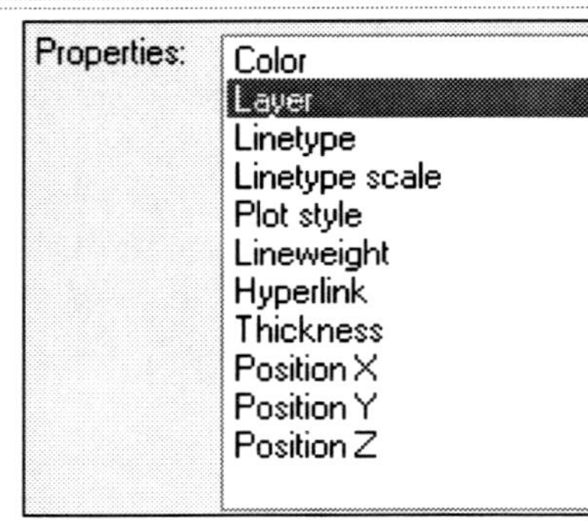


4. Leave the **Operator** box set to **= Equals**, but change the **Value** to the **OBJ5** layer.

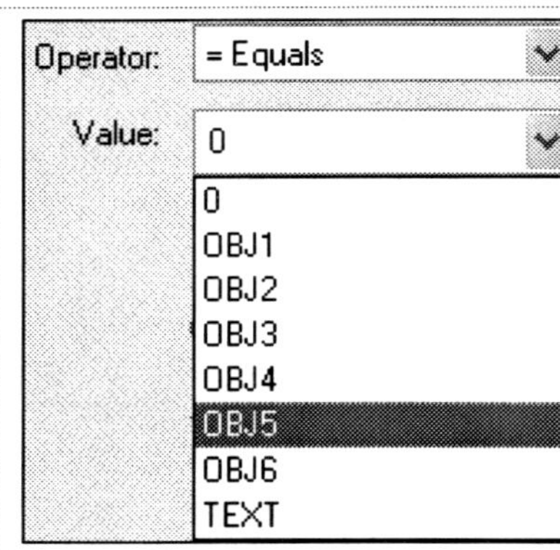


5. Pick the **OK** button 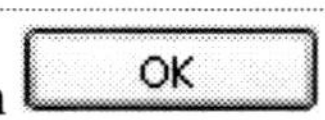

to conclude the filter process. Notice that AutoCAD highlights the same nodes we selected in Steps 2, 3, and 4 of our last exercise.

6. Enter the ***Erase*** command . (Alternately, you can use the DELETE key on your keyboard.)

   **Command: *e***

   AutoCAD erases the objects (right).

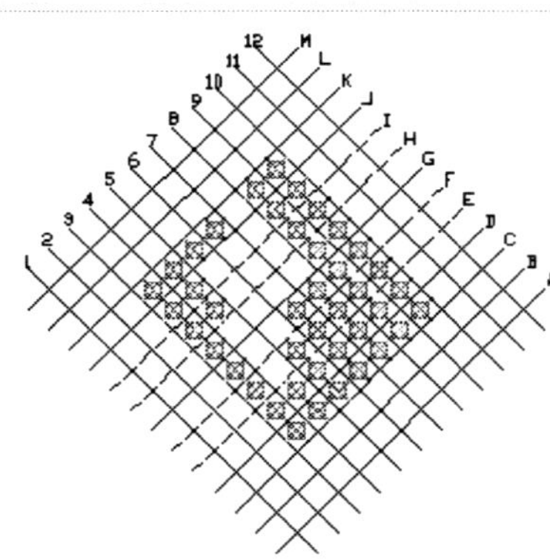

7. Quit the drawing. Don't save your changes.

   **Command: *quit***

## 10.6 AutoCAD's Calculator

The folks at Autodesk really don't like taking their eyes off the screen! But their aversion has led to some marvelous tools – like the *QuickCalc* (Figure 10.009), which we'll examine next.

Designed to take the place of your desktop calculator, the QuickCalc sports both a standard and a scientific interface. Between these, you'll find all the functionality of your typical store-bought calculator.

> I won't provide basic calculator instruction, as you can use the QuickCalc in the same way you'd use your desktop calculator. I will, however, concentrate this section of our text on how best to use QuickCalc functions in an AutoCAD environment.
>
> To learn more about how a calculator works, review the Help menu for QuickCalc. (Display the Help menu and enter "QuickCalc" on the **Search** tab.)

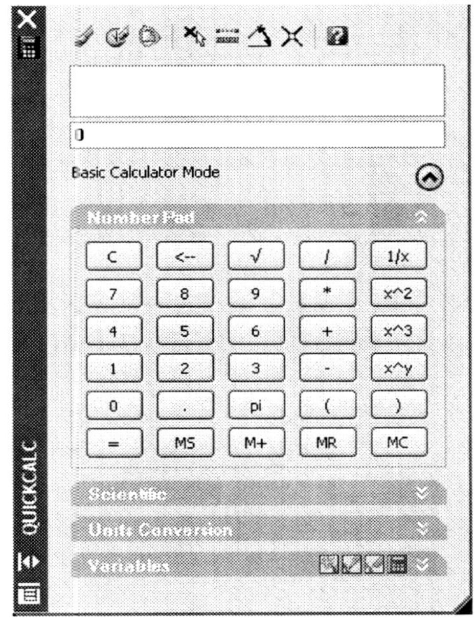


Figure 10.009

In addition to standard calculator functions (including Trig functions in the Scientific flyout), you can use QuickCalc to: convert units, modify object properties (in conjunction with the Properties palette), to calculate *and input* values at the various command prompts.

Let's take a look at the QuickCalc palette (Figure 10.009). We'll begin at the top.

- Notice the toolbar across the top. Read through the table below for the use of each button.

| BUTTON | NAME | EXPLANATION |
|---|---|---|
| | **Clear** | Clears the **Input** area (below the **History** area). |
| | **Clear History** | Clears the **History** area (below the toolbar). |
| | **Paste value to command line** | Pastes the results of a calculation on the command line. This works well when you've calculated a value in response to a command line prompt. |
| | **Get Coordinates** | Gets coordinates via a mouse-pick on the screen. |
| | **Distance Between Two Points** | Gets the distance (X,Y,Z) between two user-identified points. Once you've picked this button, AutoCAD will hide the QuickCalc and allow you to pick the points on the screen. |
| | **Angle of Line Defined by Two Points** | Gets the angle of a line between two user-identified points. As with the **Distance** button, AutoCAD will hide the QuickCalc and allow you to pick the points on the screen. |
| | **Intersection of Two Lines Defined by Four Points** | Determines the intersection between two lines by prompting you for four points (to identify both lines). |
| | **Help** | Calls AutoCAD's help window. |

- Below the toolbar lies the **History** area. Here you'll find a running account of completed calculations. The **History** area's cursor menu (Figure 10.010) allows you to customize the area (options in the top section), **Copy** listings to the Windows clipboard, **Append Expressions** or **Values to the Input Area** (useful for repeating calculations), **Clear** [the] **History** area, and **Paste** [a selection to the] **Command line**.

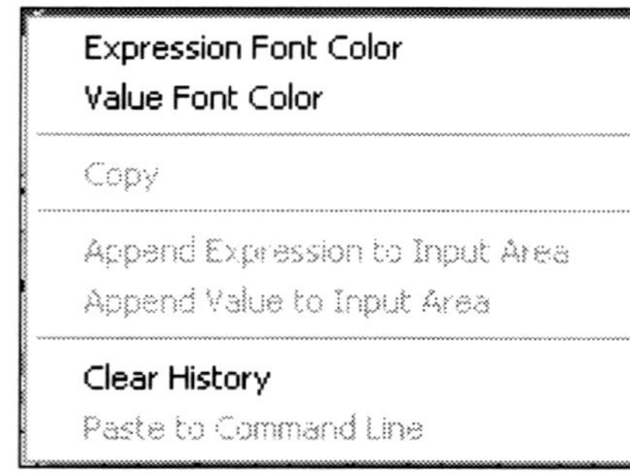


Figure 10.010

- You'll do most of your work in the **Input** area (the textbox below the **History** area). Input data (numbers and evaluation symbols) using QuickCalc's number pad, your keyboard, or the number pad on your keyboard (be sure **Num Lock** is on). Once you've entered data, tell AutoCAD to perform the calculation by picking the Equals (**=**) key on QuickCalc's number pad, or by hitting the **ENTER** key on your keyboard.
- Below the **Input** area, AutoCAD displays one of three mode settings:
  - **Basic Calculator Mode** means that you can perform any calculations just as you would on your handheld or desktop calculator. AutoCAD calls this its *modeless* mode.
  - AutoCAD's calculator has two modal approaches.
    - Access the calculator from the Properties Palette means that AutoCAD can place solutions to your calculations in the appropriate boxes on the Properties Palette. AutoCAD displays **Property Calculation** during this procedure.
    - Access the calculator transparently (***'QuickCalc***) while in a command, means that AutoCAD can place solutions to your calculations as responses to the command prompt. AutoCAD displays **Active Command** during this procedure.
- Next to the mode display, you'll find an upward or downward pointing arrow button. Use this to display or hide the flyout menus. If you're comfortable with keystrokes on a scientific calculator, hiding the flyout menus will save some screen real estate. Otherwise, or if you need to perform units conversion or examine the variables list, leave the flyout menus displayed.

Let's try our calculator.

| |
|---|
| A recent addition to AutoCAD's arsenal, the Quick Calculator functions admirably as an on-screen calculator. It's functionality as an AutoCAD tool, however, hasn't always proved reliable, is often difficult to master, and frequently tries to take the place of better-working tools (OSNAPs and such). Still, as with the young of most species, it deserves a chance. Who knows what it might grow in to?! |

| Do This: 10.6.1 | Dividing and Measuring |
|---|---|

I. Open the *Calc-prac* drawing in the C:\Steps\Lesson10 folder. The drawing looks like Figure 10.011.

II. Set running OSNAPs to endpoint and center. Clear all others.

III. Follow these steps.

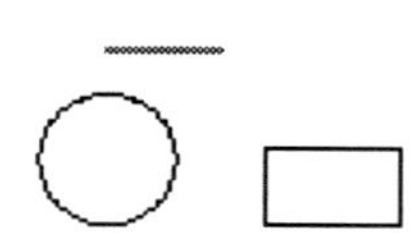

Figure 10.011

## 10.6.1: Dividing and Measuring

1. We'll begin by adding a circle that is 1¼ x the size of our existing circle. Enter the ***Circle*** command .

**Command:** ***c***

2. Select the center 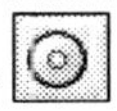 of the existing circle as our center point.

**Specify center point for circle or [3P/2P/Ttr (tan tan radius)]: _cen**

3. We don't know the radius of our existing circle, so we'll let AutoCAD calculate our new radius for us. Call the calculator. (You can use the Quick Calc button  on the standard toolbar.)

**Specify radius of circle or [Diameter]:** ***'quickcalc***

4. Tell AutoCAD to make the radius 1¼ x the radius of the existing circle as shown. When you hit ***enter***, AutoCAD will ask you to select the circle on which to base its calculations. Do that now.

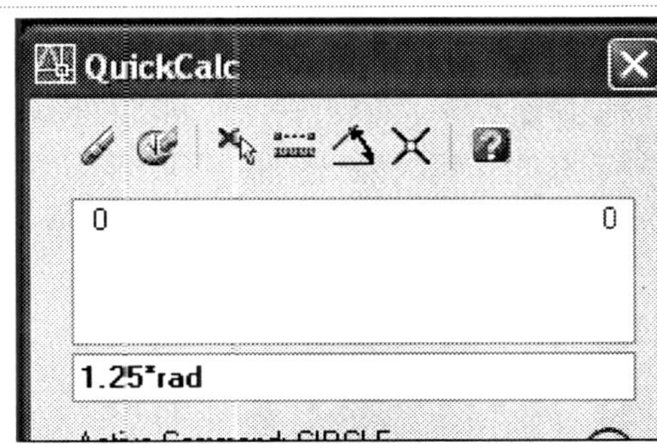


5. Select the existing circle. AutoCAD returns to the calculator with the solution to your equation (Figure 10.031).

>>>> **Select circle, arc or polyline segment for RAD function:**

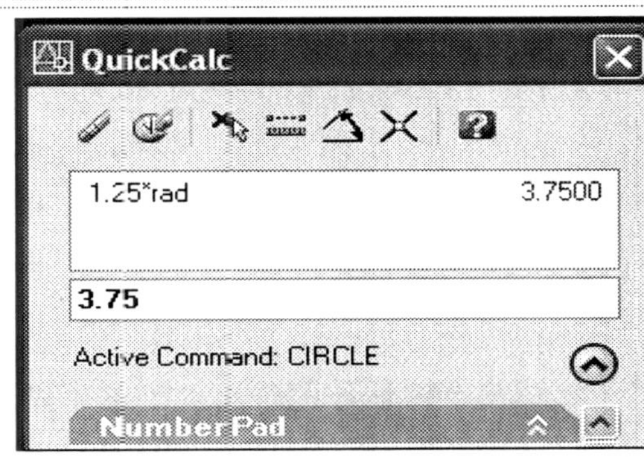


6. Pick the **Apply** button 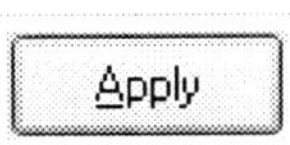 to return the calculated value to the command prompt. AutoCAD returns with the radius. Complete the command.



**Resuming CIRCLE command.**

**Specify radius of circle or [Diameter]: 3.75** ***[enter]***

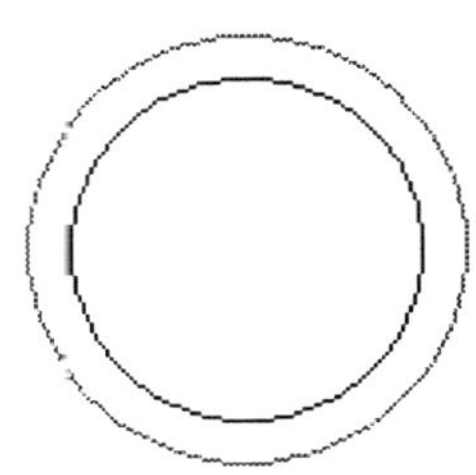

7. Now let's use the Properties palette to recalculate an area. Double click on the inner circle to open the Properties palette with the circle's data displayed.

## 10.6.1: Dividing and Measuring

8. Pick in the value column next to **Area** 

. (Scroll as needed to find **Area**.) Notice the **QuickCalc** button that appears.

9. We'll recalculate the area of the circle based on the area of the rectangle. Pick the **QuickCalc** button  next to the **Area** display. AutoCAD opens the calculator.

10. To determine the area of the rectangle, we'll need to calculate the length x width. Start by picking the **Distance Between Two Points** button 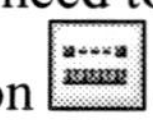 on the toolbar.

11. AutoCAD returns to the screen and asks for a first and second point. Pick the end points along the bottom of the rectangle.

**Enter a point:**

**Enter a point:**

12. AutoCAD returns to the calculator with the length of the line. Place an asterisk (*) after the length (for multiplication).

13. Repeat Steps10 and 11, but pick the end points of one of the sides of the rectangle.

**Enter a point:**

**Enter a point:**

14. AutoCAD displays the complete equation. Hit **enter** on your keyboard to complete the calculation.

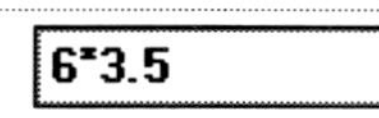


15. The calculator now displays the solution to your calculation (the area of the rectangle). **Apply** it to the circle 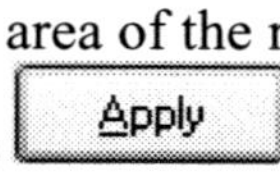

. Notice the change in the circle (Figure 10.033).

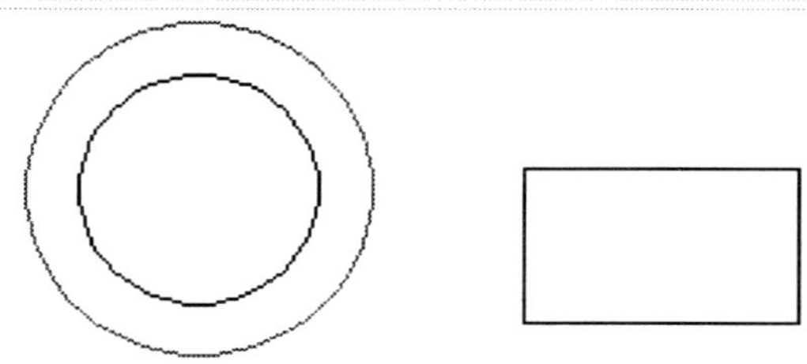

16. Quit the drawing without saving.

**Command:** ***quit***

Of course, you can also use QuickCalc as a normal calculator!

> QuickCalc will take some getting used to. Some keys may be missing and you'll have to know to use keyboard entries for them. Other helpful entries are more obvious (like OSNAPs). I suggest spending some time with AutoCAD's Help menu browsing the QuickCalc entries if you're uncomfortable with calculator use. But don't get too comfortable with it yet, I suspect that AutoCAD will be working on some changes to help QuickCalc fulfill its potential!

# 10.6 Extra Steps

I've provided another Lisp routine – this one in the C:\Steps\Lesson10 folder. Simply called *Points.lsp*, this file (when loaded) creates two new commands that you may find useful.

The first command is ***PT***. ***PT*** prompts you as follows:

**Command:** ***pt***

**PICK A BASE POINT:** ***[pick a starting point]***

**HOW FAR:** ***[how far away would you like to place an identifying point]***

**X, Y, OR P?** ***[Would you like to place the point along the X or Y axis, or polar to the base point?]***

**ANGLE?** ***[If you selected P for polar, at what angle would you like to place the identifying point?]***

PT will create a **Markers** layer and set the node style (**PDMode**) to the X we used in our first exercises in this lesson. It then places a node at the requested location. This handy tool will help locate a point relative to another point without having to draw guidelines.

The other command is ***MW***. This really cool tool will place a point midway between two user-identified points. It prompts:

**Command:** ***mw***

**SELECT THE FIRST POINT:**

**SELECT THE SECOND POINT:**

Is that simple enough? Use your OSNAPs to identify the points. This command is perfect for locating the center of rectangles or polyline ellipses. (Note: ***MW*** will also create the **Markers** layer and reset the **PDMode** to the X.)

Start a new drawing and play with these to get comfortable with them.

## 10.7 What Have We Learned?

*Items covered in this lesson include:*

- *Commands:*
  - ***Divide***
  - ***Measure***
  - ***Point***
  - ***Solid***
  - ***Donut***
  - ***Fillmode***
  - ***QuickCalc***
  - ***PT***
  - ***MW***
- *Object Selection Methods*
  - *WindowPoly*
  - *CrossingPoly*
  - *Fence*
  - *Last*
  - *All*
  - *Previous*
  - *Add and Remove*
- *Selection Filters*

We picked up some neat tricks in Lesson 10. But in your efforts to master so much material, you might easily forget some of the material in this lesson. Except for the calculator, you probably won't use most of these tools with much frequency; so, it'll take longer to fully master them. But once mastered, you'll probably wish you had done so sooner!

Work through the exercises, and then take some time to relax. The next three lessons are fairly easy to master, so this is a good time to explore and experiment with what you've learned.

## 10.8 Exercises

1. Open *MyRemote* from the C:\Steps\Lesson07 folder (or you can use the *Remote* drawing in the C:\Steps\Lesson10 folder).
   1.1. Using the ***Solid*** and ***Donut*** commands you learned in this lesson, fill in the buttons as shown.
   1.2. Save the drawing as *MyOtherRemote* in the C:\Steps\Lesson10 folder.

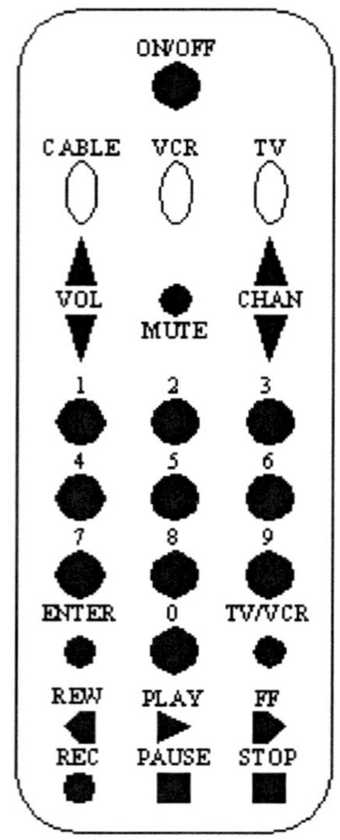


2. Setup a new drawing with the following parameters:
   2.1. Limits: [use default limits]
   2.2. Grid: .25
   2.3. Snap: as needed
   2.4. Units: architectural
   2.5. Text Height: .125
   2.6. The layers shown below.
   2.7. Create the drawing (below right).
   2.8. Save the drawing as *MyControlPanel* in the C:\Steps\Lesson10 folder.

| LAYER NAME | STATE | COL. | LINE TYPE |
|---|---|---|---|
| 0 | On | white | Cont. |
| Button-A | On | cyan | Cont. |
| Button-B | On | green | Cont. |
| Frame | On | red | Cont. |
| Infrared | On | magenta | Cont. |
| Lights | On | 32 | Cont. |
| Switch | On | 84 | Cont. |
| Text | On | yellow | Cont. |
| Vent | On | white | Cont. |

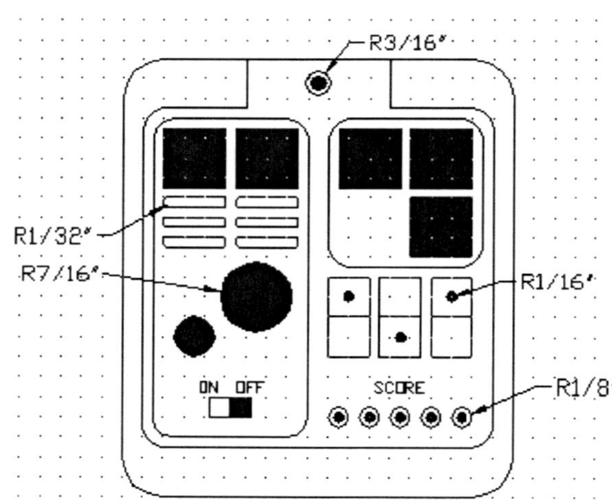


*For more exercises related to Lesson 10, please see Lesson 10 in AutoCAD 2007: One Step at a Time – Workbook.*

## 10.9 For Web-Based Review Questions, visit: http://www.uneedcad.com/2007/Files/07R10.pdf

# Lesson 11

Following this lesson, you will:

- ✓ *Know how to draw contour lines with the Spline command*
- ✓ *Be familiar with the Splinedit command*
- ✓ *Know how to create guidelines (or construction lines) using:*
  - o ***XLine***
  - o ***Ray***

# Guidelines and Splines

*Now we're moving into the more advanced aspects of basic AutoCAD. If you're not comfortable with the first ten lessons of our text, it might be a good idea to spend a couple hours going over the less familiar portions before continuing.*

*Lesson 11 will familiarize you with AutoCAD's version of guidelines – a tool missing through the first twelve releases and welcomed by many when it first appeared. We'll also cover the use of the* ***Spline*** *command to draw contour lines – like those found on topographical maps.*

## 11.1 Contour Lines with the *Spline* Command

In Lesson 8, we studied polylines and the ***PEdit*** command. I'm sure you found them as complicated as most people do the first time.

We learned that we can make a *spline* (a contour line) from a polyline using the ***PEdit*** command. Here we'll see how we can draw a spline more easily and in a way that shows a contour line as you draw it. Additionally, you'll see that a spline drawn using the ***Spline*** command takes up much less drawing memory and thus reduces the size of your drawing.

The command sequence for the ***Spline*** command is

> **Command: *spline* (or *spl*)**
>
> **Specify first point or [Object]: *[pick the starting point]***
>
> **Specify next point: *[pick the second point]***
>
> **Specify next point or [Close/Fit tolerance] <start tangent>: *[continue selecting points until you've finished]***
>
> **Specify next point or [Close/Fit tolerance] <start tangent>: *[hit enter to complete the spline]***
>
> **Specify start tangent: *[show AutoCAD how you want the beginning of the spline to curve]***
>
> **Specify end tangent: *[show AutoCAD how you want the end of the spline to curve]***

By default, you simply pick points along the spline until complete.

But let's look at some of the other options.

- The first option is the easiest. Use **Object** to convert a splined polyline into an actual spline. This reduces the drawing size considerably as we'll see. (Note: To work properly, the polyline must have been converted to a spline using the **Spline** option of the ***PEdit*** command.)
- The **Close** option works just as it does with the ***Line*** or ***Pline*** command. It simply closes the spline.
- The **Fit tolerance** option tells AutoCAD to draw the spline within a certain distance of the points selected. By default, it's set to zero (meaning, "draw the spline through the user-selected point"). Personally, I prefer leaving it at the default as it makes my drawing considerably more accurate. However, you can reset the tolerance as desired.
- The last two options – **start** and **end tangent** – enable you to control the curve of the spline at the beginning and ending points.

Let's take a look at the ***Spline*** command.

> This command is also available on the Draw pull-down menu. Follow this path:
>
> *Draw – Spline*
>
> ***Spline***'s options are also available on the cursor and dynamic input menus once the command has been entered.

| Do This: 11.1.1 | Working with Splines |
|---|---|

I. Open the *Splines* drawing in the C:\Steps\Lesson11 folder. The drawing looks like Figure 11.001.

II. Set the Running OSNAPs to **Node**; clear all others.

III. Follow these steps.

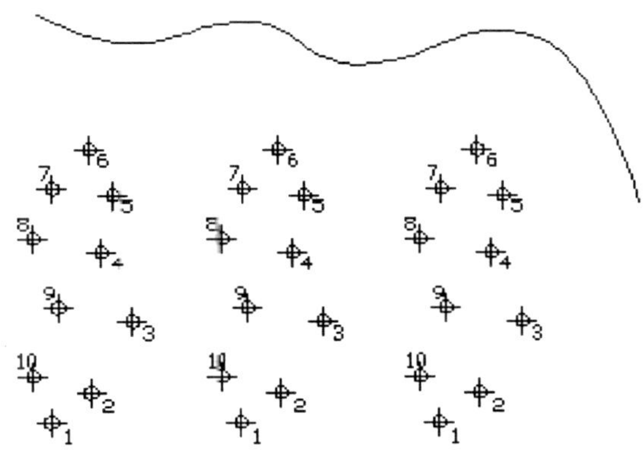

Figure 11.001

## 11.1: Working with Splines

1. Perform a ***List*** on the existing spline. See that it's a polyline (below). Note, however, that this is actually a polyline and not an lwpolyline. When AutoCAD converted it to a spline, it automatically changed it to a polyline to hold the required information to define the object.

**Command: *li***

```
                  POLYLINE   Layer: "LAYER3"
                             Space: Model space
                   Handle = FD
              Open spline
     starting width     0.0000
       ending width     0.0000
               area    34.0237
             length    22.0284

                  VERTEX     Layer: "LAYER3"
                             Space: Model space
                   Handle = 145
                at point, X=    2.0414   Y=   14.3868   Z=    0.0000
     starting width     0.0000
       ending width     0.0000
                   (Spline control point)

                  VERTEX     Layer: "LAYER3"
                             Space: Model space
                   Handle = 14D
                at point, X=    2.0414   Y=   14.3868   Z=    0.0000
     starting width     0.0000
 Press ENTER to continue:
```

2. You'll have to hit ***enter*** several times to view all the information attached to the polyline. Alternately, you can hit the ESC key on your keyboard to cancel the command.

3. Return to the graphics screen F2.

4. Enter the ***Spline*** command. Alternately, you can pick the **Spline** button on the Draw toolbar or palette.

**Command:** ***spl***

5. Tell AutoCAD you want to convert an **Object** to a spline.

**Specify first point or [Object]:** ***o***

6. Select the polyline spline.

**Select objects to convert to splines ..**

**Select objects:**

Complete the command.

**Select objects:** ***[enter]***

7. Repeat Step 1. Note the differences (below). All the information concerning the spline fits onto a single screen. There is a related reduction in the size of the drawing as well.

```
            SPLINE     Layer: "LAYER3"
                       Space: Model space
             Handle = 1B5
                      Length: 22.0422
                       Order: 3
                  Properties: Planar, Non-Rational, Non-Periodic
            Parametric Range: Start    0.0000
                                End    5.0000
   Number of control points: 7
             Control Points: X = 2.0414    , Y = 14.3868   , Z = 0.0000
                             X = 4.3990    , Y = 13.0084   , Z = 0.0000
                             X = 8.7692    , Y = 14.6740   , Z = 0.0000
                             X = 11.4143   , Y = 12.2618   , Z = 0.0000
                             X = 16.5321   , Y = 14.5017   , Z = 0.0000
                             X = 19.2922   , Y = 11.8598   , Z = 0.0000
                             X = 20.2123   , Y = 8.5287    , Z = 0.0000
```

8. Now let's draw a spline. Repeat the ***Spline*** command.

**Command:** ***spl***

9. Select nodes 1 to 10 in the left group. Use OSNAPs.

**Specify first point or [Object]:** ***[select node 1]***

**Specify next point:** ***[select node 2]***

**Specify next point or [Close/Fit tolerance] <start tangent>:** ***[this prompt repeats – continue selecting through node 10]***

10. After selecting node 10, **Close** the spline.

**Specify next point or [Close/Fit tolerance] <start tangent>:** ***c***

## 11.1: Working with Splines

11. Because you **Closed** the spline, AutoCAD only prompts once for a tangent. Hold down the SHIFT key (Ortho override) and pick a point due west.

**Specify tangent:**

Your drawing looks like this.

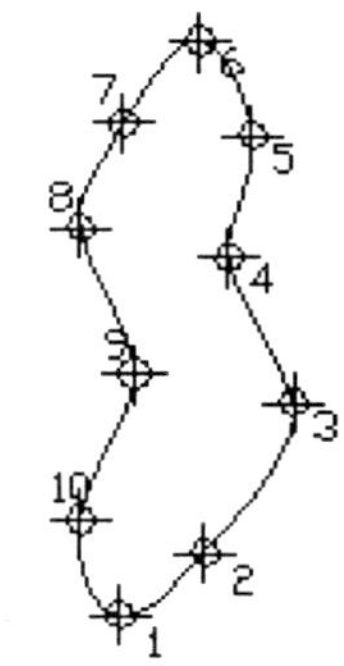


12. Repeat the ***Spline*** command.

**Command:** ***[enter]***

13. Select nodes 1 and 2 in the middle group.

**Specify first point or [Object]:**

**Specify next point:**

14. Let's change the **Fit tolerance** Fit tolerance.

**Specify next point or [Close/Fit tolerance] <start tangent>:** ***f***

15. Set the **tolerance** to ***1***.

**Specify fit tolerance <0.0000>:** ***1***

16. Continue as in Steps 9 through 11.

Your drawing looks like this. The spline has been drawn within one unit (a **tolerance** of 1) of the nodes selected.

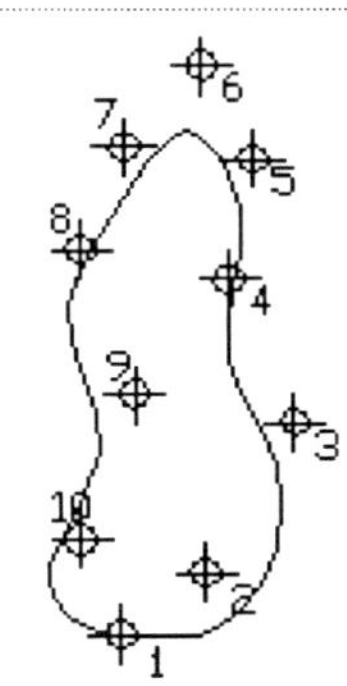


17. Repeat the ***Spline*** command.

**Command:** ***[enter]***

18. Select nodes 1 through 10 using the third group of nodes. Stop at node 10 (don't close the spline).

**Specify next point or [Close/Fit tolerance] <start tangent>:**

19. Hit ***enter*** at the last prompt.

**Specify next point or [Close/Fit tolerance] <start tangent>:** ***[enter]***

20. AutoCAD now asks for a tangent at the **start** point and **end** point. For the **start tangent**, pick a point due east; for the **end tangent**, pick a point due west.

**Specify start tangent:**

**Specify end tangent:**

Your drawing looks like this.

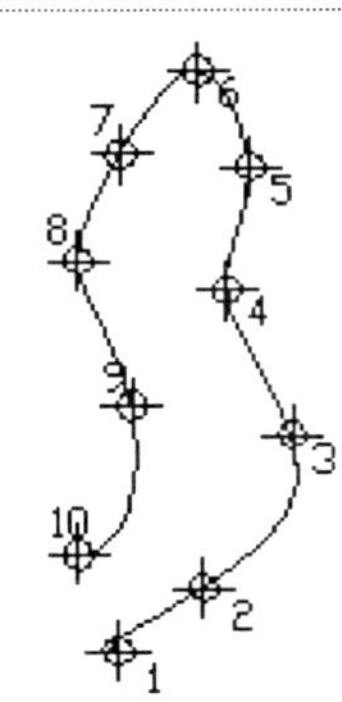


21. Save the drawing, but don't exit.

**Command:** ***qsave***

In this exercise, I've provided the location of the spline points; on the job, surveyors will provide them. Learning to do the survey as well as the drafting might mean more income for the drafter/designer.

We've seen that drawing splines isn't that difficult. Indeed, you've learned enough in this short exercise to draw some fairly complex topographical maps if the elevation points are provided. But what about editing the splines?

## 11.2 Changing Splines – The *Splinedit* Command

Like polylines, it's often easier to erase and redraw simple splines than it is to edit them. However, you'll find that some complex drawings require some knowledge of spline editing (particularly in 3-dimensional drawing). Unfortunately, also like polylines, editing is quite a multi-tiered chore.

Here's the ***Splinedit*** command sequence:

> **Command: *Splinedit* (or *spe*)**
>
> **Select spline:**
>
> **Enter an option [Fit data/Open/Move vertex/Refine/rEverse/Undo]:**

Let's look at the options.

- The **Fit Data** option enables you to edit the *fit points* of the spline. To keep this simple, think of fit points on a spline as essentially the same thing as vertices on a polyline. This option drops you into a second tier of options that looks like this:

  > **Enter a fit data option**
  >
  > **[Add/Open/Delete/Move/Purge/Tangents/toLerance/eXit] <eXit>:**

  - On this tier, you can **Add**, **Delete**, or **Move** fit points just as you did vertices in the ***PEdit*** command. You can also **Open** a closed spline or **Close** an open spline, again just as you did with polyline editing.
  - You can also change **Tangents** and **toLerances** on this level.
  - The **Purge** option removes fit point information from the drawing's database. This makes editing very difficult. So if you must use it, wait until you've finished the drawing. Its only real benefit is that it'll reduce drawing size.
- Back on the first tier of ***Splinedit*** options, we see that **Open** and **Move Vertex** also appear. These are similar to their **Fit Data** counterparts, but the **Move Vertex** option moves a single point whereas the **Fit Data – Move** option moves a curve of the spline. Note that the **Move Vertex** option may cause a closed spline to open whereas the **Move** option won't. These will become clearer in our next exercise.
- The **Refine** option also presents another tier.

  > **Enter a refine option [Add control point/Elevate order/Weight/eXit] <eXit>:**

  - **Add control point** allows you to add a single control point (points that enable you to manipulate the spline – similar to vertices on a polyline).
  - **Elevate Order** also causes more control points to appear. But this option adds control points uniformly along the spline. You determine the number of control points – up to 26. But remember, once added, control points can't be removed.
  - A control point's **Weight** is similar to tolerance. The **Weight** of a control point controls how much influence, or pull, that point has against the spline. Increasing the **Weight** of a point may cause the spline to pull away from adjacent control points.
- The **Reverse** option switches the start point and endpoint of the spline. On a large spline, you can hasten an edit using this option; it'll enable you to reach the appropriate control point a bit faster.

Is this starting to feel like the ***PEdit*** command? Let's try an exercise.

This command is also available in the Modify pull-down menu (*Modify – Object – Spline*), and the options are available on the cursor and dynamic menus once the command has been entered.

| Do This: 11.2.1 | Modifying Splines |
|---|---|

I. If you're not still in the *Splines* drawing, please open it now. It's in the C:\Steps\Lesson11 folder.

II. Freeze **LAYER1** and the **TEXT** layer. The numbers and nodes disappear from the drawing.

III. Follow these steps. (Although I don't always show them, the options are also available on the cursor and dynamic input menus.)

**11.2.1: MODIFYING SPLINES**

1. Enter the ***Splinedit*** command. Alternately, you can pick the **Edit Spline** button  on the Modify II toolbar or the Modify palette.

**Command: *spe***

2. Select the spline on the left. Control points appear as boxes.

**Select spline:**

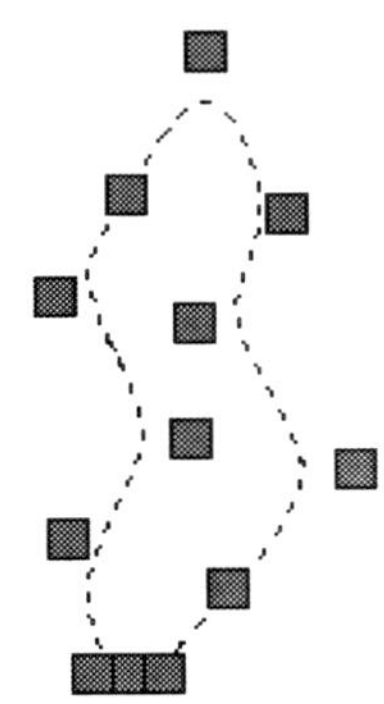

3. **Open** the spline 

. Notice that the **Open** option changes to **Close**.

**Enter an option [Fit data/Open/ Move vertex/Refine/ rEverse/ Undo]: *o***

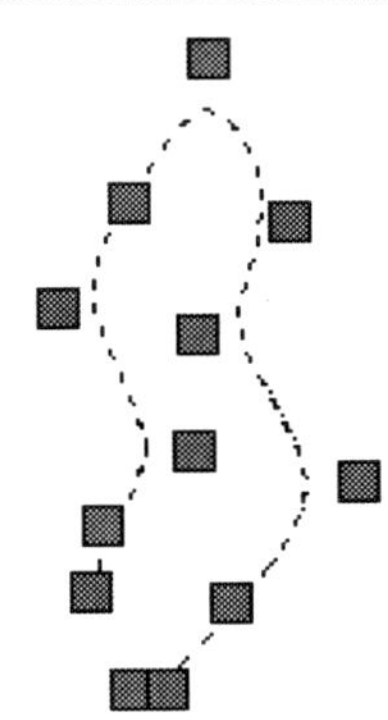

4. Move the first **Vertex** 

…

**Enter an option [Close/Move vertex/ Refine/rEverse/Undo/ eXit] <eXit>: *m***

… two units to the left.

**Specify new location or [Next/ Previous/Select point/eXit] <N>: *@2<180***

Notice the similarity between this tier of options and options in the ***PEdit*** command.

5. **eXit** this tier.

**Specify new location or [Next/ Previous/Select point/ eXit] <N>: *x***

Your drawing looks like this.

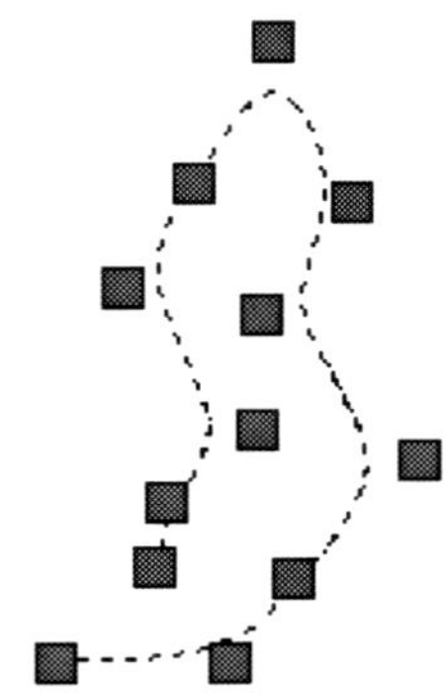

6. Select the **Refine** option.

**Enter an option [Close/Move vertex/Refine/rEverse/ Undo/eXit] <eXit>: *r***

7. Add a single **control point** …

**Enter a refine option [Add control point/Elevate order/ Weight/eXit] <eXit>: *a***

8. Select a point on the spline, as shown.

**Specify a point on the spline <exit>:**

Notice the new control point.

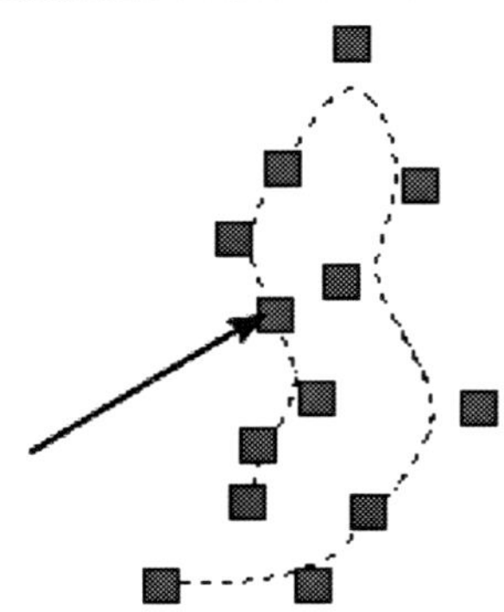

9. Exit this tier.

**Specify a point on the spline <exit>: *[enter]***

10. Tell AutoCAD you want to change the **Weight** of the new control point.

**Enter a refine option [Add control point/Elevate order/ Weight/eXit] <eXit>: *w***

11. AutoCAD makes the spline rational. (The spline becomes a NURBS – Non-Uniform Rational B-Spline. This is a smoother spline often used in 3-dimensional drawing.) Then AutoCAD allows you to select the point you want to edit. Hit ***enter*** until the new control point highlights as shown.

**Spline is not rational. Will make it so.**

**Enter new weight (current = 1.0000) or [Next/Previous/ Select point/eXit] <N>: *[enter]***

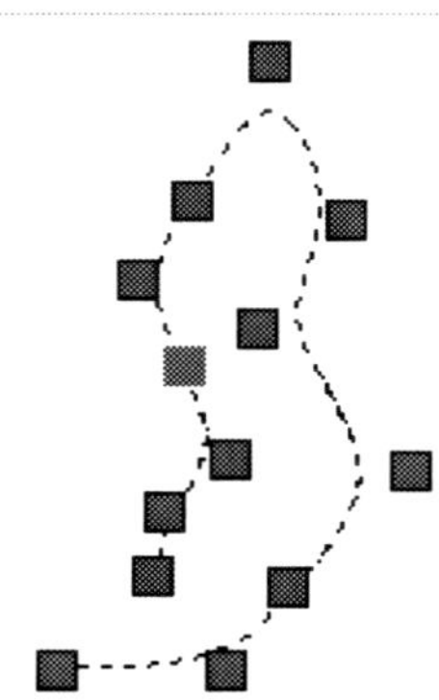

## 11.2.1: Modifying Splines

12. Change the **Weight** of this point to 4. Notice (right) the change in the spline in relation to the control points next to the one selected.

**Enter new weight (current = 1.0000) or [Next/Previous/ Select point/eXit] <N>:** *4*

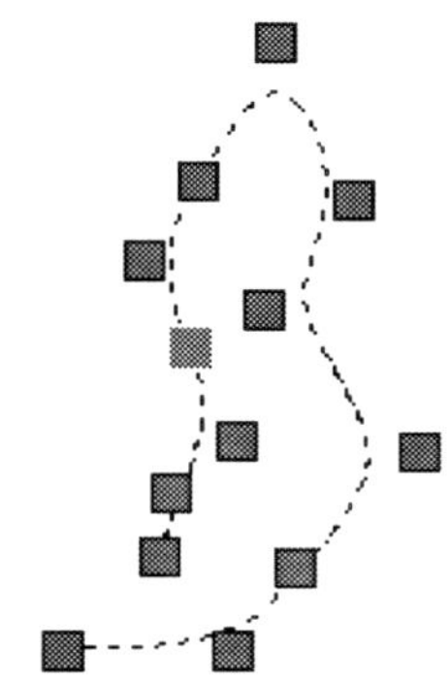

13. Exit this tier [eXit].

**Enter new weight (current = 1.0000) or [Next/Previous/ Select point/eXit] <N>:** *x*

14. Tell AutoCAD you want to **Elevate** the **order** [Elevate order] of the spline's control points.

**Enter a refine option [Add control point/Elevate order/ Weight/eXit] <eXit>:** *e*

15. Change the **order** from **4** to *5*. Notice (right) the increase in the number of control points.

**Enter new order <4>:** *5*

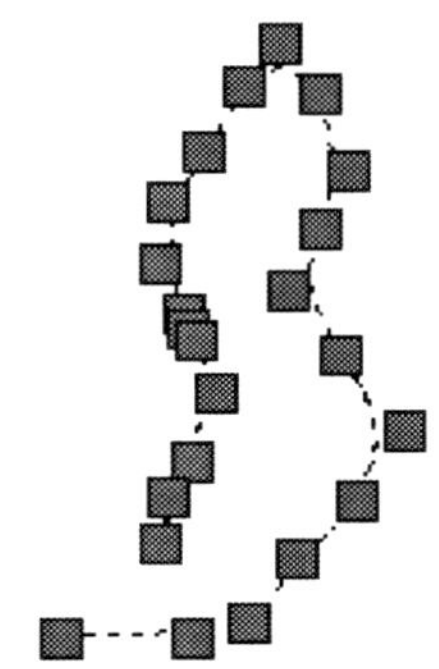

16. **eXit** the tier, then the command. All the control points disappear and your drawing looks like this.

**Enter a refine option [Add control point/Elevate order/ Weight/eXit] <eXit>:** *[enter]*

**Enter an option [Close/Move vertex/Refine/rEverse/Undo/ eXit] <eXit>:** *[enter]*

17. Repeat the ***Splinedit*** command .

**Command:** *[enter]*

18. Select the middle spline.

**Select spline:**

19. Choose the **Fit Data** option [Fit data].

**Enter an option [Fit data/ Open/ Move vertex/Refine/ rEverse/ Undo]:** *f*

20. Tell AutoCAD you want to change the **tolerance** [toLerance] for this spline …

**Enter a fit data option [Add/Open/Delete/Move/Purge/Tangents/toLerance/ eXit] <eXit>:** *l*

## 11.2.1: Modifying Splines

21. … to ***0***.

**Enter fit tolerance <1.0000>: *0***

The spline changes to look like this.

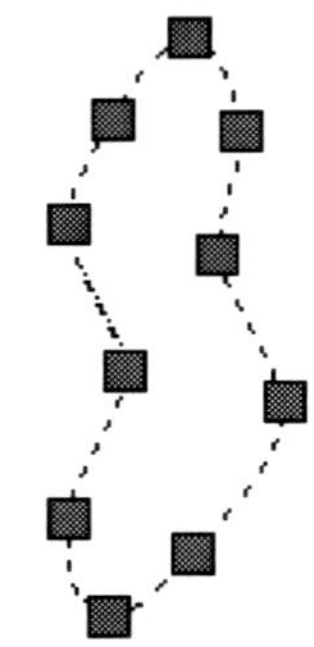

22. Now tell AutoCAD you want to change the **Tangents** 

.

**Enter a fit data option**
**[Add/Open/Delete/Move/Purge/Tangents/**
**toLerance/ eXit] <eXit>: *t***

23. Pick a point to the east this time. (Remember that we selected a point to the west when we created this spline.)

**Specify tangent or [System default]:**

Your drawing changes to look like this.

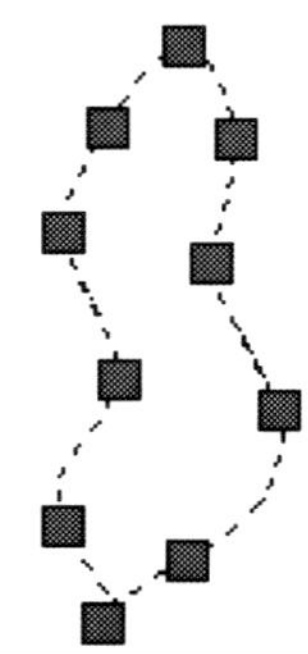

24. Now **Delete** a fit point 

.

**Enter a fit data option**
**[Add/Open/Delete/Move/Purge/Tangents/**
**toLerance/ eXit] <eXit>: *d***

25. Select the uppermost control point, then hit ***enter*** to return to the **Fit Data** prompt.

**Specify control point <exit>:**
**Specify control point <exit>: *[enter]***

Your drawing looks like this.

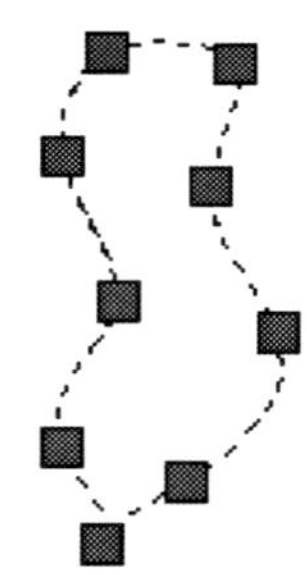

26. Lastly, let's **Move** a fit point 

.

**Enter a fit data option**
**[Add/Open/Delete/Move/Purge/Tangents/**
**toLerance/ eXit] <eXit>: *m***

27. Move the point indicated, as shown.

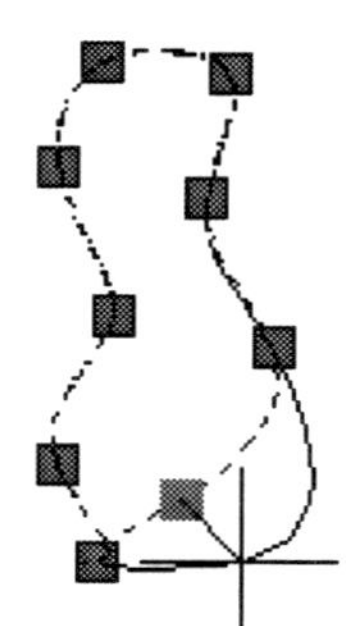

### 11.2.1: Modifying Splines

28. **eXit** this tier of options, then **eXit** the command.

    **Specify new location or [Next/Previous/Select point/eXit] <P>:** *x*

    **Enter a fit data option [Add/Open/Delete/Move/Purge/Tangents/ toLerance/ eXit] <eXit>:** *[enter]*

    **Enter an option [Fit data/Open/Move vertex/ Refine/rEverse/Undo]:** *[enter]*

Your drawing looks similar to this.

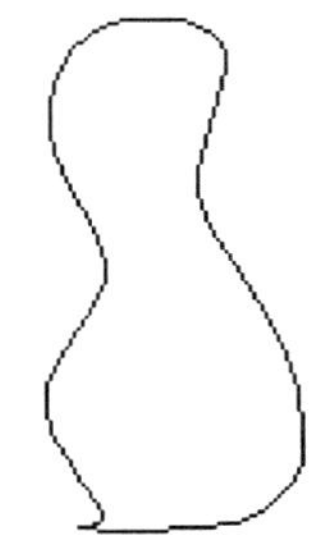

In 2-dimensional drafting, simply moving, adding, or deleting fit points isn't a problem – especially if your company has some Lisp routines that may shorten the procedures. Indeed, first-tier options are rarely a problem. And in the case of the ***Splinedit*** command, the **Fit Data** tier isn't too difficult. But the complexity of multi-tiered commands, like ***Splinedit*** and ***PEdit***, often presents a choice of erasing and redrawing rather than trying to navigate the editing command itself. Unfortunately, the only way around this is a Lisp routine (as I mentioned) or careful *study* and *familiarization* with the tools.

## 11.3 Guidelines

Beginning with this section, we'll create a multi-lesson project. We'll continue to have exercises at the end of each lesson; but in a series of *Do This* sample exercises, we'll create the floor plan of a house. We'll lay out the drawing in Lesson 11, place the walls in Lesson12, and then add some text in Lesson 13. Finally, in Lesson 15, we'll dimension the drawing.

On the drawing board, we use the *4H* lead to mark our guidelines – lines used to layout an area lightly before putting the heavier leads to paper. Precision is important, but the length of the line generally covers an area much larger than is eventually needed. This helps in locating other items on the drawing. Later, we might darken part of the guideline with an *F* or *HB* lead, or even erase it altogether.

The technical term used for these guidelines is *construction line.*

Create a construction line in AutoCAD with the ***XLine*** or ***Ray*** command. (In fact, the terms *xline* and *construction line* are used to mean the same thing.) The only real difference between an xline and a ray is that an xline is infinite in both directions, whereas a ray is infinite in only one direction. Often, the ***Ray*** command, with no options, is overlooked in favor of the more versatile ***XLine***.

Of course, we can convert the xline or ray into a drawing object just as we could darken our construction line with a heavier lead. Simply trim away what you don't need and the xline/ray becomes an ordinary line!

Let's look at each. The command sequence for ***XLine*** is

**Command:** ***xline*** **(or** ***xl*****)**

**Specify a point or [Hor/Ver/Ang/Bisect/Offset]:** ***[pick a point on the proposed line]***

**Specify through point:** ***[pick a second point on the proposed line]***

**Specify through point:** ***[AutoCAD will continue to place xlines through the initially selected point and any second point you select – hit enter to complete the command]***

- By default, AutoCAD requires you to select two points on the xline. It then draws an infinite line (a line that continues infinitely in both directions) through those two points. You may, however, select the **Hor**, **Ver**, or **Ang** options to force AutoCAD to draw horizontal, vertical, or angular xlines. Then you need only pick a single point on the xline. **Hor** and **Ver** need no further input except the location. **Ang** will prompt for the desired angle:

**Enter angle of xline (0) or [Reference]:**

You can enter the desired angle via the keyboard, or use the **Reference** option to get an angle from an existing object.

- The **Bisect** option allows you to find the bisector of an existing angle. It prompts:

  **Specify angle vertex point:** ***[select the corner of the angle – use OSNAPs)***

  **Specify angle start point:** ***[select any point on one of the lines forming the angle – again, use OSNAPs]***

  **Specify angle end point:** ***[select any point on the other line]***

  **Specify angle end point:** ***[enter to complete the command]***

  Once you've used the **Bisect** option, you'll never want to go back to the old compass method!
- The last option – **Offset** – is peculiar. It replaces the ***XLine*** command prompt with the ***Offset*** command prompt. It then behaves like the ***Offset*** command. I recommend ignoring this option in favor of the actual ***Offset*** command.

> An interesting point about xlines and rays: although they're infinite in length, neither affects a ***zoom extents*** (zooming to include all the objects in a drawing). Xlines and rays will print; but otherwise, AutoCAD treats them as background images.

The ***Ray*** command sequence is much easier:

**Command:** ***ray***

**Specify start point:** ***[pick the start point]***

**Specify through point:** ***[pick a point through which the ray will pass]***

**Specify through point:** ***[continue picking through points or hit enter to complete the command]***

Let's begin our floor plan.

> These commands are also available in the Draw pull-down menu. Follow this path:
>
> *Draw – Construction Line (or Ray)*
>
> The options for each are also available on the cursor and dynamic menus once the command has been entered.

| **Do This: 11.3.1** | **Creating Construction Lines** |
|---|---|

I. Open the *flr-pln 11* drawing in the C:\Steps\Lesson11 folder. This drawing has been set up to create a floor plan on a ¼"=1'-0" scale, on a C-size sheet of paper.

II. Follow these steps.

| **11.3.1: Creating Constructions Lines** |
|---|
| 1. Be sure the **CONST** layer is current . |
| 2. Enter the ***XLine*** command. Alternately, you can pick the **Construction Line** button 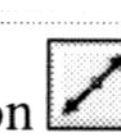 on the Draw toolbar or palette.<br>**Command:** ***xl*** |

## 11.3.1: CREATING CONSTRUCTIONS LINES

3. Tell AutoCAD you want to draw a vertical xline .


**Specify a point or [Hor/Ver/Ang/Bisect/ Offset]:** ***v***

4. Place two vertical xlines as indicated.

**Specify through point:** ***1',0***
**Specify through point:** ***87',0***

5. Complete the command.

**Specify through point:** ***[enter]***

6. Repeat the command.

**Command:** ***[enter]***

7. This time, let's draw horizontal xlines  …


**Specify a point or [Hor/Ver/Ang/Bisect/ Offset]:** ***h***

8. … through these points.

**Specify through point:** ***0,1'***
**Specify through point:** ***0,67'***

9. Complete the command.

**Specify through point:** ***[enter]***

Your drawing looks like this. (I'll turn the grid off during the rest of this exercise to make the images clearer.)

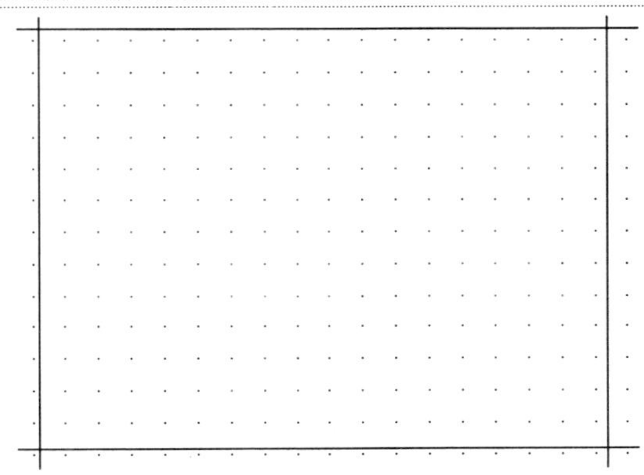

10. Use the ***Offset*** command  to offset the bottom line upward as indicated. (Use the direct distance option. Place the crosshairs above the line and enter the following numbers followed by an ***enter***: 18, 18, 21, 30.)

**Command:** ***o***
**Current settings: Erase source=No Layer=Source OFFSETGAPTYPE=0**
**Specify offset distance or [Through/Erase/Layer] <Through>:** ***[enter]***
**Select object to offset or [Exit/Undo] <Exit>:** ***[select the line]***
**Specify through point or [Exit/Multiple/Undo] <Exit>:** ***m***
**Specify through point or [Exit/Undo] <next object>:** ***18 [as the prompt repeats, enter the numbers indicated above]***
**Specify through point or [Exit/Undo] <next object>:** ***[enter]***
**Select object to offset or [Exit/Undo] <Exit>:** ***[enter]***

## 11.3.1: Creating Constructions Lines

11. Now offset the right vertical line as indicated. (Follow the procedure in Step 10. Place your crosshairs to the left and enter the numbers: 48, 84, 84.)

**Command:** ***o***

**Current settings: Erase source=No Layer=Source OFFSETGAPTYPE=0**

**Specify offset distance or [Through/ Erase/Layer] <Through>:** ***[enter]***

**Select object to offset or [Exit/Undo] <Exit>:** ***[select the line]***

**Specify through point or [Exit/ Multiple/Undo] <Exit>:** ***m***

**Specify through point or [Exit/Undo] <next object>:** ***48 [repeat with the numbers listed above]***

**Specify through point or [Exit/Undo] <next object>:** ***[enter]***

**Select object to offset or [Exit/Undo] <Exit>:** ***[enter]***

The lower right corner of your drawing now looks like figure at right.

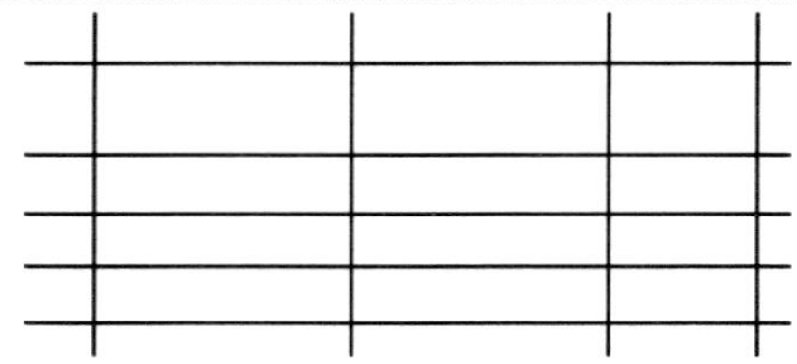

12. Use the ***Trim*** command to clean up the area to form the title block shown. (Zoom as needed to ease your view.)

**Command:** ***tr***

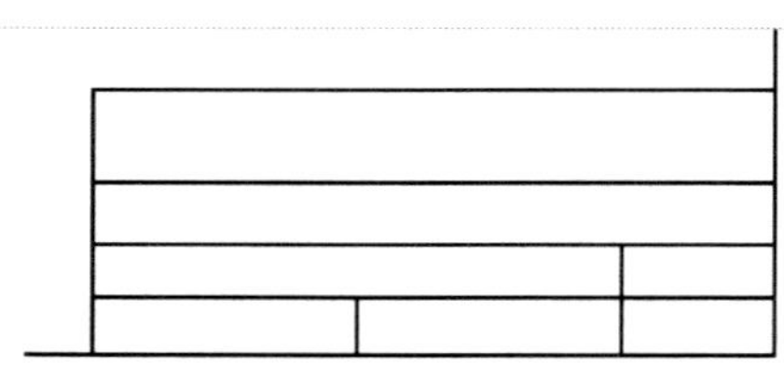

13. Finish trimming the border. Then change all the lines from the **CONST** layer to the **BORDER** layer.

**Command:** ***tr***

Your drawing now looks like this.

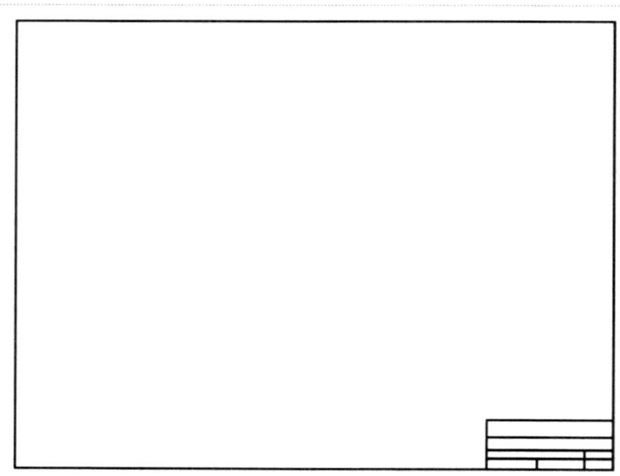

14. Remember to ***save*** occasionally.

**Command:** ***qsave***

15. Now let's locate the walls of our house. Repeat the ***XLine*** command.

**Command:** ***xl***

## 11.3.1: Creating Constructions Lines

16. Place three vertical xlines as indicated.

**Specify a point or [Hor/ Ver/Ang/Bisect/ Offset]:** ***v***
**Specify through point:** ***10',0***
**Specify through point:** ***33'4,0***
**Specify through point:** ***60',0***
**Specify through point:** ***[enter]***

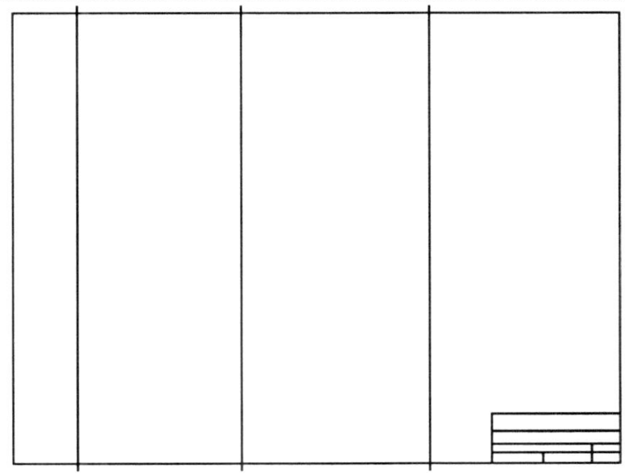

17. Place three horizontal xlines as indicated.

**Command:** ***[enter]***
**Specify a point or [Hor/ Ver/Ang/Bisect/ Offset]:** ***h***
**Specify through point:** ***0,10'***
**Specify through point:** ***0,33'***
**Specify through point:** ***0,60'***
**Specify through point:** ***[enter]***

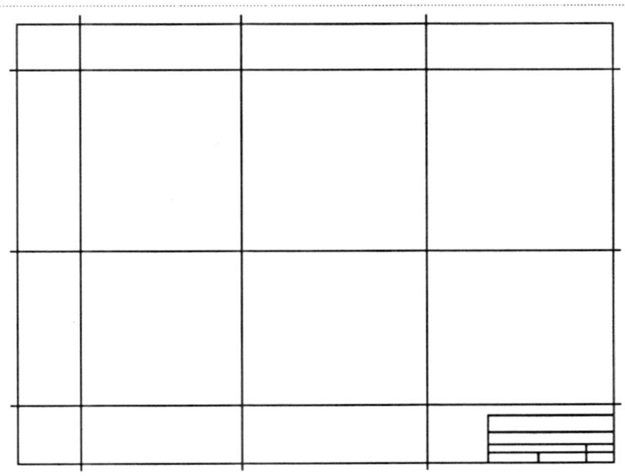

18. Trim away some of the excess lines so that your drawing looks like this.

**Command:** ***tr***

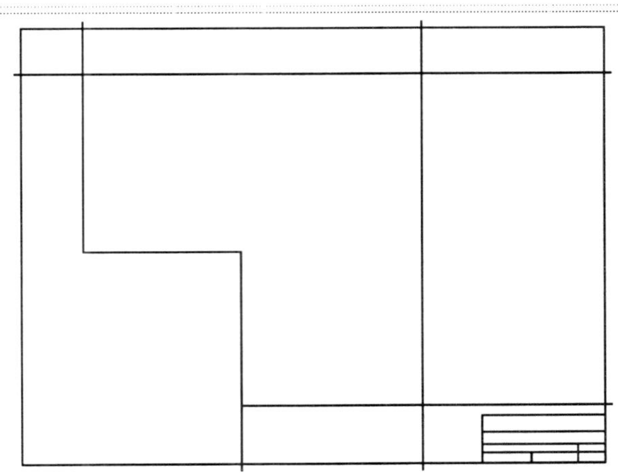

19. Now let's locate some inner walls. Make the **CONST2** layer current.

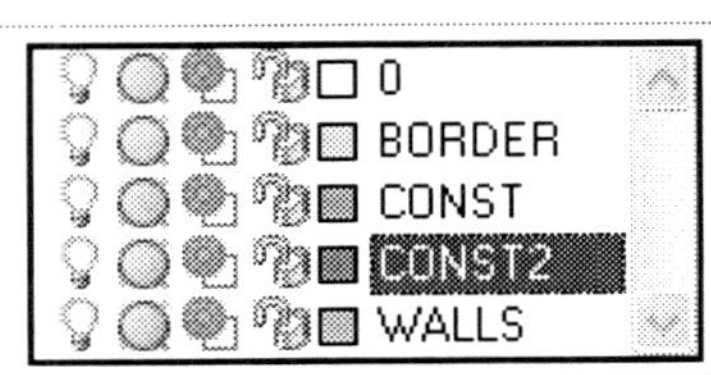

## 11.3.1: Creating Constructions Lines

20. Create vertical xlines Ver at these coordinates: ***26',0***; ***40'4,0***; ***43'10,0***; and ***47'10,0***; create horizontal xlines at these coordinates: ***0,19'10***; ***0,23'4***; ***0,28'10***; ***0,39'10***; and ***0,50'***.

**Command:** ***xl***

Now your drawing looks like Figure 11.027.

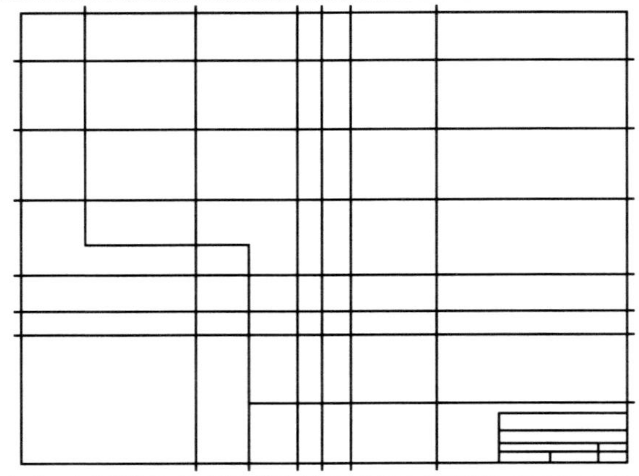

21. Let's add a bay window. With Ortho toggled on, draw a ray due west from the point indicated.

> **Command:** ***ray***
>
> **Specify start point:** ***33'4,31'***
>
> **Specify through point:** ***[pick a point to the left]***
>
> **Specify through point:** ***[enter]***

22. Offset the leftmost vertical line of the house (not the border) to the right by 3' and again by 12'.

> **Command:** ***o***

The house now looks like this.

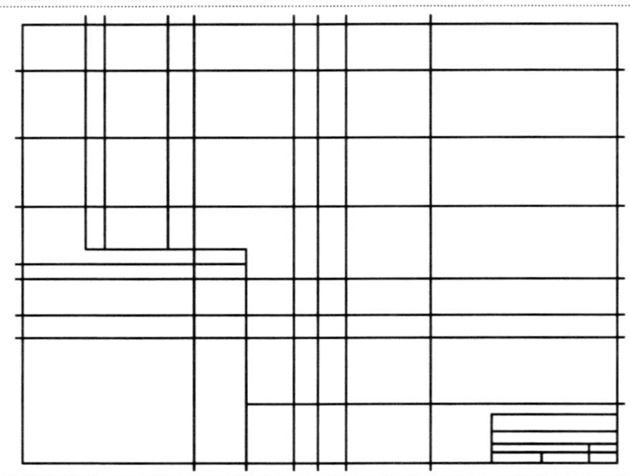

23. Use the **Angle** option to place an xline for the left wall of the bay window. Be sure to use OSNAPs to hit the intersection indicated.

> **Command:** ***xl***
>
> **Specify a point or [Hor/ Ver/Ang/Bisect/Offset]:** ***a***
>
> **Enter angle of xline (0) or [Reference]:** ***135***
>
> **Specify through point: _int of**
>
> **Specify through point:** ***[enter]***

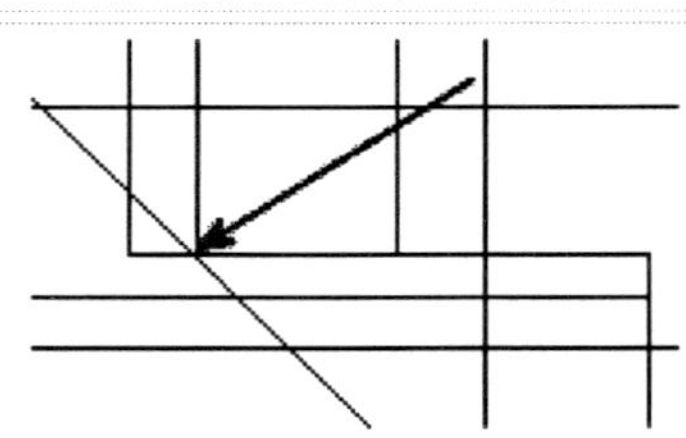

## 11.3.1: Creating Constructions Lines

24. Use the **Bisect** option to place the other wall.

**Command:** ***[enter]***
**Specify a point or [Hor/ Ver/Ang/Bisect/ Offset]:** ***b***
**Specify angle vertex point:** ***[select the intersection of the Vertex shown]*** **_int of**
**Specify angle start point:** ***[select a point nearest to Point 1]*****_nea to**
**Specify angle end point:** ***[select a point nearest to Point 2]*****_nea to**
**Specify angle end point:** ***[enter]***

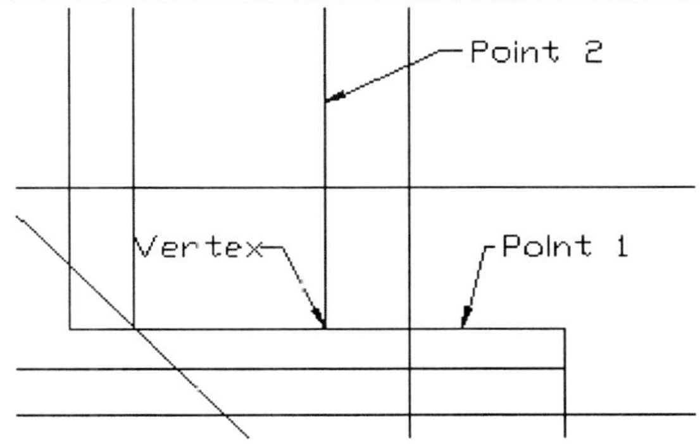


25. Use the ***Erase*** and ***Trim*** commands to complete the drawing. It'll look like this when you've finished.

26. Save the drawing as *MyFlr-Pln12* in the C:\Steps\Lesson12 folder.

**Command:** ***saveas***

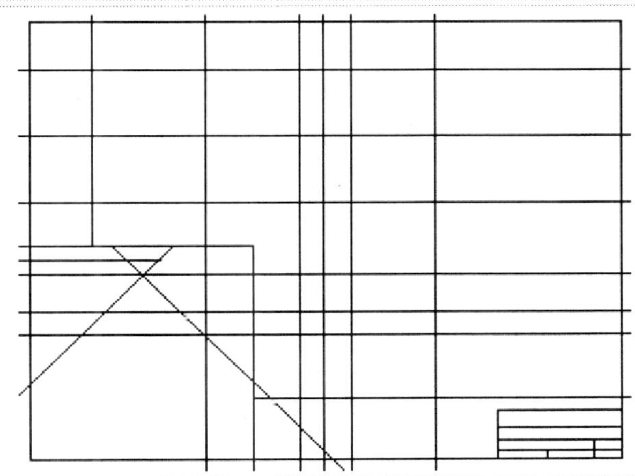

What do you think? It doesn't look much like a floor plan, does it?

Consider how a pencil layout might appear at this stage of production. All we've done is place some guidelines (construction lines) to help us locate our walls. We'll save the drawing for now and use it in our next lesson when we discuss the ***MLine*** (multiline) command.

## 11.4 Extra Steps

In the first half of this lesson, we discussed how to draw contour lines. Contour lines generally represent changes in elevation on topographical or site maps. Go to your local library, check the encyclopedia or ask your employer for some samples of topographical or marine drawings to help familiarize yourself with these fascinating tools.

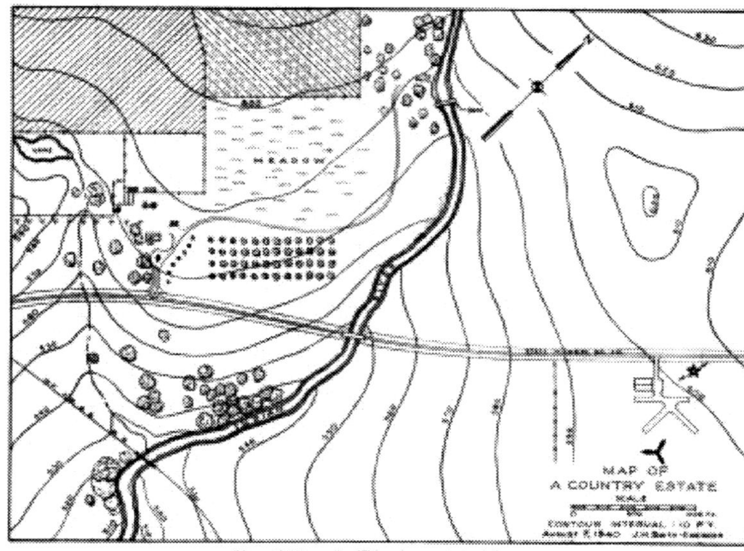


Fig. 991. A Topographic Map.

## 11.5 What Have We Learned?

*Items covered in this lesson include:*

- *Commands:*
  - ***Spline***
  - ***Splinedit***
  - ***Xline***
  - ***Ray***

We've covered some interesting tools in this lesson. Splines will prove themselves surprisingly versatile in the fields where they are used. Construction lines, while not as critical to computer drafting as they are to board work, are nonetheless quite handy in most disciplines. By the time we've finished the next few lessons, this will become apparent.

In our next lesson, we'll add walls to the *MyFlr-Pln12* drawing. After that (in Lessons 13 and 15), we'll add some notes and dimensions. By the time we complete this section of the book, you'll have accomplished quite a drawing!

## 11.6 Exercises

1. Open *topography.dwg* (next page) from the C:\Steps\Lesson11 folder.

   We shot several elevations during a survey of an area golf course The elevations for Hole # 3 are shown.

   Using the ***SPLine*** command, draw contour lines connecting like elevations. This will afford you a topographical view of the area.

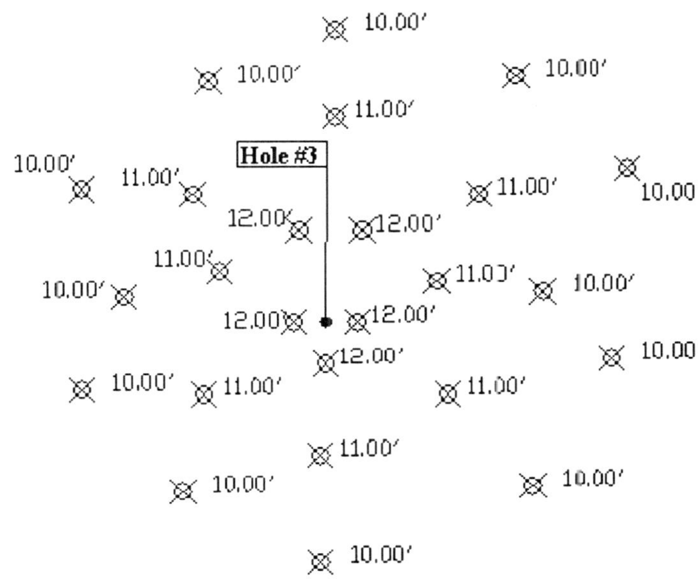


*For more exercises related to Lesson 11, please see Lesson 11 in AutoCAD 2007: One Step at a Time – Workbook.*

## 11.7 For Web-Based Review Questions, visit: http://www.uneedcad.com/2007/Files/07R11.pdf

# Lesson 12

Following this lesson, you will:

- ✓ *Know how to draw several lines at once with the **MLine** command*
- ✓ *Be able to create multiline styles with the **MLStyle** command*
- ✓ *Be able to edit multilines with the **MLEdit** command*

# Advanced Lines - Multilines

*Back in grade school, when I'd been naughty (and got caught), I was punished by being assigned to write "penance" sentences – "I will be good in school," one hundred times. Oh! The degradations of childhood!*

*But in my childish attempts to cut corners (there were always ways to cut corners), I would tape four pencils together. Then I only had to "be good in school" twenty-five times!*

*Apparently, someone at Autodesk learned a similar childhood lesson. The result was the **MLine** command. The **MLine** command does just what taping four pencils together did – it enables you to create more than one line at a time.*

*AutoCAD's multiline procecdures actually involve three commands: **MLine**, **MLEdit**, and **MLStyle**. The first actually draws the lines; the second enables you to edit, or change, the lines; the third enables you to define the lines.*

*In Lesson 12, we'll look at each.*

## 12.1 Many at Once – AutoCAD's Multilines and the *MLine* Command

The ***MLine*** command is an easy-to-use tool designed to enhance the efficiency of multiline drawing. The command sequence is

> **Command: *mline* (or *ml*)**
> **Current settings: Justification = Top, Scale = 1.00, Style = STANDARD**
> **Specify start point or [Justification/ Scale/STyle]: *[pick the start point]***
> **Specify next point: *[pick the next point]***
> **Specify next point or [Undo]: *[either continue picking points or hit enter to complete the command]***

As you can see, the actual command sequence isn't very different from drawing any other line. AutoCAD prompts **Specify start point** and then repeats **Specify next point** until you've completed the line. There are, however, some simple options you must consider.

- AutoCAD makes three choices available when you select the **Justification** option:

  **Enter justification type [Top/Zero/Bottom] <top>:**

  These involve where AutoCAD places the lines in relation to the user-identified point. (See Figures 12.001, 12.002, and 12.003 to see how these options work.)

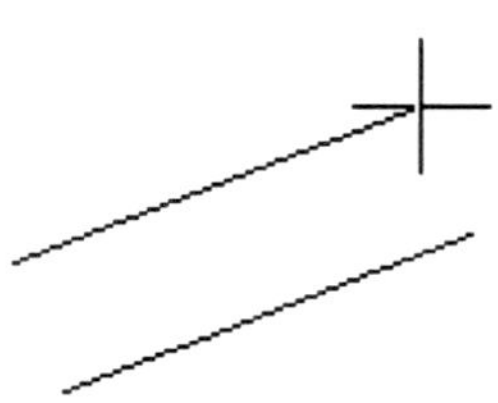

Figure 12.001: Top Justification

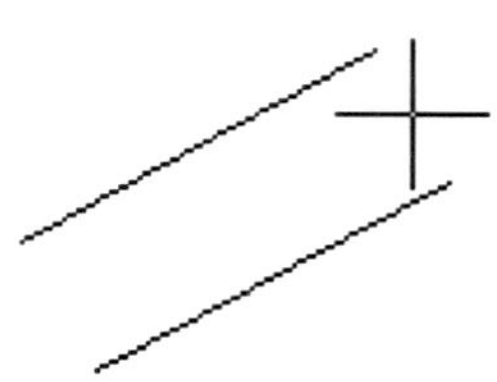

Figure 12.002: Zero Justification

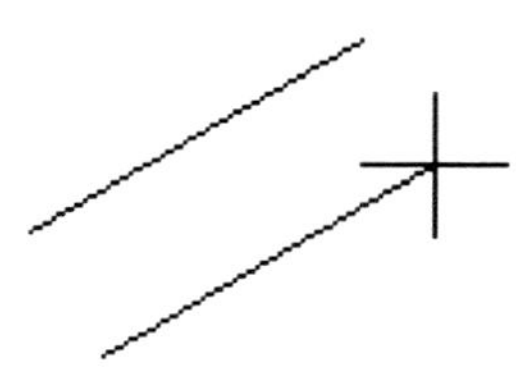

Figure 12.003: Bottom Justification

This may seem a bit strange, but it really does have its uses. For example, most pipe is drawn using centerlines. For a piper, then, the **Zero** justification would be easiest to use. But for an architect who dimensions to outer walls, the **Top** or **Bottom** justification may be just the ticket. Of course, the architect can switch to the **Zero** option if necessary!

- The **Scale** option enables you to insert a multiline at any width. For example, a piper creates a multiline style that has three lines – two outer walls and a centerline. The outer walls are one unit apart according to the style's definition. The piper needs a 3" diameter pipe, so he inserts the multiline at a **Scale** of 3.5 (the outer diameter, or OD, of the pipe). Similarly, the architect may insert a basic two-line wall at a **Scale** of 4 or 5.5 to cover different building materials for walls.
- The **STyle** option enables you to tell AutoCAD which multiline style is needed for this particular multiline. The default is **Standard**, which is a basic two-line multiline with a separation of 1 unit between the lines. We'll look at creating multiline styles in Section 12.2.

Let's draw a simple multiline using the **Standard** style.

> The ***MLine*** command is also available in the Draw pull-down menu. Additionally, the options are available on the cursor and dynamic input menus once the command has been entered.

| **Do This: 12.1.1** | **Creating Multilines** |
|---|---|

I. Start a new drawing from scratch.

II. Follow these steps. (I use Absolute coordinates in this exercise; you might want to toggle dynamic input off and on as we go.)

**12.1.1: CREATING MULTILINES**

1. Set the current color to **Blue**.

   **Command: *col***

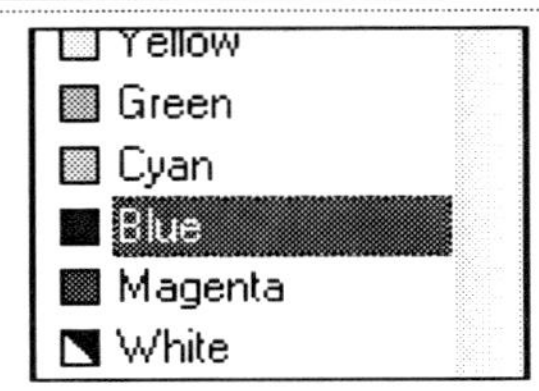


2. Enter the ***MLine*** command. (There's no button for this command.)

   **Command: *ml***

3. Accept the defaults and draw a simple multiline as indicated.

   **Current settings: Justification = Top, Scale = 1.00, Style = STANDARD**

   **Specify start point or [Justification/Scale/STyle]: *1,1***

   **Specify next point: *1,6***

   **Specify next point or [Undo]: *5,6***

   **Specify next point or [Close/Undo]: *5,1***

   **Specify next point or [Close/Undo]: *[enter]***

   Notice (right) that the color of the multiline doesn't reflect the current color setting. This is because multiline colors are set according to the Multiline Style definition (Section 12.2).

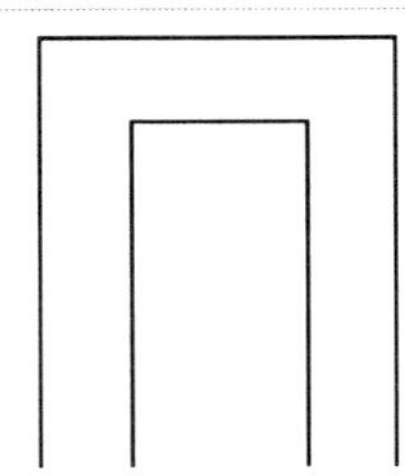

4. Set the current color back to **ByLayer**.

   **Command: *col***

5. Repeat the ***MLine*** command.

   **Command: *ml***

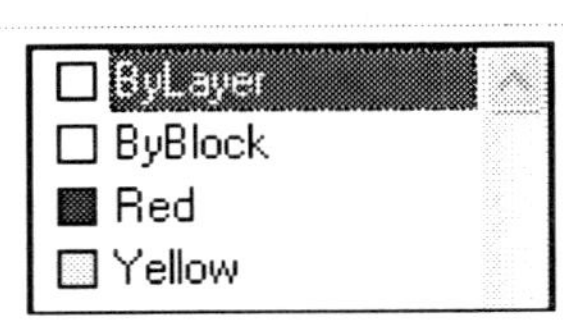


6. Tell AutoCAD you want to change the **Justification** 

…

   **Current settings: Justification = Top, Scale = 1.00, Style = STANDARD**

   **Specify start point or [Justification/ Scale/ STyle]: *j***

7. … to **Zero** Zero.

**Enter justification type [Top/Zero/Bottom] <top>:** *z*

8. Repeat Step 3 using the same coordinates. You're now locating the multiline from the center.

**Current settings: Justification = Zero, Scale = 1.00, Style = STANDARD**

**Specify start point or [Justification/ Scale/STyle]:**

Your drawing (with both multilines) looks like this.

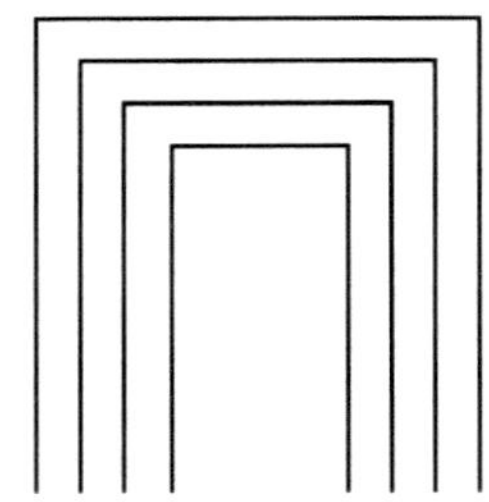

9. Repeat the ***MLine*** command.

**Command:** ***[enter]***

10. This time we'll change the **Scale** Scale …

**Current settings: Justification = Zero, Scale = 1.00, Style = STANDARD**

**Specify start point or [Justification/ Scale/STyle]:** *s*

11. … to *2*.

**Enter mline scale <1.00>:** *2*

12. Draw the multiline as indicated.

**Current settings: Justification = Zero, Scale = 2.00, Style = STANDARD**

**Specify start point or [Justification/ Scale/STyle]:** *7,1*

**Specify next point:** *7,5*

**Specify next point or [Undo]:** *12,5*

**Specify next point or [Close/Undo]:** *12,1*

**Specify next point or [Close/Undo]:** ***[enter]***

Your drawing looks like the figure below.

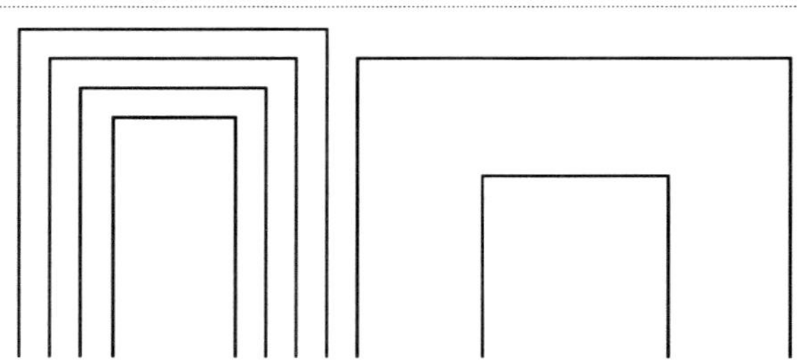

13. Exit the drawing without saving.

**Command:** ***quit***

So you see how easy it is to draw multilines. But we've only used AutoCAD's **Standard** style. Let's try something different. Let's define our own!

## 12.2 Options: The *MLStyle* Command

We define multiline styles using the ***MLStyle*** command. It can be a fairly complex task, but fortunately, AutoCAD provides dialog boxes to help. Upon receiving the ***MLStyle*** command, AutoCAD presents the Multiline Styles dialog box (Figure 12.004).

- First, you see a **Styles** list box. As with other list boxes, this one shows the styles available to you. You can select a style from this box by double-clicking or by picking and then using the **Set Current** button.
- Use the **Rename** and **Delete** buttons to do exactly what they say (that is, rename or delete a selected multiline style).
- **Load** calls the Load Multiline Styles dialog box (Figure 12.005). From here, you can load other *mln* files (multiline definition files).
- **Save** opens a standard Save File dialog box. Use this to save your drawing's multiline style definitions to a file. Then you can load the definitions into another file using the **Load** button.
- The **New** button begins the Multiline creation process by calling the Create New Multiline Style dialog box (Figure 12.006). Here you'll name your new style. You can also tell AutoCAD to begin with the setup associated with an existing style by selecting it from the **Start With** drop down menu.

  Pick the **Continue** button to move on to the New Multiline Style dialog box (Figure 12.007). You'll set up your style here. (This information will become considerably clearer with an exercise.)

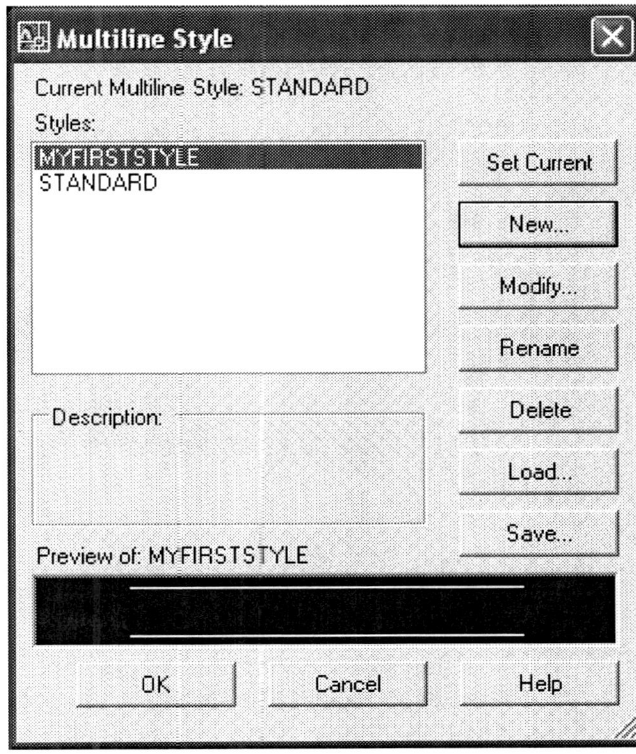


Figure 12.004

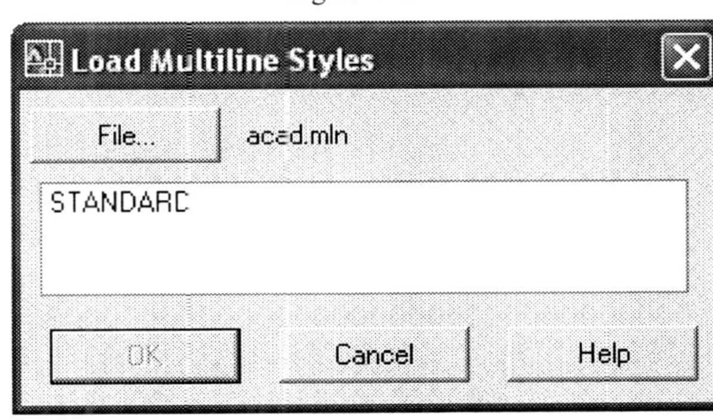


Figure 12.005

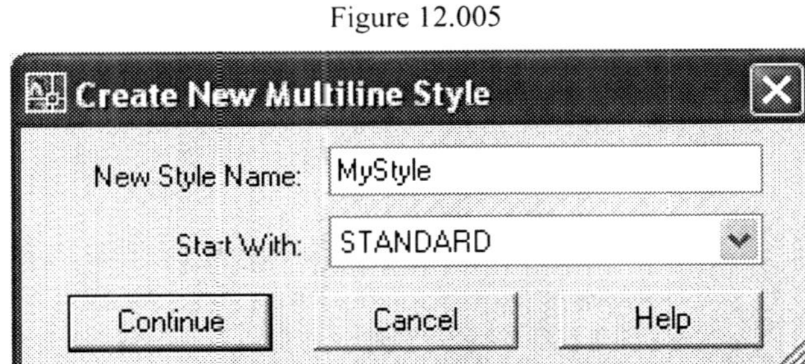


Figure 12.006

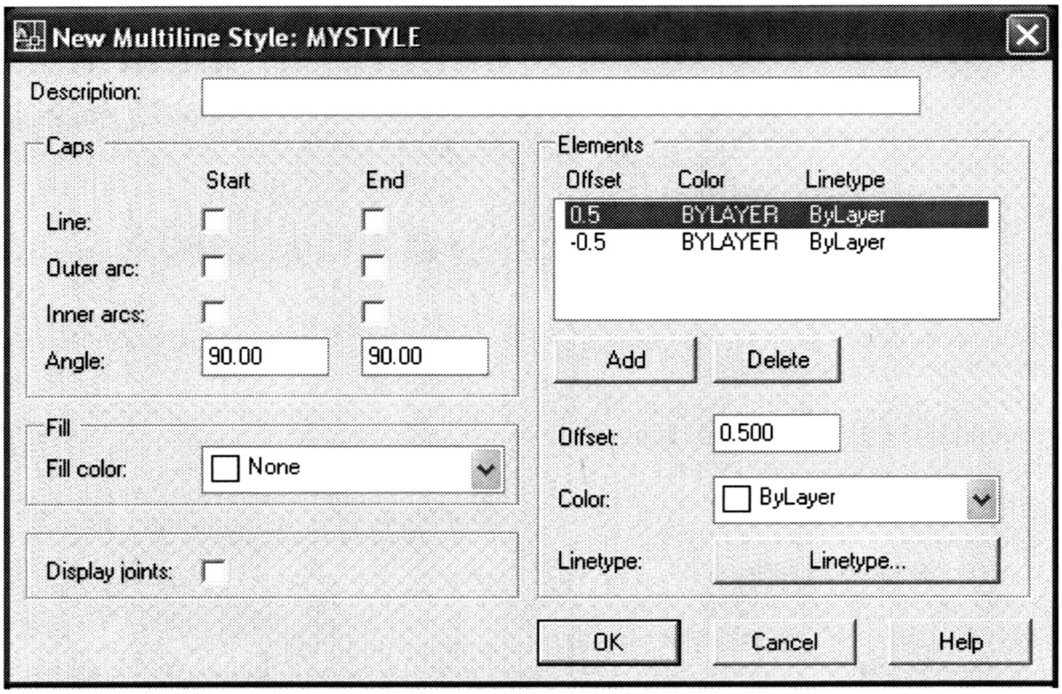


Figure 12.010

- You don't have to add a **Description**, but if you anticipate using many multilines in your drawing, it might help identify which is which later.
- The **Caps** frame allows you to add or remove caps at the end of your multiline. As you can see, you have options for a **Line**, **Outer arc**, and **Inner arcs**. (Note the difference; Outer arc – provides an arc joining the outermost lines at their endpoints; Inner arcs – provide arcs joining the endpoints of two *or more* inner lines.) You also control the **Angle** between the endpoints of the lines making up your multiline.
- Use the **Fill** color option to fill the multilines (creating something like a polyline or a solid).
- A check in the **Display joints** box means that AutoCAD will draw a line connecting the related vertices of your multiline.
- You'll control the actual parts of your multiline in the **Elements** frame.
  - First you'll see another list box. This one shows the definitions for the individual lines making up your multiline. Notice that you can control the spacing between the lines, the color and the linetype for each. You can also modify each by selecting it and using the **Offset**, **Color**, and **Linetype** tools.
  - **Add** or **Delete** lines using the buttons below the list box.
  - Confirm your creation (**OK** button) or **Cancel** it to return to the Multiline Style dialog box.

- The last button on the Multiline Style dialog box – **Modify** – calls the Modify Multiline Style dialog box. This is the same box as the New Multiline Style dialog box (Figure 12.007), but you'll use it to alter the definition of a selected multiline style.

Believe it or not, this approach to creating/modifying multiline styles beats the heck out of the old way! (We won't go into that!) Let's try an exercise.

| The ***MLStyle*** command is also available on the Format pull-down menu. |
|---|

| Do This: 12.2.1 | **Defining Multlines** |
|---|---|

I. Start a new drawing from scratch. We'll follow our procedure to create a basic style to be used in drawing pipe.

II. Follow these steps.

## 12.2.1: DEFINING MULTILINE STYLES

1. Enter the ***MLStyle*** command.

**Command:** ***mlstyle***

AutoCAD presents the Multiline Styles dialog box (Figure 12.004).

2. Pick the **New** button 

. AutoCAD presents the Create New Multiline Style dialog box (Figure 12.006).

3. Enter the name for your new multiline style.

4. Pick the **Continue** button 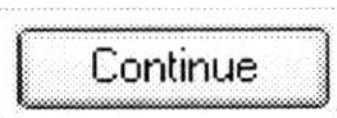

. AutoCAD presents the New Multiline Style dialog box (Figure 12.007).

5. We'll concentrate on the **Elements** frame to create our new style, which will require three lines – two outer walls and a centerline.

Pick the **Add** button 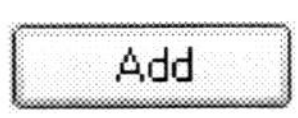

to add a line to the list box. AutoCAD places a new line at the **0** offset – in the center of the multiline.

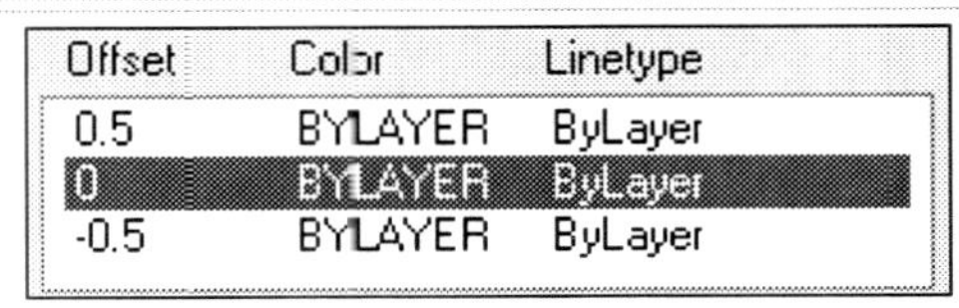


6. With the new line selected, pick the **Linetype** button 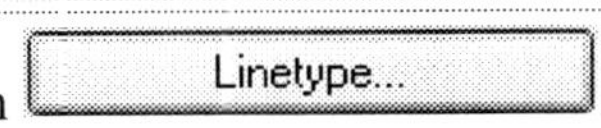

.

7. AutoCAD presents the Select Linetype dialog box (Lesson 6). Load and select the **CENTER** linetype.

8. With the center line still selected, set the **Color** to **Cyan** as shown. The list box now displays the definition.

9. Pick the **OK** button 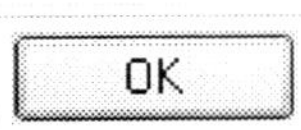

to return to the Multiline Style dialog box. Notice that your new definition appears in the list box.

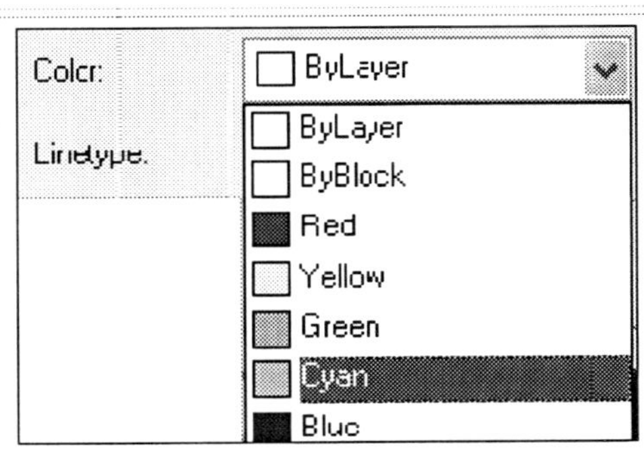


10. Now let's save the definitions in this drawing to a file so that we can use them in other drawings. Pick the **Save** button 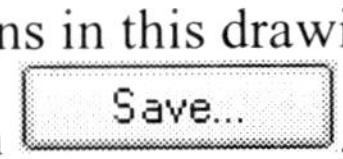

.

11. AutoCAD presents a standard Save File dialog box. Save the file as *MyMLines* in the C:\Steps\Lesson12 folder.

12. Now pick the **OK** button 

to close the dialog box.

13. Close AutoCAD completely (don't save the drawing) and reopen it. (This will clear any definitions that might linger.) We'll use the default drawing.

14. Now reopen the Multiline Style dialog box.

**Command: *mlstyle***

Notice that the **PIPE** style you create isn't listed. You haven't loaded it into the current drawing. We'll fix that now.

15. Pick the **Load** button 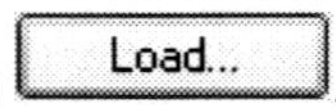

. AutoCAD presents the Load Multiline Styles dialog box (Figure 12.005).

16. Pick the **File** button 

. AutoCAD presents a standard Open File dialog box.

17. Navigate to the C:\Steps\Lesson12 folder and select the *MyMLines* file you create in this exercise. (Note: if that file is unavailable, select the *MLines* file instead.)

18. AutoCAD now shows the **PIPE** definition in the Load Multline Styles dialog box. (If you selected the MLines file, it also shows a **DEMO** style – right).

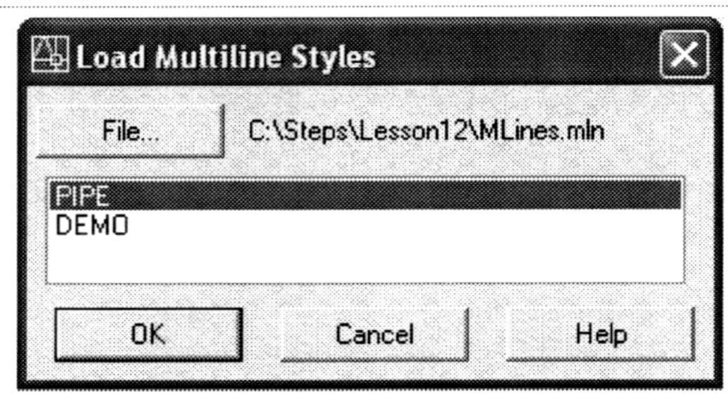


19. Select the **PIPE** style and pick the **OK** button 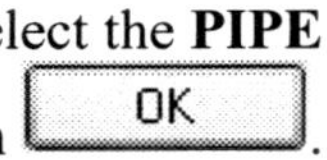

.

20. Almost done! AutoCAD returns to the Multiline Style dialog box. Select **PIPE** from the list box and pick the **Set Current** button 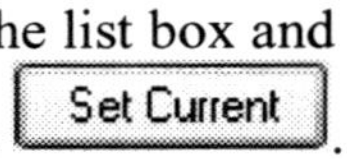

.

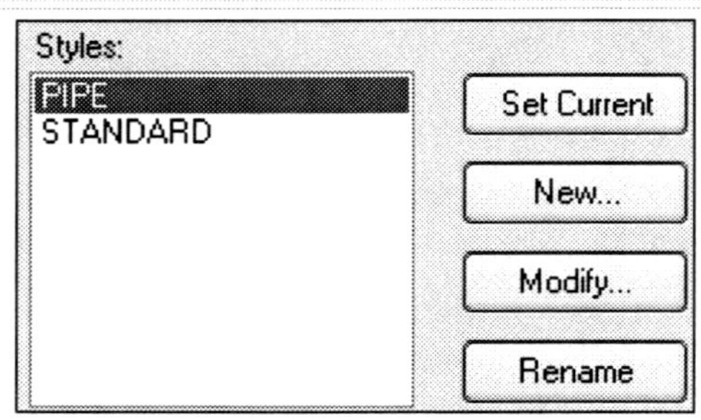


21. Pick the **OK** button 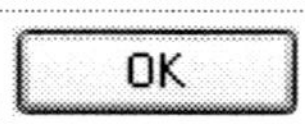

to complete the procedure.

You've done it! You've create a multiline style, saved it to a file, loaded the file into a new drawing, and set the style current in the new drawing. Any multiline you draw now will have the **PIPE** style! (Let's do that just to see. We'll create a couple of crossing, 1"ø pipes.)

22. Create a layer  called *MyPipe*. Set the color to yellow and make it current.

**Command: *la***

23. Enter the ***MLine*** command.

**Command: *ml***

## 12.2.1: Defining Multiline Styles

24. Notice that **PIPE** is the current style. Set the scale [Scale] for a 1" ø pipe as indicated.

> **Current settings: Justification = Top, Scale = 1.00, Style = PIPE**
> **Specify start point or [Justification/Scale/STyle]:** ***s***
> **Enter mline scale <1.00>:** ***1.375***

25. Draw two multilines – the first from point **6,1** to point **6,7**; the second from point **3,5** to point **11,5**.

> **Specify start point or [Justification/Scale/STyle]:**
> **Specify start point or [Justification/Scale/STyle]:** ***[enter]***

Your drawing looks like this.

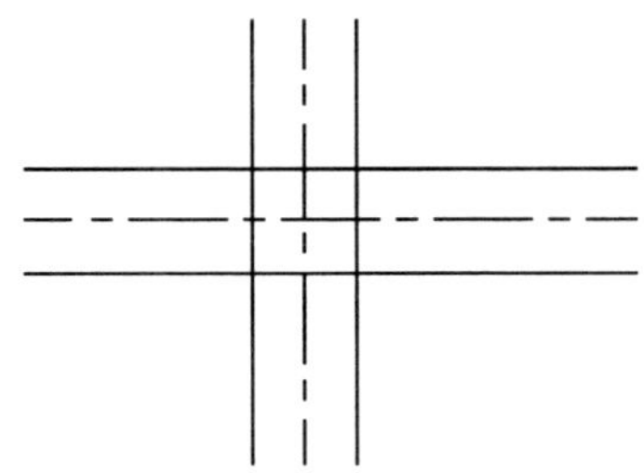

26. Save this drawing as *MyMlines* in the C:\Steps\Lesson12 folder.

> **Command:** ***save***

Notice the colors and linetypes. Lines that had their colors setup as ByLayer reflect the layer color. Lines set up with a designated color reflect that color. The same with linetypes.

Now let's take a look at the other side of the New Multiline Styles dialog box. Let's set up some properties.

| Do This: 12.2.2 | More on Multiline Styles |
|---|---|

I. Open the *MLine Properties.dwg* file in the C:\Steps\Lesson12 folder.
II. Open the MLStyle dialog box. Notice that a style called **DEMO** is current.
III. Follow these steps.

## 12.2.2: More on Multiline Styles

1. Pick the **Modify** button [Modify...]. AutoCAD presents the Modify Multiline Style dialog box (the same box as New Multiline Style seen in Figure 12.007).

2. Put a check in the **Display joints** check box.

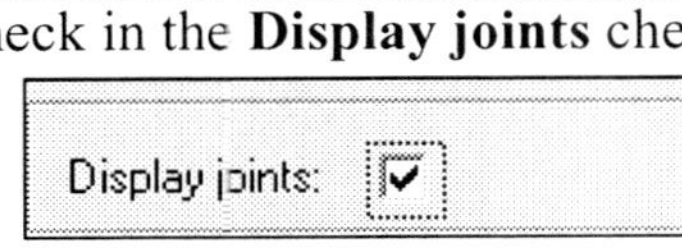


Pick **OK** to return to the Multiline Styles dialog box. Notice (right) the line in the middle of the demo box. This indicates that AutoCAD will put a line in the multiline joints.

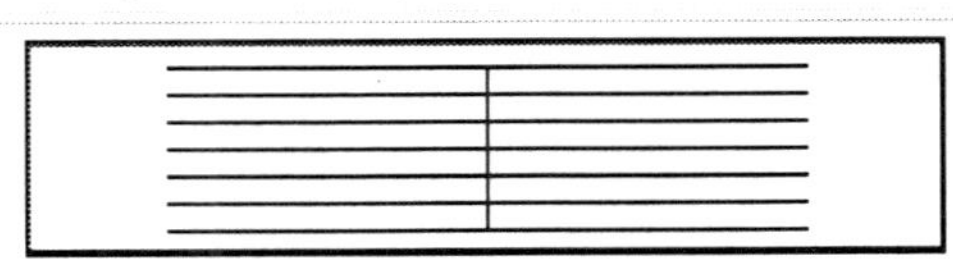

3. Complete the command [OK].

4. Enter the ***MLine*** command.

> **Command:** ***ml***

5. Accept the defaults and draw a multiline as indicated.

**Current settings: Justification = Top, Scale = 1.00, Style = DEMO**
**Specify start point or [Justification/Scale/STyle]:** ***1,1***
**Specify next point:** ***1,6***
**Specify next point or [Undo]:** ***5,6***
**Specify next point or [Close/ Undo]:** ***5,1***
**Specify next point or [Close/ Undo]:**

Notice the joints.

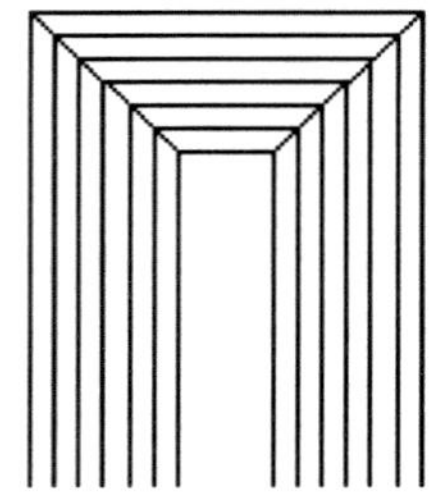

6. Repeat the ***MLStyle*** command.

**Command:** ***mlstyle***

7. Create a **New** style based on the **Demo** style – call it **Demo1**. **Continue** to the New Multiline Style dialog box.

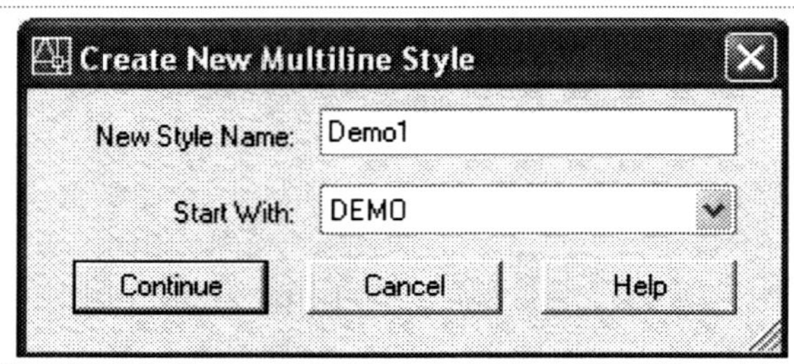


8. Make these adjustments:

- Remove the check from the **Display joints** check box.
- Add a check to the **Line** check box under the **Start** column.
- Add a check to the **Outer** and **Inner arcs** check boxes under the **End** column.
- Change the **Angle** under the **Start** column to ***45°***.

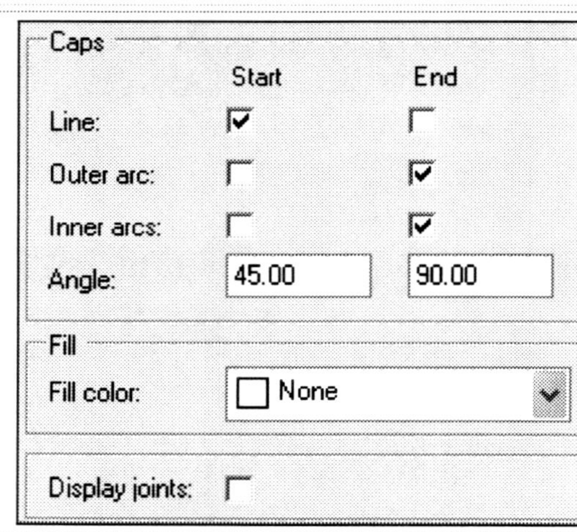


9. Pick the **OK** button 

to return to the Multiline Styles dialog box (the image in the demo box looks like this).

10. Make the **DEMO1** style current 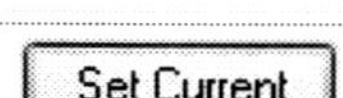

and complete the procedure 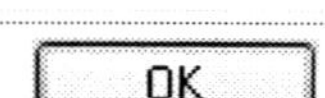

.

11. Erase  the last multiline you drew.

## 12.2.2: More on Multiline Styles

12. Draw a new multiline as indicated.

**Command:** ***ml***

**Current settings: Justification = Top, Scale = 1.00, Style = DEMO1**

**Specify start point or [Justification/Scale/STyle]:** ***2,7***

**Specify next point:** ***9,7***

**Specify next point or [Undo]:** ***9,2***

**Specify next point or [Close/Undo]:** ***[enter]***

Notice the angle of the start point is 45°. You can also see the line at the start point and the inner and outer arcs at the endpoint as you set in Step 8.

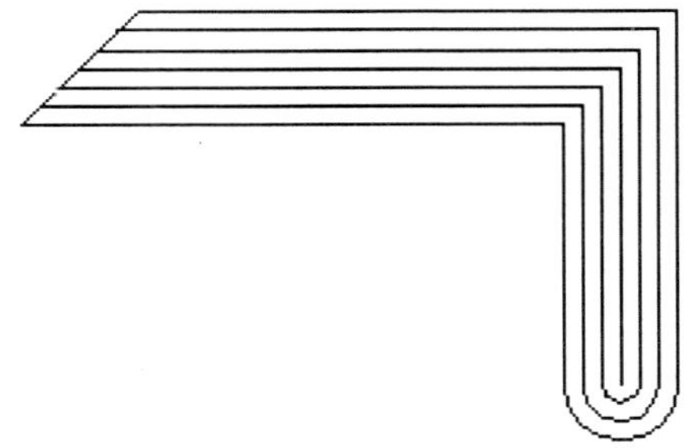

13. Repeat Steps 6 and 7 (be sure to base your new style on **DEMO**, and call your new Style **Demo2**).

14. Remove the check next to **Display joints** and set the **Fill color** to **Magenta**.

15. Complete the command 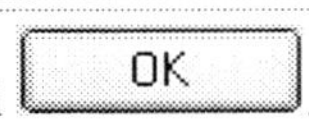

. (Be sure to set the **DEMO2** style current 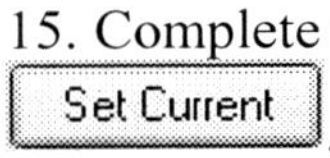

.)

16. Draw a new multiline. The multiline is filled (Figure 12.018).

16. Exit the drawing without saving.

**Command:** ***quit***

As you've seen, you can do a lot of things with multilines. You'll find them particularly useful in two fields – Piping and Architecture. But they are also quite useful in laying out multilane (or even single-lane) streets!

> And now the downside: Multilines have their limitations. The worst of these is the inability to set different layers for each of the individual lines. Because of this, centerlines can't be manipulated separately from outer lines. Another limitation is the need for a specific tool for some of the multiline modifications you'll want to make. This tool is called ***MLEdit*** and is the subject of the next section of our lesson.

## 12.3 Editing Multilines: The *MLEdit* Command

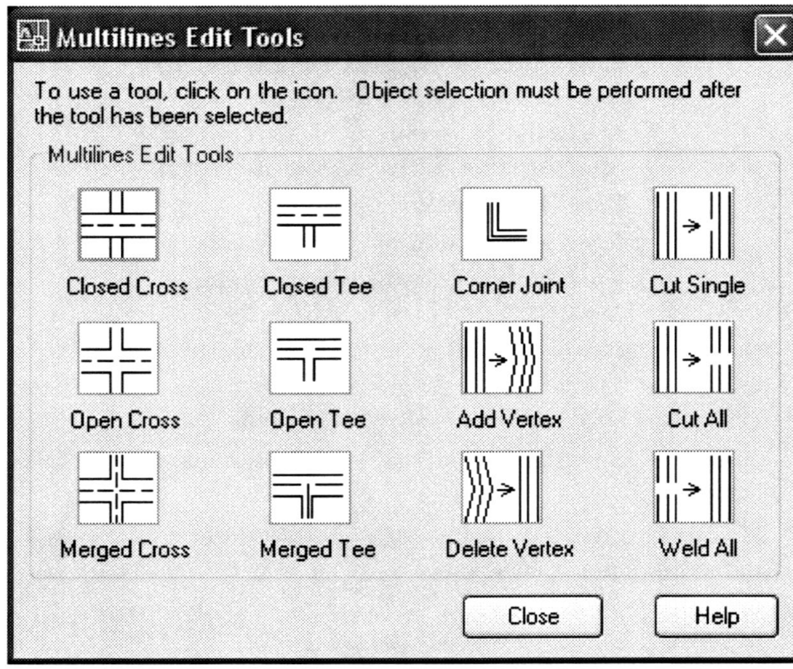


Figure 12.008

As I mentioned, editing multilines requires a special tool. Oh, some of AutoCAD's more basic modifying tools – such as ***Copy*** and ***Move*** – work on multilines, but the tools you might find most useful – ***Trim*** and ***Extend*** – work only on the multiline itself (collectively), not on the individual lines that compose it. This leaves you with two options – either ***explode*** the multiline (into individual objects as you would a polyline) or use the ***MLEdit*** command.

Exploding the multiline isn't a bad idea. In fact, once it's been drawn, there really isn't much reason to maintain its multiline definition except that, as a multiline, you can manipulate it as a single object.

But let's look at the ***MLEdit*** command. The command calls the Multilines Edit Tools dialog box (Figure 12.008). The possibilities include three types of crosses and tees, corner creation, adding or removing a multiline vertex, breaking all or part of a multiline, and welding a broken multiline.

Let's see these in action.

> The ***MLEdit*** command is also available in the Modify pull-down menu. Follow this path:
> *Modify – Object – Multiline ...*

| Do This: 12.3.1 | Editing Multilines |
|---|---|

I. Open the *MyMlines* file you created in the C:\Steps\Lesson12 folder. (If this file is unavailable, open *Mlines* in the same folder.) The drawing looks like Figure 12.009.

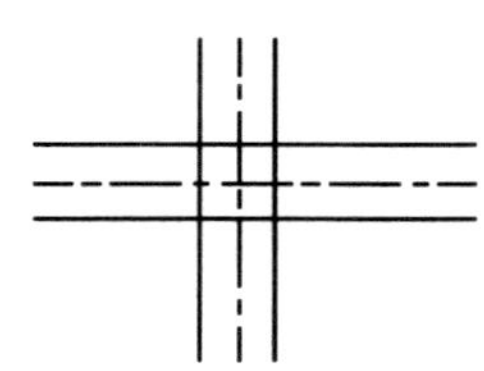

Figure 12.009

II. For this exercise, we'll again forgo the usual format in the interest of brevity (and sanity). Follow these steps for each of the options:

a. Enter the ***MLEdit*** command at the command prompt.
b. Select the editing tool you wish to use (shown in the left column of our exercise table).
c. At the **Select first mline** prompt, pick the lower part of the vertical multiline.
d. At the **Select second mline** prompt, pick the right part of the horizontal multiline. (Hit ***enter*** after this to complete the command. Your drawing will look like the image in the right column of our exercise table.

e. ***Undo*** the last modification.

f. Repeat Steps a through e for each of the tools in the left two columns of the Multilines Edit Tools dialog box, as well as for the Corner Joint tool.

| **12.3.1: Editing Multilines** | | | |
|---|---|---|---|
| **Tools** | **Results** | **Tools** | **Results** |
| 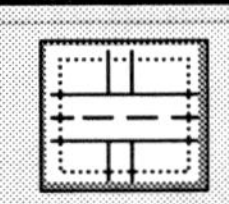 Closed Cross | 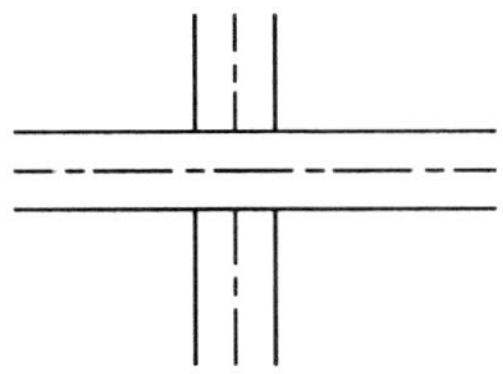 | 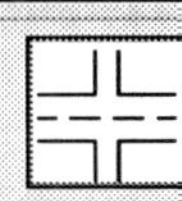 Open Cross | 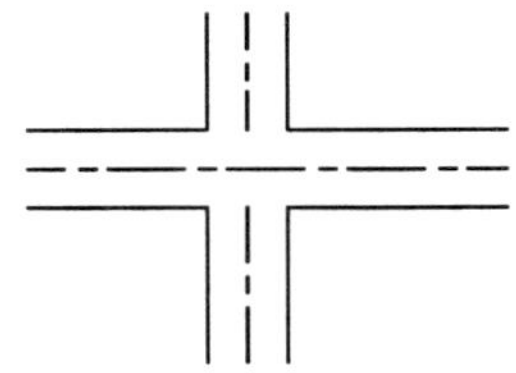 |
| 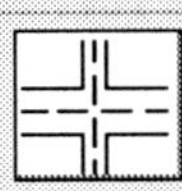 Merged Cross | 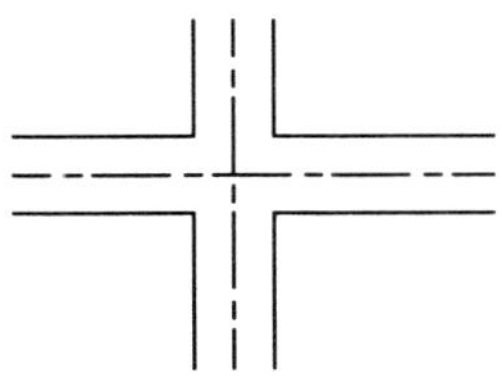 |  Closed Tee | 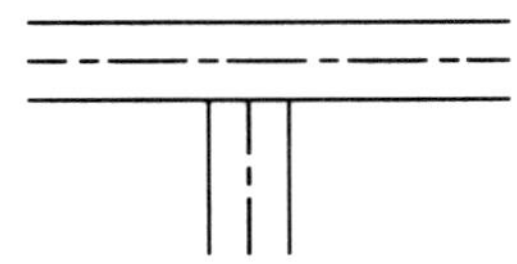 |
|  Open Tee | 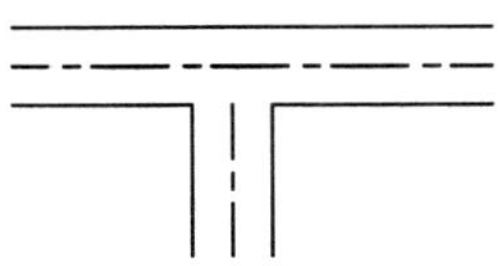 |  Merged Tee | 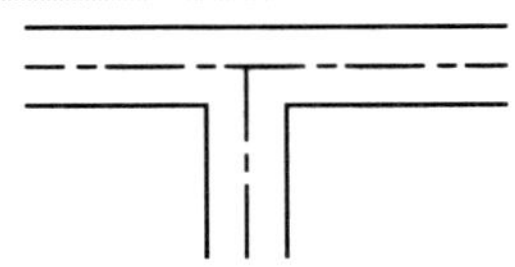 |
|  Corner Joint | 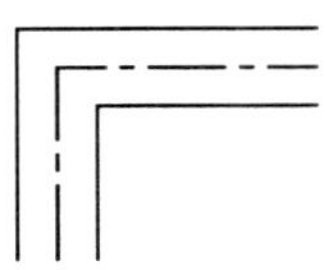 | | |

Are you getting a feel for the MLEdit tools? Let's take a more conventional look at the remaining tools.

| **Do This: 12.3.2** | **More on Editing Multilines** |
|---|---|

I. Continue in the *MyMlines* file (or *Mlines*).

II. Follow these steps.

| **12.3.2: More on Editing Multilines** |
|---|
| 1. Repeat the ***MLEdit*** command.<br>**Command:** ***mledit*** |
| 2. Select **Add Vertex** 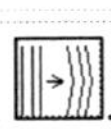. |
| 3. Pick the midpoint 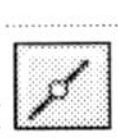 of the horizontal line.<br>**Select mline: _mid of**<br>Complete the command.<br>**Select mline or [Undo]:** ***[enter]*** |

## 12.3.2: MORE ON EDITING MULTILINES

4. Stretch the middle of the horizontal line upward one unit.

**Command: *s***

Your drawing looks like this. (Note: The ***Stretch*** procedure was to help you see the new vertex.)

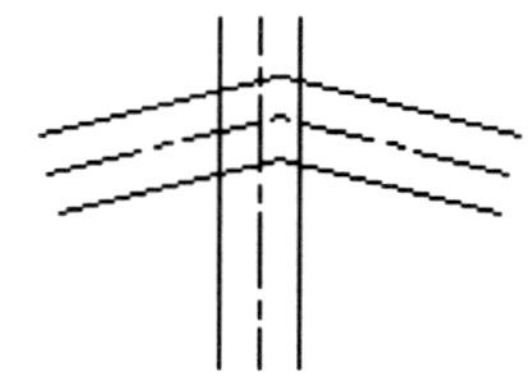

5. Repeat the ***MLEdit*** command.

**Command: *mledit***

6. Select **Delete Vertex**.

7. Select the new vertex on the horizontal multiline.

**Select mline:**

Complete the command.

**Select mline or [Undo]: *[enter]***

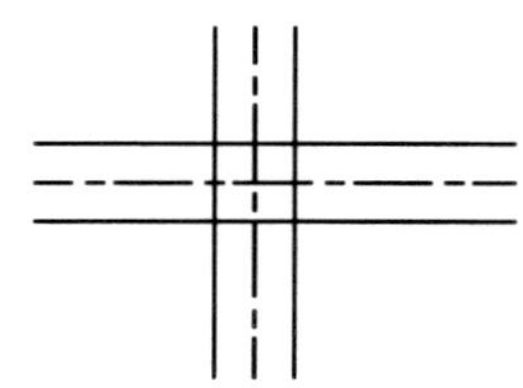

8. Repeat the ***MLEdit*** command.

**Command: *mledit***

9. Select **Cut Single**.

10. Select the left lower intersection of the two lines …

**Select mline: _int of**

11. … then the right lower intersection.

**Select second point: _int of**

**Select mline or [Undo]: *[enter]***

Your drawing looks like this.

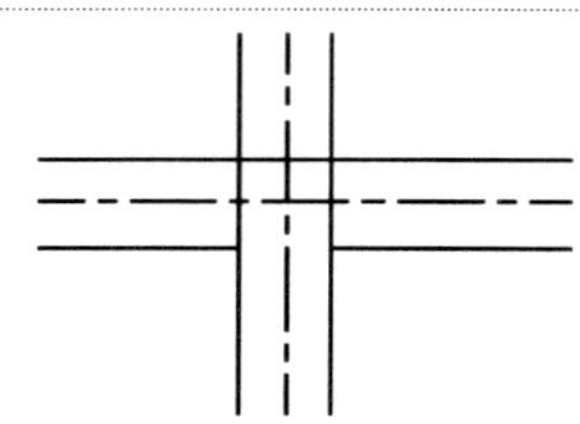

12. Undo the last command.

**Command: *u***

13. Repeat the ***MLEdit*** command.

**Command: *mledit***

14. Select **Cut All**.

15. Select the left lower intersection of the two lines …

**Select mline: _int of**

16. … then the right lower intersection.

**Select second mline: _int of**

**Select mline or [Undo]: *[enter]***

Your drawing looks like this.

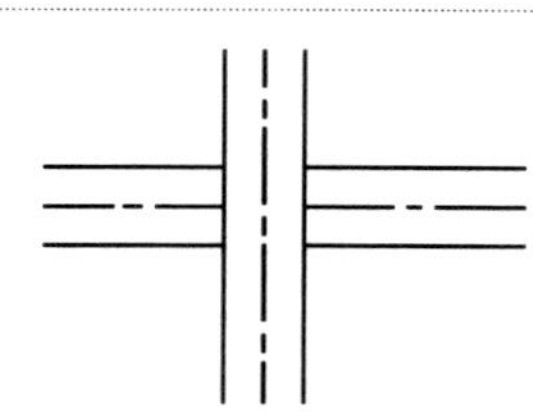

### 12.3.2: More on Editing Multilines

17. Repeat the ***MLEdit*** command.

    **Command: *mledit***

18. Select **Weld All**.

19. Select the two endpoints of the multiline you just broke.

    **Select mline:**

    **Select second point:**

    **Select mline or [Undo]: *[enter]***

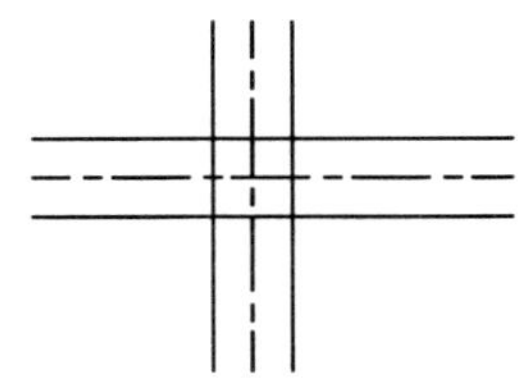

20. Quit the drawing without saving the changes.

    **Command: *quit***

## 12.4 The Project

Now that you've had some practice in drawing and editing multilines, what do you think? Perhaps it's difficult to see the full benefits of these marvelous tools without some actual experience. Let's go back to our floor plan and add some walls!

### Do This: 12.4.1 Add Some Walls

I. Open the *MyFlr-Pln 12* file you created in the C:\Steps\Lesson12 folder. (If this file is unavailable, open *flr_pln12* in the same folder.) The drawing looks like Figure 12.010.

II. Follow these steps. (Do *not* explode the multilines!)

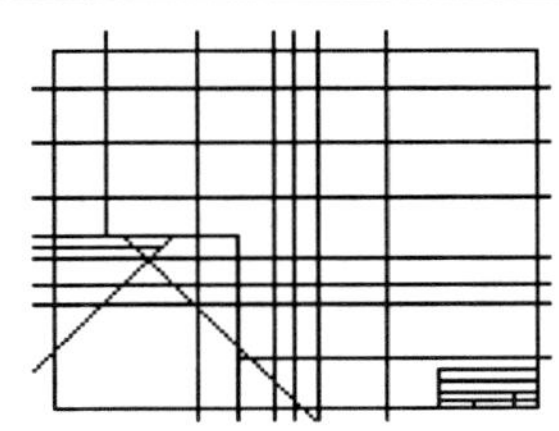

Figure 12.010

### 12.4.1: Add Some Walls

1. Enter the ***MLine*** command.

   **Command: *ml***

## 12.4.1: Add Some Walls

2. Draw a 5½" wide multiline to show the outer walls. Use the construction lines to guide you. (Hint: Set the multiline scale to ***5.5*** and use **Top** justification.)

**Specify start point or [Justify/ Scale/STyle]:**

Your drawing looks like this.

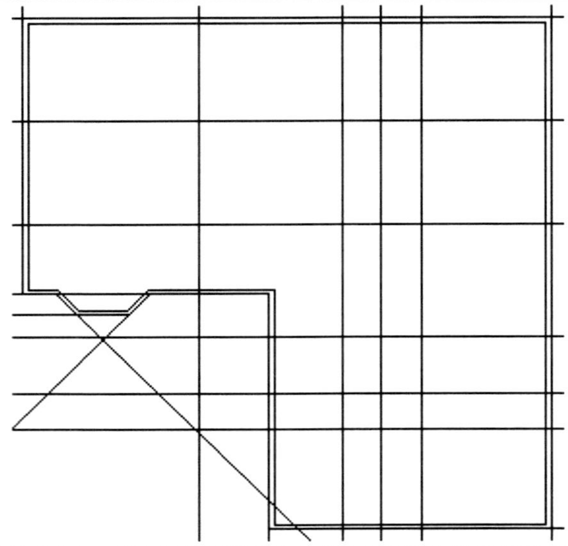

3. Draw 4" wide multilines to show the inner walls. Use the construction lines to guide you. (Hint: Set the multiline scale to ***4*** and use **Zero** justification.)

**Command: *ml***

Your drawing looks like this.

4. Erase the guidelines.

**Command: *e***

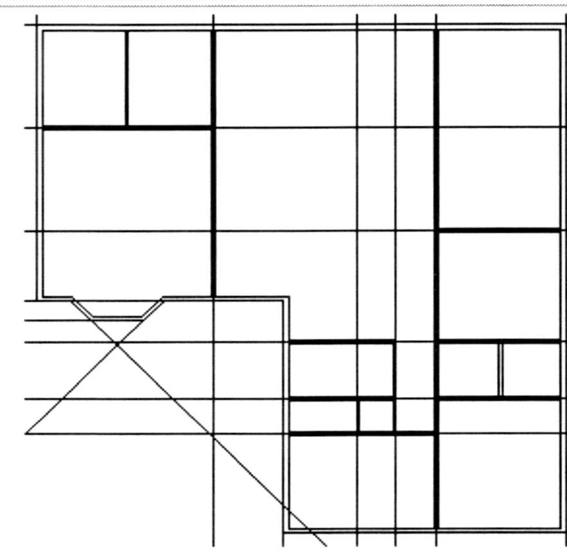

5. Cut the walls for doors and windows, as shown in Figure 12.011 (following Step 5g).

- All door openings are 36" except the smaller closet doors, which are 30".
- Window openings are 42".

There are many possible ways to locate the openings. One suggestion follows (I'll locate and size the left window on the back wall):

5a. Load the *Points* Lisp routine found in the C:\Steps\Lesson10 folder.

**Command: *appload***

5b. Enter the command ***pt*** at the command line (this command has been defined by the Lisp routine you just loaded).

**Command: *pt***

5c. AutoCAD asks you to pick a base point. Pick the left endpoint of the top wall.

**PICK A BASE POINT:**

5d. AutoCAD asks how far away to place the point. Enter the dimension given. (Be sure your running OSNAPs are off.)

**HOW FAR?** ***12'7-3/8***

5e. AutoCAD asks if the distance is along the X-plane, Y-plane, or in a Polar direction. Type *X*. .

**X, Y, OR P?** ***x***

AutoCAD places a node at that location

5f. We see by the number shown at this location that this is a 42" window. Copy the node 21" to the left and 21" to the right. The new nodes identify the edges of the window.

**Command:** ***co***

5g. Using the multiline editing tools, break the wall using the nodes placed in Step 6f as guides.

**Command:** ***mledit***

Then freeze the **Markers** layer.

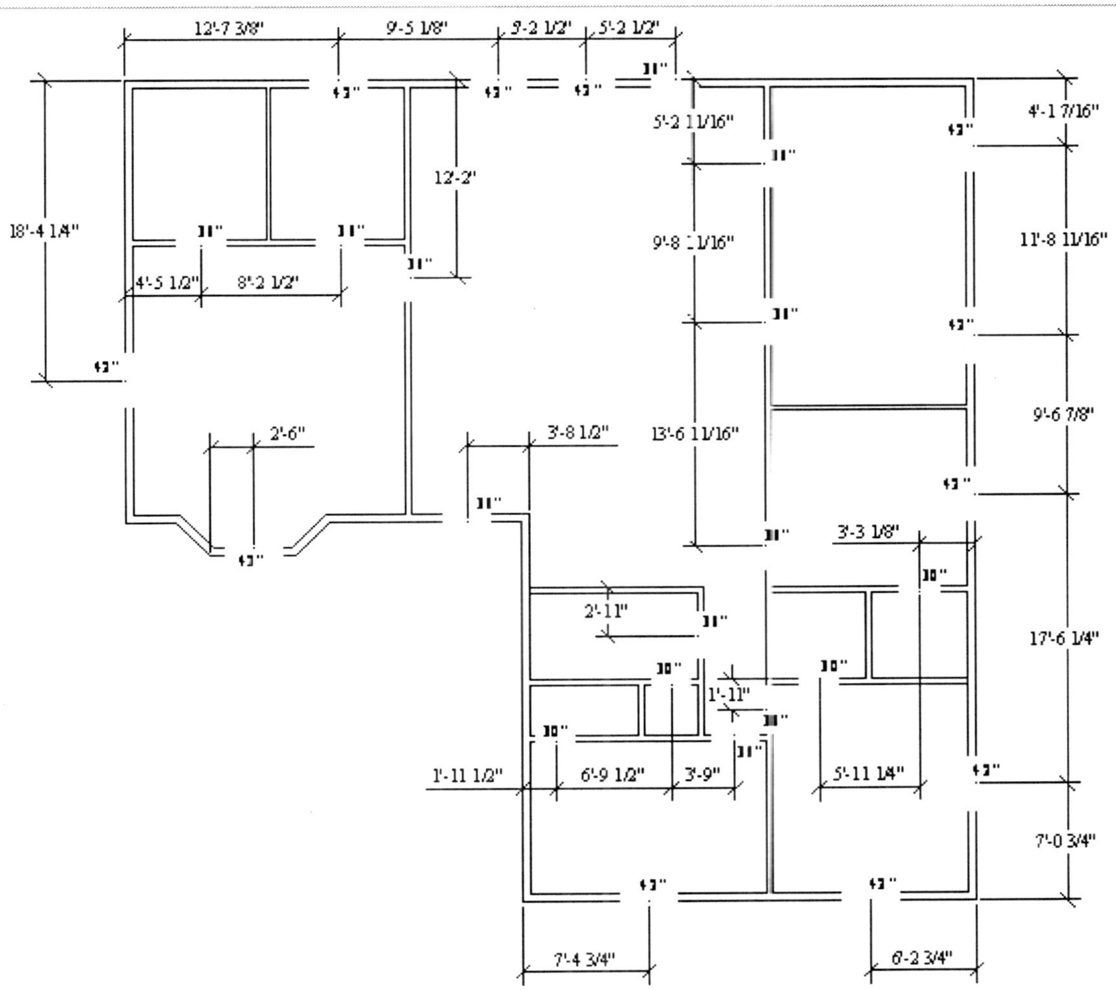


Figure 12.011

### 12.4.1: Add Some Walls

6. Open all tees (places where walls meet), as shown in Figure 12.011.
   **Command: *mledit***
7. Save the drawing as *MyFlrPln13* in the C:\Steps\Lesson13 folder, and exit.
   **Command: *saveas***

Well, that was fun! Does your drawing look more like a floor plan now? Are you beginning to feel like a CAD operator?

## 12.5 Extra Steps

- Go to a new subdivision in your area and pick up some sample floor plans from the sales office. Practice drawing them on the computer. You don't have to be exact on the dimensions (you'll only get rough dimensions on the plans anyway.)
- I know it takes a while to define styles for multilines, but now is a good time to establish a policy of never doing anything twice that can be done once and placed in a template (remember templates?). Anything that requires definition should be defined and put into a template to save time later. But does that mean you'll have thousands of templates from which to choose when creating a new drawing? Heavens, no! You should have a handful of templates – each with a lot of information. (Remember, you can also use the Design Center to milk information from one drawing or template into another!)

  Create some new templates that you might use on the job. Include units, grid and snap settings, limits, borders, and multiline definitions. But don't relax – there'll be more to add to your templates later!

## 12.6 What Have We Learned?

*Items covered in this lesson include:*

- *Commands*
  - ***MLine***
  - ***MLStyle***
  - ***MLEdit***

This has been a fun lesson – and not nearly as difficult as others have been (or will be!).

I understand that you may be a bit frustrated that the last exercise didn't go quite as fast as you might like. My instructions weren't as detailed as some earlier exercises. I'm beginning to count on you to make a necessary transition.

> Many instructors rely heavily on the step-by-step approach. Others refuse to use it at all. They argue that, in the end, all the student learns is how to follow steps. So they rely on student self-reliance to accomplish the necessary tasks.
>
> We're using a combination of the step-by-step approach and self-reliance. I lead you at first, relying more and more on what you learn as we go.

After practicing the additional floor plans in the preceding *Extra Steps* section, you probably noticed that your speed increased as your comfort with multilines increased. Eventually, multilines will prove themselves to be a timesaving tool in your arsenal.

In our next lesson, we'll add some notes to our floor plan.

## 12.7 Exercises

1. Open the *FlrPln-HVAC.dwg* file in the C:\Steps\Lesson12 folder. Add the ductwork shown below to the floor plan. Don't add the detail – it's there as a guide only.

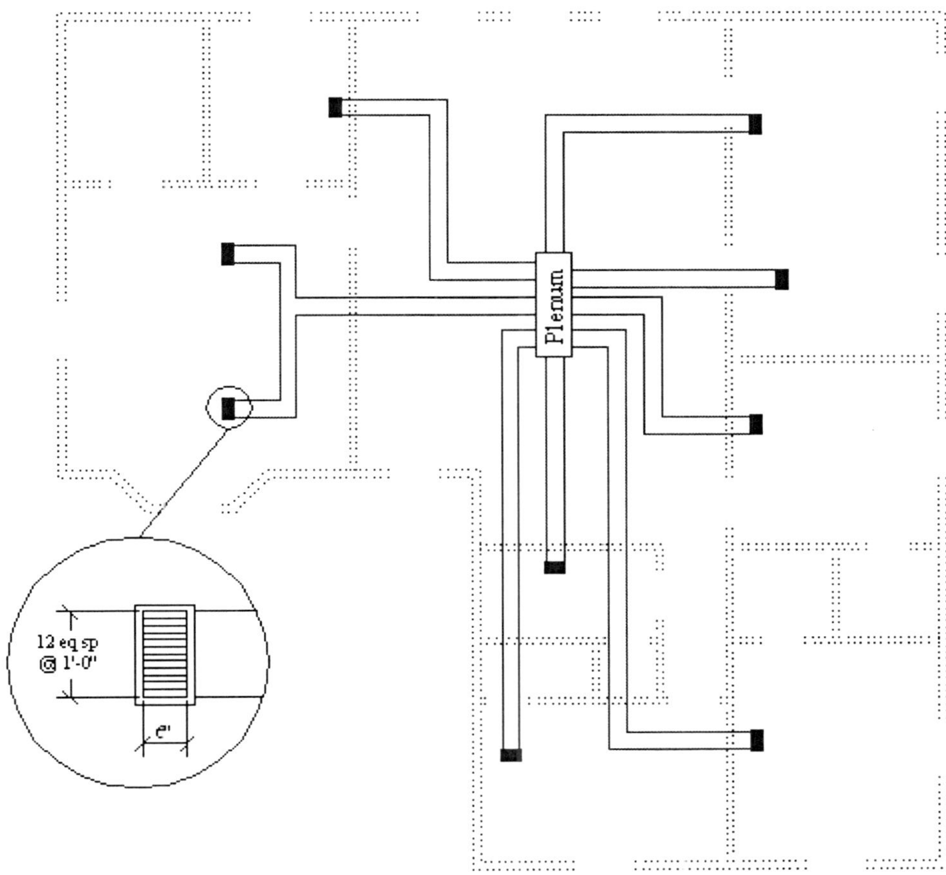


*For more exercises related to Lesson 12, please see Lesson 12 in AutoCAD 2007: One Step at a Time – Workbook.*

## 12.8 For Web-Based Review Questions, visit: http://www.uneedcad.com/2007/Files/07R12.pdf

# Lesson 13

Following this lesson, you will:

- ✓ *Know how to create and edit paragraph (multiline) text: The **MText** command*
- ✓ *Be familiar with AutoCAD's Spell Checker*
- ✓ *Know how to* Find and Replace *text in a drawing*

# Advanced Text - MText

*In Lesson 4, we learned about text, text styles, and the **QText** command. All this information will remain quite useful – indeed, **Text** will probably remain the primary method for creating call-outs on your drawings.*

*But using **Text** to create notes – that long list of construction information down the side of many drawings – can prove difficult. Editing a long list of notes can prove downright aggravating, especially if you must add or remove lines!*

*When I was on the boards, we often sweet-talked the project secretary into typing our notes. We then photocopied them onto sticky transparencies that we attached to our drawings. This worked well until revisions required additional notes or changing existing ones. Then we had to peel the sticky transparency from the drawing without damaging the paper.*

*With the **MText** command, we have the benefits of the project secretary's typing abilities without the hassles of sticky transparencies. The secretary can type the notes using a computer's word processor (MS Word, WordPerfect, etc.), and then give us the file to import into our drawings.*

*Of course, we can do the typing ourselves if the keyboard doesn't intimidate use. We can even share the secretary's dictionary to keep our spelling accurate (or at least consistent with the rest of the project). But why not take advantage of what's available – in many cases, this is a secretary's superior typing ability.*

*In this lesson, we'll see how to create, import, and edit notes in an AutoCAD drawing using the Multiline Text Editor.*

## 13.1 AutoCAD's Word Processor: The Multiline Text Editor

AutoCAD took great pains to make their word processor behave like other word processors designed for the Windows environment – and their latest effort shows some improvement over previous versions. Obviously, they couldn't incorporate the complete workings of an MS Word or WordPerfect; but the AutoCAD word processor works very much like WordPad – the simple word processor that ships with Windows. So if you're familiar with the more common word processors on the market today, this lesson will move quickly and easily.

> A word processor is the computer equivalent of a typewriter. It's what you use to type letters, notes, résumés, and even AutoCAD books. There are several on the market, but the most common are Microsoft's Word and Novell's WordPerfect.

To access the Multiline Text Editor, follow this command sequence:

**Command: *mtext* (or *mt* or *t*)**

**Current text style: "Standard" Text height: 0.2000**

**Specify first corner: *[you'll place a border around the area where you want the text to go; pick a corner of that border here]***

**Specify opposite corner or [Height/Justify/Line spacing/Rotation/ Style/Width]: *[pick the other corner of the border]***

AutoCAD first lets you know the style and text height you're using. Then it prompts for a border around the area in which to place the text. The **opposite corner** of the border is a bit tricky. There are a few options from which to choose – some refer to the bordered area, others refer to the text inside the border, and still others refer to both. Let's look at these options.

- The **Height** option allows you to set the text height. It prompts

  **Specify height <0.2000>:**

- The **Justify** option allows you to justify text within the border. The options are the same as the ***Text*** justification options, except that **Fit** and **Align** are missing.

  The **Justify** option also controls the flow of the multiline text. For example, using the default **TL** (top left) option, AutoCAD anchors the text at the topmost and leftmost corner of the user-defined border. If the text entered is too large for the border, AutoCAD will automatically expand the border downward. Using the **BC** (bottom center) option causes the anchor point to be placed at the bottom and center of the border. Expansion of the border then occurs upward. Other justifications affect expansion in a similar manner.
- The **Line spacing** option provides an opportunity to control the spacing between lines of text.
- The **Rotation** option allows you to control the rotation of the text just as it does within the ***Text*** command. It also controls the direction of expansion of the text border. For example, a downward-expanding border will actually expand toward the bottom of the text – or toward the right of the drawing when using a 90° text rotation (Figure 13.001 and 13.002).

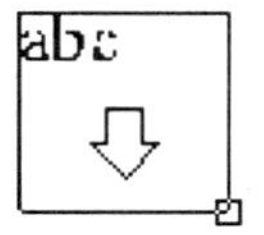

Figure 13.001

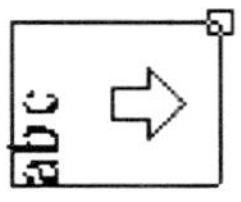

Figure 13.002

- The next option is simple enough. **Style** allows you to specify the text style AutoCAD will use in the text box. Refer to Lesson 4 for more on text style.
- The **Width** option allows you to define the width of the text border more precisely. This option is more in keeping with the precision priority of CAD use.

You can reset each of these options from within the editor, as well.

On completion of the text border, the Multiline Text Editor appears (Figure 13.003). Obviously, this odd-looking creature isn't a dialog box. Rather, it's a newly introduced interface for text entry. It includes its own toolbar (the Text Formatting toolbar – above) and a separate text-entry window. It also includes its own cursor menu, from which you can manipulate different settings.

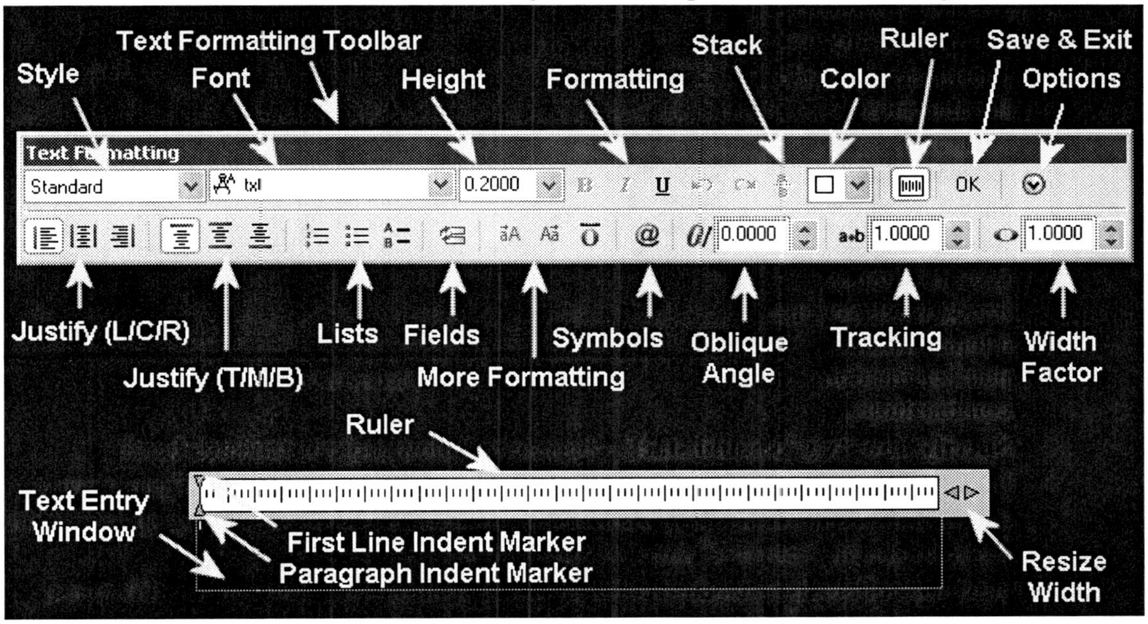

Figure 13.003

Let's start with the toolbars, which are packed with possibilities.

The most noticeable difference between these and other toolbars is that these hover independently of the Multiline Text Editor. Further, you can't dock these. They'll float until you've finished the procedure.

- We'll begin with the Text Formatting toolbar.
  - The first three items of the Text Formatting toolbar (on the top, from the left) are control boxes from which you can select or enter the text style, font, and text height. You can also use these three control boxes to change the setting of text that's currently selected in the Text Entry Window.
  - You'll recognize the next three items as standard buttons on the Formatting toolbars of most software. These common tools of emphasis are responsible for **Bold**, **Italicized**, or **Underlined** words.

    An important note to remember when formatting text is that AutoCAD fonts (those with a compass symbol next to them in the **Font** control box) can't be formatted. You can only format True Type fonts (those with a TT symbol next to them).

  - The next two buttons by now should not require much explanation – **Undo** and **Redo** buttons behave the same in word processing as they do in AutoCAD.
  - The **Stack** button **(a/b)** isn't found in most word processing applications, but is more than welcome in a CAD environment. You can highlight an area – anything that uses the front slash (/) – and pick this button to stack the text. This comes in handy when you want to stack fractions.

    If you enter fractions into the text – as in 3/8 – AutoCAD will prompt with a dialog box (Figure 13.004) allowing you the opportunity to:

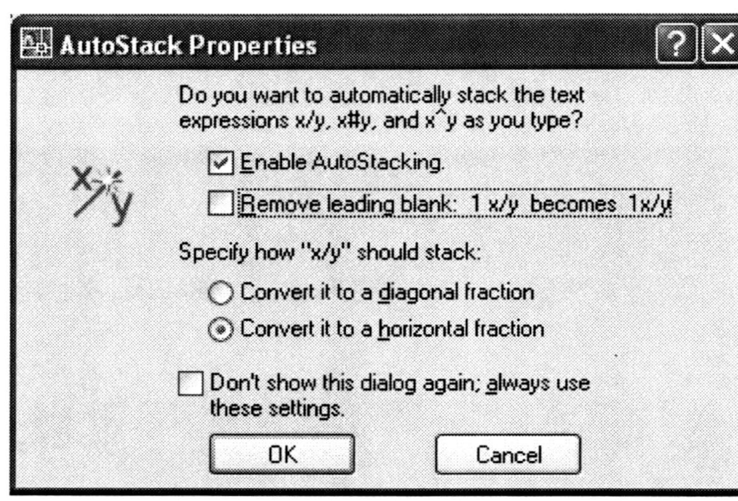


Figure 13.004

    - automatically stack the fractions **(Enable AutoStacking)**,
    - **Remove** [the] **leading blank** (you'll find this handy when you use a lot of whole number/fraction combinations,
    - **Specify how "x/y" should stack** – be sure to follow project standards here!
    - I don't recommend a check in the **Don't show this dialog again** box if you place a check in the **Remove leading blank** box; you may find yourself putting spaces before fractions (as in, "use a1/4" sheet of plywood").
  - The next control box is a standard color-selecting control box. You can use this to use color as a tool for emphasis.
  - The **Ruler** toggle controls whether or not the ruler will be visible. I use the ruler in a word processor religiously, but you can turn it off if it bothers you.

- Use the **OK** button on the Text Formatting toolbar to let AutoCAD know that you've finished and wish to save your text. If you wish to close the box without saving your changes, use the ESC key on your keyboard.
- We'll return to the **Options** button in a few minutes.

- The Options toolbar contains tools that you'll use with less frequency.
  - The Options toolbar (below the Text Formatting toolbar) begins with six buttons to assist your text justification (from the left): **Left**, **Center**, **Right**, **Top**, **Middle**, and **Bottom**.
  - The three List buttons provide quite useful tools. With these, AutoCAD can now automatically number or bullet your notes!
  - The next button allows you to **Insert Fields**. We'll discuss fields in Lesson 17.
  - The **Symbol** button calls the menu in Figure 13.005. As you can see, AutoCAD makes a wide variety of drafting symbols available to the CAD operator. Notice the programming code in the right column; entering this code will accomplish the same thing as selecting the symbol from the menu. (But why bother unless you're a typing wizard and enjoy memorizing numbers!)
  - Use the **Oblique Angle** number box to set the slant of your lettering independently of the text style you're using.
  - Use the **Tracking** number box to increase or decrease the spacing between individual letters independently of the text style you're using.
  - Use the **Width factor** number box to increase of decrease the width of individual letters independently of the text style you're using.

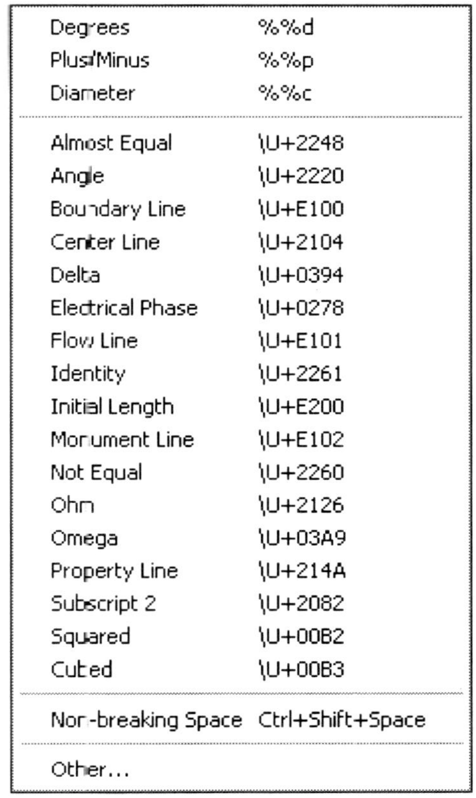


Figure 13.005

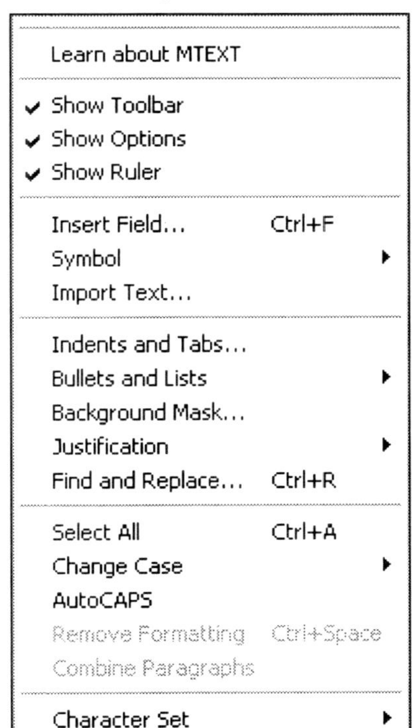


Figure 13.006

- Now let's take a quick look at the **Options** button at the right end of the upper toolbar. It calls the menu seen in Figure 13.006. (You certainly can't accuse AutoCAD's programmers of shorting you on ***MText*** options!)
  - **Learn about MTEXT** calls a tutorial to help you make the transition from your word processor to AutoCAD's way of doing things.
  - The options in the next frame toggle the visibility of the Text Formatting **Toolbar**, the **Options** toolbar, and the **Ruler**.
  - The **Insert Field** and **Symbol** options perform the same function as their button counterparts on the Options toolbar. **Import text** doesn't

appear anywhere else, however, and is the key to using notes created by that sweet project secretary. We'll see this in action in our exercise.

A file created in most word processors can be saved in simple Text (*.txt*) format. This format strips away any formatting that may have been used in creating the file. You can, however, save the file in Rich Text Format (*.rtf*), which preserves the basic formatting.

Obviously, you should opt for the *.rtf* format if it's available, when importing text from outside AutoCAD. Whenever possible, then, the project secretary should save the file accordingly. Unfortunately, it won't always be possible. Therefore, in our exercises, we'll use the more common *.txt* format when importing files so that we can study AutoCAD's methods for formatting text.

- **Indents and Tabs** calls the Indents and Tabs dialog box (Figure 13.007). Set the **First line** and **Paragraph** indentions, and the **Tab stop position**(s) here in decimal fractions. Use the **Clear** button to remove any existing settings.

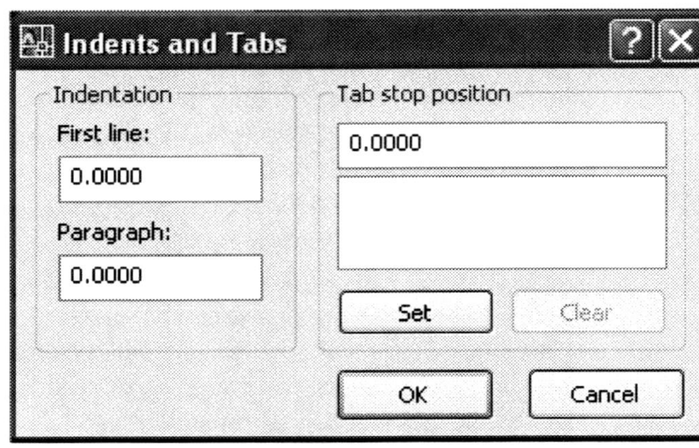


Figure 13.007

- **Bullets and Lists** calls the menu seen in Figure 13.008. This menu bears closer scrutiny.
  - **Off** removes numbering from selected text.
  - **Lettered** enables you to use letters rather than numbers. Use the flyout menu to toggle between upper and lower case letters.
  - **Numbered** enables you to use numbers rather than letters.
  - **Bulleted** replaces numbers and/or letters with bullets (much as you're seeing on this page. Change the type of bullets with the TAB key on your keyboard.
  - **Restart** does just that – it restarts the numbers or letters of your list.
  - **Continue** also does just that – it continues the previous sequence of numbers/letters in your list.

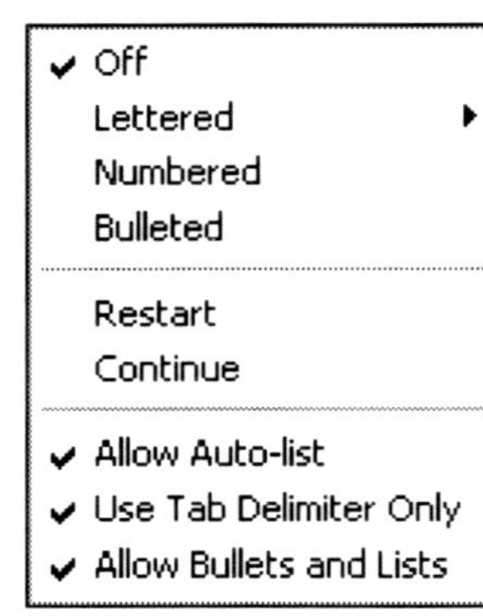


Figure 13.008

  - When **Allow Auto-list** has a check next to it, AutoCAD will attempt to recognize when you've manually begun a list and then continue the list for you. It watches for entries such as "a." or "1."
  - **Use Tab Delimiter Only** – limits the automatic creation of lists to use of the TAB key rather than the SPACEBAR.
  - **Allow Bullets and Lists** – automatically applies list formatting to anything that looks like a list. AutoCAD uses these criteria to identify lists: lines beginning with a number or symbol, use of a period after a number or letter, TAB spacing.
- **Background Mask** calls the Background Mask dialog box (Figure 13.009 – next page). Use this to place an opaque background behind your text to "mask" (hide) anything that may lie behind it. When you place a check next to **Use background mask**, AutoCAD makes the **Border offset factor** number box available. The number here determines the size of the mask (**1** means that the mask will equal the size of your text; **1.5** means that the

mask will be half again larger than your textsize). In the **Fill Color** frame, you can select a color for your mask or place a check next to **Use drawing background color** (to have your mask blend in with the background of your drawing).

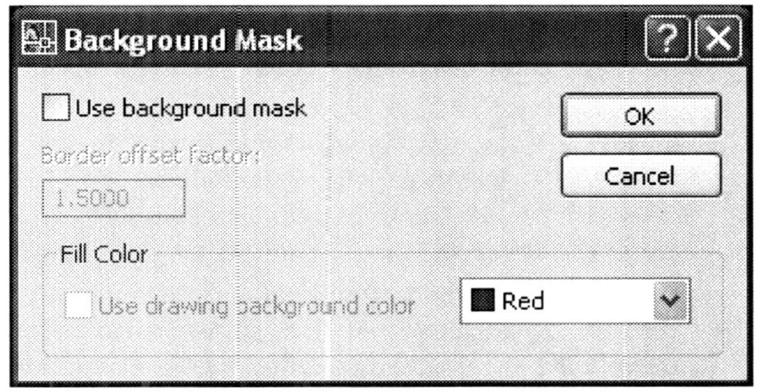


Figure 13.009

- o **Justification** provides another route to justify your text. (Although you'll find a few more options here than the buttons on the Options toolbar.)
- o **Find and Replace** calls the Find and Replace dialog box (Figure 13.010). Most of the tools in this box are fairly self-explanatory (but as with most things that are self-explanatory, they become much clearer with a bit of explanation).

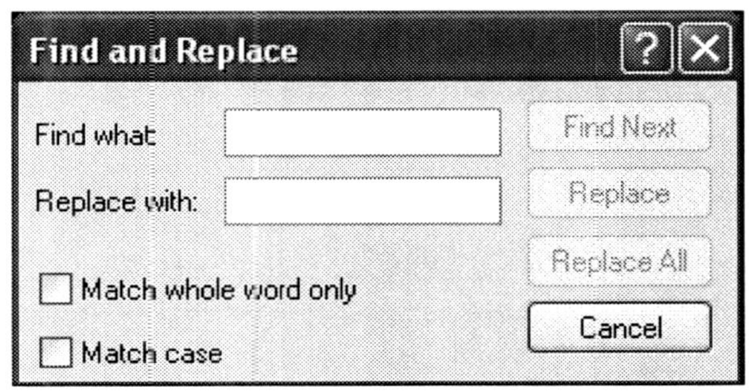


Figure 13.010

  - **Find what** enables you to find a specific bit of text. The text for which you search must be located *after the flashing cursor in the Text Entry Window.*
  - **Replace with** enables you to replace the text in the **Find what** box with a new string of text.
  - **Match whole word only** and **Match case** are filters that help streamline your search.
  - Once you've entered the text to locate in the **Find what** box and the appropriate text in the **Replace with** box (if desired), use the **Find Next** button to begin your search. If AutoCAD finds text to match your search, it'll highlight it.
  - Use the **Replace** button to replace the located text with the text in the **Replace with** box.
  - Use the **Replace All** button to replace all occurrences of the **Find what** text with the **Replace with** text.
  - Use either the **Cancel** button or the exit **X** on the title bar to complete the procedure.
- o The next frame includes some fairly straightforward formatting tools. **Select All** selects all the text in the current editing session. **Change Case** provides options for you to change from **Uppercase** to **Lowercase** lettering (or vice versa). **AutoCAPs** is the menu equivalent of the caps lock on your keyboard. **Remove Formatting** and **Combine Paragraphs** will do just what they say for selected text.
- o Use the only option in the last frame – **Character Set** – to change the character set of selected text. Okay, you probably won't need to use **Hebrew** or **Japanese** lettering (and you're probably better off just ignoring this frame), but AutoCAD provides the options for you urbane designers!

(This sure is a lot of information … and we haven't even discussed the Text Entry Window yet! Well, onward … ever onward!)

- The Text Entry Window behaves like its counter-part in most word processors. That is, it's where you'll enter your text. The window appears where your text will reside in the drawing, so you'll know exactly how it will look and fit as you enter it.
- Atop the Text Entry Window, you'll find a ruler to help you track where you are in the defined area. The **First Line Indent Marker** and **Paragraph Indent Marker** will be familiar to MS Word users. For those who are unfamiliar with MS Word, the **First Line Indent Marker** shows and controls the first line indentation of the next or selected paragraphs. The **Paragraph Indent Marker** shows and controls the indentation of the (entire) text or selected paragraphs.

  Use the left and right arrows at the right end of the ruler to resize the width of the text area. Alternately, you can right-click anywhere on the ruler and select **Set MText Width** from the menu to set the width via a more precise dialog box. (You can also call the Indents and Tabs dialog box – Figure 13.009 – from the same menu.)

Whoa, boy! That was a lot of material!

We'll look at some of these tools in our exercise. But first, if you're not familiar with word processors, please study the chart in Appendix D. This chart shows some keystrokes for maneuvering through and manipulating the text in the Multiline Text Editor. Familiarity with these keystrokes will save a considerable amount of time in Multiline Text Editing.

Let's put some text into our floor plan.

| |
|---|
| The ***MText*** command is also available in the Draw pull-down menu. Follow this path:<br>*Draw – Text – Multiline Text...* |

| **Do This: 13.1.1** | **Using Multiline Text** |
|---|---|

I. Open the *MyFlrPln13* drawin the C:\Steps\Lesson13 folder. If this isn't available, open *FlrPln13* in the same folder. The drawing looks like Figure 13.011.

II. Follow these steps.

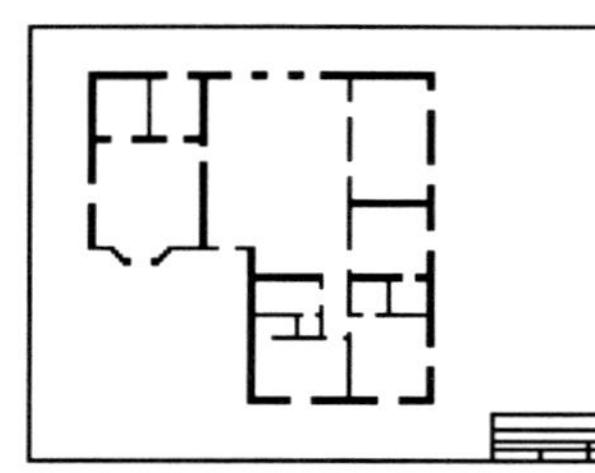

Figure 13.011

**13.1.1: MULTILINE TEXT**

1. Create a new layer called **Text** and set it current.

   **Command: *la***

2. Enter the ***MText*** command. Alternately, you can pick the **Multiline Text** button on the Draw toolbar or palette.

   **Command: *t***

3. AutoCAD displays the **Current text style** and **Text height**, then prompts for the **first corner** of the text border. Enter these coordinates.

   **Current text style: "TIMES" Text height: 3/16"**

   **Specify first corner: *69',62'***

## 13.1.1: MULTILINE TEXT

4. Tell AutoCAD you want to specify the **Width** [Width] of the text border …

**Specify opposite corner or [Height/Justify/Line spacing/Rotation/Style/Width]:** ***w***

5. … then set the **Width** to ***15'***. AutoCAD presents the Multiline Text Editor with the **TIMES** style current.

**Specify width:** ***15'***

6. Set the font size (text height) to 1'-0" [1'-0"]. (The scale factor for a ¼" drawing is 48. The desired text height at plot time is ¼". ¼" x 48 = 12".)

7. Pick the **Bold** button [B]. Notice that it appears depressed when active.

8. Type ***"The "***. (Don't worry if the text appears oversized; it'll right itself when you complete the command.)

9. Pick the **Italics** button [I].

10. Type ***"Tara II "***.

11. Deselect the **Italics** button.

12. Type ***"Floor Plan"***, and then hit enter to start a new line.

13. Pick the **OK** button [OK]. The upper right corner of your drawing looks like this.

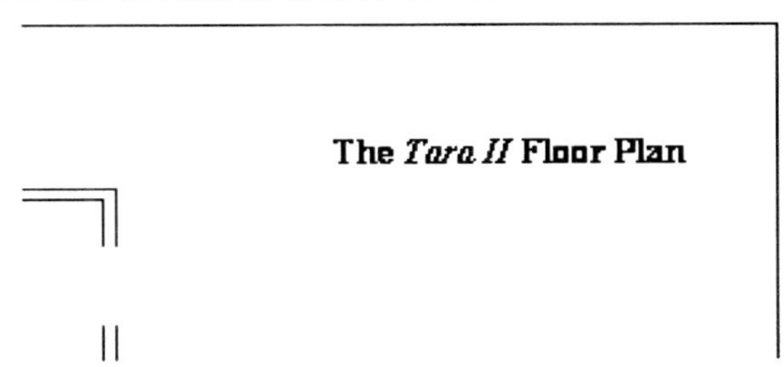


14. Remember to save occasionally.

**Command:** ***qsave***

15. To return to the Multiline Text Editor for our notes, simply edit the text. When Multiline Text is selected, ***DDEdit*** will automatically present the Multiline Text Editor. (Alternately, you can double-click on the text to edit.)

**Command:** ***ed***

**Select an annotation object or [Undo]:**

16. Hit the END key on your keyboard to go to the end of the current line; change the text height to 6" [6"] (to produce 1/8" text at plot time).

17. Deselect the **Bold** button [B].

18. Hit ***enter*** twice to locate your cursor on the second line below the text as indicated here.

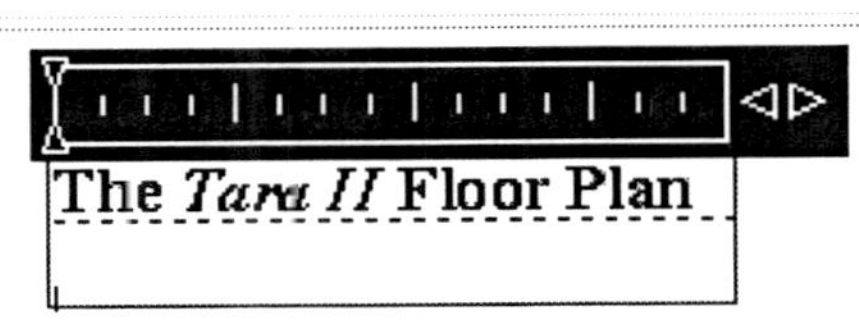


19. Pick the **Options** button and select **Bullets and Lists** from the menu.

## 13.1.1: Multiline Text

20. Remove the check next to **Allow Bullets and Lists** to turn it off. (This is an important step to ensure that the text imports properly.)

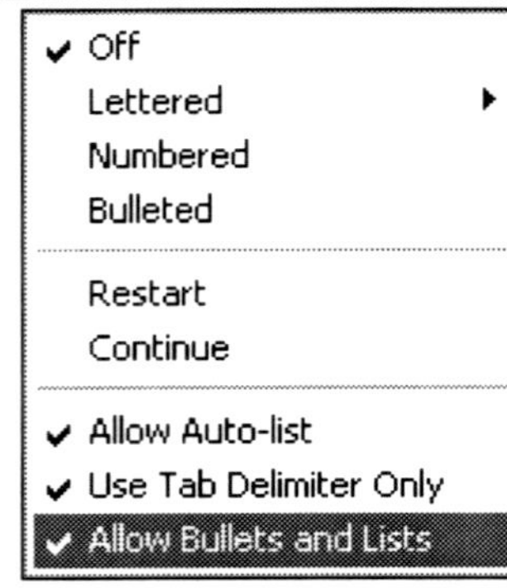


21. Now let's import some notes created by our summer intern. (Be sure your cursor is two lines below the title and that the **Bold** button is raised.) Pick **Import Text** from the fifth frame of the cursor menu. AutoCAD displays a Select File dialog box. Open the *Notes.txt* file found in the C:\Steps\Lesson13 folder.

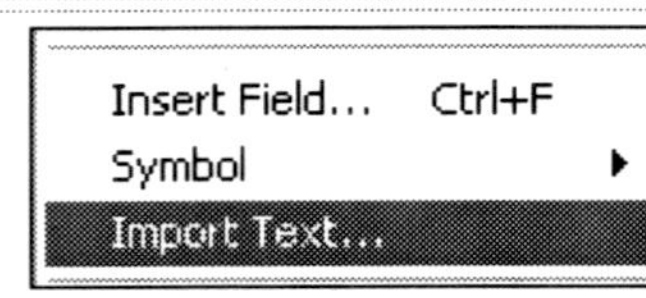


22. Complete the command [OK].

**Select an annotation object or [Undo]:**

Your text looks like this.

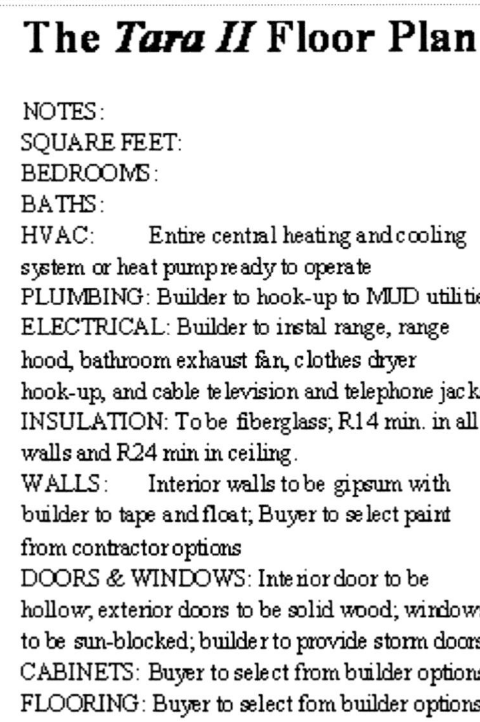

The *Tara II* Floor Plan

NOTES:
SQUARE FEET:
BEDROOMS:
BATHS:
HVAC: Entire central heating and cooling system or heat pump ready to operate
PLUMBING: Builder to hook-up to MUD utilities
ELECTRICAL: Builder to instal range, range hood, bathroom exhaust fan, clothes dryer hook-up, and cable television and telephone jacks
INSULATION: To be fiberglass; R14 min. in all walls and R24 min in ceiling.
WALLS: Interior walls to be gipsum with builder to tape and float; Buyer to select paint from contractor options
DOORS & WINDOWS: Interior door to be hollow; exterior doors to be solid wood; windows to be sun-blocked; builder to provide storm doors
CABINETS: Buyer to select from builder options
FLOORING: Buyer to select fom builder options

23. Save the drawing, but don't exit.

**Command:** ***qsave***

We've seen how easy it is to create Multiline Text both by keyboard entry and by importation. We created our text using the **TIMES** style we set up earlier, but we could just as easily have used AutoCAD's default Standard style and changed fonts in the Multiline Text Editor itself.

We've also seen that we'll use the Multiline Text Editor both to create and to edit Multiline Text. Next, we'll look at some of our options for changing, or editing, our text.

| Do This: 13.1.2 | Editing Multiline Text |
|---|---|

I. Be sure your are in the *MyFlrPln13* (or *FlrPln13*) drawing the C:\Steps\Lesson13 folder. If not, please open it now.

II. Review the material in Appendix D if you're unsure of the keystrokes required to move your cursor around the text. When unsure, use the arrow keys on the keyboard!

III. Follow these steps.

### 13.1.2: Editing Multiline Text

1. Return to the Multiline Text Editor. (Select the existing text.)

   **Command: *ed***

2. Select the text: **NOTES:**. (Be sure to get the colon, too.)

   You can do this by holding down the SHIFT key and hitting the **Right arrow** key six times. (Alternately, you can hold down the SHIFT key and hit the END key to select the whole line, or you can just hold down the left mouse button and drag over the text.)

3. Pick the **Bold** and **Underline** buttons.

4. Deselect the text. It looks like this.

5. Select the next three lines of text (including: **SQUARE FEET**, **BEDROOMS**, and **BATHS**).

   An easy way to do this is to hold down the SHIFT key while hitting the **Down arrow** three times.

6. Embolden the text.

7. Place your cursor a space to the right of **SQUARE FEET:**, and raise the **Bold** button.

8. Type ***1950***.

9. Repeat Steps 7 and 8, adding the text ***Four*** next to **BEDROOMS**, and ***Two*** next to **BATHS**.

10. Complete the command. The text looks like this.

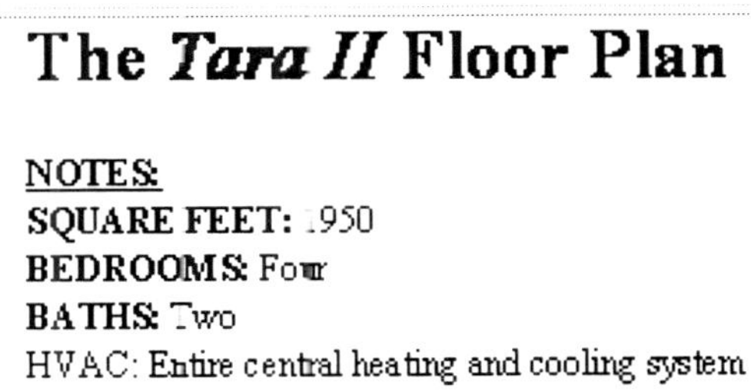


11. Remember to save often.

    **Command: *qsave***

12. Reopen the multiline text editor.

    **Command: *ed***

13. Embolden the rest of the capitalized words (and colons): **HVAC, ELECTRICAL, INSULATION**, **WALLS**, **DOORS & WINDOWS**, **CABINETS**, and **FLOORING**.

14. Complete the command [OK]. The multiline text looks like this.

# The *Tara II* Floor Plan

<u>NOTES:</u>
**SQUARE FEET:** 1950
**BEDROOMS:** Four
**BATHS:** Two
**HVAC:** Entire central heating and cooling system or heat pump ready to operate
**PLUMBING:** Builder to hook-up to MUD utilities
**ELECTRICAL:** Builder to instal range, range hood, bathroom exhaust fan, clothes dryer hook-up, and cable television and telephone jacks
**INSULATION:** To be fiberglass; R14 min. in all walls and R24 min in ceiling.
**WALLS:** Interior walls to be gipsum with builder to tape and float; Buyer to select paint from contractor options
**DOORS & WINDOWS:** Interior door to be hollow; exterior doors to be solid wood; windows to be sun-blocked; builder to provide storm doors
**CABINETS:** Buyer to select from builder options
**FLOORING:** Buyer to select fom builder options

15. Now let's number our notes. Reenter the text editor.

**Command: *ed***

16. Pick the **Options** button and select **Bullets and Lists** from the menu.

17. Pick **Allow Bullet and Lists** to enable the automatic numbering abilities of MText.

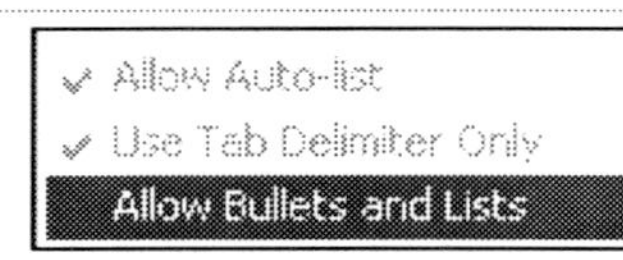


18. Select all the text below **NOTES**.

19. Pick the **Numbering** button 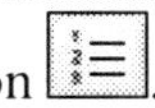. AutoCAD numbers the list, placing the tabs at its default location.

20. Let's fix the tabs. (Refer to the figure at left.) Place your cursor over the Paragraph Indent marker. Move the marker to the 1'-0" location as shown.

21. Repeat Step 20 with the **Tab** marker.

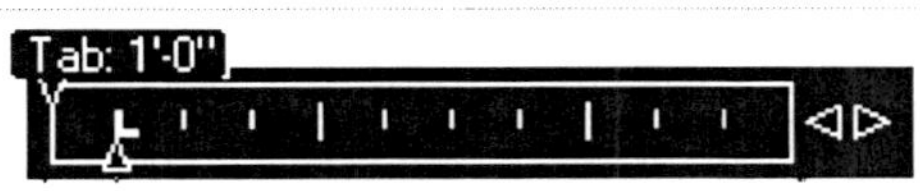


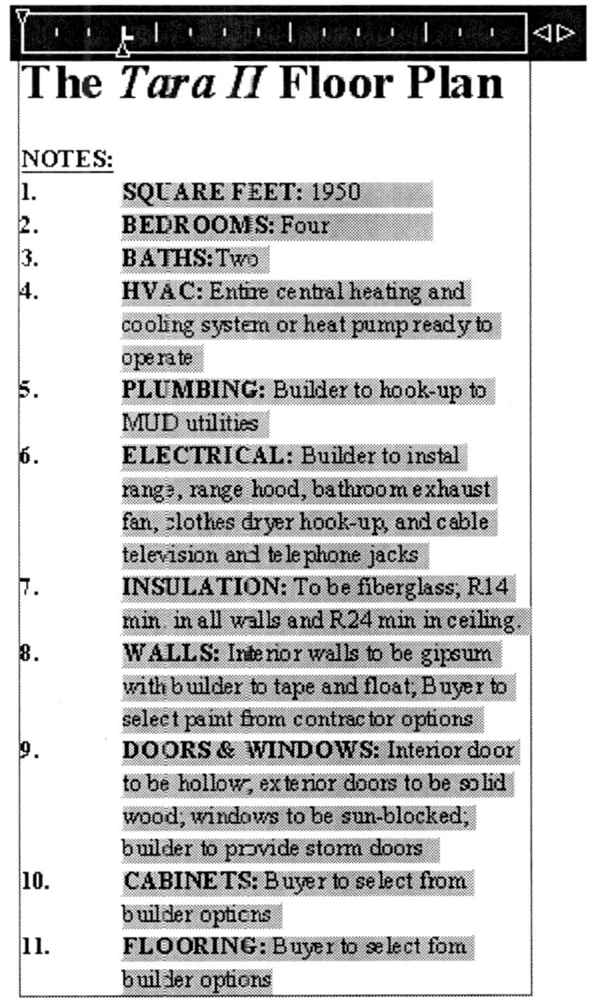

## 13.1.2: Editing Multiline Text

22. Complete the procedure [OK]. Your notes now look like this.

# The *Tara II* Floor Plan

NOTES:
1. **SQUARE FEET:** 1950
2. **BEDROOMS:** Four
3. **BATHS:** Two
4. **HVAC:** Entire central heating and cooling system or heat pump ready to operate
5. **PLUMBING:** Builder to hook-up to MUD utilities
6. **ELECTRICAL:** Builder to instal range, range hood, bathroom exhaust fan, clothes dryer hook-up, and cable television and telephone jacks
7. **INSULATION:** To be fiberglass; R14 min. in all walls and R24 min in ceiling.
8. **WALLS:** Interior walls to be gipsum with builder to tape and float; Buyer to select paint from contractor options
9. **DOORS & WINDOWS:** Interior door to be hollow; exterior doors to be solid wood; windows to be sun-blocked; builder to provide storm doors
10. **CABINETS:** Buyer to select from builder options
11. **FLOORING:** Buyer to select fom builder options

25. Save the drawing but don't exit.

**Command: *qsave***

> Note that you can also select large pieces of text by placing the cursor on one end of the text to select, holding down the left mouse button, and dragging to the other end.
>
> Note also that Windows standard hotkeys also work in the Multiline Text Editor. For example, CTRL+B will embolden selected text, CTRL+I will italicize selected text, etc.

Now that you've seen the ease with which you can edit multiline text, what do you think? Let's see what else the Multiline Text Editor can do.

| Do This: 13.1.3 | Editing Multiline Text with the Cursor Menu |
|---|---|

I. Be sure your are in the *MyFlrPln13* (or *FlrPln13*) drawing the C:\Steps\Lesson13 folder. If not, please open it now.

II. Follow these steps.

## 13.1.3: Editing with the Cursor Menu

1. Return to the Multiline Text Editor. (Select the existing text.)

**Command: *ed***

2. We want to move a section of text from one location to another. Let's take Note #4 and place it just above Note #9. First select Note #4.

### 13.1.3: Editing with the Cursor Menu

3. Right-click anywhere in the text area of the Multiline Text Editor dialog box. AutoCAD will present the cursor menu. Select **Cut** in the second frame.

The selected text disappears. (Notice that AutoCAD automatically adjusts the numbering.)

4. Move your cursor just to the left of the word **CABINETS** (now Note #9).

5. Right-click anywhere in the text area. Notice that **Cut** and **Copy** are grayed-out. These options aren't available unless some text has been selected.

Pick **Paste** on the menu. The **HVAC** text appears.

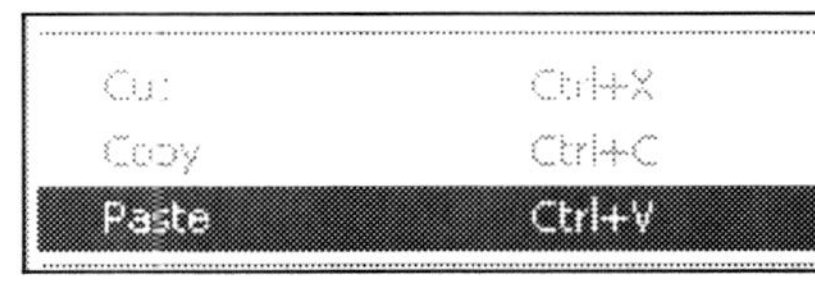


6. Save your drawing but don't exit.

**Command:** ***qsave***

> The same cursor menu technique will work for copying text rather than moving (cutting and pasting) it. You can also use the CTRL+C and CTRL+V method to copy and paste (or the CTRL+X and then CTRL+V method to cut and paste). This is actually a Windows redundancy carried into AutoCAD. It seems that nobody wants to tie you to a single approach for doing something!

Next, we'll look at the Search and Replace capabilities of the Multiline Text Editor. You'll really like this! The **Search** tool helps you find specific text. In a large group of notes, this is a real timesaver. The **Replace** tool allows you to replace that text with something new.

| **Do This: 13.1.4** | **Search and Replace Text** |
|---|---|

I. Be sure your are in the *MyFlrPln13* (or *FlrPln13*) drawing the C:\Steps\Lesson13 folder. If not, please open it now.

II. Follow these steps.

### 13.1.4: Search and Replace Text

1. Return to the Multiline Text Editor. (Select the existing text.)

**Command:** ***ed***

2. Pick **Find and Replace** option from the sixth frame of the cursor menu. AutoCAD presents the Find and Replace dialog box.

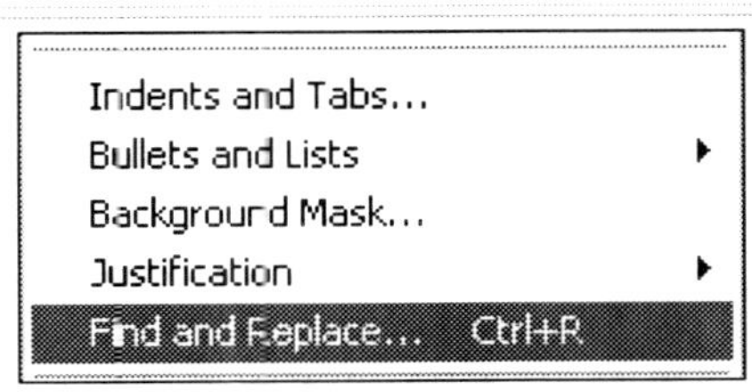

## 13.1.4: Search and Replace Text

3. Type ***builder*** into the box next to the words **Find what**. Then type ***contractor*** in the box next to the words **Replace with** as shown.

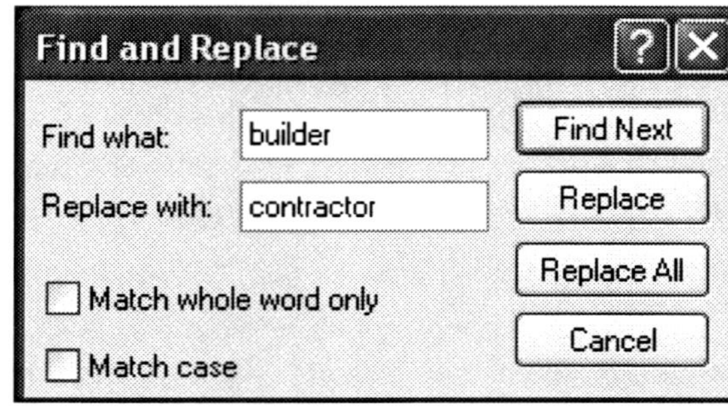


4. If we were searching for a word but didn't plan to replace that word with another, we would simply pick the **Find Next** button. But since we want to replace all instances of the word *builder* with the word *contractor*, we'll pick the **Replace All** button [Replace All]. (We won't need the filters at the bottom of the dialog box for this search.)

5. AutoCAD presents an information box telling you that it has completed its search. Pick the **OK** button [OK] to close that box, the **Exit** button [X] to close the Find and Replace dialog box, and then the **OK** button to close the Multiline Text Editor [OK]. Complete the command. The text now looks like this.

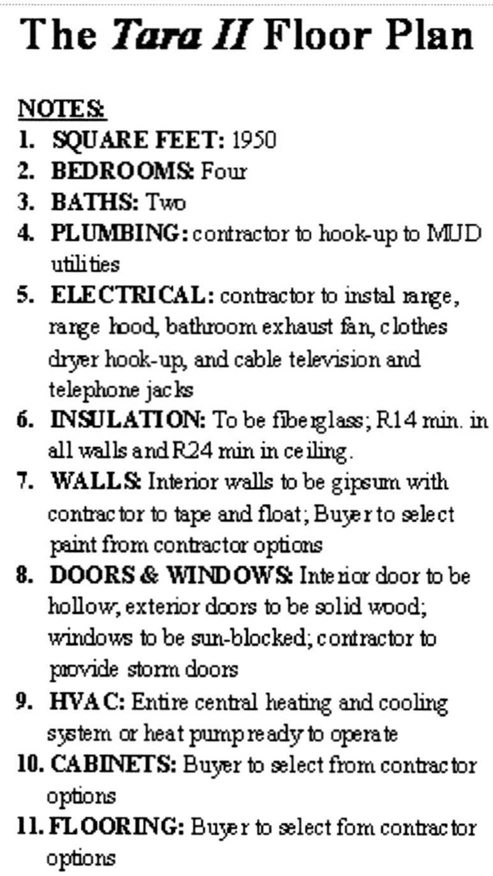
The *Tara II* Floor Plan

NOTES:
1. **SQUARE FEET:** 1950
2. **BEDROOMS:** Four
3. **BATHS:** Two
4. **PLUMBING:** contractor to hook-up to MUD utilities
5. **ELECTRICAL:** contractor to instal range, range hood, bathroom exhaust fan, clothes dryer hook-up, and cable television and telephone jacks
6. **INSULATION:** To be fiberglass; R14 min. in all walls and R24 min in ceiling.
7. **WALLS:** Interior walls to be gipsum with contractor to tape and float; Buyer to select paint from contractor options
8. **DOORS & WINDOWS:** Interior door to be hollow, exterior doors to be solid wood; windows to be sun-blocked; contractor to provide storm doors
9. **HVAC:** Entire central heating and cooling system or heat pump ready to operate
10. **CABINETS:** Buyer to select from contractor options
11. **FLOORING:** Buyer to select fom contractor options

6. Save your drawing [save icon] but don't exit.

**Command:** ***qsave***

Before we finish with the Multiline Text Editor, let's take a quick look at that **Symbol** option. As I mentioned earlier, this comes in handy when you want to insert something a bit out of the ordinary.

| Do This: 13.1.5 | Symbol Insertion |
|---|---|

I. Be sure you're in the *MyFlrPln13* (or *FlrPln13*) drawing the C:\Steps\Lesson13 folder. If not, please open it now.

II. Follow these steps.

## 13.1.5: SYMBOL INSERTION

1. Return to the Multiline Text Editor. (Select the existing text.)

   **Command:** ***ed***

2. Move your cursor to the blank area just below **The *Tara II* Floor Plan**.

3. Pick the **Symbol** button on the Options toolbar.

4. Select the **Other** option. AutoCAD presents the Windows Character Map.

5. Pick the down arrow in the **Font** control box. Scroll until you find the **Wingdings** font; select it.

6. Now select the happy face ☺ (it's located in different places depending upon the operating system you're using).

7. Pick the **Select** button 13 times, and then the **Copy** button. Windows copies the string to the clipboard.

8. Close the Character Map.

9. With the cursor located on the blank line below the title, paste the clipboard image. (You can use the cursor menu we've discussed, or use the Windows CTRL+V method.)

10. Complete the command OK. The upper part of your text now looks like this.

11. Save your drawing but don't exit.

    **Command:** ***qsave***

**The *Tara II* Floor Plan**

☺☺☺☺☺☺☺☺☺☺☺☺☺

NOTES:
1. **SQUARE FEET:** 1950
2. **BEDROOMS:** Four
3. **BATHS:** Two

## 13.2 Okay I Typed It, but I Don't Know If It's Right! – AutoCAD's *Spell* Command

The next aspect of text we must consider is AutoCAD's spell checker. This remarkably simple tool can provide an inestimable service to those of us who never made it to the national spelling bee. It works in much the same way that spell checkers work in the major word processors.

The command sequence is simply:

**Command:** ***spell*** **(or** ***sp*****)**

**Select objects:** ***[select the text object or objects]***

**Select objects:** ***[enter to complete the selection set and open the Check Spelling dialog box]***

> Rather than select individual pieces of text or multiline text, you can type ***all*** at the **Select objects** prompt. AutoCAD will then spell-check the entire drawing.

After you select some text, AutoCAD presents the Check Spelling dialog box (Figure 13.012). This box offers the same options as most spell checkers, but it also gives you the opportunity to change dictionaries. This can prove quite valuable to the project. It means that the project lead can assign a single person to control the project dictionary (usually that wonderful typist – the project secretary). That person creates the custom dictionary using a word processor. The secretary must then save the dictionary with a *.cus* extension.

AutoCAD needs this extension for recognition but your word processor should have no problem reading the file as well. (See the *Extra Steps* in Section 13.4 for a procedure to set up a custom dictionary.)

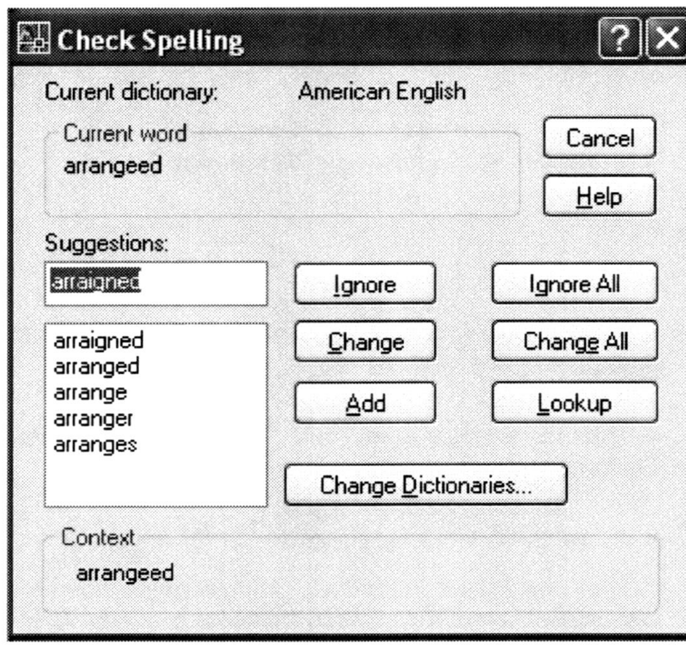


Figure 13.012

Let's take a look at the Spell Checker.

- If AutoCAD finds a word that isn't in its dictionary, it presents the word in the **Current word** frame. It makes a few suggestions as to what word it thinks you may be trying to spell in the **Suggestions** list box with the word it thinks that you're most likely trying to spell highlighted in the text box.
- You can pick a button to **Ignore** this word or **Ignore All** (ignore the word throughout this checking session), **Change** the word or **Change All** (change it every time it occurs in the selected text), or **Add** it to the dictionary.
- You can also type a word into the **Suggestions** text box and pick the **Lookup** button to have AutoCAD check its spelling.
- If you want to use the project dictionary, the **Change Dictionaries** button provides that opportunity.

Let's take a look at AutoCAD's Spell Checker in action.

> The ***Spell*** command is also available in the Tools pull-down menu. Follow this path:
> *Tools - Spelling*

| Do This: 13.2.1 | Checking Your Spelling |
|---|---|

I. Be sure you're in the *MyFlrPln13* (or *FlrPln13*) drawing the C:\Steps\Lesson13 folder. If not, please open it now.

II. Follow these steps.

## 13.2.1: CHECKING YOUR SPELLING

1. Enter the ***Spell*** command by typing ***spell*** or ***sp*** at the command prompt.

    **Command:** ***sp***

2. The spell checker works on all types of text in the drawing. Select the Multiline Text we've been using and confirm your selection.

    **Select objects:**

    **Select objects:** ***[enter]***

AutoCAD presents the Check Spelling dialog box (Figure 13.012). It identifies **Tara** as being misspelled.

3. We know that **Tara** is spelled correctly and will probably occur again somewhere in the project documents, so let's add it to the dictionary. Pick the **Add** button 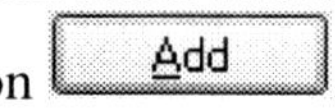

.

4. (Note: AutoCAD may identify our special font as a series of Js and indicate that it's misspelled. If so, pick the **Ignore** button.)

Next AutoCAD finds **instal**. This was probably a typo so let's just pick the **Change** button 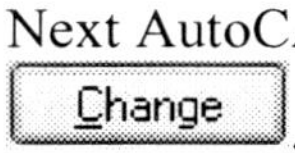

.

5. Now AutoCAD finds the abbreviation **min**. Normally, we would put a period after an abbreviation, but the project standard is to omit the period. So we'll **Ignore** 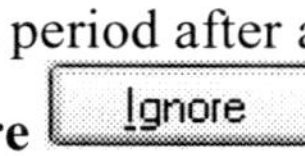

this prompt.

6. Change 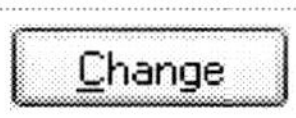

**gipsum** to **gypsum**.

7. **Ignore All** 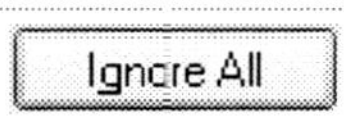

occurrences of the abbreviation **HVAC**.

8. It looks like we omitted the **r** in the word **from**. Scroll down the list box to find the correct spelling at the bottom of the list. Pick on it and notice that it appears in the text box above.

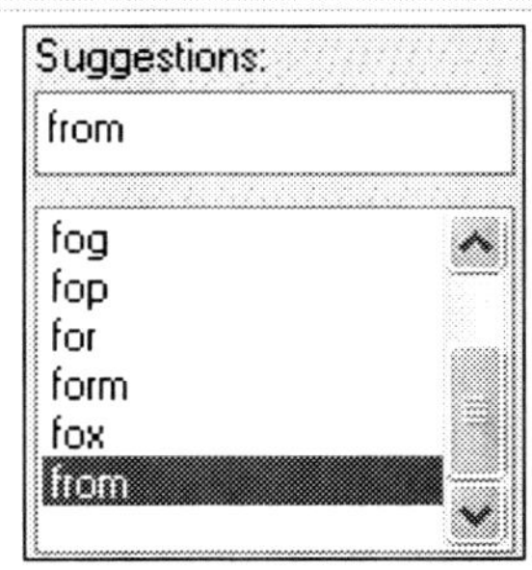


9. Pick the **Change** button 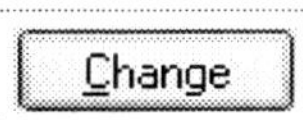

to fix the word.

10. Now AutoCAD presents a message box telling you that is has completed the spell check. Pick the **OK** button to complete the procedure.

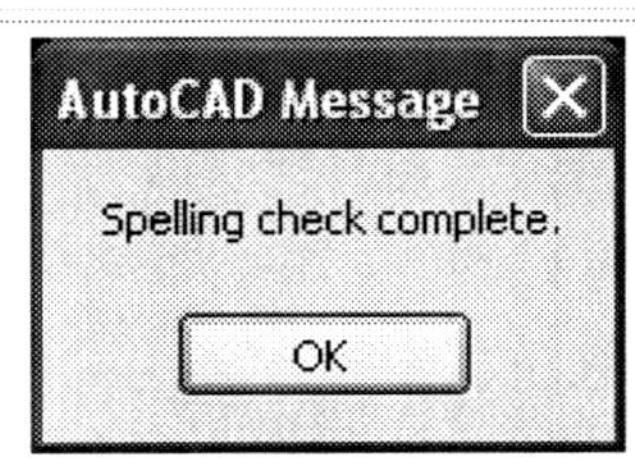


11. Save your drawing  but don't exit.

    **Command:** ***qsave***

Now complete the text as seen in Figure 13.013 as follows:

- Place all text on the **Text** layer.
- Text heights are: 12", 9", and 6".
- Put your own information into the title block (school name, your name, date, etc.).
- When you've finished, save the drawing as *MyFlrPln15* in the C:\Steps\Lesson15 folder.

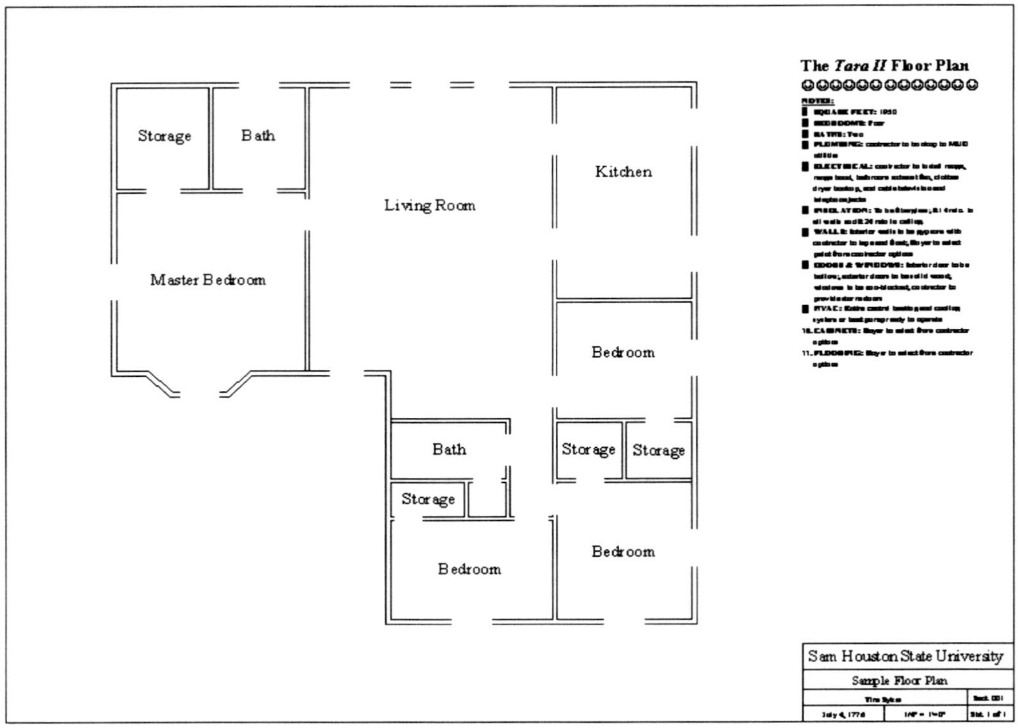


Figure 13.013

## 13.3 Find and Replace – without the Multiline Text Editor

Here's a piece of good news for those who spend a lot of time using text (rather than multiline text) for callouts – as with the spell checker, the Multiline Text Editor isn't required to perform a *Find and Replace.* The ***Find*** command will work regardless of the type of text it must search. It presents the Find and Replace dialog box (Figure 13.014).

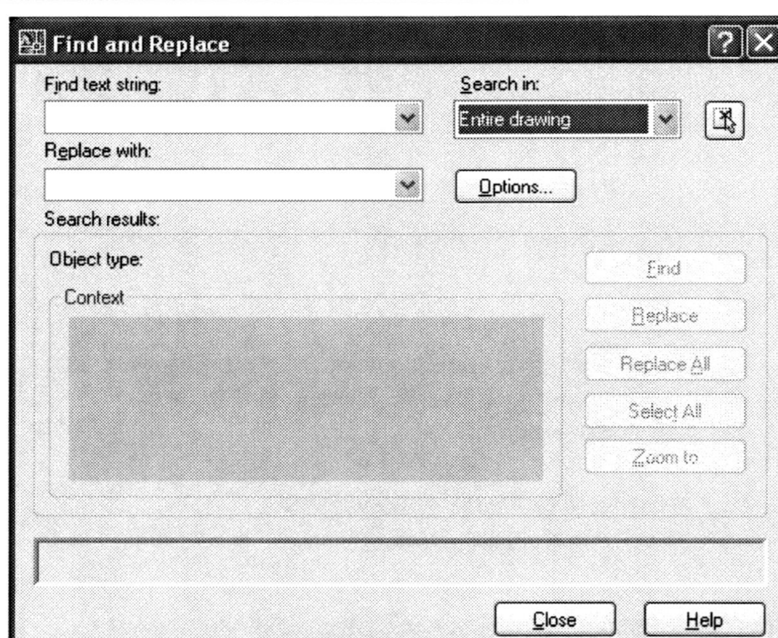


Figure 13.014

Let's take a look.

- Place the text you wish to locate in the **Find text string** control box. Text that has been previously entered can be selected using the down arrow.
- Place the new text (the text you want to use as a replacement for found text) in the **Replace with** control box. Again, text that has been previously entered can be selected using the down arrow.

- Use the **Search in** control box or the **Select objects** button (next to the control box) to define your search area. (That is, where do you want to search.)
- The **Options** button presents the Find and Replace Options dialog box (Figure 13.015). Here you can filter the selection set to include certain types of text. A great benefit is the inclusion of the **Block Attribute Value** option that allows you to find and replace attribute values (more on attributes in Lesson 20).

  You can also tell AutoCAD to **Match case** (match capital letters in the text) or **Find whole words only** in the search.
- The **Search results** frame presents the same buttons you found in the spell checker with the addition of a **Zoom to** button. I'm sure you guessed that this button will cause AutoCAD to zoom in to the located text.

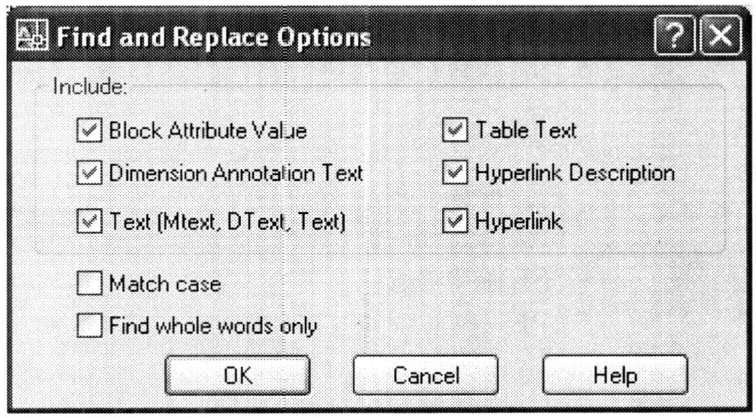


Figure 13.015

Let's try the Find and Replace tool.

| Do This: 13.3.1 | Find and Replace Text without the Multiline Text Editor |
|---|---|

I. Be sure your are in the *MyFlrPln13* (or *FlrPln13*) drawing the C:\Steps\Lesson13 folder. If not, please open it now. If you haven't finished this drawing, open *FlrPln13.3.1.dwg* in the same folder.

II. Zoom all.

III. Follow these steps.

| 13.3.1: FIND AND REPLACE TEXT WITHOUT THE EDITOR | |
|---|---|
| 1. Enter the ***Find*** command. Alternately, you can pick **Find** from the cursor menu when right-clicking in the graphics area.<br>**Command: *find*** | |
| 2. Let's replace all the **Storage** call-outs with the word ***Closet***. | 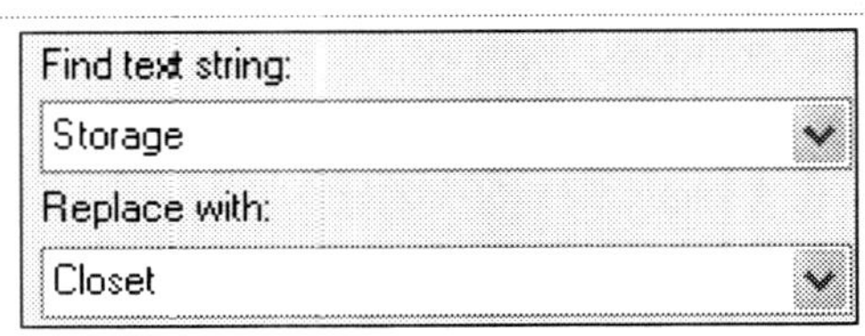 |
| 3. Tell AutoCAD to **Replace All** 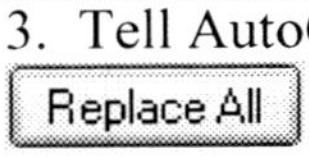 occurrences of the word **Storage**. AutoCAD responds in the message box as shown. | 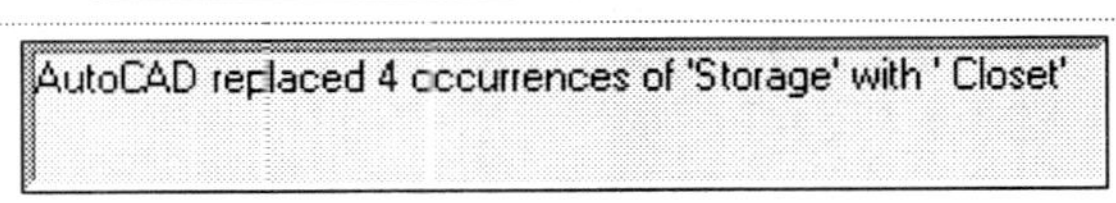 |
| 4. Let's take a look at the **Zoom to** feature. Enter the word ***Sample*** in the **Find text string** box. | 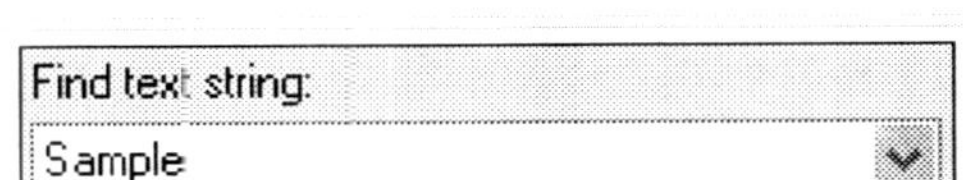 |

### 13.3.1: Find and Replace Text without the Editor

5. Pick the **Find** button [Find].

6. AutoCAD reports that it found the word as part of a string that reads: *Sample Floor Plan*. Let's seen where that string occurs. Pick the **Zoom to** button [Zoom to].

7. AutoCAD zooms to the title block and moves the Find and Replace dialog box so that you can see the text (how nice!). Pick the **Close** button [Close] to complete the procedure.

8. Zoom all to see the results of your work and then save the drawing.
   **Command: *qsave***

## 13.4 Extra Steps

You can impress the boss by being the only one on the contract capable of setting up the project to use a shared dictionary. Here's how to tell AutoCAD to use a custom dictionary.

1. On the Check Spelling dialog box you encountered in Section 13.2, pick the **Change Dictionaries** button. AutoCAD presents a Change Dictionaries dialog box.
2. Pick the **Browse** button. AutoCAD presents a Windows standard Open Files dialog box (this one is called Select Custom Dictionary). Open the *Custom.cus* file in the C:\Steps\Lesson13 folder.
3. AutoCAD returns to the Change Dictionaries dialog box. Pick the **Apply & Close** button.
4. AutoCAD returns to the Check Spelling dialog box. You can now continue with the spell check or exit the dialog box.

This little trick is guaranteed to impress the boss and save quite a bit of project time. Good luck!

## 13.5 What Have We Learned?

*Items covered in this lesson include:*

- *Multiline text creation and editing*
- *AutoCAD's spell checker*
- *How to find and replace text*
- *Commands:*
  - ***MText***
  - ***Spell***
  - ***Find***

If you were already familiar with word processors, this has probably been a fairly easy – if not downright boring – lesson. The only new thing for you would have been the *Extra Steps* part of the lesson where we learned to share dictionaries.

But if you weren't familiar with word processors, this has probably been one of the easier – almost fun – lessons.

The decision to use ***MText*** or ***Text*** won't always be an easy one. ***Text*** is less complicated (once the styles have been created); ***MText*** has more capabilities. I would suggest that any time it's a toss up, go with the easier ***Text*** (assuming, of course, that the style you need has already been created). AutoCAD, however, tends to favor the ***MText*** command. So it's really a question of preference. Do what is easier for you.

Take a break so that you'll be fresh when you start the next lesson. In Lesson 14, we'll look at dimensioning!

## 13.6 Exercises

1. Open the *MyHolder2.dwg* file you created in Lesson11. It's in the C:\Steps\Lesson11 folder. (Alternately, you can use the *holder13.dwg* in the C:\Steps\Lesson13 folder.) Create the notes shown at right.
   1.1. Use the Times New Roman font.
   1.2. Use a text height of 1/8".
   1.3. The width of the text box is 3.25".
   1.4. Save the drawing as *MyHolder13.dwg* in the C:\Steps\Lesson13 folder.

**Notes:**
1. All materials to be hot dipped galvanized steel.
2. Tube to be $\frac{3}{4}$"Ø Sch. 40 pipe.
3. Slots to be clean and filed.
4. Paint in accordance with HI spec. #HDGPS10302871.
5. All dimensions are ±.002".
6. Product to be stamped below with product code and model number: HSV5-Mod2A17.
7. Product to be stamped below with serial number.
8. Serial numbers to be sequential beginning with the number: SN001001.

2. Open the *MyDirections.dwg* file you created in Lesson12. It's in the C:\Steps\Lesson13 folder. (Alternately, you can use the *directions2.dwg* file in the C:\Steps\Lesson13 folder.) Create the notes shown at right.
   2.1. Find the arrows at top in the Wingdings font. Make them 0.15" in height.
   2.2. Find the skull and crossbones images at the bottom in the Wingdings font. Make them 0.25" in height.
   2.3. All other text uses the Times New Roman font at a height of 0.125".
   2.4. The width of the text box is 2.25".
   2.5. Save the drawing as *MyDirections2.dwg* in the C:\Steps\Lesson13 folder.

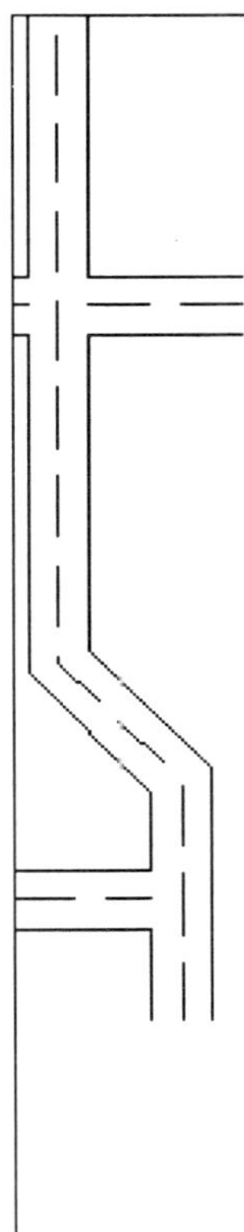

↑↓↖↗↙↘↑↓↖↗↙↘

**Getting There**

Slide eerily south on *Crane*, quietly sneaking up on *Ichobod*. Quickly now, turn right before the headless horseman sees you! Whew! You made it!

You probably won't see the *Ghostly Drive* till it's too late, so turn and ooze down the *Vampire Lane* (watch for low flying bats).

Ever so cautiously now, take a left on *Spooky St.* Don't go too far - people have gone down the *Graveyard Way* and never returned!

We're at the end of *Spooky St.* Park anywhere. Com'n in (just ignore the hooting of the owls)!

☠☠☠☠☠☠☠☠☠☠

*For more exercises related to Lesson 13, please see Lesson 13 in AutoCAD 2007: One Step at a Time – Workbook.*

## 13.7 For Web-Based Review Questions, visit: http://www.uneedcad.com/2007/Files/07R13.pdf

# Lesson 14

Following this lesson, you will:

- ✓ *Know how to create dimensions in AutoCAD using a host of dimensioning commands*
- ✓ *Know the difference between associative and normal dimensions*
- ✓ *Know how to edit dimensions using AutoCAD's* ***Dimedit*** *and* ***Dimtedit*** *commands*
- ✓ *Know how to dimension an isometric*

# Basic Dimensioning

*Creating dimensions on a drawing board requires a certain amount of expertise, a bit of patience, a scale, a calculator, and a good eye. If the dimension doesn't fit between dimension lines just right, the drafter can always scrunch it in a bit. If the drafter is experienced, he or she can often do this without the results being flagrantly noticeable. The board drafter can also cheat on a dimension fairly easily. Indeed, the company for which I worked in the early eighties maintained a 3" plus or minus tolerance for dimensioning.*

*AutoCAD dimensioning also requires a certain amount of expertise. But in contrast to board work, the CAD operator needs a lot of patience, no scale or calculator (AutoCAD will perform the calculations), and AutoCAD's "eye" for precision. If a dimension doesn't fit between dimension lines just right, some (often) complex maneuvers are required to reposition it. You can cheat on a dimension fairly easily, but it involves overriding AutoCAD's precision and is rarely a good idea.*

*AutoCAD's dimensioning tools come in three types: Dimension Creation, Dimension Editing, and Dimension Customization.*

*In the dimension Creation category, AutoCAD provides several different dimensioning commands and a* ***Leader*** *command. Use these to actually draw the dimensions.*

*The Editing category includes two dimension-editing commands. Use these to change, reposition, or reorient the dimension.*

*The Customization category is one that'll allow you to create dimension styles. Creating dimension styles involves several tabs of a dialog box for each style you create. You'll use these tabs to set at least 60 dimension variables (dimvars).*

*But as complex as dimensioning is, it's not as complicated as it seems! We'll cover the Creation and Editing categories in this lesson. We'll save Customization for Lesson 15.*

*Let's get right to it!*

## 14.1 First, Some Terminology

If you're an experienced drafter, you may already be familiar with dimension terminology. But I've provided the drawing in Figure 14.001 for the novice (and as a review for those who've been drafting for so long that dimensioning has become second nature – even though the textbook terminology has been long forgotten).

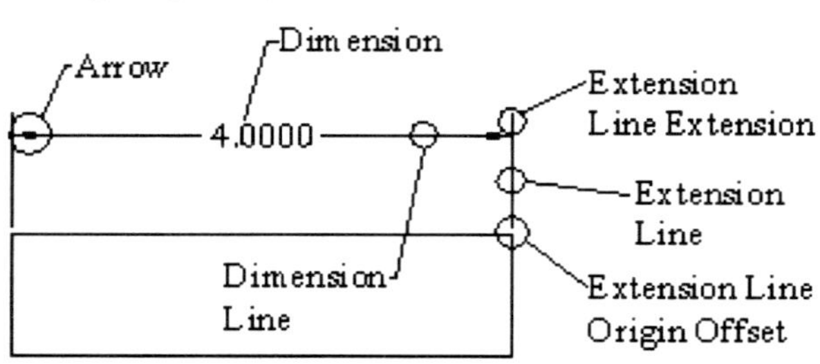


Figure 14.001

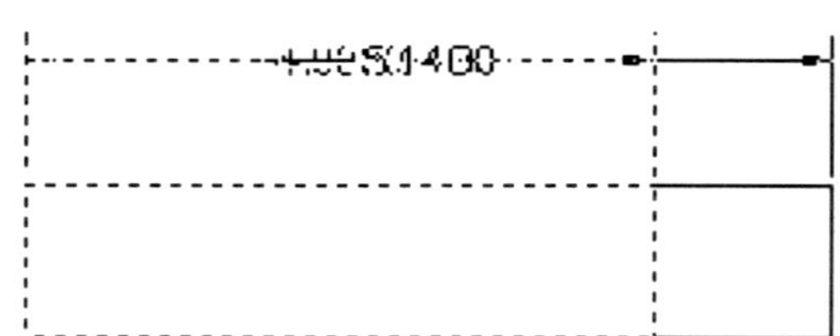

Figure 14.002

The dimension shown in this drawing, and those used throughout this lesson, use AutoCAD defaults for everything from location of the **Dimension** to the size of the **Extension Line Origin Offset**. You can see that AutoCAD uses **Arrows** by default rather than the slashes more often seen in architectural drafting. AutoCAD also defaults to decimal units (regardless of the units the drawing has been set up to use), a 0.18" text height, a 0.18" **Extension Line Extension** and **Arrow** length, and an **Extension Line Origin Offset** of 0.0625".

A new term with which you should become familiar is *Associative*. Associative dimensions are tied to the objects being dimensioned. As you stretch or move those objects, the dimension will change or move with the object. (Notice the dimension as the box is stretched in Figure 14.002.) Additionally, when associative dimensioning is active, AutoCAD uses true dimensions and doesn't prompt for verification.

But perhaps the most important thing to remember about associative dimensioning is that, like polylines and splines, associative dimensions behave as a single object. That is, a single pick will select the dimension for erasure or modification. The problem with this lies in the way the single dimension object responds to modification commands like ***Break*** and ***Trim***. Simply put, you can't break or trim the extension lines to allow room for text. The experienced CAD operator, like the experienced draftsman, knows that this is often necessary in a crowded drawing.

The **DimAssoc** system variable controls the behavior of both Associative and *Normal* Dimensions. There are three settings.

- Dimensions created with a **DimAssoc** value of **2** (the default) will be fully (truly) associative. That is, AutoCAD will invisibly connect the dimension to the dimensioned object. When you move or modify the object, the dimension will adjust accordingly. Treat these dimensions as single objects (much like polylines).
- Technically, dimensions created with a **DimAssoc** value of **1** will not be associative, although they'll behave as though they were. A setting of **1** means that AutoCAD actually associates the dimensions with definition points (*defpoints*) placed automatically at the extension line origin (see Figure 14.001). For AutoCAD to adjust the dimension when you modify the object, you must include the defpoints in the modification. You should also consider these dimensions to be single objects.
- AutoCAD will insert dimensions created with a **DimAssoc** value of **0** in an "exploded" format. That is, dimensions won't be associated with the object being dimensioned. We call these dimensions non-associative or *normal* dimensions. They are *not* single objects. Treat them as individual lines, text, and arrowheads.

> To convert from associative to normal, ***explode*** the dimension (just as you exploded a polyline into lines). You'll then find it necessary to change the layer of the separate objects to the dimension layer and the color of the object to **ByLayer**.

When associative dimensions were used in all releases prior to 2002, AutoCAD employed the defpoints method. To make legacy dimensions – dimensions created in earlier releases of AutoCAD – truly associative, use the ***DimReAssociate*** command. It looks like this:

**Command:** ***dimreassociate***

**Select dimensions to reassociate ...**

**Select objects:** ***[select the dimension object(s)]***

**Select objects:** ***[enter to complete the selection set]***

**Specify first extension line origin or [Select object] <next>:** ***[AutoCAD will identify it for you and you can accept it, or you can pick the first extension line origin]***

**Specify second extension line origin <next>:** ***[again, AutoCAD will identify it for you and you can accept it, or you can pick the second extension line origin]***

AutoCAD provides two additional commands to assist you with associative dimensions:

- ***DimDisAssociate*** allows you to change the type of association from true (a **DimAssoc** setting of **2**) to the defpoints method (a **DimAssoc** setting of **1**). Use the ***DimReAssociate*** command to convert the other way.
- Use ***DimRegen*** to regenerate just the associative dimensions in a drawing (without regenerating other objects).

Because of their single-object nature, associative dimensions required special modification tools, which we'll discuss later in this lesson. Unlike associative dimensioning, AutoCAD creates normal dimensions as separate objects (lines, arrow, text, etc.). Therefore, you can break or trim the extension lines as needed. Normal dimensioning requires that you manually update the dimension when you edit the objects dimensioned. In other words, normal dimensions won't automatically update as the object is stretched. Additionally, although normal dimensioning reads the distance between the extension lines just as associative dimensioning does, AutoCAD will automatically prompt you with the true dimension and give you the opportunity to override it with another number.

See the following chart for a comparison of associative, defpoints, and normal dimensions.

| MODIFICATION | ASSOCIATIVE OR DEFPOINT DIMENSION | NORMAL DIMENSION |
|---|---|---|
| Dimension will automatically update when stretched | Yes | No |
| Extension lines can be trimmed or broken to allow room for text in a crowded drawing | No | Yes |
| Automatically prompts to allow the true dimension to be overridden | No | Yes |

The CAD coordinator for the job (the guru) and the project manager will usually decide the question of which type of dimension to use. The CAD operator should check with one of them before entering the wrong type of dimension since, although it can be tedious to convert from associative to normal, you can't convert the other way at all!

## 14.2 Dimension Creation: Dimension Commands

One of the first things I tell my students when we study dimensioning is to use the Dimension toolbar whenever possible. AutoCAD's dimension commands can be difficult to remember, but the toolbar has pictures to show what each does. I suggest activating the Dimension toolbar and docking it above the graphics area. (See Lesson 1 if you need help).

### 14.2.1 Linear Dimensioning

The workhorse of AutoCAD dimensioning is the ***Dimlinear*** command. Use it to draw all your horizontal and vertical dimensions. The command sequence is

> **Command: *Dimlinear* (or *dli*)**
>
> **Specify first extension line origin or <select object>: *[select the first dimension point]***
>
> **Specify second extension line origin: *[select the second dimension line origin]***
>
> **Specify dimension line location or [Mtext/Text/Angle/Horizontal/Vertical/ Rotated]: *[locate the dimension line]***
>
> **Dimension text = X.XXXX *[AutoCAD reports the dimension value and places the dimension]***

- The first option AutoCAD presents is easily missed. AutoCAD prompts for the **First extension line origin**. Most users stop there, select the **first** and **second extension line origins** and proceed with the dimension. But the second part of that first prompt reads **or <select object>**. This option allows you to simply select an object to dimension. If you press ***enter*** and select an object, AutoCAD determines where the object's endpoints lie and places the extension lines accordingly.

The next set of options occurs after the extension line origins are located.

- AutoCAD will automatically determine if the dimension should be **Horizontal** or **Vertical** by the location of the crosshairs. However, you can override AutoCAD's determination by typing **H** or **V**.
- The **Text** and **MText** options allow you to override AutoCAD's automatic determination of the actual dimension.
  The dimension won't automatically update if you override here. I don't recommend doing this as it defeats the purpose of associative dimensioning.
- The **Angle** option allows you to rotate the dimension text for a better fit (Figure 14.003). This handy tool is far too often overlooked.

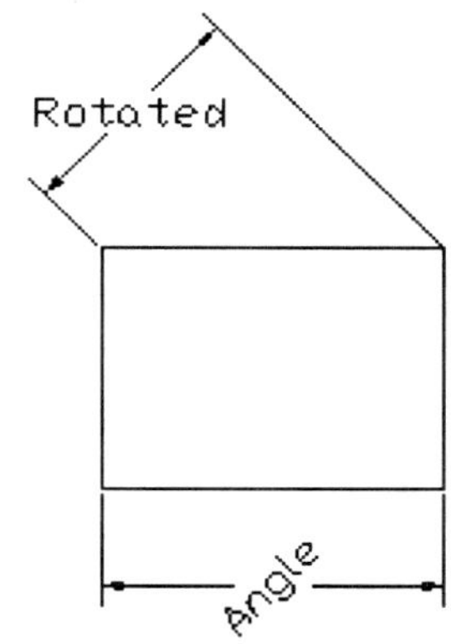

Figure 14.003

- The **Rotated** option allows you to measure a dimension at an angle to the object other than 90°. (See Figure 14.003 for a comparison of the **Angle** and **Rotated** options.)

Let's look at the ***Dimlinear*** command.

| All of the commands in this lesson can be found in the Dimension pull-down menu. |
|---|

| **Do This: 14.2.1.1** | **Linear Dimensioning** |
|---|---|

I. Open the *ex-linear.dwg* file the C:\Steps\Lesson14 folder. The drawing looks like Figure 14.004.

II. Follow these steps.

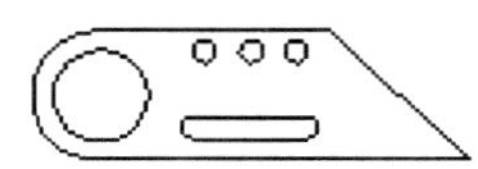
Figure 14.004

**14.2.1.1: LINEAR DIMENSIONING**

1. Enter the ***Dimlinear*** command. Alternately, you can pick the **Linear** button 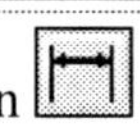 on the Dimension toolbar.

   **Command: *dli***

2. Pick the center of the circle at Point 1 …

   **Specify first extension line origin or <select object>: _cen of**

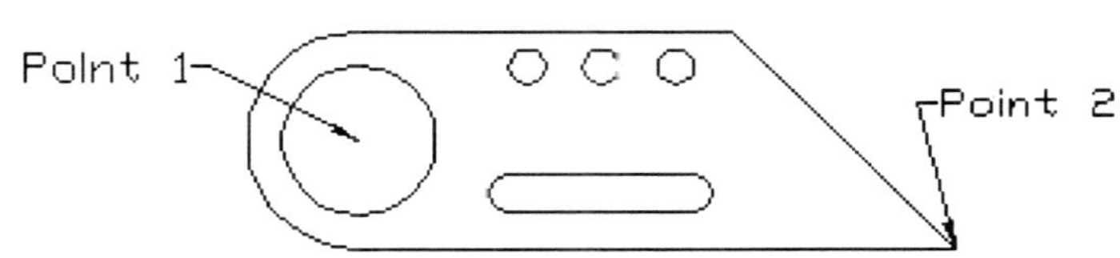


3. … then the endpoint at Point 2.

   **Specify second extension line origin: _endp of**

### 14.2.1.1: Linear Dimensioning

4. Locate the dimension line four grid points below the bottom line of the object.

   **Specify dimension line location or [Mtext/Text/Angle/ Horizontal/ Vertical/Rotated]:**

   **Dimension text = 8.0000**

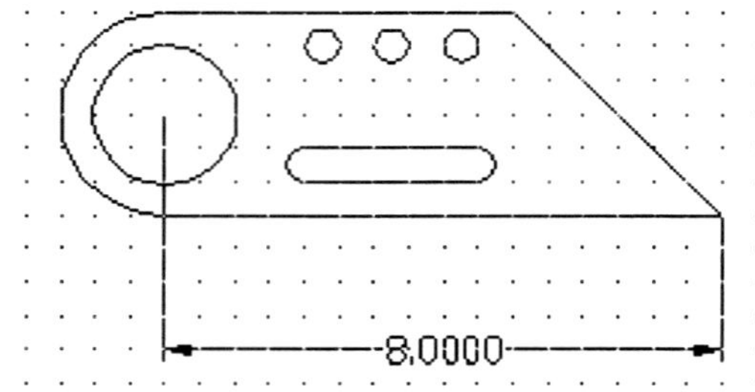


(Note: In many of these dimension examples, I've adjusted the size of the text and arrowheads for better viewing.)

5. Repeat the ***Dimlinear*** command.

   **Command:** ***[enter]***

6. Let's use the **select object** option.

   **Specify first extension line origin or <select object>:** ***[enter]***

7. Select the angled line on the right end of the object.

   **Select object to dimension:**

8. Pick a point four grid points to the right.

   **Specify dimension line location or [Mtext/Text/Angle/ Horizontal/ Vertical/Rotated]:**

   **Dimension text = 3.0000**

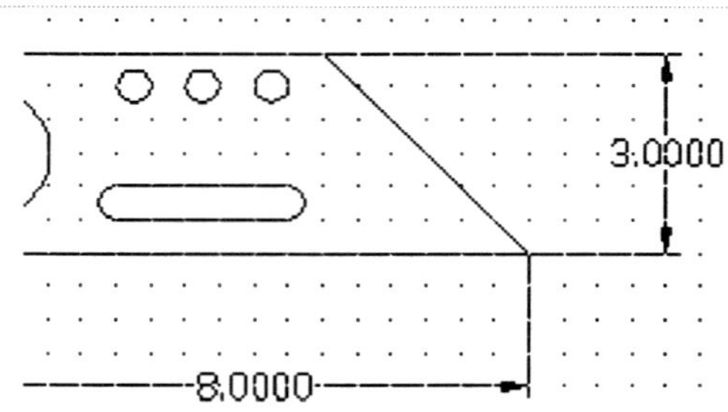


9. Save the drawing but don't exit.

   **Command:** ***qsave***

> You can use the Properties Palette (***Properties*** command) to change one or both extension lines to centerlines if you'd prefer them (at the circle, perhaps?).

## 14.2.2 Dimensioning Angles

Our next dimension command is ***Dimangular***. You'll use this to dimension angles as well as angular dimensions on circles and arcs. The command sequence for dimensioning an arc or circle is

**Command:** ***Dimangular*** **(or** ***dan*****)**

**Select arc, circle, line, or <specify vertex>:** ***[show AutoCAD what you want to dimension or hit enter to select the vertex first]***

**Specify second angle endpoint:** ***[this prompt appears only if a circle is being dimensioned]***

**Specify dimension arc line location or [Mtext/Text/Angle]:** ***[locate the dimension line]***

**Dimension text =** ***[AutoCAD reports and places the dimension]***

If you select a **line** at the first prompt, AutoCAD prompts:

**Select second line:**

Select a line that forms an angle with the first selected line, and then locate the dimension as prompted.

If you opt to select the vertex first, AutoCAD prompts:

**Specify angle vertex:** ***[select the vertex]***

**Specify first angle endpoint:** ***[select a point on the first line]***

**Specify second angle endpoint:** ***[select a point on the second line]***

The **MText**, **Text**, and **Angle** options are the same as in the ***Dimlinear*** command.

Let's look at the ***Dimangular*** command.

| Do This: 14.2.2.1 | Dimensioning Angles |
|---|---|

I. Be sure you're in the *Ex-Linear.dwg* file the C:\Steps\Lesson14 folder. If not, please open it now.

II. Follow these steps.

**14.2.2.1: DIMENSIONING ANGLES**

1. Enter the ***Dimangular*** command. Alternately, you can pick the **Angular** button 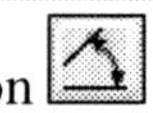 on the Dimension toolbar.

   **Command:** ***dan***

2. Select the arc on the left end of the object.

   **Select arc, circle, line, or <specify vertex>:**

3. Place the dimension at the end of the bottom linear dimension as shown.

   **Specify dimension arc line location or [MText/Text/Angle]:**

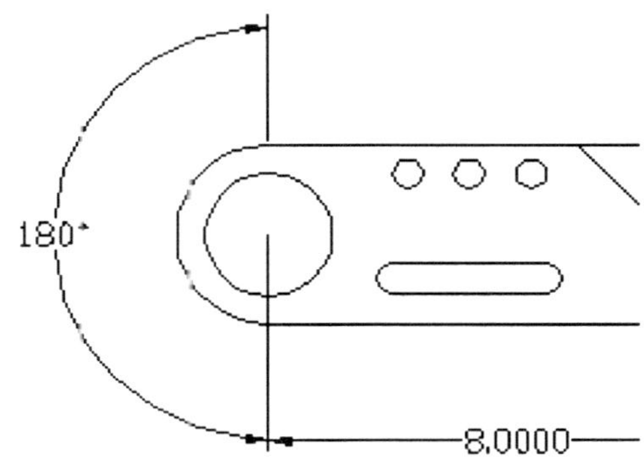


4. Now let's dimension the angle at the other end of the object. Repeat the command 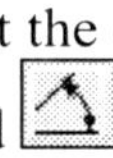.

   **Command:** ***[enter]***

5. Select the bottom line on the object …

   **Select arc, circle, line, or <specify vertex>:**

6. … then the angled line.

   **Select second line:**

7. Notice that the angle changes as you change the cursor position. Place the dimension line at the bottom arrow of the vertical dimension.

   **Specify dimension arc line location or [Mtext/Text/Angle]:**

   **Dimension text = 45**

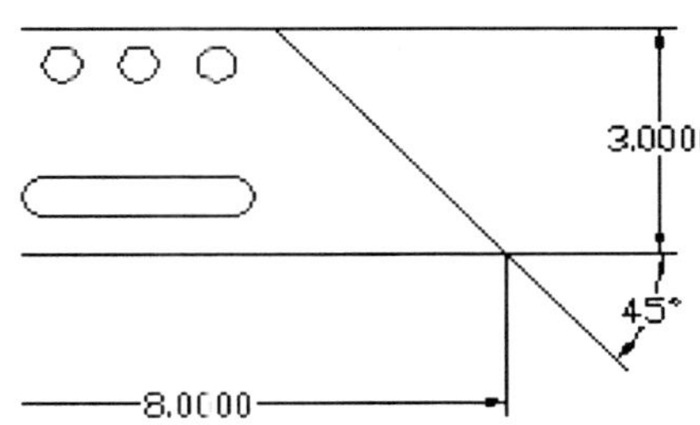


8. Save the drawing  but don't exit.

   **Command:** ***qsave***

| 14.2.3 | Dimensioning Radii and Diameters |
|---|---|

Very little difference separates dimensioning radii and dimensioning diameters. In fact, the command sequences are identical:

**Command:** ***dimradius*** **(or** ***dra*****)** **[or** ***dimdiameter*** **(or** ***ddi*****)]**

**Select arc or circle:** ***[show AutoCAD what you want to dimension]***
**Dimension text =** ***[AutoCAD reports the dimension]***
**Specify dimension line location or [Mtext/Text/Angle]:** ***[locate the dimension]***

AutoCAD will automatically place either a diameter symbol (**Ø**) or an **R** in front of the dimension to indicate what has been dimensioned.

You have one other option for placing radial dimensions – the *jogged* (or *foreshortened radius*) dimension. Here is the sequence:

**Command:** ***dimjogged*** **(or** ***jog*****)**
**Select arc or circle:** ***[select the arc or circle to dimension]***
**Specify center location override:** ***[locate the dimension in terms of distance from the arc]***
**Dimension text = 15.5322** ***[AutoCAD displays the dimension text]***
**Specify dimension line location or [Mtext/Text/Angle]:** ***[locate the dimension along the arc]***
**Specify jog location:** ***[locate the jog]***

Let's take a look.

| Do This: 14.2.3.1 | Dimensioning Diameters and Radii |
|---|---|

I. Be sure you're in the *Ex-Linear.dwg* file the C:\Steps\Lesson14 folder. If not, please open it now.

II. Follow these steps.

**14.2.3.1: DIMENSIONING DIAMETERS AND RADII**

1. Erase  the 180° arc dimension.

   **Command:** ***e***

2. Enter the ***Dimradius*** command. Alternately, you can pick the **Radius** button  on the Dimension toolbar.

   **Command:** ***dra***

3. Select the arc at the left end of the object.

   **Select arc or circle:**

4. Locate the dimension as shown.

   Notice that AutoCAD places the dimension and a *Center Mark* locating the center of the arc being dimensioned.

   **Specify dimension line location or [Mtext/Text/Angle]:**

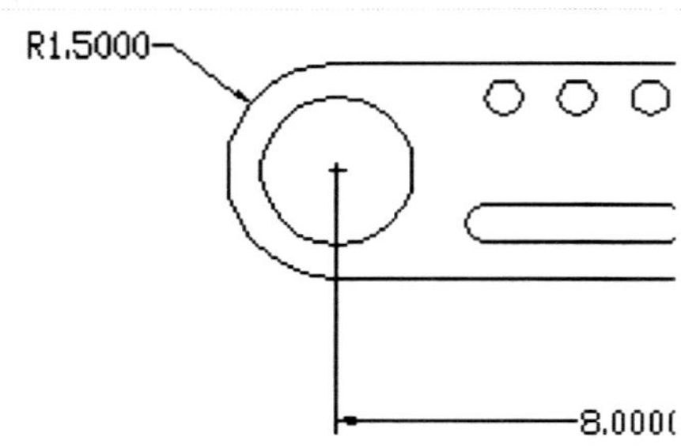


5. Enter the ***Dimdiameter*** command. Alternately, you can pick the **Diameter Dimension** button  on the Dimension toolbar.

   **Command:** ***ddi***

**14.2.3.1: DIMENSIONING DIAMETERS AND RADII**

6. Select the large circle to the left inside the object.

 **Select arc or circle:**

7. Place the dimension as shown.

 **Dimension text = 2.0616**

 **Specify dimension line location or [Mtext/Text/Angle]:**

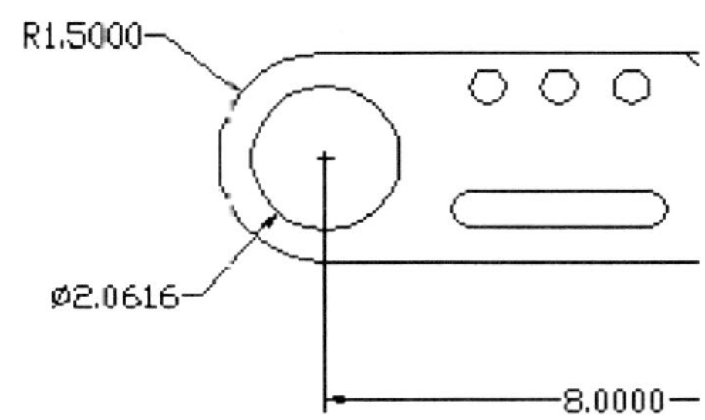


8. Now let's try a jogged dimension. Thaw the **OBJ2** layer. Notice the large arc above the object.

9. Enter the ***Dimjogged*** command. Alternately, you can pick the **Jogged** button  on the dimension toolbar.

 **Command:** ***jog***

10. Pick the new arc.

 **Select arc or circle:**

11. Locate your dimension as shown.

 **Specify center location override:**

 **Dimension text = 15.5322**

 **Specify dimension line location or [Mtext/Text/Angle]:**

 **Specify jog location:**

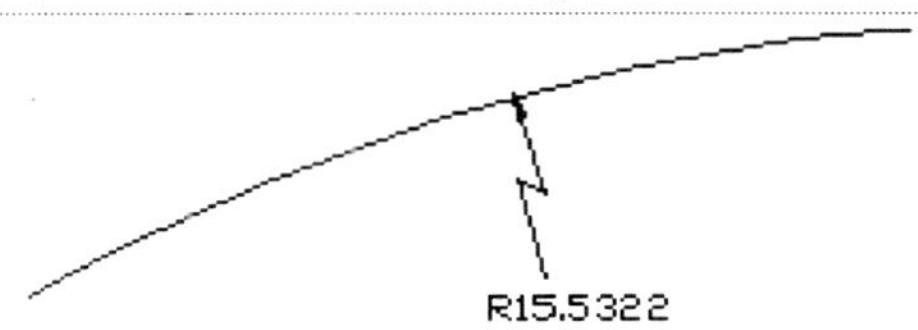


12. Undo 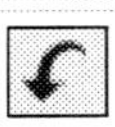 the last command and freeze the **OBJ2** layer.

 **Command:** ***u***

8. Save the drawing  but don't exit.

 **Command:** ***qsave***

## 14.2.4 Dimension Arc Lengths

You've seen two approaches to dimensioning arcs (Sections 14.2.2 and 14.2.3) – one dimensions the angle of the arc, the other dimensions the radius or diameter. These won't help, however, if you need to dimension the actual length of an arc. Luckily, AutoCAD provides a dimensioning tool specifically for this task. It's called, appropriately, ***DimArc***.

The command sequence is

 **Command:** ***dimarc*** **(or** ***dar*****)**

 **Select arc or polyline arc segment:** ***[select the arc to dimension]***

 **Specify arc length dimension location, or [Mtext/Text/Angle/Partial/Leader]:** ***[locate the dimension]***

 **Dimension text = X.XXXX**

By now, you're familiar with the first three options of the **location** prompt. **Mtext/Text/Angle** options provide the same function throughout the dimension commands. Let's look at the other two.

- **Partial** enables you to dimension between two points on an arc.
- The **Leader** option tells AutoCAD to provide a leader from the dimension text to the arc being dimensioned.

Okay, let's try the ***Dimarc*** command.

| Do This: 14.2.4.1 | Arc Length Dimensions |
|---|---|

I. Open the *ex-linear-Arc.dwg* file the C:\Steps\Lesson14 folder. The drawing looks just like the *ex-linear.dwg* file we've been using.

II. Follow these steps.

**14.2.4.1: ARC LENGTH DIMENSIONS**

1. Enter the ***Dimarc*** command. Alternately, you pick the **Arc Length** button 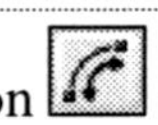 on the Dimension toolbar.

**Command: *dar***

2. Select the arc on the left end of the object.

**Select arc or polyline arc segment:**

3. Place the dimension as shown.

**Specify arc length dimension location, or [Mtext/Text/ Angle/ Partial/ Leader]:**

Notice that AutoCAD automatically inserts the arc symbol.

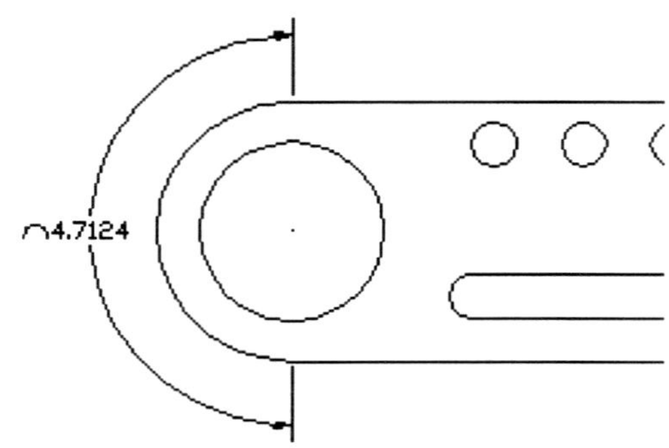


4. Erase  the dimension you created in Steps 1 through 3.

**Command: *e***

5. Thaw the **Markers** layer. Notice the nodes that appear on the arc. Let's dimension between these.

6. Repeat Steps 1 and 2.

**Command: *dimarc***

7. Tell AutoCAD to use the **Partial** option .


**Specify arc length dimension location, or [Mtext/Text/Angle/Partial/ Leader]: *p***

8. Dimension between the top and bottom nodes.

**Specify first point for arc length dimension:_nod of**

**Specify second point for arc length dimension:_nod of**

### 14.2.4.1: Arc Length Dimensions

9. Finally, locate the dimension as shown.

**Specify arc length dimension location, or [Mtext/Text/Angle/Partial]:**

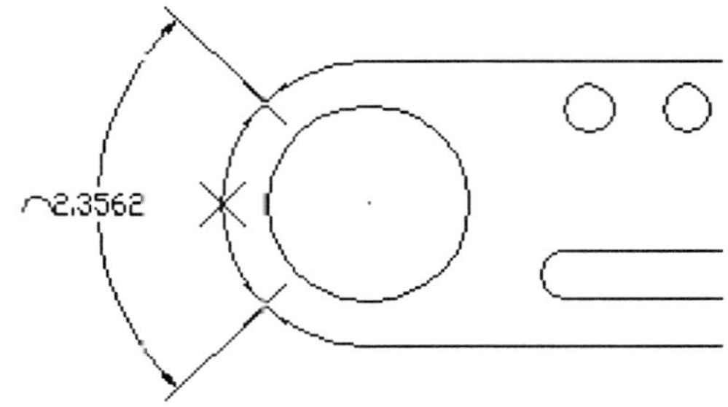


10. Erase the last dimension you created and freeze the **Markers** layer. Let's take a look at the **Leader** option.

**Command:** ***e***

11. Repeat Steps 1 and 2.

**Command:** ***dimarc***

12. Select the **Leader** option Leader.

**Specify arc length dimension location, or [Mtext/Text/Angle/ Partial/ Leader]:** ***l***

13. (Notice that the **Leader** option becomes the **No leader** option.) Place the dimension as shown.

**Specify arc length dimension location, or [Mtext/Text/ Angle/Partial/No leader]:**

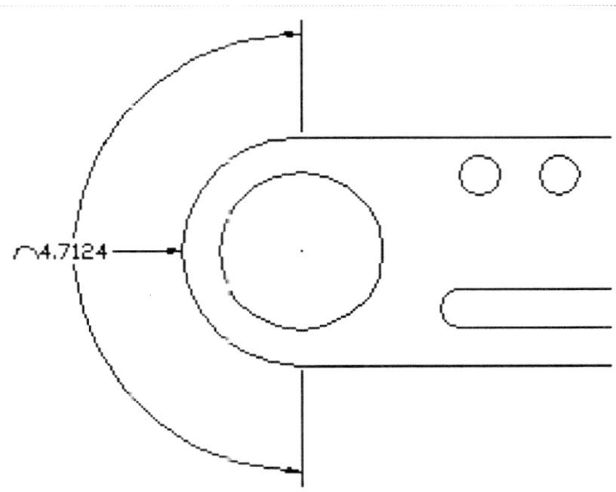


14. Exit the drawing without saving.

**Command:** ***quit***

## 14.2.5 Dimension Strings

It's often preferable to string dimensions. This makes it easier for the contractor to find and read dimensions, and it enhances the overall appearance of the drawing.

To string dimensions, we can repeat the ***Dimlinear*** command over and over, or we can begin our string with the ***Dimlinear*** command and then follow it with the ***Dimcontinue*** command. The ***Dimcontinue*** command will place dimensions along the same line begun by the ***Dimlinear*** command. With each selection, the second extension line from the previous dimension is used as the first extension line for the continued string. Some of the many benefits of this approach include:

- Not overwriting the extension line.
- You don't have to locate the dimension line with each new selection. AutoCAD simply continues along the previous string.
- The command automatically repeats until you stop it.

The command sequence is

> **Command:** ***dimcontinue*** **(or** ***dco*****)**
>
> **Specify a second extension line origin or [Undo/Select] <Select>:** ***[simply select the origin of the second extension line; AutoCAD assumes the first extension line origin to be the second extension line of the last dimension entered]***
>
> **Dimension text =** ***[AutoCAD reports the dimension]***
>
> **Specify a second extension line origin or [Undo/Select] <Select>:** ***[AutoCAD repeats the command until you hit enter to exit]***
>
> **Select continued dimension:** ***[when you hit enter at the last prompt, AutoCAD will provide the opportunity to select a different dimension from which to continue; hitting enter at this prompt will exit the command]***

| Do This: 14.2.5.1 | String Dimensions |
|---|---|

I. Be sure you're in the *Ex-Linear.dwg* file the C:\Steps\Lesson14 folder. If not, please open it now.

II. Follow these steps.

**14.2.5.1: STRING DIMENSIONS**

1. Create a linear dimension between the center of the larger circle and the center of the leftmost arc on the slot. Be sure to select the circle first.

   **Command:** ***dli***

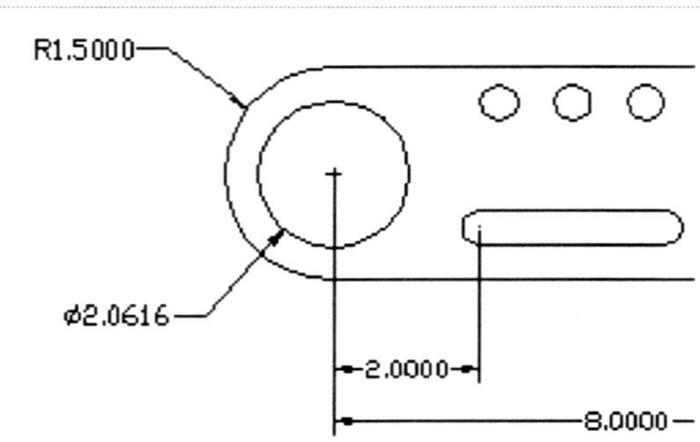


2. Enter the ***Dimcontinue*** command. Alternately, you can pick the **Continue** button on the Dimension toolbar.

   **Command:** ***dco***

3. Select the center of the arc on the other end of the slot.

   **Specify a second extension line origin or [Undo/Select] <Select>: _cen of**

4. Hit ***enter*** twice to complete the command.

   **Specify a second extension line origin or [Undo/Select] <Select>:** ***[enter]***

   **Select continued dimension:** ***[enter]***

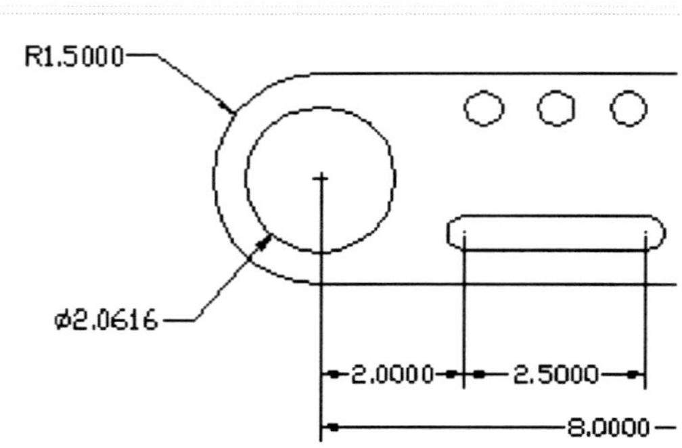


5. Now let's use what we know to dimension the upper circles. Put a linear dimension between the two left smaller circles (pick the middle one first).

   **Command:** ***dli***

   **Specify first extension line origin or <select object>: _cen of** ***[middle small circle]***

   **Specify second extension line origin: _cen of** ***[left small circle]***

## 14.2.5.1: STRING DIMENSIONS

6. **Angle** [Angle] the dimension at *60°*. Then place the dimensions as shown.

   **Specify dimension line location or [Mtext/Text/Angle/Horizontal/ Vertical/ Rotated]:** ***a***

   **Specify angle of dimension text:** ***60***

   **Specify dimension line location or [Mtext/Text/Angle/Horizontal/ Vertical/ Rotated]:**

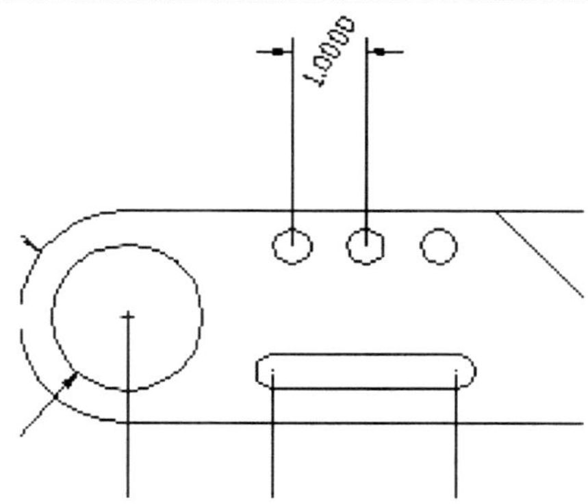


7. Continue the dimension to the center of the large circle.

   **Command:** ***dco***

   **Specify a second extension line origin or [Undo/Select] <Select>: _cen of**

8. We want to continue the dimension in the other direction now, so hit ***enter*** to go to the **Select continued dimension** prompt.

   **Specify a second extension line origin or [Undo/Select] <Select>:** ***[enter]***

9. Select the right extension line (above the smaller middle circle).

   **Select continued dimension:**

10. Select the center of the smaller right circle.

    **Specify a second extension line origin or [Undo/Select] <Select>: _cen of**

**Dimension text = 1.0000**

11. Exit the command.

    **Specify a second extension line origin or [Undo/Select] <Select>:** ***[enter]***

    **Select continued dimension:** ***[enter]***

The dimensions look like this.

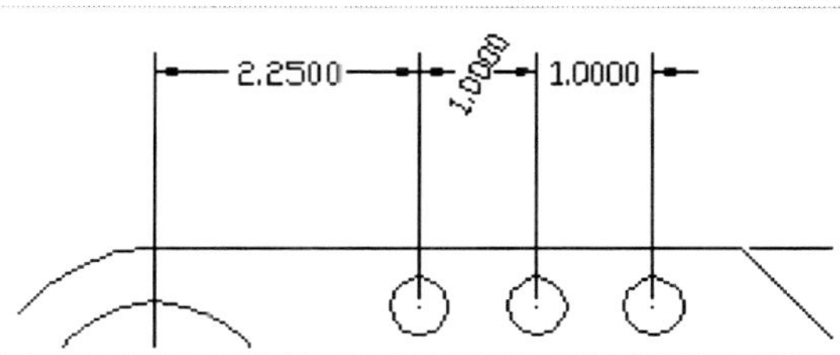


12. Now complete the dimensioning as shown in the following figure.

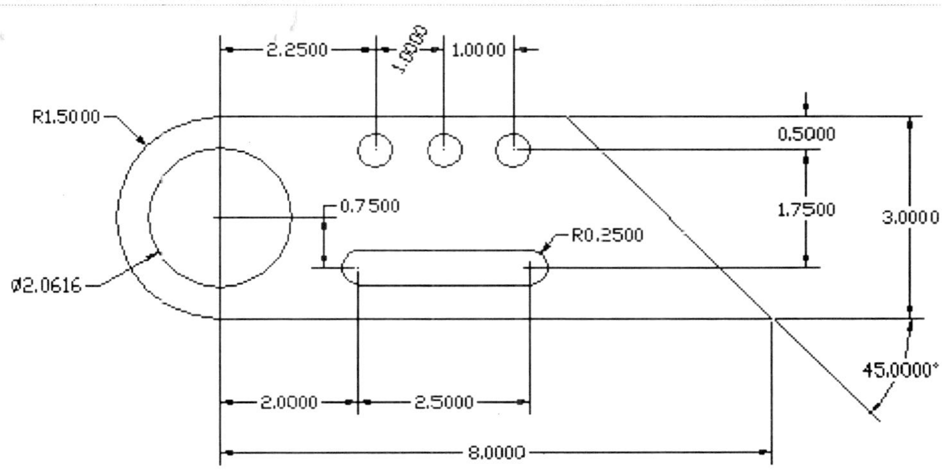

#### 14.2.5.1: String Dimensions

13. Save the drawing  and exit.

**Command:** ***qsave***

## 14.2.6 Aligning Dimensions

Nonlinear objects often require nonlinear dimensioning. This usually means that the dimension must be aligned with the object for clarity.

The ***Dimaligned*** command works almost like the ***Dimlinear*** command. The difference is that the aligned dimension parallels the first and second extension line origins.

The command sequence is

**Command:** ***dimaligned*** **(or *dal*)**

**Specify first extension line origin or <select object>:** ***[select the first dimension point]***

**Specify second extension line origin:** ***[select the second dimension point]***

**Specify dimension line location or [Mtext/Text/Angle]:** ***[locate the dimension line]***

**Dimension text =** ***[AutoCAD reports and places the dimension]***

The options are identical to those used in the ***Dimlinear*** command.

### Do This: 14.2.6.1 Aligned Dimensions

I. Open the *ex-base.dwg* file the C:\Steps\Lesson14 folder. The drawing looks like Figure 14.005.

II. Follow these steps.

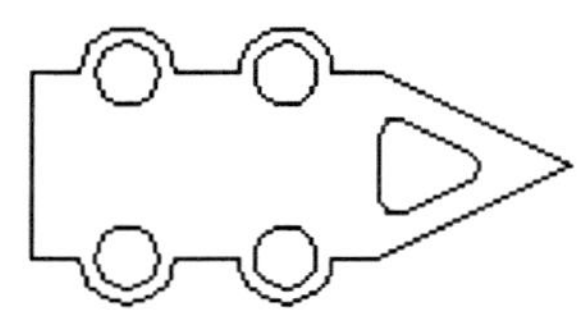

Figure 14.005

#### 14.2.6.1: Aligned Dimensions

1. Enter the ***Dimaligned*** command. Alternately, you can pick the **Aligned** button  on the Dimension toolbar.

**Command:** ***dal***

2. Hit ***enter*** to select the object to dimension.

**Specify first extension line origin or <select object>:** ***[enter]***

3. Select the upper angled line on the right end of the object.

**Select object to dimension:**

4. Locate the dimension line three grid points above the object.

**Specify dimension line location or [Mtext/Text/Angle]:**
**Dimension text = 3.3541**

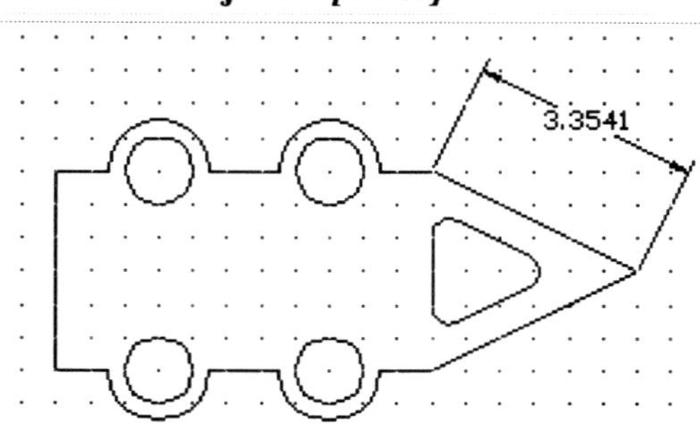

**14.2.6.1: ALIGNED DIMENSIONS**

5. Repeat the command and place a dimension for the lower angled line as shown.

**Specify first extension line origin or <select object>: *[enter]***

**Select object to dimension:**

**Specify dimension line location or [Mtext/Text/ Angle]:**

**Dimension text = 3.3541**

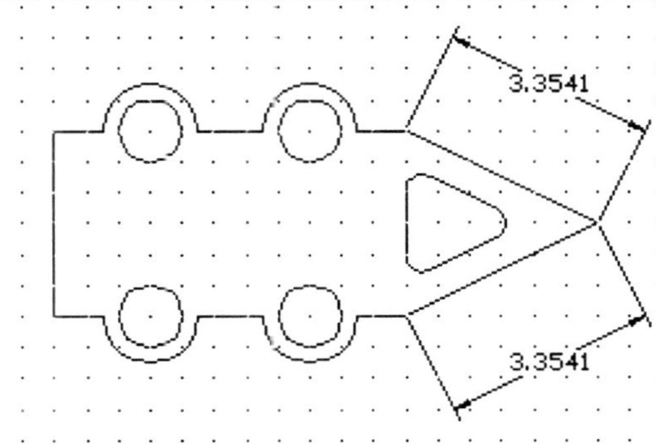


6. Save the drawing [icon] but don't exit.

**Command: *qsave***

## 14.2.7 Baseline Dimensions

Like the ***Dimcontinue*** command, ***Dimbaseline*** works from an original linear dimension. But where continued dimensions were based on the *second* extension line origin of the last or selected linear dimension, the baseline dimension starts from the same *first* extension line origin of the last or selected linear dimension.

The command sequence parallels that of the ***Dimcontinue*** command as well.

**Command: *dimbaseline* (or *dba*)**

**Specify a second extension line origin or [Undo/Select] <Select>: *[select the origin of the second extension line – AutoCAD assumes the first extension line origin to be the first extension line of the last dimension entered]***

**Dimension text = *[AutoCAD reports and inserts the dimension]***

**Specify a second extension line origin or [Undo/Select] <Select>: *[AutoCAD repeats the prompt until you hit enter to exit]***

**Select base dimension: *[when you hit enter at the last prompt, AutoCAD will provide the opportunity to select a different dimension from which to base the baseline dimensions; hitting enter at this prompt will exit the command]***

Let's try a baseline dimension.

| Do This: 14.2.7.1 | Baseline Dimensions |
|---|---|

I. Be sure you're still in the *ex-base.dwg* file the C:\Steps\Lesson14 folder. If not, please open it now

II. Follow these steps.

**14.2.7.1: BASELINE DIMENSIONS**

1. Draw a linear dimension [icon] as shown. Be sure to select the extension line origin on the right first.

**Command: *dli***

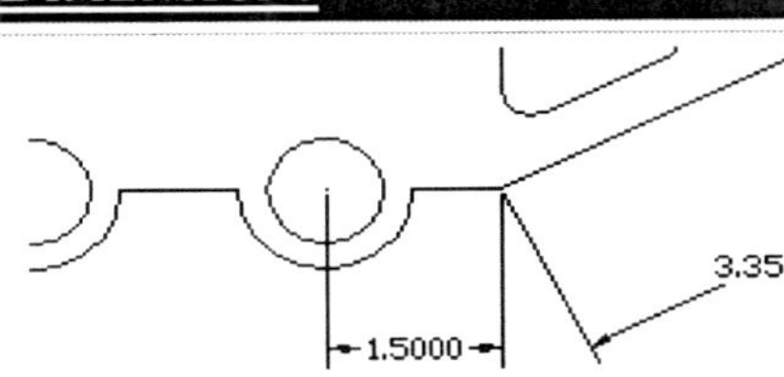

### 14.2.7.1: BASELINE DIMENSIONS

2. Enter the ***Dimbaseline*** command. Alternately, you can pick the **Baseline** button  on the Dimension toolbar.

    **Command: *dba***

3. Pick the center 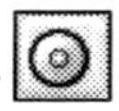 of the next bolt hole to the left. AutoCAD reports and places the dimension.

    **Specify a second extension line origin or [Undo/Select] <Select>: _cen of**
    **Dimension text = 4.0000**

4. Pick the lower left endpoint of the object.

    **Specify a second extension line origin or [Undo/Select] <Select>: _endp of**
    **Dimension text = 5.5000**

5. Hit ***enter*** twice to exit the command.

    **Specify a second extension line origin or [Undo/Select] <Select>: *[enter]***
    **Select base dimension: *[enter]***

Your drawing looks like the figure below.

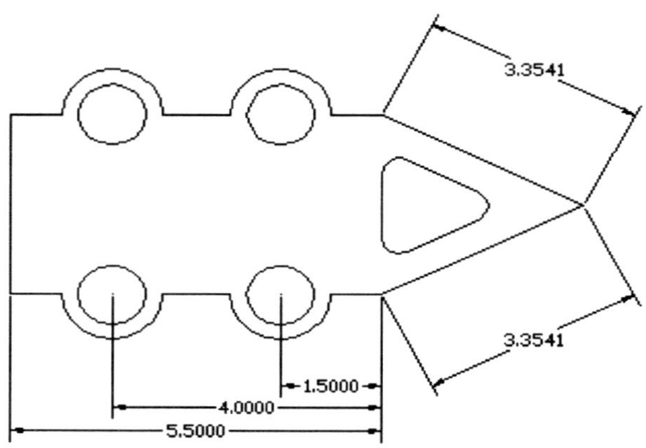


6. Save the drawing  but don't exit.

    **Command: *qsave***

## 14.2.8 Placing Leaders

Use the ***QLeader*** command to place simple callouts that require an arrow or line to reference an object.

Contrary to the way we learned to place callouts in board drafting, CAD leaders should be placed *before* the callout text. Here is the sequence:

**Command: *qleader* (or *le*)**
**Specify first leader point, or [Settings] <Settings>: *[pick the place where you want the tip of the arrow]***
**Specify next point: *[pick the outer end of the first leader line]***
**Specify next point: *[pick the end of the second leader line]***

**Specify text width <0.0000>:** ***[you can specify the width of the desired text; hitting enter at this prompt allows for unrestricted width]***

**Enter first line of annotation text <Mtext>:** ***[place your callout text – hit enter twice at the end of your text string to exit the command; if the callout requires several lines, you can hit enter before adding text to call the Multiline Text Editor]***

There are several options associated with the ***QLeader*** command. Luckily, AutoCAD has placed them in a user-friendly dialog box (Figure 14.006).

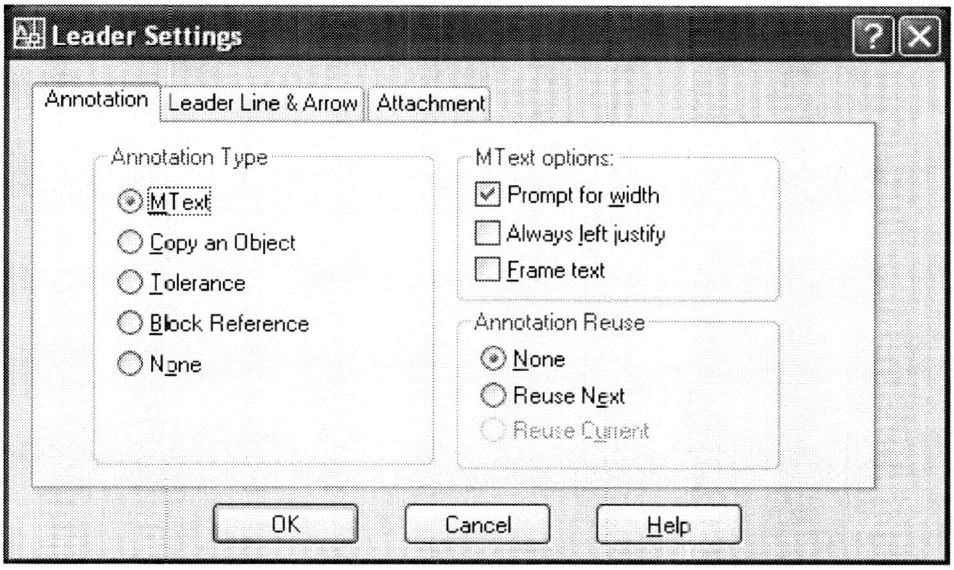


Figure 14.006

Access the dialog box via the **Settings** option at the first ***QLeader*** prompt (just hit ***enter***). Notice the three tabs. We'll look at each beginning with the default – **Annotation**.

- Three frames make up the **Annotation** tab:
  - Use the **Annotation Type** frame to determine what to place after the leader:
    - **MText** (the default) is simply the standard text entry.
    - **Copy an Object** allows you to copy text or an object from one part of the drawing to the end of the leader line.
    - We'll discuss **Tolerance** in more detail in Lesson 15.
    - **Block Reference** allows you to place a block at the end of the leader line. (We'll see more on blocks in Lessons 19 and 20).
    - **None**, of course, allows you to create a leader without text. Use this option when the callout has already been placed on the drawing (as you did on the board).
  - The **MText options** frame provides three options:
    - **Prompt for width** causes AutoCAD to prompt for the width of the MText entry (much like the ***MText*** command does).
    - **Always left justify** can be a nuisance. By default, AutoCAD will determine the text justification depending on which way the leader line goes.
    - **Frame text** will place a frame around the leader text.
  - The **Annotation Reuse** frame allows you to select options controlling whether or not (and how) you'll reuse your callouts.
- The **Leader Line & Arrow** tab (Figure 14.007 – next page) presents four frames of options.

- The **Leader Line** frame allows you to use the standard (**Straight**) leader line or a fancier **Spline** line.
- The **Arrowhead** frame contains a control box from which you can select the type of arrowhead (or no arrowhead at all) to use on the leader.
- **Number of Points** refers to the number of points allowed to define the leader line. The default (3) means that you can draw a leader with two lines. A check in the **No Limit** check box removes all limitations on the number of lines your leader can have.

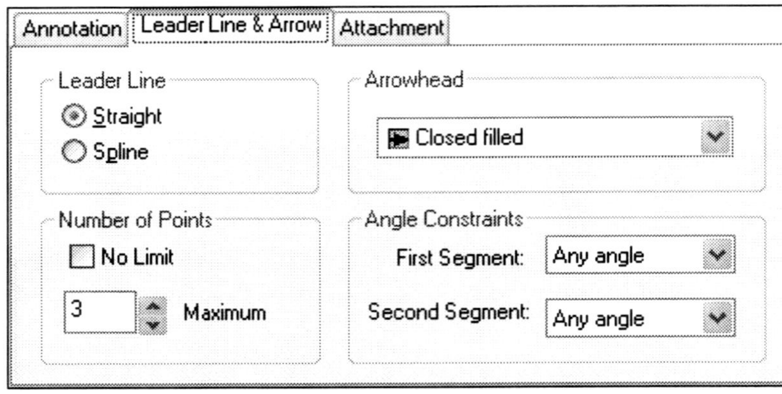


Figure 14.007

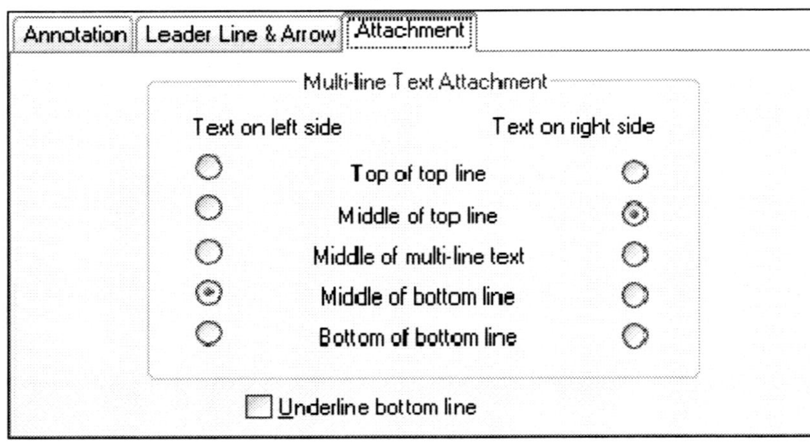


Figure 14.008

- **Angle Constraints** defines how the leader may be drawn. I prefer the default **Any angle** for the first segment; but then I require the second segment to be **Horizontal** to lead into the text.

- The last tab – **Attachment** (Figure 14.008) – allows you to position the text in relation to the leader line.

The number of options for the ***QLeader*** command reflects the importance of leaders in drafting. No one preference can be universal – although the defaults come fairly close. So you should become familiar with the Leader Settings dialog box.

Let's draw some leaders.

| Do This: 14.2.8.1 | Leaders |
|---|---|

I. Be sure you're still in the *ex-base.dwg* file the C:\Steps\Lesson14 folder. If not, please open it now.

II. Follow these steps.

**14.2.8.1: LEADERS**

1. Enter the ***QLeader*** command. Alternately, you can pick the **Quick Leader** button on the Dimension toolbar.

**Command: *le***

2. Hit ***enter*** to access the Leader Settings dialog box.

   **Specify first leader point, or [Settings] <Settings>:** ***[enter]***

3. On the **Leader Line & Arrow** tab, change the **Leader Line** to use a **Spline**.

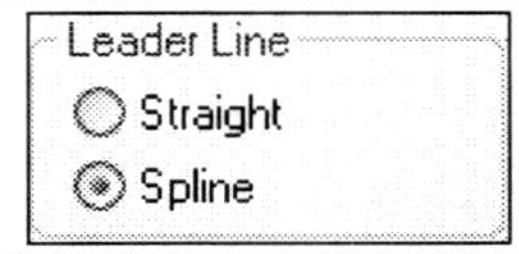


4. On the **Annotation** tab, clear the check box next to **Prompt for width**.

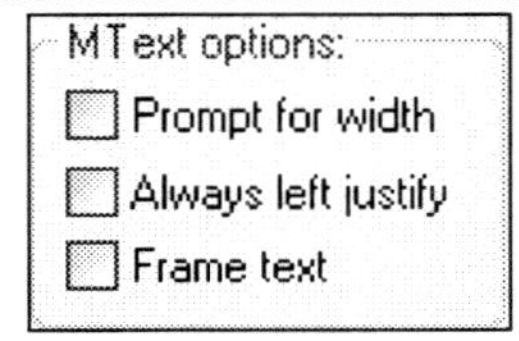


5. Pick the **OK** button OK to exit the dialog box.

6. Place the leader as shown.

   **Specify first leader point, or [Settings] <Settings>:**
   **Specify next point:**
   **Specify next point:**

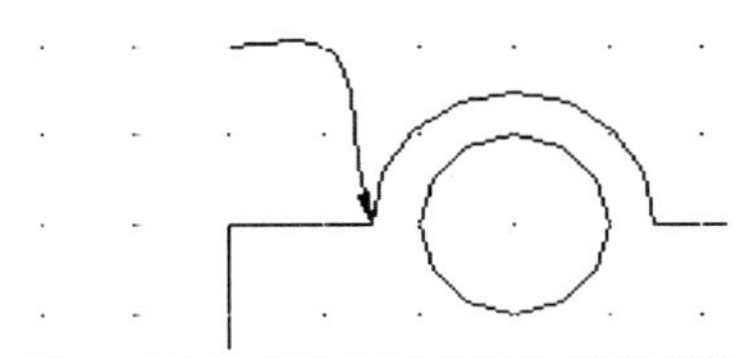

7. Type in the text indicated, and then exit the command.

   **Enter first line of annotation text <Mtext>:** ***No Fillet***
   **Enter next line of annotation text:** ***[enter]***

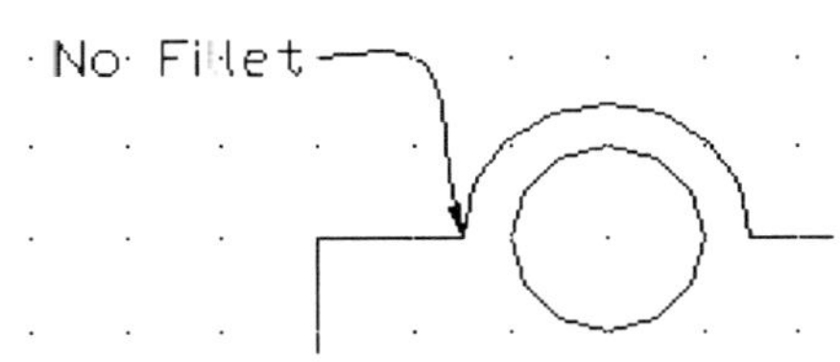


8. Save the drawing but don't exit.

   **Command:** ***qsave***

9. Complete the dimensions as shown in the following figure.

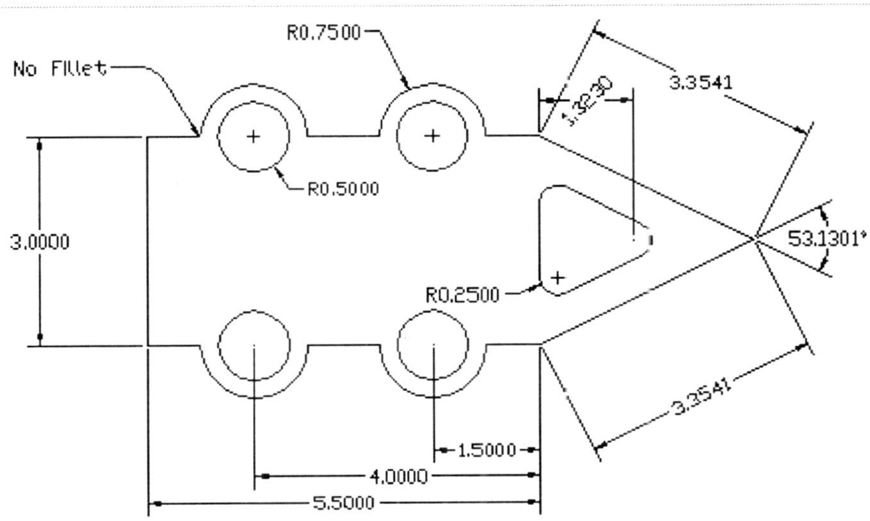

### 14.2.8.1: LEADERS

10. Save and close the drawing.

**Command:** ***qsave***

## 14.2.9 Ordinate Dimensions

Ordinate dimensioning is a valuable tool in some types of manufacturing. ***Dimordinate*** places a dimension that is actually a distance from the 0,0 coordinate of the drawing. To be useful then, 0,0 must be located somewhere on the object itself – usually the lower left corner.

The command sequence for the ***Dimordinate*** command is

**Command:** ***dimordinate*** **(or** ***dor*****)**

**Specify feature location:** ***[select the feature to be dimensioned]***

**Specify leader endpoint or [Xdatum/Ydatum/Mtext/Text/Angle]:** ***[you can specify the X or Y distance from 0,0 or identify the datum by mouse movement]***

**Dimension text =** ***[AutoCAD reports and places the dimension]***

- As indicated, you can specify an **Xdatum** (X-distance from 0,0) or a **Ydatum** (Y-distance from 0,0) by selecting that option.
- If you prefer to place **Text** or **MText** at the ordinate location, those options are also available.
- The **Angle** option behaves just as it does on other dimension tools – that is, you may define the angle of the dimension text.

Let's try an exercise.

### Do This: 14.2.9.1 Ordinate Dimensioning

I. Open the *ex-ordinate.dwg* file the C:\Steps\Lesson14 folder. The drawing looks like Figure 14.009. (We've located the 0,0 coordinate at the lower left corner of the object.)

II. Follow these steps.

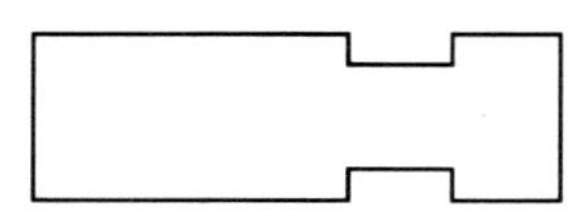

Figure 14.009

### 14.2.9.1: ORDINATE DIMENSIONING

1. Enter the ***Dimordinate*** command. Alternately, you can pick the **Ordinate** button on the Dimension toolbar.

**Command:** ***dor***

2. Select the left side of the lower indentation.

**Specify feature location:_endp of**

3. Pick a point two grid marks due south of the point selected in Step 5.

**Specify leader endpoint or [Xdatum/Ydatum/Mtext/Text/Angle]:**

**Dimension text = 4.5000**

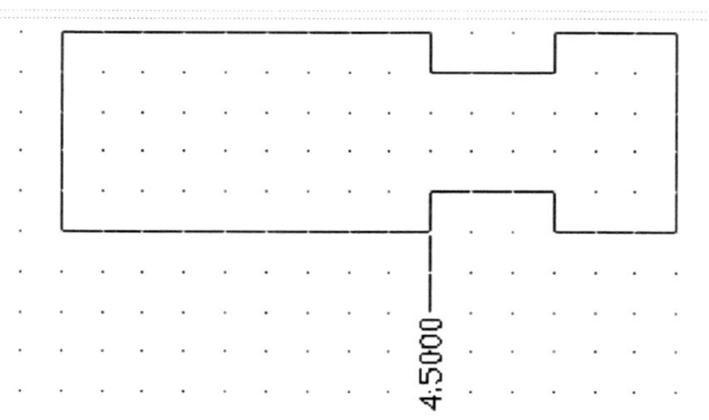

## 14.2.9.1: Ordinate Dimensioning

4. This time, specify the datum you'll use. Repeat the ***Dimordinate*** command.

   **Command: *[enter]***

5. Select the lower right corner of the object.

   **Specify feature location:_endp of**

6. Tell AutoCAD that you want an **Xdatum** [Xdatum].

   **Specify leader endpoint or [Xdatum/Ydatum/Mtext/Text/ Angle]: *x***

7. Select a point two grid marks south and two grid marks west (see the figure in Step 11). (Toggle Ortho off to make this easier.)

   **Specify leader endpoint or [Xdatum/Ydatum/Mtext/Text/Angle]:**

8. Repeat the command.

   **Command: *[enter]***

9. Select the same point selected in Step 8.

   **Specify feature location:_endp of**

10. Tell AutoCAD that you want a **Ydatum** [Ydatum].

    **Specify leader endpoint or [Xdatum/ Ydatum/Mtext/Text/ Angle]: *y***

11. Select a point two grid marks east and two grid marks north.

    **Specify leader endpoint or [Xdatum/ Ydatum/Mtext/Text/ Angle]:**
    **Dimension text = 0.0000**

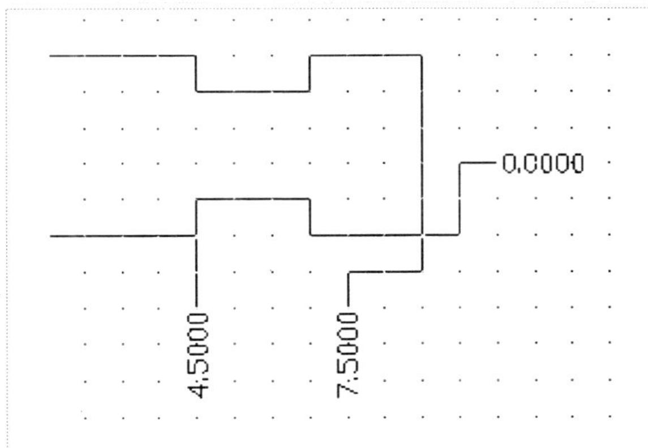


12. Complete the drawing as shown in the following figure.

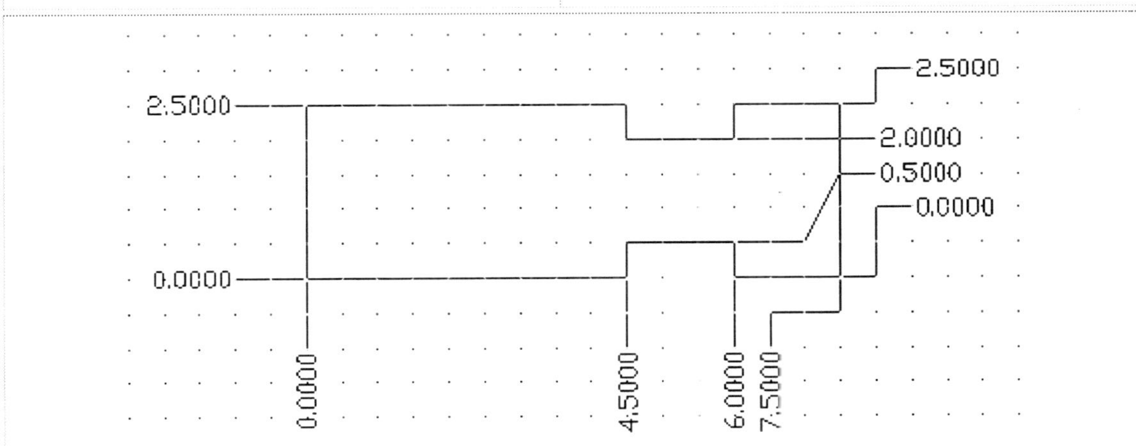

### 14.2.9.1: Ordinate Dimensioning

13. Save and close the drawing.

**Command:** ***qsave***

## 14.3 And Now the Easy Way: Quick Dimensioning (*QDim*)

AutoCAD includes a really cool dimensioning tool – *Quick Dimensioning* (***QDim***). With ***QDim***, you can create a string of dimensions using two picks to select the objects (with a window), one click to confirm the selection and one pick to locate the dimension. That's only four mouse clicks!

The command sequence looks like this:

**Command:** ***qdim***

**Select geometry to dimension:** ***[use a window or crossing window to select the objects to dimension]***

**Select geometry to dimension:** ***[hit enter to complete the selection process]***

**Specify dimension line position, or [Continuous/Staggered/Baseline/Ordinate/ Radius/Diameter/datumPoint/Edit/seTtings] <Continuous>:** ***[tell AutoCAD where to place the dimension]***

Most of the options are fairly obvious – **Continuous** for a continuous string, **Baseline** for a baseline string, **Ordinate** for ordinate dimensions, and so forth. But let's look at the last three.

- **datumPoint** allows you to define a selected point as the 0,0 coordinate of the dimension string (very handy when ordinate dimensioning).
- **Edit** prompts:

  **Indicate dimension point to remove, or [Add/eXit] <eXit>:**

  Using the **Edit** option then, you can add or remove Extension Line Origins to the selection set.
- **seTtings** prompts:

  **Associative dimension priority [Endpoint/Intersection] <Endpoint>:**

  ***QDim*** automatically dimensions to endpoints of selected objects. Using this option, you can tell AutoCAD to dimension to intersections rather than endpoints.

Let's give this nifty tool a try.

| Do This: 14.3.1 | Quick Dimensions |
|---|---|

I. Open the *ex-linear2.dwg* file the C:\Steps\Lesson14 folder. The drawing looks just like the *ex-linear.dwg* file we used earler in this lesson.

II. Follow these steps.

### 14.3.1: Quick Dimensions

1. Enter the ***QDim*** command or pick the **Quick Dimension** button on the Dimension toolbar.

**Command:** ***qdim***

## 14.3.1: Quick Dimensions

2. Use a crossing window (right) to select the bottom line, the slot, and the large circle. Don't select anything else.

   **Select geometry to dimension:**

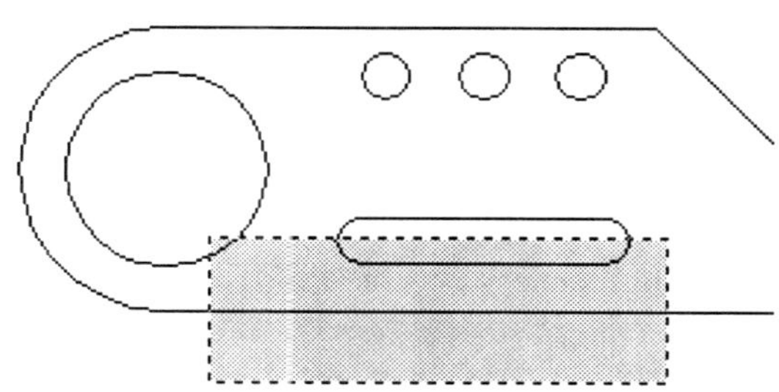

3. Confirm the selection set.

   **Select geometry to dimension:** ***[enter]***

4. Locate the dimension below the object as shown.

   **Specify dimension line position, or [Continuous/Staggered/Baseline/ Ordinate/Radius/Diameter/ datumPoint/Edit/seTtings] <Continuous>:**

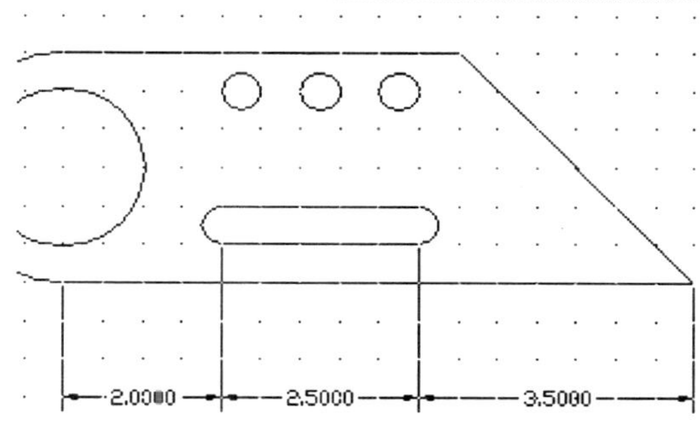


5. Now let's try a baseline dimension.

   Repeat the command .

   **Command:** ***[enter]***

6. Use a crossing window to select the upper line and the four circles as shown.

   **Select geometry to dimension:**

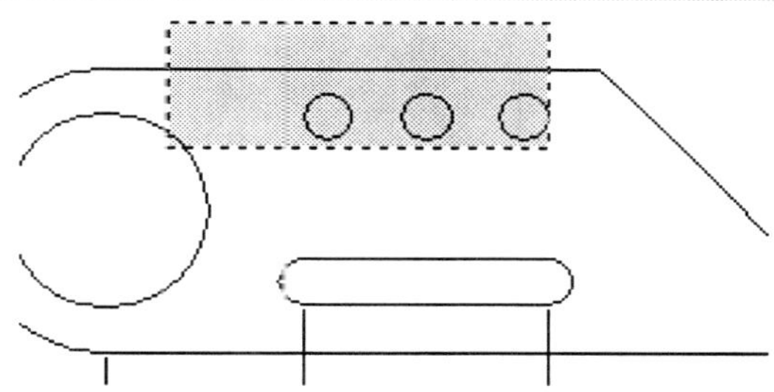

7. Confirm the selection set.

   **Select geometry to dimension:** ***[enter]***

8. Tell AutoCAD to create a **Baseline** dimension .



   **Specify dimension line position, or [Continuous/Staggered/Baseline/ Ordinate/Radius/Diameter/datumPoint/ Edit/seTtings] <Continuous>:** ***b***

9. Locate the dimensions as shown.

   **Specify dimension line position, or [Continuous/Staggered/Baseline/ Ordinate/Radius/Diameter/ datumPoint/Edit/seTtings] <Baseline>:**

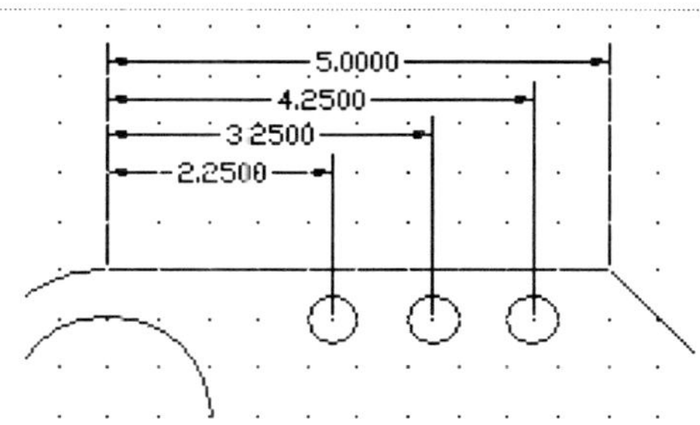


10. Exit the drawing without saving.

    **Command:** ***quit***

Doesn't that make you wonder why we ever did it any other way?

Still, by now, you may have noticed that dimensions don't always appear just the way we think they should. And sometimes (God forbid), the dimension has to change to accommodate some new design information. Our next section will show you how to modify dimensions.

## 14.4 Dimension Editing: The *Dimedit* and *DimTedit* Commands

I'll show you how to use these editing tools, but frankly, I rarely use them. You'll find your best approach to editing most dimension properties in the Properties Palette. Either double-click on the dimension to edit, or select it and pick the **Properties** button on the Standard toolbar.

AutoCAD includes two commands for editing associative dimensions. These commands show a bit of overlap in their functions (redundancy again), but you'll generally change or rotate the text or change the angle of the extension lines with the ***Dimedit*** command. With the ***DimTedit*** command, you can change the position of the text.

Although AutoCAD provides tools for editing associative dimensions, normal dimensions don't require any special tools. Use basic modification commands on dimensions as you would on any other objects. Edit the text using the text editing command (***DDEdit***).

### 14.4.1 Position the Dimension: The *DimTedit* Command

The ***DimTedit*** command sequence looks like this:

> **Command: *dimtedit* (or *dimted*)**
>
> **Select dimension: *[pick the dimension to reposition]***
>
> **Specify new location for dimension text or [Left/Right/Center/Home/Angle]: *[pick the new position or select an option]***

You can change the position of the dimension text dynamically by dragging it with the mouse, or by using AutoCAD's default **Left**, **Right**, or **Center** position. (Note: The **Left** or **Right** option redefines the **Home** position of the text next to the left or right arrow.) The **Angle** option allows you to rotate the dimension text, and the **Home** option returns the dimension text to its original position and rotation.

I realize the phrase *Dimension Text Edit* is confusing since the ***DimTedit*** command isn't used to edit the text but rather to edit the position of the text. ***Dimedit*** is actually used to edit the dimension text value. But these are AutoCAD's terms, so we'll just have to get used to them.

#### Do This: 14.4.1.1 Repositioning Dimension Text

I. Reopen the *ex-base.dwg* file the C:\Steps\Lesson14 folder. If you haven't completed this file, open *ex-base2.dwg* in the same folder.

II. Follow these steps.

**14.4.1.1: REPOSITIONING DIMENSION TEXT**

1. Enter the ***DimTedit*** command. Alternately, you can pick the **Dimension Text Edit** button  on the Dimension toolbar.

> **Command: *dimted***

## 14.4.1.1: Repositioning Dimension Text

2. Select the dimension below the right end of the object as indicated.

**Select dimension:**

3. Experiment with repositioning the text using the **Left** and **Right** options. Repeat this step until you're comfortable with these options.

**Specify new location for dimension text or [Left/Right/ Center/Home/Angle]:** ***[l or r]***

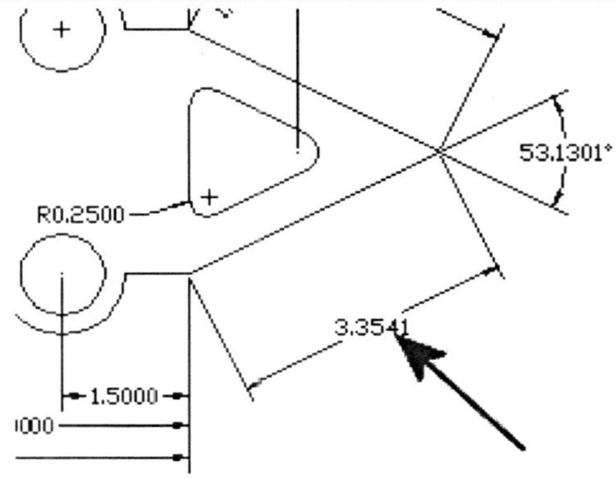


4. Use the ***Undo*** command 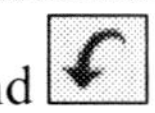 to return the text to its original position.

**Command:** ***u***

5. Repeat the ***DimTedit*** command 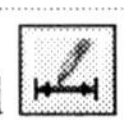 and select the same dimension.

**Command:** ***dimted***

**Select dimension:**

6. Notice that the dimension moves dynamically as you move the crosshairs. Experiment with repositioning the text manually. Repeat this step until you're comfortable with this method.

**Specify new location for dimension text or [Left/Right/ Center/Home/Angle]:**

7. Repeat the command and select the same dimension.

**Command:** ***[enter]***

**Select dimension:**

8. Use the **Home** option 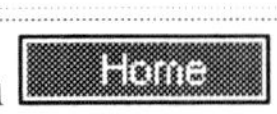 to return the text to its original position.


**Specify new location for dimension text or [Left/Right/ Center/Home/Angle]:** ***h***

9. Repeat the command and select the same dimension.

**Command:** ***[enter]***

**Select dimension:**

10. Tell AutoCAD to change the angle  of the text . . .


**Specify new location for dimension text or [Left/Right/ Center/Home/Angle]:** ***a***

11. … to 27°.

**Specify angle for dimension text:** ***27***

It now looks like this.

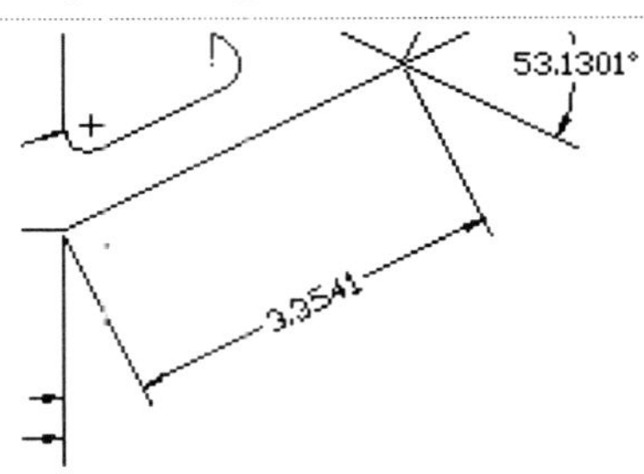


12. Save the drawing .

**Command:** ***qsave***

## 14.4.2 Changing Value of the Dimension Text: The *Dimedit* Command

The ***Dimedit*** command sequence is

> **Command: *dimedit* (or *ded*)**
>
> **Enter type of dimension editing [Home/New/Rotate/Oblique] <Home>: *[hit enter to accept the default or tell AutoCAD what you want to do]***
>
> **Select objects: *[select the object(s) to change]***

Notice that the ***Dimedit*** command uses a default (**<Home>**) for the initial prompt. Notice also that the *option* must be selected before the dimension *objects* (as opposed to the way ***DimTedit*** required selecting the *object* first).

- Most of the options are simple. **Home** returns a rotated dimension to its original state. **Rotate** does what the **Angle** option did in the ***DimTedit*** command.
- The **New** option presents the Multiline Text Editor. Just enter the desired text. When you pick the **OK** button, AutoCAD will prompt to **Select objects**. It'll then replace the dimension text with what you've typed in the Multiline Text Editor. But be aware that once you've changed the dimension text in this manner, it'll no longer automatically update when the object/dimension is modified.
- You'll find the **Oblique** option quite valuable when dimensioning isometrics. To dimension an isometric, you'll use the ***Dimaligned*** command, and then reposition the dimension in the correct isometric plane using this tool. (You'll see more on this in Section 14.5.)

### Do This: 14.4.2.1 Changing Dimension Text

I. Be sure you're still in the *ex-base.dwg* file (or the *ex-base2.dwg* file) in the C:\Steps\Lesson14 folder.

II. Follow these steps.

**14.4.2.1: CHANGING DIMENSION TEXT**

1. Enter the ***Dimedit*** command. Alternately, you can pick the **Dimension Edit** button  on the Dimension toolbar.

> **Command: *ded***

2. Tell AutoCAD to edit a dimension (select the **New** option 

).

> **Enter type of dimension editing [Home/New/Rotate/Oblique] <Home>: *n***

3. AutoCAD displays the Multiline Text Editor with a number box. Type ***4.125***. 

4. Pick the **OK** button 

.

5. Select the **4.0000** dimension indicated. Then complete the command.

> **Select objects:**
>
> **Select objects: *[enter]***

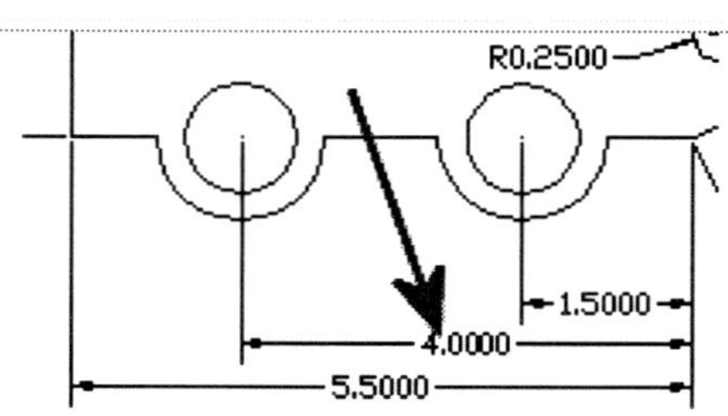

## 14.4.2.1: Changing Dimension Text

6. AutoCAD replaces the dimension text with the new text. Now try stretching the object one unit to the left.

**Command:** ***s***

Select the objects as shown here.

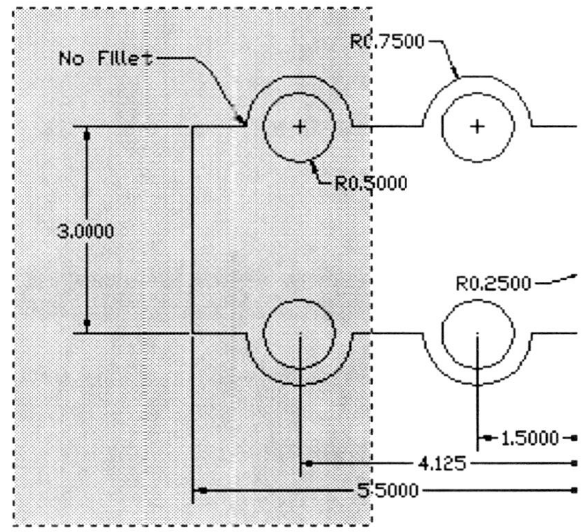


7. Notice (below) that AutoCAD automatically updated the **5.5000** dimension but the **4.125** dimension didn't change. Remember, dimensions changed made using this method are no longer associative!

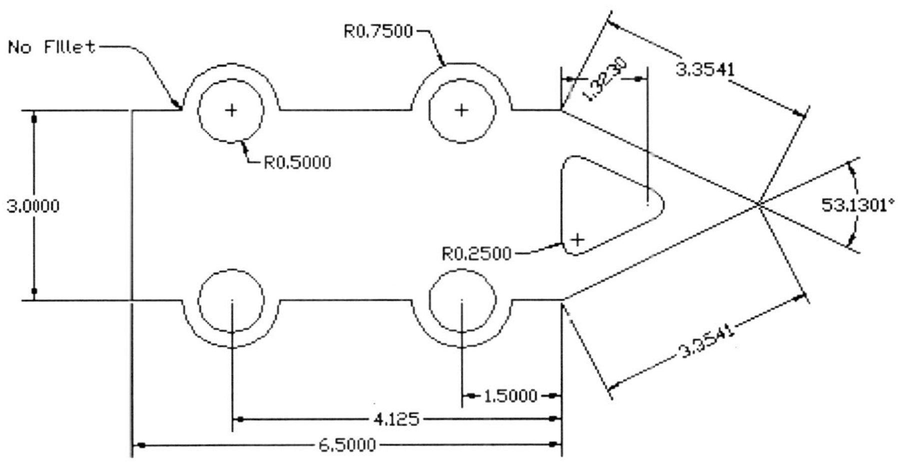


8. Save the drawing and exit.

**Command:** ***qsave***

## 14.5 Isometric Dimensioning

It might relieve you to know that there's no actual isometric dimension command. (Then again, a ***DimIsometric*** command might make this section a bit easier!)

Dimension your isometrics using the ***Dimaligned*** command. Then you must edit the aligned dimension using the **Oblique** option of the ***Dimedit*** command to adjust the aligned angle to the appropriate isometric plane.

Sound complicated? It isn't as complicated as it is tedious. Let's see how it works.

| Do This: 14.5.1 | Dimensioning Isometrics |
|---|---|

I. Open the *isodim.dwg* file in the C:\Steps\Lesson14 folder. The drawing looks like Figure 14.010.

II. Follow these steps.

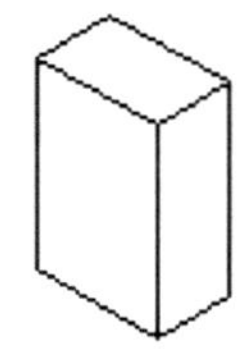

Figure 14.010

## 14.5.1: Dimensioning Isometrics

1. Use the ***Dimaligned*** command to place the dimensions shown.

   **Command: *dal***

2. Begin the ***Dimedit*** command.

   **Command: *ded***

3. Tell AutoCAD to use the **Oblique** option Oblique.

   **Enter type of dimension editing [Home/New/Rotate/Oblique] <Home>: *o***

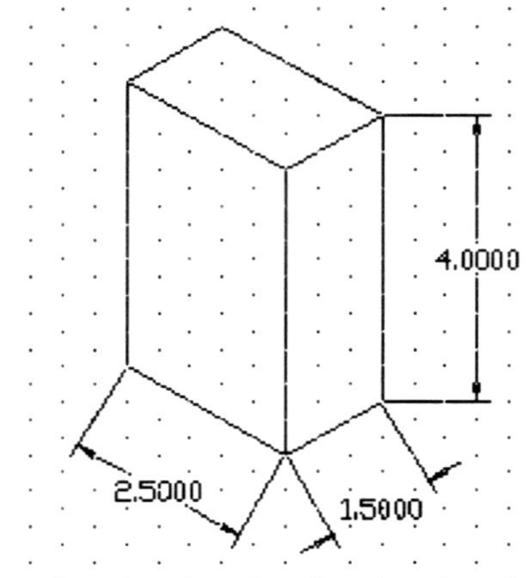


4. Select the **4.0000** vertical dimension.

   **Select objects:**

   **Select objects: *[enter]***

5. Tell AutoCAD to angle the extension lines at ***30***°.

   **Enter obliquing angle (press ENTER for none): *30***

Your drawing looks like this.

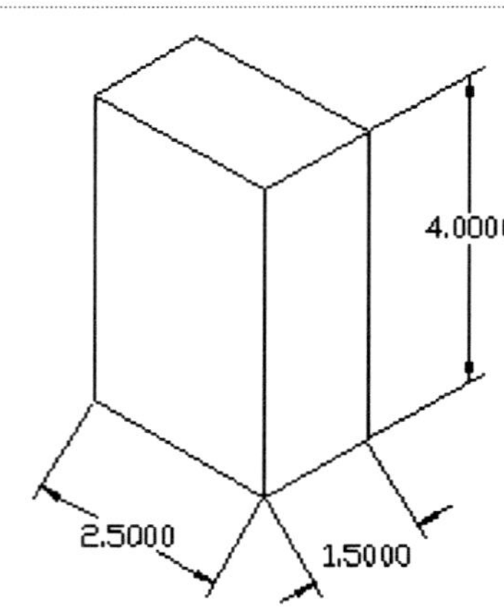

### 14.5.1: Dimensioning Isometrics

6. Now set the obliquing angle of the lower two dimensions to 270°.

   **Command:** ***[enter]***

   **Enter type of dimension editing [Home/New/Rotate/Oblique] <Home>:** ***o***

   **Select objects:**

   **Select objects:** ***[enter]***

   **Enter obliquing angle (press ENTER for none):** ***270***

   Your drawing looks like this. (Your dim arrows may be located differently.)

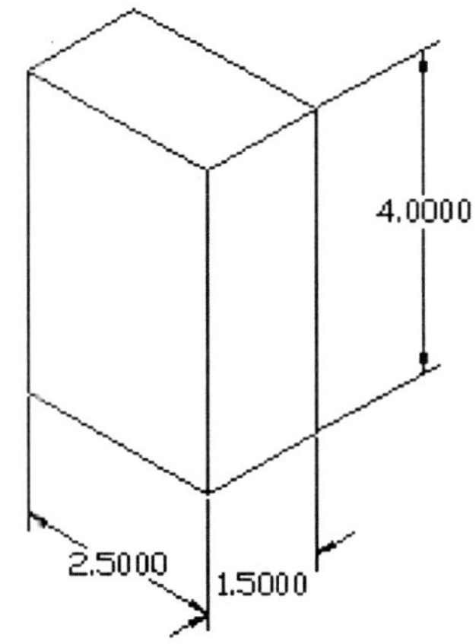


7. Save the drawing and exit.

   **Command:** ***qsave***

To change the text to an isometric format, create appropriate text styles (Lesson 4) and then use the ***Props*** command (Lesson 6) to change the style of the dimension text.

## 14.6 Extra Steps

We've used the command prompt and the toolbars throughout this lesson. Take some time to familiarize yourself with the Dimension pull-down menu. This one has the best chance of surviving the assaults of programmers because of the necessity of simplifying the dimension tools. You'll also see that the tools available on the pull-down menu are the same as those provided on the toolbar. The **Style** and **Update** options correspond to commands that we'll discuss in Lesson 15.

## 14.7 What Have We Learned?

*Items covered in this lesson include:*

- *AutoCAD Dimension Terminology*
- *AutoCAD Dimension Commands:*
  - ***Dimlinear***
  - ***Dimangular***
  - ***Dimradius***
  - ***Dimarc***
  - ***Dimdiameter***
  - ***Dimcontinue***
  - ***Dimaligned***
  - ***Dimbaseline***
  - ***QLeader***
  - ***Dimordinate***
  - ***QDim***
  - ***Dimedit***
  - ***DimTedit***
  - ***DimRegen***
  - ***DimAssociate***
  - ***DimAssoc***
  - ***DimReAssociate***

You're now familiar with the various methods of creating and editing AutoCAD's dimensions. For the most part, you can place dimensions as you would on any board. But if you spend much time with dimensioning, you'll discover some shortfalls in your understanding. This is because you're only halfway through your study of AutoCAD's dimensioning tools.

In Lesson 15, we'll discuss customizing your dimensions. This sounds difficult, but it's where you'll learn:

- to use architectural units instead of decimals,
- how to change arrow styles and text sizes,
- how to have AutoCAD insert tolerances automatically,
- and much, much more!

## 14.8 Exercises

1. Dimension the *Brake.dwg* file in the C:\Steps\Lesson14 folder.

   Remember:

   - the ***Dimaso*** command toggles associative and normal dimensioning
   - the ***Explode*** command converts an associative dimension to a normal dimension.
   - dimensions don't always fall where you want them, so remember your editing commands.

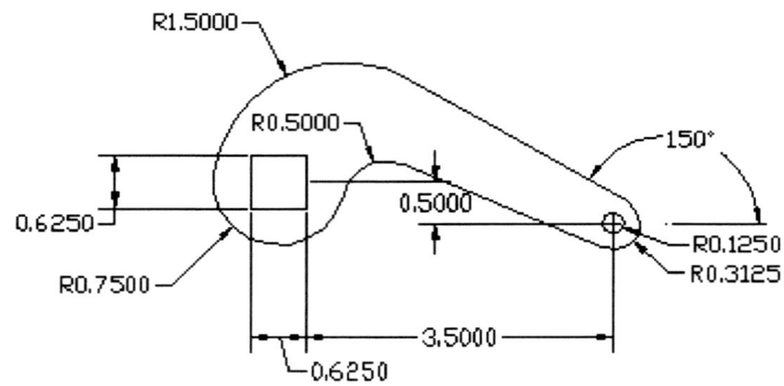


Brake

   When completed, your drawing will look like this.

2. Dimension the *Pulley-slider.dwg* file in the C:\Steps\Lesson14 folder. The drawing will look like this when completed.

*For more exercises related to Lesson 14, please see Lesson 14 in AutoCAD 2007: One Step at a Time – Workbook.*

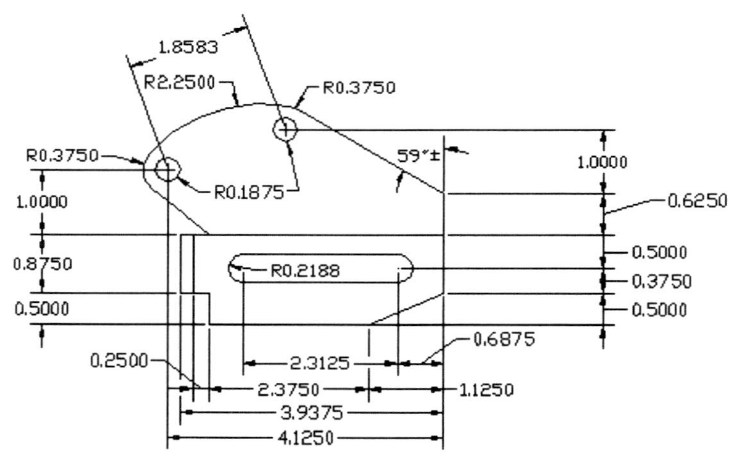


Pulley-Slider

## 14.9 For Web-Based Review Questions, visit: http://www.uneedcad.com/2007/Files/07R14.pdf

# Lesson

# 15

Following this lesson, you will:

✓ *Know how to create and use Dimension Styles*

✓ *Know how to remove unused Dimension Styles: The **Purge** Command*

# Customizing Dimensions

*Every design industry has its own preferences about such things as units, dimension arrows, text sizes, tolerances, and so forth. If all industries had to accept decimal dimensions (with four decimal places), AutoCAD would probably lose its business fairly quickly – especially from architectural and petrochemical designers who rely on the ever-present feet and inches of architectural drafting. Indeed, even metric users might wash their hands of taking millimeters to four decimal places.*

*In this lesson, we'll look at changing the way AutoCAD creates dimensions to fit different industrial standards.*

## 15.1 Creating Dimension Styles: The *DDim* Command

We'll use dialog boxes for our customization. AutoCAD will store each of our settings in a DIMension VARiable (**Dimvar**). You can adjust each dimvar manually at the command prompt (as we did in earlier releases). But take my word for it, only a programmer would want to customize dimensions this way! Still, for those who are into that sort of thing, I've included a list of AutoCAD's dimvars with their default settings in Appendix E.

Each drawing can incorporate several dimension styles, but there's rarely need for more than one. AutoCAD's clever use of the *Family* method of setup enables you to create overall dimension settings (*Parent* settings) for the drawing with different settings for each of its six children: **Linear**, **Radial**, **Diameter**, **Ordinal**, **Angular**, and **Leaders** (and **Tolerances**). This is a remarkable accomplishment when compared with other CAD systems or even earlier releases of AutoCAD. The downside of this, of course, is that you must navigate the Dimension Style Manager to create the proper settings for the parent and each child. But remember, set it up once and save it to a template, then you don't have to do it again!

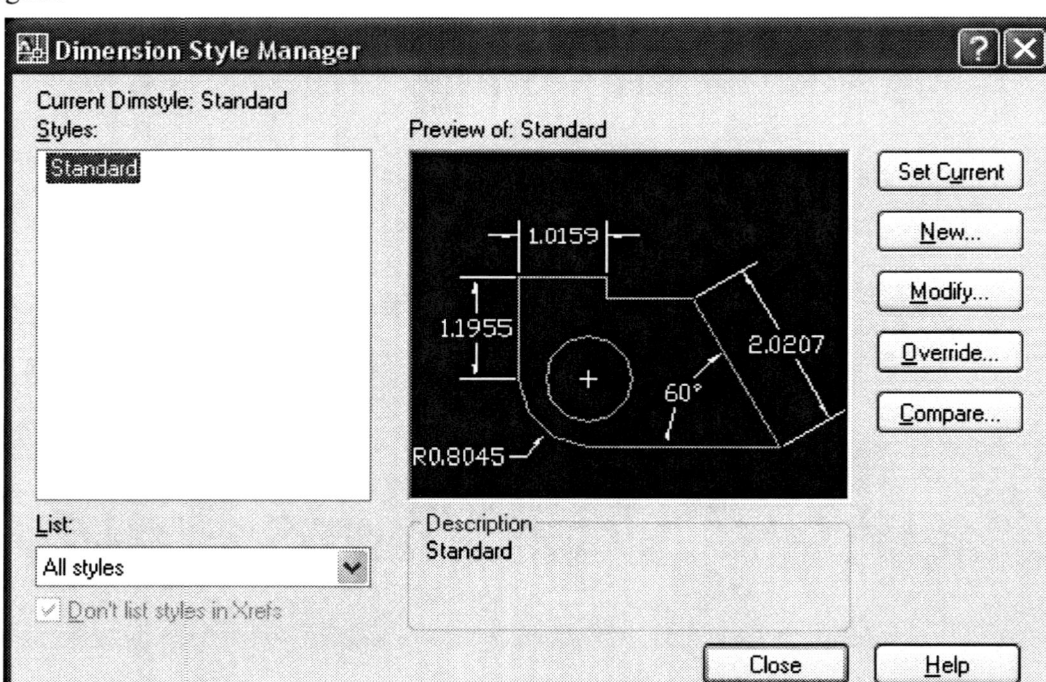


Figure 15.001

Let's look at the first step. Start a new drawing from scratch and follow along on the screen.

Access the Dimension Style Manager by typing ***DDim*** at the command prompt or picking the **Dimension Style** button on the Dimension toolbar. Alternately, you can pick **Dimension Style** from the Dimension pull-down menu. AutoCAD presents the Dimension Style Manager shown in Figure 15.001. Let's examine this.

- In the **Styles** list box, AutoCAD will display a list of all the styles currently defined in this drawing. The left-justified names are the Parent styles. The children of that parent will be listed below it and slightly indented.
- The **List** control box controls what you'll see in the **Styles** list box. Here you can tell AutoCAD to list **All styles** or just the **Styles in use** in the current drawing.
- AutoCAD shows the current dimension setup in the **Preview** display box. Following the words "Preview of:" AutoCAD will list the dimension style being displayed. A written description of the dimstyle may appear in the **Description** frame below the display box.
- The five buttons down the right side of the Dimension Style Manager allow you to **Set Current** the dimstyle highlighted in the **Styles** list box, create a **New** or **Modify** an existing dimstyle, **Override** the settings in the current dimstyle, or **Compare** two dimstyles to find the differences. Let's look at these.
  - You must set a dimension style current before you can use it (just as you do with layers). You can do that by picking the **Set Current** button here. But it's easier to use the **Dimension Style** control box on either the Dimension toolbar or the Styles toolbar (as we'll see in our exercises).
  - The **New** and **Modify** buttons both present a tabbed dialog box used to set up the dimstyle (more on these in a moment).
  - Overriding a dimension style is rarely a good idea. But selecting the **Override...** button will present the same tabbed dialog box as the previous buttons. The difference is that **Override** won't use the changes to redefine the dimstyle, although you can use the changes in your dimensioning. (More on Override in Section 15.3.3).
  - The **Compare** button presents a dialog box that allows you to compare the differences between two dimstyles.

Now that you've some idea of what the Dimension Style Manager looks like, we need to get into the specifics of exactly how to define or create a new dimension style.

How do you think you'd start a new style? Of course, you'd pick the **New...** button. When you do, AutoCAD presents the Create New Dimension Style dialog box (Figure 15.002). Let's look at our options.

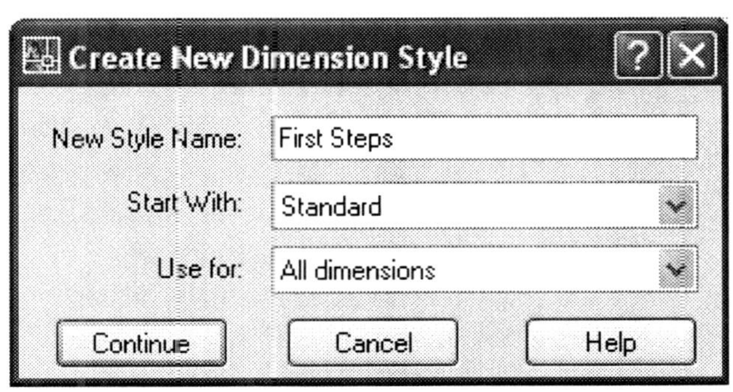

Figure 15.002

- Name your dimstyle in the **New Style Name** text box (here we've called our new style *First Steps*).
- In the **Start With** control box, you can select to use the settings from any existing dimstyle as the basis for your new style.
- The **Use for** control box is the key to the parent/child relationship of AutoCAD's dimension styles. By default, the settings you make for your new style will be used for **All dimensions** you create. However, you can create separate settings for linear, angular, radius, diameter, ordinate, or leader and tolerance dimensions (the children).

Let's start a new dimension style.

| Do This: 15.1.1 | Create a New Dimstyle |
|---|---|

I. Open the *drill-gizmo-15.dwg* file the C:\Steps\Lesson15 folder. The drawing looks like Figure 15.003.

II. Follow these steps.

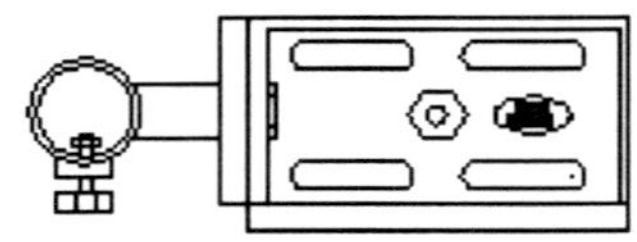

Figure 15.003

## 15.1.1: Create a New Dimstyle

1. Enter the Dimension Styles command. Alternately, you can pick the **Dimension Style** button on the Dimension toolbar. AutoCAD presents the Dimension Style Manager (Figure 15.001).

   **Command: *ddim***

2. Start a **New** style [New...].

3. Refer to Figure 15.002 – create a style called ***First Steps*** based on the **Standard** style. We'll set up this first style for **All dimension**.

4. Pick the **Continue** button [Continue]. AutoCAD presents the New Dimension Style: First Steps dialog box. (Read on before continuing.)

Once you've completed the selections in the Create New Dimension Style dialog box, you'll **Continue** to the tabbed New Dimension Style: First Steps dialog box (where *First Steps* is the name of your new style), as shown in Figure 15.004 (next page). Here you'll actually define the settings.

> You should set all the sizes in a dimension style to the actual size required on the final plot. The scale factor of the dimension objects will be set on the **Fit** tab.

Let's take a look at each tab.

- The first tab – **Lines** – contains two frames. You'll define the physical appearance of your dimensions in these.
  - Preview your setup in the upper right **Preview** area.
  - Use the first frame to set up **Dimension lines**.
    - The **Color**, **Linetype**, and **Lineweight** control boxes allow you to set the color, linetype, and lineweight of the dimension. The default for each is **ByBlock**.
    - The **Extension beyond ticks** control box remains gray unless the arrowheads have been set to tick marks (we'll look at arrowheads in a moment). If tick marks have been selected, you can tell AutoCAD how far to extend the dimension line beyond the extension line by typing a distance here (refer to Figure 15.005).

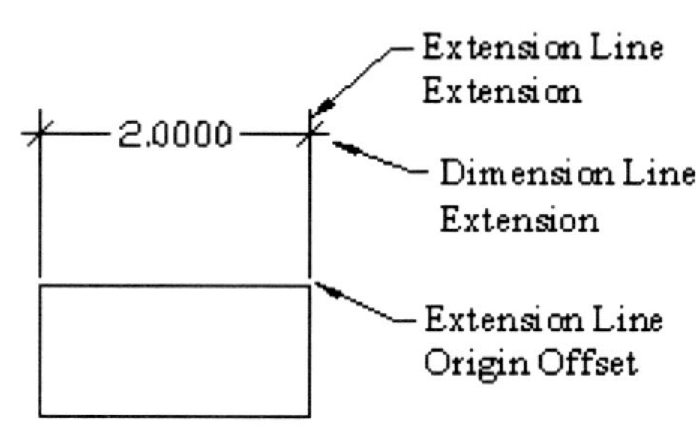


Figure 15.005

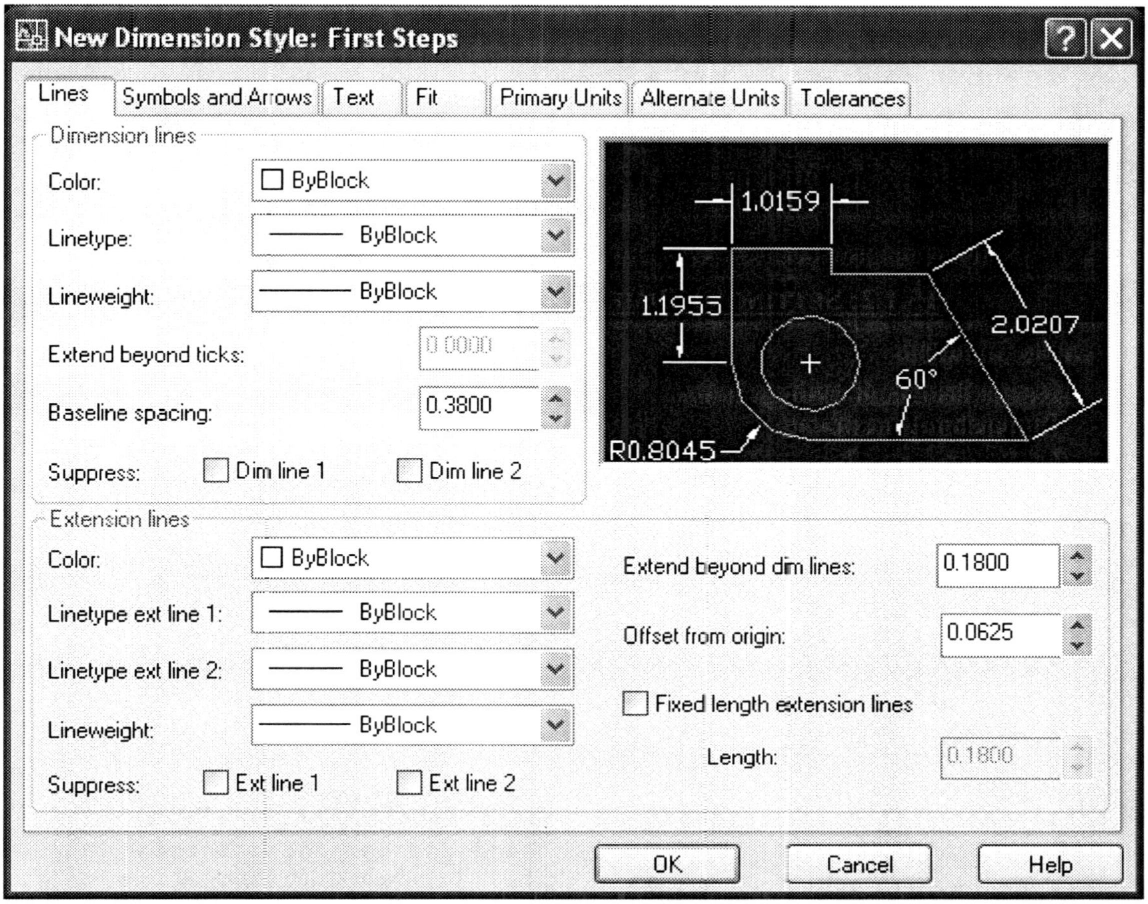


Figure 15.004

- **Baseline spacing** refers to the distance between baseline dimensions. It's probably best to leave this setting at its default unless your industry uses a different standard.
- The check boxes at the bottom of the frame allow you to **Suppress** (not draw) the dimension line on the 1st or 2nd side of the dimension. This can be useful in a crowded area.

o Set up the extension lines in the **Extension lines** frame.

- **Color**, **Linetype**, and **Lineweight** work the same as they did for dimension lines. I recommend the same setting for dimension lines and extension lines for continuity. Note, however, that you can set a different linetype for each of the extension lines.
- The **Suppress** options work on extension lines as they did on dimension lines. Use these to avoid placing one extension line atop another when stringing dimensions. I don't recommend this; AutoCAD has been programmed to avoid plotting one line atop another to prevent digging inky holes in paper (a problem in earlier releases). Besides, if you're placing more than a couple lines in one place, you might want to rethink your drafting strategy.
- The **Extend beyond dim lines** setting determine the distance the extension lines continue beyond the dimension line (the **Extension Line Extension** as seen in Figure 15.005 – previous page).

- The **Offset from origin** setting determines the distance away from the origin the extension line will begin (see the **Extension Line Origin Offset** in Figure 15.005).
- Place a check next to **Fixed length extension lines** to set the length of your extension lines to a fixed length. Use the **Length** number box to define the length.

Let's continue our exercise.

| Do This: 15.1.2 | Setting up Dimension & Extension Lines |
|---|---|

I. Continue the previous exercise. Follow these steps.

**15.1.2: SETTING UP DIMENSION AND EXTENSION LINES**

1. On the **Lines** tab:
   a. Accept the default settings in the **Dimension Lines** frame.
   b. Set the extension lines to **Extend *0.125"* beyond the dim lines**.

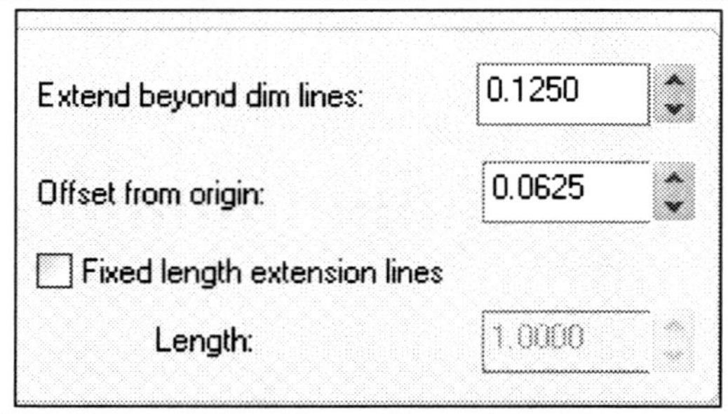


2. Pick the **Symbols and Arrows** tab [Symbols and Arrows]. (Read on before continuing.)

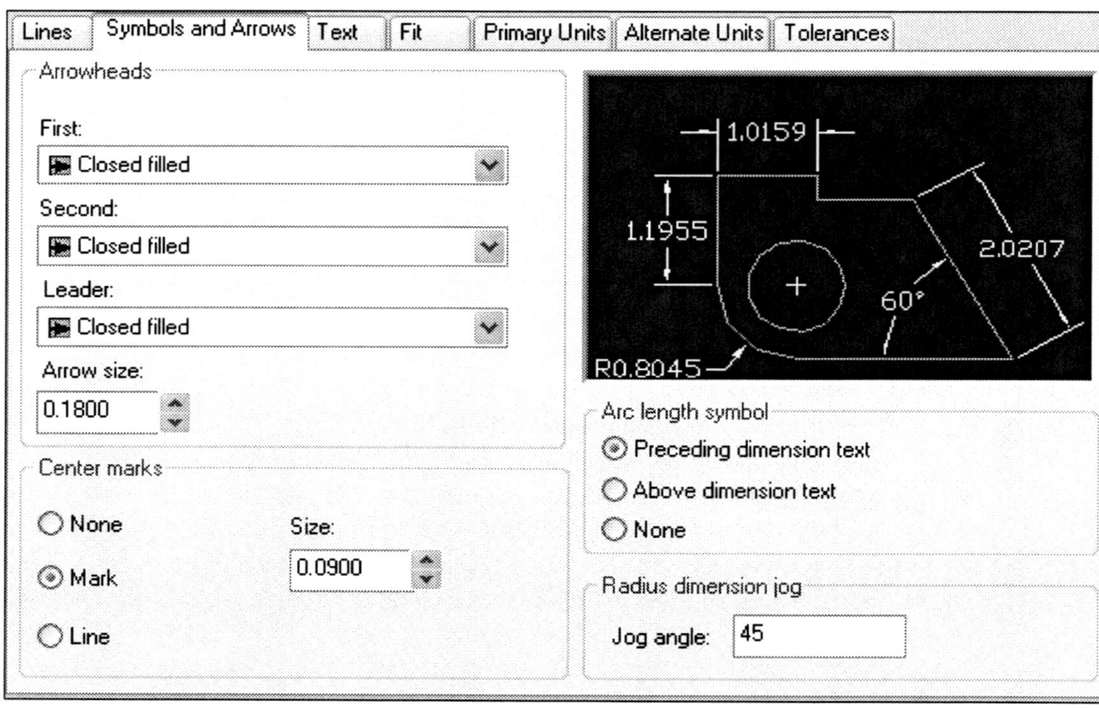


Figure 15.006

- The **Symbols and Arrows** tab (Figure 15.006) contains four frames for defining arrowheads, arcs, and radial symbols.
  - Use the **Preview** area to see what your dimension looks like as you create it.
  - You'll determine the size and style of the arrowheads in the **Arrowheads** frame.

   - AutoCAD provides sample images for each of the **1st**, **2nd**, and **Leader** arrowheads in the control boxes. AutoCAD also provides several selections as well as options to use a user-defined block or no arrowhead at all (**None**).
   - Just below the control boxes is an **Arrow size** box in which you can adjust the size of the arrowhead.
- o The **Center marks** frame allows you to use a mark (a small "+"), centerlines, or no symbol when dimensioning the center of a circle or arc. It also allows you to change the size of the center marks or the extension of the centerlines outside the circle.
- o Use the radio buttons in the **Arc length symbol** frame to define where AutoCAD will place an arc symbol when dimensioning an arc length.
- o Finally, you can change the desired **angle** of a jogged dimension in the **Radius dimension jog** frame.

Let's set up our symbols and arrowheads.

| **Do This: 15.1.3** | **Setting up Dimension Symbols and Arrowheads** |
|---|---|

I. Continue the previous exercise. Follow these steps.

### 15.1.3: Setting up Dimension Symbols and Arrowheads

1. On the **Symbols and Arrows** tab:
   c. Use **Dot small** for the 1st and 2nd arrowheads for the dimensions, but **Closed filled** arrowheads for the **Leader**.
   d. Make the arrowheads ***0.125"***.
   e. Don't use **Center marks for Circles**.
   f. Accept the default **Arc length symbol** and **Radius dimension jog**.

2. Pick the **Text** tab [Text]. (Read on before continuing.)

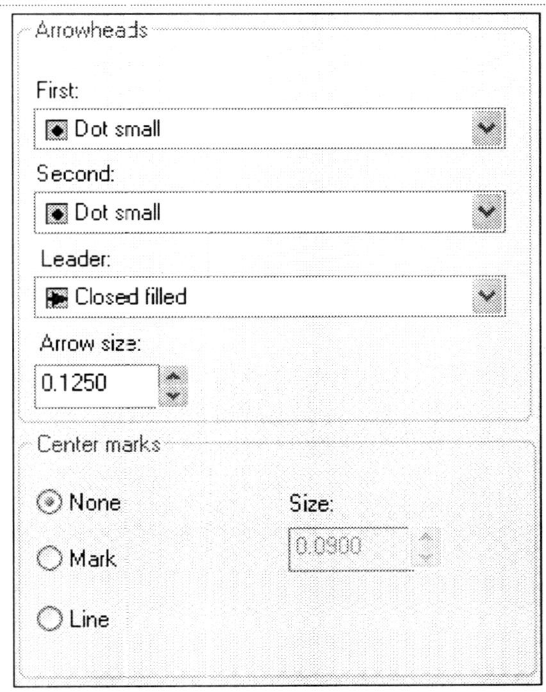


- The **Text** tab (Figure 15.007) contains three frames for defining how to use text in your dimensions.
  - o Use the **Preview** area to see what your dimension looks like as you create it.
  - o The **Text appearance** frame contains settings for the appearance of the text.
    - Set the style of text for the dimensions using the **Text style** control box. If you haven't yet created the style, use the button to the right of the control box to access the Text Style dialog box.
  - Set the **Text color** and **height** using the appropriate boxes.

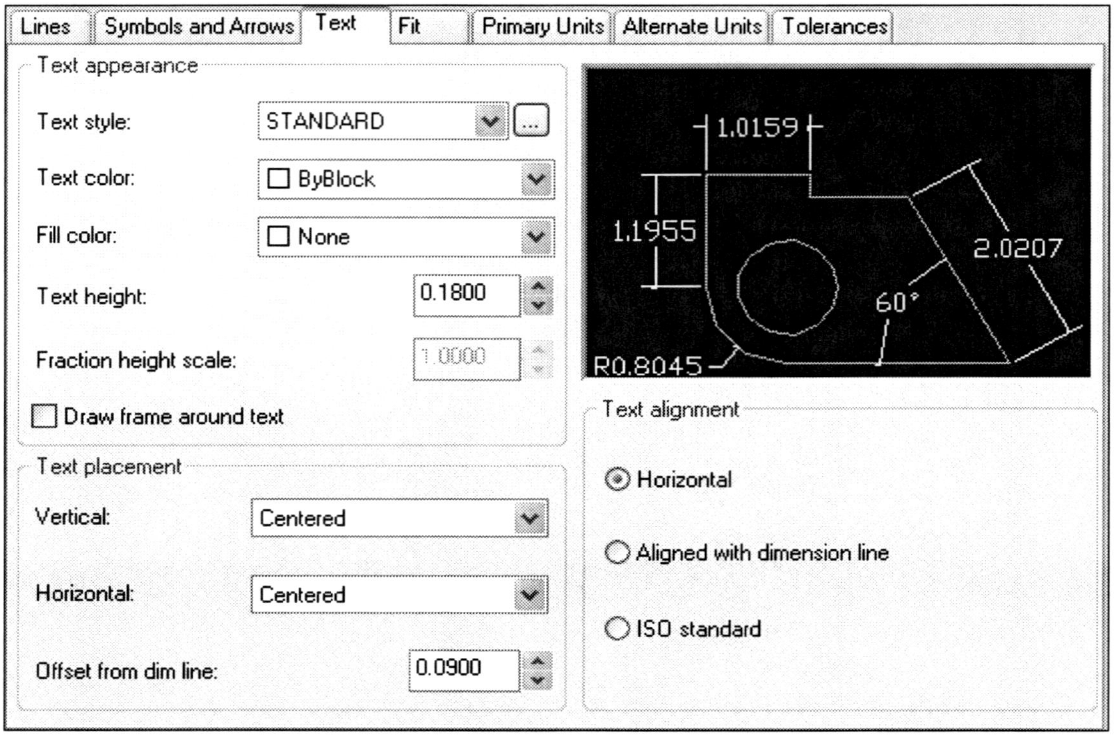


Figure 15.007

- When using fractional or architectural units, you can set the size of the fraction using the **Fraction height scale** number box.
- Place a frame around the dimension text by checking the **Draw frame around text** box.

o The **Text placement** frame allows you to control where the text will be placed in relation to the dimension line.

o In the **Text alignment** frame, determine whether to place dimension text **Horizontal**, **Aligned with** [the] **dimension line**, or in the **ISO standard** mode. (*ISO Standard* means that the text will be aligned with the dimension line if it falls between the extension lines or horizontally if it doesn't fit between the extension lines.)

Let's set up our text.

| Do This: 15.1.4 | Setting up Dimension Text |
|---|---|

I. Continue the previous exercise. Follow these steps.

| 15.1.4: SETTING UP DIMENSION TEXT |
|---|
| 1. On the **Text** tab (refer to the following figure):<br>a. Use the **TIMES** text style (it's already been set up) and a text height of ***0.125"***.<br>b. Place the text **Above** the line vertically but **Centered** horizontally.<br>c. Use the **ISO standard** alignment mode. |

## 15.1.4: SETTING UP DIMENSION TEXT

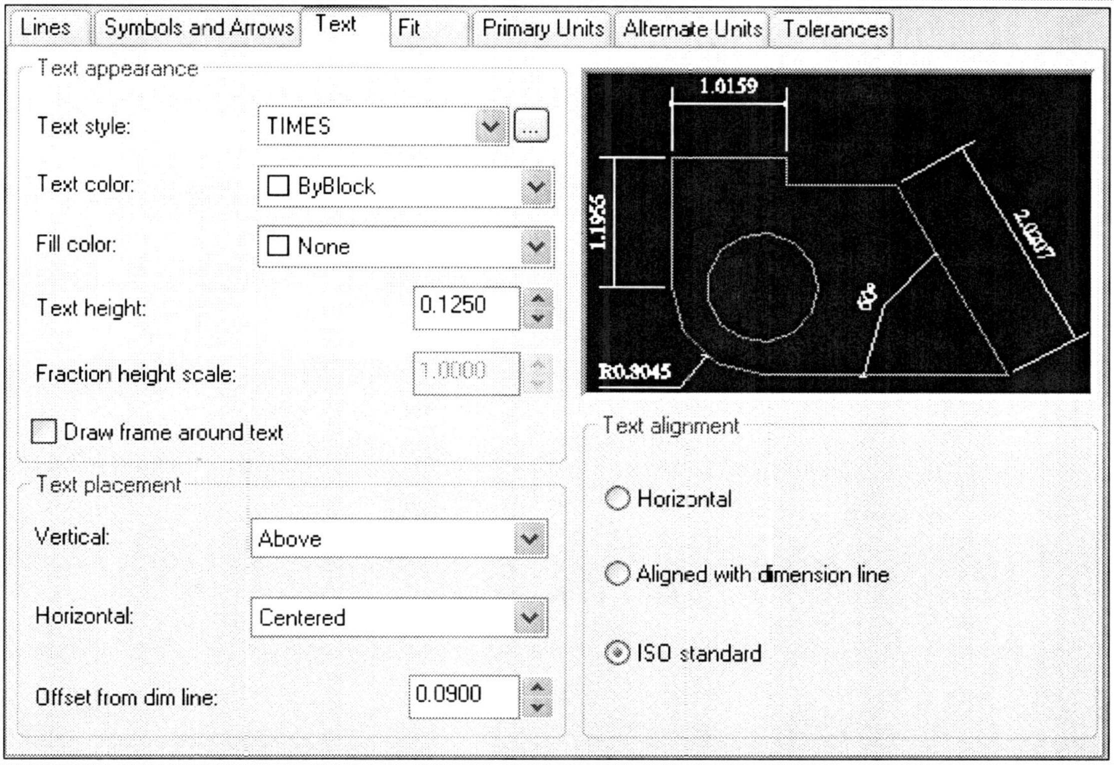


2. Pick the **Fit** tab [Fit]. (Read on before continuing.)

- The **Fit** tab (Figure 15.008) has four frames to help fine-tune your dimension style.
  - The **Fit options** frame allows you to tell AutoCAD what to do when the dimension parts don't fit between the extension lines.
    - Move text and/or arrowheads from inside to outside the extension lines.
    - Don't place arrowheads on the dimension lines.
- In the **Text placement** frame, tell AutoCAD where to place the text if it doesn't fit between the extension lines – either beside or over the dimension line (with or without a leader).
- The **Scale for dimension features** frame contains some critical settings. Scaling the dimension objects is quite a bit easier than scaling text. You should set dimension size according to the desired plot size. Simply identify the scale factor using the **overall scale** size box. AutoCAD will do the rest! That is, where you *manually* scale text (Lesson 4), AutoCAD will *automatically* scale dimension objects.

  (Ignore the **layout** option for now. We'll cover layouts in Lessons 22 and 23.)
  - The **Fine tuning** frame allows you to manually place text or to force dimension lines between extension lines (even when nothing else will fit).

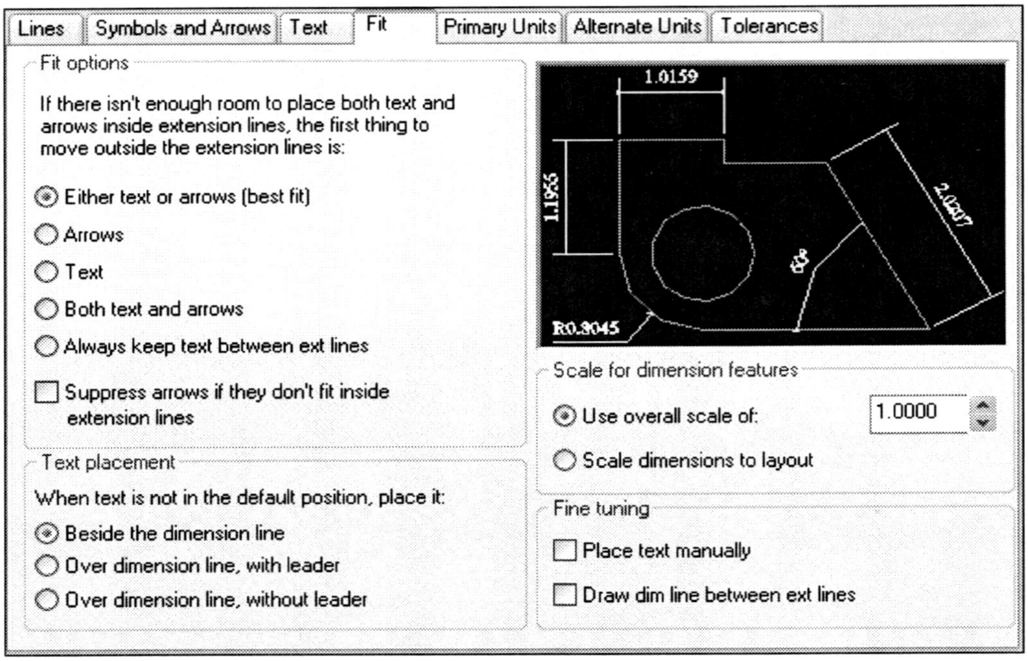


Figure 15.008

Let's continue.

| Do This: 15.1.5 | Setting up the Fit Tab |
|---|---|

I. Continue the previous exercise. Follow these steps.

**15.1.5: SETTING UP THE FIT TAB**

1. On the **Fit** tab:
   b. Allow AutoCAD to determine what to do if the text and arrows don't fit – leave the bullet in the first option of the **Fit options** frame.
   a. When text isn't in the default position, place it over the dimension with a leader (the **Text placement** frame).
   b. Accept the rest of the defaults.

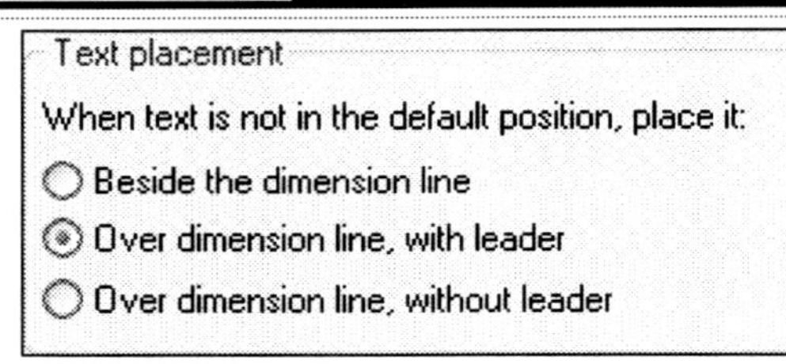


2. Pick the **Primary Units** tab [Primary Units]. (Read on before continuing.)

- The **Primary Units** (Figure 15.009) and the **Alternate Units** tabs allow you to set the dimension units separately from the drawing units. The **Primary Units** tab has two large setup frames.
  - o The **Linear dimensions** frame has several options.
    - ▪ It begins with the actual **Unit format** option. Select the type of units to use in the control box.
    - ▪ Use the **Precision** control box to set the precision of your dimensions (how many decimal places or the fractional denominator to use).

- When using **Fractional** or **Architectural** units, you can make your fractions stack horizontally or vertically, or you can choose not to stack them at all. These options will be available in the **Fraction format** control box.
- Use the **Decimal separator** control box to separate decimals from whole numbers using a period (as done in the United States), a comma (as done in Europe), or with a space.
- Tell AutoCAD how to round your dimensions in the **Round off** box. AutoCAD will round the dimensions to the nearest unit in this box. (Enter .125 and AutoCAD will round to the nearest 1/8", etc.)
- The **Prefix** and **Suffix** boxes are provided to allow you to place leading or trailing text with your dimensions (like "mm" marks).

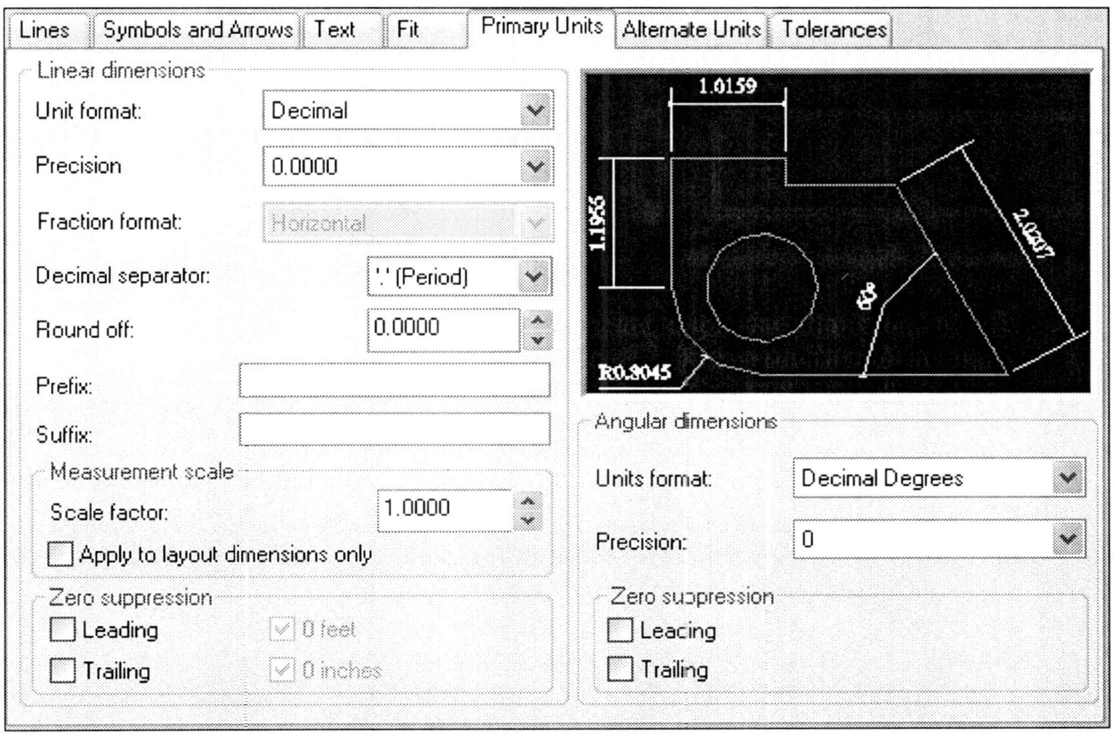


Figure 15.009

- You should probably leave the **Measurement scale** settings at their defaults. The **Scale factor** number box tells AutoCAD how to scale dimensions. Simply put, if the setting is 1.0000 (its default), dimensions reported are the same as the true distance between extension line origins. AutoCAD will take any other setting, multiply it by the true distance, and use the results as the dimension text. This is handy if you're using various details – drawn at different scales – in your drawing. On the other hand, you'll find a far better approach to different scales and detail work when we examine Paper Space in Lessons 22 and 23.
- **Zero suppression** enables you to dimension without unnecessary zeros. See the examples in Figure 15.010 to 15.013.

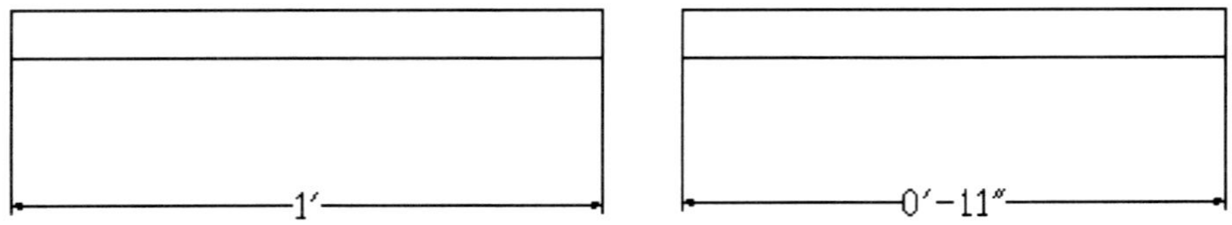


Figure 15.010: Suppress Zero Inches

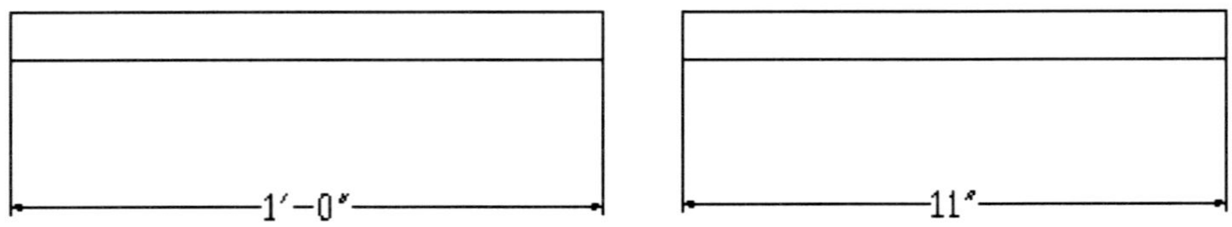


Figure 15.011: Suppress Zero Feet

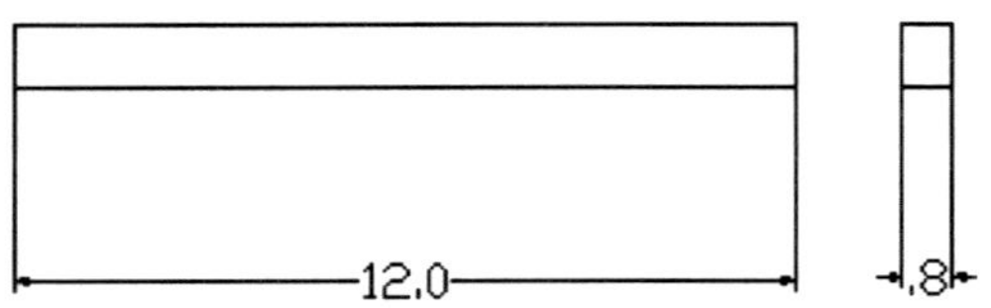


Figure 15.012: Suppress Leading Zero

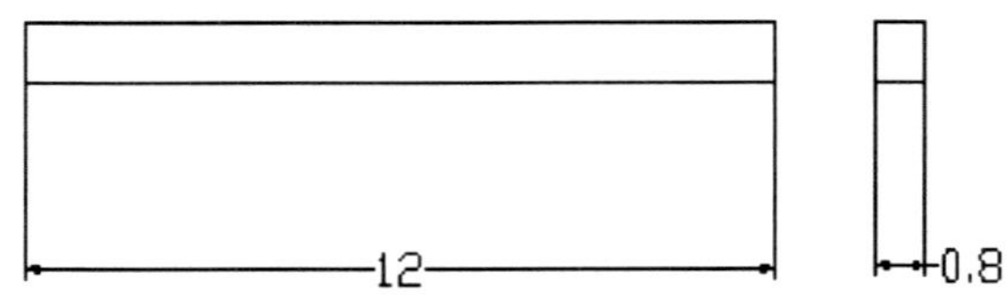


Figure 15.013: Suppress Trailing Zero

- The **Primary units** tab allows you to set up **Angular dimensions** as well. The **Alternate Units** tab doesn't allow the setup of angular dimensions, but it does provide a frame to allow you to determine the placement of alternate dimensions.

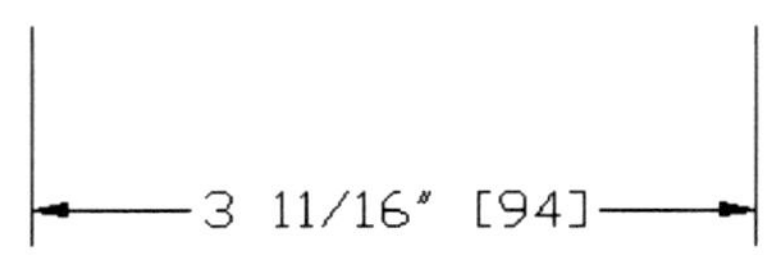


Figure 15.014: Alternate Units

  Alternate units are useful when a company in the United States is working on a European or Asian project that must show metrics as well as feet and inches. A dimension may look something like the one in Figure 15.014.

  Notice that AutoCAD places the alternate units in brackets after the primary units (by default). Also by default, AutoCAD sets the alternate to a scale of 25.4 – or *millimeters*.

Let's continue.

| Do This: 15.1.6 | Setting up the Units |
|---|---|

I. Continue the previous exercise. Follow these steps.

## 15.1.6: Setting up Units

1. On the **Primary Units** tab:
   a. Accept the decimal format, but set the precision to two decimal places.
   b. Suppress trailing zeros.
   c. Accept the **Angular dimensions** default settings.

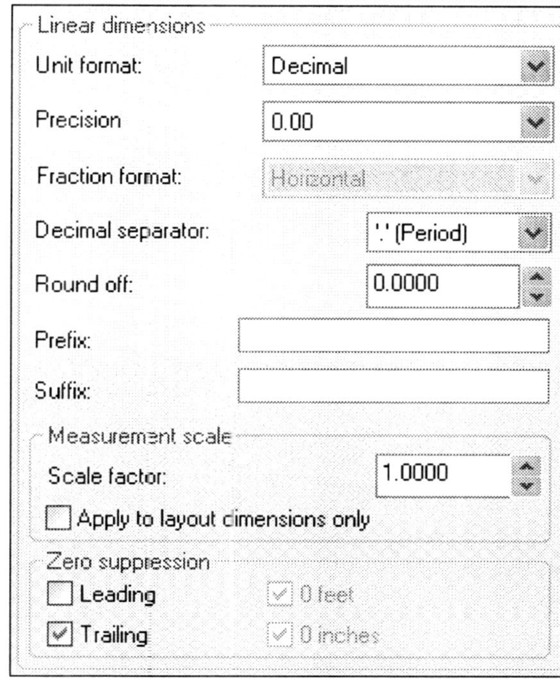


2. Pick the **Tolerances** tab [Tolerances] (we won't use alternate units in this exercise). (Read on before continuing.)

Figure 15.015

- The last tab we must examine is the **Tolerance** tab (Figure 15.015). Here you set up any tolerances that your dimensioning may require. Again, we have two large frames.
  - The first frame allows you to set up the **Tolerance format**.
    - See the examples in Figures 15.016 to 15.021 for **Method** and **Vertical position** values.

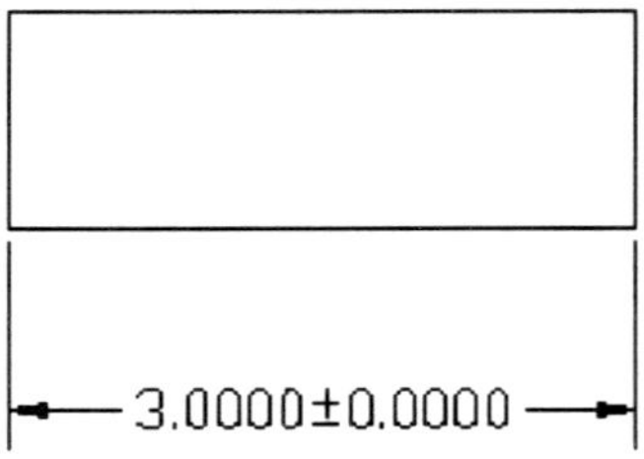


Figure 15.016: Symmetrical Tolerance

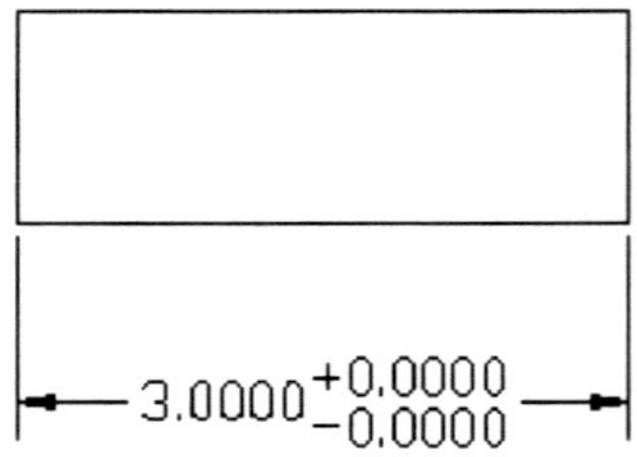


Figure 15.017: Deviation Tolerance (Middle Justification)

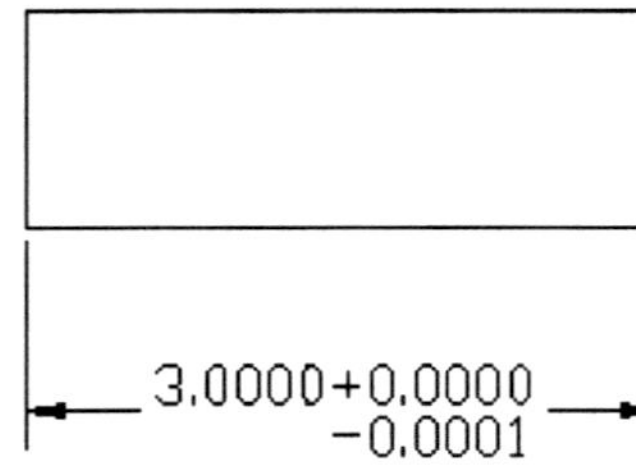


Figure 15.018: Deviation Tolerance (Top Justification)

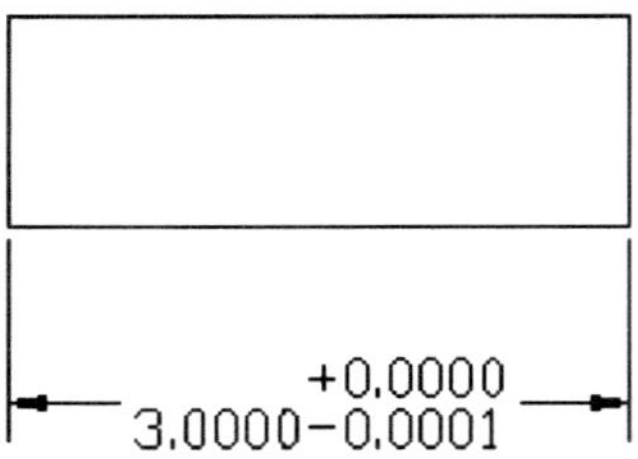


Figure 15.019: Deviation Tolerance (Bottom Justification)

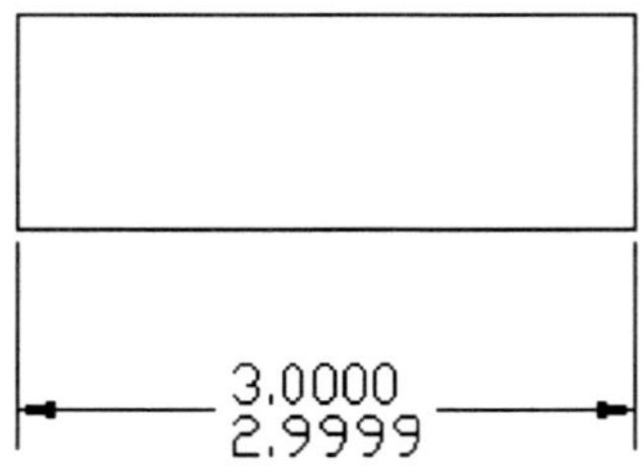


Figure 15.020: Limits Tolerance

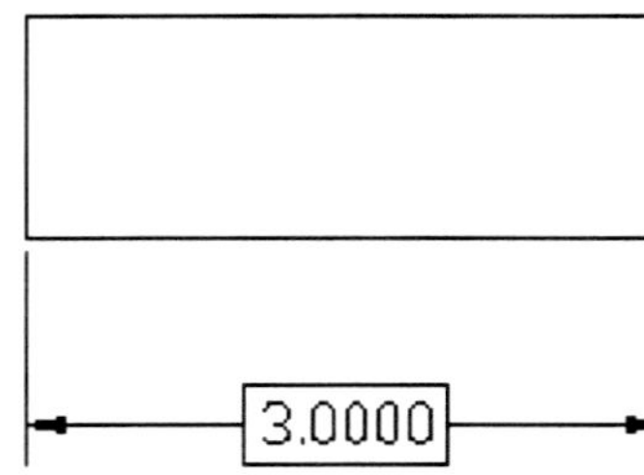


Figure 15.021: Basic Tolerance

- **Precision** works just as it did on the **Units** tabs.
- **Upper** and **Lower value** identify the value of the tolerances.
- **Scaling for height** allows you to set a separate text height (in proportion to the height set on the **Text** tab) for the tolerances.
- **Zero Suppression** works as it did on the **Units** tabs.

o **Alternate unit tolerance** controls tolerances for alternate units.

Let's complete our setup.

| | |
|---|---|
| **Do This: 15.1.6** | **Setting up Tolerances** |

I. Continue the previous exercise. Follow these steps.

## 15.1.6: Setting up Tolerances

1. On the **Tolerances** tab:
   a. Use the **Symmetrical** method …
   b. … with a precision of two decimal places …
   c. … and a value of **0.01**.
   d. Set the tolerance text height to ¾ the size of the dimension text …
   e. … and position the tolerances as shown.
   f. Suppress trailing zeros.

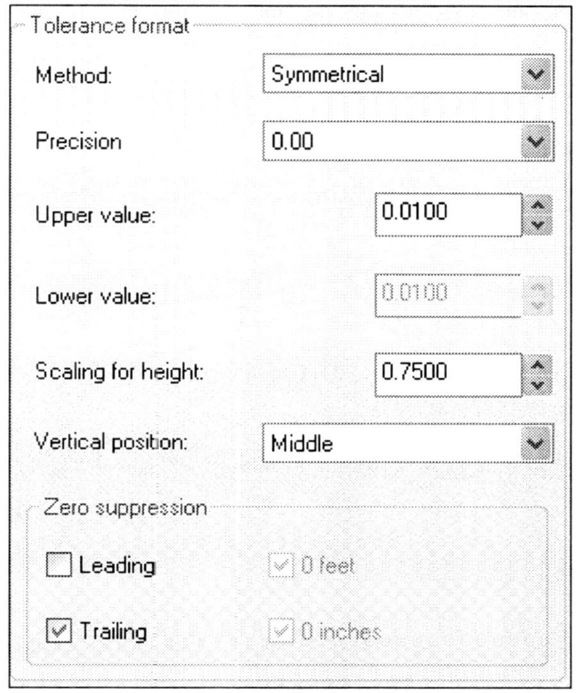


2. Pick the **OK** button 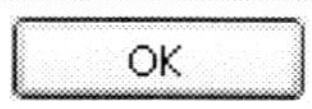 to complete the setup.

3. Pick the **Close** button 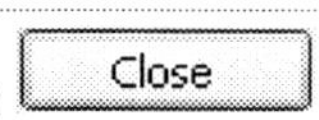 to exit the manager.

4. Save the drawing 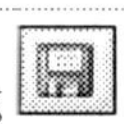 but don't exit.

   **Command: *qsave***

Remember: you can set each of the values you've studied in these last several pages separately for each member of the dimension *family*! This can prove quite handy when, for example, you want to place the dimension text *above* the dimension line, but you want to place radial text at the *end* of a leader. Alternately, you may want AutoCAD to automatically locate the dimension text for linear dimensions but allow you to manually locate it for angular dimensions.

Let's set up a child for radial dimensions.

| Do This: 15.1.8 | Setting up a Child |
|---|---|

I. Be sure you're still in the *drill-gizmo-15.dwg* file the C:\Steps\Lesson15 folder. If not, please open it now.

II. Follow these steps.

## 15.1.8: Setting up a Child

1. Reopen the Dimension Style Manager .

   **Command: *ddim***

2. Select the **First Steps** style in the list box.

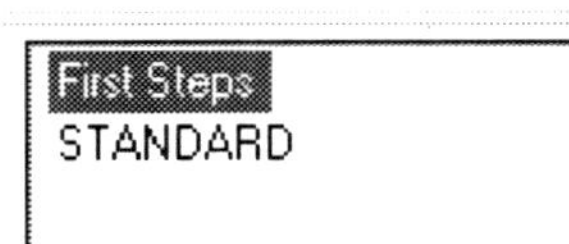


3. Pick the **New** button 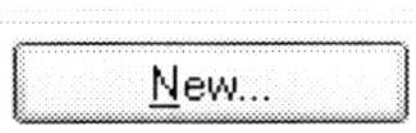 to create a new child of the **First Steps** style.

## 15.1.8: Setting up a Child

4. Use the **Use for** control box to set the child for **Radius dimensions**. Notice that the **New Style Name** box is grayed and unavailable for child styles.

Pick the **Continue** button to continue.

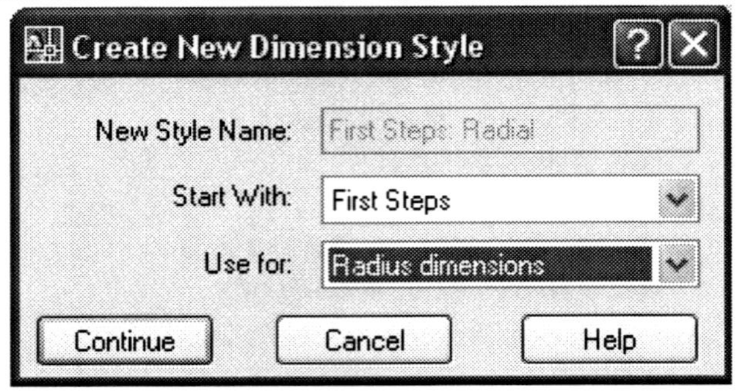


5. On the **Symbols and Arrows** tab, change the arrowheads to **Closed filled**. Remember that this will only affect radial dimensions.

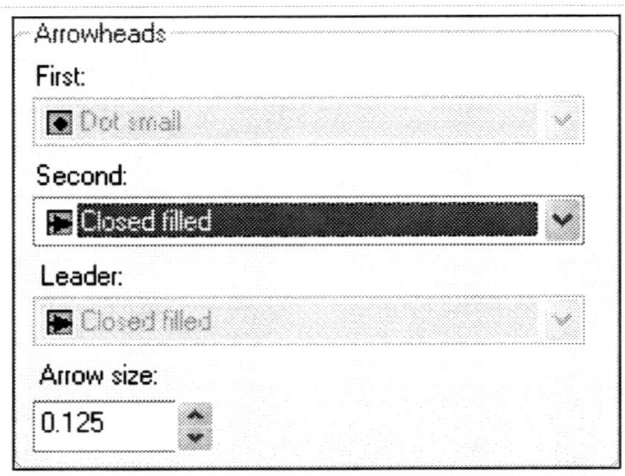


6. On the **Text** tab, set the vertical placement of the radial text as centered on the leader line …

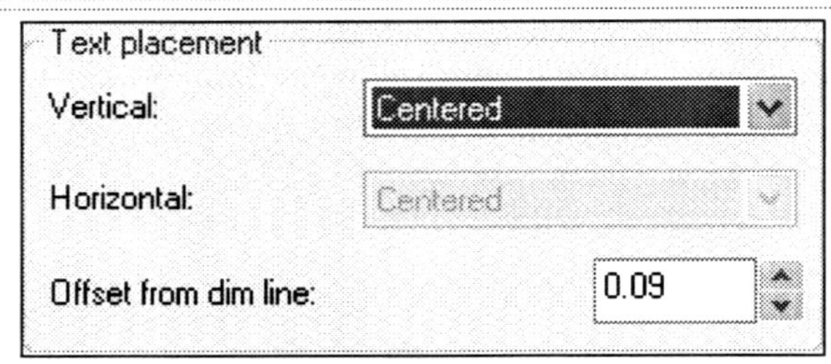


7. … and then set the text alignment to **Horizontal**. This will prevent radial dimensions appearing at oddball angles.

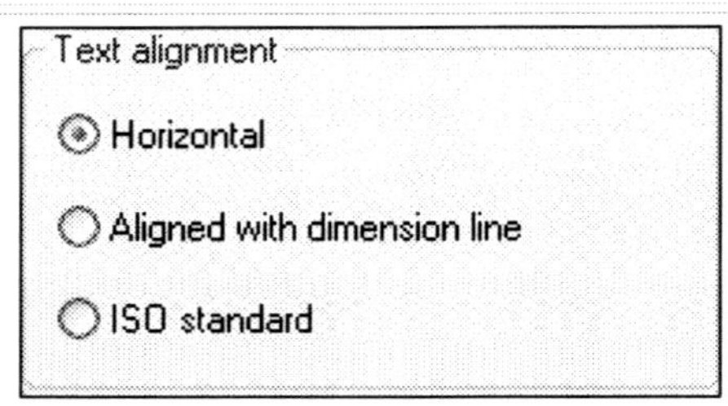


8. Complete the setup 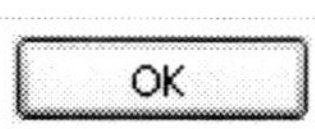

.

AutoCAD returns to the Dimension Style Manager. Notice the **Radial** child in the **Styles** list box.

9. Pick the **Close** button 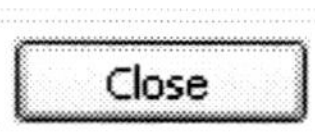

to complete the command.

10. Save the drawing 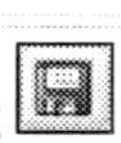 but don't exit.

**Command: *qsave***

Obviously, there's a tremendous amount of information to absorb if you want to master dimension styles. But unless you're determined to become the contract guru, it may not be necessary to memorize these dialog boxes. AutoCAD provides for everyone, even the casual user!

Your best approach to dimension styles may be to simply follow this text to set up the dimension style you prefer or the one you want to make standard for your contract. But be smart! Set up your dimension styles as part of your templates. Then you can forget them. (Another smart move will be to write down each setting as you go – computers crash and information gets lost!)

And remember – you can copy the dimstyle from one drawing to another using the AutoCAD Design Center (Lesson 6).

Let's see what our setup looks like.

| Do This: 15.1.9 | **Dimension the Drawing** |
|---|---|

I. Be sure you're still in the *drill-gizmo-15.dwg* file the C:\Steps\Lesson15 folder. If not, please open it now.

II. Dimension the drawing. It'll look like Figure 15.022 when you've finished.

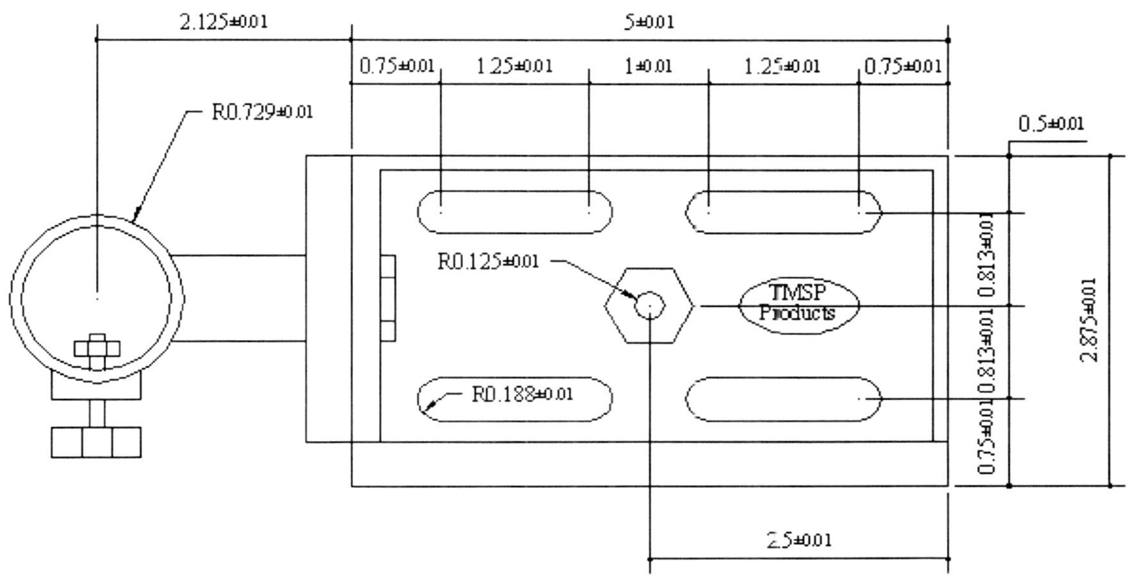


Figure 15.022

| 15.2 | Try One |
|---|---|

Now that you have some understanding of what it takes to create dimension styles and dimension a drawing, let's dimension our floor plan. As you're building experience with the software, I'm going to let you do as much as you can on your own. Refer back to the appropriate portion of the text as needed.

| Do This: 15.2.1 | **Dimension the Floor Plan** |
|---|---|

I. Open your *MyFlrPln15.dwg* file from the C:\Steps\Lesson15 folder. If it isn't available, open *FlrPln15.dwg* in the same folder.

II. Zoom all.

III. Create a dimension layer called **dim**. Assign the color **Yellow** to your new layer and make it current.

IV. Follow these steps.

## 15.2.1: Dimension the Floor Plan

1. Open the Dimension Style Manager.

   **Command: *ddim***

2. Create a new style [New...] called **Arch**. **Continue** to the New Dimension Style: Arch dialog box.

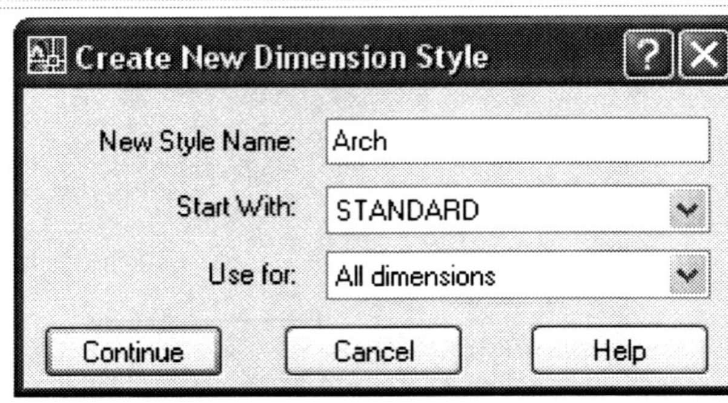


3. On the **Lines** tab:
   a. accept the default settings in the **Dimension lines** frame,
   b. set **Extension lines** to **Extend beyond dim lines** by 1/8”

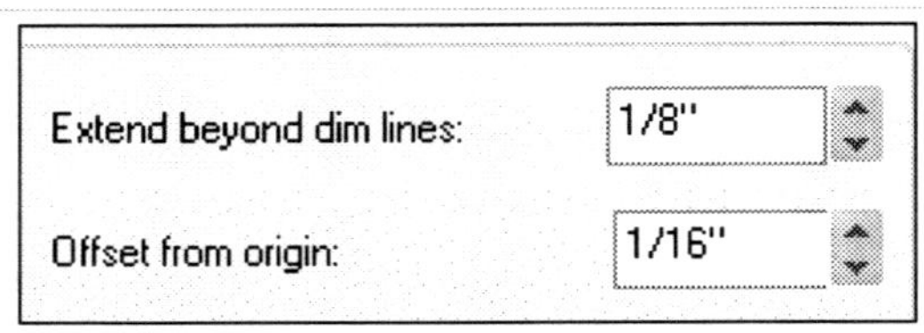


4. On the **Symbols and Arrows** tab:
   a. accept default settings for the **Arc length symbol** and the **Radius dimension jog**,
   b. use **Architectural ticks** for the **First** and **Second Arrowhead**,
   c. use **Closed filled** arrowheads for the **Leaders**,
   d. make the **Arrow size** 1/8”,
   e. don’t use **Center marks** on circles and arcs.

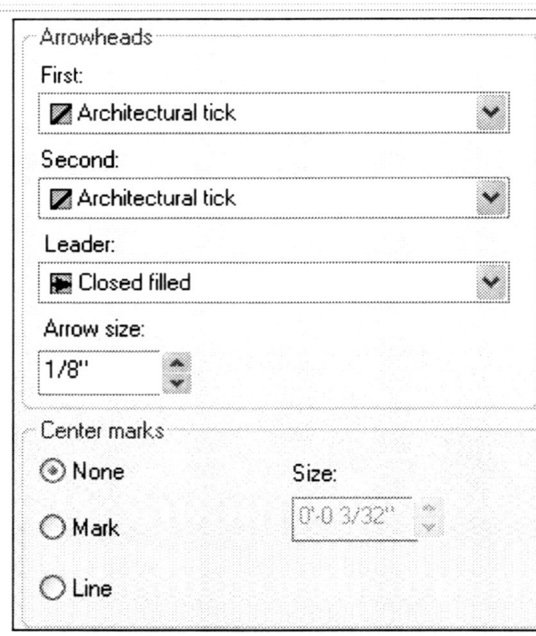


5. On the **Text** tab (see the following figure),
   a. use the **Times Text style**,
   b. use a **Text height** of 1/8”
   c. place vertical text **Above** the dimension line and **Center** horizontal text,
   d. use the **ISO standard Text alignment**.

## 15.2.1: Dimension the Floor Plan

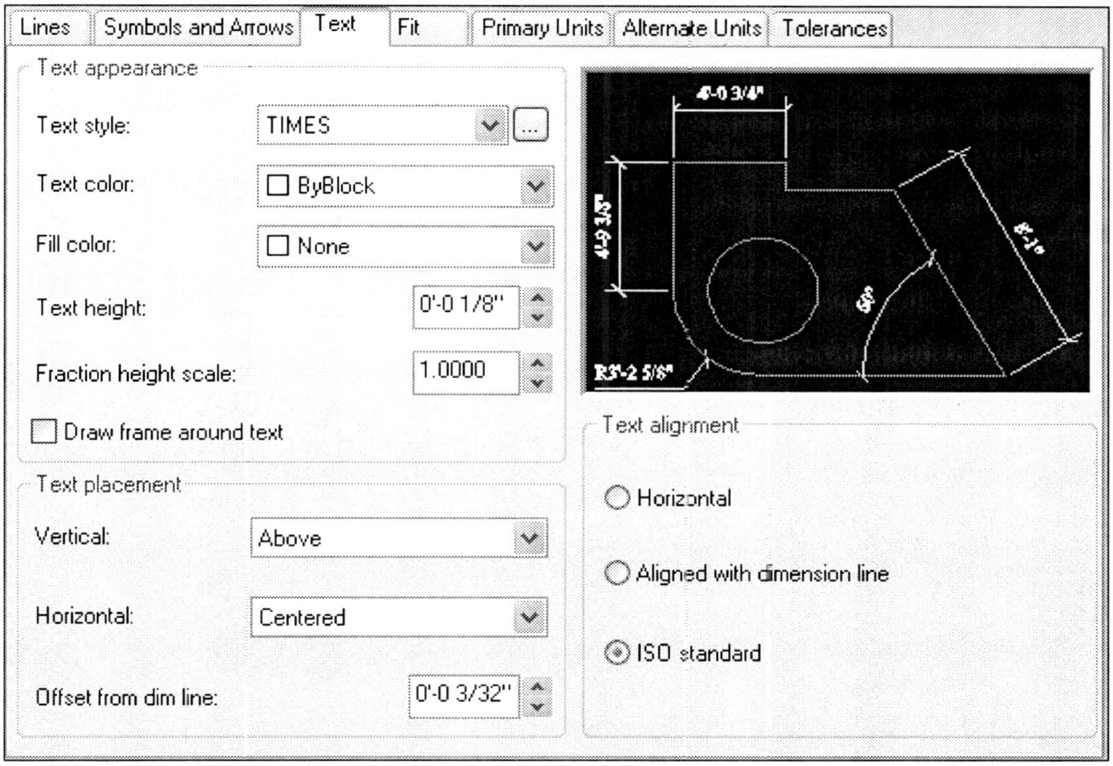


6. On the **Fit** tab (below),
   a. place the text **Over** the **dimension line, with leader**,
   b. use a dimension **scale** of 48.

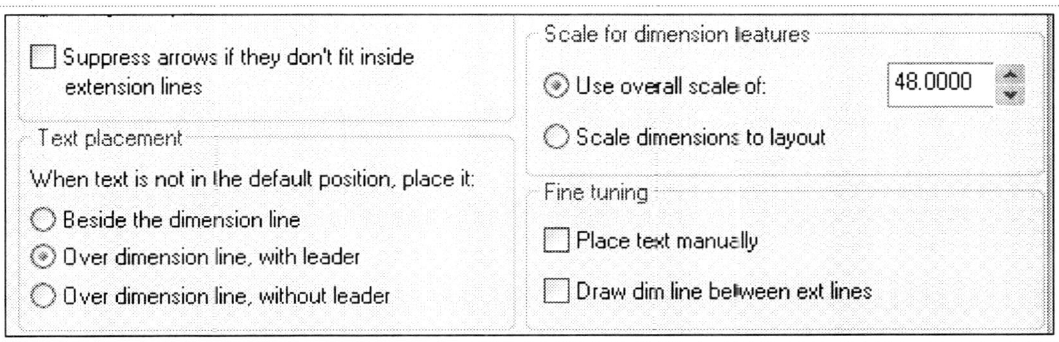

## 15.2.1: Dimension the Floor Plan

7. Set up the **Primary Units** tab as shown here.

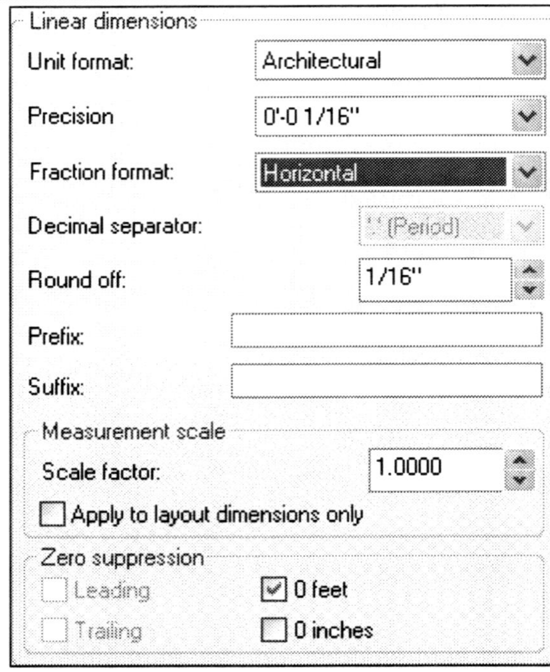


8. We won't need to do any setup on the **Alternate Units** or **Tolerances** tabs.

Pick the **OK** button 

to continue …

9. … then the **Close** button 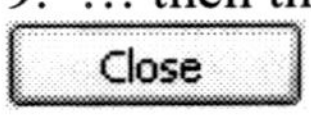

to finish the setup.

10. Use the **Dimension Style** control box on the Dimension toolbar to set the **Arch** dimstyle current.

11. Save the drawing  but don't exit.

**Command: *qsave***

12. Dimension the outer walls as shown in the following figure.

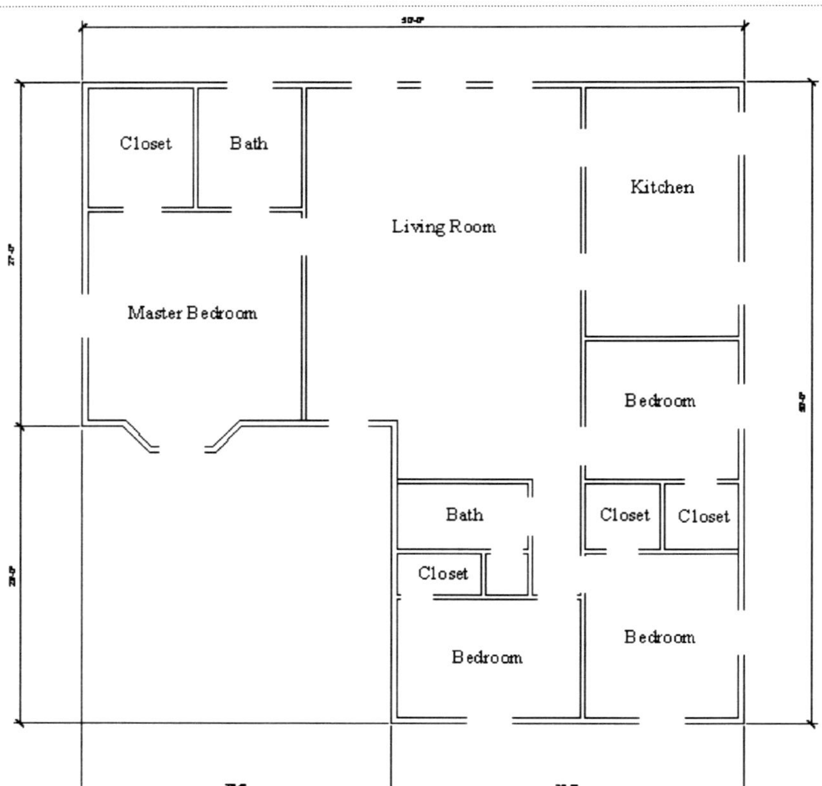

## 15.2.1: Dimension the Floor Plan

13. Now dimension the rest of the drawing. (Refer to the following figure) Notice that inner walls and door and window openings are dimensioned to their centers. There are a couple ways to do this:

   a. use the **Mid Between 2 Points** OSNAP, or

   b. load the *Points* Lisp routine in the C:\Steps\Lesson10 folder, and use its ***MW*** command to place a node midway between two points. Locate the midway point for the doors and windows and use that node for dimensioning.

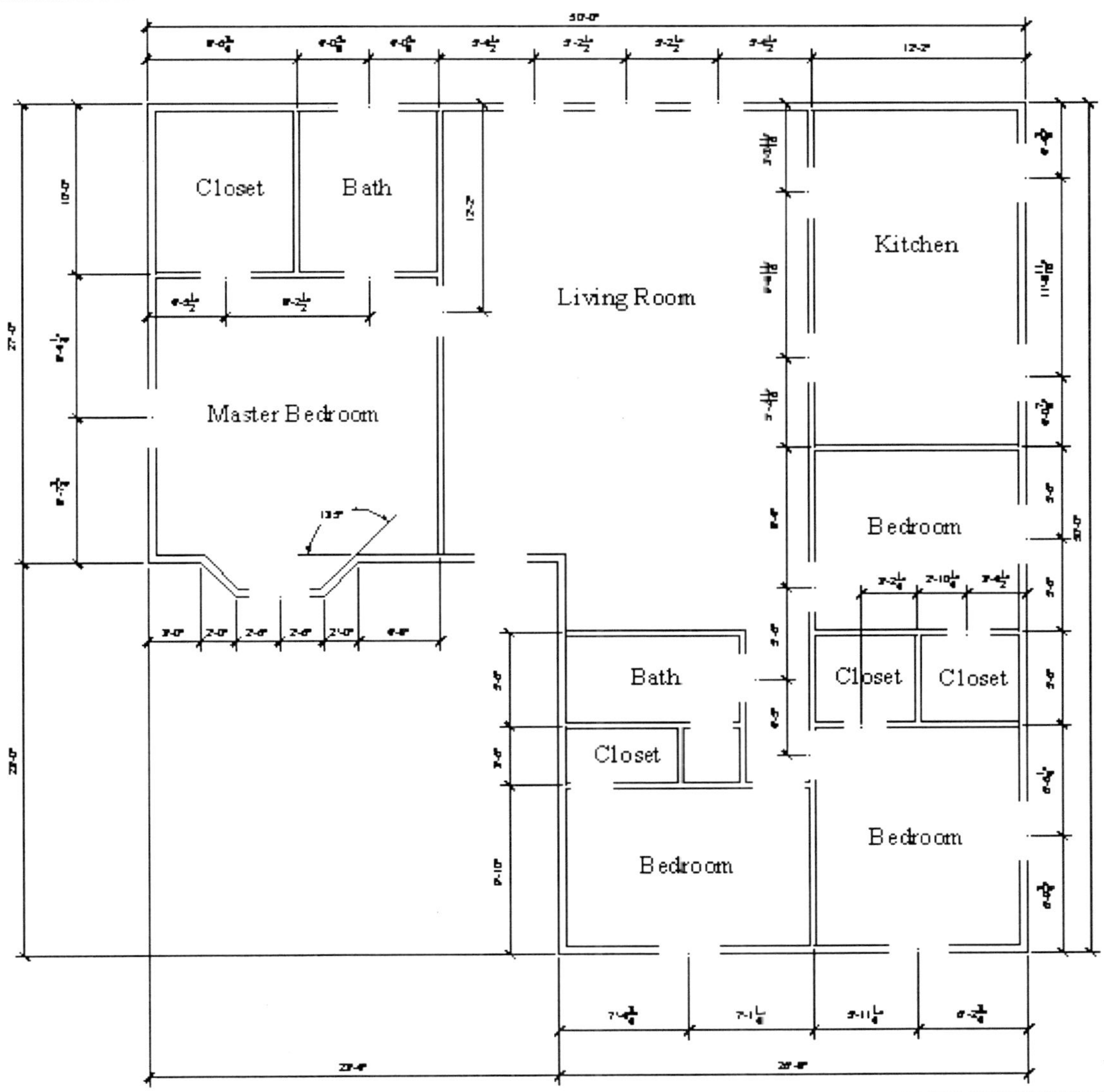


14. Save the drawing as *MyFlrPln19* to the C:\Steps\Lesson19 folder.

   **Command:** ***saveas***

## 15.3 Simple Repairs

### 15.3.1 Purging your Drawing

Setting up dimensions is no easy chore. Fortunately, AutoCAD provides some tools for accidents, boo boos, and uh, ohs!

The easiest way to rid a drawing of unwanted (and unused) dimension styles is to select the style in the list box of the Dimension Style Manager, and then hit the DELETE key on your keyboard. AutoCAD will prompt with an Are You Sure message box. Pick **Yes** to remove the style.

Another alternative for removing dimension styles – and unwanted linetypes, layers, blocks, multiline styles, and text styles (among other things) – is to use the Purge dialog box (Figure 15.023). Access the dialog box with the ***Purge*** command.

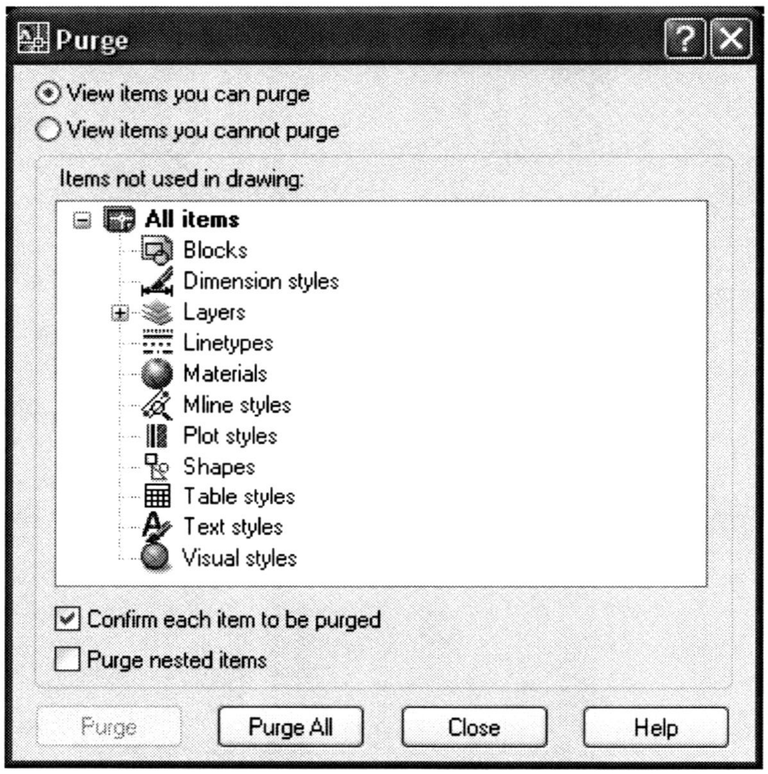


Figure 15.023

In the Purge dialog box, you can **View items you can purge** or **items you can't purge**. AutoCAD will list the items in the list box making it easy for you to decide which to remove from the drawing. Remember, once removed the item can't be recovered. However, removing unused items will lower file size.

### 15.3.2 Experimenting with Dim-Update

Occasionally, you'll find it necessary to change the setup of a dimension style. You'll notice when you do that existing dimensions don't always automatically change to reflect those changes. To change a dimension to reflect updated (or current) dimstyle settings, use the **Update** button on the Dimension toolbar.

### 15.3.3 Overriding Dimensions

You can use the **Override...** button on the Dimension Style Manager to set up dimension variables that differ from the style's settings. But if you use dimension overrides, be aware that as soon as you set a different style as current, the override settings disappear.

I advise against doing this; after all, if you need different settings once, you might need them again. It's best to set up a new style.

A better approach might be to use the Properties Paletts to adjust your dimensions' variables once they've been placed.

## 15.4 Extra Steps

Take a few minutes to go over the dimension variables (dimvars) in Appendix E. You can set each of these at the command line simply by typing the dimvar and a value.

Then take a look at the command line approach to dimension styles. It looks like this:

> **Command: *-dimstyle***
>
> **Current dimension style: arch *[AutoCAD tells you which style is current]***
>
> **Enter a dimension style option**
>
> **[Save/Restore/STatus/Variables/Apply/?] <Restore>: *[hit enter to make a different style current]***
>
> **Enter a dimension style name, [?] or <select dimension>: *[type the name of the dimension style you wish to make current]***

- Use the **Save** option to create a new style based on the current dimvar settings. Use the **Restore** option (the default) to switch from one style to another.
- The **STatus** option will show you the current settings of the dimvars.
- Using the **Variables** option, you can select a dimension and read the values of the dimvars used to create that dimension.
- The **Apply** option will change user-selected dimensions so they use the current dimvars.

This should make you appreciate the Dimension Style Manager!

## 15.5 What Have We Learned?

*Items covered in this lesson include:*

- *Defining Dimension Styles*
- *Updating Dimensions*
- *Commands:*
  - ***Ddim***
  - ***Purge***

It's important to take the time now to get comfortable with dimensioning. After all, drafting without dimensioning wouldn't be of much use to anyone. Dimensioning itself doesn't have to be difficult if you take the time to get familiar with the toolbar. But dimvars and dimension styles can easily overwhelm the AutoCAD novice.

If you don't feel comfortable with dimensioning, go back to Lesson 14 and do 14 and 15 again. Then say to yourself, "I've met the challenge and am wiser for it!"

## 15.6 Exercises

1. Open the *drillguide.dwg* file in the C:\Steps\Lesson15 folder. Create an appropriate dimension style to dimension the image as indicated below.
   1.1. Use **small dot** arrowheads but no center marks.
   1.2. Use an overall **scale** of 1.
   1.3. Use decimal units accurate to three decimal places (suppress trailing zeros).
   1.4. Use standard 1/8" text.
   1.5. Allow a tolerance deviation of 1° on all angles, and a precision of zero decimal places.
   1.6. All dimensions should be above the dimension line except radii which should be centered on the leader.

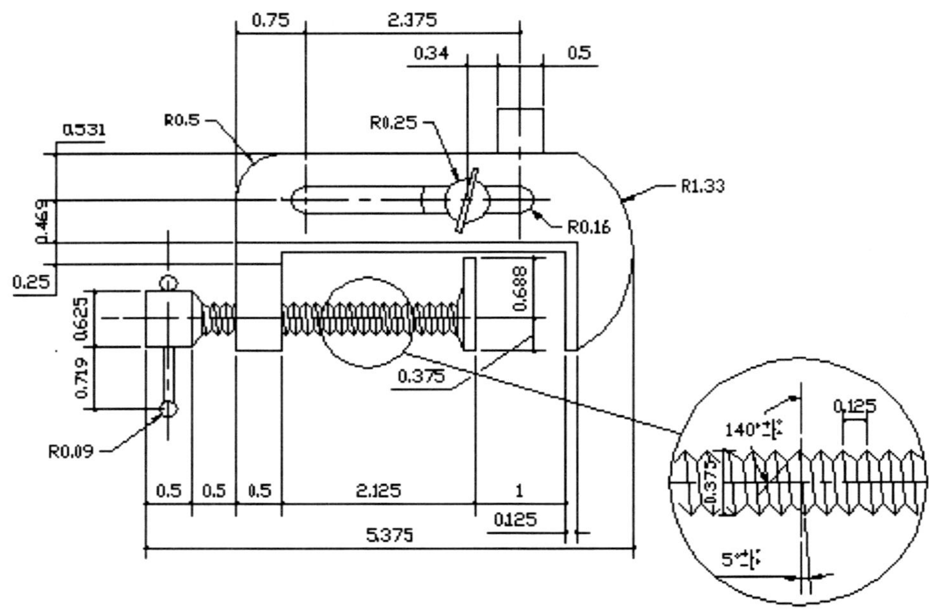


Drill Guide

*For more exercises related to Lesson 15, please see Lesson 15 in AutoCAD 2007: One Step at a Time – Workbook.*

## 15.7 For Web-Based Review Questions, visit: http://www.uneedcad.com/2007/Files/07R15.pdf

# Lesson 16

Following this lesson, you will:

- ✓ *Know how to use alternate selection techniques found in the* ***Selections*** *Tab of the Options dialog box, including:*
  - *Noun/Verb Selection*
  - *Shift to Add*
  - *Press and Drag*
  - *Implied Windowing*
- ✓ *Know how to use Grip commands to modify objects:*
  - ***Stretch***
  - ***Move***
  - ***Rotate***
  - ***Mirror***
  - ***Scale***

# Advanced Modification Techniques

*After all that effort to master dimensioning, why not take some time for something different (and much easier than the last two lessons)? Lesson 16 will deal with some nifty techniques that, although not often used by anyone other than well-trained CAD operators, can enhance your drawing speed even beyond the techniques you've already learned!*

*We'll begin with some fairly simple techniques that you may have (indeed, probably have) stumbled across already. (Have you noticed that selecting an object before picking the **Erase** button produces the same result as if you had picked the button first?)*

*Knowing how to use these techniques can help you draw faster; knowing how to turn them off if you don't want to use them can save your sanity!*

*We'll spend most of the lesson discovering grips. These are the culprits responsible for those little squares that dot an object when you select it at the command prompt instead of a **select objects** prompt. But mastering grips will put a smile on your face that a beginning CAD operator just won't understand!*

*First, however, let's take a look at some advanced object selection methods.*

## 16.1 Object Selection Settings

It'll be easier to understand selection settings and grips if they're not both active at once. Let's begin our study of the selection settings by turning off the grips. Follow this procedure:

**Command:** ***grips***

**Enter new value for GRIPS <1>:** ***0***

We'll reactivate them when we finish with this section of the text.

There are several different selection settings designed to enhance your use of AutoCAD, each with a different system variable that you can set at the command line. But AutoCAD also provides a tab on the Options dialog box that might be easier to use than half-a-dozen system variables.

Figure 16.001 (next page) shows the dialog box with the **Selections** tab on top. (*Caution: Avoid changes to the other tabs at this time.*)

Look at the frames on the left first.

- **Pickbox Size** contains a slider bar. Use this to adjust the size of the cursor box presented when AutoCAD uses a **Select objects** prompt.

  The system variable for **Pickbox Size** is **Pickbox**. I prefer a setting of **4** or **5** (an allowance for my aging eyes – many experienced users prefer **3**), but adjust it until you're happy.
- The **Selection Preview** frame has two check boxes:
  - Check **When a command is active** (the default) when you want AutoCAD to show you what you've selected in response to a **Select objects** prompt. (AutoCAD will highlight the selection.)
  - Check **When no command is active** (the default) when you want AutoCAD to show you what you've selected even if you made the selection at the command prompt. (You'll need this checked during the exercises in this lesson.)
  - The **Visual Effects Settings** button in this frame presents the Visual Effect Settings dialog box (Figure 16.002 – next page).
    - Use the radio buttons in the **Selection Preview Effect** frame to determine how AutoCAD will highlight selected objects. The **Advanced Options** button will present an Advanced Preview Options dialog box (Figure 16.003 – second page following) where you can filter exactly what AutoCAD can or cannot select.

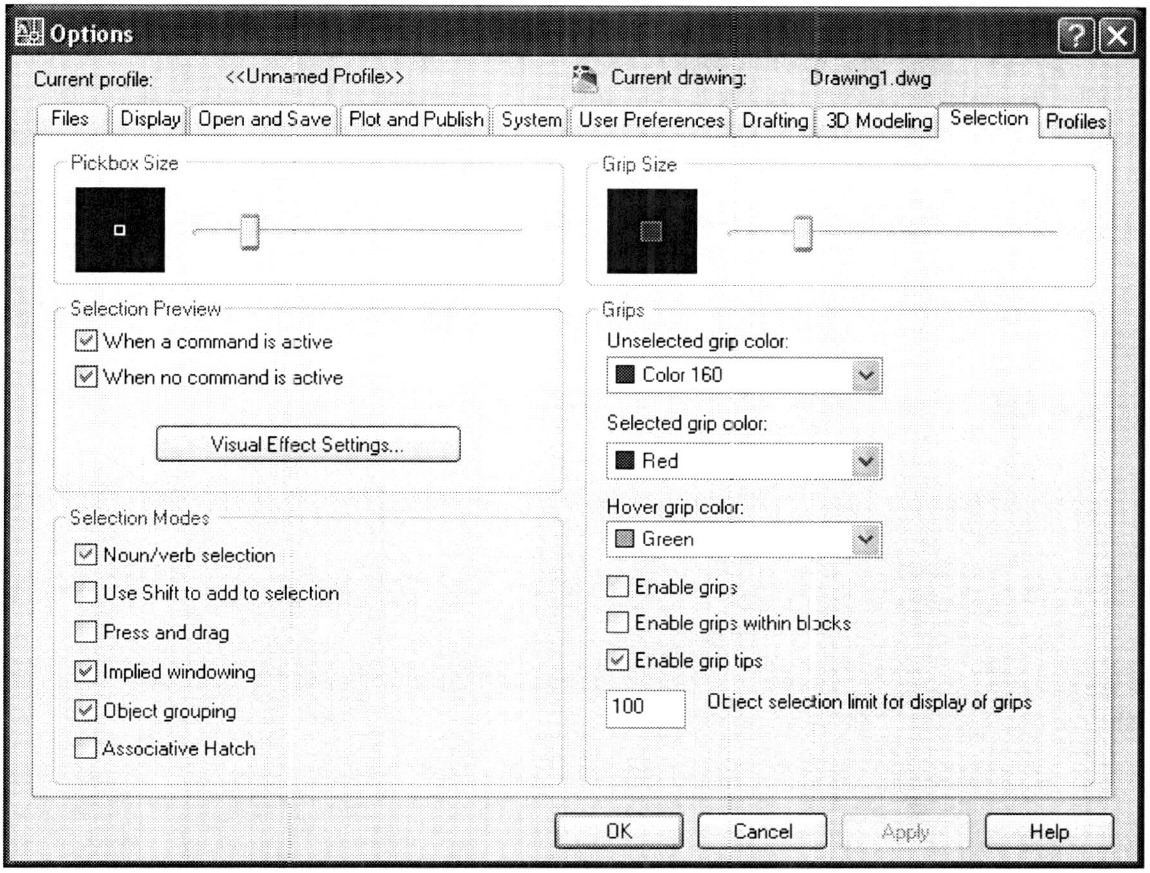


Figure 16.001

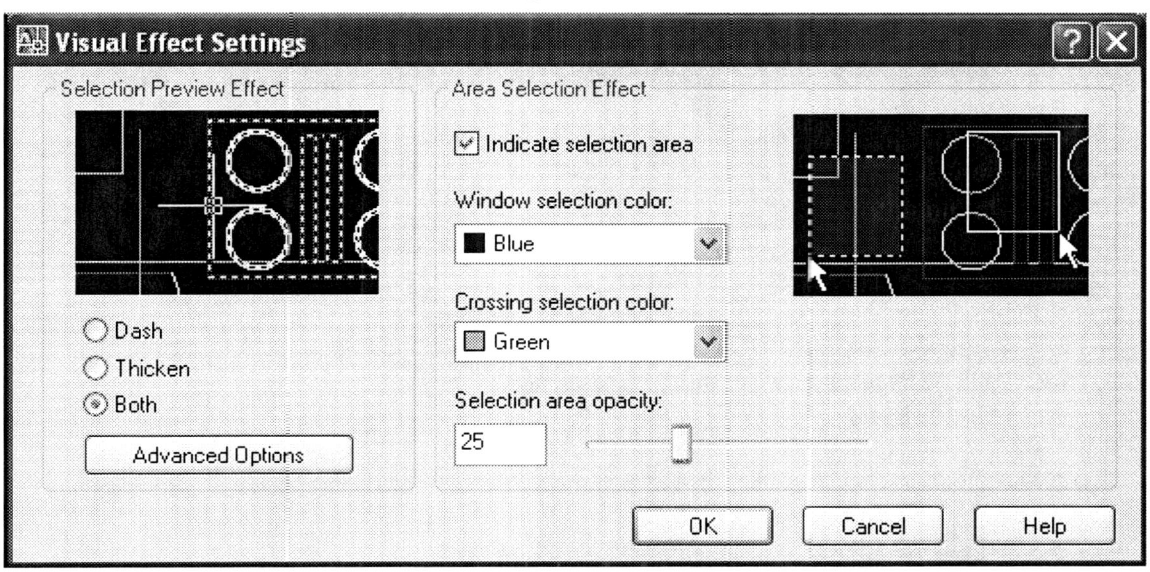


Figure 16.002

- Tools in the **Area Selection Effect** frame allow you to customize the selection windows AutoCAD uses.

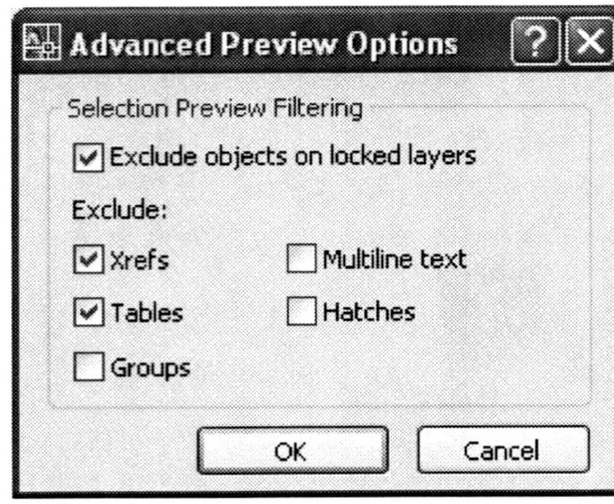

Figure 16.003

- We'll concentrate most of this section on the tools found in the **Selection Modes** frame (back on the **Selection** tab of the Options dialog box). Let's begin our study of these tools now.
  - The "normal" approach to object modification in AutoCAD is to issue a command (like ***Erase***), and then select the object(s) of that that command. This approach can be called *Verb/Noun* as the command is invariably a verb and the object is a noun. Placing a check in the box next to **Noun/Verb Selection** (as the default does) means that AutoCAD will also allow you to select the object of the command first, and then enter the command. The sequence (using the ***Erase*** command) looks like this:

    **Command: *[select an object(s)]***

    **Command: *e***

    The system variable for **Noun/Verb Selection** is **Pickfirst**. Its default setting is **1**.

| Do This: 16.1.1 | Noun/Verb Selection |
|---|---|

I. Open the *Grips.dwg* file the C:\Steps\Lesson16 folder. The drawing looks like Figure 16.004.

II. Follow these steps.

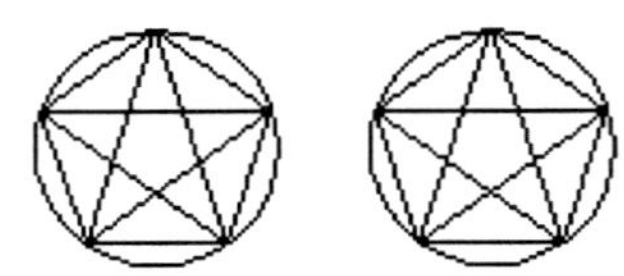
Figure 16.004

**16.1.1: NOUN/VERB SELECTION**

1. Restore the **SELECTION** view . It looks like this (grid removed for clarity).

   **Command: *v***

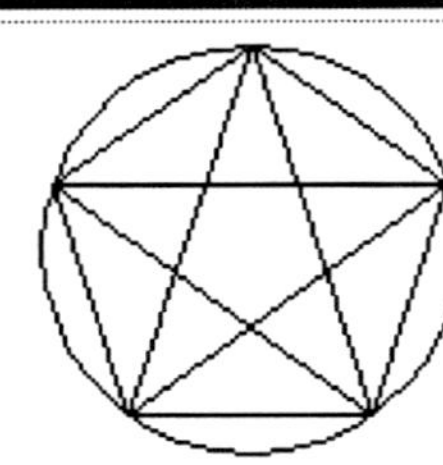

2. Enter the ***Options*** command by typing ***options*** or ***op***. AutoCAD presents the Options dialog box. Pick the **Selection** tab to put it on top (Figure 16.001).

   **Command: *op***

3. Verify that there is a check in the **Noun/verb selection** check box 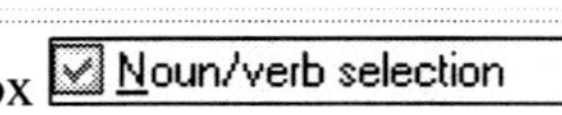

.

4. Pick the **OK** button 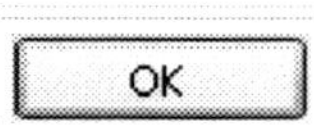

to return to the drawing.

### 16.1.1: Noun/Verb Selection

5. Select the two lines that form the topmost point of the star.

**Command:**

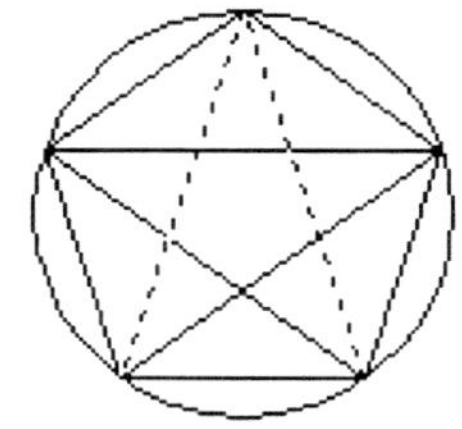

6. Enter the ***Erase*** command . Notice that the lines are erased.

**Command:** ***e***

7. Save the drawing 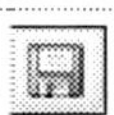 but don't exit.

**Command:** ***qsave***

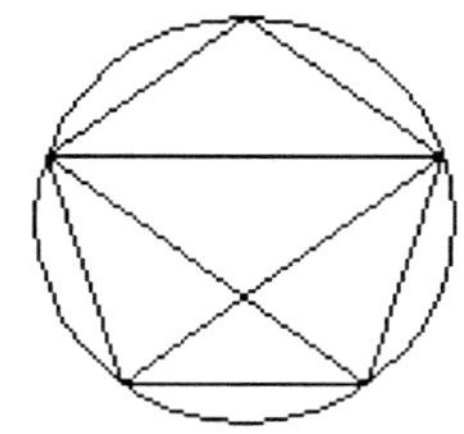

- In many Windows programs, selecting more than a single file or object requires you to hold down the SHIFT key. AutoCAD makes an allowance for users accustomed to this approach in the next option – **Use Shift to add to selection**. If this box contains a check, selecting a second object will remove all previous objects from the selection set unless you hold down the SHIFT key while selecting.

  The system variable for **Use Shift to add to selection** is **Pickadd**. Its default setting is **1**.

| Do This: 16.1.2 | Using Shift to Add |
|---|---|

I. Be sure you're still in the *Grips.dwg* file the C:\Steps\Lesson16 folder. If not, please open it now.

II. Follow these steps.

### 16.1.2: Using Shift to Add

1. Enter the ***Options*** command. Be sure the **Selection** tab is on top.

**Command:** ***op***

2. Place a check in the **Use Shift to add to selection** check box 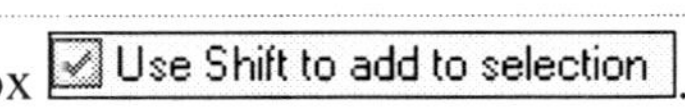.


3. Pick the **OK** button 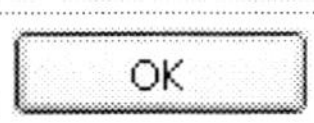 to return to the drawing.


4. Enter the ***Erase*** command 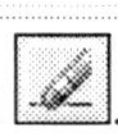.

**Command:** ***e***

5. Select the horizontal line and then the two angled lines. Notice that, as you select an object, the previously selected object is removed from the selection set (it's no longer highlighted).

**Select objects:**

6. Now select the horizontal line. Then, while holding down the SHIFT key, select the angled lines. Notice that they all highlight.

**Select objects:**

## 16.1.2: Using Shift to Add

7. Complete the command. The view now looks like this.

   **Select objects:** ***[enter]***

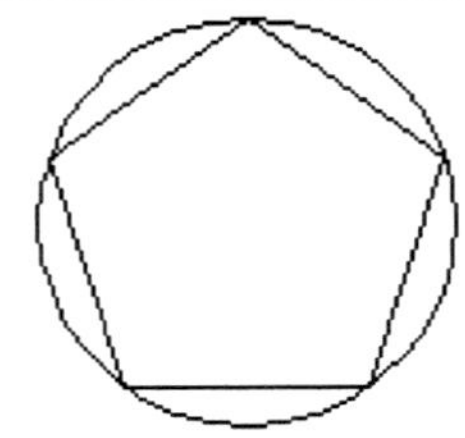

8. Save the drawing but don't exit.

   **Command:** ***qsave***

- Again, in many Windows programs, placing a window around objects requires you to hold down the mouse button between corner selections. AutoCAD doesn't require this, but it allows for those who have become accustomed to it. A check in the **Press and Drag** box will change window creation to the following procedure:
  1. Pick the first corner of the window.
  2. Hold down the mouse button while positioning the crosshairs at the opposite corner.
  3. Release the mouse button.

  The system variable for **Press and Drag** is **Pickdrag**. Its default setting is **0**.

| **Do This: 16.1.3** | **Using Press and Drag** |
|---|---|

I. Be sure you're still in the *Grips.dwg* file the C:\Steps\Lesson16 folder. If not, please open it now.

II. Follow these steps.

## 16.1.3: Using Press and Drag

1. Open the Options dialog box and place the **Selections** tab on top.

   **Command:** ***op***

2. Remove the check from the **Use Shift to add to selection** check box, and add a check in the **Press and drag** check box.

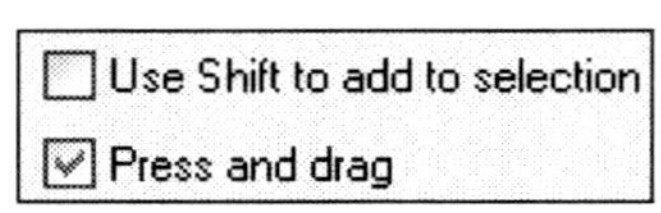


3. Complete the procedure OK.

4. Enter the ***Erase*** command.

   **Command:** ***e***

5. Try to begin an implied window as you normally would – by selecting a point around the grid mark at coordinate **6,5**. Notice that you lose the window as soon as you release the mouse button.

   **Select objects:**

6. Try it again. But this time hold down the mouse button as you move the lower right corner of the window to the grid mark around coordinate **11,0**. Now you get the window.

   **Select objects:**

7. Release the mouse button to complete the selection window.

### 16.1.3: Using Press and Drag

8. Complete the command.

   **Select objects:** ***[enter]***

The view is now empty.

9. Zoom to the limits  of the drawing,

   **Command:** ***z***

10. Repeat Steps 1 through 3, but this time, remove the check next to **Press and drag**.

11. Save the drawing  but don't exit.

   **Command:** ***qsave***

- We've been using Implied Windowing since Lesson 2. It enables us to pick an open area of the drawing to automatically begin a selection window. It's **On** by default. Removing the check will turn it off.
- The system variable for Implied Windowing is **Pickauto** Its default setting is **1**.
- A check in the **Object Grouping** option box means that AutoCAD will recognize grouped objects as a single object. We'll learn more about grouping in Lesson 18.
- The system variable for **Object Grouping** is **Pickstyle**. Its default setting is **1**. (CTRL+A will also toggle object grouping On and Off.)
- We'll look at the **Associative Hatch** option in Lesson 18 as well.

## 16.2 "A Whole New Ball Game!" Editing with Grips

Before we begin our experiments with grips, we must reactivate them. Follow this sequence:

**Command:** ***grips***

**Enter new value for GRIPS <0>:** ***1***

It'll also help if we deactivate Noun/Verb Selection. It isn't mandatory; they'll work together. But Noun/Verb Selection might confuse your study of grips, so let's turn it off for now. You can use the Options dialog box we just covered, or you can follow this sequence:

**Command:** ***pickfirst***

**Enter new value for PICKFIRST <1>:** ***0***

I've always approached grips with reluctance in my basic AutoCAD classes. It's not that they're not remarkable tools; it's just that most students in a basic class are still trying to master the "normal" modifying tools. These are fairly simple and straightforward – if you want to copy something, you type ***copy***. AutoCAD then leads you through the necessary steps by dynamic prompts at the cursor menu or by prompts at the command line. Grips, on the other hand, are more intuitive. That is, they require that you *know* how to move from one step to the next, and that you know where the specific desired modification tool is located in the grip prompts.

So, exactly what are grips?

Grips are control points located on all objects, blocks, and groups. We'll look at blocks and groups in Lesson 19, but we can gain an understanding of grips using simple lines, polylines, and circles.

Grips are assigned to specific locations on specific objects. That is, all lines and arcs will have grips at the endpoints and midpoint. All circles will have grips at the center point and quadrants. And all polylines will have grips at the vertices.

You can control all aspects of grips display using the Options dialog box (Figure 16.001). Here, you can set up different grip colors and sizes (not recommended), enable/disable grips in the drawing (the dialog box method of setting the **Grips** system variable), or enable/disable grips within blocks (more on blocks in Lesson 19).

There are five basic modification commands available using grips: ***Stretch***, ***Move***, ***Rotate***, ***Scale***, and ***Mirror***. ***Copy*** is also available as an option of each of the primary Grip commands or as a default when you hold down the CTRL key while using a grip procedure.

To access the commands, first select the object(s) you wish to modify. (Do this without entering a command.) The blue grips that display for each of the objects are called *unselected* grips. Picking on a grip will cause it to change (as shown in Figure 16.005) to a red, *selected* grip. Your crosshairs will automatically snap to a grip regardless of the **Snap** setting. You must select a grip to modify the object. (***To disable* [clear] *grips, hit the* ESC *key.*)

Note that you can select multiple objects using a window or crossing window just as you've always done. Selecting multiple objects simply means that the grips for several objects will display at once.

To remove an object from a selection set, hold down the SHIFT key and select the object to remove. Its grips will disappear and the object won't be highlighted and won't be affected by the editing procedure. (Note: In earlier releases, the grips remained visible, but the object wasn't affected by modification procedures.)

Once a grip has been selected, AutoCAD's command line presents the grip options for the ***Stretch*** command. You can toggle through the commands (***Stretch***, ***Move***, ***Rotate***, ***Scale***, ***Mirror***) by hitting the space bar.

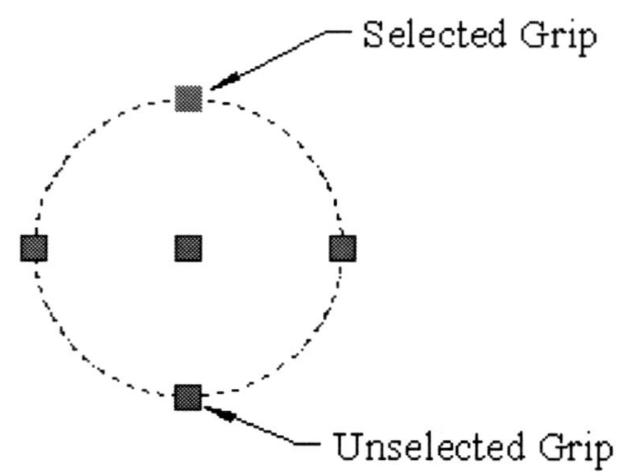

Figure 16.005

The initial grips prompt looks like this:

**** STRETCH ****

**Specify stretch point or [Base point/Copy/Undo/eXit]:**

- By default, you'll stretch the object using the opposite endpoint as an anchor.
- Selecting the **Base point** option will allow you to change the point at which you "hold" the object while stretching it. The default base point is the selected, or "hot," grip.
- The **Copy** option provides one of the great benefits of using grips – you can leave the original object as it is and create stretched copies. (You can create multiple copies by default!)
- The rest of the options are self-explanatory.

A nifty trick to using grips involves the CTRL key. Holding it down while locating the "to point" of the stretched line will automatically start the **Copy** option. Continuing to hold it down after the first "to point" is selected will cause grips to function in *offset* mode. That is, AutoCAD will determine an offset distance from the first "to point" selection; then it'll create subsequent copies at the same interval.

These techniques work as well for each of the five grips procedures.

Let's see what we can do with the ***Stretch*** grip procedure.

| Do This: 16.2.1 | Editing with Grips - Stretch |
|---|---|

I. Be sure you're still in the *Grips.dwg* file the C:\Steps\Lesson16 folder. If not, please open it now.

II. Follow these steps.

### 16.2.1: Editing with Grips - Stretch

1. Select the upper part of the star with a crossing window as shown.

   **Command:**

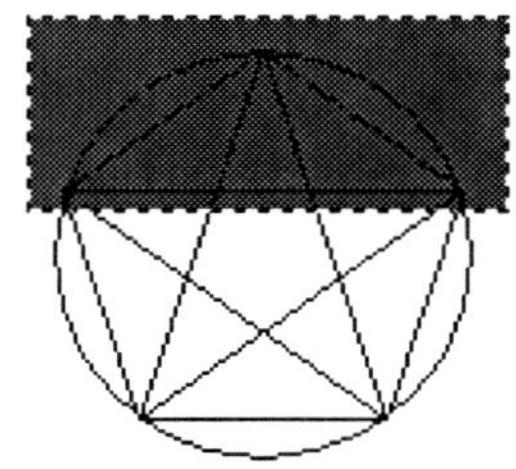

2. Notice that grips appear on each of the individual objects and that each highlights.

   **Command:**

3. Select the topmost grip.

   **Command:**

   Notice that it turns red and that the command line presents the initial grips options.

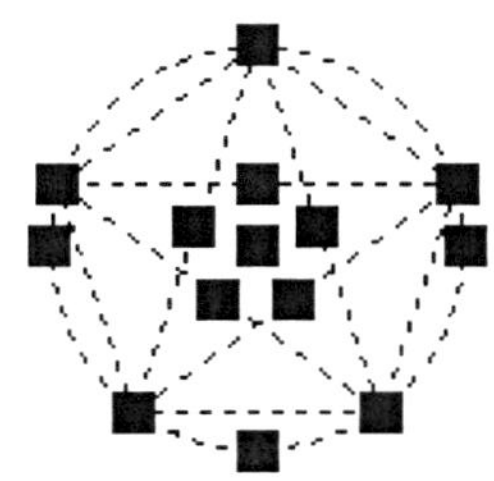

4. Pick a point three grid marks due north of the top of the star. (Turn on the snap to help you.)

   **** STRETCH ****

   **Specify stretch point or [Base point/ Copy/Undo/eXit]:**

   Notice which objects stretch. Your drawing looks like this. (Zoom or pan as necessary for a better view.)

   You've discovered the grips method of resizing a circle. You've also seen that, although it was in the selection set, the horizontal line in the star didn't change. This is because none of its grips were selected.

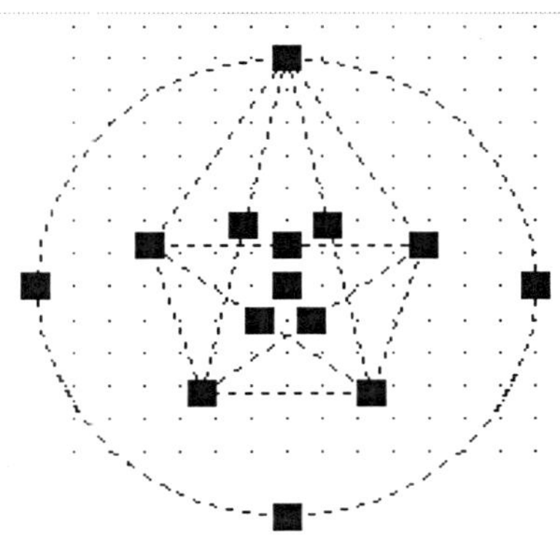

5. ***Undo*** the last modification.

   **Command: *u***

6. Repeat Step 1.

7. Let's remove the circle from the selection set. Hold down the SHIFT key and select it (select the circle, *not a grip*). Notice that its grips disappear, and that it's no longer highlighted.

8. Hit the ESC key [Esc] to clear the grips.

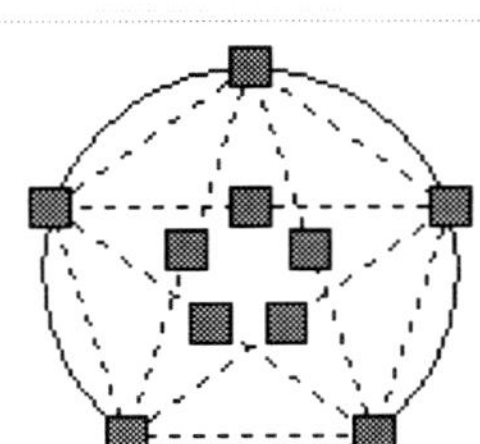

## 16.2.1: Editing with Grips - Stretch

9. This time, select just the two lines that form the upper point of the star.

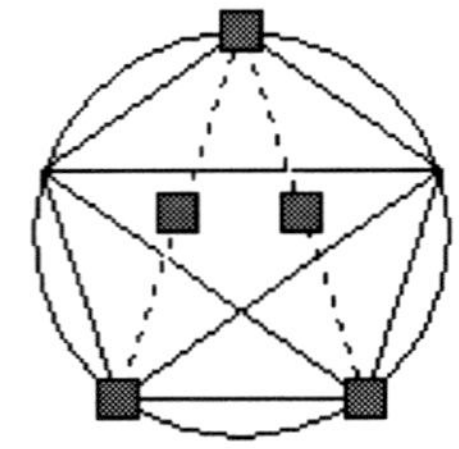

10. Select the topmost grip, then type *c* at the prompt (or select **Copy** from the menu 

) to activate the **Copy** option.

**** STRETCH ****
**Specify stretch point or [Base point/ Copy/Undo/eXit]: *c***

11. Notice how the prompt changes.
Going north, skip a grid mark and then pick the next. Do this twice.

**** STRETCH (multiple) ****
**Specify stretch point or [Base point/ Copy/Undo/eXit]:**

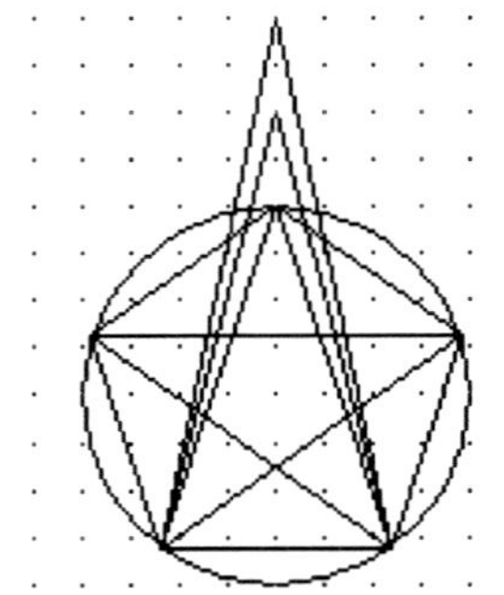

12. Hit ***enter*** to complete the procedure. (Alternately, you can pick **Exit** from the cursor menu to complete the grips procedure).

**** STRETCH (multiple) ****
**Specify stretch point or [Base point/ Copy/Undo/eXit]: *[enter]***

13. Clear the grips 

.

14. Undo the last modification 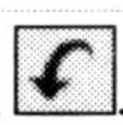.

**Command: *u***

Figure 16.006

Thaw the **TXT** layer for this next exercise. The text *My Star* appears (Figure 16.006).

We can use the command line to access the various methods used by grips. Simply use the spacebar to scroll through the options. But there's another way.

Any time the grip prompts are on the command line – that is, any time you've selected a grip – you can right-click in the drawing area to access the cursor menu that provides the same options as the command line. The menu is shown in Figure 16.007.

- The topmost option is the equivalent of its keyboard counterpart.
- **Recent Input** lists the last several responses to the current command. You can select one if you wish, or enter something else.
- The next section includes the five grips procedures (the same ones you'll see when using the spacebar to toggle through the

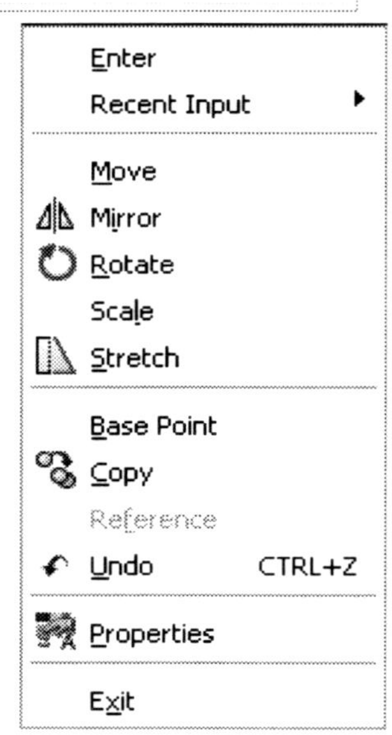


Figure 16.007

grips procedures on the command line).

- The third section shows the options available for the current grip procedure.
- **Properties** in the fourth section will cause the Properties Palette to appear.
- **Exit**, of course, returns you to the command prompt.

We'll use this menu, the dynamic input menu, and the spacebar approach to toggling grips procedures in our next exercise.

Let's examine the ***Rotate*** and ***Mirror*** Grips procedures.

| Do This: 16.2.2 | More Grips Editing |
|---|---|

I. Be sure you're still in the *Grips.dwg* file the C:\Steps\Lesson16 folder. If not, please open it now.

II. Follow these steps.

## 16.2.2: MORE GRIPS EDITING

1. Select all of the objects. Use a window or crossing window.

   **Command:**

2. Select the grip at the tip of the upper right star point. AutoCAD presents the grip options.

   **Command:**

3. Hit the spacebar twice to access the grips ***Rotate*** procedure.

   **** STRETCH ****

   **Specify stretch point or [Base point/Copy/Undo/eXit]:** ***[spacebar]***

   **** MOVE ****

   **Specify move point or [Base point/Copy/Undo/eXit]:** ***[spacebar]***

4. Type ***c*** to access the **Copy** option.

   **** ROTATE ****

   **Specify rotation angle or [Base point/Copy/Undo/Reference/ eXit]:** ***c***

5. Tell AutoCAD you wish to create a rotated copy at an angle of ***144°***.

   **** ROTATE (multiple) ****

   **Specify rotation angle or [Base point/Copy/Undo/Reference/ eXit]:** ***144***

6. Exit the procedure, and then clear the grips Esc.

   **** ROTATE (multiple) ****

   **Specify rotation angle or [Base point/Copy/Undo/Reference/ eXit]:** ***[enter]***

   Your drawing looks like this.

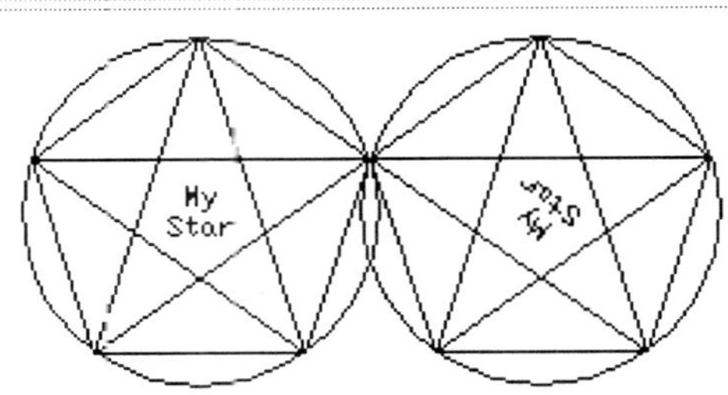


7. Undo the last modification 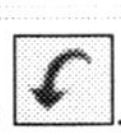.

   **Command:** ***u***

8. Let's try to rotate the objects using the **Reference** option. Repeat Steps 1 and 2.

## 16.2.2: More Grips Editing

9. Right-click in the drawing area and select the ***Rotate*** procedure.

**** STRETCH ****

**Specify stretch point or [Base point/Copy/Undo/ eXit]: _rotate**

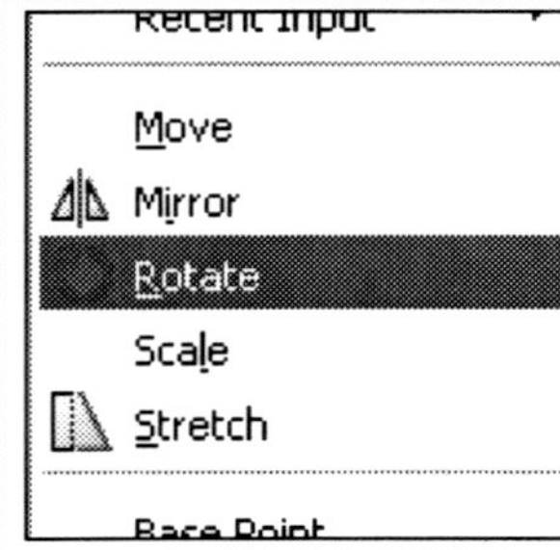


10. Right-click again and select the **Copy** option.

**** ROTATE ****

**Specify rotation angle or [Base point/Copy/Undo/ Reference/eXit]: _copy**

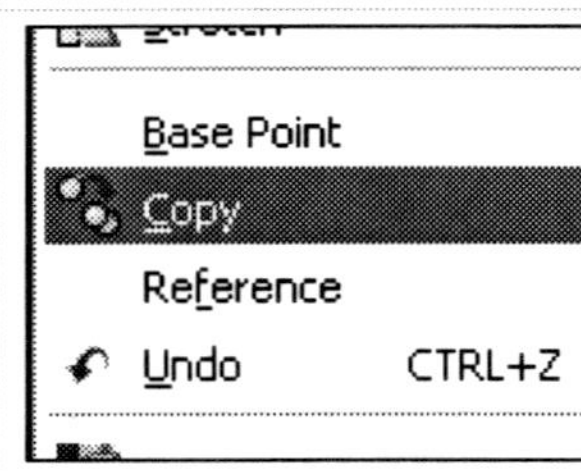


11. Right-click again and select the **Reference** option.

**** ROTATE (multiple) ****

**Specify rotation angle or [Base point/Copy/ Undo/Reference/ eXit]: _reference**

12. Accept the default reference angle of **0**.

**Specify reference angle <0>: *[enter]***

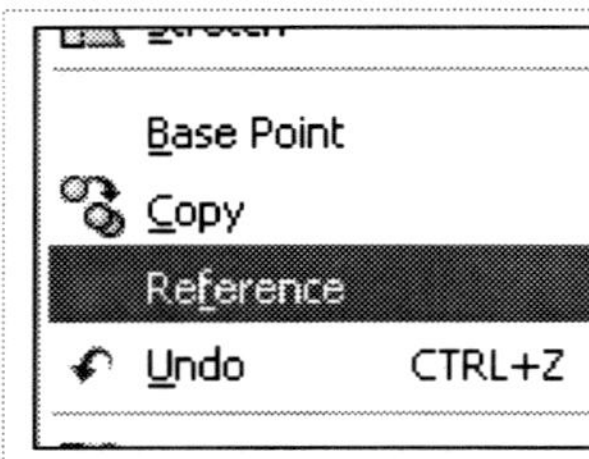


13. Tell AutoCAD you want a rotated copy at ***180°***.

**** ROTATE (multiple) ****

**Specify new angle or [Base point/Copy/Undo/Reference/eXit]: *180***

14. Complete the command; clear the grips.

**** ROTATE (multiple) ****

**Specify new angle or [Base point/Copy/Undo/Reference/ eXit]: *[enter]***

Your drawing looks like this.

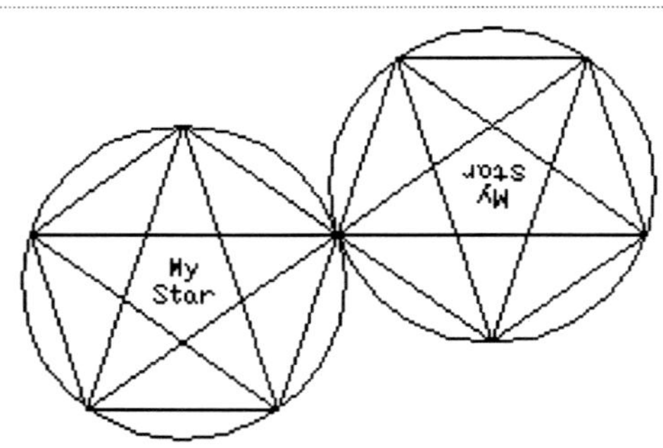


15. Undo the last modification 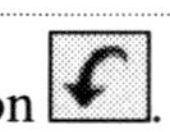.

**Command: *u***

16. Now let's look at the ***Mirror*** Grips command using dynamic input menus. Repeat Step 1.

17. Select the uppermost grip (at the upper tip of the star).

**Command:**

18. Right-click to display the Grips menu; pick the ***Mirror*** procedure.

**** STRETCH ****

**Specify stretch point or [Base point/Copy/Undo/eXit]: _mirror**

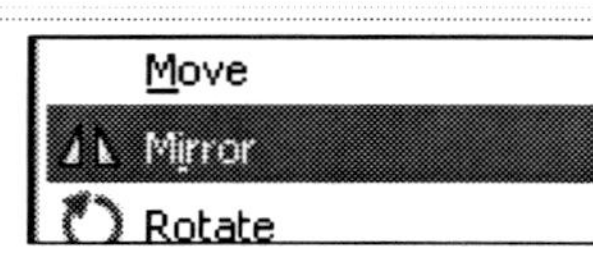

## 16.2.2: More Grips Editing

19. Use the down arrow on your keyboard to display the dynamic input grips menu, and pick the **Copy** option [Copy].

**** MIRROR ****

**Specify second point or [Base point/Copy/ Undo/eXit]: _copy**

20. Pick a point due east of the hot grip as shown. (Be sure to use Ortho.)

**** MIRROR (multiple) ****

**Specify second point or [Base point/Copy/Undo/ eXit]:**

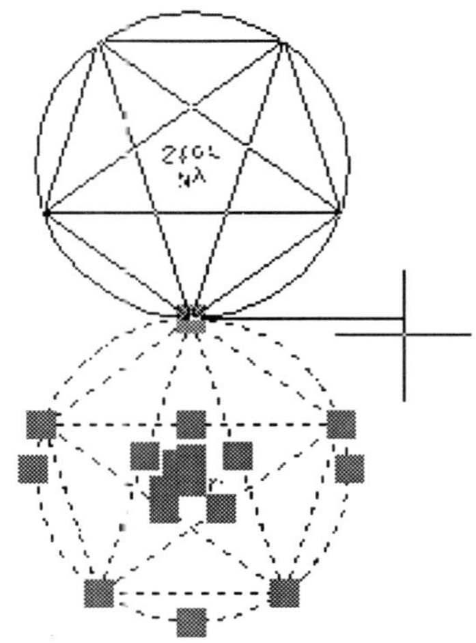

21. Pick the **Exit** option [eXit], then clear the grips.

**** MIRROR (multiple) ****

**Specify second point or [Base point/Copy/Undo/ eXit]: _exit**

Your drawing looks like this.

(Note: These objects were mirrored with the **Mirrtext** sysvar set to **1**. If yours is set to **0**, the text won't mirror.)

22. Undo the last modification.

**Command: *u***

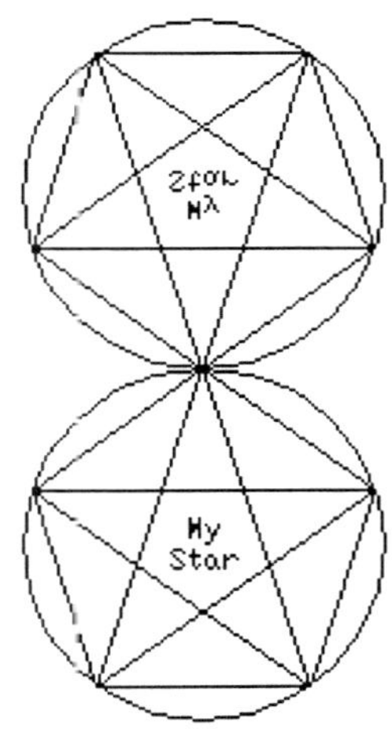


This last section will first walk you through the simple ***Move*** grips procedure. Then we'll use the ***Scale*** grips procedure to make sized copies of objects.

Let's proceed.

| Do This: 16.2.3 | Move and Scale with Grips |
|---|---|

I. Be sure you're still in the *Grips.dwg* file the C:\Steps\Lesson16 folder. If not, please open it now.

II. Follow these steps.

## 16.2.3: Move and Scale with Grips

1. Select all of the objects. Use a window or crossing window.

   **Command:**

2. Select one of the grips. (With the ***Move*** grips procedure, all the objects with active grips will move.) I'm using the grip at the topmost point of the star. (We're going to redefine the **Base point** anyway.)

   **Command:**

3. Right-click to display the Grips menu. Select the ***Move*** procedure.

   **** STRETCH ****

   **Specify stretch point or [Base point/Copy/Undo/eXit]: _move**

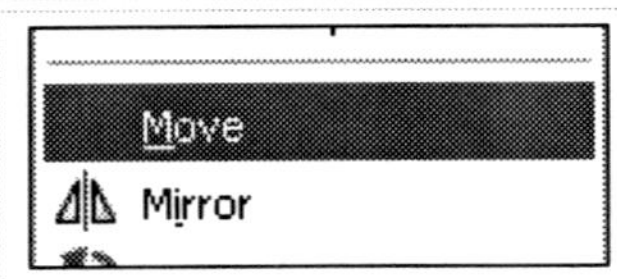


4. Select the **Base point** option Base point.

   **** MOVE ****

   **Specify move point or [Base point/Copy/Undo/eXit]: _base**

5. Pick the center of the circle as the new base point.

   **Specify base point: _cen of**

6. Tell AutoCAD to move the objects to the absolute coordinate **6,4.5**.

   **** MOVE ****

   **Specify move point or [Base point/Copy/ Undo/eXit]: *6,4.5***

   Notice that all of the objects with grips showing move even though only one grip has been selected.

7. Save the drawing but don't exit.

   **Command: *qsave***

> AutoCAD provides an easier way to move one or even a few objects with grips. Once you've selected the objects (any objects with center or midpoint grips), select the center or midpoint grip. AutoCAD will move the object(s) by default.

8. Now let's scale the objects. Select only the circle and the polygon.

   **Command:**

9. Select one of the grips. (I'll use the bottom quadrant grip.)

   **Command:**

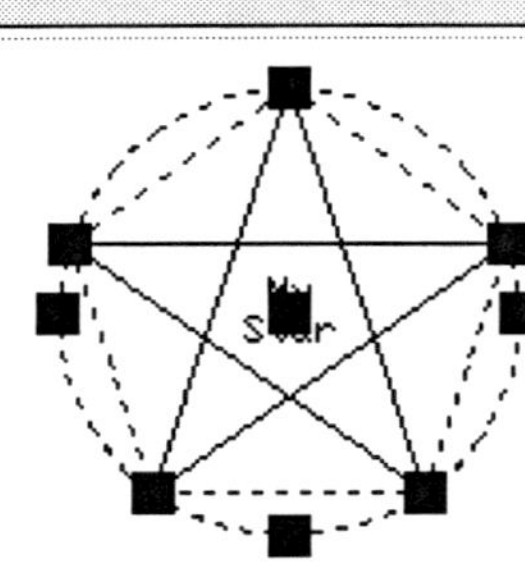

10. Call the Grips menu and pick the ***Scale*** procedure.

    **** STRETCH ****

    **Specify stretch point or [Base point/Copy/Undo/eXit]: _scale**

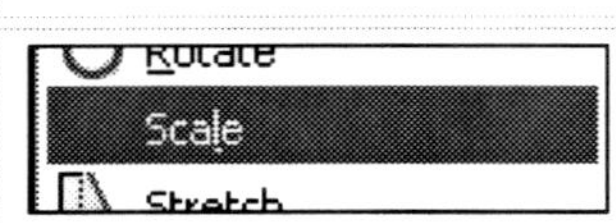

## 16.2.3: Move and Scale with Grips

11. Use the **Base Point** option [Base point].

**** SCALE (multiple) ****
**Specify scale factor or [Base point/Copy/Undo/Reference/eXit]: _base**

12. Pick the center of the circle as the base point.

**Specify base point: _cen of**

13. Hold down the CTRL key to make copies, and make two scaled copies as shown. Then clear the grips.

**** SCALE (multiple) ****
**Specify scale factor or [Base point/Copy/ Undo/Reference/eXit]:**

15. Save the drawing and exit.

**Command:** ***qsave***

So what do you think of grips?

After learning the basic modifying commands in earlier lessons, grips may be difficult at first. But practice, practice, practice! Grips will increase speed and productivity (excuse that nasty corporate word) … and your earning potential!

## 16.3 Extra Steps

As your Extra Step, I suggest returning to any of the exercises in previous lessons (Lessons 7 and 9 would be especially useful) and experimenting with the settings and methods learned in this lesson.

While you're working, ask yourself:

- Is this any faster than the first time I did it?
- Is it any easier?
- Do I prefer this setting to AutoCAD's default?
- Do I prefer the basic or grip method of modification?

Answering these questions will put you on your way to some real expertise with the software!

At this point in your training, you should begin to "customize" the software to your style of doing things. The user interface should begin to reflect your preferences for toolbars and scrollbars; the system variables should reflect your preferences for drawing styles and methods.

## 16.4 What Have We Learned?

*Items covered in this lesson include:*

- *AutoCAD Selection Tools:*
  - *Noun/Verb Selection*
  - *Shift to Add*
  - *Press and Drag*
  - *Implied Windowing*
- *AutoCAD's Grip Tools*

- *Move*
- *Stretch*
- *Scale*
- *Rotate*
- *Mirror*

In this lesson, we learned some entirely different approaches to modifying AutoCAD drawings. Now you must decide which methods and settings you, as the CAD operator, will use.

You've completed Part I of our text and accomplished quite a bit.

Tackle this lesson's exercises with confidence in your training and faith in your ability! Then approach Part II knowing that you'll soon have the knowledge necessary to succeed as a drafter or junior designer at any company in the United States!

## 16.5 Exercises

2. Start a new drawing from scratch.
   2.1. Use the setup described in 2.1.
   2.2. Save the drawing as *MySlottedGuide* in the C:\Steps\Lesson16 folder.
   2.3. Create the drawing shown.

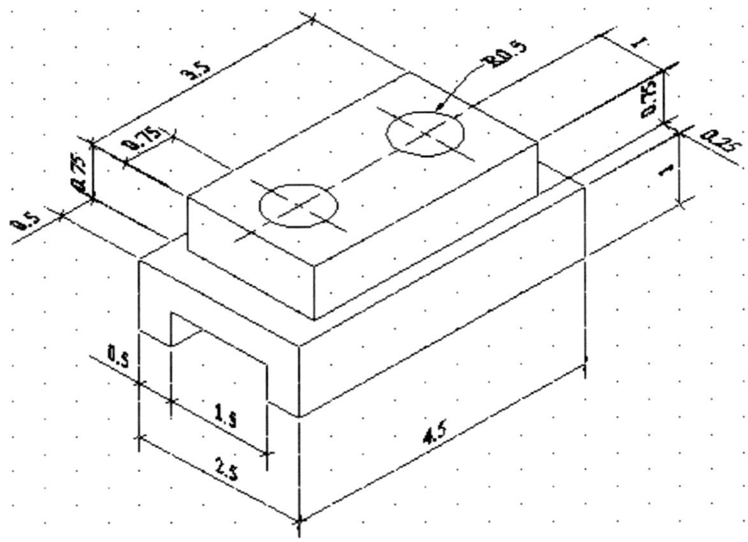


Slotted Guide

3. Start a new drawing from scratch.
   3.1. Repeat the setup you did in Exercises 2 and 3.
   3.2. Save the drawing as *MySpring* in the C:\Steps\Lesson16 folder.
   3.3. Create the drawing shown.

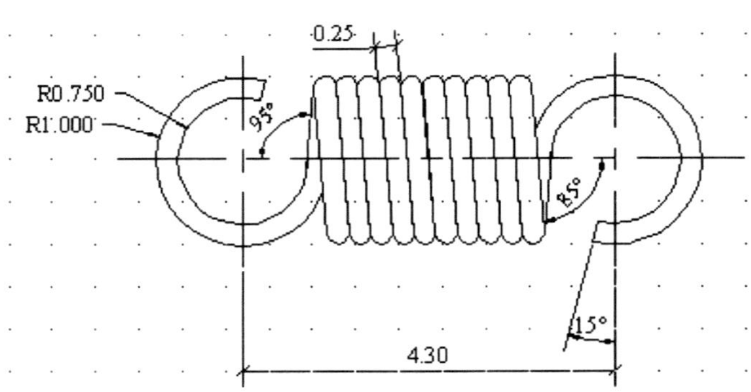


Spring

*For more exercises related to Lesson 16, please see Lesson 16 in AutoCAD 2007: One Step at a Time – Workbook.*

## 16.6 For Web-Based Review Questions, visit: http://www.uneedcad.com/2007/Files/07R16.pdf

# Lesson 17

Following this lesson, you will:

- ✓ *Know how to use tables in your drawing*
- ✓ *Know how to use fields in your drawing*
- ✓ *Know how to use these commands:*
  - ***Table***
  - ***Tablestyle***
  - ***DwgProps***
  - ***Field***

# Tables and Fields

What we humans have worked for since the dawn of time has been a way to avoid work! (And oh, how hard we've worked to succeed at this most admirable goal!)

*That's where things like tables and fields come in handy. Tables organize our world (nothing says lazy like pristine organizational skills, which of course, free up time to stare at the skyline or drift aimlessly in the pool); fields fill in those nicely organized blanks for us.*

*This section of our text will cover some razzle-dazzle tools. These are the tools that pushed CAD systems ahead of the drawing board as the preferred tool in design work. We'll begin with some text tools in this lesson; then, in subsequent lessons, we'll learn to create hatching, blocks of objects, and blocks of information.*

*So, stop yawning, and let's begin.*

## 17.1 Tables

It's amazing just how much work can be avoided by the innovative use of rows and columns (just consider how the appendices at the end of this text help you avoid wasting time trying to find solutions to some basic CAD problems)! Of course, the collective name for rows and columns is *table*. Tables have saved time and effort in virtually every industry on earth (just ask any accountant).

AutoCAD makes tables available for legends, materials lists, revision blocks, spreadsheets, and just about any other use you might require. We'll look at creating a top-down table (a legend) and then at creating a bottom-up table (a revision block). More importantly, we'll look at the ease with which you can modify a list for your own uses.

### 17.1.1 Creating a Table

To keep it simple, AutoCAD provides a dialog box (Figure 17.001) for creating tables. Let's take a look at it.

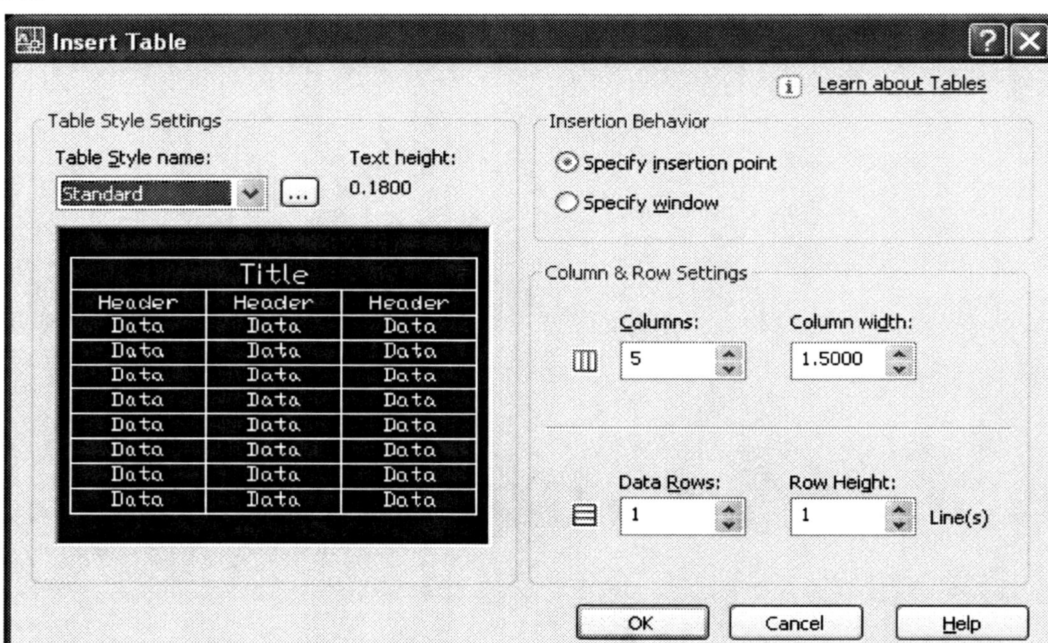


Figure 17.001

- The first frame – **Table Style Settings** – allows you to change the style you'll use to create your table. The default (**Standard**) is shown. If you'd like to change to another existing style, use the down arrow next to the **Table Style name** control box. If you need to create a new style, you can use the **Table Style dialog** button next to the control box, or you can enter the ***Tablestyle*** command at the command prompt. We'll look more at table style creation later in this lesson.
- The **Insertion Behavior** frame contains two options:
  - A bullet next to **Specify insertion point** means that AutoCAD will prompt you for a location for your table.
  - A bullet next to the other option, **Specify window**, tells AutoCAD to prompt you for a windowed area for the table (much as it does for an MText insertion).
- The **Column and Row Settings** frame allows you to set up the number of columns and rows in your table. You'll also specify the width and height of your columns and rows here.

Does that sound simple enough? Let's try one.

> The ***Table*** command is also available in the Draw pull-down menu and palette.

| Do This: 17.1.1.1 | Creating a Table |
|---|---|

I. Open the *Floor Plan Data Sheet* drawing in the C:\Steps\Lesson17 folder. The drawing looks like Figure 17.002.

II. Follow these steps.

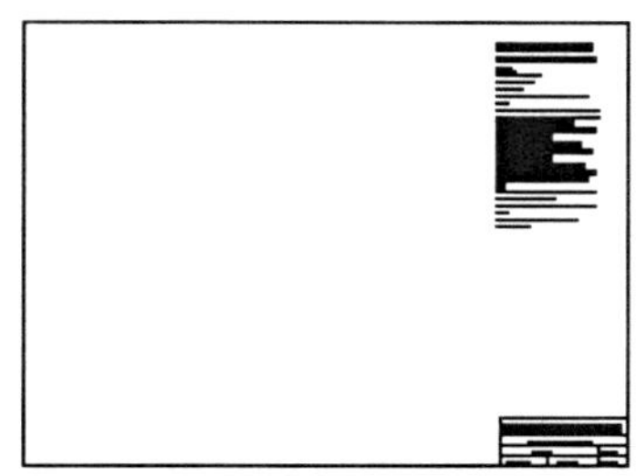

Figure 17.002

## 17.1.1.1: Creating a Table

1. Enter the ***Table*** command. Alternately, you can pick the **Table** button 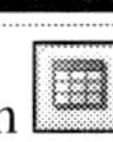 on the Draw toolbar or palette.

**Command:** ***table***

AutoCAD presents the Insert Table dialog box (Figure 17.001).

2. Use the **Standard** table style (it's the only one available to you at this time).

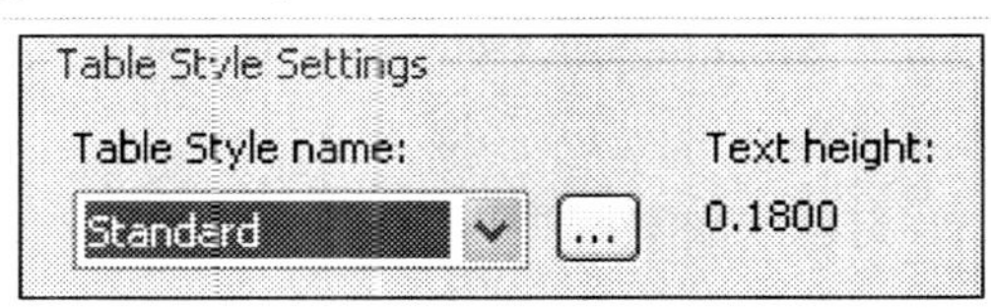


3. Tell AutoCAD you'd like to use an insertion point to insert the table.

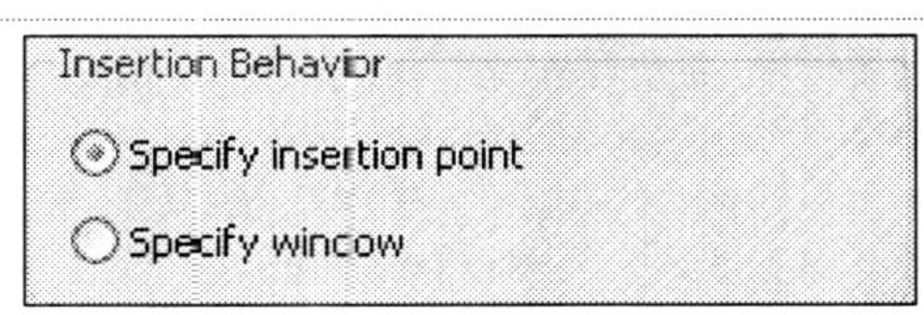

### 17.1.1.1: Creating a Table

4. Finally, give your table four **Columns** with a 1.5" width, and two **Data Rows** with a single line height.

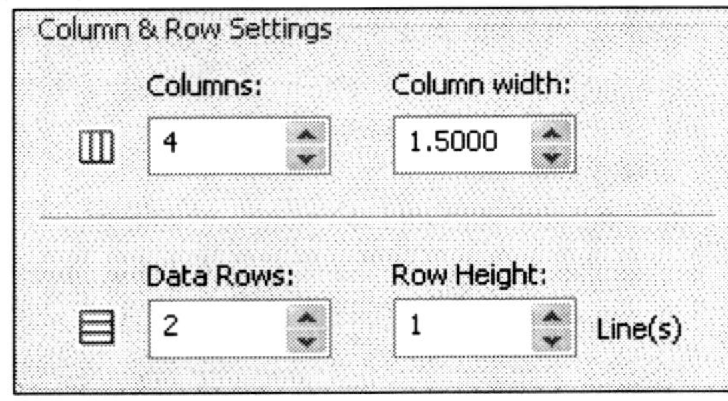


5. Complete the setup 

.

6. AutoCAD asks where you'd like to insert the table. Use the coordinates indicated.

    **Specify insertion point:** ***1,16***

AutoCAD presents the MText editor and highlights the title *cell* of your table for your input (see figure below).

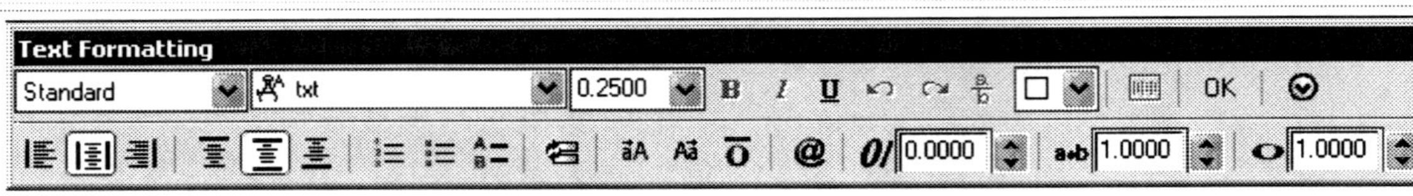


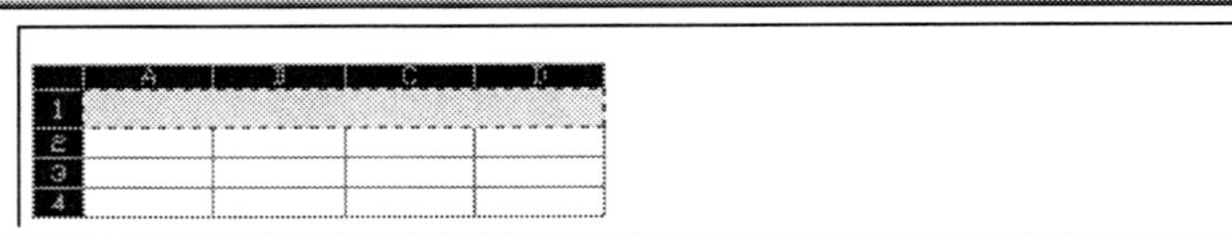

7. Enter the name of the table (***Symbols Legend***). Press the TAB key on your keyboard to continue.

8. AutoCAD highlights the first cell in the column header row. Enter the word ***Symbol*** here.

9. Using the TAB key to move to the next cells, complete the column header row as indicated. (Pick the **OK** button 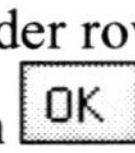

on the MText toolbar to complete the procedure.)

| Symbols Legend | | | |
|---|---|---|---|
| Symbol | Descripti on | Symbol | Descripti on |
| | | | |
| | | | |

10. Save the drawing  but don't exit.

    **Command:** ***qsave***

## 17.1.2 Editing a Table's Properties

The first thing you probably noticed about the table you just inserted was that the *Column Heads* didn't fit in the cell provided for them. In fact, both description columns are far too narrow for much of a description. Additionally, you might have noticed that the text in the table doesn't match the text we've used in the Floor Plan drawings through our last several lessons.

We'll use the Properties palette a bit, but AutoCAD makes use of cursor menus for easier editing of a table's properties (as well as values).

Let's see what we can do with our table before we start entering values.

| Do This: 17.1.2.1 | **Editing a Table's Properties** |
|---|---|

I. Be sure you're still in the *Floor Plan Data Sheet* drawing in the C:\Steps\Lesson17 folder. If not, please open it now.

II. Be sure the **Pickfirst** sysvar is set to **1**.

III. Follow these steps.

**17.1.2.1: EDITING A TABLES'S PROPERTIES**

1. First, let's change the text style in the title and header cells. Pick once in the title cell. Notice that its grips display.

2. Now hold down the SHIFT key and select a cell in the header row. Notice that both rows display grips.

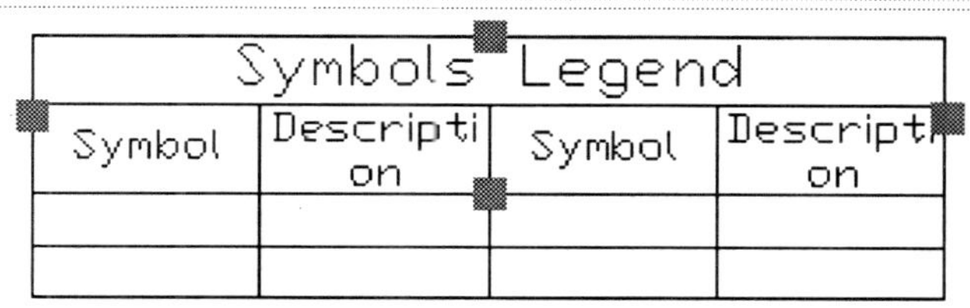


3. Now right-click in one of the selected cells. Take a moment to look over the opportunities provided on the cursor menu. We'll look at some of these, but you should make time later to experiment with the others.

Pick **Properties**.

AutoCAD presents the Properties palette.

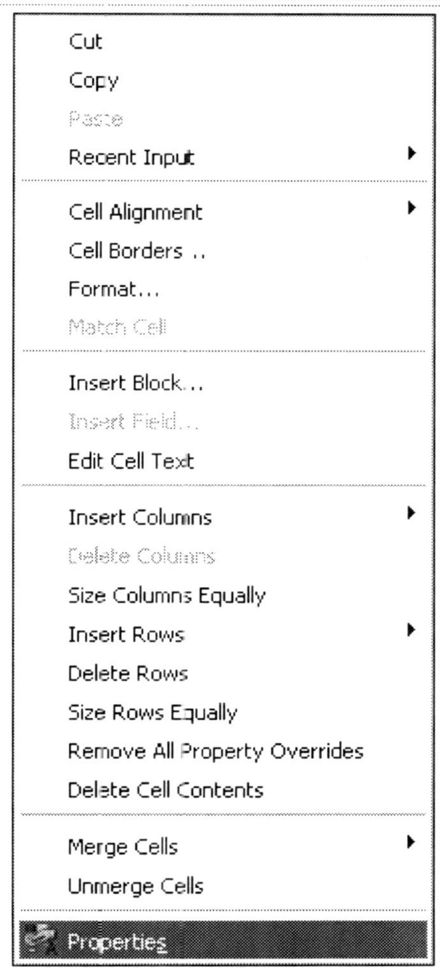


4. Under the **Content** heading on the Properties palette, select **Text style**, and then select **Times Bold** from the drop down menu. (The style has already been created for you.)

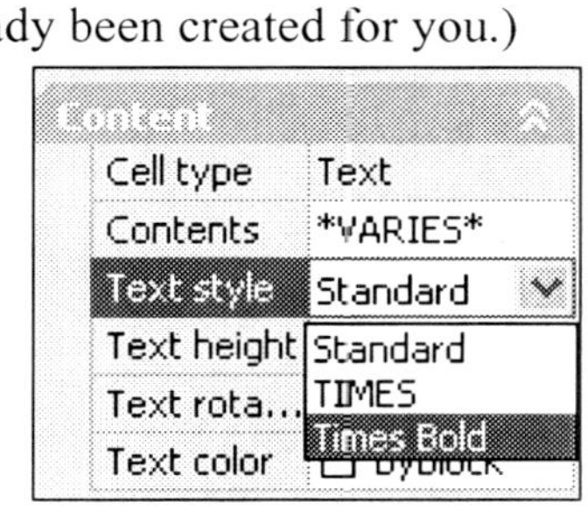

5. Close the Properties palette and clear the grips. Your table looks like this.

| Symbols Legend | | | |
|---|---|---|---|
| Symbol | Description | Symbol | Description |
| | | | |
| | | | |

6. We'll also need more rows than we originally set up. Pick inside any of the cells on the bottom row. Its grips will display.

7. Right-click inside the highlighted cell and select **Insert Rows … Below** on the cursor menu. Repeat this step until you have six empty rows. Then clear the grips.

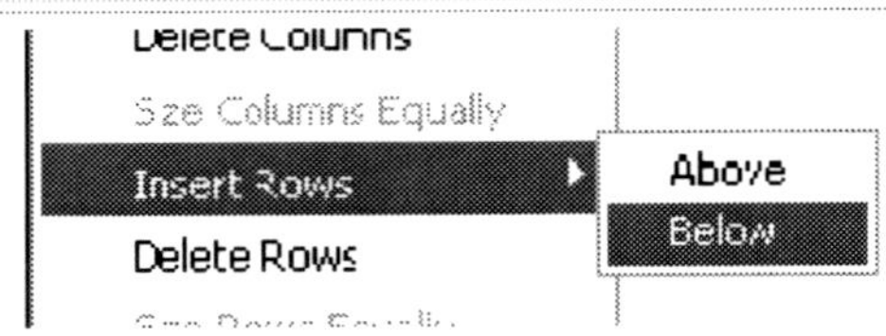


8. Now we'll make the **Description** columns wider. Select the entire table with a window. Notice that the entire table highlights and displays grips.

9. Pick on the line grip between the first **Symbol** and **Description** columns and move it to the left. Resize the other columns as well. (Move the grips left or right as needed.)

Clear the grips. Your drawing looks like this.

| Symbols Legend | | | |
|---|---|---|---|
| Symbol | Description | Symbol | Description |
| | | | |
| | | | |
| | | | |
| | | | |
| | | | |
| | | | |

10. Let's change one last property. Repeat Steps 1 and 2; but this time, select the bottom row in Step 2 (the grips appear for the outer walls of the table).

11. Right-click in one of the cells and select Properties from the cursor menu.

12. Under **Cell** on the Properties palette, select **Background … Cyan** as indicated.

Close the Properties palette and clear the grips. Your table now has a colored background (this helps it stand out a bit on your drawing.).

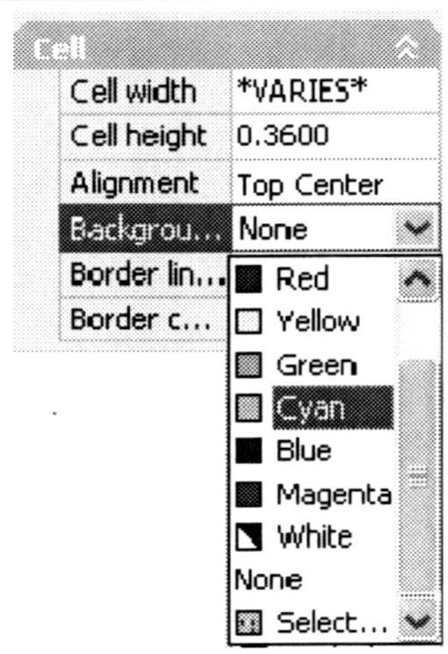


13. Save the drawing but don't exit.

**Command:** ***qsave***

## 17.1.3 Adding Values to Table Cells

Now that you've set up your table, you'll need to add some values to the cells (otherwise, the table would be pretty … but useless). Luckily, adding values is the easy part! In fact, it's just a matter of inserting MText.

### Do This: 17.1.3.1 Inserting Table Values

I. Be sure you're still in the *Floor Plan Data Sheet* drawing in the C:\Steps\Lesson17 folder. If not, please open it now.

In this exercise, you'll get a preview of those wondrous timesavers called *blocks*. We'll look at blocks in much greater detail in Lessons 19 and 20, but enjoy the preview for now.

II. Follow these steps.

**17.1.3.1: INSERTING TABLE VALUES**

1. We'll start right off with a block insertion. Pick inside the first empty cell in the first **Symbols** column. Its grips appear.

2. Right-click in the highlighted cell and pick **Insert Block** on the cursor menu. AutoCAD presents the Insert a Block in a Table Cell dialog box shown in Step 3.

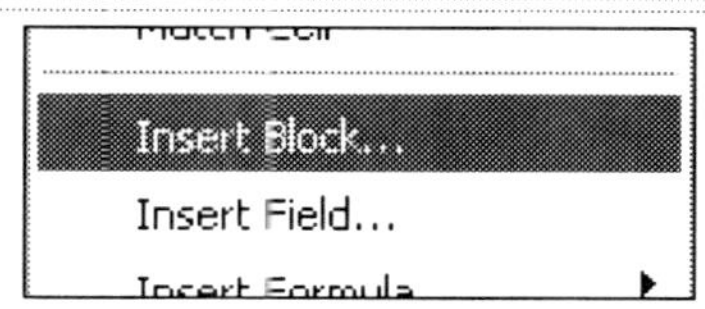


3. Fill out the dialog box as follows:
   - Select the **230 volt outlet** block in the **Name** drop down list box.
   - Use the **Middle Center** cell alignment.
   - Remove the check from the **AutoFit** check box.
   - Set a **Scale** of **1**.
   - Accept the **Rotation angle** default.

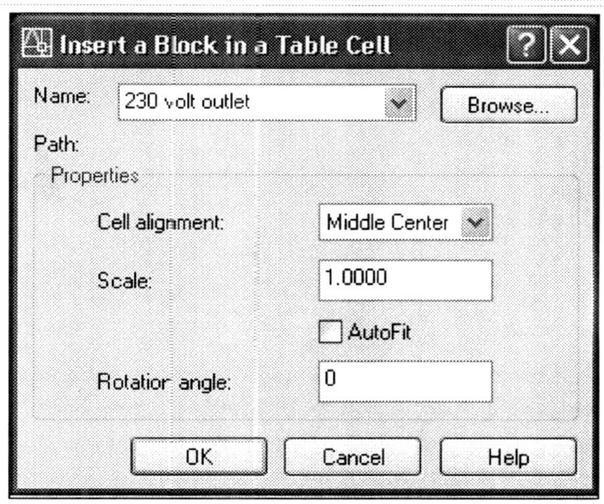


4. Complete the procedure 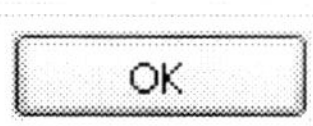.

5. Use the TAB key to move to the adjoining cell (in the **Description** column).

6. Enter the text – **230 Volt Outlet**.

## 17.1.3.1: Inserting Table Values

7. Repeat Steps 1 through 6 to complete the table. (Hint: To enter the text, simply pick in the appropriate cell and start typing. AutoCAD will automatically open the MText editor.)

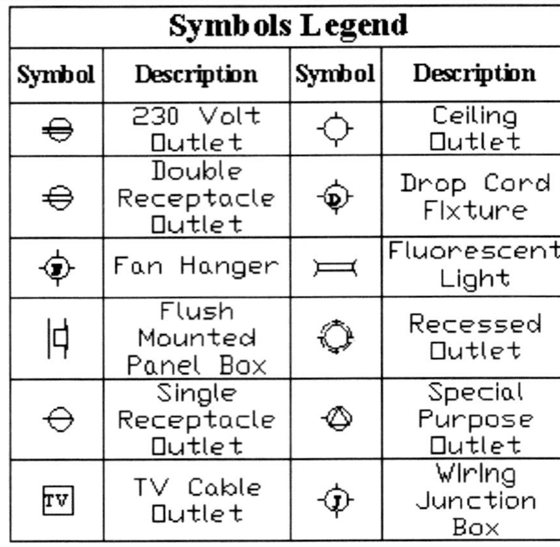

| Symbols Legend | | | |
|---|---|---|---|
| Symbol | Description | Symbol | Description |
| | 230 Volt Outlet | | Ceiling Outlet |
| | Double Receptacle Outlet | | Drop Cord Fixture |
| | Fan Hanger | | Fluorescent Light |
| | Flush Mounted Panel Box | | Recessed Outlet |
| | Single Receptacle Outlet | | Special Purpose Outlet |
| TV | TV Cable Outlet | | Wiring Junction Box |

8. Finally, use the tools you found in the last exercise to convert the text to the **Times** style and change its justification to **Middle Center**. Your table looks like this.

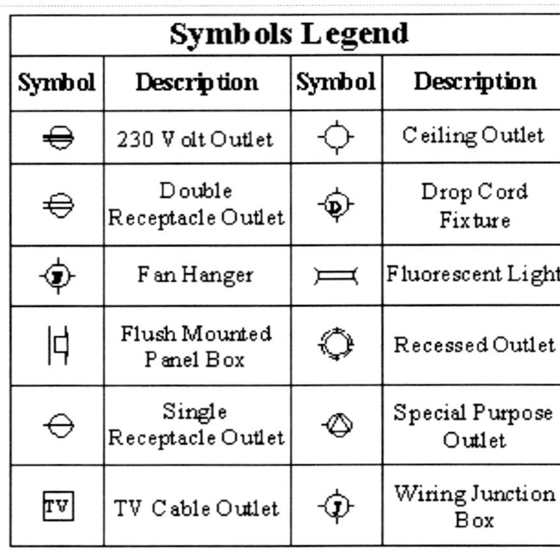

| Symbols Legend | | | |
|---|---|---|---|
| Symbol | Description | Symbol | Description |
| | 230 Volt Outlet | | Ceiling Outlet |
| | Double Receptacle Outlet | | Drop Cord Fixture |
| | Fan Hanger | | Fluorescent Light |
| | Flush Mounted Panel Box | | Recessed Outlet |
| | Single Receptacle Outlet | | Special Purpose Outlet |
| TV | TV Cable Outlet | | Wiring Junction Box |

9. Save the drawing but don't exit.

**Command: *qsave***

Did you notice how AutoCAD automatically adjusted the height of the rows to accommodate what you inserted? Did you see the text automatically wrap within the cells? If you've ever had to create a table manually (with the ***Line*** command), you'll really appreciate these automated actions!

But there is more to tables than what you've seen. What about using a table for a revision block (one that grows from bottom to top)? Or how about setting up as defaults some of the things you had to do manually (text styles, justifications, etc.)?

Let's look next at table *styles*.

## 17.1.4 Customizing Tables

Since you've already mastered dimension styles, you'll probably find table styles fairly easy to set up; they look as though the same programmers designed them.

The ***Tablestyle*** command calls the Table Style dialog box (Figure 17.003). As you can see, the dialog box closely resembles the Dimension Style dialog box.

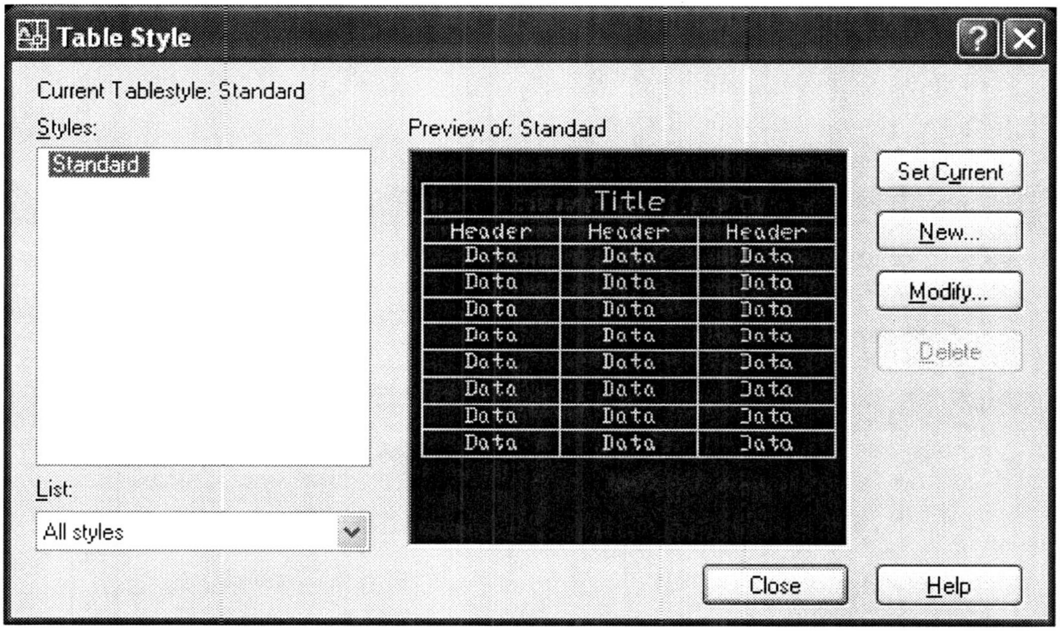


Figure 17.003

- The **Styles** list box indicates the names of styles available in this drawing. Luckily, however, AutoCAD doesn't inflict "children" styles here as it does with dimension styles, so your job is already easier!
- As with other tools, the **List** box below the **Styles** box serves as a filter for what goes in to the **Styles** box (**All styles** or **Styles in use**).
- The **Preview** box, of course, shows a preview of the selected style.
- A total of six buttons dwell on the dialog box. These are fairly self-explanatory:
    - **Set Current** sets the selected style as the one that AutoCAD will use when inserting a new table.
    - Use the **New** button to create a new table style. It calls the Create New Style dialog box (Figure 17.004). Use this familiar tool to name your new style, and then to access the New Table Style dialog box where you'll actually set up the style. (We'll see these in our next exercise.)

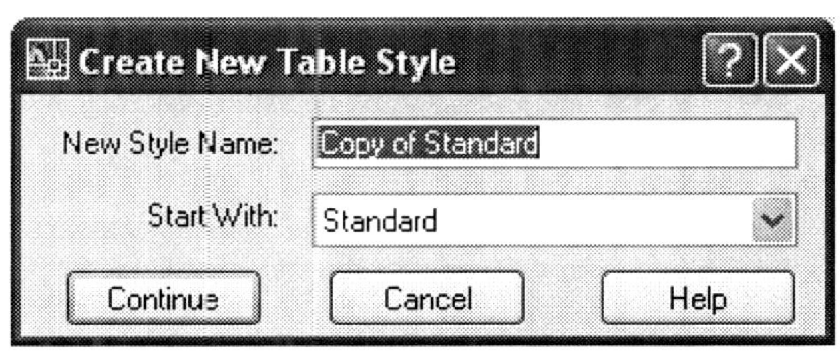


Figure 17.004

    - **Modify** allows you to alter settings for the selected style. You'll use the same dialog box as with the New Style procedure.
    - **Delete**, of course, allows you to delete the selected style. Note that you can't remove a style that's in use.
    - **Close** closes the dialog box.
    - **Help** calls AutoCAD's help window with information on the Table Style dialog box.

Let's set up table style to use in creating a revision block.

| Do This: 17.1.4.1 | **Defining a Table Style** |
|---|---|

I. Be sure you're still in the *Floor Plan Data Sheet* drawing in the C:\Steps\Lesson17 folder. If not, please open it now.

II. Follow these steps.

## 17.1.4.1: DEFINING A TABLE STYLE

1. Open the Table Style dialog box. You can enter the command at the command prompt or select **Table Style** from the Format pull down menu.

   **Command: *tablestyle***

2. Tell AutoCAD you want to create a new style .


3. Call your new style **Revision Block** and pick the **Continue** button to open the New Table Style dialog box.

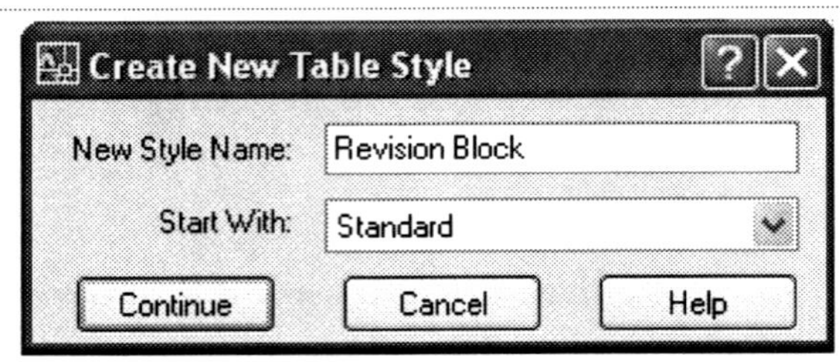


4. For Steps 4 through 6, refer to the figure following Step 6 (next page).
Notice that the dialog box contains only three tabs. Begin on the **Data** tab (this tab controls settings for the data cells of your table).
In the **Cell properties** frame:
   - Set the **Text style** to **TIMES** and the **Text height** to 1/8".
   - Set the **Text color** to match the **Text** layer's settings.
   - Set the **Alignment** as indicated.
   - Take a look at the **Format** options available to you, and then select the **General** format.

5. In the **Border properties** frame:
   - Tell AutoCAD to use grid lines for **All Borders**,
   - Accept the **Grid lineweight** default, but set the **Grid color** to **ByLayer**.

6. In the **General frame**, tell AutoCAD to expand the table **Up** (title cell at bottom), and accept the defaults in the **Cell margins** frame.

## 17.1.4.1: Defining a Table Style

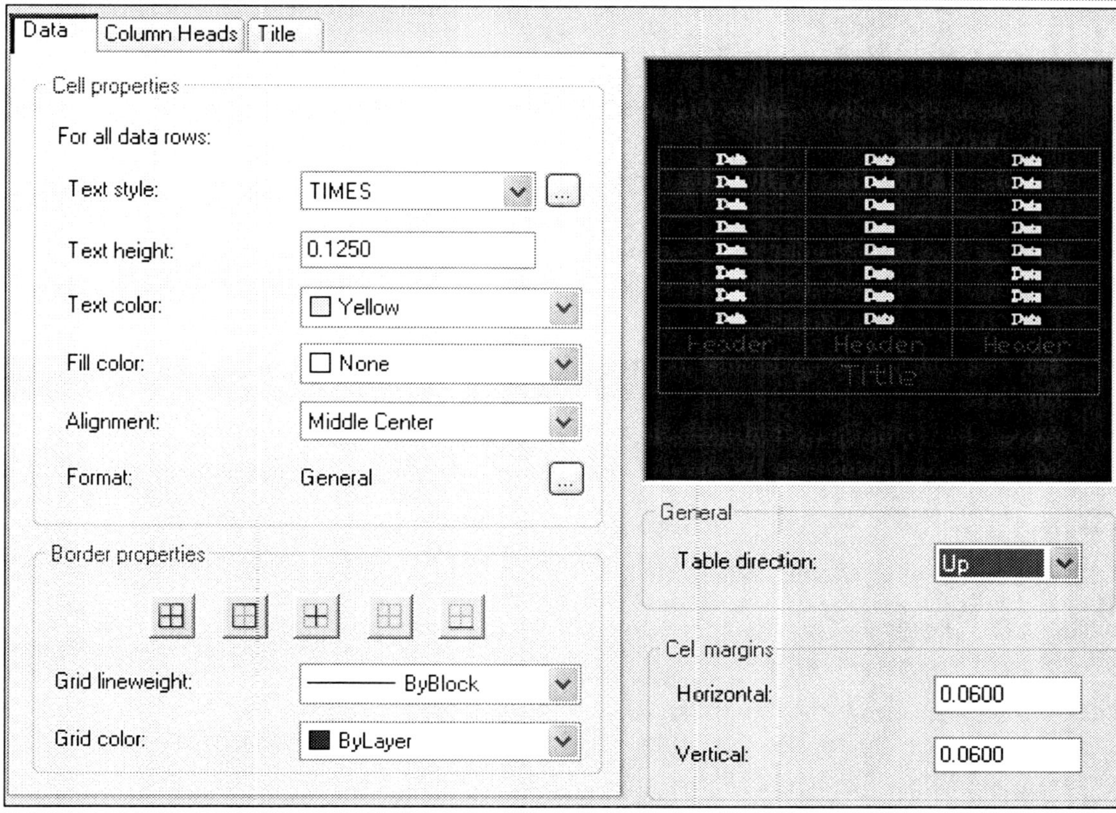


7. Pick the **Column Heads** tab to continue .

8. Refer to the image at left.

In the **Cell properties** frame:

- Be sure the **Include Header row** box is checked (this tells AutoCAD to include a header row in your table).
- Use the **TIMES Text style**, and a **Text height** of 1/8".
- Use the Text layer's color and the same **Alignment** you used for the data cells.

In the **Border properties** frame:

- Tell AutoCAD to use grid lines for **All Borders**,
- Accept the **Grid lineweight** default, but set the **Grid color** to **ByLayer**.

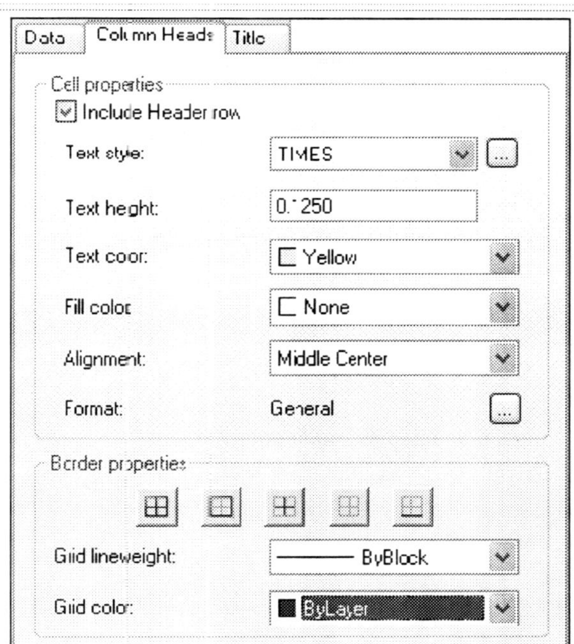


9. Pick the **Title** tab to continue 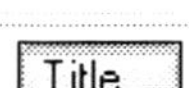.

## 17.1.4.1: Defining a Table Style

10. Refer to the image at left.

In the **Cell properties** frame:

- Be sure there's a check in the **Include Title row** box.
- Use the **TIMES Text style** and a **Text height** of 3/16".
- Use the Text layer's color and the same **Alignment** you used for the data cells.

In the **Border properties** frame:

- Tell AutoCAD to use grid lines for **All Borders**,
- Accept the **Grid lineweight** default, but set the **Grid color** to **ByLayer**.

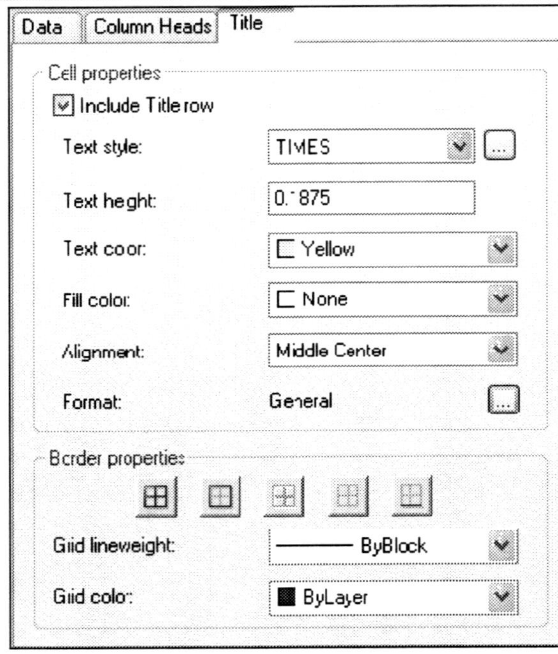


11. Complete the setup OK.

12. Notice that the **Styles** list box in the Table Style dialog box now contains your new table style. Complete the procedure Close.

13. Save the drawing but don't exit.

**Command:** ***qsave***

Now let's take a look at our new style in action.

| Do This: 17.1.4.2 | Using Your New Table Style |
|---|---|

I. Be sure you're still in the *Floor Plan Data Sheet* drawing in the C:\Steps\Lesson17 folder. If not, please open it now.

II. Zoom in just to the left of the title block.

III. Set the **BORDER** layer current.

IV. Follow these steps.

## 17.1.4.2: Using Your New Table Style

1. Begin a table.

**Command:** ***table***

2. Fill in the Insert Table dialog box as shown in the following figure, and pick **OK** OK to continue.

## 17.1.4.2: Using Your New Table Style

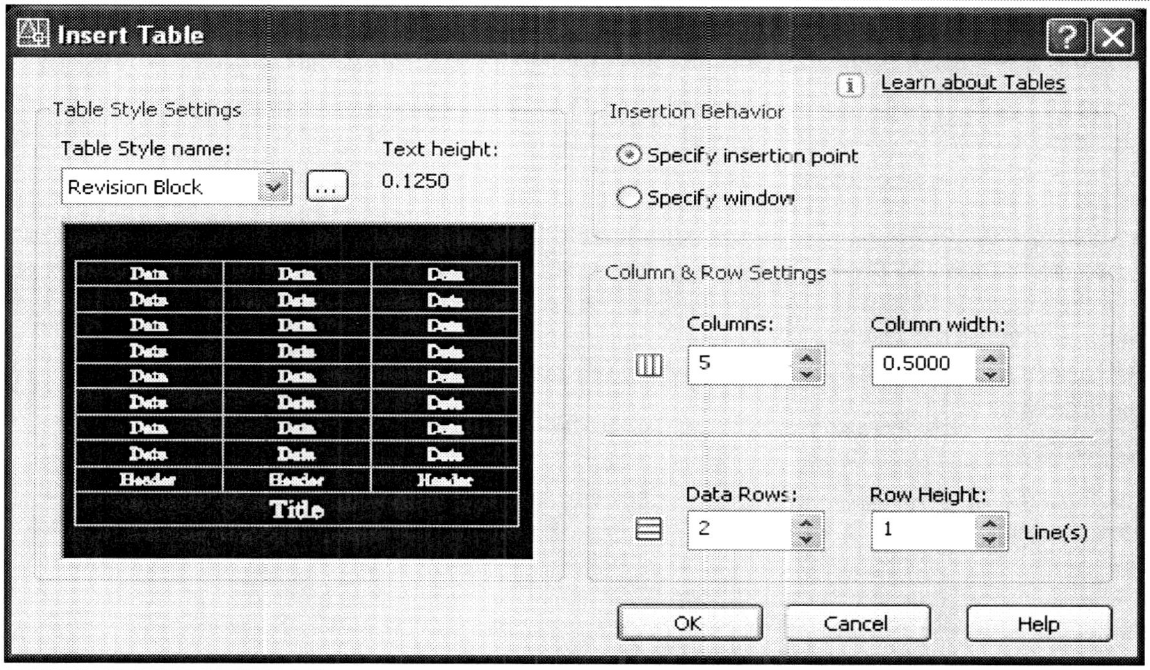


3. Insert the table next to the title block and fill in the **Title** and **Header** rows as shown.

**Specify insertion point:**

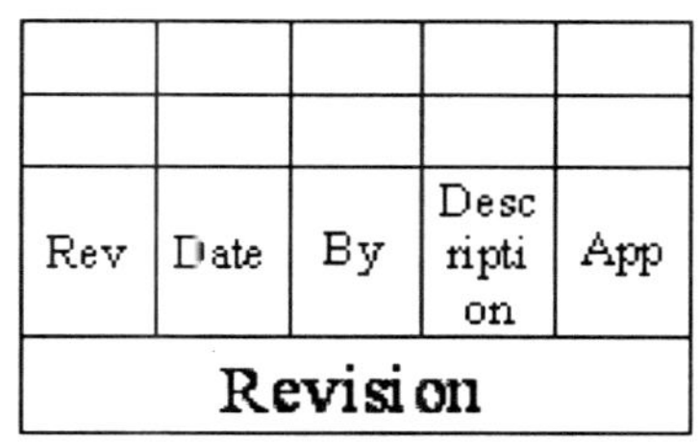


4. Pick anywhere on the revision block, select the grip between **App** and **Description** and stretch it about an inch to the right. (Polar snap will help this procedure.)

5. Pick in the **Rev** cell, hold down the SHIFT key, and pick in the **App** cell. AutoCAD highlights the row.

6. Using the Properties palette, change the height of the row to **.2876"** (the height of the data rows). (Close the Properties palette and clear the grips.)

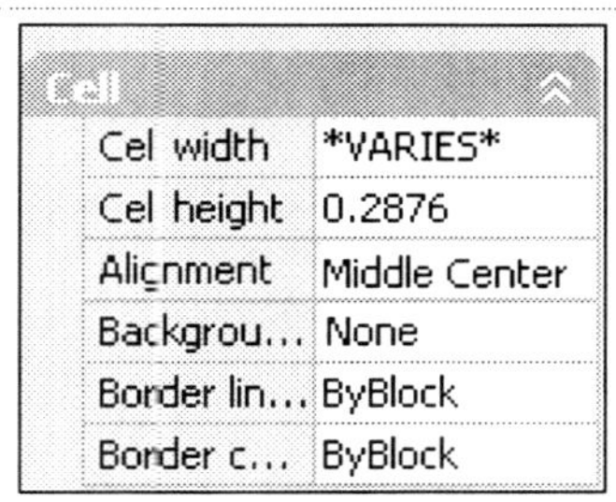


7. Reposition the revision block next to the title block.

**Command:** ***m***

The revision block now looks like this.

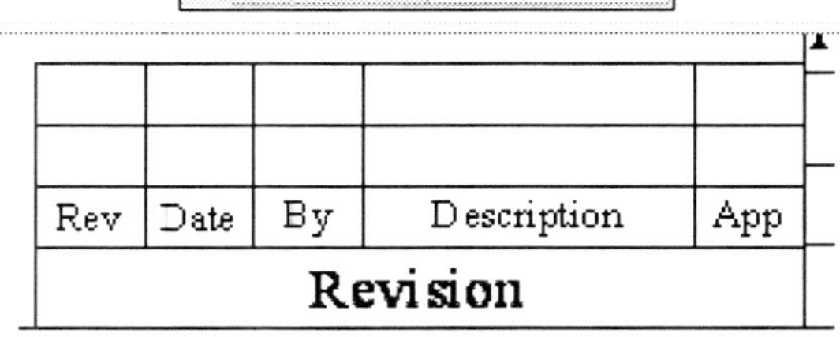

### 17.1.4.2: Using Your New Table Style

8. Fill in everything except the **Date** block with your own information.

| | | | | |
|---|---|---|---|---|
| | | | | |
| A | | TSS | For Grade | MH |
| Rev | Date | By | Description | App |
| **Revision** | | | | |

9. Save the drawing but don't exit.

**Command: *qsave***

Okay, tables were pretty easy (all things considered). They may take a bit of work to set things up, but once that's done, the rest is child's play. Try to remember as you do the setup, that you won't see the real benefit to tables until you discover later that you need to change something or (Heaven forbid!) move the entire table!

Our next tool requires less setup, and it can be even more of a timesaver!

## 17.2 The Wonders of Automation – Fields

Fields (placeholders for text) require very little setup, but they relieve the operator of some of the more mundane chores of life – automatically filling in some of the common requirements of virtually all documents (author, date, etc.). In the case of the draftsperson, they can help with the revision block we just created as well as the title block, and even provide a modifiable plot stamp for your drawings. But the usefulness of fields in a drawing goes beyond the basic documentation benefits. You can also use fields to keep track of such things as length, area, and even elevation of an object!

First, we'll look at the source of some of the information AutoCAD will use to fill in the fields you'll create. Then we'll create some fields.

### 17.2.1 Drawing Properties

AutoCAD automatically sets up many of the things you'll want to use for field values – dates, object information, and so forth. But you'll have to set up some of the other things – drawing name, author name, and so forth. Luckily, AutoCAD limits your input to a single dialog box (with four fairly simple tabs). See the [Drawing Name] Properties dialog box in Figure 17.005. (Access the dialog box with the ***DwgProps*** command.)

- The **General** tab provides information – file attributes, recent modification dates, and so forth. You can't change any of this information here, but some of it can prove useful in tracking things you may need to know (such as file size).

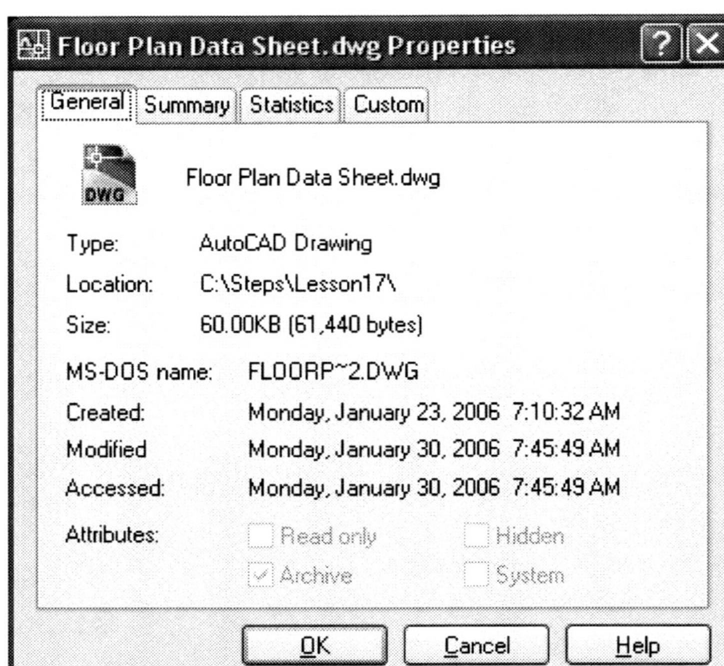


Figure 17.005

- The **Summary** tab (Figure 17.006) is your workhorse. You'll need to fill in this information. Remember, if you don't fill it in, it won't be available to you; so use your best judgment as to what to include.

  Most of the blanks are self-explanatory. But this information might help:
  - Use the **Keywords** box to include words that might be useful when searching a group of drawings for this one.
  - Use the **Comments** box to add any useful comments you'd like to make.
  - The **Hyperlink base** can be a folder or website – anywhere that drawings including or related to this one might be located.
- Like the **General** tab, you won't be able to alter the information provided on the **Statistics** tab (Figure 17.007). This one, however, has some really useful information that an operator can use to keep track of his time on a specific drawing, or when the drawing was edited last. (There's no defense before an irate employer like computer-generated facts!)
- The last tab – **Custom** (Figure 17.008) – provides an opportunity for including some of your own information.

You'll be able to see the benefits of this tool once you've set it up and we examine fields in more detail. Let's set up our drawing's properties.

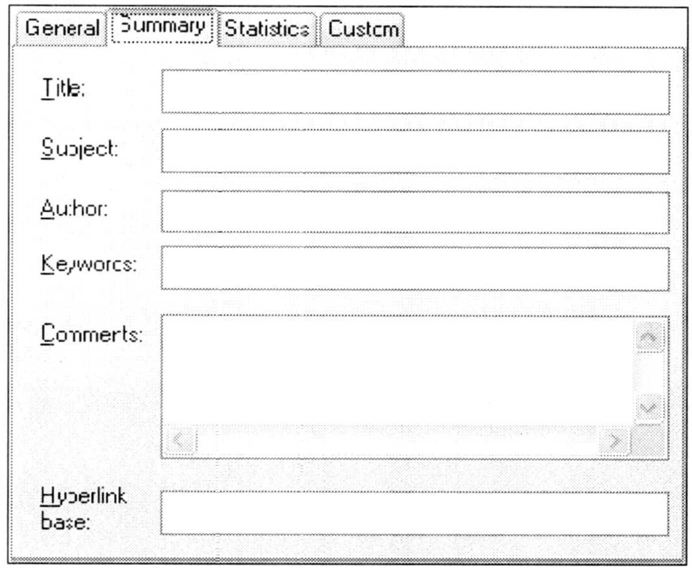


Figure 17.006

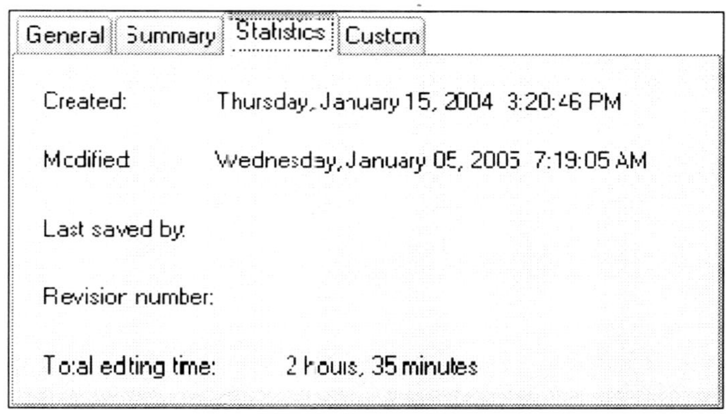


Figure 17.007

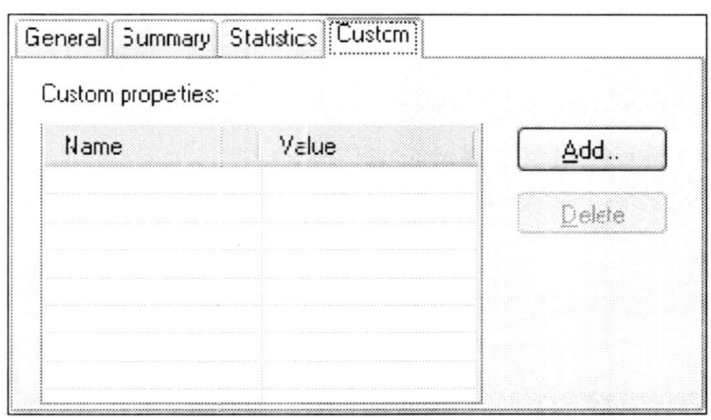


Figure 17.008

You can find an additional benefit of the properties dialog box shown here by right clicking on the file in Windows Explorer. Select **Properties** from the cursor menu, and Windows will show you the information you've provided without having to open the file!

| **Do This: 17.2.1.1** | **Setting Up Drawing Properties** |
|---|---|

I. Be sure you're still in the *Floor Plan Data Sheet* drawing in the C:\Steps\Lesson17 folder. If not, please open it now.

II. Follow these steps.

**17.2.1.1: SETTING UP DRAWING PROPERTIES**

1. Open the Floor Plan Data Sheet.dwg Properties dialog box. It opens with the **General** tab on top as shown in Figure 17.005.

   **Command: *dwgprops***

2. Pick the **Summary** tab [Summary] to move it to the top.
3. Enter the data shown.
4. Examine the **Statistics** and **Custom** tabs. These can be useful, but we won't include any custom information for this drawing.
5. Complete the procedure [OK].
6. Save the drawing but don't exit.

   **Command: *qsave***

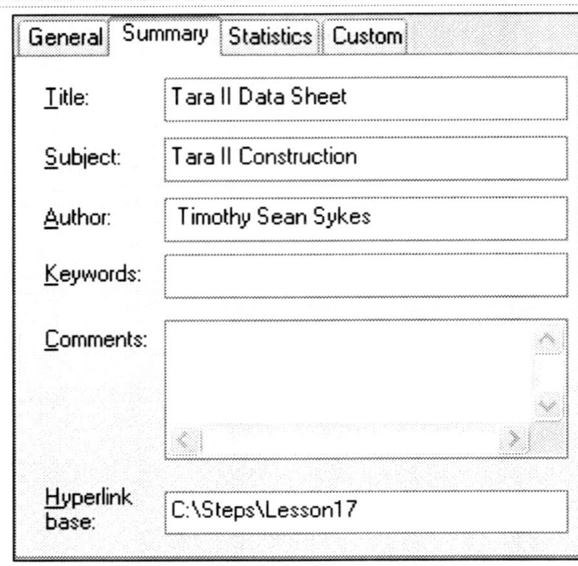


Nothing to it, right?

Now let's take a look at why we set up this dialog box. Let's look at fields.

| **17.2.2** | **Inserting Fields** |
|---|---|

You'll find two ways to insert a field – insertion via MText editor and simple insertion. (We'll use both in our next exercise.) Both methods involve the Field dialog box (Figure 17.009 – next page). The dialog box, despite its simple appearance, allows for a great number of possibilities.

- The **Field category** drop down box provides a list of the various categories available for your field. If you aren't sure which category to use, leave the **All** default, which will provide a list of all the available field names in the list box below.
- The **Field names** list box provides a list of fields available in the selected category.
- The **Field value** box (shown here as **Author**) lets you know the current value of the selected field. This box changes with the selection of different fields in the **Field names** list box. It will show dashes if no value has been assigned to the selected field or pound symbols (#) if the field is invalid.

- The **Format** box allows you to select from a list of available formats for your field. Formats change with the selection of different fields.
- To the right of the **Field value** and **Format** boxes, you'll see a large empty space. AutoCAD will fill this space with hints or additional options as your selection requires.
- The **Field expression** box just above the buttons is informational only. It shows the coding required to create the selected field. Unless you're a programmer, you can ignore this area.

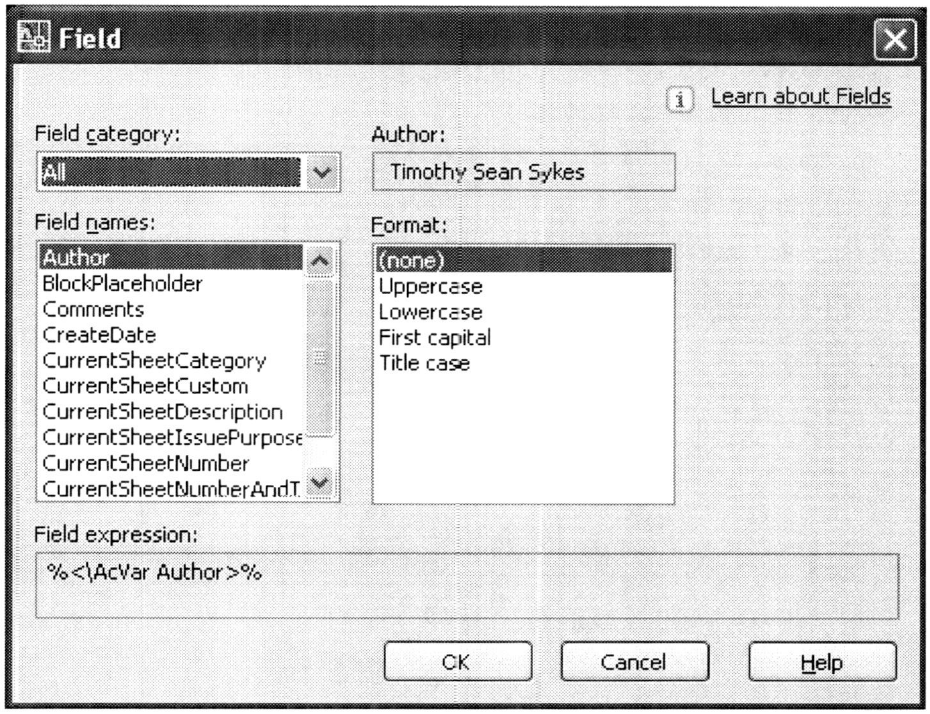

Figure 17.009

AutoCAD provides the usual buttons at the bottom of the dialog box, but I'd like to point out the **Help** button just to make sure you know it's there. This very intuitive dialog box may require some support as you get used to it.

Let's insert some fields.

| Do This: 17.2.2.1 | Inserting Fields |
|---|---|

I. Be sure you're still in the *Floor Plan Data Sheet* drawing in the C:\Steps\Lesson17 folder. If not, please open it now.

II. Set the **TEXT** layer and the **TIMES** text style current.

III. Set the **TextSize** system variable to 1/8".

IV. If you're not already zoomed in around the title/revision blocks, please do so now.

V. Increase the size of the **Date** column by ½" to the right (refer to Exercise 17.1.4.2 if you need help). Reposition the revision table as needed.

VI. Follow these steps.

| 17.2.2.1: INSERTING FIELDS |
|---|
| 1. We'll begin by putting a date in our revision block. Double-click in the cell set aside for the date. AutoCAD opens the MText editor. |
| 2. Pick the **Insert Field** button . AutoCAD presents the Field dialog box. |
| 3. Set up the dialog box as shown in the following figure. |

## 17.2.2.1: Inserting Fields

- Select **Date & Time** in the **Field category** drop down box. Notice that the **Field names** list shows just those fields in the selected category.
- Select **Date** from the **Field names** list.
- Select the format shown.

Notice the **Hints** shown to the right of the selection boxes. This box can help you make an educated decision about your field.

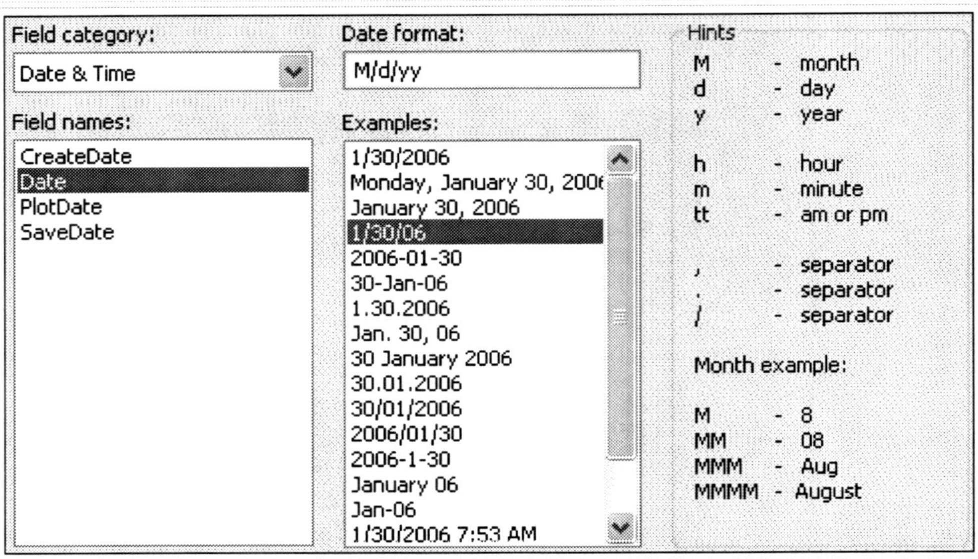


4. Complete the setup OK. Close the MText editor OK.

AutoCAD removes the dialog box and puts the field in the table.

Notice that the field has a light background. AutoCAD places this here to make it easier to find the fields in a drawing; it won't print/plot.

| | | | | |
|---|---|---|---|---|
| | | | | |
| A | [redacted] | TSS | For Grade | MH |
| Rev | Date | By | Description | App |
| **Revision** | | | | |

5. The title in the title block is incorrect. Erase it (the part that reads *Floor Plan Data Sheet*).

**Command: *e***

6. Reset the **TextSize** system variable to 3/16".

**Command: *textsize***

**Enter new value for TEXTSIZE <0.1250>: *3/16***

7. This time we'll enter the ***Field*** command at the command prompt. AutoCAD presents the Field dialog box (Figure 17.009).

**Command: *field***

## 17.2.2.1: Inserting Fields

8. In the **Document** category, select **Title**. Notice the title is the one you entered in the drawing properties dialog box (Exercise 17.2.1.1). Use the **Title case** format and pick the **OK** button to continue 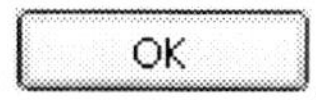.

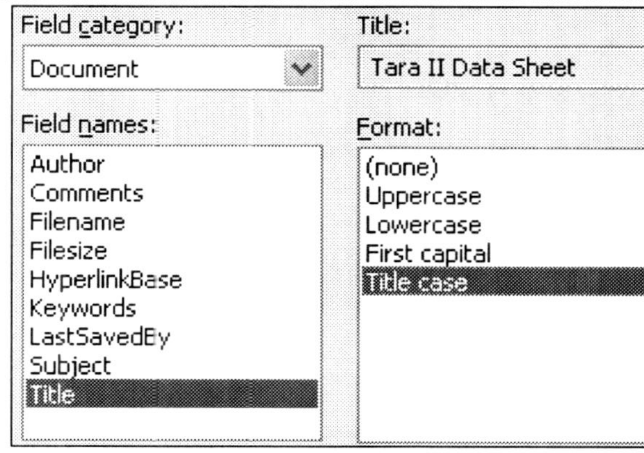


9. Place the field in the title block as shown.

10. Save the drawing as *Tara II Data Sheet* in the C:\Steps\Lesson17 folder.

**Command: *saveas***

11. Now let's look at something really cool. Adjust your view to see the text in the upper right corner of the drawing.

**Command: *p***

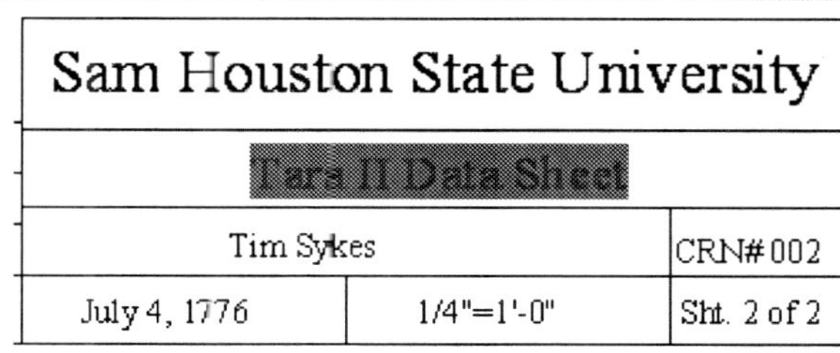


12. Double-click on the text to open the MText editor.

13. Place your cursor below the last note. (Refer to the figure next to Step 23, for a look at where we're going.)

14. Enter the text: ***This data sheet references the following drawings:***

15. Pick the **Insert Field** button .

16. On the Fields dialog box, select **Hyperlink** from the **Linked** category. Pick the **Hyperlink** button to select the drawing to which you'd like to link.

17. AutoCAD presents an Insert Hyperlink text box (more on this when we talk about Web publishing in Lesson 21). For now, pick the **File** button 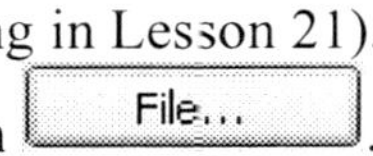.

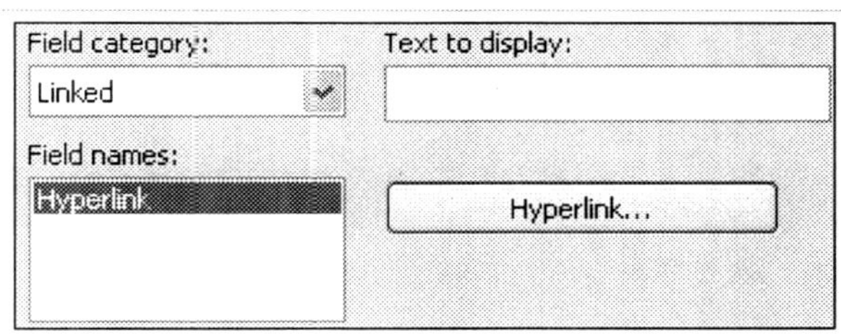


18. AutoCAD presents a standard Select File dialog box. Navigate to the C:\Steps\Lesson17 folder and double-click on the *Floor Plan 17.dwg* file.

19. AutoCAD returns to the Insert Hyperlink text box. Pick the **OK** button 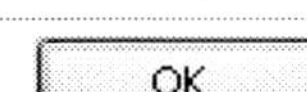 to return to the Field text box.

20. In the **Text to display** box, remove the period and the backslash as shown.

21. Complete the procedure and close the MText editor. Notice the new text.

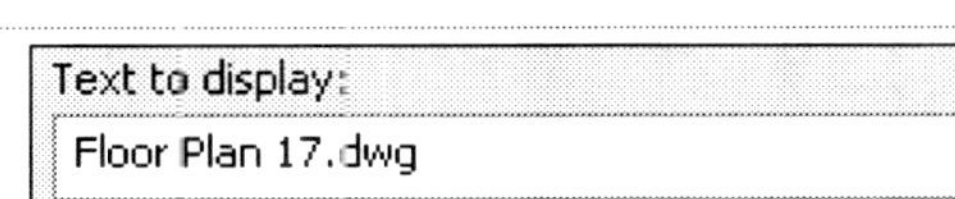

### 17.2.2.1: Inserting Fields

22. Save the drawing.

**Command:** ***qsave***

23. Move your cursor over the field you just placed in the notes. Notice that AutoCAD tells you how to use the hyperlink.

24. Follow AutoCAD's instructions (hold down the CTRL key and click to follow the link). AutoCAD opens the referenced drawing! (Pretty cool, huh?)

25. Close all open drawings.

**Command:** ***closeall***

## 17.2.3 Calculating Fields

You've really just scratched the surface of what you can do with tables. AutoCAD has incorporated some of the more useful elements of spreadsheets into their tables, too. If you've ever used MS Excel or any other spreadsheet program, you might see the potential!

We're going to use fields in an AutoCAD table to calculate the square footage of each of the rooms of our Tara II floor plan. Then we'll total the square footage … and even calculate the average square footage per room!

Let's get started right away.

### Do This: 17.2.3.1 Calculating with Fields

I. Open the *Floor Plan 17* drawing in the C:\Steps\Lesson17 folder. This is the same floor plan we've been using except that I've added a Square Footage table in the lower left corner.

II. Zoom in around the Square Footage table.

III. Follow these steps.

### 17.2.3.1: Calculating with Fields

1. Double-click on the D3 cell (last column in the first data row).

2. Pick the **Insert Field** button.

3. (Refer to the figure that follows.)
   a. Select **Objects** in the **Field Category** selection box,
   b. Select **Formula** in the **Field names** list box,
   c. Enter *B3*C3* in the **Formula** text box,
   d. Pick the **Evaluate** button (AutoCAD displays options in the **Format** list box),
   e. Select **Fractional** from the **Format** list box.

## 17.2.3.1: Calculating with Fields

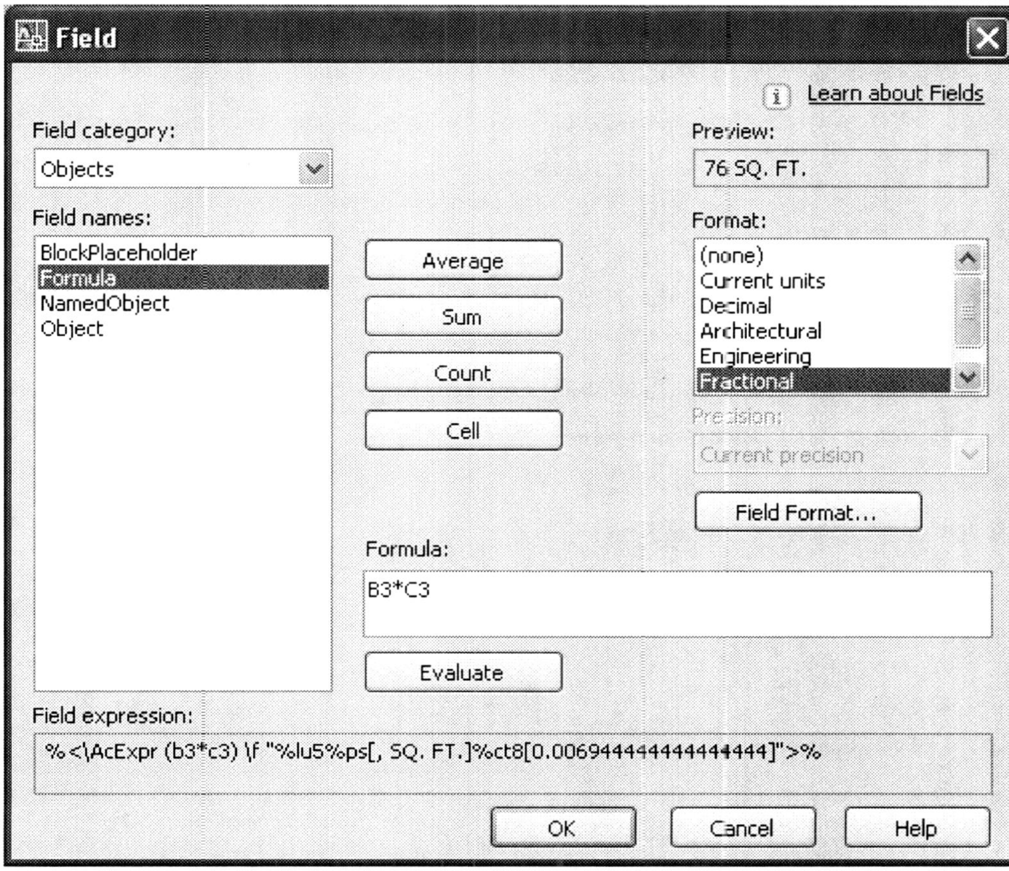


4. Pick the **OK** button 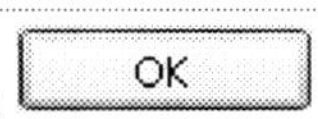 to complete the procedure. Notice that AutoCAD places the product of the values of cells B3 and C3 into cell D3. (Or put more simply, AutoCAD multiples 8 by 9.5 and puts the answer in the location you selected in Step 1.)

5. Use the down arrow key to move to cell D4.

6. Repeat Steps 2 and 3 for this cell as well as cells D5 through D14.

7. Now highlight cell D15 (down arrow into it or double-click on it if you've closed the MText editor). Here we'll sum the square feet column.

8. Pick the **Insert Field** button .

9. This time, we'll let AutoCAD do the work. Pick the **Sum** button .

10. AutoCAD returns to the graphics screen and asks you to place a window around the **table cell range** you wish to total. Put the window around the cells you've been using (D3 through D14).

**Select first corner of table cell range:**

**Select second corner of table cell range:**

## 17.2.3.1: Calculating with Fields

11. AutoCAD returns to the Field dialog box. Select the **Fractional** format you've been using, and then pick the **OK** button [OK] to complete this procedure.

12. Finally, we'll give our client an average figure for the rooms in our house. Use the down arrow to move to cell D16.

13. Pick the **Insert Field** button.

14. Again, we'll let AutoCAD do the work. Pick the **Average** button [Average] and select the same cells (D3 through D14).

15. AutoCAD again returns to the Field dialog box. Again, use the **Fractional** format, and pick the **OK** button [OK] to complete this procedure.

16. We've finished our calculations! Pick the **OK** button [OK] to close the MText editor.

Your table looks like this. (Adjust your column width if necessary.)

| Square Footage | | | |
|---|---|---|---|
| Room | Length | Width | Sq. Ft. |
| Closet - Mstr | 8' | 9.5' | [redacted] |
| Closet #1 | 10' | 3' | [redacted] |
| Closet #2 | 5.5' | 5' | [redacted] |
| Closet #3 | 5.5' | 5' | [redacted] |
| Bath - Mstr | 8' | 9.5' | [redacted] |
| Bath - Com. | 10' | 5' | [redacted] |
| BR - Mstr. | 16' | 16.5' | [redacted] |
| Br #1 | 11.5' | 10.5' | [redacted] |
| Br #2 | 11.5' | 12.5' | [redacted] |
| Br #3 | 13.5' | 9' | [redacted] |
| Kitchen | 11.5' | 19.5' | [redacted] |
| LR | 21' | 30.5' | [redacted] |
| Total | | | [redacted] |
| Rm. Avg. | | | [redacted] |

17. Save the drawing.

**Command:** ***qsave***

Cool, huh? Want to see something even cooler? Change the value in one of the **Length** or **Width** cells. AutoCAD will automatically adjust not only the value in the **Sq. Ft**. column, but the **Total** and **Rm. Avg.** values as well!

## 17.3 Extra Steps

Take a look at the **New Features Workshop** (under the **Help** pull down menu).

Specifically, follow the picks – **Create … Drafting tools … Create Fields**. Go through the exercise to see another way fields can be useful (here you'll automatically calculate and insert the area of a polygon). You'll also see how to update a field.

Remember to take advantage of AutoCAD's various training tools when you have a few extra minutes between lessons or projects at the job site; the effort will prove occasionally beneficial (but never harmful)!

## 17.4 What Have We Learned?

*Items covered in this lesson include:*

- *Field tools:*
    - ***Field***
    - ***DwgProps***
- *Table tools:*
    - ***Table***
    - ***Tablestyle***

AutoCAD makes dozens of combinations of fields and tables available to you. Hopefully, this lesson has whetted your appetite for knowledge and you'll spend some time exploring these new and innovative tools.

Try some of the exercises in Section 17.5, and then relax for a minute before tackling the lesson on hatching. It isn't difficult material, but it's always best to start a new lesson with a fresh mind.

## 17.5 Exercises

1. Add drawing properties and a revision block to the Piping Plan you've been working on. If you're not up to date on it, use *Piping Plan 17* in the C:\Steps\Lesson17 folder. (Refer to the figure below.)
    1.1. Try setting up a new field (Scale) on the **Custom** tab of the [drawing] Properties dialog box. Give it a value of 3/8"=1'-0". Insert it as a field in the title block as shown.
    1.2. When you set up the new table style for the revision block, remember to take the drawing scale factor into account when you assign text sizes. (Hint: I gave you the scale for this drawing in the previous step.)
    1.3. Save the drawing.

| | | | | |
|---|---|---|---|---|
| | | | | |
| 0 | [redacted] | TSS | For Construction | BB |
| **No** | **Date** | **By** | **Description** | **App** |
| Revision | | | | |

| | | |
|---|---|---|
| North Harris College<br>Houston, Texas | | |
| [redacted] | | |
| Tim Sykes | | PLN-002 |
| July 4, 1776 | [redacted] | Sht. 1 of 1 |

## 17.6 For Web-Based Review Questions, visit: http://www.uneedcad.com/2007/Files/07R17.pdf

# Lesson 18

Following this lesson, you will:

- ✓ *Know how to add Hatching and Section Lines to your AutoCAD drawing through:*
  - *The **Hatch** dialog box*
  - *Tool Palettes*
  - *The ADC*
- ✓ *Know how to edit hatch patterns using the **Hatchedit** command*

# Hatching and Filling

*Remember all those templates I mentioned in Lesson 5 – the ones I needed to draw ellipses? Remember how much simpler (and more accurate) it was to draw ellipses with AutoCAD?*

*Here's another drawing tool that puts those pieces of plastic to shame. No longer will the drafter need to spend hours drawing each line or symbol to show section lines, a brick façade, concrete, and so forth. With AutoCAD's hatch commands, you can fill a large area with lines or symbols in a matter or seconds!*

## 18.1 Hatching and Filling

There are actually two ways to draw hatch patterns. (Section lines and fills are created as styles of hatch pattern. Therefore, I'll refer to all as hatch patterns.) There's a dialog box approach and a simple drag-n-drop approach that utilizes the tool palettes. We'll begin with the Hatch and Gradient dialog box (Figure 18.001).

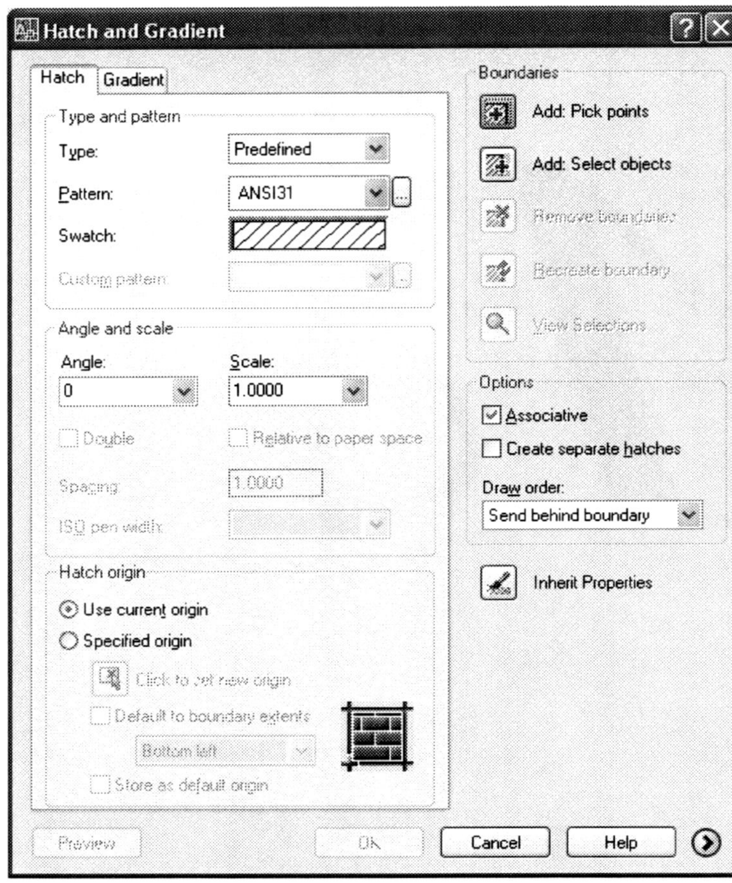


Figure 18.001

The first tab you see **(Hatch)** allows you to set up the **Type**, **Pattern**, **Scale**, **Angle**, and **Origin** of your desired hatching.

The second tab – **Gradient** – allows you to create some interesting gradient fills – similar to the solid option but with more clout.

Additionally, you'll find a series of five buttons in the **Boundaries** frame. These allow you to identify where the hatch pattern will go.

Below the **Boundaries** frame, an **Options** frame helps you define how your hatch pattern or fill will behave.

- An **Associative** hatch pattern, like associative dimensions, dynamically updates when the defining boundaries change.
- A check next to **Create separate hatches** allows you to hatch several things at once, while maintaining the independence of each pattern when it comes to editing.
- **Draw order** lets you define where your pattern will lie – in **front** of or **behind** the boundaries. (This usually won't matter, but AutoCAD allows for the exception to most rules.)

Finally, you'll find an **Inherit Properties** button. Use this to duplicate an existing hatch definition.

Let's look at the tabs.

- The Hatch and Gradient dialog box defaults to the **Hatch** tab.
  - The **Type and pattern** frame contains four different tools you can use to select a hatch pattern: the **Type** control box (which filters your selections), a **Pattern** control box (which lists the patterns available), a **Swatch** box (which you can pick to access a visual listing of available patterns), and a **Custom pattern** control box (which will list any custom patterns loaded into AutoCAD by the CAD guru on your job).
    - The **Type** control box allows you to select a **Predefined** pattern, a **User defined** pattern, or a **Custom** pattern.
      - ∴ **Predefined** patterns accompany AutoCAD. You'll see a sample of the selected pattern in the **Swatch** box or by picking the button next to the **Pattern** control box.
      - ∴ The **User defined** option allows you to set the **Angle** and **Spacing** of hatch lines in the **Angle and scale** frame. Use these tools to define your own hatch pattern. The **User defined** option also makes the **Double** check box available (also in the **Angle and scale** frame). A check here will cause AutoCAD to duplicate your hatch pattern within the same boundaries *but at 90° to the first pattern.*
      - ∴ Selecting **Custom** in the **Type** control box makes the **Custom pattern** control box available. A custom pattern is also predefined, but the definition is stored in a file other than the *Acad.pat* (the file where AutoCAD keeps hatch pattern definitions by default). The CAD guru will provide custom patterns if needed. If you select the **Custom** option in the **Pattern** control box, you must enter the name of the desired pattern in the **Custom Pattern** control box.
    - The **Pattern** control box allow you to scroll through the patterns one at a time; or you can pick the button to the right of the control box to display the Hatch Pattern Palette, which displays visual representations of several patterns at a time. (This is the same palette displayed when you pick in the **Swatch** box.)
  - The **Angle and scale** frame contains tools for defining (or customizing) the pattern you've selected in the **Type and pattern** frame.
    - The **Angle** control box defaults to zero. This doesn't mean that the lines of the hatch pattern will be horizontal. It means that AutoCAD will draw the lines of the selected hatch pattern as they appear in the pattern's definition. Changing the angle here will cause AutoCAD to rotate the pattern (which may have defined the lines at an angle already) by the angle specified.
    - Use the **Scale** control box to set the scale of your pattern. I suggest you start with the scale factor for your drawing. You can adjust it later using the ***Hatchedit*** command.
    - AutoCAD makes **Spacing** available only when you're creating a user defined hatch pattern. Use it to tell AutoCAD how far apart to place the lines.
    - Ignore the **Relative to paper space** check box for now. We'll discuss paper space in Lessons 22 and 23.
    - The **ISO pen width** option becomes available only when you've selected an ISO pattern. This control box allows you to select the width of the ISO lines.
  - You won't find the **Hatch** origin frame in earlier releases of AutoCAD, but its tools have been needed for quite some time.

    Normally, the hatch origin defaults to the 0,0 coordinates. Theoretically, bricks, grating, etc. will begin there even if you only see the portion of the hatch within the boundaries you've designated. This can result in partial bricks (or grating, etc.) along the bottom of the "wall" you're bricking. I doubt that a mason will cut bricks in half to start a new row just to make a building look like your hatching, so AutoCAD decided to allow you to start with a whole brick – by allowing you to redefine the hatch origin.

- A bullet next to **Use current origin** (the default), will lay out hatching based on the 0,0 coordinate of your drawing. This works fine for most hatching.
- You can set a new origin for your hatching by picking the **Click to set new origin** button. But this is the hard way (unless you want to put the origin in an odd place).
- For fancier hatching (like bricks, grating, etc.), put your check next to **Default to boundary extents**. When you do, AutoCAD makes the boundary extents control box available to you (just below the **boundary extents** option). Here you can opt to locate your hatch origin in relation to the boundary (**Bottom left**, **Bottom right**, **Top left**, **Top right**, or **Center**).
- Finally, you can put a check next to **Store as default origin** if you wish to use these settings by default.

• The other tab – **Gradient** (Figure 18.002) – allows you to apply a color or colors with graduated intensity; that is, you can create colors that get more or less intense from one part of the colored area to another.

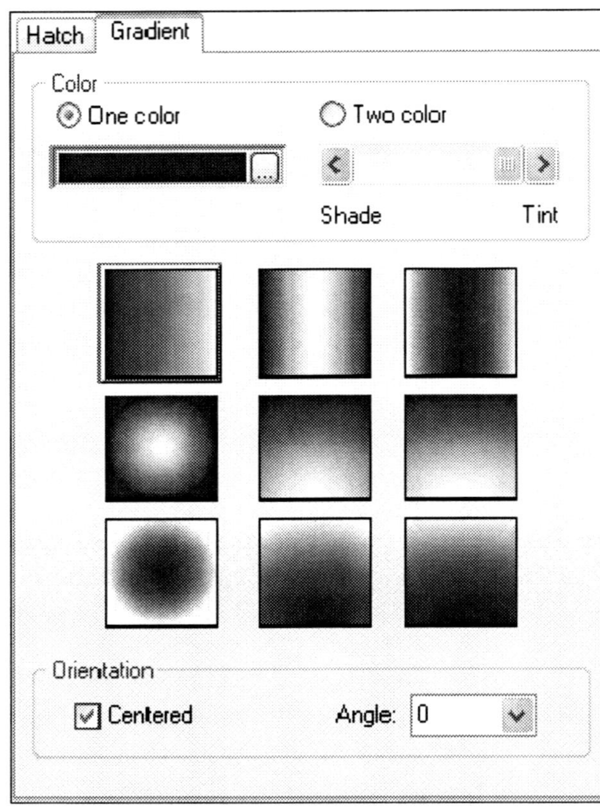

Figure 18.002

  o You can select between a **One color** or a **Two color** gradient with the radio buttons at the top of the tab.

    If you opt for one, AutoCAD presents a color selection box (below the radio buttons) and a **Shade/Tint** slider bar to help you control the intensity of the color.

    If you opt for two colors, AutoCAD replaces the **Shade/Tint** slider bar with a second color selection box to allow you to select the second color.

  o In the lower half of the tab, AutoCAD presents nine selections for how you'd like your gradient to behave. Select the one you prefer.

  o Below the gradient selections, you'll find the **Orientation** frame.
    - The **Centered** check box controls how the graduations behave – remove the check and the intensity grows from mild in the upper left corner (appearing something like a light source) to more intense as you move away from the upper left corner.
    - The **Angle** selection box, of course, controls the angle of the gradients.

Once you've made your selections on the tabs, you must tell AutoCAD what to hatch using one of the buttons on the right side of the dialog box. Here, you'll find two frames, a button, and a quiet arrow button to assist you.

- Define the edges of your hatching with tools in the **Boundaries** frame (Figure 18.003).
  - When you use the **Add: Pick points** button, AutoCAD returns to the graphics screen and prompts:

    **Pick internal point or [Select objects/remove Boundaries]:**

    Pick anywhere within the boundaries (where you want to place your hatching). Be sure the area is closed; AutoCAD will *not* hatch an open area unless the gap tolerance has been properly set (more on that in a few minutes)! Alternately, you can enter an ***S*** and select an object to use as a boundary, or a ***B*** to remove boundaries from your selection set. (Remember to hit enter to complete the selection set.)

Figure 18.003

  - Use the **Add: Select objects** button to go straight to the **Select objects** option.
  - Use the **Remove boundaries** button to go straight to the **remove Boundaries** option.
  - You'll use **Recreate boundary** to redefine existing hatching.
  - **View selections** returns you to the graphics screen and highlights the boundaries you've selected to use to create a new hatching.
- Below the **Boundaries** frame lies the **Options** frame (Figure 18.004).
  - **Associative** hatching means that hatch patterns will update automatically when the boundaries change (much as associate dimensions do).

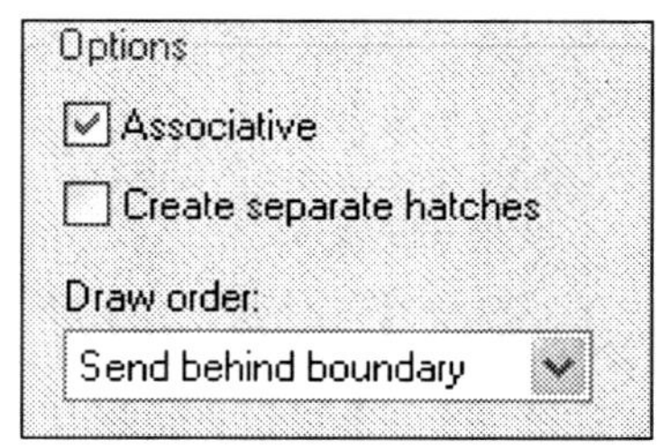


Figure 18.004

> You can convert a hatch pattern (associative or nonassociative) into its constituent lines using the ***Explode*** command. You cannot convert the other way, however, so do this with caution.

  - Normally, if you hatch within several boundaries at once, AutoCAD treats the different hatches as a single object. (That is, if you erase one, they all go.) Place a check next to **Create separate hatches** to avoid problems that this might present.
  - Use the **Draw order** control box to place the hatching in relation to the boundaries. We'll discuss more on draw order in Lesson 26.
- Don't over look the solitary button – **Inherit Properties** – resting below the frames on the right side of the Hatch and Gradient dialog box. This handy tool makes it possible to duplicate any existing hatching in your drawing – even if you don't know how it was set up! Pick the button; AutoCAD will return to the graphics screen and prompt you to **Select hatch object**. Pick the one you wish to duplicate and voila! AutoCAD automatically adjusts the settings in the Hatch and Gradient dialog box to duplicate it! (Way cool!)
- You'll find another solitary button in the bottom left corner of the dialog box – **Preview**. This button allows you to see the hatched object before completing the command. This way, you can make any necessary adjustments before applying the hatching.

Think you're finished? Not quite yet! Notice that insignificant arrow button next to Help (at the bottom of the dialog box). Pick it now. Gadzooks! More options (Figure 18.005)!

- Islands are boundaries within boundaries. By default, AutoCAD recognizes islands and uses an island hopping approach to hatching. That is, hatch – skip – hatch. It does, however, allow other approaches in the **Islands** frame.
    - Leave the check next to **Island detection** for AutoCAD to recognize islands. Remove it, and AutoCAD will ignore any islands and hatch within the outer boundary. (Note: AutoCAD treats text as an island and will not hatch over it unless told to do so with the **Ignore** option.)
    - Use the three radio buttons below the check box (and the graphic representations) to determine how you wish AutoCAD to respond when it finds islands.
- Tools in the **Boundary retention** and **Boundary set** frames work together. Let me explain.

  You'll notice that, in larger drawings, it may take AutoCAD a while to locate boundaries when using the **Pick points** method. This is because AutoCAD must search the drawing database for information on all visible objects. Using the **New** button in the **Boundary set** frame can really hasten this process. When picked, AutoCAD will prompt you to **Select objects** on the screen, and then return to the Hatch and Gradient dialog box. AutoCAD will then restrict its search to the objects selected. You can make the new boundary set from the **Current viewport** or from an **Existing set** by selecting your choice from the control box in the **Boundary set** frame.

  When defining a new boundary set, you should use a window or crossing window; other methods will work, but these are faster in a large drawing. In the **Boundary retention** frame, you can tell AutoCAD to retain the defined area as a **Polyline** or a **Region** (an object similar to a 2-dimensional solid). Simply place a check in the **Retain boundaries** check box and then make your selection in the **Object type** control box.

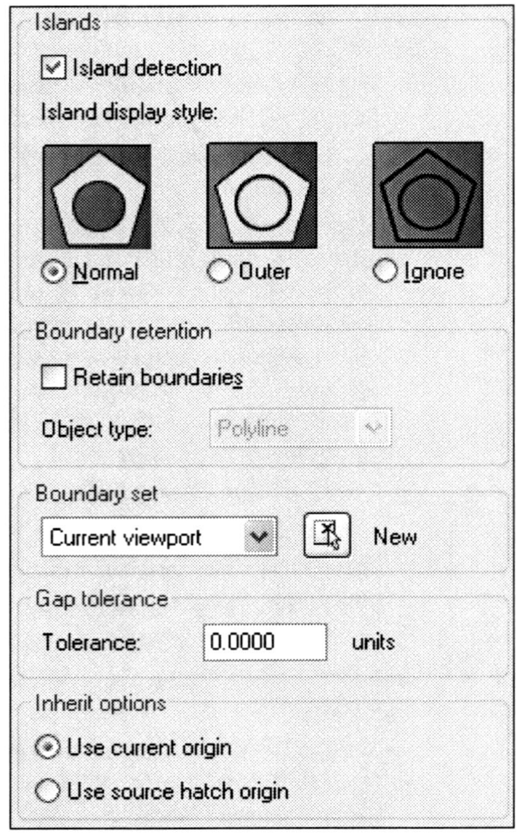

Figure 18.005

> Tools available in the **Boundary retention** and **Boundary set** frames can make a tremendous difference in the amount of time required for AutoCAD to hatch objects in larger drawings. However, you must decide if it's necessary to use these tools by considering how long you're willing to wait for the hatching and how long AutoCAD is taking to do the job.

- **Gap tolerance** can prevent temper tantrums! (I know, designers don't have tempers, right?) When trying to hatch an open grouping of objects, AutoCAD has always run into problems (okay, it wouldn't work). But set this to a number greater than 0. If the ends/edges of the objects fall within that tolerance, AutoCAD will hatch it without grief.
- The final frame (whew!) to consider in creating hatches – **Inherit options** – gives you the opportunity to adjust the hatch origin when you inherit hatch properties.

Are you thoroughly confused? Let's try an exercise.

| Do This: 18.1.1 | Hatching |
|---|---|

I. Open the *demo-hatch.dwg* file the C:\Steps\Lesson18 folder. The drawing looks like Figure 18.006.

II. Follow these steps.

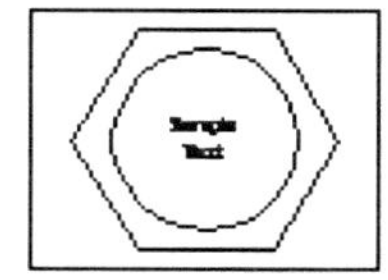

Figure 18.006

## 18.1.1: Hatching

1. Open the Hatch and Gradient dialog by entering the ***Hatch*** command – type ***hatch*** or ***h*** at the command prompt. Alternately, you can pick **Hatch** button  on the Draw toolbar or palette.

**Command: *h***

2. On the **Hatch** tab, **Type and pattern** frame, pick the **Pattern** button.

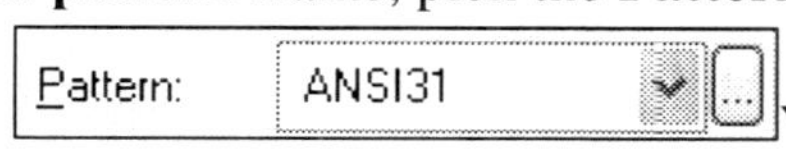


The Hatch Pattern Palette dialog box appears (below).
Here you can select a pattern in one of two ways:

- double-click on it;
- click on the desired pattern and then pick the **OK** button.

Pick the tabs and use the scroll bar to see other patterns.

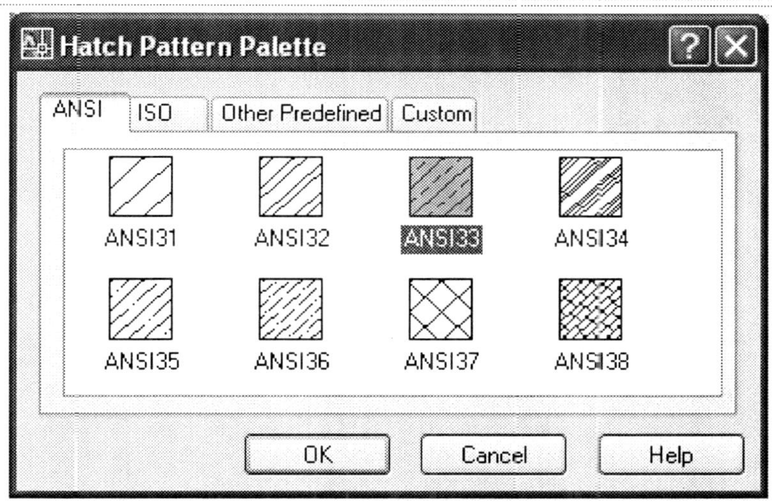


3. Double-click on the **ANSI33** pattern (first tab, first row, third column – see the above figure).
AutoCAD returns to the Hatch and Gradient dialog box. The ANSI33 pattern is now shown as current in the **Pattern** and **Swatch** control boxes.

4. Set the **Scale** to ***1.5*** and the **Angle** to ***0***.

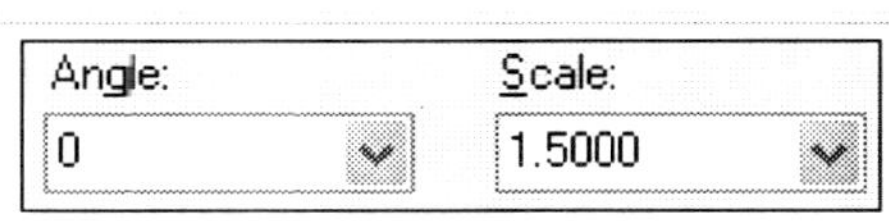


5. Pick the **More options** button  (next to **Help**). AutoCAD displays the frames seen in Figure 18.005.

## 18.1.1: Hatching

6. Set the **display style** to **Outer** in the **Island** frame.

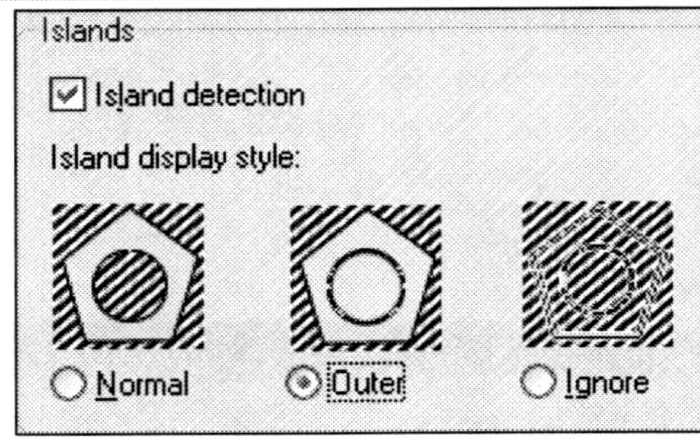


7. Pick the **Add: Pick points** button . AutoCAD returns to the graphics screen.

8. At the prompt, pick any point between the rectangle and the polygon.

**Pick internal point or [Select objects/remove Boundaries]:**

9. AutoCAD tells you what it's doing, and then repeats the prompt. Right click to display the cursor menu.

**Selecting everything...**
**Selecting everything visible...**
**Analyzing the selected data...**
**Analyzing internal islands...**
**Pick internal point or [Select objects/remove Boundaries]:**

10. We could return to the Boundary Hatch dialog box and pick the **Preview** button to see the hatching before applying it. But let's use the **Preview** option on the cursor menu .


Your drawing looks like this.

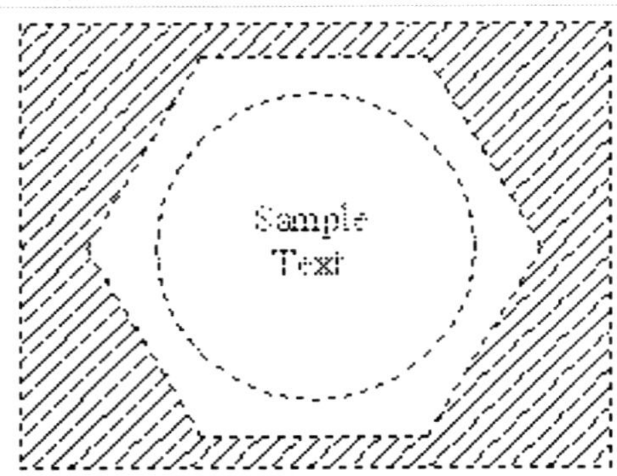


11. Pick anywhere to return to the dialog box.

**<Previewing the hatch>**
**Pick or press Esc to return to dialog or <Right-click to accept hatch>:**

12. Complete the command 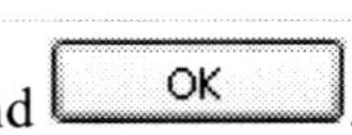.

AutoCAD returns to the graphics screen and the command prompt.

Your drawing looks like this.

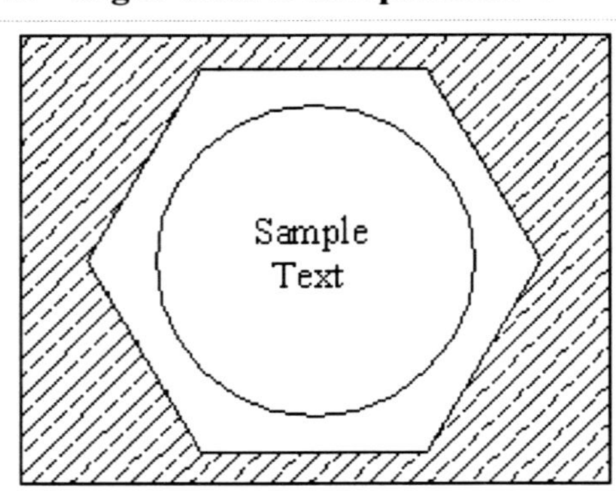

13. Repeat Steps 1 through 12, but hatch between the polygon and the circle with the ANSI37 pattern . Use a **Scale** of ***2.0*** and an **Angle** of ***45°***.

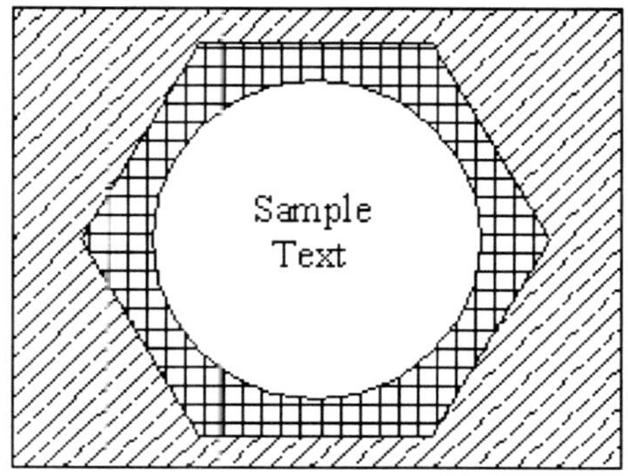


14. Now we'll use the **Inherit Properties** button to hatch the circle using the ANSI33 pattern we used between the rectangle and the polygon. Repeat the ***Hatch*** command .

**Command:** ***[enter]***

Notice that the settings default to the last settings used.

15. Pick the **Inherit Properties** button . AutoCAD returns you to the graphic screen.

16. At the prompt, pick a line on the hatch pattern between the rectangle and the polygon.

**Select hatch object:**

17. Pick a point inside the circle.

**Inherited Properties: Name <ANSI33,_O>, Scale <1.5000>, Angle <0>**
**Pick internal point or [Select objects/remove Boundaries]:**

18. Hit ***enter***. AutoCAD returns to the Boundary Hatch dialog box. Notice that the settings have changed to match those used when you created the first hatching.

**Selecting everything...**
**Selecting everything visible...**
**Analyzing the selected data...**
**Analyzing internal islands...**
**Pick internal point or [Select objects/remove Boundaries]:** ***[enter]***

19. Change the **Angle** setting to ***90°***.

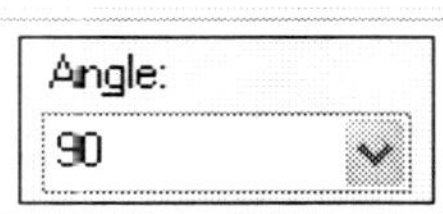


20. Pick the **View Selections** button . AutoCAD returns to the graphics screen and highlights the boundaries you selected in the previous step.

21. Hit ***enter*** (or right-click) to return to the dialog box.

**<Hit enter or right-click to return to the dialog>**

## 18.1.1: Hatching

22. **Preview** the hatching if you wish, then **OK** it.
Your drawing looks like this.

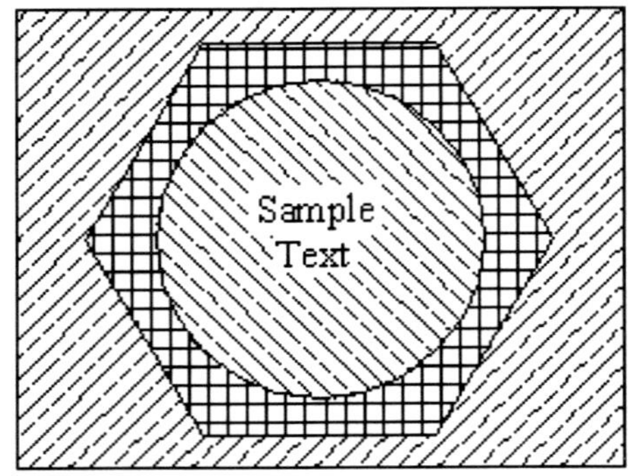


22. Now for a real treat, try stretching the rectangle or the polygon. Note the effects of *Associative* hatching!

**Command: *s***

23. Undo the ***Stretch*** command and save the drawing.

**Command: *qsave***

24. Now let's look at some other options. Thaw the **OBJ2** layer (but leave **HATCH** current). Notice the new rectangles. (Adjust your view as necessary.)

25. Repeat the **Hatch** command.

**Command: *h***

26. Select the AR-B816 pattern from the Hatch Pattern Palette. (Refer to Step 2 if you need help.)

27. Set the **Angle** and **Scale** as indicated.

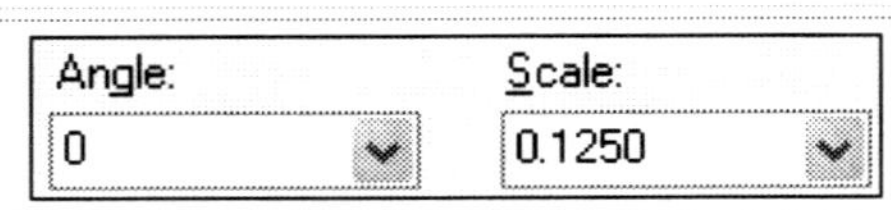


28. Tell AutoCAD to use **Normal Island detection** …

29. … and **Use** [the] **current origin** (Use current origin).

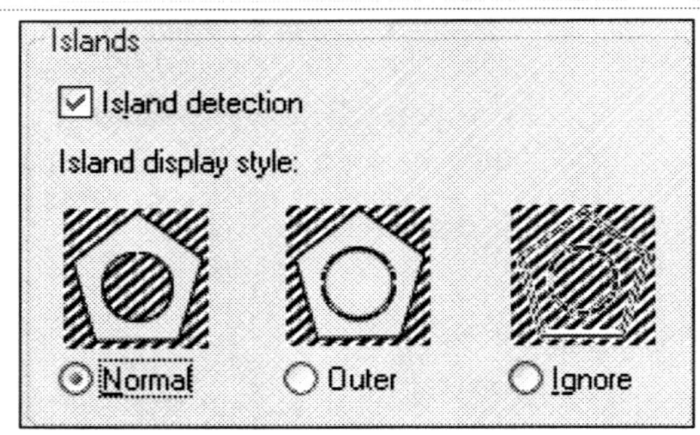


30. Now pick a point between the two outer rectangles.

**Pick internal point or [Select objects/remove Boundaries]:**

**18.1.1: Hatching**

31. And finally, complete the procedure [OK].

Your rectangles look like this. Notice the **Normal** hatching (island hopping: hatch – skip – hatch). Notice also where the bricks start.

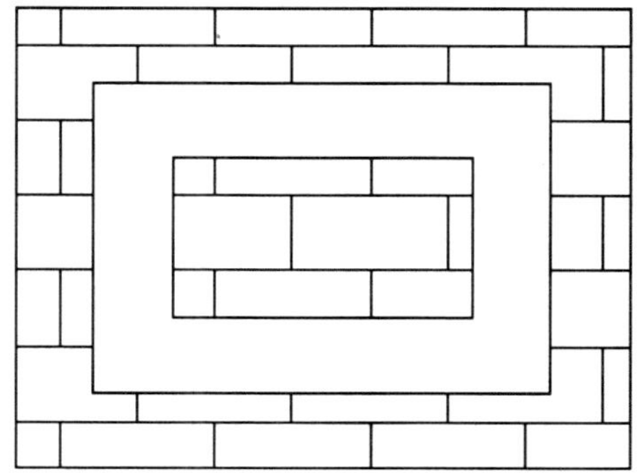

32. Erase the brick pattern.

**Command:** ***e***

33. Repeat Steps 25 through 31, but this time, **Specify** that you want the **origin** to **Default to boundary extents**, and select the **Bottom left** boundary as shown.

See the difference (below)?

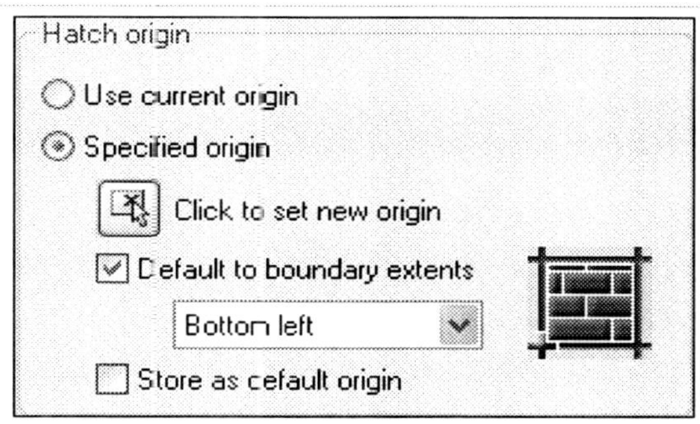


23. Save the drawing.

**Command:** ***qsave***

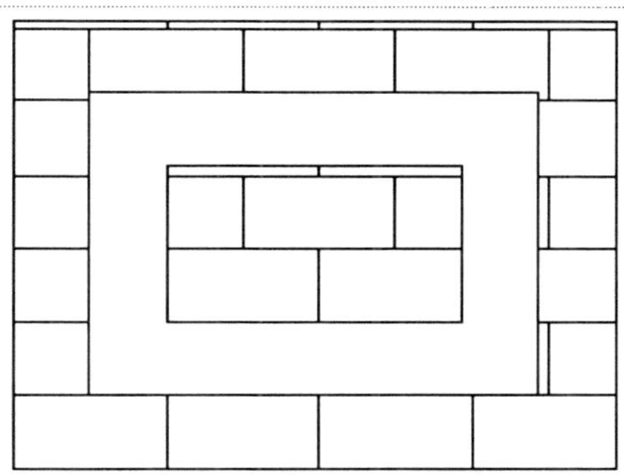

Those familiar with the *One Step at a Time* series might recognize that I've removed instructions for the command line approach to the ***Hatch*** command. Some will welcome the removal; others may not. There are few things that can be done on the command line that you can't do better with the dialog box, but those who know how to use it will miss the direct hatch option (available only on the command line). For those of you interested in this tool, I posted the appropriate sections of the '05 text on the web (www.uneedcad.com/Files).

## 18.2 Editing Hatched Areas

We have a couple other ways to apply hatching, but before we look at them, let's take a quick look at editing the pattern once you've applied it. (This may seem a bit out of order, but it'll help in later explanations.)

Remember how the ***DDEdit*** command, when used on MText, returned you to the Multiline Text Editor? Once there, editing the text was as easy – and followed the same rules and procedures – as creating the text. The ***Hatchedit*** command works the same way on hatching. Simply enter the command and select the hatch pattern to be edited. AutoCAD returns you to the Hatch and Gradient dialog box (but calls it the Hatchedit dialog box). Then you can proceed as though you were creating the hatching for the first time.

Let's try it.

> ***HE*** will also access the ***Hatchedit*** command. Alternately, you can pick **Hatch** on the Modify pull-down menu (*Modify – Object – Hatch*), pick the **Hatch** button on the Modify II toolbar or Modify palette, or select the hatching to be edited and then select **Hatch Edit** from the cursor menu. Still too complicated? You can also double-click on the hatching you want to edit!

| **Do This: 18.2.1** | **Hatch Editing** |
|---|---|

I. Be sure you're still in the *demo-hatch.dwg* file in the C:\Steps\Lesson18 folder. If not, please open it now.

II. Follow these steps.

## 18.2.1: Hatch Editing

1. Enter the ***Hatchedit*** command .

**Command: *he***

2. Select the hatching inside the circle. AutoCAD presents the Hatch Edit dialog box (below). Notice that the settings reflect those you used to create the pattern.

**Select hatch object:**

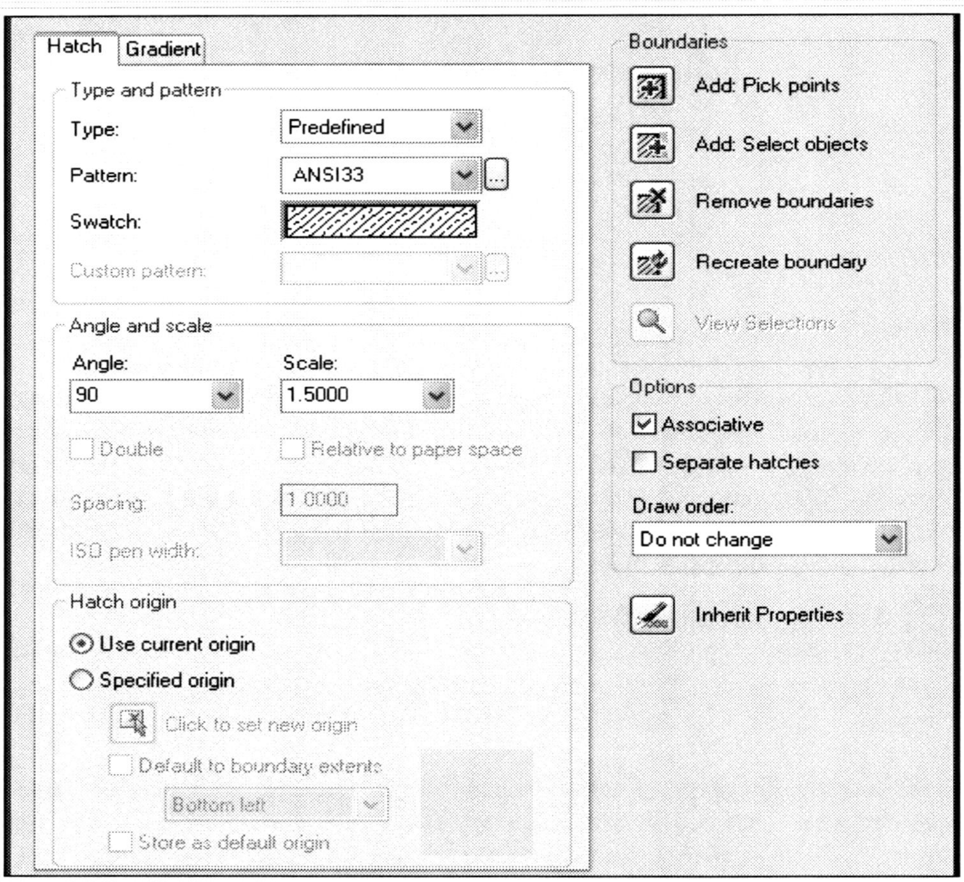

## 18.2.1: Hatch Editing

3. Pick the **Gradient** tab Gradient.

4. Select the lower left gradient fill pattern 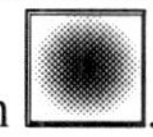.

5. Pick the **OK** button OK. AutoCAD returns to the graphics screen
The drawing now looks like this.

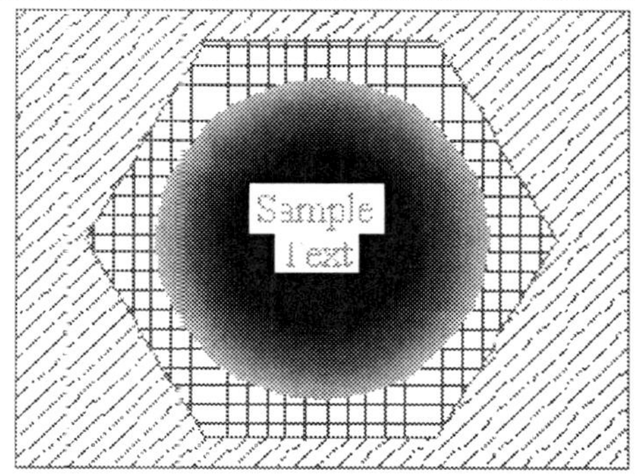


6. Save  and close the drawing.
**Command:** ***qsave***

## 18.3 Drag-and-Drop Hatching – Using the ADC and Tool Palettes to Hatch

### 18.3.1 Using the ADC to Hatch

You've seen how to drag-and-drop layers into a drawing using the AutoCAD Design Center (Lesson 6). Although the procedure is slightly different, the same principle applies to drag-and-drop hatching. The difference in the procedures results from having different sources from which you mine desired objects. You mine layers from existing drawings or templates; you mine hatch patterns from a pattern file (a file with a .pat extension).

> What exactly does drag-and-drop mean and how do I do it?
>
> Drag-and-drop means to pick something up (with your mouse), carry it somewhere, and drop it into place.
>
> The term *drag-and-drop* is actually quite illustrative of the procedure. To pick up the object to be dragged, place your cursor over it. Pick (generally with the left mouse button, but in AutoCAD hatching procedures, you'll use the right mouse button more often than the left) and *hold the button down*. Move the cursor to the target area (you'll notice that you're dragging the object you picked up) and release the button. That's really all there is to drag-and-drop. If you've used the left mouse button for your drag-and-drop procedure, the object will be placed without further ado. If you've used the right mouse button, AutoCAD will ask you what to do by presenting a cursor menu like that shown in Figure 18.007.

You also have more options when mining hatch patterns via the ADC as indicated in the right-click cursor menu (Figure 18.007). Let's consider these.

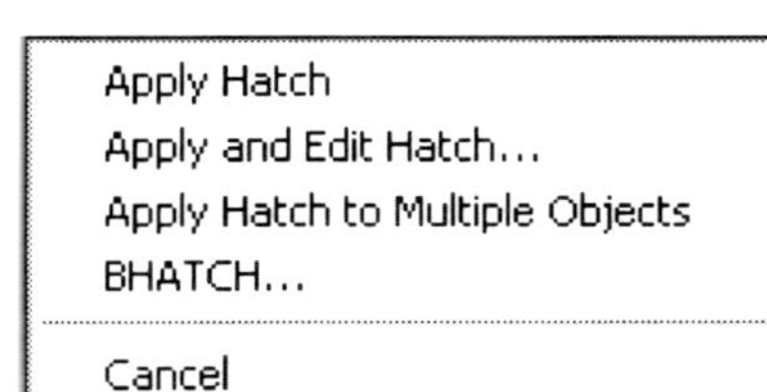


Figure 18.007

- The **Apply Hatch** option behaves as if you had performed the drag-and-drop with the left mouse button (see the previous insert).
- **Apply and Edit Hatch** applies the hatch pattern as if you'd used the **Add: Pick points** button in the Hatch and Gradient dialog box. It then immediately opens the Hatch Edit dialog box where you can adjust the settings

as you did in our last exercise.

- **Apply Hatch to Multiple Objects** allows you to place the hatch pattern as if you'd used the **Add: Pick points** button – picking as many different locations as you like – except that each location will contain individual hatch patterns (not a single pattern in multiple areas). Hit the ESC key on your keyboard to complete this procedure.
- The **BHatch** option calls the Hatch and Gradient dialog box with the selected pattern shown in the **Pattern** control box. This allows you to insert the hatch with whatever settings you wish.

The last option doesn't appear on the cursor menu. You can drag-and-drop using the left mouse button just as drag-and-drop procedures work in most other applications. When you do this, AutoCAD hatches with the selected pattern as if you had used the **Add: Pick Points** button in the Boundary Hatch dialog box, using the last scale and angle settings entered in the dialog box or on the command line.

Let's see how some of these options work in an exercise.

| Do This: 18.3.1.1 | Drag-and-Drop Hatching with the ADC |
|---|---|

I. Open the *d&d-hatch.dwg* file the C:\Steps\Lesson18 folder. It looks like Figure 18.008.

II. Open the AutoCAD Design Center.

III. Follow these steps.

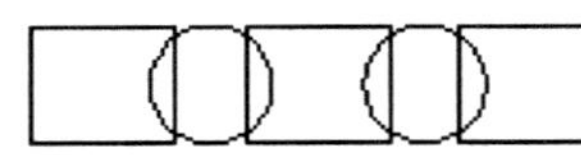

Figure 18.008

### 18.3.1.1: Drag-and-Drop Hatching with the ADC

1. (Refer to the following figure).

Scroll to the *\AutoCAD 2007\UserDataCache\Support\acad.pat* file as indicated. This file contains the default hatch patterns that ship with AutoCAD. Notice the list on the right.

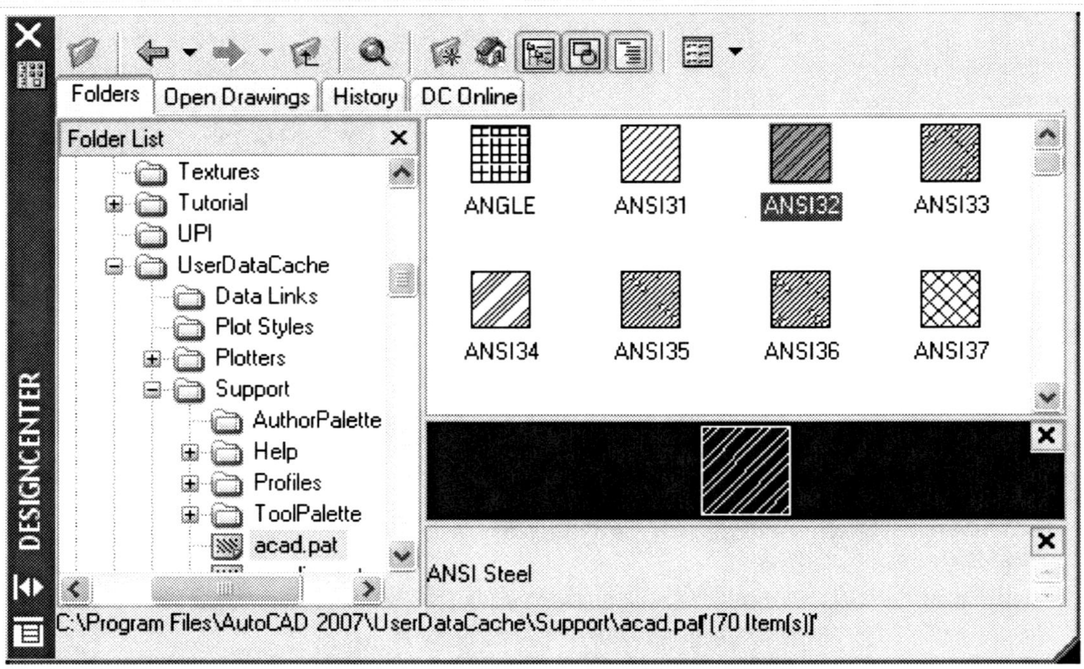

## 18.3.1.1: Drag-and-Drop Hatching with the ADC

2. Using the left mouse button, drag-and-drop the ANSI31 pattern into the center of the leftmost circle.

Your drawing looks like this.

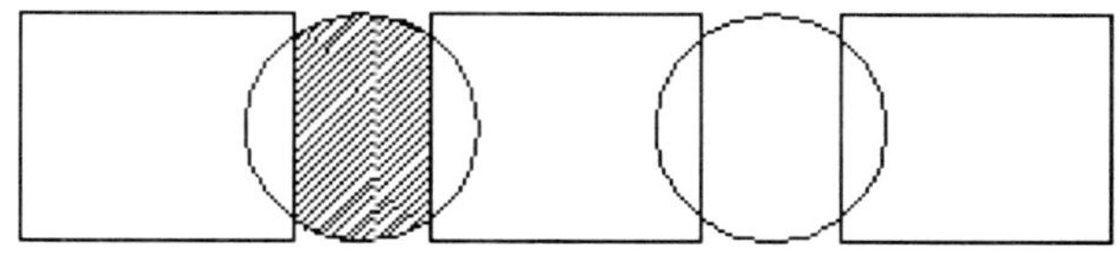

3. Now, using the right mouse button, drag-and-drop the ANSI33 pattern into the center of the right circle. AutoCAD presents the cursor menu when you release the mouse button.

4. Select **Apply and Edit Hatch**. AutoCAD applies the hatch to the circle and opens the Edit Hatch dialog box.

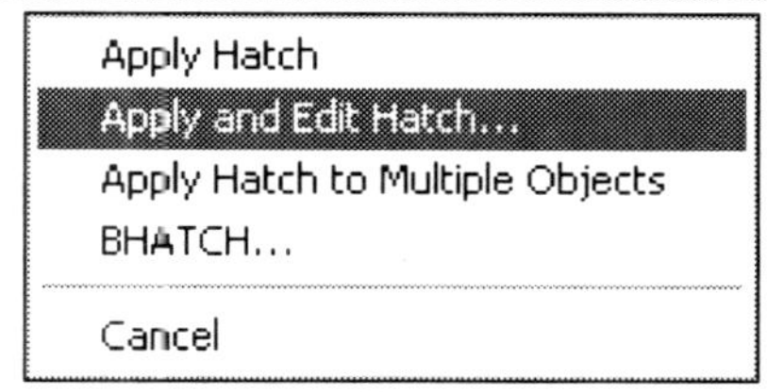


5. Set the scale of the pattern to ***2***, and then complete the procedure.

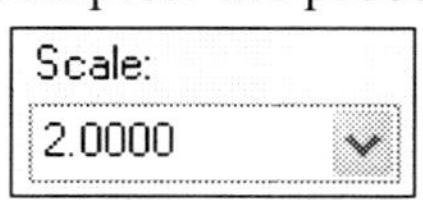


Your drawing looks like this.

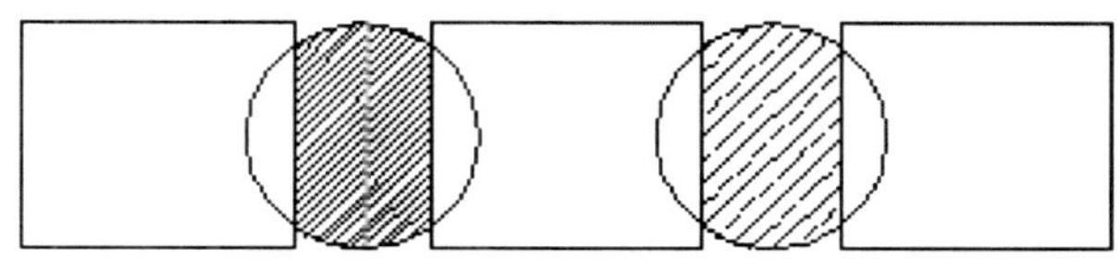

6. Now let's apply the ANSI35 pattern to multiple objects. Using the right mouse button, drag-and-drop this pattern into the first rectangle.

7. On the cursor menu, select **Apply Hatch to Multiple Objects**.

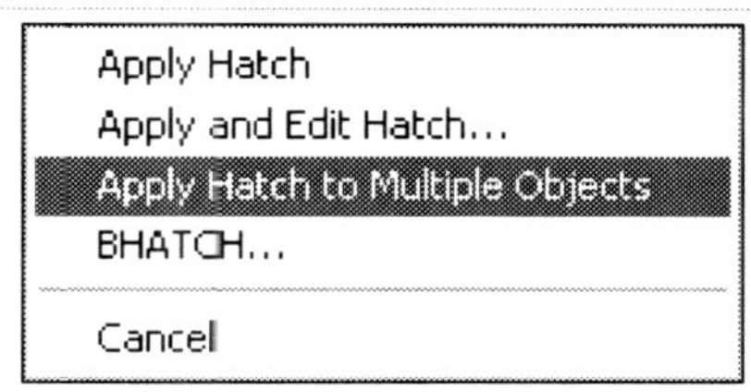


8. AutoCAD inserts the pattern and then prompts for another insertion point. Place the pattern in the center of the other two rectangles.

**Specify insertion point:**

Hit the ESC key 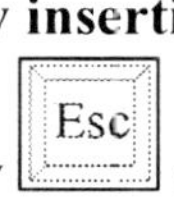

on your keyboard to complete the procedure.

Your drawing looks like this.

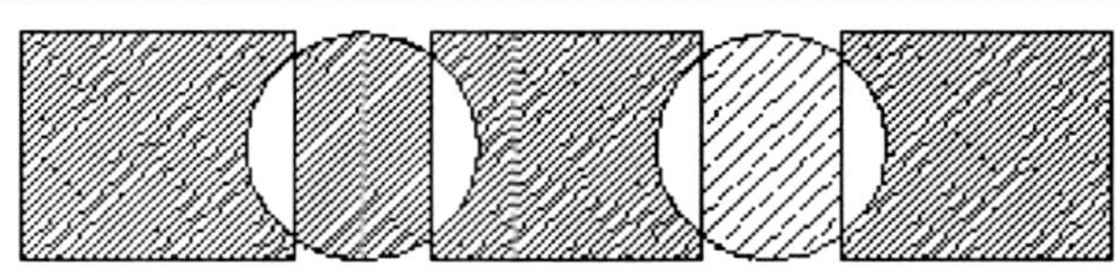

9. Now let's try the **BHatch** option. Drag-and-drop the ANSI37 pattern (right mouse button) into the first circle-rectangle overlap and select **BHatch** on the cursor menu. AutoCAD presents the Hatch and Gradient dialog box.

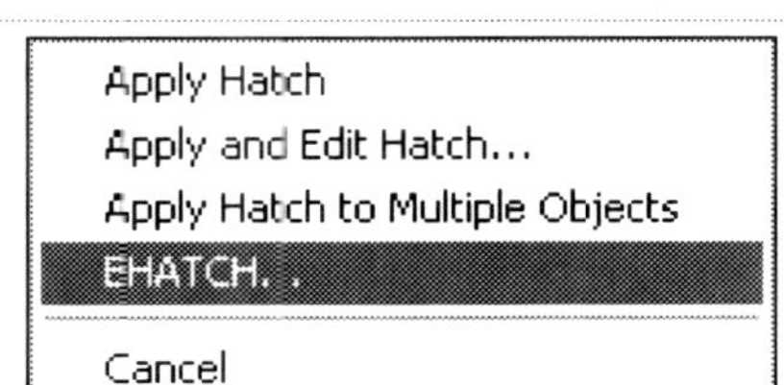


10. Set the scale to ***2*** and pick the **Add: Pick points** button 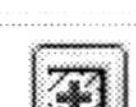.

### 18.3.1.1: Drag-and-Drop Hatching with the ADC

11. Place the hatch pattern into all the overlapping spaces.

Your drawing looks like this.

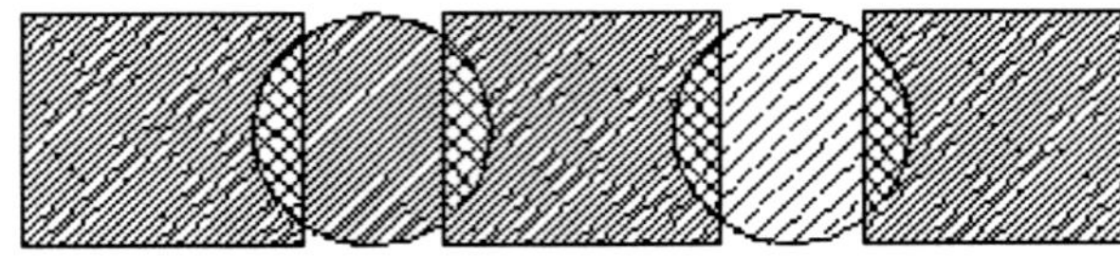

12. Remember that you placed multiple patterns using the **Apply to Multiple Objects** option of the cursor menu in Steps 7 and 8. These are the patterns in the rectangles. You also placed several patterns at once in Step 11.

Try to erase an individual pattern in a rectangle. Try to erase an individual in one of the overlapping spaces. Notice that the drag-and-drop procedure created separate pattern definitions that can be treated as individual objects. The Hatch and Gradient dialog box method did not.

13. Erase  the hatch patterns and close the ADC, but don't exit the drawing.

**Command: *e***

## 18.3.2 Using Tool Palettes to Hatch

Using tool palettes is a bit easier, although they're not radically different from the ADC methods for applying hatch patterns. The most obvious difference is that the patterns are already visible without having to scroll around looking for the pattern (.pat) file.

But a more important difference lies in the cursor menus. Whereas the ADC allows a right click drag-and-drop procedure to call a cursor menu with the various procedural options, the tool palettes has no right-click procedure … no application cursor menus. The tool palette procedure relies on the Properties palette to modify hatch pattern definitions before you insert them, or the ***Hatchedit*** command to modify patterns after they've been inserted.

Let's see how this works.

**Do This: 18.3.2.1 Drag-and-Drop Hatching with Tool Palettes**

I. Be sure you're still in the *d&d-hatch.dwg* file the C:\Steps\Lesson18 folder. If not, please open it now.

II. Open the Tool Palettes.

III. Follow these steps.

### 18.3.2.1: Drag-and-Drop Hatching with Tool Palettes

1. The first procedure compares quite favorably to the left-button method in the ADC.

Using the left mouse button (the right one won't work for these procedures), drag-and-drop one of the brick patterns from the **Hatches** tab of the tool palette into the left rectangle.

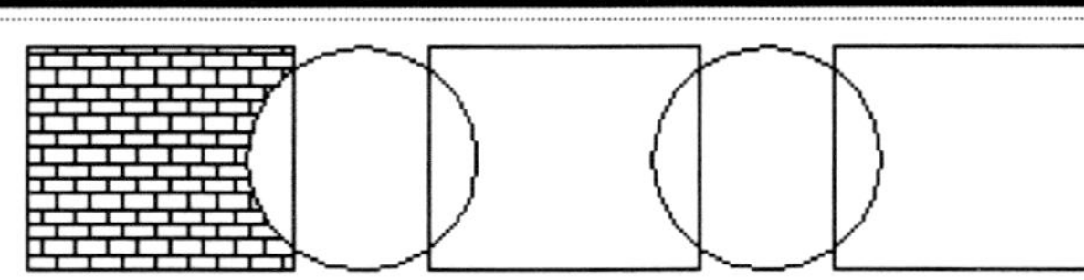

2. Right click on the same pattern on the tool palette. AutoCAD presents a cursor menu.

### 18.3.2.1: Drag-and-Drop Hatching with Tool Palettes

3. We'll customize our pattern before we apply it. Select **Properties** 

. AutoCAD presents a Tool Properties dialog box for this pattern (similar to the Properties Manager).

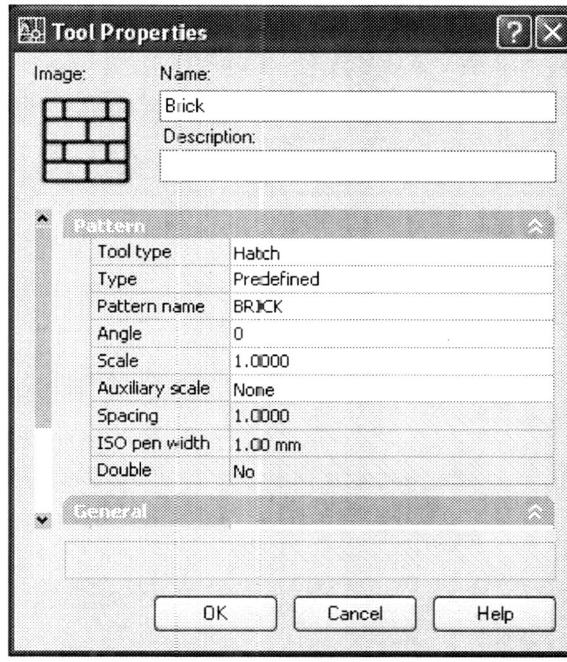


4. Look over the properties you can customize, and then change the **Scale** of the pattern to **2**.

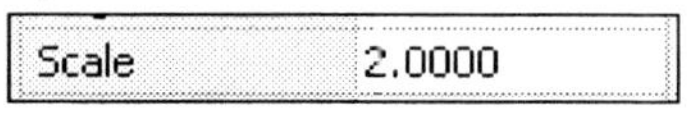


5. Complete the procedure 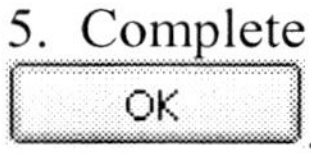

.

6. Repeat Step 1, but this time, insert the pattern into the center of both the circles.

Your drawing looks like this.

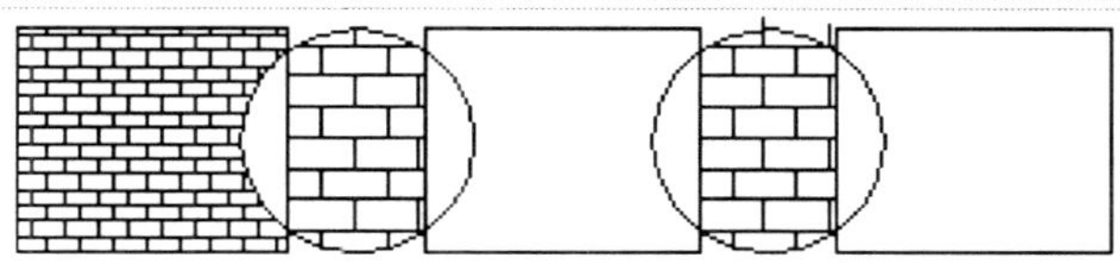

7. Exit the drawing without saving it.

**Command:** ***quit***

So which method do you prefer? Obviously, you prefer the easiest!

## 18.4 Extra Steps

Experiment with the command line approach to the ***Hatch*** command. Begin by placing a dash before the command (***-hatch***). (For a more detailed explanation of the command line approach, download *CmdLineHatch* from www.uneedcad.com/Files.

## 18.5 What Have We Learned?

> *Classroom acquired skills are to the mind what paint is to pottery – nothing but surface fluff that fades and disappears with the passing of time. For the skills to become actual knowledge, they must be tempered into the mind's clay through the repeated pounding of experience.*
>
> *PRACTICE PRACTICE PRACTICE*
>
> Anonymous

*Items covered in this lesson include:*

- *Hatching Tools:*
  - ***Hatch***
  - ***HatchEdit***
  - ***Drag and Drop Hatching***

By now you should be growing more comfortable with AutoCAD procedures and routines. You've passed beyond basic drawing and can create more complex objects in a few keystrokes or mouse picks. The one thing you still need – and need plenty of – is practice!

Work through the exercises at the end of this lesson. They may take a bit longer than earlier exercises, but that's because the drawings are becoming more complex. Additionally, I'm expecting more from you while providing less.

Our next two lessons will teach you to use the first tools that make AutoCAD something more than a very expensive drafting tool. We'll cover blocks in Lesson 19; we'll attach *information* to blocks in Lesson 20.

## 18.6 Exercises

1. Start a new drawing from scratch.
   1.1. Create the following setup:
      1.1.1. Use a 1½"=1'-0" scale on an A-size sheet of paper (8½x11)
      1.1.2. Grid: 1" (snap as needed)
      1.1.3. The layers in the table.
   1.2. Use this information for the Grade hatching:
      Pattern: EARTH
      Scale: 8.0000
      Angle: 45
   1.3. Use this information for the sand hatching:
      Pattern: AR-SAND
      Scale: 0.5000
      Angle: 0
   1.4. Use the Times New Roman font. Large text should plot at ¼"; small text should plot at 1/8".
   1.5. Create the Exterior Slab drawing shown here. Save it as *MySlab* in the C:\Steps\Lesson18 folder.

| LAYER NAME | COLOR | LINETYPE |
|---|---|---|
| 0 | 7 (white) | Continuous |
| Border | 5 (blue) | Continuous |
| Cl | 6 (magenta) | Center2 |
| Dim | 2 (yellow) | Continuous |
| Const | 1 (red) | Continuous |
| Hidden | 42 | Hidden |
| Obj1 | 4 (cyan) | Continuous |
| Obj2 | 3 (green) | Continuous |
| Obj3 | 1 (red) | Continuous |
| Obj4 | 6 (magenta) | Continuous |
| Text | 2 (yellow) | Continuous |

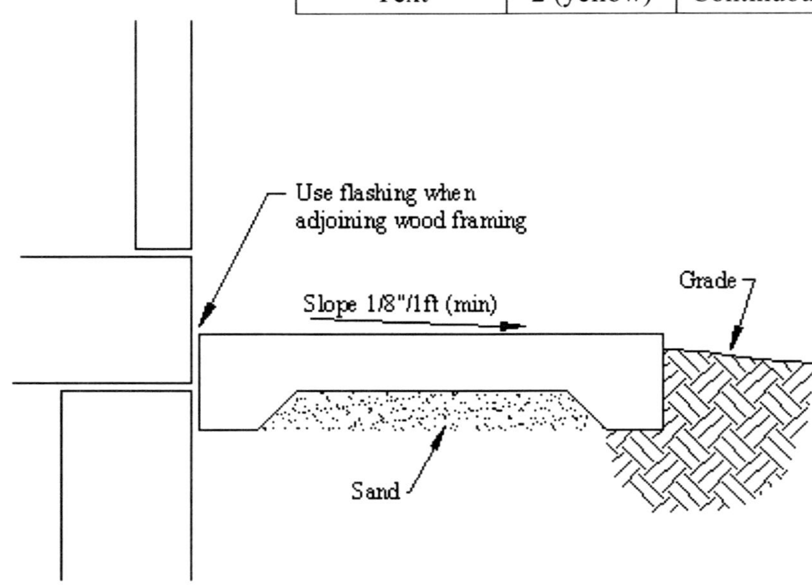


**Exterior Slab**

2. Start a new drawing from scratch. Using the same information you used in the *Exterior Slab* drawing in Exercise 2, create the *Concrete Pier Footing* drawing.
   2.1. Use this information to hatch the concrete:

      Pattern: AR-CONC

      Scale: 0.5000

      Angle: 0

   2.2. Save the drawing as *MyFooting* in the C:\Steps\Lesson18 folder.

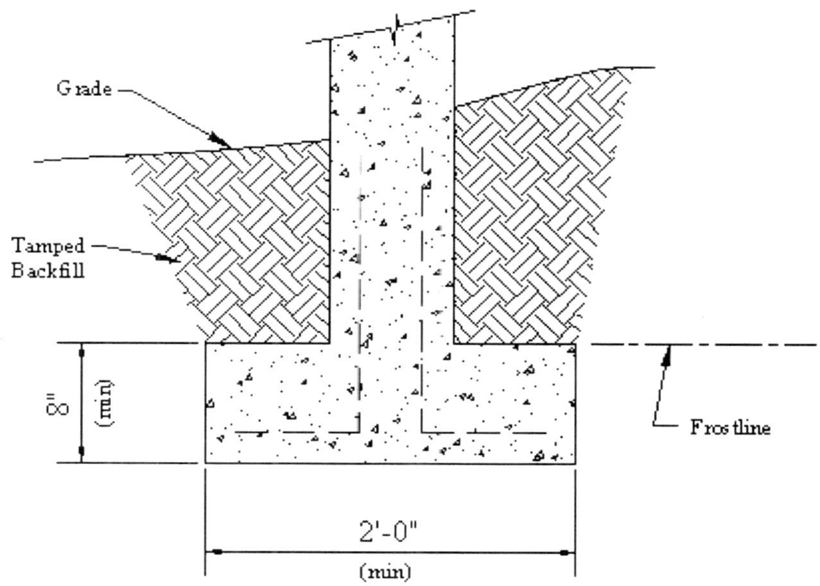


Concrete Pier Footing

*For more exercises related to Lesson 18, please see Lesson 18 in AutoCAD 2007: One Step at a Time – Workbook.*

| 18.7 | **For Web-Based Review Questions, visit: http://www.uneedcad.com/2007/Files/07R18.pdf** |
|---|---|

# Lesson 19

Following this lesson, you will:

- ✓ *Know how to create and manipulate Groups*
- ✓ *Know how to use blocks in a drawing*
    - o *The **Block** command*
    - o *The **WBlock** command*
    - o *The **Insert** Command*
- ✓ *Know how to create libraries of blocked objects*
- ✓ *Know how to share blocks between drawings using the AutoCAD Design Center and Tool Palettes*

# Many as One – Groups and Blocks

*One of the great benefits of using a computer to create design plans lies in the ability of the operator to create something once, and then duplicate or manipulate it as desired. We've used several modification commands, techniques, and procedures throughout the course of this text and have become fairly comfortable with the basic tools. But there are still two modification routines that can increase speed and make your work easier. These are the* ***Group*** *and* ***Block*** *commands.*

*We'll look at these in Lesson 19. Although they often behave in a similar manner, each has its niche in the drawing world and it'll be important to know when to use them. Then, in Lesson 20, we'll learn why blocks are one of the most valuable design tools ever created.*

## 19.1 Paper Dolls: The *Group* Command

Have you ever done a furniture layout for an office or an equipment layout for a shop or plant? You may know then that the easiest way to accomplish the layout (in such a fashion that the equipment can be moved around as the plan develops) is to use the "paper dolls" approach. That is, you create a scaled drawing of the room or work area, make a blue line of it, and then move scaled representations (paper dolls) of the equipment around the blue line until you're satisfied with the locations. Once you're satisfied, you tape the dolls to the blue line for reference and draw the objects in your layout.

It's easy work *if* you keep the windows closed and nobody slams a door. A slight breeze, however, sends people scrambling for the paper dolls and mumbling things that might make a sailor blush. Of course, this is only after the hours spent reminiscing about kindergarten while cutting paper dolls out of construction paper.

Once again, AutoCAD has created tools that provide the benefits of construction paper and tape (combined with a few new benefits) while removing the hassles. Enter ***Groups***.

What is a group? Simply put, a group is a collection of objects treated as a single unit.

Let's take a look.

| Do This: 19.1.1 | Working with Groups |
|---|---|

I. Open the *groups.dwg* file the C:\Steps\Lesson19 folder. The drawing looks like Figure 19.001.

II. Follow these steps.

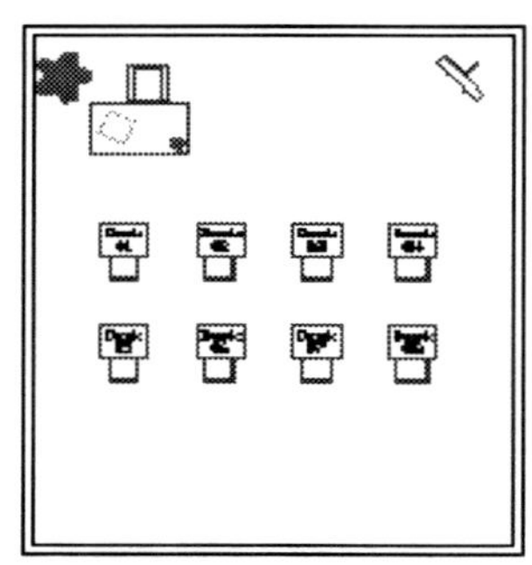

Figure 19.001

| 19.1.1: Working with Groups |
|---|
| 1. We'll switch the tree (in the upper left corner of the screen) with the easel pad (in the upper right corner). Enter the ***Move*** command. <br> **Command: *m*** |

## 19.1.1: Working with Groups

2. Select anywhere in the tree as shown. Complete the selection.

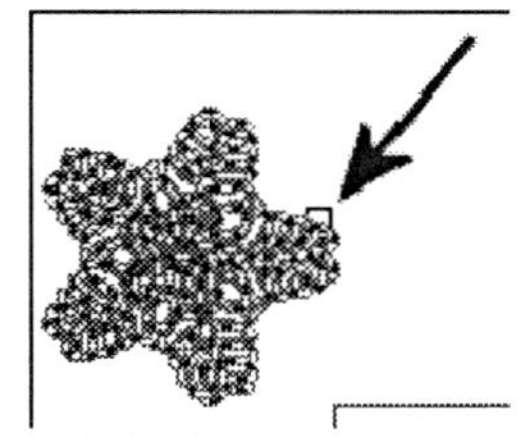

**Select objects: 80 found, 1 group**

**Select objects:** ***[enter]***

(Notice how easy it is to select these 80 objects!)

3. Move the tree 21 feet to the right.

**Specify base point or [Displacement] <Displacement>:** ***21',0***

**Specify second point or <use first point as displacement>:** ***[enter]***

4. Repeat Steps 1 through 3 to move the easel pad 21 feet to the left. Your drawing looks like the figure below.

Notice that, in each instance, you selected the objects with a single pick and AutoCAD indicated the number of objects *and the number of groups* found.

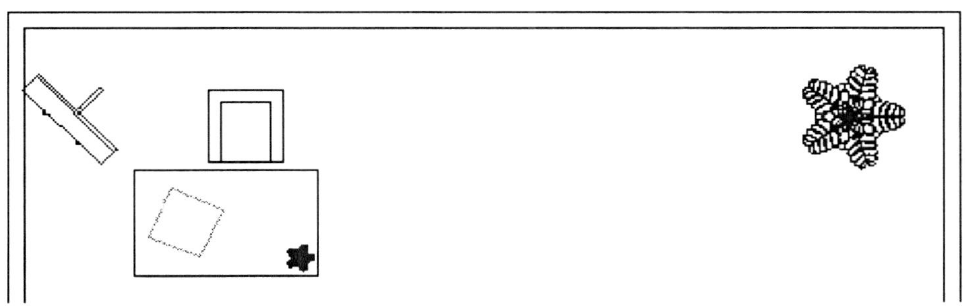

5. Now rotate the easel pad 90° to face the correct direction.

**Command:** ***ro***

This part of your drawing now looks like this.

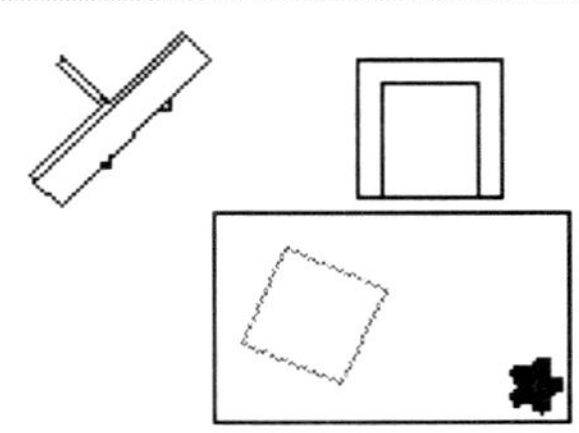

6. Save the drawing but don't exit.

**Command:** ***qsave***

You can see how easy it is to manipulate grouped objects. And before you ask, yes, you can manipulate individual objects within a group (but *not* within a block – well, at least not easily).

Let's take a look at how you can create groups yourself and at how you can work with individual parts of the group.

When you enter the ***Group*** command, AutoCAD provides the Object Grouping dialog box to assist you (Figure 19.002 – next page).

- The upper list box shows the names of existing groups (under **Group Name**) and whether or not the group is currently **Selectable** (**Yes** or **No**). Selectable simply means that you can manipulate the group as a single object. You'll want the group to be selectable to do what we did in the last exercise; but you won't want it selectable if you need to modify something within the group (like pruning the branches of the tree we moved). You can't change the **Selectable** setting in the list box. We'll see how to do that shortly.

- The **Group Identification** frame holds several useful items.
  - o Appearing in the appropriate text box, you'll find the name and description (if any) of the group highlighted in the list box at the top of the dialog box. You'll begin to create a new group by typing a new **Group Name** and **Description** (if desired) into these boxes. (We'll create some new groups in our next exercise.)

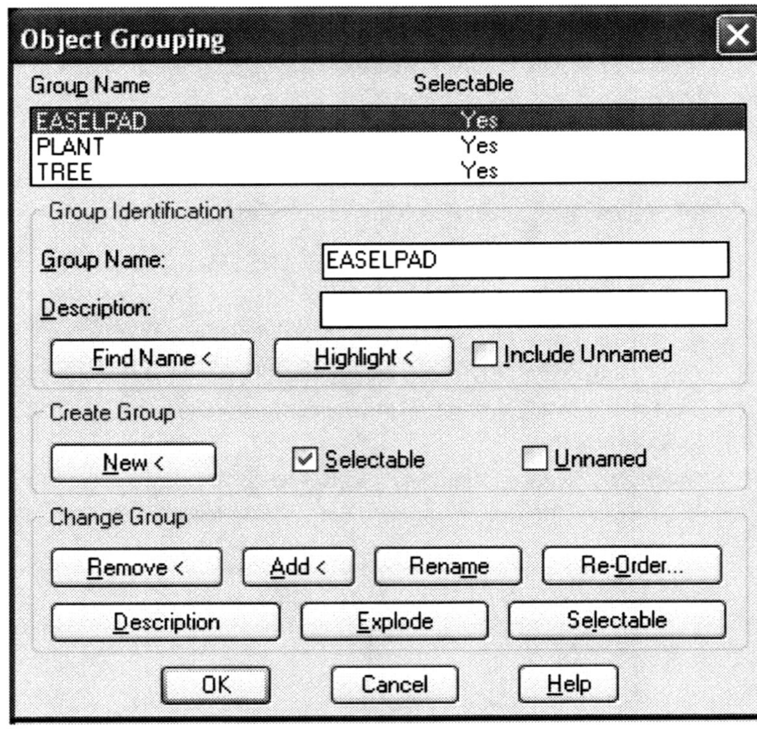


Figure 19.002

  - o To find the name of an existing group, begin by picking the **Find Name** button. AutoCAD returns to the graphics screen and prompts you to **Pick a member of a group**. It then displays the Group Member List Dialog box (Figure 19.003) showing a list of all the groups to which that object belongs.

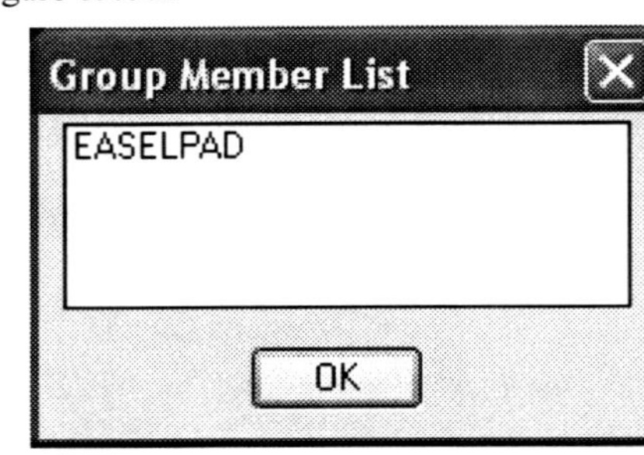


Figure 19.003

  - o To find which objects belong to a certain group, begin by selecting the name of the group in the upper list box, and then pick the **Highlight** button. AutoCAD returns to the graphics screen, highlights all the objects belonging to that group, and presents a **Continue** button to return to the Object Grouping dialog box.
  - o Sitting inconspicuously in the lower right corner of the frame, you'll find a check box next to the words **Include Unnamed**. When a group is copied, the copy is also a group. You haven't named the copy, but AutoCAD has assigned a temporary name to it. Placing a check in this box tells AutoCAD to display the temporary names as well as the user-assigned names. You can then rename the copies to something more appropriate.
- You'll use tools in the **Create Group** frame to create a new group. After typing a name for your new group in the **Group Name** text box (or placing a check in the **Unnamed** check box if you want AutoCAD to assign the name), pick the **New** button. AutoCAD will return to the graphics screen and prompt **Select objects for grouping**. When you've finished selecting the objects, hit enter to return to the Object Grouping dialog box. Be sure there's a check in the **Selectable** check box if you want to manipulate the selected objects as a group.
- Use the seven buttons in the **Change Group** frame to modify a group. First, select the group to be modified in the list box. Then pick one of the buttons in the **Change Group** frame.
  - o Add or remove objects from a group with the **Add** and **Remove** buttons.

- Use the **Rename** button to change the name of a group. For example, to change the temporary name assigned by AutoCAD to a more recognizable name, highlight the temporary name in the list box, type the new name in the **Group Name** text box, and then pick the **Rename** button.
- Type some text into the **Description** text box, and then pick the **Description** button to update the description of the highlighted group.
- The **Explode** button will remove the definition of the group from the drawing's database. All objects in the group will then behave as individual objects (not as part of a group).
- The **Selectable** button is a toggle for treating a group as a group or for suspending the group definition so you can modify one or more of the objects within the group. When **Selectable** is toggled off, the word **No** appears in the **Selectable** column of the list box, and all the objects within a group behave as individual objects. To manipulate the objects as part of the group, simply toggle **Selectable** back on.
- The **Re-Order...** button presents the Order Group dialog box (Figure 19.004). Here you can change the order in which AutoCAD reads the objects in a group. Type the number of the object you wish to change in the **Remove from position** text box. Type the position to which you wish to move the object in the **Enter new position number for the object** text box. Type the number or range of objects to reorder in the **Number of objects** text box.

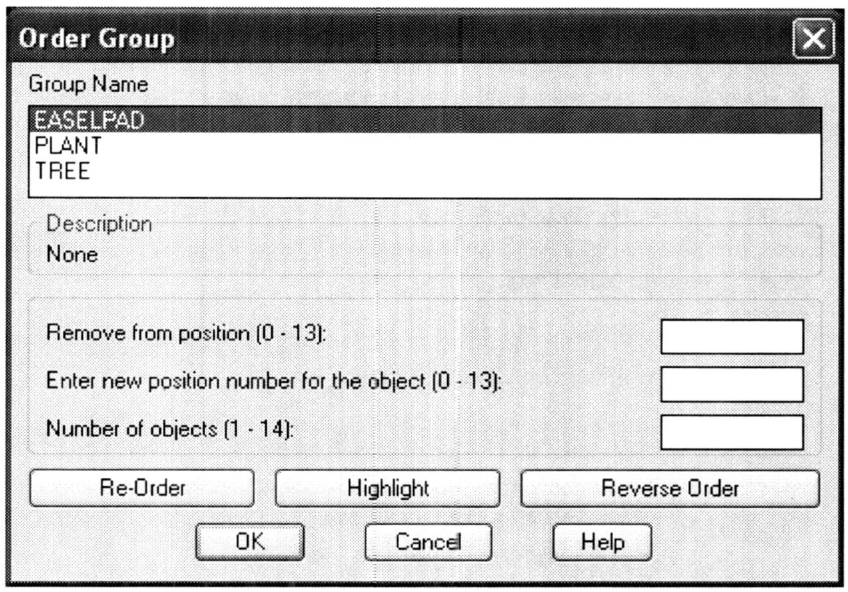

Figure 19.004

  Pick the **Reverse Order** button to simply reverse the order of the objects within the group.

> You'll rarely (if ever) need the **Order** options of the ***Group*** command. In the few brief years since AutoCAD included this tool, I haven't found a need or even a use for reordering objects in a group. However, this doesn't mean that you won't find a need or use. A corollary to AutoCAD's Redundancy Rule might be the Overkill Rule. Both rules simply and correctly state that *More is Better*. In other words, *if it might be useful, make it possible!*

If you're unsure of the position of the object you wish to reorder, pick the **Highlight** button. AutoCAD will present the Object Grouping dialog box shown in Figure 19.005, and highlights the objects making up the group you selected.

Let's play with the ***Group*** command!

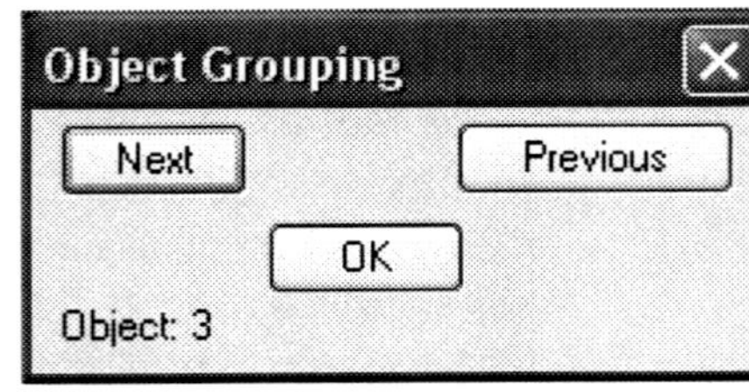


Figure 19.005

| Do This: 19.1.2 | **Creating and Manipulating Groups** |
|---|---|

I. Be sure you're still in the *groups.dwg* file the C:\Steps\Lesson19 folder. If not, please open it now.

II. Follow these steps.

**19.1.2: CREATING AND MANIPULATING GROUPS**

1. Enter the ***Group*** command by typing ***group*** or ***g*** at the command prompt. AutoCAD presents the Object Grouping dialog box (Figure 19.002).

**Command: *g***

2. We'll group the teacher's desk, chair, computer, and the plant on the desk. Enter the name and description shown.

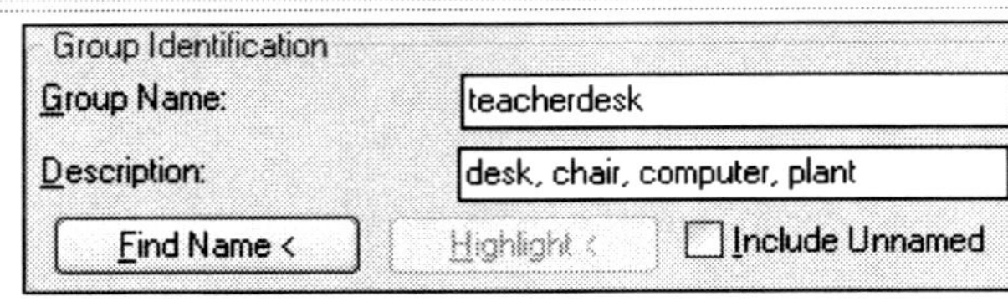


3. Pick the **New** button 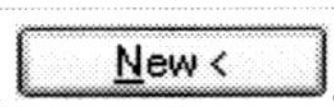

.

4. Select the teacher's desk and the other objects. Hit **enter** (or right-click) to return to the dialog box.

**Select objects for grouping:**

**Select objects: 86 found, 1 group**

**Select objects: *[enter]***

5. AutoCAD now lists the **TEACHERDESK** in the list box as shown.

Complete the command 

.

6. Move 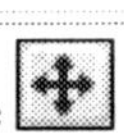 the **TEACHERDESK** group next to the tree as indicated.

**Command: *m***

**Select objects: 86 found, 1 group**

**Select objects:**

**Specify base point or [Displacement] <Displacement>: *13',0***

Your drawing looks like this.

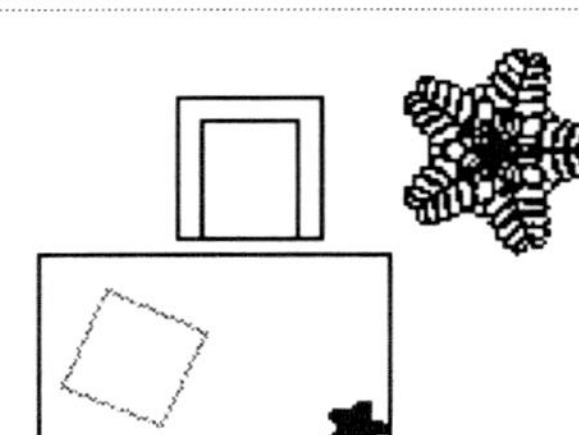

7. Reopen the Object Grouping dialog box.

**Command: *g***

## 19.1.2: Creating and Manipulating Groups

8. Now we'll list all the groups to which an object belongs. Pick the **Find Name** button [Find Name <].

9. AutoCAD returns to the graphics screen. Pick the plant on the teacher's desk.

**Pick a member of a group.**

10. AutoCAD presents the Group Member List dialog box showing that the object selected belongs to the **Plant** and **Teacherdesk** groups. You see now that groups can be *nested* – that is, one group can contain another group. Objects can also be shared by more than one group.

Pick the **OK** button to return to the Object Grouping dialog box.

11. Let's see which objects are in the **Plant** group. Pick **PLANT** in the list box. Notice that the name appears in the **Group Name** text box.

12. Pick the **Highlight** button [Highlight <]. AutoCAD returns to the graphics screen and highlights the plant on the teacher's desk.

13. Return to the Object Grouping dialog box [Continue].

14. Complete the command [OK].

15. Let's give the teacher two new plants. Try to copy  the **Plant** group.

**Command: *co***

Notice that the entire desk highlights when you select the plant. We must first make the desk *unselectable*.

16. Hit the ESC key [Esc] to cancel the command.

17. Return to the Object Grouping dialog box.

**Command: *g***

18. Pick **TEACHERDESK** in the list box and then pick the **Selectable** button [Selectable] in the **Change Group** frame. Notice (right) that the word **No** appears in the **Selectable** column of the list box.

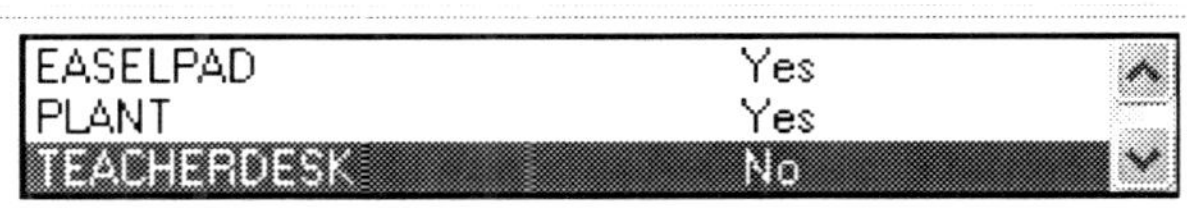


19. Complete the command [OK].

## 19.1.2: Creating and Manipulating Groups

20. Now make two copies of the plant on the teacher's desk.

**Command: *co***

Your drawing now looks something like this.

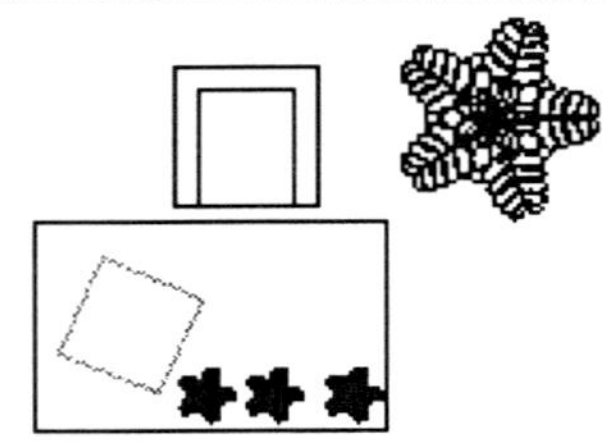

21. Return to the Object Grouping dialog box.

**Command: *g***

22. Place a check in the **Include Unnamed** check box in the Group Identification frame. Notice that two new groups appear in the list box – ***A1** and ***A2**.

23. Select ***A1**.

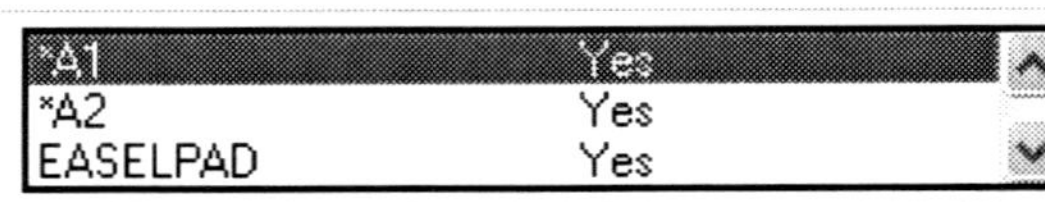


24. Enter the name ***PlantB*** into the Group Name text box.

25. Now pick the **Rename** button. AutoCAD renames the group.

26. Repeat Steps 22 through 25 to rename ***A2** to ***PlantC***.

27. Now let's add these new plants to the **Teacherdesk** group. Select the **Teacherdesk** group in the list box (you may have to scroll down a bit to find it).

28. Pick the **Add** button in the **Change Group** frame.

29. AutoCAD returns to the graphics screen and prompts you to **Select objects to add to group**. Select the two new plants, and then return to the Object Grouping dialog box.

**Select objects to add to group...**
**Select objects: 80 found, 1 group**
**Select objects: 80 found, 1 group, 246 total**
**Select objects: *[enter]***

30. Pick the **Selectable** button to make the **TEACHERDESK** group selectable again. Notice that the word **Yes** appears in the **Selectable** column of the list box.

31. Complete the procedure.

32. Save the drawing but don't exit.

**Command: *qsave***

We've seen how groups can benefit our work by simplifying object selection and manipulation. We've also seen how to manage our groups through some of the buttons in the **Change Group** frame of the Object Grouping dialog box. Now let's remove a group definition from a drawing.

| **Do This: 19.1.3** | **Removing a Group Definition** |
|---|---|

I. Be sure you're still in the *groups.dwg* file the C:\Steps\Lesson19 folder. If not, please open it now.

II. Follow these steps.

### 19.1.3: Removing a Group Definition

1. Enter the ***Group*** command.

   **Command: *g***

2. Select the **EASELPAD** group in the list box.

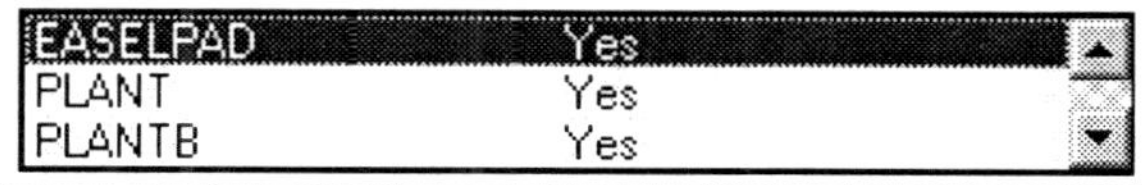


3. Pick the **Explode** button 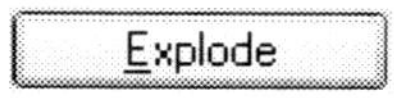

in the **Change Group** frame. Notice that **Easelpad** disappears from the list box.

4. Complete the command 

. AutoCAD returns to the graphics screen.

5. Try to move 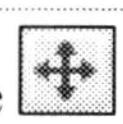 the easel pad now.

   **Command: *m***

   Notice that you can't select the entire pad with a single pick. The pad is no longer a group.

6. Save the drawing 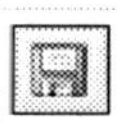 and exit.

   **Command: *qsave***

I've frequently used groups in my capacity as a piping designer to manipulate (particularly moving and copying) items such as control stations and pipe configurations. Architects and interior designers can also use groups as we've done in these exercises. Other disciplines can make use of groups when dealing with layouts, circuitry, boltholes, windows, and many other items.

The only limitations to groups are simple – their use is limited to a single drawing (you can't share groups between drawings), the group definition is permanently lost once the group is exploded or erased from a drawing, and you can't attach information to a group. To overcome these limitations, use blocks instead of groups.

## 19.2 Groups with Backbone – The *Block* Commands

No single aspect of CAD has served as a stronger selling point than blocks. In fact, all quality CAD systems have blocks (or cells, or something that behaves like blocks). No other single command or routine can speed the drawing process as well, and none has a greater potential for cost cutting or streamlining design management.

What is a block? A block is a single object made up of several other objects. You can manipulate blocks, like groups, as single units. But you can share blocks *between* drawings. More importantly, *blocks can contain user-defined data.* We'll discuss creation and manipulation of blocks here. In Lesson 20, we'll discuss attaching data to blocks and exporting that data to other computer applications (such as spreadsheets or databases).

> Be aware that much of the block details you will learn in this edition of the *One Step at a Time* series ***does not hold true for releases earlier than 2006!*** Dynamic blocks, as you will learn about them, are one of those rare giant leaps for Autodesk. (Be glad you're here!)

There are two important block commands – ***Block*** (which creates blocks within a drawing) and ***WBlock*** (which creates a block as a separate drawing file). Mercifully, both use dialog boxes. But to keep it even simpler, you'll use the ***Block*** command to create blocks and the ***WBlock*** command to copy your blocks into a *Folder library*.

What's a library?

Groups of blocks are often assembled in useful packages called libraries (Figure 19.006). A library is a group of blocks used as inserts in a drawing. Use of blocked objects saves the time you might otherwise need to create the objects. There are two types of libraries: *Template* files – associated with the ***Block*** command, and *Folders* – associated with the ***WBlock*** command. Both libraries are useful (each has its pluses and minuses), but each project should use only one type.

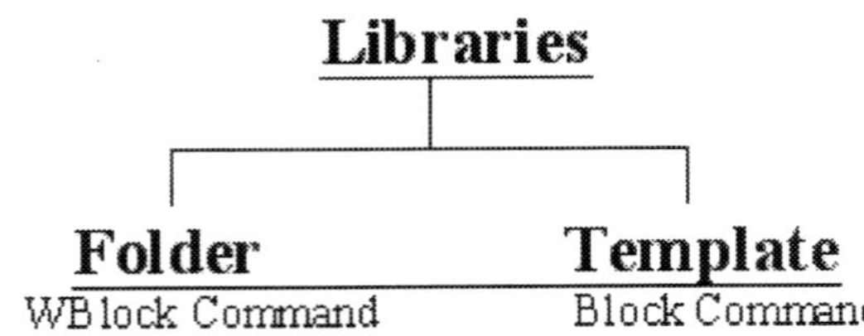

Figure 19.006

- The project guru (CAD coordinator) should create (or oversee) the folder library – a collection of standardized drawings to be used on the contract – and store it on a network. The path to the folder should be defined in the *Support File Search Path* section of the **Files** tab of the Options dialog box. This will make insertion much easier. [Note: The Options dialog box isn't a place for AutoCAD novices to experiment!]

  The folder library is easy for a single person (the guru) to maintain. Adding, deleting, or changing a project standard involves modifying only one file for each change.
- Blocks can be included as part of the templates used on a project (creating template libraries). Accessing blocks that are part of the original template is a bit faster than the folder method, but the size of the template can become quite large (heavy with block definitions) before any actual drafting begins. Additionally, any changes in project standards require that all the templates be updated. Even if the templates are centrally stored on a network, this may involve several files.

The decision as to which type of library to use should be universal for the project and is best made by the guru and the design supervisor. This doesn't mean that the operator can't create and use blocks on the fly. But the operator should take care not to duplicate (or overwrite) project standards.

> Most libraries consist of drawings associated with a single design discipline. For example, an architectural library may contain drawings of doors, windows, toilets, tubs, and so forth, whereas a piping library will contain drawings of valves, elbows, tees, etc. Library creation has become quite a business alongside CAD industries.

Another thing that must concern the CAD operator, both in the creation and insertion of blocks, is how blocks relate to layers. This can sound complicated, so let's use a chart (after all, a chart is worth a thousand words – give or take).

| IF THE OBJECTS USED TO MAKE THE BLOCK ARE ON: | WHEN INSERTED, THE BLOCK HAS THE CHARACTERISTICS OF: | WHEN INSERTED, THE BLOCK EXISTS ON: |
|---|---|---|
| Layer 0 | The current layer | The current layer |
| Any other layer | The layer on which it was created | The current layer |

Let me try to explain this by using some examples (and fewer than a thousand words).

Generally speaking, you should always create objects for blocks on layer **0**. Then when inserting the block on another layer (let's say, layer **obj**), all the objects that went in to creating the block will appear on – and share the characteristics of – the current layer (layer **obj**). When this layer (**obj**) is frozen, turned off, or locked, the block will be affected accordingly.

Text might be an exception to this rule (and is rarely a good idea in a block – generally speaking). When part or all of the objects used to create a block exists on a layer other than 0 (say, **text**), those objects in the inserted block will appear with the characteristics of the layer on which they were created. (If that layer doesn't exist in the drawing, AutoCAD will create it.) This will be true regardless of the layer that's current (say, **obj**) when you insert the block. Now, when the **obj** layer is frozen, turned off, or locked, the block will be affected accordingly because the block exists on (was inserted on) layer **obj**. *Additionally*, when the text layer is frozen, turned off, or locked, the block will also be affected because that is the layer on which it was created.

Sound complicate? Use the chart!

### 19.2.1 Template Library Creation

We use the ***Block*** command to create template libraries or to create blocks on the fly. We'll use the ***WBlock*** command to convert template library blocks to folder libraries.

When completed, the newly defined block has become part of the current drawing's database and can be inserted into the current drawing at any time. Save this drawing as a template, and the block will be available to any drawing using this template.

***Block*** presents the Block Definition dialog box (Figure 19.007) where you can enter the information you'll need to create a block.

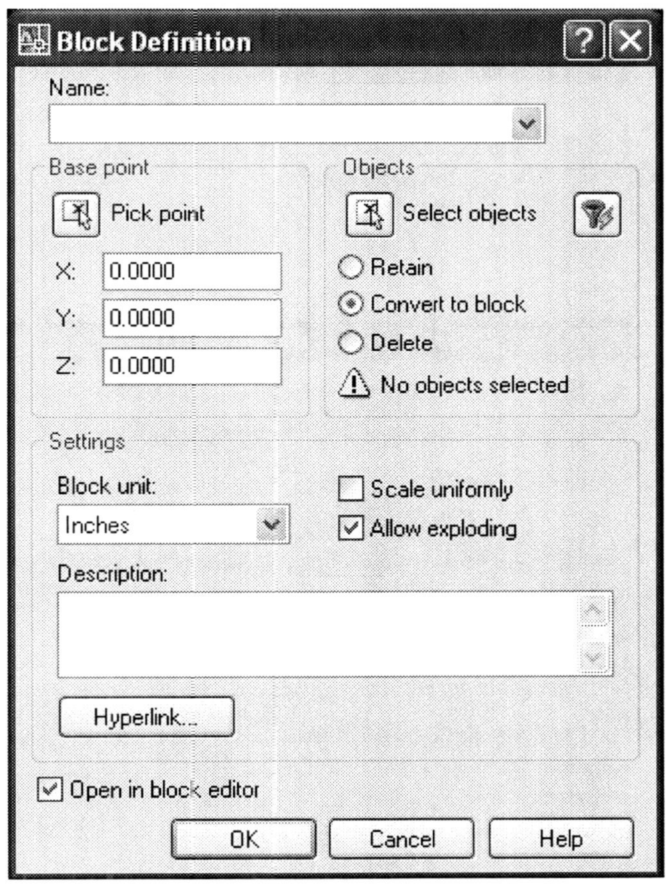

Figure 19.007

- Place the name of the block in the **Name** control box.
- Although you can enter an insertion point's coordinates in the **Base Point** frame (X, Y, and Z text boxes), it's easier to use the **Pick point** button. AutoCAD hides the dialog box and prompts:

  **Specify insertion base point:**

  You can then pick a base point on the screen.
- Use the **Select Objects** button (in the **Objects** frame) to return to the graphics screen and select objects to include in the block. Alternately, you can use **Quick Select** filters by picking the "funnel" button to the right of **Select objects**.

  Once you've selected the objects, you must tell AutoCAD what to do with them after it makes the block. Simply place a bullet next to the appropriate option:
  - **Retain** tells AutoCAD to keep the selected objects in their current state. That is, AutoCAD won't automatically delete the objects after creating the block.
  - **Convert to block** tells AutoCAD to convert the objects from individual objects to the first insertion of the newly defined block.
  - **Delete** will delete the objects used to create the block.

- In the **Block unit** control box (**Settings** frame), you should define what units to use when inserting the block (preferably the units used by the drawing in which the block will be inserted). AutoCAD will use these units when it inserts a block via the ADC or tool palettes (more on this in Section 19.4.2).

  Place a check next to **Scale uniformly** to restrict scaling of the block to uniform X, Y, and Z scaling.

  Place a check next to **Allow exploding** if you wish to allow this option. Exploding a block loses all the block's definitions and leaves only the objects that went in to creating it.

  Enter a description of the block in the **Description** text box.

  The **Hyperlink** button at the bottom of the frame allows you to associate a hyperlink with the block using an Insert Hyperlink dialog box.
- The inconspicuous check box at the bottom of the dialog box – **Open in block editor** – provides access to a wonderful new world of block control! We'll discuss this in more detail in Section 19.3.

First, let's create some simple blocks. You can use simple blocks on the fly, but these instructions will also help to get your feet wet.

| Do This: 19.2.1.1 | Creating Simple Blocks |
|---|---|

I. Open the *blocks.dwg* file the C:\Steps\Lesson19 folder. The drawing looks like Figure 19.008.

II. Follow these steps.

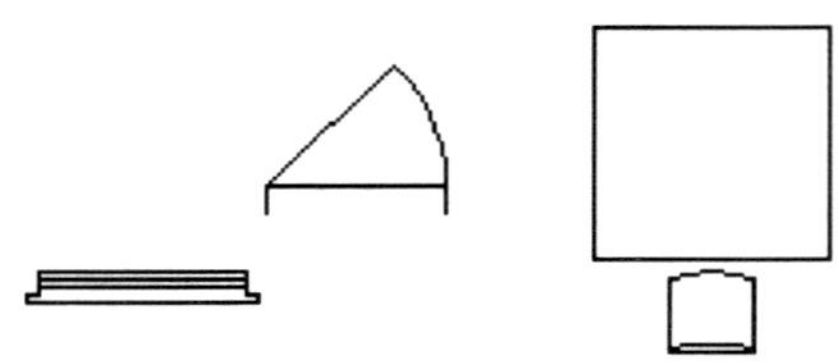

Figure 19.008

### 19.2.1.1: Creating Simple Blocks

1. (Refer to the door seen in the center of the drawing.)

Enter the ***Block*** command by typing ***block*** or ***b*** at the command prompt. Alternately, you can pick the **Make Block** button 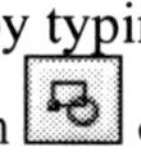 on the Draw toolbar or palette.

**Command: *b***

AutoCAD presents the Block Definition dialog box (Figure 19.007).

2. Enter the name (***door***) in the **Block name** text box.

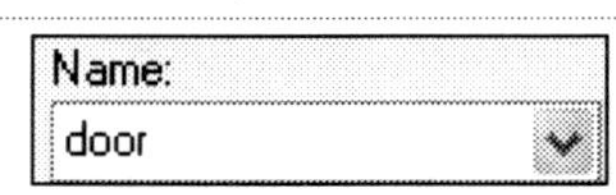


3. Pick the **Pick point** button  in the **Base point** frame. AutoCAD returns to the graphics screen.

**19.2.1.1: CREATING SIMPLE BLOCKS**

4. Pick the insertion point indicated.

   **Specify insertion base point: _mid of**

   AutoCAD returns to the dialog box.

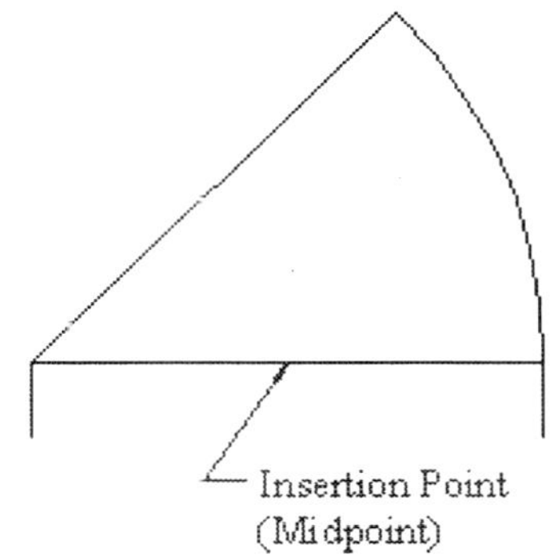


5. Pick the **Select objects** button. AutoCAD returns to the graphics screen.

6. Select the arc, the vertical lines, and the angled line. Do *not* select the horizontal line. Confirm your selections.

   **Select objects:**

   **Select objects:** ***[enter]***

   AutoCAD returns to the dialog box.

7. Place a bullet next to the **Convert to block** option [Convert to block] in the **Objects** frame. (We're going to do more with this drawing later.)

8. Complete the block definition by identifying the **Block unit** and providing a **Description.** We'll also restrict this block to a uniform **Scale** and allow it to be exploded.

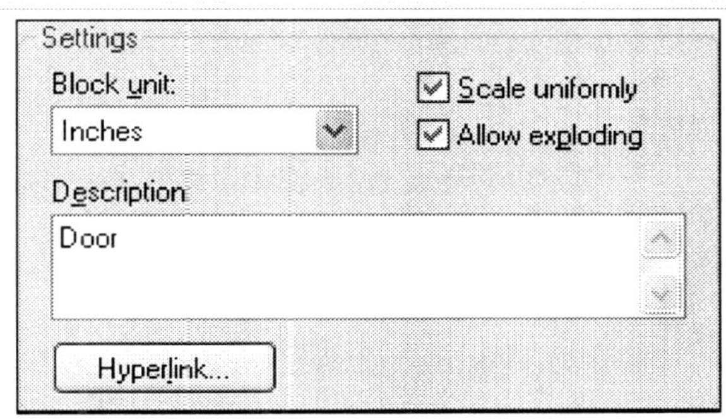


9. Clear the **Open in block editor** box [Open in block editor] (no sense complicating things just yet).

10. Complete the command [OK].

11. Save the drawing but don't exit.

    **Command:** ***qsave***

In this exercise, we've begun a template library. We could continue to add dozens of drawings as needed (deleting the drawings as we go). Then, when we've finished, we would save this drawing with the .dwt extension and use it as a template for any number of future drawings. But let's use what we have to start a Folder library.

## 19.2.2 Folder Library Creation

Use the ***WBlock*** (**WriteBlock**) command to create folder libraries. The procedure can be very similar to creating blocks, but it also allows you to convert template library files to folder library files.

As with the ***Block*** command, AutoCAD also provides a dialog box interface to ease creation of WBlocks. Access it by entering the ***WBlock*** command (or the ***W*** hotkey). The Write Block dialog box appears (Figure 19.009 – next page).

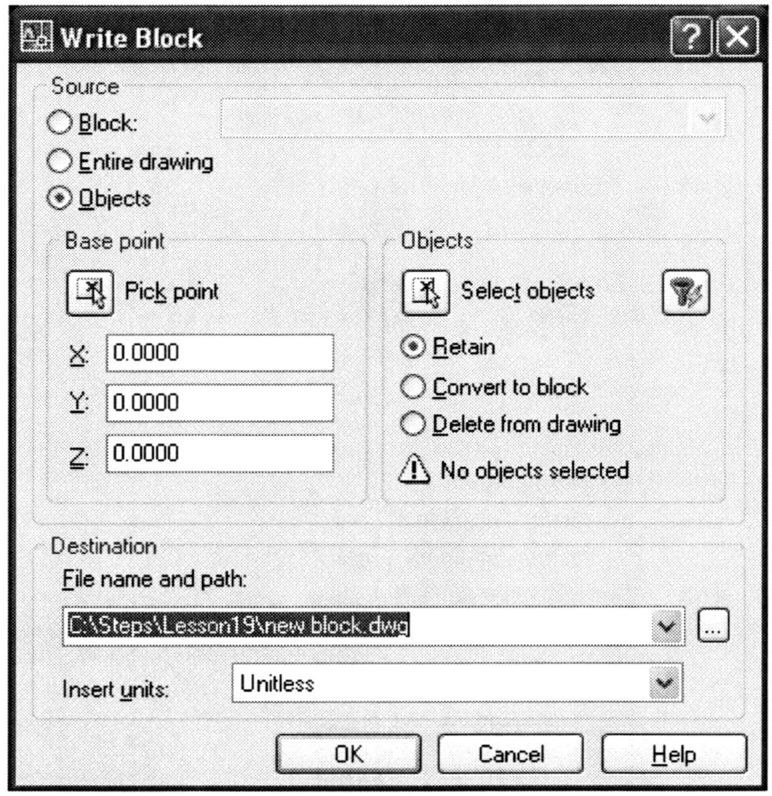


Figure 19.009

Does it look familiar? It should. Two of the frames are identical to the Block Definition dialog box. Let's examine the other frames.

- In the **Source** frame, AutoCAD gives you three options:
  - The **Block** option opens the control box next to it. Here you can select from a list of blocks existing in the drawing to be saved as separate drawing files (WBlocks).
  - Of course, the **Entire drawing** option allows you to create a separate drawing file using all of the objects in the drawing.
  - The **Objects** option (the default) behaves like the ***Block*** command and allows you to select objects just as you did using the Block Definition dialog box.
- The **Base point** and **Objects** frames are identical to their namesakes found on the Block Definition dialog box.
- In the **Destination** frame, you'll:
  - name and locate the new block (**File name and path** text box).
  - identify the **Insert units** of the new block (this is the same thing as the **Block unit** found on the Block Definition dialog box).

In our next exercise, we'll create a WBlock to begin a folder library by converting the block created in our template library to a file we can use in our folder library.

| Do This: 19.2.2.1 | Creating Blocks for a Folder Library |
|---|---|

I. Be sure you're still in the *blocks.dwg* file the C:\Steps\Lesson19 folder. If not, please open it now.

II. Follow these steps.

| 19.2.2.1: Creating Blocks for a Folder Library |
|---|
| 1. We'll use the ***WBlock*** command to export our earlier block to our Folder Library. Enter the ***WBlock*** command.<br>**Command: *w*** |
| 2. (Refer to the following figure.) Do this:<br>a. Place the **Source** bullet in the **Block** option and then select **door** from the control box. |

### 19.2.2.1: Creating Blocks for a Folder Library

(This is the block you created in our last exercise.) Notice that the **Base point** and **Objects** frames are no longer available. (This information was provided when you defined the original block.)

b. Be sure the **Destination** information in your dialog box saves the new file as Door in the C:\Steps\Lesson19 folder.

c. Pick the **OK** button to complete the command.

How simple!

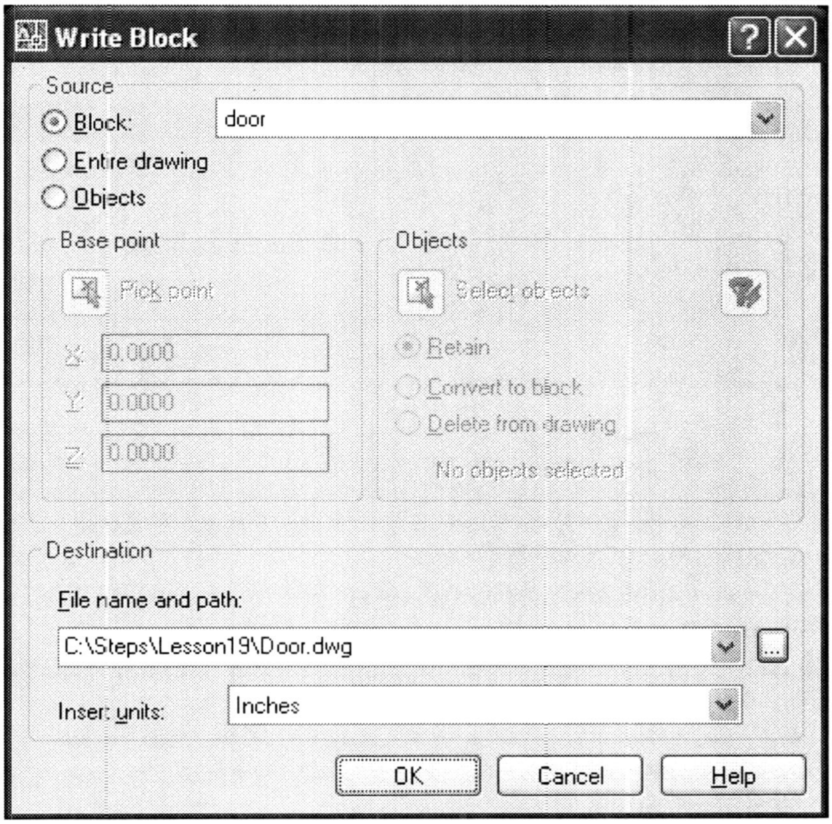


8. Save and close the drawing.

**Command:** ***qsave***

The block you just created will appear in the C:\Steps\Lesson19 folder as a new drawing that you can insert into other drawings as blocks!

## 19.2.3 Using Blocks in a Drawing – The *Insert* Command

Before we continue, we must know how to insert a block into a drawing once we've created it. We'll do this, appropriately enough, with the ***Insert*** command.

The ***Insert*** command calls the dialog box shown in Figure 19.010.

- The **Name** control box will list all of the blocks currently associated with the drawing (by definition, previous insertion, or template). To insert a WBlock not currently associated with the drawing, use the **Browse** button to locate the file. AutoCAD will show the path next to the **Path** statement.

- In the **Insertion point** frame, you can identify the **X/Y/Z** coordinates for the insertion or (preferably) leave the check in the **Specify On-screen** box. Then you can identify the insertion point on the screen with a mouse pick and OSNAP.

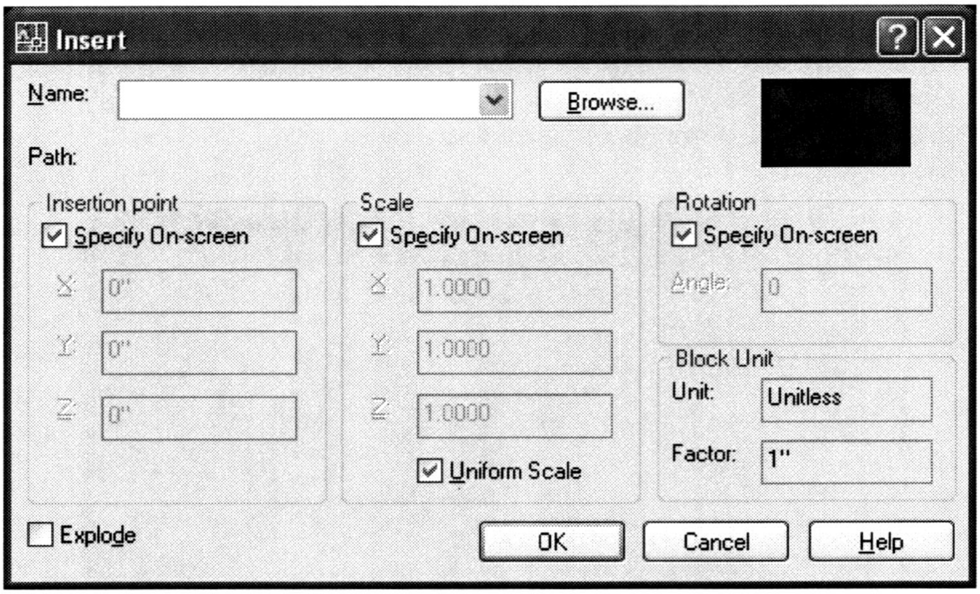


Figure 19.010

- The **Scale** frame also has a **Specify On-screen** box. But it may be preferable (unless you must see the scaled block to be sure of its size) to enter the **X/Y/Z** scale in the text boxes provided. A check in the **Uniform Scale** box will ensure the **X/Y/Z** scales remain proportional to the original block definition.
- The **Rotation** frame also has a **Specify On-screen** box. Like the **Scale** data, it's up to you to decide what's easiest to use.
- The **Block Unit** frame displays information about the block currently identified in the **Name** control box. This frame is informational only.
- The last item in the Insert dialog box – the **Explode** check box in the lower left corner – enables you to place all the objects of a block without the definition of the block. In other words, you can insert the block pre-exploded.

Let's insert a block into a drawing.

| |
|---|
| You can also access the ***Insert*** command from the Insert pull-down menu. |

| | |
|---|---|
| **Do This: 19.2.3.1** | **Inserting Blocks** |

I. Open the *cab-pln.dwg* file the C:\Steps\Lesson19 folder. The drawing looks like Figure 19.011.

II. Follow these steps.

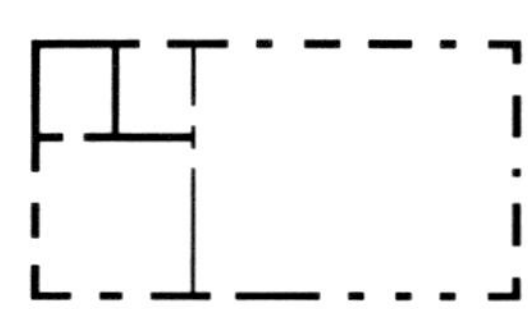

Figure 19.011

## 19.2.3.1: Inserting Blocks

1. Adjust the display on your screen to see the front door opening.

   **Command: *z***

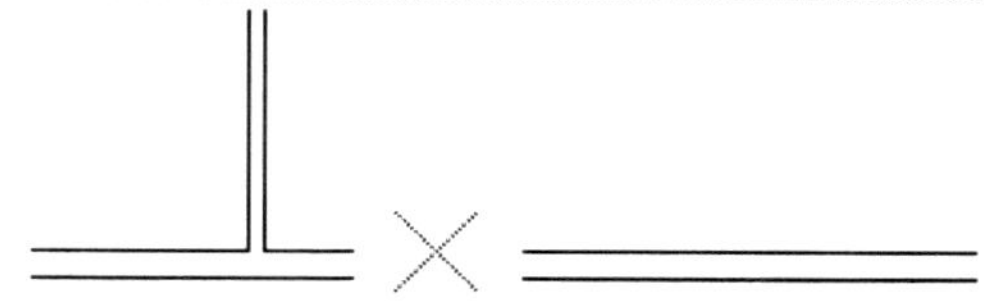

2. Enter the ***Insert*** command by typing ***insert*** or ***i***. Alternately, you can pick the **Insert Block** button on the Draw toolbar or palette.

   **Command: *i***

   AutoCAD presents the Insert dialog box (Figure 19.010).

3. We'll have to get our block. (It isn't part of this drawing yet.) Pick the **Browse** button Browse... .

4. Navigate to the C:\Steps\ Lesson19 folder and select the *Door.dwg* file you created in Exercise 19.2.1.1.

   Pick the **Open** button Open . (AutoCAD returns to the Insert dialog box and displays the *Door* block in the **Name** control box.

5. (Refer to the following figure.) Be sure the **Insertion point**, **Scale**, and **Rotation** are set as indicated. (Be sure the **Explode** check box is empty.)

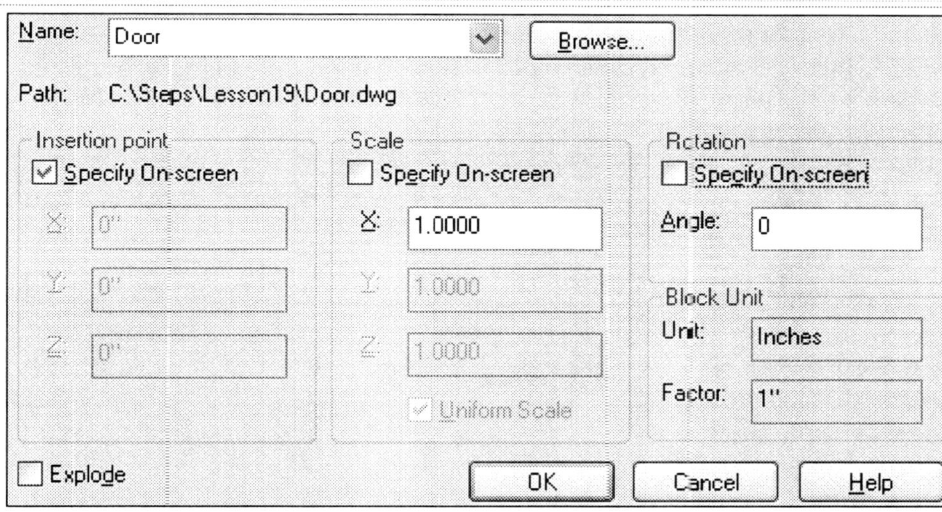


6. Pick the **OK** button OK . AutoCAD will continue the prompts on the command line.

7. Use the node as your **Insertion point**. AutoCAD won't prompt for **Scale** or **Rotation** because you entered that data in the dialog box. The door looks like this.

   **Specify insertion point or [Basepoint/Scale/Rotate]:**

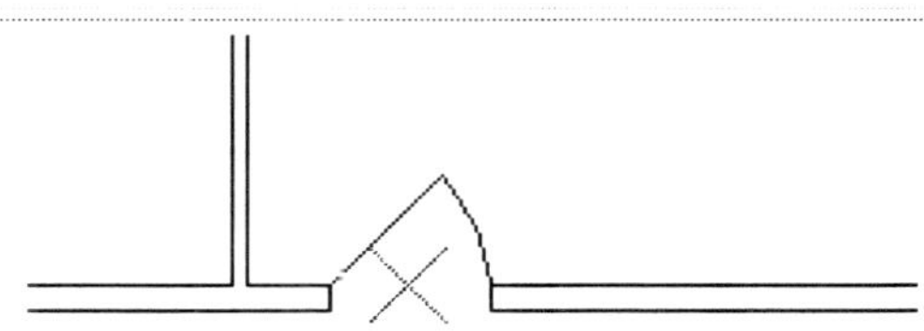

## 19.2.3.1: Inserting Blocks

8. Save the drawing and exit.

   **Command:** ***qsave***

## 19.3 Dynamic Blocks

*Wow! Look what I made it do!*

*Novice CAD Operator*

I've been working with AutoCAD now for about a million years. They don't come up with new things anymore that really evoke a "way cool!" out of me (at least not very often), but dynamic blocks even make me capitalize the expression – *WAY COOL!*

Dynamic blocks will take a bit of time to master, but the time will be well spent.

*What is a dynamic block?*

Well, a dynamic block has at least one *parameter* (a tool that generally looks like a dimension but acts as a control for selected object properties). The CAD operator can manipulate the block objects associated with the parameter through grips which drive user-defined actions which, in turn, can change the geometry of the block.

By making them *dynamic*, AutoCAD has given us the power to manipulate the objects that compose a block. By manipulate, I mean that you can insert a single table & chairs combination (block), adjust its size, adjust its *style* (that's right, change the drafting symbol to any predefined style), flip parts of it, rotate parts of it, move parts around (like the chairs), and more! The same holds true for valve stations, doors and windows, electrical boxes, landscaping, and so forth! (*The dickens, you say!*)

The size of your libraries just got radically smaller!

As you can imagine, creating these blocks requires a bit more effort than the simple blocks you've already done. We'll do the work in the *block editor*. Remember that check box at the bottom of the Block dialog box? It takes you directly to the block editor. Alternately, you can get there by entering ***BEdit*** at the command prompt or by double-clicking on an existing block.

AutoCAD responds to the ***BEdit*** command with the Edit Block Definition dialog box (Figure 19.012). Pick the block you wish to edit from the list, and then pick the **OK** button to open the editor.

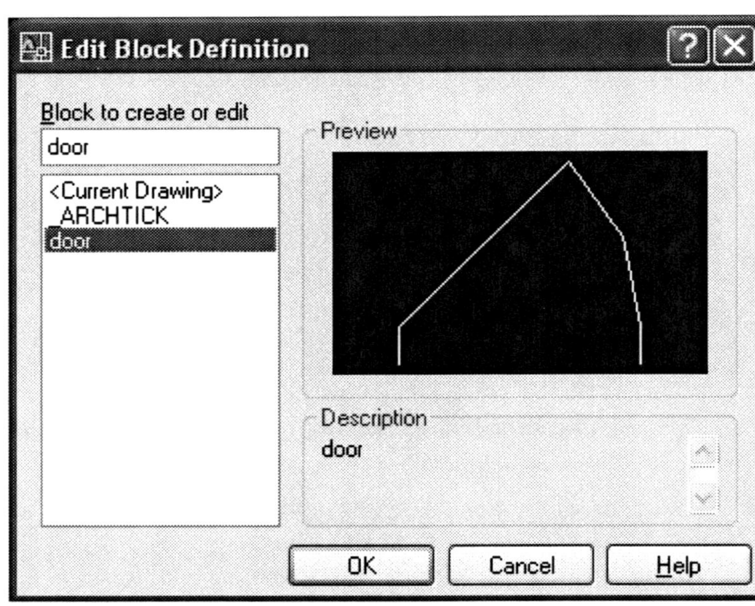


Figure 19.012

When entering the Block Editor, you may encounter a message box inviting you to view a tutorial on dynamic block creation. Take a few minutes to look this over if you have the time. (I strongly recommend it; it'll make the rest of this section much easier to understand.)

If you don't see the message box, you can find the tutorial by way of the Help pull down menu:
*Help – New Features Workshop – Produce – Dynamic Blocks*

You'll immediately notice a marked change in your screen – the background becomes white, a new toolbar appears (Figure 19.013) and the Block Authoring Palettes appear (Figure 19.016). Let's spend a few minutes with each of these treasure houses of tools.

We'll begin at the left end of the new Block Authoring toolbar (Figure 19.013) and use a table for clarity.

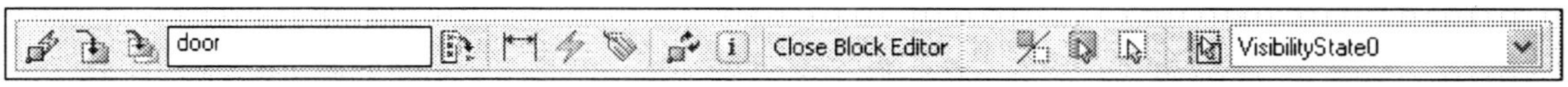


Figure 19.013

| ITEM | DESCRIPTION |
|---|---|
|  | The **Edit or Create Block Definition** button returns you to the Edit Block Definition dialog box (Figure 19.012). |
| 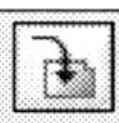 | Use the **Save Block Definition** button to save your block work before exiting the block editor. |
|  | Use the **Save Block As** button to save your work as a different block name before exiting the editor. |
| door | The **Block Name** box reminds you on which block you're working. |
|  | The **Authoring Palettes** button toggles the display of the Block Authoring Palettes. |
| 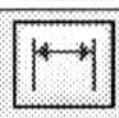 | The **Parameter** button enters the ***BParameter*** command. This is the keyboard approach to creating parameters in your block. The prompt looks like this:<br>**Enter parameter type [Alignment/Base/pOint/Linear/Polar/Xy/ Rotation/Flip/Visibility/looKup]: *[select an option]***<br>You're probably better off using tools on the Block Authoring Palettes (which we'll examine shortly), but all the options appear in both locations. |
|  | The **Action** button enters the ***BAction*** command. This is the keyboard approach to creating actions for your parameters. The prompt looks like this:<br>**Select parameter: *[you must associate actions with parameters]***<br>**Enter action type [Array/Move/Scale/Stretch/Polar Stretch]: *[select an action to associate with the parameter]***<br>The prompts that follow will depend on the action you've selected. |
|  | The **Define Attribute** button is the key to even richer possibilities within the world of blocks. We'll dedicate most of Lesson 20 to these! |
| 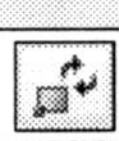 | **Update Parameter and Action Text Size** simply regenerates the drawing. |
| 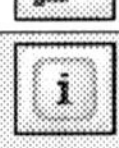 | **Learn About Dynamic Blocks** launches the New Features Workshop – Dynamic Blocks introductory tutorial. |
| Close Block Editor | Use the **Close Block Editor** button to conclude your block editing session. If you haven't saved your work, AutoCAD will prompt you to do so.<br>If you've already inserted blocks into the drawing, AutoCAD will display a message box giving you the opportunity to update the block definition for those blocks as well. |

You could consider the remaining tools as part of a Visibility toolbar. Since they're next to the Block Authoring toolbar, however, and since we're here, we'll look at them now. These tools

| ITEM | DESCRIPTION |
|---|---|
| | provide the method for toggling through styles of objects (simple round sinks vs. fancy oval sinks, desk chairs vs. kitchen chairs, etc.). The tools become available only when you've inserted a **Visibility** parameter into the block. (We'll do this in our next exercise.) |
| 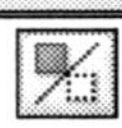 | **Visibility Mode** serves as a toggle for the **BVMode** system variable. **On** (a setting of **1**) means that hidden objects will appear visible but dimmed. **Off** (a setting of **0**) means that hidden objects will not appear at all. This is a working tool and won't affect the actual insertion of the block. |
|   | **Make Visible** and **Make Invisible** enable you to "add" and "remove" objects from your blocks. To enable your user to toggle between different styles of sinks (or other objects) within a single block, you'll draw both sinks and make one visible and the other invisible. You'll then associate the visibility with a visibility state. |
|  | Use the **Manage Visibility** button to access the Visibility States dialog box (Figure 19.014). You'll set up your visibility states there. (We'll look at this in more detail in a moment. |
| 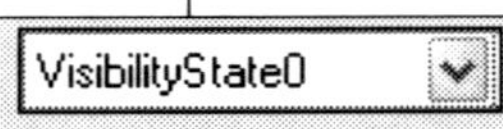  | Use the **Visibility States** control box much as you use the control boxes on the Layer and Properties toolbars to make a selected visibility state current. As with other layers, colors, and linetypes, work performed while in a selected visibility state is associated with that visibility state. |

Luckily, you won't find visibility states as complicated as layers. Take a look at the Visibility States dialog box (Figure 19.014). Most of it is fairly clear.

- The **Visibility states** list box lists all the states available in the block. Select one and use the **Set current** button to make it current.
- The buttons down the right side and across the bottom of the box are self-explanatory.
- The **New** button calls the New Visibility State dialog box (Figure 19.015). Here you'll name your new state and decide what, if anything, should be hidden in it. I recommend leaving the bullet next to **Leave visibility of existing objects unchanged in new state**. You can then adjust what is visible using the **Make Visible** and **Make Invisible** buttons on the toolbar.

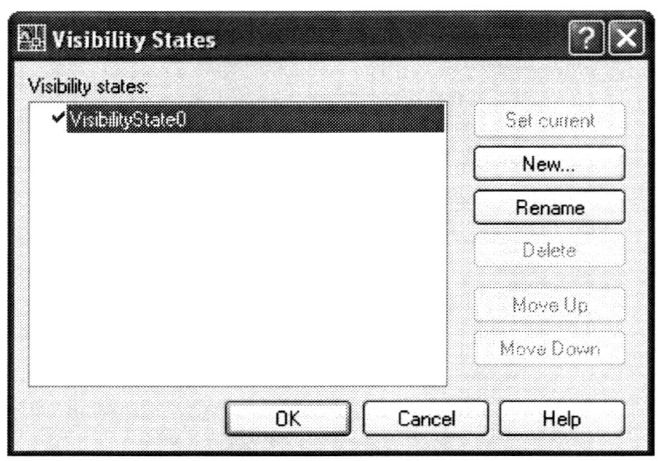


Figure 19.014

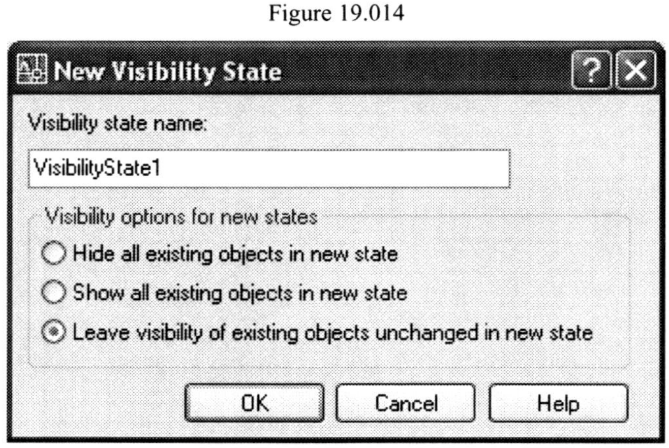


Figure 19.015

Now let's look at Block Authoring Palettes (Figure 19.016 – next page).

- We'll begin with the Parameters palette (Figure 19.016). Remember, for a block to be dynamic, it must contain at least one parameter (control object).

The type of action you intend will govern which type of parameter you'll need to add. (All items on this palette invoke the associated option of the ***BParameter*** command.)

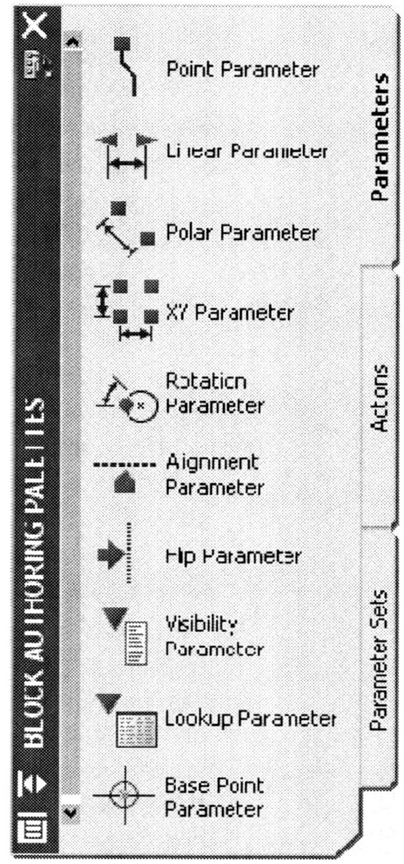

Figure 19.016

We'll start at the top.

- Associate a **Point Parameter** with a **Move** or **Stretch** operation, although it also works quite well for defining additional insertion points for your block. You can move or stretch specific points of the block when you've added a point parameter.

  The **Point Parameter** will prompt:

  > **Specify parameter location or [Name/Label/Chain/Description/Palette]:** ***[locate the point]***
  >
  > **Specify label location:** ***[locate the label – this can go anywhere but for organizational purposes, should go fairly close to the point]***

  The first prompt offers you several options (which repeat for some of the other parameters).

  - Assigning a **Name** to the parameter helps you locate it later in the Properties palette where you'll go to edit it.
  - The **Label** should reflect the **Name**. The label helps you keep track of where you've located the parameter.
  - You may find the **Chain** concept a bit difficult to understand at first. When you include the point parameter in the selection set of an action associated with a different parameter (call it parameter B), an edit of parameter B in the block will affect the point parameter. Now suppose you have a separate action associated with the point parameter. (That's two actions – the point parameter action and the parameter B action.) If the **Chain** option setting is **Yes**, any editing done with parameter B will also cause the action associated with the point parameter. If the **Chain** option setting is **No** (the default), the parameter B action will not cause the point parameter action to occur.
  - Any **Description** you enter will appear in the Properties palette when you select the parameter in the block editor.
  - The **Properties** option controls whether or not the parameter will appear in the Properties palette when the block is selected.

- Associate a **Linear Parameter** with a **Move**, **Stretch**, **Scale**, or **Array** action. You can move, stretch, scale, or array a group of objects when you've included a **Linear Parameter**. (Like a linear dimension, this is a workhorse. You'll use it as one way to resize tables, windows, doors, and other objects.) It prompts:

  > **Specify start point or [Name/Label/Chain/Description/Base/Palette/Value set]:** ***[pick the first endpoint of the parameter or another option]***
  >
  > **Specify endpoint:** ***[pick the other endpoint of the parameter]***
  >
  > **Specify label location:** ***[locate the label]***

  You've seen most of the options of the first prompt, but let's look at the rest.

    - The **Base** option will ask you for a **Base location** (either a **start point** or a **midpoint**). The **start point** will remain fixed when you edit the end points in the block editor. The **midpoint** will also remain fixed and both endpoints will react simultaneously to any editing.
    - The **Value set** option provides a valuable key to block insertion. Its options include:
        - ∴ **None** means that a block edit of this parameter has no limits.
        - ∴ **List** means that, when a user edits the block, he can select from a list of available options (such as: window sizes, valve sizes, etc.).
        - ∴ **Increment** means that the user doesn't have to select from a list of different sizes, but resizing is restricted to incremental adjustments defined by the block editor. The editor can define the increment and a minimum and maximum adjustment.
- Associate a **Polar Parameter** with a **Move**, **Scale**, **Stretch**, **Polar Stretch**, or **Array** action. It's prompt is simple:

    **Specify base point or [Name/Label/Chain/Description/Palette/Value set]:** ***[pick base (or anchor) point of the parameter or another option]***

    **Specify endpoint:** ***[pick the other endpoint of the parameter]***

    **Specify label location:** ***[locate the label]***

    You've already seen these options.
- Associate an **XY Parameter** with a **Move**, **Scale**, **Stretch**, or **Array** action. Use this parameter to move, scale, stretch, or array objects a set distance along the X- or Y-axis. (Set the distance with the **Value set** option.) It prompts:

    **Specify base point or [Name/Label/Chain/Description/Palette/Value set]:** ***[pick base point of the parameter or another option]***

    **Specify endpoint:** ***[pick a point that will define both the X- and Y-distance]***
- Associate a **Rotation Parameter** with a **Rotation** action only. Use it to rotate objects within a block (like the hands of a clock). It prompts:

    **Specify base point or [Name/Label/Chain/Description/Palette/Value set]:** ***[pick the base (or anchor) point of the parameter or another option]***

    **Specify radius of parameter:** ***[specify the radius or pick anywhere on the arc of the rotation]***

    **Specify default rotation angle or [Base angle] <0>:** ***[identify the base angle; zero indicates the current location of the object which will be rotated]***

    **Specify label location:** ***[locate the label]***
- You won't associate an **Alignment Parameter** with an action. Its location, however, is important as it will align the identified points with an object upon insertion. It prompts:

    **Specify base point of alignment or [Name]:** ***[pick a point along the path which will align with the drawing object]***

    **Alignment type = Perpendicular**

    **Specify alignment direction or alignment type [Type] <Type>:** ***[pick a second point along the path for a*** **Perpendicular** ***alignment or use the*** **Type** ***option to create a*** **Tangent** ***alignment]***
- Associate a **Flip Parameter** with a **Flip** action only. Use this to mirror a block insertion. It prompts:

    **Specify base point of reflection line or [Name/Label/Description/Palette]:** ***[pick a base point of the parameter (the first point of your mirror line) or another option]***

**Specify endpoint of reflection line:** ***[pick a second point to identify the mirror line]***

**Specify label location:** ***[locate the label]***

- Like the **Alignment Parameter**, you won't associate a **Visibility Parameter** with an action. It is, however, required to use Visibility States, which makes it required for a multiple styles block. It prompts:

  **Specify parameter location or [Name/Label/Description/Palette]:**

- Associate a **Lookup Parameter** with a **Lookup** action. This cool tool allows the user to select the size of an object from a lookup box. (We'll see this one in action in our exercise, too.) It prompts:

  **Specify parameter location or [Name/Label/Description/Palette]:**

  In this case, the location is fairly important as the grip for the lookup box will appear here.

- The **Base Point Parameter** is another parameter that isn't associated with an action. It locates a point within the block which other objects in the block will use as a base point. It prompts:

  **Specify parameter location:**

- Next we'll look at the Actions Palette (Figure 19.017). Here, you'll assign actions to the parameters you added using the Parameters palette. This is the actual block modification setup. (All items on this palette invoke the associated option of the ***BAction*** command.)

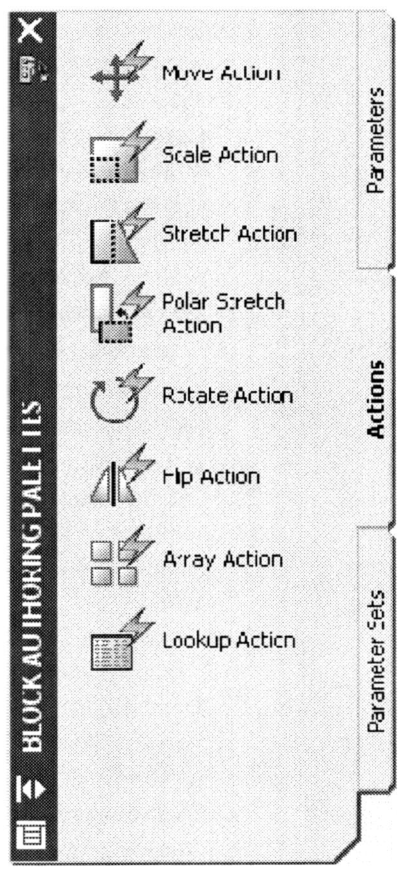


Figure 19.017

  - You can associate the **Move Action** with a **Point**, **Linear**, **Polar**, or **XY** parameter. Use it to allow a user to move a block object(s). It prompts:

    **Select parameter:** ***[select the parameter with which you'll associate the action]***

    **Specify parameter point to associate with action or enter [sTart point/Second point] <Second>:** ***[pick one of the points of the parameter with which you'll associate the action – hit enter to use the second parameter point]***

    **Specify selection set for action**

    **Select objects:** ***[select the objects that will be affected by the action]***

    **Select objects:** ***[enter]***

    **Specify action location or [Multiplier/Offset]:** ***[locate the action symbol; you can locate it anywhere, but try to keep it close to the parameter for organizational purposes]***

    The second prompt allows you to select a **sTart point** or a **Second point**. You can ignore these options if you wish as the **sTart point** is the default and hitting ***enter*** will automatically select the **Second point** option.

    You'll notice two other options – **Multiplier** and **Offset** – at the last prompt. When the action is triggered (when the user selects the associated grip), the **Multiplier** will multiply the action by a number you enter here. The **Offset** option has a similar result except that it factors the angle of the action by the number you enter in response to its prompt.

- You can associate the **Scale Action** with a **Linear**, **Polar**, or **XY** parameter. Use it to allow the CAD operator to scale selected objects within the block. **Scale Action** prompts:

  **Select parameter:** ***[select the parameter with which you'll associate the action]***

  **Specify selection set for action**

  **Select objects:** ***[select the objects that will be affected by the action]***

  **Select objects:** ***[enter]***

  **Specify action location or [Base type]:** ***[locate the action symbol; as always, you can locate it anywhere, but try to keep it close to the parameter for organizational purposes]***

  The only option that concerns you in this action is the **Base type** option of the last prompt. When selected, AutoCAD will prompt you to select either a **Dependent** base point (scaling done from the associated parameter's base point) or an **Independent** base point (scaling done from a user-identified base point).

- You can associate the **Stretch Action** with a **Point**, **Linear**, **Polar**, or **XY** parameter. Use it to allow the CAD operator to stretch selected objects within the block. **Stretch Action** prompts are similar to both the **Scale** and **Move Action** prompts:

  **Select parameter:** ***[select the parameter with which you'll associate the action]***

  **Specify parameter point to associate with action or enter [sTart point/Second point] <Second>:** ***[pick one of the points of the parameter with which you'll associate the action – hit enter to use the second parameter point]***

  **Specify first corner of stretch frame or [CPolygon]:** ***[create a typical crossing window]***

  **Specify opposite corner:**

  **Specify objects to stretch**

  **Select objects:** ***[select the objects to stretch]***

  **Select objects:** ***[enter]***

  **Specify action location or [Multiplier/Offset]:** ***[locate the action symbol]***

- You can associate the **Polar Stretch Action** only with a **Polar** parameter. Use it to allow the CAD operator to stretch selected objects within the block. **Polar Stretch Action** prompts are nearly identical to **Stretch Action** prompts:

  **Select parameter:** ***[select the Polar parameter with which you'll associate the action]***

  **Specify parameter point to associate with action or enter [sTart point/Second point] <Second>:** ***[pick one of the points of the parameter with which you'll associate the action – hit enter to use the second parameter point]***

  **Specify first corner of stretch frame or [CPolygon]:** ***[create a typical crossing window]***

  **Specify opposite corner:**

  **Specify objects to stretch**

  **Select objects:** ***[select the objects to stretch]***

  **Select objects:** ***[enter]***

  **Specify objects to rotate only**

  **Select objects:** ***[select objects that will rotate only (not stretch)]***

  **Select objects:** ***[enter]***

**Specify action location or [Multiplier/Offset]:** ***[locate the action symbol]***

- You can associate the **Rotate Action** only with a **Rotation** parameter. Use it to allow the CAD operator to rotate selected objects within the block. Compared to other actions, **Rotate Action** prompts are simple (and familiar):

  **Select parameter:** ***[select the Rotation parameter with which you'll associate the action]***

  **Specify selection set for action**

  **Select objects:** ***[select the objects that will rotate]***

  **Select objects:** ***[enter]***

  **Specify action location or [Base type]:** ***[locate the action symbol]***

- You can associate the **Flip Action** only with a **Flip** parameter. Use it to allow the CAD operator to "flip" or mirror objects within the block. This works much like the **Mirror** command (with the original objects removed). These prompts are also simple:

  **Select parameter:** ***[select the Flip parameter with which you'll associate the action]***

  **Specify selection set for action**

  **Select objects:** ***[select the objects that will flip]***

  **Select objects:** ***[enter]***

  **Specify action location:** ***[locate the action symbol]***

- You can associate the **Array Action** with a **Linear**, **Polar**, or **XY** parameter. Use it to allow the CAD operator to array selected objects within the block. **Array Action** prompts:

  **Select parameter:** ***[select the parameter with which you'll associate the action]***

  **Specify selection set for action**

  **Select objects:** ***[select the objects that will array]***

  **Select objects:** ***[enter]***

  **Enter the distance between rows or specify unit cell (---):** ***[as with the* Array *command, you must enter a distance between rows and cells; AutoCAD will limit the block object's array to these distances]***

  **Enter the distance between columns (|||):**

  **Specify action location:** ***[locate the action symbol]***

- You can associate the **Lookup Action** only with a **Lookup** parameter. Use it to allow the operator to select specific property values from a predefined list. **Lookup Action** prompts are very simple:

  **Select parameter:** ***[select the Lookup parameter with which you'll associate the action]***

  **Specify action location:** ***[locate the action symbol]***

  Once you've located the action symbol, AutoCAD presents the Property Lookup Table dialog box (Figure 19.018 – next page). Here you'll define the properties that will appear in the lookup box.

  - The name of the action associated with the table appears in the **Action name** box (upper left corner of the dialog box).
  - The **Input Properties** list box contains columns of user-selected parameters associated with the dynamic block. When a parameter appears here, the corresponding name (found in the **Lookup Properties** list box) will appear in the lookup box.

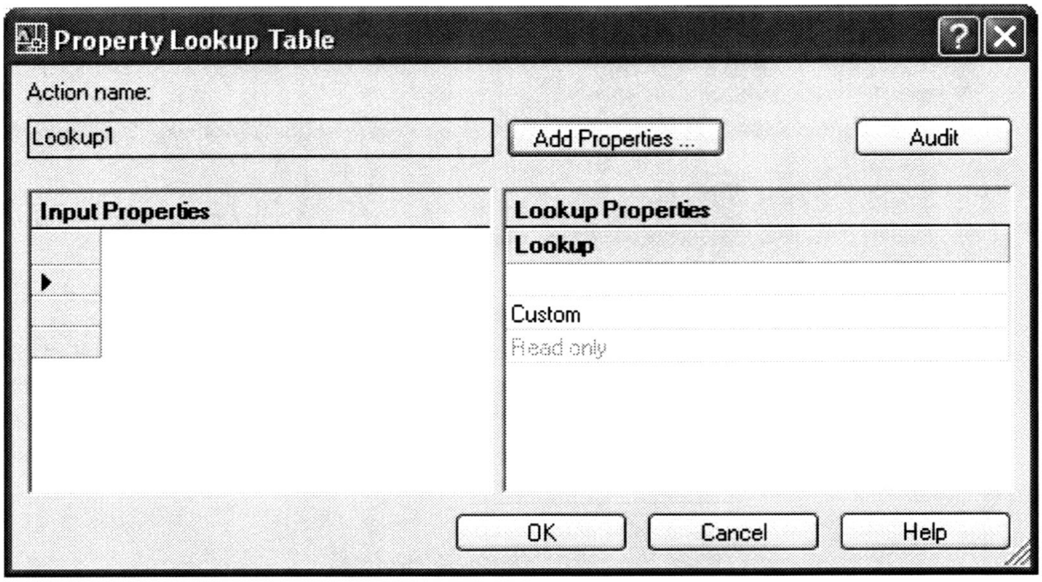


Figure 19.018

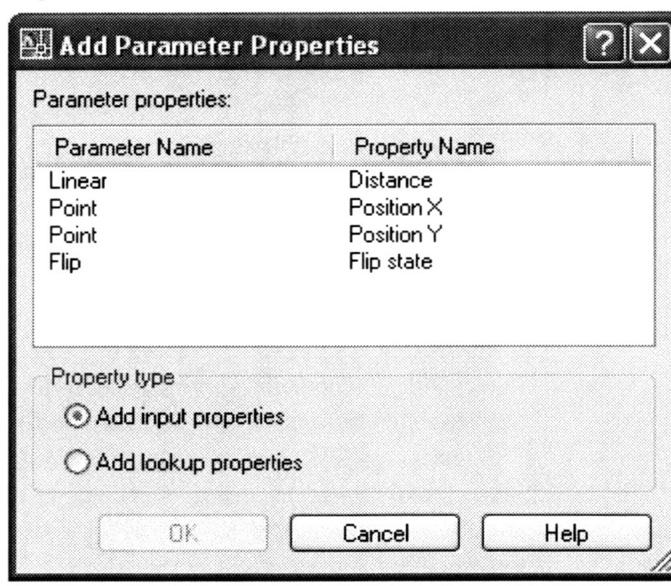


Figure 19.019

- Use the **Add Properties** button to call the Add Properties dialog box. (Figure 19.019). Here you'll find a list of parameters already associated with the dynamic block. Select the property you'd like to add to the lookup box. (Use the **Add … properties** radio buttons to set what can be added to each of the list boxes.)

  We'll see lookup boxes in action in our exercises.

- After taking so many pages to describe the Parameter and Action palettes, you might expect more from the Parameter Sets palette (Figure 19.020 – next page). These clever tools combine a parameter with an action, thus saving you the hassle of using both the Parameter and Action palette tools. (Notice the slider bar to the left; there are more tools available on the palette than can be shown here.)

| Appendix G contains a chart to help you keep track of which actions and parameters can be paired. |
|---|

Well that was a lot of pages of fun! I know, most of you fully understand dynamic blocks now, but let's try a couple exercises for those suffering that glazed look in their eyes.

In the next two exercises, we'll create three blocks – a door (we'll edit our door to make it much more efficient), a window, and a dining table.

- The window must be resizable. (We'll need 36" and 42" windows for the insertion exercise that follows.) We'll make it stretchable to predefined lengths.
- The door must be also resizable. (We'll need 30" and 36" doors.) We'll use a lookup box for this one. We must also be able to flip it to open in different directions. While we're there, let's give it another insertion point, too.
- The table will be our coup-de-grace. It'll be resizable to predefined lengths, have two styles of movable chairs, and align with a wall when we insert it.

Take a deep breath, put on some soft mood music, clear your calendar, and let's go …

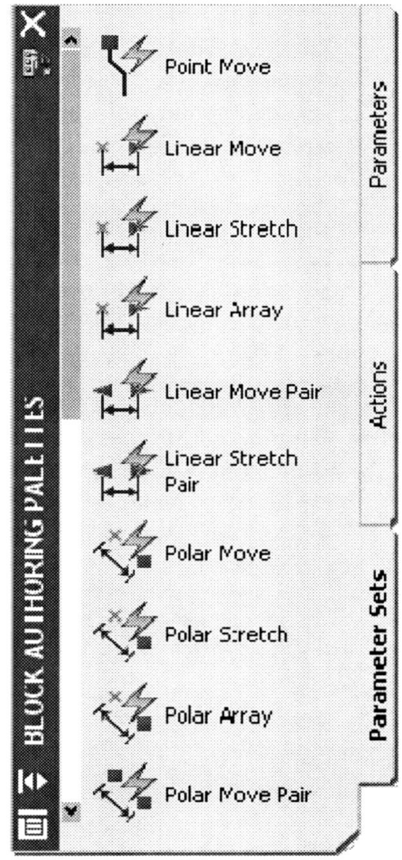


Figure 19.020

| Do This: 19.3.1 | Creating Dynamic Blocks |
|---|---|

I. Reopen the *blocks.dwg* file the C:\Steps\Lesson19 folder.
II. Erase the horizontal line associated with the door block you created in Exercise 19.2.1.1.
III. Follow these steps.

| **19.3.1: CREATING DYNAMIC BLOCKS** |
|---|
| 1. Let's start with the easy one (the window), enter the ***Block*** command . AutoCAD presents the Block Definition dialog box (Figure 19.007.)<br>**Command: *b*** |

2. Enter the information shown (use the upper left corner of the window as the insertion point). Be sure the **Open in block editor** check box is checked.

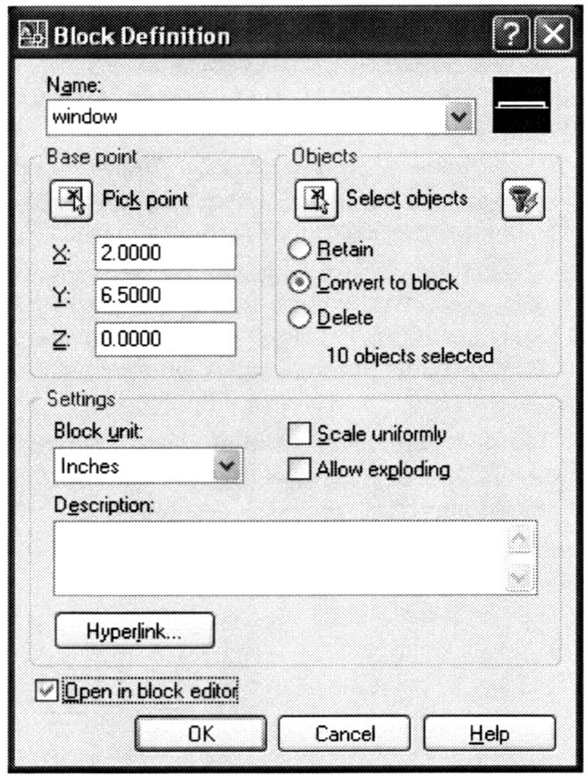


3. Pick the **OK** button to continue. Because you checked **Open in block editor**, AutoCAD opens the new *window* block in the block editor. (Resize the drawing as needed for a better view.)

4. We want to be able to stretch the window, so pick the **Linear Stretch** tool on the Parameter Sets palette. (This tool will insert a Linear parameter and a Stretch action.)

5. AutoCAD begins the parameter prompt. Tell it you'd like to set up a **Value set**.

**Specify start point or [Name/Label/Chain/ Description/Base/Palette/ Value set]:** ***v***

6. We'll use the **Incremental** option to limit the size of our window.

**Enter distance value set type [None/List/Increment] <None> :** ***i***

7. We'll allow windows from 24" to 42", sized in 3" increments.

**Enter distance increment:** ***3***

**Enter minimum distance:** ***24***

**Enter maximum distance:** ***42***

8. Now AutoCAD needs to know where to place the parameter.

**Specify start point or [Name/Label/Chain/ Description/Base/Palette/ Value set]:**

**Specify endpoint:**

**Specify label location:**

Place it as shown (start point on the left). When you use a parameter set, AutoCAD will locate the label for you.

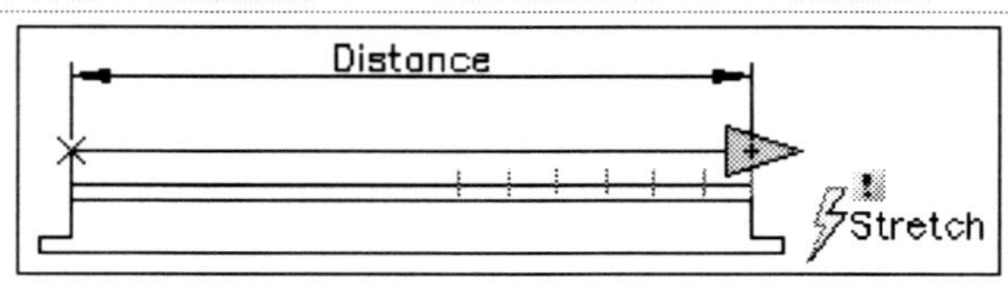

## 19.3.1: CREATING DYNAMIC BLOCKS

Notice the increment identifiers locating the sizes you identified in Step 7. Notice also the **Stretch** label. The exclamation symbol indicates that you haven't identified the action yet. We'll do that now.

9. Double click on the **Stretch** action label 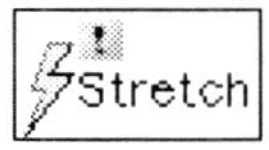

to define the action.

10. First, you'll create the stretch window (as you would with the ***Stretch*** command). Create the crossing window shown.

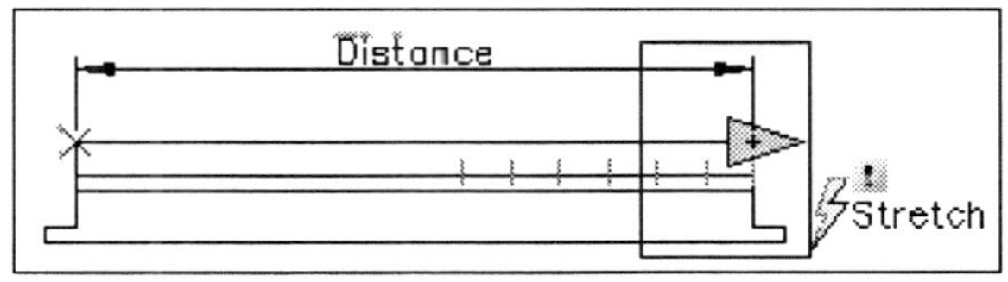


**Specify first corner of stretch frame or [CPolygon]:**

**Specify opposite corner:**

11. Then you'll actually select the objects to stretch. Recreate the crossing window in Step 10. (Hopefully, AutoCAD will correct this redundancy in future releases.)

**Specify objects to stretch**

**Select objects:**

**Select objects: *[enter]***

12. Notice that the **Stretch** label no longer bears the exclamation point.

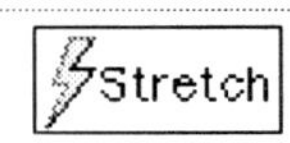


13. Save your work in the block editor 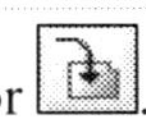. Then close the editor Close Block Editor.

14. Since you selected **Convert to block** in Step 2, AutoCAD has converted the window objects into a window block. Pick it now.

15. Notice the grips on the window block. The arrow grip is a *block stretch* grip. Select it.

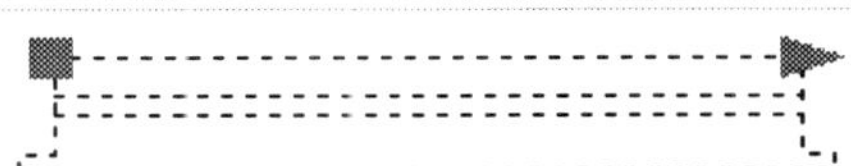

16. Notice that when you selected the block stretch grip, AutoCAD showed you the available increments.

Move the arrow back and forth. Notice that you can only resize the block to the available increments!

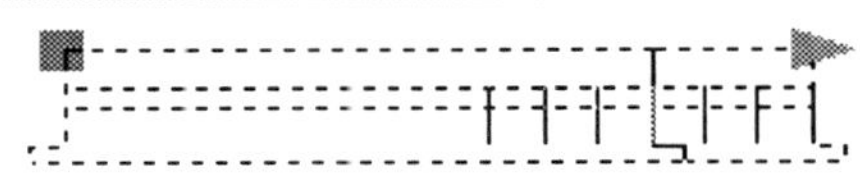

17. Clear the grips and save the drawing . Don't exit.

**Command: *qsave***

18. Ready for something harder? Let's edit our door block to make it resizable … and flip-able. Double click on the door block you created in Exercise 19.2.1.1. (Alternately, you can enter the ***BEdit*** command or use the **Block Editor** button  on the Standard toolbar.)

**Command: *be***

Select the **door** block from the Edit Block Definition dialog box. AutoCAD opens the door block in the block editor.

## 19.3.1: Creating Dynamic Blocks

19. Let's start by adding a **Point** parameter that AutoCAD can use as a second insertion point.

Pick **Point Parameter** on the Parameters palette .


20. Select the **Label** option , and call the parameter: **Insertion Point 2**.


**Specify parameter location or [Name/Label/Chain/Description/ Palette]:** ***L***

**Enter position property label <Position>:** ***Insertion Point 2***

21. Locate it as shown. As we have no action to associate with this parameter, we'll ignore the exclamation mark symbol.

**Specify parameter location or [Name/Label/Chain/ Description/Palette]:**

**Specify label location:**

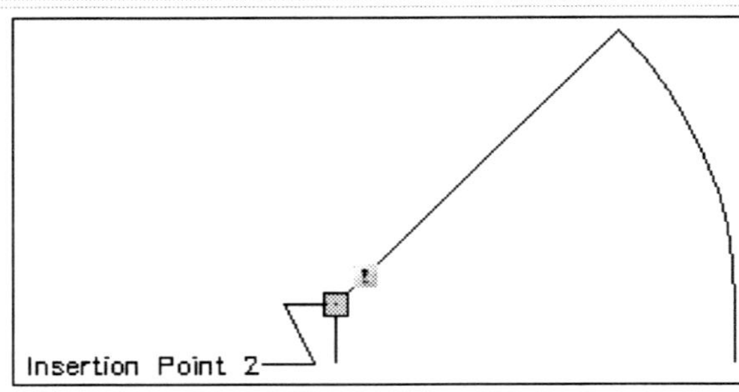


22. We'll make the door flip-able next. Select the **Flip Set** tool  on the Parameter Sets palette. (You may have to scroll down a bit.)


23. Use the midpoint of the eastern vertical line as the **base point of reflection**.

**Specify base point of reflection line or [Name/Label/Description/Palette]:**

24. Place the **endpoint of reflection line** (second point of the mirror line) anywhere to the west (use ORTHO).

**Specify endpoint of reflection line:**

**Specify label location:**

Locate the label as shown.

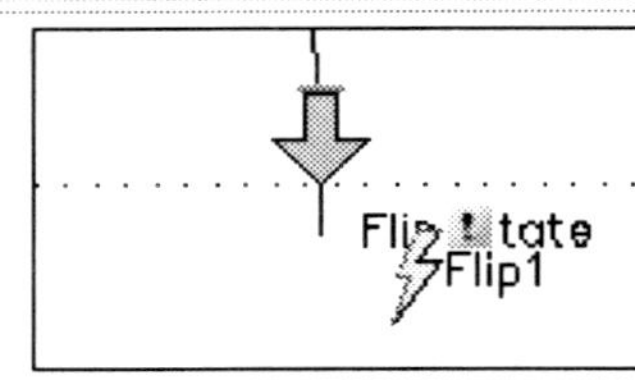


25. We still need to define the **Flip** action. Double click on the action label 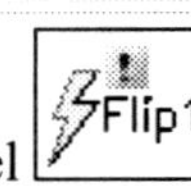.


26. Select all the objects in the block.

**Specify selection set for action**

**Select objects:** ***all***

**Select objects:** ***[enter]***

27. Repeat Steps 22 through 26 using a **base point** midway between the midpoints of the two vertical lines. Make your **reflection line** vertical.

28. Now we'll make the block resizable and list the available sizes in a lookup box. Begin insertion of a Linear parameter 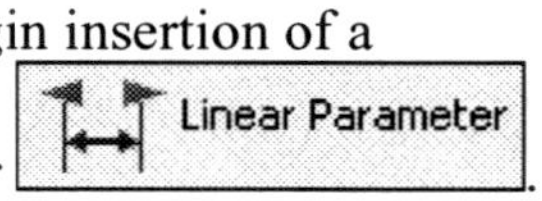.


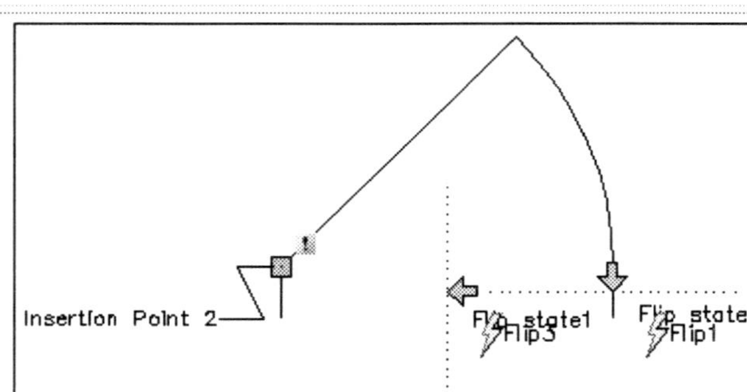

29. This time, we'll use a **List Value set** 

, 

. **List** is very similar to **Increment**, but it makes a list available for our use in the lookup box.

**Specify start point or [Name/Label/Chain/ Description/Base/Palette/Value set]:** ***v***

**Enter distance value set type [None/List/Increment] <None> :** ***l***

30. Enter the values shown.

**Enter list of distance values (separated by commas):** ***24,30,36***

31. Finally, locate the parameter as shown.

**Specify start point or [Name/Label/Chain/ Description/Base/Palette/ Value set]:**

**Specify endpoint:**

**Specify label location:**

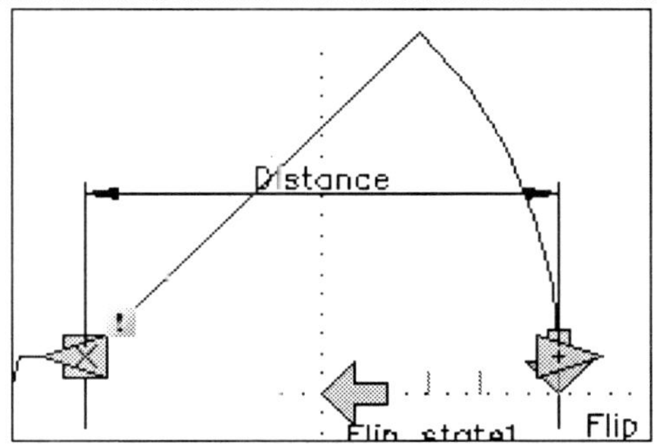


32. Now add your **Scale** action. Begin by picking **Scale Action** 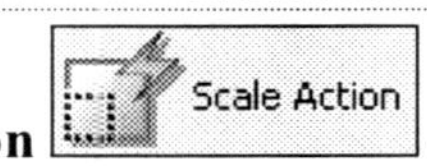

on the Actions palette.

33. Select the parameter you created in Steps 28 – 31.

**Select parameter:**

34. Place a crossing window around the objects shown. Also, select the bottom left vertical line. (Locate the label next to the parameter.)

**Specify selection set for action**

**Select objects:**

**Select objects:** ***[enter]***

**Specify action location or [Base type]:**

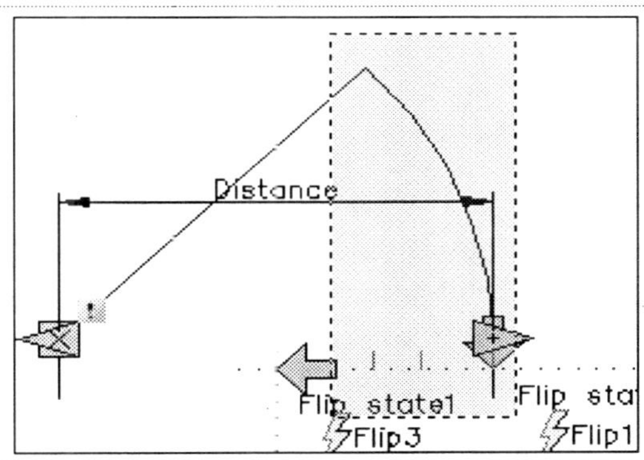


35. Finally, we'll create our lookup box. Begin by picking **Lookup Set** 

on the Parameter Sets palette.

36. Place the label just above the door.

**Specify parameter location or [Name/Label/ Description/Palette]:**

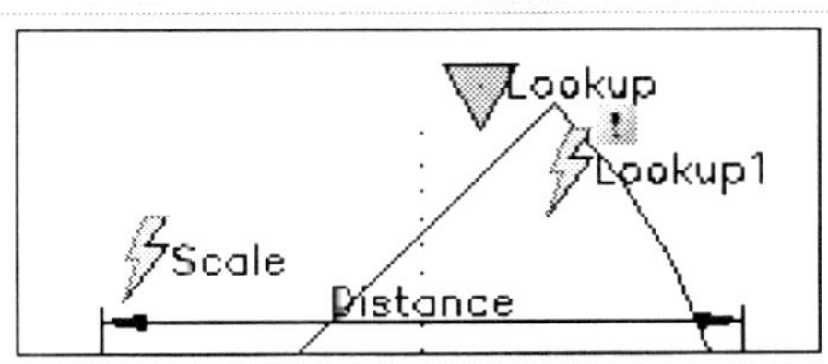

## 19.3.1: Creating Dynamic Blocks

37. Double click on the action label 

. AutoCAD opens the Properties Lookup Table dialog box (Figure 19.018).

38. Pick the **Add Properties** button 

. AutoCAD opens the Add Parameter Properties dialog box (Figure 19.019).

39. Pick the **Linear** parameter and then the **OK** button to return to the Properties Lookup Table dialog box.

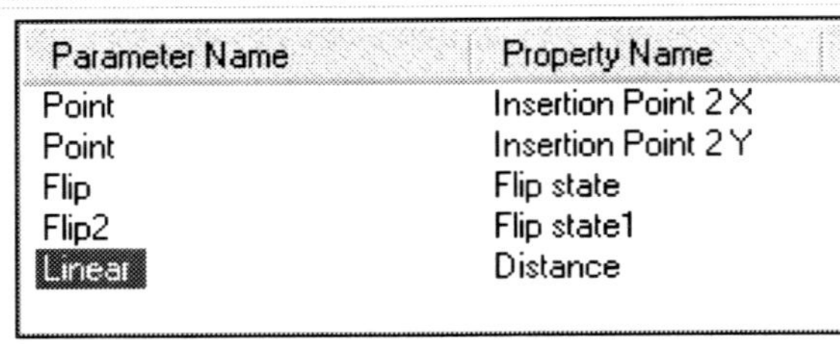


40. Under **Input Properties**, select the empty text box beside the arrow. A selection box will appear with the list you created in Step 31. Select the first item in the list.

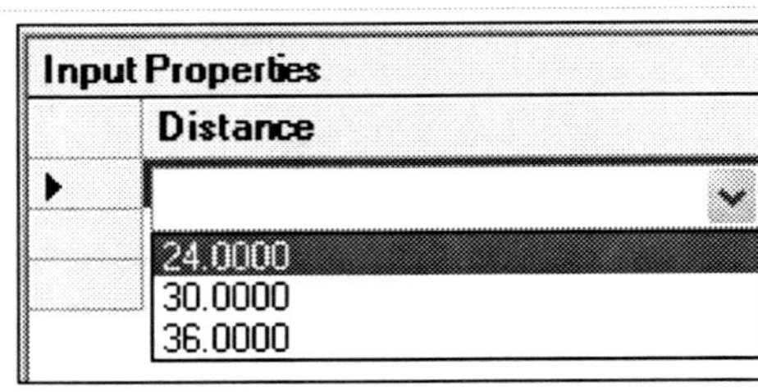


41. In the corresponding row under Lookup Properties, enter ***24" Door***. (This is the text that will appear in the list box.)

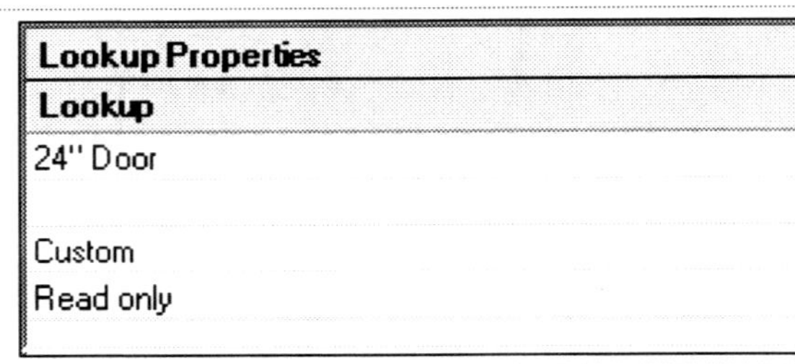


42. Repeat Steps 40 and 41 for the remaining items in the list.

43. Finally, pick the **Read only** row under **Lookup Properties** and select **Allow reverse lookup** from the selection box that appears. (This step is necessary to make the list box available to the operator.)

The box will look like the following figure when you've finished.

## 19.3.1: Creating Dynamic Blocks

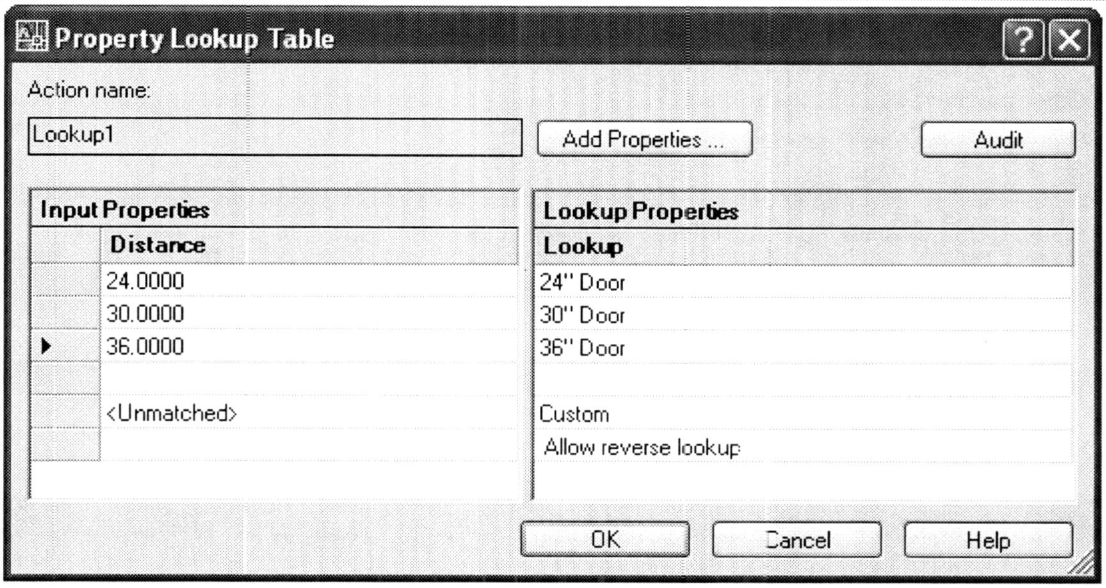


43. Complete the command OK.

44. Save your work in the block editor . Then close the editor Close Block Editor.

45. Pick the **Door** block. Notice the grips.

46. Experiment with the two flip grips (the two bottom arrows) to see how they affect the block.

47. Experiment with the scale grip (the right pointing arrow). See that you can resize the block as you defined (to 24" and 30").

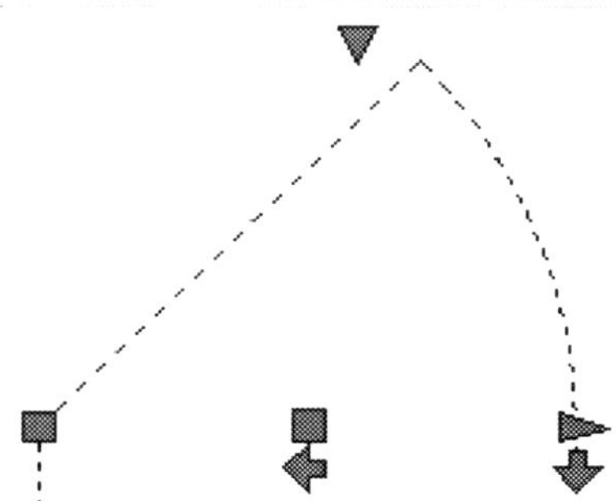

48. Now experiment with the list box grip (the downward pointing arrow above the block). Notice that it shows the available sizes for the door. Notice also that you can resize the door by selecting the size you want.

49. Begin to insert the *door* block . (Remove all checks in the Insert dialog box except the **Insertion point – Specify On-screen** box.)

**Command: *i***

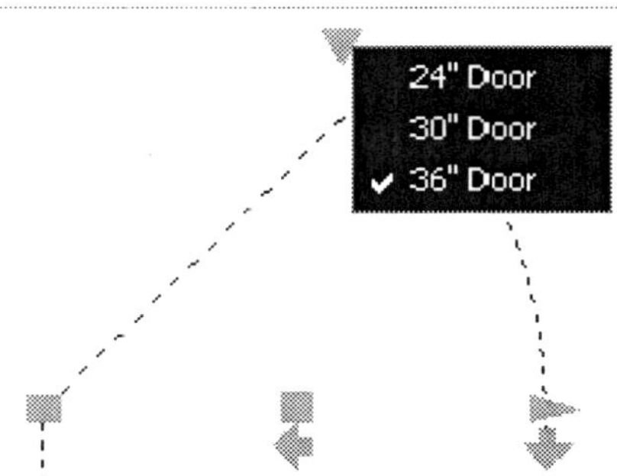


50. When AutoCAD prompts you for an insertion point (notice you're dragging the block on the screen), hit the CTRL key to toggle between the blocks insertion points.

## 19.3.1: Creating Dynamic Blocks

51. Abort the insertion.

52. Save the drawing  but don't exit.

**Command: *qsave***

Are you beginning to see the benefits of dynamic blocks? Catch your breath and then move on to the next exercise – creating the dynamic table; it's another long one!

| Do This: 19.3.2 | Creating Dynamic Blocks (Continued) |
|---|---|

I. Be sure you're still in the *blocks.dwg* file the C:\Steps\Lesson19 folder. If not, please open it now.

II. Restore the **Table** view.

III. Follow these steps.

## 19.3.2: Creating Dynamic Blocks (Continued)

1. Enter the ***BEdit*** command  and select the *table* block.

**Command: *be***

2. Create a **Linear Stretch** Parameter Set 

with listed increments 

of 36, 48, 60, 72, and 84. Select the right end of the table to stretch. (Refer to our last exercise and to the figure following Step 7 if you need assistance.)

3. Create a **Lookup Set** 

to go with the Linear parameter list you created in Step 2.

4. Now let's set up our block so we can move the chair around after it's inserted. Begin a **Point Move** Parameter Set 

.

5. Call the parameter, ***Chair Location***.

**Specify parameter location or [Name/Label/Chain/ Description/ Palette]: *L***
**Enter position property label <Position>: *Chair Location***

6. Place the parameter at the northern quadrant of the chair.

**Specify parameter location or [Name/Label/Chain/ Description/ Palette]: _qua of**
**Specify label location:**

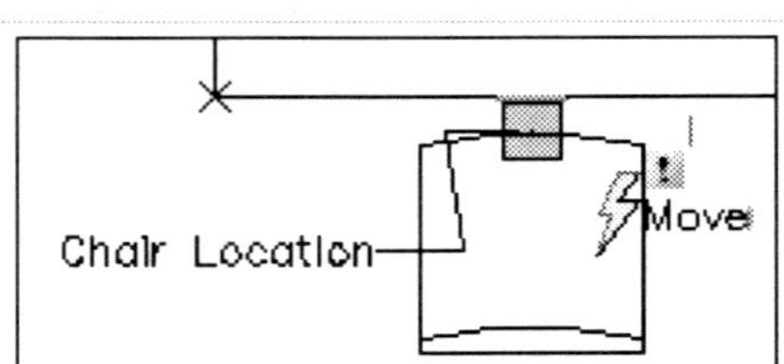

## 19.3.2: CREATING DYNAMIC BLOCKS (CONTINUED)

7. Double click on the **Move** action 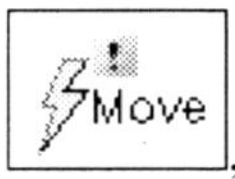

, and create a selection set consisting of the objects that make up the chair.

**Specify selection set for action**

**Select objects:**

The block looks like this.

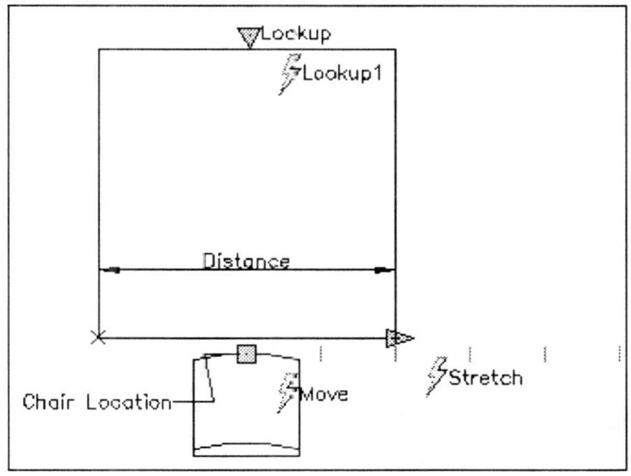


8. Add a **Flip** action for the chair 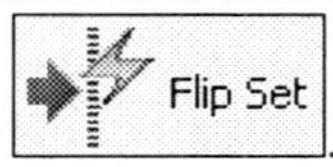

. Use these guidelines:

a. Select a **base point of reflection** in the center of the table

**Specify base point of reflection line or Name/Label/Description/ Palette]:**

b. Pick an endpoint of reflection on the horizontal.

**Specify endpoint of reflection line:**

c. Locate the label next to the reflection line.

**Specify label location:**

d. Select the objects that compose the chair 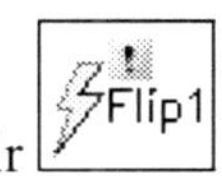


**Specify selection set for action**

**Select objects:**

9. Let's enable our operator to align the table upon insertion. Place an **Alignment Parameter** 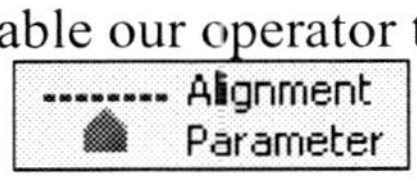

along the top of the table.

**Specify base point of alignment or [Name]:**

**Alignment type = Perpendicular**

**Specify alignment direction or alignment type [Type] <Type>:**

Now we're going to provide for two really cool tricks. First, we'll tell AutoCAD to increase the number of chairs when the table is resized. Then, we'll set up our block so the operator can select a different style of chair.

9. Before we begin, draw a two point circle  over the chair using the midpoint of the chair sides as the two points.

**Command:** ***c***

10. Now here's a handy trick. We need to add the circle to the selection set for the **Flip** action.

Double click on the action symbol. AutoCAD assumes you wish to add objects to the selection set and prompts you to do so. Select the circle.

**Specify selection set for action object [New/Modify] <New>: _m**

**Select object to add to action set or [Remove]:**
**Select object to add to action set or [Remove]:** ***[enter]***

11. Repeat Step 10 to add the circle to the **Move** action next to the chair. (Isn't editing actions a breeze?!)

12. We'll use the **Array** action with an existing parameter to have AutoCAD increase the number of chairs as the table stretches. Pick **Array Action** on the Action palette 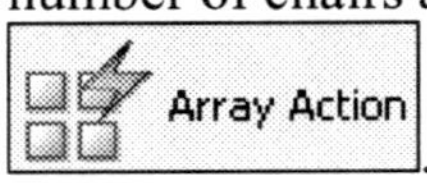

.

13. Select the Linear parameter you created in Step 2. (It looks like a **Distance** dimension.)

**Select parameter:**

14. Select the objects that compose the chair and the circle you drew in Step 9.

**Specify selection set for action**
**Select objects:**
**Select objects:** ***[enter]***

15. Tell AutoCAD to place the chairs 25" apart, and place the label next to the chair.

**Enter the distance between columns (|||):** ***25***
**Specify action location:**

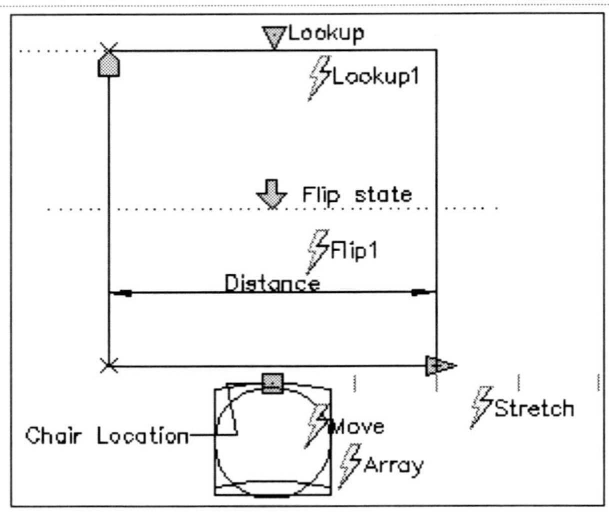


16. Finally, we'll set up our block so an operator can select a stool rather than a chair. Begin by adding a **Visibility** parameter 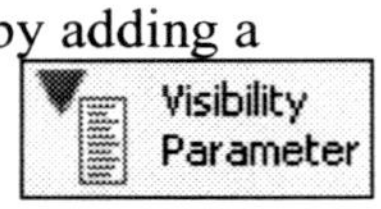

from the Parameters palette. Place it next to the **Lookup** symbol.

**Specify parameter location or [Name/ Label/Description/ Palette]:**

17. Now we'll create some Visibility States. Double click on the **Visibility** symbol 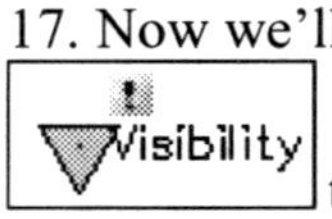

to display the Visibility States dialog box (Figure 19.014).

18. Select the only existing visibility state and rename 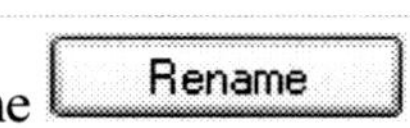

it to *Chair*.

19. Pick the **New** button 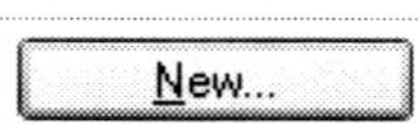

to display the New Visibility State dialog box.

20. Create a new **Visibility state** called *Stool*. Leave the **Visibility options for new states** bullet next to **Leave visibility of existing objects unchanged in new state**, and pick the **OK** button twice to complete the command.

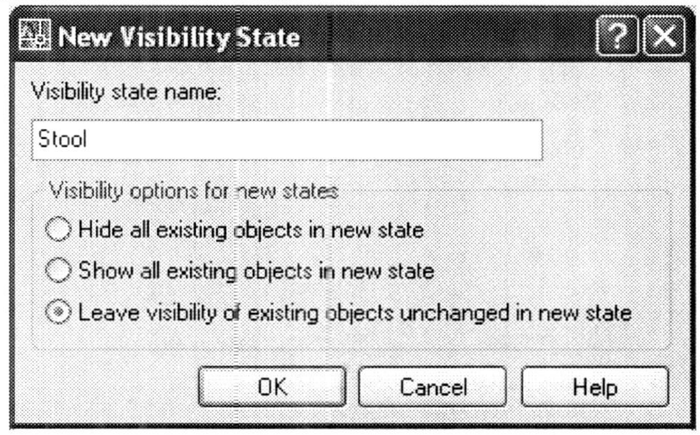


21. Set the **Chair** visibility state current in the **Visibility State** control box (right end of the Visibility toolbar).

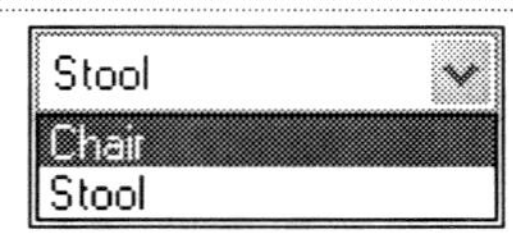


22. Pick the **Make Invisible** button 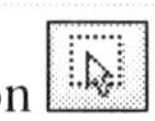 (next to the **Visibility State** control box), and select the circle.

**Select objects to hide:**
**Select objects:**
**Select objects:** ***[enter]***

23. Repeat Steps 21 and 22, making the chair objects invisible on the **Stool** visibility state.

24. Save your work in the block editor 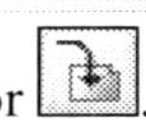. Then close the editor .


25. Select the table. Your grips should look something like these in.

26. Experiment with flipping the chair (use the arrow grip in the center of the table).

27. Experiment with the chair location (use the grip on the chair).

28. Select the different table sizes from the list box grip (the down arrow on the left). Notice that AutoCAD adds more chairs as the table gets longer.

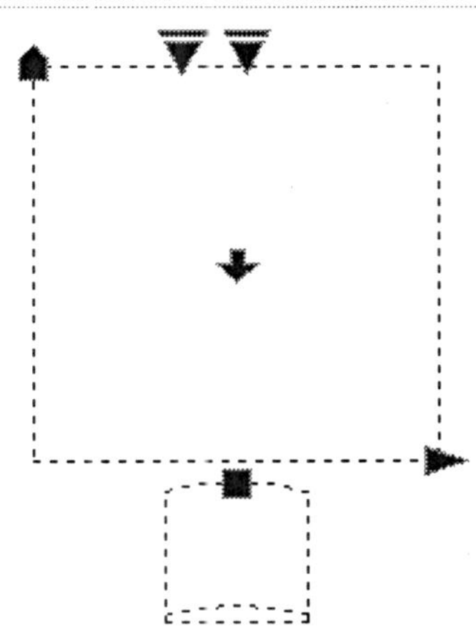

29. Use the other down arrow grip to select the stool. Notice how the type of chair changes.

30. Save the drawing 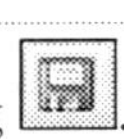.

**Command:** ***qsave***

31. Use the ***WBlock*** command to save the blocks to the C:\Steps\Lesson19 folder. (Refer to Exercise 19.2.2.1 if you need help.)

Now use the blocks you've created to complete the *cab-pln.dwg* file you began earlier. It will look like Figure 19.021 when you've finished.

Let's take a look now at a couple other cool tools that make blocks nearly indispensable.

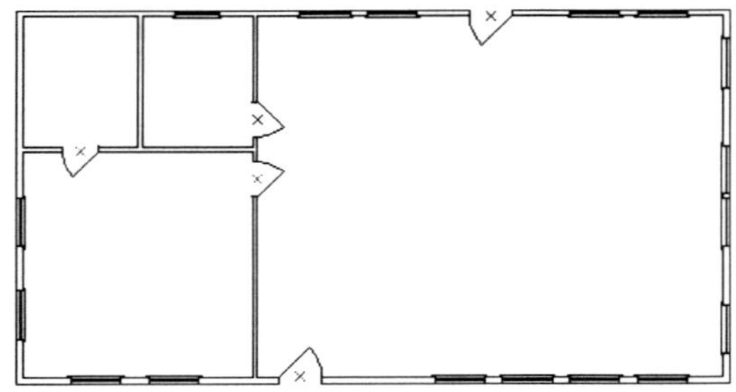

Figure 19.021

## 19.4 Other Insertion Methods

### 19.4.1 Getting Blocks from a Folder Library on a Web Site via AutoCAD's iDrop

AutoCAD has a marvelous toy called *iDrop*, and it bears closer examination before we proceed.

What is iDrop?

iDrop is the name given to a simple procedure for grabbing drawings (Write Blocks) from an iDrop enabled web site (folder) library and then dragging and dropping them into your drawing.

Why bother when I can create my own blocks?

Taking iDrop drawings from a manufacturer's site means that you have the exact item you want. It greatly reduces any possibility of error during the exchange of information between manufacturer and designer, including dimensional errors and engineering data provided through attributes. (We'll look more at attributes in Lesson 20.) It also saves the designer/draftsperson drawing time as well as research time.

Before you get too excited, however, let me give the downside. iDrop is fairly new. To date, not all manufacturers have iDrop-enabled blocks for you to use (although the list is growing). Additionally, the programmers at Autodesk designed the plug-in for Internet Explorer 5 or better. So you may need to change or upgrade your web browser. Finally, all insertions use a command line interface.

Let's take a look at that command line interface.

When you insert a iDrop, AutoCAD will prompt:

> **Specify insertion point or [Basepoint/Scale/X/Y/Z/Rotate]:** ***[using coordinates or picking a point with the mouse, tell AutoCAD where to put the block (you're precisely locating the block's insertion point)]***

We're presented with a few new options.

- AutoCAD asks for an **insertion point**. This sounds simple enough but the list of options that follows the prompt can be quite confusing. Let's take a look at these:
  - Selecting the **Basepoint** option will allow you to temporarily drop the block into the drawing where it's currently located. It then prompts:

    **Specify base point:** ***[select a new base point]***

    AutoCAD will then allow you to insert the block using your new base point. (This procedure *does not* redefine the base point of the block.)
  - The **X/Y/Z** options allow you to scale along the selected axis.
  - **Scale** allows you to scale the block uniformly.

Once you're ready, proceed with the next exercise. (This exercise requires Internet access and Internet Explorer.)

| Do This: 19.4.1.1 | iDrop and Block Insertions |
|---|---|

I. Open the *cab-pln.dwg* file the C:\Steps\Lesson19 folder. We'll iDrop some bathroom fixtures from our uneedcad site.

II. Freeze the **MARKER** layer and create a new layer for fixtures. Make the new layer current.

III. Open Internet Explorer and go to this site: *http://www.uneedcad.com/2007.*

IV. Follow these steps.

**19.4.1.1: IDROP AND BLOCK INSERTIONS**

1. If your browser is maximized, pick the **Restore** button in the upper right corner of the window to float it over the AutoCAD window.

2. Scroll down until you see the tub, sink, and WC.

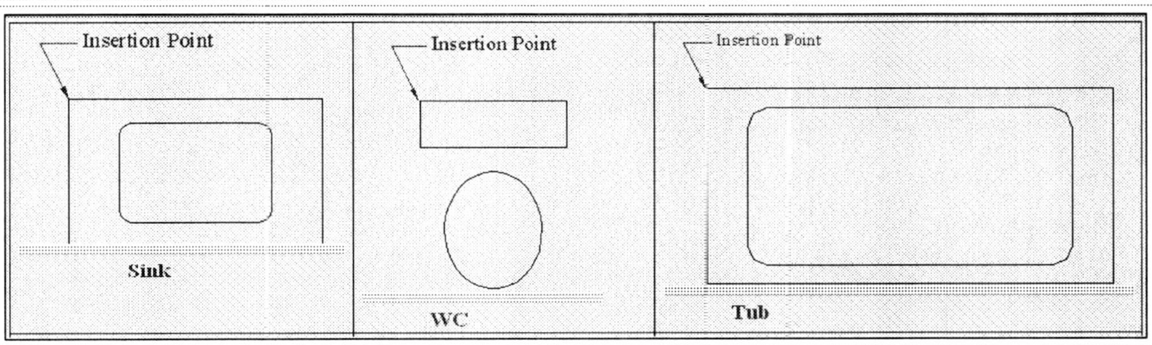


3. Notice the cursor when you pass over one of these items. It takes the shape of a tiny eyedropper.

4. Pick anywhere in the AutoCAD window to make it active.

5. Zoom in around the bathroom. Your screen should look something like this.

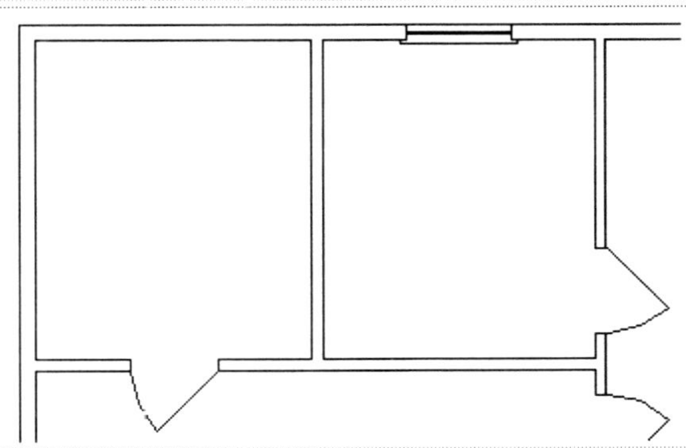

6. Hold down the ALT key on your keyboard and press the TAB key until your browser highlights on the menu. Release the ALT key. Windows floats the Internet Explorer window over AutoCAD again. (Use this procedure for toggling between AutoCAD and Internet Explorer.)

**19.4.1.1: iDrop and Block Insertions**

7. Place the iDropper over the tub. Pick with the left mouse button and, holding the mouse button down, drag the object into the bathroom.

Release the button.

8. Place the tub as shown. (The block has an alignment action attached to it to make insertion easier.)

**Specify insertion point or [Basepoint/Scale/X/Y/Z/Rotate]:**

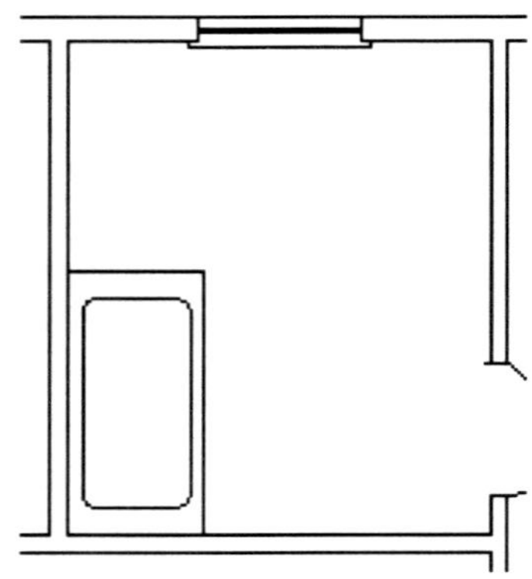

9. Repeat Steps 6, 7, and 8 to insert the sink and WC. Then change the sink to **oval** and the WC to **Smooth**. Your drawing looks like this.

10. Save your work 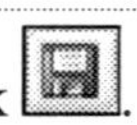.

**Command:** ***qsave***

Close Internet Explorer.

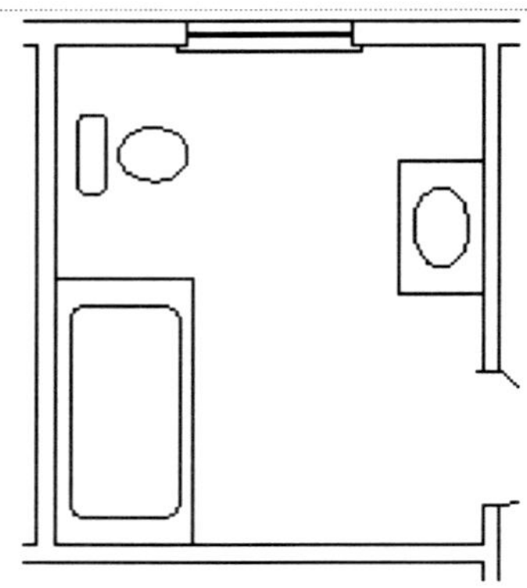

## 19.4.2 Adding Blocks with the ADC or Tool Palettes

We first met the ADC (AutoCAD Design Center) back in Lesson 6 when we saw that we could share layer definitions between drawings. Well, sharing blocks between drawings is just as easy! In fact, with AutoCAD, you can view objects in a template library (or another drawing) as easily as you could view the different types of hatch patterns using the ***Hatch*** command.

In our next exercise, we'll take advantage of several things – first, we'll use the ADC to access a block on the web. We'll use the ADC to insert a block directly into our drawing (we'll use iDrop to do this); then we'll create a new tool palette in which to put our block so that we can access it more quickly and easily in the future (and to give us some experience creating tool palettes). Last, we'll use the tool palettes to insert another block into our drawing. (This exercise also requires Internet access.)

Let's give it a try.

| Do This: 19.4.2.1 | Sharing Blocks |
|---|---|

I. Be sure you're still in the *cab-pln.dwg* file the C:\Steps\Lesson19 folder. If not, please open it now.

II. Zoom to display the bedroom (the large room to the left of the drawing).

III. Create a **Furniture** layer and make it current.

IV. Follow these steps.

## 19.4.2.1: SHARING BLOCKS

1. Open both the tool palettes  and the ADC 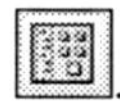.

    **Command: *toolpalettes***

    **Command: *adc***

2. Pick the **DC Online** tab on the ADC DC Online. AutoCAD accesses the Design Center web site.

3. Scroll until you've located the \2D Architectural\Furniture\Beds folder. Select **Queensize Bed** as indicated below.

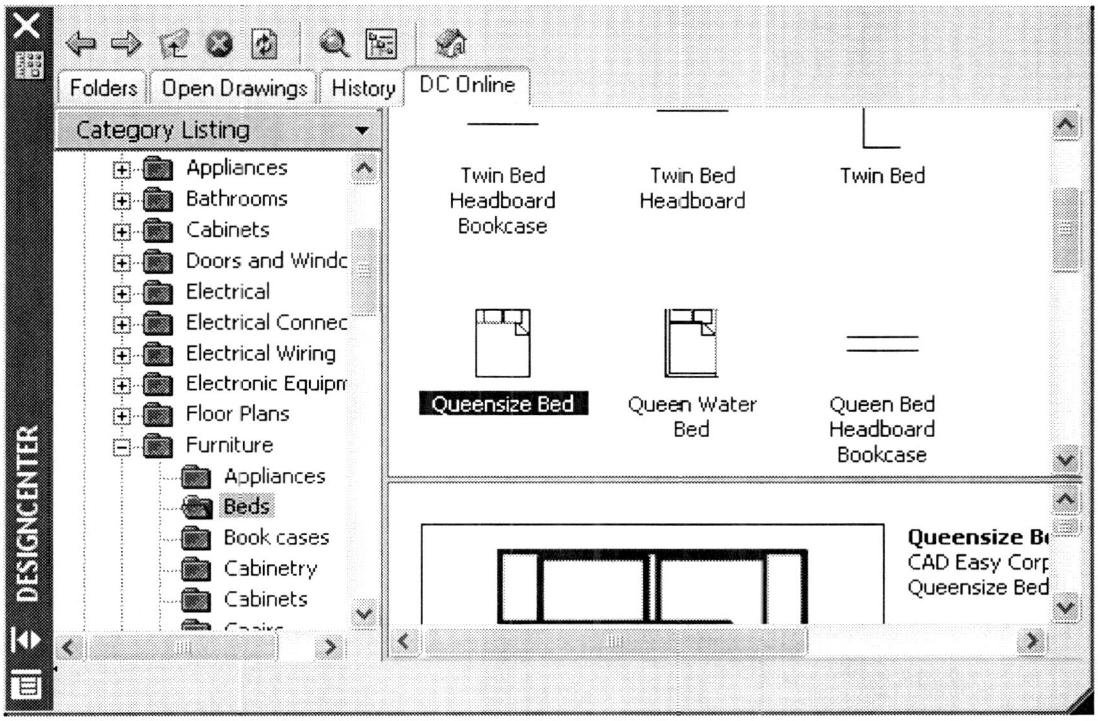


4. Using the iDrop technique you learned in our last exercise, drag the bed and place it into the bedroom.

    **Specify insertion point or [Basepoint/Scale/X/Y/Z/Rotate]: *r***

    **Specify rotation angle: *270***

    **Specify insertion point:**

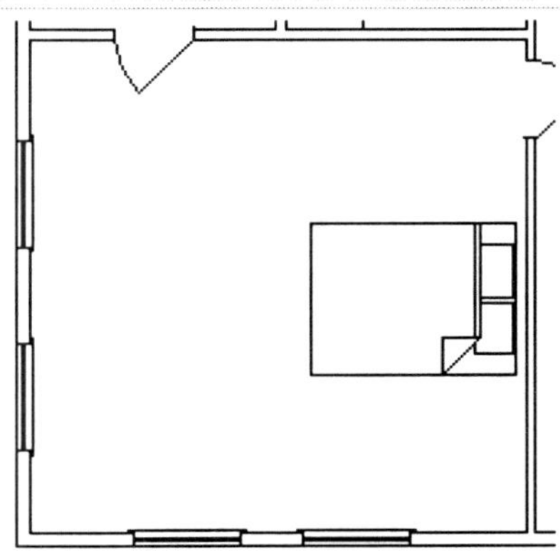

5. Save the drawing .

    **Command: *qsave***

6. Now let's create a tool palette and put the bed on it so that we can access it later without Internet access. Pick the **Properties** button  at the base of the Tool Palettes title bar.

### 19.4.2.1: Sharing Blocks

7. Select **New Palette** from the menu. AutoCAD creates a new tool palette and asks you to name it.

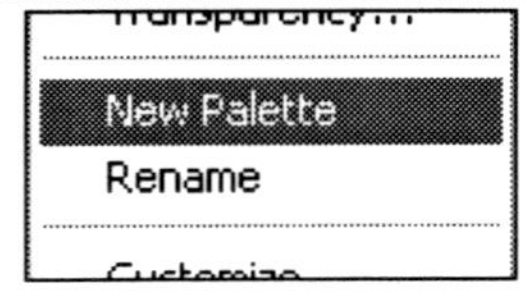


8. Call it **MyPalette** [MyPalette].

9. Now drag-and-drop the **Queensize Bed** from the drawing into the new tool palette. The palette shows the bed.

10. Now we'll insert a block from the tool palettes into the drawing. Pick the **Architectural** tab on the tool palettes and select the tree [Trees - Imperial].

10. Place the **tree** into your drawing (at ½ scale) outside the window. Your drawing looks like this.

11. Add some more furnishings if you wish, and then save the drawing [save icon] and exit.

**Command:** ***qsave***

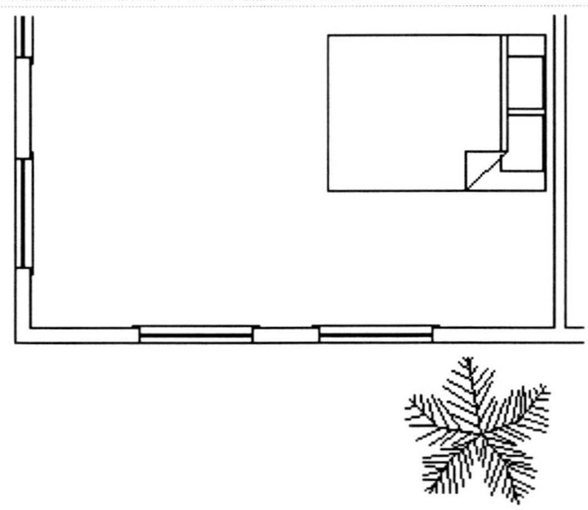

These procedures save quite a bit of time by showing the CAD operator exactly what's available for insertion from any library!

## 19.5 Extra Steps

1. Familiarize yourself with the following chart to help you know when to use groups and when to use blocks.

| Ability | Blocks | Groups |
|---|---|---|
| Can be shared between drawings | Yes | No |
| You can work on objects within the block/group | Yes | Yes |
| Can be treated as a single object | Yes | Yes |
| Can carry information (data) | Yes | No |
| Retrievable after erasure (without the Undo command) | Yes | No |
| May contain (other) blocks | Yes | Yes |
| May contain (other) groups | No | Yes |

2. Experiment with inserting blocks into tables. Use the ***TInsert*** command. Use AutoCAD's Help menu if you have trouble.

## 19.6 What Have We Learned?

*Items covered in this lesson include:*

- *Working with groups*
- *Folder & template libraries*
- *Block creation, insertion, and editing*
- *Using iDrop, the ADC, and tool palettes to share blocks between drawings*
- *AutoCAD Commands:*
    - ***Block***
    - ***Explode***
    - ***WBlock***
    - ***Insert***
    - ***BEdit***
    - ***BParameter***
    - ***BAction***
    - ***BVMode***
    - ***TInsert***

After 18 lessons of learning *How*, we've begun to answer the question *Why*. *Why* is CAD a better design tool than paper and pencil? *Why* should I spend thousands of dollars to do on a computer what I can do for a lot less on a board? *Why* must I educate myself (or in many cases, reeducate myself) to work with a computer?

Hopefully, the answers began to dawn on many of you in this last lesson.

We'd already seen throughout this book that CAD drawings are neater and easier to read than many pen or pencil drawings. But up to the beginning of Lesson 18, it all seemed like a lot of work – often more than a comparable board drawing might require.

Then in Lesson 19, we found ways to manipulate large numbers of objects at once. With blocks, once created (or purchased), *no further drawing is necessary!* Additionally, a project (often a company and occasionally an entire industry) can expect standard symbols!

But believe it or not, we've only begun to scratch the surface of what we can accomplish using blocks. Wait until you see what we do in Lesson 20!

## 19.7 Exercises

1. Start a new drawing from scratch.
   1.1. Set the limits for a full scale drawing on an 8½" x 11" sheet of paper.
   1.2. Grid: ¼"
   1.3. Create the layers indicated (all layers use a continuous linetype).
   1.4. Use the Times New Roman font. Text sizes are ¼", 0.2", and 1/8."
   1.5. Create the blocks shown in the *Legend* (below right). (Remember to create all blocks on layer 0.)
   1.6. Create the drawing (be sure to insert blocks on the appropriate layer). Use a table for the legend. Save it as *MyBridge* in the C:\Steps\Lesson19 folder.

| LAYER NAME | COLOR |
|---|---|
| Battery | 56 |
| Border | 5 (white) |
| Coil | 4 (cyan) |
| Copperwire | 3 (green) |
| Galvanometer | 7 (white) |
| Pin | 7 (white) |
| Resistor | 6 (magenta) |
| Switch | 1 (red) |
| Text | 2 (yellow) |

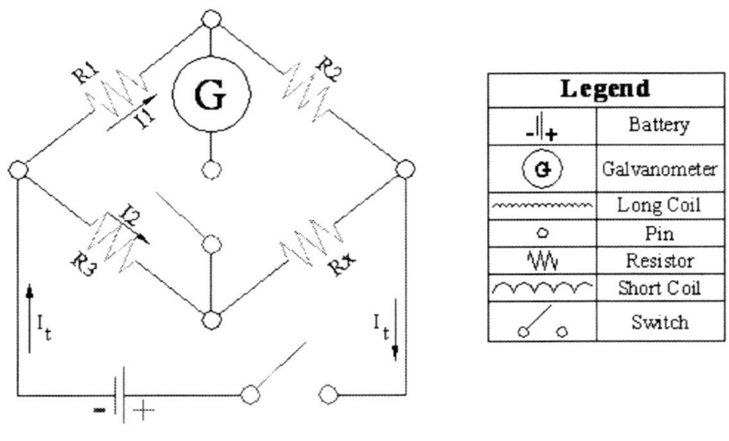


Bridge

2. Start a new drawing from scratch.
   2.1. Repeat the setup you used for Exercise 2 with the following exceptions:
      2.1.1. Add a layer called *Loop* using color 32.
      2.1.2. Grid: ½
      2.1.3. Use the standard text style with ¼" and 0.2" text heights.
      2.1.4. Use the battery block you created in Exercise 2 and create a block for the wire loop.
   2.2. Create the *ElectroMagnet Circuitry* drawing. Save it as *MyMagnet* in the C:\Steps\Lesson19 folder.

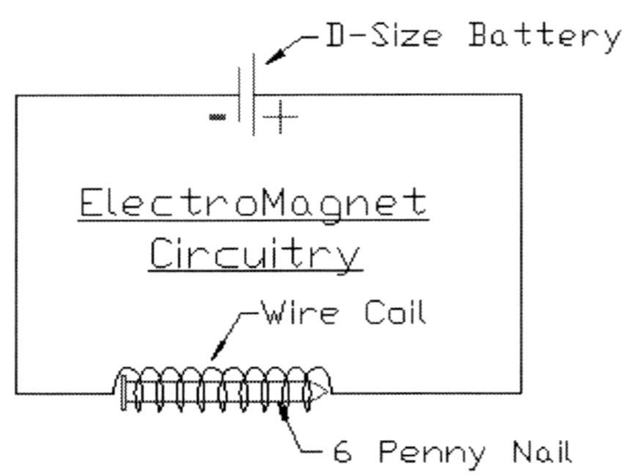


ElectroMatnet

*For more exercises related to Lesson1 9, please see Lesson 19 in AutoCAD 2007: One Step at a Time – Workbook.*

## 19.8 For Web-Based Review Questions, visit: http://www.uneedcad.com/2007/Files/07R19.pdf

# Lesson 20

Following this lesson, you will:

- ✓ *Know how to create and manipulate Block Attributes*
  - o *The **Attdef** command*
- ✓ *Know how to insert blocks with attributes*
- ✓ *Know how to control the display of attributes*
  - o *The **Attdisp**, **Attreq**, and **Attdia** system variables*
- ✓ *Know how to edit attribute information*
  - o *The **-Attedit** command and the Properties palette*
- ✓ *Know how to redefine a block with attributes*
  - o *The Block Attribute Manager*
- ✓ *Know how to extract attribute data to another program or for a bill of materials*
- ✓ *The **Eattext** command*

# Advanced Blocks

*One of the most important jobs a CAD operator may have involves the politics of convincing his or her supervisor (and often the supervisor's supervisor) of the importance of using AutoCAD as its creators intended. This will inevitably mean that the initial job setup will take more time than a non-CAD-oriented person might consider necessary. But the delay will be repaid "seven-fold" at the end of the project.*

*The operator might explain that AutoCAD isn't, as is commonly believed, simply a very expensive drafting tool. Rather, AutoCAD should be considered the backbone of the overall project. Indeed, a design properly created in AutoCAD serves not only as an outline for construction but also reduces material take-off and purchasing chores from weeks to minutes.*

*To cut large pieces of time from the end of the project, smaller pieces of time must be spent at the setup phase. Part of this time is required to create your libraries or to adjust purchased libraries to project standards. This adjustment should involve the addition of project-specific attributes to your blocks. You'll use these attributes to generate bills of materials and to share material information with material take-off (MTO) and purchasing programs.*

*This lesson will cover how to create and edit attributes and how to share attribute data with other programs.*

*Let's begin.*

## 20.1 Creating Attributes

*What exactly is an attribute?*

Think of an attribute as a vessel that carries information. This information can be AutoCAD generated or user defined. We've learned that all objects in a drawing contain information kept in the drawing's database. This information identifies the object using such things as type, style, color, linetype, layer, position, and so forth. An attribute allows you to attach this information (and other types of information) to a block and to retrieve it later.

### 20.1.1 Defining Attributes

AutoCAD provides a simple, straightforward dialog box (Figure 20.001) for creating attributes. Access it from within Model Space or the block editor with the ***Attdef*** command (or the ***att*** hotkeys). Understanding this dialog box will go a long way toward helping you understand how attributes work.

Let's take a look.

- As you can see in the upper left frame (**Mode**), AutoCAD provides four modes from which to choose. These control how the attributes function. By default, all modes are toggled off (the check boxes are clear). Let's see what happens when you toggle each one on.

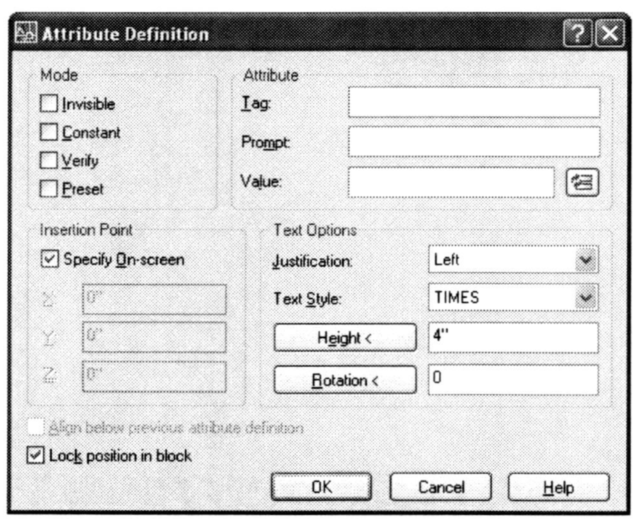


Figure 20.001

- An **Invisible** attribute holds data that won't show on the screen or drawing. This setting is ideal for most information. (Use visible data for information you wish to see on the drawing – such as valve sizes or title block data.)
- A **Constant** attribute contains information that doesn't change. AutoCAD won't prompt for this information when you insert the block, and you can't edit the value of the constant attribute after inserting the block.
- When you insert a block with an attribute that was created in **Verify** mode, AutoCAD will first prompt you to enter a value for the attribute and then prompt you again to *verify* that value.
- AutoCAD won't prompt for an attribute value (except those requiring verification) when you create it in the **Preset** mode. AutoCAD assumes default values for all the attributes when the block is inserted.

- The **Attribute** frame provides a convenient location for you to easily place other important information.
  - Enter the name of the attribute in the **Tag** text box. Make this something simple but descriptive so that the operator can easily identify it.
  - Place the prompt – what you want AutoCAD to say when asking you for a value to assign to this attribute – in the **Prompt** text box. Follow the advice of the old English professor: "Be brilliant; be brief." (In other words, keep your prompts short, concise, and to the point.)
  - You can place a default value for the attribute in the **Value** text box. AutoCAD doesn't require a default value, but it'll provide you with the ability to respond to the prompt with an ***enter*** keystroke or a right click of the mouse.
  - To the right of the **Value** box, you'll find an **Insert field** button. This handy tool can even increase the incredible usefulness of attributes! Add a field into the **Value** box and AutoCAD will automatically update the attribute value even after you've inserted the block!
- The **Insertion Point** frame works exactly as it did on the Insert dialog box. But remember, this insertion is for the attribute not the block.
- In the **Text Options** frame, you'll use control boxes to select the **Justification** and **Style** of the attribute's text. You can also place the **Height** and **Rotation** of the text into the appropriate text box, or pick a button to select each from the screen.
- When creating several attributes, a check in the **Align below previous attribute** box will help keep the attributes organized.
- You can also **lock** [an attribute's] **position in** [a] **block**, although it's not always a good idea.

To edit or change an attribute before creating the block or within the block editor, use the standard text editor command (***DDEdit***) or double click on it. AutoCAD will present the Edit Attribute Definition dialog box shown here.

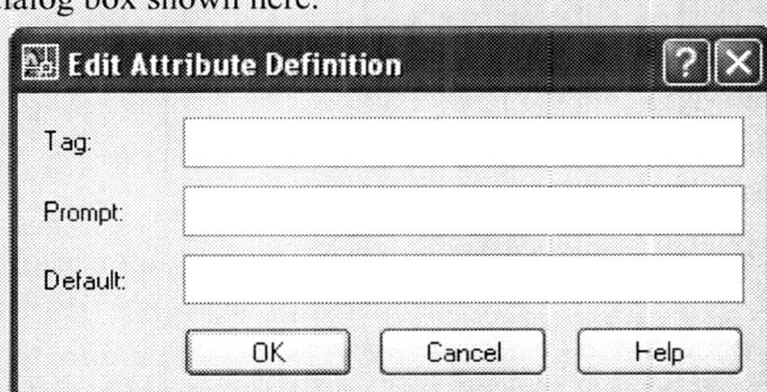

Here you can change the **Tag**, **Prompt**, or **Default** value from here, but you can't change the mode of the attribute. You can, however, change all the attribute's properties using the Properties manager.

Remember this handy method when you have several similar attributes to create. Simply copy your attributes to the blocks you wish to create, edit them as needed, and then create the block.

Let's add some attributes to a few blocks.

You can create attributes before creating a block. Just include them in the objects selected to create the block.

You can also access the ***Attdef*** command from the Draw pull-down menu. Follow this path:

*Draw – Block – Define Attributes…*

| **Do This: 20.1.1.1** | **Creating Attributes** |
|---|---|

I. Open the *blocks-pipe2006.dwg* file the C:\Steps\Lesson20 folder. The drawing looks like Figure 20.002.

II. Follow these steps.

Remember: If you discover an error in an attribute after you've created it, edit the definition with the Properties palette.

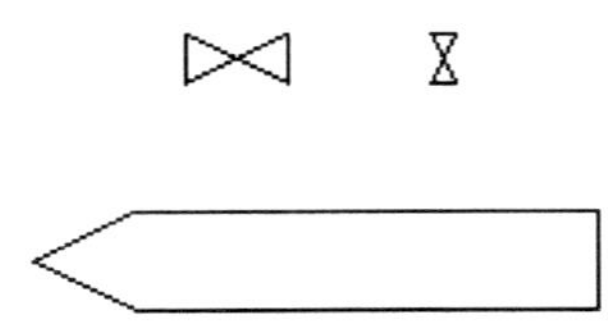

Figure 20.002

**20.1.1.1: CREATING ATTRIBUTES**

1. Open the left valve in the block editor.
   **Command: *be***

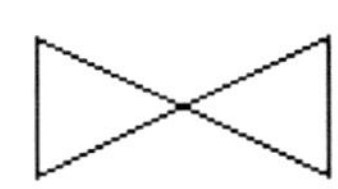

2. Change the current layer to **TEXT**.

3. We're going to create five attributes to attach to this valve. Enter the ***Attdef*** command.

Alternately, you can pick the **Define Attribute** button on the Block Editor toolbar.
   **Command: *att***

4. Fill in the dialog box as shown in the following figure.
   a. Accept the default modes for this block.
   b. Call the attribute ***Size***.
   c. The prompt should read as shown.
   d. Give the attribute the default value indicated.
   e. Center-justify the text.
   f. Use a text height of 1/8".
   g. Enter the **Insertion Point** shown.
   h. Clear the **Lock position in block** check box.

## 20.1.1.1: CREATING ATTRIBUTES

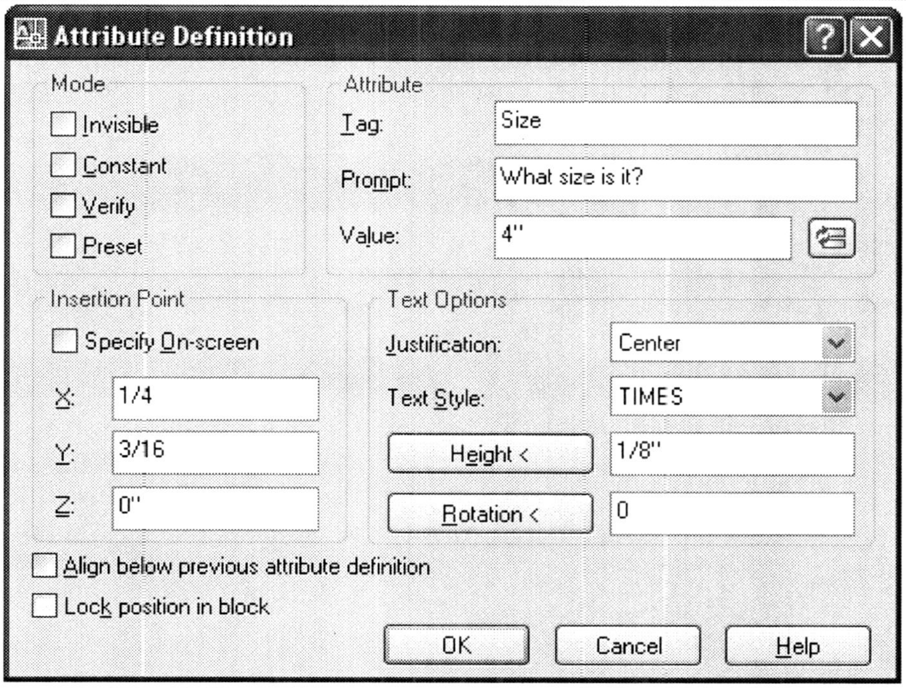


5. Pick the **OK** button to complete your first attribute definition. Your screen should look like this.

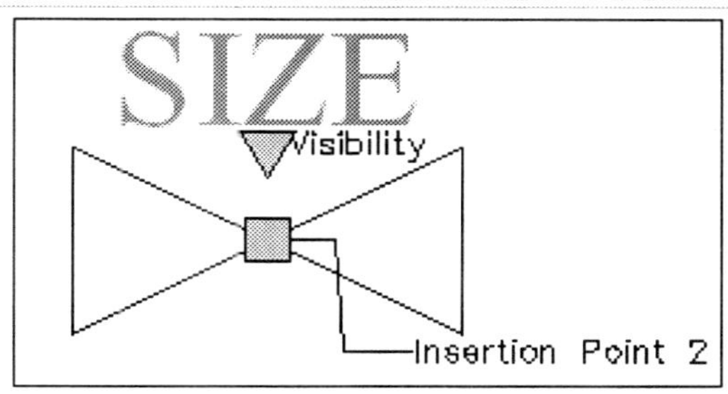


6. Save the block  and drawing 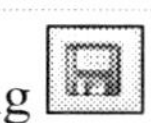 but don't exit. (Update the reference when prompted.)

**Command: *qsave***

7. Repeat Steps 3 through 6 to create a **Rating** attribute. All the modes for the attribute should be toggled off, the tag should be ***rating***, the prompt should read, ***What is the rating?***, and the default attribute value should be ***150#***. Center the tag below the valve at coordinates .25,-.25.

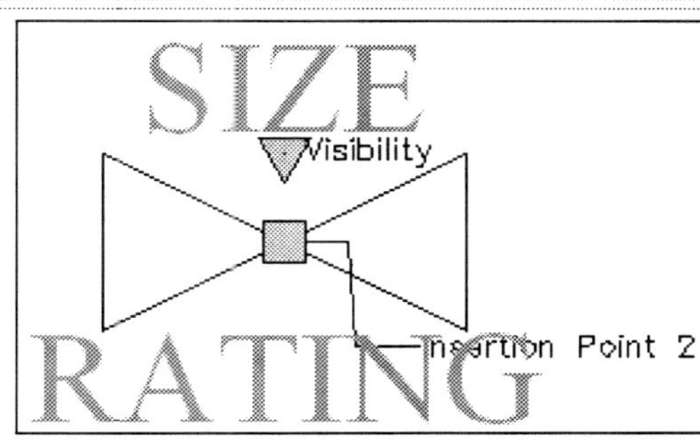


8. Now let's create a **Constant**, **Invisible** attribute. Repeat the ***Attdef*** command.

**Command: *[enter]***

9. Create the settings shown (Figure "A" – next page).
   a. Begin by placing checks next to **Invisible** and **Constant**. Notice that the other modes become unavailable.
   b. Call the attribute ***Filename***. Notice that, with a constant attribute, you don't need a prompt.
   c. Pick the **Insert Field** button next to the **Value** control box
      Select **Filename** in the **Field Names** box and use the **Lowercase** format (Figure "B").

Pick the **OK** button to close the Field dialog box.

d. Place a check in **the Align below previous attribute** definition option. Notice that AutoCAD removes the options to locate and define text types. It assumes this information from the previous definition.

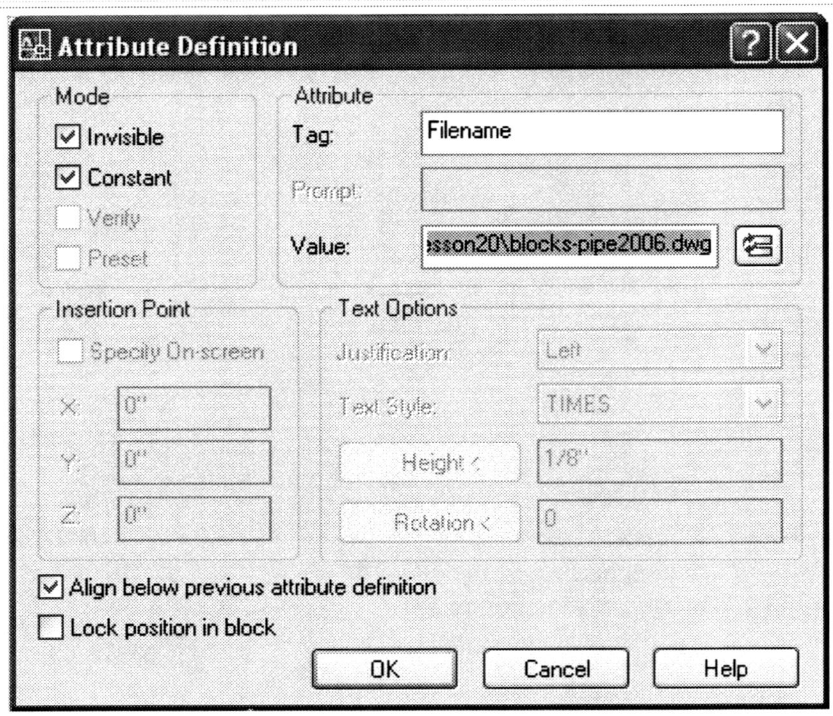


"A"

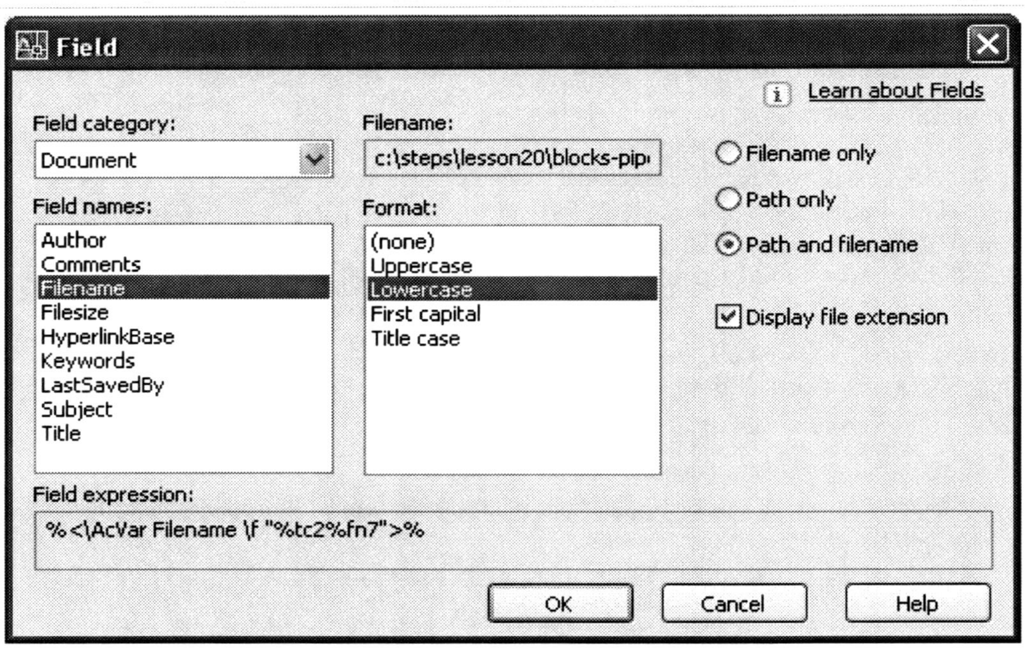


"B"

## 20.1.1.1: CREATING ATTRIBUTES

10. Complete the definition [OK].

11. Save the block and drawing but don't exit.

**Command:** ***qsave***

12. Now create an **Invisible** ***Type*** attribute as shown. Align the tag beneath the **Filename** tag.

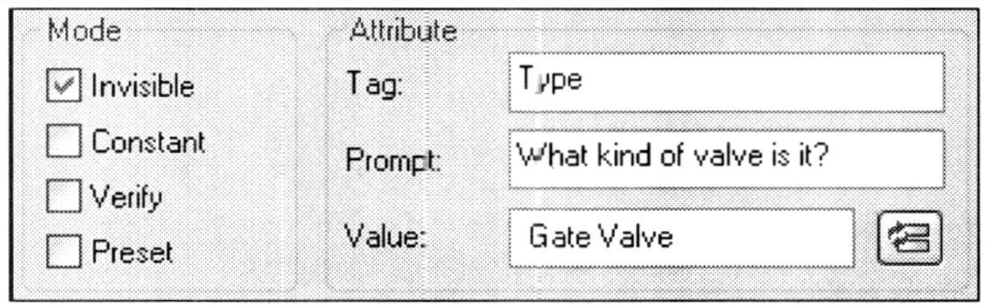


13. Create a final attribute – this one for the price of the valve.

   a. Call the attribute ***Price***.
   b. Have it prompt for the cost as indicated.
   c. It should be invisible, but you should verify the value entered.
   d. Align it below the previous attribute.

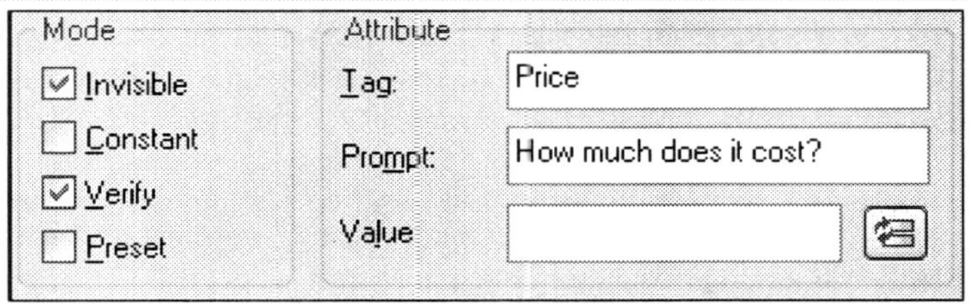


14. Save the block and drawing but don't exit.

**Command:** ***qsave***

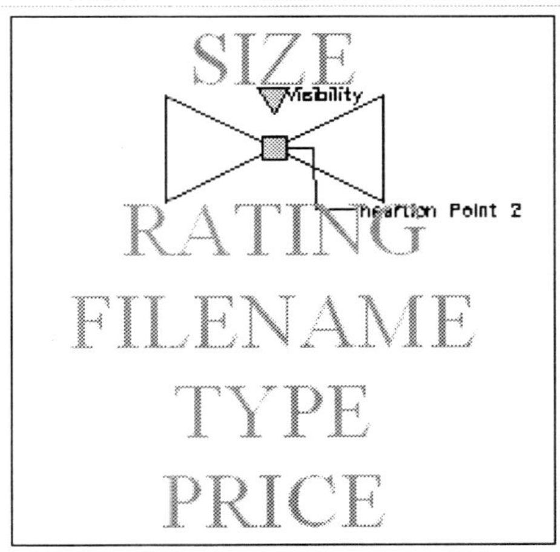


15. Notice that you've been working in the **Gate Valve** visibility state. (Look in the **Visibility State** control box.) Use the control box to change to the **Globe Valve** visibility state.

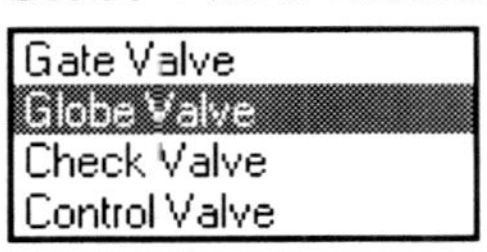


Notice that all the attributes have disappeared! Let's fix that.

16. Toggle the **Visibility Mode** so that you can see the attributes. (They'll appear gray.)

**Command:** ***bvmode***

**Enter new value for BVMODE <0>:** ***1***

17. Now, with the **Globe Valve** visibility state current, use the **Make Visible** button to make the attributes visible.

**20.1.1.1: CREATING ATTRIBUTES**

18. Repeat Step 17 for the **Check Valve** and **Control Valve** visibility states.

19. Save the block and close the block editor Close Block Editor.

20. WBlock the valve block as *Valve* to the C:\Steps\Lesson20 folder.

    **Command: *w***

21. Save the drawing but don't exit.

    **Command: *qsave***

## 20.2 Inserting Attributed Blocks

When you insert an attributed block into a drawing, the attribute prompts will follow the standard insertion prompts. This can occur in one of two ways – command line prompts or the Enter Attributes dialog box.

Let's look at the command line method first; then we'll look at the dialog box in Exercise 20.2.2.

> AutoCAD includes a system variable – ***Attreq*** – which controls whether or not you'll be prompted for attribute values. If the variable is set to **1** (the default), AutoCAD prompts on the command line or with a dialog box. If you set this system variable to **0**, however, AutoCAD won't prompt at all for attribute values and you must use the attribute editor to add the values.
>
> Whether or not AutoCAD prompts for attribute values at the command line or with a dialog box is controlled by the ***Attdia*** system variable. A setting of **0** (the default) means that you'll receive prompts on the command line, whereas a setting a **1** calls a dialog box.

**Do This: 20.2.1 — Inserting Attributed Blocks Using the Command Line**

I. Open the *pid-20.dwg* file the C:\Steps\Lesson20 folder. The drawing looks like Figure 20.003.

II. Be sure the ***Attdia*** system variable is set to **0**. (This means that attribute prompts will appear on the command line.)

III. Set **VA** as the current layer.

IV. Follow these steps.

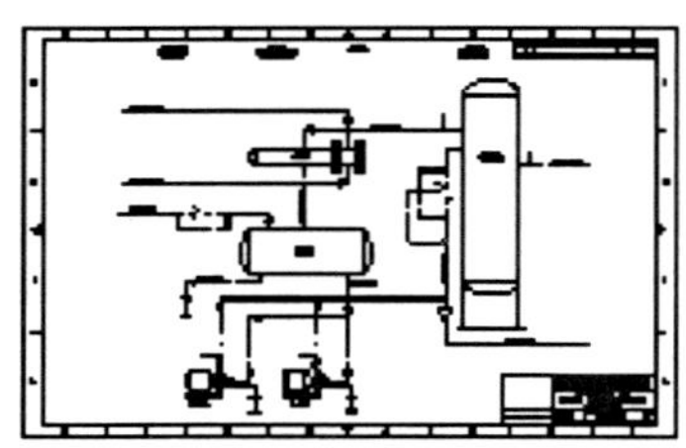

Figure 20.003

**20.2.1: INSERTING ATTRIBUTED BLOCKS – COMMAND LINE**

1. Restore the **Cont_Station1** view. The view looks like this.

    **Command: *v***

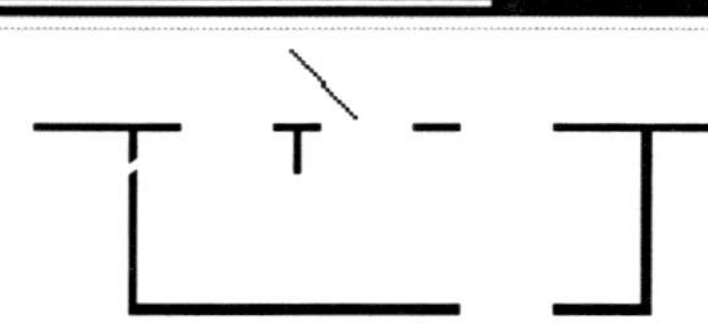

2. Insert the block you created in the last exercise. (Find it in the C:\Steps\Lesson20 folder.) Insert it at the leftmost endpoint (arrow). Accept the default size and orientation.

    **Command: *i***

## 20.2.1: INSERTING ATTRIBUTED BLOCKS – COMMAND LINE

3. Once you've located the block, AutoCAD asks you to **Enter attribute values**. Accept the default **rating** and **size**, and enter a price of ***55.00***. (Note that you assigned these defaults in our last exercise.)

*The prompts may appear in a different order. They'll reflect the order in which you created them.*

**Enter attribute values**
**What size is it? <4">:** ***[enter]***
**What is the rating? <150#>:** ***[enter]***
**What kind of valve is it? <Gate Valve>:** ***[enter]***
**How much does it cost?:** ***55.00***
**Verify attribute values**
**How much does it cost? <55.00>:** ***[enter]***

4. Save the drawing but don't exit.

**Command:** ***qsave***

It looks like this.

Notice that the **Type**, **Filename**, and **Price** attributes aren't visible. Notice also that the valve assumed the characteristics defined by the **VA** layer, and the attribute text assumed the characteristics defined by this drawing's **Text** layer.

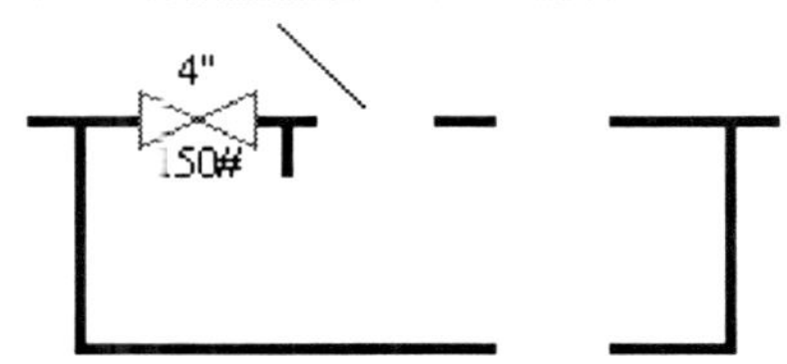


5. Repeat Steps 3 through 6 to place the other block valve. The drawing looks like this. (Can you think of an easier way to have achieved the same results?[*])

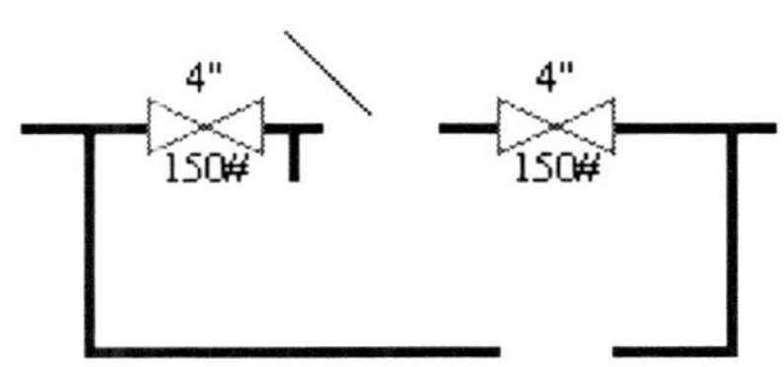


6. Save the drawing but don't exit.

**Command:** ***qsave***

We'll look at the dialog box approach next. Note that, although the dialog box presents a comfortable user interface, familiarity with the command line approach will prove quite handy when you use AutoCAD's iDrop tools.

| Do This: 20.2.2 | Using a Dialog Box to Insert Attributed Blocks |
|---|---|

I. Be sure you're still in the *pid-20.dwg* file the C:\Steps\Lesson20 folder.
II. Be sure the **Cont_Station1** view is still current.
III. Set the ***Attdia*** system variable to **1**. (This tells AutoCAD to use a dialog box for its attribute insertions.)
IV. Follow these steps.

[*] You could simply have copied the existing attributed valve

## 20.2.2: Inserting Attributed Blocks – Dialog Box

1. Insert the valve 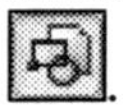. Put it at the endpoint of the opening in the bypass line. Accept the size and orientation defaults.

**Command: *i***

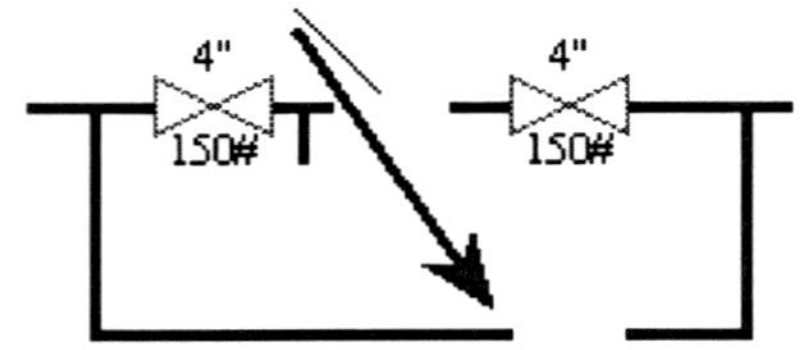


2. AutoCAD presents the Enter Attributes dialog box (below). The box shows the command line prompts with their defaults (yours may appear in a different order). Notice that no prompts are given for the **Filename** attribute. Remember that you created this one as a **Constant**; it can't be changed.

Enter the data shown, in the appropriate text boxes.

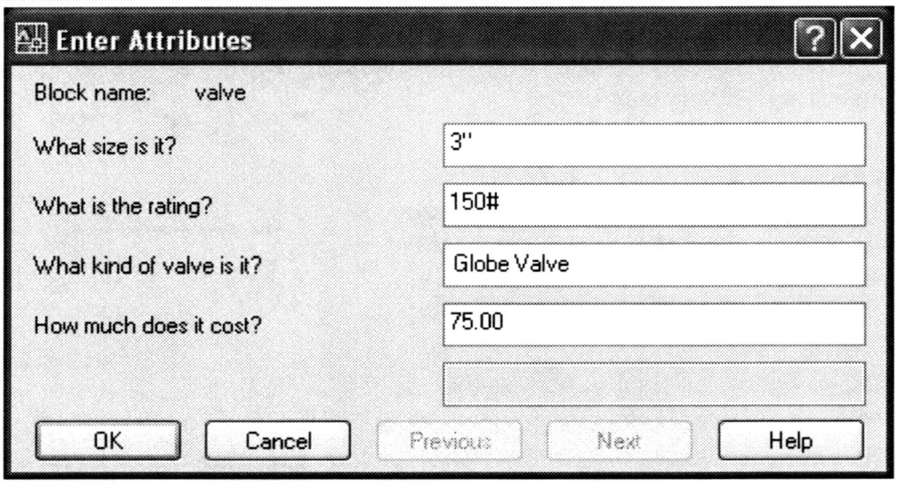


3. Pick the **OK** button  to complete the command.

4. Select **Globe Valve** from the list box. (Pick the down grip to display the list box.)

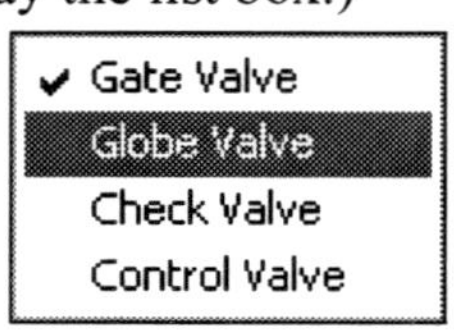


Your drawing looks like this.

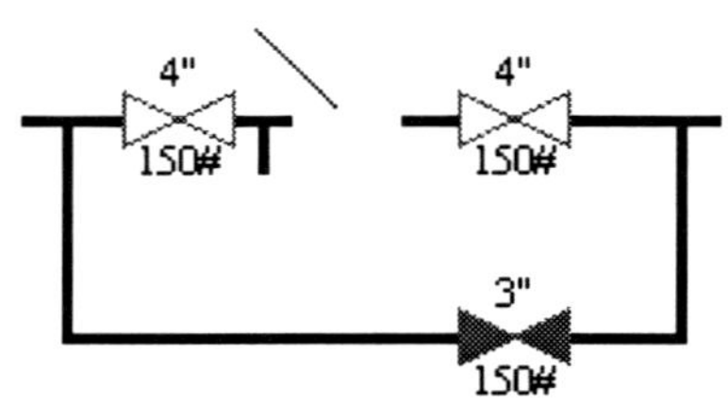


5. Save the drawing  but don't exit.

**Command: *qsave***

6. Insert  the valve (use the **Control Valve** selection) and the drain. (I created this already as *DrainVent*; it's in the C:\Steps\Lesson20 folder.)

- You'll need to move some of the visible attributes. Use grips.
- The price of the control valve is 175.00.

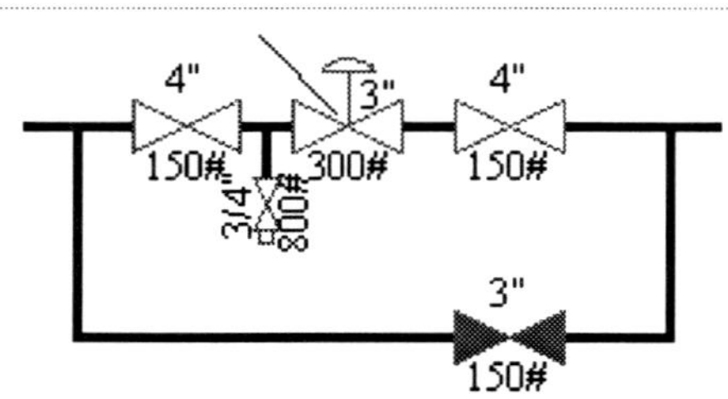

## 20.2.2: Inserting Attributed Blocks – Dialog Box

- Use a capped drain (list box).
- The price of the drain is 35.00.

**Command:** ***i***

The drawing looks like the one at right.

7. Save the drawing but don't exit.

**Command:** ***qsave***

8. Use these blocks to complete the drawing. (The blocks have already been created and can be found in the C:\Steps\Lesson20 folder.) See the completed drawing sections in Figures 20.004 through 20.008. Use the price list shown here to assign attribute values.

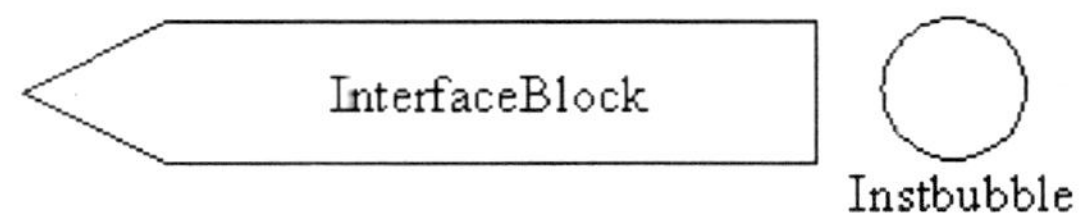


| SIZE/VALVE | GATE | GLOBE | CONTROL | CHECK |
|---|---|---|---|---|
| ¾" | 35.00 | | | |
| 2" | 55.00 | | | |
| 4" | 85.00 | 175.00 | 275.00 | |
| 6" | 127.00 | | | 195.00 |
| 8" | 385.00 | | | |
| 10" | 585.00 | | | |

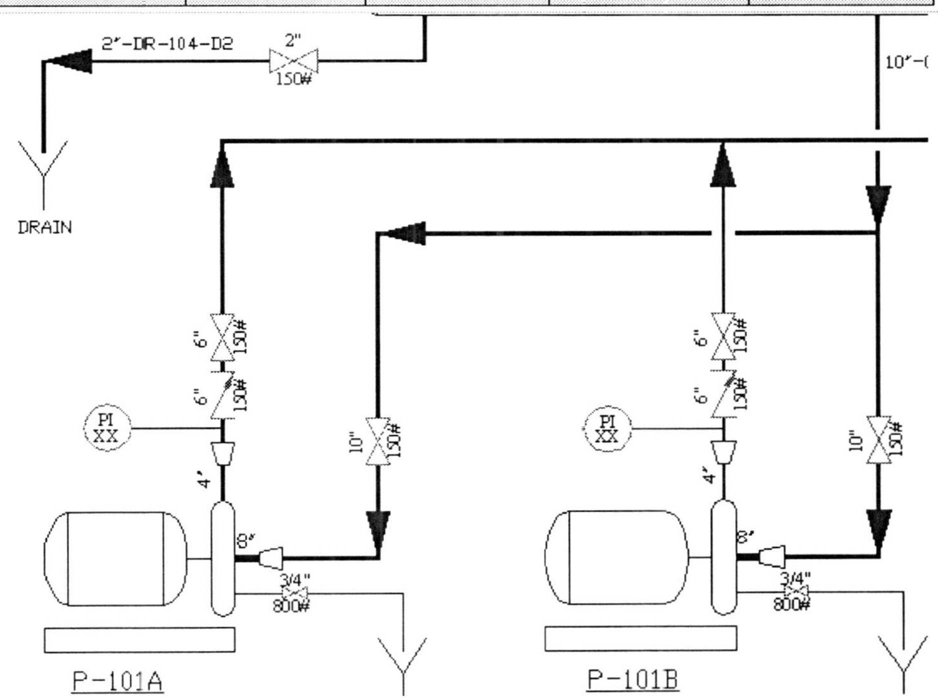


Figure 20.004

## 20.2.2: Inserting Attributed Blocks – Dialog Box

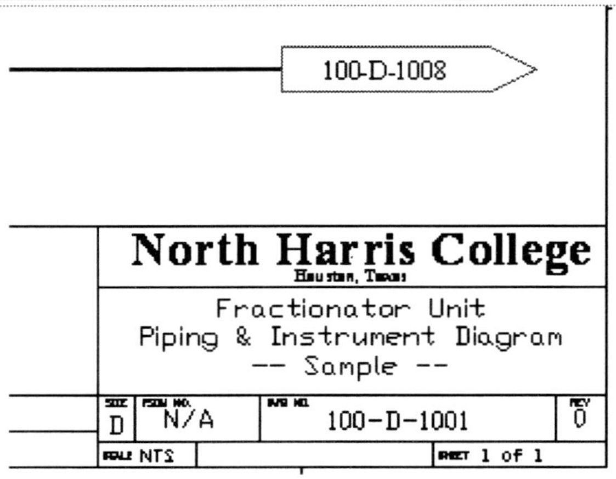


Figure 20.005

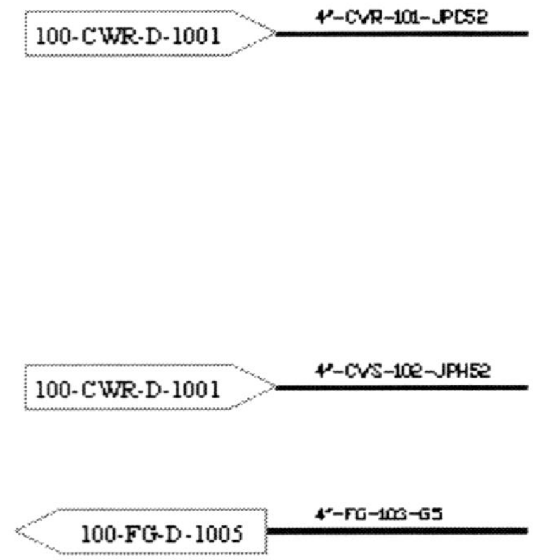


Figure 20.006

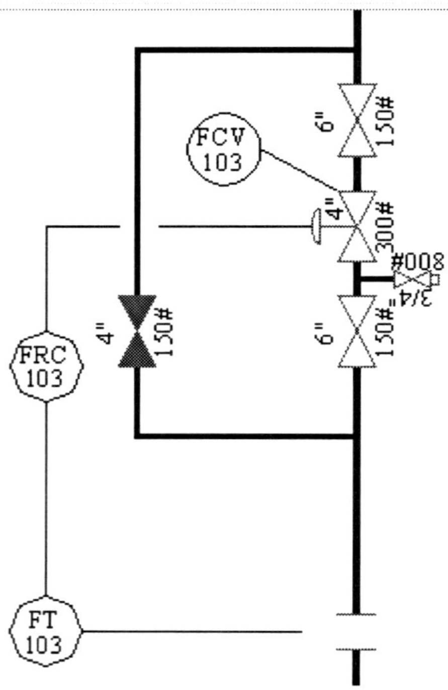


Figure 20.007

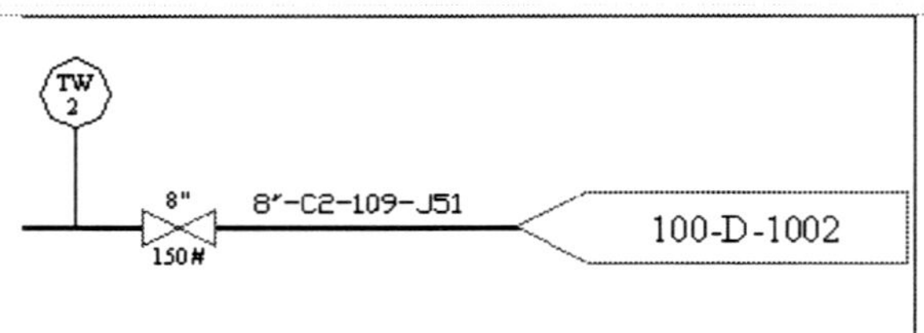


Figure 20.008

## 20.3 Editing Attributes

In previous editions of this text, I provided many pages of discussion for a couple block editing tools (***EAttEdit*** and ***DDAtte***). But this is a new release and blocks have become complicated enough without these monsters. So to keep life simple, I'm going to show you how to accomplish all the editing you'll need using a familiar tool – the Properties palette – and one really old command line tool – ***-ATTEdit*** (we'll need that one for universal changes).

For those of you who insist on doing things the hard way, I've placed this section of the '05 edition of *One Step at a Time* on the website. Go to: http://www.uneedcad.com/2006/Files . You'll find details on ***EAttEdit***, and ***DDAtte*** in a file called *EditingAttributes.pdf.* (Knock yourself out!)

## 20.3.1 Editing Attribute Values

Editing attribute values is as easy as calling the Properties palette.

### Do This: 20.3.1.1 Editing Attribute Values

When we inserted the gate valves, we assigned a price value of 55.00. According to the chart at the end of our last exercise, the price should be 85.00. Let's fix that.

I. Be sure you're still in the *pid-20.dwg* file the C:\Steps\Lesson20 folder. If you haven't finished this one, open *pid-20 Phase 2.dwg* instead.

II. Open the Properties palette and move it to the side of the screen.

III. Be sure the **Cont_Station1** view is current.

IV. Follow these steps.

**20.3.1.1: EDITING ATTRIBUTE VALUES**

1. Select both gate valves. The Properties palette changes to reflect this block's properties.

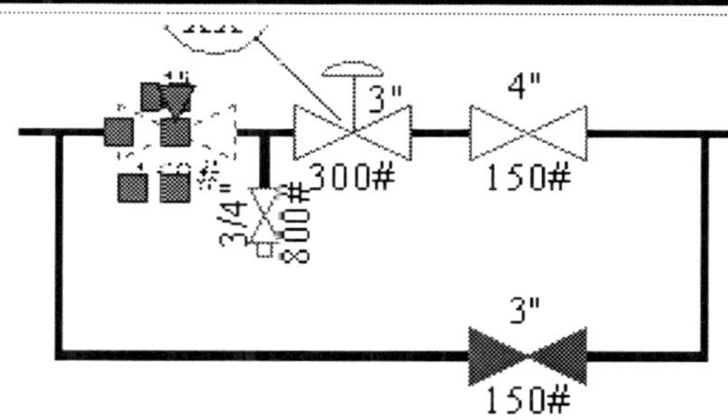


2. Scroll to the **Attributes** group and pick in the text area next to the **PRICE** attribute. Enter the correct value (shown).

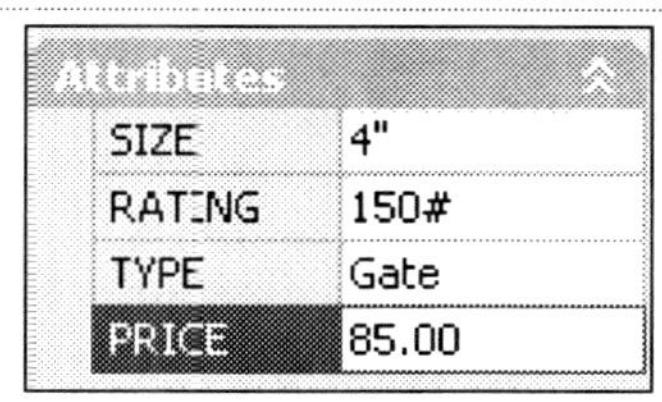


3. Save the drawing but don't exit.

**Command: *qsave***

Was that easy enough for you? (That same exercise contained 11 steps when we discussed ***DDAtte*** and ***EAttEdit***!) Take a moment and look over the other properties listed in the palette. Remember, you can edit the white values; the gray values are informational.

But what if you have several attributes to edit at once?

It's possible, using an older command line AutoCAD tool, to edit the values and some of the properties of attributes in multiple insertions of a block. The command sequence is:

**Command: *-attedit* (or *–ate*)**

**Edit attributes one at a time? [Yes/No] <Y>: *[enter]***

**Enter block name specification <*>: *[enter]***

**Enter attribute tag specification <*>: *[enter]***

**Enter attribute value specification <*>: *[enter]***

**Select Attributes:** ***[select the attributes to change]***

**Select Attributes:** ***[enter to complete the selection set]***

**1 attributes selected.** ***[AutoCAD reports how many attributes were selected]***

**Enter an option [Value/Position/Height/Angle/Style/Layer/Color/Next] <N>:** ***[tell AutoCAD what you want to do]***

- The first option – **Edit attributes one at a time?** – allows you to change attributes globally (or several at once).
- The next three lines ask for some specifics about what you wish to edit. You can simply hit ***enter*** at each prompt if you'll edit the attributes individually. The default is to accept all selected attributes for possible editing. But you can use these prompts to act as filters in a global selection set. For example, you can edit just the gate valves in our *PID-20* drawing by responding ***valve*** to the **Enter block name specification** prompt.
- After you select the attributes to edit, AutoCAD presents a line of options to help specify what type of editing to perform.
  - The **Value** option allows you to change the value of the attribute. Use this if you need to globally change a value. For example, assume the price of 4" globe valves has just changed. You could edit your drawing globally to change the value of the **Price** attribute for all 4" globe valves. It's easier to use the Properties palette to change individual values.

> An easy way to see the values of all the attributes attached to a block is to set the **Attdisp** system variable to **On**. The command sequence looks like this:
>
> **Command:** ***attdisp***
>
> **Enter attribute visibility setting [Normal/ ON/OFF] <Normal>:** ***on***
>
> It can be useful to display all the attributes when searching for errors, but the display can quickly become quite crowded.
>
> - The **Normal** option tells AutoCAD to display only those attributes created with the **Invisible** mode off.
> - Turning **Off** the ***Attdisp*** tells AutoCAD to hide all the attributes regardless of the **Invisible** mode setting. This setting will speed regeneration, but be careful not to place objects where they'll overlap the attributes when they're displayed again.

  - The **Position** option comes in quite handy when the value of an attribute is physically too large to fit in the area allotted for it (it overlaps something else). The ***Move*** command will move the entire block, but the **Position** option of the ***Attedit*** command (command line method) allows you to move just a single attribute. (Then again, so do grips!)
  - The **Angle** option is also quite handy for making attributes read properly despite the insertion rotation of the block.
  - The other options – **Height**, **Style**, **Layer**, and **Color** – allow you to edit these properties of attributes. If it's necessary to change any of these, however, it may be better to redefine the block(s) so that it inserts properly in the first place.

Let's try multiple attribute editing.

| Do This: 20.3.1.2 | Editing Attribute Values Globally |
|---|---|

I. Be sure you're still in the *pid-20.dwg* file (*or pid-20 Phase2.dwg*) in the C:\Steps\Lesson20 folder.

II. Be sure the **Cont_Station1** view is still current.

III. Follow these steps.

**20.3.1.2: EDITING ATTRIBUTE VALUES GLOBALLY**

1. Our project engineer has determined that this control station requires a higher rating for the block and bypass valves. Enter the ***-Attedit*** command.

    **Command: *-ate***

2. We want to edit all the 150# valves. Tell AutoCAD that you don't want to **Edit attributes one at a time**.

    **Edit attributes one at a time? [Yes/No] <Y>: *n***

AutoCAD responds that this will be a global edit.

    **Performing global editing of attribute values.**

3. We'll want only the valves on the screen to be affected by this editing.

    **Edit only attributes visible on screen? [Yes/No] <Y>: *[enter]***

4. We'll be editing more than one type of block, so leave this default at the global setting.

    **Enter block name specification <*>: *[enter]***

5. We want to edit only the **RATING** attributes. If we tell AutoCAD this, it won't change any other type of attribute.

    **Enter attribute tag specification <*>: *rating***

6. We don't need any further filtering for our edit.

    **Enter attribute value specification <*>: *[enter]***

7. Put a window around the entire control station; let AutoCAD sort things out for the **RATING** attributes.

    **Select Attributes:**

    **Select Attributes: *[enter]***

8. AutoCAD wants to know what to change …

    **Enter string to change: *150#***

9. … and what to make it.

    **Enter new string: *300#***

Your drawing looks like this.

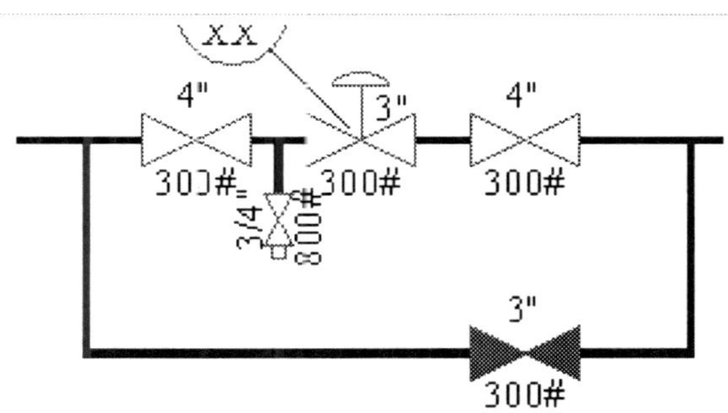


10. Save the drawing but don't exit.

**Command: *qsave***

Let's take a look at how we can edit an attribute's *definition* after creating the block.

## 20.3.2 Editing Attribute Definitions

With the Block Attribute Manager (Figure 20.009 – next page), AutoCAD has made editing attribute properties after block creation almost easier than editing them before you make the block! Access the manager with the ***BAttMan*** command, but exercise some caution when editing block properties. Remember that *modifications may affect all insertions of the block (current and future).*

Let's take a look.

- You'll probably notice the large list box first. Here AutoCAD lists the various attributes associated with the block shown in the **Block** control box above it. You can select another block from the control box, or you can use the **Select block** button to select a block from the drawing. The button is handy when you don't know the name of a particular block that needs editing.

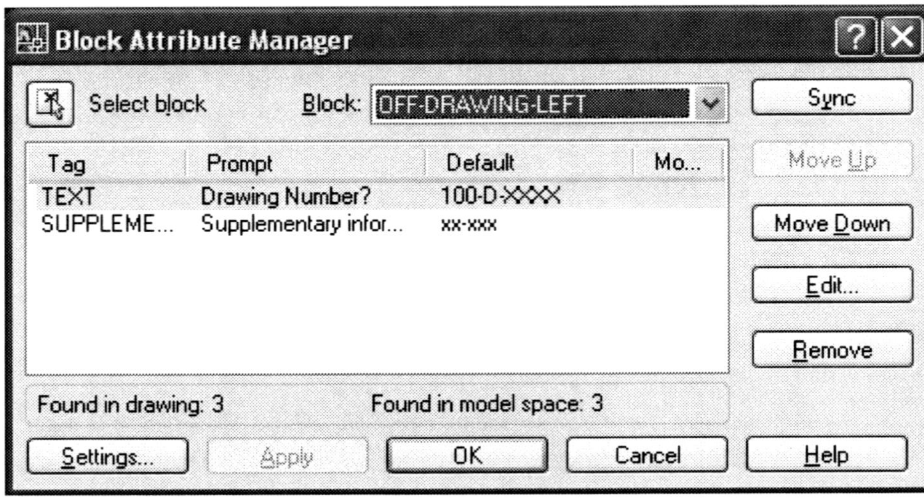


Figure 20.009

- For its size, this dialog box contains quite a few buttons.
    - Use the **Sync** button to update all insertions of the selected block with the currently defined attribute definitions. AutoCAD does this automatically when you edit but provides this manual procedure for those who prefer it.
    - AutoCAD lists the attributes in the list box in the order in which it prompts for values (when you insert the block). Use the **Move Up** and **Move Down** buttons to change the order of the prompts.
    - Use the **Remove** button to remove an attribute from a block definition. Be careful with this one. By default, AutoCAD will remove the attribute definition *and values* from all the insertions in the drawing; you may lose some information.
    - The **Apply** button (along the bottom of the box) applies your changes but leaves the dialog box open.
    - The **OK** button also applies your changes but closes the dialog box.
    - **Cancel** closes the dialog box without saving your changes.
    - **Help** calls the Help dialog box.
- The two buttons we omitted – **Edit** and **Settings** – each call additional dialog boxes.
    - The **Edit** button calls the Edit Attribute dialog box (Figure 20.010). Its three tabs provide access to the attribute definitions.
        - The **Attribute** tab (shown) allows you to change the **Mode**, **Tag**, **Prompt**, and **Default** settings.

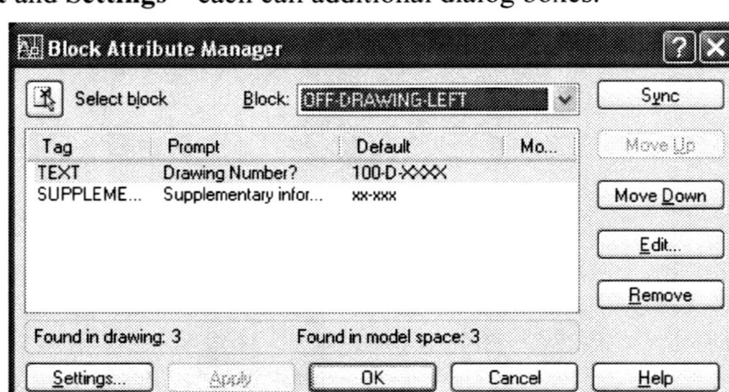


Figure 20.010

- The **Text Options** tab (Figure 20.011) allows you to
- change the **Text Style**, **Justification**, **Height**, Rotation, **Width Factor**, and **Oblique Angle**.

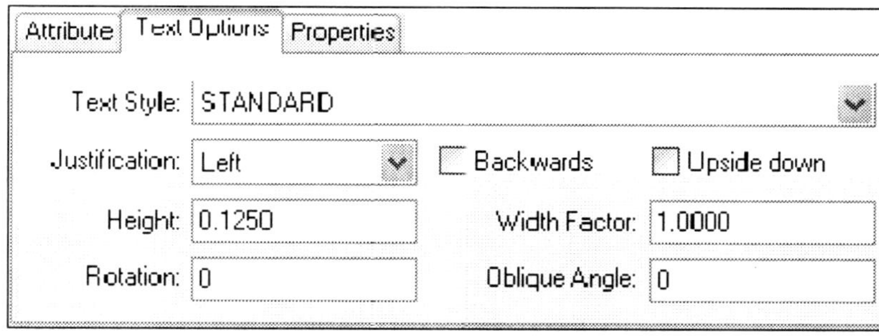


Figure 20.011

- The **Properties** tab (Figure 20.012) allows you to change the **Layer**, **Linetype**, **Color**, **Lineweight**, and **Plot style**.

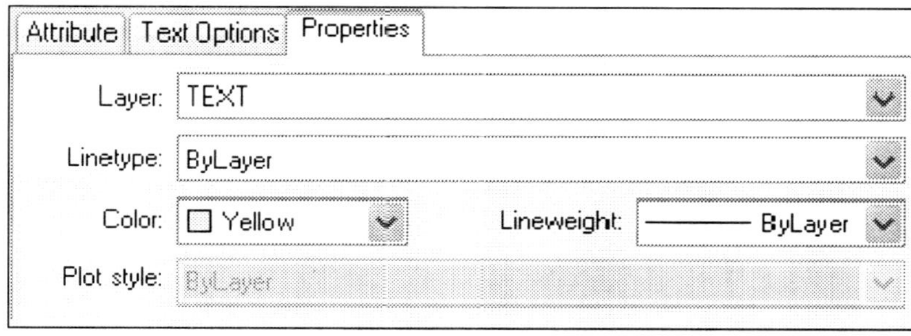


Figure 20.012

> The bottom of the Edit Attributes dialog box contains a simple check box that might save you some time and grief. Put a check next to **Auto preview changes** and you can see the changes take place on your screen as you make them. This nifty tool enables you to catch errors before locking yourself into them.

- The **Settings** button (back on the Block Attribute Manager) calls the Settings dialog box (Figure 20.013). Here you can tell AutoCAD exactly what (and what not) to show in the Block Attribute Manager.

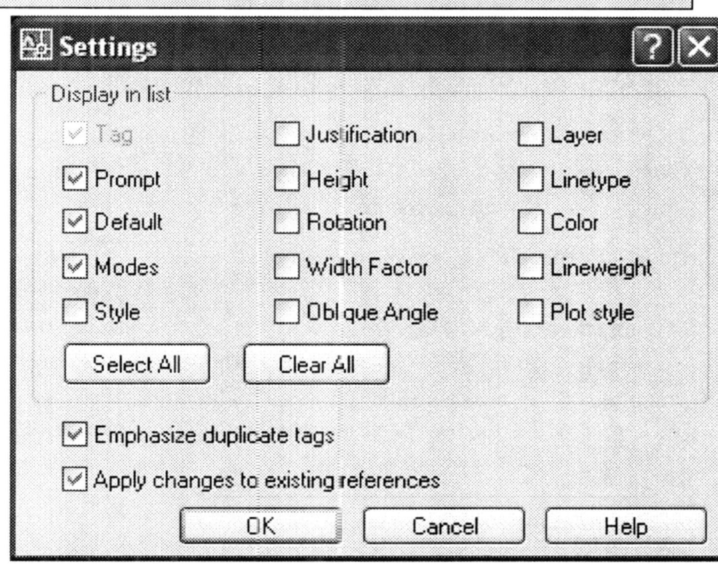


Figure 20.013

  - Use the check boxes in the **Display in list** frame to customize the list box of the Block Attribute Manager. A check next to an item tells AutoCAD to display that information in BAttMan's list box; a clear check box tells AutoCAD not to display it. When too many items are checked for AutoCAD to display them all, a scroll bar will appear in the bottom of the list box to allow you to see everything.
  - Use the **Emphasize duplicate tags** check box to have AutoCAD let you know if a block has attributes with duplicate tags in it. AutoCAD will highlight the duplications

where they occur. When that happens, you might want to change one of the tags for clarity.

- The purpose of **Apply changes to existing references** might seem a bit confusing, but understanding its use is quite important. A check next to this tool means that AutoCAD will update all current insertions of the block with the modifications you're making. Clear this box and AutoCAD will use the modifications for any new insertions but won't update existing blocks.

Let's see what BAttMan can do!

| Do This: 20.3.2.1 | Editing Attribute Definitions |
|---|---|

I. Open the *pid-20-done.dwg* file the C:\Steps\Lesson20 folder.

II. Restore the I_O_LEFT view. Your drawing looks like Figure 20.014.

III. Follow these steps.

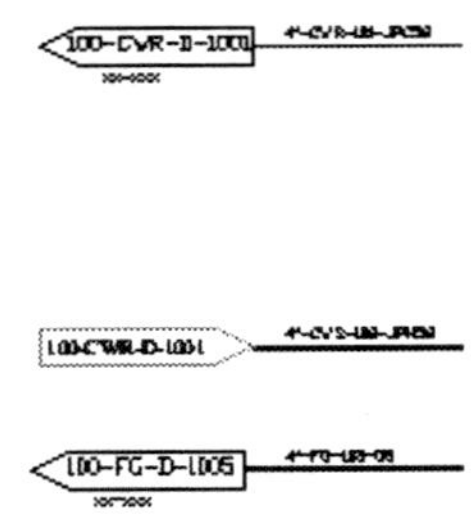

Figure 20.014

**20.3.2.1: EDITING ATTRIBUTE DEFINITIONS**

1. Open the Block Attribute Manager by entering ***battman*** at the command prompt.

Alternately, you can pick the **Block Attribute Manager** button on the Modify II toolbar or the Modify palette.

**Command: *battman***

2. On the Block Attribute Manager, pick the **Select block** button.

3. AutoCAD returns you to the graphics screen and prompts you to select a block. Select the upper block with the text that reads *100-CWR-D-1001*.

**Select a block:**

4. Select the **TEXT** attribute.

5. Pick the **Edit** button Edit... .

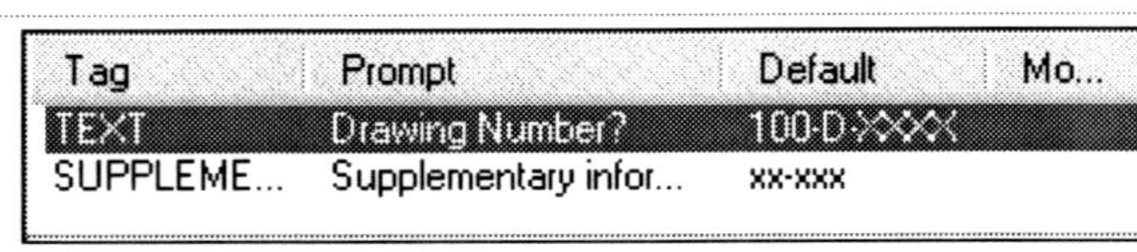


6. AutoCAD presents the Edit Attribute dialog box (Figure 20.010). Go to the **Text Options** tab Text Options .

7. On the **Text Options** tab, change the **Text Style** to **TIMES**.

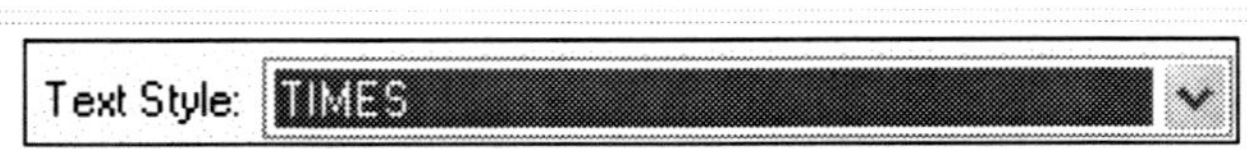


8. Go to the **Properties** tab Properties .

### 20.3.2.1: EDITING ATTRIBUTE DEFINITIONS

9. Notice that the attribute was placed on the **txt** layer rather than the **TEXT** layer that is standard in this drawing. Change it to the proper layer. (Be sure the **Color** control box is set to **ByLayer**.)

If there's a check next to **Auto Preview Changes**, you can already see your changes.

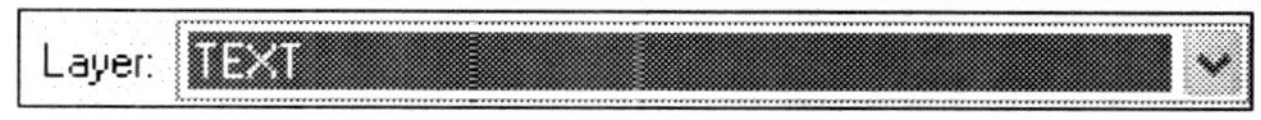


10. Pick the **OK** button 

to return to the Block Attribute Manager.

11. Now let's do something about that extra attribute. Select the **Supplementary** attribute in the list box and then pick the **Edit** button 

.

12. Go to the **Attribute** tab 

.

13. Rather than delete the extra attribute (there's always a chance we might need it later), we'll simply make it invisible. Place a check in the proper **Mode** box.

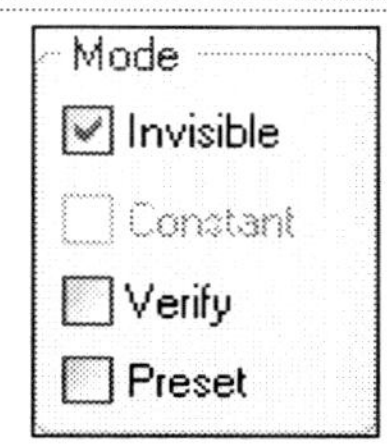


14. Pick the **OK** button 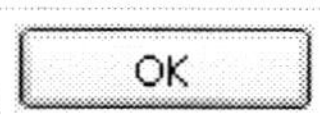

to return to the Block Attribute Manager, and again to complete the procedure.

15. Save the drawing 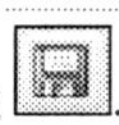.

**Command:** ***qsave***

Oh, yeah.

## 20.4 The Coup de Grace: Using Attribute Information in Bills of Materials, Spreadsheets, or Database Programs

This nifty stuff is guaranteed to move you to the head of the class!

One of the most useful and timesaving devices available to AutoCAD users lies in AutoCAD's ability to save steps along the road to project completion. In this section of our lesson, we'll discover how to use the information we've attached to our blocks. We'll extract the data into a table, *and* we'll simultaneously export the table and import it into a Microsoft Excel spreadsheet (for the folks in the Materials department).

> Again, there's an older procedure involving the ***ATText*** command. But I'm not even going to post that procedure as the one we're about to discuss is infinitely easier.

After so much work creating blocks, dynamic blocks, and attributes, extracting the data might seem almost anticlimactic. You just have to follow instructions in a wizard! (Access the wizard using the ***EAtText*** command.)

Let's give it a shot.

> You can also access the ***EAtText*** command using the Tools pull down menu. Follow this path:
> *Tools – Attribute Extraction*

| Do This: 20.4.1 | Extracting Attribute Data |
|---|---|

I. Reopen the *pid-20 Phase 2.dwg* file (or the *pid-20 Phase 2-2006.dwg* file) the C:\Steps\Lesson20 folder.

II. Set the **TEXT** layer current and zoom all.

III. Follow these steps.

## 20.4.1: EXTRACTING ATTRIBUTE DATA

1. Enter the ***EAtText*** command. Alternately, you can pick the **Attribute Extraction** button  on the Modify II toolbar or the Modify palette.

**Command: *eattext***

AutoCAD begins the Attribute Extraction wizard.

2. You'll find two options on the Begin page (figure below):

- **Create table or external file from scratch**
- **Use template**

You haven't created a template yet (although you'll have a chance soon), so select the **Create table** option, and the pick the **Next** button to continue.

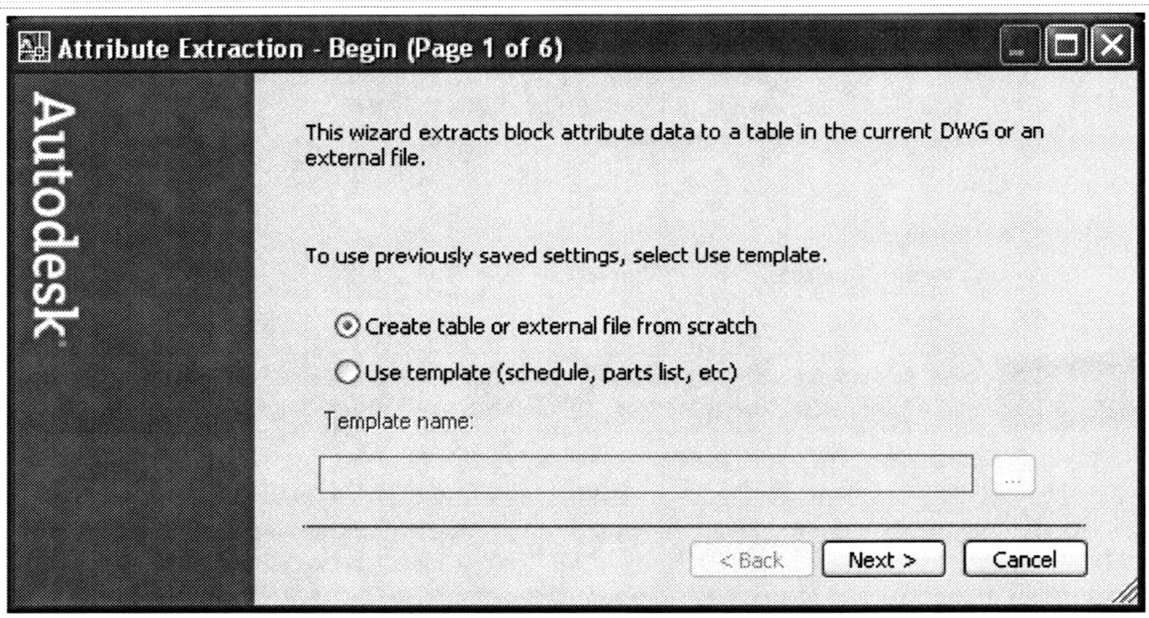

## 20.4.1: Extracting Attribute Data

3. The Select Drawings page presents some options in the **Data source** frame:

- **Select objects** allows you to select the blocks you'd like to include in your table. You'll use the **Select blocks** button to return to the screen.
- A bullet next to **Current drawing** tells AutoCAD to use all the blocks in the drawing.
- Finally, if you wish to create a table from multiple drawings or sheet sets (more on sheet sets in Lesson 24), place your bullet next to **Select drawings/sheet sets**. AutoCAD will include all blocks in the selected drawings or sheet sets. Use the **Click to browse** button to select the drawings/sheet sets.

The Additional Settings button calls an Additional Settings dialog box where you can filter for: **Nested blocks**, **Xrefs** (more on Xrefs in Lesson 25), or **Model Space**.

We'll create our table from the blocks in the current drawing only. Place the bullet as shown, and pick the **Next** button to continue.

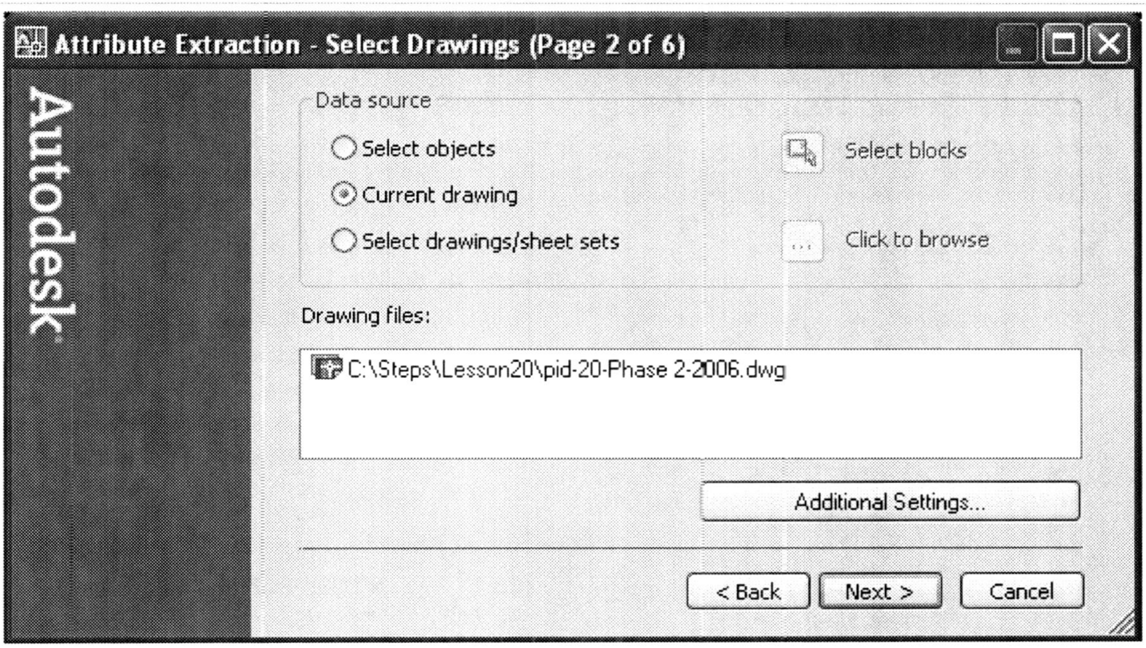

4. Now we come to the key page – Select Attributes.

- You'll find two check boxes across the top:
  - **Exclude blocks without attributes** simply means that you won't have extra blocks to clutter up your selection boxes.
  - **Exclude general block properties** means that AutoCAD won't display information relating strictly to drawing properties (color, layer, linetype, etc.)

  Check both of the boxes for now.
- Next you'll find two selection list boxes:
  - The **Blocks** box lists the blocks available for your table. We'll select only the valve blocks (**valve** and **DrainVent**). Clear the rest.
  - The **Properties for checked blocks** lists all the properties (Attributes) available for the blocks you checked in the Blocks list. Select the ones shown.

Pick the **Next** button to continue.

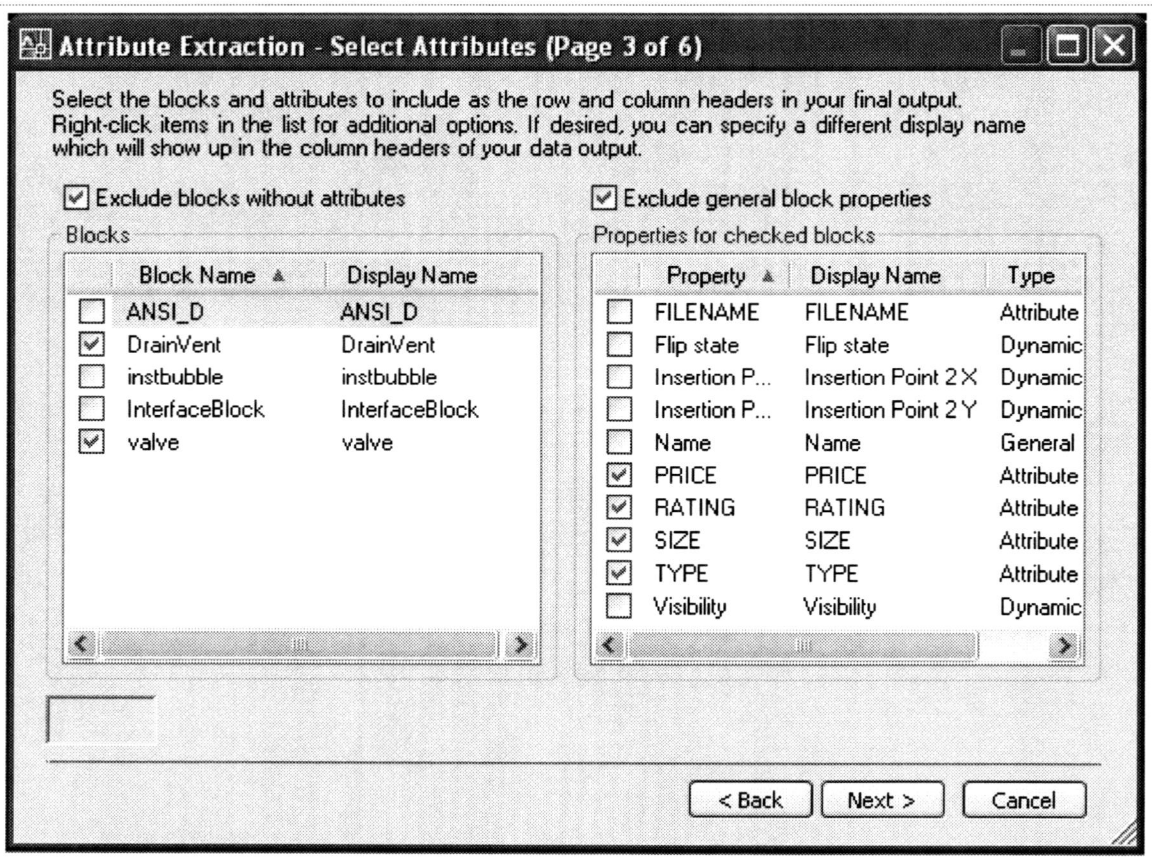

5. On the Finalize Output page, you'll set up your table's data.
    - Adjust the grid by dragging the column headers to the desired position. Adjust yours to look like the image below.
    - Adjust the order by picking in a column header – pick in **TYPE** until the arrow points upward, as shown.
    - Below the list box, notice the **Extract attribute data to** frame. Here you'll tell AutoCAD to extract to a table or to an external file. Pick both.

      You'll have to pick the **...** button next to the text box to name and locate the extraction file. Your file type options include: **csv** (comma delimited format suitable for importing into many other applications), **xls** (Microsoft Excel file), **mdb** (Microsoft Access file), and **txt** (simple text file).

      Create the extraction file indicated.
    - You can use the **Full Preview** button to see the data if you wish.

Pick the **Next** button to continue.

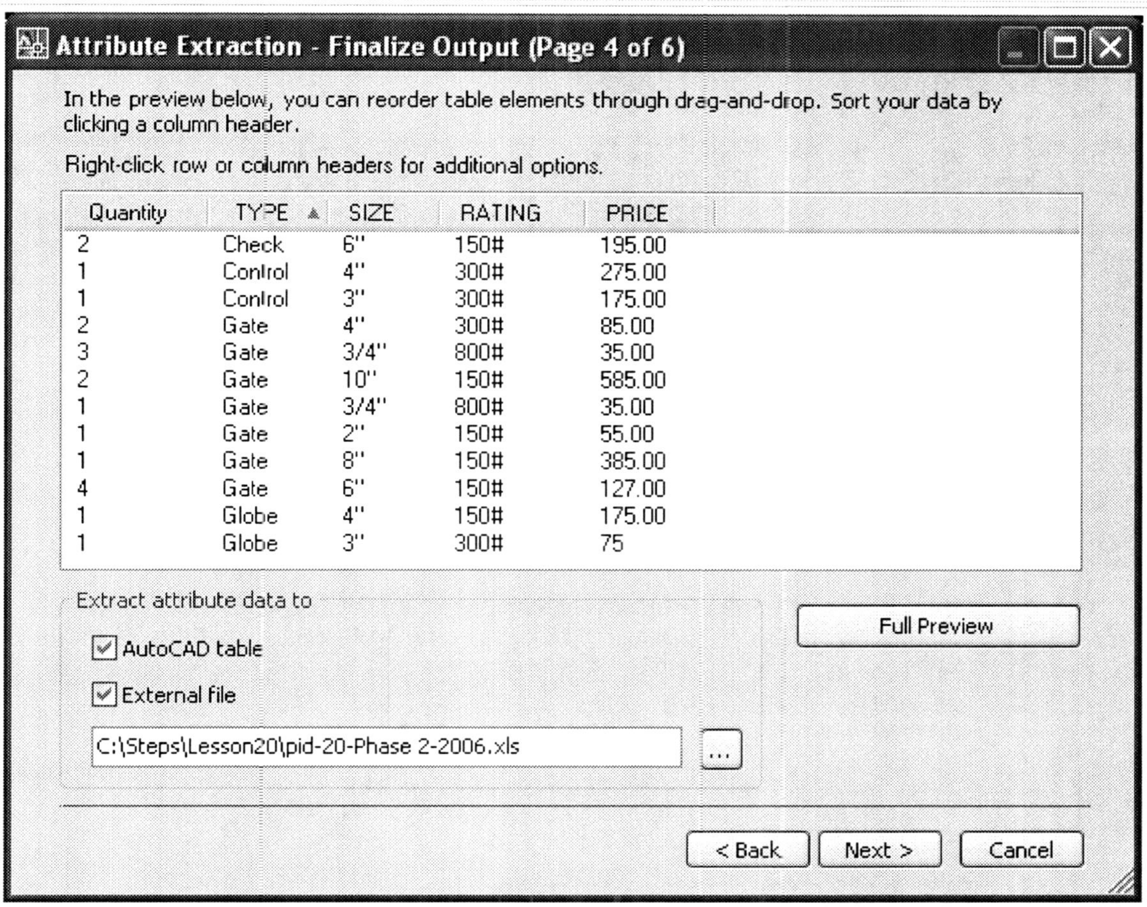

6. Now you'll select the Table Style. In the Table Style settings frame of the Table Style page:
   - **Enter a title for your table** (we'll call ours Valves List).
   - **Select a table style** (I provided the **Valve Table**, but you can use the **Table Style** button next to the control box to open the Table Style dialog box and create your own).
   - Leave the check next to **Display tray notification when data needs refreshing** so that AutoCAD will notify you in the status tray when your table needs updating.

(This really is easy, isn't it?) Pick the **Next** button to continue.

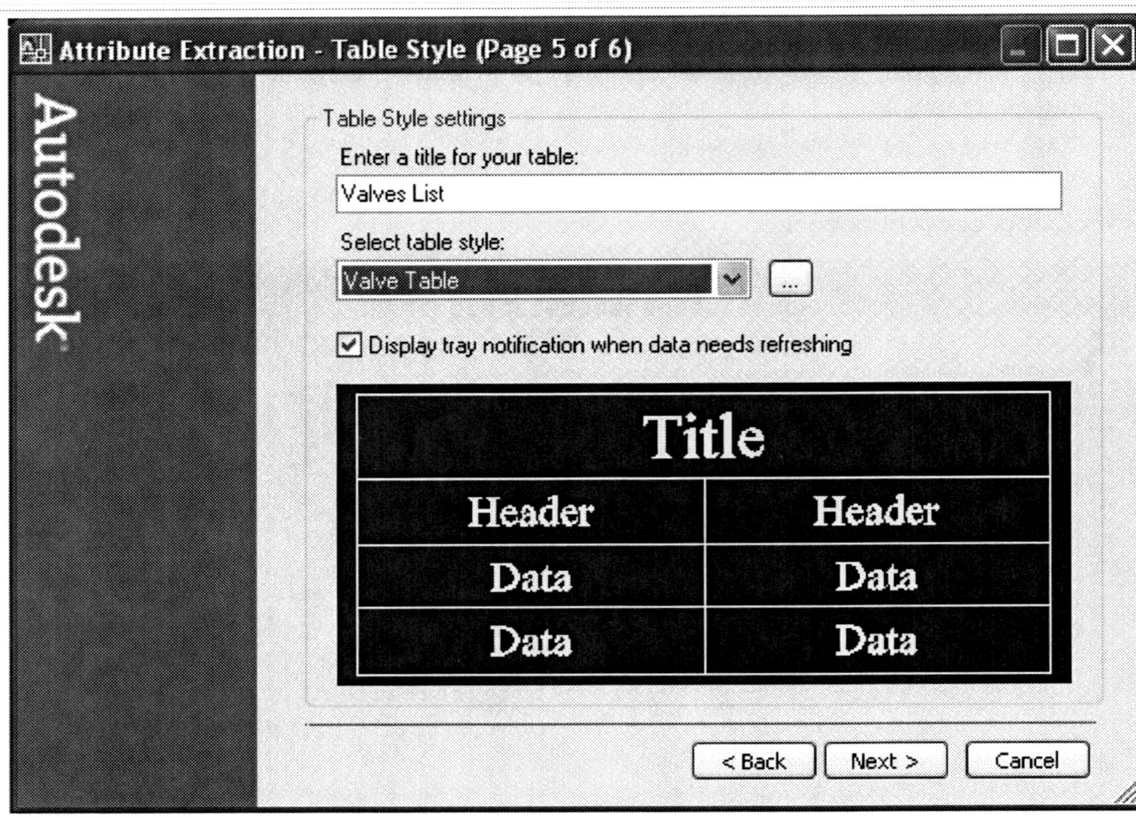


7. The only option left is to save your setup as a template. Go ahead and do that now (pick the **Save template** button). Save the template as *PID-20.blk* to the C:\Steps\Lesson20 folder. Then pick the **Finish** button to insert the table. (As the window says, once you finish, AutoCAD will automatically generate your spreadsheet and place it in the appropriate folder.)

## 20.4.1: Extracting Attribute Data

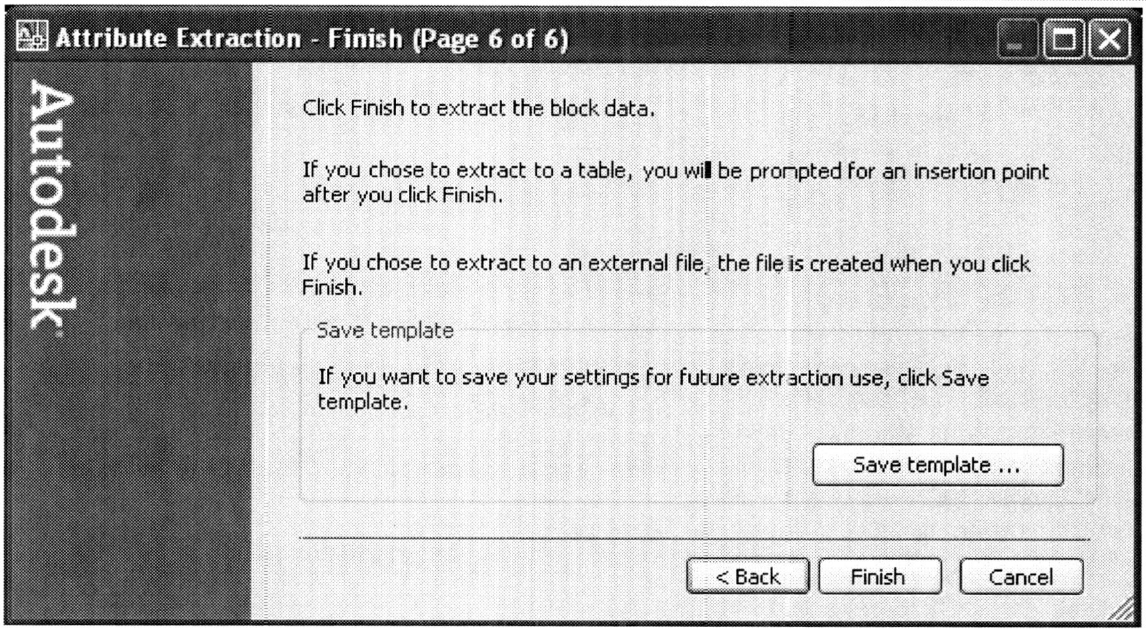


8. Locate the table around coordinates 3,7.

    **External file "C:\Steps\Lesson20\pid-20-Phase 2-2006.xls" was successfully created.**

    **Specify insertion point:** ***3,7***

    The table looks like this.

| Valve List | | | | |
|---|---|---|---|---|
| Quantity | TYPE | SIZE | RATING | PRICE |
| 2 | Check | 6" | 150# | 195.00 |
| 1 | Control | 4" | 300# | 275.00 |
| 1 | Control | 3" | 300# | 175.00 |
| 3 | Gate | 3/4" | 800# | 35.00 |
| 2 | Gate | 4" | 300# | 85.00 |
| 1 | Gate | 2" | 150# | 55.00 |
| 1 | Gate | 3/4" | 800# | 35.00 |
| 1 | Gate | 8" | 150# | 385.00 |
| 2 | Gate | 10" | 150# | 585.00 |
| 4 | Gate | 6" | 150# | 127.00 |
| 1 | Globe | 3" | 300# | 75 |
| 1 | Globe | 4" | 150# | 175.00 |

9. Save the drawing but don't exit.

    **Command:** ***qsave***

That may get a "way, cool," but you're not finished yet! Let's do one more thing.

| Do This: 20.4.2 | Updating Attribute Data in a Table |
|---|---|

I. Continue in the *pid-20 Phase 2.dwg* file.

II. Zoom in to the lower left quadrant of the screen so you can see the table and the pump next to it.

III. Follow these steps.

## 20.4.2: Updating Attribute Data in a Table

1. Erase the ¾" drain valve indicated.

**Command: *e***

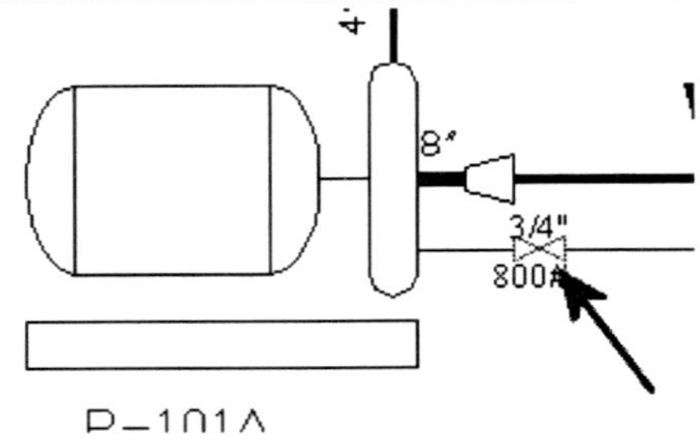


2. Notice the balloon letting you know that the table needs refreshing and offering you a chance to do so. Pick **Refresh table data**. (Note: If you do not get the message balloon, right click on the selected table and pick **Update Table – Refresh Only** from the cursor menus.)

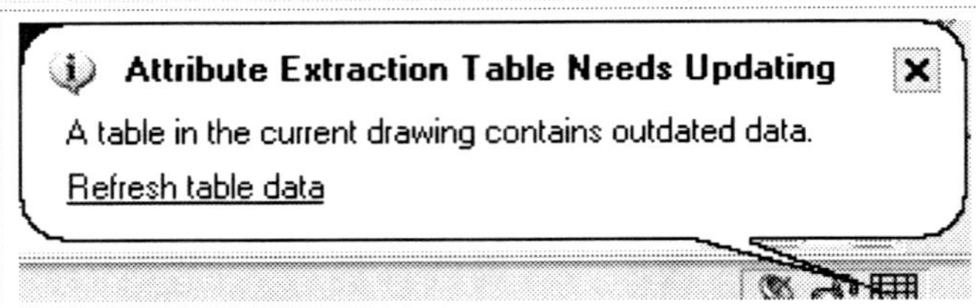


3. Now examine the table (Figure 20.040. Notice that it now lists only two ¾"-800# Gate valves!

| | | | | |
|---|---|---|---|---|
| 2 | Gate | 10" | 150# | 585.00 |
| 2 | Gate | 3/4" | 800# | 35.00 |
| 1 | Gate | 2" | 150# | 55.00 |

4. Save the drawing .

**Command: *qsave***

You can edit what you've created by selecting **Update Table – Edit Extraction Settings** from the cursor menu when you right click in the selected table.

Okay, now you can do the "Way, COOL!"

## 20.5 Extra Steps

Check out the Excel spreadsheet you created in Exercise 20.4.1 (if you have a copy of MS Excel). You'll notice a couple things:

- Both number columns (**Quantity** and **Price**) are formatted as text. You'll have to select the columns and use the Excel converter to turn the data into numbers so you (or your Materials rep.) can total the **Price** column.
- The quantity of ¾"-800# valves did not update as did the table in your drawing. You'll still have to notify the Materials folks when there's a change. (There's a thought for future releases; you listening, Autodesk?)

## 20.6 What Have We Learned?

*Items covered in this lesson include:*

- *Creating, Inserting, and Manipulating Block Attributes*
  - ***Attdef***
  - ***Insert***
- *Attribute display commands:*
  - ***Attdia***
  - ***Attdisp***

- *Attreq*

- *Editing Attributes*
  - ***Attedit***
  - *The Properties Palette*
  - ***BAttMan***
- *Extracting Attribute Data*
  - ***Eattext***

In this lesson, we learned what makes AutoCAD worth the price you (or your company) paid for it. Here we saw how we can shave weeks from a project by spending a day or two in additional setup time. This savings translates into increased profit for the company by cutting production time (thus increasing the amount of work possible in a given period of time). It means more money for the trained operator because it's his or her training that makes the savings possible.

What we've done in this lesson is to cover the methods and techniques available that can accomplish these savings. But it's often up to you, the CAD operator and designer, to explain, demonstrate, and even sell these possibilities to the people and companies for whom you work. Remember that CAD is still relatively new to many people. They are relying on your expertise to show them what can be done!

## 20.7 Exercises

2. Using what you've learned, create the drawing at right.
   2.1. Place the drawing on an appropriate title block (it was created on a 34"x22" sheet of paper and is NTS).
   2.2. Using attributes, create a BOM.

*For more exercises related to Lesson 20, please see Lesson 20 in AutoCAD 2007: One Step at a Time – Workbook.*

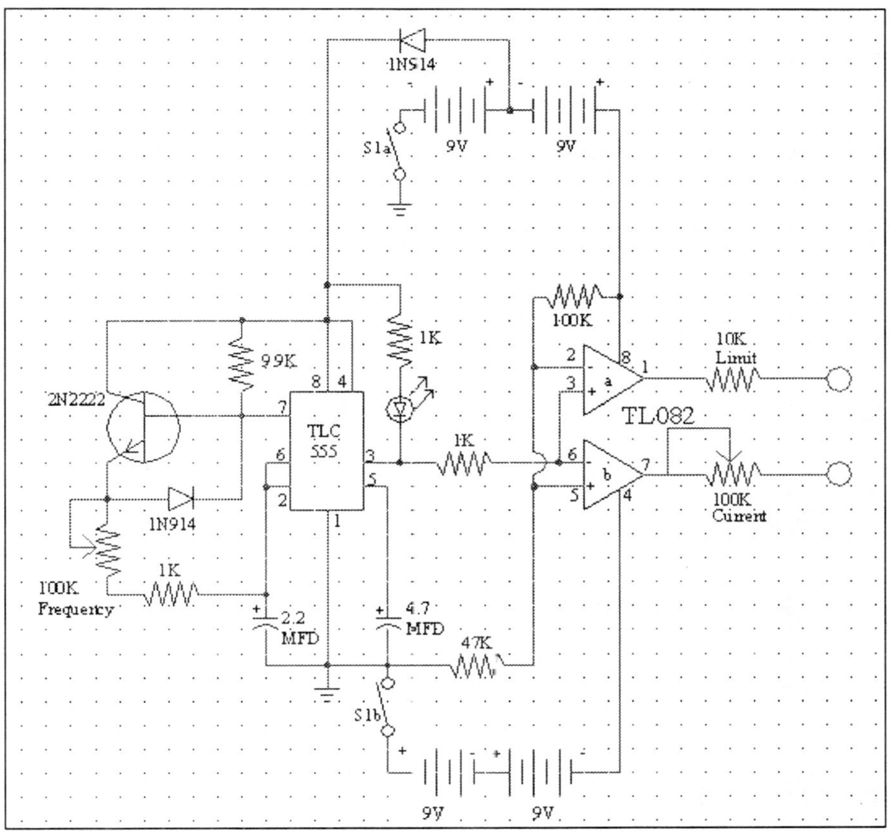


Design Courtesy of Thomas Miller or Richmond, Indiana

## 20.8 For Web-Based Review Questions, visit: http://www.uneedcad.com/2007/Files/07R20.pdf

# Lesson 21

Following this lesson, you will:

- ✓ *Know how to plot a drawing*
    - o *Setting up a drawing (page)*
    - o *Plotting*
- ✓ *Know how to plot multiple drawings at one time*
- ✓ *Know how to create an eTransmittal*
- ✓ *Know how to publish a drawing to the web*

# Sharing Your Work with Others

*A General Note to Students and Instructors:*

Many instructors prefer to cover plotting early in a course; others prefer to cover it at the end. For this reason, we've made this lesson completely modular. The instructor might choose to cover this material earlier in the course.

However, I don't recommend covering this material later than this. Material in the next few chapters assumes familiarization with plotting.

*Goods which are not shared are not goods.*

*Vernando de Rojas,* **La Celestina**, *Act 1*

*Sharing. This simple word might carry different meanings for different people. Indeed, it might mean something different for the same person depending on the circumstances.*

*Certainly, you must share the results of your labor – at least if you want to get paid for it – and for this purpose, AutoCAD provides the tried-and-true* ***Plot*** *command as well as the eTransmit tools and the newer* ***Publish*** *command.*

*We'll start with the* ***Plot*** *command and explore the ways AutoCAD has provided for you to share the work and then share the fruit.*

*Let's begin.*

The terms print and plot are used interchangeably in industry – and in this lesson.

## 21.1 The Old-Fashioned Way – Putting It on Paper (Plotting)

*It seems that we'll never escape our paper world!*

*Lamentations for a Pine Tree*

*Anonymous*

The ironic thing about CAD is that, after all the wonders of the computer world have created this marvelous drawing; in the end, you still need that paper for construction. After all, it might be a bit clumsy to fold a PC and stick it in your tool belt down at the job site (and not many companies are ready to provide those cool pocket computers to their field workers … yet!)

Fortunately, AutoCAD has made it fairly painless to make the transfer from computer to paper. We'll use a series of dialog boxes that will guide us through the process – *One Step at a Time*.

Let's get started!

### 21.1.1 First Things First – Setting Up Your Printer (or Plotter)

Before actually printing a document in any application, you must first tell the application which printing device you'll use. The reasons are technical and involve those driver gizmos about which you've probably read. All printers ship with their own drivers. You must help the application – in this case, AutoCAD – to figure out which one to use.

Fortunately, that isn't as complicated as it might seem, and it only needs to be done once for each plotting device.

Since most people won't have plotters available to them, I've moved the printer/plotter setup section of this chapter to a supplemental pdf file. (Download *PlotterSetup.pdf* from here: *http://www.uneedcad.com/Files/PlotterSetup.pdf*.) If you don't have a plotter, you can ignore it. If you or your company will use a plotter, you might want to go through those instructions first.

I must distinguish between printers and plotters here (as opposed to printing and plotting). *Printers* are comparatively inexpensive devices that usually sit on a desk or table and use letter or legal size paper. *Plotters* are much larger and are generally used to create drawings on C, D, or E size sheets of paper.

As a rule, AutoCAD can print to a printer using the computer's settings; you won't need to do any additional set up. Plotters, on the other hand, will require some efforts on your part.

### 21.1.2 Plot Styles

Believe it or not, there will be times when you must ask yourself, "Do I want to print it the way I drew it or some other way – different lineweights, linetypes, colors, etc.?" Personally, I've always been a firm advocate of *WYSIWYG* technology (see the insert), but there will be times when a change at plot time is necessary. (Some folks even prefer to set lineweights and linetypes at plot time!?) For example, my printer uses color. I like that, but I can't afford the cost of printer cartridges when I must print working drawings in full color. So I prefer to print in black-and-white until the final product is ready. With plot styles, I can do that without affecting the drawing. (Of course, for those of you who would rather wait until you create a plot to see what it looks like, you can always set weights and types using plot styles.)

**WYSIWYG** (pronounced "whiz-ee-wig") – literally, "What You See Is What You Get" – simply means that what appears on your screen is what will appear on your paper. This may seem obvious (and generally is for other types of documents). But some gurus prefer to assign (or change) such things as lineweights, linetypes, or colors at plot time rather than during the drawing setup.

As with plotters, you're fairly unlikely to need this information. However, I understand that once I say that .... Anyway, I've put details on setting up plot styles in a supplemental pdf file for those who'll need it. (*Download PlotStyleSetup.pdf* from here: *http://www.uneedcad.com/Files/PlotStyleSetup.pdf*.)

### 21.1.3 Setting Up the Page to Be Plotted

As with plotter setups and table setups, you don't absolutely have to know how to set up a page for printing/plotting. However, in this case, it's a good thing to know as it may save you a lot of time as using named page setups means that you won't have to repeat the setup every time you plot.

It isn't difficult; although it isn't as easy as the initial dialog box (the Page Setup Manager – Figure 21.001 – next page) might indicate.

When you access the Page Setup Manager with the ***PageSetup*** command (or by picking Page Setup Manager from the File pull down menu), AutoCAD presents Figure 21.001. Here you see two frames – one in which you'll work and one for information. Additionally, there are two fairly standard buttons and a check box.

- Most of your work will occur in the **Page setups** frame. Here, AutoCAD begins by telling you the **Current page setup** (**None** in our figure) and presents a list of existing setups from which you can select. Selecting a setup from the list means that your work here is finished. But if that was all there was to it, you wouldn't need those buttons down the side of the frame.
    - Use the **Set Current** button to use the selected setup to do your printing.

- The **New** and **Modify** buttons present dialog boxes. **New** gives you an opportunity to name the new setup before continuing (Figure 21.002). After you name the new setup, AutoCAD presents the Page Setup dialog box. (**Modify** takes you directly to the Page Setup dialog box and makes the selected setup's information available for modification.) We'll look at the Page Setup dialog box in more detail in a moment.

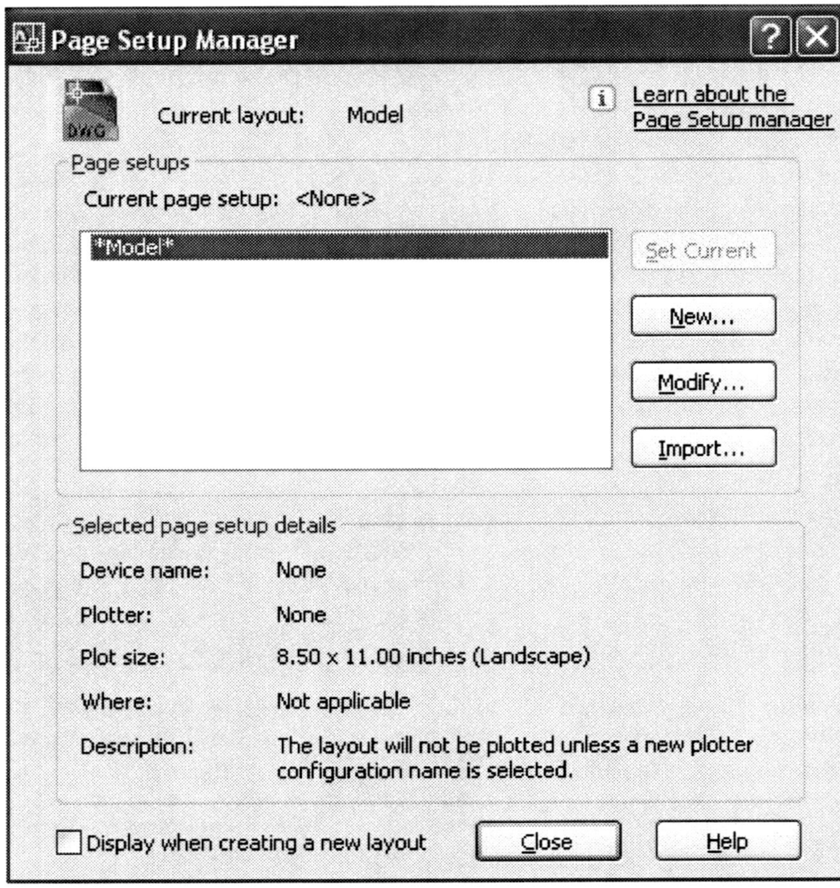


Figure 21.001

- **Import** allows you to take the page setup definition from another drawing and make it a definition in your drawing. You'll use a common Select File dialog box for this one and select a DWT file (a template).

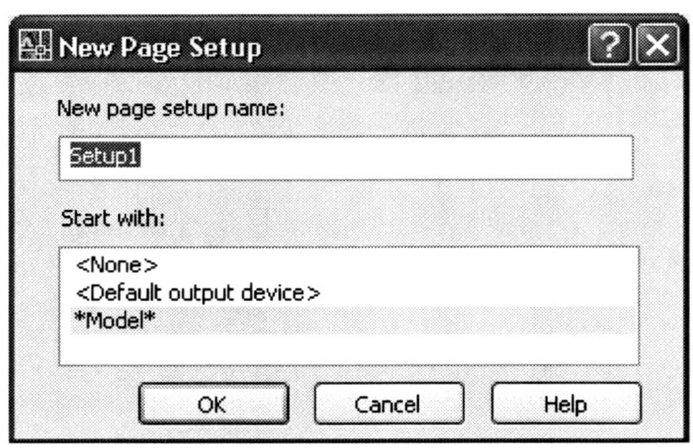


Figure 21.002

- The **Selected page setup details** frame provides information about the selected setup. Use this information to be sure you've selected the correct setup for your plot.
- Placing a check next to **Display when creating a new layout** won't mean anything to you at this point – even if you've gone through the twenty chapters ahead of this one. It will, however, prove useful when you begin using Paper Space. We'll look at Paper Space in Lessons 22 and 23.

You can also remove a setup using the Page Setup Manager. Simply select the setup and use the DELETE key on your keyboard.

The important thing to remember about the manager you've just seen is that it provides only the opportunity to select an existing setup for use, or to create or modify a setup. It doesn't create the setup for you. You'll need the Page Setup dialog box for that (Figure 21.003) ... and it's a ten-frame doozy! Let's begin in the upper left corner and take a look.

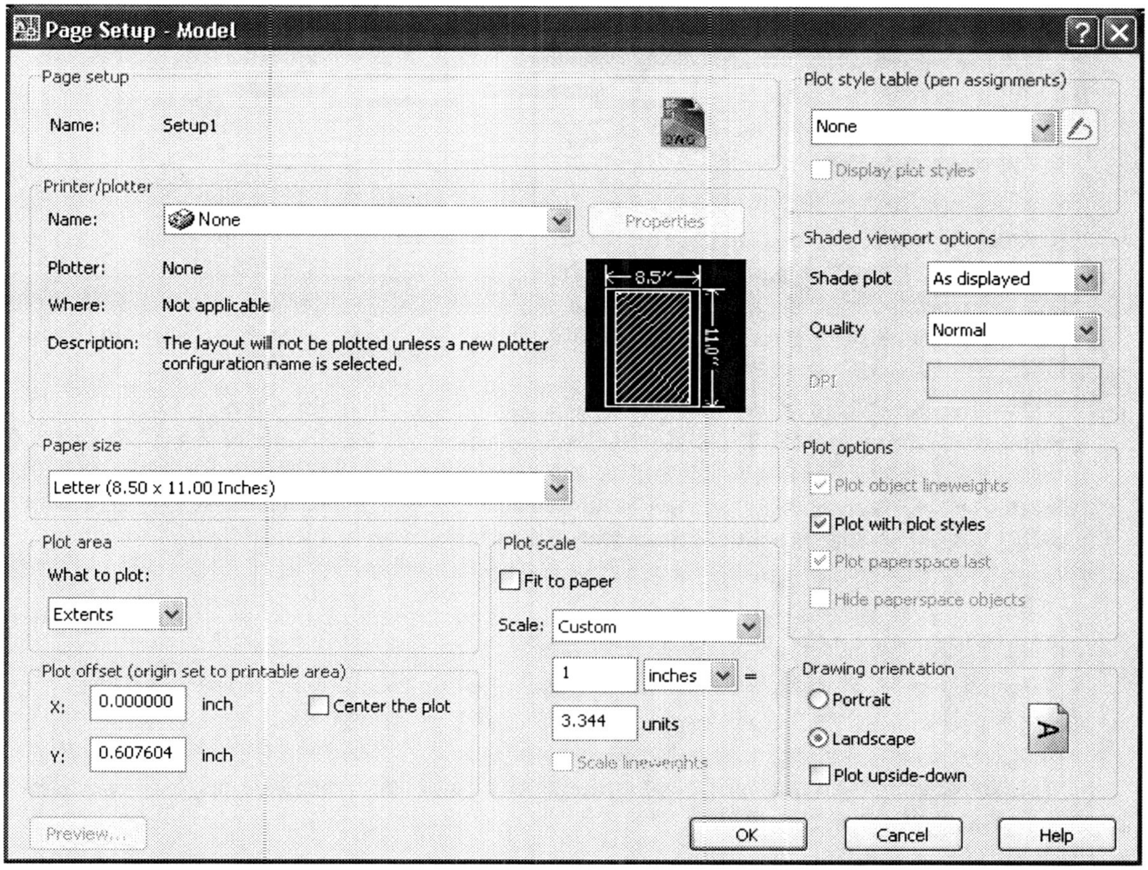


Figure 21.003

- The first frame – **Page setup** – is harmless enough. It tells you the name of the setup you're creating or modifying.
- The next frame down – **Printer/plotter** – allows you to select the device you'll use for this setup. Select the device from the **Name** drop down box and set any properties you want on the device via the **Properties** button just to the right of the control box. This is fairly simply stuff (and standard for most computer applications) as long as the device you want to use is on the list. If it isn't, you'll need to set it up. Refer to the plotter setup supplement for this. AutoCAD fills the rest of the frame with useful information about the selected device and the orientation of the setup.
- Below the **Printer/plotter** frame, you'll find the **Paper size** frame, which you'll use for selecting the size of the paper on which you wish to print.
- The **Plot area** frame also contains only a single drop down box. Use it to select exactly what you want to plot on the drawing. AutoCAD allows you to plot just the currently displayed portion of the drawing, the drawing's extents, limits, or an area defined by a window. (If you've opted to complete this lesson out of order, these options will become clearer as you complete the first few lessons.)
- Use the tools within the handy **Plot offset (origin set to printable area)** frame to adjust where your drawing lands on the page. I've found that a check in the box next to **Center the**

**plot** works well for my printing, but you can adjust the position manually using the **X** and **Y** boxes if you wish.

- The **Plot scale** frame contains some critical options.
    - o A check next to **Fit to paper** eliminates any effort to plot to scale and forces the drawing onto the page. The results are reduced\enlarged by ratio to fit on the paper. Use this setting for creating small, working drawings.
    - o If you don't place a check in the **Fit to paper** box, AutoCAD allows you to select the scale from the **Scale** drop down box, or to enter a customized scale in the boxes below the drop down box.
    - o **Scal**[ing] **lineweights** is a good idea if you've used lineweights (Lesson 6).
- The **Plot style table (pen assignments)** frame (back at the top, on the right) allows you to select a style table. You can use plot style tables to convert a color drawing to black and white or to assign specific colors to specific pens on a multi-pen plotter. Use the **Edit** button next to the drop down selection box to modify the selected table. For more information on plot style tables, see the supplement.
- The next frame – **Shaded viewport options** – contains controls for plotting three-dimensional drawings. We'll discuss shaded three-dimensional drawings in the *3D AutoCAD 2007: One Step at a Time* text. (Look for this one in the spring of 2006.) Don't mistake the **Quality** option as something that might be useful in a two-dimensional drawing; it controls quality of shaded or rendered three-dimensional objects.
- The **Plot options** frame provides four check boxes.
    - o Use **Plot object lineweights** only if you've set the drawing up to use lineweights (Lesson 6). If you haven't, you can ignore this box.
    - o Again, use **Plot with plotstyles** only if you've set up the drawing to use plot styles.
    - o Normally, AutoCAD plots Paper Space objects first. If you prefer to plot Model Space objects first, place a check in the **Plot paperspace last** box. I haven't seen where this is necessary, but you might discover a need for it. (As I've mentioned, we'll discuss Paper Space in Lessons 22 and 23.)
- You'll tell AutoCAD how to position the drawing on the paper in the last frame (Whew!) – **Drawing orientation**. Your options are the standard **Portrait** and **Landscape** orientations, and a **Plot upside-down** option that you can use to print sepias.
- Finally, there's a **Preview** button at the bottom of the dialog box that will help you see what your settings will produce.

I know this has been a lot of material, but it might hearten you to know that it's less that has been required in previous releases. Let's set up a page and plot a drawing.

| Do This: 21.1.3.1 | Setting Up a Page and Plotting |
|---|---|

I. Open the *pid-21.dwg* file in the C:\Steps\Lesson21 folder.

II. Follow these steps.

| 21.1.3.1: SETTING UP A PAGE AND PLOTTING |
|---|
| 1. Open the Page Setup Manager by entering the command at the command prompt.<br>Alternately, you can pick the Page Setup Manager button on the Layouts toolbar or select **Page Setup Manager** from the cursor menu presented when you right click on the **Model** tab.<br>AutoCAD presents the Page Setup Manager (Figure 21.001).<br>**Command: *pagesetup*** |

## 21.1.3.1: Setting Up a Page and Plotting

2. Create a new page setup 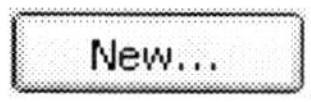

.

3. AutoCAD presents the New Page Setup dialog box. Select the **Model** setup in the **Start with** list box, and then enter the name of your new setup as shown.

Pick the **OK** button to continue.

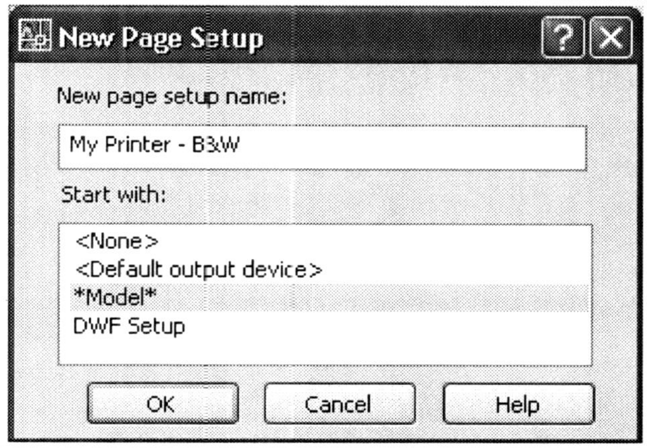


4. AutoCAD presents the Page Setup dialog box (Figure 21.003). We'll go through the frames to set up our printer.

Begin in the **Printer/Plotter** frame and select the printer you wish to use from the **Name** drop down selection box. (I'll use my Minolta magicolor.)

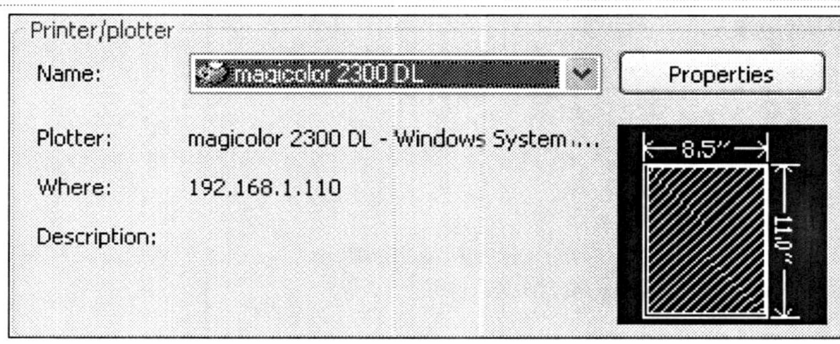


5. Select the paper size you wish to use. My Minolta only goes to legal, but I'll use **Letter** for this setup.

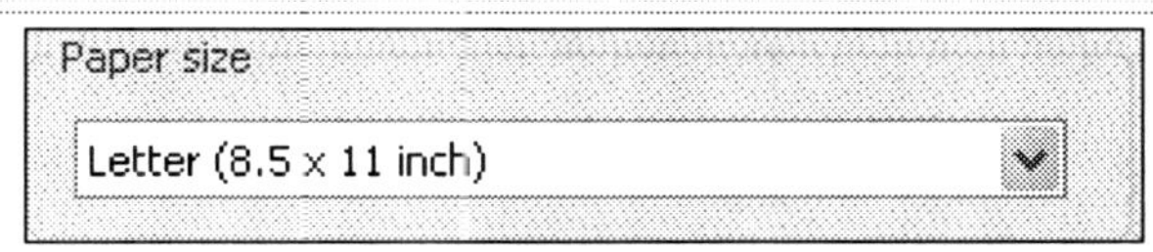


6. I want to fit the entire drawing on the page, so I'll plot the **Extents**. (More on **Extents** in Lesson 4.)

I'll **center the plot** on the page as well.

Since I designed the drawing for a D-size sheet, I'll have to make it **Fit** on this smaller size. (This will suit my purposes for a working drawing.)

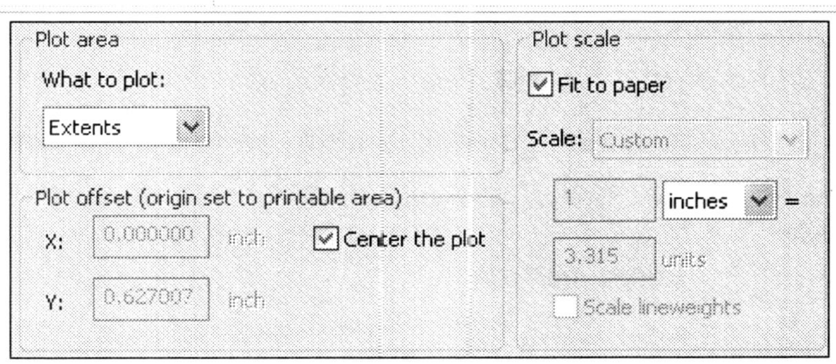

## 21.1.3.1: Setting Up a Page and Plotting

7. I could've use the **Properties** button in the Printer/plotter frame to access my printer's settings, but I'll use tables to tell AutoCAD to convert all the geometry in my drawing to black and white.

8. AutoCAD wants to know if I'd like to assign this table to all the layouts in my drawing. We're not using layouts, but I may decide to use some Paper Space technology in later lessons, so I'll tell it to go ahead by picking the **Yes** button.

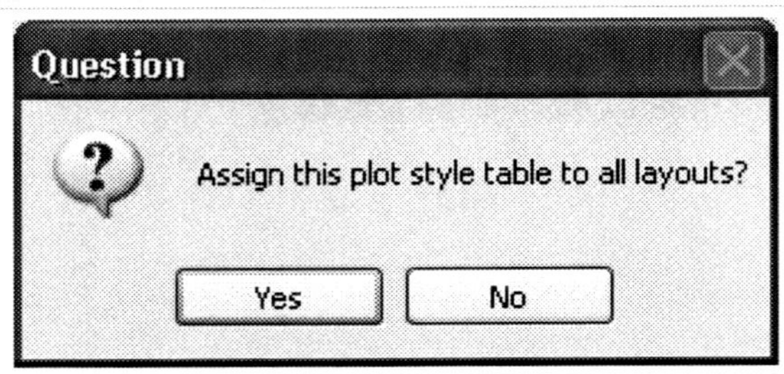


9. Since I told AutoCAD to use a styles table in Step 7, I need to select that in the **Plot options** frame.

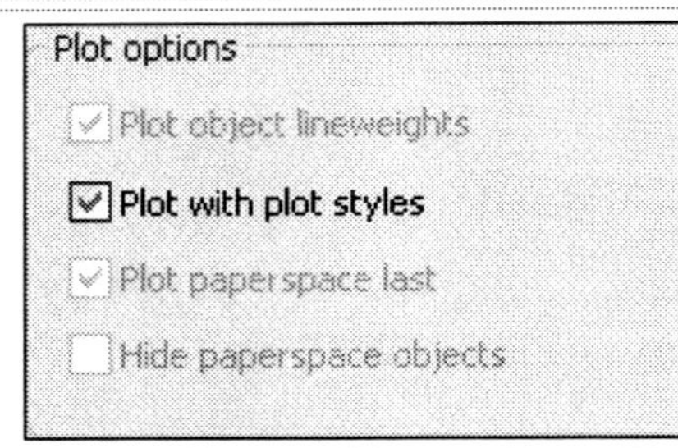


10. Finally, I'll let AutoCAD know how to position the drawing on the paper.

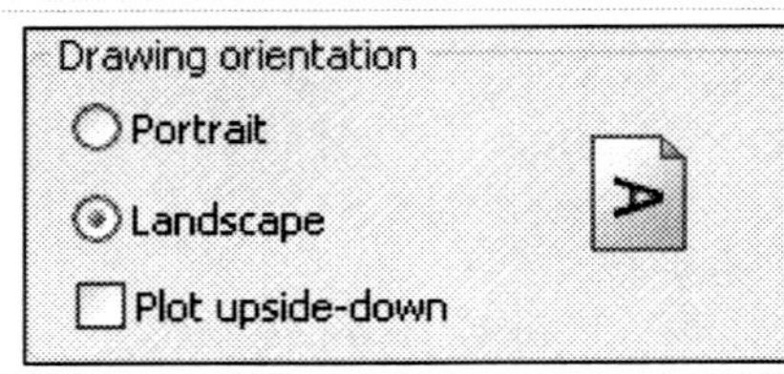


11. That's it for my page setup 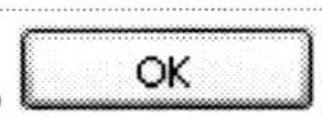! I'm ready to print.

12. Back at the Page Setup Manager, set the new style current 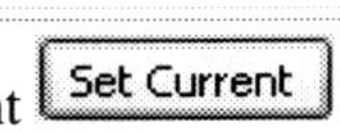 (select it and pick the appropriate button).

13. Close the Page Setup Manager 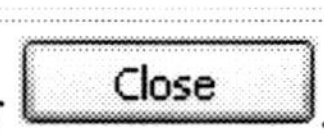.

14. Now we can print the drawing. Enter the command at the command line. Alternately, you can pick the **Plot** button 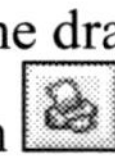 on the Standard toolbar or select **Plot** from the File pull down menu.

**Command:** ***print***

15. Notice that the Plot dialog box is just a simplified version of the Page Setup dialog box. This time, however, because we set our new page setup as current (Step 12), all of our settings have been made for us. Use the **Preview** button 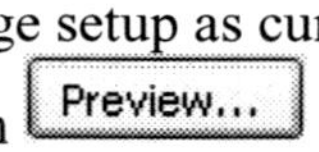 to be sure that this setup will work for our drawing.

### 21.1.3.1: Setting Up a Page and Plotting

16. Our drawing looks okay on the paper, so we'll pick the **Close Preview Window** button to leave the preview.

17. Pick the **OK** button [OK] to start the print.

18. AutoCAD will let you know that it has completed your printing job. It'll also let you know of any problems! Pick the **X** to close the bubble.

19. Save your drawing but don't exit.

**Command:** ***qsave***

## 21.2 Sharing Your Drawing with the *Plot* Command – and *No Paper*!

*"Gettin' paid a check's okay, I s'pose, 'cept it don't leave me nuttin' to jingle in my pocket."*

*from* A Geezer's Lament

*Anonymous*

Ah, progress! Just as our poor geezer lost the joy of jingling pocket change, so we must eventually say goodbye to paper drawings – at least as much as we've said goodbye to cash!

AutoCAD has provided a special type of file that you can use to share design information via the Internet – without the need to send paper. This new file type also loads considerably faster than a drawing file, but it contains the ability to manipulate layers and views, and to be printed like any other web document.

AutoCAD called the file a Drawing Web Format file (DWF, pronounced "DWIF"), gave it the capability to contain hyperlink jumps (just like any other web document), and made its creation as simple as plotting a document (in fact, you use AutoCAD's ***Plot*** command to create it!).

> With Autodesk's DWF Composer, you can even use DWFs for review issues with clients. Visit the Autodesk website – http://www.autodesk.com – for more information on DWF Composer.

Let's see how it works.

### 21.2.1 Viewing a Drawing Web Format (DWF) File Using Your Browser

The AutoCAD installation includes a tool called the DWF Viewer. This tool, like its many predecessors, enables you to view an AutoCAD DWF file. The DWF file is a wonderful innovation that allows AutoCAD users – *and clients without access to the AutoCAD program* – to view AutoCAD drawings!

The DWF Viewer ships with the AutoCAD program, but for those clients who don't have access to AutoCAD, the viewer is a free download (2Mb) at the Autodesk web site: http://www.autodesk.com/. With the DWF Viewer, you can view files from within your browser or through the viewer program itself – the interface is the same.

Let's take a look.

| Do This: 21.2.1.1 | Viewing a DWF File |
|---|---|

I. You can start a new drawing from scratch or continue from any drawing you have open.

II. Follow these steps.

**21.2.1.1: VIEWING A DWF FILE**

1. Launch your browser by entering the ***Browser*** command at the command line. Alternately, you can pick the **Browse the Web** button  on the Web toolbar.

    **Command: *browser***

    **Enter Web location (URL) <http://www.autodesk.com>: *[enter]***

2. Enter the address indicated to view our *Web.dwf* file. (Remember, your browser is case-specific.)

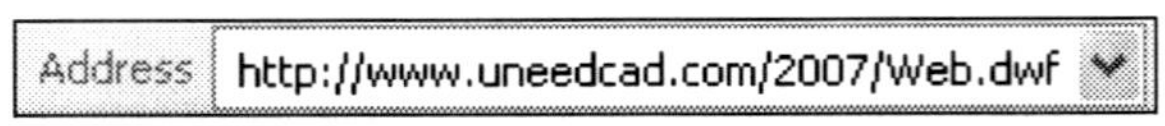


[You may get notification that Internet Explorer has **restricted this file from sharing active content**. If you do, just pick on the notice (below the address bar) and select **Allow Blocked Content** from the pop up menu.]

Your browser presents the DWF file with the DWF Viewer's toolbar across the top (see the following figure). [Something to consider when sharing a drawing: the drawing file is 47.8k; the DWF file is 7.24k. It's much faster to download a DWF file.)

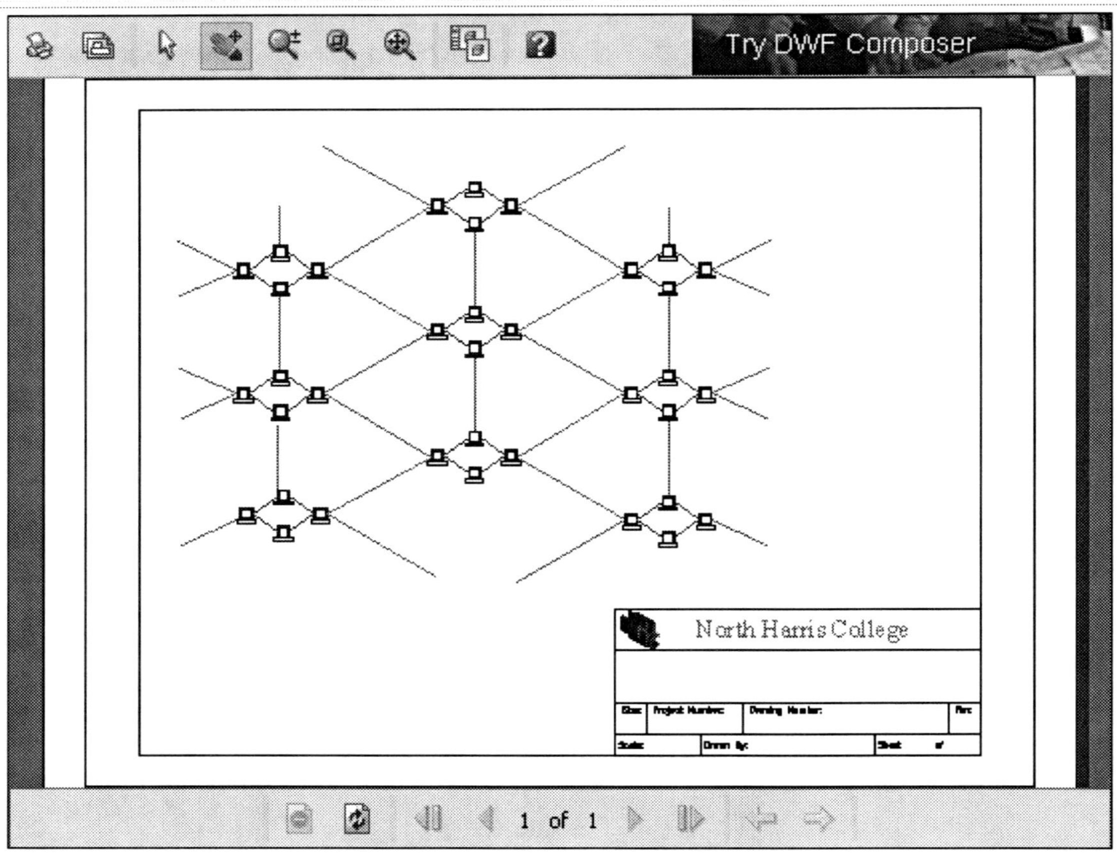

## 21.2.1.1: Viewing a DWF File

3. Let's take a look at some of the possibilities DWF files offer.

There are view buttons on the DWF Viewer toolbar: **Print**, **Copy**, **Select** (for selecting an object to view extended information that may be attached to it), **Pan**, **Zoom**, **Zoom Rectangle**, **Pan**, **Zoom**, **Fit to Window**, and **Show/Hide Navigator**.

[The **Pan** and **Zoom** options behave like their realtime counterparts in the AutoCAD program – see Chapter 4. **Fit in Window** behaves like a zoom extents.]

Alternately, each of these view options appears on the cursor menu.

There are also tools across the bottom of the viewer. These include buttons to stop the load and to refresh (reload) the file. The bottom buttons also include typical document navigator buttons.

4. Pick the **Zoom Rectangle** button on the upper toolbar.

5. Notice that your cursor changes to a magnifying glass with a rectangle behind it. Pick just northwest of the title block and drag (holding the mouse button down) to the south and east. Release the mouse button when the entire title block has been highlighted.

Your browser presents the view shown.

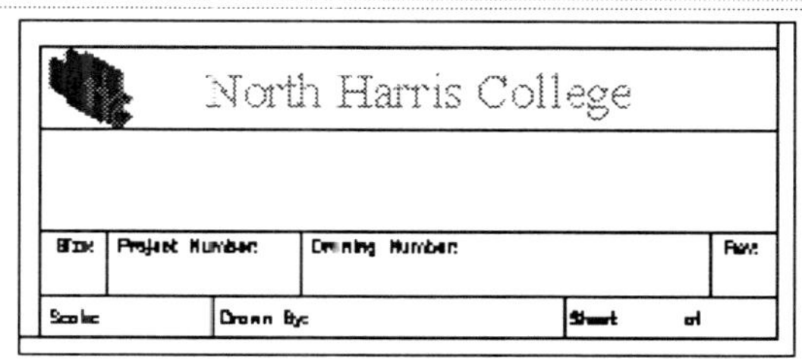


6. Notice that the magnifying glass cursor remains. You could continue to use **Zoom Rectangle** if you wished.

Pick the **Fit to Window** button to return to the original view.

7. Let's take a look at the cursor window. Right-click and pick the **Layers** option from the **Navigator Items** flyout (Figure "A" below). The DWF Viewer presents the Navigator dialog box with the **Layer** frame open (Figure "B" below).

Notice the light bulb symbol. When yellow, objects residing on that layer are visible. Pick on a light bulb to turn it gray (**Off**). Objects residing on that layer are now hidden.

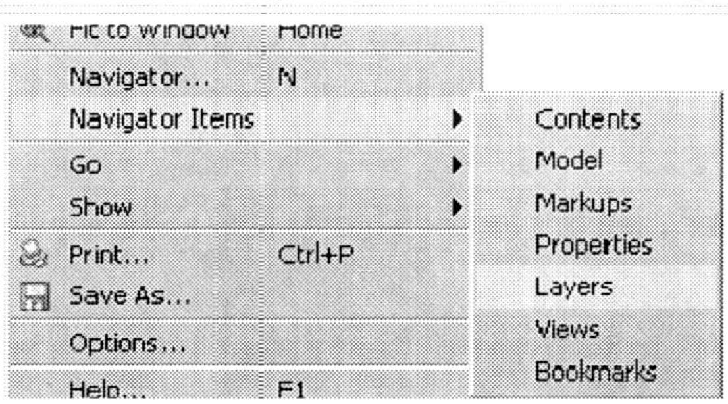


Figure "A"

7. Toggle the layers **On** and **Off** to see how the display is affected. Then pick the "X" in the upper right corner of the Layers dialog box to close it.

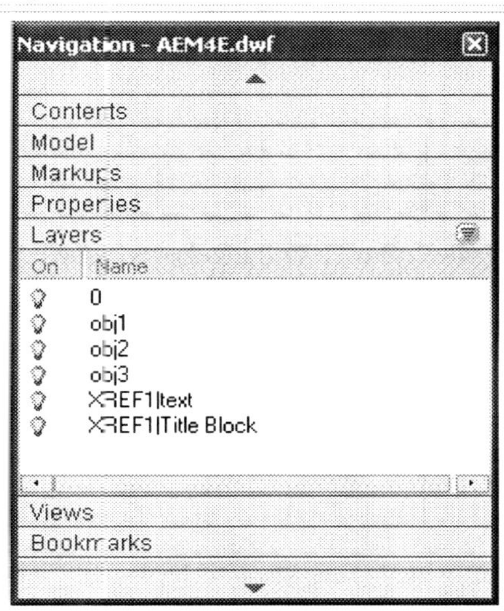


Figure "B"

## 21.2.1.1: Viewing a DWF File

8. Examine the rest of the cursor menu.

- The top two frames provide another approach to buttons we've discussed.
- The **Views** option presents a similar box that enables you to switch between previously saved views.
- **Navigation** displays a navigation window that shows **Contents, Model, Markups, Properties, Layers, Views,** and **Bookmarks** frames (much like the Adobe Reader that you're using to follow this text.) Use these frames to view different sheets of a multi-sheet DWF file.
- **Go** provides another approach to the button on the bottom toolbar.
- **Show** presents options to view hyperlinks, markups of the DWF, the toolbars, or a paper background for your drawing image.

The rest of the options are self-explanatory.

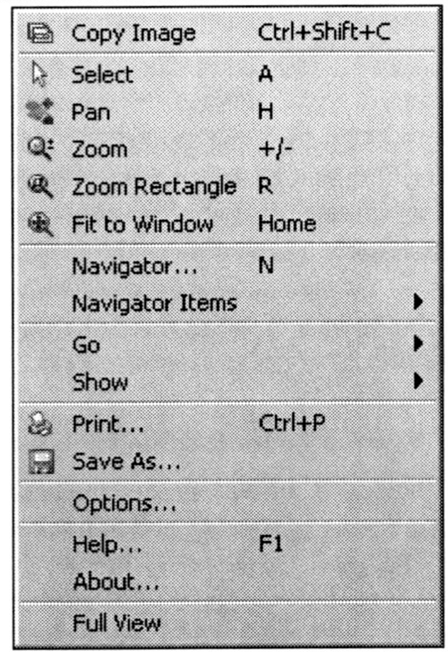


9. Let's take a look at printing your DWF file. Pick the **Print** button  on the toolbar. DWF Viewer presents a Print dialog box (see the following figure) very similar to the **Print** tab of the Plot dialog box discussed earlier in this lesson.

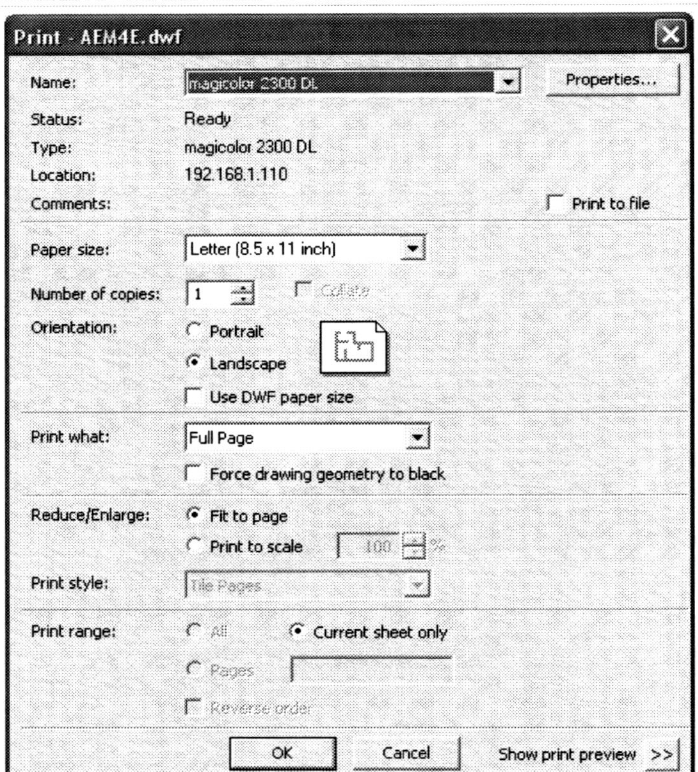

10. Select your printer and make whatever other adjustments you wish to make (I usually set my prints to **Force all geometry to black** to save my printer's color cartridges.) Then pick the **OK** button 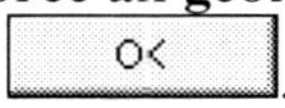. DWF Viewer prints your drawing.

The rest of the menu options are self-explanatory. Use the **Help** option if you have any problems with these.

You can also copy the DWF file from the web site to your hard drive using the **Copy** option on the cursor menu.

So, now you can see what a remarkable tool a DWF file can be – shared information without compromising the security of your drawing files! Let's create a DWF file for ourselves.

## 21.2.2 Multiple Plots and Creating a DWF File – with Hyperlinks!

In previous versions of AutoCAD, we created DWF files using some different settings in our plotting procedure. It was simply a question of selecting the DWF device on the **Plot Device** tab of the Plot dialog box.

We can still use this approach – simply select the **DWF6** plotting device – or we can opt for the newer ***Publish*** command and dialog box (Figure 21.004).

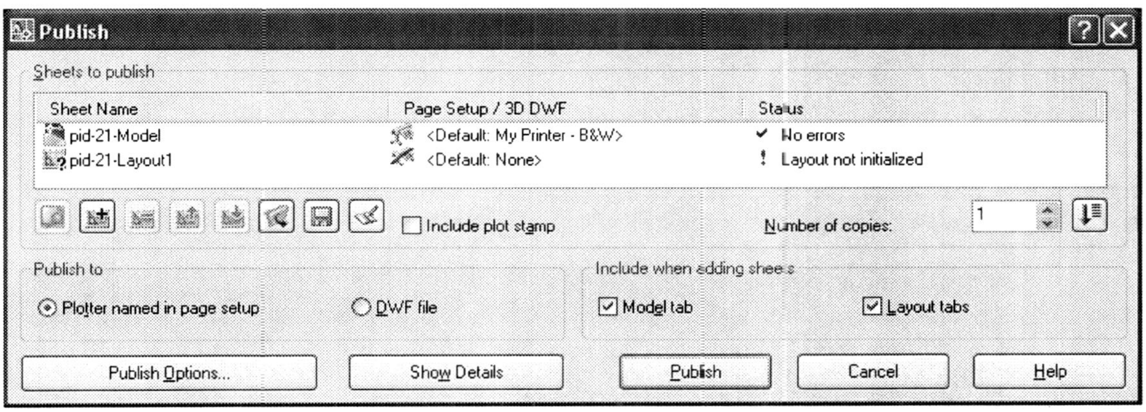


Figure 21.004

Let's take a look.

- The first thing you see – the **Sheets to publish** list box – shows the various sheets associated with the current drawing file, their current page setups, and their status. As we haven't discussed Paper Space and **Layout** tabs yet, we'll concentrate on the **Model** sheet.
- Below the list box, you'll find several buttons and a couple frames. Let's look at these.

| | |
|---|---|
| **Preview** presents the same plot preview you saw in our last section. It enables you to preview the plot. |  |
| **Add sheets** enables you to add drawing sheets to the multi-sheet DWF file. | 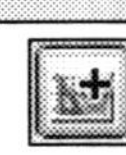 |
| **Remove** allows you to remove sheets from the list. |  |
| **Move Sheet Up** and **Move Sheet Down** allow you to change the order in which the sheets will appear in the DWF file. |   |

| | |
|---|---|
| **Load Sheet List** allows you to select a sheet list (a batch plot file - .bp3 – or a DSD file) to either append to or replace the current sheet list. This option uses a standard select file window. | |
| **Save Sheet List** allows you to save the current list as a DSD file. | |
| The **Plot Stamp Settings** button calls the Plot Stamp dialog box (Figure 21.005). Here you can set the parameters for a plot stamp via check boxes or by selecting a parameter file. We'll see more on this in a moment. | |

- Turn the plot stamp on by putting a check in the **Include plot stamp** check box (Publish dialog box).
- Use the **Number of copies** box to plot multiple copies of a drawing.
- You have a couple choices to make in the **Publish to** frame. You can plot to the device in the selected setup (**Plotter named in page setup** column); or you can create a **DWF file**.
- In the **Include when adding sheets** frame, you'll tell AutoCAD what to include in your plot – either the **Model tab** (where you've been working thus far in this text), the Layout tabs (Paper Space) or both.
- Use the **Publish Options** button to tell AutoCAD where to place the DWF file, whether or not to password protect the file, and whether or not to include layer or block information.
- The **Show Details** button presents two data frames for the selected sheet.
- Finally, the **Publish** button tells AutoCAD to proceed with the plot.

Stamping a plot provides useful information for tracking the particulars of when and what was plotter. Picking the Plot Stamp Settings button in the Publish dialog box produces the Plot Stamp dialog box (Figure 21.005). Let's look at this.

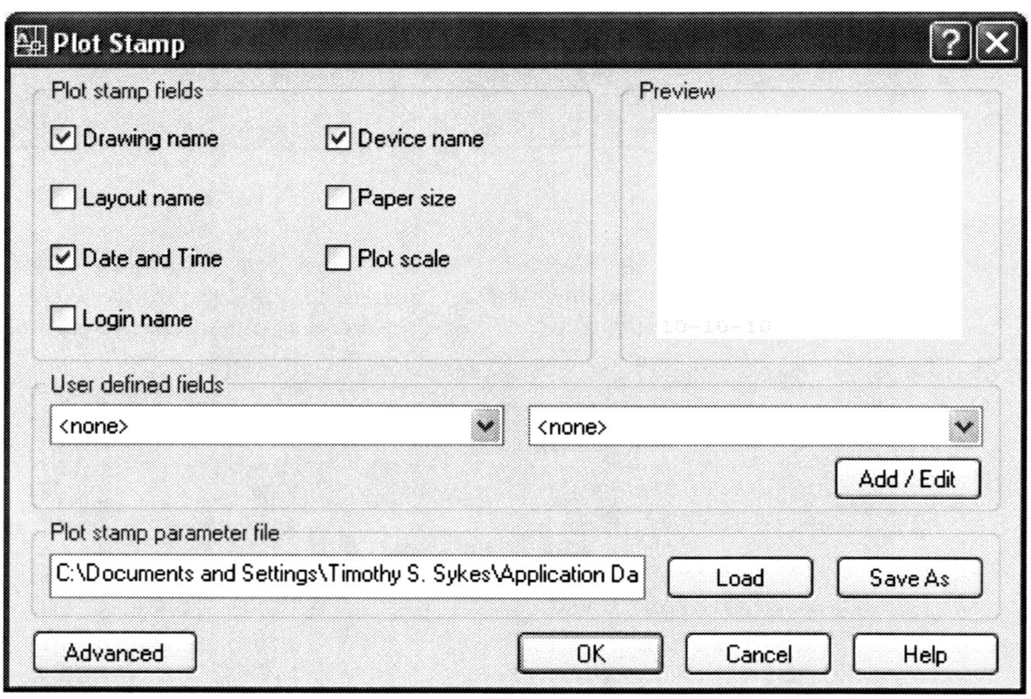


Figure 21.005

- Select what your stamp should include in the **Plot stamp fields frame**. Preview your selections in the **Preview** frame.
- Pick the **Add / Edit** button to add **User defined fields**. AutoCAD provides a simple dialog box to assist you (Figure 21.006).

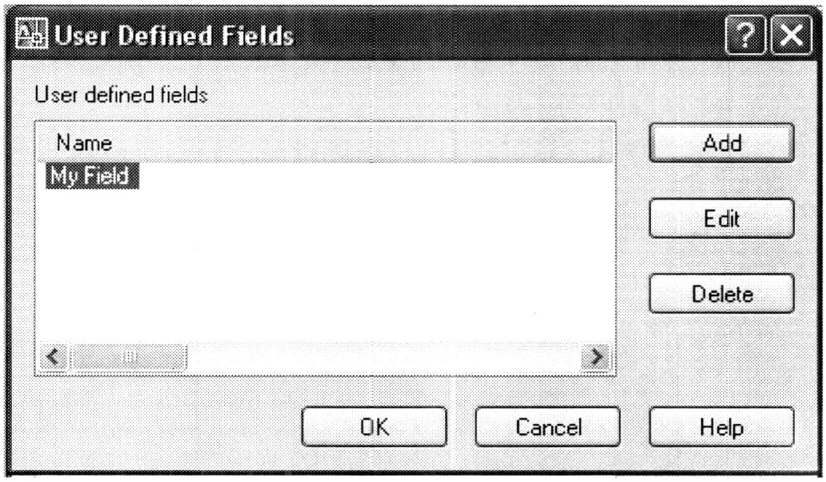


Figure 21.006

- Simplify your efforts by saving your setup and then loading it in the **Plot stamp parameter file frame**.
- The **Advanced** button calls another useful dialog box (Figure 21.007). Here you can set the **Location**, **Orientation**, and **offset** of your stamp, as well as **Text properties**. You can even tell AutoCAD to keep a log of your plots. Pretty handy, don't you think?

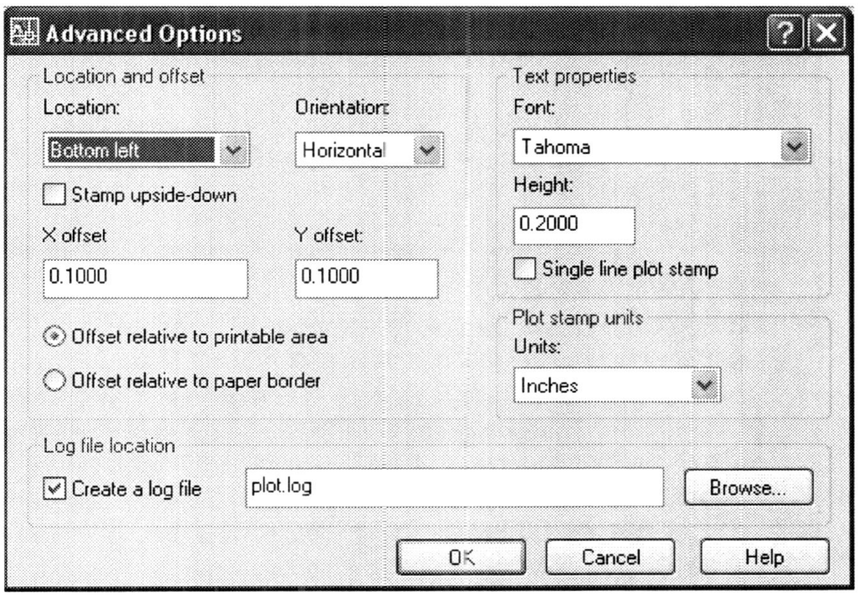


Figure 21.007

## 21.2.3 Hyperlinks

If you plan to use hyperlinks in your DWF file, you must assign them before plotting. Let's look at how to do that now.

Begin by entering the ***Hyperlink*** command and selecting the object(s) to which you want to assign the jump (the thing you want to pick to go to another web address). AutoCAD will present the Insert Hyperlink dialog box (Figure 21.008 – next page).

The dialog box looks considerably more complicated than it actually is. Let's look at one piece at a time.

- At the top of the dialog box, you'll find a text box with the words **Text to display** next to it. What you enter here will display in a small tooltip whenever a viewer passes his cursor over the hyperlink.

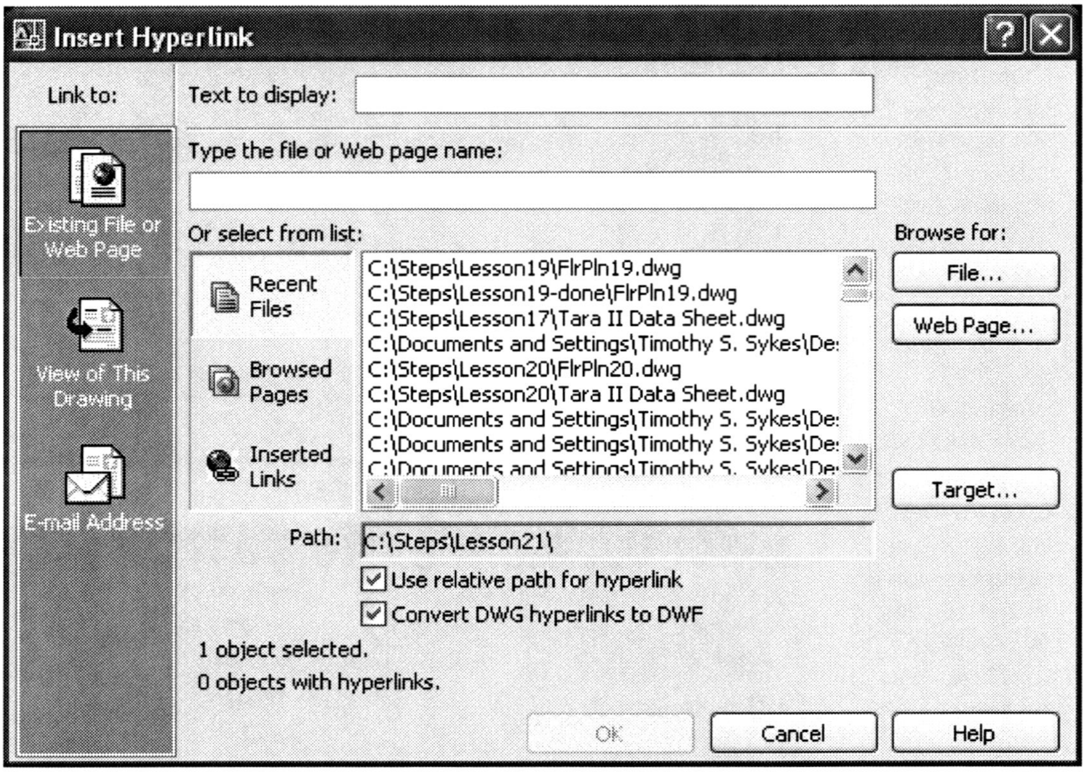


Figure 21.008

- Down the left side of the box, you'll see three **Link to** picks. These control the methods you'll use to identify the target hyperlink (the place to which you wish to jump).
- The first **Link to** pick – **Existing File or Web Page** – provides the dialog shown in Figure 21.008. Use it to create a link to a file, layout, or web site that already exists. (The other links change the dialog box as you'll see shortly.) Let's look at how to do this.
  - Below the **Text to display** box, you see a **Type the file or Web page name** text box. This provides the key to your hyperlink and the easy way to identify your web site or target file. Enter the page name and address of the target site in this box.
  - In the **Or select from list** box, AutoCAD has provided a selection list from which you can pick the data that will go into the **Type the file or Web page name** text box. Selecting a target here saves you from having to type in a target (and deal with typos). Three option buttons help organize your choices into these groups:

    **Recent Files** – files you've recently opened in AutoCAD.

    **Browsed Pages** – Internet pages to which you've browsed.

    **Inserted Links** – recently inserted hyperlinks.

    Each of these option buttons changes the list to accommodate the choice.
  - To the right of the list box are three buttons that also provide an easy method of filling the **Type the file or Web page name** text box.
    - The **File** button opens a standard Open dialog box where you can select the name of the target file.
    - The **Web Page** button works just like the **File** button but opens AutoCAD's browser where you'll select the name of the target web site.

- The **Target** button allows you to select a layout or preset view within the drawing as a target.

- The second **Link to** pick – **View of This Drawing** – provides the same thing the **Target** button provides when the **Existing file or Web page** button has been selected.
- With the last **Link to** pick – **Email Address** – you can place a hyperlink in the drawing that will allow the reader to send an email to a predefined address. AutoCAD provides the simple interface shown in Figure 21.009 for this task. (It even provides a list of recently used email addresses from which to choose.)

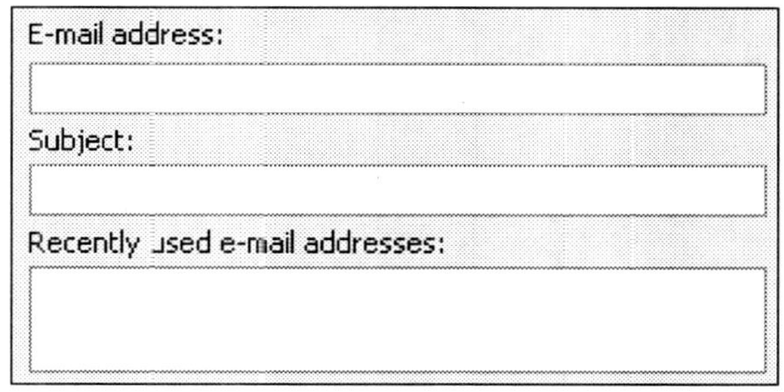

Figure 21.009

Let's create a DWF file with a hyperlink.

| Do This: 21.2.2.1 | Creating a DWF File with Links |
|---|---|

I. Be sure you're still in the *pid-21.dwg* file in the C:\Steps\Lesson21 folder. If not, please open it now.

II. Zoom in around the title block.

III. Follow these steps.

**21.2.2.1: CREATING A DWF FILE WITH LINKS**

1. First, we must create our hyperlinks. Enter the ***Hyperlink*** command.

   **Command: *hyperlink***

2. Select the **North Harris College** text in the title block. (Remember to hit ***enter*** to complete the selection set.)

   **Select objects:**

   **Select objects: *[enter]***

3. Link to the North Harris College web site by entering the web address in the **Type the file or Web page name** text box as shown. (The address is: *http://www.northharriscollege.com.*) Notice that the name appears in the **Text to Display** text box as well. You can change this to something more descriptive or simply leave it as is. (I'll call it *North Harris College Website.*)

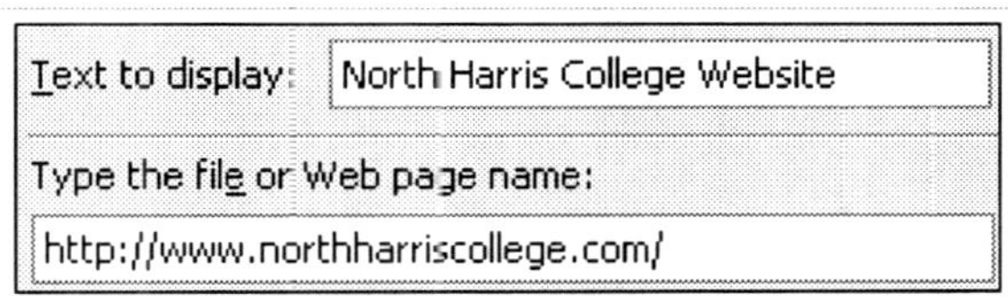


4. Pick the **OK** button 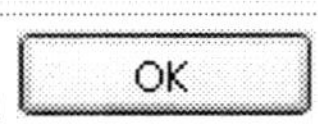 to complete the command.


5. Now let's provide an email hyperlink. Repeat Step 1, but select the name in the title block. (Zoom as necessary.)

6. Pick **Email Address**  in the **Link to** column.

## 21.2.2.1: Creating a DWF File with Links

7. Enter an email address as shown. (Note: The address shown isn't real – enter one of your own.) AutoCAD will place the *mailto:* part before the address.

Place a subject in the appropriate text box.

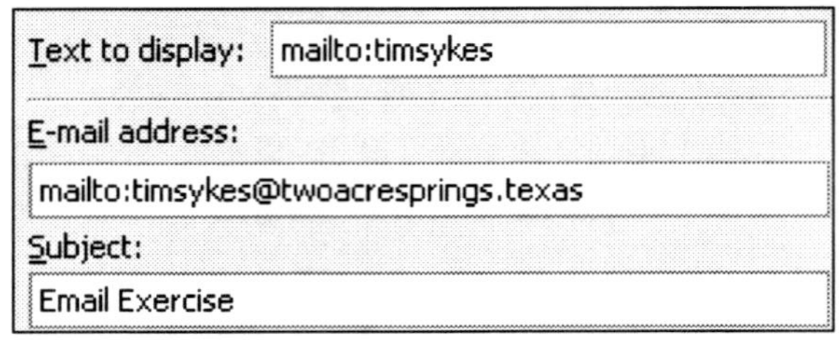


8. Pick the **OK** button  to complete the command.

9. Run your cursor over the North Harris College text in the title block. Notice (right) how it changes to indicate the presence of a hyperlink jump. The tooltip gives you the description of the link and tells you how to follow it.

10. Now we'll publish the drawing to create the DWF file. (Hint: It might be a good idea to save the drawing first.) Zoom all, and then enter the ***Publish*** command. Alternately, you can pick the **Publish** button  on the Standard toolbar.

**Command: *publish***

AutoCAD presents the Publish dialog box (Figure 21.004).

11. We haven't set up to use the **Layout** tabs, so select **Layout1** in the list box and pick the **Remove sheets** button . (Repeat this step for everything in the List box except the *PID-21-Model* listing.

12. Select **DWF Setup** from the drop down selection box in the **Page setup** column.

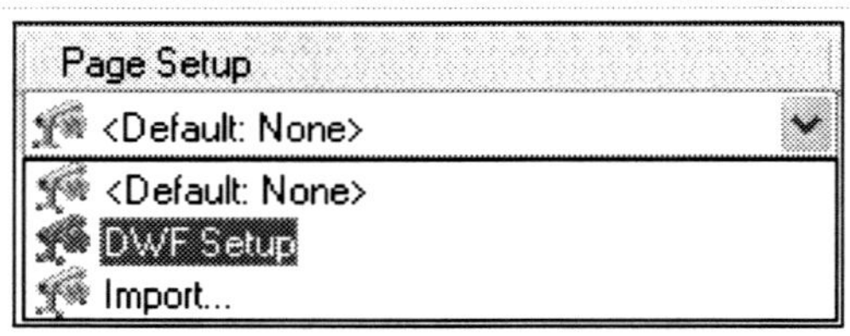


13. Put a bullet next to DWF file in the **Publish to** frame.

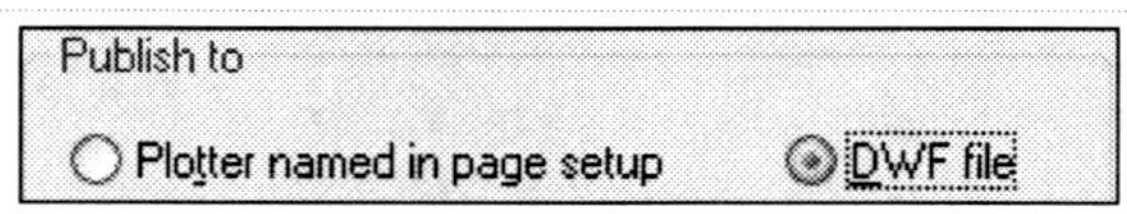


14. Pick the **Publish Options** button 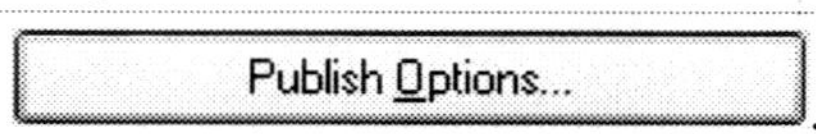.

15. On the Publish Options dialog box, locate the output directory as indicated.

16. Tell AutoCAD that you want to plot only a single sheet.

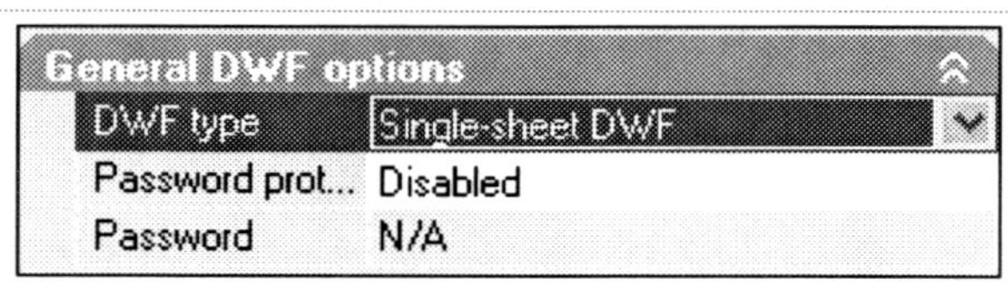


17. Return to the Publish dialog box 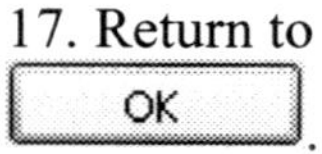.

## 21.2.2.1: Creating a DWF File with Links

18. Pick the **Publish** button  to complete the command. (Don't save the current list of sheets if prompted.)

19. AutoCAD lets you know when it has finished the publishing job. Close the bubble.

20. Launch your browser from within AutoCAD.

**Command: *browser***

21. Enter the address of the file you just created: *C:\Steps\Lesson21\pid-21-Model.dwf.*

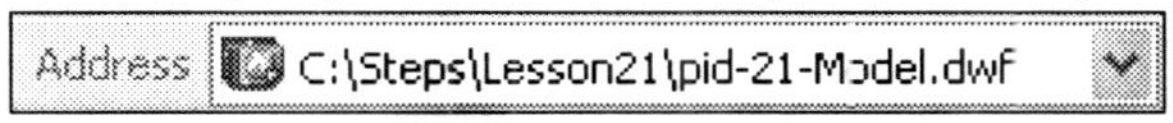


(The spelling and case must be precise.) Your browser presents your first DWF file!

22. Run your cursor over the text in the title block. Notice that it changes to indicate a hyperlink. Pick on the text. Your browser opens the North Harris College web site in a fresh window!

23. Close the new window.

24. Pick the name in the title block. Your email software will launch with the address and subject filled in as you indicated back in Step 7!

25. Close all the windows except AutoCAD.

26. Save your drawing  but don't exit.

**Command: *qsave***

Wow!

## 21.2.4 AutoCAD can Create Full Web Pages, Too!

Your efforts so far in this section have been to create and manipulate files that a programmer can place at a web site for you. But AutoCAD has also provided a way to cut that middleman – the extremely well paid web-programmer – out of the loop and save yourself (or The Company) some money. With the *Publish to Web* tool, AutoCAD enables you to create (or edit) your own web page! The tool even works in the form of a wizard so that you can do the job in no time at all!

Let's take a look.

### Do This: 21.2.4.1 Creating Your Own Web Page

I. Be sure you're still in the *pid-21.dwg* file in the C:\Steps\Lesson21 folder. If not, please open it now.

II. Follow these steps.

## 21.2.4.1: Creating Your Own Web Page

1. Begin by entering the ***PublishToWeb*** command at the command prompt. Alternately, you can select **Publish to Web** from the File pull down menu.

**Command:** ***publishtoweb***

AutoCAD begins the Publish to Web wizard with the dialog box shown in Step 2.

2. Notice that AutoCAD allows you the option of creating a new web page or editing an existing page (below). The second option will come in handy when you need to make adjustments to an existing page. We'll **Create** [a] **New Web Page** for now. Be sure the bullet is next to that option and pick the **Next** button to continue.

(Note: This tool will work only on a saved drawing.)

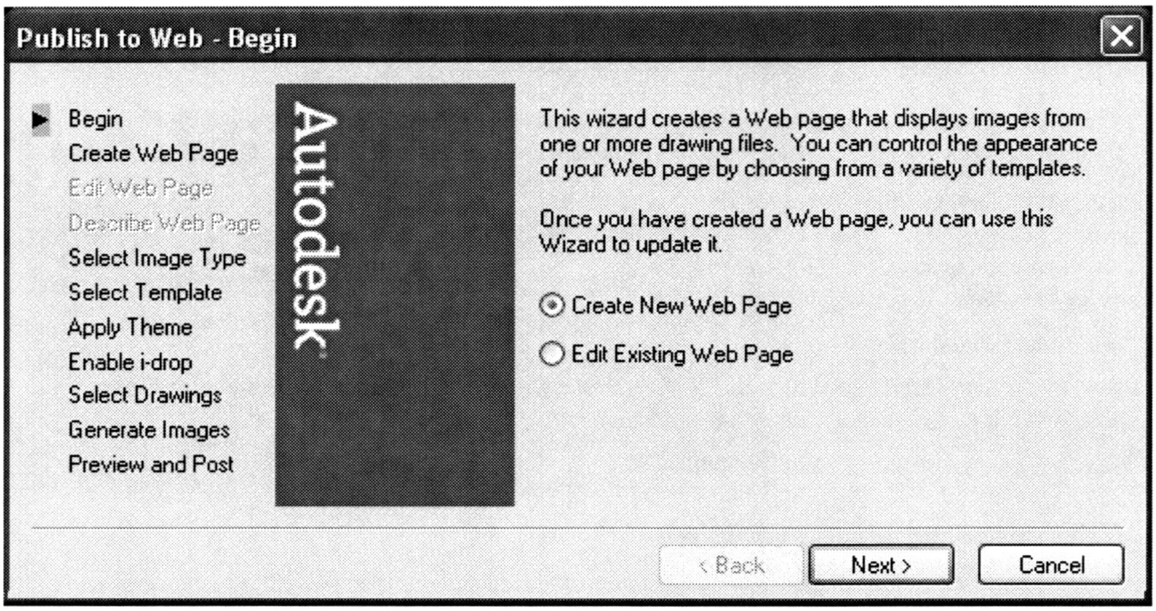


3. AutoCAD presents the Create Web Page dialog box (see the following figure). Here you'll name your web page. AutoCAD will create a new subfolder with the name of the web page.

- To begin, enter the name of your web page as indicated (I'll call mine *PID21WebPage*). Don't place a file extension on the name; AutoCAD will do that for you. (Note: Don't use spaces in the name of the page. Although they won't bother AutoCAD, the Internet won't like them.)
- Use the browse button (**...**) to locate the web page folder in the C:\Steps\Lesson21 folder.
- Add the description shown in the figure.
- Pick the **Next** button to continue.

## 21.2.4.1: Creating Your Own Web Page

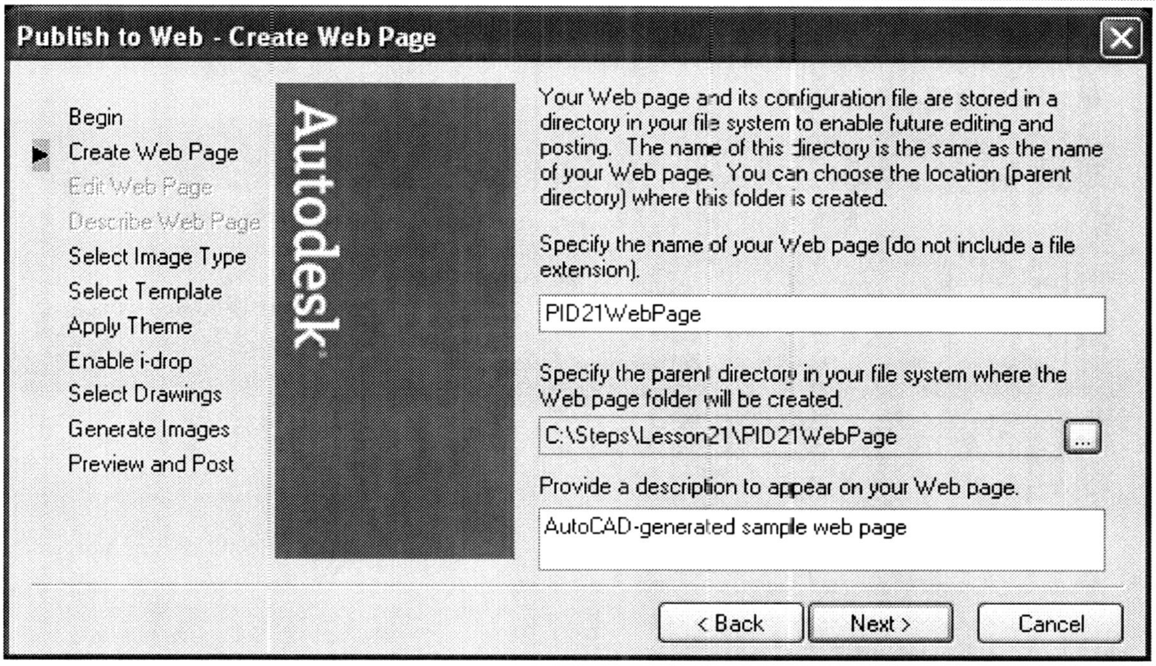


4. AutoCAD presents the Select Image Type dialog box (below). Here you'll decide what type of image to place on your web page. You've already seen the many uses of DWF files, but AutoCAD allows you to use a JPEG (.jpg) file or a PNG (.png) file as an alternative to DWF. These files are generally smaller and load faster. Their chief benefit is that they require no special programming or plug-in for proper viewing. However, they lack the quality of a DWF file.

Select the layout you wish to use for your web page; we'll use the **DWF** image option.

Pick the **Next** button to continue.

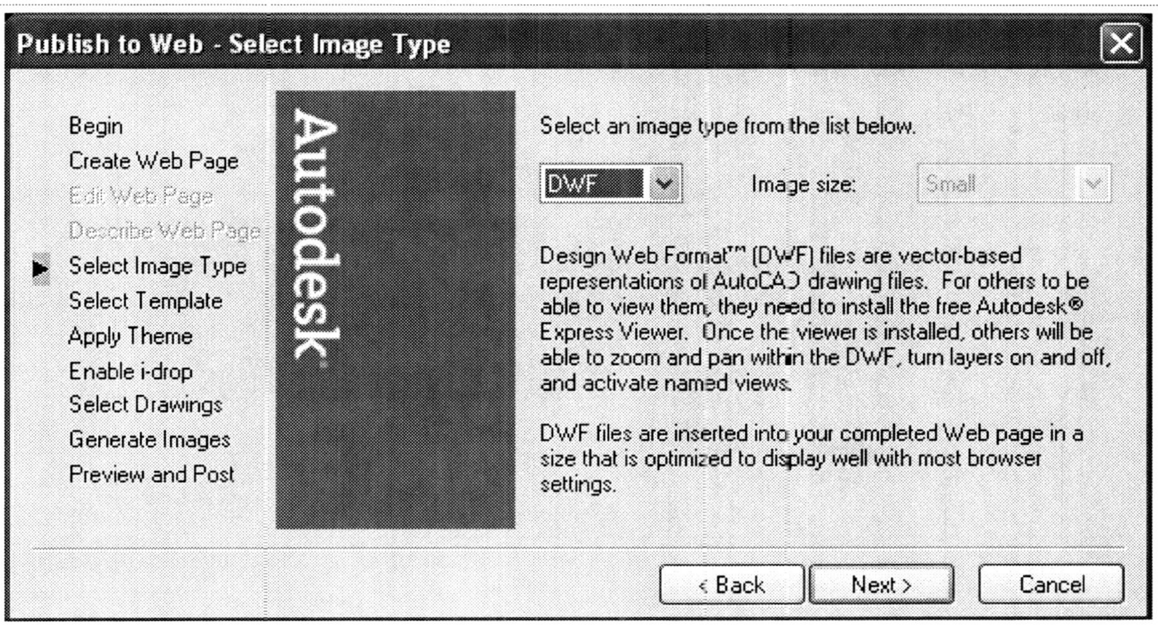

## 21.2.4.1: Creating Your Own Web Page

5. Now AutoCAD wants to know how to lay out your web page. Pick each of the four options to view samples of the layouts, and then select **List Plus Summary**.

Pick the **Next** button to continue.

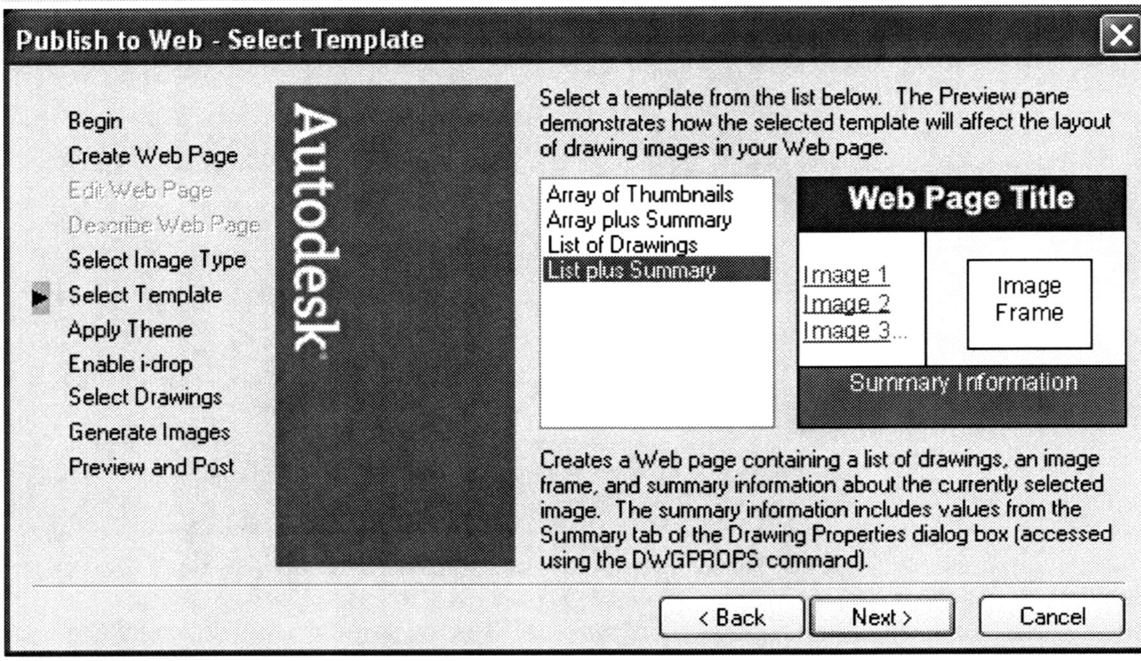


6. Select the **Theme** (color scheme and fonts) you'd like to use. I'll use **Rainy Day** as indicated.

Pick the **Next** button to continue.

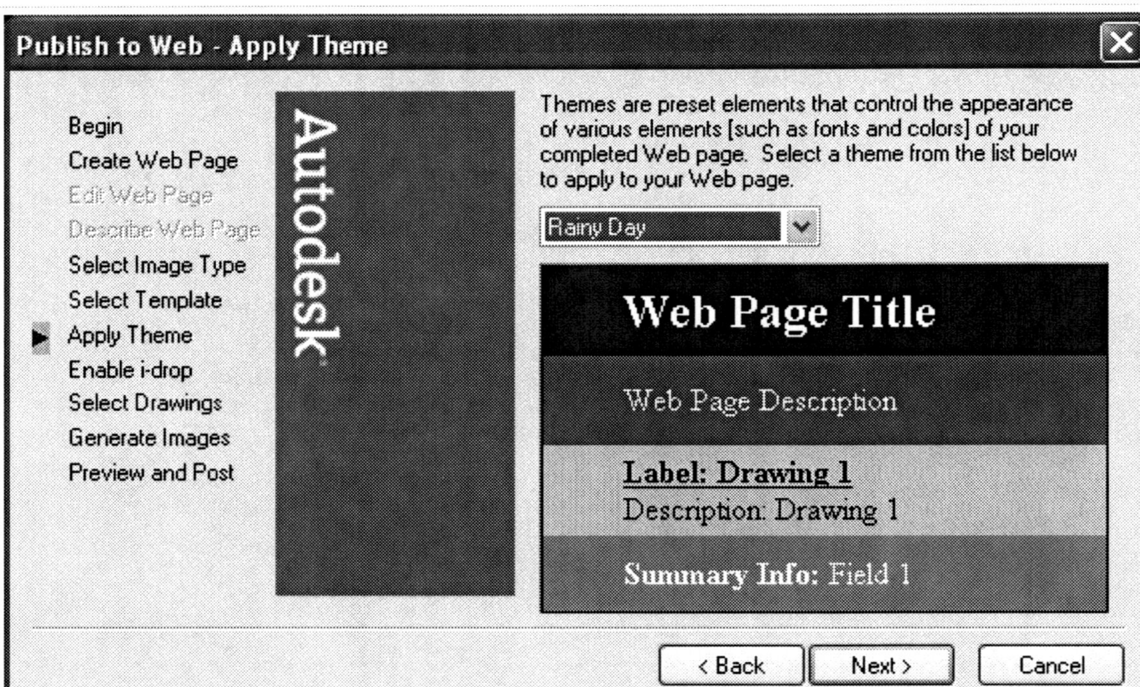

## 21.2.4.1: Creating Your Own Web Page

7. AutoCAD offers you an opportunity to make your drawings I-Drop available. We won't use iDrop for now; its value lies in the ability to drop blocks into current drawings. (Be sure you read the explanation at the top of the page.)

Pick the **Next** button to continue.

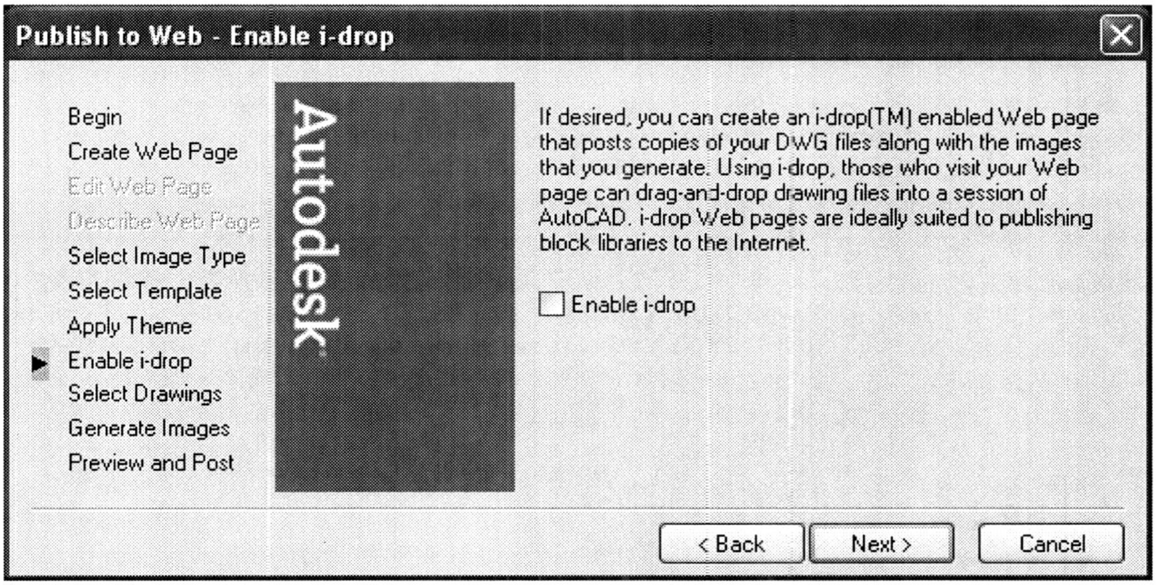


8. AutoCAD needs to know what to include in your web page.

- In the **Label** text box, enter a label for the image selected.
- The **Description** box allows you to annotate the image. Place a description there as indicated.

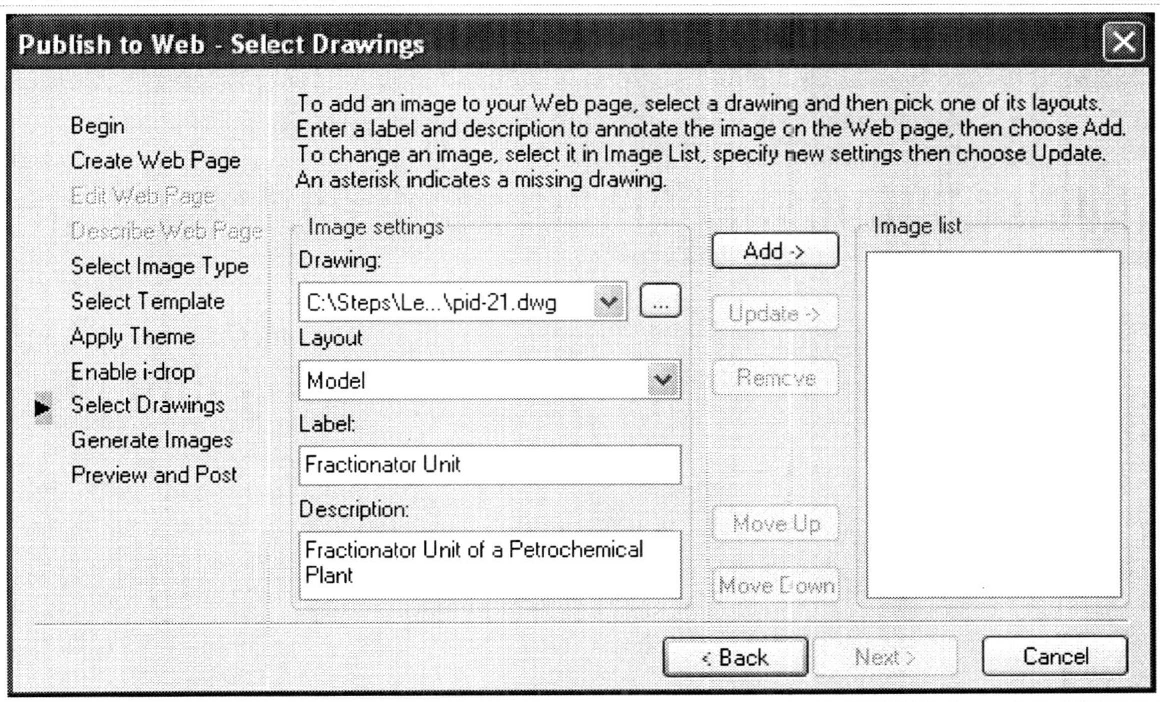

9. Once you've finished the **Image settings**, pick the **Add** button 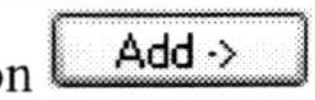

to add the image to the **Image list**.

You can add more images if you wish by picking the browse button next to the **Drawing** control box. I'll add the *Floor Plan* drawing from the C:\Steps\Lesson21 folder.

10. Pick the **Next** button 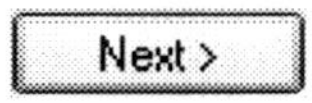

to continue.

11. Now AutoCAD will generate the web page. First it would like to know how much regeneration to do. Remember, regeneration insures that what's on the screen is what's in the drawing's database (what you see is what's actually there). It's safest to regenerate the entire drawing before creating the web page. Put a bullet there and pick the **Next** button to continue.

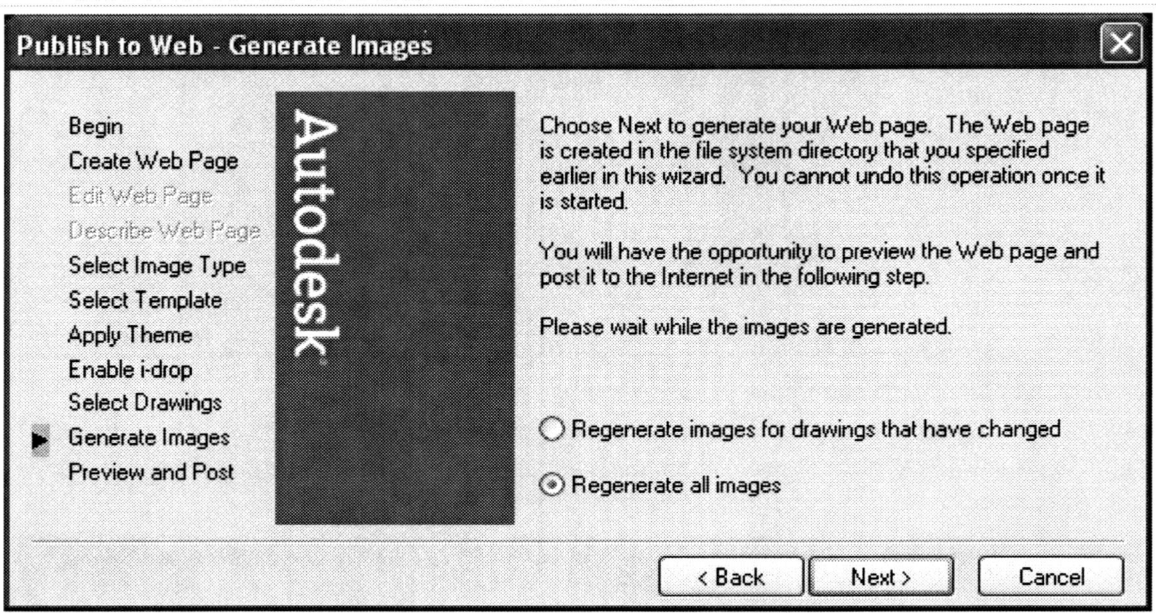


12. Now AutoCAD tells you it has finished creating the web page and offers you the chance to view it or post it to a web site (see the figure on the next page).

Posting the page requires an ftp site (a place to put the files on the Internet or an Intranet) – usually involving permissions and passwords. If you don't post it now, you can always post it later by copying all the files created during this procedure (found in the folder you told AutoCAD to create earlier) to the web site.

For now, pick the **Preview** button to see your new web page.

## 21.2.4.1: Creating Your Own Web Page

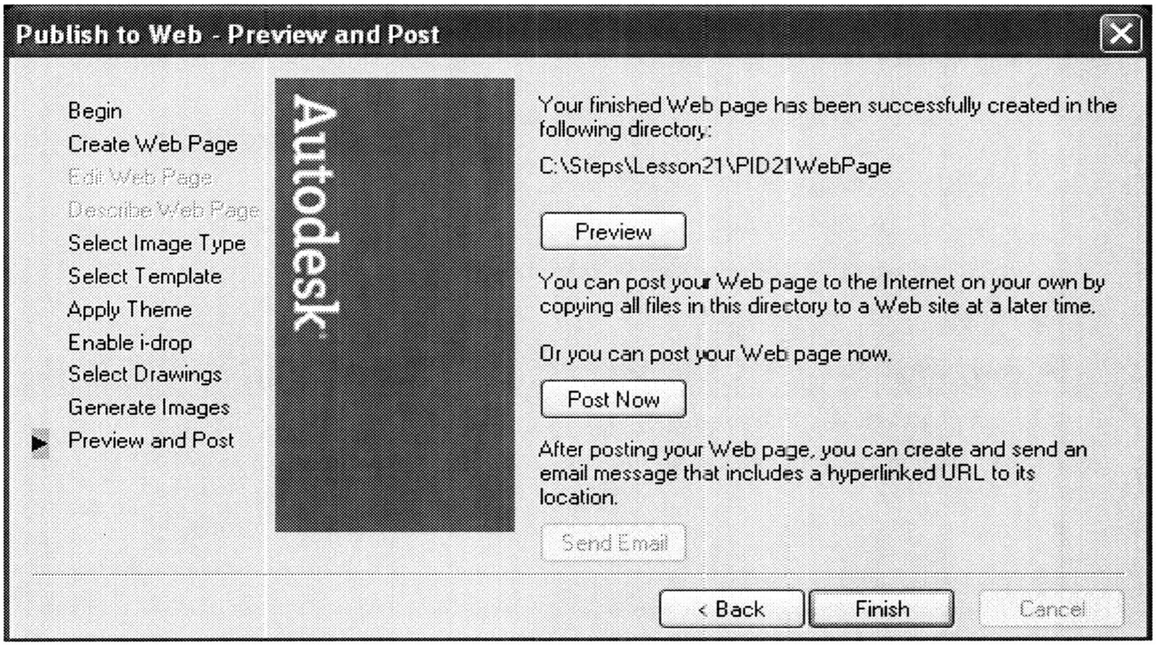


13. Take a few minutes to explore the web page. Notice that the hyperlink jumps you created in our last exercise still work here (you can create hyperlinks prior to creating a web page just as you did prior to creating the DWF file).

14. When you've finished with the web page, close your browser and pick the **Finish** button 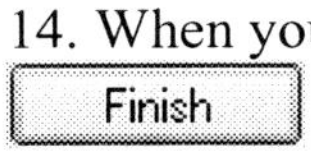

on the wizard.

15. Save your drawing 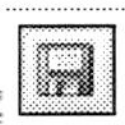 but don't exit.

**Command:** ***qsave***

## 21.3 Sending the Package over the Internet with *eTransmit*

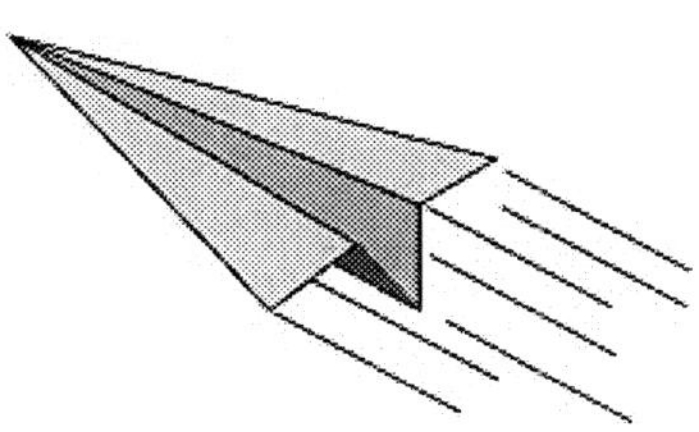

Times will undoubtedly occur when you need to share an actual drawing file with someone – that is, you'll need to send the drawing to someone for changes or even as a final product to a client. In the past, difficulties have occasionally arisen with incompatible or missing support files (such as fonts, linetypes, and so forth). At other times, you may need to share secure data with a client or co-worker and posting information to a web site simply won't do. With AutoCAD's **eTransmit** tool, these difficulties need no longer concern you.

**eTransmit** groups a drawing file with all the necessary support files (and any other files you wish to attach) into a single self-extracting executable or .zip file. You can protect this data with an encrypted password and transmit it to a friend or client via web site, email, CD, or even a good old-fashioned floppy disk!

To make things even easier, AutoCAD uses a dialog box (Figure 21.010) to help create the transmittal. Just answer a few questions!

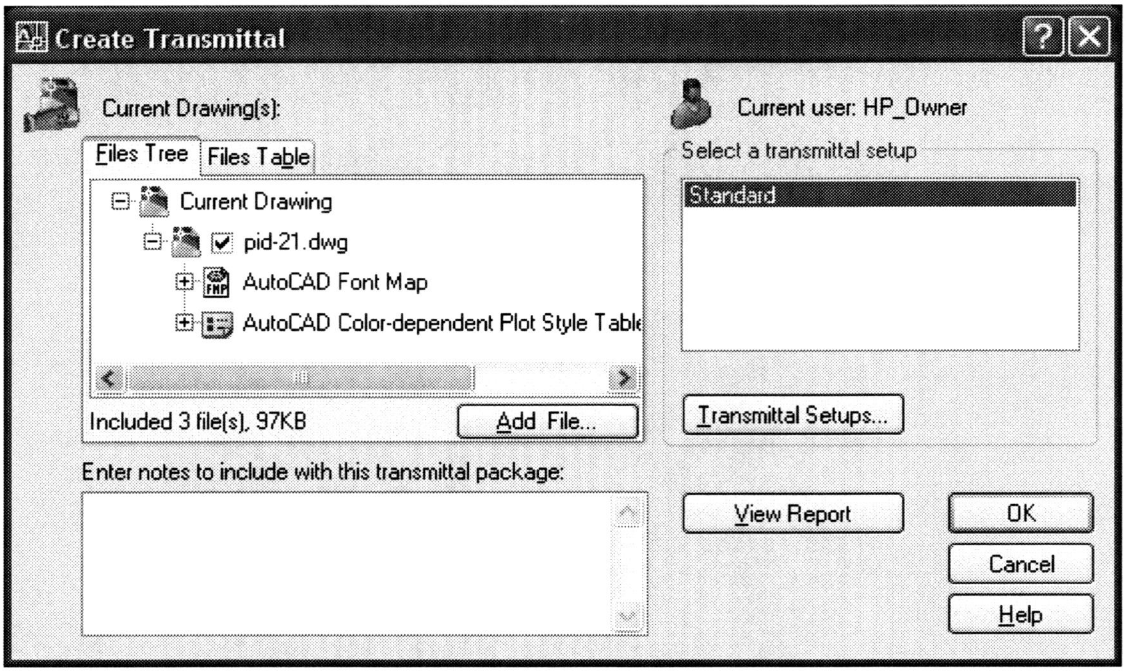


Figure 21.010

Let's take a look.

The Create Transmittal dialog box presented by the ***eTransmit*** command contains two tabs. (Note: There will be a third tab – Sheets – when sheet sets are open. More on sheet sets in Lesson 24.)

- The **File Tree** tab displays all the files included in the transmittal.
- The **Files Table** tab displays the same thing, but in table format.
- Use the **Add File** button at the bottom of the tab to add files to the transmittal using a standard Open File dialog box.
- Below the tabs, you'll find a text box. Use this to **Enter notes to include with this transmittal package**.
- Just to the right of the notes text box, AutoCAD has placed a **View Report** button. This will present the report that'll accompany your eTransmittal. The report contains details about what AutoCAD has included in the transmittal. You can save this file or print it for your records.
- Above the **View Report** button is the **Select a transmittal setup** frame. Here, you'll select the format for your transmittal, or pick the **Transmittal Setups** button to create a new one.

To set up a transmittal, you'll follow a procedure very similar to that which you used to set up a dimension style or a page (for plotting).

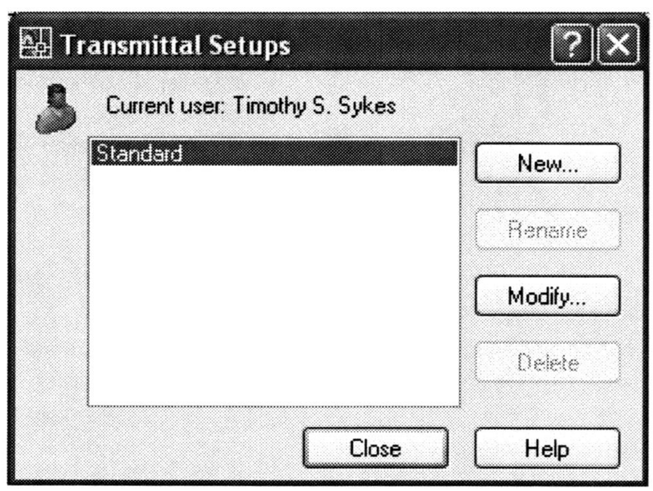


Figure 21.011

The first thing you'll see after you pick the **Transmittal Setups** button is the Transmittal Setups dialog box (Figure 21.011). Use the buttons on the right of this box to create a **New** transmittal, **Rename** an existing transmittal, **Modify** an existing transmittal, or **Delete** an existing transmittal.

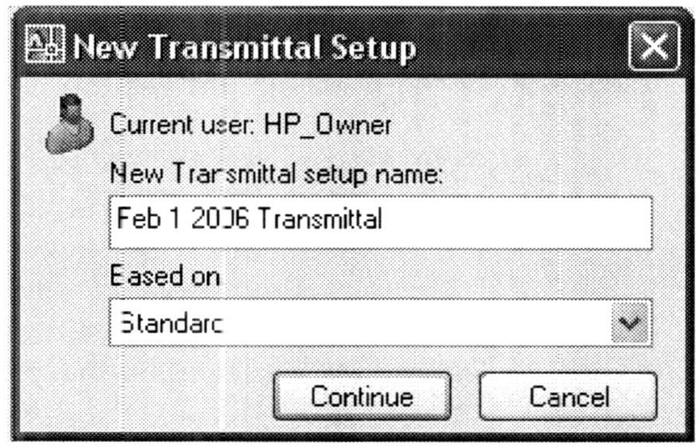


Figure 21.012

- The **New** button calls the New Transmittal Setup dialog box (Figure 21.012). Use this to name the new transmittal (use something that you can trace later). You can even base the settings for the new transmittal on those of an existing transmittal by selecting the existing one from the **Based on** list box.
- The **Continue** button on the New Transmittal Setup dialog box calls the Modify Transmittal Setup dialog box (Figure 21.013). (Note: The **Modify** button on the Transmittal Setups dialog box will take you directly to the Modify Transmittal Setup dialog box.)

  Let's look at this frightening dialog box!

  - The **Transmittal type and location** frame (at top) provides many options:
    - Select the type of transmittal (how it will be compressed for electronic transmittal) from the **Transmittal package type** drop down list box. Your options include:

      **Self-extracting executable (*.exe)** files. This option compresses all files into a single file with an EXE extension. Executing this file (double-clicking on it) will cause it to extract (decompress) the files necessary to open and edit your drawing.

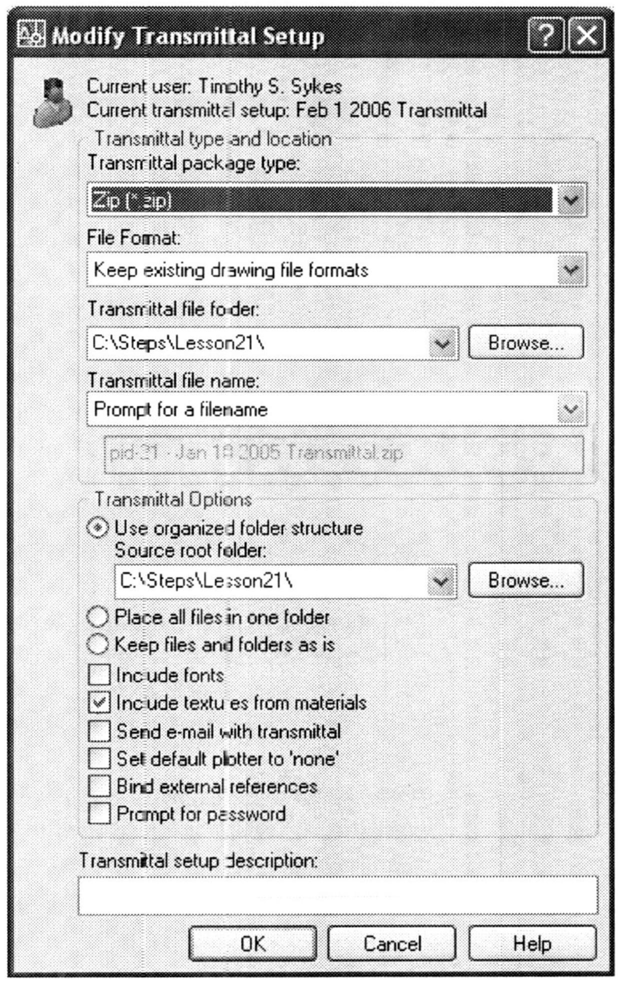


Figure 21.013

      **Folder (set of files)**. This option copies all the necessary files for opening and editing your drawing into a single folder. You can copy this folder to a disk or web site for your client or co-worker to retrieve.

      **Zip (*.zip)** files. Like self-extracting executable files, zip files compress the appropriate files into a single file (this time with a ZIP extension). Most Windows operating systems can read the zip file, or you can pick up an application (*WinZip* or *Zip*) to extract the files.

    - Use the **File format** list box to change the drawing file type to be more compatible with previous releases of AutoCAD (if necessary).
    - The **Transmittal file folder** is where AutoCAD will create the transmittal. Use the **Browse** button to select an alternate location.
    - Your best option in the **Transmittal file name** box is the default (**Prompt for a file name**). The **Overwrite if necessary** option means that you'll run the risk of accidentally overwriting an existing transmittal; the **Increment file name if necessary** option means that you may end up with a lot of unnecessary files on your computer.
    - The last box in the **Transmittal type and location** frame simply lists the name of the transmittal.
- The second frame – **Transmittal options** – requires that you make some formatting decisions.
    - **Use organized folder structure** forces AutoCAD to use the folder structure for the files being transmitted.
    - The **Source root folder** is the relative path for drawing-dependent files (like Xrefs or images – we'll see more on Xrefs and images in later lessons).
    - **Place all files in one folder** negates the previous options and forces AutoCAD to include all transmittal files in a single folder.
    - **Keep files and folders as is** negates the previous options and tells AutoCAD to retain the existing hierarchical structure of transmitted files. (Don't use this one if you intend to save the transmittal package to an Internet location.)
    - A check next to **Include fonts** tells AutoCAD to transmit the fonts used in the drawing with the package. This isn't necessary unless you've used some non-standard fonts in your drawing.
    - You'll learn about **materials** and **textures** in the 3D text. Ignore them for now.
    - **Send email with transmittal** means that AutoCAD will launch your email program so that you can send an email with the transmittal as an attachment.
    - It's a courtesy to **Set default plotter to none** before sending the transmittal. Your printer/plotter settings won't mean anything to your client (unless he happens to be using the same printer/plotter).
    - We'll learn about Xrefs and binding Xrefs in Lesson 25. For now, you can ignore this option.
    - **Prompt for password** is yet another acknowledgement of the paranoia of most companies. Adding a password to your package insures that no one but your designated recipient can open it.
- Use the **Transmittal setup description** box to give a brief description of this setup. AutoCAD will present this in the Create Transmittal dialog box when you select this setup.

*JEEPERS*; that was a lot of information!

Let's create an eTransmittal.

| Do This: 21.3.1 | Creating an eTransmittal |
|---|---|

I. Be sure you're still in the *pid-21.dwg* file in the C:\Steps\Lesson21 folder. If not, please open it now.

II. Follow these steps.

## 21.3.1: CREATING AN ETRANSMITTAL

1. Begin by entering the ***eTransmit*** command. Alternately, you can pick **eTransmit** under the File pull-down menu.

**Command: *etransmit***

AutoCAD presents the Create Transmittal dialog box (Figure 21.010).

2. We'll create a new transmittal setup; pick the appropriate button 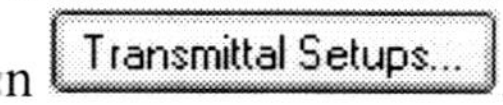

.

3. AutoCAD presents the Transmittal Setups dialog box (Figure 21.011). Pick the **New** button 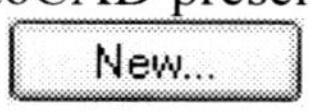

to continue.

4. Now AutoCAD asks for a name for the new transmittal. Give it a name you can remember and pick the **Continue** button to proceed.

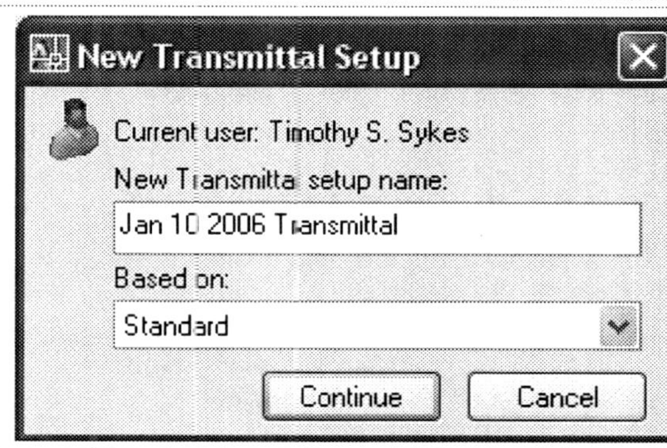


5. AutoCAD presents the Modify Transmittal Setup dialog box (Figure 21.013). In the **Transmittal type and location** frame:

- Create a Self-extracting executable file.
- Keep the existing drawing file formats.
- Save the transmittal in our C:\Steps\Lesson21 folder.
- Tell AutoCAD to ask us for a file name when it creates the transmittal.

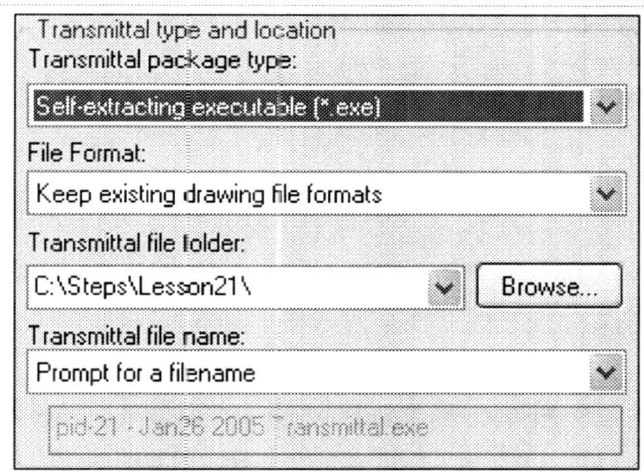

## 21.3.1: CREATING AN ETRANSMITTAL

6. In the **Transmittal options** frame:
   - **Use** [the] **organized folder structure** and set the **Source root folder** to our C:\Steps\Lesson21 folder.
   - Include our fonts with the transmittal just in case our client needs them.
   - Send our transmittal with an email.
   - Courteously set our default plotter to **none**.

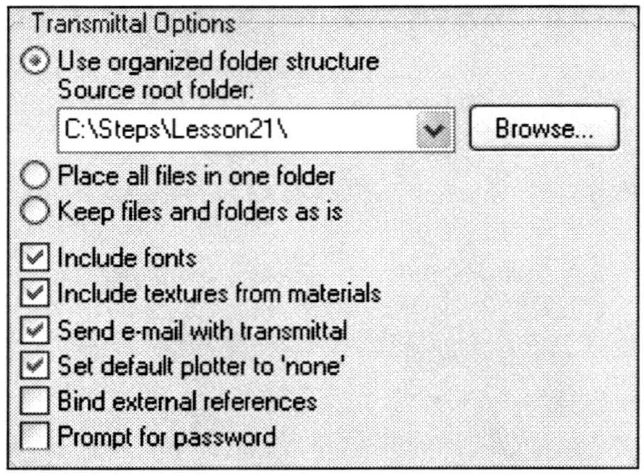


7. Let's give our setup a description so we'll know which one it is in the future.

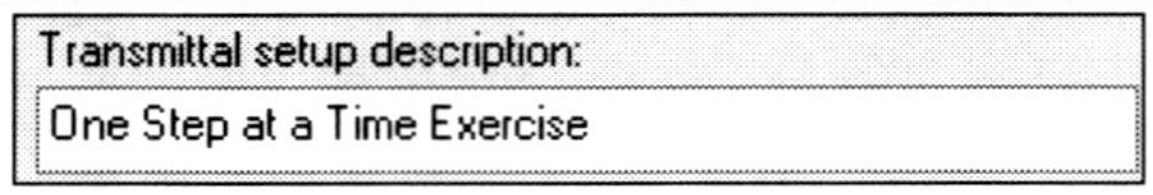


8. Now complete the setup… 

9. … and close 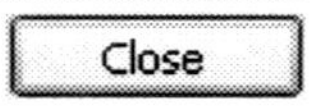

the Transmittal setups dialog box.

10. In the Create Transmittal dialog box, notice that the new setup is available and that a description appears below the list box in the **Select a transmittal setup** frame.

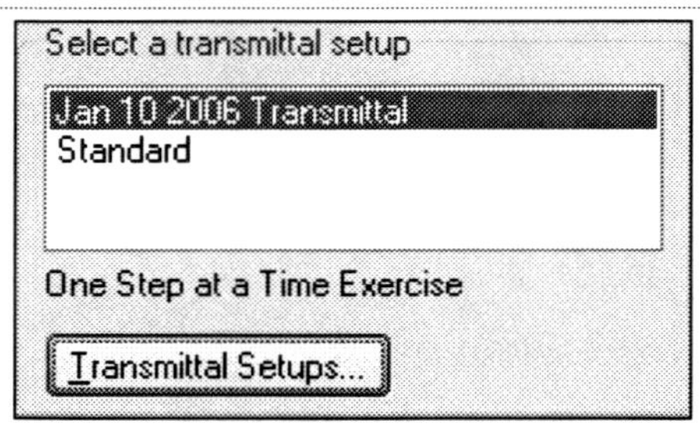


11. Select your new transmittal in the **Select a transmittal setup** frame, and pick the **OK** button 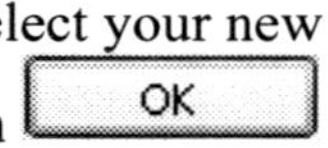

to create your transmittal.

12. As instructed in Step 5, AutoCAD prompts for a name for the transmittal file. Accept the default (below) and pick the **Save** button to continue.

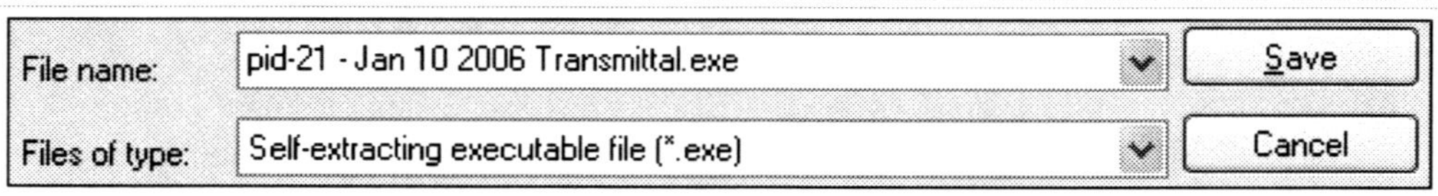


13. AutoCAD creates the transmittal and, again as instructed in Step 6, and opens your email software with the transmittal and a text file attached. (The text file is the report we discussed at the beginning of this section.)

All you have to do is fill in the recipient's address and send the email!

The recipient of the transmittal will receive a file that, once executed, will create a folder with all the files and data required for your client to open, read, and modify the drawing you've sent him! (If you want to check this out, the files are located in the C:\Steps\Lesson21 folder. Feel free to execute it; for this exercise, I'd extract the files to a separate directory just to see exactly what was included in it.)

## 21.4 Extra Steps

- If you haven't looked at the supplementary material for this lesson, it would be helpful for you to do so.
- Autodesk offers a unique approach to sharing project drawings and other information. It works something like a web host and operates for an addition fee. Visit their Buzzsaw site (http://usa.autodesk.com/) for more information.

## 21.5 What Have We Learned?

*Items covered in this lesson include:*

- *Setting up a printer/plotter*
- *Setting up a Plot Style*
- *Setting up a drawing page*
- *Creating an eTransmittal*
- *AutoCAD plot commands:*
    - ***Pagesetup***
    - ***Plot & Print***
    - ***Browser***
    - ***Hyperlink***
    - ***PublishToWeb***
    - ***Publish***
    - ***eTransmit***
- *Creating a DWF file*
- *Adding hyperlinks to a drawing*
- *Creating a web page through AutoCAD*

I strongly suggest printing at least two of the assignments for each of the lessons you'll complete throughout the remainder of this text. Then, when you've finished the course, review this lesson once again. After all, you really can't roll up the PC and stick it in your tool belt down at the job site. Your drawings must, eventually, be put on paper.

## 21.6 Exercises

*Before trying these exercises, familiarize yourself with your printer and / or plotter by reading the appropriate manuals.

1. If you've a plotter available, plot the *Floor Plan* drawing found in the C:\Steps\Lesson21 folder. Use these parameters:
    - Plot to a ¼"=1'-0" scale;
    - Plot to a C-size (22"x17") sheet of paper.
2. Using a printer, plot the *Floor Plan* drawing to fit on a 17" x 11" sheet of paper.
3. Using a printer, plot the *Floor Plan* drawing to fit on a 11" x 8.5" sheet of paper.
4. Create a hyperlink from the title of the *Floor Plan* drawing to your company's or school's web site.
5. Create a DWF file for the *Floor Plan* drawing.
6. Create a web page for the *Floor Plan* drawing.

*For more exercises related to Lesson 21, please see Lesson 21 in AutoCAD 2007: One Step at a Time – Workbook.*

## 21.6 For Web-Based Review Questions, visit: http://www.uneedcad.com/2007/Files/07R21.pdf

# Lesson 22

Following this lesson, you will:

- ✓ *Be familiar with Viewports*
- ✓ *Know the difference between Model Space and Paper Space (aka. Layout Space)*
- ✓ *Know how to set up a drawing in the Paper Space environment*

# *Space for a New Beginning*

*By now, you've printed (or plotted) a drawing in Model Space. You understand, then, the complexity of the mathematics involved ...*

- *How large is the area to plot?*
- *How large is the paper?*
- *At what scale will I want to plot?*

*... and a host of other questions that must be answered. And then you have to consider stuff like text and dimensions – plotted size and drawing scale factor. AGHH!*

*Does it have to be that difficult!?*

*The answer is a resounding, NO! ("Now I tell you!")*

*We begin this section of our text by simplifying these tasks with a remarkable tool called Paper Space.*

*When it comes to drawing display and arrangement, there exist two distinct groups of CAD operators – those who've used Paper Space and would never use anything else, and those who (generally for lack of training) haven't used Paper Space.*

*This lesson will familiarize you (painlessly) to the wonders of Paper Space and Viewports so that you may join the ranks of enlightened operators! To keep it simple, we'll remain in the two-dimensional world throughout this lesson. However, you'll continue to discover the benefits of these tools even as you explore the third dimension in our next text – 3D AutoCAD 2007: One Step at a Time.*

*Let's begin by answering the basic questions.*

## 22.1 Understanding the Terminology

*What is a viewport?*

My *New American Dictionary* defines a port as a window in the side of a ship. Similarly, a viewport is a window into your drawing.

If you imagine viewing an object that's resting in the center of a box through holes in the sides, top, and bottom of the box, you'll get a fairly good idea of what viewports are. Essentially, viewports are openings into your drawing, each presenting a different view of the drawn object(s).

AutoCAD provides two types of viewport from which to choose – simple *tiled* viewports and more complex *floating* (or untiled) viewports. We'll look at each of these.

*What is Paper Space?*

Paper Space is a plotting tool. (You'll like this one!) It provides a method for creating a finished drawing that uses more than one scale and/or view of a drawing. In other words, this is how you can create a drawing with separate details shown at larger scales for ease of viewing (and dimensioning).

You'll create the drawing as you always have – in *Model Space* (the *space* where you create your drawing or three-dimensional *model*). But before you plot, you'll place the drawing and details in their own spaces on an imaginary sheet of *paper*.

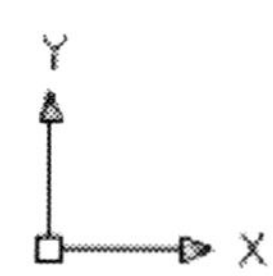

Figure 22.001

*How do I know which space I'm using?*

There are a few ways to know.

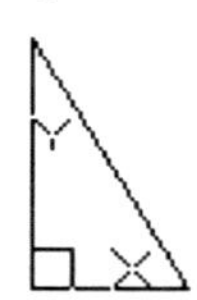
Figure 22.002

First, look at the UCS icon. The standard XY icon (Figure 22.001) indicates Model Space; the triangular icon (Figure 22.002) indicates Paper Space.

If you have the UCS icon turned off, you can look at the **Model/Paper** toggle on the status bar. If **MODEL** appears, you're in Model Space. Conversely, if **PAPER** appears, you're in Paper Space.

*How do I switch between Model Space and Paper Space?*

The keyboard approach is simply to type ***MSpace*** (or ***MS***) for Model Space or ***PSpace*** (or ***PS***) for Paper Space at the command prompt. Alternately, you can pick the toggle on the status bar.

All of this will become clearer as we proceed.

## 22.2 Using Tiled Viewports

Use tiled viewports in Model Space (what you might at this point consider "normal" drawing space) to enhance your ability to see several parts of the drawing at once. This ability will become particularly important when drawing in three dimensions. You can place a three-dimensional view of the object in one viewport while drawing on a single, two-dimensional plane (one side of the object) in another.

Create tiled viewports using the Viewports dialog box (Figure 22.003). Access the dialog box using either the ***Viewports*** or ***VPorts*** command.

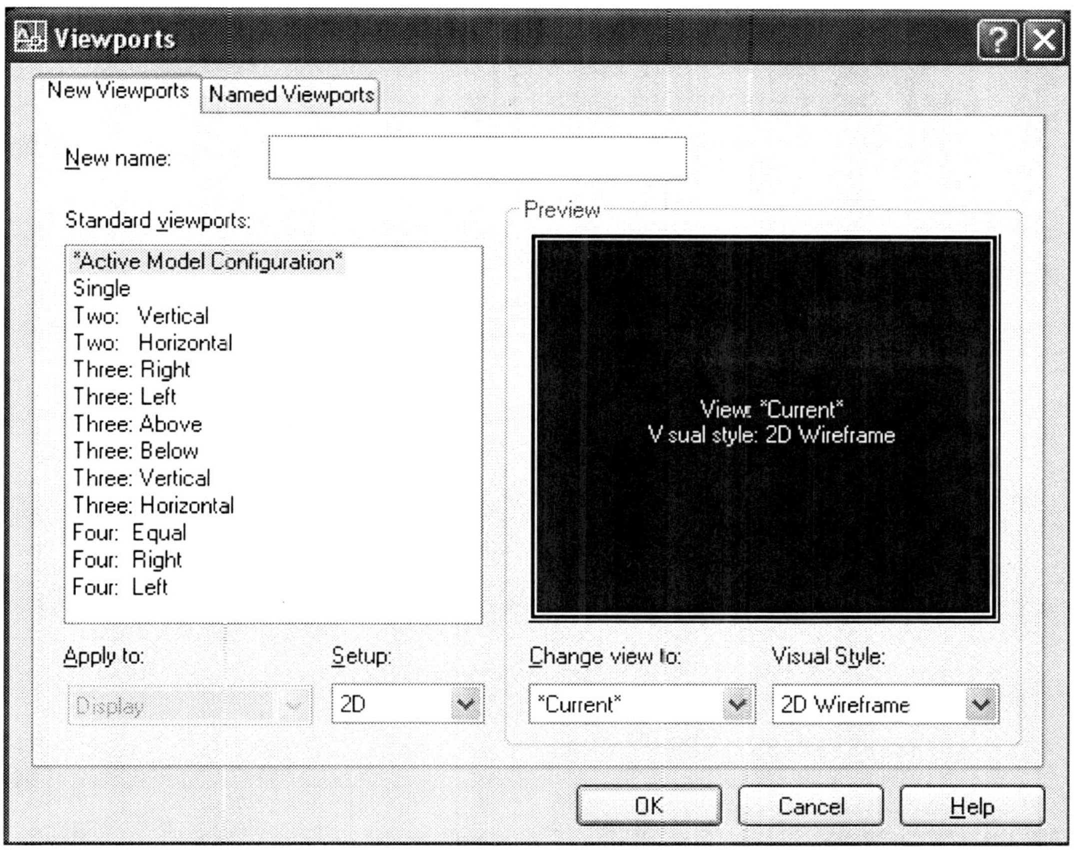


Figure 22.003

Let's look at our options.

The names of the two tabs indicate their function; use **New Viewports** to create new viewports and **Named Viewports** to activate or set current a saved viewport configuration.

We'll begin with the **New Viewports** tab.

- Place a name or title in the **New name** text box at the top if you wish to save a current configuration. (You won't need to use a name if you don't want to save the configuration.) You'll be able to recall your configuration later using the **Change view to** control box (lower-right) or the **Named Viewports** tab.
- The **Standard viewports** list box provides a list of the more common viewport setups. Select each and see the configuration in the **Preview** frame.
- Once you've selected a viewport configuration, you can choose to apply your selection to the **Display** or the **Current Viewport** using the **Apply to** control box. Using the **Display** option will replace the drawing's current configuration with the new selection. Using the **Current Viewport** option will place the new configuration inside the currently active viewport. This is how you customize your viewports.
- The **Setup** control box offers two choices: **2D** or **3D**.
  - The **2D** option will place the drawing's current view in each of the viewports.
  - The **3D** option will create the viewports using standard 3D views (top, front, side, isometric).

  Once selected, you can adjust the view using display commands (***Zoom***, ***Pan***, ***View***).
- Leave the Visual Styles control box set to **2D Wireframe** for your 2D work. We'll discuss the other options in the 3D text.
- The **Named Viewports** tab (Figure 22.004) presents the **Named viewports** list box and a **Preview** frame.

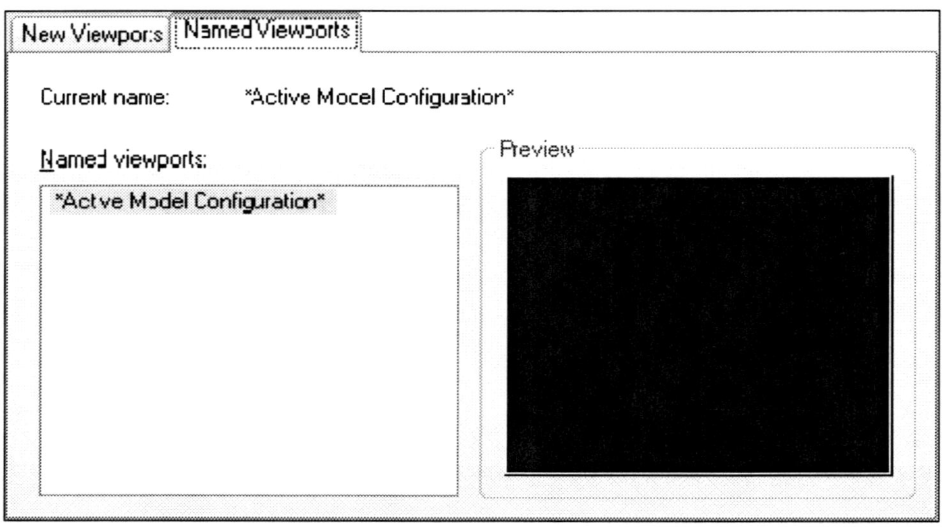


Figure 22.004

  - The **Named viewports** list box offers the names of any viewport configurations that have been saved. You can set a viewport configuration current by selecting its name and picking the **OK** button.
  - The **Preview** frame allows you to see the setup of the selected viewport configuration.

Let's experiment a bit.

> You can also access the Viewports dialog box by selecting it from the pull-down menus. Follow this path:
>
> *View – Viewports – New [or Named] Viewports ...*

| Do This: 22.2.1 | Working with Tiled Viewports |
|---|---|

I. Open the *flr-pln22a.dwg* file in the C:\Steps\Lesson22 folder. The drawing looks like Figure 22.005.

II. Follow these steps.

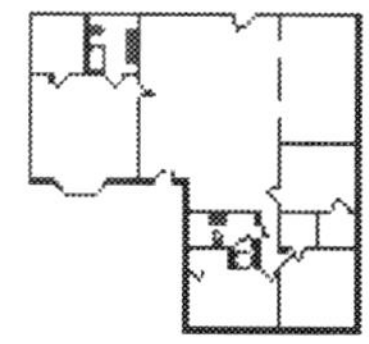

Figure 22.005

## 22.2.1: Working with Tiled Viewports

1. We'll begin by creating some viewports. Enter the ***Viewports*** command by typing ***viewports*** or ***vports*** at the command prompt. Alternately, you can pick the **Display Viewports Dialog** button  on either the Viewports or the Layouts toolbar.

**Command: *vports***

2. Select the **Three: Right** configuration. Notice the **Preview** window (below).

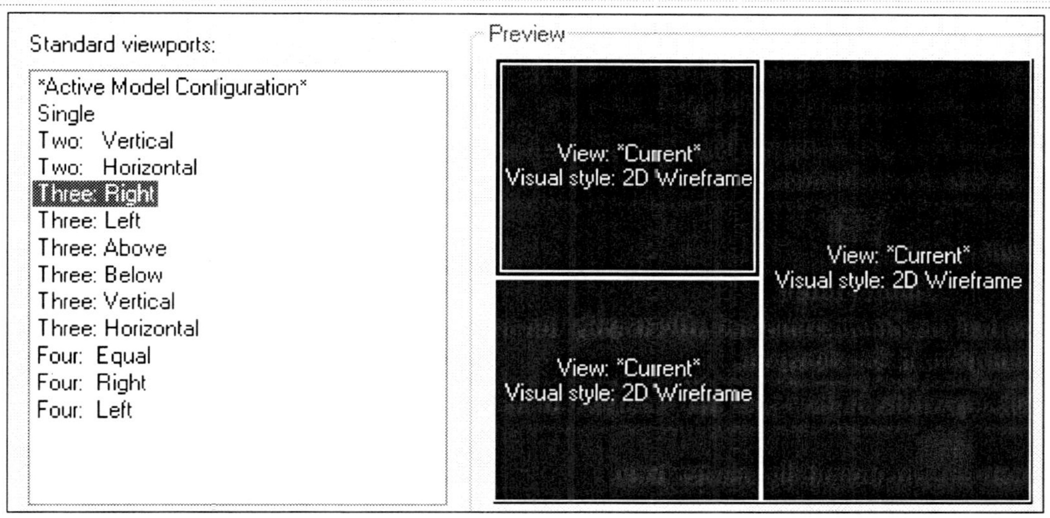


3. Pick the **OK** button 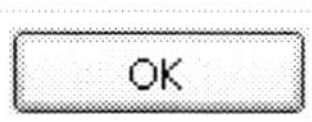

to continue. Your drawing looks like the following figure.

## 22.2.1: Working with Tiled Viewports

4. Place your cursor into each of the viewports. Notice that only the right (active) viewport presents crosshairs. Other (inactive) viewports present a cursor arrow. Activate a viewport by placing the cursor in the desired viewport and picking once with the left mouse button. Notice that you can activate only one viewport at a time.

Notice also that each viewport contains the UCS icon (Figure 22.001). You can manipulate each viewport separately as though it were your entire drawing screen.

5. Be sure the right viewport is active. (Place the cursor in the right viewport and pick once with the left mouse button.)

5. ***Zoom*** extents.

**Command: *z***

Notice that the ***Zoom*** command affects only the active viewport. If necessary, ***Pan*** to center the floor plan in the viewport.

6. Pick anywhere in the upper left viewport to activate it.

7. Zoom in around the master bath.

**Command: *z***

The viewport will look like this.

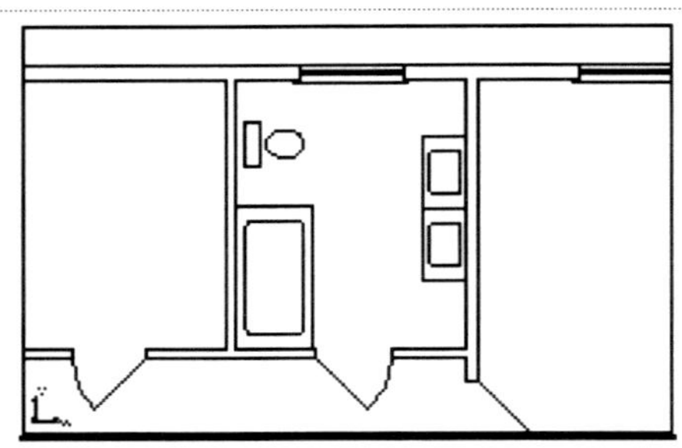

8. Now activate the lower left viewport.

9. Zoom in around the common bath.

**Command: *z***

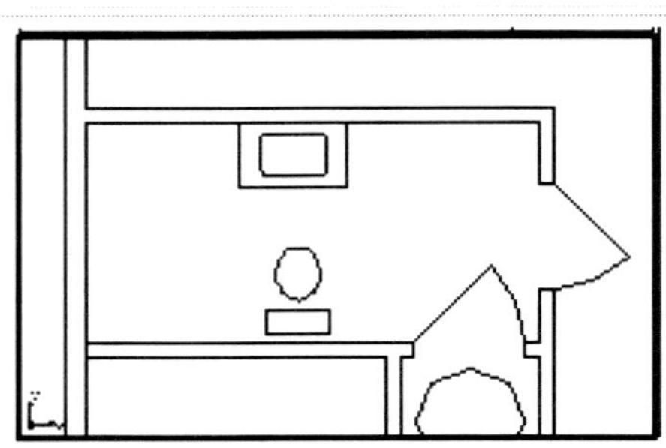

10. Let's place a tub in the common bath. Enter the ***Copy*** command.

**Command: *co***

## 22.2.1: WORKING WITH TILED VIEWPORTS

11. Pick once in the upper left viewport to activate it; then select the bathtub. Select the lower left endpoint of the tub as your base point.

**Select objects:**

**Specify base point or [Displacement] <Displacement>: _endp of**

12. Pick once in the lower left viewport to activate it, and then place the tub in the lower left corner of the bathroom.

**Specify second point or <use first point as displacement>: _endp of**

Your screen now looks like the figure below. Notice that the changes are reflected in the right viewport as well as the lower left.

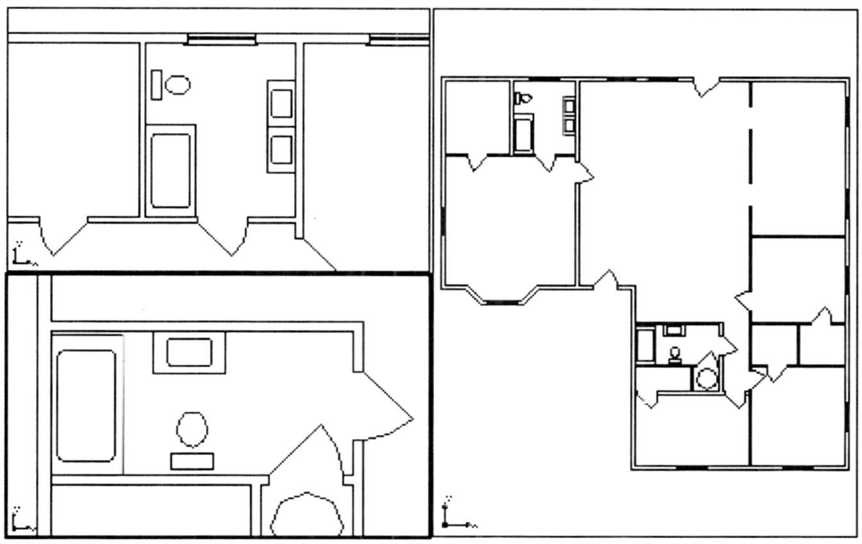

13. Remember to save the drawing 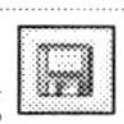 occasionally.

**Command: *qsave***

14. Now let's save our viewport configuration. Open the Viewports dialog box 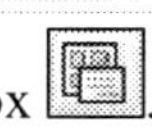.

**Command: *vports***

15. Enter the name *Baths* in the **New name** text box.

16. Complete the procedure 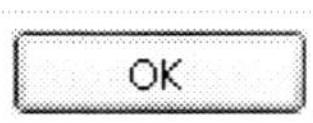.


17. Now let's reset the screen to a single viewport. Reopen the Viewports dialog box 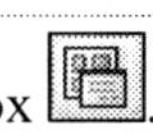.

**Command: *vports***

18. Select the **Single** configuration and then pick the **OK** button  to continue. AutoCAD presents a single viewport displaying the view of the current (lower left) viewport.


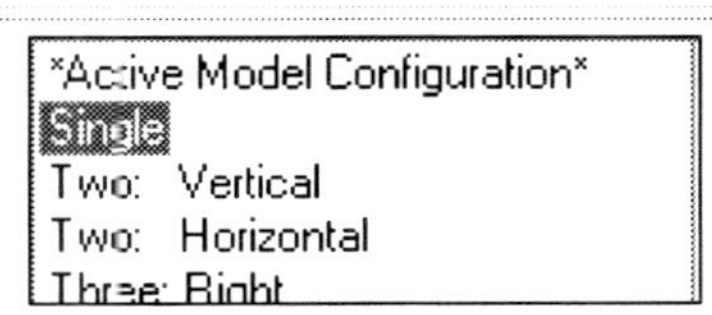

## 22.2.1: Working with Tiled Viewports

19. ***Zoom*** extents .

**Command:** ***z***

20. Now restore the **Baths** configuration. Open the Viewports dialog box .

**Command:** ***vports***

21. Pick the **Named Viewports** tab and select the **Baths** configuration in the **Named viewports** list box (below).

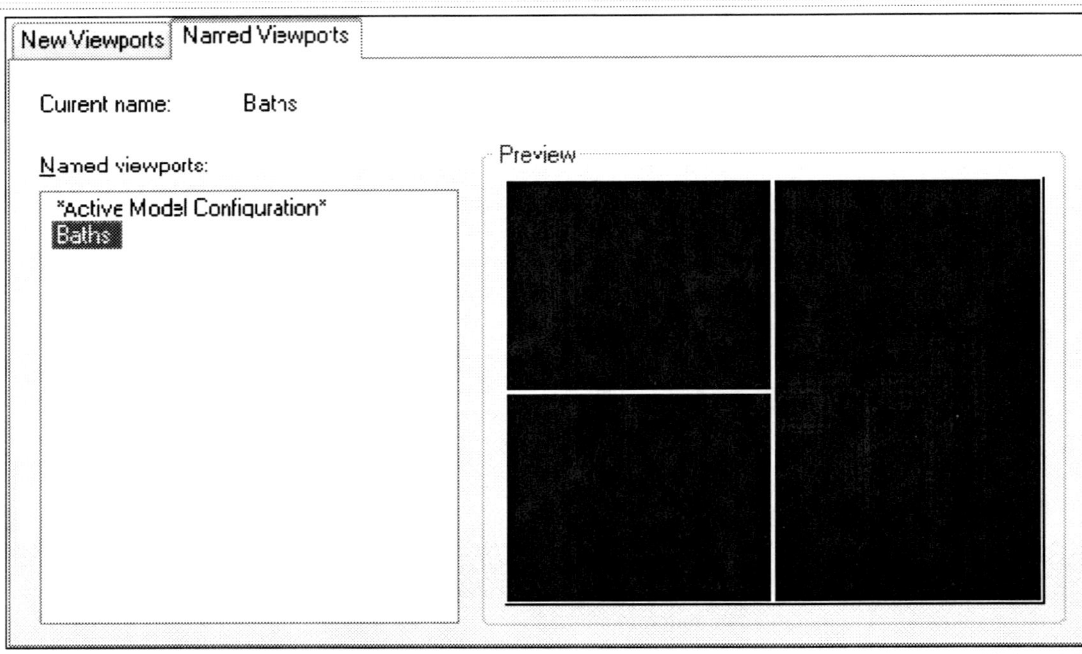


22. Pick the **OK** button to complete the command [OK]. AutoCAD presents the **Baths** configuration (see the Step 12 figure).

23. Save the drawing  but don't exit.

**Command:** ***qsave***

You can see the benefits of using viewports when manipulating several smaller parts of your drawing at one time. But when we consider the limitations of tiled viewports, we can see that they were designed as drawing aids, not plotting tools.

Some things to remember about tiled viewports include:

- Tiled viewports were designed for use in Model Space.
- Tiled viewports are not objects and won't plot. Your plot will show only the view in the *active* viewport.
- Only one viewport is active at a time. This means that you can draw only in one viewport at a time, but you can activate a new viewport transparently (while using another command).
- The active viewport will show crosshairs while inactive viewports will show a cursor. Place the cursor in the viewport you wish to activate and click once to activate it.

- Layers behave universally in tiled viewports. You can't freeze or thaw a layer just for one viewport as you can with floating viewports. (You'll see how to use layers in floating viewports in Lesson 23.)
- While you can control the number and position of tiled viewports, you can't easily control the size. You can't control the shape at all (all tiled viewports are rectangular).
- You can create viewports within viewports, but you should consider the size of the viewports and the size of your monitor before attempting this.
- Manipulation of viewports doesn't affect the actual drawing.

To see how you can use viewports to assist in plotting a drawing that uses multiple scales, we'll take a look at floating viewports in Section 22.4. But first, we must set up our Paper Space environment.

> You'll occasionally see the term *Paper Space* written as *paperspace*. Both refer to the same thing, though *paperspace* is generally a programmer's term.

## 22.3 Setting Up a Paper Space Environment

Entering Paper Space is as easy as picking a **Layout** tab just above the command line. When you select a **Layout** tab for the first time, AutoCAD will create a single floating viewport in the center of the page.

Like Model Space, Paper Space must be set up. But it's quite a bit easier with Paper Space. Let's set up a Paper Space layout for our floor plan.

> Note: This procedure will utilize my printer. You may have to adjust the settings to match your printer or plotter setup.

### Do This: 22.3.1 Creating a Paper Space Layout

I. Be sure you're still in the *flr-pln22a.dwg* file in the C:\Steps\Lesson22 folder. If not, please open it now.

II. Set **VPORTS** as the current layer.

III. Follow these steps.

**22.3.1: CREATING A PAPER SPACE LAYOUT**

1. Pick the **Layout1** tab just above the command line. AutoCAD opens the layout and creates a floating viewport (see the following figure).

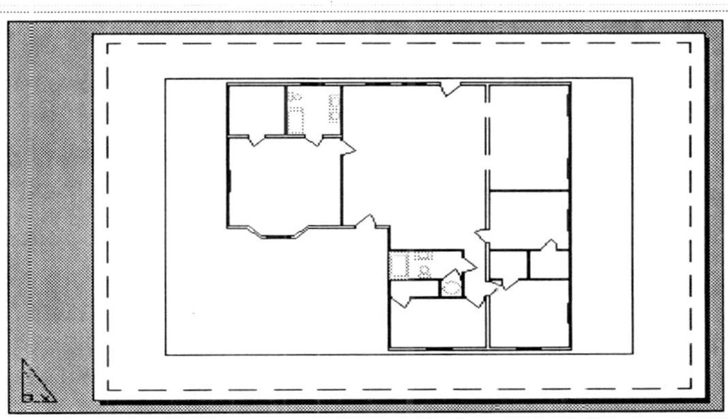

## 22.3.1: Creating a Paper Space Layout

2. Let's rename the tab for better understanding. Right-click on the **Layout1** tab and select **Rename** from the cursor menu.

3. Call the layout *Tara II Layout* (as indicated), and then pick the **OK** button to continue. Notice the new name on the tab.

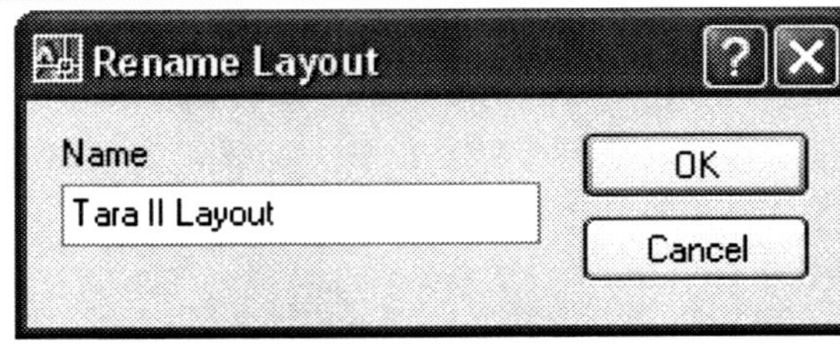


4. Save the drawing.

**Command: *qsave***

5. Try erasing different parts of the drawing. Notice that only the frame around the floor plan (the floating viewport) is selectable.

Erase the floating viewport.

**Command: *e***

Notice that the entire floor plan disappears. There is no longer a hole (a viewport) in the paper through which to see the model (your drawing).

6. Save the drawing but don't exit.

**Command: *qsave***

You've seen how to start a Paper Space layout – just go to the **Layout** tab and let AutoCAD do the rest. AutoCAD presents a sheet of paper with a floating viewport (a hole in the page) that's the only thing that exists on the page. (The dashed outline shows the margins of the working area on the page.)

You can place objects on the paper that won't affect the model (title block, text, and so forth). Alternately, you can return to Model Space to work on the model. You can even work on the model through the viewport by entering the ***MSpace*** command! We'll look at this in more detail in later sections of this lesson; but first, let's examine floating viewports.

> You can have more than one layout in your drawing – each set up differently for different printing needs. Use the ***Layout*** command to add, remove, or copy layout tabs. It presents the following options:
>
> **Command: *layout***
>
> **Enter layout option [Copy/Delete/New/Template/Rename/SAveas/Set/?] <set>:**
>
> Most of these options are self-explanatory. However, the **Save** option might not do what you expect. It replaces the default layout with the current setup (all future layouts will begin with the current setup).
>
> The command line isn't difficult, but you'll probably find it easier to simply to right-click on a tab and select the desired option from the cursor menu.

## 22.4 Using Floating Viewports

Floating, or untiled, viewports, although more complex than tiled viewports, offer considerably more flexibility. But how are floating viewports different from tiled viewports? Let's take a look.

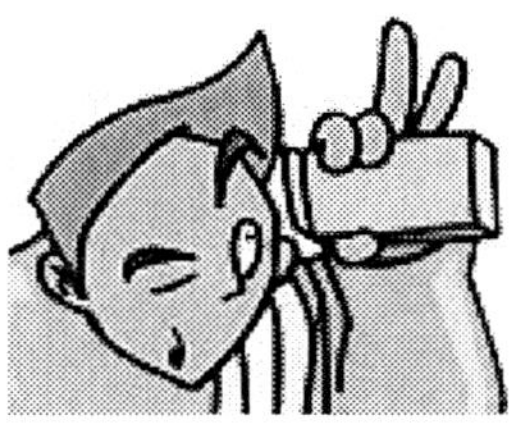

As we saw in Section 22.2, AutoCAD designed tiled viewports as *drawing* tools for a Model Space environment. Tiled viewports act like holes in an imaginary box through which you view different parts of your drawing. The location and size of the hole determine what you see, how much you *see*, and at what angle you see the drawing objects. Tiled viewports don't affect how the drawing will be plotted.

Floating viewports were designed as *plotting* tools in a Paper Space environment. Floating viewports also act like holes, but this time they're holes in a sheet of paper covering the drawing objects. The location and size of floating viewport holes determine what will be *plotted*, how much will be plotted, and at what angle the drawing objects will be plotted.

Some things to remember about floating viewports include:

- Floating viewports are objects and can be moved, stretched, and erased like any other object on a drawing. Consequently, you can place them on a separate layer that can be frozen at plot time.
- Unlike tiled viewports, floating viewports don't have to be rectangular.
- Floating viewports can overlap.
- You can control layers within each viewport independently of the rest of the drawing. This is a key benefit since you often won't want details shown in one viewport reflected in another.
- Use floating viewports to show different views of one or more objects on a single plot.
- Like tiled viewports, only one floating viewport is active at a time.
- Floating viewports live in Paper Space (on a **Layout** tab). Although they're not available in Model Space, you can work in Model Space *through* a floating viewport (much as a doctor works on a kidney or gall bladder through a hole in the skin).
- Sizing text on Paper Space is really quite easy. Since you're working on the actual plotted page, simply enter the text at the desired plotted size. No need for scale factors!

## 22.4.1 Creating Floating Viewports Using *MView*

Creating floating viewports using the ***MView*** command appears more daunting than it actually is. The command sequence looks like this:

**Command: *mview* (or *mv*)**
**Specify corner of viewport or**
**[ON/OFF/Fit/Shadeplot/Lock/Object/Polygonal/Restore/2/3/4] <Fit>: *[begin a window]***
**Specify opposite corner: *[complete the window]***

Let's look at each option.

- The **ON/OFF** options allow you to "open" or "close" the viewport through which you see the drawing. If the viewport is **OFF**, it's closed and you can't see through it. Thus, that part of the drawing is hidden.
- When you select one of these options, AutoCAD will prompt you to select the viewport to turn **ON** or **OFF**.
- The **Fit** option will create a single, maximum-size floating viewport within the display area.
- **Shadeplot** controls exactly what plots within a viewport. It prompts

  **Shade plot? [As Displayed/Wireframe/Hidden/Visual styles/Rendered] <As Displayed>:**

AutoCAD presents several options (mostly stuff you'll see in the 3D text). For our 2D purposes, leave the **As Display** default. If you change it accidentally, re-enter the **2D Wireframe** setting.

- The **Lock** option allows you to lock a viewport. It prompts

  **Viewport View Locking [ON/OFF]:** ***[enter ON or OFF]***

  **Select objects:** ***[select the viewport to lock or unlock]***

  When a viewport is locked, you can't (intentionally or accidentally) change the scale factor within it. This is a handy tool if you intend to work on the Model Space within a viewport.
- The **Object** option allows you to select any existing closed polyline, ellipse, spline, region, or circle (existing in Paper Space) and turn it into a floating viewport.
- The **Polygonal** option allows you to create a floating viewport with any number of sizes and in any shape. It prompts

  **Specify start point:** ***[pick a start point]***

  **Specify next point or [Arc/Length/Undo]:** ***[create the shape just as you would a polyline]***
- The **2/3/4** options tell AutoCAD to create two, three, or four viewports. AutoCAD will prompt you to locate the viewports.
- **Restore** is a very useful tool. It allows you to translate tiled viewports into floating viewport objects. When selected, AutoCAD allows you to enter the name of a saved tiled configuration or to translate the current tiled configuration into floating viewports.
- Of course the default option – **Specify corner of viewport** – allows you to manually create viewports one at a time.

Let's insert a title block into our drawing and then set up some floating viewports.

| Do This: 22.4.1.1 | Creating Floating Viewports |
|---|---|

I. Be sure you're still in the *flr-pln22a.dwg* file in the C:\Steps\Lesson22 folder. If not, please open it now.

II. Set the **BORDER** layer current.

III. Follow these steps.

**22.4.1.1: CREATING FLOATING VIEWPORTS**

1. Insert  the *ANSI-A title block* drawing that came with AutoCAD. (Find it in the **Documents and Settings\[Timothy S. Sykes]\Local Settings\Application Data\Autodesk\ AutoCAD 2007\ R17.[X]\enu\Template** folder. (This is on a Windows XP computer.)

   Put it at the 0,0 coordinates.

   **Command:** ***i***

2. Set the **VPORTS** layer current.

3. Enter the ***MView*** command by typing ***mview*** or ***mv*** at the prompt.

   **Command:** ***mv***

4. Place the first floating viewport as indicated.

   **Specify corner of viewport or**

   **[ON/OFF/Fit/Shadeplot/Lock/ Object/Polygonal/Restore/2/3/4] <Fit>:** ***.5,7.5***

   **Specify opposite corner:** ***4.75,4.25***

## 22.4.1.1: Creating Floating Viewports

5. Place a second floating viewport as indicated.

    **Command:** ***[enter]***
    **Specify corner of viewport or [ON/OFF/Fit/Shadeplot/Lock/ Object/Polygonal/Restore/2/3/ 4] <Fit>:** ***5,6.5***
    **Specify opposite corner:** ***10,2.5***

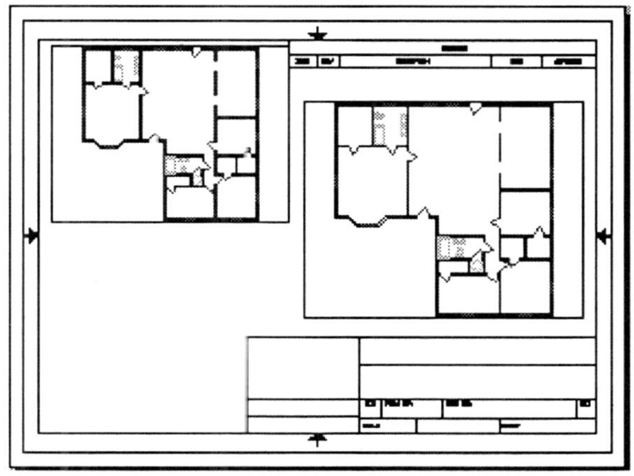

6. Now let's make a nonrectangular viewport – the easy way. Draw a circle as indicated.

    **Command:** ***c***
    **Specify center point for circle or [3P/2P/Ttr (tan tan radius)]:** ***2.25,2.25***
    **Specify radius of circle or [Diameter]:** ***1.75***

7. Now we'll convert the circle to a floating viewport. Enter the ***MView*** command.

    **Command:** ***mv***

8. Use the **Object** option Object.

    **Specify corner of viewport or [ON/OFF/Fit/Shadeplot/ Lock/Object/Polygonal/ Restore/2/3/4] <Fit>:** ***o***

9. Select the circle.

    **Select object to clip viewport:**

Your drawing now looks like this. Notice that the round viewport shows only part of the drawing. It began with the full drawing and then clipped away the part that didn't fit into the circle.

10. Save the drawing but don't exit.

    **Command:** ***qsave***

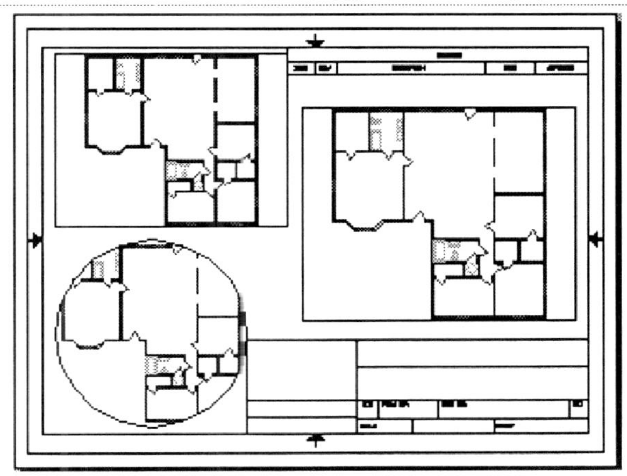

## 22.4.2 The Viewports Toolbar

*The one common thread that permeates the thrills of life – your first kiss, your first child, your first paycheck ...– is that each results from the* ***discovery*** *of something new and wonderful.*
*Never miss an opportunity to explore or you may miss an opportunity to discover.*
*Anonymous*

We've made a good start with Paper Space and floating viewports. But have you discovered the viewports toolbar yet (Figure 22.006)?

Figure 22.006

This handy item provides single-button selection of some of the ***MView*** options as well as some other tools.

Let's take a look.

- The first button – **Display Viewports Dialog** – does just that. It displays the Viewports dialog box that we used to create tiled viewports in Section 22.2 of this lesson. You can also use this dialog box to create *floating* viewports in Paper Space! Simply follow the same procedures you learned for tiled viewports.

  (Notice that the viewports dialog box presented when in Paper Space doesn't have the **New name** text box. Floating viewport configurations are saved as layouts.)
- The second button – **Single Viewport** – enables you to create a single viewport much as you created the first two viewports in our last exercise.
- The third button – **Polygonal Viewport** – allows you to create a viewport with any number of sizes and in any shape by executing the **Polygon** option of the ***MView*** command.
- The fourth button – **Convert Object to Viewport** – executes the **Object** option of the ***MView*** command as we did in our last exercise.
- The last button – **Clip Existing Viewport** – is a modifying tool used to redefine viewport boundaries. We'll learn more about it in Lesson 23.
- On the right end of the toolbar, you'll find the **Viewport Scale** control box. You'll use this to set the scale of the image seen through the floating viewport. We'll look at this procedure next.

## 22.4.3 Adjusting the Views in Floating Viewports

Once you've created floating viewports, you'll need to adjust what you see through them. This means adjusting the scale and then panning to achieve the appropriate view for your plot. Before we do either, we must tell AutoCAD to allow us to work in the Model Space we see through the floating viewport. Do this by simply entering ***MSpace*** or ***MS*** at the command prompt and then selecting the viewport you wish to use (see the insert below).

> To toggle between Paper Space and Model Space, simply type ***PSpace*** (or ***ps***) or ***MSpace*** (or ***ms***) at the command prompt. Alternately, you can pick on **PAPER** or **MODEL** on the status bar. You can also double-click in a Paper Space area to activate Paper Space, or in a viewport to activate Model Space (simultaneously making that viewport current).

We'll begin by setting the scale for the viewport. AutoCAD provides two methods of doing this – the **XP** option of the ***Zoom*** command, or the **Viewport Scale** control box on the Viewports toolbar.

- The Zoom Approach: While at the ***Zoom*** prompt, simply type ***1/[SF]xp*** (where ***SF*** is the scale factor for the scale you wish to use in this particular viewport – refer to Appendix A).
- The Control Box Approach: Pick the down arrow and select the appropriate scale. Alternately, you can type a scale into the box.

Let's try it.

### Do This: 22.4.3.1 Scaling Floating Viewports

I. Be sure you're still in the *flr-pln22a.dwg* file in the C:\Steps\Lesson22 folder. If not, please open it now.

II. Follow these steps.

## 22.4.3.1: Scaling Floating Viewports

1. Open Model Space by typing ***mspace*** or ***ms*** at the command prompt. Alternately, you can pick **PAPER** on the status bar 

.

**Command:** ***ms***

2. Select anywhere in the upper left viewport to activate it. Notice that the boundary darkens to indicate that it's active.

3. Use the ***Pan*** command  to center the master bath in the viewport.

**Command:** ***p***

4. Now we'll set the scale for this viewport. Enter the ***Zoom*** command on the command line.

**Command:** ***z***

5. We wish to set the scale of this viewport to ¼"=1'-0". The scale factor for this scale is 48 (see Appendix A). So enter the scale factor, as shown, using the ***xp*** suffix to indicate that you are scaling Paper Space.

**Specify corner of window, enter a scale factor (nX or nXP), or [All/Center/Dynamic/Extents/Previous/Scale/ Window/ Object] <real time>:** ***1/48xp***

AutoCAD scales the viewport. (You may have to pan slightly to center the view again.) This viewport now looks like this.

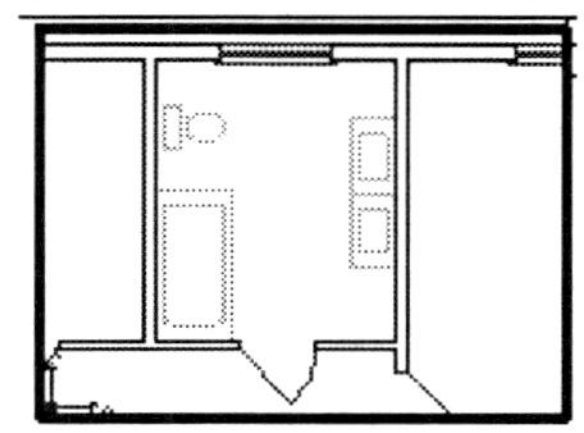

6. Now let's use the control box method. Pick anywhere in the right viewport to activate it.

7. Pick the down arrow in the **Viewport Scale** control box on the Viewport toolbar, and then scroll down until you can see the 1/16"=1' selection. Pick that one.

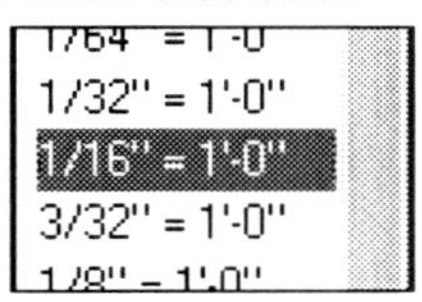


Easy? This viewport now looks like this.

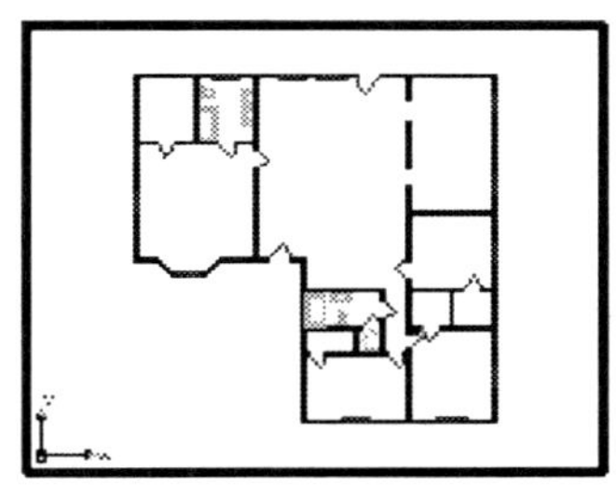

8. Activate the round viewport and center the bay window in the view. Use the ***Zoom – Center*** option .

**Command:** ***w***

9. Use either of the methods we've discussed to set the scale in this viewport to ¼"=1'-0".

10. Return to Paper Space 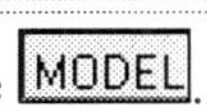

.

**Command:** ***ps***

11. On the **TEXT** layer, add the geometry shown in the following figure.

### 22.4.3.1: Scaling Floating Viewports

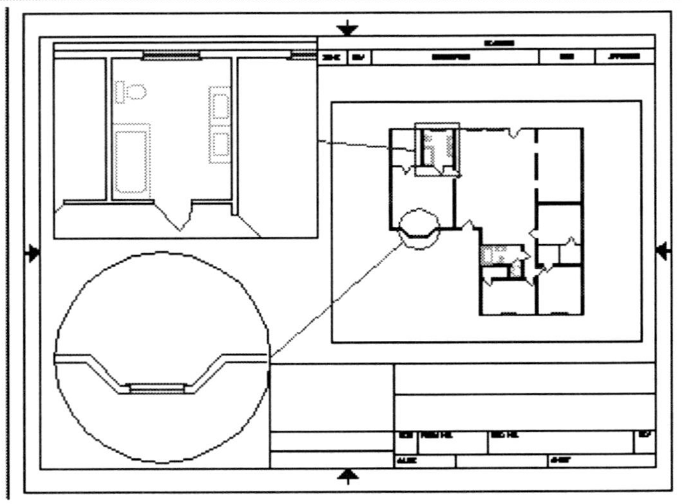

12. Save the drawing as *MyFlr-pln23a* in the C:\Steps\Lesson23 folder.

    **Command: *saveas***

Close the drawing.

The drawing now shows the full plan at a 1/16"-1'-0" scale and the common bathroom and bay window at a ¼"=1'-0" scale.

We've completed the Paper Space setup of our drawing. Let's review what we've accomplished.

- We began with a floor plan drawn in Model Space. The limits of Model Space had been set to produce a ¼"=1'-0" drawing on a C-size sheet of paper.
- We opened the layout tab of our drawing and set it up to print our Model Space drawing on an A-size sheet (AutoCAD's default). We used an AutoCAD title block designed for this page size and added three floating viewports – two rectangular and one converted object (circle).
- We set different views of the same model in each of the floating viewports – each viewport having its own scale.

## 22.5 And Now the Easy Way – The *LayoutWizard* Command

We've explored several steps in creating and setting up a Paper Space layout. But as you know, I always save the best for last.

I briefly discussed the ***Layout*** command in Section 22.3. That command allowed you to create new layouts. But AutoCAD's Layout Wizard does the same thing and more!

Using the ***LayoutWizard*** command, you can create a new layout and set it up as well.

Let's take a look at the wizard.

| Do This: 22.5.1 | Using the Layout Wizard |
|---|---|

I. Open the *flr-pln22b.dwg* file in the C:\Steps\Lesson22 folder. This is the same file as *flr-pln22a*, but hasn't had the layout set up yet.

II. Set the **VPORTS** layer current.

III. Follow these steps.

## 22.5.1: USING THE LAYOUT WIZARD

1. Enter the ***LayoutWizard*** command by typing ***layoutwizard*** at the command prompt. Alternately, you can use the Tools pull-down menu. Follow this path:

*Tools – Wizards – Create Layout…*

**Command: *layoutwizard***

2. AutoCAD presents the Create Layout – Begin dialog box (below). Enter the name *My Wizard Layout* in the text box as shown.

Pick the **Next** button to continue.

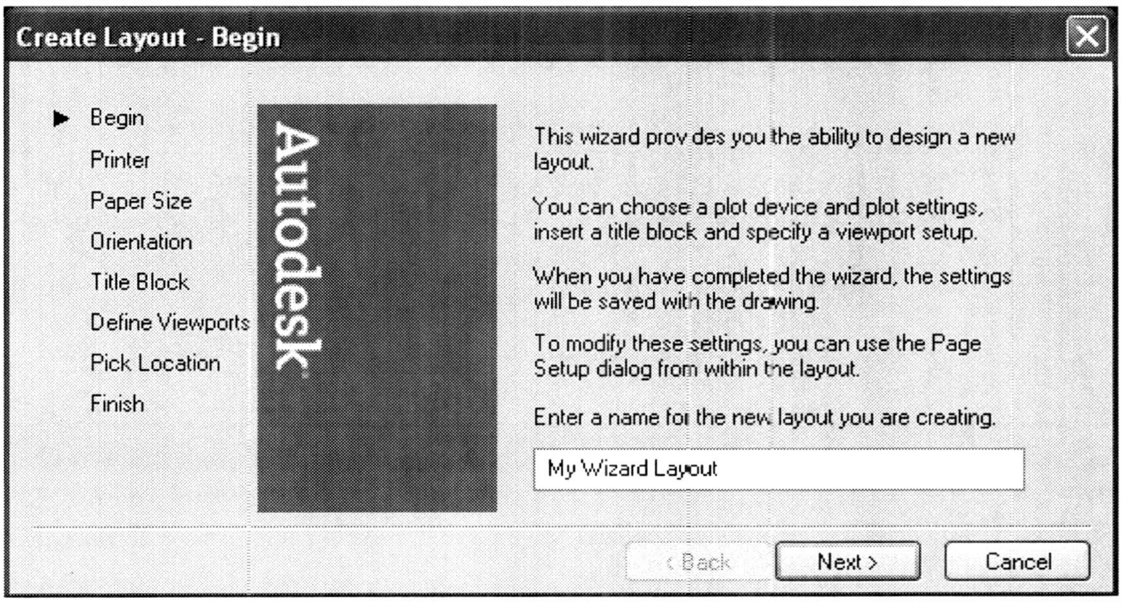


3. Select the printer or plotter you wish to use (below). (Your options may differ from mine.)

Pick the **Next** button to continue.

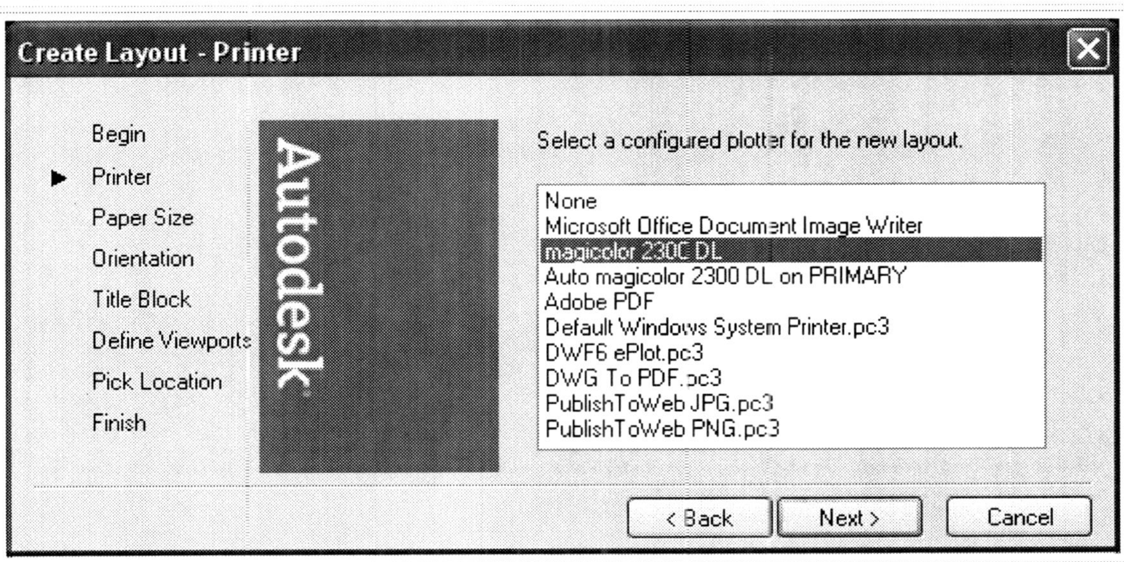

## 22.5.1: Using the Layout Wizard

4. Select a paper size for the layout (I'll use the **8½" x 11"** size). Remember to tell AutoCAD to set up the layout in **Inches** or **Millimeters**. Here we'll use **Inches** (below).

Pick the **Next** button to continue.

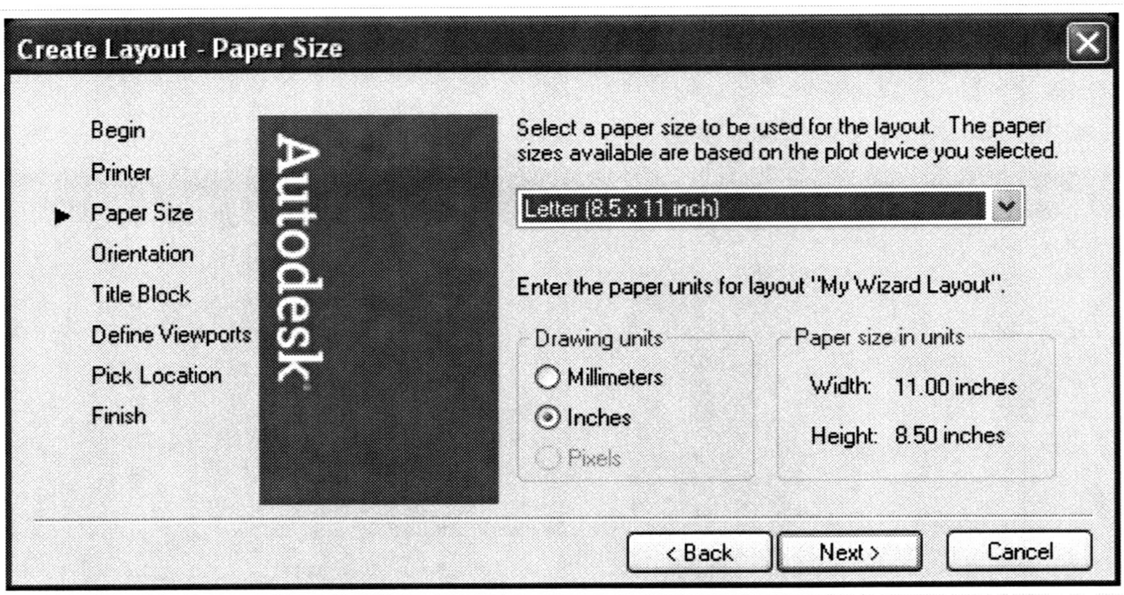


5. You'll probably want to leave the layout set to **Landscape** as we will here. Use **Portrait** when you wish to print to an upright sheet of paper (the longer dimension vertical rather than horizontal).

Pick the **Next** button to continue.

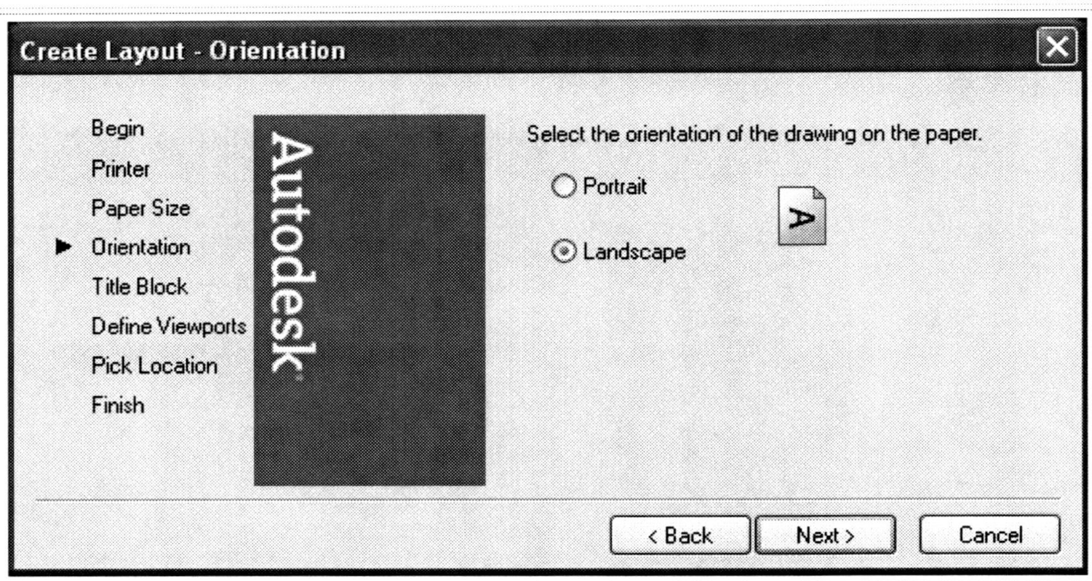

6. Select the title block you wish to use or choose **None** if you want to insert one later. I'll use the **ANSI A title block**.

Below the list box, you'll find a **Type** frame. Tell AutoCAD you wish to insert the title block as a **Block**. (We'll discuss Xrefs in Lesson 25.)

Pick the **Next** button to continue.

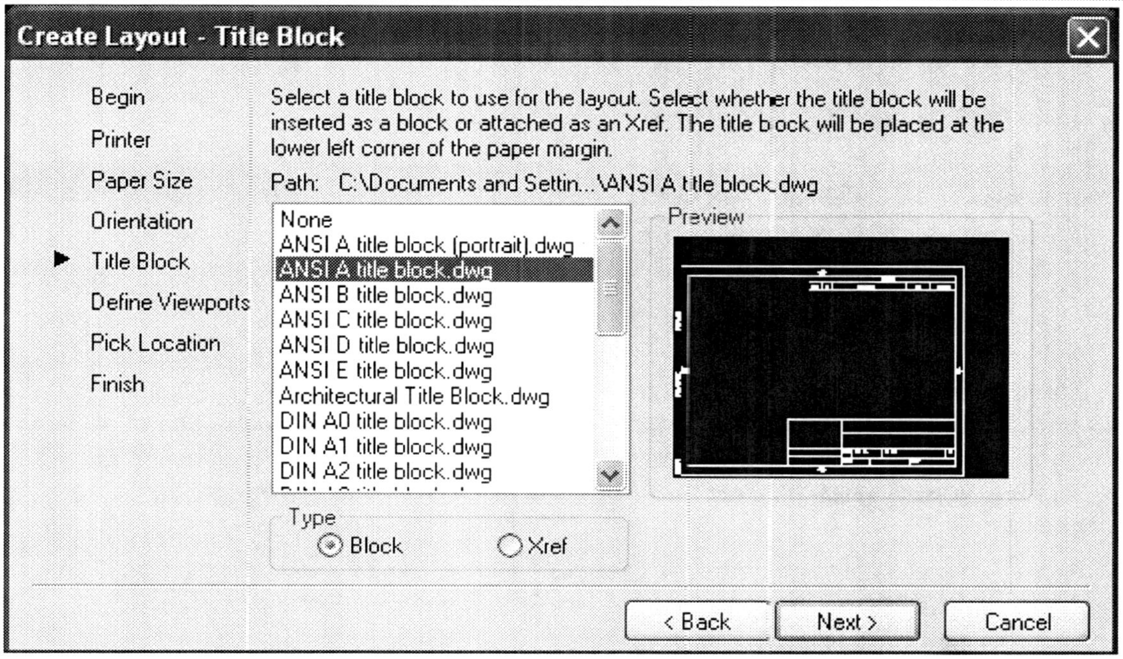


7. Now we can create a rough setup for our viewports.

In the **Viewport setup** frame (see the following figure), select the **Single** option to create a single viewport. You can use the other options to create the standard three-dimensional engineering views (four viewports – three with orthographic views and one three-dimensional view) or an **Array** of viewports. The **Array** option displays the **Rows/Columns** and **Spacing** boxes below the **Viewport setup** frame.

In the **Viewport scale** control box, set the scale for our single viewport as 1/16"=1'-0".

Pick the **Next** button to continue.

## 22.5.1: Using the Layout Wizard

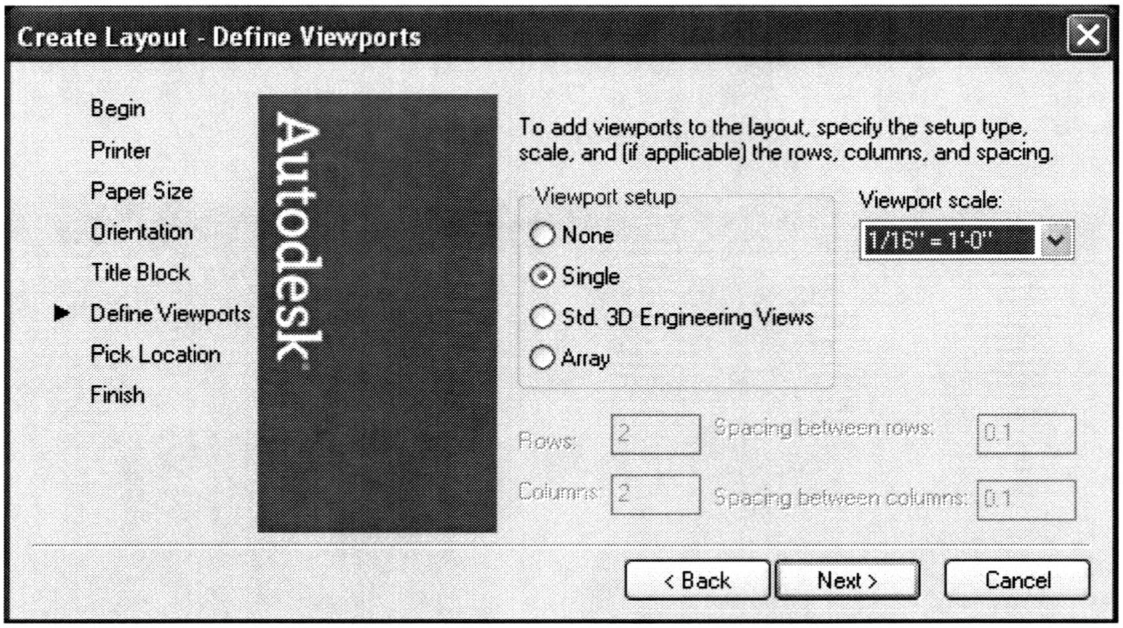


8. Pick the **Select Location** button 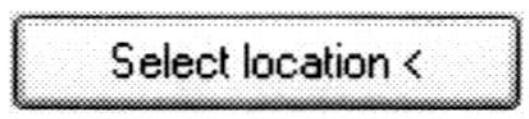

on the next screen to locate the viewport.

9. AutoCAD takes you to the graphics screen of your new layout, shows the title block you selected, and prompts for the corners of the viewport. Enter the coordinates indicated.

**Specify first corner: *4.75,6.5***

**Specify opposite corner: *10,2.25***

10. AutoCAD returns to the wizard. Pick the **Finish** button 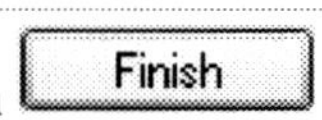

to complete the command.

AutoCAD returns to the graphics screen with the new layout visible.

11. Save the drawing 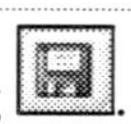.

**Command: *qsave***

Wasn't that easier than our previous exercises? You can use the ***MView*** command to add additional viewports as desired, but the bulk of the work has been accomplished in fewer steps and with less effort.

How will you set up your layouts?

We've accomplished quite a lot in such a short lesson. But we haven't finished learning the basics of Paper Space. We must consider how dimensions, layers, text, and plotting relate to Paper Space, as well as some methods of editing our layout. We'll look at these in Lesson 23, but for now, let's take time for some projects.

We've used the ***MView*** command to set up our floating viewports. We've also seen an easier approach to creating layouts – using the ***LayoutWizard*** command. But wait! There is another approach.

AutoCAD provides a method that incorporates all aspects of Paper Space setup into a single command – the ***MVSetup*** command. You may experiment with this command if you like, but be warned that consolidation doesn't always make a task easier! We'll explore ***MVSetup*** as an editing tool in Lesson 23.

## 22.6 Extra Steps

If you have access to a printer or plotter, try to plot the results of the last exercise. Don't worry if you have problems; we'll cover plotting in Paper Space in Lesson 23. This is just a preview.

Some important things to remember when plotting include:

- Be sure to plot the **My Wizard Layout** tab.
- Plot to a 1=1 scale.
- Use an A-size sheet of paper (ANSI A is 11" x 8½").

Examine the scale. Designers use Paper Space to create drawings at industry standard scales while showing details at whatever scale is necessary for clarity.

## 22.7 What Have We Learned?

*Items covered in this lesson include:*

- *Tiled viewports (Model Space)*
- *Floating viewports (Paper Space)*
- *The Layout Wizard*
- *Commands:*
    - ***PSpace***
    - ***MSpace***
    - ***Viewports***
    - ***MView***

We've seen the basic setup of Paper Space in two-dimensional drawings.

While the setup may seem somewhat confusing at first, the benefits of practice can't be overemphasized. In the two-dimensional world, Paper Space provides convenience when using multiple drawing scales and details. In the three-dimensional world, you'll find Paper Space an essential tool for printing the same object from different angles simultaneously!

Try some of the exercises at the end of this lesson to make yourself more comfortable with Paper Space. Then move on to the next lesson where you'll discover more about how to work in Paper Space.

## 22.8 Exercises

1. Open the *needle.dwg* file in the C:\Steps\Lesson22 folder. Create the drawing configuration for plotting found in the *needle* drawing atop the next page. Some helpful information includes:
    1.1. The page size is A4 (metric – 210mm x 297mm).
    1.2. The title block is the *ISO-A4* file found in AutoCAD's Template folder. (You may need to adjust its position on the sheet.)
    1.3. The title block text is attributed.
    1.4. Watch your layers (place viewports on the **VPorts** layer).
    1.5. The radius of the large circle is 60mm; the radius of the smaller circle is 36mm.

1.6. Remember that floating viewports can overlap.
1.7. The scale of each viewport (from top to bottom) is 10:1, 8:1, 2:1.
1.8. Fill in the title block as desired.
1.9. Save the drawing as *MyNeedle* in the C:\Steps\Lesson23 folder.

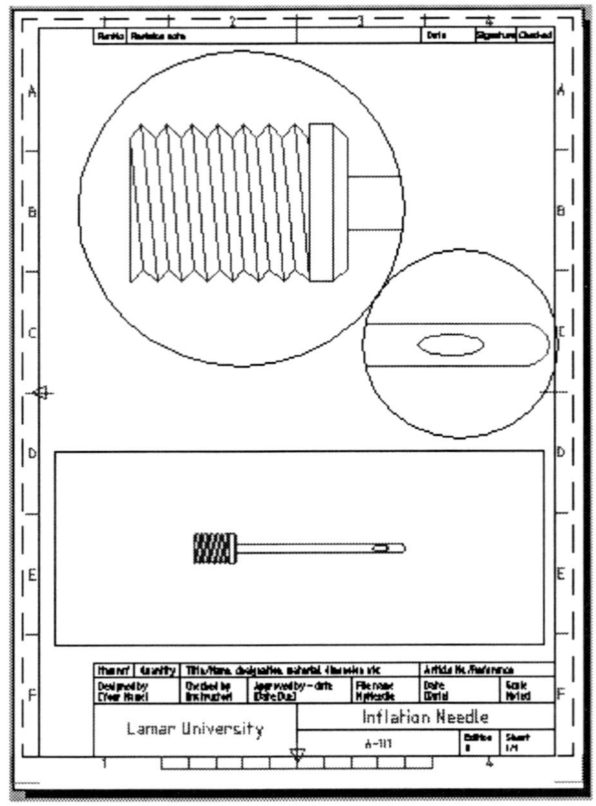

Inflation Needle

2. Open the *cable splitter.dwg* file in the C:\Steps\Lesson22 folder. Create the drawing configuration for plotting found the *cable splitter* drawing. Some helpful information includes:
   2.1. The page size is 11 x 8½".
   2.2. Watch your layers (place viewports on the **VPorts** layer).
   2.3. The radius of the circle is 1.75".
   2.4. The title block is the *ANSI A title block* file found in AutoCAD's Template folder.
   2.5. The scale of each viewport is 4:1 (upper left), 4:1 (lower left), and 1:1 (right).
   2.6. Fill in the title block as desired.
   2.7. Save the drawing as *MySplitter* in the C:\Steps\Lesson23 folder.

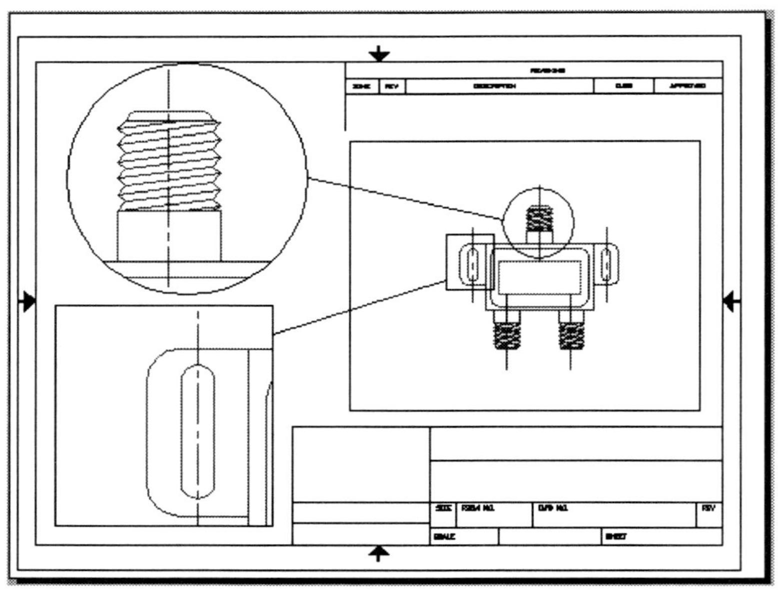
Cable Splitter

*For more exercises related to Lesson 22, please see Lesson 22 in AutoCAD 2007: One Step at a Time – Workbook.*

## 22.8 For Web-Based Review Questions, visit: http://www.uneedcad.com/2007/Files/07R22.pdf

# Lesson 23

Following this lesson, you will:

- ✓ *Know how to work with a Paper Space drawing*
  - *Know how to use layers in Paper Space*
  - *Know how to use text in Paper Space*
  - *Know how to dimension in Paper Space*
  - *Know how to plot a Paper Space drawing*
- ✓ *Know how to use* ***MVSetup*** *as a floating viewport editor*
- ✓ *Know how to use* ***Regenall*** *and* ***Redrawall*** *to refresh viewports*

## The New Beginning Continues ...

*You've seen how to show a drawing (a model) at different scales on the same page. But what'll happen to text and dimensions when the scale changes? What'll happen when you need to show information in a detail that you don't want to see on the plan (after all, that's why we use details)?*

*Up until now, you've determined text and dimension sizes using a mathematical formula based on the desired size at plot time and the drawing scale factor. An undiscovered error in your math might have wreaked havoc when you went to plot the drawing and discovered that all the text and dimension elements had to be resized.*

*In creating Paper Space, AutoCAD took these problems into consideration and provided some clever solutions. In Lesson 23, we'll investigate these solutions as well as some tricks to control the display both inside and outside of your viewports.*

*Let's begin.*

## 23.1 Dimensioning and Paper Space

AutoCAD has two ways to create dimensions when Paper Space is involved – the *Olde Way* and the *New Way*. The *Olde Way* takes considerably more work and will, no doubt, eventually pass the way of Beta VCRs and the two-dollar bill. Still, you'll probably find yourself editing older drawings from time to time; knowledge of how it was done "in olden times" will be beneficial. You'll almost certainly prefer the New Way.

Let's take a look at both.

### 23.1.1 Dimensioning and Paper Space – the Olde Way

The Olde Way of setting up dimensioning for a Paper Space drawing is almost identical to setting up dimensioning for Model Space. The subtle difference involves the scale factor on the **Fit** tab of the Dimension Style Manager. For Model Space dimensioning, you must enter the scale factor, but for Paper Space dimensioning, you have to put a check in the **Scale dimensions to layout (paperspace)** check box. AutoCAD will scale the arrowheads, text, and other dimension objects accordingly.

The confusing part is answering the question of just where to place the dimensions. When thinking about dimensioning and Paper Space, it helps to remember that old adage: *Dance with the one what brung you.* In other words, if you draw it in Model Space, place your dimensions in Model Space; if you draw it in Paper Space, place your dimensions in Paper Space.

This will become clearer with an example. Let's step back in time, play some Beatles tunes on the 8-track, and try one.

| Do This: 23.1.1.1 | Adding Paper Space Dimensions – The Olde Way |
|---|---|

I. Open the *MyFlr-pln23a.dwg* file in the C:\Steps\Lesson23 folder. (If this drawing wasn't completed in the last chapter, open the *flr-pln23a.dwg* file instead.)

II. Set the **DIM** layer current.

III. Follow these steps.

| 23.1.1.1: Adding Paper Space Dimensions – The Olde Way |
|---|
| 1. Double click in the upper left viewport to activate it in Model Space. |
| 2. Call the Dimension Style Manager.<br>**Command: *ddim*** |

## 23.1.1.1: Adding Paper Space Dimensions – The Olde Way

3. Select the **Arch** parent style…

4. …and pick the **Modify** button [Modify...].

5. In the **Scale for dimension features** frame of the **Fit** tab, place a bullet next to **Scale dimensions to layout**.

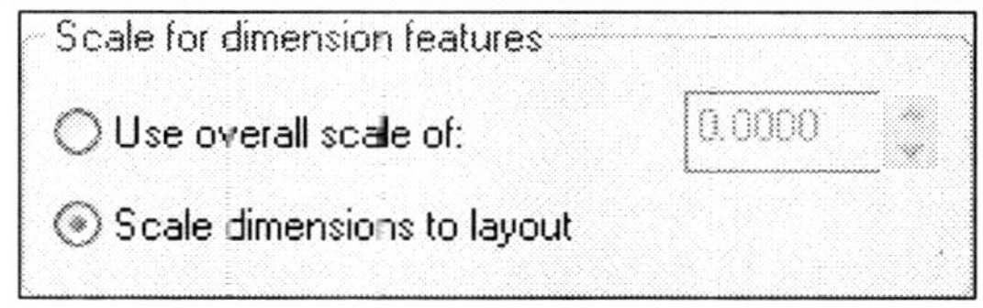


6. Pick the **OK** button [OK] and then the **Close** button [Close] to continue. (The rest of the setup has been done for you.)

7. Place the dimensions shown. (Use grips or the ***Stretch*** command to adjust the size and shape of the viewport as necessary.)

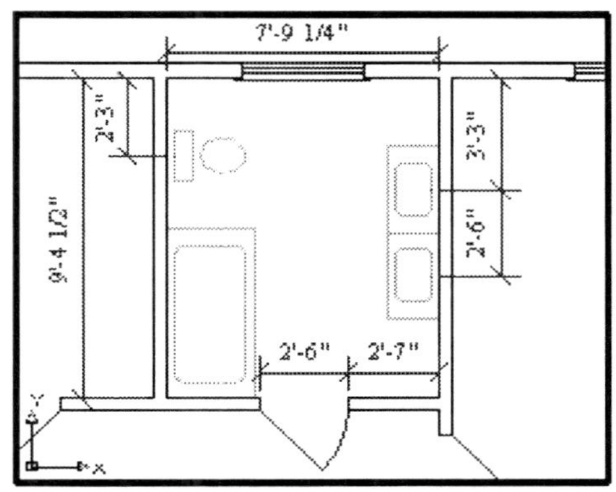


8. Now place the dimensions in the round viewport as shown. (Hint: You may have to use ***DimTedit*** to help you.)

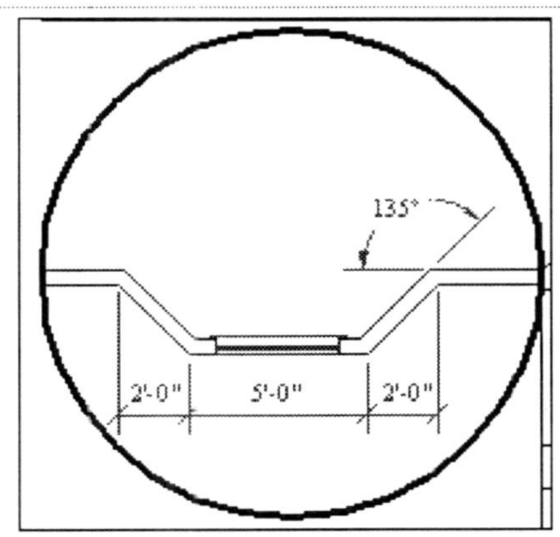


9. Return to Paper Space by double-clicking outside the viewports.

10. Save the drawing as *MyFlr-pln23a*, but don't exit.

**Command: *saveas***

> You'll find a useful tool on the status bar next to the Paper/Model toggle. Use the **Minimize Viewport** button  to toggle between the view in an active viewport and the same view on the **Model** tab. Use the arrows on the sides to toggle between viewport views while still on the **Model** tab.

As you can see, the only problem presented by dimensioning in Paper Space was one of room. But if dimensions didn't fit into the viewport, you could use standard modifying tools (grips or the ***Stretch*** command) to resize it. (Remember that the viewport exists in Paper Space. So any modifying on the viewport itself must be done there.)

Did you notice that the dimensions appeared not only in the active viewport but also in the other viewports as well? (Look in the large viewport where you can see both the bath and bay window.) This presented a problem that users of older AutoCAD releases would fix with careful manipulation of layers. Regardless of how you place dimensions, the techniques used to manipulate those layers are still quite useful today for a host of other reasons. You'll learn the how-tos of layers in Paper Space in Section 23.2, but first, let's take a look at the modern approach to Paper Space dimensioning.

## 23.1.2 Dimensioning and Paper Space – the New Way

Despite the name, the new way of Paper Space dimensioning really involves no new techniques at all. With some programming adjustments, you simply place dimensions in Paper Space rather than Model Space (regardless of where the objects to be dimensioned reside). AutoCAD automatically interprets in which space the objects exist and adjusts the dimension accordingly. Using this new program, all dimensions exist in Paper Space – even if the object dimensioned exists in Model Space.

You should remember some general rules when using this new approach:

- The **Dimassoc** system variable must be set to **2**. Since this is the default for new drawings, you won't have a problem with them. However, if you're working with a drawing created in an earlier release, you'll have to change the variable setting.
- The new programming may have a problem recognizing multilines. If this occurs, you'll find it necessary to either explode the multilines or use the Olde Way as detailed in Section 23.1.1.

## Do This: 23.1.2.1 Adding Paper Space Dimensions – The New Way

I. Open the *flr-pln23a-new.dwg* file in the C:\Steps\Lesson23 folder.
II. Be sure the **Dimassoc** system variable is set to **2** and the **DIM** layer is current.
III. Be sure you're in Paper Space (the toggle on the status bar should read **PAPER**).
IV. Follow these steps.

### 23.1.2.1: Adding Paper Space Dimensions – The New Way

1. Place the dimensions indicated for the upper left viewport. Do *not* change to Model Space except to make adjustments in the display as needed. Use grips to resize the viewport as needed.

**Command: *dli***

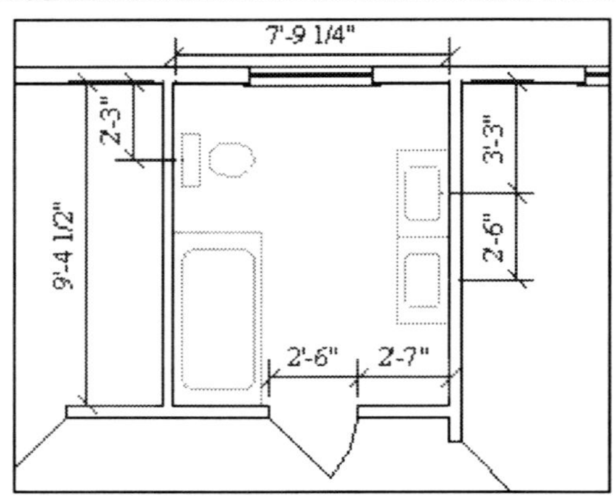

## 23.1.2.1: Adding Paper Space Dimensions – The New Way

2. Now dimension the bay window as shown. Again, don't change to Model Space except to make adjustments in the display.

3. Now Zoom all and look at the drawing. Compare it to the drawing you did in the last exercise (reopen that drawing if necessary and view the two side by side).

4. Save the drawing and exit.

**Command:** ***qsave***

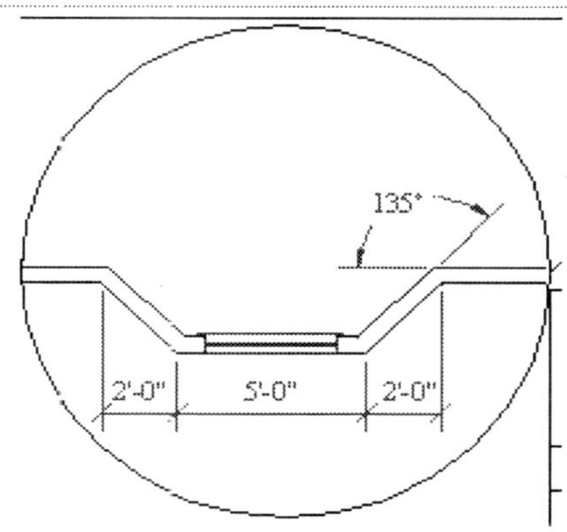


Did you notice the difference between the two drawings?

You should have seen that the dimensions placed in the first exercise appeared both in the viewport being dimensioned and in the full viewport at right. This happens because the dimensions exist in Model Space, which appears through the viewports. In the drawing you created in the second exercise, the dimensions appear only in paperspace where you created them. These dimensions, although detailing objects that live in Model Space, exist in Paper Space.

It won't be necessary to manipulate layers to hide dimensions in the second drawing, but you'll have to do so in the first. You'll see how in our next section.

## 23.2 The Benefits of Layers in Paper Space

One of the real wonders of Paper Space has to be the ability to manipulate layers in a single viewport independently of other viewports. In other words, you can freeze (or thaw) layers in one viewport while leaving them thawed (or frozen) in another! The trick lies in using the ***VPLayer*** command instead of the ***Layer*** command in your manipulations. Alternately, you can use the **Freeze or Thaw in Current Viewport** column on the **Layer Control** box.

Thawed/ Frozen Layer in Current Viewport

The ***VPLayer*** command sequence goes like this:

**Command:** ***vplayer***

**Enter an option [?/Freeze/Thaw/Reset/ Newfrz/Vpvisdflt]:** ***[tell AutoCAD what you want to do]***

Let's look at each option.

- The **?** option prompts you to select a viewport. Then AutoCAD shows the layers that are frozen in that particular viewport. If the command is given from Model Space, AutoCAD will switch to Paper Space just long enough to complete the procedure.
- The **Freeze/Thaw** options allow you to enter the name(s) of a layer(s), and then prompt you to select the viewports in which the layer(s) will be frozen or thawed. The command sequence looks like this:

  **Enter layer name(s) to freeze or <select objects>:**

  **Enter an option [All/Select/Current] <Current>:** ***[tell AutoCAD to freeze/thaw the layer in all the viewports, Selected viewports, or the Current viewport]***
- The **Reset** option sets layers to their default settings. Use the **Vpvisdflt** option to create the default settings. The **Vpvisdflt** option will prompt as follows:

**Enter layer name(s) to change viewport visibility or <select objects>:** ***[name the layer(s) – use commas to separate several layer names]***
**Enter a viewport visibility option [Frozen/Thawed] <Thawed>:** ***[tell AutoCAD how you wish this layer to behave by default]***

- The **Newfrz** option will create a new layer that is frozen in all viewports.

Let's take a look at how layers interact with viewports.

| Do This: 23.2.1 | Manipulating Layers in Floating Viewports |
|---|---|

I. Go back to the *MyFlr-pln23a.dwg* file in the C:\Steps\Lesson23 folder. Reopen it if necessary.
II. Be sure you're in Paper Space.
III. Follow these steps.

## 23.2.1: Manipulating Layers in Floating Viewports

1. Enter the ***VPLayer*** command. There's no hotkey, button, or pull-down menu selection for this command.

   **Command:** ***vplayer***

2. Tell AutoCAD you wish to freeze 

the **DIM** and **FIXTURES** layers.

   **Enter an option [?/Freeze/Thaw/Reset/ Newfrz/Vpvisdflt]:** ***f***
   **Enter layer name(s) to freeze or <select objects>:** ***dim,fixtures***

3. AutoCAD asks you to identify the viewport in which you want the layers frozen. Tell it that you'll select one 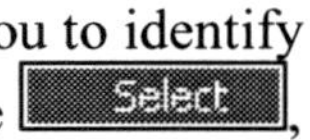

, and then select the right viewport.

   **Enter an option [All/Select/Current] <Current>:** ***s***
   **Select objects:** ***[select the right viewport]***

4. Confirm the selection and complete the command.

   **Select objects:** ***[enter]***
   **Enter an option [?/Freeze/Thaw/Reset/Newfrz/ Vpvisdflt]:** ***[enter]***

The drawing now looks like the following figure.

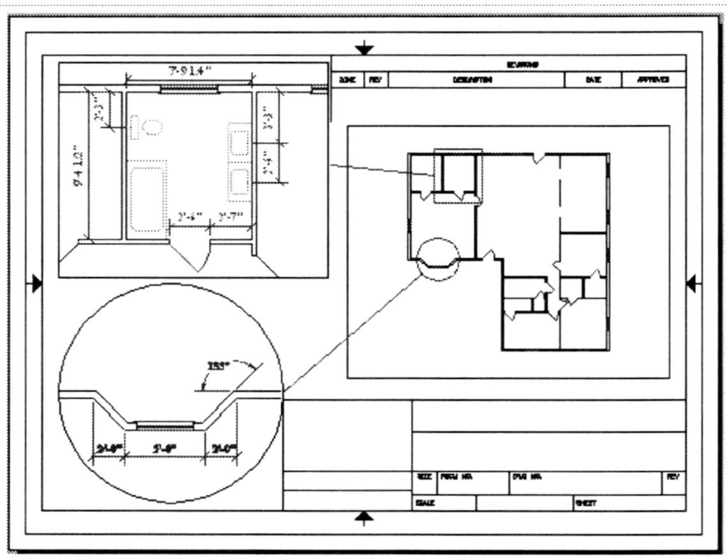

## 23.2.1: Manipulating Layers in Floating Viewports

5. Let's crosshatch the master bath area (the area shown in the detail) in the right viewport. First, create a hatch layer. Make it a dark color, and make it current.

**Command:** ***la***

6. Return to Model Space [PAPER] and activate the right viewport.

**Command:** ***ms***

7. Now enter the ***Hatch*** command.

**Command:** ***h***

8. In the **Angle and scale** frame of the **Hatch** tab, set the **Scale** to ¼" and place a check in the **Relative to paper space** box. Accept all other defaults.

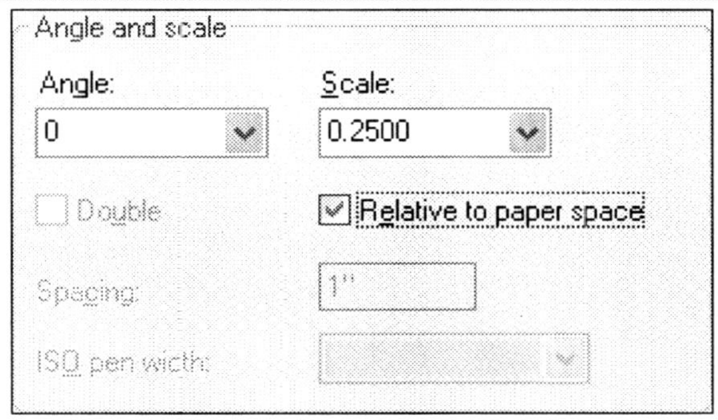


9. Pick the **Add: Pick points** button and select a point inside the master bath. Hit ***enter*** to return to the dialog box.

**Pick internal point or [Select objects/remove Boundaries]:**

10. Pick the **OK** button [OK] to continue. Notice that the hatch pattern appears in both viewports that show the master bath.

11. Let's try an easier way to freeze layers. Make the upper left viewport current.

12. Now use the viewport toggle in the **Layer Control** box to freeze the **Hatch** layer in the current viewport. Your drawing looks like the following figure.

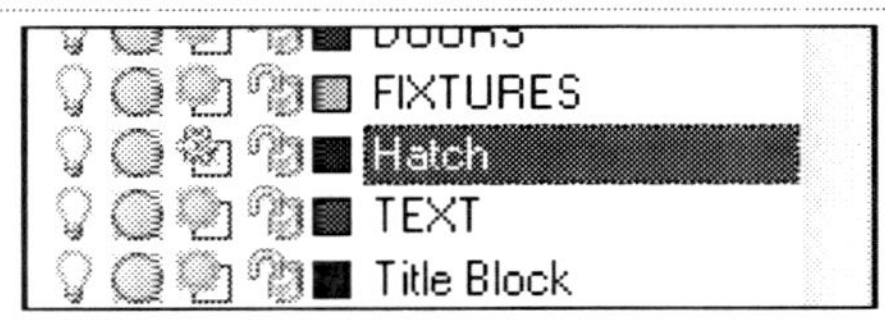


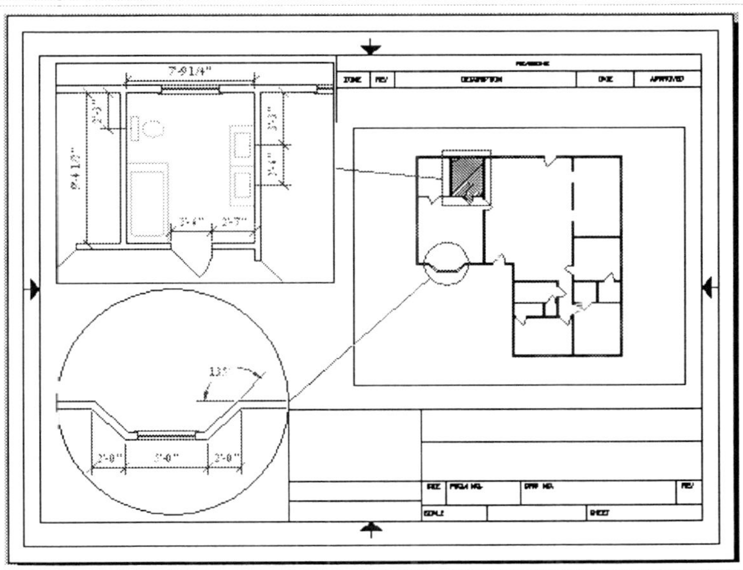

## 23.2.1: Manipulating Layers in Floating Viewports

13. Return to Paper Space.

    **Command:** ***ps***

14. Change the two viewports on the left to the **TEXT** layer.

    **Command:** ***props***

15. Now freeze the **VPORTS** layer. Your drawing now looks like the figure below.

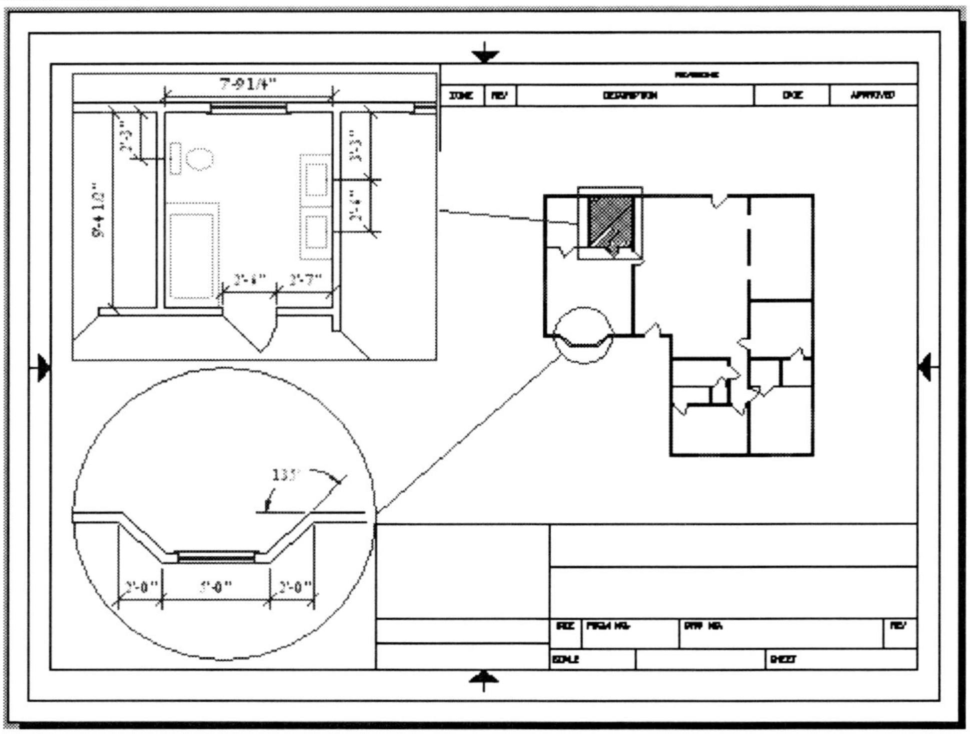


16. Save the drawing  and exit.

    **Command:** ***qsave***

This is a much finer image for plotting, but there's still more to do. We must add some callouts to the drawing before we plot it.

## 23.3 Using Text in Paper Space

In a drawing that uses Paper Space, place all text in Paper Space unless it's part of the model. The reasoning behind this general rule is this: *Placing text in Paper Space is easier than placing text in Model Space.*

Let me explain.

Remember how difficult you found sizing text in Model Space? You had to consider the size that you wanted the text to be at plot time and the scale at which you would plot. Then you had to work some mathematical wizardry to determine the size of the text to use in your drawing. You had to do all of this before placing any text.

Try this formula to determine text height in Paper Space:

*The height you want the text to be when you plot = the height you make your text*

It just can't get any simpler than that!

But wait! AutoCAD has included a tool that greatly simplifies the Paper Space to Model Space (and vice versa) translation of text sizes. When you determine that text simply must go into Model Space, use the ***SpaceTrans*** command to help you determine its size. This transparent command works anytime AutoCAD asks you for a size. Look at its sequence (this sequence is seen when the command is given from Model Space):

> **Command:** ***dt***
>
> **Current text style: "TIMES" Text height: 0'-0"**
>
> **Specify start point of text or [Justify/Style]:**
>
> **Specify height <0'-0">:** ***'spacetrans***
>
> **>>Specify paper space distance <1">:** ***[tell AutoCAD how large you'd like the text to be in Paper Space]***
>
> **Resuming TEXT command.**
>
> **Specify height <0'-0">:** ***[AutoCAD automatically translates the size into Model Space increments]***
>
> **Specify rotation angle of text <0>:** ***[continue with the* Text *command]***
>
> **Enter text:**

***Spacetrans*** determines the appropriate Model Space size for the text and responds to the Specify height prompt for you. (The prompts are slightly different when translating from Paper Space to Model Space.)

| Note: **Spacetrans** is *not* available on the **Model** tab. (Oh, *that's* why we didn't cover it earlier!) |
|---|

You'll see this in action in our next exercise. Let's add a bit of text to our drawing.

| **Do This: 23.3.1** | **Adding Text in Paper Space** |
|---|---|

I. Open the *flr-pln23b-new.dwg* file in the C:\Steps\Lesson23 folder.

II. Be sure you're in Paper Space.

III. Follow these steps.

### 23.3.1: ADDING TEXT IN PAPER SPACE

1. On the **TEXT** layer, add the callouts 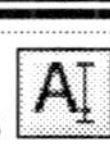 shown in the following figure. Large text is 3/16" and smaller text is 1/8". (Use the **Times** text style that has already been set up for you.)

> **Command:** ***dt***

## 23.3.1: Adding Text in Paper Space

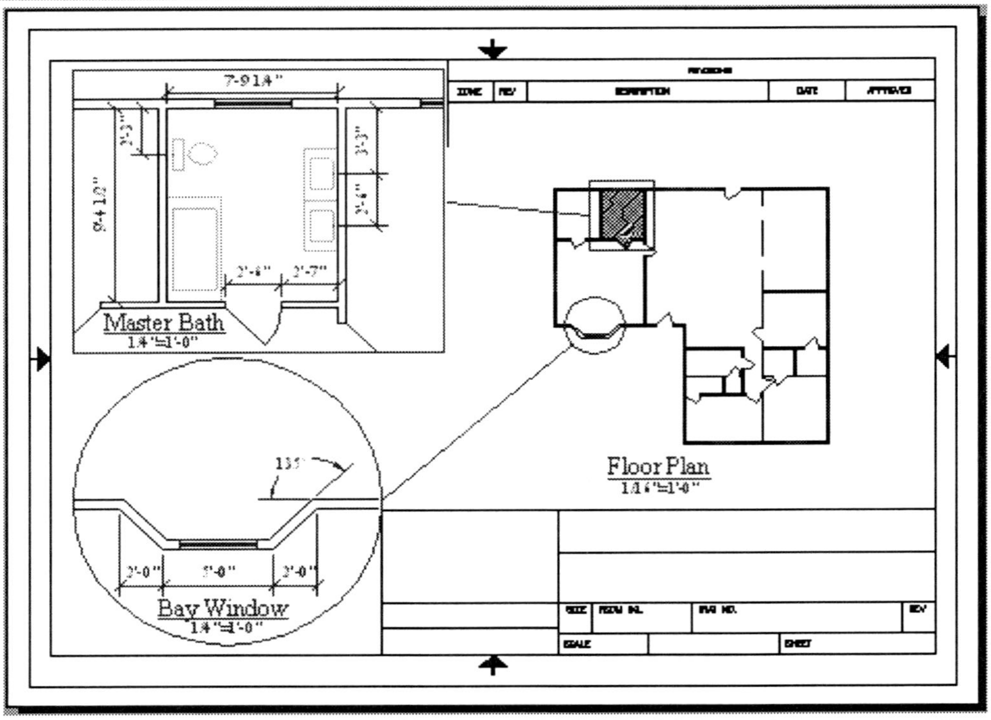


2. Now fill out the title block as shown below. Text sizes are ¼", 3/16", and 1/8". Feel free to use your own school's name.

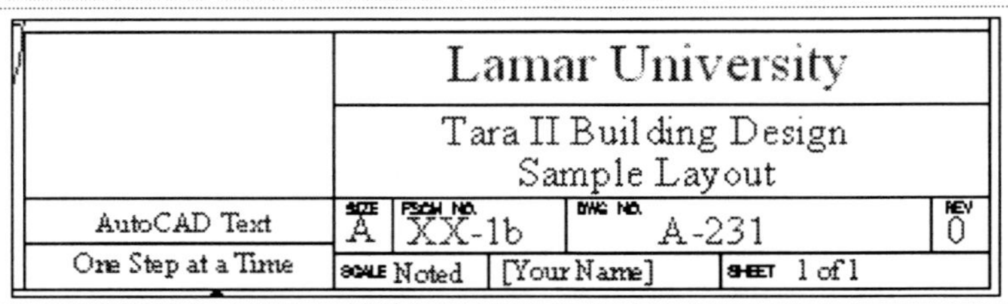


3. Save the drawing but don't exit.

**Command:** ***qsave***

## 23.3.1: ADDING TEXT IN PAPER SPACE

4. Now let's add some text to Model Space. Open Model Space and set the right viewport current.

Begin the ***Text*** command and center the text in the den.

**Command:** ***dt***

**Current text style: "TIMES" Text height: 0'-0 1/8"**

**Specify start point of text or [Justify/ Style]:** ***c***

**Specify center point of text:**

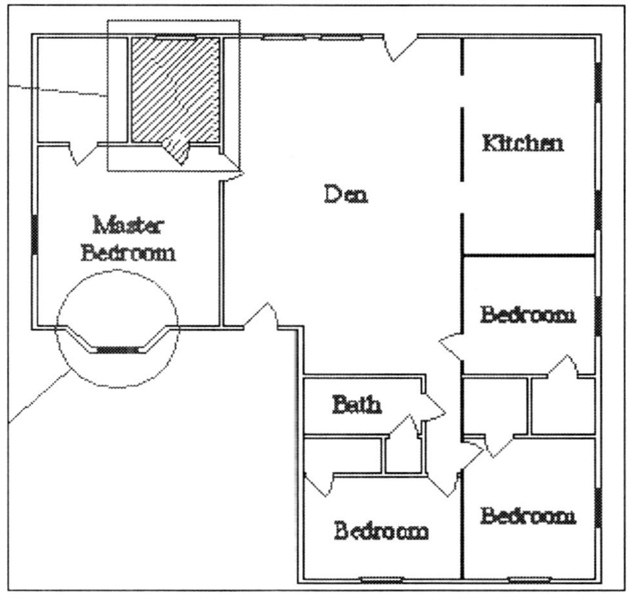


5. Now enter the ***SpaceTrans*** command transparently.

**Specify height <0'-0 1/8">:** ***'spacetrans***

6. Tell AutoCAD to make the text height 3/32". AutoCAD makes the translation and enters the text height for you.

**>>Specify paper space distance <1">:** ***3/32***

**Resuming TEXT command.**

**Specify height <0'-0 1/8">: 18.00000000**

8. Complete the command, entering the text ***Den*** as shown above.

**Specify rotation angle of text <0>:** ***[enter]***

9. Complete the text entries as detailed above.

10. Save the drawing .

**Command:** ***qsave***

Take a moment and toggle between the **Model** tab and the Layout (**Tara II Layout**) tab of your drawing. Notice which objects exist as part of the model and which don't. Only those objects that you created through the viewports in Model Space exist on the **Model** tab. Everything else exists as part of the paper on which you'll plot your model.

Once the dimensions are drawn and the text placed – the *i*'s dotted and the *t*'s crossed – it's time to plot the drawing. Let's look at that next.

## 23.4 Plotting the Layout

It's funny that, after all the setting up, creating, and manipulating, it always comes back to getting it on paper. Perhaps that's why AutoCAD has put so much time and money into making printing as user-friendly as possible.

Printing a layout isn't very different from printing Model Space (although it is a bit easier). Let's print our floor plan layout.

| Do This: 23.4.1 | Printing/Plotting the Layout |
|---|---|

I. Be sure you're still in the *flr-pln23b-new.dwg* file in the C:\Steps\Lesson23 folder. If not, please open it now.

II. Follow these steps.

### 23.4.1: PRINTING/PLOTTING THE LAYOUT

1. Enter the ***Plot*** command.

**Command: *plot***

AutoCAD presents the Plot dialog box.

2. In the **Printer/Plotter** frame, use the **Name** control box to select the plotter or printer you wish to use.

3. Select **Layout** in the **What to plot** drop down box (**Plot area** frame) to plot the current layout.

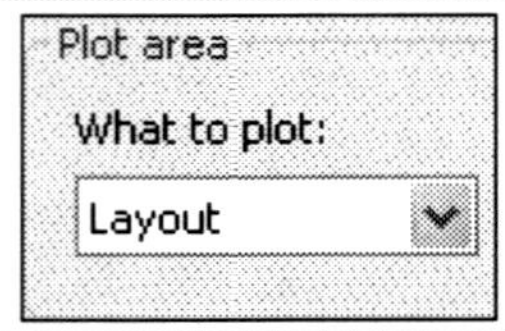


4. Be sure your **Plot scale** is set to 1:1.

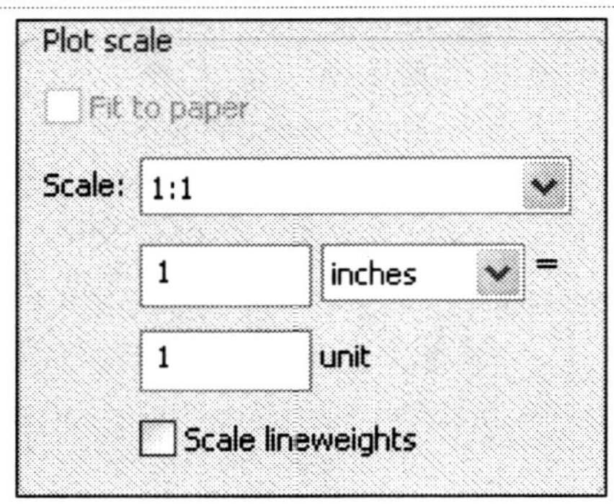


5. Use the **Preview** button [Preview...] to help set the Plot offset to properly center your drawing on the page.

6. When you're satisfied with the offset, pick the **OK** button [OK] to print the drawing.

7. Save the drawing.

**Command: *qsave***

Use a drafting scale to check the dimensions on your plot. How did you do?

As with any print job, it's inevitable that something must be modified after the plot. Despite the ability to preview a drawing before plotting, some things simply don't show up until you see it on paper.

You can make changes in Model Space through the viewports or on the **Model** tab. You can make changes in Paper Space on the **Layout** tab. However, changes to the viewports themselves may require some additional tools. We'll look at these next.

## 23.5 Tweaking the Layout

Generally speaking, modifying the layout is as easy as modifying any other part of a drawing. The basic modifying tools – ***Move***, ***Copy***, ***Stretch***, and so forth – will work in Paper Space as well as Model Space. However, adjusting the view through a viewport or adjusting the shape or scale of a viewport will require some new modifying procedures. These include two commands: ***MVSetup*** and ***VPClip***.

## 23.5.1 Modifying Viewports with the *MVSetup* Command

AutoCAD originally designed the ***MVSetup*** command to perform the same function as the layout wizard. Using the single ***MVSetup*** command, we can insert the title block and create/scale the viewports just as we did with the wizard. But the wizard is so much easier to use than ***MVSetup***'s command line approach that ***MVSetup*** might have been removed. But AutoCAD chose to leave it (it's so hard to lose a good tool) because of its use as a modifying tool.

We'll look at all parts of the ***MVSetup*** command, but we'll use the command as a modifying tool.

The command sequence looks like this:

**Command:** ***mvsetup***

**Enable paper space? [No/Yes] <Y>:**

When entered while on the **Model** tab, the ***MVSetup*** command initially asks if you wish to enable Paper Space. What follows depends on your answer.

- If you respond ***No***, you'll set up the drawing for Model Space. AutoCAD prompts as follows:

  **Enter units type [Scientific/Decimal/Engineering/Architectural/Metric]:**

  Tell AutoCAD which type of units you wish to use. AutoCAD will respond with a list of scale factors available. Select one. Then AutoCAD will ask for the width and height of the sheet of paper to which you will plot. When it has all the information, it will place a polyline border around the limits of the drawing.

  This approach is a bit quicker for someone who is comfortable with AutoCAD and the keyboard, but an AutoCAD novice might wish to use the **Setup Wizard** in lieu of the command line.

- If you respond ***Yes*** to the **Enable paper space** prompt (or if you enter the command while on a layout tab), AutoCAD flips to the first layout tab, creates a single viewport (if none currently exist), and then prompts as follows:

  **Enter an option [Align/Create/Scale viewports/Options/Title block/Undo]:**

  The first line simply lets you know what AutoCAD is doing.

  The last line presents several options. These include:

  - The **Align** option allows you to align a view in one viewport with the view in another.
  - **Create** allows you to create (or delete) floating viewports. It prompts:

    **Enter option [Delete objects/Create viewports/Undo] <Create>:**

    - The **Delete objects** option, of course, allows you to remove a viewport.
    - The default option – **Create** – offers these choices:
      - **Available layout options: . . .**

        **0: None** ***[for no viewports]***

        **1: Single** ***[for a single viewport]***

        **2: Std. Engineering** ***[This option creates four viewports with standard three-dimensional views (plan, front, side, isometric).]***

        **3: Array of Viewports** ***[This option allows you to create a rectangular array of viewports – you define the number of rows and columns to use and the spacing between them]***
      - **Enter layout number to load or [Redisplay]:** ***[Make your selection or hit enter to return to MVSetup's first option line.]***
  - Scaling the viewports can be done one at a time or uniformly. You'll find setting the scale one viewport at a time more easily accomplished using the **Viewport Scale** control

box on the Viewports toolbar, or the ***Zoom*** command. If you select more than one viewport to scale, AutoCAD will prompt as follows:

**Set zoom scale factors for viewports. Interactively/<Uniform>:**

**Set the ratio of paper space units to model space units...**

**Enter the number of paper space units <1.0>: *[usually hit enter]***

**Enter the number of model space units <1.0>: *[enter a scale factor]***

- The **Options** prompt allows you to set the following:

  **Enter an option [Layer/LImits/Units/ Xref] <exit>:**

  Most of these are obvious. You can set the current layer and Paper Space units, or you can allow AutoCAD to set the limits according to the drawing you've created. (We'll look at Xrefs in Lesson 25.)

- The **Title Block** option allows you to insert a title block in Paper Space.

Let's change the scale in one of our viewports. We'll use the ***MVSetup*** command to change the actual scale. Then we'll use more conventional commands to adjust the viewport.

| Do This: 23.5.1.1 | Using MVSetup as a Modifying Tool |
|---|---|

I. Be sure you're still in the *flr-pln23b-new.dwg* file in the C:\Steps\Lesson23 folder. If not, please open it now.

II. Follow these steps.

### 23.5.1.1: Using MVSetup as a Modifying Tool

1. Enter the ***MVsetup*** command.

   **Command: *mvsetup***

2. Choose the **Scale viewports** option  and select the upper left viewport (the master bath). Hit ***enter*** to complete the selection.

   **Enter an option [Align/Create/Scale viewports/Options/Title block/Undo]: *S***

   **Select the viewports to scale...**

   **Select objects: *[select the upper left viewport]***

   **Select objects: *[enter]***

3. Now you'll set the ratio of Paper Space to Model Space. Accept **1** as the number of **paper space units**.

   **Set the ratio of paper space units to model space units...**

   **Enter the number of paper space units <1.0>: *[enter]***

4. We'll change the scale from ¼"=1'-0" to 3/16"=1'-0". Enter the scale factor for the 3/16" scale (***64***). Notice how everything is rescaled.

   **Enter the number of model space units <1.0>: *64***

5. Complete the command. Notice that the dimensions automatically update – even though they're in Paper Space.

   **Enter an option [Align/Create/Scale viewports/Options/Title block/Undo]: *[enter]***

6. Use ***DimTedit*** 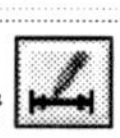 or grips to adjust the locations of the dimensions as needed.

   **Command: *dimtedit***

### 23.5.1.1: Using MVSetup as a Modifying Tool

7. Using grips or other modifying tools, resize and reposition the viewport. Then edit the text as shown below.

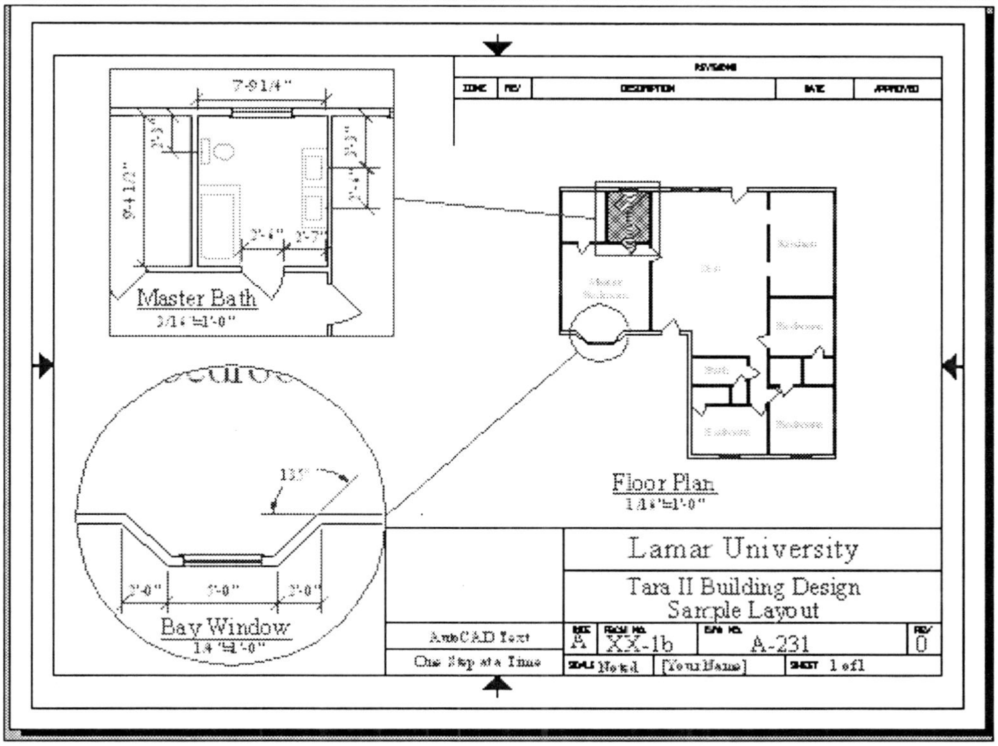


8. Save the drawing [save icon] but don't exit.

**Command:** ***qsave***

> When working with several viewports, you may notice that the ***Redraw*** and ***Regen*** commands only affect the one that is currently active. To use these commands to refresh all of the viewport simultaneously, use the ***Redrawall*** and ***Regenall*** commands.

Now that we've created our viewports and set up Paper Space, let's see what comes next.

## 23.5.2 Changing the Shape of a Viewport with the *VPClip* Command

Occasionally you'll discover that the shape you chose for your viewport doesn't satisfy the needs of that particular view. If you created the viewport using the **Object** option of the ***MView*** command to convert a polygon, closed polyline, or spline to a viewport, you can use the ***PEdit*** or ***Splinedit*** commands to reshape the viewport. If you used any other method to create the viewport, modifying the shape won't be so easy.

Fortunately, AutoCAD has provided the ***VPClip*** command. You can use this to reshape the view in a standard rectangular viewport. The command sequence looks like this:

**Command:** ***vpclip***

**Select viewport to clip:** ***[pick the viewport you wish to reshape (clip)]***

**Select clipping object or [Polygonal/Delete] <Polygonal>:** ***[enter]***

**Specify start point:**

**Specify next point or [Arc/Length/Undo]:** ***[this line operates like the* PLine *command and repeats until the polyline is closed]***

Let's look at each of the prompts.

- The first line is simple enough. It asks which viewport you wish to clip. Select one.
- The next line gives you a couple options:
  - o The default option – **Polygonal** – allows you to place the clipping border manually with a closed polyline (a polygon).
  - o The **Delete** option allows you to remove a clipping border. It'll return the view to its original shape.
  - o Enter **S** to use the **Select clipping object** option (or just select the object) if you've created a new boundary around the view using a polyline, spline, and so forth. It prompts:

    **Select object to clip viewport:**

    Simply select the object you wish to use as the new viewport.

> You can also access the ***VPClip*** command by selecting the viewport to clip, opening the cursor menu, and selecting **Viewport Clip**.

Let's clip the round viewport in our drawing. (Notice that it has some unwanted text in it.)

| Do This: 23.5.2.1 | Reshaping a Viewport |
|---|---|

I. Be sure you're still in the *flr-pln23b-new.dwg* file in the C:\Steps\Lesson23 folder. If not, please open it now.

II. Be sure you're in Paper Space and the **VPORTS** layer is thawed and current.

III. Follow these steps.

**23.5.2.1: RESHAPING A VIEWPORT**

1. Draw a rectangle around the bay window similar to the one shown.

   **Command:** ***rec***

2. Enter the ***VPClip*** command or pick the **Clip existing viewport** button on the Viewports toolbar.

   **Command:** ***vpclip***

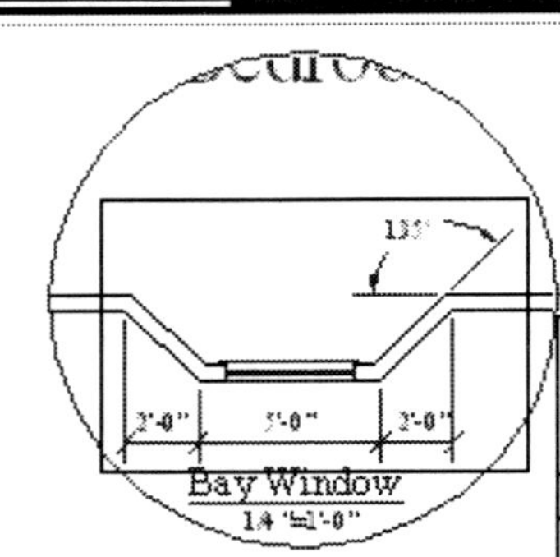


3. Select the viewport (the circle).

   **Select viewport to clip:**

4. Select the rectangle.

   **Select clipping object or [Polygonal/ Delete] <Polygonal>:**

AutoCAD replaces the circle with a new viewport based on the shape of the rectangle.

5. Set **TEXT** as the current layer and freeze the **VPORTS** layer.

### 23.5.2.1: Reshaping a Viewport

6. Redraw a circle around the viewport. The viewport now looks like this.

**Command:** ***c***

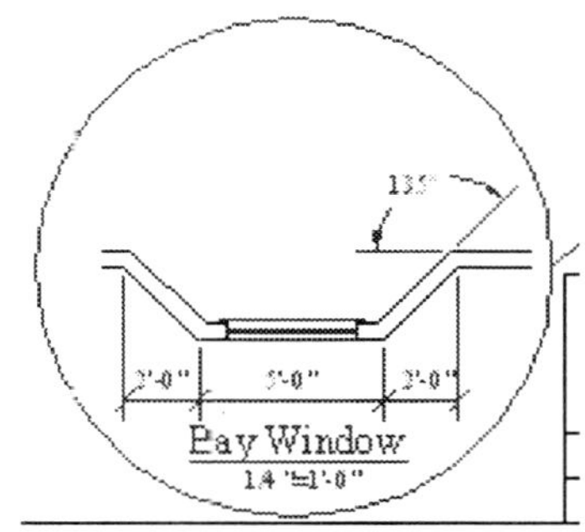


7. Save and close the drawing.

**Command:** ***qsave***

## 23.6 Putting It All Together

We've learned quite a bit about Paper Space and viewports. Let's try a project from the beginning (well, almost the beginning – I'll provide the drawing).

### Do This: 23.6.1 From Setup to Plot – A Project

I. Open the *table saw.dwg* file in the C:\Steps\Lesson23 folder. The drawing looks like Figure 23.001 (I've hidden the grid for clarity.)

II. Set the **VPORTS** layer current.

III. Follow these steps.

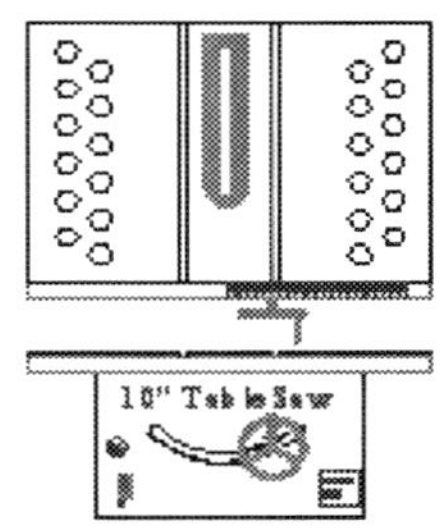

Figure 23.001

### 23.6.1: From Setup to Plot – A Project

1. Let's start the easy way. Enter the ***LayoutWizard*** command.

**Command:** ***layoutwizard***

2. Call the layout *MasterLayout*.

Pick the **Next** button to continue.

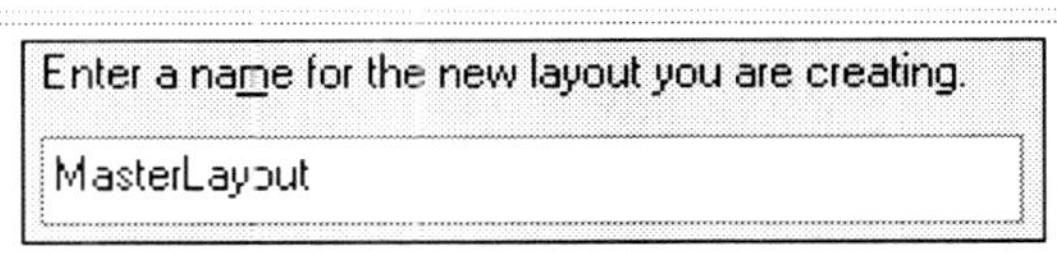


3. Select a plotter if one is available. Otherwise, select **None**.

Pick the **Next** button to continue.

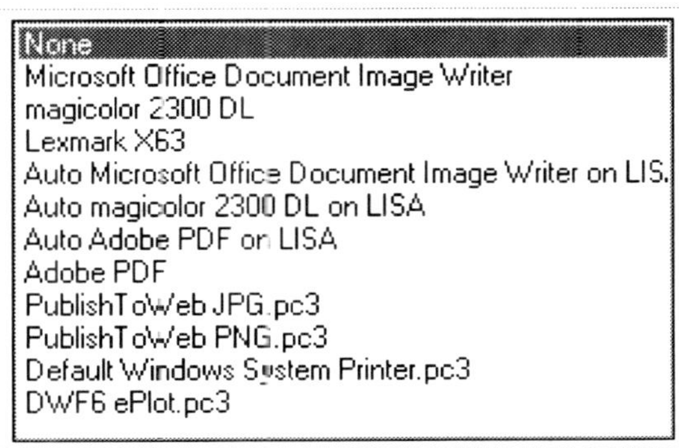

## 23.6.1: From Setup to Plot – A Project

4. Select an **ANSI D** size sheet and use **Inches** for your drawing units.

Pick the **Next** button to continue.

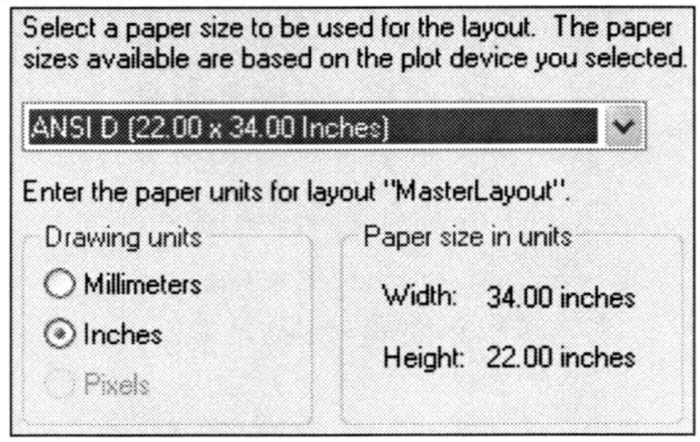


5. Tell AutoCAD to plot a **Landscape** drawing.

Pick the **Next** button to continue.

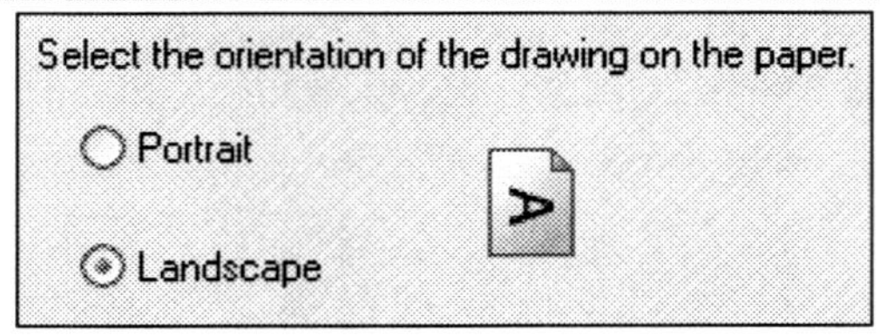


6. Select an appropriate title block for the sheet of paper you selected in Step 4 (**ANSI D**). Use a **Block** insertion.

Pick the **Next** button to continue.

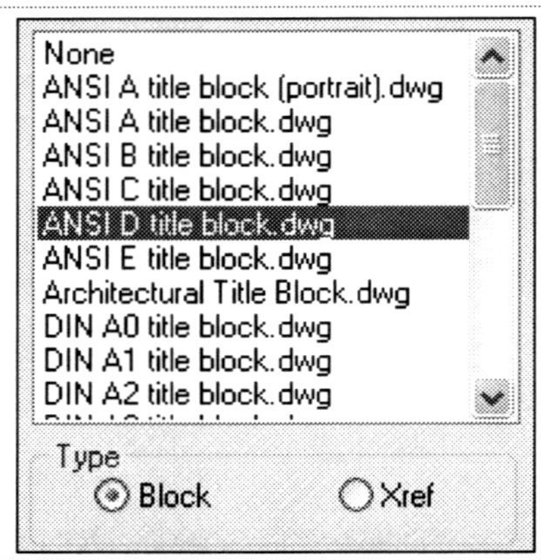


7. Define the viewports by **Array**. Use **2** rows and **3** columns and accept the default spacing.

Pick the **Next** button to continue.

8. Pick the **Select Location** button 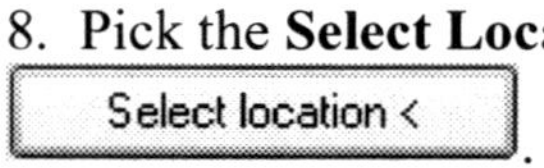.


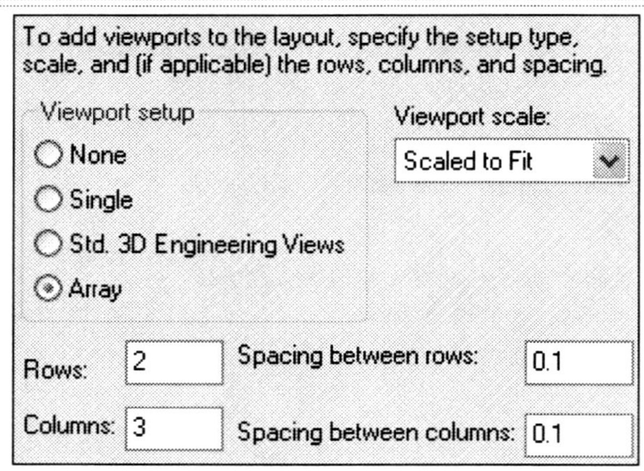


9. Specify the area for the viewports.

**Specify first corner: *1.5,19***

**Specify opposite corner: *31,3***

10. Pick the **Finish** button  to complete the command.

11. Remember to save  occasionally.

**Command:** ***qsave***

Your drawing looks like the figure below.

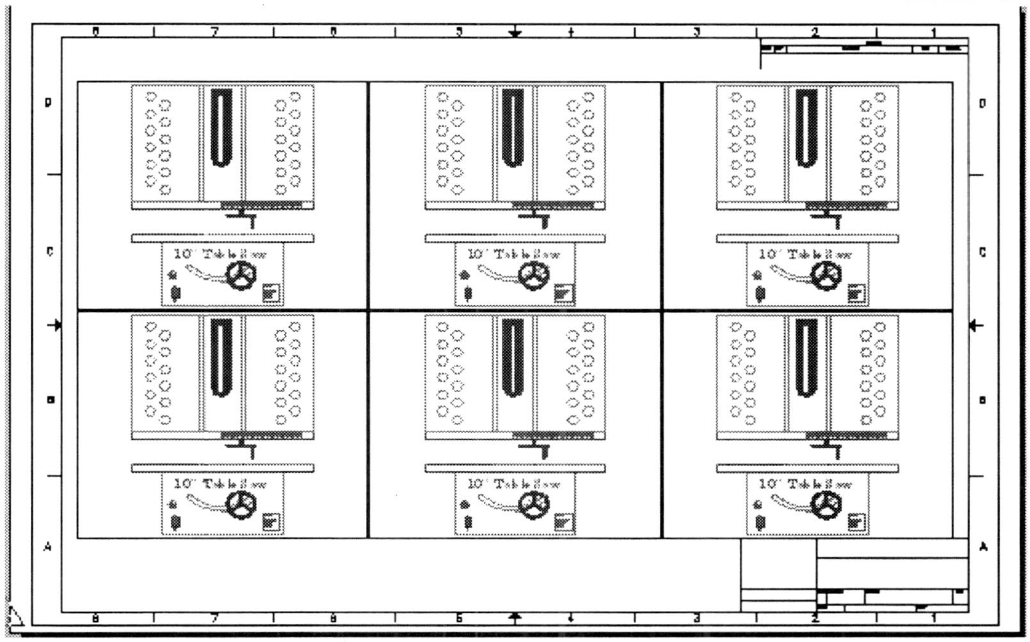

12. Let's turn the UCS icon off in all of the viewports. Enter the ***UCSIcon*** command.

**Command:** ***ucsicon***

13. Use the **All** option …

**Enter an option [ON/OFF/All/Noorigin/ ORigin/ Properties] <ON>:** ***a***

14. … and turn the icon **OFF**.

**Enter an option [ON/OFF/Noorigin/ ORigin/Properties] <ON>:** ***off***

15. Set the scale in each viewport as follows: (use either the **Viewport Scale** control box on the Viewports toolbar or the ***MVSetup*** command):

First row: 1:1, 1:2, 2:1

Second row: 1:1, 1:2, NTS

## 23.6.1: From Setup to Plot – A Project

16. Resize and relocate each viewport using grips and/or the ***Stretch*** and ***Move*** commands. (*Readjust the views in each port as shown in the following figure.*) The lower left and upper right coordinates for each viewport follow. (Hint: Grips and absolute coordinates make this job much easier.)

| Viewport (Row/Col) | Handwheel Plan (1/1) | Saw Plan (1/2) | Switch (1/3) | Handwheel Elev. (2/1) | Saw Elev. (2/2) | Spec. Plate (2/3) |
|---|---|---|---|---|---|---|
| Lower left coordinate | 1.5,15.1 | 7.25,8.25 | 2,1.75 | 1.5,10 | 7.25,1 | 23.75,4 |
| Upper right coordinate | 7.75,19 | 23.5,20 | 5.75,7.75 | 7.75,15 | 23.5,11 | 31,11.75 |

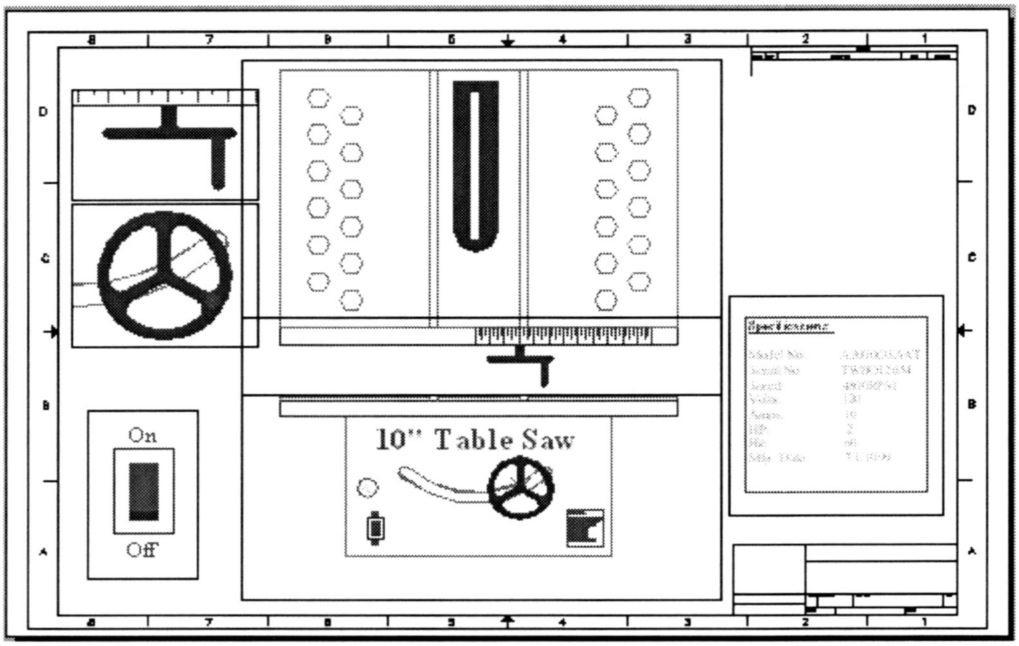


17. Use the ***VPLayer*** command to freeze unwanted layers as follows. (Hint: It might be faster to freeze all layers with the * and then thaw the few you wish visible.)

| Viewport: | Handwheel – Plan & Elev. | Switch | Saw – Plan & Elev. | Specs |
|---|---|---|---|---|
| Freeze All Layers Except: | Obj3<br>Obj3a | Obj2<br>Obj2a<br>Obj3<br>Text | (Don't freeze any layers) | Text |

18. Remember to save  occasionally. Your drawing looks like the following figure.

**Command: *qsave***

## 23.6.1: From Setup to Plot – A Project

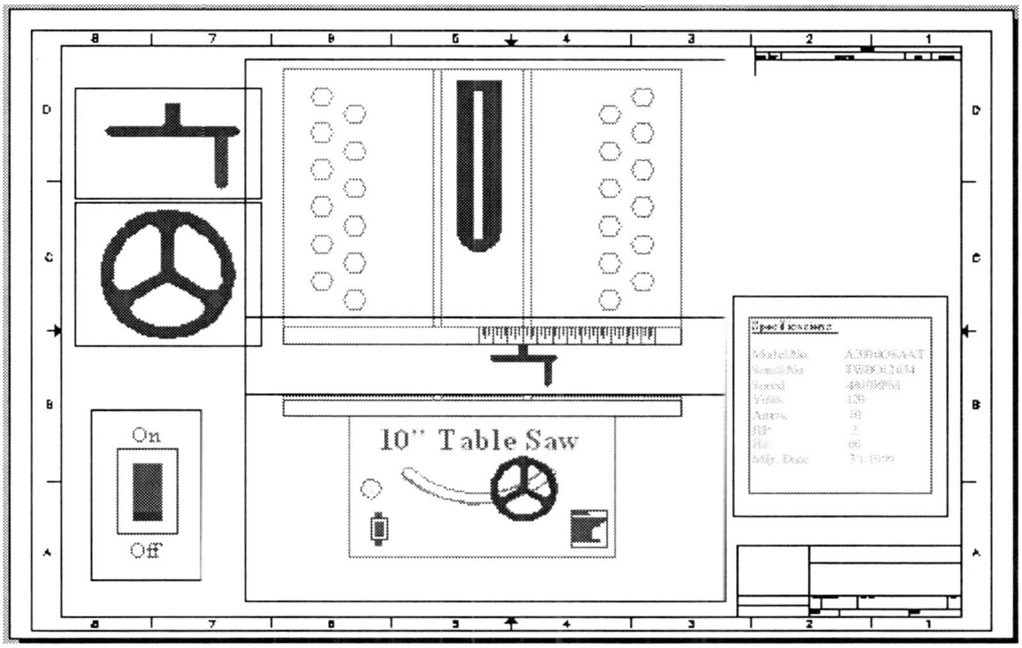


19. Now use the ***MVSetup*** command to align the views in the handwheel plan and elevation. Begin by entering the command.

**Command: *mvsetup***

20. Select the **Align** option 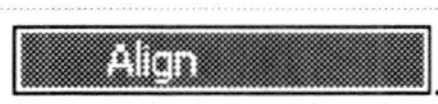

.

**Enter an option [Align/Create/ Scale viewports/ Options/Title block/Undo]: *a***

21. We'll align the objects vertically 

.

**Enter an option [Angled/Horizontal/Vertical alignment/Rotate view/Undo]: *v***

22. Select the leftmost quadrant of the handwheel in the plan view ..

**Specify basepoint: _qua of**

23. ... and the corresponding quadrant in the elevation view

**Specify point in viewport to be panned: _qua of**

24. Complete the command.

**Enter an option [Angled/Horizontal/Vertical alignment/Rotate view/Undo]: *[enter]***

**Enter an option [Align/Create/Scale viewports/Options/Title block/Undo]: *[enter]***

25. Repeat Steps 19 through 24 to align the plan and elevation views of the saw.

26. We'll use the ***VPClip*** command to set the saw plan and elevation viewports so that all you see is the plan in the plan viewport and the elevation in the elevation viewport.

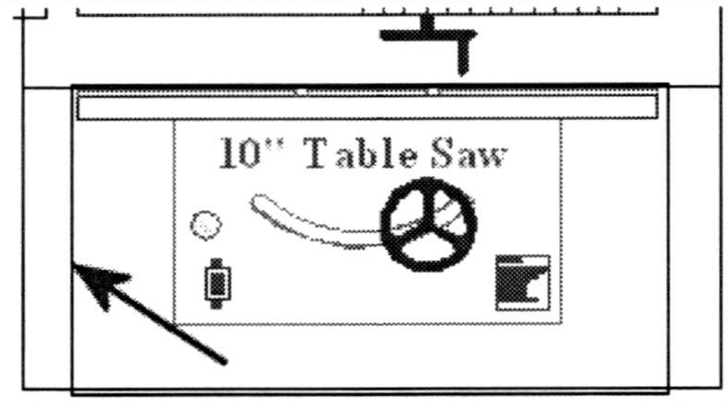


Begin by drawing a rectangle  around the elevation in the bottom viewport. (Be sure you're in Paper Space and that the **vports** layer is current.)

**Command: *rec***

27. Enter the ***VPClip*** command .

**Command: *vpclip***

28. Select the viewport with the saw elevation in it.

**Select viewport to clip:**

29. Select the polyline you drew in Step 26.

**Select clipping object or [Polygonal] <Polygonal>:**

30. Move the title block to the **Title Block** layer. Set the **text** layer current and freeze the **vports** layer.

31. Remember to save 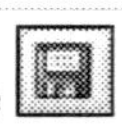 occasionally.

**Command: *qsave***

Your drawing looks like the figure below.

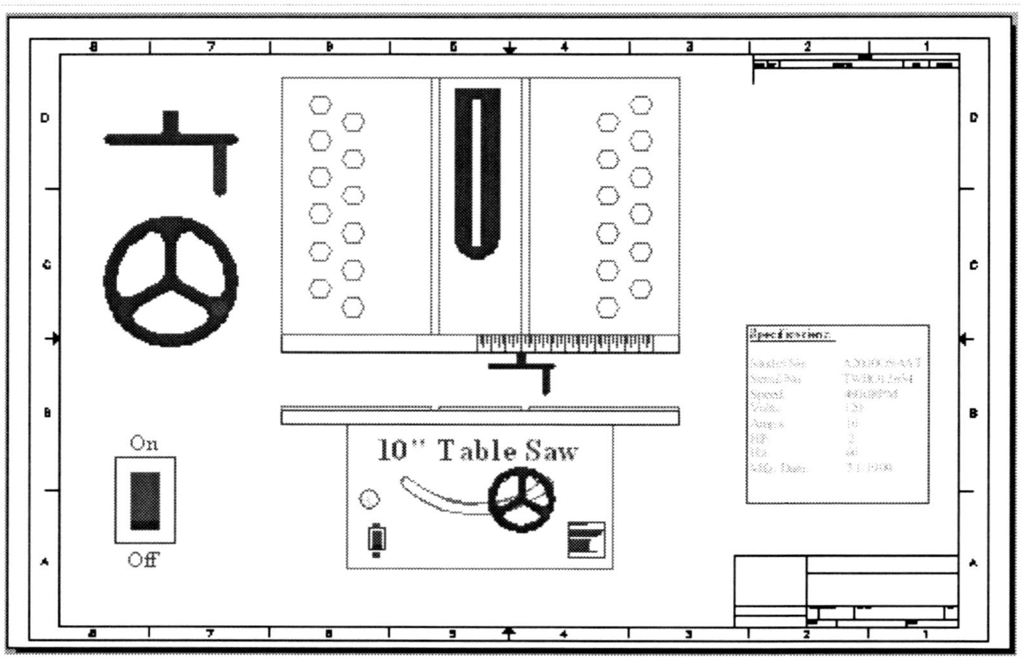


32. Add the text and detail markings as shown in the following figure. Text heights are ¼" and 3/16". The text style is **simple**. (Place the detail markings on the **details** layer.)

## 23.6.1: From Setup to Plot – A Project

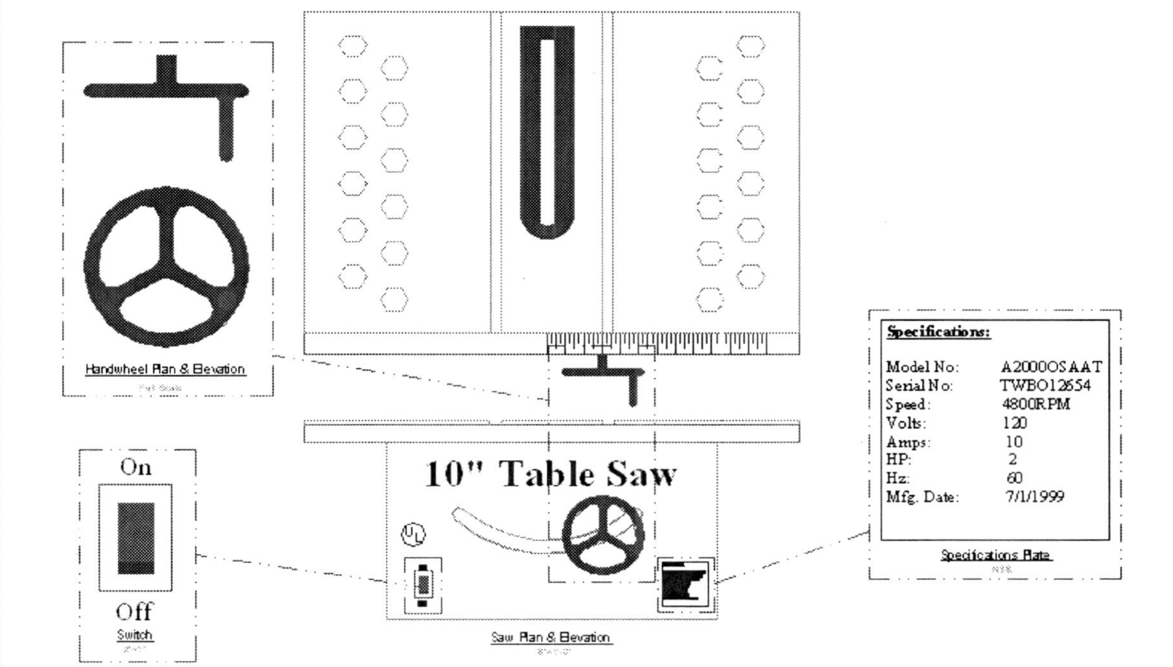


33. Fill in the title block as shown below. Text sizes are ¼", 3/16", and 1/8". Styles are **Timesbold** and **Times**.

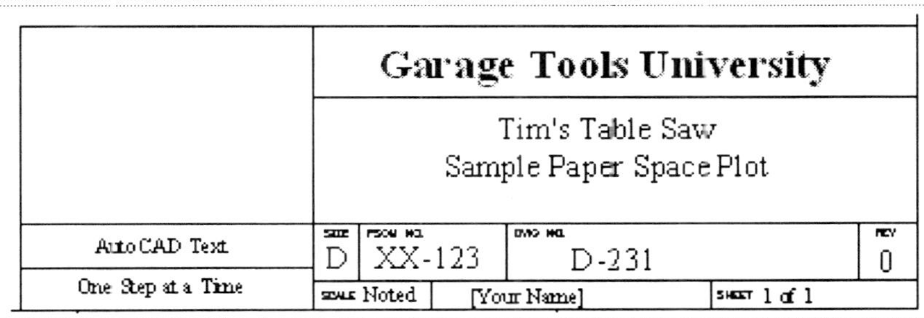


34. Remember to save occasionally.

**Command:** ***qsave***

35. Now we must plot the drawing. (Note: If you haven't a plotter available, you can print to your own printer – just make sure you print to fit.) Begin by entering the ***Plot*** command.

**Command:** ***plot***

36. Your Plot dialog box should resemble the one in the following figure. (Note: I'm printing to fit on a printer, as I don't have a plotter available.) Your plotter may vary and the **Plot offset** may vary. Use the **Preview** button to be sure you have set up the plot correctly and then plot the drawing.

## 23.6.1: From Setup to Plot – A Project

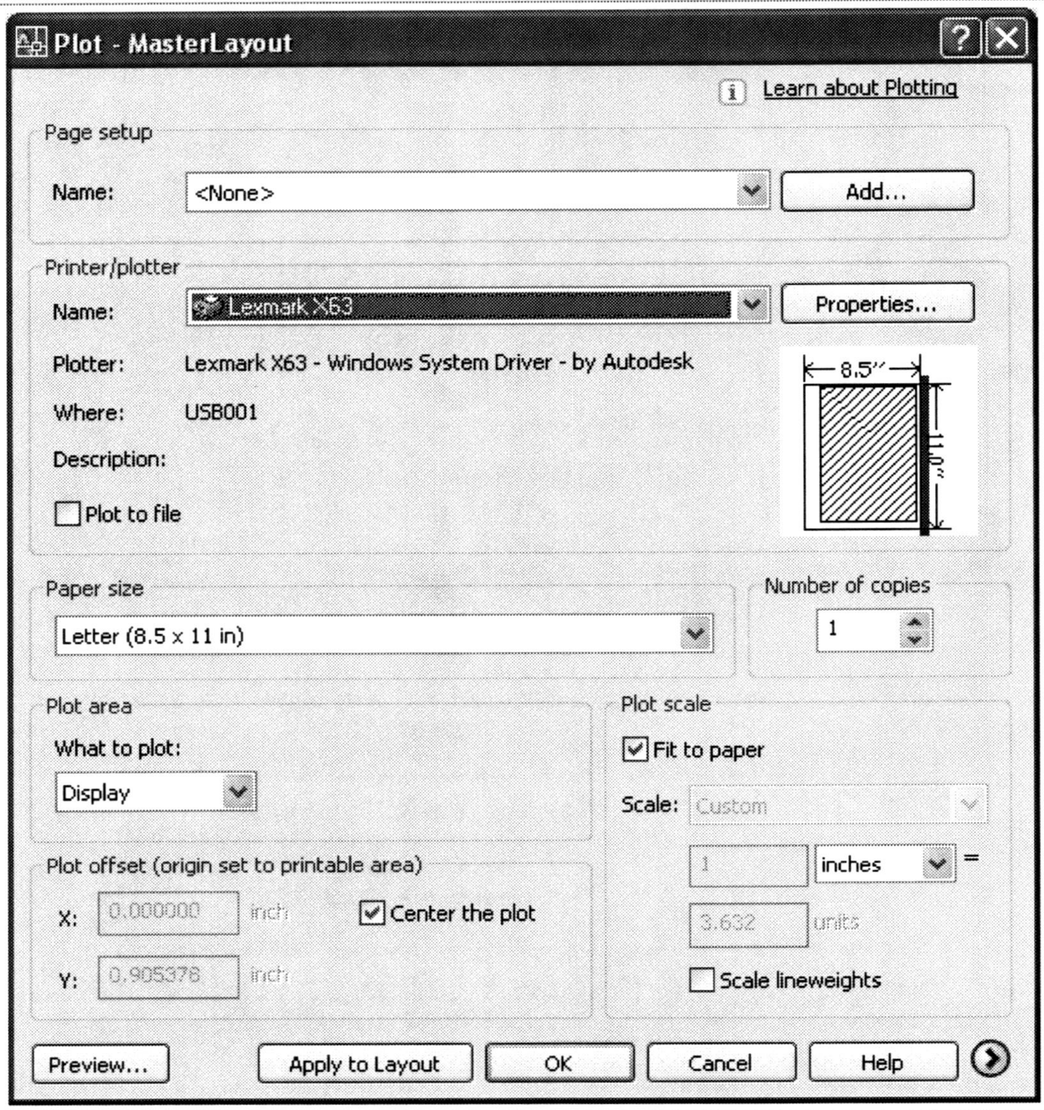


37. Save the drawing  and exit.

**Command:** ***qsave***

How was that? Just 37 easy steps to completion!

I know what that sounds like, but most of these steps will become second nature in time. Where it probably took 45 minutes to complete the exercise, with experience it'll take about 15 minutes to complete a similar project. This text can help you acquire some of that experience. Try some of the projects at the end of this lesson!

## 23.7 Extra Steps

- Try setting up and plotting some of your own drawings in a Paper Space environment.
- Try plotting the drawing from Exercise 23.6.1 to **Fit** on an 11" x 8½" sheet of paper.

## 23.8 What Have We Learned?

*Items covered in this lesson include:*

- *Using layers in Paper Space*
- *How to use text in Paper Space*
- *How to dimension in Paper Space*
- *How to plot a Paper Space drawing*
- *Commands*
    - ***MVsetup***
    - ***VPLayer***
    - ***VPClip***
    - ***Regenall***
    - ***Redrawall***
    - ***Spacetrans***

Remember the first paragraphs of Lesson 22? You may now step into that group of CAD operators who have used Paper Space and would never use anything else!

In Paper Space, you've taken your first steps into a whole new AutoCAD world! With experience, you'll soon wonder why we don't teach Paper Space from the beginning. But think back to what you knew when you began your first AutoCAD class. So much of what you learned in the last two lessons requires that you already have a foundation in the basics. And now, with Paper Space (and viewports) under your belt, you have a foundation for what comes next.

## 23.9 Exercises

1. Open the *MyNeedle.dwg* file in the C:\Steps\Lesson23 folder. (If that drawing isn't there, use the *needle 23.dwg* file in the same folder.) Create the drawing configuration for plotting found in the figure at right. Some helpful information includes:
    - 1.1. The text height is 5mm and 2.5mm; the font is Times New Roman.
    - 1.2. The title block text is attributed.
    - 1.3. I used two dimension layers (create new layers as required).
    - 1.4. Dimension text is 3mm.
    - 1.5. Remember that Floating viewports can overlap.
    - 1.6. Save the drawing as *MyNeedle23.dwg* in the C:\Steps\Lesson23 folder.

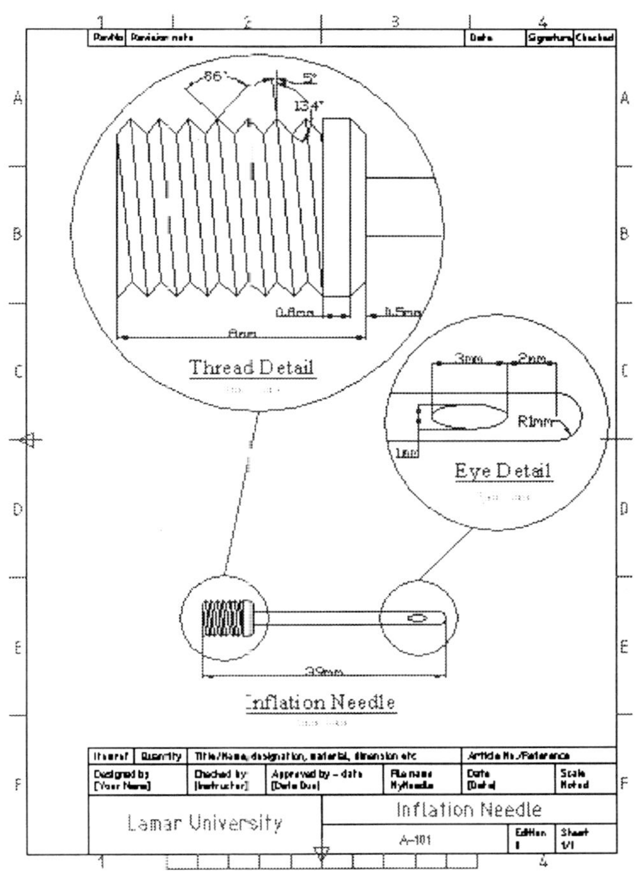


Inflation Needle

2. Open the *MySplitter.dwg* file in the C:\Steps\Lesson23 folder. (If this drawing isn't there, open the *cable splitter 23.dwg* file instead.) Create the drawing configuration for plotting found in the figure below. Some helpful information includes:
   2.1. The text height is 3/16" and 1/8"; the font is Times New Roman.
   2.2. The title block text is ¼", 3/16", and 1/8"; the font is Times New Roman.
   2.3. I used two dimension layers (create new layers as required).
   2.4. Dimension text is 1/8".
   2.5. Remember that floating viewports can overlap.
   2.6. Save the drawing as *MySplitter23.dwg* in the C:\Steps\Lesson23 folder.

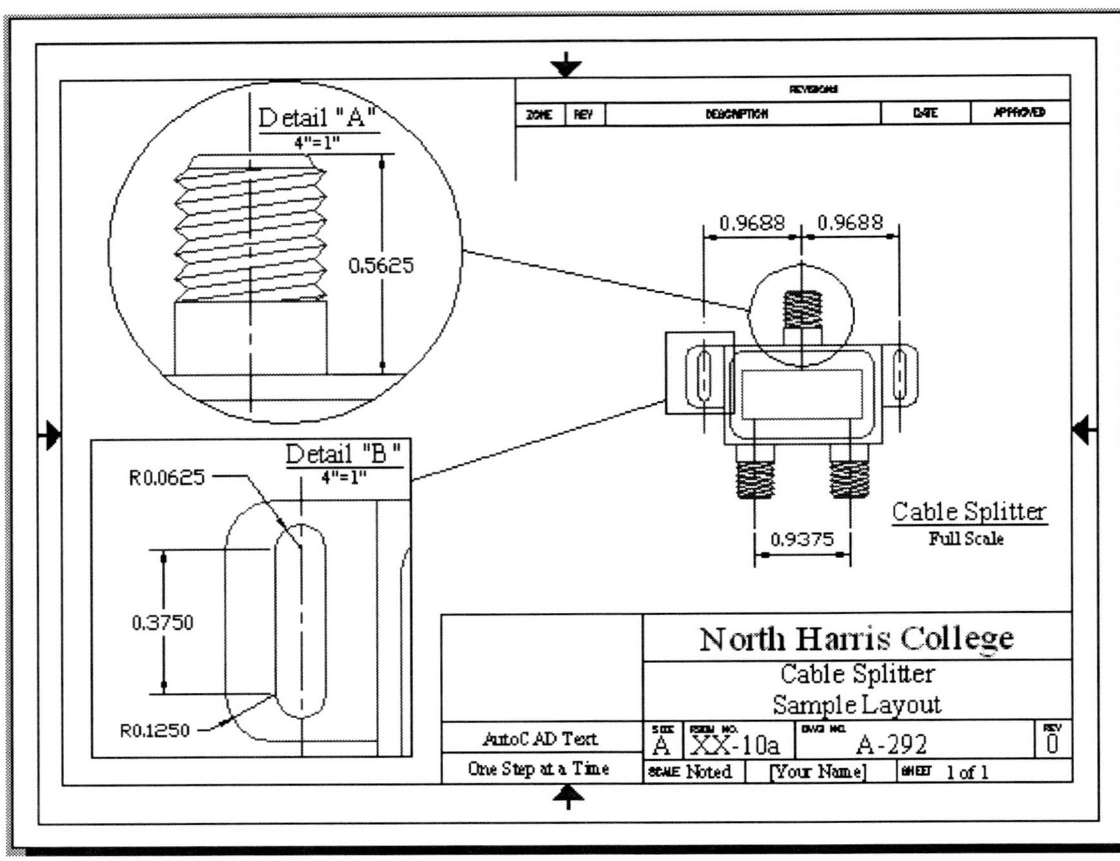


Cable Splitter

*For more exercises related to Lesson 23, please see Lesson 23 in AutoCAD 2007: One Step at a Time – Workbook.*

**23.10** **For Web-Based Review Questions, visit: http://www.uneedcad.com/2007/Files/07R23.pdf**

# Lesson 24

Following this lesson, you will:

- ✓ *Know how to organize your Paper Space Drawings into Drawing (Sheet) Sets*
    - ***SheetSet***
    - ***NewSheetSet***
    - ***OpenSheetSet***
- ✓ *Know how to transmit your sheet set to a client*
- ✓ *Know how to archive a project*
- ✓ *Know how to create multiple-sheet DWF files*

# Drawing Sheet Sets

*If the last couple lessons frightened you or you didn't see where Paper Space would do you any good, you can skip this chapter altogether. If, on the other hand, you saw the potential of this remarkable "plotting tool", then by all means, please continue. What you find in Lesson 24 will place the icing on the cake of your Paper Space aspirations! (Be warned, however; if you have an employer who lacks foresight – as many do – he or she will no doubt resist sheet sets. They are, after all, the bane of the sedentary boss ... they're an innovation – something completely new!)*

## 24.1 Sheet Sets – A Primer

*Knowledge isn't what you know ... it's what you know how to find out!*
*Hickory*

> Let me warn you before we start; the Sheet Sets palette, although benign in appearance, contains an amazing amount of opportunity (as you can tell from the amount of explanation before we even begin our first exercise). But don't feel as though you have to learn it all at once; take your time and repeat a section if you become confused. Remember what Hickory said at the beginning of this section. In other words, keep this text handy and make reference to it when you need help!

AutoCAD doesn't make it easy to find a definition for sheet sets. In fact, the Preview Guide refers both to drawing sets and sheet sets, but further reading indicates that both names essentially refer to the same thing (but like *print* and *plot*, don't expect them to settle on one name any time soon!). That being said, "sets" actually include both drawings and "sheets" (or Paper Space layouts).

*So, what exactly are drawing/sheet sets?*

Often, you'll find yourself with a bundle of drawings that need to be numbered and cataloged properly so that you (and your client) can keep track of them. Usually, this means keeping a log of some sort with drawing numbers assigned by discipline, and then running plots that we store in separate drawers of a large cabinet … or folders on someone's hard drive (or network).

Sheet sets (we'll settle on one name to keep it simple) are a systematic approach to organizing the package you're creating for your client – plans, details, electrical, plumbing, data sheets, etc. Further, the Sheet Set Manager greatly simplifies locating, opening, and editing any drawing or any layout in the set.

In this lesson, I'll walk you through the set up and use of sheet sets using the Sheet Set Manager. But bear in mind that this relatively new tool warrants greater exploration than we can do in these few pages. Once you've gotten your feet wet, feel free to head on into the deep end of the pool. (By now, you should be able to swim fairly well!)

## 24.2 Using the Sheet Set Manager to Organize Your Project

### 24.2.1 The Sheet List Tab

Unlike other managers, the Sheet Set Manager appears as a palette (Figure 24.001). (This should probably fill us with a sense of foreboding for what other managers will look like in future releases.) This handy palette – accessed with the ***SheetSet*** command or ***SSM*** hotkeys – will prove its value in more complex projects.

Let's take a look at its three tabs.

- The **Sheet List** tab (Figure 24.001) presents a list of the sheets in the set (under the **Sheets** heading), and either specific information about the selected sheet (**Details**) or a preview of the drawing (**Preview**). You can decide which of the latter two you'll see by picking the appropriate button on the title bar of the lower section. Right-click on any selected sheet and pick open to open the drawing to that layout.

  The top of this tab presents a selection box and three buttons.

  - o Use the selection box to **Open** an existing set, create a **New Sheet Set** (to launch the New Sheet Set wizard – see Exercise 24.2.1.1), or view a list of **Recent**[ly] opened sets.
  - o The first button – **Publish to DWF** – works much like a print button except that it tells AutoCAD to create a DWF file. This button works automatically and uses the defaults set up in the **Publish** command.

Figure 24.001

  - o The second button – **Publish** – calls a menu (Figure 24.002) with several options.
    - ▪ **Publish to DWF** operates the same as the button to the left. **Publish to Plotter** does the same thing, but plots to the default plotter.
    - ▪ **Publish using Page Setup Override** publishes the sheet using the selected overrides. The overrides come from drawing templates with their own setups.
    - ▪ The toggle **Include Plot Stamp** tells AutoCAD whether or not to place a stamp on the plot you're about to make.

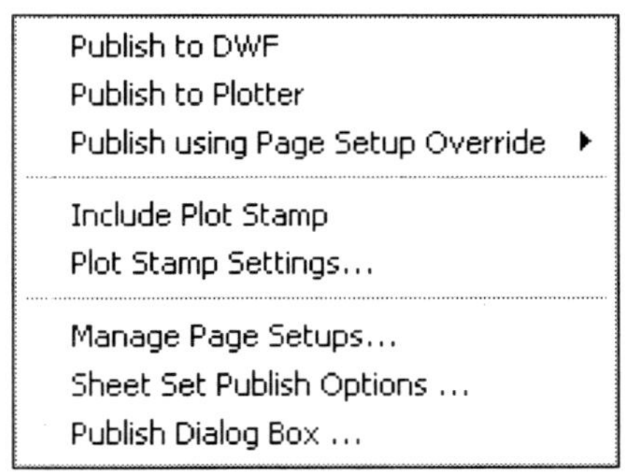


Figure 24.002

    - ▪ **Plot Stamp Settings** calls the Plot Stamp dialog box that will help you set up the stamp. (For more on the Plot Stamp dialog box, see Section 21.2.2.)
    - ▪ **Manage Page Setups** displays the Page Setup Manager. (For more on the Page Setup Manager, see Section 21.1.3.)
    - ▪ **Sheet Set Publish Options** calls the Publish Options dialog box but the settings are specific to the current sheet set. (For more on the Publish Options dialog box, see Section 21.2.2.)
    - ▪ Finally, **Publish Dialog Box** calls the Publish dialog box (Section 21.2.2).
  - o The last button on the **Sheet List** tab – **Sheet Selections** – enables you to either **Manage** or **Create** sheet selections. Use this tool to group several selected sheets for simultaneous publishing or transmitting action. AutoCAD will ask you for a name for the sheet selection. (Use something descriptive as there is no opportunity to describe the set anywhere else.) Once you've identified the sheet selection, you can publish or transmit the grouping. Use the **Manage** option to rename or delete the sheet selection.

- The **Sheets** list box presents a list of the drawings and sheets (layouts) currently listed in the sheet set. AutoCAD presents the cursor menu shown in Figure 24.003 when you right-click on one of the listings. (Note: The options will vary according to where your cursor is when you right-click. I produced the menu in the image by right-clicking on the sheet set name – at the top of the palette.) Let's look at these options.

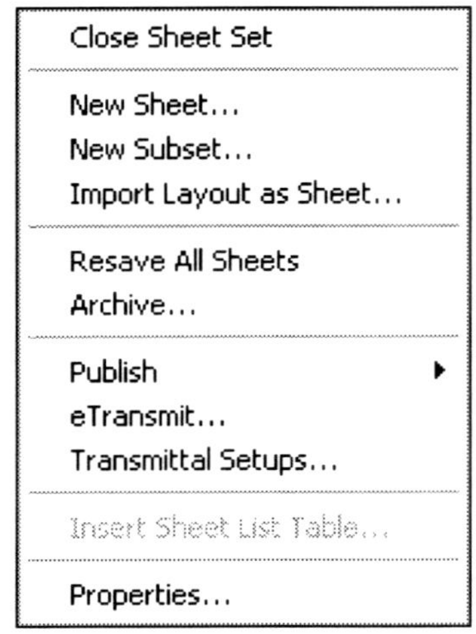


Figure 24.003

  - Use **Close Sheet Set** to close the current sheet set. You can't delete the DST file (sheet set data file – the file that contains the setup information for your sheet set) while the sheet set is open.
  - Create a **New Sheet** set with the next option. First, create your new drawing with a layout, and then this option will present the New Sheet dialog box (Figure 24.004), which will allow you to number and identify (**File name**) the new sheet in the current set.

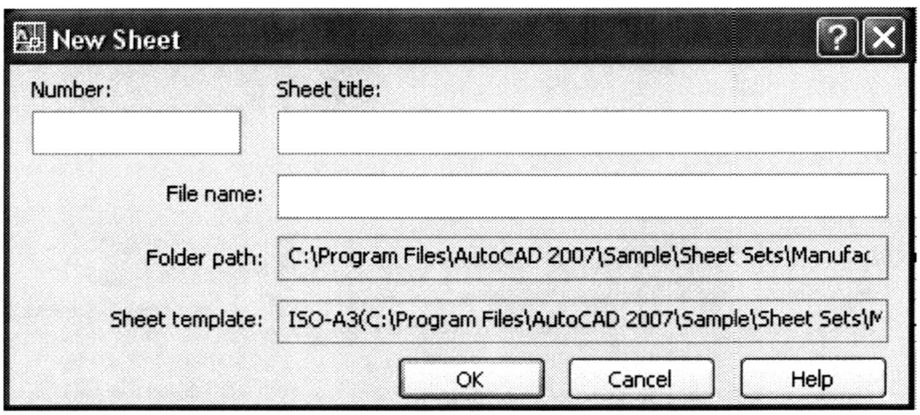


Figure 24.004

  - Use the **New Subset** option to call the Subset Properties dialog box (Figure 24.005). It'll help organize your list with a subset of an existing set. The Subset Properties dialog box provides options for naming (**Subset name**), storing (**Store new sheet DWG files in**), and even providing

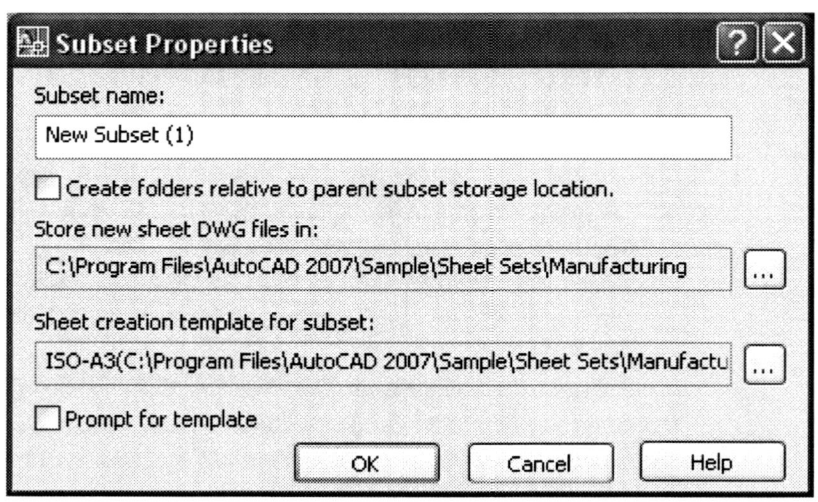


Figure 24.005

a template to create the new subset (**Sheet creation template for subset**). A check in the **Prompt for template** box tells AutoCAD to ignore the default template and ask you which template to use. A check next to **Create folders relative to parent subset storage location** helps you better organize your efforts.

- **Import Layout as Sheet** presents another dialog box (Figure 24.006). Use the **Browse for Drawings** button to select drawings to include in your sheet set. Once you've selected drawings, the list box will provide the layout names available for import. Put a check next to those rows that contain layouts you want to use.

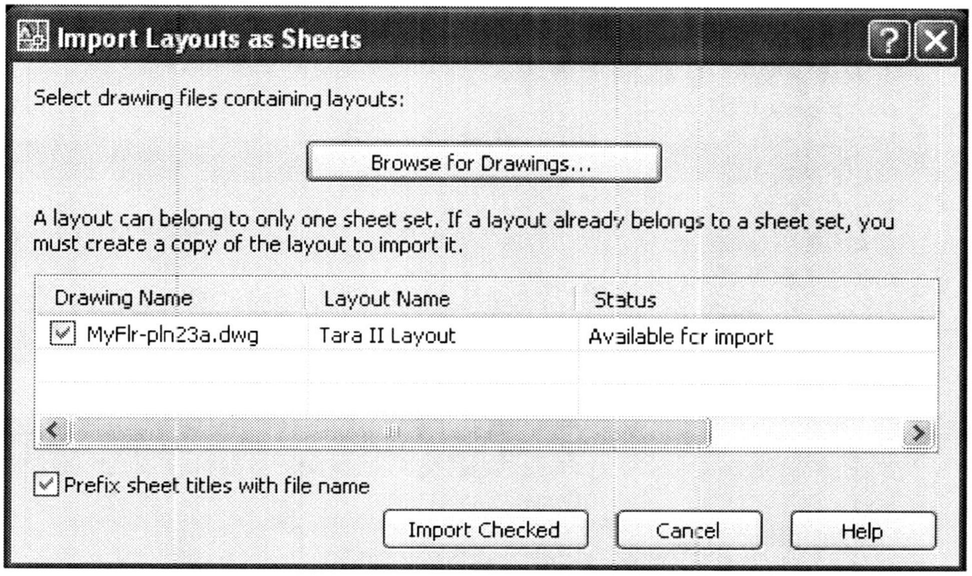


Figure 24.006

- **Resave All Sheets** opens and saves all the sheets associated with the sheet set. Use this tool to save any new sheet set information to the sheets, but be sure all the sheets are closed first.
- The **Publish** option presents the same cursor menu seen in Figure 24.002.
- **eTransmit** presents the Create Transmittal dialog box we discussed in Section 21.3.
- **Transmittal Setups** presents the Transmittal Setup dialog box. We also discussed this one in Section 21.3.
- Use **Insert Sheet List Table** to insert a table listing the sheets in the set. You'll usually insert this table on the data sheet for a project. (You can use the ***SheetSet*** command to accomplish the same purpose.) AutoCAD simplifies this procedure with a dialog box.
- The **Properties** option will display a Properties dialog box with information about the sheet set or the selected sheet.
- **Archive** presents the Archive a Sheet Set dialog box (Figure 24.007 – next page). (Reach the same dialog box with the ***Archive*** command.) You can use this to archive (store) all the drawings associated with a project at critical stages (Issued for Approval, Issued for Construction, Issued for Review, and so forth).

You'll notice three tabs in this dialog box. The first, **Sheets**, creates an archive package from your sheet set. The other two list the files in that package – the **Files Tree** tab does it in a tree view while the **Files Table** tab does it in a table view. You can remove any sheet or file by removing the check in the box to its left.

Use **Enter notes to include with this archive** to add your own notes to the report that accompanies the archive. (The **View Report** button will display the report for you.)

The **Modify Archive Setup** button calls the Modify Archive Setup dialog box (Figure 24.008). This box is almost identical to the Modify Transmittal Setup dialog box we discussed in Section 21.3. Please refer to that section for explanations of the various options.

Figure 24.007

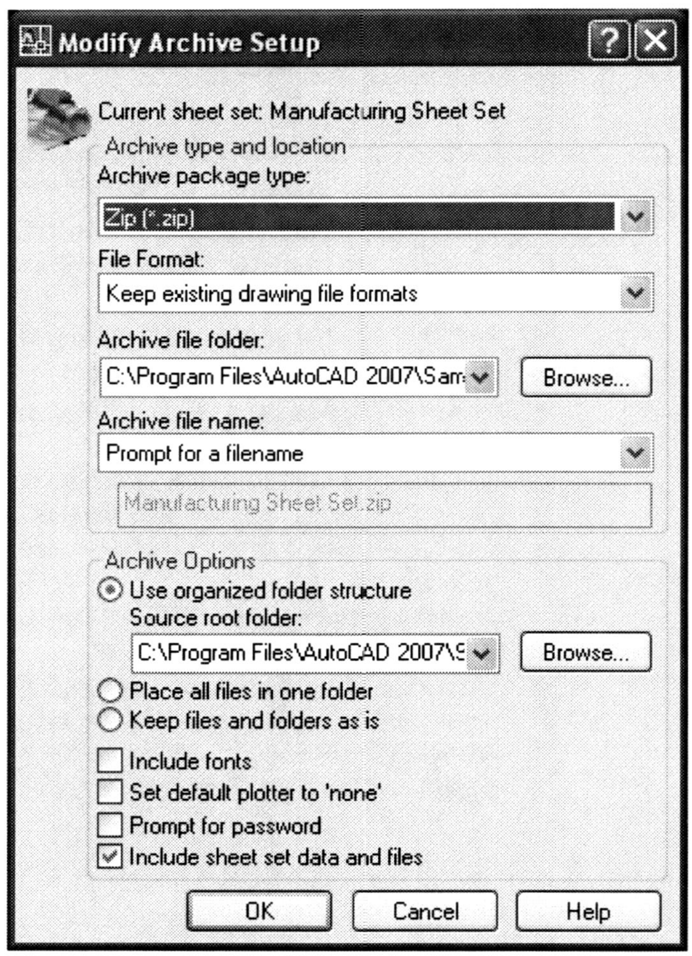


Figure 24.008

- The cursor menu presented when you right-click over a sheet in the sheet set looks like Figure 24.009. We haven't discussed two of these options.
    - The **Rename and Renumber** option calls a dialog box similar to the New Sheet dialog box (Figure 24.004). Here, however, you have a couple check boxes that enable you to **Rename associated drawing file to match sheet set title** or to **Prefix** [a] **sheet number to** [the] **file name.**
    - **Remove Sheet** removes the selected sheet from the set; it does not delete the drawing.

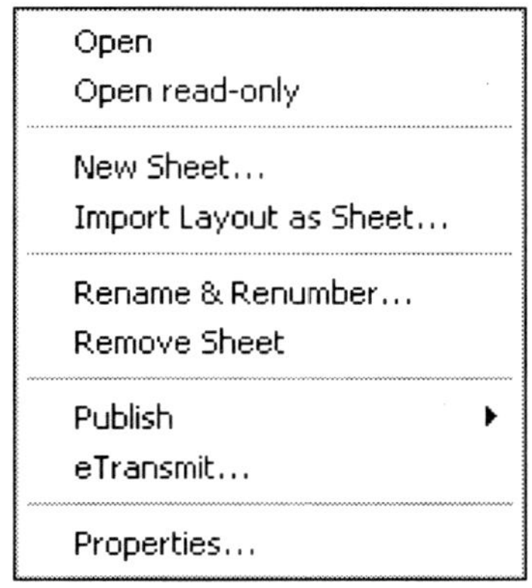

Figure 24.009

That's a tremendous amount of material for the first tab of a palette! But wait, there's more to come! (This might be a good time to shake the cobwebs loose and go get some coffee before you continue.)

Let's try an exercise with what we've learned so far.

| Do This: 24.2.1.1 | Creating Sheet Sets |
|---|---|

I. Open the *Tara II Data Sheet* drawing in the C:\Steps\Lesson24\Sheet Sets folder. Notice that I've set up this drawing in Paper Space. We'll create a sheet set for this project.

II. Follow these steps.

**24.2.1.1: CREATING SHEET SETS**

1. Open the Sheet Set Manager. You can use the command prompt or the **Sheet Set Manager** button on the Standard toolbar.

   **Command:** ***ssm***

2. We'll use the Create Sheet Set wizard. You can start it by either entering the ***NewSheetSet*** command at the command line, or selecting **New Sheet Set** from the drop down selection box at the top of the palette.

   **Command:** ***newsheetset***

3. AutoCAD begins the New Sheet wizard with an option to create your new sheet set using **Existing drawings** or **An example sheet set**.

   Using existing drawings allows you to select a folder(s) with files in it. AutoCAD will use the layouts from these drawings in the new sheet set.

   Using **An example sheet set** tells AutoCAD to use the structure from the sample in creating the structure for the new set. It won't add any drawings to your set.

   We'll use the **Existing drawings** option for this exercise.

   Pick the **Next** button to continue.

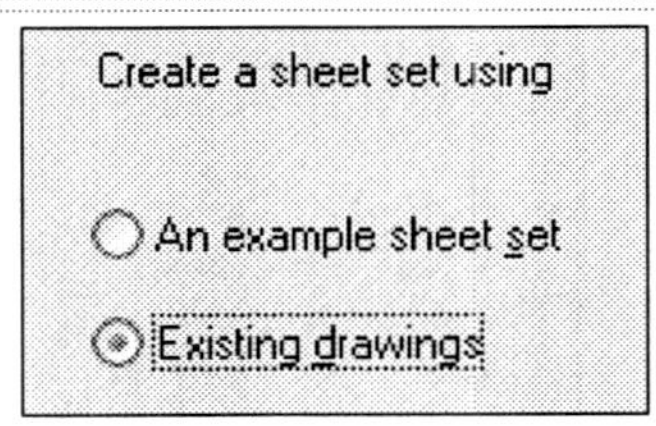

4. On the second page of our wizard, we can name the new set (call it ***Tara II Project***). Add a description if you wish and tell AutoCAD to store the data file for the sheet set in the C:\Steps\Lesson24\Sheet Sets folder.

Notice the **Sheet Set Properties** button. Use this to create custom properties for your project. (We'll ignore it for this exercise.)

Pick the **Next** button to continue.

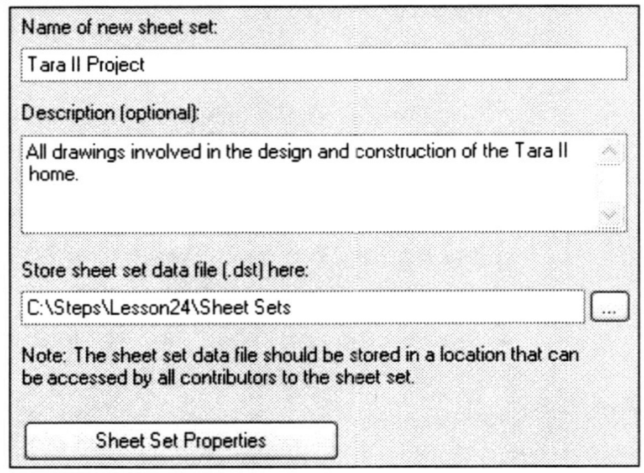


5. Pick the **Browse** button on the next screen to select the folder where the drawings for your sheet set reside (C:\Steps\Lesson24\Sheet Sets).

Notice the **Import Options** button. This will call a dialog box where you can tell AutoCAD to **Prefix the sheet titles with the file name** (a good idea to help keep track of things) and/or to **Create subsets based on the folder structure**.

We'll ignore the import options for now.

Pick the **Next** button to continue.

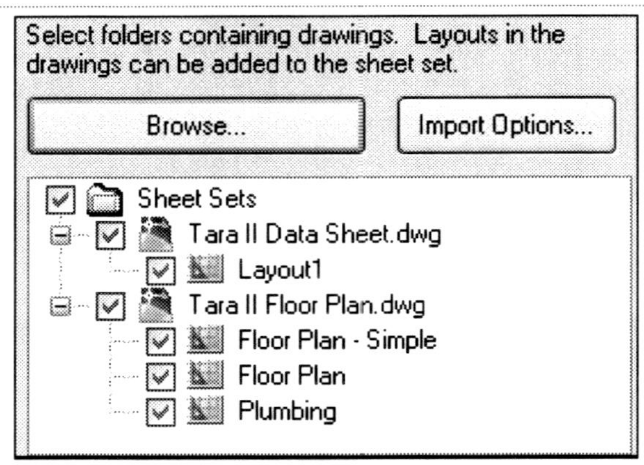


6. AutoCAD finishes with a preview of your sheet set properties (below) and asks you to confirm your setup. Pick the **Finish** button to complete the wizard.

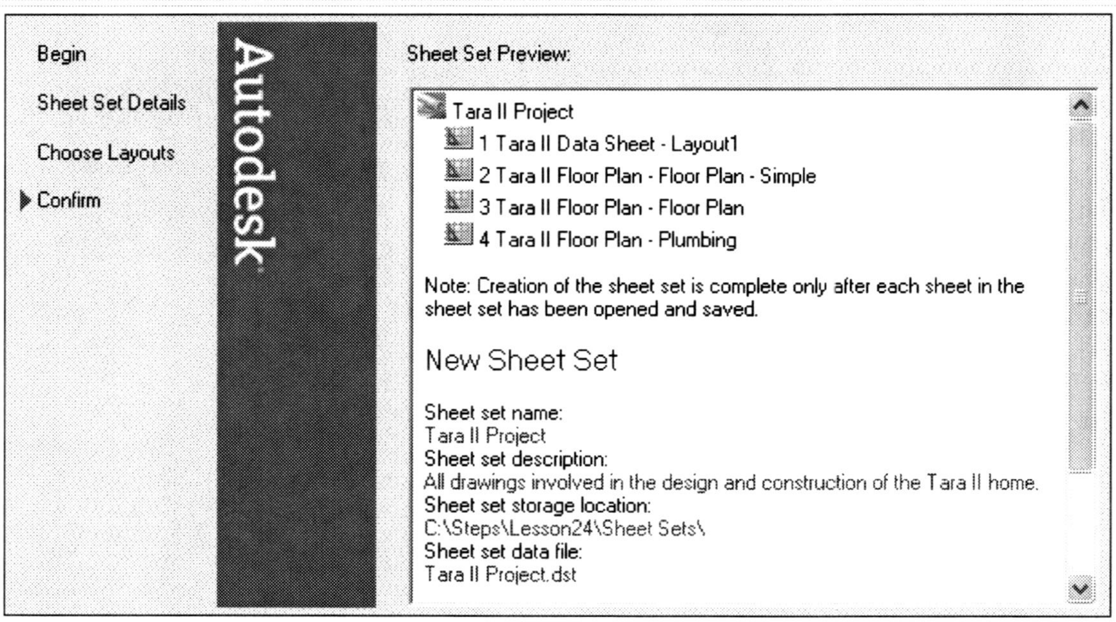

## 24.2.1.1: Creating Sheet Sets

7. Notice (right) that AutoCAD has created your sheet set.

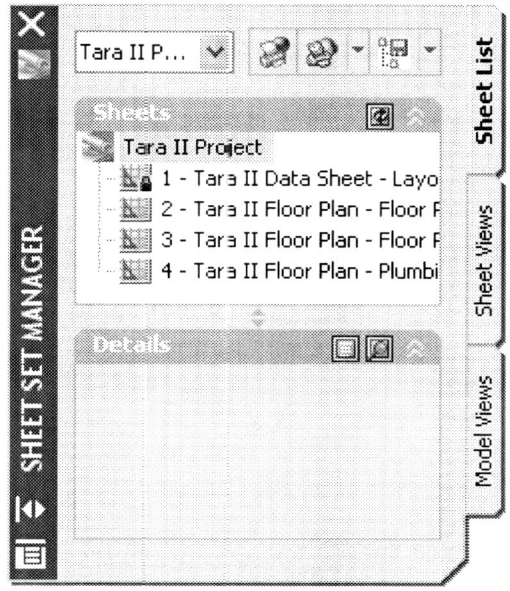


8. Now let's see what we can do with the cursor menus. Right-click on **Tara II Data Sheet** and select **Rename and Renumber**.

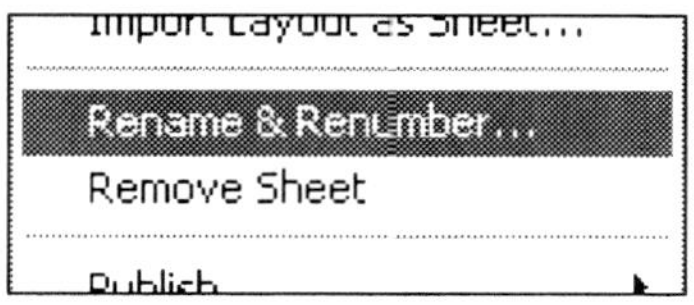


9. Rename the sheet ***Data Sheet*** and be sure it's drawing #1 as indicated below. Then pick the **Next** button to rename/renumber the rest of the sheets as follows:
   - call sheet #2 ***Simple Floor Plan***
   - Sheet #3 ***Floor Plan***
   - Sheet #4 ***Plumbing***

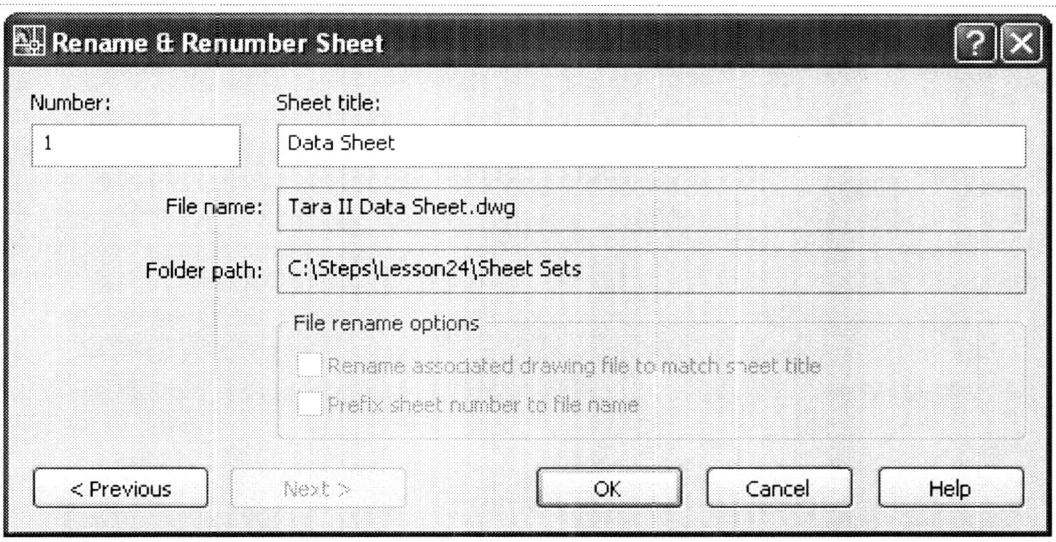


10. Complete the procedure 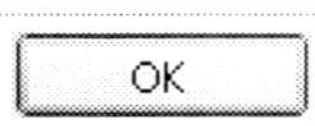.

11. Save the drawing 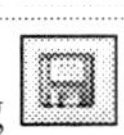 but don't exit.

**Command: *qsave***

In this exercise, AutoCAD has created a sheet set using the two drawings available in the C:\Steps\Lesson24\Sheet Sets folder (*Tara II Data Sheet.dwg* and *Tara II Floor Plan*). Bear in mind that I created both with Paper Space layouts (these are versions of the files you've been using), views, and blocks. But this simple four-step wizard has done so much more than is readily visible.

Take a moment and explore the **Sheet List** in the light of what we've discussed so far. Then let's continue our discussion and see what else this complex tool has to offer!

### 24.2.2 The View List Tab

The **Sheet Views** tab of the Sheet Set Manager (Figure 24.010) presents a list of available views. In the upper list box (**View by sheet**), AutoCAD organizes the views under the name of the sheets in the set. Use the two buttons on the section's title bar to toggle between **View by category** and **View by sheet**. You can even use the button at the top of the palette (**New View Category**) to create your own categories. Once you have your own category, just drag and drop the views where you want them.

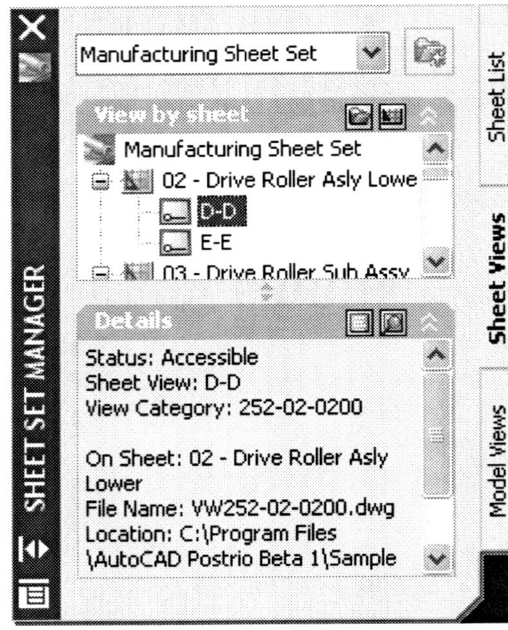

Figure 24.010

You can also use this tab to mine drawings for their blocks (and use the blocks in the current drawing).

Let's look at the three cursor menus for this tab.

- The first (Figure 24.011) displays when you right-click on the title of the sheet set (when in **View by category** mode). Use this one to either create a **New View Category** (just as the button does) or to check the **Properties** of the sheet set.

Figure 24.011

If you select the **New View Category** option (or pick the button at the top of the palette), AutoCAD will present the View Category dialog box (Figure 24.012). Here you can name your new category (**Category name** text box) or **Select the callout blocks to be used in this category**. The list box shows the blocks that are currently available in the sheet set. Use the **Add Blocks** button to add additional blocks or remove existing ones (you'll see this in our next exercise).

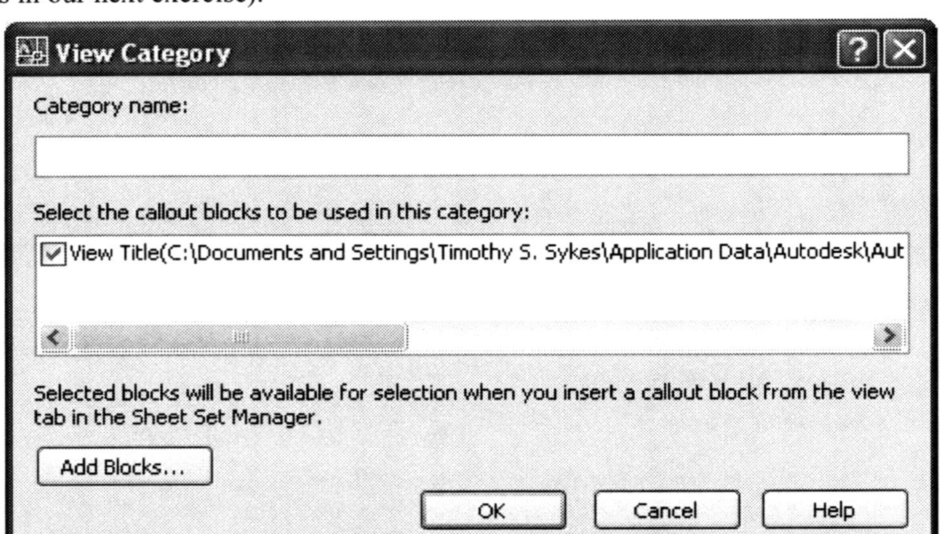

Figure 24.012

- The second cursor menu (Figure 24.013) appears when you right-click on one of the folders. Use it to **Rename** a category, **Remove** [a] **Category**, or view the **Properties** of that category. You can also add blocks to the category via the Properties dialog box.

Figure 24.013

- The last (Figure 24.014) appears when you right-click on one of the views.

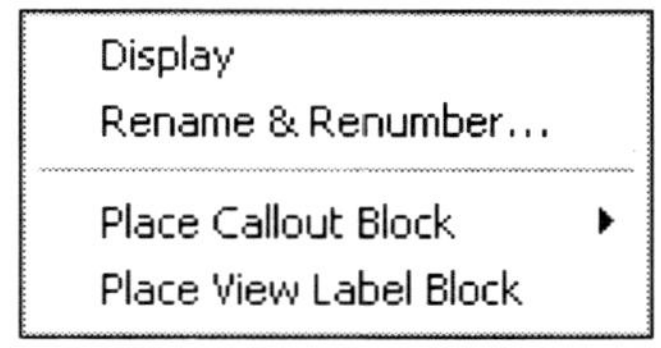


Figure 24.014

  - The **Display** option is one of AutoCAD's finest. It opens the appropriate drawing with the selected view displayed. How's that for handy?! (Show some restraint with this one. You can wind up with several drawings open at once ... and wonder why your system has slowed so much!)
  - **Rename and Renumber** (when selected from this menu) will present the Rename and Renumber dialog box seen in Figure 24.015. Here you can rename and/or renumber the selected view.

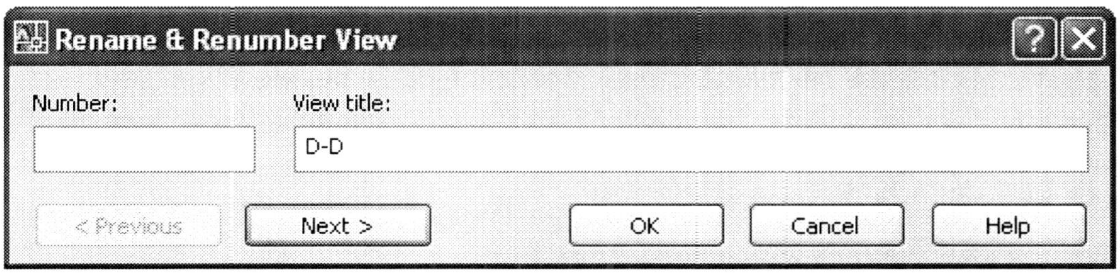


Figure 24.015

  - **Place Callout Block** presents a list of blocks available from the sheet set drawing that contains the selected view. You can insert these blocks into the current drawing. If no blocks are available, AutoCAD displays a **Select Blocks** option. Use this to call the View Category dialog box (Figure 24.012). From there, pick the **Add Blocks** button to add blocks to the list.
  - The **Place View Label Block** inserts a standard view label (we'll see this in our next exercise).

Let's try another exercise before we continue to the last tab.

| **Do This: 24.2.2.1** | **Working with the Sheet Views Tab** |
|---|---|

I. Begin a new drawing from scratch.

II. Use architectural units and set the limits for a ¼" scale, C-size sheet of paper (upper left limits of 88',68').

III. Follow these steps.

**24.2.2.1: WORKING WITH THE SHEET VIEWS TAB**

1. If the Tara II sheet set isn't open, use the drop down selection box at the top of the palette to open it. (Select **Open** from the list, navigate to the C:\Steps\Lesson24\Sheet Sets folder, and then select the *Tara II Project.dst* file.) Alternately, you can use the ***OpenSheetSet*** command.

   **Command:** ***opensheetset***

2. Pick the **Sheet Views** tab and then the **View by category** button to adjust the list. Notice the categories with and without a list of views. Let's make these more manageable.

## 24.2.2.1: WORKING WITH THE SHEET VIEWS TAB

3. Use the cursor menu to **Renumber and Rename** the three views in the Border Data category as follows:

- rename **FP - Block Border Data** to **Floor Plan Title Block**; make it #**001**;
- rename **FP – Simple Title and Revision Block** to **Simple Plan Title Block**; make it #**002**;
- rename **Plumbing – Block Border Data** to **Plumbing Title Block**; make it #**003**.

4. Right click on the **Project** title and select **New View Category**.

5. Create a new category called **Details**. (Don't add any blocks at this time.)

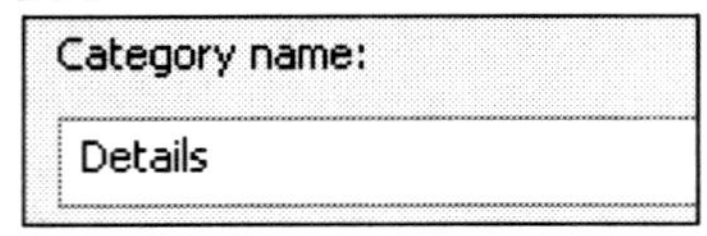


6. Move both of the views listed under the **Plumbing Views** category to the **Details** category. (Drag the listing with the left mouse button and release it under the **Details** category title.)

7. Right click on the empty **Plumbing Views** category and pick **Remove Category** from the cursor menu.
The **Views** section of the palette looks like this.

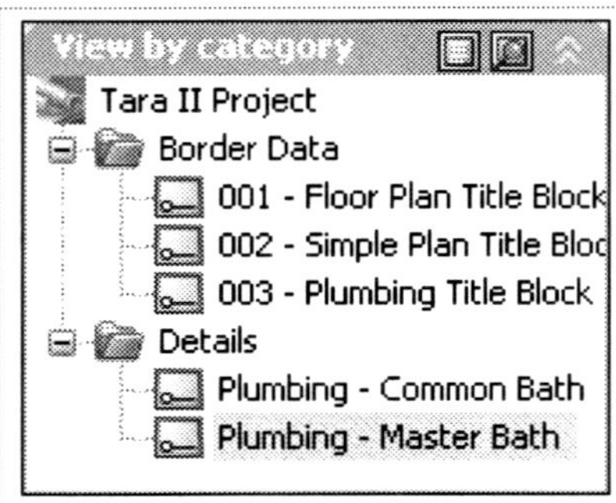


8. Use the cursor menu to open the View Category dialog box of the **Details** category (pick **Properties**).

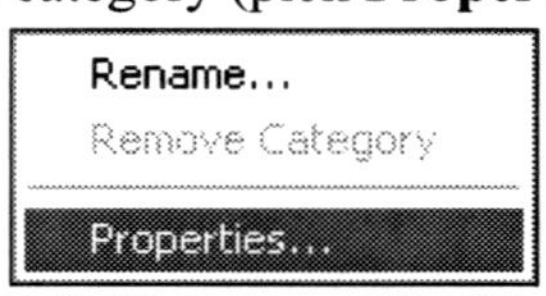


9. Pick the **Add Blocks** button 

.

10. AutoCAD presents a List of Blocks dialog box. The blocks we need aren't in this list, so pick the **Add** button 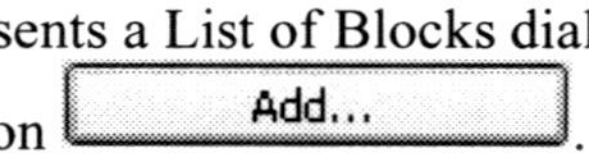

.

11. AutoCAD presents the Select Block dialog box (below). Pick the **Browse** button next to the **Enter the drawing file name** text box.

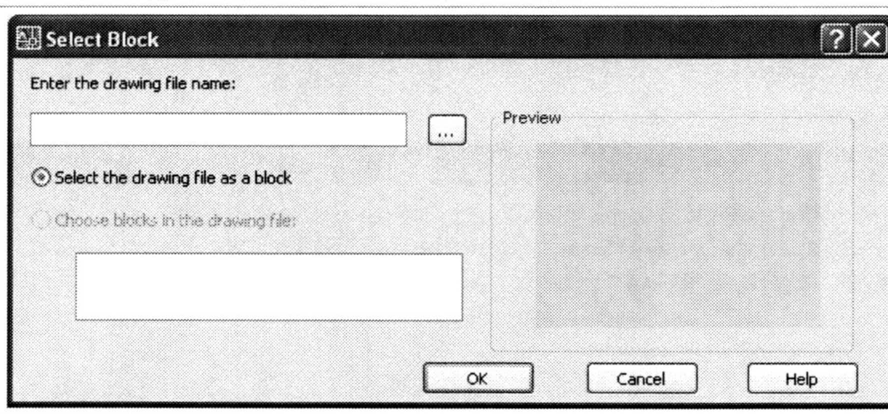

## 24.2.2.1: Working with the Sheet Views Tab

12. AutoCAD presents a standard Open File dialog box. Navigate to the C:\Steps\Lesson24\Sheet Sets folder and open 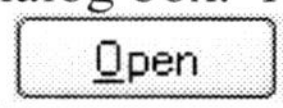

the *Tara II Floor Plan* drawing.

13. AutoCAD returns to the Select Block dialog box. Notice (below) the difference. Now AutoCAD lists the source file for your blocks in the **Enter the drawing file name** text box.
Put a bullet next to **Choose blocks in the drawing** file. This makes the individual blocks in the listed drawing available for your selection.
Select the **Sink**, **Tub**, and **WC**, as shown.
Pick the **OK** button here and on the List of Blocks dialog box to return to the View Category dialog box.

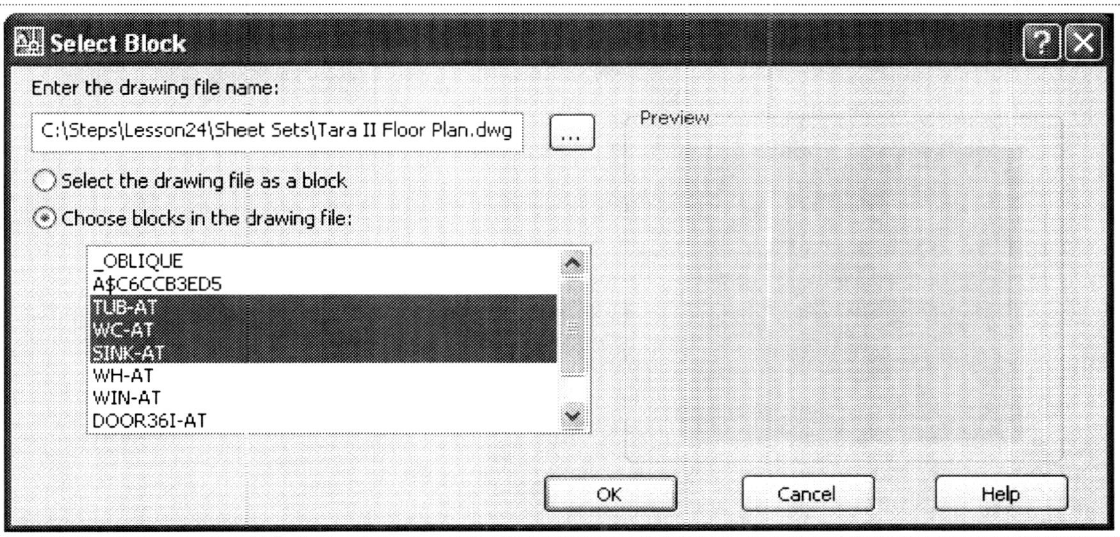


14. Put checks in the boxes next to our new blocks (below) and pick the **OK** button to complete the procedure. Your blocks are now available for insertion into the current drawing (or any drawing while the Tara II Project is open in the Sheet Set palette).

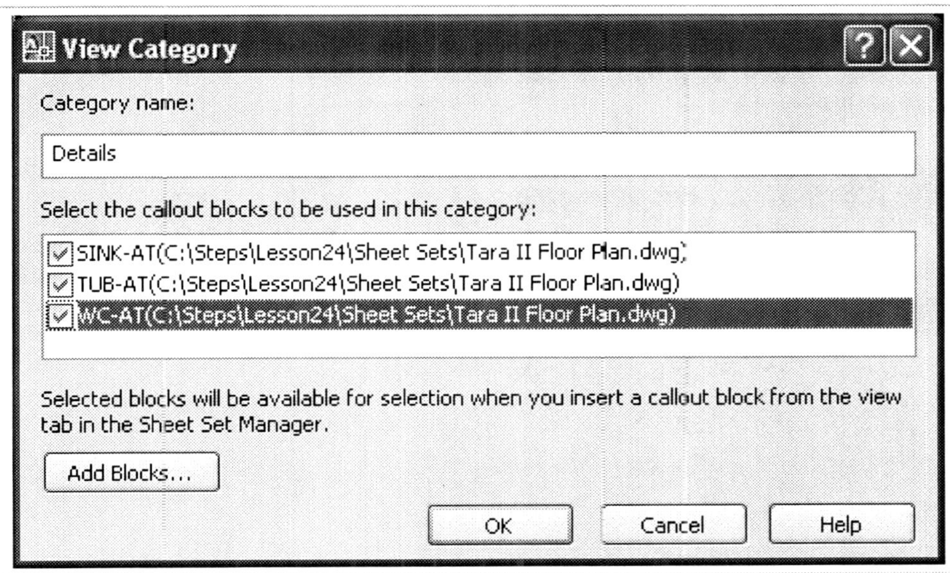

## 24.2.2.1: Working with the Sheet Views Tab

15. Just to see it work, right-click on one of the views in the **Detail** category, select **Place Callout Block** and then **WC-AT** from the flyout menus. Follow block insertion procedures to insert the block anywhere in your drawing.

(Pretty cool, huh?)

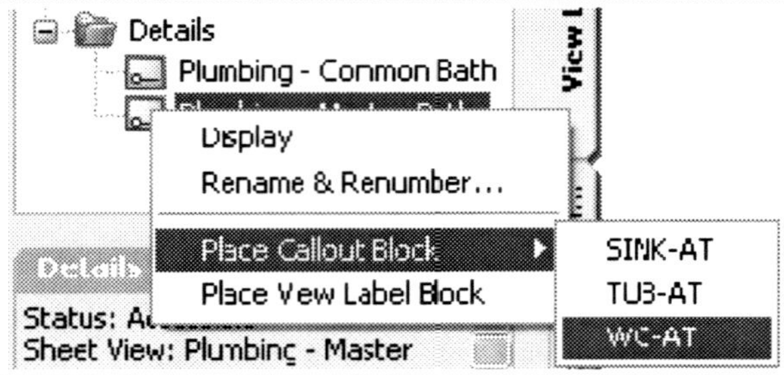


16. Next, we'll insert a label block.
Right click on the same view, but this time, select **Place View Label Block**. Since we haven't set up for this yet, AutoCAD again presents the Select Block dialog box.

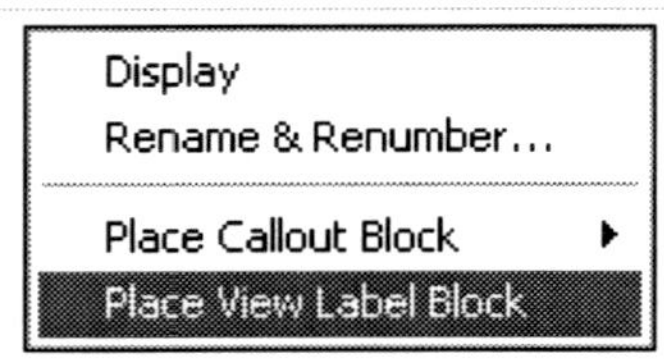


17. This time we won't select a drawing; we'll select a template that contains the block. Pick the **Browse** button 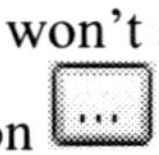 next to the **drawing file name** text box.

18. AutoCAD opens a standard file open dialog box. Navigate to this file (be sure to browse for DWT files – not DWGs): *Template\SheetSets\Architectural Imperial.dwt.* (Note: AutoCAD begins in the *Template* folder when you browse for a *.dwt* file.)

Pick the **Open** button 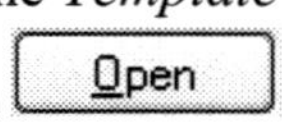 to continue.

19. Back on the Select Block dialog box, put a bullet next to **Choose blocks in the drawing file**, and select the **Drawing Block Title**. (AutoCAD will now use this block whenever you place a view label.)

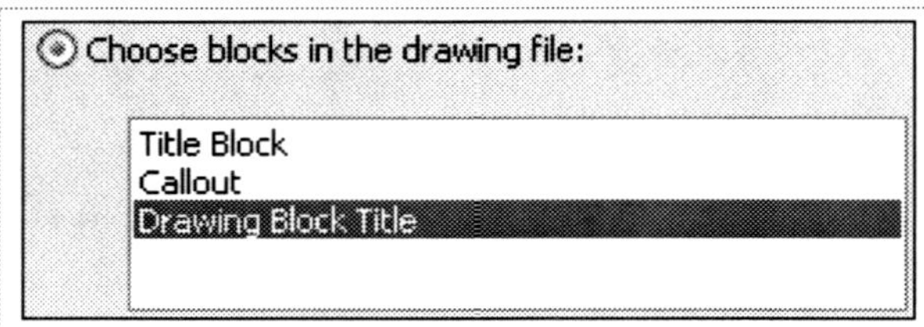


20. Complete the procedure 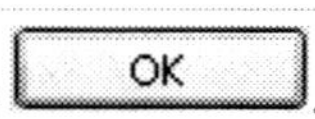.

21. Now AutoCAD asks for an insertion point. Pick a point near the block you inserted in Step 15. The label looks like the figure below.

22. You can use standard block editing tools (Enhanced Attribute Editor) to edit the attributes of this block.

Wasn't that neat? Of course, you won't have to do the setup in Steps 17 through 20 every time.

## 24.2.3 The Model Views Tab

One more tab! And we can relax … this one's fairly easy.

The **Model Views** tab (Figure 24.016) contains a single option – **Add New Location**. You'll use this to add the location (folder) where you've located additional drawings that you wish to be associated with the current sheet set.

In our next exercise, we'll use this third tab to add an additional folder to our sheet set. Then we'll import a layout into our sheet set and place a sheet list onto our *Tara II Data Sheet*.

Let's begin.

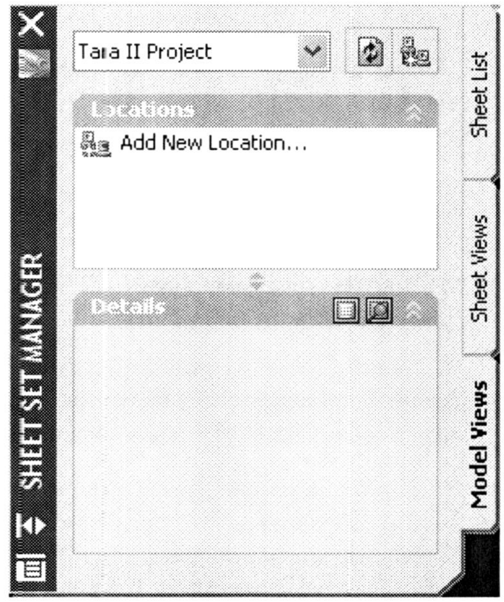


Figure 24.016

## Do This: 24.2.3.1 Working with the Model Views Tab & Some Final Touches

I. Open the *Tara II Data Sheet* drawing in the C:\Steps\Lesson24\Sheet Sets folder. If not, please open it now.

II. Set the **TEXT** layer current, and pick on the **Model Views** tab to put it on top of the Sheet Set palette.

III. Follow these steps.

| 24.2.3.1: WORKING WITH THE MODEL VIEWS TAB & SOME FINAL TOUCHES |
|---|

1. First, let's associate the new folder. Double-click on the **Add New Location** option in the **Locations** list box. Alternately, you can pick the **Add New Location** button 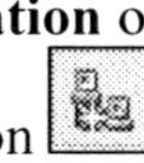 at the top of the palette.

2. AutoCAD presents a standard Open dialog box. Navigate to the C:\Steps\Lesson24\ Resource Drawings folder and pick the **Open** button [Open].

Notice (right) that the palette now shows the new folder and the drawing file within it. This drawing is now associated with the sheet set and may be plotted, archived, or transmitted with it.

3. Next, we'll import a new sheet into our set. Return to the **Sheet List** tab.

## 24.2.3.1: Working with the Model Views Tab & Some Final Touches

4. Right-click on the **Tara II Project** title (at the top of the **Sheets** section) and pick the **Import Layout as Sheet** option.

AutoCAD presents the Import Layouts as Sheets dialog box (Figure 24.006).

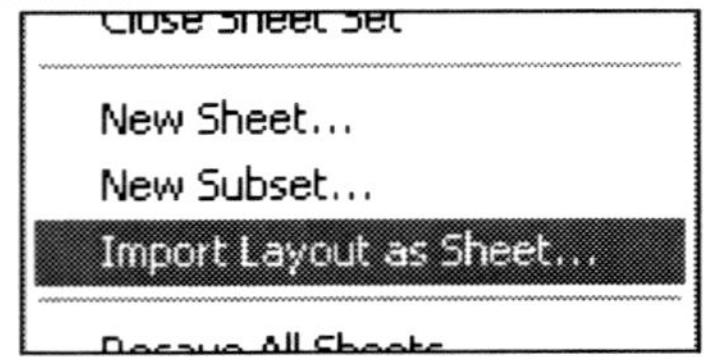


5. Pick the **Browse for Drawings** button 

. AutoCAD presents a standard Open File dialog box.

6. Navigate to the C:\Steps\Lesson24\ Resource Drawings folder and select the *Architectural Symbols – 2005.dwg* file. AutoCAD returns to the Import Layouts as Sheets dialog box, which now shows the Architectural drawing.

7. Complete the procedure 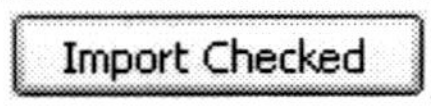

. Notice that the new sheet appears in the **Sheets** section of the palette.

8. Use the **Rename and Renumber** option in the cursor menu to give this sheet the number ***5*** and the title ***Architectural Electrical Symbols***.

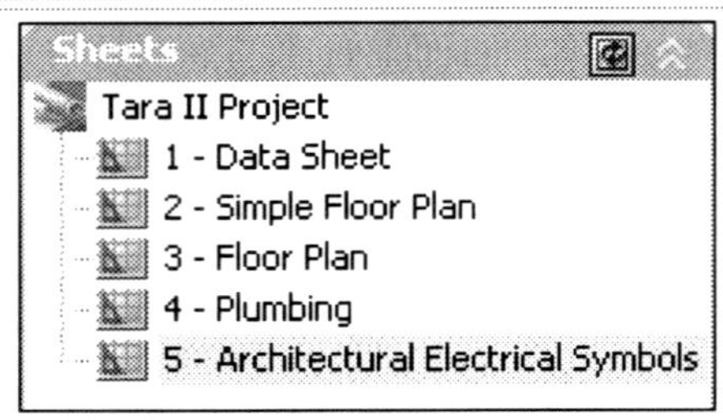


9. Finally, let's place a drawing sheet list on our *Tara II Data Sheet*. Begin by picking the **Insert Sheet List Table** option on the cursor menu presented when you right-click on the **Tara II Project** title.

AutoCAD presents an Insert Sheet List Table dialog box (below).

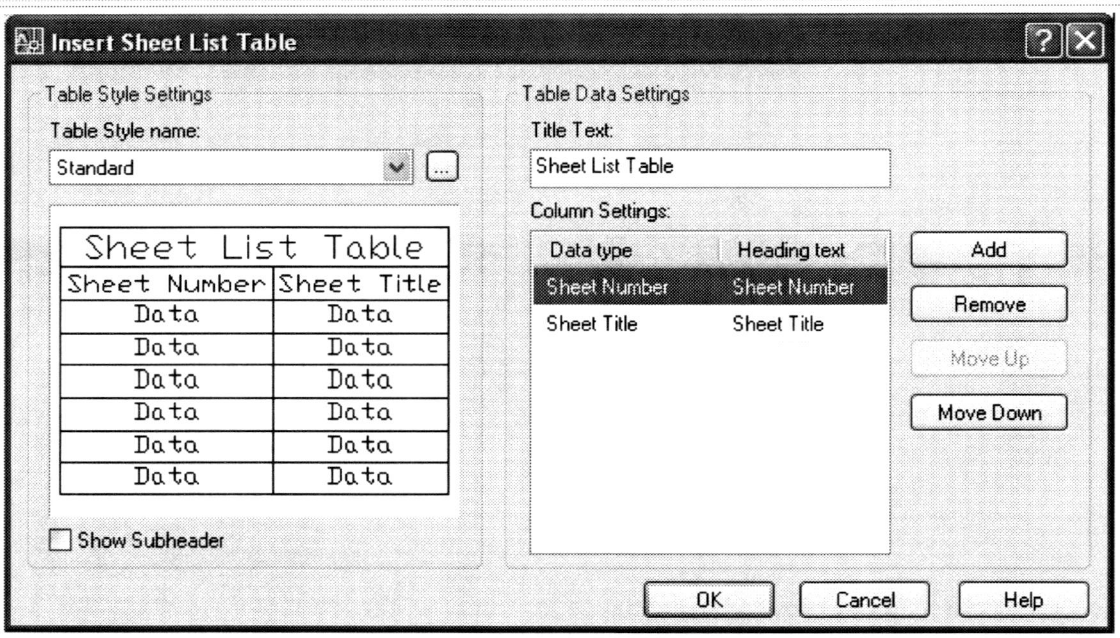


10. This dialog box is very similar to others you've used to insert tables. Accept the defaults and pick the **OK** button 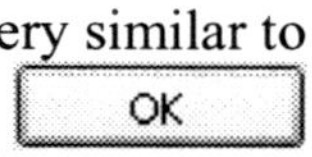

to proceed.

## 24.2.3.1: Working with the Model Views Tab & Some Final Touches

11. AutoCAD warns you that you shouldn't modify this table manually (it's produced automatically from the sheet set). Pick the **OK** button [OK] to continue.

12. AutoCAD removes the dialog box and asks you to specify an insertion. Place the table below the text (on the right side of the sheet). Your drawing now looks like the figure below.

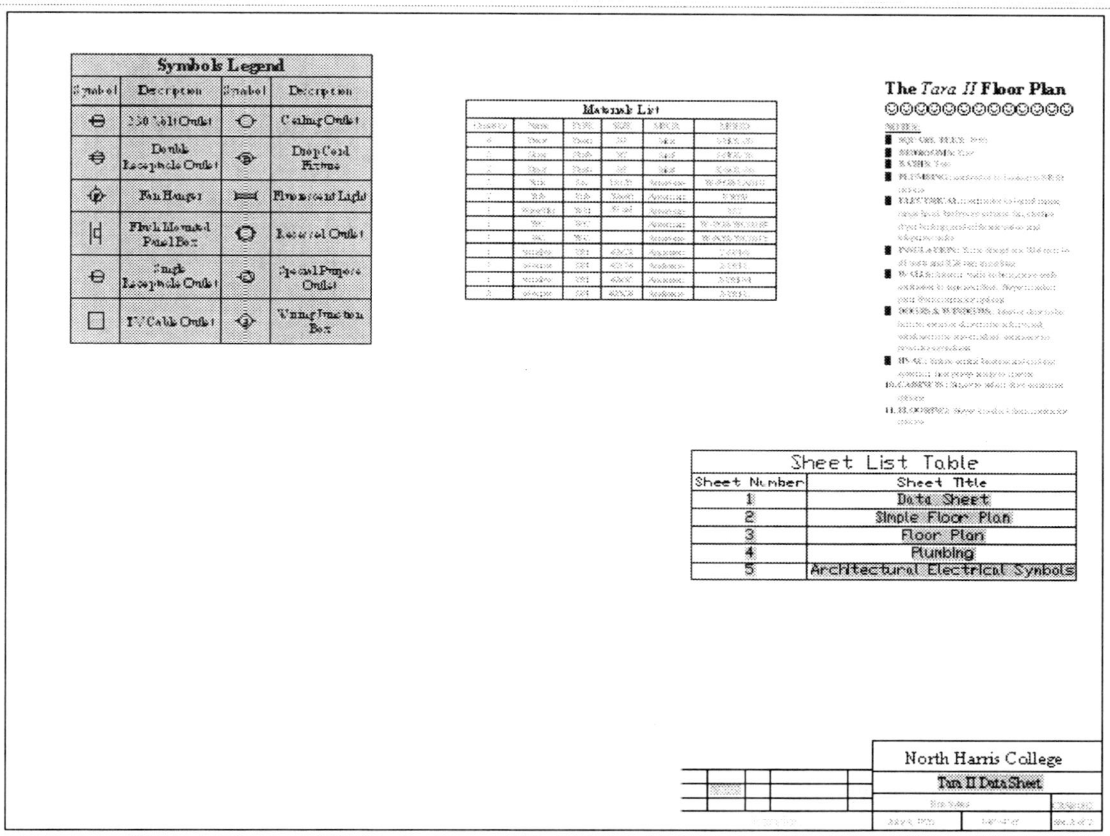


13. Save the drawing.

**Command:** ***qsave***

The table is filled with fields that contain hyperlink jumps. These will translate to the PDFs you'll create shortly.

## 24.3 Using Your Sheet Sets to Share Information

You've seen how to set up your sheet sets, but what's the purpose? Aside from making the transition between drawings and sharing blocks (which you do as easily with other tools), what good are sheet sets?

Sheet sets help you share *project* information (as opposed to information about a specific drawing or discipline). Use them to communicate project status to clients or employers and to archive your project at predetermined stages of development.

Let's do some exercises that'll walk you through plotting (as we don't have a plotter, we'll plot to a DWF), transmitting information to our client/employer, and archiving our project.

| Do This: 24.3.1 | Sharing Information with Sheet Sets – Creating a Multi-Sheet DWF File |
|---|---|

I. Be sure you're in the *Tara II Data Sheet* drawing in the C:\Steps\Lesson24\Sheet Sets folder. If not, please open it now.

II. Be sure the Sheet Set Manager and the **Tara II Project** are open.

III. Follow these steps.

## 24.3.1: Sharing Information with Sheet Sets – DWFs

1. We'll begin by creating a DWF file. Right-click on the project title and select the **Publish** option from the cursor menu (see the figure below). Then pick the **Publish to DWF** option from the Publish menu.

AutoCAD presents a standard Select File Dialog box.

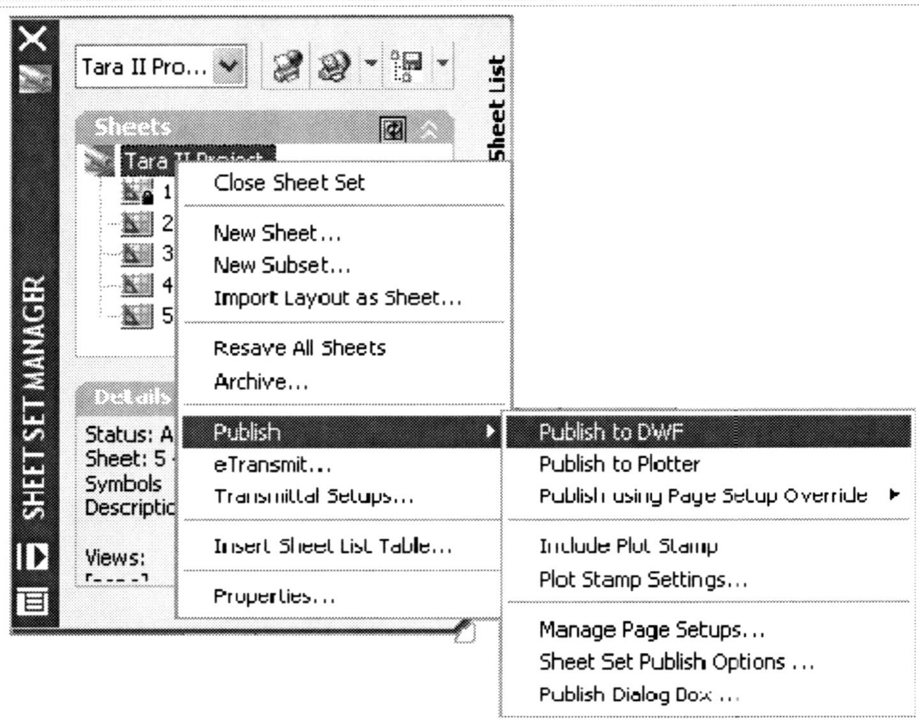


2. Save the DWF file as *Tara II Project.DWF* in the C:\Steps\Lesson24\ DWFs folder. (Create the DWFs folder if it isn't there.)

3. Pick the **Select** button 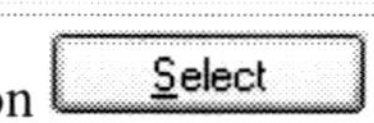

to complete the procedure. (AutoCAD may take a few minutes to complete the procedure, but it works in the background so you can continue to work on the drawing if you wish.)

4. AutoCAD let's you know when it's finished, and it gives you a chance to see the details of what it did. You can look at this if you wish, then close the bubble.

## 24.3.1: Sharing Information with Sheet Sets – DWFs

5. Let me show you a quick way to view your most recently published DWF. Right-click on the plotter icon on the right end of the status bar and select **View DWF File**. AutoCAD will launch the DWF Viewer with the DWF file (see below).

Take a few minutes to look thing over. Scroll down to the properties area at the lower left corner of the window. This offers details about the currently selected sheet.

You can select different sheets to view in the **Content** frame at the upper left area of the window. (You can also pick the titles in the Sheet List Table you created in the last exercise!)

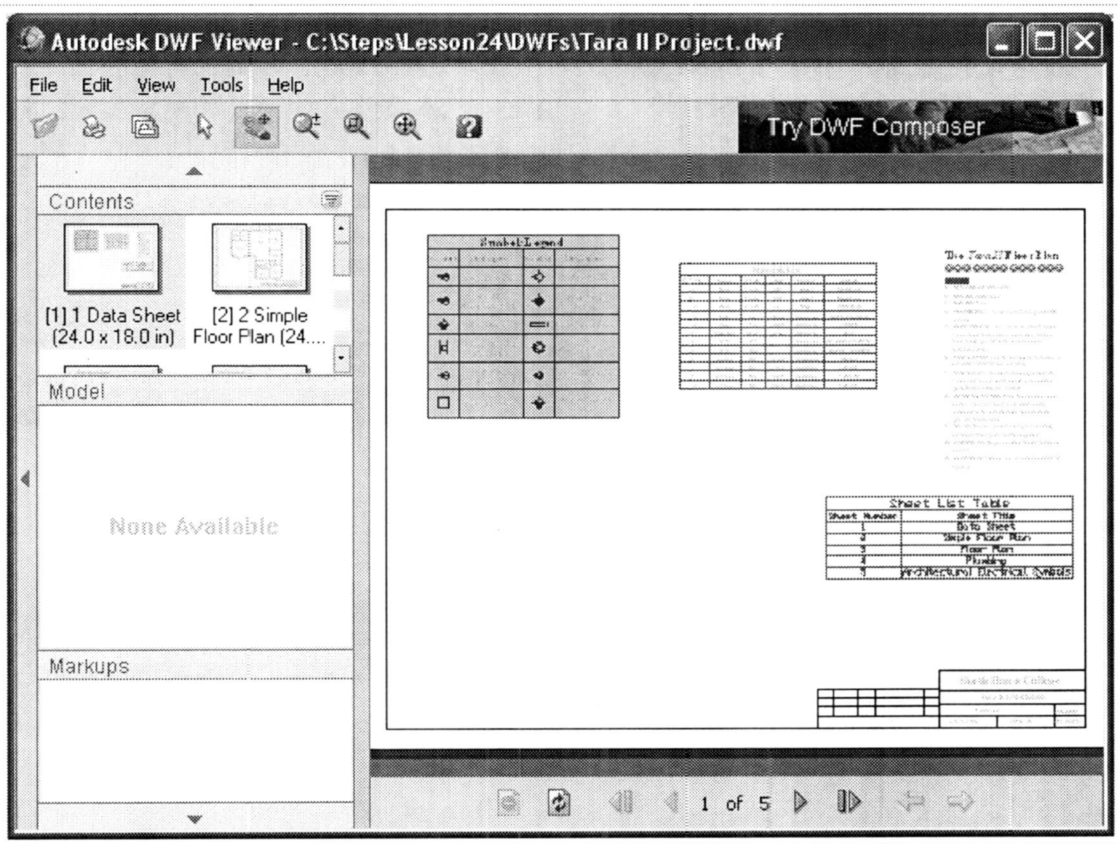


You see that creating a DWF file for a multi-sheet set is really quite easy. But remember that the Publish to DWF option uses defaults set up in the Publish dialog box, so you'll need to go there to change any settings.

The client liked our project; so let's transmit it to him.

| Do This: 24.3.2 | Sharing Information with Sheet Sets – Using eTransmit for a Multi-Sheet Set |
|---|---|

I. Be sure you're in the *Tara II Data Sheet* drawing in the C:\Steps\Lesson24\Sheet Sets folder. If not, please open it now.

II. If the DWF viewer is still open, close it.

III. Be sure the Sheet Set Manager and the **Tara II Project** are open.

IV. Follow these steps.

### 24.3.2: Sharing Information with Sheet Sets - eTransmit

1. First, we'll have to create a setup for our transmittal. Right-click on the project title and select **Transmittal Setups** from the cursor menu. AutoCAD presents the Transmittal Setups dialog box.

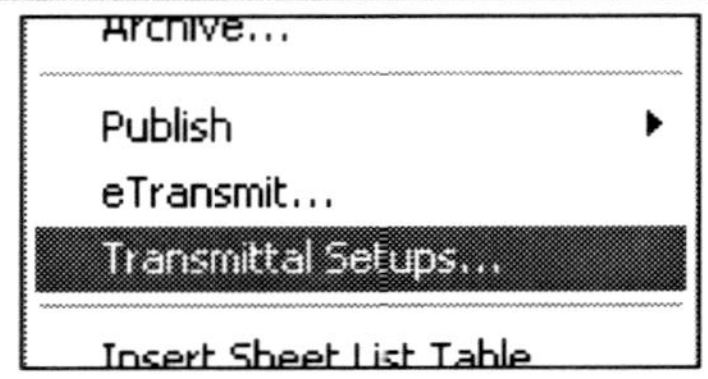


2. Pick the **New** button 

to create a new setup.

3. AutoCAD asks for a name for the new setup. I'll call mine *Construction Issue Transmittal.*

**Continue** to the Modify Transmittal Setup dialog box. (You're familiar with this from Lesson 21, Exercise 21.3.1.)

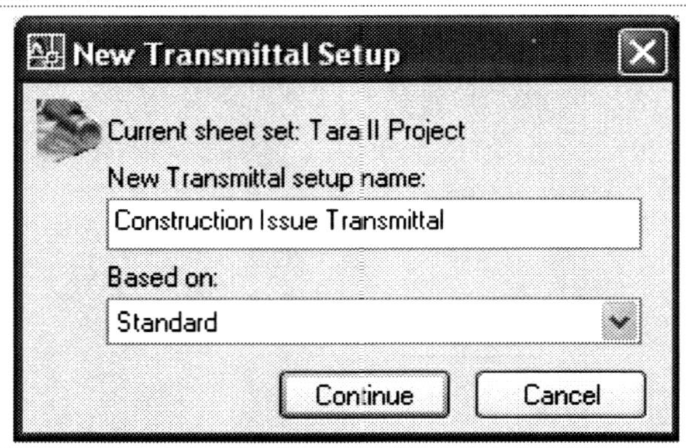

## 24.3.2: Sharing Information with Sheet Sets - eTransmit

4. Set up the transmittal as indicated, and then **OK** the setup to continue.

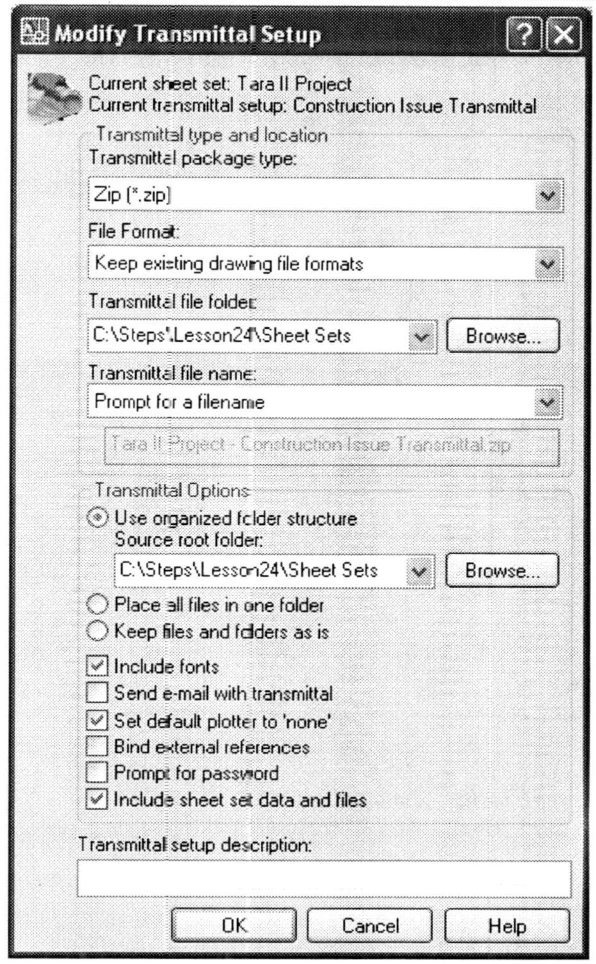


5. **Close** 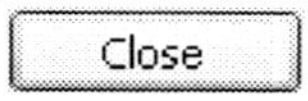

the Transmittal Setups dialog box.

6. Save the drawing .

**Command:** ***qsave***

7. Now we can create the transmittal. (This is the easy part.) Select **eTransmit** from the project title's cursor menu.

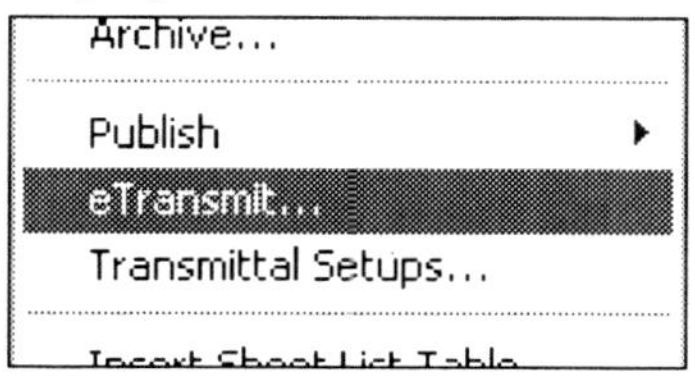


8. AutoCAD prepares the transmittal, and then presents the Create Transmittal dialog box (see the following figure).

You're familiar with this dialog box from your studies in Lesson 21, but notice that AutoCAD has included a **Sheets** tab. This tab lists the drawings that AutoCAD will include in the transmittal (you can remove the check from the check box to exclude a drawing).

Notice that not all of the sheets have checks. These sheets are included as layouts in a checked drawing.

Select the **Construction Issue Transmittal** setup (or whatever setup you created) and pick the **OK** button to continue.

**24.3.2: SHARING INFORMATION WITH SHEET SETS - ETRANSMIT**

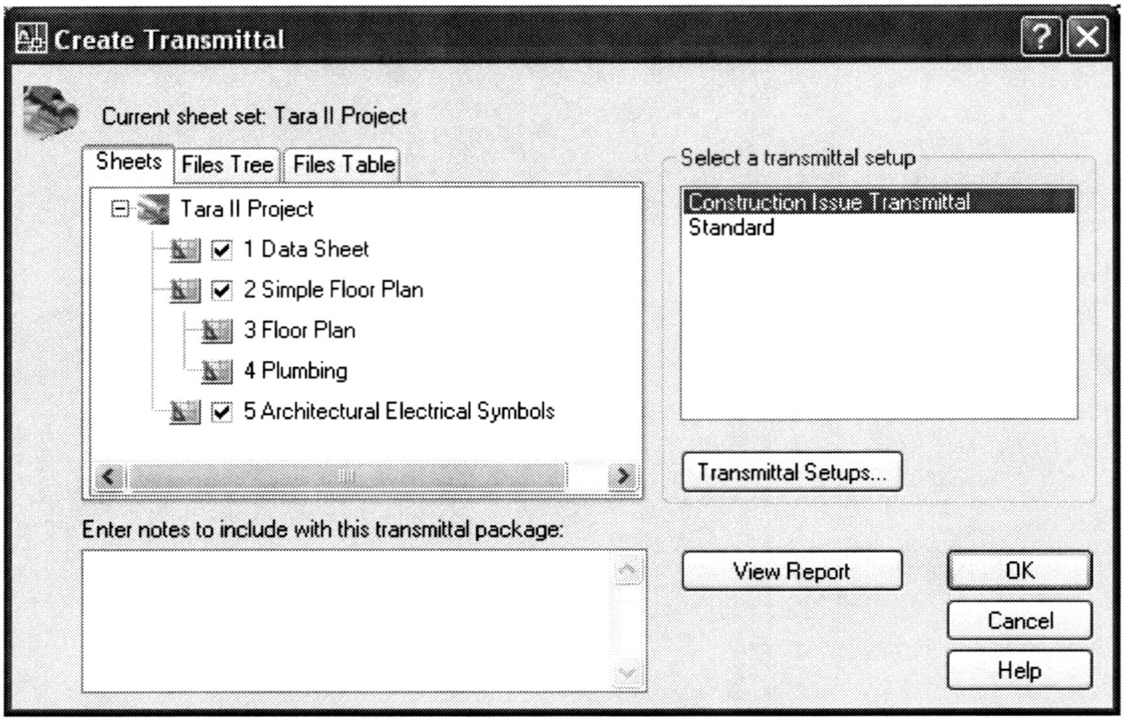


9. AutoCAD asks for a name for the transmittal file. Accept the default and pick the **Save** button 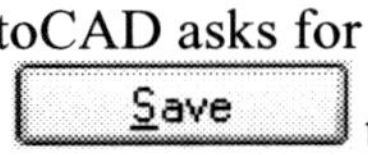

to continue.
AutoCAD creates the transmittal and closes the dialog box.

10. You should check your transmittal before sending it. Go to the C:\Steps\Lesson24\Sheet Sets folder to make sure your transmittal file was created. (You can open it if you have a program capable of opening a zip file, and check the files that were included.)

Okay, we've plotted our project (created a DWF) and sent it to the client. Now we need to archive it – put it away so we can start working on something else.
Here we go.

| Do This: 24.3.3 | Sharing Information with Sheet Sets – Archiving Your Project |
|---|---|

I. Be sure you're in the *Tara II Data Sheet* drawing in the C:\Steps\Lesson24\Sheet Sets folder. If not, please open it now.
II. Be sure the Sheet Set Manager and the **Tara II Project** are open.
III. Follow these steps.

**24.3.3: SHARING INFORMATION WITH SHEET SETS - ARCHIVING**

1. Select **Archive** from the project title's cursor menu. AutoCAD presents the Archive a Sheet Set dialog box.

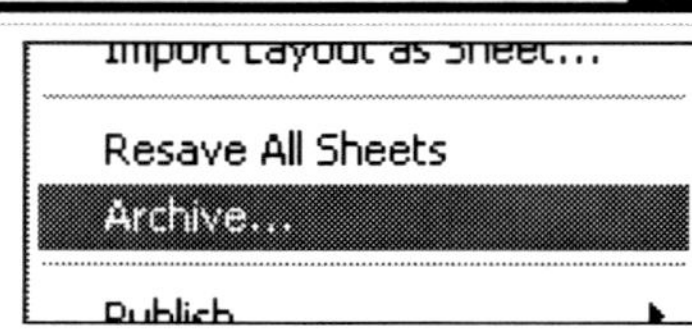

## 24.3.3: Sharing Information with Sheet Sets - Archiving

2. We'll need to set up the archive so pick the **Modify Archive Setup** button [Modify Archive Setup...].

3. AutoCAD presents the Modify Archive Setup dialog box. Set it up as indicated and pick the **OK** button to continue.

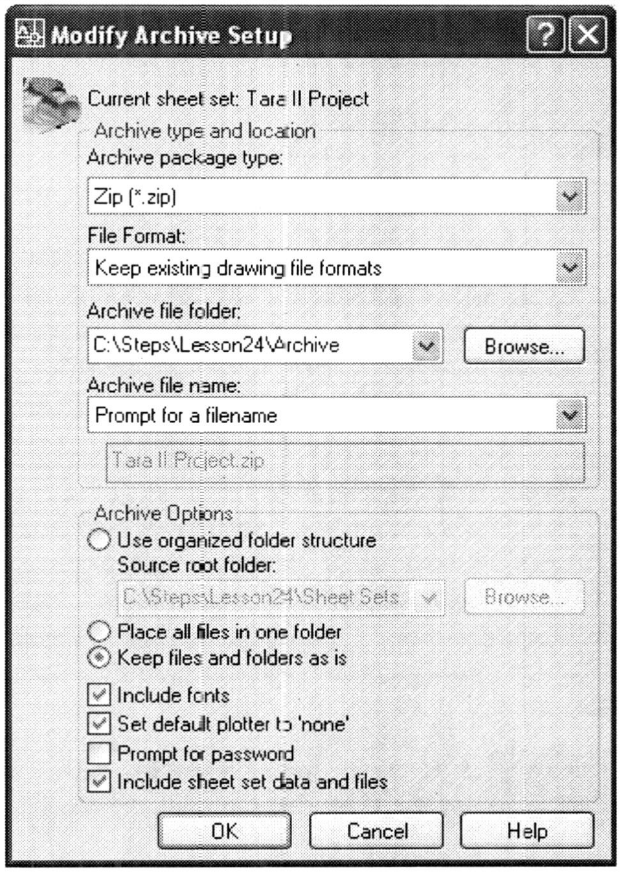


4. AutoCAD returns to the Archive a Sheet Set dialog box. Pick the **OK** button [OK] to complete the procedure.

5. AutoCAD presents a standard Save File dialog box. Accept the file name and pick the **Save** button.

It takes a moment or two for AutoCAD to complete the procedure, but when it's finished, close the drawing. (Don't make any changes or save anything after archiving or you may have to repeat the procedure!)

## 24.4 Extra Steps

- Since this is a fairly new tool, call up AutoCAD's help window and explore the entries under the **Sheet Set** category.
- Launch the New Features Workshop under the Help pull down menu and let AutoCAD walk you through the Sheet Set tutorials. (There's nothing quite like a demonstration to help you see things you might have missed!)

## 24.5 What Have We Learned?

*Items covered in this lesson include:*

- *Sheet Sets*
  - *creation*
  - *transmittals*
  - *archiving*
  - *publishing*

This has been a tough lesson. For a palette with such a simple appearance, AutoCAD has created a bit of a monster ... but like Godzilla, it's a monster that can be quite helpful. (Okay, so Godzilla helped mostly in urban renewal efforts for a model Tokyo ... but you get the idea.)

I do encourage you to take some time to get comfortable with sheet sets. Like most complex tools, those who demonstrate mastery are the ones who make the money.

This completes the fifth section of our text (whew!). Our next (last!) section will explain how AutoCAD gets along with others (including other AutoCAD programs).

## 24.6 Exercises

Open the *Sample Unit Data Sheet* in the C:\Steps\Lesson24\Exercises folder. Follow these instructions.

1. Add the table shown below.

| | | | | |
|---|---|---|---|---|
| | | | | |
| | | | | |
| 0 | 2-6-04 | TS | Issued for Approval | BB |
| Rev | Date | By | Description | App |
| Revisions | | | | |

   1.1. Items in the **Reference Drawings** table are hyperlink jumps to their respective drawings. The *Sample Unit.dwg* file is in the C:\Steps\Lesson24\Exercises folder; the other two drawings are in the C:\Steps\Lesson24\Exercise Resource Drawings folder.

   1.2. Locate the **Reference Drawings** table in the upper right corner of the drawing.

   1.3. Locate the **Revision block** next to the title block.

   1.4. Position the other tables as you wish. (All blocks are part of the drawing.)

*For more exercises related to Lesson 24, please see Lesson 24 in AutoCAD 2007: One Step at a Time – Workbook.*

## 24.7 For Web-Based Review Questions, visit: http://www.uneedcad.com/2007/Files/07R24.pdf

# Lesson 25

Following this lesson, you will:

- ✓ Know how to reference a drawing or DWF from another drawing
  - o Know how to use the External Reference Palette
  - o Know how to attach, detach, overlay, and underlay a reference drawing or DWF
  - o Know how to clip a reference to see just what you want to see
  - o Understand reference drawings' dependent symbols
  - o Know how to load, unload, and reload a reference
  - o Know how to edit a referenced drawing from within the primary drawing
- ✓ Know how to open a reference from within the primary drawing
- ✓ Know how to permanently bind a referenced drawing to the primary drawing

# Externally Referenced Drawings & DWFs

*Think way back to our discussion of layers in Lesson 6. I explained layers by referring to the presentation method* Encyclopedia Britannica *used to detail the human body (plastic overlays with the different systems of the body). This is also the idea behind externally referenced drawings – Xrefs.*

*There is, however, quite a difference between layers, Xrefs, and attached DWFs. We use layers, as you know, to control the display of, and differentiate between, objects in a drawing (much as we used linetypes and widths on the drawing board). On the other hand, we use Xrefs to save drawing time and computer memory by sharing information (much as* Britannica *shared the outline of the human body among the various system overlays). We use attached DWFs much as we use Xrefs, but they're easier (if not as accessible) and considerably more secure.*

When working with Xrefs and attached DWFs, file location is a critical consideration. For the exercises in this lesson to work properly with the files provided, the files must be located in one of two places:

1. The best location is the C:\Steps\Lesson25 folder. This site has been thoroughly tested to be sure the files work properly.
2. The files may be placed on a network or other location *provided the path is defined in the* ***Project File Search Path*** (**Files** tab of the Options dialog box). If you're not comfortable with the Options dialog box, however, and don't have a CAD guru who can help, *please don't attempt to make changes in the Options dialog box.* Use the first choice instead.

## 25.1 Working with Externally Referenced Drawings (Xrefs) and DWFs

*We've seen DWFs before, but what are Xrefs?*

Xrefs – externally referenced drawings – are drawings called into another drawing as a referenced background or object. They are, in fact, quite similar to blocks with some notable exceptions:

- Unlike blocks, Xrefs and DWFs occupy very little space within a drawing. That is, you'll find the drawing's increase in size negligible with the inclusion of an Xref or DWF (slightly more of an increase with a DWF than an Xref).
- Whereas a block may contain attributed information, an Xref/DWF can't. However, the referenced drawing file may contain blocks with attributes, and the values of these attributes may be extracted from the primary drawing (the one doing the referencing). This doesn't hold true, however, for DWFs.
- The primary drawing automatically reloads the referenced drawing whenever the primary drawing is accessed. Additionally, when the referenced drawing is updated, AutoCAD will let you know with an information bubble in the lower right corner of the window. So, the reference is as current as the last time the primary drawing was opened.

*What are the benefits of using Xrefs? DWFs?*

- An important benefit of using Xrefs is that another operator may edit the referenced drawing without tying up your primary drawing. The changes he makes become available to you as soon as you reload the reference. (This may prove more difficult with a DWF unless you have software to edit the DWF.)
- Like blocks, any number of primary drawings may use a single referenced drawing or DWF. But unlike blocks, updating the references is automatic.

  Consider a refinery unit. Each unit requires civil, structural, piping, and electrical plans. Generally, the structural designer will copy the civil drawing for a "foundation" for his work. Likewise, the piper and electrical designer will use the structural plan. Changes to the structural plan may go unnoticed for days or weeks by others (unless some extraordinary communication occurs). However, if the pipers and electrical designers Xref the structural plan,

- they won't have to draw the background themselves, and
- they'll be automatically notified of any changes made to the referenced drawing, and
- any changes made by the structural designer will automatically show on the others' drawings with the next loading or reloading.

- On the other hand, your client may want you to use an existing drawing as a background but may be uncomfortable with actually giving you the drawing. The client can, instead, give you a DWF "print" of the drawing (thus keeping his pristine original) and allow you to use the DWF as an unchangeable background for your work.

Let's take a look at how to use Xrefs & DWFs.

## 25.1.1 Attaching and Detaching External References to Your Drawing

Although you can use individual commands for each manipulation of a referenced drawing or DWF, AutoCAD provides an External Reference palette (Figure 25.001) – to help.

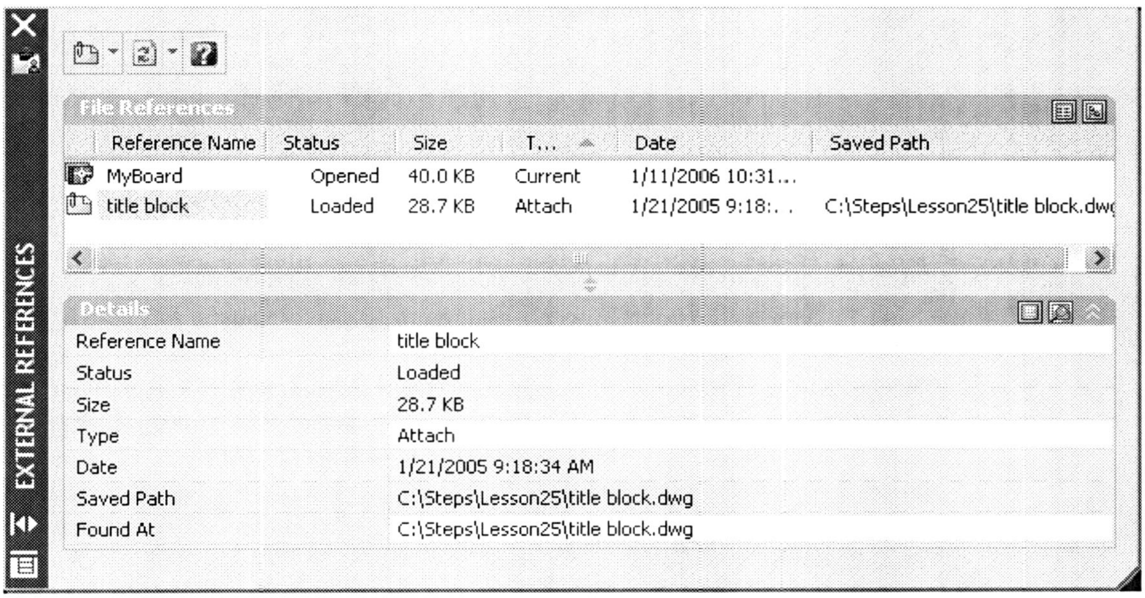


Figure 25.001

Let's take a look.

- Across the top of the External Reference palette (Figure 25.001), you'll find a couple flyout buttons. Let's look at these.
  - The **Attach Drawing** button 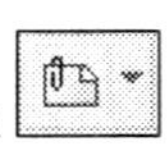 begins the ***XAttach*** command.

    The ***XAttach*** command begins with a standard Select File dialog box. There you'll follow the path to the file you wish to reference. Once you've selected a file and picked the **Open** button (on the Select File dialog box), AutoCAD presents the External Reference dialog box (Figure 25.002 – next page).
    - The **Name** control box indicates the file you're attaching. You may pick the **Browse** button to select another file.
    - In the **Reference Type** frame, tell AutoCAD if you want your reference to be an **Attachment** or **Overlay**.

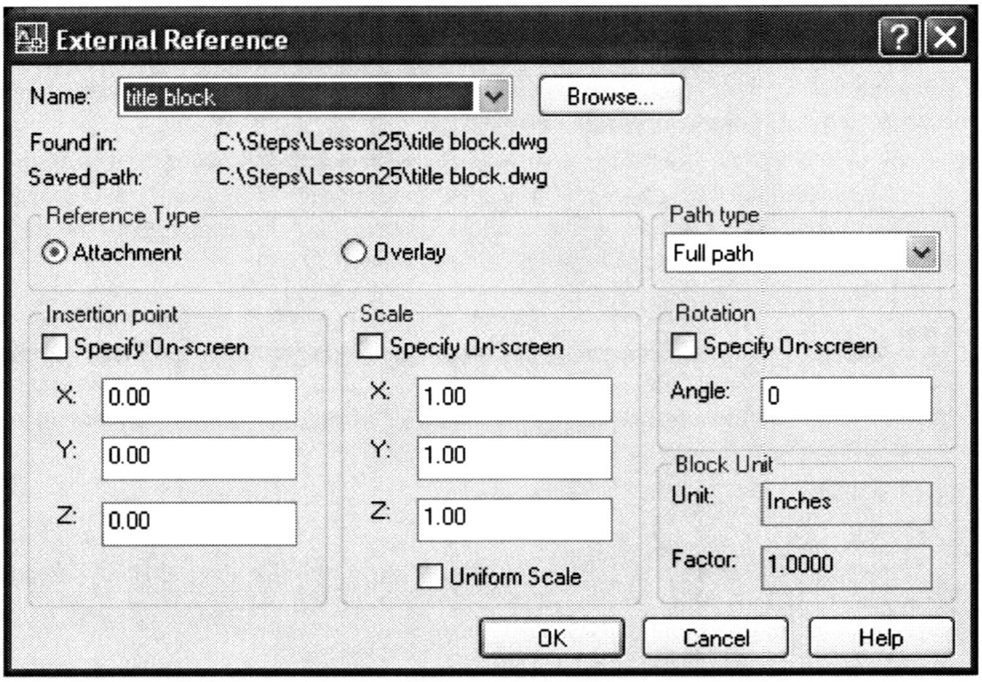


Figure 25.002

- The **Path type** provides three options to make location of the reference a bit easier.
  - ∴ Using **Full path** (the default) means that AutoCAD will use the full path (drive & location) when searching for the reference.
  - ∴ The **Relative path** option tells AutoCAD that the referenced file may be located in a subfolder of the folder in which the primary drawing is located. Relative paths won't work if the referenced drawing is on another drive.
  - ∴ **No path** means that the referenced drawing must be located in the same folder as the primary drawing or in a path identified in the **Project File Search Path** in the Options dialog box.
- The **Insertion**, **Scale**, and **Rotation** frames are identical to their counterparts on the Insert dialog box.

o The **Attach DWF** button 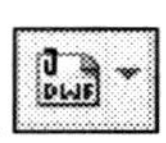 (reached via the Attach Drawing flyout) begins the ***DWFAttach*** command.

The ***DWFAttach*** command also begins with a standard Select File dialog box where you'll follow the path to the file you wish to reference. Once you've selected a file, AutoCAD presents the Attach DWF Underlay dialog box (Figure 25.003 – next page). The options presented here correspond to their counterparts on the External Reference dialog box already discussed (Figure 25.002). Notice, however, that you cannot overlay or attach the DWF; DWFs can only be "underlain" – that is, they're for background reference only.

> You'll find another button under the Attach flyouts –**Attach Image** – which we'll discuss in Lesson 26.

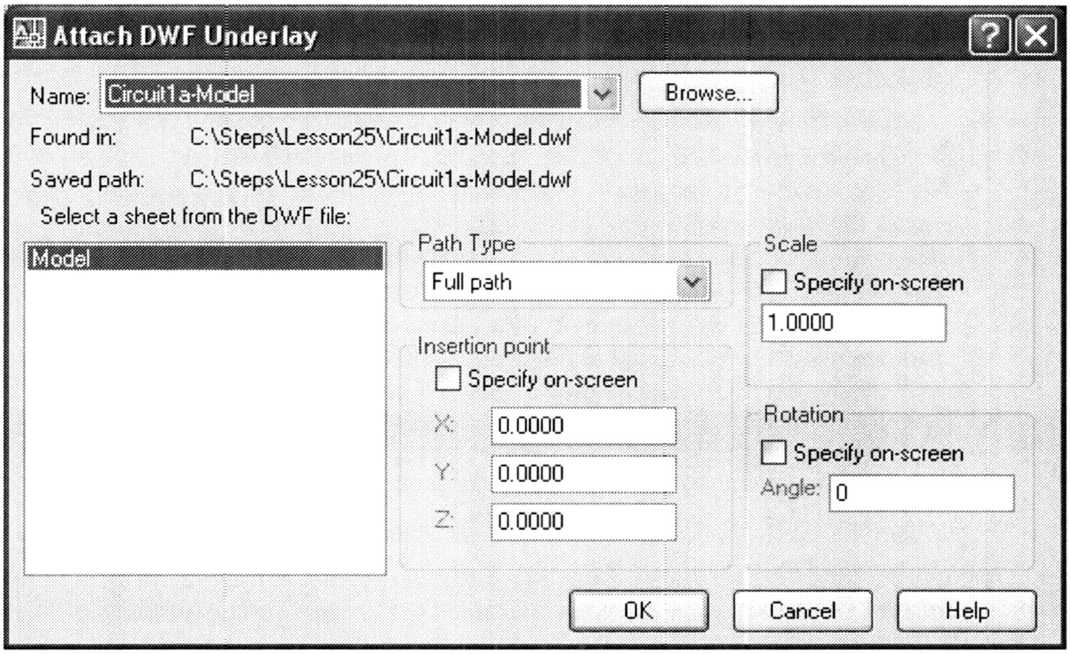

Figure 25.003

- The flyout buttons next to the **Attach** flyouts contains two buttons – **Refresh** 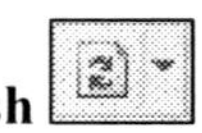 and **Reload All Xrefs** 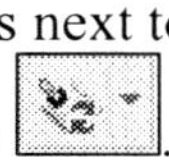. These do exactly what their names imply but provide a convenient way to perform these tasks without resorting to the keyboard.
- The final button along the top of the palette calls AutoCAD's help window.

- AutoCAD allows you to view the items in the **File References** frame (of the External Reference palette – Figure 25.001) using either a **List View** (the default) or a **Tree View**. Toggle between types of views using the buttons in the upper right corner of the frame. (We'll use the default list view in this lesson).
  - In the **File References** frame, AutoCAD provides several columns of information:
    - The **Reference Name** is the file name of the referenced drawing or DWF.
    - The drawing's **Status** will fall into one of several categories:
      - ∴ **Loaded** simply means that the drawing or DWF is currently attached.
      - ∴ An **Unloaded** reference is removed from the primary drawing. This isn't a permanent condition. The reference remains intact and may be reloaded as desired.
      - ∴ An **Unreferenced** drawing or DWF is attached to the primary drawing but has been erased. It can be reattached.
      - ∴ A drawing or DWF that no longer resides in the folder from which it was originally referenced (or in the search path defined in the Options dialog box) is marked in the **Status** column as **Not Found**.
      - ∴ If AutoCAD can't read the reference, it marks it as **Unresolved**.
      - ∴ Xrefs can be nested. An **Orphaned** reference was nested into a reference that is unreferenced, unloaded, or not found.
    - The **Size** column indicates the size of the referenced drawing or DWF.

- You can either **Attach** or **Overlay** (see the **Type** column) a referenced drawing (but not a DWF). An attached drawing will go with the primary drawing if another drawing references it; an overlaid drawing won't (more on this in Section 25.1.4).
- The **Date** column indicates when the referenced drawing or DWF was last modified.
- The **Saved Path** column is a bit misleading. The path refers to the location of the drawing when it was originally referenced but *not necessarily where the reference is found.* Let me explain.

  When AutoCAD begins a drawing, it searches for a referenced drawing in the **Saved Path** location. If it doesn't find it there, it searches the **Project File Search Path** defined in the Options dialog box. Then it searches the folder in which the current drawing resides. It'll use the first file it finds with the appropriate name regardless of its location. But it won't change the information in the **Saved Path**.

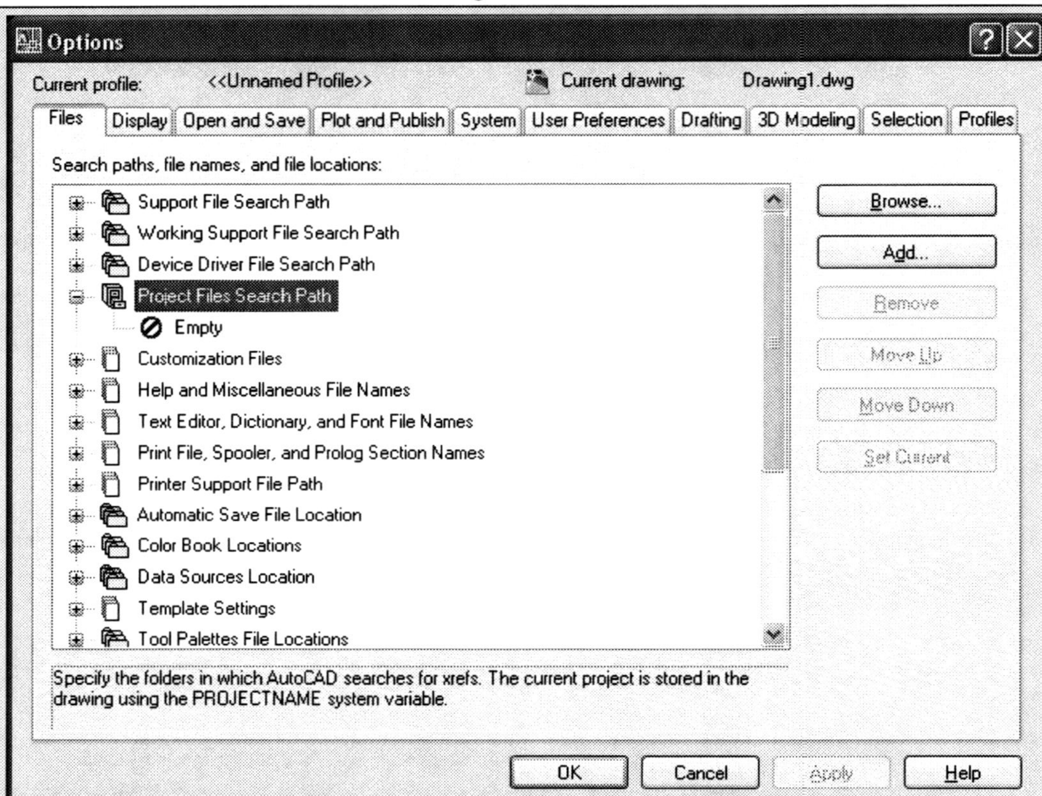


The **Project File Search Path** is defined on the **Files** tab of the Options dialog box (above). Pick the "+" beside the **Project File Search Path** listing to see the folders AutoCAD will search. To add a folder, select the **Project File Search Path** listing and pick the **Add** button. AutoCAD will add a listing, and you must type in the desired name.

Then pick the plus beside the new project name, double-click on the **Empty** slot, and select the folder you wish to add to the search path.

*Warning: Don't make changes in the Options dialog box without first consulting the CAD guru on your project.*

- AutoCAD may provide different cursor menus within the **File Reference** frame, depending upon where you right click. Right clicking in an open area produces a menu that includes the same tools called by the buttons we've already discussed. Right clicking on a referenced file, however, calls a menu (Figure 25.004) that proves useful in managing your references.

- The **Open** option opens the selected reference. Drawings open in a new AutoCAD window where you can edit them (we'll look at another way to edit referenced drawings later in this lesson); DWFs open in the DWF viewer.
- The **Attach** option reopens the appropriate Attach dialog box. We've already discussed these.
- **Unload** a drawing to remove a reference that you may want to use later. Unloading doesn't permanently remove the reference from the drawing, but it does remove it from display.

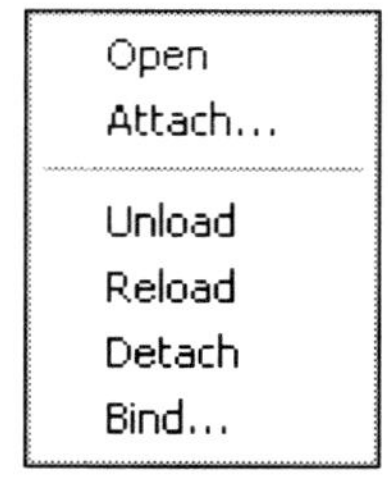


Figure 25.004

- Use the **Reload** option to update a reference without having to reopen your primary drawing, or to display an unloaded drawing.
- Use the **Detach** option to remove references to the selected drawing or DWF. (Note: You can't detach a nested reference. You must detach its primary drawing.)
- Use the **Bind** option only on a referenced drawing; it isn't available for DWFs. It will permanently attach a reference drawing to a primary drawing. (This isn't the same as the ***XBind*** command, which we'll discuss in Section 25.1.3.) AutoCAD presents the Bind Xrefs dialog box (Figure 25.005).

Figure 25.005

As referenced information, *dependent symbols* are identified by the name of the referenced drawing followed by a bar and the symbol's name (i.e., **board|slots** is the **slots** layer on the referenced *board* drawing). The two options in the Bind Xrefs dialog box determine how Xref dependent symbols will be treated.

> *Dependent symbols* are the layers, blocks, text styles, dimension styles, and linetypes that are part of a referenced drawing. To be available in the primary drawing, these symbols require that the referenced drawing be attached. DWFs do not include dependent symbols and, although they will reflect the freeze/thaw/on/off settings of the layer on which they're inserted, they won't reflect color or linetype settings.

∴ **Binding** a referenced drawing causes AutoCAD to rename the dependent symbol but retain the referenced drawing's name in the new name. Thus, the **board|slots** layer will become **board$0$slots**. This approach means that you'll always be able to trace where the symbol originated. [If the **board$0$slots** already exists, the number between the dollar signs increases (**board$1$slots**, **board$2$slots**, etc.).]

∴ **Inserting** a referenced drawing changes the referenced drawing into a block with the name of the referenced drawing becoming the name of the block. Dependent symbols become a part of the drawing but drop the name of the referenced drawing (i.e., **board|slots** becomes **slots**).

- The **Details** frame of the External Reference palette (Figure 25.001) can provide details about the reference selected in the **File References** frame. Most of the details are for reference, although some can be modified (such as the **Attach/Overlay Type** of referenced drawing or the **Found At** location of the reference). The **Found At** box indicates where the selected drawing was found when AutoCAD loaded. This is where AutoCAD actually found the drawing and may not be the same as the saved path. Use the **Browse** button (to the right of the selected box) to select a different copy of the reference.

Alternately, you can have the **Details** frame provide a preview of the selected reference by using the buttons on the right end of the frame's title bar.

Whew! That was a lot of material to cover! Let's try our hands at referencing.

Here's the scenario for this lesson:

*Your employer is developing a new product – a kit designed to help children learn about electricity. The kit will contain a circuit board where the child can attach a battery pack, switches, lights, resistors, and a galvanometer (kids love those big scientific words). The kit must be capable of creating any of several different wiring layouts.*

*Your job is to lay out some wiring diagrams of things the child can build using the objects listed. You have the initial board and component designs from the engineer, but some of these objects may change as the project develops. You don't have time to wait for engineering (what a surprise!), so you'll begin your layouts now using Xrefs so you can easily modify the component designs as they develop.*

> You can also access the External Reference palette by selecting **External Reference** on the Insert pull-down menu.

| Do This: 25.1.1.1 | Working with Xrefs |
|---|---|

I. Start a new drawing using the *Start* template found in the C:\Steps\Lesson25 folder.

II. Save the drawing as *MyBoard* in the C:\Steps\Lesson25 folder.

III. Follow these steps.

### 25.1.1.1: WORKING WITH XREFS

1. We'll begin by referencing our title block. Enter the ***ExternalReferences*** command to open the External Reference palette. (An easier command entry is ***XR*** – the hotkeys for ***Xref***.)

Alternately, you can pick the **External References** button on the Reference toolbar.

**Command: *xr***

2. AutoCAD presents the External Reference palette. Pick the **Attach DWF** option (under the **Attach** flyouts).

3. AutoCAD presents the Select DWF File dialog box. Select the *title block-Model.dwf* file in the C:\Steps\Lesson25 folder. (Double-click on the file name or pick the **Open** button [Open] to continue.)

4. AutoCAD presents the Attach DWF Underlay dialog box. Be sure the selections match those shown in the following figure.

- Use a **Relative path**.
- Remove the checks from the boxes in the insertion frames.

Pick the **OK** button [OK] to continue.

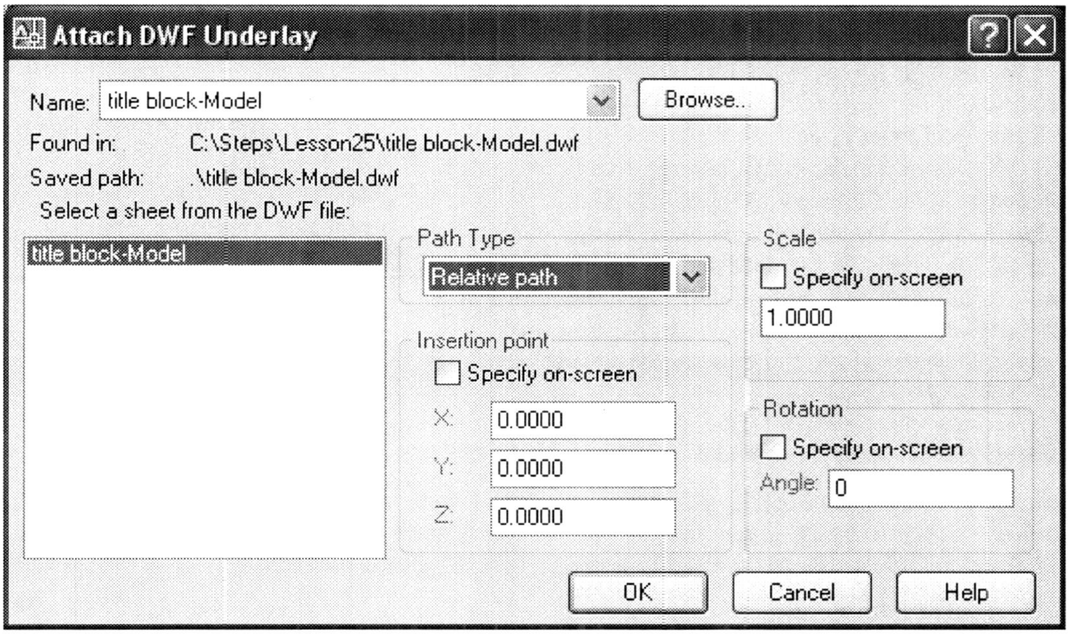


5. Draw the board shown.
   - The board is on the **board** layer.
   - The rectangle's corners are at coordinates ***1,1*** and ***8.5,9***.
   - The fillets are ½".
   - The slots are on the **slots** layer.
   - The slots are 3/16"dia., ½" apart, and begin at coordinate ***1.5,1.5***.
   - There are 15 rows and 14 columns of slots.

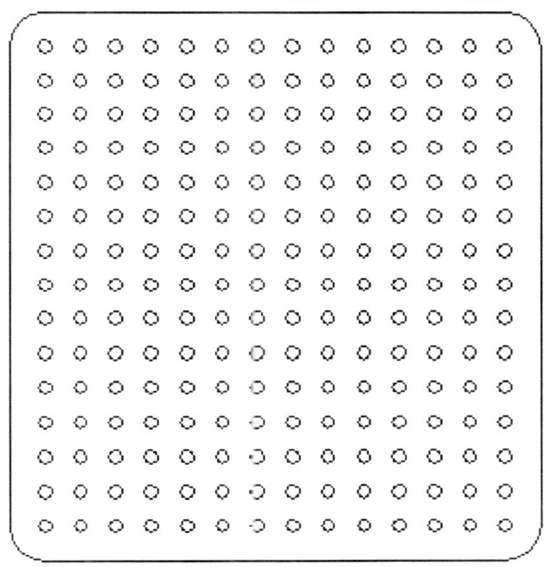

6. Save 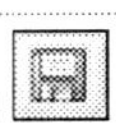 the drawing and close it.

**Command: *qsave***
**Command: *close***

7. Start a new drawing using the Start template found in the C:\Steps\Lesson25 folder. Save the drawing as *MyCircuit1* in the C:\Steps\Lesson25 folder.

8. Repeat Steps 1 to 4 using the **Attach Dwg** button 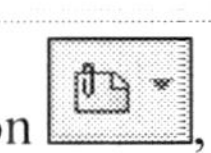, but this time, reference the *MyBoard.dwg* you created earlier in this lesson. (If you have a problem with this one, you can attach the *board.dwg* file instead.) Be sure to use an **Attachment Reference Type** and a **Relative** path.

9. Save the drawing 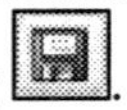.

**Command:** ***qsave***

10. Check the **Layer** control box. Notice that AutoCAD has added the layers **board| board**, and **board|slots.** (The other layers were part of the template.) These are the layer included in the referenced drawing. Notice that the layers are gray – you can turn them off, freeze them, lock them, or plot them; but they can't be made current. Nor can you draw on these layers, as they aren't actually part of the primary drawing.

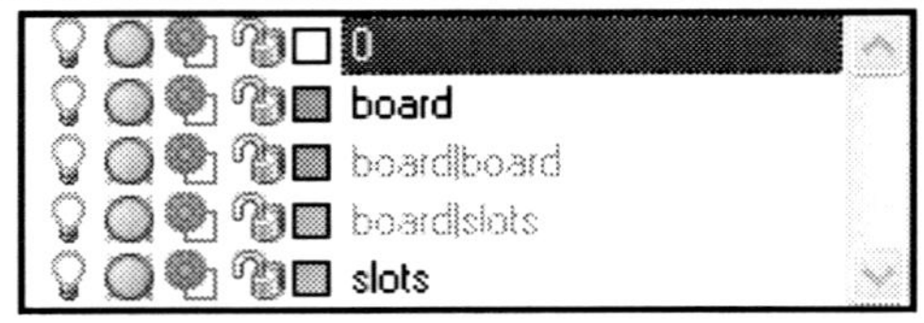


11. Using the ***XAttach*** command, we'll attach the battery and switch drawings. Begin by entering the ***XAttach*** command. Alternately, you can pick the **Attach Xref** button 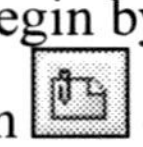 on the Reference toolbar. (You'll notice that this procedure is identical to the one we used to attach the *MyBoard.dwg* file except that we skip the External Reference palette.)

**Command:** ***xa***

12. AutoCAD presents the Select Reference File dialog box. Select the *battery.dwg* file in the C:\Steps\Lesson25 folder.

13. Insert the file at coordinates ***2.5,4*** as shown below. (Be sure to use a **Relative** path.)

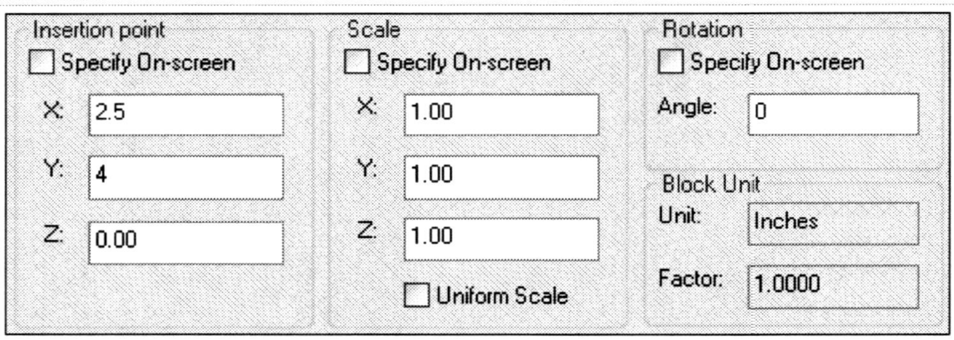

**25.1.1.1: WORKING WITH XREFS**

14. Repeat Steps 11 through 13 to insert the *switch.dwg* file at coordinates 2.5,5.5. Be sure to insert this file at 90° (see the figure below Step 15). Your board looks like this.

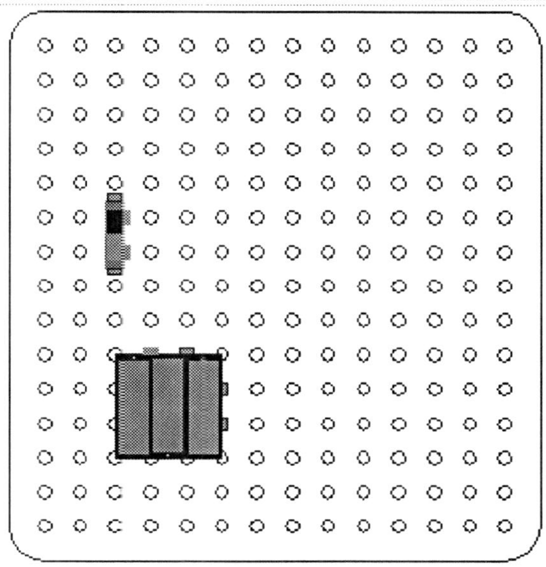

15. Save the drawing [save icon] but don't exit.

**Command:** ***qsave***

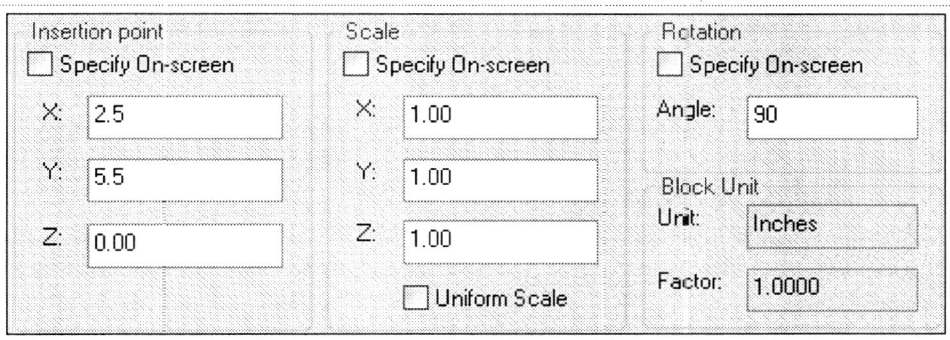


Notice the two pairs of wire connections on both the switch and the battery. Our engineers haven't decided where to put the single required pair, so they've created two for now. We have a fair idea which ones they'll eventually use, but we don't want to change the actual component drawings yet. We can, however, alter the reference to show only those connections we want to show.

## 25.1.2 Removing Part of a Reference – the *XClip* and *DWFClip* Commands

To remove part of a reference, use either the ***XClip*** command (for referenced drawings) or the ***DWFClip*** command (for referenced DWFs).

- The ***XClip*** command sequence looks like this:

  **Command:** ***xclip*** **(or** ***xc*****)**

  **Select objects:** ***[select the reference(s) to clip]***

  **Select objects:** ***[enter]***

  **Enter clipping option**

  **[ON/OFF/Clipdepth/Delete/generate Polyline/New boundary] <New>:** ***[tell AutoCAD what you want to do – accept the default to clip a reference]***

  **Specify clipping boundary:**

  **[Select polyline/Polygonal/Rectangular] <Rectangular>:** ***[tell AutoCAD what type of clipping boundary you wish to use]***

- The first line of options presents several choices:
  - The **ON/OFF** options determine whether AutoCAD will present only those portions of the referenced drawing visible through the clipping window (**ON**) or the entire referenced drawing (**OFF**).
  - **Clipdepth** allows you to set the front/back clipping planes of three-dimensional objects. A two-dimensional boundary must exist before you can define front or back clip points. Identify the clip points by coordinate or distance from the two-dimensional clipping boundary.
  - Use **Delete** to remove a boundary.
  - **Generate Polyline** will automatically draw a polyline along the clipping boundary. Again, a boundary must exist before AutoCAD can generate the polyline.
  - **New boundary** (the default) permits you to identify a new clipping boundary.
- The next line of options (**[Select polyline/Polygonal/ Rectangular] <Rectangular>:**) offers some choices for how to create the new boundary.
  - Use the **Select polyline** option to use an existing polyline to define the boundary. The polyline doesn't have to be closed, but it must not intersect itself. (To create a "round" clipping boundary, use a polygon with a large number of sides.)
  - Use the **Polygonal** option to create a multisided or nonlinear shape for a boundary (much like using a poly-window to create a selection set).
  - Use the **Rectangular** option (the default) to use a window to define the clipping boundary.

- The ***DWFClip*** command sequence is very similar to the ***XClip*** command … but easier!

  **Command: *dwfclip***

  **Select DWF to clip: *[select the reference to clip]***

  **Enter DWF clipping option [ON/OFF/Delete/New boundary] <New boundary>: *[tell AutoCAD what you want to do – hit enter to accept the default and create a clip boundary]***

  **Enter clipping type [Polygonal/Rectangular] <Rectangular>: *[tell AutoCAD what type of clipping boundary you wish to use]***

  The ***DWFClip*** options are the same as the ***XClip*** options.

> AutoCAD provides a system variable to allow you to see a boundary even when it isn't a polyline. The system variable for Xrefs is **XClipFrame**, for DWFs, it's **DWFFrame**. A setting of **0** (the default) means the boundaries will be hidden. A setting of **1** will show the boundaries. AutoCAD provides a button – **Frame** – on the Reference toolbar to help you toggle the **XClipFrame** system variable on and off. A setting of **2** (**DWFFrame** only) means that AutoCAD will display the DWF, but it won't plot it.

We'll remove the extra wire connectors from the views of our battery and switch.

> You can also access the ***XClip*** command on the Modify pull-down menu. Follow this path:
> *Modify – Clip – Xref*

| Do This: 25.1.2.1 | Clipping Xrefs |
|---|---|

I. Be sure you're still in the *MyCircuit1.dwg* file. If not, please open it now.

II. This exercise is easier if you zoom in around the battery and switch.

III. Follow these steps.

## 25.1.2.1:Clipping Xrefs

1. Enter the ***XClip*** command. Alternately, you can pick the **Clip Xref** button  on the Reference toolbar.

    **Command:** *xc*

2. Select the battery.

    **Select objects:**
    **Select objects:** ***[enter]***

3. Accept the default **New boundary** option 

.

    **Enter clipping option**
    **[ON/OFF/Clipdepth/Delete/ generate Polyline/New boundary] <New>:** ***[enter]***

4. Tell AutoCAD that you'll create a **Rectangular** 

clipping boundary (the default).

    **Specify clipping boundary:**
    **[Select polyline/Polygonal/ Rectangular] <Rectangular>:** ***[enter]***

5. Place the first corner at the lower right corner of the battery (use OSNAPs).

    **Specify first corner: _endp of**

6. … and the opposite corner northward and westward of the battery.

    **Specify opposite corner:**

AutoCAD clips the reference, and the battery now looks like this. (Note that you haven't actually modified the battery, just how much of it you can see through the reference window.)

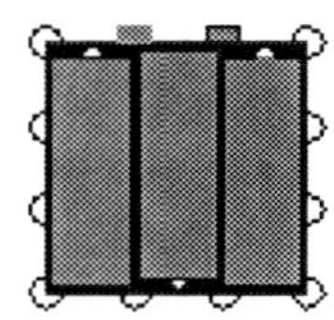

7. Repeat Steps 1 to 6 to clip the side connections from the switch. Your board looks like this.

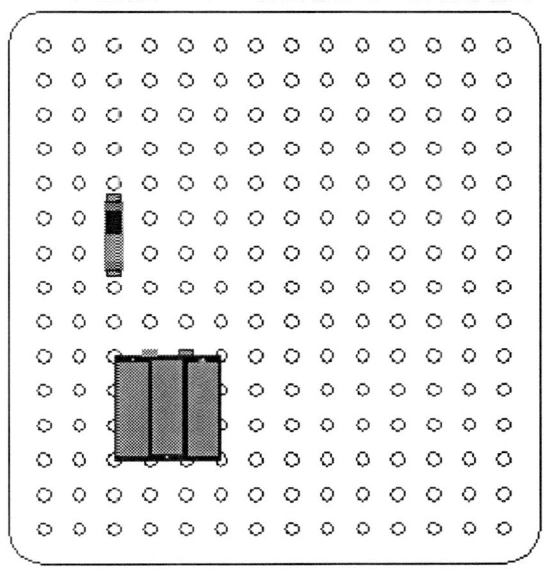

8. Have you noticed that the title block affects your ability to zoom in and out on the board with ease? Let's remove it temporarily while we work on our board.

Open the External Reference palette .

    **Command:** *xr*

9. Notice (see the following figure) that all the referenced drawings are now listed – even the nested title block drawing (remember, it was part of the *Board* drawing).

Right click on **board|title block** and select **Unload** from the cursor menu.

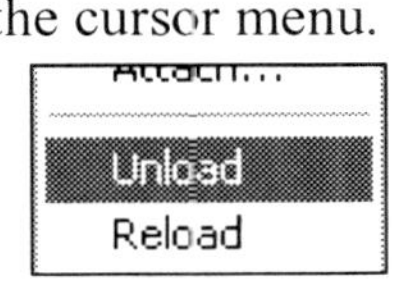

## 25.1.2.1: Clipping Xrefs

| Reference Name | Status | Size | Type | Date | Saved Path |
|---|---|---|---|---|---|
| MyCircuit1 | Opened | 41.4 KB | Current | 2/3/2006 7:20:3... | |
| battery | Loaded | 41.5 KB | Attach | 1/13/2006 8:19:... | .\battery.dwg |
| board | Loaded | 43.8 KB | Attach | 1/12/2006 2:02:... | .\board.dwg |
| switch | Loaded | 40.8 KB | Attach | 1/13/2006 8:20:... | .\switch.dwg |
| board\|title block-M... | Loaded | 6.52 KB | DWF | 1/12/2006 1:36:... | .\title block-Model.dwf |

10. Zoom extents now to see that, although it's still attached, the *title block* drawing is no longer loaded into our *MyCircuit1* drawing.

**Command: *z***

13. Save the drawing but don't exit.

**Command: *qsave***

## 25.1.3 Xrefs and Dependent Symbols

AutoCAD allows two methods of permanently attaching referenced drawing data to the primary file – Binding and Xbinding. You'll use the **Bind** button on the Xref Manager to permanently attach, or bind, an entire referenced drawing to the primary drawing. We discussed this in Section 25.1.1 and will demonstrate it in Section 25.4. But you can also attach parts (specific dependent symbols) of the referenced drawing individually to the primary drawing. The command for this is ***Xbind*** (or ***xb***), and it presents the Xbind dialog box (Figure 25.006).

The Xbind dialog box is one of AutoCAD's easiest. Simply select the dependent symbol you wish to bind in the Xrefs frame, pick the **Add** button, and **OK** your changes! Let's try one. The battery drawing has a **wire** layer and a **times** text style; we'll add these to our primary file.

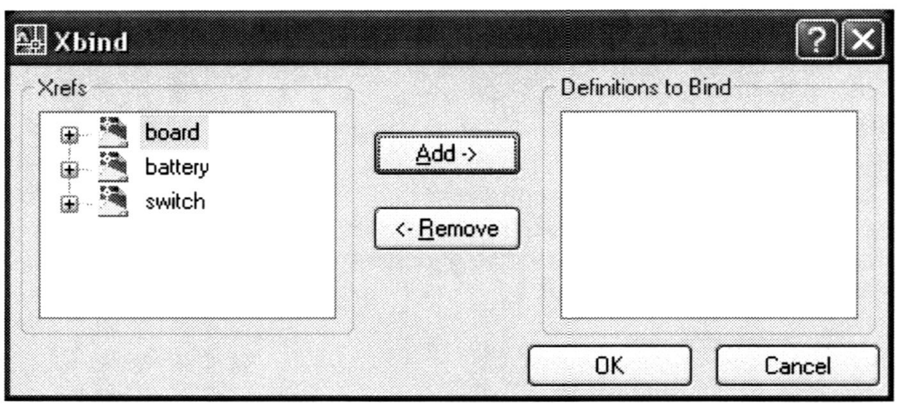


Figure 25.006

You can also access the ***Xbind*** command on the Modify pull-down menu. Follow this path:

*Modify – Object – External Reference – Bind...*

## Do This: 25.1.3.1 Xbinding Dependent Symbols

I. Be sure you're still in the *MyCircuit1.dwg* file. If not, please open it now.

II. Follow these steps.

## 25.1.3.1: XBINDING DEPENDENT SYMBOLS

1. Enter the ***Xbind*** command. Alternately, you can pick the **XBind** button  on the Reference toolbar.

**Command:** ***xb***

2. AutoCAD presents the Xbind dialog box (Figure 25.006). Pick the "+" beside the battery reference. AutoCAD presents a list of dependent symbol categories. Categories with symbols available for binding have a "+" beside them.

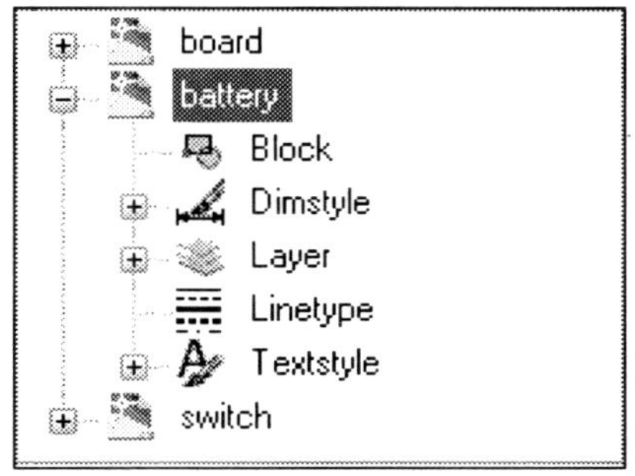


3. Pick the "+" beside the **Layer** category, and then select the **battery|wire** layer.

4. Pick the **Add** button 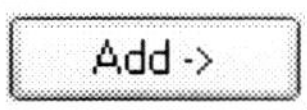

. Notice that the **battery|wire** layer disappears from the **Xrefs** frame and appears in the **Definitions to Bind** frame (below).

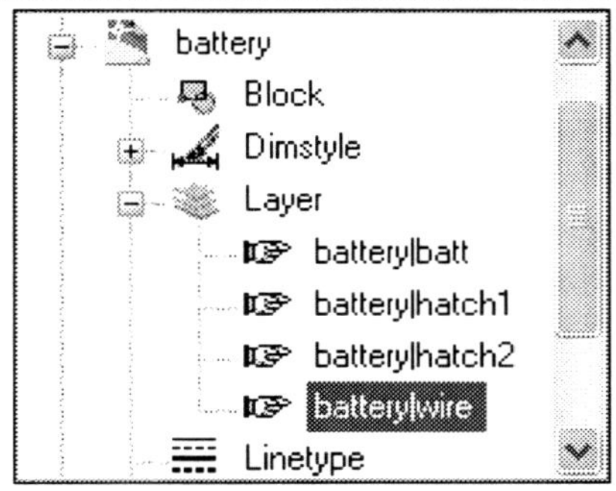


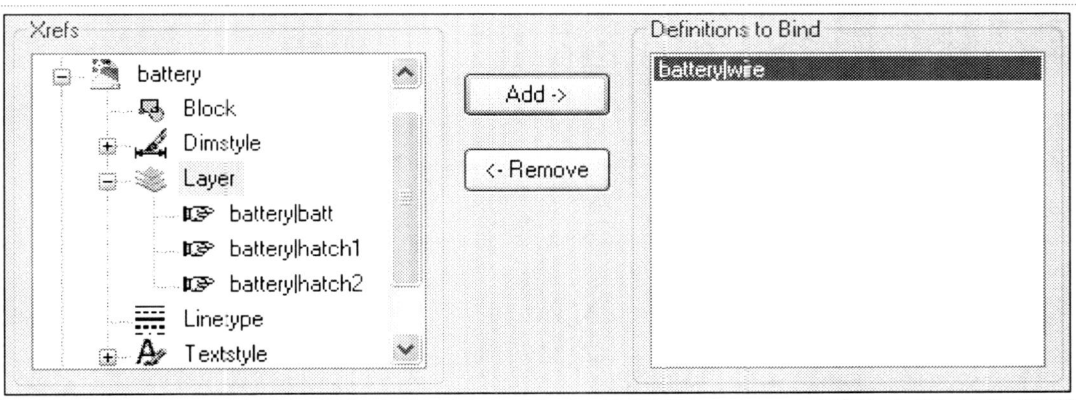


5. Pick the **OK** button 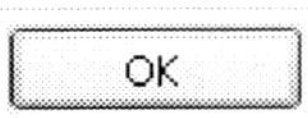

to complete the command.

6. Check the **Layer** control box. Notice that the **battery|wire** layer has been replaced with **battery$0$wire**. You can now use this layer as you would any other layer in the primary drawing.

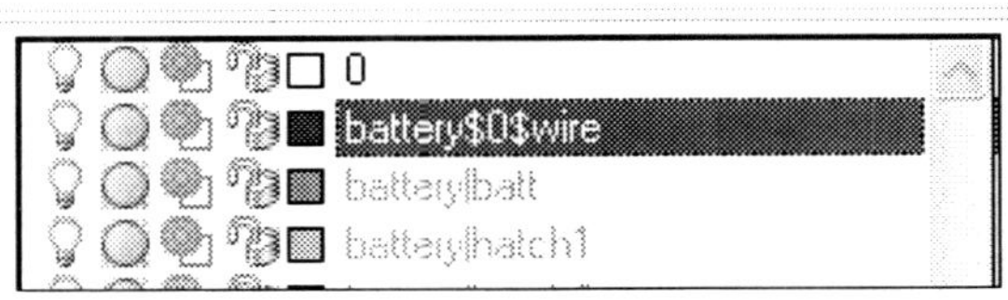

## 25.1.3.1: XBINDING DEPENDENT SYMBOLS

7. Repeat Steps 1 to 5 to bind the **battery|times** text style to the primary drawing. [Check your success by looking in the **Style Name** control box in the Text Style dialog box to be sure you have the **battery$0$times** style (Figure 25.016).

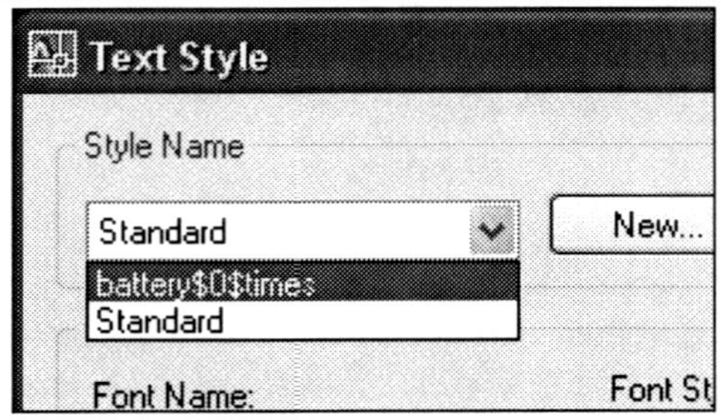


8. Save the drawing but don't exit.

**Command:** ***qsave***

## 25.1.4 Unloading, Reloading, and Overlaying Xrefs

In Exercise 25.1.2.1, we unloaded the *title block* reference to make our work easier. All we had to do was to select the reference to unload (*title block*) in the External Reference palette, and then pick the **Unload** button in the cursor menu. Unloading a reference can speed work by reducing regeneration time. And as we saw, unloading a reference can remove unnecessary, distracting, and even obstructing objects from the display. But eventually, you'll probably have to reload the unloaded reference.

Reloading an unloaded reference is as easy as unloading it. Simply select the drawing to reload and pick the **Reload** option in the same cursor menu. We'll reload the title block in our next exercise.

But first, let's consider the **Attach** versus **Overlay** types of reference. Consider the diagram in Figure 25.007.

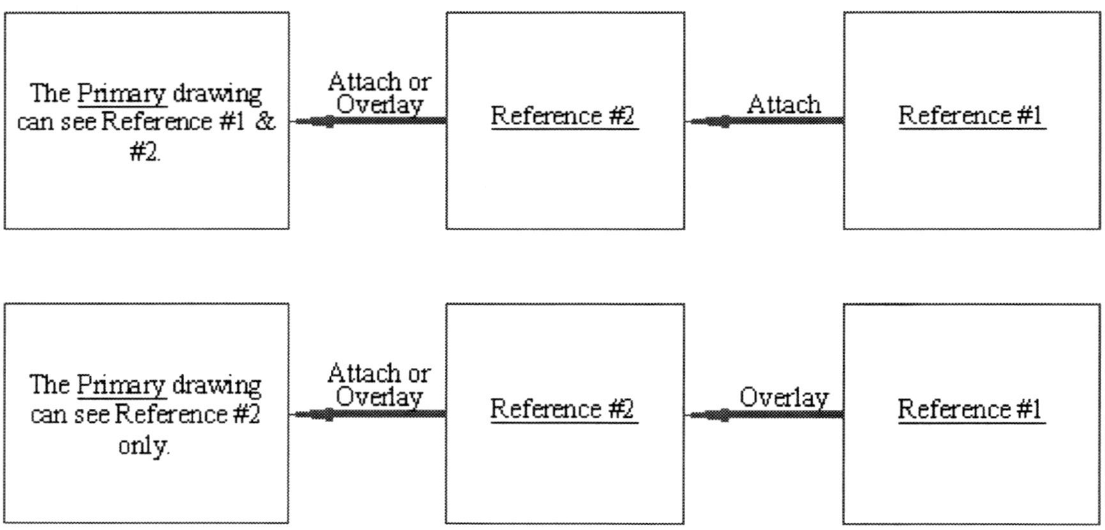


Figure 25.007

As you can see, the **Overlay** type of reference is effective only when used on a nested reference. In other words, overlaying a reference into the primary drawing won't affect the nested reference's visibility. To hide the nested reference, it must be overlaid into the drawing being referenced by the primary drawing. We'll see this in our next exercise.

This is what we'll do: We'll save our drawing and insert it as a reference into a new drawing. The new drawing will be the Primary drawing in our schematic (Figure 25.007), and *MyCircuit1* will be Reference #2). Since *MyBoard* (or *board*) is referenced by MyCircuit1 (using the **Attach** type of

Let's begin.

| Do This: 25.1.4.1 | Overlaying References |
|---|---|

I. Be sure you're still in the *MyCircuit1.dwg* file. If not, please open it now.

II. Reload the title block (repeat Steps 8 – 10 in Exercise 25.1.2.1, but pick **Reload** in Step 9). Save and close *MyCircuit1*.

III. Start a new drawing using the *Start* template in C:\Steps\Lesson25.

IV. Follow these steps.

**25.1.4.1: OVERLAYING REFERENCES**

1. Open the External Reference palette.

   **Command: *xr***

2. Reference the *MyCircuit1* drawing in the C:\Steps\Lesson25 folder. (If *MyCircuit1* isn't available, use *Circuit1*.) Use the **Attachment Reference Type**.

3. Save the drawing as *MyCiruitA*.

   **Command: *saveas***

4. Leave *MyCircuitA* open, but open *MyCircuit1* (or *Circuit1*), too.

   **Command: *open***

5. In the External Reference palette of the *MyCircuit1* (*Circuit1*) drawing, select *board* (or *MyBoard*). Then change the **Reference Type** in the **Details** frame as shown below.

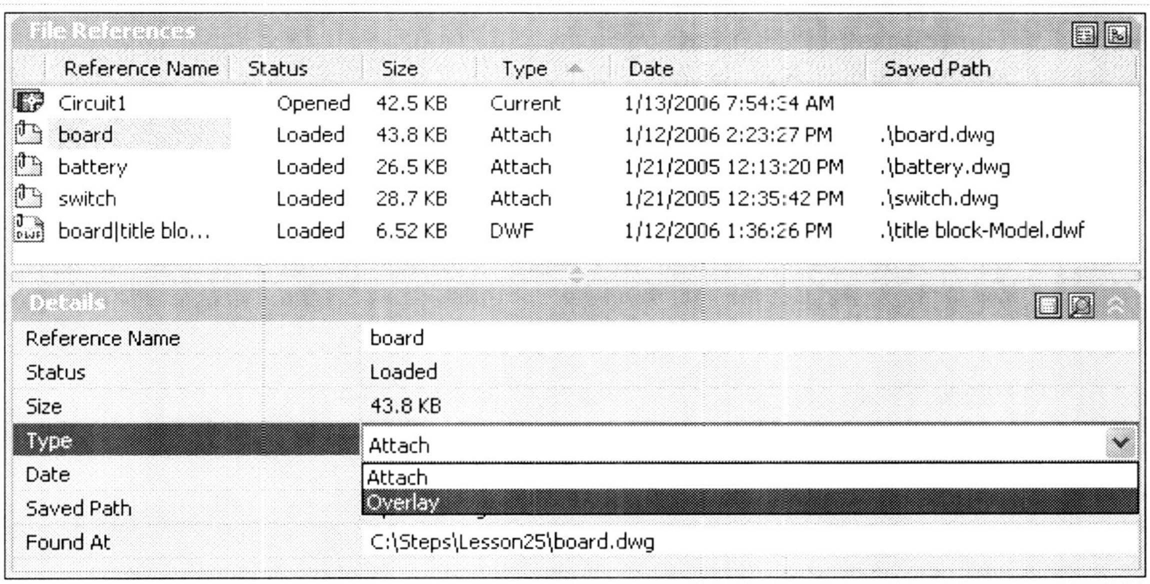


6. Save *MyCircuit1* (or *Circuit1*) …

   **Command: *save***

… and return to *MyCircuitA*. (You can use the Window drop down menu and select the drawing you wish to be current.)

## 25.1.4.1: Overlaying References

7. AutoCAD returns to the *MyCircuitA* drawing and presents a bubble message telling you that a referenced drawing has changed. Pick on the link to reload the changed drawing.

Notice that the *board* reference disappears.

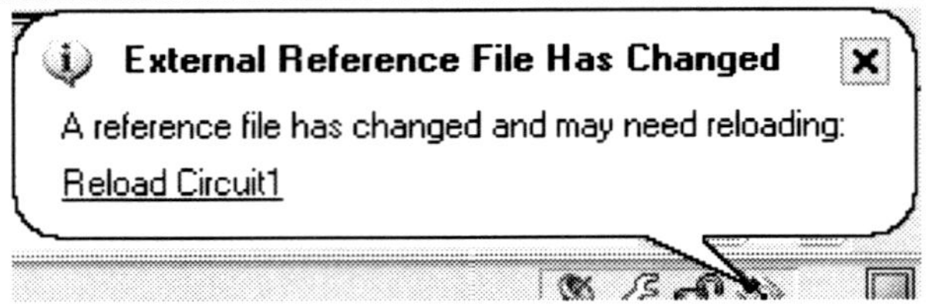


8. Repeat Steps 4 through 7, but this time set the **Reference Type** back to **Attach**. You'll notice that the *board* reference returns to the *MyCircuitA* drawing.

9. Save and close any open drawings.

**Command: *qsave***

## 25.2 Editing Xrefs

Although AutoCAD has made it quite simple to edit a referenced drawing, you should do so with caution. Remember that others may have referenced the same drawing and any changes made to it will reflect in their drawings as well.

We've already seen how simple it is to open a referenced drawing for editing. But there's another tool available for this purpose – one of the nicest tools in the AutoCAD command family. It provides the ability for us to edit a referenced drawing (or a block!) without having to leave the primary drawing. Even better is the fact that it's so easy to do.

Three commands make up the reference editing tools.

- ***Refedit*** begins the editing session. It prompts you to select the referenced objects to edit, like this:

  **Command: *refedit***

  **Select reference: *[select the referenced drawing]***

  ***[Here, AutoCAD presents the Reference Edit dialog box (Figure 25.008). Complete the options and pick the* OK *button to continue. AutoCAD then closes the dialog box and makes the referenced drawing available for editing.]***

  **Use REFCLOSE or the Refedit toolbar to end reference editing session.**

  ***[AutoCAD lets you know how to end the reference editing session.]***

  - The **Identity Reference** tab of the Reference Edit dialog box (Figure 25.008) provides a list box showing the name of the selected reference and a **Preview** frame where you can see the referenced drawing. It also provides two options:

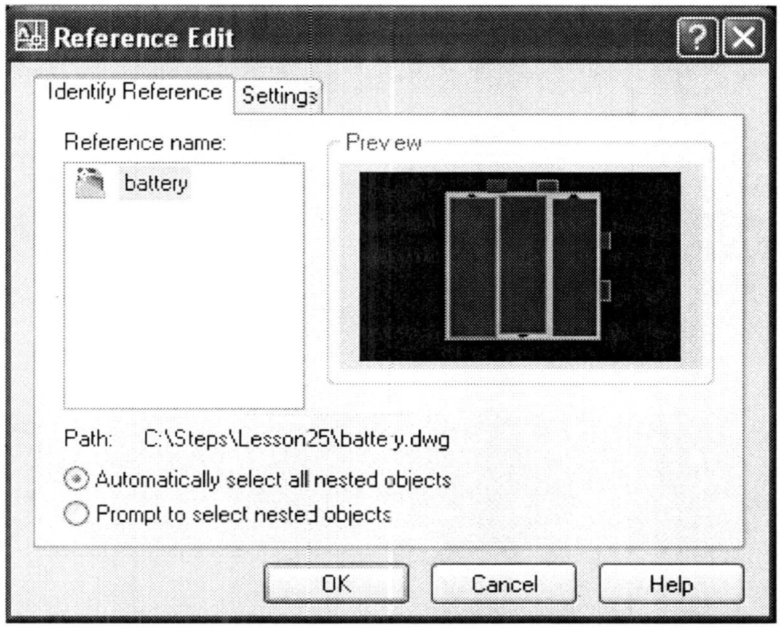

Figure 25.008

- **Automatically select all nested objects** controls whether or not AutoCAD will automatically include nested references in the editing session.
- A bullet next to **Prompt to select nested objects** lets AutoCAD know that you'd rather individually select nested objects in your editing session.

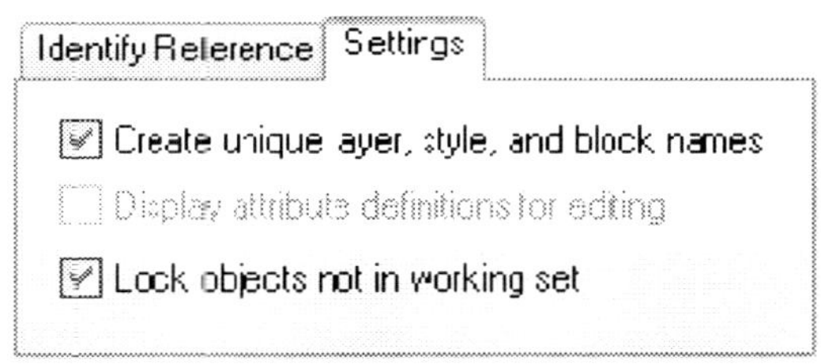

Figure 25.009 (not actual size)

- The **Settings** tab of the Reference Edit dialog box (Figure 25.009) provides some options that may make your editing session run more smoothly.
  - A check next to **Create unique layer, style, and block names** tells AutoCAD to use the $#$ procedure for dealing with symbols much as it does when binding an Xref. If unchecked, layer, style, and block names remain the same as in the referenced drawing.
  - Selecting **Display attribute definitions for editing** means that the attribute definitions of blocks within the referenced drawing will be available for your editing.
  - It's best to leave the check next to **Lock objects not in working set**. This prevents you from accidentally editing something in the primary drawing when you're editing your referenced drawing.

- Use ***Refset*** to add or remove referenced objects from the editing session. It prompts:

  **Command: *refset***

  **Transfer objects between the RefEdit working set and host drawing...**

  **Enter an option [Add/Remove] <Add>: *[enter to add or type R to remove objects from the set]***

  **Select objects: *[select the object(s) to add or remove]***

- ***Refclose*** ends the editing session. It prompts

  **Command: *refclose***

  **Enter option [Save/Discard reference changes] <Save>: *[enter to save the changes or type D to discard the changes]***

AutoCAD presents a warning box (Figure 25.010) telling you what you're about to do. Pick **OK** to continue or **Cancel** to prevent saving.

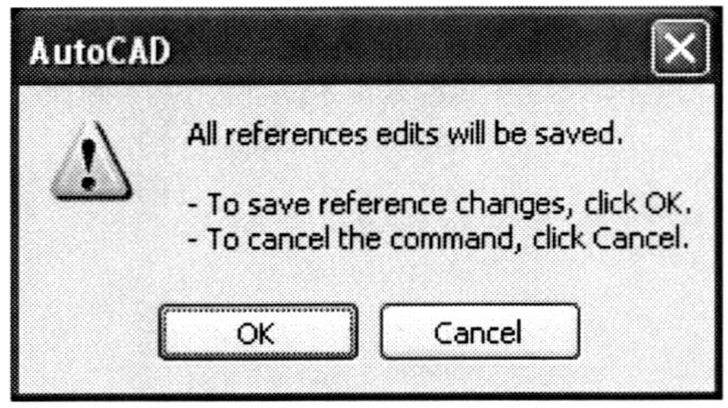

Figure 25.010

AutoCAD also provides buttons on the Refedit toolbar to add or remove objects from the editing session (***Refset***) and to close the session saving or discarding your changes (***Refclose***).

Let's try ***Refedit***.

*Our engineer has determined where the wire connections should be on our battery and switch. We could open those drawings for the changes, but we're in the MyCircuit1.dwg file now and can make the changes here using* ***Refedit****.*

| Do This: 25.2.1 | Editing Referenced Drawings |
|---|---|

I. Open the *MyCircuit1.dwg* file.

II. Follow these steps.

**25.2.1: EDITING REFERENCED DRAWINGS**

1. First, let's remove the clipping planes. Enter the ***XClip*** command.

 **Command:** ***xc***

2. Select the battery and the switch.

 **Select objects:**

 **Select objects:** ***[enter]***

3. Tell AutoCAD you want to **Delete** [Delete] the clipping plane.

 **Enter clipping option**

 **[ON/OFF/Clipdepth/Delete/ generate Polyline/New boundary] <New>:** ***d***

AutoCAD presents both references in their entirety.

4. Now we begin the editing session. Enter the ***Refedit*** command at the command prompt. There's no hotkey for this command, but you can pick the **Edit Reference in-Place** button on the Refedit toolbar.

 **Command:** ***refedit***

5. Select the battery.

 **Select reference:**

6. AutoCAD presents the Reference Edit dialog box (Figure 25.008). We'll use the default settings, so pick the **OK** button [OK].

7. Erase the wiring connections on the right side of the battery. (There are actually three objects – a hatching and two rectangles.)

 **Command:** ***e***

**25.2.1: EDITING REFERENCED DRAWINGS**

8. Complete the ***Refedit*** command with the ***Refclose*** command. Hit enter to accept the **Save** option. Alternately, you can pick the **Save Reference Edits** button on the Refedit toolbar.

   **Command:** ***refclose***

9. AutoCAD presents a warning box (Figure 27.010). Pick the **OK** button OK to complete the procedure.

10. Repeat Steps 4 through 9 to remove the right set of wiring connections on the switch.

11. Save and close the drawing.

   **Command:** ***qsave***

## 25.3 Using Our Drawing as a Reference

Now that we've created a drawing with circuit board, battery, and switch, we can begin to create our wiring diagrams. We'll plan on three layouts using the battery and switch in these locations, so we'll use the *MyCircuit1.dwg* file as a reference over which we'll create our layouts.

Let's begin.

### Do This: 25.3.1 Using Xrefs to Create Three Wiring Diagrams

I. Start a new drawing using the *Start* template in the C:\Steps\Lesson25 folder. Save the new drawing as *MyCircuit1a.dwg* in the C:\Steps\Lesson25 folder.

II. Follow these steps.

**25.3.1: USING XREFS TO CREATE THREE WIRING DIAGRAMS**

1. Begin by attaching the *MyCircuit1* (or *Circuit1* if *MyCircuit1* isn't available) drawing as an xref. Attach as an **Attachment Reference Type** with a **Relative path**. Accept the other defaults.

   **Command:** ***xa***

2. Xbind the **battery|wire** layer and the **battery|times** text style to your new drawing. (Use the procedure detailed in Exercise 25.1.3.1.)

   **Command:** ***xb***

3. Rename the new layer to **Wire** and the new text style to **Times**.

4. Save the drawing.

   **Command:** ***qsave***

5. Reference the *lamp.dwg* file in the C:\Steps\Lesson25 folder and place it at coordinates ***6.5,6***.

   **Command:** ***xa***

## 25.3.1: Using Xrefs to Create Three Wiring Diagrams

6. Using splines, draw the wire shown in the following figure. (Be sure to use the **Wire** layer.) Add the text on an appropriate layer. (Text size is 3/16" and uses the **Times** style.)

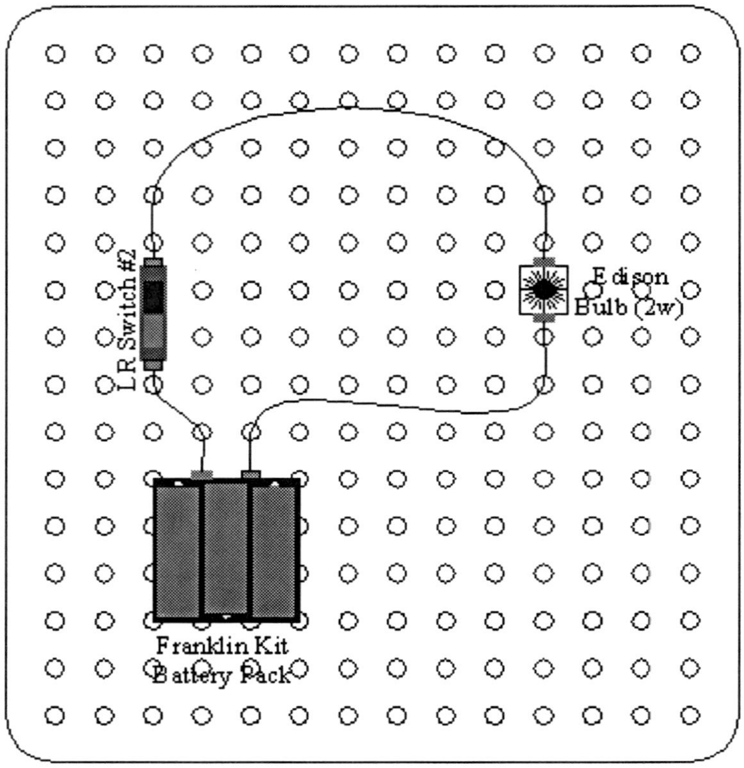


7. Insert the block file *title info* at the lower left corner of the title block (below). (Place it on its own layer, and fill in the data as appropriate for your situation.)

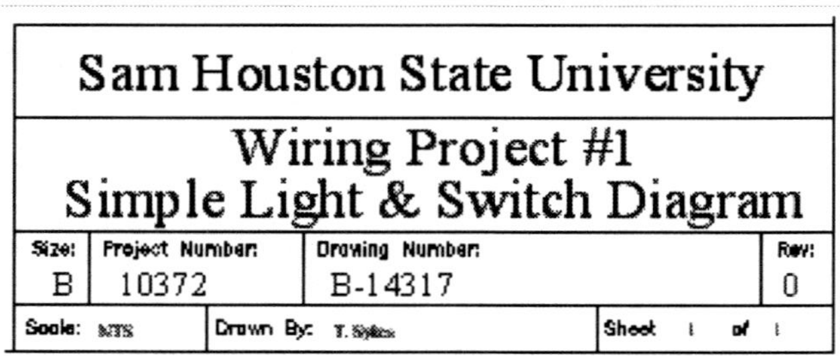


8. Save  and close the drawing.

**Command:** ***qsave***

9. Repeat Steps 1 through 8 (as needed) to create the drawings shown in the following figures. Adjust the title blocks to read *Wiring Project #2*, *Galvanometer Diagram* (drawing number) *B-14319a*, and *Wiring Project #3*, *Resistor Diagram* (drawing number *B-14319b*. (Appropriate reference drawings have been provided in the C:\Steps\Lesson25 folder.)

## 25.3.1: Using Xrefs to Create Three Wiring Diagrams

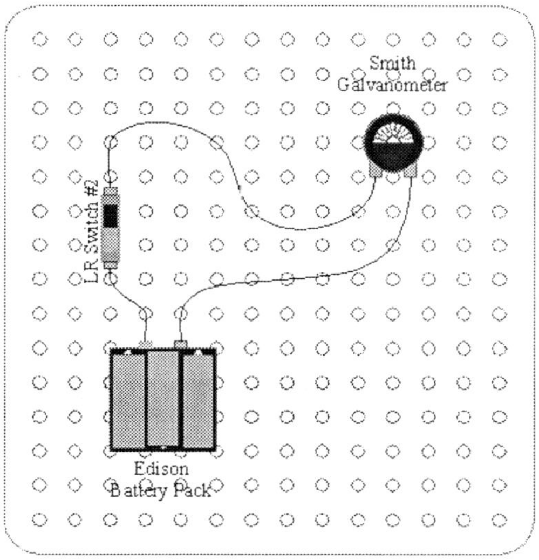


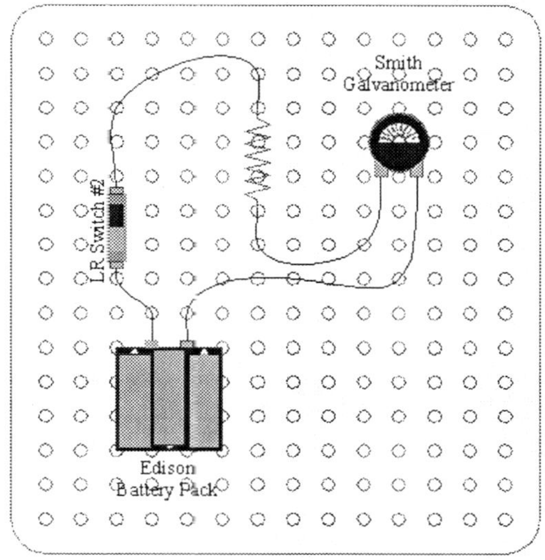


10. Save the drawings as *MyCircuit1b* and *MyCircuit1c* in the C:\Steps\Lesson25 folder.

Congratulations! You've completed three diagrams according to your original job requirements! (I've included DWFs of the referenced electronics if you wish to repeat the exercise using DWFs rather than Xrefs.)

You'll have an opportunity to create other diagrams at the end of this lesson. First, however, let's take a look at some special requirements for sending your referenced drawings to your client.

## 25.4 Binding an Xref to Your Drawing

The biggest problem that arises from the use of Xrefs lies in the location of the referenced file and how AutoCAD keeps track of that location.

By default, AutoCAD will look for referenced files in the **Saved Path** first, and then in folders listed in the **Project Files Search Path**. Again, by default, the **Project Files Search Path** is empty. Therefore, you'll need to add the location (path) of your references to the **Project Files Search Path** or rely on the **Saved Path**. Of course, you could put all the drawings in the same folder, but that's not very organized.

A problem develops, however, when you decide to send your drawing to the client (or somewhere else). First, you must remember to send all the reference files along with the primary file. But even when you do this, the client may not (indeed, probably won't) place the files in a folder with the same name you were using. The result will be that the primary drawing won't be able to locate the references (your client gets frustrated and you look for another job).

You could solve the problem by fully documenting necessary project/folder/path information and sending the documents along with the files (much as eTransmit does). But this means that the client must read instructions about how to view your work – probably not a strong selling point for giving you more business.

You might use the eTransmit tool and/or sheet sets. Indeed, that's probably the best approach, but there is another way. AutoCAD allows you to bind all the references to the primary drawing as blocks. Then you simply send the one file, and the client reads it with any AutoCAD program or viewer.

Binding references, however, dramatically increases the size of the drawing. So you need to wait until the project is complete before doing it. It might even be a good idea to archive the project before binding in case you need to do additional work on the original(s).

As we saw in our study of the External Reference palette (Section 25.1.1), binding isn't difficult. Simply select the references to bind and pick the **Bind** button on the cursor menu. AutoCAD will ask if you wish to **Bind** or **Insert** (via the Bind Xrefs dialog box (Figure 25.005). (See the discussion of these options in Section 25.1.1.)

Let's see what happens when we bind our references.

> Although you can bind referenced drawings, you cannot bind DWFs. Keep this in mind when creating your referenced drawings. It might be a good idea to insert DWFs without a path – then keep the DWF in the same location as the drawing you're creating.

| Do This: 25.4.1 | Binding References |
|---|---|

I. Open the *MyCircuit1a.dwg* file in the C:\Steps\Lesson25 folder. (If this file isn't available, you can open *Circuit1a* instead.)

II. Follow these steps.

### 25.4.1: Binding References

1. Before we bind our references, let's see how large our drawing file is. Enter the ***dwgprops*** command.

    **Command: *dwgprops***

2. AutoCAD presents the [Drawing Name] Properties dialog box.
Note the size of the drawing (it's on the **General** tab), and then exit the dialog box.

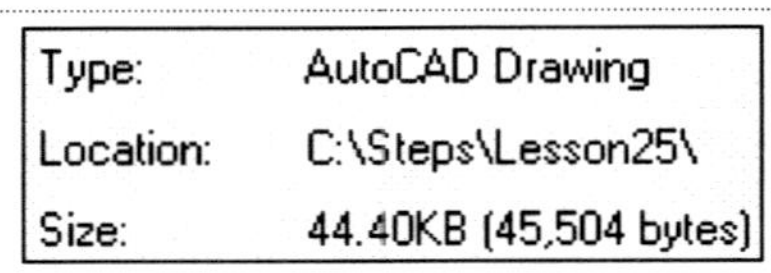


3. Open the External Reference palette .

    **Command: *xr***

4. Select the *MyCircuit1* (or *Circuit1*) drawing and then pick **Bind** on the cursor menu.

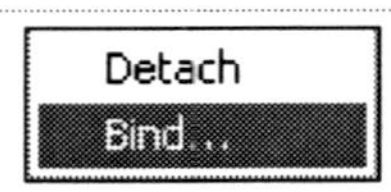


5. AutoCAD presents the Bind Xrefs dialog box. Remember, if you use the **Bind Bind Type**, dependent symbols adopt this format: **[ref name]$[#]$[layer]** (as in **battery$0$hatch1**). If you use **Insert**, dependent symbols drop the reference drawing name and **$[#]$** from their name.
Put a bullet next to **Insert** and pick the **OK** button.

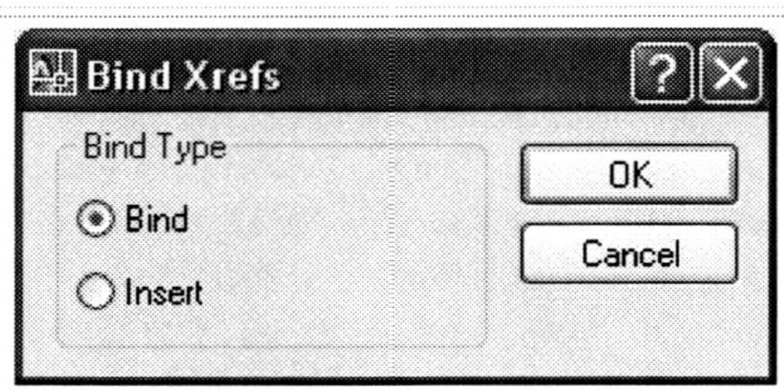


6. AutoCAD returns you to the palette. Notice that all the drawing references except **lamp** and the attached DWF have been removed. All the other references were nested into our primary drawing via the *MyCircuit1.dwg* file. When it was bound, its references were also bound into the primary drawing.

7. Repeat Steps 4 through 6, this time binding the **lamp** reference.

## 25.4.1: Binding References

8. Close the palette.

9. AutoCAD has attached the references to the drawing as blocks. Look at the **Layer** control box to see the changes in how layers are identified. Notice that the reference drawing has been dropped from the name.

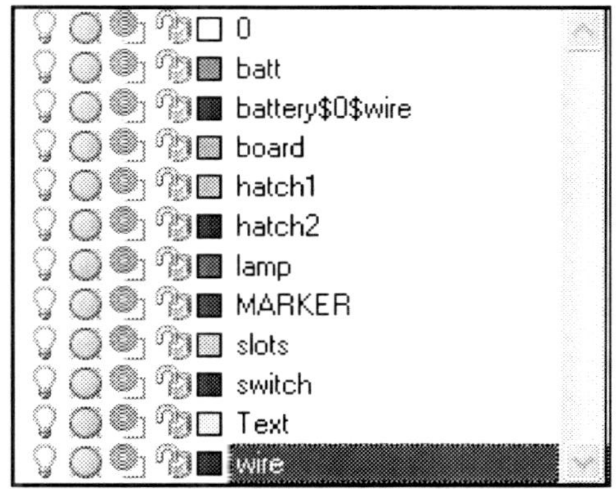


11. Save the drawing but don't exit.

**Command:** ***qsave***

12. Repeat Steps 1 and 2 and compare the drawing size now with the size before binding the Xrefs. Notice the size increase; this is how much drawing space you saved by using Xrefs. (Imagine how much help they'll be in a 2Mb or 3Mb drawing file!)

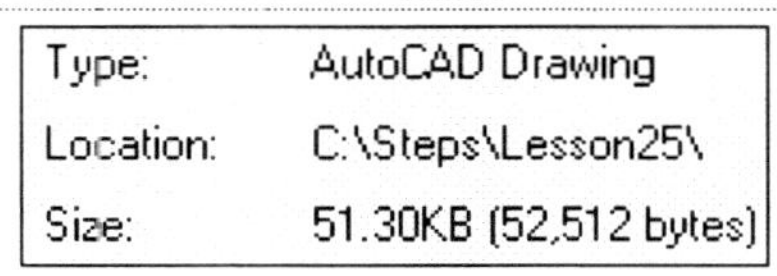


13. Now explode all the blocks (except the title block information) and save the drawing. We do this for a comparison of drawing sizes (how large the drawing would have been had we simply drawn each object.)

**Command:** ***x***

14. Repeat Steps 11 and 12. Notice how large the drawing file is now!

15. Close the drawing. (Save the changes.)

**Command:** ***close***

You can now send the drawing to your client without fear of losing something in the transmittal!

## 25.5 Extra Steps

*Asking is only half the battle. Listening to the answer reveals the path to success.*

Anonymous

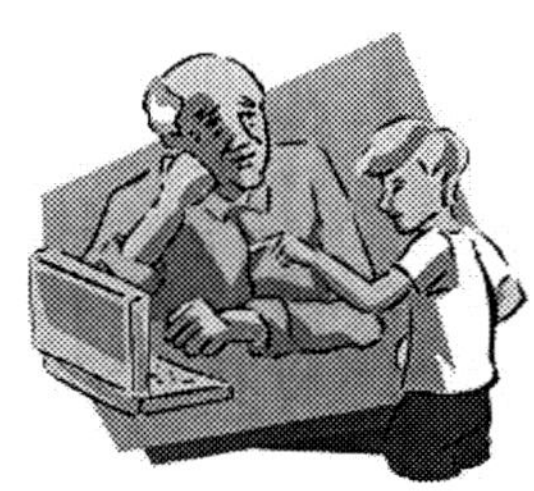

So, what do you think of External References? When used properly, they can be tremendous timesavers. But something else is required. Let me tell you a story.

When I was working for one of the big petrochemical companies in Houston a few years ago, a friend of mine (another guru) was assigned to a new project. He was to set up the CAD system for the project.

For some wild reason (wild reasoning isn't uncommon in petrochem), he decided to buck the norm and set up the project the way AutoCAD was designed to work – using things like attributes to track materials and Xrefs to save time. Jim worked diligently for weeks setting up and starting the project.

Then the company fired him. It seemed the project's lead knew nothing about Xrefs and very little about attributes. All he saw was weeks gone with only a few drawings created (remember that proper setup of an AutoCAD project takes time in the beginning but saves time in the end).

The project lead hired a beginning CAD operator, had him teach himself about Xrefs and attributes, and then spent more weeks disassembling, binding, exploding, and so forth all of the drawings and setups which Jim had created.

What is the moral of this story? Jim forgot one crucial fact of CAD operations. That fact involves communication. Many supervisors are simply not aware of AutoCAD's potential or proper use (yet). Jim didn't explain to the boss what he was doing, nor did the boss bother to learn Jim's "new" system. He replaced it with something he understood (more expensive and time consuming, but also more comfortable for him).

Your Extra Steps exercise is this: Go to your supervisor (or contact a supervisor in the industry in which you hope to work) and set up an interview. Ask if the company uses Xrefs and/or attributes to track materials. Then ask why or why not. If they're using Xrefs, try to convince them to stop (explain that this is an assignment and don't get too combative) and listen closely to their arguments. If they're not using Xrefs, try to convince them to do so. Again, listen closely to their arguments.

## 25.6 What Have We Learned?

*Items covered in this lesson include:*

- *The Xref Manager*
- *Dependent Symbols*
- *Manipulating Xrefs – unloading, reloading, overlaying, and binding*
- *Editing Xrefs*
- *Commands:*
    - ***Xref***
    - ***DWFAttach***
    - ***XAttach***
    - ***Xbind***
    - ***XClip***
    - ***DWFClip***
    - ***DWFFrame***
    - ***XClipFrame***
    - ***Refedit***
    - ***Refclose***
    - ***Refset***
    - ***Dwgprops***

While only a fraction of the people to whom I've spoken about Xrefs actually use them, the number seems to be growing. Xrefs rank well behind blocks in popularity, but they can be almost as useful in their own way. Take some time to get comfortable with them in the exercises at the end of the lesson. Then talk it over with your employer and make an educated decision about how you'll proceed.

The objects of our next lesson – raster images and OLE – closely resemble Xrefs. There we'll discuss referencing other forms of graphics into our drawings. The procedures and dialog boxes resemble those of Xrefs, so the lesson should go fairly smoothly.

But first, let's try a few more Xrefs.

## 25.7 Exercises

1. Using Xrefs and DWFs whenever possible, create the drawing in the following figure.
    1.1. Use the following references (included in the C:\Steps\Lesson25 folder):
        1.1.1. *Title block*
        1.1.2. *Battery*
        1.1.3. *Lamp*

1.1.4. *Galvanometer*

1.1.5. *MyBoard* (you created this in Exercise 25.1.1.1) or *Board*

1.1.6. *title info* (insert this as a block to use the attributes)

1.2. Create layers as needed (you'll need a wire and a text layer)

1.3. Save the drawing as *MyCircuit1d.dwg* in the C:\Steps\Lesson25 folder.

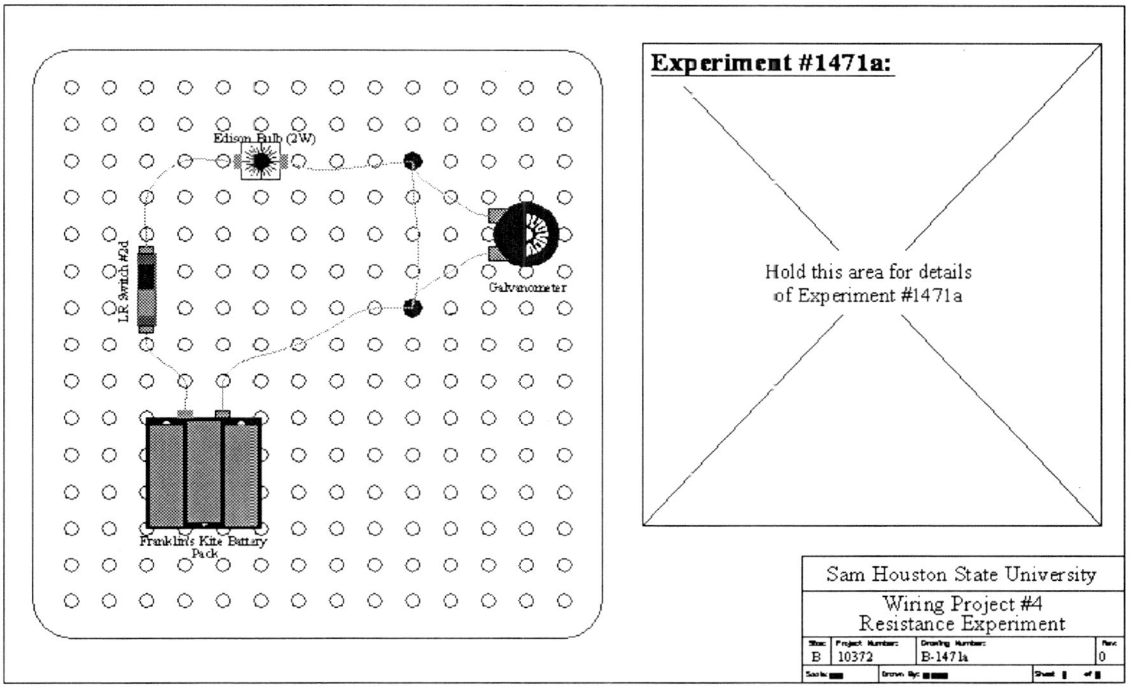


*MyCircuit1d.dwg*

2. Create the drawings in the following two figures, using Xrefs and DWFs whenever possible.

2.1. Use the following references (included in the C:\Steps\Lesson25 folder):

2.1.1. *Title block-a*

2.1.2. Other drawings you might wish to create

2.1.3. *title info* (insert this as a block to use the attributes)

2.2. Create layers as needed (you'll need a pipe and a text layer)

2.3. Save the drawings as *Pump Config 1.dwg* and *Pump Config 2.dwg* in the C:\Steps\Lesson25 folder.

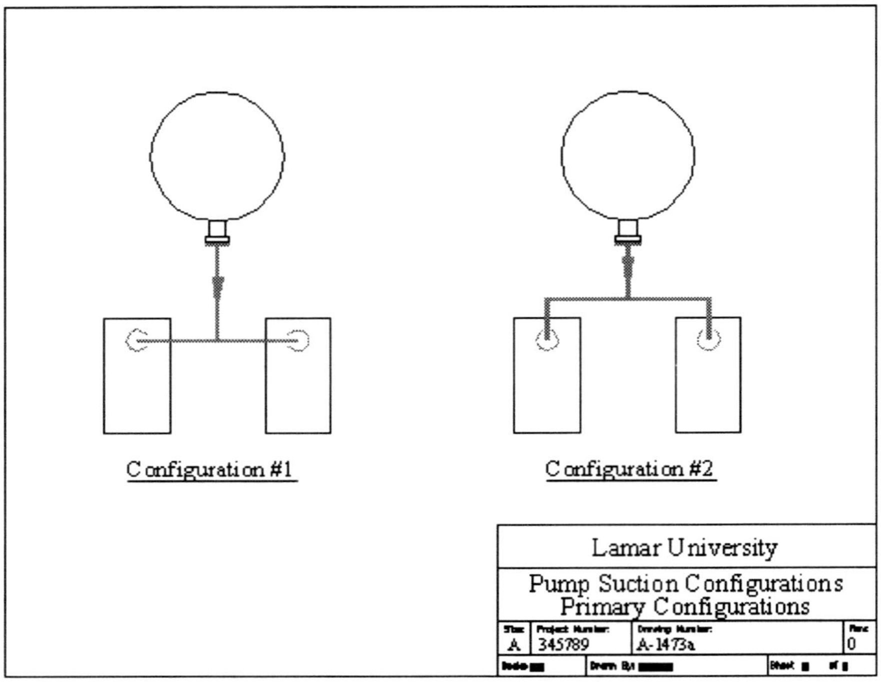


*Pump Config 1.dwg*

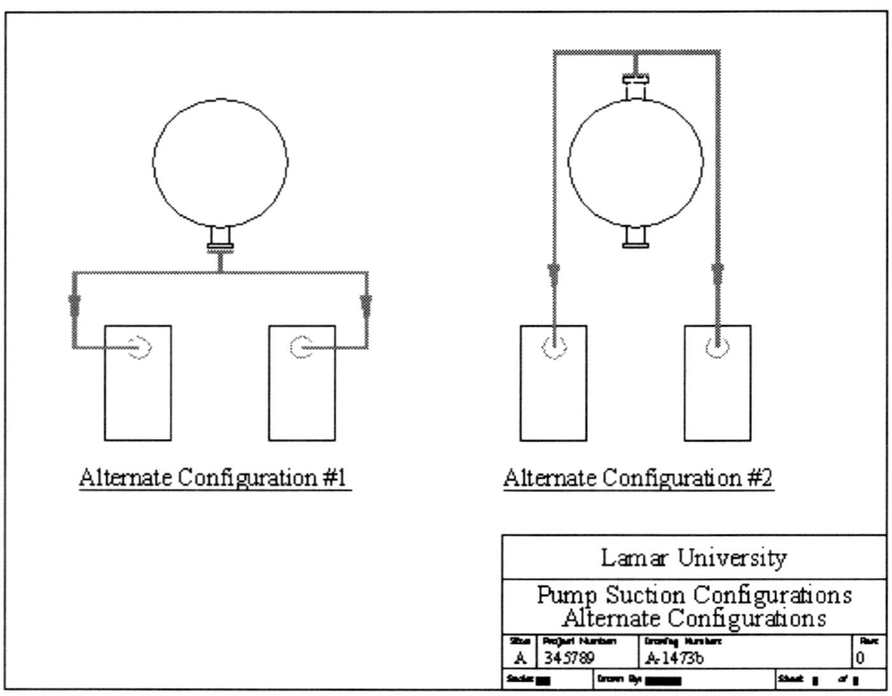


*Pump Config 2.dwg*

*For more exercises related to Lesson 25, please see Lesson 25 in AutoCAD 2007: One Step at a Time – Workbook.*

| 25.8 | **For Web-Based Review Questions, visit: http://www.uneedcad.com/2007/Files/07R25.pdf** |
|---|---|

# Lesson 26

Following this lesson, you will:

- ✓ *Know how to use graphic images from other applications in AutoCAD drawings*
- ✓ *Know how to use AutoCAD drawings in other applications*
- ✓ *Be familiar with raster and vector images*
- ✓ *Know how to use Object Linking and Embedding to share information with other applications*

# Other Application Files and AutoCAD

*I can think of several reasons why you might want to use other application files in an AutoCAD drawing. How about including a photograph of a completed project on a mechanical drawing? I've used them to show completed pieces of furniture I designed. Or perhaps you might want to include a corporate logo in the title block of your drawing. If you can find a nice, colorful scan of the logo, your employer might be pleased to find it on the design! Architects and plant designers might show an outline of the proposed new building or unit against an aerial photograph of the area.*

*You can probably think of many uses for other applications' files in your drawings. Thank goodness that the thinkers and doers at AutoCAD also considered the possibilities.*

## 26.1 Two Types of Graphics

Two categories of graphic files are associated with AutoCAD: *Vector Images* and *Raster Images.*

- Vector Images

  By default, AutoCAD creates vector images. In fact, you've been drawing vector images since you began using AutoCAD.

  Vector images locate geometry by definition and coordinate. For example, a line has two defined endpoints. AutoCAD treats it as a single object – a line – by definition.

  Vector images hold their definition regardless of the resolution of the screen or drawing view. Since they only have to define coordinates and objects, their size is quite small compared to a raster image of the same objects.

  Types of files found in this category include:

  - *DWG* – You're already familiar with how AutoCAD shares its drawing files within the AutoCAD program (blocks and Xrefs).
  - *DWF* – The Drawing Web Format is a 2D vector file designed for publishing AutoCAD drawings on the web.
  - *3DS* – This is another Autodesk file. This one works with 3D Studio.
  - *DXF* – ASCII version of the image file.
  - *SAT* – The ACIS file format.
  - *EPS* – Adobe graphic file. Useful for sharing information with Adobe's publishing applications.
  - *WMF* – Windows MetaFiles were created by Microsoft for use in its graphics programs. You can use them to share information with most Microsoft publishing software. (Note: A WMF file actually contains both vector and raster imaging.)

- Raster Images

  Most non-CAD programs use raster images. These images locate geometry by screen pixel coordinate. In other words, objects aren't defined as circles, lines, and so forth, but are the result of the color definition of a series of pixels.

  This method of graphics creation generally requires more memory and tends to lose image quality (sharpness) as the viewer gets close to the image.

  The more popular types of files in this category include:

  - *GIF* – An ideal Internet file because of its small size, the GIF file is no longer supported in AutoCAD drawings.
  - *JPG* – Also good for Internet use, the JPG (pronounced "jay'-peg") file doesn't have the GIF's color limitations, making it perfect for photographs. However, the JPG file can become quite large.
  - *TIF* – Microsoft had a hand in developing this file type, so its acceptability in various graphics programs is almost universal.

- *BMP* – Microsoft's original bitmap, this file type also is almost universal in acceptability. Virtually all IBM-type computers (all those with the Windows operating system) use BMPs in the Windows' Paint program.
- *PCT* – Use this Apple graphics file for easy exchange with the Apple-type computer.

Other and lesser-known file types include *RLE*, *DIB*, *RST*, *GP4*, *MIL*, *CAL*, *CG4*, *FLC*, *FLI*, *BIL*, *IG4*, *IGS*, *PCX*, *PCT*, *PNG*, RLC, AND *TGA*.

Since we're already familiar with the important vector images, let's look at raster images.

## 26.2 Working with Raster Images: The Image Manager

For working with raster images, AutoCAD uses the External Reference palette you studied in our last lesson (so this one should be easy!). You can access it with the ***Image*** command, the ***IM*** hotkeys, or using the methods you learned in Lesson 25.

You'll find very little difference in the way you manage images and the way you manage DWFs.

### 26.2.1 Attaching, Detaching, Loading, and Unloading Image Files

You can use the External Reference palette to attach, detach, load, or unload image files just as you did Xrefs and DWFs. Use the **Attach Image** option on the toolbar (with the **Attach** flyout) to select an image to load (again, just as you did with Xrefs and DWFs), and then proceed to the Image dialog box in Figure 26.001. Notice the similarity between the Image dialog box and the External Reference dialog box we discussed in our last lesson (Figure 25.002). They're almost identical and the function of each button/frame is the same.

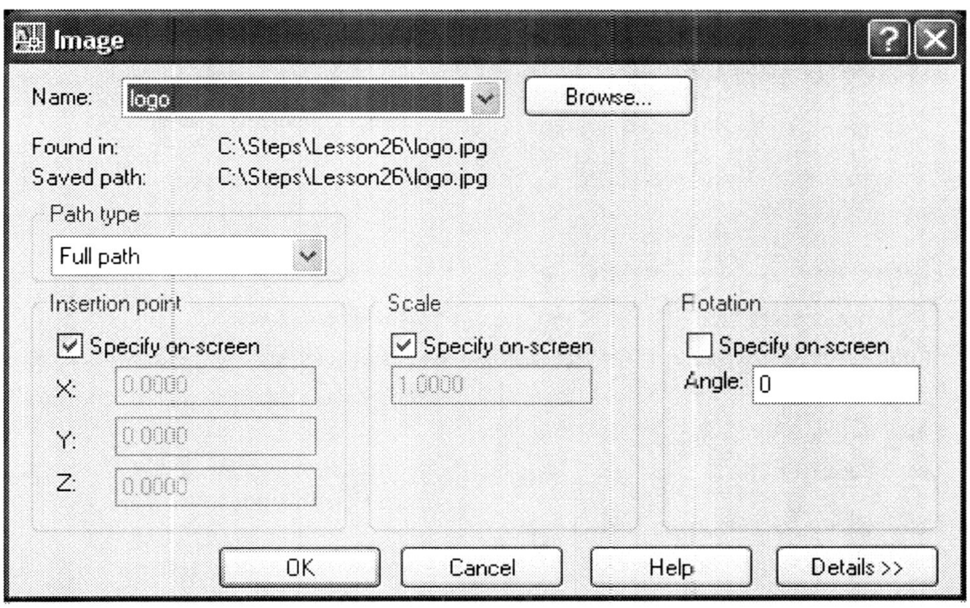


Figure 26.001

There're two notable exceptions; the **Scale** frame of the Image dialog box has only one text box. The reason for this is simple: while you could scale a reference drawing file along the XYZ axes, a raster image has no XY or Z-axis along which to scale. Therefore, AutoCAD restricts us to a uniform scale for raster images. Additionally, images are underlain, as were DWFs, and you have no **Reference Type** choices.

Let's reference some images into a file.

Just as Xrefs have a more direct ***XAttach*** command, so images also have an ***ImageAttach*** command. You can enter it at the keyboard or via the Insert pull-down menu. Follow this path:

*Insert – Raster Image Reference…*

| Do This: 26.2.1.1 | Working with Images |
|---|---|

I. Open the *cutting table26.dwg* file in the C:\Steps\Lesson26 folder. The drawing looks like Figure 26.002.

II. Thaw the **MARKER** layer.

III. Enter the following command sequence:

**Command: *imageframe***

**Enter image frame setting [0, 1, 2] <1>: *0***

[We'll discuss image framing after this exercise, but for now, it's best to have it turned off.]

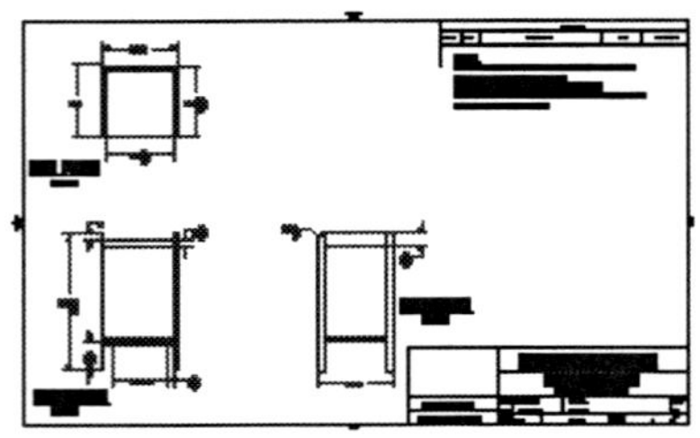

Figure 26.002

IV. Follow these steps.

## 26.2.1.1: Working with Images

1. Open the External Reference palette with the ***Image*** command.

**Command: *im***

2. We'll attach a logo in the title block, so pick the **Attach Image** option in the **Attach** flyouts.

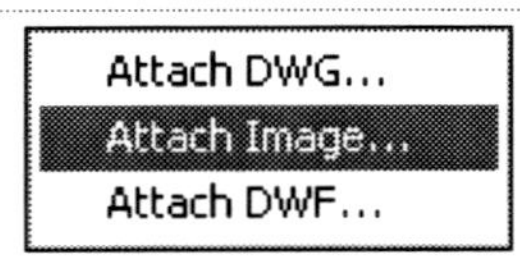


3. AutoCAD presents a Windows Select… File dialog box. Select the *logo.jpg* file in the C:\Steps\Lesson26 folder.

Pick the **Open** button 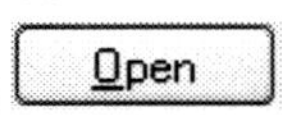

to continue.

4. AutoCAD presents the Image dialog box (see the following figure).

- Be sure there is a check in the **Specify on-screen** check box in the **Insertion point** frame. Clear the check boxes in the other frames.
- Enter ***0.2*** into the Scale frame's text box.
- Use a **Relative path**.

Pick the **OK** button 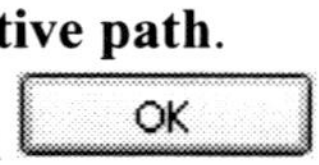

to continue.

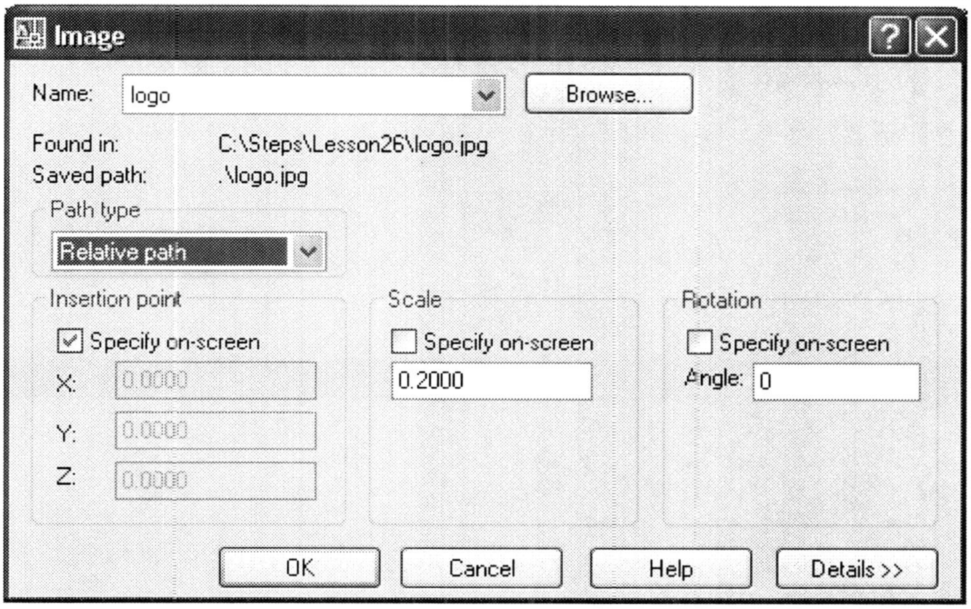


5. Insert the image at the node in the title block (just left of the words "AutoCAD Text").

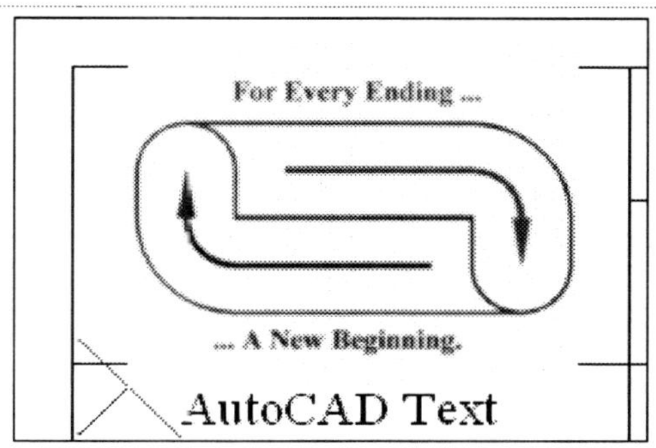


6. Now let's use the ***ImageAttach*** command to insert a photograph of the cutting table. Enter ***imageattach*** or ***iat*** at the command prompt. Alternately, you can pick the **Attach Image** button on the Reference toolbar.

**Command: *iat***

7. Select the *cutting table.jpg* file, and then pick the **Open** button Open to continue.

8. This time enter a scale of **.75**.

Pick the **OK** button to continue and insert the image at the node in the middle of the screen (~6,5).

Your drawing looks like the figure atop the next page.

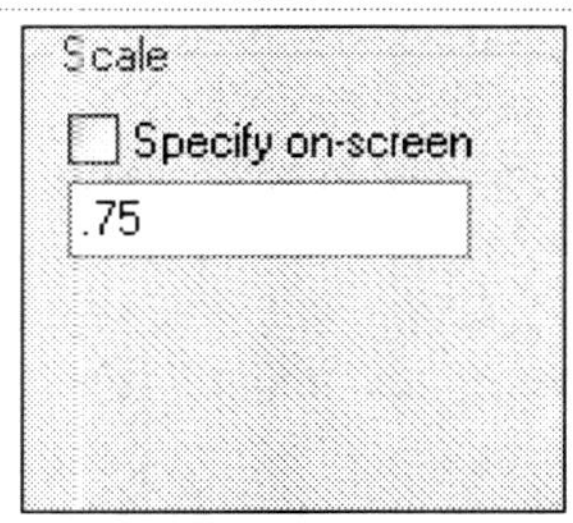

## 26.2.1.1: Working with Images

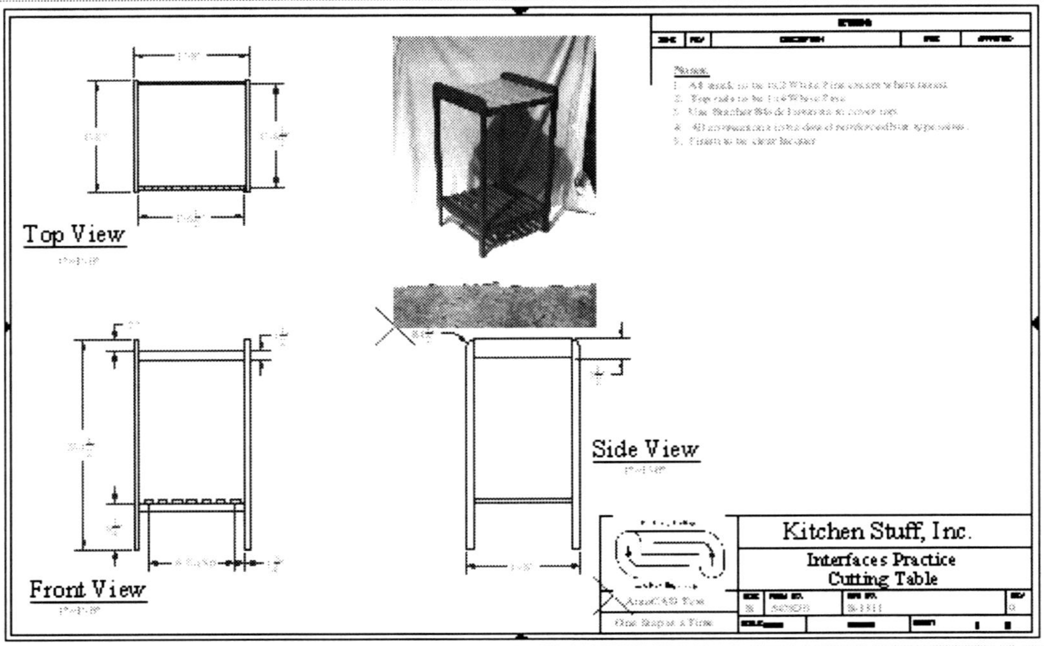


9. Save the drawing but don't exit.

**Command:** ***qsave***

> Note: Images attach on the current layer. You can freeze them, turn them off, lock them, and so forth just like any other object.

Over the course of this exercise, did you try to adjust either of the images we referenced? Did you notice that you couldn't select either one? If not, try to erase one of them now.

Unlike Xrefs and DWFs, which allow you to use OSNAPs and other modifying tools, images have no vector geometry to select. But AutoCAD doesn't leave you with something you can't modify. It provides a system variable – called **ImageFrame** – that reveals a selectable frame around the image. The command prompts:

**Command:** ***imageframe***

**Enter image frame setting [0, 1, 2] <1>:**

When set to **0**, images in the drawing are not selectable; that is, you can't modify them. When set to **1** or **2**, AutoCAD shows a frame around the image. You can select this frame to move, scale, or otherwise modify the image. (When set to **1**, the frame will plot; when set to **2**, it won't.)

In our next exercise, we'll use the frame to adjust our view of the photograph.

> You can also pick the **Image Frame** button on the Reference toolbar to access the **ImageFrame** system variable. Alternately, you can access the **ImageFrame** system variable via the Modify pull-down menu. Follow this path:
>
> *Modify – Object – Image – Frame*

| 26.2.2 | Clipping Image Files |
|---|---|

Clipping an image is no different from clipping an Xref or DWF. The command sequence is identical:

**Command:** ***imageclip*** **(or** ***icl*****)**

**Select image to clip:** ***[select the image you wish to clip]***

**Enter image clipping option [ON/OFF/ Delete/New boundary] <New>:** ***[tell AutoCAD what you want to do]***

**Enter clipping type [Polygonal/Rectangular] <Rectangular>:** ***[tell AutoCAD what type of clipping boundary you wish to use]***

**Specify first corner point: Specify opposite corner point:** ***[identify the corners of the rectangle or the vertices of the polygon]***

The ***ImageClip*** command automatically activates the **ImageFrame** system variable so that you can select an image.

Let's clip our photograph.

> You can also access the ***ImageClip*** command via the Modify pull-down menu. Follow this path:
> *Modify – Clip – Image*

| Do This: 26.2.2.1 | Clipping Images |
|---|---|

I. Be sure you're still in the *cutting table26.dwg* file in the C:\Steps\Lesson26 folder. If not, please open it now.

II. Follow these steps.

**26.2.2.1: CLIPPING IMAGES**

1. Enter the ***ImageClip*** command. Alternately, you can pick the **Clip Image** button 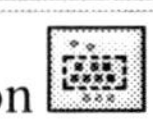 on the Reference toolbar.

   **Command:** ***icl***

2. (Notice that AutoCAD activates the **ImageFrame** system variable.) Select the frame around the cutting table photograph.

   **Select image to clip:**

3. Hit ***enter*** twice to accept the **New** and **Rectangular** boundary defaults.

   **Enter image clipping option [ON/OFF/Delete/New boundary] <New>:** ***[enter]***
   **Enter clipping type [Polygonal/ Rectangular] <Rectangular>:** ***[enter]***

4. Place a rectangle around the image of the cutting table as shown in the following figure (left). AutoCAD clips the photograph.

   **Specify first corner point:**
   **Specify opposite corner point:**

The results look like the right figure.

**26.2.2.1: Clipping Images**

5. Repeat Steps 1 through 4 for the logo image.

6. Save the drawing but don't exit.

   **Command: *qsave***

Let's continue.

## 26.2.3 Working with Image Files

AutoCAD provides four tools for use with graphic images that aren't available (nor would they be useful) for Xrefs. These include: ***ImageAdjust***, ***ImageQuality***, ***Transparency***, and ***DrawOrder***.

- The ***ImageAdjust*** command calls the Image Adjust dialog box (Figure 26.003). Here you can adjust the brightness, contrast, or fading effect (how well the image blends with the background color of the drawing) of the image. The dynamic preview image helps you see the results of your modifications before you accept them with the **OK** button.

  Like ***ImageClip***, ***ImageAdjust*** automatically activates the **ImageFrame** system variable.

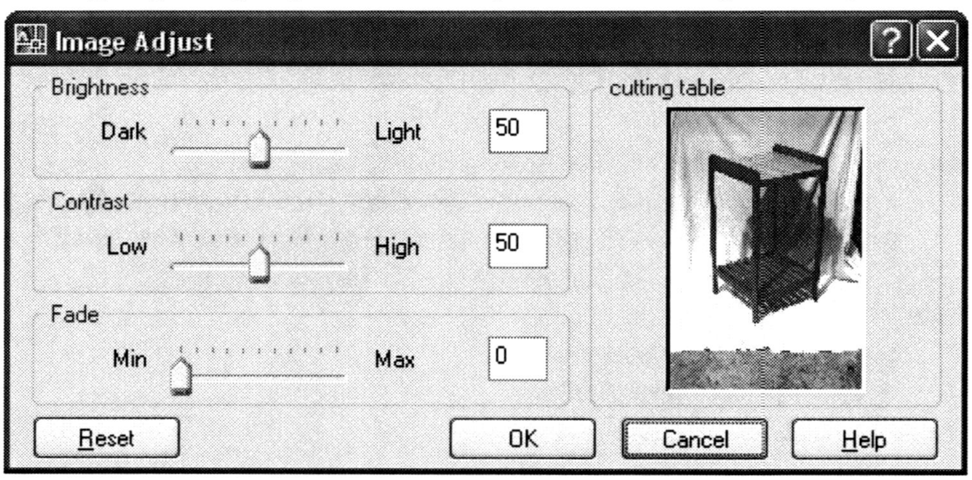


Figure 26.003

- **ImageQuality** is a system variable that affects only the display of your graphic images. It presents the following prompt:

  **Command: *imagequality***

**Enter image quality setting [High/ Draft] <High>:**

**High** quality presents the best possible image in the display, but it may cause some delay in the initial display or redraw/regen time. Draft quality isn't quite as pretty, but it allows for much faster displays. AutoCAD will always use **High** quality when plotting despite this setting.

- The ***Transparency*** command works only on certain types of graphics that have a transparency property.

  You can set transparency on a per-image basis.

- [We'll discuss ***DrawOrder*** after the next exercise.]

Let's experiment with these commands before looking at our last tool.

> You can also access the ***Transparency***, ***ImageQuality***, and ***ImageAdjust*** commands via the Modify toolbar. Follow this path:
>
> *Modify – Object – Image – [command]*

| **Do This: 26.2.3.1** | **Image Quality** |
|---|---|

I. Be sure you're still in the *cutting table26.dwg* file in the C:\Steps\Lesson26 folder. If not, please open it now.

II. Follow these steps.

**26.2.3.1: IMAGE QUALITY**

1. We'll begin by adjusting the cutting table photograph. Zoom in a bit closer to it.

   **Command:** *z*

2. Enter the ***ImageAdjust*** command. Alternately, you can pick the **Adjust Image** button on the Reference toolbar.

   **Command:** ***iad***

3. Notice that ***ImageAdjust*** activates the **ImageFrame** sysvar. Select the frame around the photograph.

   **Select image(s):**

   **Select image(s):** ***[enter]***

4. AutoCAD presents the Image Adjust dialog box (Figure 26.003). Work with the three settings until you're pleased with the preview image. (Use the **Reset** button in the lower left corner if you need to return to the original settings.)

   Pick the **OK** button when you're satisfied.

5. Now we'll set the ***ImageQuality*** to speed our display time. Enter the command. Alternately, you can pick the **Image Quality** button on the Reference toolbar.

   **Command:** ***imagequality***

6. Tell AutoCAD to use a **Draft** Draft quality. Notice the change in the photograph. Remember that the ***ImageQuality*** setting affects only the display.

7. Zoom all.

   **Command:** *z*

## 26.2.3.1: Image Quality

8. Add the *Product* text, freeze the **MARKER** layer, and save the drawing.

**Command: *qsave***

It now looks like the following figure.

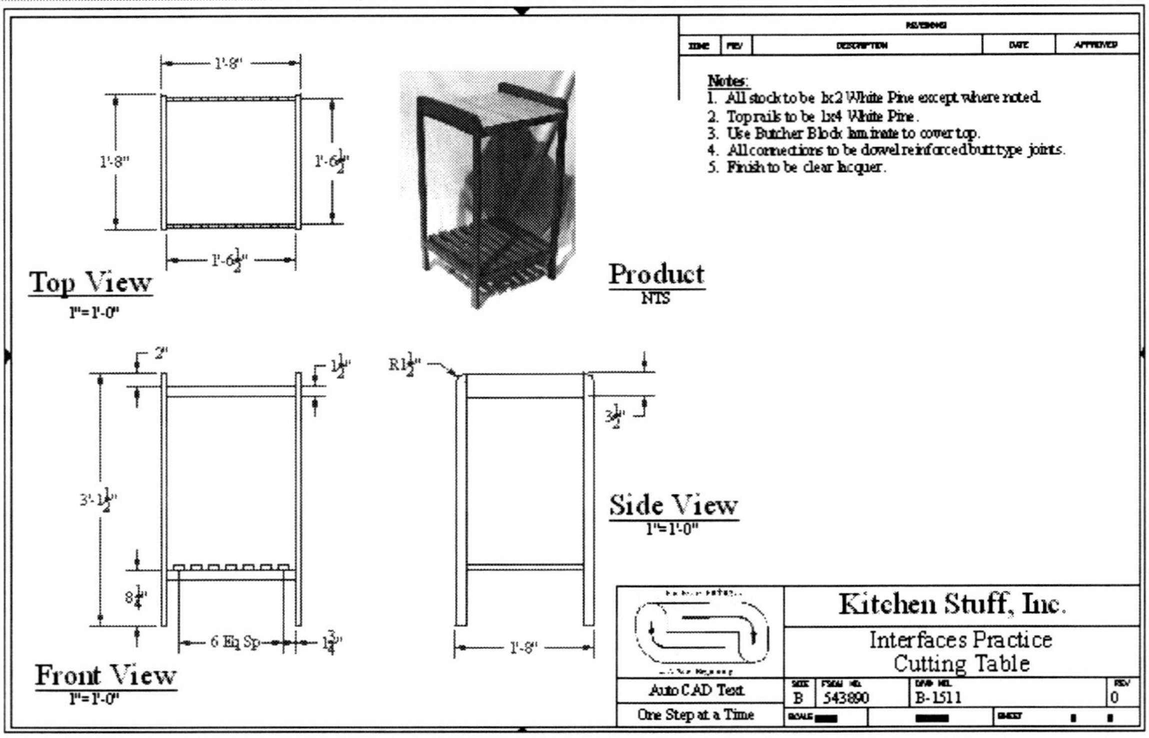


- Our last image modification tool is called ***DrawOrder***. By default, AutoCAD displays the last object drawn or inserted atop (or over) previously drawn objects. This may cause certain objects to "hide" behind other objects. ***DrawOrder*** allows you to control the order in which objects are displayed. In other words, use ***DrawOrder*** to control which object appears on top. It presents the following sequence:

  **Command: *draworder* (or *dr*)**

  **Select objects: *[select an object to modify]***

  **Select objects: *[select more objects or hit enter to confirm the set]***

  **Enter object ordering option [Above object/Under object/Front/Back] <Back>: *tell AutoCAD how to reposition the image/object]***

The options are best explained in an exercise, so let's begin.

> You can also access the various options of the ***DrawOrder*** command via the Tools pull-down menu. Follow this path:
>
> *Tools – Draw Order – [option]*

| Do This: 26.2.3.2 | Controlling Drawing Order |
|---|---|

I. Open the *DrawOrd.dwg* file in the C:\Steps\Lesson26 folder. The drawing looks like Figure 26.004. (The drawing has two polylines and an image.)

II. Follow these steps.

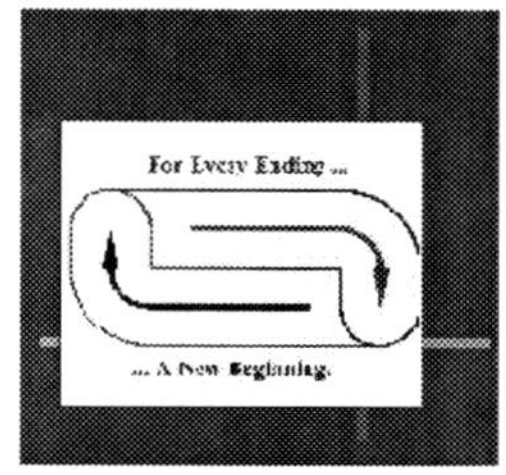


Figure 26.004

**26.2.3.2: CONTROLLING DRAWING ORDER**

1. Enter the ***DrawOrder*** command. Alternately, you can pick the **Draw Order** button  on the Modify II toolbar or the Modify palette.

   **Command: *dr***

2. Select the red horizontal polyline.

   **Select objects:**

   **Select objects: *[enter]***

3. Move it to the front 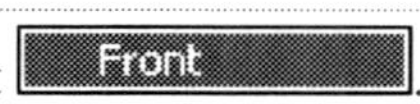.

   **Enter object ordering option [Above object/Under object/Front/Back] <Back>: *f***

   Notice the change in the display.

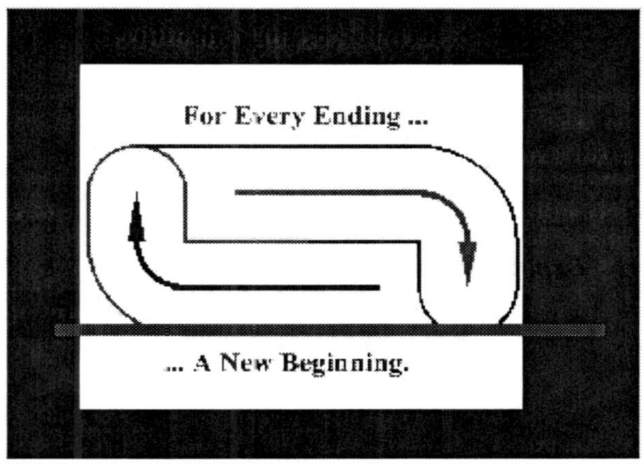


I created this file to give you a chance to play with the various options of the ***DrawOrder*** command. Take a few minutes to experiment with each of the options. (Note: You can also use the buttons on the Draw Order toolbar.)

## 26.3 Exporting Image Files

It seems that there are almost as many ways to export image files as there are types of image files to export. Luckily, AutoCAD has also provided a single command that covers the spectrum. That command is ***Export***, and it works with a Windows standard Save-type dialog box.

The Export Data dialog box works as easily as the Save dialog box. Simply select the type of file you wish in the **Save as type** control box, and then pick the **Save** button.

Let's give it a try.

> You can also access the ***Export*** command via the File pull-down menu. Follow this path:
>
> *File – Export ...*

| Do This: 26.3.1 | Exporting Image Files |
|---|---|

I. Be sure you're still in the *DrawOrd.dwg* file in the C:\Steps\Lesson26 folder. If not, please open it now.

II. Follow these steps.

### 26.3.1: Exporting Image Files

1. Enter the ***Export*** command.

    **Command: *export***

2. AutoCAD presents the Export Data dialog box. Pick the down arrow next to the Files of type control box, and select **Bitmap (*.bmp)**.

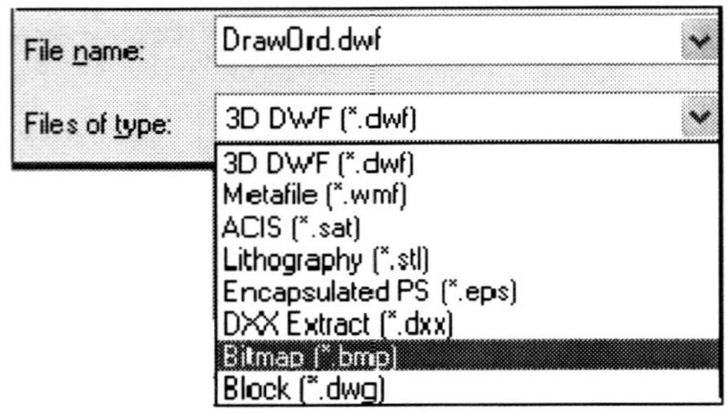


3. Pick the **Save** button   to return to the command line.

4. Hit ***enter*** to select all the objects in the drawing.

    **Select objects or <all objects and viewports>: *[enter]***

5. Use Windows' Paint (or any other graphics program) to view the *DrawOrd.bmp* file you just created in the C:\Steps\Lesson26 folder.

Try repeating the last exercise using the *Cutting table26.dwg* file. Does it work?

The ***Export*** command usurps several graphics-type-specific commands including the following:

| Command | File Type | Command | File Type |
|---|---|---|---|
| ***WMFOut*** | *WMF* | ***ATText*** | *DXX* |
| ***ACISOut*** | *SAT* | ***BMPOut*** | *BMP* |
| ***STLOut*** | *STL* | ***3DSOut*** | *3DS* |
| ***PSOut*** | *EPS* | ***WBlock*** | *DWG* |
| ***JPGOut*** | *JPG* | | |

## 26.4 Working with Linked Objects – Object Linking and Embedding (OLE)

Let's begin with the obvious: Exactly what is OLE? You've probably heard the term since you began using computers, but what does it mean?

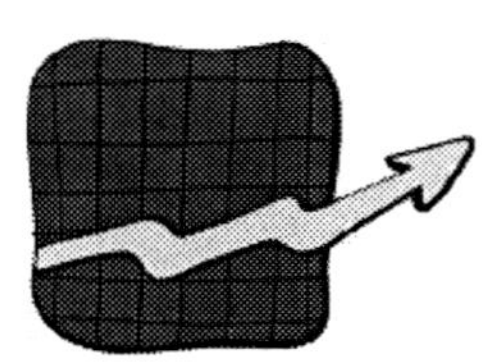

OLE stands for *Object Linking and Embedding*. It refers to the method of creating a compound document – a document that requires more than one application (program) to create. In other words, you might use OLE to show a bill of materials on an AutoCAD drawing by linking directly to the Excel spreadsheet or MS Access database file where the information is stored. (These are Microsoft examples; other programs can be used as well.)

There are actually three *Object* terms. The first – *OLE Object* – I explain below. The second – *OLE Server* – refers to the source program that originated the object. The third – *OLE Container* – refers to the program to which you wish to link or embed the object.

The *Object* part of OLE refers to something that you'll add to your drawing (or other Windows program file). The object is actually a file, part of a file, or graphic image that originated in another program.

The *Linking and Embedding* part of OLE refers to how you wish to attach the OLE Object from the OLE Server to the OLE Container document. A linked document maintains its ties with the server file. Any changes made to it will reflect in the original linked document. An embedded document has no ties with the server file. Changes made to it are unique within your compound document.

Both linked and embedded documents require the OLE Server application (program) for editing.

## 26.4.1 Inserting Other Application Data into AutoCAD Drawings

Microsoft and AutoCAD each provide a method for inserting an OLE Object into a document/drawing. The Microsoft method utilizes the clipboard and an AutoCAD dialog box. It gives greater control over exactly what will be inserted but requires that the server file be opened in the server application. The AutoCAD method utilizes two dialog boxes and doesn't require that the server application be opened, but in the past, it didn't offer as much control over what would be inserted.

We'll see each of these methods in our exercise. But first, let's take a look at the AutoCAD dialog boxes.

AutoCAD presents the Insert Object dialog box (Figure 26.005) when you enter the ***InsertObj*** command (or ***io*** hotkey). Here you find two options for creating the image you wish to insert, and a **Display As Icon** check box.

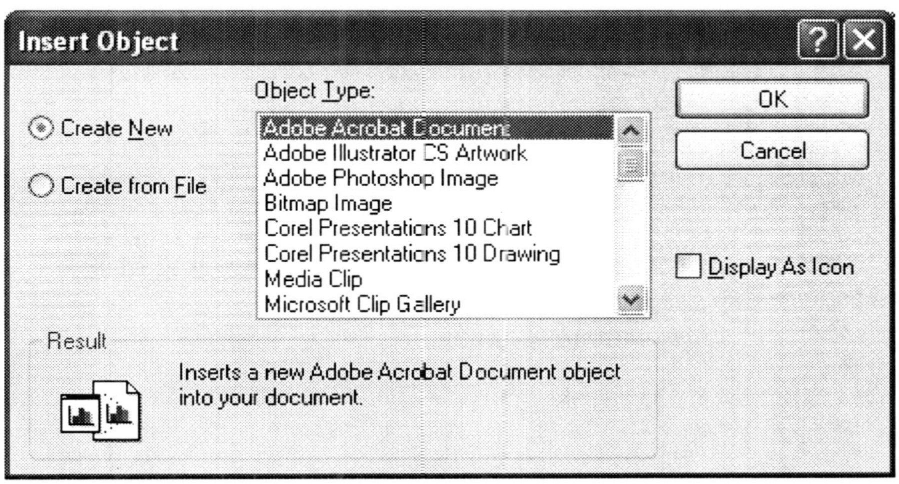


Figure 26.005

- When you place a check in the **Display As Icon** box, AutoCAD displays the server application's icon in the drawing instead of the file itself. Double-clicking on the icon calls the object file for editing. This can speed display time.
- A bullet in the **Create New** option causes the **Object Type** list box to display a list of all the programs on the computer available for OLE communication. Use this approach when an OLE Object doesn't exist and you want to create one. AutoCAD

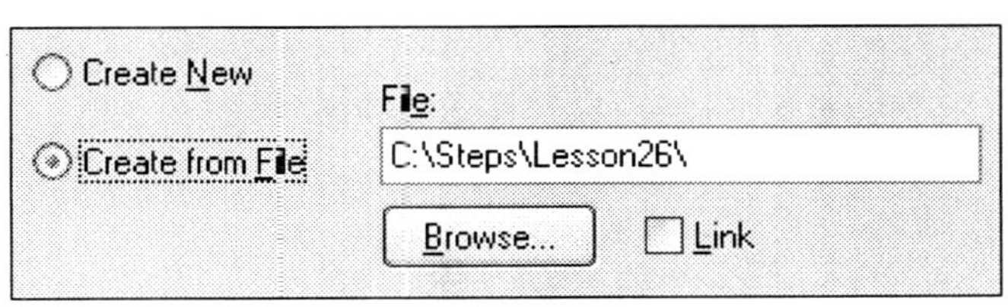


Figure 26.006

automatically embeds objects created using this method.

- A bullet in the **Create from File** option will cause AutoCAD to switch the **Object Type** list box with the **File** text box, **Browse** button, and **Link** check box shown in Figure 26.006 (previous page).

  You'll use the **File** text box to enter the name and location of the file you wish to insert. Alternately, you can pick the **Browse** button to use a Windows standard Open File dialog box to select the file you wish to insert.

  A check in the **Link** box will link the object to your drawing rather than embedding it.

Let's insert an Excel spreadsheet into our cutting table drawing. (Note: This exercise requires the use of MS Excel – Office 97 release or better. If you don't have this software on your computer, read through the exercise, but don't try to do it.)

> OLE Objects are hidden in a rendered drawing.
>
> You can also access the Insert Object dialog box using the **OLE Object** selection on the Insert pull-down menu.
>
> Additionally, you can edit OLE properties using the Properties palette.

| **Do This: 26.4.1.1** | **Inserting OLE Objects** |
|---|---|

I. Reopen the *cutting table26.dwg* file in the C:\Steps\Lesson26 folder. If you haven't completed work on that drawing, open the *cutting table-done.dwg* file in the same folder.

We'll insert the OLE Object (an Excel spreadsheet) twice to see both methods of insertion and both types of insertion.

- Using the AutoCAD method, we'll embed the object.
- Using the Microsoft method, we'll link the object.

II. Zoom extents.

III. Follow these steps.

### 26.4.1.1: Inserting OLE Objects

1. Enter the ***InsertObj*** command. Alternately, you can pick the **OLE Object** button on the Insert toolbar.

   **Command:** ***io***

2. On the Insert Object dialog box, pick the **Create from File** option Create from File. AutoCAD presents the dialog box you saw in Figures 26.005 and 26.006.

3. Pick the **Browse** button Browse... .

4. AutoCAD presents the Browse dialog box (a Windows Select File dialog box). Select the *Cutting List.xls* file (an Excel spreadsheet) in the C:\Steps\Lesson26 folder.

   Pick the **Open** button Open to continue.

5. AutoCAD returns to the Insert Object dialog box. We'll embed the spreadsheet object into our drawing, so be sure the **Link** check box is clear Link.

6. Pick the **OK** button OK to complete the command. AutoCAD places the OLE Object in the upper left corner of the screen.

## 26.4.1.1: Inserting OLE Objects

7. Select the OLE object, and then pick the **Properties** button on the Standard toolbar.

8. In the **Geometry** section of the Properties palette, change the width of the object to **5.5**. Close the Properties palette.

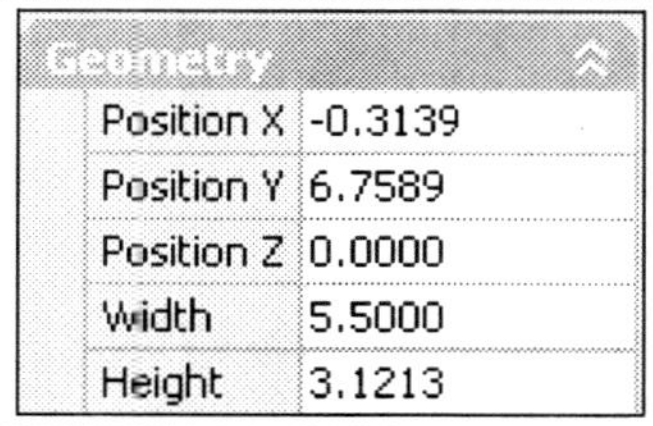


9. Move the object to the open area on the right side of the drawing.

**Command:** ***m***

10. Open the *Cutting List.xls* file in Excel.

11. Return to AutoCAD. (You can pick the **AutoCAD** button on the task bar or hold down the ALT key while tabbing to AutoCAD.)

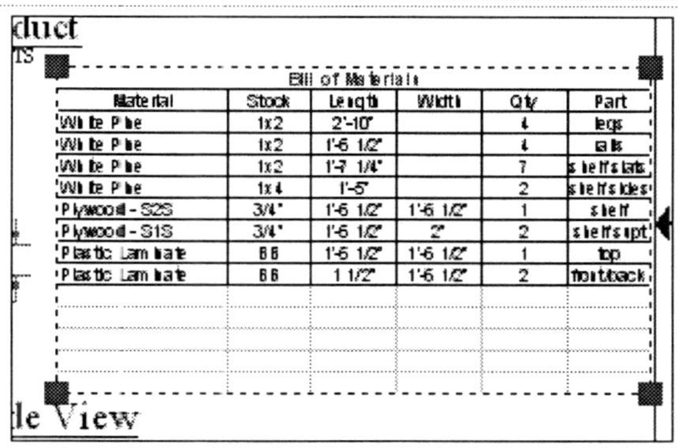


12. Double-click on the OLE Object to edit it. Notice that the object opens in Excel for editing (below). But notice also that the name of the file being edited is *Worksheet in … cutting table.dwg*.
Change the value of cell A3 to read ***Red Oak***. (Be sure to hit ***enter*** to finish the procedure.)

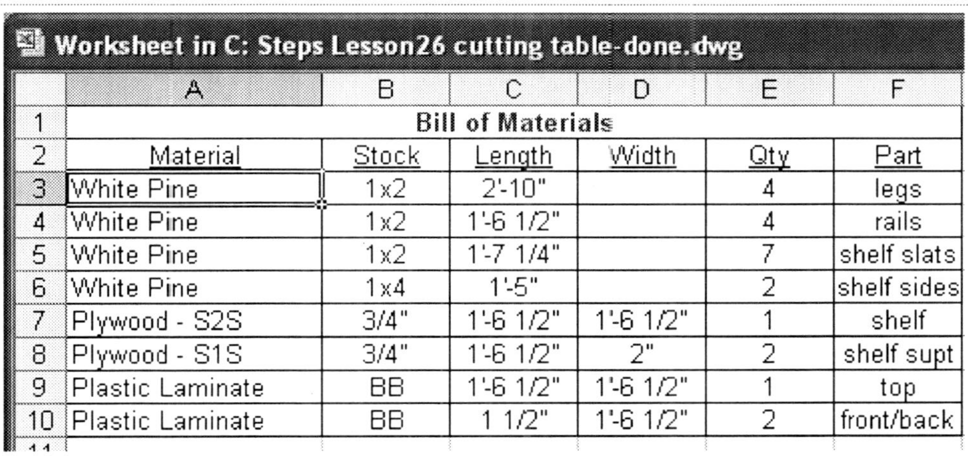
Worksheet in C: Steps Lesson26 cutting table-done.dwg

| | A | B | C | D | E | F |
|---|---|---|---|---|---|---|
| 1 | Bill of Materials | | | | | |
| 2 | Material | Stock | Length | Width | Qty | Part |
| 3 | White Pine | 1x2 | 2'-10" | | 4 | legs |
| 4 | White Pine | 1x2 | 1'-6 1/2" | | 4 | rails |
| 5 | White Pine | 1x2 | 1'-7 1/4" | | 7 | shelf slats |
| 6 | White Pine | 1x4 | 1'-5" | | 2 | shelf sides |
| 7 | Plywood - S2S | 3/4" | 1'-6 1/2" | 1'-6 1/2" | 1 | shelf |
| 8 | Plywood - S1S | 3/4" | 1'-6 1/2" | 2" | 2 | shelf supt |
| 9 | Plastic Laminate | BB | 1'-6 1/2" | 1'-6 1/2" | 1 | top |
| 10 | Plastic Laminate | BB | 1 1/2" | 1'-6 1/2" | 2 | front/back |

13. Repeat Step 11. Notice that the value of the material in the first row has changed. (You may need to Regen the drawing to see the change.) This is how you'll edit embedded OLE Objects.

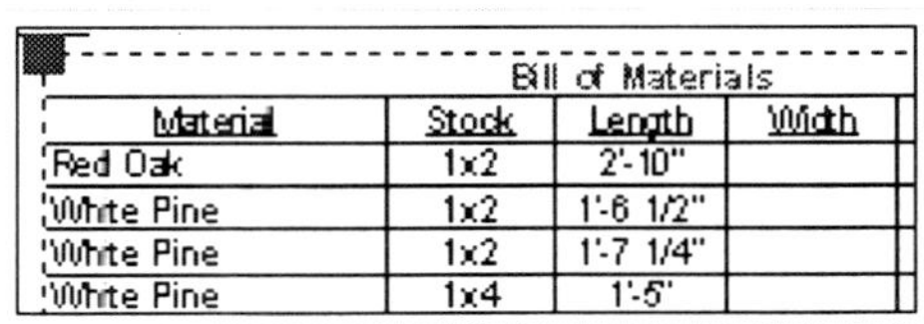


14. Return to Excel and close the *Worksheet in cutting table.dwg* file. Excel then presents the original *Cutting List.xls* file. Notice that it hasn't changed. Remember that the OLE Object was embedded into the OLE Container, not linked to the original file.

## 26.4.1.1: Inserting OLE Objects

15. Leave Excel running, but return to AutoCAD and undo all the changes (until the OLE Object is no longer in the file).

**Command: *u***

16. Now we'll use the Microsoft method for inserting an OLE Object. Return to the spreadsheet and highlight the data cells (A1:F10) as shown below.

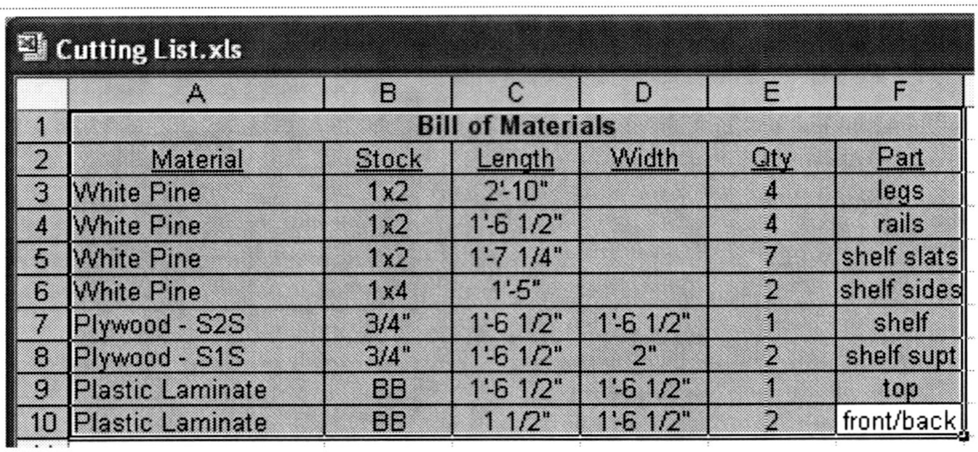
Cutting List.xls

| | A | B | C | D | E | F |
|---|---|---|---|---|---|---|
| 1 | Bill of Materials | | | | | |
| 2 | Material | Stock | Length | Width | Qty | Part |
| 3 | White Pine | 1x2 | 2'-10" | | 4 | legs |
| 4 | White Pine | 1x2 | 1'-6 1/2" | | 4 | rails |
| 5 | White Pine | 1x2 | 1'-7 1/4" | | 7 | shelf slats |
| 6 | White Pine | 1x4 | 1'-5" | | 2 | shelf sides |
| 7 | Plywood - S2S | 3/4" | 1'-6 1/2" | 1'-6 1/2" | 1 | shelf |
| 8 | Plywood - S1S | 3/4" | 1'-6 1/2" | 2" | 2 | shelf supt |
| 9 | Plastic Laminate | BB | 1'-6 1/2" | 1'-6 1/2" | 1 | top |
| 10 | Plastic Laminate | BB | 1 1/2" | 1'-6 1/2" | 2 | front/back |

17. On Excel's Edit pull-down menu, select **Copy** to copy the highlighted section to the Windows clipboard.

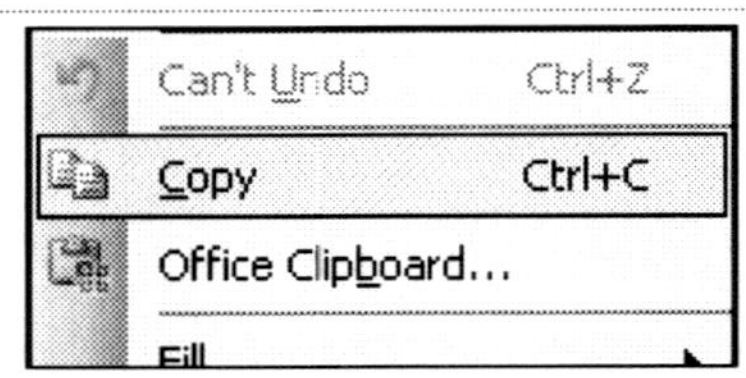


18. Return to AutoCAD.

19. On AutoCAD's Edit pull-down menu, select **Past Special**. (Notice that there is also a **Paste** option. This one will embed the clipboard material into the document/drawing.) Alternately, you can enter the ***Pastespec*** command at the command prompt.

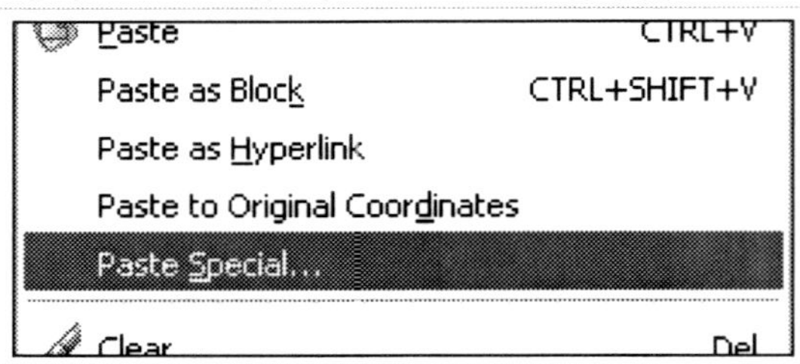


20. AutoCAD presents the Paste Special dialog box. By default, it'll embed the objects. Notice the formats available for embedding objects.

Pick the **Paste Link** option. Notice that, when linked, the image must be in the format of the OLE Server application (below).

## 26.4.1.1: INSERTING OLE OBJECTS

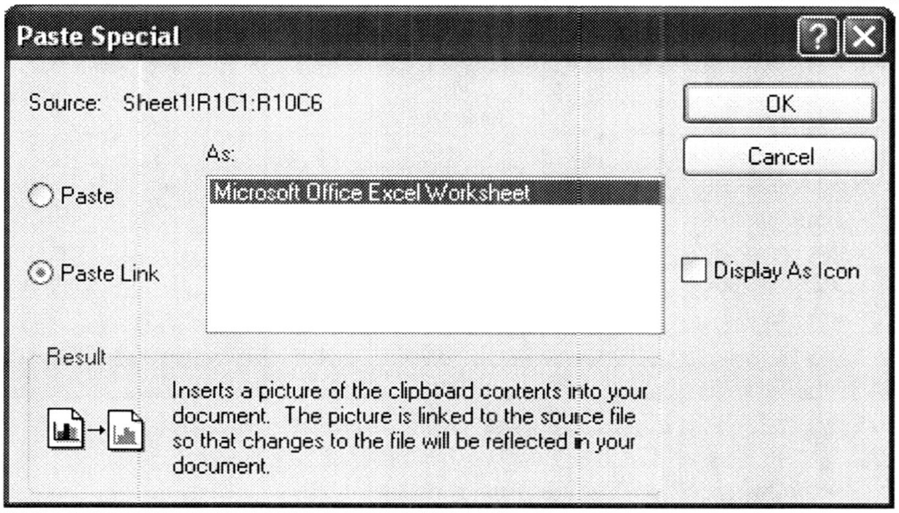


21. Pick the **OK** button 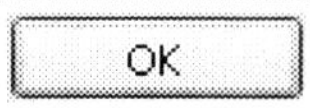 to link the clipboard object (the Excel spreadsheet) into your AutoCAD drawing.

22. AutoCAD asks where to place the object. Put it under the **Product** callout (where we put in previously).

23. Select the OLE object and open the Properties palette .

**Command:** ***props***

24. Resize the object as you did in Step 8.

25. Close the Properties palette.

26. Return to Excel and exit the program .

27. Now let's see what happens when we edit a linked object. Double-click on the OLE Object. AutoCAD opens the OLE Server application (Excel) with the appropriate file. (Notice that the name of the file is *Cutting List.xls* – our original file, not an embedded copy.)

28. To make our OLE Object consistent with our drawing, change the font to **Times New Roman** (in Excel).

29.Now change the **White Pine** materials to **Ponderosa Pine (**see the following figure).

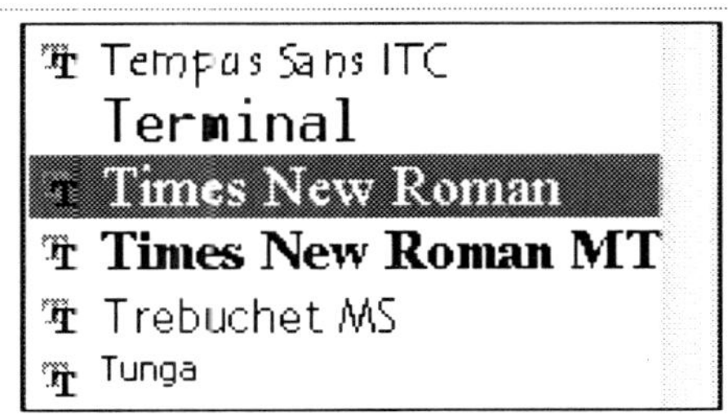

## 26.4.1.1: INSERTING OLE OBJECTS

**Cutting List.xls**

| | A | B | C | D | E | F |
|---|---|---|---|---|---|---|
| 1 | Bill of Materials | | | | | |
| 2 | Material | Stock | Length | Width | Qty | Part |
| 3 | Ponderosa Pine | 1x2 | 2'-10" | | 4 | legs |
| 4 | Ponderosa Pine | 1x2 | 1'-6 1/2" | | 4 | rails |
| 5 | Ponderosa Pine | 1x2 | 1'-7 1/4" | | 7 | shelf slats |
| 6 | Ponderosa Pine | 1x4 | 1'-5" | | 2 | shelf sides |
| 7 | Plywood - S2S | 3/4" | 1'-6 1/2" | 1'-6 1/2" | 1 | shelf |
| 8 | Plywood - S1S | 3/4" | 1'-6 1/2" | 2" | 2 | shelf supt |
| 9 | Plastic Laminate | BB | 1'-6 1/2" | 1'-6 1/2" | 1 | top |
| 10 | Plastic Laminate | BB | 1 1/2" | 1'-6 1/2" | 2 | front/back |

30. Save the changes in Excel and exit the program.

31. Return to AutoCAD and notice the changes. These changes have been incorporated both in the original document and in the AutoCAD link.

32. Save the drawing.

**Command: *qsave***

It now looks like the figure below.

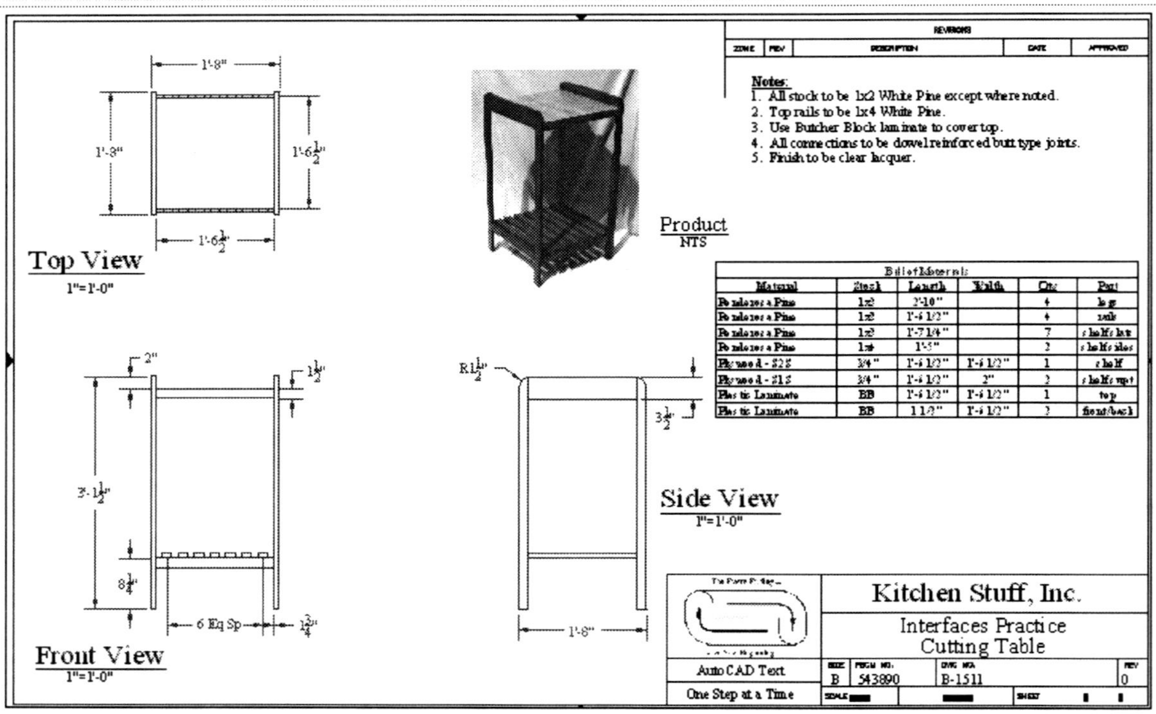


You have now practiced inserting OLE Objects. You've seen the difference between embedding and linking, but you haven't seen some of the OLE editing tools AutoCAD provides. Let's take a look at these now.

## 26.4.2 Modifying OLE Objects

For many reasons, I prefer OLE to imaging via the External Reference palette. I particularly enjoy the versatility offered by being able to edit an OLE Object using its source application. I'm no longer restricted to AutoCAD's commands and procedures. (Although an impressive program, AutoCAD can't do all things.) But thanks to some brilliant programmers at both Autodesk and Microsoft, I can use all of the programs and applications on my computer in a holistic approach to providing my client with a more complete product.

AutoCAD does, however, provide some additional tools for controlling the OLE image once it becomes part of our drawing. Let's look at these now.

- **Olehide**. You can use any of four settings for the **Olehide** system variable to control the display of an OLE Object both on the screen and when plotting. A setting of
  - **0** (the default) makes all OLE Objects visible and printable.
  - **1** makes only OLE Objects in Paper Space visible and printable.
  - **2** makes only OLE Objects in Model Space visible and printable.
  - **3** hides all OLE Objects and none are printable.
- **Olelinks**. The ***Olelinks*** command presents the Links dialog box (Figure 26.007). Here you find several options.

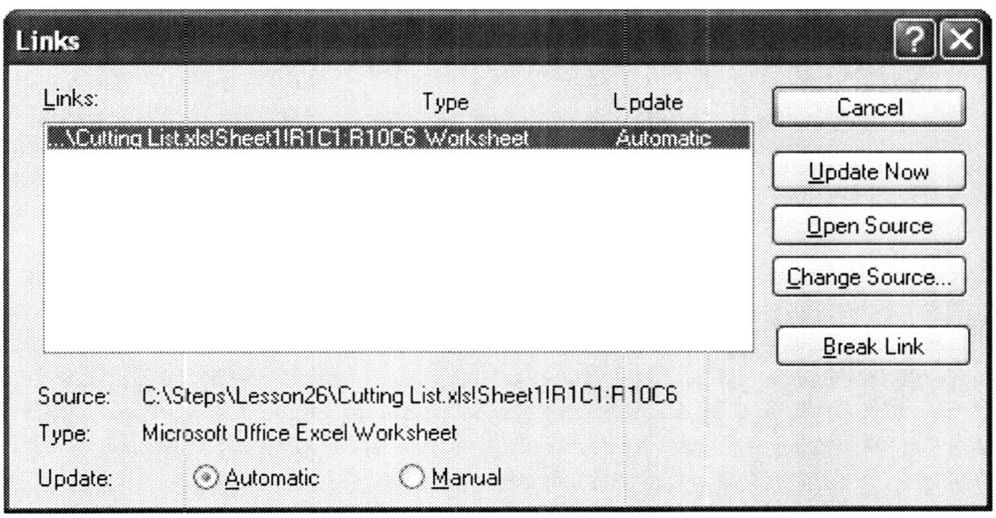


Figure 26.007

  - The list box shows all the linked OLE Objects in the drawing. Select the one with which you want to work.
  - The **Update Now** button will update the OLE Object by reading the source file and making any necessary adjustments.
  - **Open Source** opens the OLE Object in its source application.
  - **Change Source** provides an opportunity to change the source of the link.
  - **Break Link** converts the selected OLE Object into a picture of the object. Use caution when doing this because you can't modify the picture. It's a handy way, however, to send the drawing to a client who might not have the OLE Server application. Remember: *The OLE Server application must be loaded on the computer for an OLE Object to be visible!*
  - At the bottom of the dialog box, you'll find two radio buttons. Selecting **Automatic** means that AutoCAD will update the links as they change. Selecting **Manual** means that

you must update the links yourself (using the **Update Now** button) whenever you want them updated.

- **Olescale**. ***Olescale*** calls an OLE Text Size dialog box (Figure 26.008) where you can adjust the size and font of the OLE text. (You have to select an OLE object *before* entering the ***Olescale*** command.)

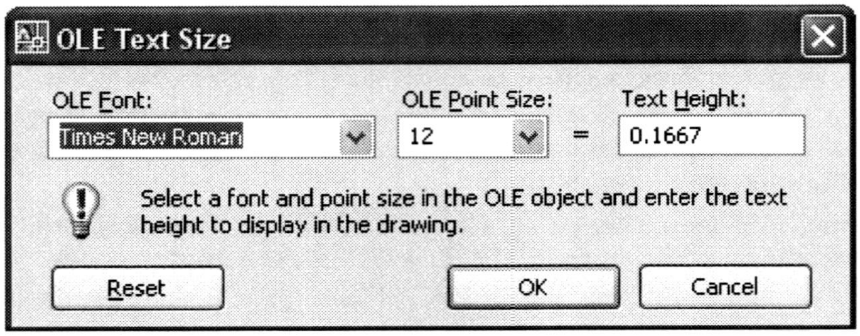


Figure 26.008

- **Olestartup**. This system variable controls whether or not the OLE Server application loads when you plot the drawing. A setting of **0** (the default) won't load the application. A setting of **1** will load the application. Loading the application often improves the quality of a plot.
- **Olequality**. This system variable controls the plot quality of the OLE objects. The possible settings and their meanings follow:
  - **0** produces a monochrome plot. This is the lowest quality but is appropriate for embedded spreadsheets.
  - **1** (the default) produces low graphics (text) quality. Use this for text documents (like Word or WordPad). (I prefer a setting of **1** for spreadsheets as well, since a spreadsheet is mostly text.)
  - **2** produces high graphics quality. It works well for charts, bitmaps, or simple artwork.
  - **3** tells AutoCAD to automatically select the quality based on the type of object being plotted.

## 26.4.3 AutoCAD Data in Other Applications

The methods and procedures for using an AutoCAD drawing in another application (such as Word or Excel) don't differ from what you've already seen. The only limitation involves Paper Space and Model Space views. Remember that you can't select objects in Paper Space if Model Space is active (and vice versa). This presents a problem when copying objects to the clipboard. But let's try an exercise copying our cutting table drawing into a Wordpad document.

### Do This: 26.4.3.1 Using AutoCAD Drawings in Other Applications

I. Be sure you're stil in the *cutting table26.dwg* (or *cutting table26 – done.dwg*) file in the C:\Steps\Lesson26 folder. If not, please open it now.

II. Follow these steps.

| 26.4.3.1: Using AutoCAD Drawings in Other Applications |
|---|
| 1. Pick on the **Model** tab 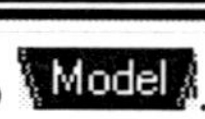. |
| 2. Without entering a command, select all of the objects on the screen. |
| 3. Hold down the CTRL key and type ***C***. This places all of the selected objects on the Windows clipboard.<br>**Command: ^*c*** |

#### 26.4.3.1: Using AutoCAD Drawings in Other Applications

4. Open WordPad. Follow this path from the **Start** button on Windows' desktop: *Start – All Programs – Accessories – Wordpad*

5. In Wordpad, pick the **Paste Special** option on the Edit pull-down menu.

6. WordPad presents the Paste Special dialog box (below). Highlight **AutoCAD Drawing** in the list box, and make sure there is a bullet next to **Paste**. Then pick the **OK** button.

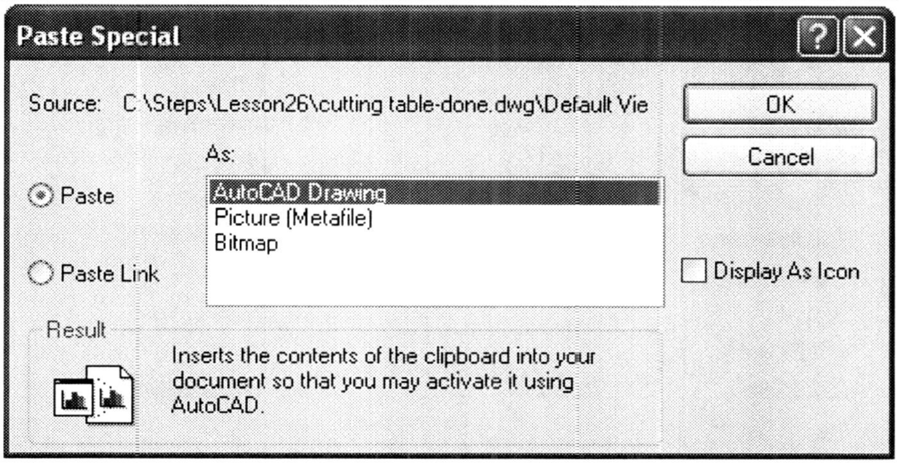


7. Return to AutoCAD and close the cutting table drawing. (Don't save changes, but leave the application running.)

8. Back in Wordpad, double-click on the drawing image. Notice that AutoCAD launches with *Drawing in Document* on the title bar. You've embedded an AutoCAD drawing into a Wordpad document!

9. Close both applications without saving.

Of course, linking an AutoCAD drawing into another application's document is as easy!

## 26.5 Extra Steps

Return to the *MyCircuit* series of drawings (*1a* through *1d*) you created in Lesson 25. Create a bill of materials in Excel to include all of the block objects in *MyCircuit1a*. Be sure to save the spreadsheet outside of AutoCAD (save as *MyMats.xls* in the C:\Steps\Lesson26 folder). Then insert the spreadsheet into each of the drawings as an OLE Object, changing the list as necessary to reflect the materials in the drawing. Will you embed or link the spreadsheet?*

* You'll need to embed the OLE Object so that your changes are specific to the individual drawings.

## 26.6 What Have We Learned?

*Items covered in this lesson include:*

- *Differences between raster and vector imaging*
- *The Image Manager*
- *Exporting image files*
- *Object Linking and Embedding*
- *Using Windows' clipboard in AutoCAD*
- *AutoCAD Commands:*
    - ***Image***
    - ***ImageAttach***
    - ***ImageFrame***
    - ***ImageClip***
    - ***ImageAdjust***
    - ***ImageQuality***
    - ***Transparency***
    - ***DrawOrder***
    - ***Export***
    - ***WMFOut***
    - ***ACISOut***
    - ***STLOut***
    - ***PSOut***
    - ***ATText***
    - ***BMPOut***
    - ***3DSOut***
    - ***InsertObj***
    - ***Olehide***
    - ***Olelinks***
    - ***Olequality***
    - ***Olescale***
    - ***Olestartup***

In this lesson you learned how to use material from several types of applications in your drawing – and even how to use your drawings in other applications! These steps toward publication-quality drawings will serve you well in almost any industry.

## 26.7 Exercises

1. Open the *Wine Rack.dwg* file in the C:\Steps\Lesson26 folder. Create the layout shown in the following figure. Use the following to guide your setup:
   1.1. Set up to plot on a B-size (17x11) sheet of paper.
   1.2. Use the *ANSI B Title Block.dwg* file in the \Template folder as your border/title block.
   1.3. Use the *title info26.dwg* file to insert data into the title block.
   1.4. The photograph is *winerack.tif* and can be found in the C:\Steps\Lesson26 folder.
   1.5. Embed the BOM using the *Winerack.xls* Excel file.
   1.6. The logo in the title block is *logo.jpg* and can be found in the C:\Steps\Lesson26 folder.
   1.7. Complete the layout and dimension the viewports as indicated.
   1.8. Save the drawing as *MyWineRack.dwg* in the C:\Steps\Lesson26 folder.

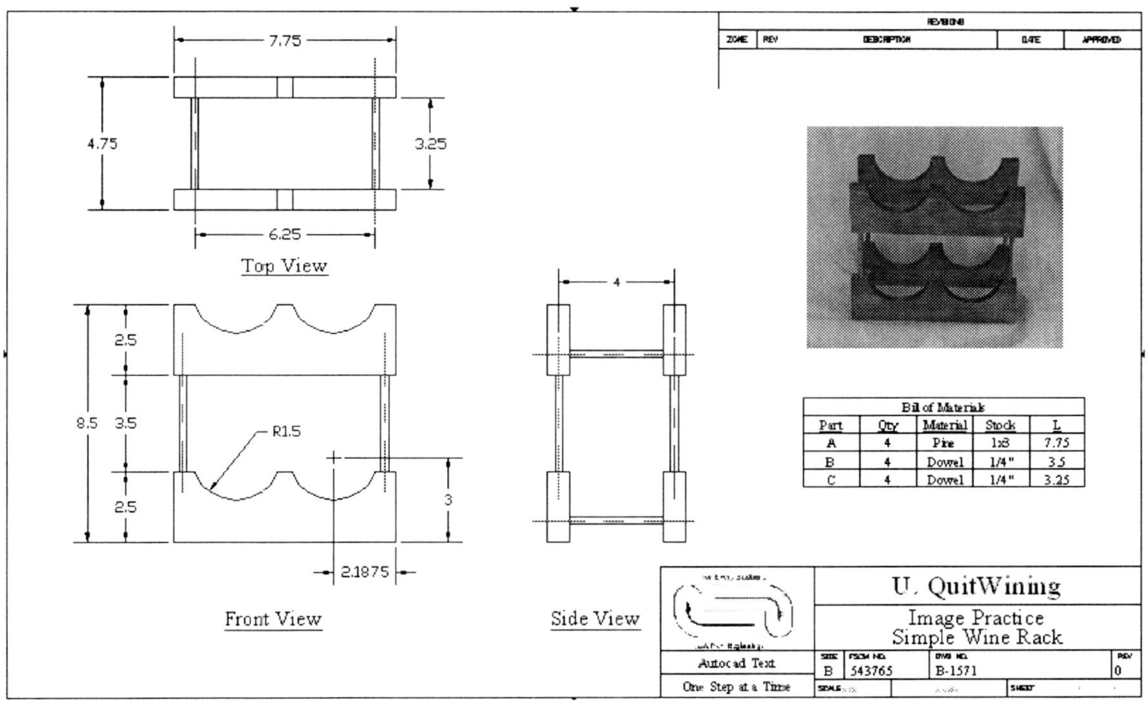

2. Open the *Jewelry Box.dwg* file in the C:\Steps\Lesson26 folder. Create the layout shown. Use the following to guide your setup:
   2.1. Set up to plot on a B-size (17x11) sheet of paper.
   2.2. Use the *ANSI B Title Block.dwg* file in the \Template folder as your border/title block.
   2.3. Use the *title info26.dwg* file to insert data into the title block.
   2.4. The photograph is *jewlery box.tif* and can be found in the C:\Steps\Lesson26 folder.
   2.5. Embed the BOM using the *JBox.xls* Excel file.
   2.6. The logo in the title block is *logo-mini.jpg* and can be found in the C:\Steps\Lesson26 folder.
   2.7. Complete the layout and dimension the viewports as indicated.
   2.8. Save the drawing as *MyJewelryBox.dwg* in the C:\Steps\Lesson26 folder.

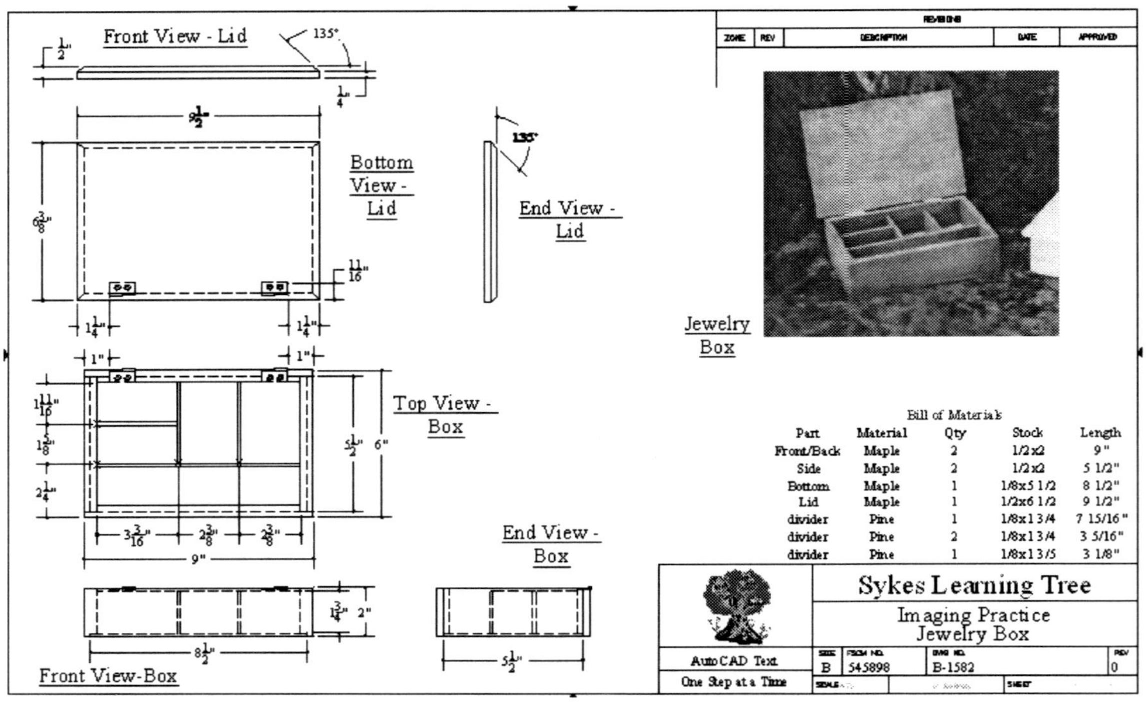


Figure 26.027: Jewelry Box

*For more exercises related to Lesson 26, please see Lesson 26 in AutoCAD 2007: One Step at a Time – Workbook.*

| 26.8 | **For Web-Based Review Questions, visit: http://www.uneedcad.com/2007/Files/07R26.pdf** |
|---|---|

**To continue, please pick up a copy of *3D AutoCAD 2007: One Step at a Time*.**

## 3D AutoCAD 2007: One Step at a Time

## Contents

## Appendix – A: Drawing Scales

| SCALE (= 1') | SCALE FACTOR | DIMENSIONS OF DRAWING WHEN FINAL PLOT SIZE IS: 8½"x11" | 11"x17" | 17"x22" | 22"x34" | 24"x36" |
|---|---|---|---|---|---|---|
| **1/16"** | 192 | 136'x176' | 176'x272' | 272'x352' | 352'x544' | 384'x576' |
| **3/32"** | 128 | 90'8x117'4 | 117'4x181'4 | 181'4x234'8 | 234'8x362'8 | 256'x384' |
| **1/8"** | 96 | 68'x88' | 88'x136' | 136'x176' | 176'x272' | 192'x288' |
| **3/16"** | 64 | 45'4x58'8 | 58'8x90'8 | 90'8x117'4 | 117'4x181'4 | 128'x192' |
| **¼"** | 48 | 34'x44' | 44'x68' | 68'x88' | 88'x136' | 96'x144' |
| **3/8"** | 32 | 22'8x29'4 | 29'4x45'4 | 45'4x58'8 | 58'8x90'8 | 64'x96' |
| **½"** | 24 | 17'x22' | 22'x34' | 34'x44' | 44'x68' | 48'x72' |
| **¾"** | 16 | 11'4x14'8 | 14'8x22'8 | 22'8x29'4 | 29'4x45'4 | 32'x48' |
| **1"** | 12 | 8'x6'11 | 11'x17' | 17'x22' | 22'x34' | 24'x36' |
| **1½"** | 8 | 5'8x7'4 | 7'4x11'4 | 11'4x14'8 | 14'8x22'8 | 16'x24' |
| **3"** | 4 | 34"x44" | 3'8x5'8 | 8'x6'11 | 7'4x11'4 | 8'x12' |
| **(1" =)** | | | | | | |
| **10'** | 120 | 85'x110' | 110'x170' | 170'x220' | 220'x340' | 240'x360' |
| **20'** | 240 | 170'x220' | 220'x340' | 340'x440' | 440'x680' | 480'x720' |
| **25'** | 300 | 212'6x275' | 275'x425' | 425'x550' | 550'x850' | 600'x900' |
| **30'** | 360 | 255'x330' | 330'x510' | 510'x660' | 660'x1020' | 720'x1080' |
| **40'** | 480 | 340'x440' | 440'x680' | 680'x880' | 880'x1360' | 960'x1440' |
| **50'** | 600 | 425'x550' | 550'x850' | 850'x1100' | 1100'x1700' | 1200'x1800' |
| **60'** | 720 | 510'x660' | 660'x1020' | 1020'x1320' | 1320'x2040' | 1440'x2160' |
| **80'** | 960 | 680'x880' | 880'x1360' | 1360'x1760' | 1760'x2720' | 1920'x2880' |
| **100'** | 1200 | 850'x1100' | 1100'x1700' | 1700'x2200' | 2200'x3400' | 2400'x3600' |
| **200'** | 2400 | 1700'x2200' | 2200'x3400' | 3400'x4400' | 4400'x6800' | 4800'x7200' |

## Appendix – B: Function Keys and Their Uses

| KEY | FUNCTION | KEY | FUNCTION | KEY | FUNCTION |
|---|---|---|---|---|---|
| F1 | AutoCAD's Help | F5 | Isoplane toggle | F9 | Snap toggle |
| F2 | Toggle between graphics & text screen | F6 | Toggle coordinate indicator on or off | F10 | Polar Tracking Toggle |
| F3 | OSNAP settings | F7 | Grid toggle | F11 | Object Tracking Toggle |
| F4 | Tablet (Digitizer) toggle | F8 | Ortho toggle | F12 | Dynamic Input Toggle |

[Note: Appendix C has been replaced with web addresses for chapter review questions and their answers.]

## Appendix – D: MText Keystrokes

| | These Keys: | Do This: |
|---|---|---|
| POSITION | ← → ↑ ↓ | Move the cursor through the text one space at a time |
| | Ctrl + ←<br>Ctrl + → | Move the cursor through the text one word at a time |
| | Home | Move the cursor to the beginning of the line |
| | End | Move the cursor to the end of the line |
| | Page Up<br>Page Down | Move the cursor through the document up to 28 lines at a time |
| | Ctrl + Home | Move the cursor to the beginning of the document |
| | Ctrl + End | Move the cursor to the end of the document |
| | Ctrl + Page Up<br>Ctrl + Page Down | Move the cursor to the top or bottom of the screen |
| SELECTION | Ctrl + A | Selects all the text in the mtext object |
| | Shift + ←<br>Shift + → | Selects / deselects text one character at a time |
| | Shift + ↑<br>Shift + ↓ | Selects / deselects text one line at a time |
| | Ctrl + Shift + ←<br>Ctrl + Shift + → | Selects / deselects text one word at a time |
| ACTION | Delete | Deletes the character to the right of the cursor |
| | Backspace | Deletes the character to the left of the cursor |
| | Ctrl + Backspace | Deletes the word to the left of the cursor |
| | Esc | Leaves the text editor without saving the changes |
| | Ctrl + C | Copy the selected text to the Windows clipboard |
| | Ctrl + V | Paste text from the Windows clipboard into the text editor |
| | Ctrl + X | Remove the selected text and place it on the Windows clipboard |
| | Ctrl + Z | Undo the last edit |
| | Enter | Starts a new paragraph |

## Appendix – E: Dimension Variables

| DIMENSION VARIABLE | DEFAULT SETTING | EXPLANATION |
|---|---|---|
| DIMADEC | -1 | Angular decimal places (set from 0-8); a setting of –1 tells AutoCAD to use the DIMDEC setting |
| DIMALT | Off | Use of alternate units |
| DIMALTD | 2 | Decimal places in alternate units |
| DIMALTF | 25.4 | Scale factor in alternate units |
| DIMALTTD | 2 | Decimal places in tolerances of alternate units |
| DIMALTTZ | 0 | Suppression of zeros in alternate units (0 or 1) |
| DIMALTU | 2 | Units format for alternate units (except angular) |
| DIMALTZ | 0 | Suppression of zeros in tolerance values |
| DIMAPOST | “” | Identifies a text suffix / prefix to be used with alternate dim |
| DIMASO | on | Associative dimensioning (on or off) |
| DIMASZ | 0.18 | Arrowhead size |
| DIMAUNIT | 0 | Format for angular dimensions |
| DIMBLK | “” | Specify a block to place on the dimension line rather than an arrowhead |
| DIMBLK1<br>DIMBLK2 | ““<br>”” | Specifies blocks for both ends of the dimension line (if the DIMSAH variable is **on**) |
| DIMCEN | 0.09 | Controls what, if any, center marks are placed in circles and arcs (Centerlines are drawn if the number is less than 0; Center marks are drawn if the number is above 0; no center marks/lines are drawn if value equals 0) |
| DIMCLRD | 0 | Color for dimension lines, arrowheads, and leaders |
| DIMCLRE | 0 | Color for extension lines |
| DIMCLRT | 0 | Color for dimension text |
| DIMDEC | 4 | Primary units decimal places |
| DIMDLE | 0.0 | Extension of dimension line beyond extension line |
| DIMDLI | 0.38 | Spacing of baseline dimension lines |
| DIMEXE | 0.18 | Extension of extension line beyond dimension line |
| DIMEXO | 0.0625 | Distance from origin to beginning of extension line |
| DIMFIT | 3 | This controls whether or not a dimension line will be placed between the extension lines if there is enough space. Settings are: 0 – arrows and text; 1 – just text; 2 – just arrows; 3 – best fit (puts text and arrows between the extension lines as space is available); 4 – leader (when no space is available for the text, it is placed aside and connected to the dimension line with a leader line); 5 – no leader (same as 4 but will not use a leader line). |
| DIMGAP | 0.09 | Space around the text when it is placed inside the dimension line or between bottom of text and dimension line when text is placed above the line |
| DIMJUST | 0 | Horizontal position of dimension text. Possible settings include: 0 – centered between extension lines; 1 – next to the first extension line; 2 – next to the second extension line; 3 – next to and aligned with the first extension line; 4 – next to and aligned with the second extension line |

| DIMENSION VARIABLE | DEFAULT SETTING | EXPLANATION |
|---|---|---|
| DIMLFAC | 1.0 | Global scale factor for dimensioning |
| DIMLIM | off | Places dimension limits as default dimension text |
| DIMPOST | "" | Identifies a text prefix or suffix for the dimension text |
| DIMRND | 0.00 | Rounds the dimension distances to this value |
| DIMSAH | off | Determines whether or not blocks will be used instead or arrowheads |
| DIMSCALE | 1.0 | Sets an overall scale factor for all dimension variables requiring size settings |
| DIMSD1<br>DIMSD2 | off<br>off | Suppression of the first and second dimension line |
| DIMSE1<br>DIMSE2 | off<br>off | Suppression of the first and second extension line |
| DIMSHO | on | This actually controls whether or not the dimension will be redefined as the dimension is dragged |
| DIMSOXD | off | Controls whether or not dimension lines will be drawn outside the extension lines |
| DIMSTYLE | "Standard" | Current dimension style |
| DIMTAD | 0 | Vertical position of text. Possible settings are: 0 – centered inside the dimension line; 1 – place text above the dimension line; 2 – on the side of the dimension line farthest from the defining point; 3 – Japanese standard |
| DIMTDEC | 4 | Decimal places in tolerance value |
| DIMTFAC | 1.0 | Scale factor the text height of tolerance values |
| DIMTIH | on | Whether (**on**)or not (**off**) text inside the dimension lines will be horizontal |
| DIMTIX | off | Force text between the extension lines |
| DIMTM | 0.0 | Sets the minimum tolerance limits when either DIMLIM or DIMTOL is **on** |
| DIMTOFL | off | Force a dimension line between extension lines |
| DIMTOH | on | Position of text outside dimension lines (**on** forces horizontal text) |
| DIMTOL | off | Add tolerances to dimension text |
| DIMTOLJ | 1 | Vertical justification of tolerance values (0 – bottom; 1 – middle; 2 – top) |
| DIMTP | 0.0 | Upper tolerance limit |
| DIMTSZ | 0.0 | Size of ticks used instead of arrowheads |
| DIMTVP | 0.0 | Vertical position of text above / below dimension line |
| DIMTXSTY | "Standard" | Text style used for the dimension text |
| DIMTXT | 0.18 | Height of dimension text |

| DIMENSION VARIABLE | DEFAULT SETTING | EXPLANATION |
|---|---|---|
| DIMTZIN | 0 | Suppression of zeros in tolerance values. Possible values: 0 – suppresses zero feet and zero inches; 1 – includes zero feet and inches; 2 – includes zero feet but suppresses zero inches; 3 – includes zero inches but suppresses zero feet; 4 – suppresses leading zeros in decimals; 8 – suppresses trailing zeros in decimals; 12 – suppresses both leading and trailing zeros in decimals. |
| DIMUNIT | 2 | Dimension units for everything but angular dimensions. Possible settings are: 1 – Scientific; 2- Decimal; 3 – Engineering; 4 – Architectural (stacked); 5 – Fractional (stacked); 6 – Architectural; 7 – Fractional; 8 – windows settings |
| DIMUPT | off | If **on**, the cursor controls placement of both dimension and text; if **off**, the cursor controls placement only of the dimension |
| DIMZIN | 0 | Suppression of zeros in the primary units. . Possible values: 0 – suppresses zero feet and zero inches; 1 – includes zero feet and inches; 2 – includes zero feet but suppresses zero inches; 3 – includes zero inches but suppresses zero feet; 4 – suppresses leading zeros in decimals; 8 – suppresses trailing zeros in decimals; 12 – suppresses both leading and trailing zeros in decimals. |

## Appendix – F: Hotkeys

| COMMAND | HOTKEY |
|---|---|
| ADCenter | ADC |
| Align | AL |
| Area | AA |
| Array | AR |
| Attdisp | ATT |
| Attedit | ATE |
| Block | B, -B |
| Break | BR |
| Chamfer | CHA |
| Circle | C |
| color | COL |
| Copy | CO, CP |
| DDEdit | ED |
| Dimaligned | DAL |
| Dimangular | DAN |
| Dimbaseline | DBA |
| Dimcontinue | DCO |
| Dimdiameter | DDI |
| Dimedit | DED |
| Dimlinear | DLI |
| Dimordinate | DOR |
| Dimradius | DRA |
| Dist | DI |
| Divide | DIV |
| Donut | DO |
| Dsettings | DS |
| Ellipse | EL |
| Erase | E |
| Explode | X |
| Extend | EX |
| Fillet | F |
| Filter | FI |
| Grid | F7 |
| Grips | GR |
| Group | G |
| Hatch | H |
| HatchEdit | HE |
| Insert | I |
| Layer | LA, -LA |
| Leader | LE |
| Lengthen | LEN |
| Line | L |
| Linetype | LT, -LT |

| COMMAND | HOTKEY |
|---|---|
| List | LI |
| LTScale | LTS |
| Lweight | LW |
| MatchProp | MA |
| Measure | ME |
| Mirror | MI |
| MLine | ML |
| Move | M |
| MText | MT, T |
| Offset | O |
| Open | ^O |
| Ortho | F8 |
| OSNAP | OS, -OS |
| Pan | P, -P |
| Pedit | PE |
| Pline | PL |
| Point | PO |
| Polygon | POL |
| Properties | PROPS |
| Purge | PU |
| QSave | ^S |
| Rectangle | REC |
| Redraw | R |
| Regen | Re |
| Rotate | RO |
| Save | ^S |
| Scale | SC |
| Snap | SN |
| Solid | SO |
| Spell | SP |
| Spline | SPL |
| Splinedit | SPE |
| Stretch | S |
| Style | ST |
| Text | DT |
| Trim | TR |
| Units | UN |
| View | V |
| WBlock | W, -W |
| Xline | XL |
| Zoom | Z |

## Appendix – G: Actions & Parameters Chart for Dynamic Blocks

| Parameters | Actions | | | | | | | | |
|---|---|---|---|---|---|---|---|---|---|
| | Move | Stretch | Scale | Array | Polar Stretch | Rotation | Flip | Lookup | No Action |
| Point | ■ | ■ | | | | | | | |
| Linear | ■ | ■ | ■ | ■ | | | | | |
| Polar | ■ | ■ | ■ | ■ | ■ | | | | |
| XY | ■ | ■ | ■ | ■ | | | | | |
| Rotation | | | | | | ■ | | | |
| Alignment | | | | | | | | | ■ |
| Flip | | | | | | | ■ | | |
| Visibility | | | | | | | | | ■ |
| Lookup | | | | | | | | ■ | |
| Base Point | | | | | | | | | ■ |

## Appendix – H: 2D Drawing Setup

During Beta testing, AutoCAD started with a 3D screen known as a *workspace*. If your screen (AUI) doesn't look like the one if Figure 1.001, follow this procedure so we all begin at the same place.

| Do This: H1 | Starting With a 2D Workspace |
|---|---|

II. Follow these steps.

**H1: Starting With a 2D Workspace**

1. In the upper left corner of the window (just below the File pull down menu), you'll find a control box with the words "3D Modeling" in it. Select the down arrow next to the box.

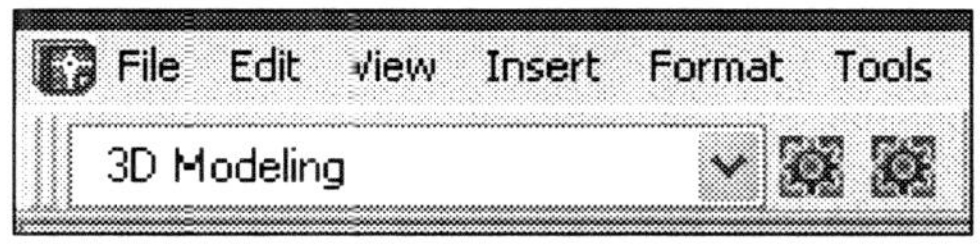


2. Select "AutoCAD Classic" from the menu that appears.

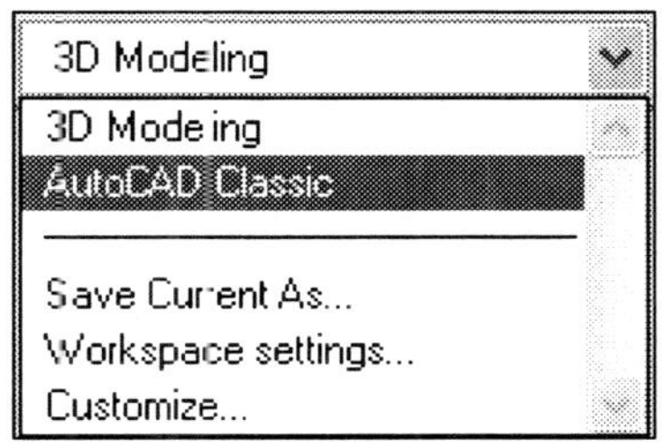


3. Now select **Options** from the **Tools** pull down menu. Alternately, you can enter the word ***Options*** on the keyboard (it'll appear next to your crosshairs/cursor).

An Options dialog box will appear.

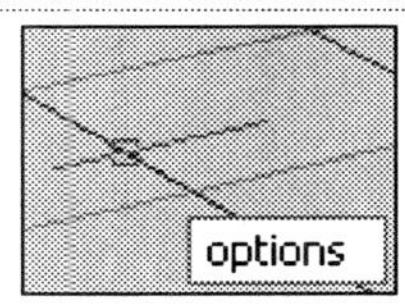


4. In the Options dialog box, select the plus (+) next to the following (as shown in the following figure):

a) Template Settings

b) Default Template File for QNEW

## H1: Starting With a 2D Workspace

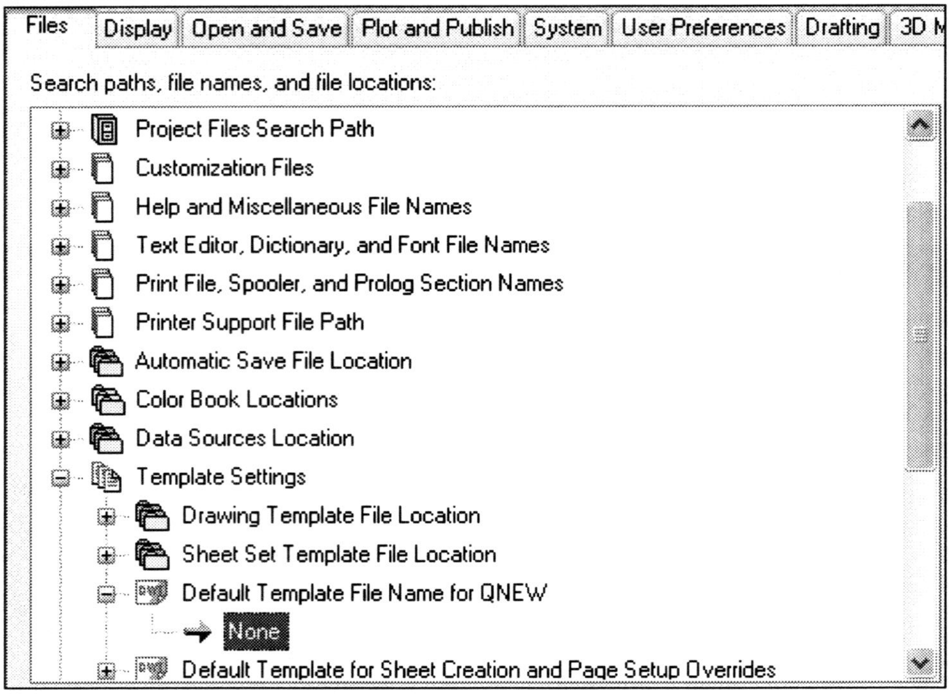


5. Double click on **None**. AutoCAD will present a file selection dialog box. Select **Acad.dwt**.

6. Pick the **Open** button 

to close the select file dialog box.

7. Pick the **OK** button 

to finish the procedure.

8. Close 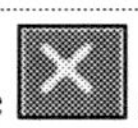 any open palettes or windows that hover over the drawing area.

9. Close and reopen AutoCAD.

You're now ready to continue the text.

AutoCAD will open in this "AutoCAD Classic" mode until you change the workspace back to 3D. We'll look at that in more detail shortly.

Printed in the United Kingdom
by Lightning Source UK Ltd.
123634UK00001B/10/A

9 780976 588863